The Roman Empire of Ammianus

The Roman Empire of Ammianus

With a New Introduction

John Matthews

Michigan Classical Press

Revised edition copyright © 2007 by John Matthews
All rights reserved.
Library of Congress Control Number 2007940076
ISBN 978-0-9799713-2-7

Printed in the United States of America
2010 2009 2008 2007   4 3 2 1

First edition published 1989 by Gerald Duckworth & Co. Ltd.

∞ Printed on acid-free paper

No part of this publication may be reproduced, stored in a retrieval system, or transmitted in any form or by any means, electronic, mechanical, or otherwise, without the written permission of the publisher.

Michigan Classical Press
PO Box 130194
Ann Arbor, MI 48113 USA

www.michiganclassicalpress.com

Contents

Preface		ix
List of illustrations		xiv

Part One. Res Gestae

I	Introduction	3
II	Ammianus and his History	8
	(1) The political setting	8
	(2) Composition	17
III	Ammianus and Constantius: Civil Dissension and Foreign War	33
IV	North-East Frontier	48
	(1) The satrapy of Corduene	48
	(2) The siege of Amida	57
V	The Young Ammianus: Social and Cultural Setting	67
VI	The Rise of Julian	81
VII	Julian and the Philosophers	115
VIII	The Invasion of Persia	130
	(1) Historical perspectives	130
	(2) Historical geography	140
	(3) Ammianus and other sources	161
IX	Legitimacy and Usurpation: Jovian to Procopius	180
X	Valentinian and Valens: Sex, Magic and Treason	204

Part Two. Visa vel Lecta

XI	The Office of Emperor	231
XII	The Character of Government	253

XIII	The Practice of War	279
XIV	Barbarians and Bandits	304
	(1) Farmers: Alamanni and Goths	306
	(2) Nomads: Huns and Saracens	332
	(3) Rebels: Isaurians and Moors	355
	(4) Conclusion: Ammianus and his sources	376
XV	The Physical Environment: Town and Country	383
XVI	Social Relations	404
XVII	Religion and Philosophy	424
	(1) Divination and *daimones*	424
	(2) Christianity in Ammianus	435
XVIII	The Roman and the Greek	452
	Notes	473
	Bibliography	554
	Index	572

To my friends

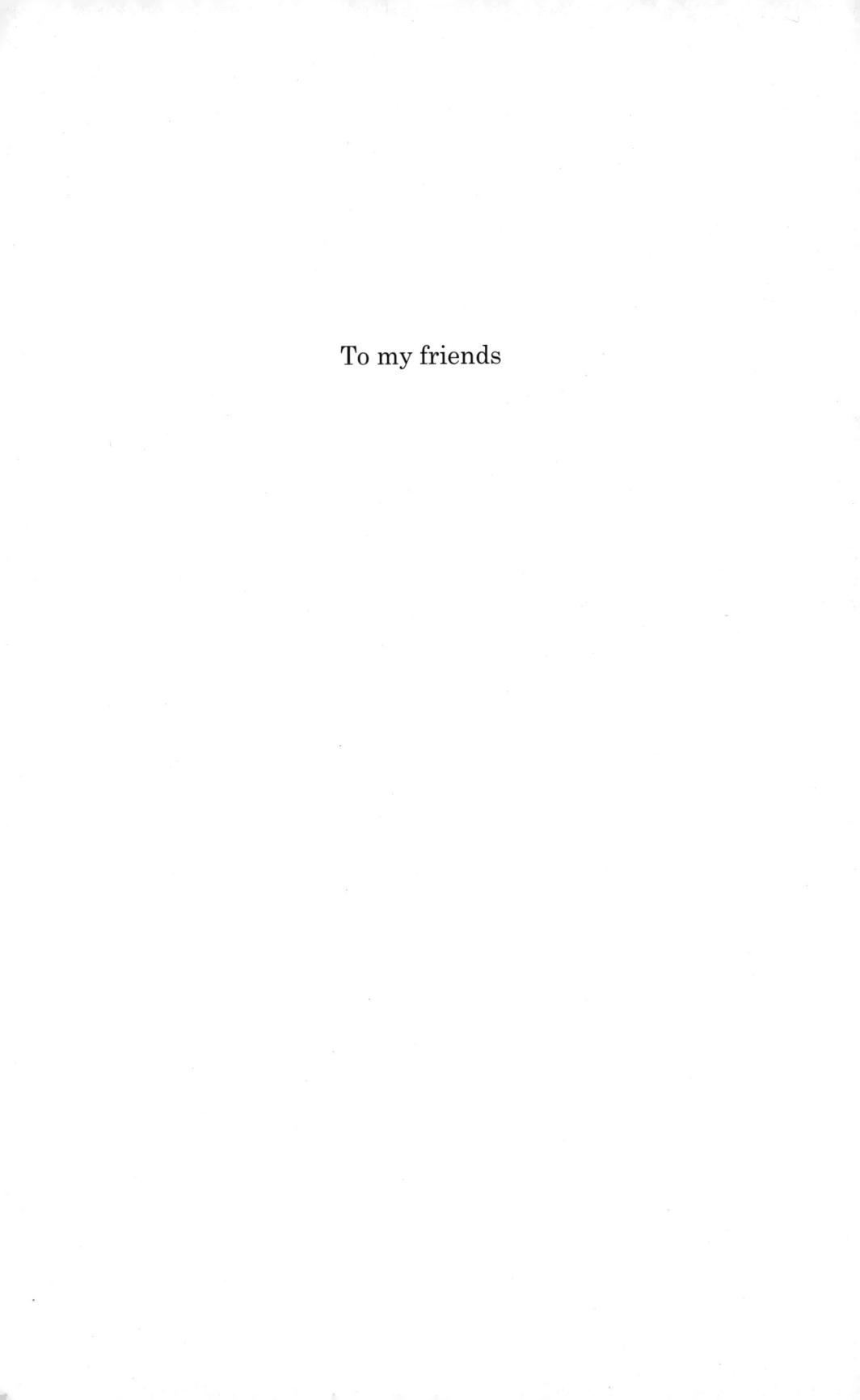

Think, when we talk of horses, that you see them
Printing their proud hoofs i' th' receiving earth;
For 'tis your thoughts that now must deck our kings,
Carry them here and there, jumping o'er times
Turning th' accomplishment of many years
Into an hour-glass; for the which supply,
Admit me Chorus to this history...
Shakespeare, Henry V

If personality is an unbroken series of successful gestures....
Scott Fitzgerald, The Great Gatsby

To most of us the movements of the soul are so mysterious that we seize upon events to make them explicable.
William Cooper, Scenes from Provincial Life

Preface to 2008 Reprint

It is almost twenty years since, on the first appearance of this book, I reflected on the effect upon a new graduate student of late Roman history of a reading of Ammianus Marcellinus, and on the impression made by Edward Thompson's pioneering book, *The Historical Work of Ammianus Marcellinus*, published in 1947 – sixty years from the time that I write this! I still remember, too, the citation in the third volume of J. C. Rolfe's Loeb edition, of Ernest Stein's judgment of Ammianus as the greatest literary genius the world had seen between Tacitus and Dante, unmatched among historians in his power to move the reader's heart. Such an extravagant leave-taking was a contrast to that of Gibbon, whose better-known regret at parting from his 'accurate and faithful guide' was tempered by distaste for 'the vices of his style, the disorder and perplexity of his narrative', and, in another passage, for 'his love of ambitious ornaments [that] frequently betrayed him into an unnatural vehemence of expression'. One can see how Gibbon's more Classical discernment led him to this verdict; it is not the only occasion on which his historical judgment was infected by the aesthetic taste of his own age. Still more remarkably, it appeared (still from Rolfe's preface), that Stein had declared Ammianus, in his greater objectivity and wider horizons, the superior of Tacitus himself. This was a powerful claim, for had not Gibbon described Tacitus as the greatest of philosophic historians, whose writings would instruct the last generations of mankind? Also cited was Otto Seeck, who in a standard reference article set against Ammianus' admitted shortcomings an unrivalled ability to portray human character, that set him in the front rank of historians of any age.

Setting these judgments aside, one only had to open the pages of Ammianus to see that this was a source for late Roman history that, to one undertaking research after study of the great Classical historians, was a wonderfully effective introduction to a new age, combining the unexpected features of this new age with a more or less traditional way of describing them. After the well-practised regularities of early imperial history, what was striking about the later Roman empire was its richness and diversity, and its massive and varied documentation; and here was a writer prepared to address it in the familiar terms of the Classical historian, with the repertoire one was used to – high politics, conspiracies and civil war, battles and sieges, social satire and moral judgments, learned digressions, vivid portrayals of character, a multiplicity of names and places – together with much that one was not – eunuchs in politics, Germans in the high command, bishops in the cities, frank despotism and religious bigotry in the world at large. Criticise as one may Ammianus' opinions and choices of emphasis, it is hard to imagine a writer more responsive to the issues and personalities of his time, and hard to think of a topic on which he does not make some contribution to our understanding.

As I also remarked in my first preface, *The Roman Empire of Ammianus* is a much longer book than the one I promised to its publisher. I have one sort of explanation for this, when I remember how, at some time in the mid-1980s, I had taken with me on vacation a more or less complete draft of the smaller book I had undertaken to write. Reading through the draft after a fine lunch, sitting under the hot sun of southern France, and replenished by the red wine of the region, I saw that I had a choice: to round off and finish the book I had in my hands, or spend an extra two or three years and write the much larger book that Ammianus did by now seem to deserve. Some readers may say (in fact, have said) that in the process the book has lost focus, that it is self-indulgent, that it is too large for its purpose (whatever this might be), and so on. I have to say that, whatever the truth of these criticisms, I have never for one minute regretted my decision; I so much enjoyed writing it, and enjoyment has a great way of lowering the defences. Others have remarked on my over-identification with the subject, but I do not regret that either. Ammianus is a marvellous writer, alive on every page, and, as Ronald Syme said so beautifully and memorably of Tacitus, it is good fortune and a privilege to spend time in his company.

The structure of the book expresses the two elements in its title. In Part One, 'Res Gestae', Ammianus' work and career are combined in a survey of the history of his time as he saw and experienced it, narrative chapter alternating with excursus in a manner intended to reflect his own. In these earlier chapters, Ammianus figures prominently, as participant in and observer of events. Here, too, the figure of the emperor Julian is increasingly prominent, to the extent, almost, of forming a separate monograph within the design of the book (chapters VI-VIII). Ammianus' personal role diminishes after this early phase of intensive involvement, and the last two chapters of Part One (IX and X) follow the history to its conclusion with only intermittent participation from the historian. Although they are intelligible in their own right, readers will understand these chapters better (and understand how derivative they are) if they also equip themselves with a text or translation of Ammianus. Part Two, 'Visa vel Lecta' (a phrase directly borrowed from Ammianus), consists of a series of descriptions of topics for which Ammianus is a chief source, and on which his views are of interest. These chapters are arranged in groups, connected thematically or in sequence: XI-XIII present the office of emperor and his functions in government and war, the last of these leading (in XIV) to a description, considerably enlarging on the text of Ammianus, of the main foreign, and some internal, enemies of the Roman order. From here Chapter XV, on town and country, leads to XVI, social relations in Ammianus, and this

Preface

in turn to a discussion of the historian's attitude to matters of religion (XVII). These two chapters draw the attention progressively back to Ammianus himself, in a fashion that begins to mirror on an intellectual plane the more circumstantial emphasis on the historian in the earlier chapters of Part One, and the concluding chapter (XVIII) recapitulates and addresses in a more fully developed historiographical dimension questions of the composition, structure and cultural identity of the history that are raised in formal terms at the beginning of the book (II).

Each chapter can be read independently, though better, of course, in the context of the book as a whole, or at least of its immediate neighbours. References to Ammianus himself, and to other particular sources under review, are, at the cost of some visual untidiness, given in parenthesis in the text of the book. More elaborate references, and all supporting argumentation, are presented in the notes. These are placed at the end of the book. Footnotes or endnotes, one has to choose one or the other, and my decision allowed me to write some more extensive notes and bibliographical essays, rather in the nature of small appendices, of a length that would be obtrusive if they were to compete with the main text for room on the page. I am not much in favour of those bottom-heavy presentations, in which three or four lines of text at the head of the page are supported by massive foundations of footnote references and bibliography.

My earlier remarks, echoing those of Thompson, about the lack of interest evinced by Classical scholars in Ammianus, and about the attention paid by them to less interesting and less important writers from what some are still happy to call more 'central' periods of Roman history, have been somewhat allayed by the continuing appearance of much excellent work (though to judge by the appearance of recent monographs there still seems to be more interest in Statius). Without attempting to give a thorough update (my book has to remain as it was when it was written), I mention some important work that has appeared in the meantime, beginning with the continuation of the impressive *Philological and Historical Commentary on Ammianus Marcellinus*, edited by J. den Boeft, J. W. Drijvers, D. den Hengst and H. C. Teitler, of which the latest volume to be published covers Book 25 and is therefore of special interest, this being the last book of Ammianus' history largely devoted to the emperor Julian (Leiden & Boston, 2005; Book 26 follows shortly). In the meantime, the Budé edition of Ammianus has been brought to a splendid conclusion by G. Sabbah, with Books 29-31 (Vol. 6, 1999). In addition to his survey, *The Historians of Late Antiquity* (London, 2003), David Rohrbacher has published a study of 'The Sources for the lost books of Ammianus Marcellinus', *Historia* 55 (2006), 106-24, which gives some idea of what those books would actually have looked like, and there are excellent comments on Ammianus as part of the classical historiographical tradition in John Marincola, *Authority and Tradition in Ancient Historiography* (Cambridge, 1997), and a fine introduction by Sabbah, in G. Marasco (ed.), *Greek and Roman Historiography in Late Antiquity: fourth to sixth century A.D.* (Leiden,

2003), 43-94. I advanced more fully the arguments for Ammianus' Antiochene origin in 'The Origin of Ammianus', *CQ*, n.s. 44 (1994), 252-269, and said a little on a topic in which my interest has grown in recent years, in 'Ammianus on Roman law and lawyers' in den Boeft, den Hengst and Teitler (edd.), *Cognitio Gestorum: the Historiographic Art of Ammianus Marcellinus* (Amsterdam, 1992), 47-57. The newest treatment of Ammianus in his literary dimension is Gavin Kelly, *Ammianus Marcellinus: the Allusive Historian* (Cambridge, 2008), following his fine article, 'Ammianus and the Great Tsunami', *JRS* 94 (2004), 141-67; while given my own present interests, I would have been especially interested (for Chapter XV) in his 'The new Rome and the old; Ammianus Marcellinus' silences on Constantinople', *CQ*, n.s. 53 (2003), 588-607. Without changing my basic position on Ammianus' relations with earlier literature, I would have been happy to give weight to the arguments of Charles Fornara, 'Ammianus' knowledge and use of Greek and Latin literature', *Historia* 41 (1992), 420-37, and, in an area where many different points of emphasis are possible, those of F. Paschoud, '"Se non è vero, è ben trovato": tradition littéraire et vérité historique chez Ammien Marcellin', *Chiron* 19 (1989), 37-54.

Many criticisms of the book, combined with what in my view are unsupported assertions of alternative positions (for example that the extant books are misnumbered in the manuscripts and by Priscian and should run from 19 to 36, with 1-18 lost, that Ammianus came from Tyre or Sidon, and that he was an apostate from Christianity), are offered by T. D. Barnes, *Ammianus Marcellinus and the Representation of Historical Reality* (Ithaca, 1998). One can safely say of this book that it offers a choice of approaches, but I must restate a view expressed more than once in *The Roman Empire of Ammianus*, that factual description and rhetoric are not clearly separable features of Ammianus' writing. The issue, and what makes it interesting, is how the one is deployed in relation to the other. A feature of Ammianus' style, which he can use to stunning effect, is the way in which he can shift from a rhetorically framed narrative to a moment of personal experience, or a personal observation that gains all the more power from its rhetorical setting.

Among books on the period covered by Ammianus that bear significantly on the historian, especially notable are Peter Heather's *Goths and Romans, 332-489* (Oxford, 1991) and his later writings on the barbarians, Noel Lenski's *Failure of Empire: Valens and the Roman State in the Fourth Century A.D.* (Berkeley and Los Angeles, 2002), R. Malcolm Errington's *Roman Imperial Policy from Julian to Theodosius* (Chapel Hill, 2006) and of general works, on a grand and richly detailed scale that Ammianus would have appreciated, David Potter's *The Roman Empire at Bay, A.D. 180-395* (London, 2004).

This reprint of *The Roman Empire of Ammianus* is unchanged from the first edition except for the correction of a few specific errors of which I became aware or which were pointed out to me. T. D. Barnes noted that the date of the death of Constantius II was on November 3rd 360, not October 5th, as Ammianus and I said (p. 101, cf.

Preface

21.15.3 'tertium nonarum Octobrium' MSS; Seeck emended the text to give the correct date, but it would be better to leave it as an error of Ammianus'). More conspicuous, at least in its location in the book, is my description of Ephraim of Nisibis as a priest. I have made an appropriate correction, which again I owe to a remark of T. D. Barnes, and in doing so cannot resist observing that he and I share a rare distinction, of having made a mistake at the very beginning of a book. It is indeed impossible to check everything. The exposure of a book to possible error grows by the square of what it attempts to cover, and the reader may decide whether it more serious to think that Ephraim was a priest (in fact, just a deacon), or that the city of Naissus was on the Danube. For some other corrections, and advice on later bibliography and for lively conversations about Ammianus and other late Roman topics, I thank Gavin Kelly, whose new book is referred to above.

In order not to remind them, or myself, of the passage of time (in fact I am saddened to see the number of them who are no longer living), I will not repeat the many individual acknowledgments that I offered in my original Preface. The debts are real all the same, and I am honoured to acknowledge them collectively, adding the names of the graduate students, now young colleagues and friends, whose work has invigorated mine and whose own publications are already making their mark: from Yale, Joel Allen, Serena Connolly, Kimberly Kagan, Joshua Levithan, Scott McGill, Josiah Osgood, Cristiana Sogno and Edward Watts; still from Oxford days, Neil McLynn and Mark Vessey; and, for his constant inspiration, energy and exuberance, David Potter. As always, my debt and sense of gratitude to my wife Veronika Grimm are immeasurable. For some time this book has been hard to find and very expensive, and I am especially grateful to Ellen Bauerle and Michigan Classical Press for undertaking the reprint.

October 2007

John Matthews
Department of Classics
Yale University

Illustrations

Maps

1.	The Roman East	42
2.	The city of Antioch	73
3.	Julian in Gaul, 356-60	82
4.	Seleucia and Ctesiphon	142
5.	Julian in Mesopotamia	150
6.	The territory of the Alamanni	307
7.	Gothia and the Roman Danube	319
8.	Isauria and its neighbours	356

Figures

1.	The Emperor Constantius	232
2.	The Face of Battle (1)	289
3.	The Face of Battle (2)	292
4.	Herding and hunting in southern Russia	338-9

Chart

The rise of Julian, 359-62   102-3

Part One
Res Gestae

CHAPTER I

Introduction

I went and came, my brethren, to the bier of the defiled one
and I stood over it and I derided his paganism.
I said, Is this he who exalted himself
against the living name and forgot that he is dust?

For a time in the high summer of 363 a Christian cleric, Ephraim of Nisibis, could look down from the walls of his ancient city to see an army encamped on the plains below.[1] For inhabitants of the cities of northern Mesopotamia it was not an unfamiliar sight, often repeated during a quarter-century of active warfare between the eastern and western powers that disputed their territories, as they and their predecessors had disputed them since time immemorial. Roman armies advanced by these cities to engage the Persians in the north-eastern corner of Mesopotamia that was their regular theatre of conflict, or to repel Persian invasion directed across the Tigris to strike at the Roman cities of Osrhoene and Syria. Persian armies, their progress measured by the fires which marked the advance of raiding parties, were viewed with sombre anxiety by the inhabitants of the cities, as they wondered for how long their defences would sustain a siege, speculated how soon a Roman field army might arrive to relieve them, or watched them pass on their way for some other immediate object of hostilities. In a recent invasion in 359, the Persian king Sapor II had passed by Nisibis without attacking it, as he made for Amida to the north-west, captured and sacked after a siege of seventy-three days and the loss, it was said, of thirty thousand Persian fighting men. Between the death of Constantine the Great in 337 and 350, Nisibis had been besieged no less than three times, the river Mygdonius (the Oued Jaghjagha) being on the third of these occasions diverted by massive earthworks and dykes to form a lake around the city in order to undermine the city walls and expose them to attack. These events too were described, with much vivid circumstantial as well as rhetorical detail, in the hymns of Ephraim — waters lapping round the city as it stood there like a beleaguered Noah's Ark, the sudden collapse of dykes, the breaching by the floodwaters and the repair overnight of a section of the city walls, Persian elephants sinking in the mud, Sapor leaving disconsolate after his third unsuccessful attempt to take the city.[2]

Now, in 363, circumstances were different. The army outside Nisibis was the Roman army of the Emperor Julian, not advancing on Persia but already defeated there and now pausing in its retreat, safe on what was still for the moment Roman soil. Julian himself had been killed in a skirmish, after turning back from the Persian capital of Ctesiphon unable to attempt its siege. In the fields of Nisibis, Ephraim could stand by the emperor's hearse, escorted back to Roman territory by his army in a sort of bizarre parody of a funeral procession. Julian's death had left his hastily chosen successor, Jovian, in the position of having to treat for terms in order to secure the safe departure of the harried Roman army from Persian territory. The Persians had seized their opportunity, demanding the cession of a large tract of northern Mesopotamia, including the cities of Singara and Nisibis itself, all the fortified sites in the region and five satrapies, or semi-independent principalities, along the upper Tigris. Observing the strict letter of his agreement, Jovian refused to allow his men to enter Nisibis, but kept them encamped outside, in spite of the pleas of the inhabitants that they should not be unprotected. Their resentment burst out in the retort of an envoy who came from the city to present to Jovian the 'crown gold' due to an emperor on his accession – a normal civic duty, which in the circumstances had acquired an only too obvious irony: 'And so, emperor,' said the envoy, a leading citizen of Nisibis, 'may you be crowned by the other cities of your empire!' His anger is not surprising, for a Persian commander and garrison arrived to take possession of Nisibis, which was to be handed over empty. Its people were evacuated, to be re-resettled in other Roman cities (Ephraim went to the famous Christian city of Edessa), and the Persian standard was run up on the citadel:[3]

> the banner which was sent from the East wind
> the Magian took and fastened on the tower
> so that a flag might point out for spectators
> that the city was the slave of the Lords of that banner.

It was a pitiful scene, as weeping families were parted from their homes with whatever they could carry, and for the Roman government a moment of humiliation not endured in living memory.

Somewhere in the midst of that army which Ephraim viewed from his city walls and walked among was a young officer from Syrian Antioch, who after service in both east and west had joined the Persian campaign of Julian, witnessed its failure and shared the painful retreat across the desert. In the magnificent history which he brought to completion at Rome a quarter of a century later, Ammianus Marcellinus described his and the army's experiences, presenting the surrender of Nisibis – Persian flag and all – in language as intensely emotional within its own conventions as that of Ephraim, and sparing no words of condemnation for the emperor whom he considered responsible for it.[4] On this point Ammianus differed sharply from his Christian counterpart. Against all reason and justice, he attributed to Jovian's action in treating with the Persians the blame surely more properly deserved by the emperor whose overwrought ambition and impulsive death had made acceptance of their terms inevitable. The extent of Ammianus' misjudgment will become clearer when these events are discussed later in this book (Chapter IX). We can understand, however, why Ammianus, and others of his mind, viewed the situation as they did. For them, much more was at stake than the acceptance of military defeat. The death of Julian was nothing less than the death of their hero, and a fatal blow to their hopes that the Roman empire might be renewed upon the principles of an earlier age. Turning from the Christian religion of the house of Constantine in which he had been brought up, and espousing the cause of the ancestral gods, Julian had thrown the energies of his short reign into the restoration, by legislation, inducements and personal example, of the traditional civic, religious and cultural practices of the Roman empire. How far he might have succeeded had he lived longer is a question which fascinates historians – and rightly, for it exposes deeper questions about late Roman society and the nature of its acceptance of Christianity. In the summer of 363, however, the question would have seemed bitterly ironic. The failure of the Persian campaign and the death of Julian meant the end of his attempt to restore the traditional religion, as surely as they meant the end of his attempt to restore the traditional military practices of the Roman empire in its confrontations with its ancestral enemy.

If he were to be successful, Julian should have returned to the Roman empire with the title 'Conqueror of Persia' (*Parthicus*) to which he aspired, and the prestige of a great foreign victory to put behind his religious and cultural policies. But the fates were not in his favour. The emperor lay dead under the Mesopotamian sky whose omens against the campaign he had ignored, and had been succeeded by a Christian emperor. After Jovian (who died the next year), the brothers Valentinian and Valens, then Valentinian's son Gratian, and particularly Theodosius I, made emperor after the death of Valens at the battle of Hadrianople in 378, brought with them a further generation's government in favour, and ultimately in aggressive support, of Christianity. These same years saw Ammianus himself progress from his vigorous youth of the time of the Persian campaign, to late middle and early old age. To Ammianus at sixty, looking back in his imagination from late fourth-century Rome to Mesopotamia, across a generation of Christian government to a pagan emperor, the death of Julian and the scenes before Nisibis must have seemed very distant. It would be surprising if he had viewed these events with an unchanging eye, or if his reactions had remained fixed and unaltered as the person and reign of Julian receded ever further into the past, behind another twenty-five years' tumultuous political events and further entrenchment of the Christian order.

The evolution of Ammianus' personal attitudes over these years is as fundamental an aspect of his interpretation as a historian, as it must remain in all but the most hesitant terms beyond the reach of his reader. This is not because Ammianus is an evasive writer. He is in many respects the most self-revealing of ancient historians, as he describes in great detail his role during his active years both in east and west, and alludes from time to time to his later travels in the time between his departure from the army in 363 and his arrival at Rome about twenty years later. He is by no means sparing of his personal reactions to the events and situations which he describes, and he expresses his moral and political views with force, sometimes with prejudice and not always consistently. He allows the time and place of his writing to appear quite precisely, and he says much – little of it favourable – about the nature of the society in which, as a late arrival at Rome, he found himself. Indeed, the prominence that Ammianus allows himself as a participant in his own history is one of its most interesting features. It is important too in defining the historiographical tradition in which he is best understood, and in answering the question why he turned to the writing of history. Yet for all this, little is known of the precise milieu in which Ammianus – the historian, not the military officer – moved. He remains obstinately unattached. He does not belong to any particular intellectual or social circle of which we know, nor, with a single exception discussed below, does any other writer mention or address him by name.[5] Any literary influence exerted by Ammianus on other writers of the age is extremely difficult to establish. On the best possible showing, it is severely limited, and involves an author and a work of which Ammianus himself would not have approved, namely the collection of second- and third-century imperial biographies, mixed in value and obscure in intention, known as the *Historia Augusta*.[6] Later, Ammianus is cited by the grammarian Priscian, writing in the early sixth century at the eastern capital of Constantinople. Interest among eastern literary circles in the last great Latin historian of the Roman empire is not surprising in that period, when Constantinople was full of western emigrés and others with an interest in Latin literature, and Latin itself still had an important role, at least as a ceremonial and official language, at the imperial court; but that Priscian's citation, on a not uncommon point of orthographic interest, is chosen from Book 14 of the history of Ammianus has long been taken to suggest that this was already in his day the first book available to him.[7] The oldest manuscript of Ammianus is a ninth-century text originally from the monastery of Fulda in Germany, copied from a slightly earlier manuscript from Hersfeld, of which only six leaves now survive. If this is a tradition of descent independent of that known to Priscian, then the loss here too of the first thirteen books would indicate that the history was already incomplete when it was transmitted to Constantinople at some time in the fifth or early sixth century. The situation does not suggest that Ammianus, for all his apparent contemporary success, retained a wide readership, even in the generations immediately after his own day.[8] We note with frustration the manuscripts, numbered in hundreds, of the fifth-century Christian apologetic historian Orosius, of which a round twenty precede the tenth century – such representation of a writer whose qualities as a historian, when compared with those of Ammianus (and even when not compared with them), are an embarrassment to the profession.

Much can be learned of Ammianus from his own writing, and from the study of the political, social and geographical milieux in which he moved, and this book is concerned as much with the Roman empire of his day, as Ammianus saw it, as with the historian himself. But it is right to begin with the single item of direct external evidence for the life and work of Ammianus himself. This will take us at once to the time and place at which the history was nearing completion, the city of Rome in the time of Theodosius, around the year 390. Ammianus is looking back at the reign of Julian and his own active career at a distance of more than twenty-five years since that dreadful day at Nisibis, and more than thirty-five since his first appearance as a participant in his history. It is between these poles of attraction that Ammianus' interpreter must be prepared to move in his imagination – between his career as a young man and the recollections of the retired soldier, between the Middle East in which most of this active career was pursued and the ancient capital of the Roman empire in which he determined to settle in order to complete his history and, not least important, between the Greek language of his eastern background and the Latin in which he chose to write. The reader of this book should try to bear all these aspects in mind. Of all ancient historians, Ammianus deserves to be treated, not as the unreflecting spokesman of set ideas, to be neatly encapsulated by bland statements about social class and upbringing, but as the living product of tensions of time, place and memory.

CHAPTER II

Ammianus and his History

(1) The political setting

For a man to visit Rome and live there quietly, attending its famous teachers and admiring their eloquence, is an enviable privilege. That such a man should undertake literary composition, offer it to the public of that incomparable city and be acclaimed the equal or superior of the great writers of the past – this puts Rome herself in his debt and enhances the honour both of the visitor and of his own city and compatriots. For it is the mark of a distinguished citizen to glorify by his achievements the place from which he comes.

Around such sentiments did the late Roman literary world revolve. They came in this instance from the aged sophist, Libanius of Antioch, as he wrote to a fellow-citizen who was winning just such a reputation at Rome by giving readings from his newly-composed historical work.[1] Libanius' letter was written late in the year 392, and the name of the successful historian from Antioch was Marcellinus. The identity of Libanius' correspondent as Ammianus Marcellinus is inescapable, and the letter makes it possible to reconstruct in some detail the political and social setting in which Ammianus' work was nearing completion.

Libanius mentioned in his letter that he had been told of his compatriot's fame by men returning to Antioch from Rome, an apparently casual remark that could turn out more helpful than it seems. In the summer of the previous year, the Emperor Theodosius, after suppressing rebellion in the west and restoring legitimate power there, had brought his army and court back to the eastern empire. On 19 June 391 the emperor was still at Aquileia in north Italy, ready for his journey through the Balkans to Constantinople, but by 18 July he had already reached the eastern capital of the Roman empire.[2] From here, his supporters would over the next months scatter farther afield, pursuing their various employments and interests in the eastern provinces. There were no doubt other visitors from Antioch to Rome in these years, who might upon their return have brought back news of a fellow-citizen there. Other reasons for a visit can easily be imagined, and some are known; on one occasion for instance, just a few years later, a delegation of city councillors from Antioch passed through Rome on its way to Spain, to acquire horses to show at public games in their city (Symmachus, *Ep.* 4.62). But if Libanius' informants had after all returned with the emperor from the

II. Ammianus and his History

campaign in the west, they would have been able to bring news to Antioch in the course of 392. The historical readings of which they informed Libanius will in this case have taken place not actually in 392, but earlier. They could be ascribed to the more general setting of the presence of Theodosius and his court in the west, which had lasted for almost three years from the late summer of 388. It is natural to think of the emperor's official visit to Rome in June 389 and to locate Ammianus' readings in that year or the next, when the court, as other sources such as the letters of Symmachus show, was in constant and close contact with Rome. Ammianus sometimes affected a certain modesty about his achievement as a historian, but he would not have persisted in such work without confidence in his abilities. Nor do historians write without any conception of their possible public, and Ammianus would have shown a distinct lack of opportunism if he had failed to exploit the presence of Theodosius and his courtiers to bid for the audience which they offered for the first major history of Rome to appear in Latin for nearly three hundred years. Senators, on Ammianus' own account, lacked interest in such things, and it may be that visiting imperial courtiers offered the prospect of a more receptive and more open-minded audience: possibly Ammianus put on his readings with them in mind rather than the parochial, ill-educated senators – though not all were like this – whom he so effectively exposed in his digressions on Rome.[3]

On any account, Ammianus was living at Rome, to adapt one of his own metaphors, during a period of rapidly turning fortunes.[4] The usurper Maximus, proclaimed in Britain in the summer of 383, had crossed the Channel and put an end to the young emperor Gratian. Settling at Trier, Maximus had opened diplomatic relations with an imperial court at Milan headed nominally by the even younger Valentinian II, and with his colleague Theodosius at Constantinople. He hoped, with some reason based on their previous acquaintance and military service together, and perhaps also their common Spanish origin, to win Theodosius' acceptance, but with only transient success. After a moment of recognition in 386, by summer 387 diplomatic relations between the usurping and legitimate regimes had collapsed. Valentinian abandoned Italy to Maximus, and went to Thessalonica to meet Theodosius and, with the help of a dynastic marriage to his sister Galla, secure his help. By the following year Theodosius was ready to undertake the campaign to the west. Once Theodosius had moved against him, Maximus offered little resistance. After two military setbacks, he was surrendered by his own men to Theodosius and executed at Aquileia (28 August 388). Theodosius pressed on to Milan and was established there by 10 October, sufficiently confident to extend clemency to those who, from bad luck or judgment, had opposed him.[5] Among those forgiven for their indiscretion was the leading orator and Roman senator of the day, Q. Aurelius Symmachus, who had acted as senatorial envoy to Maximus' court and there delivered a panegyric. An emperor should know the difference between active support of a usurper and the satisfaction of ceremonial requirements such as the delivery of official orations; but there were certain appearances to be kept up, and Symmachus had to excuse himself for his panegyric to Maximus before receiving Theodosius' pardon (Symmachus, *Epp.* 2.30-1). If, as one writer claimed, Symmachus had been obliged to seek asylum in a church of schismatic Christians and owed his pardon to their bishop's intervention before Theodosius, this would have doubled the embarrassment of one who was not only the leading senator of his day, but, since his unsuccessful petition of 384 for the restoration of the altar of Victory to the senate-house, the most prominent spokesman for the ancestral religion. But the unsupported word of an ecclesiastical writer on such a matter cannot be taken as authoritative.[6] Symmachus' restoration to favour, and the consulship which he held in 391, are more convincingly put down to the influence of a powerful friend at the imperial court – Virius Nicomachus Flavianus, the emperor's quaestor and praetorian prefect, and himself some sort of historian. He was the author of a work entitled 'Annales', which he consented at the emperor's request to dedicate to Theodosius. Unfortunately the content and quality of these Annales are unknown, and their relevance to Ammianus Marcellinus is at best insubstantial. Theodosius is reported to have liked history, particularly that of great figures of the Roman Republic (*Epit. de Caes.* 48.11f.); perhaps it was to these, rather than to contemporary history, that Flavianus' work was devoted. He and his friends, including Symmachus, are known for their work as editors of Livy, especially the earlier books of that voluminous author.[7]

All these events fell beyond the terminal point of Ammianus Marcellinus' history, and he had nothing to say of them. Nor, for whatever reason, did he find occasion to mention Symmachus. This is interesting, for the orator's father does figure occasionally in events described by Ammianus, and it would not have been impossible, had Ammianus felt obliged to him, to have contrived a reference to the younger and more famous man; Q. Aurelius Symmachus had been senatorial legate to the court of Valentinian in 369-70, and proconsul of Africa in 373.[8] Ammianus did, however, take note of another supporter of Maximus, his prefect of Rome Julianus Rusticus. Rusticus had made a brief appearance in Ammianus' history in events of the year 367, when he was the favoured candidate of a group of Gallic officials at the court of Valentinian I in the event (as seemed quite likely at the time) that the emperor should die (27.6.1f.). In later years, wrote Ammianus in that context, Rusticus governed Africa – he was Symmachus' predecessor as proconsul – with savage violence: a facet of his temper which he was obliged to suppress as prefect of Rome through fear of the 'tyrant' under whose uncertain regime he held the office. The 'tyrant' was Magnus Maximus, and Rusticus' prefecture of Rome, during the tenure of which he died, can be placed in 387/8. He had risen to these heights, pronounced Ammianus, in the absence of worthy candidates.[9]

Ammianus was living at Rome during Julianus Rusticus' prefecture of the city, and knew what (and whom) he was writing about. It was by no

II. Ammianus and his History

means the only occasion on which he briefly mentioned the later careers of personalities who occurred in his narrative – no doubt (in most cases) for their own satisfaction, and for the benefit of those to whom they were known at Ammianus' time of writing; perhaps, also, because he happened to know them himself. Whatever the reason, these allusions, as we shall see in the second part of this chapter, are helpful to the reader of Ammianus in providing points of reference for the period of time between the latest events described in the history, in summer 378, and its publication about twelve years later.

Ammianus was at Rome, also, for another, more auspicious occasion in these highly eventful years. On 13 June 389 Theodosius himself entered Rome to celebrate his victory over Maximus, on one of those, now rare, occasions on which the ancient capital received its emperor in a personal visit. A panegyrist from southern Gaul, Pacatus, evoked the setting in a speech delivered before senate and emperor, recalling some of the most striking moments (*Paneg. Lat.* 12, ed. Galletier): the emperor's reception by senate and people, his conduct at ceremonial processions, his visits to the great monuments of Rome and to the private residences of senators.[10] It is an attractive notion that one of Ammianus' most famous pieces of writing reached its final version with Theodosius' State Visit in mind: this is his description of the triumphal entrance to Rome of the Emperor Constantius more than thirty years before, in 357 (16.10.1ff.) Constantius' procession, like that of Theodosius, came into Rome along the Via Flaminia as if lined up in battle array, along roads crowded with people who had come from all parts to see the display. The emperor sat motionless as a statue, moving his face neither to right nor left, not spitting nor wiping the sweat off his face or nose (he must have been incredibly hot in his ceremonial regalia), nor even allowing his head to shake when his carriage jolted on the road. Around him were the ranks of imperial household troops, their figured standards billowing in the breeze – or, as Ammianus wrote with a brilliant touch of imagery that will be pursued later, 'hissing' like the dragons whose images appeared on them.[11] Acclamations swelled and echoed all around, before which Constantius showed himself majestically imperturbable.

There is no need to assume that Ammianus was here deliberately and in direct fashion referring to the entry to Rome of Theodosius in 389. He included such criticisms of Constantius' conduct as could hardly have been made so directly of Theodosius. Moreover, the language and the actual forms of ceremony are by their nature conventional and apt for repetition. Ammianus, who in his life had seen many an imperial 'adventus', could have composed his account of Constantius' visit some years before that of Theodosius took place. Yet if he were giving readings from his work in or soon after 389, it would be perverse to deny the impact of this passage in relation to the more recent visit. In reading Ammianus' account of Constantius' reaction to the public monuments of Rome, we may even have a glimpse of Ammianus' own sentiments, as he first set eyes on the wonders of the city which, for his later years, he made his own. Wherever Constantius looked, he saw a wonder to surpass the last, his amazement conveyed by Ammianus by hyperbole piled on hyperbole to a point touching the absurd: the temple of Capitoline Jupiter, superior in magnificence as divine things are to human; baths as big as provinces; the Colosseum, its summit scarcely visible, so high it was; the Pantheon, like a lofty, rounded city district in its own right; the columns of Trajan and his successors, with imperial statues surmounting them and spiral staircases inside, leading to platforms from which one could view the city. Most impressive of all was the Forum of Trajan, a work (wrote Ammianus) unique in the world, never to be surpassed by the hands of men, a marvel even to the gods (16.10.15). Constantius' declaration that if he could not rival the Forum he might erect there an equestrian statue of himself to match that of Trajan, was countered by an associate, the Persian exile Hormisdas, with a suitably clever remark − or perhaps it is just *ben trovato* for this wily Oriental: the emperor should first order to be built a stable to compare with this − if he had the power.[12] The horse that he had it in mind to make might then range as widely as the one he saw (16.10.16)! In the end, Constantius was content, after long deliberation, with the raising of an obelisk, the description of which Ammianus deferred to its proper place in his text (17.4.12-23). In all this, Ammianus is clearly looking beyond the factual circumstances of Constantius' visit, to give an image of Rome such as would impress itself on any observer.

What must be appreciated from the outset is the depth of penetration of the ideals of Rome into the mental outlook of this Greek from Antioch. Not that the present realities of the city matched the ideals. About to embark, in a passage near the beginning of the surviving part of the history, on a scathing description of the manners of the nobility and people of Rome, Ammianus invited his readers to consider why it should be that whenever his narrative turned to Rome, there was nothing to tell but of 'riots, drunkenness and other such common matters' (14.6.2). In Ammianus' view, this was the contribution of a frivolous minority to the life of a city, whose incomparable greatness was enshrined in its history and institutions. It is particularly notable that Ammianus puts himself forward at this moment as one writing for outsiders. He addressed his remarks to such foreigners ('peregrini') as he might be lucky enough to have as the readers of his book; 'mirari posse quosdam peregrinos existimo haec lecturos forsitan, (si contigerit)...' (14.6.2).

It is beyond belief that Ammianus could write like this without recalling his own position as a foreign visitor to Rome. He touched on the experience of a newcomer to the city only a few sentences later in his digression, in which he reflected on the reception of such a stranger as he first approaches the houses of the great men of Rome. You are then greeted with such an amazing display of concern, he wrote, 'that you regret not coming to Rome ten years before'; 'miraberis ... summatem virum tenuem te sic enixius observantem, ut paeniteat ob haec bona tamquam praecipua non vidisse ante decennium Romam' (14.6.12). This interest is however not repeated at later visits, when you are likely to be

II. Ammianus and his History

treated as a total stranger or, if ultimately invited to dinner, find yourself placed at table below gamblers, charioteers and fortune-tellers (6.14). The air of grievance in this passage may be deceptive, for it is influenced by an old tradition of satire on the moral unworthiness of the great and their failure to recognise honest virtue. More revealing may be the informality of the address in the second person, with its invitation to the reader to imagine himself in the situation pictured by Ammianus. Had not Ammianus himself once regretted 'not coming to Rome ten years before', only to find his initial reception not borne out by the outcome?

Pursuing the same theme, Ammianus recalled the occasion when, at a time of a severe food shortage, foreign visitors had been expelled from Rome, including those men (and they were few enough) who were there for the pursuit of liberal arts. At the same time, attendants of mime actresses and any who could masquerade as such were kept in the city, together with three thousand dancing girls with their trainers and supporting troupes. Allowance must again be made for some rhetorical exaggeration, but this does not weaken the force of Ammianus' remark that the event in question had taken place 'not so very long ago'; 'haud ita dudum' (14.6.19). The famine, and the expulsion of visitors which it occasioned, were well-known events, mentioned by other writers, and appear to have taken place in 383 or, perhaps better, 384.[13] Symmachus regretted the necessity of the expulsion in a letter dated to one of these two years (*Ep.* 2.7). Ammianus, as a visitor to Rome and as a student of the liberal arts, fell on both counts within the categories of those whom he said were expelled at that time. To explore the suspicion that he was himself among those made to leave the city, we must turn back to an earlier phase in the historian's career, and in particular to his movements since his retirement from active military service some twenty years before his arrival at Rome.

*

In the summer of 363 the broken army of Julian had endured its retreat from Persian territory to the safety of the Roman empire. After the traumatic surrender of Nisibis, Ammianus returned with Jovian to Antioch, marking his arrival with an account of the portents seen there (25.10.1ff.); but when, in mid-winter, Jovian pressed on towards Constantinople (10.4ff.), Ammianus seems not to have been with the army but to have stayed behind at Antioch. The use of the first person with which he marked his arrival there ('Antiochiam venimus', 10.1) does not recur in the succeeding narrative.

For the next two decades, Ammianus was able to travel, to explore, to seek out witnesses of events whose testimony he would add to his own experiences in order to write a history of his times. As he explained in the preface to Book 15, he recorded as faithfully as possible what he was old enough to have witnessed himself and what he could learn by the close questioning of participants in events.[14] Ammianus' movements in these years can be picked out only intermittently, from allusions inserted from time to time into his narrative. He had been to Greece, or at least to the Peloponnese, for he had seen at Mothone in Laconia the wreck of a ship cast two miles inland by the tidal wave caused by a major earthquake in 365. Ammianus had seen the stranded vessel while 'passing through' ('transeundo') on a journey, its hulk gaping apart from long decay; 'diuturna carie fatiscentem' (26.10.19). At Alexandria, the same disaster had landed ships on the roofs of houses; although Ammianus did not specifically say so, there is no reason to doubt that he had been told of or seen this phenomenon during a visit there. He described Alexandria in a long digression, with particular attention to its great temple, the Serapeum, and to the intellectual life, especially in medical studies, which still flourished there (22.16.7ff.). In all likelihood, Ammianus passed by Alexandria in order to gain access to the upper Nile. He introduced a digression on Egypt by referring back to previous discussions, in the lost books, in which he had described at length many things he had seen there; 'quarum notitiam ... digessimus late, visa pleraque narrantes' (22.15.1).[15] He observed that the temples and pyramids were among many things 'worth seeing' in Egypt (22.15.28), and in the city of Thebes, he recalled having seen obelisks standing and lying around, complete with hieroglyph inscriptions (17.4.6). Later, after an engaging digression on the cunning of the hippopotamus, he reported a speculation of the inhabitants of the region as to where these beasts had disappeared to; they had fled to the land of the Blemmyes, through weariness at being hunted (22.15.24). Ammianus was writing now of the regions around Memphis; it is difficult to imagine a better source for this speculation than the local inhabitants themselves. In such passages, Ammianus stands square as a Greek historian in the tradition of Herodotus – whom he names in this very context (22.15.28); travelling widely, curious in everything he sees, eager for information about it.[16]

Ammianus at some time visited the Black Sea. Introducing a digression on the regions of Pontus and Thrace, he wrote that he would set down accurately what he had seen and read of them, 'visa vel lecta quaedam' (22.8.1). The digression, like others, bears more traces of what Ammianus had read than of what he had seen;[17] but one wonders whether he had himself set eyes on one of the sights of the Pontus, the Symplegades, or 'Clashing Rocks', of the legend of the Argonauts. Since the Argo had passed through the rocks, they had stood motionless and united, their force spent, so that, unless the ancient poets had agreed on the story, no one who now looked at them would believe that they had ever been separated; 'eos aliquando fuisse diremptos *nulli nunc conspicantium* credant, nisi super hoc congruerent omnes priscorum carminum cantus' (22.8.15). Ammianus is not here being ironic or having a joke: it is rather that, for events of legendary times, poets were, after all, the proper authority.

What cannot be determined is the date of these various visits, their relationship to each other, or the nature of the larger journeys of which they may have formed part. The 'passing visit' to Laconia will have fallen several years after 365 – but where was Ammianus travelling to when he saw it? and how long does it take for a stranded ship to decay and fall apart? It is clear in any event that Ammianus was in his home city of Antioch in and shortly after 370. He described in dark colours prosecutions of Antiochene notables on charges of magic and treason. The charges arose from a curious affair in which some men had used magic spells to tell the future, and had turned up the first part of the name of a threatened successor to Valens. The letters revealed to them seemed sufficient to identify a Gallic secretary named Theodorus, then working at Antioch.[18] Theodorus was unfortunate enough also to possess links with Julian the Apostate, and in consequence the prosecutions took on the character of a witch-hunt of literary men and philosophers, some of whom had been connected with Julian. In the panic, men destroyed their libraries to avoid the suspicion of possessing books on magic; and in the same passage Ammianus spoke of himself and his fellow Antiochenes as 'creeping around in deathly gloom' while the emperor and his associates used the courts of law to grab men's fortunes and satisfy personal grudges (29.2.4). Among those in danger was a man described by Ammianus as 'our' Hypatius, an individual of calm and noble virtues, who brought credit to his ancestry and to his descendants by his conduct of two prefectures (29.3.16). Hypatius was prefect of Rome in 379, being summoned from Antioch to hold the office, and praetorian prefect of Italy in 382-3.[19] In describing him as 'our' Hypatius, Ammianus was associating himself with the dangers suffered by his Antiochene compatriot, and claiming for his city some of the credit won by his later distinction – much as Libanius laid claim to a share in Ammianus' reputation, won at Rome by the recitation of his history.

It is likely also that Ammianus was at Antioch during the last years of the reign of Valens, when the Goths, pressed on by the Huns and Alans, came up against the Danube frontier of the Roman empire and were permitted to cross it by the emperor. At the battle of Hadrianople, with which this phase culminated (9 August 378), only a third of the Roman army survived the encounter with the Goths. Many generals and officers were killed and the emperor himself disappeared from sight, presumed dead. Ammianus had remarked that the dangers in the remoter Danubian regions tended to be dismissed by the Roman government; because of the distances involved, they were not usually heard of until after they were suppressed, or at least subdued for a time (31.4.3). He might have pondered on this with particular irony when he reflected on the Gothic admission to the Roman empire, for at that moment the emperor was very far indeed from the spot – precisely, in Ammianus' own city of Antioch, at a time when the more pressing danger for the empire seemed to come from Persia. It was only when it had become clear that the crossing of the Danube had gone wrong that Valens came to an arrangement with the Persians over Armenia and left for Constantinople and Thrace.

The episode with which Ammianus actually concluded his history was indeed very close to home. The *magister militum* in the east, Julius, issued orders that the Goths already in service with the Roman armies should be assembled in the suburbs of the cities where they were stationed, in the expectation that they were to receive arrears of pay. The 'wisdom' of Julius' plan was revealed when the Goths, once so assembled, were massacred to a man. The risk that they might join forces with their compatriots victorious at Hadrianople was averted, and the eastern provinces were 'saved from great dangers'; 'orientales provinciae discriminibus ereptae sunt magnis'. These are the very last words of Ammianus' historical narrative.[20] In describing Julius as 'magister militiae *trans* Taurum', Ammianus places himself to the west of that mountain barrier between Roman Asia and the Orient, but this is a facet of the literary perspective of his text.[21] In terms of contemporary experience, the relevance of Julius and his action to the historian's city and region takes on a rather different aspect. Julius is otherwise attested at Antioch (in the writings of Libanius) and active, through the work of a subordinate, in the province of Arabia (*ILS* 773). For Ammianus, it is more or less local history.

Ammianus' attitudes to the disaster of Hadrianople and to the prospects of Roman recovery after it, are not a matter for discussion now, save in one respect. He was composing his history in the time of an emperor, Theodosius, whom he described on an appearance as a young general in the province of Moesia as 'later a most distinguished *princeps*' (29.6.15). Theodosius was raised to the throne in January 379 to repair the catastrophe of Hadrianople. After three years' campaigning, of which only the most fragmentary outlines are discernible, he made an alliance with the Goths, by which they were settled in certain areas of the lower Danubian provinces, with military obligations to the Roman government. The agreement was finalised in early October of 382; before that, on 11 January 381, Theodosius had gained much good will among the Goths by receiving their king Athanaric with honour at Constantinople.[22] When Athanaric died after a fortnight, the emperor buried his guest with full honours. Ammianus mentioned the burial of Athanaric early in 381 'with splendid pomp, in the Roman style' – 'ambitiosis exsequiis, ritu ... nostro' – in the context of Athanaric's first encounter with Valens in the Gothic campaign of 367 (27.5.10). He will have derived his knowledge of the occasion, which fell outside the narrative scope of his history, from those 'participants in events' whom he mentioned in his preface to Book 15 – if indeed he was not himself at Constantinople in 381 to witness the funeral of Athanaric.

Whether or not Ammianus was at Constantinople at this time, it is likely that he was still in the east. He may possibly, though it is not a necessary inference, have visited Thrace and seen one of the battlefields of the terrible years 376-8. From the battle, near the town of Ad Salices by the Danube delta, Romans and Goths had parted on level terms after heavy bloodshed. Those of the dead who were of any distinction were properly buried, as well as circumstances allowed. The rest were left where they had fallen, to be devoured by the vultures – as was shown 'to the present day' by the piles of bones whitening the field; 'ut indicant *nunc usque* albentes ossibus campi' (31.7.16). Ammianus' Vergilian allusion at this point (*Aen.* 12.36) heightens the impact of the scene, lending to his words a touch of epic style without quite presupposing that he had observed it himself. It is not clear how precisely Ammianus intended his phrase 'nunc usque' to be taken, nor from what present point in time he meant it to be understood, and he could certainly have gained an impression of the scene as well as a mere description of it from someone else who had been there. Yet it is impossible not to wonder whether his description of the battlefield reveals Ammianus' own acquaintance with it, not too many years after the battle was fought.

It was only after Theodosius' treaty of 382 with the Goths that the Thracian regions were really safe to visit. Now and in the previous year, bishop Ambrose of Milan noted that communications between Thessalonica and north Italy were broken by the hostile occupation of Thrace, impeding the summoning of a church council.[23] Bishops were accustomed to the advantages of the imperial transport system, the *cursus publicus*, and their more sedate expectations ought not necessarily to be applied to Ammianus, who – as the experiences which he recounted in his history well show – was in his earlier years a man of considerable vigour and enterprise, well able to look after himself. We should be foolish to rule out the possibility that Ammianus visited the Thracian battlefield before the region was safe for regular travel, but it would be more natural to suppose that if he visited Ad Salices, it was after Theodosius' peace treaty of 382. The Danube delta is not on any normal route from the eastern empire to Rome. We would best assume that, if Ammianus visited Thrace, he would return to Constantinople before embarking on a journey to the west. It would then be a possible speculation, but no more than this, that the 'passing visit' to Mothone in Laconia mentioned earlier formed part of a voyage made by the sea route from the east to the Peloponnese and across the Adriatic to Brundisium, before travelling through Italy by the main road to Rome. The alternative route, by land through the Balkans and down into Italy through Aquileia – the route taken by Theodosius' army in 388 – is an equal possibility; in which case it would be still more unlikely, given the state of the country in the years after Hadrianople, that Ammianus would make the journey to the west before 383.

(2) Composition

It is not much to go on: personal knowledge of Laconia, Egypt and the Black Sea, time spent in Antioch, conjectured visits to Constantinople and Thrace – such things hardly offer the basis for a reconstruction of Ammianus' life and movements in the years between his retirement from active service and his arrival at Rome some twenty years later.

Ammianus springs into his history in 354 and disappears from it nine gregarious, exciting and well-documented years later; yet even of these nine years almost three, ending in April 363 with the closely narrated Persian campaign of Julian, are void of any personal reference. For his life before this period of active service we must resort to generalised inferences from social background and cultural milieu, after it to the assembling of scattered allusions in some rational order; for the movements sketched in the first part of this chapter are only among many possible sequences of visits and journeys that could have brought Ammianus to Rome in the early 380s. Yet it must on any account be clear that Ammianus came to Rome with much material for his history already collected, his guiding ideas already formed, no doubt with selections of his work already drafted for presentation to some great literary patron, some well-informed politician or socially prominent figure willing to be convinced of his visitor's promise and good faith as a historian and thinking, possibly, of his own commemoration in the eyes of posterity. We can assume that Ammianus did not come to Rome entirely unprepared for the work he had it in mind to do, whatever the disappointment his actual reception there may have caused him.

On the narrowest and least ambitious criterion of good historical writing, that of accurate, plain narrative, there is little in the earlier of the surviving books that Ammianus could in principle not have known and recorded before he came west in the 380s.[24] It is clear from allusions in the earliest of these books that Ammianus had described the first years of the reign of Constantius in detail comparable to what now survives. He gives references back to the Persian campaigns of Constantius in the 340s, the visit to Britain of Constans in 343, his overthrow by the usurper Magnentius, and Magnentius' suppression by Constantius in 353. The name is given of the man who had closed the gates of Trier against Magnentius' Caesar Decentius (15.6.4), and a chapter in Book 14 tells of the punishments of the supporters of Magnentius in a tone grimly expressive of the aftermath of civil war.[25]

Book 14 is otherwise dominated by the bloody regime at Antioch of Gallus Caesar, whom Constantius had installed there while he marched west to deal with the usurpation. The arrest of Gallus and his execution at Pola in Dalmatia formed the dark climax of this book; for the whole narrative, Ammianus will have had little difficulty in finding sources of information in the east for such events of this period as he was not able to describe from actually living in the city which Gallus had terrorised, and from serving under the general ordered to preside over Gallus' courts of law. In the west, the problems of security demonstrated by the rebellion of Magnentius were further shown by the proclamation at Cologne of another usurper, Silvanus, in whose suppression Ammianus took part as a young officer and which he described in Book 15 from his personal knowledge of it. Unable to ignore this repeated evidence of the physical unwieldiness of the empire, Constantius overcame his dislike and appointed his nephew Julian to maintain the imperial presence in the

II. Ammianus and his History

northern sector of the provincial frontiers: and for the ensuing sequence in Ammianus' history (Books 16-20), the exploits of Julian and Constantius are described in parallel. Ammianus stayed in Gaul for nearly two years (355-7) after the suppression of Silvanus, and so witnessed the achievements of Julian in the first, magnificent, period of his imperial career. To this phase, the more remarkable because it was so unexpected, Ammianus devoted literary skills touching the panegyrical, its climax being Julian's victory over the Alamanni at Strasbourg, with which he concluded Book 16; but the visit of Constantius to Rome in 357 and his subsequent campaigns on the Danube frontier were also narrated fully, and with recognition of their importance.

The danger to the empire now shifted to the eastern frontier, to which Ammianus had been transferred in 357 (before the battle of Strasbourg); and the later part of Book 18 and almost the whole of 19 are taken up with events that he witnessed at very close hand indeed, the fighting on the eastern front and (in Book 19) the siege and capture of the city of Amida. Ammianus was among the besieged, and this part of the history shows his narrative skill at its very finest, and his concentration on his personal experience at its most intense.

In Book 20, the activities of Julian in Gaul and of Constantius on the eastern frontier are balanced, the proclamation of Julian as Augustus bringing to a crisis the relations between them; and 21 describes the open declaration of war on Constantius by Julian, his march against him and Constantius' death, opportune in that it averted yet another destructive civil war, from which it is not likely that Julian would have emerged successful. In this book (and more especially at the beginning of Book 22), Julian's emergent pagan sympathies begin to attract attention, and it ends with another demonstration of Ammianus' literary technique, his obituary notice of Constantius. This is skilfully contrived in its presentation of virtues and vices to make that emperor's merits seem insignificant beside the suspicion, judicial cruelty and civil dissension that clouded his reign.

With Julian as sole emperor, the narrative structure of Ammianus' exposition became simpler, it being possible to devote Books 22-25 to an integrated account of his reign with few interruptions from events in distant parts of the empire; these books of Ammianus' history are more noted for the learned digressions by which he enlarged the scale of a narrative that is rather less expansive when taken in isolation than seems apparent when it is read in context. If, during this phase, certain parts of the Roman empire appear to be neglected by Ammianus, then this was because they were neglected also by Julian, to make room for the greater designs that now appeared. The reign is followed from its early hopes of a renaissance of traditional civic, religious and military ideals, through the doomed ambition of the invasion of Persia in which Ammianus took part, to its ignominious collapse and the emperor's death on the retreat. Jovian, made emperor in Julian's place, had to cede territory to the Persians in order to gain safe passage back to the Roman empire. It was with the army's return to Antioch, as we saw, that Ammianus left active service, never to return to it. He had followed the campaign like many others of an enterprising and curious nature, and sometimes of less conspicuous military abilities than were possessed by Ammianus. There was always, in these eastern adventures, something of an air of exploration and government-sponsored travel alongside the strictly military objectives which it may (or, as in this case, may not) be possible to identify.[26]

The death of Jovian early in 364 and the succession of the brothers Valentinian and Valens posed new difficulties of structure and arrangement; for the emperors divided the empire and its administration into eastern and western portions, which they governed independently. Even the proclamation of Procopius at Constantinople in September 365 failed to distract Valentinian from the Rhine frontier to which he had devoted his attentions; and Valens was obliged to repel from his own resources this last resurgence of the dynastic tradition of Constantine the Great. With the usurpation of Procopius, which in the event was easily resolved in Valens' favour, Ammianus filled the latter part of Book 26 of his history, having now, as he had explained in the preface to this book, arrived at the threshold of the present age; 'ad usque memoriae confinia propioris' (26.1.1).

*

Such a bare summary of Books 14-26 of Ammianus' history leaves out much of what is most essential to its special quality and character. It takes no account of the wealth of detail which Ammianus invested in his story, nor of the control of structure with which he organised a wide-ranging narrative covering the Classical and near eastern worlds from the Rhine to the Euphrates and beyond, the proliferation of sub-plots and rivalries that defined the nature of the political life, the importance of individual character, the richness of imagery, and the illustrative role of anecdote. It ignores the breadth of Ammianus' conception of history, as shown especially in the digressions with which he varied his narrative and provided the full context necessary for its understanding. It therefore omits the central part of Ammianus' case to be considered as a Classical historian in the grand tradition. Nor does it touch so fundamental an aspect of his approach as his choice of Latin for a history that, in terms both of his own background and the contemporary historiographical tradition, might more naturally have been written in Greek. Its purpose is limited and strictly practical: to give a working survey of the actual contents of the history, and to suggest that, as far as concerns the plain narrative of these books, there is little in them that Ammianus could not have compiled, annotated and in part drafted in the years before his visit to the west.

Once the decision was made to carry the history beyond the rebellion of Procopius, a visit to the west became however a clear necessity. The eastern regime of Valens could of course be narrated on the strength of Ammianus' presence there. As we have seen, he felt himself threatened by Valens' prosecutions on charges of magic and treason, conducted at Antioch in the early 370s: he was living there at the time and saw some of his friends and acquaintances fall under suspicion. Equally, if an inference made earlier is justified, Ammianus saw the battle of Hadrianople and its aftermath from the point of view of one living in the east: and he was surely living there when he compiled material for the digression on the Huns and the Alans with which he began the last book of his history. Valens' earlier, successful Gothic war (367-9) and his subsequent involvement with Persia and Armenia around 370 would, equally, have caused little difficulty for an alert enquirer living in the east, and for much of the time sharing residence at Antioch with the emperor and his supporters.

But it was well known that of the imperial brothers it was Valentinian who was the driving force. He had chosen Valens against the implied advice of his associates, and in the division of the empire which took place later in 364 it was Valentinian who nominated the personnel and the military establishment to be assigned to each emperor and chose for himself the western part of the empire. The division of the empire imposed a narrative apportioned between eastern and western events, while the degree to which the parts of the empire were now separately governed would imply that a historian – not that Ammianus would be unwilling – must be prepared to travel in order to gain his information.

The most cursory glance at Ammianus' account of the reign of Valentinian will show that its author must have come to the west to compose such a narrative as he presents of these years. The argument might rest on his descriptions of Valentinian's campaigns on Rhine and Danube, with treatment both of military exploits and engineering works, and his accounts of court life and politics. In these matters, Ammianus far surpasses any other source in accuracy, richness of incidental colour and supporting anecdote. But he ranges far beyond the setting of the imperial court and the enterprises connected with it. He offers, in the most careful detail, two episodes in widely separated parts of north Africa. One of these, which brought the citizens of Tripolitanian Lepcis into dispute with their military governor and subsequently into complex and hazardous diplomatic relations with the imperial court, concludes with mention of a report on the affair submitted to Valentinian's successor by the then proconsul and *vicarius* of Africa (28.6.1ff.). Then, further west in Mauretania, a narrative of military operations against a native rebel names not only individuals but whole regions, towns and peoples in a form suggesting use of documentary sources – perhaps a campaign report or reports which are highly unlikely to have been available in the eastern empire (29.5.1ff.). Ammianus narrated trials for magic and adultery among senatorial circles at Rome – the account balancing that of Valens' prosecutions at Antioch, although the circumstances and nature of the accusations were different in each case.

Ammianus' version of these events (28.1.1ff.) contains details and personal knowledge, not to say attitudes, which are best explained by the notion that he had pursued his enquiries among those affected.

It scarcely needs argument that the quality and detail of Ammianus' descriptions of western events in his latest books (27-31) assume his active presence in the west for the purpose of basic historical enquiry – the pursuit and scrutiny of witnesses, to which he referred in his preface to Book 15 – as well as for the more advanced processes of planning and composition. It now becomes important to determine as closely as we can the time of these more advanced stages of composition, for without this we shall find it difficult to approach the question of Ammianus' evolution as a historian, or to understand the choices of emphasis and presentation with which he finally expressed his conception of his undertaking. Self-evidently the later books, especially those parts concerning the west, will be the more closely involved with this period of final composition, in that Ammianus will have had to wait until his evidence was well in hand before embarking on their writing. It will be more interesting if for his earlier books also, parts of which he could have drafted before he came to the west, Ammianus was in a position to make extensive insertions and revisions at a later stage of composition.

To proceed in order from the later to the earlier books, the prefecture of Rome held under the usurper Maximus by Julianus Rusticus has already been mentioned (p. 10). The prefecture fell in 387/8, being anticipated in Book 27, under events of the year 367 (27.6.1). More substantially, also in Book 27, Ammianus mentioned the death of a notable individual of the time, the senator Petronius Probus, four times praetorian prefect and, after the emperors themselves, the most powerful man in the late fourth-century west. Probus makes several appearances in Ammianus' account of the reign of Valentinian. On the first of these occasions, under the year 368, the historian took the opportunity to provide a portrait of this remarkable figure, a fascinating combination of obsessive personal and family ambition, love of power, and nervous tension (27.11.1ff.; p. 277). Ammianus wrote of Probus that he 'possessed immense power, while he lived': 'potuit, quoad vixit, ingentia' (27.11.2). Now the death of Petronius Probus fell in or very near to 390.[27] Ammianus' reference to his death is no trivial or superficial insertion, consisting of a few words only. The whole substantial passage reads like a formal obituary. It is integral to the context, contains measured reflections on the nature of power, and was clearly not made public before the death of its subject. It is of course possible that Ammianus had for years been cherishing his words in anticipation that Probus would die by the time he came to publish his history; best however to assume that the entire passage was written, as it was certainly inserted, in or after 390.

We will find no difficulty in assuming that Ammianus was completing the last five books of his history in the years around 390. So much is implied, not only by references to events of that time such as the death of Probus, but by the practical difficulties of compiling, arranging and

II. Ammianus and his History

composing a narrative of the reign of Valentinian in the few years since Ammianus' arrival in the west. The same argument applies, with reducing but still considerable force, to the years previous to Valentinian's reign, and to books earlier than 27. Ammianus' knowledge of events before 365 may in essentials have been complete before he came to the west, but that is not to say there were no improvements to make, no new sources to consult, no additional details that might throw light on those years. At the time of the outbreak of Procopius' rebellion in 365, for instance, Valentinian was making for Rheims to take his stand against the Alamanni. Not allowing himself to be deflected by civil war in the east, he sent three chosen agents to secure Africa against seizure by Procopius. Two of them were military officers, one of them well known to Valentinian, the other with experience of the terrain from previous service in the province. The third agent was Neoterius, at that time an imperial secretary (*notarius*), later consul; 'postea consulem, tunc notarium'.[28] The consulship was, indeed, very much later, falling precisely in 390. The reference comes in Book 26 of Ammianus' history (5.14).

Book 26 stands, for Ammianus, at the threshold of the present age (p. 204), but the argument can be extended to earlier books. Writing of the Emperor Julian in Book 22, Ammianus related a series of anecdotes about the emperor's behaviour at Constantinople (22.7.1ff.). He processed on foot at the inauguration of the consuls of the year; some praised this, others thought it cheap and affected. Catching himself out in a violation of protocol, Julian levied on himself a fine of ten pounds of gold. When a meeting of the senate was interrupted by news of the arrival of an old associate, the philosopher Maximus, Julian leapt from his seat, ran from the senate-house and led him inside. Ammianus thought this untimely ostentation, unsuitable for a philosopher (let alone an emperor). Finally, two imperial agents came forward with information on the whereabouts of a condemned former praetorian prefect now in hiding, but were rejected by Julian. Ammianus remarked that 'all these events' were witnessed by a visitor to Constantinople, the Roman senator Praetextatus, whom Julian had found there on private business and appointed proconsul of Achaia. Surely Praetextatus was Ammianus' source for these stories – only one of which, the arrival of Maximus, is mentioned elsewhere.[29] If so, and if, as is likely though not of course certain, it was at Rome that Ammianus first met Praetextatus, then this passage on Julian will not only reflect a time of final composition for Book 22 in the middle or later 380s, but will provide a secure limit in time for Ammianus' arrival at Rome. To the distress of his friends and the Roman populace, Praetextatus died as consul designate towards the end of 384.

Equally interesting is an episode from Book 21. Marching against Constantius in 361, Julian had encountered at Sirmium Aurelius Victor, an imperial official whom he then summoned to Naissus to receive appointment as governor of Pannonia Secunda (21.10.6). Julian also honoured Victor by the award of a bronze statue in the Forum of Trajan, for he was not only an imperial functionary but a literary man of note, a historian of the Roman empire from the time of Augustus to 360 – as it turned out the last year of the reign of Constantius. Many years later, wrote Ammianus, Victor was prefect of Rome, an office which can be assigned to 389/90. Aurelius Victor was a person of some interest to Ammianus, less perhaps as a fellow-historian than for what he might tell of the circumstances of Julian's advance upon Sirmium, on which Ammianus was clearly well informed.[30] It would be reasonable to suppose that Ammianus knew Aurelius Victor during his tenure of the prefecture of Rome – and that he was a source of Ammianus' information on those events of almost thirty years earlier.

So, to combine these allusions, Books 26 (the consulship of Neoterius) and 27 (the urban prefecture of Julianus Rusticus and the death of Petronius Probus) attained their final form in 388/90 or later. Material for Book 22 became available to Ammianus from Praetextatus in 383 or 384, and for Book 21 from Aurelius Victor perhaps as late as 389. Whatever stage of composition these books had reached, Ammianus was able to make insertions and revisions which were sometimes quite substantial, and to add materially to the information available to him.

Ammianus included at various points of his text accounts of the tenures of office of the prefects of Rome. Whatever his sources for these notices, written, oral, or a combination of the two, Ammianus' access to such material assumes his presence in the west. It is unlikely that even an official record of the prefectures, if it existed (and it does not look as if Ammianus derived his information from such a document), was widely available in the empire.[31] The first such passage, narrating the prefecture of Rome of Memmius Vitrasius Orfitus in 353-6, comes as it happens in the earliest of the surviving books (14.6.1ff.). It is this prefecture that provided the opportunity for Ammianus' first long digression on the habits of the senators and people of Rome – a digression in which, as was proposed earlier, are reminiscences both of Ammianus' own arrival at Rome and of the expulsion of foreigners at the time of the corn shortage of 383 or 384. Ammianus' remark that the expulsion had occurred 'not so very long ago' ('haud ita dudum') places the final preparation even of Book 14 of the history some few years after 383/4. Again, it is no trivial addition, the insertion merely of a few words with some sort of marginal indication; the allusion is relevant and integral to its context, and in making it Ammianus must have considered the effect of the entire passage in which it came.

It begins to look as if the whole of the surviving part of Ammianus' history reached its final form towards the year 390; that is to say, whatever he had written or drafted earlier, he was able to make substantial additions and amendments at that late stage. This conclusion, scarcely contentious for the latest books (27-31) in view of the extensive information on recent western events assembled in them, seems also to hold for Book 14, as well as for 21, 22 and 26. As to these earlier books, it is true that Ammianus' information was already very full

II. Ammianus and his History

for events which he had witnessed at first hand or for which he had been able to find witnesses in the east: at the same time, relevant details remained to be gathered from western sources, and some quite emphatic and integral passages (like the prefecture of Orfitus and the advance upon Sirmium) in different ways reflect the historian's later presence in the west. It is possible even to suggest that this applies also to passages in books of the history no longer extant.

Introducing his narrative of the trials for magic arts and adultery conducted at Rome under Valentinian, Ammianus remarked that they were the most dreadful event to afflict Rome in the fifteen years or more since the rebellion of Nepotianus.[32] The Goddess of War, he wrote, raged through the Eternal City and laid everything in flames; 'saeviens per urbem aeternam urebat cuncta Bellona' (28.1.1). The uprising at Rome of Nepotianus, a subsidiary event to the revolt of Magnentius, had been suppressed by him in 350. The intensity of Ammianus' comparison must surely owe something to the Roman circles in which he moved when assembling information on the trials conducted by Valentinian's agents. We may infer that in narrating the rebellion and fall of Nepotianus in Book 13 or earlier, Ammianus would have used Roman sources for his information.

Lastly, in Book 16 Ammianus had occasion to describe the support given to Julian before Constantius by the eunuch Eutherius (16.7.2f.; p. 83). The episode prompted Ammianus to reflect on a prodigious fact, the probity and courage of a eunuch. Adding an account of Eutherius' career, Ammianus remarked that he had in old age retired to Rome, where he still lived, secure in the possession of a good conscience, and loved and admired by all classes of men. Ammianus noted a particular gift of Eutherius, his amazing memory; 'immensum quantum memoria vigens' (7.5). Eutherius had served Julian, whose inconsistency of judgment he sometimes corrected; before this, he had attended the Emperor Constans, whose faults, claimed Ammianus, Eutherius would have mitigated had Constans listened to his advice. Still earlier, he had been acquainted with the court of Constantine, for he had been captured as a boy by Armenian tribesmen and sold as a eunuch to Roman traders and so brought to Constantine's palace, where his keen intelligence soon brought him to notice. If Ammianus did not use Eutherius' 'immense memory', not only in his researches on the recent age but on the earlier emperors with whom the eunuch had been acquainted, he would have been guilty of an unbelievable waste of an opportunity. Ammianus is telling us, as directly as he can, that Eutherius was one of his sources. He was therefore in a position during his stay at Rome to gather material on events and personalities of a time substantially before the first extant book of his history, as far back as the reign of Constantine the Great. A eunuch supporter of Julian on Constantine – that would have been worth reading, as Ammianus surely thought it worth hearing.[33]

The internal indications provided by Ammianus himself converge therefore with Libanius' letter to him, written late in 392 but referring to a slightly earlier time, to suggest that the final stages of composition of the history should be assigned to the years up to and shortly after 390. As to how long after 390 the work was completed, only one passage offers guidance. In his digression on Alexandria in Book 22, Ammianus mentioned its great temple, the Serapeum, comparing it to the Capitol, 'by which venerable Rome lifts herself to eternity'; 'quo se venerabilis Roma in aeternum tollit' (22.16.12). He could hardly have written in this way, explicitly comparing the Serapeum with a symbol of eternity at Rome, had he known of the destruction of the great temple by gangs of monks, possibly abetted and certainly not discouraged by the imperial authorities. This catastrophe took place in the summer of 391. If it is assumed that news of the event carried quickly round the Roman world, it is a natural inference that Book 22, in which the allusion occurs, was completed before 392.

There are various possible objections to such a straightforward inference. Perhaps news of the destruction did not carry round the Roman world as quickly as we would have expected. Possibly Ammianus thought it less necessary to revise digressions than he would narrative passages in the light of new information more relevant to the latter. He sometimes seems to apply different criteria to the two forms of writing (p. 389f.), and his words on the Serapeum may have been written earlier and left as they stood in a digression, despite the tragedy of 391. It is not impossible that Ammianus' history came out in instalments, the latest books (say 26-31) appearing after 391, the earlier, including the reference to the Serapeum, before that date. Libanius in his letter to Ammianus expresses hopes of a further contribution from the historian, and his words are sometimes taken to imply that he knew of a further instalment, soon to follow what had already been made public in the recitations of which he had been informed. Perhaps then Libanius anticipated the publication of Books 26-31, beginning as they do with a preface that seems, to some, to hint at a change of approach.[34] Yet we cannot be sure that Libanius knew enough about the scope and character of the history to validate this inference. Libanius had learned from his informants of recitations recently given from it. When a work of contemporary history was being presented to the public it was natural to wonder what its terminal point would be, and Libanius may simply have been expressing the polite, or even the self-interested, hope – for he himself was a considerable figure in Antiochene society in the 380s – that Ammianus would continue his story to the present day. Both literary convention and common tact would however advise Ammianus against this, and in an epilogue to the history he firmly assigned the continuation of his work to a new generation of writers (31.16.9).

Ammianus shows that he was up to the year 390 still engaged in compiling material for and at least revising, if not actually composing, parts of the earlier as well as the later books of his history. That these indications converge upon the later 380s, but that none falls after 390, suggests that completion of the history followed closely upon the latest datable allusion (the consulship of Neoterius) which it contains. In terms of the evidence, a date of publication for the entire work in 390 or 391 remains the most convincing hypothesis.[35] It is also perfectly compatible with the letter of Libanius, written at the end of 392 but with information relevant to a slightly earlier time. If, as suggested earlier, Libanius' informants were returning to the east with the court of Theodosius, they had left Italy in the summer (late June) of 391.

*

The lost books of Ammianus pose many problems, not least that of their scale in proportion to what survives. The eighteen extant books cover the twenty-five years from 353 to 378, a ratio (to leave aside complications such as the incidence of digressions and the peculiar narrative intensity of certain books) of less than one-and-a-half years per book. The first thirteen books, covering the period of two hundred and fifty-seven years from AD 96 to 353 at a rate of twenty years per book, present a sharp contrast, made still more acute by the need to allow for the likelihood, argued above from the nature of Ammianus' back-references to them, that the books immediately preceding Book 14 were written on a comparable scale to what now survives. It would be reasonable to assume that the more detailed mode of writing began at least as early as the accession of Constantius in 337. If the expansion began, let us say, at Book 11 (giving a ratio of five years per book in the eventful first half of the reign of Constantius), the first ten books will have covered just over two hundred and forty years, at an average of almost twenty-five years for each book. If the expansion came earlier, for example with the conquest of the east by Constantine from Licinius in 324, the earliest books will have been still more compressed; six books from 96 to 324 would give an average of nearly forty years per book. It makes no substantial difference if we assume a gradual rather than a sudden expansion of treatment as Ammianus' account approaches the range of living memory; the contrast of scale, and therefore of manner, between the lost and the extant books will in any case have been conspicuous. The early books were not much more than introductory to what follows, and Ammianus' history remains in essentials a history of the present age, its nature defined by the methods outlined in the preface to Book 15; the recording of what Ammianus had himself seen, supported by the rigorous questioning of eye-witnesses.

This reconstruction of Ammianus' history has been questioned, and the suggestion made that the whole of the history of which we have Books 14-31 was devoted to the present age, the period from the principate of Nerva to where it began (whether the death of Constantine, or his conquest of the east from Licinius) being covered in a separate lost work of unknown but generous dimensions.[36] Introducing a digression on Egypt in Book 22, Ammianus remarks that he had twice before, in his accounts of the reigns of Hadrian and Septimius Severus, given full descriptions of that country, basing his accounts in large part on what he had seen himself; 'quarum notitiam in actibus Hadriani et Severi principum digessimus late, visa pleraque narrantes' (22.15.1). If we can judge Ammianus' definition of a 'long' digression by reference to those that survive (including the excursus on Egypt in Book 22), then we must take his words seriously; and it is argued that for his accounts of Hadrian and Severus to contain such digressions, the narratives themselves must also have been too substantial to have been comprised in a mere thirteen books from Nerva to 354 (or whatever variation of these proportions is accepted from the previous paragraph). To meet these objections, a separate history was postulated, derived from written sources, to complement the one which we in part possess, based on verbal enquiries and personal experience. It is from a literary point of view an intriguing possibility, for Ammianus, a Greek, could have exploited Greek histories of the second and third centuries in order to make good the deficiencies of the poor Latin accounts of that period that were available; but it is more than this, for it affects our understanding not only of the formal nature of Ammianus' historical writing, but of the sort of individual he was. To the man of action and writer of memoirs, drawing on personal experience, travelling, searching out and questioning eye-witnesses, we must add the literary scholar and man of books, the author of a history quite different in kind from that which in part survives.

It is by no means an impossible image of Ammianus. The combination in a historian of man of affairs and man of letters was familiar to ancient opinion, which indeed expected it. It was designed to ensure that a historian had access to the best contemporary information, to guarantee the authority of the judgments expressed by a man with a general experience of politics and human affairs, and to offer the resources of literary culture necessary for their communication to an educated public – expectations no less relevant to the history of previous ages than to that of the present.[37] As for the literary erudition of Ammianus, the surviving books leave no doubt of that.

But there are difficulties with this view of his history. Little can safely be inferred from Ammianus' allusion to the 'long' digressions on Egypt in the books about Hadrian and Septimius Severus. There are no rules as to the 'proper' length of digressions in relation to their narrative contexts, and if there were such rules we could not apply them to Ammianus without knowing how he organised these passages of his earlier books. It is possible, for instance, that his account of the earlier empire was based not so much on direct or continuous narrative as on descriptions of its various regions, no doubt with emphasis on the wars conducted in them. He surely chose the reigns of Hadrian and Severus for his earlier descriptions of Egypt because of these emperors' famous visits to the province, but it does not follow either that the visits themselves or their narrative contexts were described in any great detail. Ammianus writes also of having described Trajan's and Severus' attacks on the desert city of Hatra 'when I digressed on these regions in my descriptions of their deeds'; 'ut in eorum actibus has quoque digessimus partes' (25.8.5). In all these passages, the scale of the digressions may have been more ample than that of the narrative to which Ammianus took the opportunity to link them, his main purpose being to describe the regions of the empire rather than give a detailed narrative of the political history of the second and third centuries.

Further, when Ammianus refers back to events described in the lost books, he uses expressions like 'as I wrote above', 'as I said before', not seeming to imply that the reader had to look up a separate work in order to find the passages mentioned; and his expressions do not distinguish between the remoter and the more recent of the lost books. He can allude to the Parthian campaigns of Lucius Verus in the second century with the same phrase as that used of the conduct of a Roman general in the 340s ('ut ante rettulimus', 23.6.24; 14.7.7), or an event of the later years of Constantine ('ut dudum rettulimus plene', 24.4.23).[38] Moreover, it is sometimes implied that accounts of earlier events given in those books were not very detailed. An important, and certainly interesting, aspect of the reign of the Emperor Maximinus (235-8), the soothing influence of his wife upon his savage character, was described in Ammianus' account of the Gordians, suggesting that he did not assign to Maximinus the separate account one would have thought he deserved (14.1.8).[39] His recollection in Book 31 of the wars between Romans and Goths in the mid-third century is so confused in its chronology that it is hard to believe he had described them in any detail before, and he does not mention having done so, referring only to the possibly excessive claims made in unspecified historical works, or in the general historical tradition ('nisi fingunt annales'), as to the numbers of men killed in the sack of Philippopolis (31.5.15ff.).[40] He appears not to have described earlier the Persian attack on Antioch led by the traitor Mareades in the time of Gallienus, despite the evident interest and significance of that event (23.5.3; p. 170f.). It would be surprising if in a lengthy account he had omitted to mention the ruin of a considerable part of Alexandria in urban disorders in the time of Aurelian, or had said nothing about the execution of Crispus Caesar by Constantine the Great in 324; but he writes of both these events as if for the first time in the extant books (22.16.15; 14.11.20). In referring to Diocletian's introduction of Persian ceremonial to Roman court behaviour Ammianus does not indicate that he had written at any length on that most important subject in his discussion of the reign of Diocletian. He remarks only that 'we have read' that this was the case (15.5.18). Examination of his language in this passage suggests that his source was a standard Latin history of the period used also by the epitomators Eutropius and Aurelius Victor.[41] This is an important point, for in general Ammianus' back-references do not indicate a much wider range of subject-matter, greater knowledge of historical detail, or superior judgment than that of the other sources that we possess. The majority of his references to the history of the earlier period can, where they are not commonplace, be explained in terms of the use of standard sources like Cassius Dio, Herodian and the Latin history just mentioned. If Ammianus were able to cite a major work of his own on the second and third centuries, we would expect to learn much more from his back-references of what we do not otherwise know, than is actually the case.[42] It still seems best therefore to regard the early books of Ammianus as little more than a substantial introduction to the history of the present age. An account of the period from Nerva to the death of Constantine in as few as nine or ten books, and even six books from Nerva to 324, would however be fuller than survives in any other non-biographical Latin source available to us.

*

The argument set out in this chapter has been very formal in character and has said little in substantive terms about the intellectual and literary character of Ammianus' history. This is deliberate, in order not to allow the interpretation of our author to be influenced at the outset by subjective impressions, but first to set out as neutrally as possible the objective framework within which his work evolved. For the present, certain possibilities may be stated briefly, if it is remembered that they are provisional statements only, subject to revision as we become more familiar with the actual content and manner of the history.

First, if Ammianus was able at a relatively late stage of composition to make significant additions to his material, not only as relevant to the history of his own day but also to that of earlier periods, then it is possible that his opinions also, as he set them down, are an expression of what he thought at the time of final composition rather than an array of unrevised attitudes from different periods of his life. Perhaps this should be put more cautiously: Ammianus had the opportunity to express himself more carefully if he felt that his earlier views were very different from what he now thought. What this implies for our understanding of Ammianus' historical perspectives is illustrated by the reflection that when he completed his work his opinion, for example, of the Emperor Julian was informed by the passage of nearly thirty years since Julian's death. Ammianus' admiration for Julian – modified, as we shall see, by criticisms of a disquieting accuracy – must be seen in the context not only of his acquaintance with the emperor as a young man but of his advance through the middle years of his life to the verge of old age, and of the demonstration in time of the failure of Julian's ambitions and the rejection by the emperors, and by Roman society at large, of his ideals. These are two variable factors – in Ammianus himself and in the society around him – that must not be ignored as we read his text.

Second, the process of the final composition of Ammianus' history – if by this we mean the gathering of the last of the information required, its arrangement or insertion into a planned overall design, and the presentation to the public of a definitive literary version – may for the entire work have been relatively short. It is impossible to calculate how much preliminary writing and planning a historian may do before he reaches this stage, and obvious that much of Ammianus' material (especially in the digressions) was the product of many years' reading and annotation.[43] It would be absurd to imagine that no drafting was done in this period, the development of historical style requiring of all things time, practice, the willingness to experiment and to discard the unsuccessful. The Greek historian Cassius Dio noted that he had spent ten years collecting material for his history of Rome from the earliest times to the death of Septimius Severus in 211, and a further twelve years composing it (72.23.5).[44] Now, there are from every point of view many differences between Dio and Ammianus Marcellinus. Dio's planning was affected by the fact that contemporary history continued to be made after his originally envisaged terminal point and during the twelve-year period of composition, and that he attempted, as he had promised, to keep abreast of it. Ammianus stopped his narrative in 378. The question of continuation beyond that point did not arise, though he had no doubt begun writing before it, and his plan was not subject to revision in the same way or on the same scale as that of Dio. He would have to allow for the discovery of more material than he had expected to find, and may have changed his mind as to the emphasis he would give to certain subjects (the battle of Hadrianople, carrying the total of books to thirty-one rather than a round thirty, is an obvious possibility), but he was not liable to be overwhelmed by an ever-increasing flood of current events down to the actual moment of writing. Further, on the assumption made here that the earlier part of Ammianus' narrative did not constitute an entirely separate work but was contained within the thirty-one attested books, the proportion of contemporary to earlier historical material was very much higher in the case of Ammianus than in that of Cassius Dio. Given these different patterns of their works, it is only by the crudest of calculations that one can reduce the twelve years spent by Cassius Dio 'composing' his eighty books to the time required by Ammianus to compose his thirty-one; but the result, something of the order of five years, would be consistent with the indications set out in this chapter, suggesting a period of final composition beginning later than 383/4 and ending in 390 or very soon after that date. One could allow Ammianus longer, on the grounds that it is more difficult and takes more time to write history from primary sources than from books, but five years may not be a gross underestimate of the time taken for composition within a framework devised, and attitudes evolving, over the preceding twenty years.

Third, if Ammianus was engaged in composition in the later 380s, and prepared then to make substantial additions and insertions to material he had assembled earlier, then certain literary influences postulated in his evolution may also have exerted themselves relatively late. We do not know when he decided to extend his account back from his own day to begin with the accession of the Emperor Nerva in AD 96, nor why he chose that date precisely. Nor – another way of putting the same question and an obvious answer to the second part of it – do we know when Ammianus became aware of the earlier Latin historical tradition to that point, as represented by Tacitus and Suetonius. Their contemporary, the satirist Juvenal, and Suetonius' successor as a historian, Marius Maximus, are mentioned by Ammianus in unflattering terms in his digression on the intellectual tastes of late Roman senators (28.4.14); of Suetonius and Tacitus themselves, not a word. Perhaps they were mentioned and their influence put on record in an early book now lost, but, on the arguments presented above, these early books do not seem central to Ammianus' historical conception. Given the dominance in the surviving books of recent eye-witness material, and the likelihood that this was true also of the immediately preceding books as far back as Book 10 or 11 if not earlier, it is not clear that the decision to start at AD 96 need have been of more than formal significance. One might choose it because it happened to be the point at which Tacitus and Suetonius ended, thereby asserting a certain continuity in the tradition, but it seems at least possible that the influence of these writers, and so Ammianus' standing in the Latin historiographical tradition, were secondary to a decision to write history originally conceived in rather different terms. Ammianus' acquaintance with Tacitus, if taken as proved (as it may not be) by the parallels of expression detected between them, does not seem to provide more than touches of stylistic colouring, with no apparent intention to evoke in any systematic way the substance or moral purpose of his predecessor's work.[45] If Tacitus were in any more profound sense Ammianus' model, his writing would be more remarkable for opportunities missed, than opportunities taken, to show it. The influence of Sallust is far more pointedly relevant, and it is to Sallust, if indeed to any single author, that we must look in considering the broader issue of Ammianus' conception of the 'dignity and character' of Roman history.

There is little to be gained at present by pursuing these reflections, whose purpose is merely to indicate the formal conditions within which Ammianus' work should be considered. In order to do justice to the substance of Ammianus' intellectual and literary evolution, we must try in more empirical terms to identify the origins of his decision to write history and to define the manner of writing that it entailed. To this theme my final chapter will return, after the description of Ammianus as participant in and observer of the Roman empire of his day that is the real subject of this book. We may start by looking in closer detail at his earlier life and career, beginning with his experiences as a young officer under Constantius and at the social and cultural milieu in eastern, and Antiochene, society from which he came.

CHAPTER III

Ammianus and Constantius: Civil Dissension and Foreign War

The first extant page of Ammianus' history plunges the reader into a sentence of a length and complexity entirely typical of Ammianus, and into an atmosphere of military and political crisis equally typical of the reign of Constantius.[1] No break is apparent from what has preceded, nor any expansion of scale, only a brief reminder of the point reached in the story. The context is the aftermath of the rebellion of Magnentius, and in particular of the battle of Mons Seleucus, after which Magnentius committed suicide (10 August 353). The war is over, the participants exhausted, but the clamour of trumpets is not yet quieted, nor the troops dispersed to winter quarters (14.1.1). The subject now changes abruptly. With dramatic effect as telling as the metaphor with which he makes the transition, Ammianus turns to the regime of Gallus Caesar at Antioch and judicial atrocities committed there; these were the 'strong blasts of raging fortune' afflicting the east, as the rebellion of Magnentius had the west (14.1.1-10). Diversions follow on the Isaurians and Saracens, divided, geographically as in sequence, by a Persian raid on Mesopotamia (14.2-4); but immediately Ammianus brings his narrative back to the west, it is to tell of the inquisitions conducted in Britain and Gaul to root out and punish the supporters of Magnentius (14.5). It was above all the suspicion of treason, wrote Ammianus, that stirred Constantius to anger and laid him open to the influence of his associates, who by bloody insinuations ('cruentae blanditiae') built up incidental events into matters of state security and persuaded the emperor that the well-being of the whole world hung, as it were, by the thread of his personal safety: 'velut filo pendere statum orbis terrarum' (14.5.4).

Constantius' suspicion of political dissent, and his dependence on supporters who exploit his weakness to further their own ambitions, are central themes in Ammianus' judgment of this emperor. The intensity of his narrative of Constantius' inquisitions in Britain and Gaul is deliberately heightened by the implied comparison with the regime of Gallus at Antioch. But it is not enough simply to explain the whole affair as a product of the emperor's personal character. In his previous book, Ammianus has narrated a serious rebellion in the western provinces. Political dissension was not a figment of Constantius' brooding imagination or his supporters' invention, but present reality. Political trials were the least to be expected, with torture, death sentences and exiles, and false as well as true accusations their normal counterpoint. For those involved, it was an unpleasant time in which to be living, but the emperor was not alone responsible for that.

Ammianus' presentation of the atmosphere as one of suspicion and uncertainty, and of the emperor's character as the main cause of it, was however a true reflection of his own experience. If the civil war had thrown into doubt the loyalty of Constantius' western provinces, the conduct in the east of Gallus Caesar had proved far from reassuring. Early in 354, Ammianus' superior, the *magister equitum* Ursicinus, was recalled from Nisibis by Gallus to take part in investigations into treason pursued at Antioch.[2] Someone, it was not known who or for what purpose, had ordered a cloak of imperial purple from the dye-works at Tyre. Employees in the workshops confessed under torture to preparing also a purple tunic; and a letter was found from a Christian deacon to a weaving factory at Tyre, asking for a job, of an unspecified nature, to be hurried along. The deacon was tortured to the point of death but revealed nothing. Others were executed, including an orator from Emesa in Syria and a Cilician philosopher, together with the provincial governor of Phoenicia and his son, an imperial official (14.9.1-9). The orator and the philosopher were cases of mistaken identity, their informer (now dead) having meant to incriminate two managers of arms factories with the same names (14.7.18).

This was the authentic stuff of treason trials in the Roman empire. But there were serious issues behind these messy allegations. The provincial governor's son had been sent by his father-in-law to Mesopotamia, to find out from the troops there whether incriminating messages had been received from Gallus Caesar, suggesting that he might be aiming at imperial power for himself (14.7.19). The father-in-law was the late praetorian prefect, Domitianus, another recent victim – if he was not also an agent – of the suspicions that attended Constantius' relations with his Caesar. On his arrival at Antioch, Domitianus had snubbed Gallus and threatened to cut off his supplies, but had been lynched by Gallus' soldiers (7.16).[3] The delicacy in the situation lay in the fact that the prefect was an agent of Constantius, sent to Antioch specifically to restrain Gallus' behaviour and to induce him, if possible, to return to the court in Italy (7.9). It is likely too that Domitianus' enquiries among the soldiers in Mesopotamia were made on Constantius' instructions. In his investigations at Antioch, Gallus was enquiring, consciously or not, into the intelligence activities of Constantius' own agents in the east. From a western point of view, suspicion of treason fell upon Gallus Caesar.

Ursicinus, who on Ammianus' account took a reluctant part in the proceedings at Antioch, was described by the historian as a man of war, a soldier and a leader of soldiers, ill at ease with disputes at law and outclassed in cunning by those with whom he was now associated (14.9.1). At the trials, Ursicinus was the mere shadow of a judge

III. Ammianus and Constantius

('imaginarius iudex'), surrounded by court attendants who had been told in advance what was required, and by secretaries who wrote everything down and took it straight to Gallus (9.3). One can well understand Ursicinus' action in writing 'secret letters' to Constantius, in the hope that an intervention from him might do something to restrain his Caesar (9.1f.). Ammianus took the view that Ursicinus should have been bolder in justifying his conduct to Constantius, for his participation in the trials, seen from the west, was highly suspect. He was caught in a most difficult conflict of loyalties. He had no choice, short of declaring rebellion against his immediate master, but to obey Gallus' summons to come to Antioch; while, taking the broader view of his situation, it is unlikely that Ursicinus or anyone else had a true impression of the extent of Constantius' intelligence operations in the east. But on any account, as *magister equitum* and – so it seems – presiding officer at the trials, Ursicinus carried some responsibility for the sentences inflicted after the hearings. Ammianus himself regarded the sentences as no better than judicial murder (9.5f.).

It was no doubt Gallus' conduct of these investigations which finally brought Constantius to the conclusion that he must be removed – by direct methods where indirect ones had failed. The arrest and execution of Gallus are narrated by Ammianus with an intensity and sense of atmosphere which it would be pointless to attempt to match (14.11.1-24). For the development of Ammianus' own career, the attitude of Constantius to Ursicinus is a more fruitful line of enquiry.[4] Again, Ammianus' interpretation is made to hang on Constantius' character, in particular his obsessive fear of conspiracy. He is said to have been convinced that, with Gallus once removed, Ursicinus would be likely to make his own bid for power – he was popular and well known in the east, and possessed two active and able sons, whom he might use to support his claims as a rival (11.2f.). He was therefore replaced for the time being by another general and summoned to Milan for 'consultations' with the emperor. Ammianus went with him, the party travelling with all possible speed by the imperial transport service (11.4f.). Only after Ursicinus' departure was Gallus removed from Antioch, stripped of his support and placed under arrest, and finally executed at Pola in Istria (11.20ff.).[5]

Ammianus' portrayal of the events which he witnessed under Constantius, and indeed of the general character of his reign, was influenced by considerations of a rather personal nature. First was his close relationship to Ursicinus, to whose staff he had been assigned, with implications that will be considered later, by imperial commission; 'cui nos obsecuturos iunxerat imperiale praeceptum'. Then, there was the atmosphere of suspicion and tension in which this phase of Ursicinus' career was enveloped. This, as we have seen, was not simply a matter of the invention of the emperor and his associates, although it certainly allowed scope for this, but of the actual situation of the time – with civil war only recently suppressed in the west and growing doubts as to the intentions of Gallus Caesar.

To this extent, Ammianus' explanation of the political climate as the expression of Constantius' obsessive and easily intimidated temperament is less than just. But given the nature of Ammianus' involvement with Ursicinus, a 'just' assessment of Constantius would be more than we could reasonably expect. Beyond the immediate circles of those openly involved in rebellion, the detection of political dissidence is at all times a question of interpretation, of the constructions placed by others upon the attitudes and intentions of those suspected. As Ammianus admitted, Ursicinus might have done more to put himself on the right side of Constantius' opinion in the matter of Gallus' trials at Antioch, and it takes little imagination to suppose that there were men at court who would welcome the opportunity to remove a long-serving general in favour of some other candidate, one perhaps closer to themselves and a possible source of political favour. Whether, in the prevailing atmosphere, Ursicinus survived or fell might depend less upon any objective assessment of his attitudes than on the interpretation of them put about by some such individual or group in the emperor's entourage, and on Constantius' response to it. If Ammianus' view of Constantius' behaviour and mentality is a less than dispassionate analysis of the situation, it is a true reflection of Ursicinus' and so of Ammianus', standing in it.

At Milan, the position of Ursicinus was indeed no less precarious than before. After the arrest and execution of Gallus, he became the object of accusations of treason, to which the emperor was receptive (15.2.1). Ammianus portrayed his patron as courageous and firm, but saddened because his previously numerous friends had begun to leave him for men of more promising influence. He alleged a secret plot to seize Ursicinus from the company of the soldiers and assassinate him; all was ready, claimed Ammianus, but at the last moment the plan was postponed by the emperor's intervention (2.5). The allegation is untestable and need not be taken very seriously; yet, again, it vividly reflects the anxious state of mind of Ursicinus and his protégé as they awaited the resolution of the emperor's uncertainty. At this point, Ammianus compared Ursicinus to Domitius Corbulo, the general of the early empire who, after defending Nero's provinces loyally and with care, was killed on his instructions. With the reservation that Corbulo was not executed but forced to suicide by Nero, the parallel is a close one. Corbulo, like Ursicinus, had achieved his renown on the eastern frontier of the empire and was involved with political dissidence, if at all, only indirectly and by association.[6]

By process of natural insinuation, the suspicion at Constantius' court came to involve Gallus' half-brother, Julian, who was in danger of falling victim to the machinations of Constantius' advisers and was brought to Comum near Milan; suspected because he had seen Gallus Caesar on his doomed journey through Constantinople, but defended by the Empress Eusebia, Julian was allowed to leave for academic studies at Athens (15.2.7f.). Meanwhile the governor of Pannonia Secunda was brought down after indiscreet conversations at a dinner-party at Sirmium

(3.7-11). Ursicinus waited on at Milan while the emperor went on a campaign in Raetia against the Alamanni, but in the late summer of 355 was unexpectedly given the opportunity to restore his standing.

The opportunity arose, ironically, from yet another rebellion in the west. The *magister peditum* at Cologne, Silvanus, became the object of an immensely complicated plot at Milan involving letters forged above his signature, on paper from which the rest of his handwriting had been erased (15.5.3f.).[7] The plot, set up by various minor officials and – so rumour had it – the praetorian prefect of Gaul and others in the highest state offices, was uncovered by enquiries at Milan undertaken at the insistence of Silvanus' Frankish colleagues there. The forgeries were incompetently done and easily detected, but in the meantime Silvanus, embroiled in suspicion and knowing the times, embarked upon rebellion as his only means of defence; it was a case of suspicion actually bringing about what was suspected. Ammianus' narrative conveys vividly the speed and tension of subsequent events (5.17ff.). News of the proclamation arrived at Milan one evening, and a council of state was summoned. The high officials hurried along to the palace at the second watch of night. The discussion in the consistory, at first confused, in time brought hesitant, then more confident mention of Ursicinus as a man equipped by military experience to undertake the suppression of Silvanus, and unjustly under a cloud of suspicion. He was sent for and introduced into the consistory. It was a difficult moment. Beginning a speech of self-defence, Ursicinus was checked by the emperor's mild rejoinder that this was no time for recrimination, the necessity of empire requiring unanimous and decisive action before any more harm could develop (5.20).[8]

As to tactics, it was decided that Ursicinus should go to Cologne pretending to know nothing of the proclamation, but that he had simply come with letters appointing him to succeed Silvanus. With him was sent a group of tribunes and ten *protectores domestici*, and they were to handle the situation in the light of what they should find. Ammianus (and, no doubt, Ursicinus) could not help thinking that, behind all the talk of Ursicinus' abilities and loyal service, it was really in Constantius' mind that he would in any event get rid of one of his dangerous subjects, Silvanus or Ursicinus (15.5.19). It was a natural reflection, but unfair, for it takes no account of the immense problem facing Constantius if Silvanus should succeed in establishing his regime.

Ammianus himself was one of the ten *protectores* in attendance on Ursicinus (15.5.22). He had little hope of returning alive from the mission. Each member of the party thought only, as he measured out the long journey to the north, of his own prospects of survival. In somewhat contradictory fashion, Ammianus also claimed that all reflected, as they travelled, on Cicero's sentiments on the relief brought by the restoration of good fortune after bad (5.23). One would imagine that this is a touch that occurred to Ammianus later, as he looked back on his experience.[9]

The arrival of the party at Cologne brought no improvement in their prospects. It was evident that Silvanus was popular there, and that unless Ursicinus and his men employed the very greatest circumspection they were liable to be condemned and executed 'under a single proclamation'; 'constabat nos omnes sub elogio uno morte multandos' (15.5.26). The whole situation was beyond their control; 'cuncta nostris conatibus altiora' (5.24). Yet, given time, stealth might pay off. Under guise of friendship and sympathy with Silvanus, Ursicinus' men tested the loyalty of his supporters. While Ursicinus was honoured and dined by Silvanus, sharing treasonable confidences on the state of the empire and their own frustrations, soldiers from the Bracchiati and Cornuti were found ready, for money, to attack Silvanus early one morning, haul him from the Christian chapel where he took refuge and kill him (5.31).[10]

Ammianus, no doubt reflecting Ursicinus' opinion, expressed admiration for Silvanus. He was a general of distinction who had supported Constantius loyally, as his father, a Frank called Bonitus, had supported Constantine. Like Ursicinus, Silvanus had received less recognition than his services merited. Men of lesser deserts were raised to the consulship, while Silvanus – again, comparison with Ursicinus is implied – unjustly suspected of disloyalty, was forced into it. Yet Ammianus had no comment to make, no scruple to express, on the manner of Silvanus' suppression. Having with Ursicinus successfully performed Constantius' commission, he wrote of the outcome with detachment, as merely a question of expediency and efficiency. Viewing their accomplishment in this light, they had indeed done very well.

Even after the suppression of Silvanus, the incorrigibly suspicious emperor complained to Ursicinus that the Gallic treasuries had been interfered with (15.5.36). Ammianus asserted that no one had touched them, and, in any event, Ursicinus was instructed to succeed Silvanus as commander-in-chief of the Rhine armies, and retained that command after the arrival of the new Caesar, Julian, appointed by Constantius late in 355. His position was somewhat anomalous. Since his recall for consultations at court, Ursicinus had neither been relieved of nor promoted from his post as *magister equitum* in the east, where a deputy, Prosper, held office as *comes* until he should return (14.11.5). In 356, Ursicinus received a successor, Marcellus, in Gaul, but again was instructed to remain there until the end of the campaigning season (16.2.8). In fact, he was in Gaul for eighteen months, until the early summer of 357 (16.10.21), and Ammianus was with him for all that time.

Ammianus recalled aspects of his stay beyond the Alps, some of them surely from personal experience. He mentioned inscriptions which he had read on the mythical origins of the country (15.9.6). He had apparently seen the remains of Aventicum (Avenches), 'now a deserted city, but once of some distinction, as its half-ruined buildings demonstrate to the present day' (15.11.12). A description of the decayed walls of Augustodunum (Autun) need in itself owe nothing to personal knowledge on Ammianus' part, though it is likely enough that he had been there (16.2.1). Other allusions prompt more speculative inferences. Ammianus narrated at one point an accusation of treason which arose out of an opulent dinner-party in Aquitania, 'such as are very often given in those parts' (16.8.8). Perhaps the reputation of this part of Gaul for wealth and elegance, expressed in its many literary productions of the fourth century, explains Ammianus' information on this matter. But it might be simpler to believe that he had some personal knowledge, having himself been to such parties. A common stereotype, rather than personal experience, was presumably behind another of Ammianus' livelier pictures, that of the enraged Gallic housewife entering the fray in support of her man, baring mighty arms and levelling blows 'like a catapult' (15.12.1)![11] Gauls in general, Ammianus went on, are loud and threatening in manner, even when in good humour, but they are proud of their appearance and one will rarely see a Gallic man or woman, however poor, in ragged or dirty clothes. Again, Ammianus thought of Aquitania as particularly bearing out the truth of this remark (15.12.2).

*

Ammianus witnessed in Gaul the first phase of Julian's achievement as Caesar, which he believed to be even more remarkable than what followed later – above all, because it was so unexpected (16.1.5). But he did not himself see the climax of this phase, the battle of Argentorate (Strasbourg) at which Julian's army routed the confederation of Alamannic tribes led by king Chnodomarius; for, by then, Ursicinus, still attended by Ammianus, had at last been relieved of his command in Gaul and allowed to take up his appointment in the east. Constantius had just completed his visit to Rome, from where, on 29 May 357, he departed to march to Sirmium by way of Tridentum (Trento), in the valley of the Adige. It was to Sirmium that Ursicinus was summoned, to resume his commission as *magister equitum* in the east. The more senior of his companions were promoted to independent commands of their own. The younger members ('adolescentes'), among whom Ammianus classed himself, were directed to stay with Ursicinus 'to perform whatever public service he should assign to us' (16.10.21). Relations between the Romans and the Persian king had recently developed in the light of the latter's difficulties with the rebellious eastern regions of his empire. The praetorian prefect of the east had judged that it might be possible to use the moment to conclude peace, and it was with this in view that Constantius sent Ursicinus, the best known of his generals on the eastern frontier, to resume his service there.

At the beginning of 358, the Persian king was still occupied with rebellion in the east. But he heard of Constantius' interest in a settlement just as he had resolved his difficulties there. Guessing that the emperor would not have made overtures unless he were himself in difficulties, Sapor was inspired to write aggressively to Constantius, demanding the return of his 'ancestral dominions' in Mesopotamia and Armenia. There was little Constantius could do, in the exchange of letters whose general purport is recorded by Ammianus (17.5.1ff.),[12] other than inform him that the usurpations in the Roman empire were suppressed, utter some sort of warning and meanwhile try to delay the Persians' preparations (5.15). But an embassy, the first of two that were sent to achieve this, returned unsuccessful (14.1f.).

After these diplomatic skirmishes, which occupied the summer of 358, events began to move very quickly. During the winter, Sapor was assembling his army, and preparing supplies and equipment for an offensive into the disputed provinces. At this time Ammianus, still no doubt with Ursicinus, was at Samosata, a strategic crossing of the upper Euphrates (18.4.7). Even at this distance, Ursicinus was not safe from his enemies at court, 'night and day banging away at the same anvil', who were still portraying the general as a threat to the emperor's position; chief among them was the eunuch Eusebius, annoyed with Ursicinus because he refused to make over to him his house at Antioch (4.3). Ursicinus therefore received his recall to court, where he would be more exposed to his enemies, and less likely to rebel. This was Ammianus' explanation; in fact, Ursicinus was recalled to replace Barbatio as *magister peditum* in the west. Barbatio had just been beheaded for treason, and Ursicinus' recall to serve near the emperor should undoubtedly be construed as a promotion, as indeed Ammianus states; 'dignitate adficiendus superiore' (6.1). It also seems evident that, once at court, Ursicinus should have found it easier, not more difficult, to defend himself against the attacks of rivals there.

Ammianus claimed that, far from being taken from the Persian front, Ursicinus should have been assigned to it, even if he had to be summoned from the ends of the earth (18.6.1). Nor did he think much of Ursicinus' successor Sabinianus, of whom he wrote with hearty dislike as a cultivated and well-heeled old gentleman, but obscure and quite unfitted for matters of war (5.5):[13] small in stature and narrow in mind, he could scarcely tolerate even the noise of a banquet, let alone battle (6.7). But Ursicinus obeyed the summons and set out on the long road west, turning aside the decrees and acclamations of cities trying to retain him as their protector (6.2); in such apparently spontaneous, but in fact calculated, expressions of sentiment by local communities, one gains some idea of the danger which an emperor might feel from a long-serving and popular general in a particular region (below, p. 405). The party had not far passed the Bosphorus when yet more letters were received from Constantius, instructing Ursicinus to return to the eastern front. This mandate was received by Ursicinus at the river Hebrus in Thrace (the Maritza, in European Turkey), and after some baffled hesitation he obeyed it (6.5-7).[14] To Ammianus', and presumably to Ursicinus', disgust, Sabinianus was left in office. Ammianus again saw this as an attempt to undermine Ursicinus, since if the Persians were repelled Sabinianus would be given the credit, and Ursicinus disgraced if they were not (6.6); but this view ignores the different military functions to be filled by the two men.[15] Ursicinus was to take local measures for frontier defence,

Sabinianus to manage the larger deployments and to preserve intact the main body of Constantius' army in case a major engagement with the Persians had to be fought (cf. 19.3.2).

Nor were Constantius' changes of plan as wilful as they seemed to Ammianus and Ursicinus. The situation in the east was developing very fast, and the government had to respond to its changing phases as well as it could at the considerable distance – over 1,500 miles – at which it was placed from the scene of action. Just at the time that Ursicinus was recalled to court, a Roman from Syria, named Antoninus, defected to Persia with intelligence on Roman military dispositions. Received with delight at the Persian court, Antoninus encouraged Sapor's intention to attack the Roman provinces. It was the intensification of Sapor's preparations in the light of the intelligence brought by Antoninus that prompted Ursicinus' re-assignment to the Mesopotamian theatre of war. That he should have received notice of this re-assignment in what were to him such puzzling circumstances is a measure of the time needed by a government in the west to receive information from the eastern frontier and to react to it by sending instructions to participants who were nearer the sources of information than was the emperor himself.

Returning east, Ursicinus left Sabinianus to his slumbers at Edessa and rode to Nisibis to prepare it for a siege. Events were indeed developing rapidly, for the first stages of the invasion had already begun. From the walls of Nisibis, fires could be seen burning in the country as far as the Tigris: Persian raiding parties had crossed the river and were on their way (18.6.9). Ursicinus left Nisibis and pressed on to make arrangements elsewhere. Two miles from the city, the party encountered in the road a little boy, wailing because his mother, distracted by terror of the enemy and hurrying to get to the safety of the city, had lost him. The boy was well dressed and apparently came from a good family; so Ammianus was detailed to take him back to Nisibis. He rode with the boy to the city walls and put him down inside a postern gate. Persian raiders were already surrounding the city, and Ammianus did not want to get caught up in a siege, so he galloped off to catch up his party. Slipping pursuit, he saw Ursicinus and his party resting at a weak fortification called Amudis, their horses put out to graze around it.[16] He warned them of the Persians' approach by waving his cloak in the air and joined the party, which hurried on, Ammianus and his now weary horse keeping up with difficulty (6.13).

Night came and with it a full moon, and the group was confronted by an open, treeless plain; so they employed the classic device of fixing a light to a pack animal and driving it off in another direction as a decoy. Only this stratagem, thought Ammianus, had saved them from capture. Pausing only to seize, interrogate and put to death a Roman soldier (a Gaul from Paris) who had deserted to the Persians and was sent back by them as a spy, Ursicinus and his followers reached Amida (18.6.16).

Here, Ammianus' narrative takes on still more of the air of an

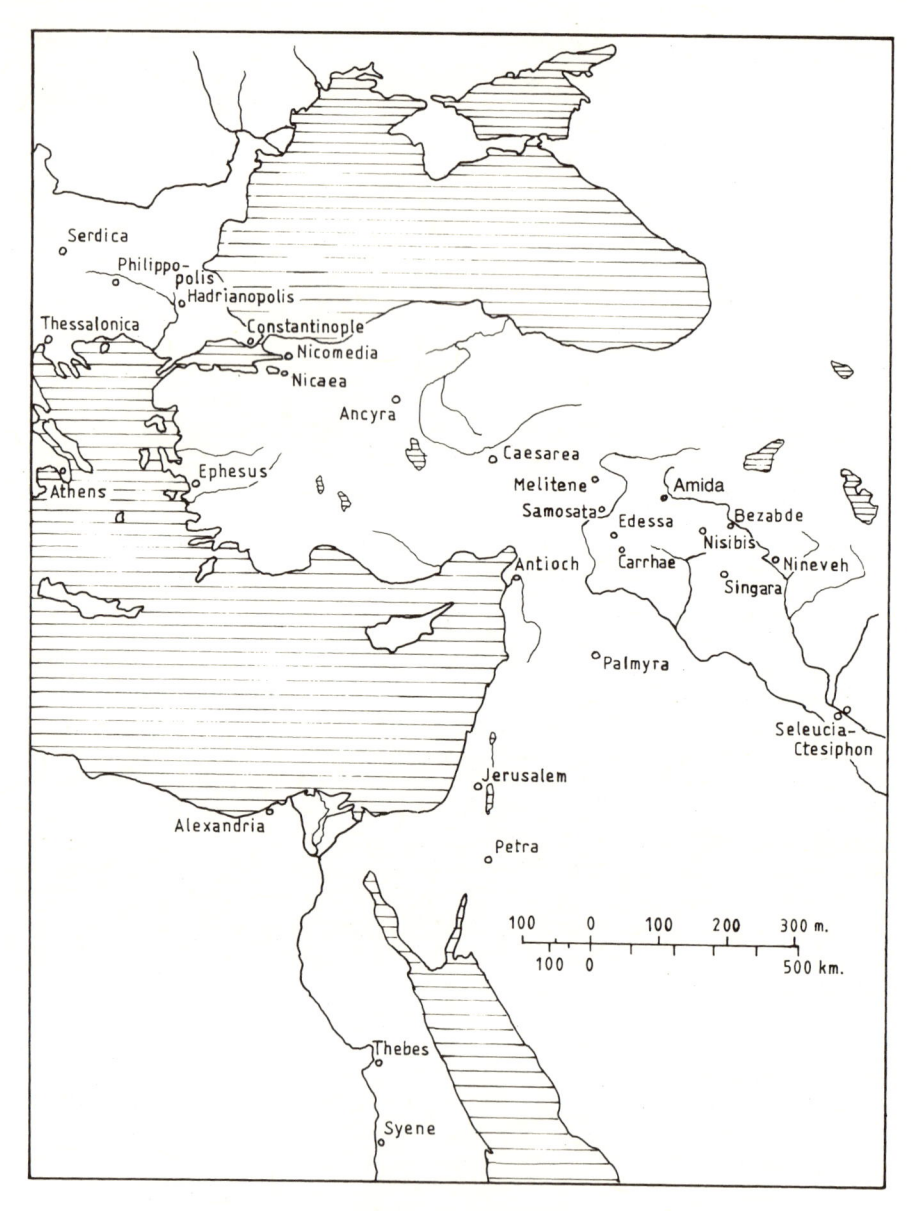

Map 1. The Roman East.

adventure story. Scouts returning to the city brought with them, hidden in a sword-scabbard exactly as recommended by Frontinus three centuries earlier (*Strat.* 3.13.5), a ciphered letter from the second group of ambassadors whom Constantius had sent to the Persian court (cf. 17.14.2). The envoys of the Greeks, ran the message, given by Ammianus in a Latin version of a presumably (once deciphered) Greek original, had

III. Ammianus and Constantius 43

been sent away, perhaps to their deaths; 'while that aged king, not satisfied with the Hellespont, will join bridges over the Granicus and Rhyndacus and invade Asia with many peoples. He is by nature prone to anger and very cruel, and is urged on and provoked by the successor of Hadrian, a Roman emperor of former times'. Unless Greece took care, the message ended, she was finished and her funeral rites sung (18.6.18).

Ammianus recalls that the cipher was found very difficult to understand – an observation that sounds more surprising than it should, partly because Ammianus has already given the text and its interpretation when he makes it. The message in the scabbard was written in symbols ('notarum figuris', 18.6.7) which, even when deciphered, yielded a second code describing the present situation by allusion to a historical parallel that was not totally obvious, and indeed has only recently been fully interpreted.[17] The message attests favourably the historical culture of its senders, as well as some optimistic assumptions on their part as to the culture of those to whom it was sent. It should have been enough to baffle the intelligence, though it would no doubt have raised the suspicions, of any Persian who intercepted it and managed to get any sense from its coded symbols; and it may be that even Ursicinus and his advisers did not appreciate every nuance. It referred, not as one might suppose to the great invasion of Greece by Xerxes in 480 BC, but to the invasion of the Roman province of Asia by King Mithridates VI (Eupator) at the beginning of the third Mithridatic War in 74/3 BC. Mithridates, not Xerxes (or Alexander the Great) was the 'aged king' of fierce temper who would bring many foreign allies against Asia (Appian, *Mithr.* 69-71). Beyond this point, and even without understanding all the historical allusions of the message, it was relatively easy to interpret Mithridates' objective 'Asia' as the Roman province of Syria, and a matter of basic historical knowledge to identify the 'successor of Hadrian' as Antoninus, who had deserted to Persia and was now supplying Sapor with the military intelligence he was using in the preparations for his invasion. As for the 'bridges over the Granicus and Rhyndacus', Mithridates would have crossed these rivers in his march from the Hellespont to Asia: they were identified by Ursicinus and his aides with the Anzaba (the Greater Zab) and the Tigris. Sapor was therefore intending to cross both the Greater Zab and the Tigris, presumably (to make the double crossing worth while) at some distance above the confluence of the two rivers. Even if this were correct (and it might not be), much remained open. The Persians might take a line along the hills of Sinjar, passing the city of Singara, where Constantius and Sapor had fought a drawn battle in the 340s, and then – with difficulty – march north-west to Nisibis or Carrhae: they might, on the other hand, follow the Tigris another forty or fifty miles upstream, crossing it somewhere south of Bezabde and then marching into the Roman empire along the flank of the Tur Abdin. For a general concerned with local defence, these alternatives made a considerable difference. It is true that raiding parties had reached Nisibis; but who could tell what was happening meanwhile at Singara?

To try to verify and put more precise detail into their information,

Ursicinus and his colleagues devised a plan to send Ammianus himself on a spying mission to the satrapy of Corduene in northern Mesopotamia. It happened that the governor, or satrap, of Corduene was known to Ammianus. His name was Jovinianus — at least this was the name he assumed on Roman soil, since he had earlier been sent to Syria as a hostage, and was there filled with such a love of liberal studies that he wished for nothing more than to return to the Roman empire (18.6.20).[18] He is described by Ammianus as a young man, 'adolescens', and so was the same sort of age as himself; and Ammianus' recognition and warm reception by Jovinianus after his journey to him 'through trackless mountains and precipitous passes' in the company of a loyal centurion, may suggest that the two men had known each other quite well. It is an obvious conjecture that they had been educated together at Antioch (below, pp. 55ff.).

Jovinianus provided his visitor with a discreet native guide, with whose help Ammianus reached a vantage point in the mountains from which, he wrote, even the smallest objects were visible at fifty miles' distance, 'if only the human eye was keen enough' (18.6.21). Ammianus waited there for two days and on the morning of the third saw what he had come for: the entire country filled to the horizons with the vast army of the Persian king, as he led it over the Zab and past the site of ancient Nineveh against the Roman empire (18.7.1). The array seemed to Ammianus to put to shame the boastful legends of the Greeks on the invasion of Xerxes, who in the famous story had counted his troops by corralling them in batches of ten thousand. The total of that army, so counted, was alleged to have come to a million and seven hundred thousand men (Herodotus 7.60ff.). Ammianus' literary flourish — this is of course what it is — may seem extravagant, but it is how one might expect to find conveyed to an educated Graeco-Roman public an impression of the sheer scale of the threat now facing the east Roman empire.

Ammianus judged that the army would take a full three days to pass over into the Roman empire. He had also established, as the ciphered message had indicated but despite Roman fears to the contrary, that the Persians were in fact taking a more northerly route rather than crossing the Tigris directly — below its junction with the Greater Zab — by a single bridge of boats (18.7.2).[19] He therefore allowed himself to rest a little and be entertained by Jovinianus — the two men doubtless recalling in their conversations old times together at Antioch as well as matters closer at hand. He then returned to Ursicinus, who immediately sent fast dispatch-riders with orders to the military and civil governors of Mesopotamia to evacuate Carrhae and clear the country people off the land. The Romans set fire to the grasslands to deprive the Persians of fodder, and sent detachments to fortify the west bank of the Euphrates with manned fortifications, palisades and artillery (7.6).

So Ursicinus pursued his instructions to supervise the local preparations for war, while Sabinianus remained inactive, conducting military exercises among the graveyards outside the walls of Edessa 'as if

III. Ammianus and Constantius

he had made peace with the dead' (18.7.7).[20] Meanwhile, the Persian army had after crossing the Tigris skirted the hills (the southern edge of the Tur Abdin) to avoid the scorched plains, and passing Nisibis without attacking it turned further to the north; they had learned that the Euphrates was in spate and must be crossed higher up. Sapor was evidently still directing his invasion against the cities of northern Syria. Ursicinus countered this by making for Samosata, with the intention of breaking the bridges at Zeugma and Capersana (8.1), but he was frustrated at the outset of this manoeuvre by the failure of a recently arrived Illyrian detachment, set to guard the road near Amida. Ursicinus and Ammianus found their party surprised by Persian cavalry, and were forced to fight their way out of it. At the beginning of the skirmish, which went on for half an hour (8.7), Ursicinus and the renegade Antoninus actually met and, in a curiously ceremonious scene, exchanged words; at the end of it, more Persians arrived, and the Romans had to meet their danger as best as each man could, fighting in scattered groups right up to the steep banks of the Tigris (8.9). Some fell in and were drowned, dragged down by their armour or pulled under by the current. Others got away and made for the mountains. Ursicinus himself escaped with a tribune and a single attendant.

Separated from his party, Ammianus looked around him and saw a *protector* struggling up, with an arrow in his thigh. It was Verinianus, also named as one of the party sent to suppress Silvanus at Cologne and so an old comrade of Ammianus (15.5.22). Ammianus stopped to help him but was again threatened by Persians and made his way alone towards Amida. Verinianus is not mentioned again nor is his fate described, and it does not look as if Ammianus waited to see what it was. Rushing frantically towards the city, he joined crowds of others, Romans and Persians, all struggling to reach the higher ground where Amida stood. Only a single approach to the city was open – a narrow track, further constricted by artificial obstructions placed there precisely to prevent easy access.[21] All night they waited without moving, so closely packed together that corpses were propped upright, unable to fall: in front of Ammianus, a hideous companion, a soldier with his head split from top to bottom by a ferocious blow from a sword and gaping apart, but standing there like an upright post or tree stump.[22] Above, the defensive artillery thundered and howled, hurling its missiles over the heads of the refugees as they huddled below the city walls. So Ammianus edged his way into the city through a postern gate. Inside, too, he found great crowds; the Persian attack had happened to coincide with an annual fair, and thousands of the country folk had come to the city as innocent visitors. Here it was the confused noise of human voices that Ammianus recalled, of people wailing for their dead, crying with pain from their wounds, calling out for their families, lost in the narrow, crowded streets (8.14).

When Ammianus came to describe the siege of Amida, it seemed to him, in a memorable expression, that the city and its region had attracted to themselves the sufferings of the entire Roman world; 'Romanae rei totius aerumnas intra unius regionis... ambitum' (19.1.4). It was left to face them without much help from the Roman authorities. Despite Ursicinus' complaints, Sabinianus refused to commit his forces to the relief of Amida. Perhaps he was right to do so, and he was certainly fulfilling the letter of his instructions from Constantius not to risk his forces in a major engagement before the emperor himself could reach the scene (3.2). In any event, it seems unlikely that, had he sent 'all his light-armed troops' to Amida, as Ursicinus suggested, these forces would have had much impact on the huge Persian army around the city. Ammianus should have reminded himself, as he set out his judgment on Sabinianus' behaviour, that he had compared this army to the hosts of Xerxes (18.6.23).

Ammianus' description of the siege of Amida, and of his own part in it, is one of the high points of his history (indeed, of all Latin historical writing), and is discussed in detail in the next chapter (IV.2). After more than two months, the defence of the city finally yielded to the Persian attack. Ammianus, seeing the end as the Persians overran the defences, slipped out (in a masterpiece of under-statement as well as cunning) as he had entered the city, by a postern gate.[23] After more adventures, he came with his two companions to Melitene. There he found Ursicinus, whom he accompanied back to Antioch: he had thought that he would never see it again (19.8.12). Among the defenders of Amida, the count and tribunes in charge of the defence of the walls were crucified by the Persians, and the *protectores* were led off into captivity, hands bound behind their backs (9.1). Ammianus must have found this out later. Had he stayed in the city, he would have been among them – and our knowledge of late Roman history would have been immeasurably the poorer.

Sapor's anger is easy to understand. The siege of Amida had detained him for seventy-three days, diverted him from his main object and cost the lives of thirty thousand soldiers (19.9.9). On the Roman side Constantius, stunned by the loss of the city, appointed two senior officers to enquire why it had happened. For Ammianus and Ursicinus, the reason was obvious. Sabinianus had been implored by Ursicinus to send help to Amida, but had refused from inertia and envy, and was therefore to blame for its loss (20.2.3). As we have seen, this was not a balanced assessment of the situation, and it took no account of Sabinianus' instructions from Constantius. Ammianus was certainly entitled to ask himself what more he personally could have done, but that is not quite the same question.

By this time, Constantius had returned from the west to Constantinople to take on the Persian threat at close hand (19.11.17),[24] and Ursicinus had joined him to assume his appointment as *magister peditum* at the imperial court, held over since his temporary reassignment to the eastern frontier. He had clearly not so far been held responsible for the loss of Amida; but now he felt that the commission of enquiry was against him, in refusing to see the obvious and accept his denunciations of Sabinianus. Placing the blame, as he was inclined to, with his personal

III. Ammianus and Constantius

enemies and especially with the eunuch Eusebius, Ursicinus demanded that his case could properly be heard only by the emperor in person. This was not unreasonable, but Ursicinus added tactless aspersions against Constantius' advisers, finally proclaiming that if the emperor continued to submit to the judgment of eunuchs, nothing could prevent the total seizure of Mesopotamia the following year, even if he came with an army himself to defend it (20.2.4). His sentiments were conveyed to the emperor. It was enough, and Ursicinus was dismissed.

In 360 the Persians did renew their attack, and Constantius was present to meet them. Yet he was unable to prevent the siege and capture of Singara and Bezabde (20.6-7), and his efforts to recover Bezabde late in the season were cut short by the onset of bad weather (20.11).

It has been suggested that Ammianus remained in active service between 360 and 363, and even that the vividness of his account of the siege of Bezabde shows that he was present under the command of Constantius at the operations there.[25] But compared with what precedes, his narrative of this event gives no real indication of personal involvement, and it seems more likely that whatever happened to him – whether like Ursicinus he was dismissed the service, whether he was given some remote, inhospitable posting, or whether he was able simply to recede from view and live for a while in private life out of the public eye – the removal of Ursicinus from active life was the end too of Ammianus' privileged view of contemporary affairs.[26] Until the renewal of his ambitions with the arrival of Julian at Antioch and the excitement of the Persian campaign in 363, Ammianus' interest in events was as an observer rather than as a participant. In fact, even taking into account the Persian campaign it is doubtful whether he ever again achieved the familiarity with the highest counsels of state that he had enjoyed in the service of Ursicinus. His partisan commitment to Ursicinus is an obvious consequence of this relationship, while his failure to consider other points of view is a small price to pay for the realism, the living tension and the sense of involvement of this part of his history.

CHAPTER IV

North-East Frontier

(1) The satrapy of Corduene

One of the most intriguing personal episodes in Ammianus' history is his journey to Corduene briefly described in the previous chapter, and one of its most vivid individual moments is the description of his towering view over the plains of northern Mesopotamia to see the Persian army assembling beyond the Tigris. Both aspects merit further reflection.[1] We cannot expect to know exactly where Ammianus stood to get his view. A glance at a relief map will show that in every sector of their northern and eastern limits these wide plains are overlooked by such commanding vantage points. Just such a view as that enjoyed by Ammianus is described by the Englishman Austen Layard, while narrating his journey made in 1849 along the upper Tigris from Redwan (Ridvan) to Nineveh. Layard followed the Tigris through its gorges east of Ridvan, but then diverged from the river and began to climb towards the summit of a ridge from which, he was assured by his guide Cawel Yusuf, they were to 'behold all the world'. His impression when they did so is worth reading, as an echo of the feelings which a similar view must have evoked in Ammianus, and as a telling brief account of the physical geography of northern Mesopotamia:

> and certainly [wrote Layard], when we reached the summit, there was about as much of the world before us as could well be taken in at one ken. We stood on the brink of the great platform of Central Asia. Beneath us were the vast plains of Mesopotamia, lost in the hazy distance, the undulating land between them and the Taurus confounded, from so great a height, with the plains themselves; the hills of the Sinjar and of Zakko, like ridges on an embossed map; the Tigris and the Khabour, winding through the low country to their place of junction at Dereboun; to the right, facing the setting sun, and catching its last rays, the high cone of Mardin; behind, a confused mass of peaks, some snow-capped, all rugged and broken, of the lofty mountains of Bohtan and Malataiyah.... (*Nineveh and Babylon*, p. 51)

The hills of the Sinjar, on whose southern slopes, and so out of Layard's (as of Ammianus') view, stood the Roman city of Singara, were a full sixty miles to the south of his vantage point, while the mountains of Malataiyah, or Malatya – Roman Melitene, by the upper Euphrates – were no less than 150 miles to the west. Later in his expedition, Layard

IV. North-East Frontier

journeyed from east to west along the hills of Sinjar. He travelled along their southern edge, but on one occasion crossed over to the northern side to settle a village feud, and there too recorded the impact of the view which opened up when he came to the summit of the pass:

> The Sinjar hill is a solitary ridge rising abruptly in the midst of the desert; from its summit, therefore, the eye ranges on one side over the vast level wilderness stretching to the Euphrates, and on the other over the plain bounded by the Tigris and the lofty mountains of Kurdistan. Nisibis and Mardin were both visible in the distance. I could distinguish the hills of Baadri and Sheikh Adi, and many well-known peaks of the Kurdish Alps....
> I have rarely seen any prospect more impressive than these boundless plains viewed from a considerable elevation. (*Nineveh and Babylon*, pp. 251-2)

From the Jebel Sinjar, Nisibis is about sixty, and Mardin eighty, miles – distances which even show as unduly cautious Ammianus' estimate that he could see up to fifty miles from the vantage point to which he was directed by Jovinianus (18.6.21).[2]

The particular question of where Ammianus stood to get his view of the plains of Mesopotamia is not solved by the comparison with Layard. Layard, after all, produces two different vantage points, from near Findik and from the Sinjar hills, which are very similar in their general effect, and there were others (in a footnote he compares the view from Sinjar favourably with a third, better known view from Mardin).[3] It is unlikely that Ammianus was anywhere near Layard's first position just north of Findik, since this was only a few miles across the Tigris from the fortress of Bezabde, still in Roman hands at the time of Ammianus' visit to Jovinianus. He could hardly have described such a location as remote and distant, nor need he have taken quite so much trouble to get there.

In his review of the Persian army massing beyond the Tigris, Ammianus mentioned the sacrifices made by the Persians in the middle of the bridge over the Anzaba, and of their passage by the city of Nineveh; 'postquam reges, Nineve Adiabenae ingenti civitate transmissa, in medio pontis Anzabae hostiis caesis extisque prosperantibus, transiere laetissimi...' (18.7.1). It has often been noted that the sacrifices, which are in fact no part of Persian ritual, can hardly have been seen by Ammianus but were a product of his literary imagination.[4] No more need we suppose that he actually saw with his own eyes the Persian king at the head of his host, dressed in brilliant attire, with Grumbates, king of the recently rebellious Chionitae, beside him – 'a man of only moderate physical strength and with wasted limbs, but with a certain grandeur of mind and distinguished for his many famous victories' (18.6.22). The figures of Grumbates, and of Sapor himself, were better known to Ammianus from their later appearances before the beleaguered city of Amida (below, p. 61). Yet we should need no reminder that the use of literary artifice to heighten dramatic effect is part of the accepted technique of an ancient historian. Ammianus' flourish can be recognised for what it is, without throwing his entire account into discredit. If he took back to Ursicinus the information that the Persians had to cross two rivers (the Greater Zab and the Tigris) rather than just one before they could enter the Roman empire (18.7.2), his knowledge, and therefore his viewpoint, must relate to the regions around the Zab.[5] He must have stood on an eminence to the south of Bezabde and of Layard's vantage point, perhaps an outlying ridge of the mountains of Zakho somewhere north-east of Nineveh.

It is a nice coincidence that Ammianus should have described the Persian king as passing by Nineveh, that 'great city of Adiabene' (18.7.1), while Austen Layard should be confronted by his view of 'all the world' while on his way to resume his explorations in its ruins. It was another of Layard's many strands of interest in northern Mesopotamia to trace the course of one of those confrontations between east and west, of which its plains had seen, and would again see, so many – the route taken by the Ten Thousand Greeks of Xenophon in their retreat from Persia in 401 BC. Both Ammianus and Layard were in their times gazing down onto the very place where the Ten Thousand had paused and decided what best now to do, in the light of their information on what lay before them. They had just passed the ruins of two great cities once held by 'the Medes'. The first of these, Larisa, was Assyrian Nimrud or Khalhu, with its mighty brick walls and stone base, and its perimeter of two parasangs, or six miles (so according to Xenophon; the actual perimeter is 4½ miles). The nearby 'pyramid of stone' on which the local villagers had taken refuge from the Ten Thousand, was evidently the Assyrian citadel, or ziggurat.[6] The second city, Mespila, was ancient Nineveh, situated at six parasangs (the distance is in fact twenty miles) north of Nimrud (*Anabasis* 3.4.7-12).

The choice which lay before the Ten Thousand, as they paused not far north of Nineveh, was either to retreat westwards, to Lydia and Ionia (that is to say, along the route through northern Syria envisaged by Sapor in 359), or to the north, through the mountains of the 'Kardouchoi' – the Kurdish mountains of Bohtan, whose 'well-known peaks' were viewed by Layard from the distant hills of Sinjar. What Xenophon heard of the inhabitants of these mountains was, to say the least, disconcerting. An army of 120,000 Persians, he was told, had once penetrated their fastnesses and never been heard of again; though sometimes they made peace with the satrap in the plains and then there was mutual contact (*Anabasis* 3.5.16). Xenophon's Kardouchoi were warlike mountain folk, defending their passes fiercely against the intruding Greeks. Yet in the first century AD the geographer Strabo, discussing the territory of the 'Gordyaioi', gives a rather different view of its inhabitants (16.1.24). The Gordyaioi, he wrote, in ancient times called the Kardouchoi, lived near the Tigris and were especially skilled as building engineers and in the operation of siege machinery, and were used for their expertise in the armies of King Tigranes of Armenia. They possessed three main cities, Sarisa (this will be Charich, south of the Tigris in the Tur Abdin), Satalka

IV. North-East Frontier

(possibly Chattakh or Çatak), and Pinaka. The last of these was a strong defensive position, with three mountain peaks each separately fortified, to produce a sort of 'triple city'.[7]

Sarisa, Satalka and Pinaka were undoubtedly not the only cities, or fortified settlements, in Strabo's land of the Gordyaioi. They were not necessarily the same as the chief cities of Ammianus' time, and it does not help that all cannot be located with certainty. Yet in setting off for Corduene under Ursicinus' instructions, Ammianus must have known, or been able to find out, where he was likely to find Jovinianus, and it would no doubt be to the same place that he returned, to rest and be entertained after his journey of reconnaissance (18.7.1). It is something to be able to visualise it as some sort of city or castle which served as a chief place of Jovinianus' satrapy.

*

Roman occupation of northern Mesopotamia had followed in the tracks of the Macedonians, both civilisations conforming to the conditions laid down by the geography and climate of the region.[8] Such cities as Carrhae, Edessa, Nisibis, Resaina (later Theodosiopolis) and Singara with their territories represent the possibilities, and the limits, of sedentary cultivation. All are enclosed by the 200mm rainfall limit (isohyet), sufficient to permit the cultivation of cereal crops by dry-farming techniques; although these possibilities are rather more stringently defined by local conditions, and by the reliability of rainfall in an individual year, to which figures based on a sequence of years may not be an accurate guide. Marginal land, both inside and outside the 200mm isohyet, would be cultivated as opportunity arose by transhumant or semi-sedentary Arab tribesmen seizing 'catch-crops', otherwise put to use as seasonal pasture for stock-raising – sheep, horses and, in the more arid zones, camels. The potential for more regular and systematic cultivation of the marginal areas depended also, where the expectation of rainfall justified it, on the active encouragement and stable conditions provided by a political authority, on one side or the other. This was sometimes forthcoming, sometimes not. War between Rome and Persia was doubly prejudicial to the sedentary way of life, for it was an obvious deterrent against the investment of labour required for agricultural exploitation, and, on both sides, offered greater incentives and opportunities for licensed banditry (below, p. 351f.).

Looking beyond the possibilities of agricultural exploitation, the essential condition for urban development was of course the availability of continuous sweet water (whatever surface water is found on the plains is frequently impure and made saline by evaporation). Edessa had its famous sacred pools with their shoals of fish, described by a Christian pilgrim in the 380s (*Itin. Egeriae* 19.7) and still to be seen today – 'nunc usque', as Ammianus would say.[9] The modern Arabic version of the name of Resaina, Ras el Ain, records the water-point which sustained the ancient city (ᶜain, a common element in Arabic place-names, is 'well' or 'spring'). Coins commemorating its settlement under the Severi as a veteran colony of Legio III Parthica show the symbolic act of breaking up the land with the plough.[10] The coins are not literal evidence of agricultural exploitation, but the site would not have been colonised at all had not this been possible, and Resaina is an example of genuine settlement, not simply the upgrading in status of an existing community. Singara, another Roman colony of the Severan period, and a site much fought over in the fourth century, exploited the water catchment of the Jebel Sinjar, at the southern, and more fertile, base of which it stands; south-easterly winds bring up moisture from the Persian Gulf and the marshes of the lower Tigris-Euphrates basin, to fall on the southern side of the range.[11] This is a feature rather specific to Singara, for most of the rain in northern Mesopotamia comes in from the Mediterranean to fall on the higher land to the north and east: the tract between Singara and Nisibis is accordingly described by Ammianus as arid and waterless (20.6.9). Nisibis, the key Roman city of the region, was fed by the river Mygdonius (the Oued Jaghjagha) from the catchment area of the Tur Abdin, and could live comfortably on the produce of its fields (devoted in modern times to the production of cotton). At Nisibis as at nearly all cities of the Roman empire it was agriculture which sustained the wealth of its upper class, of which Ammianus provides an interesting example in the person of the renegade *curialis*, Craugasius. He possessed a country estate eight miles from the city (19.9.7; below, p. 387).

From a different point of view, the deliberate burning of the grasslands running along the southern edge of the Tur Abdin between the Tigris and the Euphrates, as reported by Ammianus (18.8.4), is another indication of the nature of the cultivation and possibilities of settled life in the area, good cereal country; to which he adds a comment no less illuminating of the natural history of northern Mesopotamia in ancient times. The fires, notes Ammianus, caused the death of many of the fierce lions which roamed the area.[12] Their habitat was the swampy country (to be seen on modern maps in the depression between Nisibis and Singara), where they live quietly in winter, but in summer are plagued by hordes of mosquitoes which attack their eyelids. Tormented by their bites, they leap into watercourses to rid themselves of the insects and drown, or else scratch out their own eyes in fury. Were it not for this, concluded Ammianus in a fine piece of ecological observation, the whole of the east would be infested by the beasts (18.7.5)!

The limits of the Romans' influence to the south are shown by their earlier inability to control Hatra, a once important Arab city in the desert beyond Singara; its abandoned ruins were seen by Ammianus during the retreat of Julian's army from Babylonia in 363 (25.8.5; below, p. 186). To the east of Singara, equally, extended a tract of territory towards the river Tigris, to which the Romans did not lay claim. The direction of their occupation was north-eastwards, where the Roman empire marched with the Tigris in the region north of ancient Nineveh, an occupation

IV. North-East Frontier

represented by the fortress of Bezabde and supported by their influence over the northern satrapies, of which Corduene was one. When the Romans ceded Nisibis and Singara to the Persians in 363, they had also to give up the fifteen fortified points by which they had controlled this region (25.7.9). It is interesting as further indirect evidence for the agricultural exploitation of the area, that when Ammianus describes the surrender of these fortifications and their occupation by Persian commanders he mentions also the territories attached to them; 'munimenta praesidiaria cum regionibus' (25.9.12). The region formed the Persian province, and in due course the ecclesiastical district based on Nisibis, of Arbaye or Arabia.[13]

It would be banal to describe this as the far eastern frontier of the Roman empire. Equally important, within their local context the satrapies extending along the eastern Taurus towards the Tigris formed a barrier between north and south. Corduene and its neighbours might protect the cities of northern Mesopotamia from an attack mobilised from Armenia, if Armenia should be induced to be be disloyal to Rome; or, in different circumstances, if the Persians were to overrun Mesopotamia as they threatened to in 359, the satrapies might protect Armenia against attack from the south. Their status and loyalties were thus matters of great importance both to Roman and to Persian governments.

In the mid-third century, control of northern Mesopotamia had been wrested from the Romans by the reinvigorated Sasanian regime in Persia; but it had been recovered under the Tetrarchs, especially by the spectacular campaign of Galerius in 298.[14] Galerius had redeemed the Persians' capture of Valerian by seizing the harem of the Persian king Narses. In consequence he was able to dictate his terms, which were essentially that the Roman frontier was set at the Tigris, while Rome acquired five principalities in the north. The westernmost of these principalities, Ingilene, was centred on the Armenian fortress of Egil, not far north of Amida. The next, Sophanene, later contained Justinian's fortress of Pheison, or Fis, and three days' journey to the east of this was the Roman city of Martyropolis (Mayferqat), ancient Tigranocerta. Beyond this, the river Nymphios (Batman Sou) divided the satrapy from Arzanene, which in Procopius' day was where Persian territory began; the centre of this principality was the fortress of Arzen. Then came Corduene, where the Tigris turns the eastern limit of the Tur Abdin to run down into the plains of Mesopotamia; and the fifth region was Zabdicene, with its city of Bezabde (Syriac Beth Zabde). The place is described by Ammianus, in narrating its siege by Sapor in 360. It stood on a slight elevation on the banks of the Tigris, fortified by a double wall where the terrain gave less protection. It was defended by three legions and a large number of local troops – 'archers of the Zabdiceni, then loyal to us, in whose territory this town is situated' (20.7.1). To give some idea of the importance of Bezabde, the regular garrison of Amida was only one legion, together with substantial local forces (18.9.3).

Such a formal account of the Tigris frontier of the Roman empire gives no real idea of the local ambiguities within which it functioned. The frontier won by Galerius, for instance, is said to have lain on the Tigris; yet the five regions ceded to Rome in 298/9 lay largely beyond it. This difficulty is resolved by supposing direct military occupation by the Romans as far as the Tigris, and an area of influence, maintained by alliances, beyond it; some sources do in fact speak of the frontier as standing on the far side of the river, 'supra ripam Tigridis', assuming Roman dominance, if not direct control, of the five principalities to the north. At the same time, it is clear that some parts at least of the five districts came over to the strictly 'Roman' banks of the Tigris. Bezabde itself, standing as Ammianus says 'in the territory of the Zabdiceni', was actually on the Roman west bank; while if Strabo's town of Sarisa, one of the three chief places of the Gordyaioi, can be identified with Charich in the Tur Abdin, then at least the earlier equivalent of Ammianus' Corduene also extended to the Roman side.

A fuller impression of the actual functioning of the frontier zone is given by Ammianus, and by a later Syriac source, in their accounts of the foundation of the city of Amida. According to Ammianus, Amida was established as a fortified place by Constantius, while he was still Caesar – that is, before 337. It had previously been insignificant, but Constantius, to give the neighbouring peoples a secure place of refuge,

> surrounded Amida with solid towers and walls, and equipping it with a battery of defensive artillery, made it formidable to the enemy and wished it to bear his own name. (18.9.1)

This last is a puzzling statement, possibly to be explained by confusion with Antoninupolis/Constantina or Constantia (modern Viranşehir) mentioned by Ammianus in the same passage, as another city founded by Constantius.

The Syriac *Life of James the Hermit* describes the same event in more colourful detail. After building Amida, Constantius is said to have come to love it more than all the other cities of his empire, and to have submitted to its control many lands –

> from Ris Aina as far as Nisibis, and also the territory of Mayferqat [Martyropolis] and Arzoun [Arzanene] and as far as the limits of Qardou [Corduene]. Because these lands were at the frontier, Persian raiding parties were constantly attacking and plundering them. Tur Abdin was in the midst of these lands, and so the emperor built there two great fortresses to protect the lands against the Persian raiders. He built one of them at the frontier of Beth Arbaye at the summit of the mountain, and the other on the Tigris. This he called the 'Castle of the Rock' [Syriac Hisn Kef], and he made it the chief place of the land of Arzoun....[15]

If this is so, Constantius had established forts in and around the plateau of the Tur Abdin, namely Amida, the 'Castle of the Rock', and the fortress in the mountains. As to Amida, Ammianus gives a formal description (18.9.1ff.), a curious feature of which is that it reverses the orientation of two of the faces of the city. According to his description, the river Tigris washes the southern (it should be the eastern) side, while the eastern (in fact, the southern) side faces the plains of Mesopotamia: presumably a moment of confusion on Ammianus' part when he came later to write up his account of the city, for no one will doubt that he knew it intimately.[16] Ammianus was mistaken, also, in thinking that the Tigris rises close by (18.9.2). To the north, Ammianus goes on to say, Amida looks towards the river Nymphius (true if he means its upper reaches) and the Taurus mountains, and to the west the fertile, farmed country of Gumathena, in which is the township of Abarne with the thermal springs for which it was well known (18.9.2). Abarne is modern Çermik, from the Armenian Djermuk, 'baths'.

Hisn Kef or Kiphas, the 'Castle of the Rock', lies on the south bank of the Tigris about 70 km below Amida. An infantry detachment, Legio II Parthica, is listed there in the late fourth century by the *Notitia Dignitatum* (*Or.* 36.30) under the command of the *dux Mesopotamiae*; it had been transferred from Bezabde, where Ammianus makes it part of the garrison in 360 (20.7.1). The *dux* of Mesopotamia in office at the time of Ammianus' involvement on this frontier, Cassianus, is mentioned on a few occasions by the historian; he receives the orders from Ursicinus to clear the land, evacuate Carrhae and burn the grasslands (18.7.3), is later found stationed at Nisibis (19.9.6) and turns up in 363 to meet Julian's army on its retreat from Persia towards that city, somewhere in the desert south of Singara (25.8.7).

The unnamed 'castle on the mountain' has been persuasively identified with the fortress Rhabdion, and this associated with the name of Tur Abdin itself. Mentioned frequently in Byzantine sources and a site of obvious importance, Rhabdion is surprisingly not mentioned by Ammianus: hence a speculative identification with Ammianus' 'castra Maurorum', equally important but not named by other sources, surrendered to the Persians with Nisibis and Singara in 363 (25.7.9); one name will reflect a Roman, the other an indigenous, form.[17] At the southern edge of the plateau of the Tur Abdin, as Hisn Kef is to the north, Rhabdion does indeed, as indicated by the *Life of James the Hermit*, stand at the southern limit of the district, and later Persian province, of Beth Arbaye.

The eastern culmination of these strong points was Bezabde, besieged and taken by Sapor in 360. The military frontier, so traced, falls on the river Tigris, as the cessions made to Galerius require. At the same time, the frontier runs through and impinges upon native territories whose relationships with Rome, and indeed with each other, are far more complex and changeable than the formal situation may suggest.

In terms of the peace treaty of 298/9, Corduene, the satrapy of Jovinianus, ought to have been subservient to Rome, Galerius having then won it from Persia. But it had slipped away. Ammianus regarded Jovinianus as a Persian nominee – his time spent in Syria had been as a hostage, evidently to secure the good behaviour of his family or people, and Jovinianus now gave the allegiance of his satrapy to the Persians, as Ammianus makes clear; 'satrapa Corduenae, quae obtemperabat potestati Persarum' (18.6.20). When Julian's supporter Procopius led a division into Persian territory in the great campaign of 363, he was ordered to march through Corduene before devastating Chiliocomum and invading Assyria (23.3.6). At a later stage, the Roman army in their retreat from Ctesiphon by the Tigris route resolved to 'seize' Corduene, and from there make for safety in the Roman empire (24.8.4f.; below p. 159).

In all these situations, Corduene is envisaged as in effective Persian territory; yet this was still not so in formal terms, since Jovian's peace treaty with the Persians made later in 363 involved the surrender to them of Corduene, together with four other 'Transtigritane regions' then in hands of Rome: Arzanene, Moxoene, Zabdicene, Rehimene (25.7.9). Together, as we have seen, they were to constitute the Persian administrative district of Arbaye (p. 53). The 'surrender' of Corduene in 363 is formally incompatible with Ammianus' statement that it already, four years earlier, gave its allegiance to Persia; 'obtemperabat potestati Persarum'. The ambiguities in the position of Corduene can be resolved only by a more flexible understanding of how it and its neighbouring 'satrapies' behaved in their social and political setting.

The status of the northern satraps in relation to Rome is well illustrated by a law of Theodosius addressed to the 'satrap of Sophanene' in 387 (*CTh* 12.13.6). Sophanene was still at that time within the Roman sphere of influence; but it is most unusual to find a recipient of imperial legislation addressed with the Persian title of 'satrap', and the conditions under which he is supposed to offer crown gold (*aurum coronarium*) to the Roman emperor are equally revealing of his special position. According to the law, the gold, traditionally offered by all satraps as a gift to the emperor, was to be paid from the satrap's own resources and not raised in levies from his subjects. It was not a form of taxation – as it would be in a normal Roman province – but a personal gift, after the ancient custom whereby the satraps showed their 'devotion, which is due to the Roman empire'.

Whatever the ambiguities of their status in the Roman empire, the view taken by the Persian king of these 'Transtigritane regions' was quite unambiguous. After the capture of Amida in 359, Sapor had the Roman soldiers recruited from these regions rounded up and killed to a man, with no distinction of rank (19.9.2). The districts from which they came were treated by the Persians as theirs by right, and the service to Rome of the Transtigritani was thus a simple case of treachery. This was however clear only in the context of Persian pretensions to ownership of these regions. In general, it was an area of complex local loyalties that do not always fit into the tidy categories of 'Roman' or 'Persian'. Ammianus' friendship with the satrap Jovinianus was formed, we can assume, in the setting of the literary schools of Antioch. Jovinianus had been educated

IV. North-East Frontier

there and become a lover of Greek culture, and longed – or so he gave Ammianus to believe – to return to the Roman empire. An eastern source, the Syriac *Life* of a Persian martyr saint, shows Jovinianus in a very different light. He is here found supervising the settlement in the region of Beth Arbaye – as we have seen, the territory east of Nisibis towards the Tigris – of peoples from Arzoun, Beth Zabde and 'Arabia' itself, with the permission of Julian the Apostate 'who then resided at Mahoze'.[18]

Mahoze is the Persian capital of Ctesiphon (below, p. 155f.); the circumstances of Julian's residence in that region hardly seem to permit of his alleged role in Jovinianus' settlements, and other details in the narrative are confused and self-contradictory (despite the connection with Julian, for instance, the text has Jovinianus already dead at the time of Sapor's attack on Bezabde in 360, before Julian had come to the east). It is possible that the emperor, if one was involved at all, was Constantius rather than Julian, but if the main outlines of the situation envisaged are authentic – and Jovinianus' presence at all in the document is evidence of his local prestige – a most interesting picture emerges. Beth Arbaye is an area where sedentary occupation was possible in the terms outlined earlier (p. 51), but one of uncertain political control, more usually inhabited by transhumant groups of tribesmen raising catch-crops and exploiting the pasturage as it was available. In settling this area with peoples from Arzanene, Zabdicene and Beth Arbaye or 'Arabia', Jovinianus was exercising pretensions beyond the confines of Corduene, on land that formed part of the territory, if not of the Roman empire itself, then of its clients the Zabdiceni. It is not clear at whose expense or with whose (if anyone's) permission Jovinianus' aggrandisement was taking place, but we begin to see Ammianus' friend for what he was: a local chieftain, whose cultural horizons had been enlarged by his education as a hostage in Syria, respecting a friendship made there by receiving Ammianus and offering assistance for his mission, but sufficiently sensitive to the balance of power on the frontier of the two empires to have carried his satrapy into the Persian sphere of influence without quite losing touch with the Roman, while seizing the opportunity to enhance his own position as patron of peoples beyond the rather flexible limits of his own satrapy. Perhaps one of the motives for his kindly reception of Ammianus was that he, as much as his guest, wished to know the true scale of the Persian preparations; for Jovinianus cannot have been the only local potentate to await with interest the outcome of the invasion of 359 and of the siege of Amida. If it is true that Jovinianus, a young man of Ammianus' age, was dead by 360, it may even be that something went badly wrong with his calculations.

(2) The siege of Amida

Looking back at the siege of Amida, as it were through the eyes of king Sapor, Ammianus counted it as another instance of the great losses he had sustained in siege warfare against the Romans, citing the sieges of Singara and – more than once – Nisibis (19.9.9).[19] Amida had held him up for seventy-three days and cost him 30,000 men. If the second part of this information, based though it was on observation, seems doubtful, there is no need to question the first. Ammianus several times states or implies that Sapor's main objectives lay elsewhere – Ursicinus, it will be recalled from the previous chapter, had gone to break the upper Euphrates crossings at Zeugma and Capersana. Antoninus' advice to the king, supported by his commanders, was to the same effect (19.1.3,6), and the reduction of Amida, forced upon Sapor by the refusal of his ally king Grumbates to leave the place without avenging his son's death before its walls (2.1), was a frustrating diversion of the aims of his invasion. The anger obvious in Sapor's treatment of the city and its defenders after its fall can be understood. He had arrived before Amida with his strategic purpose intact and his main options still open to him; when he left the destroyed city it was already the month of October, too late to advance further and time to take his army, captives and booty back into Persia (9.1).

Ammianus' account of the siege of Amida is one of the high points of his narrative and a classic passage in Roman historical writing. Despite this, or because of it, it is easy not to realise that it presents certain difficulties of interpretation, and especially of chronology. Even if, against the natural reading of his text, we take the seventy-three days attributed by Ammianus to the siege to include the two days' marching required by Sapor to arrive at Amida from the captured forts of Reman and Busan (19.1.1), a surprisingly small proportion of the operation is actually covered by his narrative. At the opening of the siege Sapor approaches the walls, evidently hoping that the defenders will immediately agree to surrender, but is shot at and retires in a flurry of disorder (1.5). Dissuaded by his commanders from a wasteful display of anger, he decides to try again. On the second day the Chionite king Grumbates comes up to the city on his behalf, but a skilled marksman picks off his son with a bolt from a *ballista*. Fighting breaks out, but from the next day a truce is observed, culminating in the funeral of the young man with native rites; these ceremonies last for seven days (1.10). After two further days of rest, the Persian army surrounds the city in a massed demonstration of strength, which lasts all day though no attack is made (2.4). The first two assaults come on the next two days, the second of which Ammianus gives as the 'fifth day', counting this from the end of the seven days' truce (2.12).

At the end of the siege, six more days are registered in a similarly careful fashion. They begin with the return of the Gallic troops at Amida from a night attack on the outposts of the Persian camp (19.6.7ff.). A truce of three days is observed, before the Persians press their final assault. This lasts three days (7.1; 7.6; 8.1), and on the third day the city falls (8.1).

Between these extremes, the first fourteen and the last six days of the siege, Ammianus provides only two further episodes relating to its chronological development. A pestilence breaks out, which is settled on the night after the tenth day of its incidence by a light shower of rain. The episode provides Ammianus with an opportunity, hardly justified by the relative scale of the events in question, to mention Thucydides and other authorities in a short digression on the origins and causes of plagues (19.4.2-7). It was caused, in Ammianus' view, by the decomposition of corpses, aggravated by the torrid heat and the poor physical state of the occupants of Amida (4.1). As to when the pestilence broke out, Ammianus gives little indication, but his attribution of cause would lose its point if the outbreak were long delayed. There were many fatalities in the first two Persian assaults on the city (2.14f.), and the corpses of Romans, as he remarked in discussing the aftermath of the siege, decomposed beyond recognition after four days (9.9).[20]

The second episode was the occupation of one of the defensive towers of the city by seventy Persian archers, who were installed there by a deserter; he led them to it by way of the hidden staircase linking the city with the Tigris, as Ammianus had observed was the case in all cities of that region that adjoined rivers (19.5.4f.). The repulse of the threat by skilled artillery fire from five small *ballistae* lined up against the tower, and of the assault on the walls which was co-ordinated with the occupation of the tower, took until mid-day (5.8). On the next morning the defenders of Amida could see from their citadel columns of prisoners from the captured city of Ziatha being led away into Persia. This in particular angered the Gallic troops in Amida, who demanded with threats that they be allowed to attack the Persian army (6.3). It was agreed that if they were prepared to wait for a while they might do this, the night sortie being the result.

That the occupation of the tower, a major event in Ammianus' account of the siege, came near its end is indicated by what he had written of the mood and character of the Gallic troops (19.5.2). Raised by the usurper Magnentius but transferred by Constantius to the east because of doubts about their loyalty (18.9.3), they were brave and quick, well-suited to pitched battles but not to the style of warfare in which they were now involved. They made several sorties ('aliquotiens') against the Persians, to no significant effect – as if one man, in the popular saying, were to try to extinguish a burning city with water carried in the palm of the hand (19.5.2). In the end ('postremo') the Gauls were locked inside the city, the gates being barred against them; though their effectiveness as fighters was demonstrated in days to come ('secutis diebus') in their heroic night attack on the Persian camp. Ammianus' indications of time, and his statement that the Gallic troops had made repeated earlier assaults until as a last resort they were confined, suggest that the occupation of the tower and the night attack against the Persians were not far separated. Ammianus presents the night attack, which closely preceded the fall of the city, as being due to the Gauls' refusal to tolerate any more delay after the promise had been given them that they might make an attack ('morarum impatientes', 6.7).

Ammianus' account of the siege of Amida is therefore concentrated on certain major episodes. He accounts for the first fourteen days of the siege and, with little detail, ten days of pestilence which perhaps ensued quite soon; then, towards the end of the siege, the occupation of the tower, on the next day the sight of the prisoners from Ziatha and, soon after this, the six days leading to the final assaults on the city and its fall. Of Ammianus' seventy-three days during which Sapor was at Amida we must presumably assign some for the thorough sacking and burning of the city at the end of the siege; yet even so, a clear thirty or thirty-five days, occupying the central phases of the operation, remain unaccounted for and there is no episode that can be assigned to any particular part of them.

The omission is not so surprising, in a history concerned with 'res gestae' – with great deeds, heroic and ingenious exploits, violent emotion and suffering.[21] It may even reflect reality. Protracted sieges actually were like this, with initial assault and final outcome separated by large tracts of time involving occasional initiatives by one side or the other, and much general preparation and waiting. In two or three passages, Ammianus indicates this less distinctive level of activity. In the first, he describes how 'while the fighting was going on' ('dum pugnatur') Ursicinus tried persistently but in vain to persuade Sabinianus – stationed, it will be recalled, at Edessa – to release troops for the relief of Amida. The fighting here referred to was, to judge by the context, in the early stages of the assault, but Ammianus' presentation assumes that Ursicinus' efforts to awake Sabinianus were persistent. Failing in this, he 'often' ('saepe') sent scouts to the city, who were usually unable to penetrate the ring of Persian besiegers (19.3.2).

There is also the necessary, and necessarily protracted, preparation of siege works. Ammianus makes a transition from his description of the end of the pestilence, to the 'unquiet Persian's' surrounding of the city by wickerwork mantlets, and the preparation of mounds and ironclad towers designed to overtop the city walls and drive the defenders from the battlements by missile fire from a higher level (19.5.1). While this was going on, though there is no major assault, the city is kept under continuous fire from slingers and archers; it was during this period of light engagements, too, that the Gallic soldiers made their earlier sorties against the Persian forces. At a later stage – immediately before the Gauls made the night attack which ushers in the final assault on Amida – Ammianus again describes the piling up by both Persians and Romans of high mounds to serve as fighting platforms; these were the 'slow works' ('operibus lentis'), through which the fall of the city was being devised (6.6). When the Roman mound suddenly collapses during the final assault, Ammianus refers to it with almost proprietorial feeling as 'that mound of our men, built with such long labour': 'diu laborata moles illa nostrorum' (8.2). This long, unremitting preparation and toil form the essential background, indicated so briefly by Ammianus, to the high points of drama and action that can seem to the reader to dominate his narrative. The siege of Amida, like any other, consisted largely of hard

IV. North-East Frontier

work and careful preparation, and the anxious waiting for something to happen. This even, relatively unspectacular level of activity is less easy to describe, but Ammianus is careful to indicate its presence.

As we should by now expect of him, Ammianus' account is at all levels full of momentary impressions, presented with an acute sense of their visual impact.[22] The view from the walls and citadel of Amida, as the city is encircled by the vast array of Persian arms, the entire landscape reflecting the glitter of weaponry and the glint of the famous armoured cavalry, the *cataphracti* who feature in the first of the final assaults on Amida (19.1.2; 7.4): as Sapor approaches so close to the walls with his escort that his features can be clearly recognised, and hastily retreats when fired on (1.5);[23] the shooting next day of the son of king Grumbates by the skilled *ballistarius* (1.7); the long column of prisoners from Ziatha being led away into Persian captivity, a sight which so angered the Gallic soldiers in Amida (6.1); the dizzying heights of the tower commanding a view of the Tigris over broken, rocky cliffs, from which it was impossible to look down without suffering from vertigo (5.4); and so on. Sometimes Ammianus' remarks go beyond what he could personally have known at the time. He is unlikely to have known positively when he actually saw them that the columns of prisoners were from Ziatha, and Ammianus does in fact take the opportunity to remark that other fortifications also were taken in these same days and their inhabitants, including old men and women, led off into captivity or left with their tendons cut if they could not keep up (6.2). He discovered these details later or could safely infer them, and inserted them where they belonged. Conversely, his description of king Grumbates, inserted in the course of his narrative of his visit to Corduene, may, as we have seen, derive from what Ammianus saw later before the walls of Amida; he thought it worth while to introduce in good time a man whose influence on the course of events was to be so decisive.

There is no need to doubt that Ammianus, like the skilled marksman who took aim and shot him, saw the death before Amida of Grumbates' young son. He would obviously be on the walls with other colleagues of relatively senior rank. One wonders how much Ammianus could actually see of the native burial rites of the prince, his body laid 'ritu nationis propriae' in military dress on a raised bier, surrounded by the effigies of ten young men on litters, sad feasts of soldiers 'per contubernia et manipulos' (a very Roman touch), dances and songs of mourning and the wails of women, compared by Ammianus for his Roman audience with the performance of the cult of Adonis by priestesses of Venus (19.1.10f.). Yet, if the Persian outposts were just beyond a bowshot's range (6.5), perhaps these events after all took place not so very far away, and Ammianus' description contains items of more than circumstantial interest, which are surely the result of observation. The effigies of the ten young men on litters – there would in the original rite have been, not effigies, but young men killed for their master's funeral – were no doubt appointed to serve the dead prince after death, in a funerary practice widely documented, from the *Iliad* of Homer (the funeral of Patroclus; 23.175f.) and Herodotus' Royal Scythians (4.71f.) to the Fiji Islands, the Kayans of Borneo, the native tribes of Central and South America, the kingdoms of India and China, in fact anywhere that anthropologist has set foot.[24] Further, for all its 'Roman' colouring, Ammianus' description of the funeral of Grumbates' son distinguishes the Chionitae in religious belief from the Zoroastrian Persians, whose rite involved neither cremation nor burial (which would pollute the elements) but the exposure of the dead in high places, to be consumed by birds of prey.

These matters merit a few moments' reflection. The Chionitae, coming from the north-east, had occupied the valleys between the river Oxus and the Hindu Kush in northern Afghanistan, and so bordered over the mountains the once powerful Kushans of the Kabul and upper Indus valleys. The Kushans, under the name 'Cuseni' in Ammianus, also fought as vassals in the army of Sapor (16.9.4; 19.2.3); in fact, the distinctive head-dress of their king, with its image of a ram's head, was mistakenly attributed by Ammianus to the Shah of Shahs himself (19.1.3).[25] Whether the Chionitae were identical with the settled, law-abiding and honourable people known to Procopius in the sixth century as the Hephthalites or 'White Huns' (*Wars* 1.3.1-7), and whether either really were Hunnish, are difficult questions, debated among specialists.[26] Procopius is at pains to point out the great differences in appearance and way of life between Hephthalites and 'regular' Huns, and it is hard to feel convinced that the differences can be entirely explained by changes in lifestyle from the nomadic to the sedentary; on the other hand it is possible that the assemblage of central Asian tribes that threw off the Huns as they became known to the west was actually much more varied in character than Graeco-Roman authors, who only saw part of them, suspected (below, p. 341). Procopius describes a Hephthalite custom whereby upon the death of a noble his living 'friends' or boon-companions, up to twenty or more, were entombed with him, but this again is inconclusive, for it might either suggest the identity of the Hephthalites with Ammianus' Chionitae, or simply reflect the wide diffusion of the funerary practice (*Wars* 1.3.7). Procopius' information on the Hephthalites expresses an antiquarian, somewhat 'Herodotean' spirit, and may not be accurate in every detail for his own day. The ceremony witnessed near Amida already represents a substitution of effigy for actual human sacrifice, while the fact that Ammianus indicates a rite of cremation but Procopius one of inhumation might be explained by a change in time from one mode to the other, or by some local variation of custom within the same ethnic group. Ammianus in any case gives as a fact Grumbates' decision that his son's ashes be taken to his homeland for burial in a silver urn; so, too, he may have had positive knowledge of the advice given to Sapor by his generals not to be deflected from his major objectives in the war by delaying at Amida through mere anger at being shot at (1.6), and of Grumbates' refusal to move from the city before his son's shades were avenged – and those who had killed him were by their

IV. North-East Frontier

own death reduced to his service in the after-life (2.1). It is a curious posture in which to imagine the shade of Ammianus Marcellinus.

In many details of the actual fighting at Amida Ammianus shows himself as clearly an eye-witness of what he describes, again with that sense of occasion which he can convey so marvellously; as in the first encirclement of the city by no less than five ranks of shields (the largest number he records in any siege that he describes) – the army filling the landscape, it seemed to Ammianus, as far as the eye could reach (2.2), with the Chionitae of Grumbates ranged opposite the wall by which his son had been killed (2.3). The whole day long they stood there immobile and absolutely silent, not a foot being moved nor the whinny of a horse being heard. At evening they withdrew in the same order, to eat and sleep before the sound of trumpets announced that the attack was to begin. Only then does Grumbates cast the blood-stained spear which to the Persians, as to the Romans, consecrated the start of the battle (2.5). The whole occasion is a splendid expression of the 'ritualistic' aspects of ancient warfare, Ammianus presenting it in the measured, rhythmic terms of ceremonial so characteristic of Roman, as well as Persian, public life; and he passes with calculated abruptness to the unceremonious brutality of the actual fighting; 'proinde diffractis capitibus...' (2.7).

Ammianus conveys the varied sounds of fighting, the blast of trumpets signalling a Persian attack (19.2.12) or raising the alarm in the Persian camp (6.9), answered on the latter occasion by the distinctive tones of the horns (*lituae*) in the city (6.10); the din of the artillery, operated unloaded to confuse the Persian outposts and cover the retreat of the Gauls from their night attack (6.10); the confused clamours of the countrymen of Grumbates' stricken son, summoning help from the 'numerous peoples' in the Persian camp to prevent his body being seized by the Romans. Ammianus' expression for 'confused' shouting – 'clamoribus *dissonis*' (1.8) – is used elsewhere to suggest the diverse cultures and languages of an army of Moorish rebels in north Africa;[27] a nuance which, unless it is a mere rhetorical gesture, would respond well to the diverse nationalities comprising the Persian army – notably Albani and Segestani (from Sistan in eastern Iran) and the Kushans and Chionitae just mentioned (19.1.6; 2.3). In the acclamations which accompanied the first (and, no doubt, every other) day's fighting at Amida, the Romans extol Constantius as 'Lord of the world and of all things' ('dominum rerum et mundi'), the Persians praise Sapor in their own language as 'Saansaan' and 'Pirosen'. Ammianus gives the meaning of these words. 'Saansaan' is 'King of Kings' (Shah of Shahs) – overlord of all the vassal princes of his empire – and 'Pirosen', 'Victor in wars' (2.11). The latter word provides the first element in the name of a great Mesopotamian city besieged and taken by Julian in 363, Pirisabora or Peroz-Shapur – 'Sapor Victorious' (24.2.9).[28]

Irrationally, it might seem, given the other dangers surrounding him, Ammianus harboured a particular dread of the elephants which formed a regular part of the Persians' armament. He describes them at the outset of the siege, as their hideous wrinkled bodies lumbered forward, laden with armed men – a spectacle, Ammianus thought, beyond any other in its dire horror, 'as I have often explained'; 'ultra omnem diritatem taetri spectaculi formidanda, ut rettulimus saepe' (19.2.3). This would have been in the lost books, but Ammianus returns to the subject again in much the same spirit while describing Julian's Persian campaign (25.1.14), and he is not averse from repeating his sentiments even sooner, during the last assaults on Amida. The attack was joined by the elephants, 'than whose shrill screeching and monstrous bodies the human mind knows of nothing more terrible'; 'quorum stridore immanitateque corporum nihil humanae mentes terribilius cernunt' (19.7.6). Like the elephants of Hannibal, the beasts did not always live up to their reputation; on this occasion, surrounded and scorched by the burning wreckage of the Persian siege-towers which the Romans had destroyed, they backed away and could not be controlled by their drivers (7.7).

Ammianus' personal involvement in the siege of Amida can be seen at its various levels in his use of the first person to describe his, and his colleagues' and fellow-sufferers', experiences.[29] The most commonplace of these, needing no documentation, is in his use of the first person to denote the Roman as opposed to the Persian side in the fighting, as in his contrast between the offensive and defensive siege works erected by the two armies (19.6.6). More interesting are the passages in which Ammianus associates himself with the others inside the city, seen at large. The vast Persian forces assembled outside the city, previously devoted to the overthrow of the entire Roman world, seemed now to be directed at 'our destruction'; 'in nostrum conversos exitium' (2.4). All we could now hope for, writes Ammianus, was a glorious end to our lives, and this we strove to achieve – a sentiment repeated a few sentences later (2.13). The heavenly powers had decreed, it seemed, that the miseries of the entire Roman world were to be concentrated within this single region; 'ut Romanae rei totius aerumnas intra unius regionis concluderet ambitum' (1.4).

Ammianus sometimes uses the first person to associate himself more closely with the group of officers responsible for the direction of the defence of Amida. The occupation of the tower by the Persian archers, with the co-ordinated attack on the walls, 'made us uncertain and doubtful which threat to face first'; 'inter incertos nos et ancipites quibus occurri deberet' (19.5.6). The work was divided between those who would operate the light *ballistae* brought up against the tower and those who would defend the walls against the attempt to scale them. Here Ammianus writes as one who was involved in the decision, as he does later in describing how the 'scorpions' were brought up to oppose the Persian siege-towers with their *ballistae*. This was determined, he writes, after much discussion on 'our' part; 'et tandem multa versantibus nobis, sedit consilium...' (7.6). Though Ammianus here remarks on the technical difficulties involved in moving the machines to their new emplacements, he is not writing in particular as an expert on artillery, but as an officer

IV. North-East Frontier

who, being as it happened in Amida, was necessarily involved in planning its defence.[30] The Gallic troops confined in the city, he noted, were quick and brave, but inept in 'those arts of war, by which we were encompassed' and indeed rather a nuisance; 'ad eas vero belli artes, quibus stringebamur, non modo inhabiles, sed contra nimii turbatores' (5.2). They could give no help in constructing siege machinery or defensive earthworks but could only make unproductive excursions against the Persian forces. If Ammianus uses the first person here as one of those generally besieged in Amida, in describing what it was eventually agreed to do with the Gauls he again puts himself in the company of those who made the decision; 'inopes nos consilii, et ... ambigentes, tandem elegimus...' (6.5).

As we have seen, Ammianus must have felt a particular sense of anger when he described how the *protectores* captured in Amida by the Persians were led off into captivity, hands bound behind their backs (19.9.2). He comes near to expressing it when he states how the *comes* Aelianus and the *tribuni* taken with him were wickedly ('sceleste') crucified by the Persians. It was through their practical initiative, wrote Ammianus, that the walls had been defended for so long and so many Persians brought to grief; 'quorum efficacia diu defensa sunt moenia stragesque multiplicatae Persarum' (9.2). He was certainly in a position to know at first hand the extent of their skill and enterprise.

The sudden collapse of the Roman defensive mound ultimately opened the way for the Persians to enter the city. Ammianus, seeing its fall imminent, hid with two companions near an unguarded postern gate and, when evening fell, escaped with them from Amida (19.9.5). Ammianus has never, throughout the entire siege, referred to himself in the first person singular; he always associates himself with others, whether the entire population or a smaller group, in the city. At the point of his escape he suddenly breaks into the singular ('evado'), as he used it also in earlier enterprises involving himself as an individual, such as his visit to Corduene, his departure from Nisibis and subsequent experiences when separated from Ursicinus, to his entry to Amida among the crowds of refugees inching their way up the steep path into the city (pp. 41ff.). Narrating the departure from Amida, Ammianus returns to this manner of writing. He uses the first person plural to associate himself with the two companions travelling with him, the singular to distinguish his experiences from theirs, as in their capture of a runaway horse ten miles from the city (8.6f.);[31] Ammianus gets on to ride, the companions continue on foot. The journey was not without incident and it was to combine speed with safety that Ammianus and his companions made through wooded country for the higher mountains and Melitene; they would thereby avoid the attentions of Persian cavalry, which naturally preferred to operate on the plains. Finding there 'the general' (identified by most commentators as Ursicinus) about to depart, they accompanied him and came to Antioch.

The fall of Amida, as we saw earlier, brought about the retirement of

Ursicinus after his tactless remarks on the emperor's reliance on eunuch advisers (20.2.4f.). It brought a worse fate for the Count of the Sacred Largesses, Ursulus, who, moved by the sight of the ruined city when Constantius came to visit the scene in 360, allowed himself to pronounce on the lack of spirit shown by soldiers, for whose provision the empire's financial resources were gaping asunder – an interesting point of view, which secured his execution at the trials conducted under Julian at Chalcedon two years later (20.11.5; cf. 22.3.7f.). Ammianus deplored the execution, for Ursulus had supported Julian in the difficult times of his Caesarship under Constantius (below, p. 88). He was destroyed without Julian's knowledge and against his wishes, wrote Ammianus, by the resentment of the military ('militaris ira'), mindful of what he had said when he saw the ruins of Amida. Ursulus' remark was indeed unjust to the defenders of Amida, as Ammianus obviously realised. He ascribed it to Ursulus' bitterness, brought on by his grief at the sight of the ruins (20.11.5). So Ammianus reconciled the injustice done by Ursulus to the defenders of Amida, with the injustice done to him at Chalcedon.

Amida was rebuilt. Its strategic position, important before, was still more so after the surrender of Nisibis and the advance of the Persian frontier to the west of that city. The Roman population of Nisibis had to be found new homes, and it is likely that Amida received many of them. It had previously, according to Ammianus, been a city of relatively modest extent: 'intra civitatis ambitum non nimium amplae' (19.2.14). He means not just that it was a small place in relation to the 20,000 souls crowded into it in 359, but that it was made intolerable by the influx of such numbers. The surviving walls of Amida (Diyarbakir), built of forbidding dark basaltic stone, date originally from the sixth century. They represent a Justinianic rebuilding, with some enlargement, of a city whose main expansion in the time of Valens, transforming it from the city known to Ammianus, had taken place after its siege and sack by king Sapor, and in consequence of the surrender to him of Nisibis in 363.[32]

CHAPTER V

The Young Ammianus: Social and Cultural Setting

Ammianus' narrative of the Persian invasion of 359 expresses vividly the sense of personal adventure and action which are an essential aspect of this part of his history. At the same time, in ranging with such vigorous effect over this complex and fascinating country between his own city of Antioch and the Tigris, the narrative reveals something of no less interest and importance, the regional and cultural setting of Ammianus' experience as a young man. A single phrase shows how well at ease was Ammianus in the landscape of this theatre of war. Escaping from Amida after its fall to the Persian attack, he made his way with his two companions to a distance of ten miles from the city. He did so, as he wrote, helped by his knowledge of the desert terrain: 'squalentium peritia locorum' (19.8.5).

Seen in a longer perspective, this was a region of ancient and great civilisations, of cultural complexities deriving from millennia of history.[1] The city of Carrhae, which Ursicinus evacuated against the Persian invasion of 359, was Biblical Harran, the home of the family of Abraham. Almost seven hundred years before Ammianus' time, it had been re-founded by the Macedonian settlers of Mesopotamia. Edessa, where the general Sabinianus 'made peace with the dead' (p. 44f.), bore the name of a Macedonian city, and was alternatively known as Antioch-upon-Callirhoe after the abundant, pure springs mentioned in the previous chapter: though it is the original Syrian name, Orhai, which has survived to denote the modern town of Urfa. The great city of Nisibis had been settled by the Macedonians and called by them Antioch-in-Mygdonia. Now known as Nusaybin, the place is mentioned, as Nasabina, in Assyrian records. Batnae in Osrhoene, as Ammianus remarked, had been settled 'by a band of the ancient Macedonians' (14.3.3). At the sites of these Macedonian settlements in Syrian territory, the Romans too had placed their colonies in the second and early third centuries. So Carrhae, Edessa, Nisibis, Singara and other places bore in their titulature the names of the Antonine and Severan emperors, representing Roman control, established in that period, of northern Mesopotamia.

The two great empires of west and east, Graeco-Roman and Sasanian, met over an area in which other civilisations had preceded them both.

Relations between them were fluid and ambiguous, often belying the notion of a fixed frontier. The renegade Antoninus, who had deserted to the Persians with intelligence on Roman dispositions, had formerly been a prosperous trader, later an accountant on the staff of the military commander of Mesopotamia, finally *protector*. In one or all of these capacities, he was a familiar figure in Mesopotamia – 'very well known in those regions', as Ammianus remarked; 'per omnes illas notissimus terras' (18.5.1). Knowing Latin as well as Greek, he was able to make researches into the military establishment of the empire in preparation for his defection. He escaped by acquiring a farm at Iaspis by the Tigris; it was situated, wrote Ammianus, 'at the extreme limits of the Roman world' (5.3). If correctly identified as Isfis (or Hespist), lying by a tributary of the Tigris (the Oued Haltan or Khaltan), it was not far from Bezabde, whose surviving inhabitants were led off into captivity by Sapor after its capture in 360 (20.7.15).[2] Having acquired his farm, Antoninus installed there his wife and children and visited them frequently to allay suspicion. He then arranged his departure from the Roman empire by being ferried with his family over the Tigris at dead of night: he achieved this with the collaboration of the satrap of the adjacent Persian province, Tamsapor, whom he already knew; 'et antea cognitus' (18.5.3).

At a later stage, when Antoninus and Ursicinus met face to face in the strange encounter near Amida described by Ammianus, and Ursicinus denounced him for his treachery, Antoninus responded in a way which in outward manner was already totally 'Orientalised' (18.8.5ff.). He dismounted, removed the tiara which he wore as a mark of honour among the Persians, and bowed low, his face nearly touching the ground, to salute Ursicinus, addressing him as 'patron' and 'lord' and joining his hands together behind his back in 'Assyrian' fashion to indicate his suppliant status. Having defended his conduct – or more precisely, as Ammianus says, while still speaking – he slowly withdrew from Ursicinus' presence, stepping backwards with dignity ('verecunde retrogradiens'); almost, one might say, as if he were in an Iranian audience-hall. Ammianus, with his late Roman sense of character portrayed in social action and gesture, must have been fascinated by the performance. It was pure theatre from start to finish – which is not to question the more general relevance of Antoninus as an example of that adaptability which characterised social relations and conduct in this frontier zone, between two empires and two cultures. Antoninus, after all, was a former merchant who knew the local Persian satrap. He is as good an example on the Roman side as is the former hostage Jovinianus on the Persian, parading his Roman name and love of Greek culture, while in his capacity as local potentate settling tribesmen from the northern satrapies on the cultivable grasslands of Beth Arbaye.[3] There is more here than theatrical declarations or nimble changes of political allegiance, granted that these were involved; the actions of Antoninus and Jovinianus are genuine expressions of the deeper ambiguities implicit in this meeting-place of Graeco-Roman and Iranian empires.

The ramifications in the confrontation are still further complicated by the use among the local populations of a dialect of the Aramaic language, Syriac, throughout the so-called 'Fertile Crescent' which runs from Palestine through Syria and down the Euphrates valley into Babylonia.[4] This situation is well appreciated, if not always sufficiently emphasised, by historians: well understood too is the fact that direct evidence of it, from Classical Graeco-Roman sources, is very slender. In the early third century the jurist Ulpian discussed the validity of verbal agreements made by parties using different languages from each other, as between Latin and Greek (which raised no problem), or other languages such as Punic or 'Assyrian', that is Aramaic – Sabinus having written that an obligation might be contracted in any language, provided that both parties understood what was said, either directly or through a reliable interpreter (*Dig.* 45.1.1.6). Elsewhere Ulpian allows the validity of 'fideicommissa' expressed in Punic, Celtic or 'the language of any other people' (*Dig.* 32.11 pr.); but such references are like isolated voices in a massive conspiracy of silence mounted by the urban upper classes of the Roman empire against the native hinterland of their cities. Ammianus' compatriot, Libanius, became involved in a dispute over jurisdiction and patronage relating to a community of Jewish peasants which had for generations worked land belonging to his family (*Or.* 47.13). At no point did he ever suggest what must almost certainly have been true, that the peasants spoke their own language, nor should we expect him to have done so; the matter was of no importance to Libanius, despite the social relations and the need for communication with the lower classes implied by the institutions of landowning and patronage. It requires the more open social perspectives revealed in the sermons of the Antiochene cleric, John Chrysostom, or *Lives of Saints* by a writer such as Jerome or, in the fifth century, Theodoret of Cyrrhus, to tell us openly that the common spoken language of the peasantry was Syriac. Chrysostom implies that this situation prevailed immediately outside the gates of Antioch, for he remarks in a sermon how at Easter the city was crowded by Christian peasants who entered it from the surrounding country, speaking a strange language 'though in faith united with us'.[5] The Syriac language is of course universally reflected in the place-names of the area, even in the immediate neighbourhood of Antioch. Ammianus gives an example which, as it happens, is relatively remote from Antioch, in the Tur Abdin not far from Amida. Describing the settlement, he remarked that its name, Meiacarire, meant 'place of cool waters'; 'cui fontes dedere vocabulum gelidi' (18.6.16). He did not explain, perhaps thinking that his readers would find it obvious (or not thinking about it at all), that the meaning derived not from Greek but from Syriac. What this implies as to Ammianus' own knowledge of Syriac is unclear; it is surely unlikely that a man whose familiarity with the landscape helped him escape from Amida was entirely without acquaintance with the most widespread of the languages spoken in it. On any view of Ammianus' knowledge of Syriac, it is important to recognise the relevance to his experience of the social dimension represented by the Syriac language, and of the social exclusiveness implied by the failure of Classical sources to say anything about it.

Antoninus, as a once prosperous merchant known throughout Mesopotamia, must have known the annual fair held at the beginning of September at Batnae in Osrhoene. To this fair came just such wealthy merchants, to trade in the merchandise brought there – through Persian territory – 'from India and China and many other parts, by land and sea' (14.3.3). The great crowds assembled at Batnae for the September fair of 354 attracted the interest of a Persian commander instructed to raid Mesopotamia at any given opportunity (14.3.1). It is simply not possible that at such a time only Greek and Latin were to be heard in the streets of Batnae; yet when Ammianus wrote of Antoninus that he 'knew both languages' – 'utriusque linguae litteras sciens' (18.5.1) – it was Greek and Latin that he meant. The context, that of Antoninus' espionage activities in the east, does not encompass Syriac, but Ammianus' phrase 'both languages' does not consider it even as a theoretical possibility.

It has been well remarked that among the Graeco-Roman upper classes of this region of a Syriac-speaking peasantry there must have been a degree of 'more or less shamefaced bilingualism' in Greek and Syriac, as members of the urban elites coped with the practical problems of running their estates while maintaining what another writer has most aptly called their 'intellectual disdain for the parochial', that is to say the culture of the countryside.[6] Whether Antoninus (or Ammianus) did not know Syriac, whether their knowledge of this language happens only not to be recorded, or whether it is simply dismissed as unimportant for their roles as participant in or writer of history, the same observation holds true; that Ammianus' view of the 'two languages' as Greek and Latin was in itself an assertion of social values – the values of culture and administration imposed in successive ages, through the cities of the east, upon a native Syriac hinterland.

In his festival speech in praise of Antioch, the *Antiochikos* (*Or.* 11), Libanius was at pains to present his city as a creation of Alexander and his successors – as a Greek city to which the contribution of Rome was late in its history and peripheral to its true character.[7] Libanius abandoned his historical survey of Antioch with the fall of the Seleucid kings to Rome, with feeble excuses for omitting what followed: this, he suggested, could be seen all around and needed no exposition. So the Romans themselves need scarcely be mentioned, except to acknowledge the superiority of Antioch over their cities and of Greek culture over their own. Having once seen the lovely suburb of Daphne, its temple, trees and gardens, they will give up their praises of Italy. Antioch may yield to Constantinople in the length of its ramparts, but it enjoys a more gentle climate, civilised customs and the practice of wisdom; if this was a jibe at the new Christian capital, it underestimated the extent to which Antioch too was now a Christian city. As for the claims of Rome, they are outshone by Antioch's possession of Greek culture and eloquence. As we have seen

V. The Young Ammianus

(p. 12), Libanius could play a different tune when writing to Ammianus of the distinction won for Antioch by his historical readings given at Rome. That much of Libanius' discourse on Antioch echoes the rules for praising cities found in rhetorical handbooks such as that of Menander Rhetor is not to say that he was insincere in his choice of the genre, and only emphasises further his dependence upon the cultural traditions of the Greek east.

As rhetorician and teacher, Libanius insulated himself from the Latin language and culture, choosing instead, at some cost to his sense of reality, to operate within an exclusively Greek tradition. That he enjoyed the considerable success that he did, is itself a tribute to the Greek conservatism of the eastern provinces, to which a Latin government based first at Nicomedia, then at Constantinople, was a still relatively recent innovation.[8] In his loyalty to Greek, Libanius did of course represent an ancient and still lively cultural tradition, and one with centuries of history still before it; but fourth-century Antioch offers a far more complex picture than he allowed to appear in the *Antiochikos*. It was a cosmopolitan city, strongly influenced by the imperial court and its agents, and thereby exposed to cultural pressures studiously ignored by Libanius.

The first of these pressures was, precisely, the Latin language. If beyond the gates of the city Greek, the language of culture and education, yielded to the Syriac of the peasantry, within the walls and among the upper echelons of Antiochene society it was Latin that offered the challenge. Latin was the language of the military, and of the civil administration of the eastern empire in its relations with the imperial court. It was recognised that knowledge of Latin was essential for advancement in the imperial civil service. 'Look at this man', wrote John Chrysostom, setting out possible careers that a man might choose; 'he has learned the language of the Italians, and shines in the imperial service' (*PG* 47.357)! Ammianus mentioned Antoninus' knowledge of 'both languages' in the context of his espionage in the military dispositions of the eastern provinces – for which, again, much of the documentation would be in Latin. In an earlier generation an associate of Constantine the Great, by name Strategius, had assisted the emperor with his enquiries into various religious sects, 'Manichaeans and suchlike' (15.13.2). Called Musonianus at the emperor's behest to commemorate his erudition, Strategius became in 354 praetorian prefect of the east, an eminence which Ammianus attributed to his eloquence in 'both languages'; 'facundia sermonis utriusque clarus' (13.1). With more precise emphasis, it was to his knowledge of Latin in addition to his native Greek that Strategius owed his rise to the highest administrative office in the eastern empire.[9] Coming as prefect to Antioch, he entered friendly relations with Libanius, who attended him assiduously, composed a panegyric in his honour and pressed tirelessly the interests of justice (Libanius, *Or.* 1.106ff.). This at least is Libanius' version of his friendship with this notable member of the imperial governing class, but there is far more than this to Strategius' qualifications. He also pursued enquiries into the regime of Gallus Caesar (15.13.2) and opened tentative peace negotiations with Persia (16.9.2ff.).

In his *Antiochikos* (177ff.), Libanius recognised that Antioch was the place from which Persian campaigns were organised and resistance to Persian attacks co-ordinated: hence, of course, the emperors' interest in the city. The Tetrarchic palace stood on the foundations of an earlier such project of the third century, begun but left unfinished.[10] Ammianus had occasion to mention the palace, when describing how the orb placed in the hand of a statue of Galerius Caesar in its vestibule fell off and toppled to the floor; it was one of the ill-omens to greet the Emperor Jovian when he arrived at Antioch on his return from Persia in 363 (25.10.2). Libanius expounded the grandeurs of the palace and its surroundings, which formed a sort of royal precinct on an island in the Orontes on the north side of the city. There the emperors resided while they prepared their wars, bringing to Antioch all the vast impedimenta of their office – 'potestatum culmina maximarum et fortunae principalis insignia thesaurosque', as Ammianus later described them, referring to the presence of Valens at Hadrianople before the fateful engagement with the Goths in 378 (31.15.2). Libanius vividly portrayed the preparations at Antioch for a Persian campaign – the city noisy and bustling, crowded with men under arms and animals for war and transport, with soldiers being taken in gladly to private homes like members of the family (*Antiochikos* 178). How idealised was Libanius' picture is shown by Ammianus' description of the troops brought by Julian for the Persian campaign of 363. Undisciplined, disorderly and drunken, and stuffed with the leftovers from Julian's sacrifices, these troops, the Celtae and Petulantes, had to be carried through the city squares to their billets to sleep it off (22.13.6).

So the population of Antioch included large numbers of people associated with the imperial government, further swollen at quite regular intervals by the residence there of the emperor with his court and army. The presence of the court establishments of Gallus Caesar in 354 and of Julian in 362 certainly aggravated, if they did not create, serious food crises leading in both cases to public demonstrations, and in the first to considerable violence.[11] Even when the emperor was not there in person, the praetorian prefect, and also the civil and military governors of the Oriental provinces had their residences and office staffs at Antioch. All, to a greater or lesser extent, represented links with the Latin government of Constantinople. Of these officials, the *consulares Syriae* enjoyed the closest affinities with Antioch itself and were usually themselves easterners by origin (not that their relations with the city were therefore invariably harmonious). At the diocesan level – intermediate between the *consularis* and the praetorian prefect – there was the *comes Orientis*; on the military side the *dux* of the province of Syria and, above all, the *magister militum Orientis*, who might be found anywhere in the eastern provinces, but whose headquarters and main office staff were at

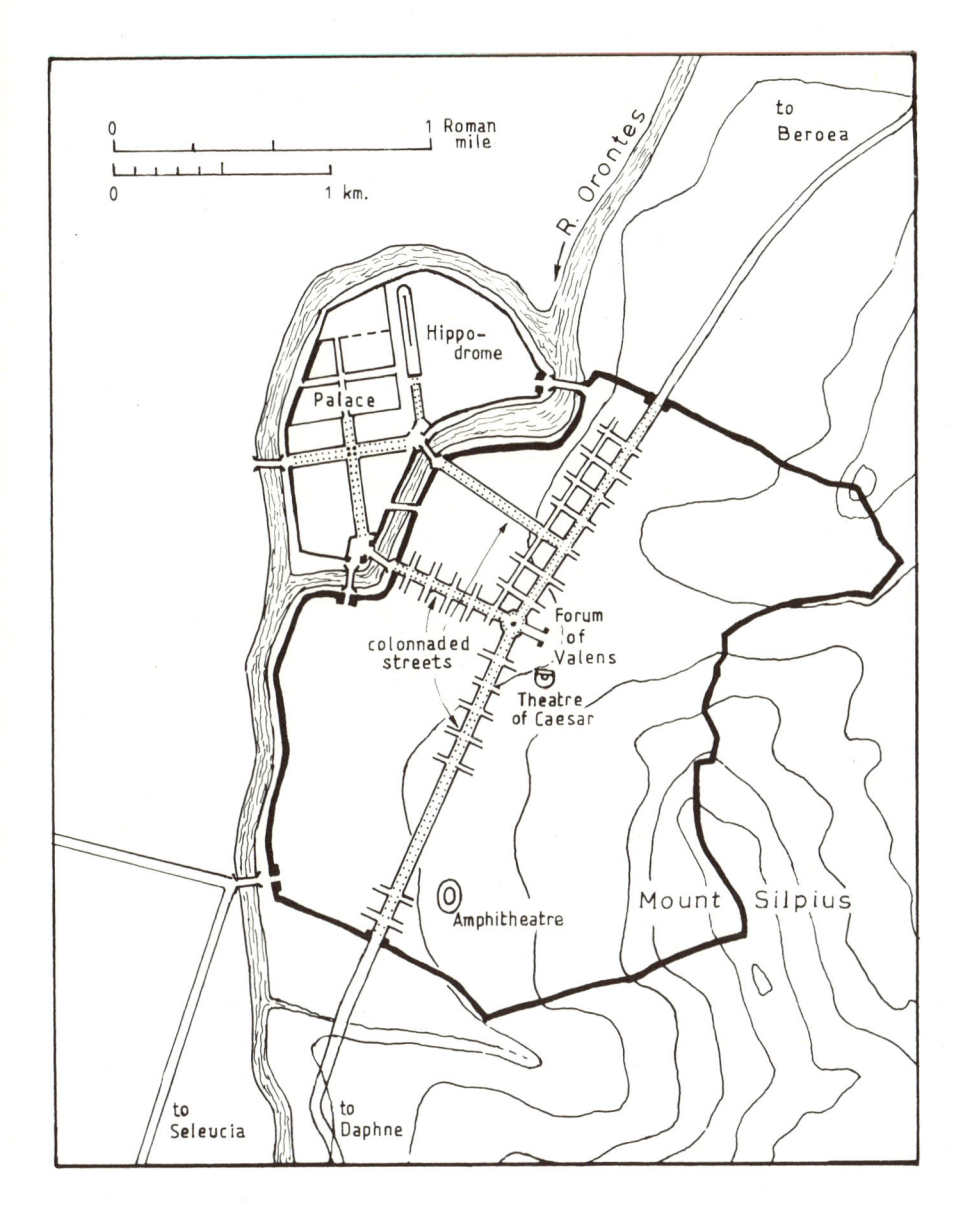

Map 2. The City of Antioch. Drawn from G. Downey, *A History of Antioch*, fig. 11, with reference also to Downey's sources and to P. Petit, *Libanius et la vie municipale*, 127

Antioch.[12] Ammianus' patron Ursicinus owned a house there – a fact known because, significantly, it was coveted by a courtier, the eunuch Eusebius, who at that moment was far away in the west, at the court of Constantius (18.4.3). Some years later another *magister militum*, Hellebichus, built a fine house at Antioch, together with baths to add to the numerous such establishments already mentioned in Libanius' *Antiochikos* (220, 244f.). Hellebichus' baths, in the centre of the city, drew men, young and old, from every quarter, wrote Libanius in a letter to the general (*Ep.* 898). It is not clear whether any but the broadest sense can be attached to Libanius' claim that Hellebichus had 'given' these amenities to the people of Antioch; what is clear is the sophist's eagerness to 'enrol' his correspondent – to judge by his name a general of Germanic descent – among the traditional munificent classes of his city.

The office staffs of the governors of the Oriental diocese, the praetorian prefecture, and the commanders of the eastern armies, provided therefore a steady flow of 'honorati' – men of wealth and influence deriving from imperial service – whose presence in the community not only diversified its character but was coming more and more to undermine traditional civic institutions. Libanius complained of the intervention of such men in the judicial process (*Or.* 47); and, while it cannot be pursued here, there was also the increasing influence of the bishop of Antioch, whose partisan use of the judicial prerogatives granted by the emperors was fiercely deplored by Libanius (*Or.* 30.11). In fact, despite Libanius' assertion in the *Antiochikos* of its essentially Greek character, his city was an imperial metropolis, sharing to a less extreme but still considerable degree the fluid, cosmopolitan character of Constantinople. It is against this background that Ammianus' social standing, and his entry into imperial service and career are to be understood.

*

The origins of the rank of *protector* belong, like so much else in the late Roman military system, to the pressures of warfare in the third century, and particularly to the emergence during that time of a mobile field army serving directly under the emperor and moving around with him wherever its services were required.[13] 'Protectores Augusti' begin to appear regularly in the time of Gallienus (253-268). They were men of tried experience who had risen to the rank of centurion or tribune and were chosen, as their full title implies, to defend the person of the emperor. One such officer made a dedication to secure the safe journey and return of an emperor, probably Gallienus, describing himself as 'protector divini lateris Augusti nostri' (*ILS* 4002). So *protectores* formed in the first instance an élite of officers of known capacity, chosen to serve under the eyes of the emperor himself. In practice, they are often found enjoying a rather more varied existence. They might be detailed to serve on especially important campaigns: so, an inscription mentions the 'special detachments and *equites*, commanders and *protectores*' present in Gaul for Claudius Gothicus' campaign against the rebellious Gallic empire (*ILS* 569). They might serve on the staffs of provincial military governors, and sometimes received promotion to legionary commands and to governorships. This development was a counterpart to the

V. The Young Ammianus

progressive disappearance of senators from military commands and governorships which is one of the most interesting features of the later third century; *protectores* thereby form a pool of senior officers of equestrian rank, among those qualified to be appointed to these more senior positions. Before his promotion as Caesar in the western empire, Constantius the father of Constantine the Great had been *protector*, tribune, then governor of Dalmatia (*Anon. Vales.* 1.2).

By Ammianus' time, the corps of *protectores* consisted of men from a variety of backgrounds. There were still the real 'professionals', long-serving *protectores* who had won their status by loyalty and industry – men such as Gratian, the father of the future emperor Valentinian. Gratian, from Cibalae in Pannonia, had attracted attention by his physical strength and skill at wrestling;[14] after promotion from the ranks to *protector* and tribune, he became field commander as *comes* in Africa and then in Britain (30.7.3f.). At a less elevated level, Fl. Abinnaeus had served for thirty-three years in the garrison of Upper Egypt when he received promotion as *protector*, having escorted foreign ambassadors to the emperor at Constantinople (*P. Abinn.* 1.6ff.). After three years' service as *protector*, Abinnaeus was then made prefect of the garrison at Dionysias and – once he had secured the appointment against a rival who also claimed it – served out his active years in this employment.[15]

At the other extreme, the corps was invaded by sinecure hunters with no military interest or qualifications whatever – for example palatine officials who had advanced themselves by patronage and corruption, and members of curial orders who had set themselves up with letters of honorary appointment so as to secure the tax immunities conveyed by the rank of *protector*. The emperors' legislation reveals their efforts to rid the ranks of these idle incumbents – men who, as one law put it, had 'never seen a line of battle, set eyes on military standards, or carried arms' (*CTh* 7.21.1). Another law, of 393, was inspired by a petition of loyal and industrious *protectores domestici*. They were resentful at the devaluation of the title earned by their strenuous efforts for the emperor if it was given by graft and corruption to men whose only concern was to feather their nest (*CTh* 6.24.5-6).

Mention of *protectores domestici* introduces a distinction of some importance for the understanding of Ammianus' career. The activities of such *protectores* as Fl. Abinnaeus were pursued entirely in the provinces, as often as not in duties resembling police or security work rather than military operations. Such duties involved, as in the case of Abinnaeus, the escort of recruits (*CTh* 7.22.2; *P. Abinn.* 1.9f.), rounding up deserters and vagrants (*CTh* 7.18.10; 22.2), conducting prisoners, convicted or awaiting trial (*CTh* 9.27.3), the inspection of the cargoes of merchant vessels (*CTh* 7.16.3), and of wagons and post-horses, to prevent overloading (*CTh* 7.5.30). Such officers, plain *protectores*, must be distinguished from the more select corps of *protectores domestici*, commissioned in the first instance to serve at the imperial court. While *protectores* fell under the command of the *magistri militum*, *protectores domestici* were commanded by the Count of the Domestics (*comes domesticorum*). By the end of the century, and presumably before, they were divided into regiments (*scholae*) of horse and foot. Their duties were ceremonial as well as strictly military, and they possessed a particularly resplendent shield device, symbolising their position in the emperor's service. It showed two winged Victories bearing crowns, one to each side of the imperial image, all emblazoned in gold on a purple field.[16]

Although they were formally attached to the imperial court, *protectores domestici* could be assigned to specific duties under a field commander such as a Master of the Soldiery (*CTh* 6.25.5). This was exactly what Ammianus meant when he recalled that he had been attached to Ursicinus' service by imperial commission: 'cui nos obsecuturos iunxerat imperiale praeceptum' (14.9.1). The assignment explains Ammianus' attendance upon Ursicinus during the trials conducted at Antioch at the orders of Gallus Caesar (above, p. 34f.), and it continued when Ursicinus was summoned to the west in 355 and Ammianus went as one of Ursicinus' company to suppress Silvanus at Cologne (p. 38f.).

The group assembled for this operation had consisted of some tribunes and ten *protectores domestici* together, though Ammianus does not mention them, with their personal attendants (15.5.22). It was a carefully chosen group, which had to present itself to Silvanus as Ursicinus' escort rather than as a force with hostile intentions, and its members would need to feel secure and at ease with each other; they can most readily be seen as already members of the personal staff of Ursicinus. Among Ammianus' colleagues as *protector domesticus* was Verinianus, named both as a participant in this enterprise (15.4.22) and later, still serving under Ursicinus, in what was surely his final encounter with the enemy near Amida (18.8.11; above, p. 45). Ammianus and Verinianus were among the younger members of Ursicinus' entourage, who were instructed to accompany him on his recall to the eastern front in 357 while the senior members received military commands; 'provectis e consortio nostro ad regendos milites natu maioribus, adolescentes eum sequi iubemur' (16.10.21). This, for Ammianus and Verinianus, amounted to a renewal of their assignment by the emperor to the staff of the *magister equitum*.

The term 'adolescens' is not always employed precisely. Formally, it should refer to the stage between the years of childhood ('pueritia') and youthful maturity ('iuventus'), the time of a man's introduction to public life and his first offices – say, between the ages of fourteen and thirty.[17] It is sometimes used, in specific contexts, to designate men in their thirties and even, on occasions, in their forties; but normal practice, and the force of Ammianus' contrast with 'natu maiores', make it unlikely that he intended to suggest his own age at this moment as more than thirty, and probably even a few years younger than this. 'Natu maiores' is in itself no more precise than 'adolescentes', which is its point of reference in Ammianus' text; but it would be natural to suppose that the appointments received by these senior members of Ursicinus' staff were

V. The Young Ammianus

assignments of unattached tribunes ('tribuni vacantes') to specific commands held at this rank, rather than to any more elevated employments. The future emperor, Valentinian, was tribune of the second Schola Scutariorum in 363, by which time he was forty-two years old (25.10.9); but his promotion would have looked rather better had he not unluckily been cashiered six years before, when he was already tribune, serving under Julian in Gaul (16.11.6f.). Ammianus' 'natu maiores' one imagines, similarly, as men in their thirties and early forties.

If Ammianus was no more than thirty in 357 – even rather younger – it becomes of interest to ask how long before 354, when he first appears on Ursicinus' staff, he was admitted to the rank of *protector domesticus*.

Admission to the rank of *protector* involved the ceremony of 'adoration of the Purple', a ceremony in which the candidate made obeisance before the emperor and was offered the edge of the imperial purple robe to touch with his lips.[18] In his petition to the emperor to confirm him in the post of prefect of the garrison of Dionysias, Fl. Abinnaeus recalled that he had gone to Constantinople and there been instructed to 'adore the sacred purple from the rank of *ducenarius*' (*P. Abinn.* 1.7f.); the term 'ducenarius', originally indicating the salary of 200,000 sesterces drawn by the holder of the title, normally a procurator, had come for historical reasons to indicate the rank of *protector*.[19] In another case, a letter authorising four *protectores* to draw rations from imperial granaries mentioned how their superior officer, the tribune Fl. Gaiolus, had 'sent them to the sacred *comitatus* to adore the divine purple of the emperors' (*Cod. Pap. Lat.* 267.4ff.). If such relatively obscure officers attended the emperor in person to receive promotion to the rank of *protector*, we can hardly imagine that a *protector domesticus*, about to be deputed by the emperor to serve on the personal staff of the *magister equitum Orientis*, was not required to do the same.

The Emperor Constantius had spent much of the 340s in and around Antioch, constantly beset by the threat from Persia; but his latest residence in the east had been in the late summer of 350, when he was obliged to move west to prepare for the campaign against Magnentius. It is not likely that Ammianus would have attended the emperor after this date to kiss the purple and receive promotion to *protector* and attachment to Ursicinus. If this is right, and if he was thirty or less in 357, then he will have received the rank of *protector* at the age, say, of twenty-two or twenty-three. At that age, he entirely lacked the military experience possessed, for instance, by long-serving *protectores* like Gratian the father of Valentinian, or Fl. Abinnaeus.[20] Ammianus' claims were of a different order: like many a well-bred young man in many an army, Ammianus took the high road to officer's rank, entering a fashionable regiment almost from his teens. It may even be that Ammianus was commissioned as *protector domesticus* without serving in the ranks at all; for it is necessary to allow in his upbringing for that literary education shared, and envied, by his friend Jovinianus the satrap of Corduene.

Possession of this literary culture in itself shows Ammianus to have come from the more elevated sector of Antiochene society, since, in a very important sense, the function of this culture was precisely to define an elite against the ordinary run of mankind (as we saw earlier, it effectively distinguished the Graeco-Roman from the Syriac layer of eastern society). If this should seem a doctrinaire assumption, then it may be added that Ammianus himself reveals his social origin, in narrating a well-known episode.

Leaving Nisibis with Ursicinus in 359, Ammianus had been detailed to take a forlorn child back to the city (above, p. 41). Not any child was worth such attention, but this one had a well-bred look and wore a neck-band indicating social rank: 'liberalis formae puerum torquatum' (18.6.10). The word then attributed to the boy to denote his father's standing, 'ingenuus' – 'a man of breeding' – is that used by Ammianus to define his own social position. This emerges a little later. Escaping from Amida with two companions at the moment of its fall, Ammianus travelled on foot for a distance of ten miles from the city. By this time, he was very tired – overcome, as he nicely put it, 'by the excessive walking, to which as a man of breeding I was unaccustomed'; 'incendendi nimietate iam superarer ut insuetus ingenuus' (19.8.6). At this point a runaway horse came into view, dragging the lacerated corpse of its rider, a groom who had tied the halter too firmly to his wrist and so was unable to free himself when thrown (the horse was without saddle or harness, and it appears that the groom should have been leading and not riding it). The animal was tired and easily caught; and Ammianus got on it and was conveyed to some natural springs not far away. With him went the same two companions ('cum isdem sociis', 8.7) – men clearly more used to walking than was Ammianus himself! The episode is a telling illustration of distinctions of social rank, revealed with the artless innocence of a man who never questions them.[21]

Ammianus' attachment to the staff of Ursicinus explains both his own highly adventurous personal experiences and his obviously partisan commitment to Ursicinus' cause, both military and political – not to mention his eclipse from the scene at the time of Ursicinus' dismissal (above, p. 46f.). It will not be misleading, either, to look for Ursicinus' influence at the outset of Ammianus' career as it is now taking shape, as the patron of an active young Antiochene of good family in quest of adventure and experience. Ursicinus had been *magister equitum* in the east since 349, and Ammianus' attachment to his service could be seen as an instance of the age-old Roman practice of 'tirocinium' – the 'apprenticeship' by which a young aspirant to a career in public life would sit at the feet of an acknowledged master to learn the skills and gain some practical experience of what was involved. At the same time, one would imagine that Antioch was full of just such adventurous and well-born young men, and it is worth asking whether Ammianus had a special claim upon Ursicinus' attention.

In other recorded cases of *protectores domestici* commissioned without

V. The Young Ammianus

long previous service, a relevant consideration seems to have been that their fathers had risen before them in military service. The son of a Master of the Cavalry murdered in 342 was serving as *protector domesticus* twelve years later (14.10.1), and could still be described as a 'young man' in 363 (Libanius, *Ep.* 828). A future emperor, Jovian, was senior officer (*primicerius*) of the *protectores* in his early thirties; he was the son of Varronianus, who had recently retired as *comes domesticorum*. As Ammianus wrote, his father's merits gave Jovian some claim to recognition when he was chosen as emperor after Julian's death; 'paternis meritis mediocriter commendabilis' (25.5.4).[22] Presumably the same had been true earlier in his career. If these were especially conspicuous cases of nepotism (that is, of the normal workings of the system), Ammianus' early promotion remains difficult to understand without something like it. Perhaps his father was known to Ursicinus, whose contemporary he would be, as a colleague in military service in the east. A further refinement is suggested by a law issued by Valentinian in 364. According to its terms, sons and other relatives of *protectores domestici* may be enrolled on the lists of the corps while still children and too young for active service, and may even draw rations (*CTh* 6.24.2). It is unclear whether the law initiates a new procedure or regularises an established one. If the latter, then this is a further possible explanation for Ammianus' appearance, at such an early age, as *protector domesticus* assigned to the service of the *magister equitum* in the east. Enrolled in boyhood by a father in active service, he simply presented himself, having reached a suitable age, to assume a commission.

These are conjectural possibilities; but they are based on what seems to be implied by the pattern of Ammianus' military career – that his connection with army circles should go back in one way or another to his father's generation. Some important consequences for the understanding of Ammianus' history may be stated briefly at this point.

First, Ammianus, an 'ingenuus' of Antioch, appears more precisely as a member of the military and administrative class which the imperial service had established there and which had acquired a position of influence in the society of the metropolis.[23] Ursicinus' house at Antioch is a sign of his membership of this class – and incidentally, also of the social aspirations of the court eunuch who was said to covet it (18.4.3). If it be assumed that Ammianus was by descent a native of Antioch rather than from a family which had migrated to the city in an earlier generation, his affinities were still with the court and government establishment there as much as with the strictly 'civic' element in the population (as represented for instance by Libanius): for more than half of Ammianus' early years to the age of twenty, the emperor himself was regularly resident in the city, with the consequences for its social life outlined in the first part of this chapter. Such a perspective might help to explain the complexity of Ammianus' attitudes to the curial class of Antioch and other cities. As a member of a socially well-placed family, Ammianus may have felt a general sympathy with the economic interests of the landed upper class without wishing to associate himself with every aspect of their situation. In narrating, in so far as he did so, the economic crises at Antioch under both Gallus Caesar and Julian, Ammianus unreservedly took the part of the *curiales* of the city against the imperial authorities (p. 406). On the other hand he more than once deplored the attempts made by the Emperor Julian to impose curial obligations on men who possessed established and proper exemptions. It has often been suspected that as a long-serving officer he possessed them himself.

Second, and of particular importance in considering the style of Ammianus' historical writing, his command of Latin as an instrument of such elaborate complexity will not be his own unique achievement, nor yet a reflection in any narrow sense of the Latin of the military circles in which he moved. Ammianus may have had Latin from boyhood, as a member of a family connected with the Roman administration based at Antioch. His knowledge of it was in that case a natural (if outstanding) expression of the 'cultural bilingualism' discussed earlier in this chapter; of the fluency in Latin as well as Greek which, to those who accepted it, was the particular contribution of the late Roman governing order to the cultural life of the Greek east.

Third, Ammianus' interest in the military history of the previous generation will gain a new depth of perspective. In entrusting to Ursicinus the mission to overthrow Silvanus, the Emperor Constantius was influenced (said Ammianus) by reminders of his service under Constantine the Great (15.5.19). The reported conversations of Ursicinus with Silvanus at Cologne were clearly intended by Ammianus to imply comparison between the two generals, whose services were inadequately rewarded by an ungrateful emperor. Alone among all the generals, complained Silvanus, were he and Ursicinus so despised after their labours for the state (5.27). In summarising Silvanus' character after his assassination, Ammianus again referred to his past services, and in particular to his father Bonitus' part in the civil war of Constantine against Licinius (5.33). These, and other passages in which Ammianus referred to events and personalities of the time of Constantine, would be the more telling if Ammianus' own father were a military officer or government official of the generation of Ursicinus and Silvanus. They would also provide a link between Ammianus' narrative of his own times and his views on the earlier fourth century. With this in mind, we may return to his narrative, moving back a few years to the elevation and the early career, which was witnessed by Ammianus, of Julian Caesar.

CHAPTER VI

The Rise of Julian

After the suppression of Silvanus, Ursicinus had been instructed by Constantius to remain in the Gallic provinces (p. 38). Despite the fact that he still held office as *magister equitum* in the Orient, seconded to the western court first 'for consultations' and then to lead the enterprise against Silvanus, he was in effect to replace Silvanus until some more permanent arrangement was made.[1] In the spring of 356 Ursicinus received a successor, Marcellus, but was directed to remain in Gaul for the duration of the campaigning season, 'ad usque expeditionis finem' (16.2.8). The new Caesar, Julian, was totally without military experience and, loth though he would prove to admit it, needed all the help and advice that he could get.[2] At midsummer Julian was instructed to join a field army being assembled at Rheims by the two *magistri*, and marched there from Vienne, where he had spent the winter, by hazardous routes leading by way of Augustodunum, Autessiodurum and Tricasini (Autun, Auxerre, Troyes). All these towns he found troubled by a barbarian occupation extending, in his own later words, for 300 stades, or nearly forty miles, west of the Rhine along its entire length to the North Sea. A further band of territory three times that width was rendered unusable for agriculture or grazing, and forty-five cities had been stripped of their defences, not counting the smaller settlements and fortifications that had been taken (*Ep. ad Ath.* 279A-B). Ammianus' narrative of this first march bears out the essential truth of Julian's remarks. The walls of Autun, surrounded by marauding Alamanni, were defended by veteran soldiers gathered there from their homes in the vicinity, the resident garrison being inactive and useless; the route from Autun to Auxerre was beset by danger of barbarian attack, and the inhabitants of Troyes, surprised by the suddenness of Julian's arrival, were at first reluctant to admit him, in case they let in the barbarians milling about their walls (16.2.1-7).

Despite his own presence on Ursicinus' personal staff, Ammianus defines neither the military nor the political role of his patron during the season of 356. It would however be reasonable to suppose that, beginning at Rheims where the field army assembled to wait for Julian, it permitted Ammianus to know something of the recovery of Cologne, achieved at the end of the campaign (16.3.1f.). As for the political scene, the preceding winter was marked by more sinister activities, namely the punishment of the supporters of Silvanus, a leading part in this being taken by the

82   Part One: Res Gestae

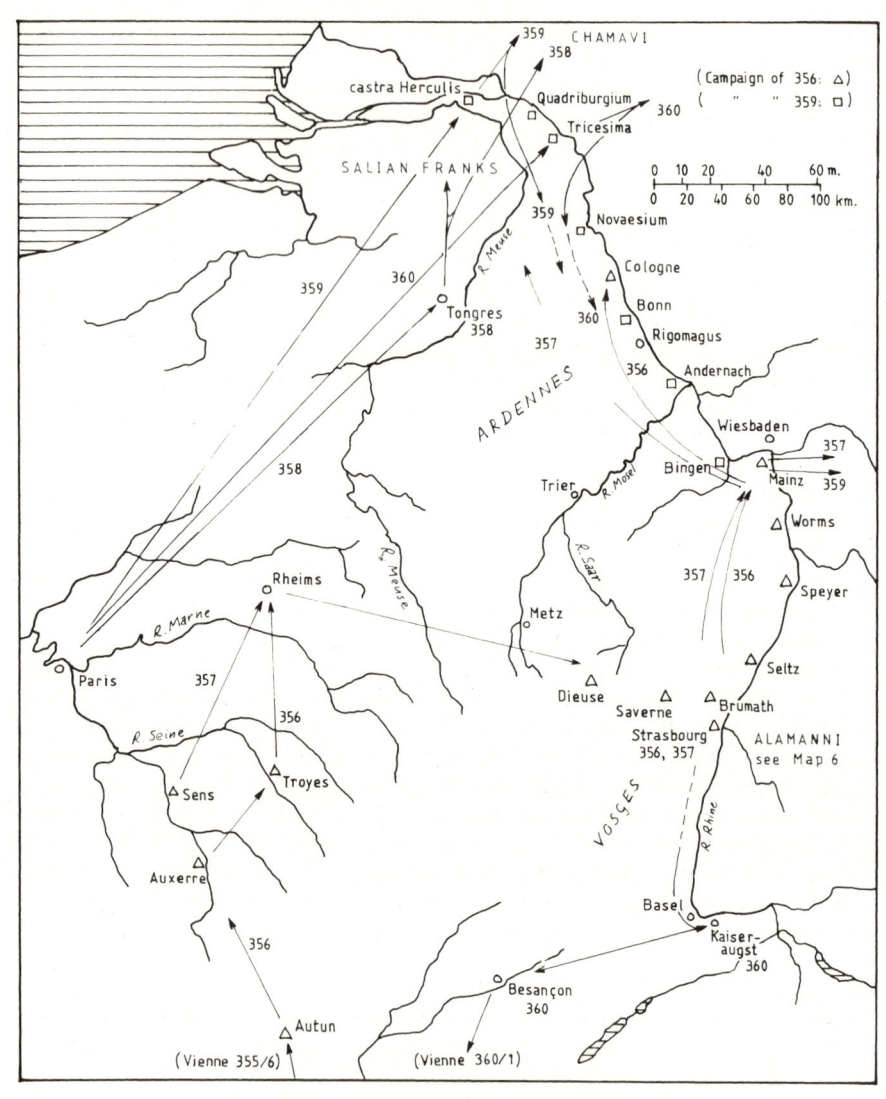

Map 3. Julian in Gaul, 356-360

infamous agent of Constantius, Paulus known as 'the Chain' because, according to Ammianus, of his skill in 'linking together' criminal accusations; 'ut erat in complicandis negotiis artifex dirus' (15.6.1-4, cf. 14.5.8). Given the role of Ursicinus in the enquiries for treason conducted by Gallus Caesar at Antioch, and his recent part in the suppression of Silvanus, one is led to wonder whether the general may have been associated more closely with the activities of Paulus 'Catena' than Ammianus wished to reveal. A certain elusiveness attends Ammianus'

VI. The Rise of Julian

description of Ursicinus' judicial role under Gallus Caesar, and we may surely assume that the general had some contribution to make to the broader aspects of the restoration of loyalty to the Gallic provinces. The inquisition by 'consistoriani and militares' of one supporter of Silvanus called Proculus is reported with a particularly vivid sense of occasion. A slight, sickly man, Proculus gave grounds for fear that the torture to which his slender frame was subjected would cause him to name names indiscriminately, but he remembered a dream in which he had been forbidden to incriminate any innocent person. Racked to the point of death, he named no one, and even made a good case for the innocence of Silvanus himself.[3] Four days before his proclamation, the usurper had made a payment of coin to his troops in the name of Constantius – curious behaviour if he had intended to rebel (15.6.1-3). If Ursicinus were there, Ammianus might himself have witnessed the interrogation.

The following winter, that of 356/7, saw the removal from office of the *magister militum* Marcellus, ostensibly for his refusal to relieve Julian when the latter was trapped for thirty days by the Alamanni in the town of Sens (16.4.1-5). The sequel of Marcellus' dismissal – his recriminations against Julian at the court of Constantius and the Caesar's defence against them – involved the faithful eunuch Eutherius, a presumed acquaintance of Ammianus when living in later years at Rome.[4] It is likely that Ammianus' knowledge of the scenes at Constantius' court, as well as of the situation at Sens in 356/7, derived from first-hand, or very close to first-hand, information.

Marcellus' successor was Severus, a modest, co-operative man ('nec discors nec arrogans', 16.11.1) with whom Julian established far better working relations than he had with the more temperamental Marcellus – 'strepens et tumultuans, ut erat vanidicus et amenti propior', as Ammianus writes of the latter's appearance before Constantius to denounce his Caesar. Ammianus mentions the appointment of Severus in the same sentence that describes the recall of Ursicinus to join Constantius at Sirmium, to be assigned to the eastern theatre of war with the results described in earlier chapters of this book (III-IV). The dispatch of Severus to Gaul and the recall of Ursicinus took place in June or July 357 (cf. 16.10.20). The regular campaigning season in Gaul began only in July (17.8.1), and Ursicinus and Ammianus took no part in the military operations leading to the victory of Strasbourg over the Alamanni in the late summer of the year; Ammianus was not, as has been asserted, a witness of the battle but derived his knowledge of it from very different sources.[5] His first encounter with Julian was therefore brief; it covers only the first military campaign of the Caesar, still submissive to the commands of his Augustus, with the first hints of his unsuspected genius for military and administrative action. This aspect of Julian's achievement – his triumphant emergence from the peaceful shades of the academy to the bloody turmoil of war – is given full rhetorical amplification at the outset of Ammianus' narrative of his regime as Caesar (16.1.1-5). In the very first sentence of this narrative, Julian enters the consulship at Vienne as the colleague of Constantius, already 'dreaming of the clash of battle and barbarian slaughter' (16.1.1). In fact, he had hardly seen an army in his life.

Despite this recognition of the sheer unexpectedness of Julian's achievement after the seclusion of his early years, Ammianus makes no attempt to explore the personality or to explain the rise of Julian in biographical terms, and he says very little of the actual nature of his background in childhood and youth. In this respect as in others, Ammianus differs from those contemporary Greek sources – Eunapius, Libanius, and Julian himself – that form the basis of most modern accounts of Julian and his reign, based on biographical reconstruction with a strong element of speculative psychology.[6] What to writers in this vein is the formative influence upon Julian's personality, the murder of his father, elder brother and other male relatives in the dynastic carnage that followed the death of Constantine in 337, is in Ammianus' extant books not connected with Julian at all, but adduced as evidence of Constantius' cruelty in his obituary of that emperor. This is compared to the cruelty of Caligula, Domitian and Commodus – as was shown at the outset of his reign, when at one fell swoop he murdered all his relations; 'cunctos sanguine et genere se contingentes stirpitus interemit' (21.16.8).[7] An obituary notice, which is explicitly a summary of an emperor's reign, need include no back-reference to any specific episode, and we may assume that Ammianus had mentioned the murders in an earlier passage of his work – especially if it was at that point that his treatment began to enlarge in scale (p. 27). In his attribution of the blame to Constantius alone (other views were possible), Ammianus agrees with Julian, in the *Letter to the Athenians* in which he justified his declaration of civil war against Constantius (270C-D). Yet Ammianus' failure to make any reference to the tragedy in any context actually relating to Julian differs markedly from the *Letter to the Athenians*, in which Constantius' responsibility for the murders looms very large in Julian's personality. As he implies in the case of Julian, referring on the occasion of his elevation as Caesar to those 'ancient books', in which one could read how 'the secrets of the mind are revealed by signs of the body' (15.8.16), Ammianus is interested, indeed pre-eminently interested, in character as expressed in action and gesture. He is less concerned as to how and under what pressure from external experience the character itself is formed, and in this respect stands apart from that more philosophical tradition of biographical writing in which the development of character as such was a central preoccupation. The personality of Julian is seen in terms of his conduct as Caesar and Augustus, not vice versa: 'res gestae', not biography.[8]

After the death of his relatives, Julian passed a secluded childhood at Nicomedia and subsequently at the imperial estate of Macellum in Cappadocia,[9] attended by various guardians and teachers whose diverse influence upon the impressionable boy is a main theme in most modern accounts of Julian. Three men in particular are mentioned; bishop

VI. The Rise of Julian

Eusebius of Nicomedia; the learned George, later a hated bishop of Alexandria; and the Armenian eunuch Mardonius, to whom Julian owed his early love of the classics. Ammianus mentions Julian's sojourn at Nicomedia only incidentally, in connection with the partial destruction of the city by an earthquake in 358 (cf. 17.7.1-8); Julian recognised some people there when four years later he passed through the city, because he had been educated there by bishop Eusebius, his distant relative (22.9.4). He nowhere refers to Mardonius, and in describing the murder of bishop George in 362 (below, pp. 442ff.), had nothing to say of his earlier connection with Julian. Macellum is mentioned once only, as the estate in Cappadocia which Julian left in order to pursue liberal studies in Asia. Ammianus recounts this in explanation of certain charges laid against Julian by calumniators, namely that he had left Macellum without permission and had had unauthorised contact with Gallus Caesar as he passed through Constantinople, and he gives no indication that he had made any earlier reference to the place (15.2.7). Julian was at that time recalled to Italy and lived at Comum near Milan before being allowed to go to Greece, again for the sake of intellectual study (15.2.8). As often, the *Letter to the Athenians* gives more specific details of this period of residence in Italy, notably in Julian's recollection that he lived 'in the same city' as Constantius (not strictly true) for six months and only received a single audience with him, a second being promised but never given; and that when he was sent to Greece he had been on the point of setting off for his mother's estates in Asia but was diverted to Athens when news arrived of the rebellion of Silvanus (*Ep. ad Ath.* 273D). It seems likely that in choosing this relatively accessible place of seclusion Constantius already anticipated the role that awaited his young nephew.

Within a matter of weeks, Julian was recalled from Greece, in the event to be made Caesar, but neither in this nor in the earlier passage does Ammianus even name Athens as the city in which Julian spent this short, and often over-emphasised, fragment of his life. Ammianus' words are less exact, as if what mattered was not that Julian was specifically at Athens, but merely that he was not in north Italy at this time; 'ad Graeciam ire permissus est' (15.2.8), and later, 'ab Achaico tractu accitus' (15.8.1). It is further acknowledged that both in Asia and in Greece Julian was involved in those academic pursuits for which he had a passion; 'liberalium desiderio doctrinarum ... procudendi ingenii causa, ut cupidine flagrabat' (15.2.7f.). Nothing is however said of the intellectual and personal contacts made in both places by Julian, nor of the distinctive character of the traditions of learning, especially in Neoplatonist philosophy, which were prevalent there. The omission by Ammianus of any specific reference to philosophy, particularly striking in the light of our other evidence for Julian's actions in Asia Minor and their later influence upon his reign, again denies us the opportunity to consider at this stage a most powerful influence in the development of Julian's personality.

Ammianus is equally reticent on another aspect of his experience in

Italy that seemed very important to Julian himself. The help given him by the emperor's wife Eusebia in protecting him from the suspicions of Constantius and his supporters is described in the *Letter to the Athenians* and evoked an entire oration in her praise from the grateful Caesar (*Or.* 2 Bidez). Julian thanks the empress for the wedding-gifts bestowed on him on the occasion of his marriage to Helena the sister of Constantius – that wife who, in the words of Joseph Bidez, 'passed like a shadow into Julian's life' (*Vie de l'empereur Julien*, p. 131) – and above all for the 'travelling library' of Classical texts which Eusebia gave him as he set out on his journey to Gaul (*Or.* 2.15; 123D-124D). In Ammianus' account the role of Eusebia is indicated but not explored. She was 'inspired by heaven' to get Julian recalled to Italy rather than leave him exposed abroad to the suspicions of his enemies (15.2.8), and later steadied the wavering determination of Constantius to make him Caesar (15.8.3). After this it comes as a discreditable shock, and can only be an unsupported fragment of court gossip, later to find Eusebia accused of using poison to prevent Helena from bearing a child to Julian (16.10.18). Eusebia's inability to conceive for Constantius was well known, and interpreted by the emperor, it is alleged in the *Letter to the Athenians* (270D-271A), as a punishment for his murder of his relations in 337. It is a sign of Julian's own sense of priorities, that in his *Letter to the Athenians* he omits even to mention in its proper context his marriage to Helena, giving it only a single incidental allusion to explain a later, unrelated event (284C).[10]

Ammianus is only in retrospect explicit even about that most significant personal aspect of Julian's early life, his disaffection from Christianity; and again, it forms no part of any explanation of his early character. In a text of late 362 (*Ep.* 111 Bidez; 434D), Julian himself wrote that he had been for eleven years a secret believer in the gods, a persuasion given vivid circumstantial quality by Eunapius' account of the young man's activities, which were indeed not all that secret, in the cities of Asia Minor.[11] For Ammianus, looking back from the vantage point of 361, Julian's commitment to the gods derived, without any implication of a conscious apostasy from Christianity, from his earliest boyhood, became more intense as he grew up and finally, on his succession to Constantius, achieved full freedom of expression (22.5.1f.). None of this is directly stated by Ammianus at the time of its occurrence, nor is it put in any relation to the character of Julian. The importance of the theme is made plain not so much by explicit statement as by the steadily more emphatic patterning of Ammianus' narrative. An old woman prophesies, upon Julian's entering Vienne on his first arrival as Caesar in Gaul and before anything has been said of Julian's paganism, that 'this man will restore the temples of the gods' (15.8.22). On the eve of his proclamation Julian is addressed in his quarters by the figure of the 'genius publicus', again telling him to look to the future (20.5.10), and after it he is presented as an expert on dreams and divination, accepts omens and conducts other rites of the gods (21.1.6-2.5). He hides his adherence to the gods by attending church – again, as it happens, at Vienne – to celebrate

VI. The Rise of Julian

Epiphany (21.2.4), and, while on the road to attack Constantius, performs with certain associates rites of divination (22.1.1-3). Despite this steady amplification of Julian's religious character, the issue never displaces Julian's military and political development from the first plane in Ammianus' narrative. Even his open declaration of faith after the death of Constantius and his accession as sole Augustus is preceded, in Ammianus' text, by other transactions of the new reign, such as the accusation and punishment of supporters of Constantius in capital trials held at Chalcedon, and the elimination of waste and ostentation in the palace administration (22.3-4).

Ammianus' narrative of the actual elevation of Julian in 355 is in sharp contrast with the brevity of his allusions to intellectual and religious matters. Here we find a detailed exposition of Constantius' hesitation and motives, resolved in part by the advice of Eusebia, for accepting so uncongenial a solution to the crisis of his reign, together with Julian's presentation to the army and speeches by Constantius – these being dramatically presented in three sections, punctuated by the favourable reception by the soldiers of the proposed elevation and the actual placing of the purple robe on Julian's shoulders (15.8.9; 11). There is a reference to Julian's marriage to Helena, and a full description of his journey over the Alps to Gaul and his reception at Vienne (15.8.18-22). At this point of an already detailed narrative, Ammianus adds a digression on the Gallic provinces, beginning with the allusion to Vergil that neatly balances Julian's Homeric quotation about 'purple death and fate imperious' that he was heard muttering to himself as he was conveyed with Constantius to the imperial palace (15.8.17; 9.1). The Vergilian reference is intended to lift the reign of Julian to a higher level, and, by reminding us of the Italian wars of Aeneas in the second half of Vergil's epic, to define Ammianus' subject also as essentially military. The following book maintains the effort, its prologue comparing Julian to great emperors of the past, with citation of Cicero and renewed appeal to the greatness of its hero, seized from the life of a student and immersed in that of a soldier and general; all this achieved in a fashion that might seem to consign Ammianus' account to the level of mere panegyric, were not everything based on the authentic testimony of true facts (16.1.1-5).

*

It was Constantius' intention on raising Julian to the rank of Caesar that he would act as a figurehead in the Gallic provinces, carrying around the image of the emperor but leaving the civil and military administration in the hands of others. This is the picture presented both by Ammianus and by Julian, who in his *Letter to the Athenians* complains bitterly about the restrictive character of Constantius' supervision. Even after his elevation he was allowed only four slave attendants, in addition to the doctor Oribasius, to whom Julian entrusted the care of his books; and Oribasius' presence was only tolerated because Constantius was not aware that he and Julian were friends (*Ep. ad Ath.* 277B-278A). Julian mentions with unjustified contempt the guard of 360 soldiers given to accompany him to Gaul, as if it were intended as a field army rather than a personal guard – that 'comitatus parvus' which in Ammianus' narrative escorted the new Caesar from Milan on 1 December 355, accompanied by Constantius as far as the two columns flanking the road between Laumellum (modern Lomello) and Ticinum; 'ad usque locum duabus columnis insignem' (15.8.18). Ammianus had seen the place a few months earlier, on his mission with Ursicinus to suppress Silvanus; it is the staging post ('mutatio') known as Duriae (modern Dorno) mentioned by a fourth-century itinerary twelve miles beyond Ticinum (Pavia) on the road to Turin.[12] Only upon his entry to Turin on the road that crosses the Alps by the pass of Monte Cenisio and descends into Gaul by way of Modane and Chambéry, was news passed to Julian of the capture of the city of Cologne in Germania Secunda; Constantius had known but suppressed the information so as not to disturb his arrangements, 'ne parata diffluerent' (15.8.19).

Julian's conduct as Caesar was defined by instructions given to himself, and to the generals and other high officials assigned to him; the generals were supposed, as he put it, to watch Julian as carefully as they did the enemy (*Ep. ad Ath.* 277D). The mandate was conveyed to Julian in a 'libellus' written out in the emperor's own hand, 'as if he were sending Julian like a stepson to University' (16.5.3) – all things considered, not a bad description of his position. Julian recalls how he begged Constantius at the outset, if he were determined to make him Caesar, to give him exact guidance what he must do and what avoid, in order to make clear where his and his advisers' responsibilities lay (*Ep. ad Ath.* 282A-B). The emperor even specified, in the only detail preserved by Ammianus of what was evidently a lengthy document, what could be spent on his Caesar's table. The delicacies that Constantius thought permissible were rejected by Julian in favour of regular soldier's fare and whatever food was offered; 'munificis militis vili et fortuito cibo contentus' (16.5.3). It is a small but not insignificant detail, as Julian acquired not only the taste for a basic soldier's diet – that was after all not so different from a philosopher's – but for a soldier's profession and way of life, to an extent that would have astonished anyone meeting for the first time this intense and over-active young man, characterised more by the excitability of an intellectual than by the steady nerve of a fighting man (15.8.1).[13]

Ammianus' most explicit statement of the subordinate position of Julian is given in retrospect, when he describes the unjust fate of Ursulus in the trials of Chalcedon (this was the man who had bewailed the fate of Amida and thereby incurred the enmity of the military). Serving Constantius as *comes sacrarum largitionum* at a time when his Caesar was 'to be held in check by every constraint' ('omni tenacitate stringendus'), Ursulus had written to the official in charge of the Gallic treasuries that he was to issue to Julian without question everything he asked for (22.3.7). Julian's best publicised disputes of authority turn

VI. The Rise of Julian

however on his relations with the praetorian prefect of Gaul Florentius, and similarly involve demarcations of competence, in this case of the *praefectus praetorio* in the fields of taxation and supply. In the most fully narrated of these disagreements, Julian opposed Florentius' instructions to remedy a tax shortfall by extra requisitions, and when the prefect objected to this slight to his authority, showed him by careful calculations that the regular assessment, or 'capitatio', provided more than enough for the needs of the state without the superimposition of extra burdens; 'scrupulose computando et vere docuit non sufficere solum, verum etiam exuberare capitationis calculum' (17.3.2-4).[14] Whatever the force of Julian's arguments, few things can be imagined more annoying to a senior bureaucrat with the explicit endorsement of Constantius, than to be lectured on finance by his novice Caesar. Both sides were obdurate. When the prefect some time afterwards persisted in imposing an additional assessment ('indictionale augmentum'), Julian refused to sign or even listen to it, but hurled it to the ground in contempt. To Constantius, who responded to Florentius' complaint by writing to Julian not to interfere so much ('non agere ita perplexe') as to show lack of respect for his prefect, Julian replied with characteristic directness that the emperor should be thankful to receive even the regular tax from his devastated provinces, without expecting supplements such as no threats of punishment could extort from men reduced to poverty. His point of view was apparently accepted, and Gaul was exempted from superindictions (17.3.5). Julian's actions form part of that radical approach to taxation whereby, according to Ammianus in an earlier passage, the standard 'capitatio' in Gaul was reduced from the twenty-five *solidi* he found there at the time of his arrival in Gaul to seven *solidi* when he departed (16.5.14). Enlarging upon this achievement, Ammianus adds a detail of some general interest in considering the operation of the late Roman tax system. To the end of his life, he states, Julian opposed the giving of so-called 'indulgences' or remissions of overdue tax, knowing that this was simply money in the pockets of the rich, while the poor had to pay in full, immediately and without alleviation (16.5.15). To suggest more precisely how this came about, it appears that the upper classes of the provinces, whom the law made responsible through membership of their town councils for the collection of taxes, exacted the dues from the rural peasantry at the beginning of the 'indictio', or tax assessment period, and then petitioned for indulgences to avoid passing it on to the authorities. The poor were oppressed and the rich became richer, additional taxes were imposed to meet the shortfall, and the cycle was repeated.

Julian also achieved from Florentius what Ammianus rightly describes as an unprecedented arrangement, whereby he was personally entrusted with the administration of Belgica Secunda, on the understanding that no official either of prefect or governor should coerce anyone in the province to pay his tax.[15] Even while doubting the literal truth of Ammianus' statement that the provincials were so relieved that they actually paid all their dues without reminders before the appointed day (17.3.6), we have to admire the patience of Constantius in striving to reconcile Julian and his praetorian prefect. One hesitates to say the same of Florentius' ceding of Belgica Secunda to Julian, if only because of the suspicion that his purpose in agreeing to the experiment was to provide the Caesar with an opportunity to demonstrate incontrovertible failure. At the very least, it might restrict Julian's opportunities for interference in more important areas of the administration.

Another dispute between Julian and Florentius is described by Julian in the *Letter to the Athenians*. It concerned an arrangement made by the prefect to pay two thousand pounds' weight of silver to the Chamavi and Salian Franks, in return for which they would permit access to the lower Rhine waterways for 600 supply ships from Britain (*Ep. ad Ath.* 280A). Again, Constantius allowed his Caesar some discretion in the matter, for, informed by Florentius of the proposed payment, he wrote to Julian to tell him to make it, unless he thought it totally disgraceful (ibid. 280B). This was not simply a formal right of veto with no practical consequences, for its exercise would commit Julian to the alternative policy to that of Florentius, a military expedition. This, the campaign of 358, is described by Ammianus (17.8.2-9.7), and was indeed marked by serious difficulties of supply, Julian having hoped that corn grown by the Chamavi would be ripe for his use but being disappointed by the lateness of the harvest in these northerly regions (17.9.2f.). Despite this conflict with his Caesar, Florentius turned up loyally in the following season, bringing supplies to be stored in the granaries built after the campaign of 358 for the corn shipped across from Britain (18.2.3f.).

*

It was in the sphere of military action that Julian felt himself to be most severely restricted by the controls imposed upon him by Constantius: a situation that it requires little imagination to appreciate from the point of view of Constantius rather than that of his Caesar. To revert to the first season of his campaigns, Julian was instructed to take the field in midsummer 356 with the army assembled at Rheims by Marcellus and Ursicinus, and after the operations described by Ammianus (16.2-3), was required to disperse his troops for the winter, and allowed only a small force for his own protection (*Ep. ad Ath.* 278B). It was when he assigned the majority even of these forces for the protection of neighbouring towns who asked for them, that Julian found himself isolated at Sens (16.3.1-4.3; *Ep. ad Ath.* 278B).[16] If Julian had been given no specific authority so to assign his troops, then Marcellus' complaint to Constantius that the Caesar was wilfully exceeding his powers can be seen to be well-founded (16.7.2). With a cocksureness that is even in retrospect amazing, Julian wrote of the campaign that – after this, the first military expedition of his entire life – he was 'thought to be not at all a serious or talented general' merely because he had shown himself to be

VI. The Rise of Julian

mild and tolerant. The proof of this was that he had resolved not to exceed his instructions or contradict any general unless he saw (from his position of profound experience) that something was being omitted that should be done in a dangerous situation, or something being done that should not be. After meeting disrespect from one or two individuals, he decided to confine himself to the ceremonial role that had been assigned to him (*Ep. ad Ath.* 278C-D). This came from the leader who had marched through treacherous wooded country with cataphract horsemen and 'ballistarii' or artillerymen totally unsuited to the purpose – 'parum ad tuendum rectorem idoneos' as Ammianus says (16.2.5) – and who through excessive haste on a foggy morning had nearly lost two legions to the enemy's superior knowledge of the country (16.2.9f.). Only from that moment, we may infer from Ammianus, did Julian appreciate the dangers of ambush (16.2.9-11).[17]

Julian goes on in his *Letter to the Athenians* to assert that Constantius was sufficiently sure of an improvement in the state of Gaul to entrust to him command of the field army in the spring of 357 (278D). This would be surprising on the evidence shown so far, and it may be that the choice of the elderly Severus as *magister equitum* to replace the anomalous joint command of Marcellus and Ursicinus is as much a part of Constantius' decision as any confidence in his Caesar's burgeoning military genius. That Severus, apart from his long experience of war, is described as 'neither contentious nor arrogant' ('nec discors nec arrogans'), might suggest that an improvement in personal relations between Julian and his senior general was expected to avert the conflicts of authority that were already emerging in the conduct of the Gallic administration. Julian, who liked professors, might respect the experience of old age in a general. Every policy has its risks, however, and those inherent on this occasion became clear when Severus, after two seasons' successful collaboration, suddenly lost energy and faded away; 'bellicosus ante haec et industrius repente commarcuit' (17.10.1).

The campaign of 357 was marked instead by Julian's conflicts of opinion with Constantius' *magister peditum* Barbatio – conflicts presented by Ammianus in favour of Julian but which, on closer inspection, may yield a different interpretation (p. 299f.); its culmination was the great battle of Strasbourg in late summer of the year, in which, because of the failure of his co-operation with Barbatio, Julian faced the Alamanni with far fewer troops than they had expected (16.12.1-70). The character of this battle, which drew from Ammianus one of his most elaborate rhetorical compositions, is described in a later chapter of this book (Chapter XIII), but it is worth pausing on a detail that again throws light on the nature of Julian's authority in Gaul, and perhaps also on his military judgment. Having marched to the field of battle, Julian proposed to delay the engagement until the following day in order to give his men time to rest. He was however overruled by his senior advisers, among whom Florentius is specifically named (16.12.14). Severus, who fought in command of the left wing of the Roman forces (16.12.27), must also be presumed to have formed part of the 'celsarum potestatum assensus' in favour of joining battle without delay. Ammianus has obscured the issue by presenting the decision to fight in the context of the alacrity of the soldiers, inspired by Julian's speech urging caution and a victory on the morrow – as if it were designed precisely to have the opposite effect (16.12.9-12).

Although Ammianus gives due weight to the considerations recommending an immediate engagement (16.12.14f.), this detail is a salutary reminder that the battle, Julian's greatest single military triumph and the event that more than any other transformed his position in Gaul, was fought in circumstances in which he was overridden by his advisers. After the battle Julian's army acclaimed him as Augustus, and although he angrily refused the title ('petulantius milites increpabat', 16.12.64), the event, and the victory that inspired it, conveyed a threat to Constantius as to the standing of his Caesar, from which he would never now be free.

Julian's discontent at the restrictions exercised over him by Constantius' agents appears in a more sympathetic light when we consider the actual identity of some of the men to whose care the emperor entrusted his Caesar. Three of the unpleasant bunch (there were others) are named together in the *Letter to the Athenians* (282B): Pentadius, Paulus, Gaudentius.[18] Gaudentius was a former *agens in rebus* whose information had brought down Africanus the governor of Pannonia Secunda after indiscreet conservations overheard at a dinner-table (15.3.7f., cf. 16.8.3). Promoted as *notarius* and sent to Gaul with the specific instructions to inform on the Caesar's actions (17.9.7, cf. 21.7.2), Gaudentius returned to the court of Constantius and, after the proclamation of Julian, was sent by the emperor to secure Africa against attack by the usurper's forces (21.7.2-4). Paulus 'Catena' is familiar to us. He had sought out supporters of the usurper Magnentius, figured in the trials held after the execution of Gallus Caesar, and played a similar role after the suppression of Silvanus (14.5.6ff.; 15.3.4; 6.1). He was in 359 summoned to the east by Constantius, to conduct trials held at Scythopolis in Palestine on accusations of magic arts and high treason, based on records found at an Egyptian shrine (19.12.1-18; below, pp. 217f.). Pentadius, Julian's *magister officiorum* in 358-60, was earlier implicated as a *notarius* in the inquisition of Gallus Caesar at Pola, and with others conveyed the sentence of execution against him (14.11.21; 23). The only official with whom Julian felt a positive sympathy was Saturninius Secundus Salutius, an elderly Gaul with a distinguished public career and an interest in philosophy, who was removed from Julian's entourage by Constantius because he and the Caesar were friends (*Ep. ad. Ath.* 282C). Julian wrote an essay to console himself on the departure of Salutius (*Or.* 4 Bidez) and, when he reached Constantinople in 361, made him praetorian prefect of the east. In this capacity, Salutius presided over the trials of Constantius' supporters conducted at Chalcedon, at which Florentius was condemned to death in

VI. The Rise of Julian

absence and Paulus 'Catena' burned at the stake (22.3.6; 11).[19] Pentadius, also brought to trial at Chalcedon, defended himself successfully against a charge of complicity in the death of Gallus and was set free; all he had done was take notes of the Caesar's replies to his interrogators (22.3.5). The third of the 'paid sycophants' of the *Letter to the Athenians*, Gaudentius, was later arrested in Africa, brought in chains to the east and executed (22.11.1).

In view of the company he was forced to keep among these agents of Constantius, several of them implicated in the regime and ruin of Gallus Caesar and in the tracking down and punishment of conspiracy by traditional late Roman methods, it is not surprising that Julian should have sought the company of men more congenial to his taste, Greek philosophers and intellectuals. The significance of these men and their interests in the rise of Julian may be left for discussion in the next chapter of this book. The most important of them, the doctor Oribasius, has already been mentioned; Constantius allowed him and Julian to stay together because he did not know of their friendship (*Ep. ad Ath.* 277C), and Oribasius was at Julian's side to the very end of his life (below, p. 182). There was an African named Euhemerus, Priscus, an Athenian philosopher, and the Eleusinian hierophant Nestorius, all of whom Julian had visit him at least for a short time in Gaul. These men were alleged by Eunapius to have plotted the overthrow of Constantius, a claim that may relate more to the supernatural than to the strictly secular means by which Julian came to the imperial power. Ammianus has nothing to say of them, possibly more through distaste than ignorance (pp. 127ff.).

*

The context of Julian's proclamation in 360, in terms both of his own situation and of broader aspects of recent history, makes it a relatively unproblematic event; the surprise would rather have been had it not come about, and the scenario that actually occurred is one among many that might be imagined. In the context of recent history, the sequence of usurpations in the western provinces had established a pattern that might well be repeated. Nothing in the background – Germanic aggression and the need, on the Roman side, for large armed forces, freedom of action among their commanders and sufficient authority in their hands to conduct recruitment, raise finance and negotiate settlements – none of this had changed, and it remained impossible to guarantee that generals who were granted such powers would, or could, be content with them. The history of Gallus Caesar showed the difficulty, even with the most careful constraints, of confining a Caesar's role within the limits laid down for him, while Gallus' fate made clear what lay in wait for a nominee who failed to observe them.[20] At the end of Julian's very first campaigning season the general Marcellus had accused him of arrogance and of harbouring designs above his station, while Eutherius was obliged to state in his Caesar's defence that he was a loyal servant, staking his own life on the truth of what he said; 'apparitoremque [sc. Caesarem] fidum auctori suo, quoad vixerit, fore obligata cervice sua spondebat' (16.7.3). Both the asseveration that Julian would be loyal and the force of Eutherius' oath express the opposite possibility. It would in practice be impossible to limit public recognition of Julian's successes to those advisers who were responsible for them; while the acclamation of Julian as Augustus after Strasbourg, despite his strenuous refusal of the title, was bound to inspire speculation as to the ultimate outcome, and comparisons between him and Constantius. The emperor's lack of success in foreign war was too widely believed for such comparisons not to be made and, for all Constantius' insistence in the protocol of his dispatches that he himself was responsible for the victory, everyone knew that it was Julian who had won it and that Constantius' general, whatever the explanation, had not even taken the field.

Julian's own description in his *Letter to the Athenians* of the events leading to his proclamation at Paris in 360 shares much, in general outline and in detail, with that of Ammianus, and there is no need to recount either narrative in detail. However, Ammianus, who presumably knew Julian's account (though he neither mentions nor shows any sign of having used it), enables us to view the event from a wider variety of standpoints, and with a greater diversity of motives on the part of more participants. In this respect he gives what is by far the most authentic picture of the circumstances.

The crisis broke when Constantius, after his losses at Amida in late summer 359, wrote to Julian ordering the transfer to the east of substantial numbers of his troops – namely the Heruli and Batavi, Celtae and Petulantes of the 'auxilia palatina', together with three hundred men selected from the other 'numeri' in Julian's command, and the pick of the Scutarii and Gentiles of the palace guard (20.4.2f.). The instructions were to be implemented by Julian's *magister militum*, Severus' successor Lupicinus, and in respect of the Scutarii and Gentiles by an officer of Julian, a *tribunus stabuli* called by Ammianus 'Sintula' and by Julian 'Gintonius', certainly the same man (20.4.5; *Ep. ad Ath.* 282D). Julian was told to do nothing to oppose Constantius' orders, which were conveyed to the west by a *tribunus et notarius* named Decentius (20.4.2; *Ep. ad Ath.* 283C).

Enquiries as to motive may begin with Constantius, and with the question whether his need for troop reinforcements was genuine, or part of an excuse to deprive Julian of his military support in order either – to borrow a metaphor from the general Marcellus – to clip his wings (16.7.2), or even to facilitate his removal altogether; the deposition of Gallus Caesar, a constant precedent, had been achieved by progressively isolating him from possible supporters. Introducing Constantius' request, Ammianus gives both motives but with more weight to the less creditable, adding the stimulus of the praetorian prefect Florentius, who was said to have written to Constantius recommending that troops be withdrawn from the Gallic theatre (20.4.2; 7). It has been argued that

VI. The Rise of Julian

Constantius' motive cannot have been genuine since he could not in practice get the troops to the east in time for their use in the early spring of 360 ('primo vere', 20.4.2) and since in any case his conduct of the campaign of 360 shows no particular urgency;[21] yet in the earlier context of the loss of Amida Ammianus presents Constantius' need for reinforcements as perfectly serious, without any indication that he doubted it (19.11.17).

Similar ambiguity attaches to the motives of Julian, especially in light of a suggestion that his German campaign of 359 shows a deliberate drawing back from a normally aggressive military policy, in order (it is argued) to provide himself with a secure base for a declaration of war against Constantius.[22] It is true that in 359 Julian concentrated on the rebuilding of captured forts and the construction of granaries (18.1.2-6), but he also crossed the Rhine into Alamann territory, in a campaign that does not seem in principle less ambitious than its predecessors. As Julian's campaigns won for him an increasing military dominance, there will in any case have been a shift of emphasis from aggression to consolidation: that is precisely what successful campaigning is meant to ensure. The building of the granaries was a natural product of the campaign of 358 against the Chamavi and Salian Franks, conducted, at Julian's insistence against his praetorian prefect's less aggressive policy, in order to secure access to the Rhine waterway for supply ships from Britain (above, p. 90). The argument that Julian's change of policy indicates his preparation for civil war might be turned by the observation that, if his Caesar's campaign pattern had in fact shifted from one of military aggression to one of consolidation, Constantius might feel the more justified, on receiving reports to this effect from his praetorian prefect in Gaul (cf. 20.4.7), to request the transfer of troops for use in the east.

When Decentius arrived with his orders for the troop withdrawal, any hopes of a smooth implementation of his instructions were thrown into disarray by the fact, which he now discovered for the first time ('nondum compertus', 20.4.3) that Lupicinus, to whom the administration of the task was entrusted, was absent on campaign in Britain. The dispatch of Lupicinus is another factor that has seemed to betray Julian's complicity in an approaching coup d'état.[23] Again, suspicion is one thing, reasoned proof another. Ammianus' introduction of the British campaign gives no indication that there were not sufficient grounds for it – indeed rather the contrary, as he evokes in rhetorical terms the irruptions in the frontier zone of the 'wild nations' of the Picts and Scots (20.1.1). It is unjustified to argue, on the basis of Ammianus' brief description of Lupicinus' first move, a march to London (20.1.3), that he seemed unsure of what he should do, or that his force was excessive for the task in hand. Both his caution and the size of his force might be an indication of the seriousness of the situation and the need to plan carefully the Roman response, and Ammianus indicates that Lupicinus justifiably wished to take the field as quickly as he could; 'ut exinde suscepto *pro rei qualitate* consilio festinaret ocius ad procinctum' (20.1.3). His first move is the same as that made, admittedly with more difficulty, by Theodosius a few years later, and the importance of this campaign is not usually underestimated, at least by historians of late Roman Britain (27.8.6-8; 28.3.1).[24] The size of Theodosius' force, four 'numeri', was the same as that assigned to Lupicinus (two of the units, Heruli and Batavi, were used on both occasions) and there are no grounds for belittling the seriousness of the latter's task. It was a quite different situation when, after the proclamation of Julian, Lupicinus was isolated in Britain and arrested once he set foot at Boulogne (20.9.9, cf. *Ep. ad Ath.* 281A).

Ammianus presents Julian, not as keeping Lupicinus out of the way, but as lacking his advice, which he sorely needed on the arrival of Decentius at his winter quarters at Paris (20.4.6; 9). This is not an absurd presentation of the position. The 'auxilia' required by Constantius were under the command of the *magister militum* (*Not. Dig., Occ.* 5.160-3), and their removal could hardly be achieved without his knowledge and consent – indeed, we have just seen that of the troops requested by Constantius, the Heruli and Batavi were actually in Britain with Lupicinus. No such formal problem arose with the picked troops from the Scutarii and Gentiles also demanded by Constantius. These units of the palace guard fell under the authority not of the *magister militum* but of the *magister officiorum* (*Not. Dig., Occ.* 9.4-8); this would be Pentadius, whom Julian connects with Decentius and Nebridius (the *quaestor sacri palatii*) in his account of these transactions (*Ep. ad Ath.* 283C). Pentadius may be assumed to have approved the transfer and the tribune Sintula, correctly paying more attention to Constantius' instructions than to Julian's complaints, took them off without difficulty and in the hope of receiving promotion from Constantius, 'spe potiorum erectus' (20.4.5). He brought them back when news of the proclamation overtook him on his journey (20.5.1).

The most difficult question of motive attends the conduct of Julian's praetorian prefect, that Florentius with whom his relations had been so fraught. Decentius' problems on arriving at Paris were in fact even greater than indicated so far.[25] Not only was the *magister militum* absent in Britain; Florentius was at Vienne in southern Gaul, ostensibly to organise supplies but in fact, according to Ammianus, because he feared military disorder (20.4.6). The reason for this was that he 'was believed' ('putabatur') to have sent to Constantius a report advising the withdrawal of high-quality troops from the defence of Gaul. His conduct is more intelligible if he had in fact sent such a report and assumed that this would be known, than if he had not sent it but assumed that he would be believed to have done so; in any case, he refused to move from Vienne at Julian's request, even when the Caesar urged on him the public interest, and the duty of a *praefectus praetorio* to stand by his *imperator*, threatening to lay aside the insignia of rank if Florentius did not come (20.4.8). Such an approach was perhaps not best calculated to induce the prefect to rush to Julian's side, but this is not to say that Julian actually intended to deter him; nor, in view of his mandate from Constantius to supervise his Caesar, was Florentius necessarily obliged to perform every action that Julian suggested to him. Whatever the explanation of his conduct, the result of Florentius' absence was that Julian can again be presented, in Ammianus' as in Julian's own account, not as cleverly keeping the heads of his civil and military administration away from the scene of a conspiracy, but on the contrary, as deprived of the advice from them by which it might have been avoided.

Julian's own actions are at least compatible with his categorical profession, made before the gods, of good faith and innocence (*Ep. ad Ath.* 284B). To the withdrawal of the men from the Scutarii and Gentiles he had made no objection, 'yielding in all matters to the will of his superior'; 'acquieverat Iulianus, potioris arbitrio cuncta concedens' (20.4.4). He allowed himself the observation that men who had been recruited on the understanding that they would not have to serve outside Gaul should not suffer inconvenience, adding his fears that unless the understanding were respected it would prove difficult in future to recruit barbarian volunteers who often joined Roman service on these conditions. Despite his remarks, the troops departed (20.4.4). It was concerning the 'other troops' ('residui') requested by Constantius that difficulties arose, through the absence of the *magister militum* and praetorian prefect; these considerations, Julian's anxieties and the competing claims in his mind of the barbarian enemy and imperial authority, are well set out by Ammianus in a single, concentrated sentence (20.4.6).

In the end, and in the absence of his advisers, Julian decided to comply with Constantius' demands (20.4.9). From this point, the usurpation was under way as surely as if he had refused to obey them. The soldiers had received orders to leave winter quarters when what Ammianus calls a 'famosum libellum' – not a 'famous' or 'notorious' letter but a broadsheet containing unattributed allegations, or 'famae'[26] – was thrown onto the ground near the standards of the Petulantes, reciting among much else the grievances already put to Sintula by Julian on behalf of the Scutarii and Gentiles; they were to be compelled to serve abroad, leaving to the mercy of the Alamanni those wives and families whom their first campaigns had liberated – interesting sentiments, coming from mainly Germanic troops (20.4.10)! The contents of the broadsheet were no doubt widely known, but Julian treated it as in effect a formal petition brought in to the 'comitatus' and read; in response to the 'reasonable complaints' which he judged to be contained in it, he permitted the men's families to travel with them by the official transport service (one wonders how Constantius would regard this variation on his orders, when he received in the east not only battle-hardened soldiers but a migratory column of wives and children). Julian, who agrees with Ammianus that only one pamphlet was involved, adds that Constantius' agents pressed on him the need to dispatch the troops quickly, before similar documents could be broadcast among the other units and in order to avoid suspicions of disloyalty in addition to those that were already held (*Ep. ad Ath.*

283B-C). If they really said this, they were behaving like men who saw which way the wind was blowing but still hoped that the situation might be controlled, and Julian himself had given no indication to the contrary. The next step was to decide by which route the troops should go, and it was the tribune Decentius who recommended – according to Julian, against his own advice (ibid. 283D-284A) – to direct them by way of Paris, where Julian himself resided (20.4.11). In another fateful but perfectly innocent step, it was then natural for Julian to receive them when they arrived in the parade-ground outside the city, greeting the men whom he knew (it is important to note that he did not make a speech to their assembled company) and encouraging them to proceed to the court of Constantius, 'whose power was great and generous, and where their rewards would match their achievements'. As both Ammianus and Julian indicate, this reception by Julian of his fellow-soldiers was customary practice, and there is nothing inherently suspicious about it (20.4.12, cf. *Ep. ad Ath.* 284A). Equally unremarkable in itself, though its consequences were immediate, was Julian's invitation on the same day to the leaders of the Petulantes to a dinner at which, with no need for treasonable talk, their sense of resentment was intensified. This, we all know, is how usurpation comes about, and Julian is disingenuous in his *Letter to the Athenians* in omitting all mention of the dinner-party while at the same time calling the gods to witness that only in the course of this evening did he have any inkling of what was going to happen (*Ep. ad Ath.* 284B). A significant detail in this part of Ammianus' account is his implied confirmation that the leaders of the troops, and the soldiers themselves, were barbarians recruited into Roman service. The leaders are described not as generals or officers but as nobles, 'proceres', and the ground for their resentment was that they would be separated from their 'homelands', 'terris genitalibus' (20.4.13).[27] This phrase connects with that attributed to Julian himself in referring to the Scutarii and Gentiles led away by Sintula, 'relictis laribus transrhenanis' (20.4.4).

The acclamation of Julian as Augustus by soldiers surging at night around the palace, Julian's demurral, slowly weakening in face of the sustained force of their demands, and his own sense, confirmed by his prayers for a sign, that this was the will of the gods; his raising on a soldier's shield in the manner of proclamation of a German chieftain and his 'crowning' with the neck-chain of a standard-bearer of the Petulantes (20.4.14-18) – all this is a release into action of the accumulating tensions that have preceded. The question remains, whether it was more than this.

Certain elements in the sequence leading up to the proclamation – the broadsheet in the camp of the Petulantes, their reception at the parade-ground at Paris, the dining of their officers – are compatible with, but none actually presupposes, a premeditated conspiracy. What is disingenuous about the dinner-party is not that Julian held it but that he failed to mention it in the *Letter to the Athenians*. There may well have existed, at intermediate rather than at the highest levels of the court and

VI. The Rise of Julian

army establishment, groups of officers who saw the public interest or private advantage in a promotion of their Caesar's interests against Constantius, and who were prepared to exploit to their ends the resentment caused by the emperor's demands. The intellectual friends of Julian had caught the mood when, as will be explained in the next chapter, they conducted their secret rites in order to 'gain the courage to abolish Constantius' tyranny' (below, p. 115). To one of these friends, Oribasius, Julian had already divulged his all-too-explicit dream of the young sapling springing from the roots of a fallen tree, in response to the telling of a dream, the content of which is not imparted, of Oribasius' own (*Ep.* 14 Bidez).[28] The similarity between them seemed to Julian to show that both dreams were of the true variety. But this only shows that men were able to see, and to dream about, the obvious. As far as Julian was concerned, the proclamation was less an outcome of conspiracy than of a growing recognition in his mind, as in the minds of others, of what had from the first seemed possible, then likely, and now seemed bound to happen. To this recognition, and to his sense that, just as he owed to them his survival and his successes, so too his prospects for the future lay in the hands of the gods, we may assign the dream and other 'supernatural' experiences reported by Julian that have seemed, to some, to show his explicit designs against Constantius. They are rather to be seen as a projection of Julian's realisation that the inevitable – that is to say the will of the gods – would come about, and an expression of the need to justify to himself and to the public his own part in it.

The following sequence of events is described in similar terms by both Ammianus and Julian, and there is no need to paraphrase it in its entirety. Julian's offer to share power with Constantius, accepting a praetorian prefect of his nomination but appointing all other officials himself, was rejected outright by the emperor, who received Julian's envoys at Caesarea in Cappadocia with undisguised fury, told Julian to be content with his former status and appointed new officials for his Caesar (20.9.1ff.). Of these officials, Julian accepted Nebridius as praetorian prefect but rejected the other nominations in favour of his own (20.9.8). Nebridius' predecessor, Florentius, upon hearing of Julian's proclamation had left Vienne and taken himself with some difficulty to Constantius' court, where he denounced Julian as a rebel 'with many accusations' relating, no doubt, to more than the most recent events. In a gesture both true to his own character and good for public relations ('bene cogitans et prudenter'), Julian allowed the prefect's family, whom he had abandoned in his flight to Constantius, safe conduct to the east using the public transport service (20.8.20-2). Florentius was a little later appointed praetorian prefect of Illyricum, from which office he was uprooted by Julian's lightning advance to Sirmium (21.6.5; 9.4).

Both parties then devoted themselves studiously to their foreign wars, Julian to an expedition against the Atthuarian Franks before returning by way of Kaiseraugst to winter at Vienne, while Constantius renewed his alliance with Arsaces of Armenia and, travelling by way of Amida, addressed himself, late in the season and without success, to the recovery of Bezabde on the Tigris (20.10.1-3; 11.4-32). With the return of Constantius to winter quarters at Antioch Ammianus ends Book 20 of his history, beginning Book 21 with an ominous reflection. It was ordained, so it seemed, that as long as Constantius engaged personally in war with Persia he was never successful, though his generals sometimes were; in civil war he never failed. There was also the constant reminder of Gallus Caesar, destroyed through his own inertia and the treachery of others (20.11.32; 21.1.2). Inertia was the very last quality one would attribute to Julian, but these were anxious thoughts to occupy his mind at the end of his first year as a free agent, having exchanged Constantius' suspicions for his open enmity. Ammianus presents their implications in Julian's reflections on the coming year. Should he continue to attempt reconciliation with his 'bloody friend', or should he strike first, to gain the advantage of terror in a war in which his forces were so palpably inferior (21.1.1)?

*

The civil war of 360-1 is instinctively seen by historians from the point of view of Julian rather than Constantius: the rising rather then the setting star. That is natural. Not only was Julian the victor in the outcome (historians like a story with a future); to most of them, intellectuals like himself, he is the more attractive character, and, as can be seen from the first part of this chapter, he is articulate and, one must admit, not unpersuasive in his own defence. Seen however from Constantius' point of view, the situation provided yet another instance of the eternal choice with which his reign had confronted him, the choice between foreign and domestic war (cf. 20.9.3).

In making his choice, he was without the counsel of Ursicinus, whose outspoken criticisms of Constantius' conduct of military affairs on the eastern frontier, made early in the year at Sirmium, had already secured his dismissal (20.2.1). With him, presumably, departed Ammianus, whether for some other (no doubt unfavoured) assignment or whether for a spell of private life as an officer without posting (and largely forgotten) remains a matter of speculation: as does the intriguing possibility that, but for the dismissal of Ursicinus, Ammianus could have found himself preparing in 361 to take the field against Julian. Ammianus could easily, through Ursicinus, have picked up an account of Constantius' motives in writing to Julian for reinforcements after the loss of Amida – we have seen that in this context at least, Ammianus took quite seriously the need for reinforcements in the east (19.11.17). He would however rely on others 'versati in medio' for his knowledge of subsequent relations between Constantius and his Caesar: notable among them, again, is the eunuch Eutherius, whose authority might well lie behind Ammianus' knowledge of the rancorous secret letters addressed to Constantius by Julian in addition to the more dignified communications intended for

VI. The Rise of Julian

public circulation. Eutherius was one of Julian's two envoys to Constantius, and the account of their reception at Caesarea is told with a certain terse vigour for which he was probably the source.[29] The emperor's white-hot display of anger — 'ultra modum solitae indignationis excanduit imperator' — had scared the life out of them (20.8.18f.; 9.1f.).

In 361, despite Julian's preparations against him, Constantius again decided, after some hesitation, to devote himself to the eastern frontier, thinking that he could more safely attack Julian without an external enemy at his back and still hoping to catch his rival before his undertaking had gained momentum; this at least is what he told his associates, to reassure them (21.7.1). In the meantime he secured Africa by sending there the *notarius* Gaudentius, a manoeuvre which, as Ammianus makes clear, worked very well. As long as Constantius lived, none of his adversaries landed there (21.7.2-5). Constantius again enlisted the kings and satraps of the Transtigritane regions, together with the kings of Armenia and Hiberia, crossed the Euphrates at Capersana and waited at Edessa for Sapor to decide whether or not the omens would permit him to invade that year (21.6.7f.; 7.6; 13.2). The emperor was dismayed to learn that Julian had already occupied the pass of Succi (21.13.6), though he presumably also knew that his *comes Thraciarum*, Martianus, was preparing to amass troops to the east of Succi and prevent Julian from advancing further (21.12.22). It was nevertheless an immense relief when Constantius heard that Sapor had yielded to the omens and taken his army away from the frontier without attempting a crossing (21.13.8). The emperor at once returned to Hierapolis and devoted his attention to the suppression of Julian. Ammianus — who, we must remember, was in the east at the time — remarked that no one doubted for a moment that Constantius would win the war (21.7.3). He later has occasion to mention one Theodotus of Hierapolis, who had escorted Constantius from his city among the 'honorati' and flattered the emperor with gross effusiveness ('deformiter') as the certain victor — an act which many people later reported to Julian, who forgave him (22.14.4). Theodotus' conduct is a sure measure of what people expected the outcome would be.

Not for the first or last time in Julian's career, Fortune took a hand. Constantius led his army from Hierapolis to Antioch and from there on to Tarsus and into Cilicia; and there, at Mopsucrena in the shadow of the Taurus mountains, on 3 November 361 he succumbed to a fever that he had contracted at Tarsus but hoped with typically stolid determination to shake off by travelling. Whether truthfully or by a useful fiction, he was said while his mind was still lucid to have named Julian as his successor. He then lapsed into silence and passed away after a long death-struggle; 'diuque cum anima colluctatus iam discessura abiit e vita' says Ammianus, bringing Constantius' life to an end with words of a ceremonious, almost liturgical dignity (21.15.2).

The operations of the partisans in the civil war of 360 and 361 are summarized in the chart overleaf, which is designed not to supplant

The Rise of Julian, 359–62

The chart shows the movements of Julian and Constantius from late 359 to early 362: every detail shown is either stated or directly implied by Ammianus. Its purpose is to present an integrated view of events in different theatres of action; to illustrate the difficulty of the task of narrative reconstruction and co-ordination faced by Ammianus; and to show how successfully he achieved it, working from such individual items of information as those shown on the chart.

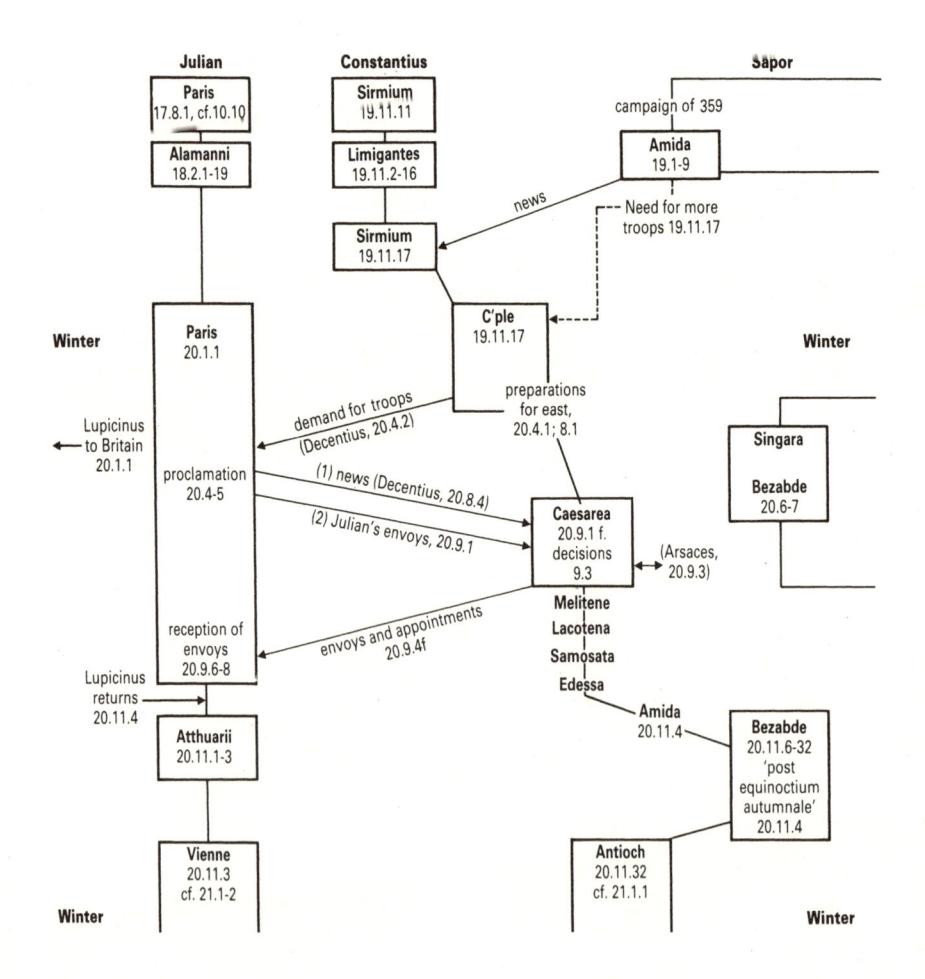

Julian	Constantius	Sapor
Paris 17.8.1, cf.10.10	Sirmium 19.11.11	campaign of 359
Alamanni 18.2.1-19	Limigantes 19.11.2-16	Amida 19.1-9
	Sirmium 19.11.17 ← news	---Need for more troops 19.11.17
	C'ple 19.11.17 ←---	

Winter (left) — **Winter** (right)

- Paris 20.1.1
- Lupicinus → to Britain 20.1.1
- proclamation 20.4-5 — demand for troops (Decentius, 20.4.2) →
- (1) news (Decentius, 20.8.4) →
- (2) Julian's envoys, 20.9.1 →
- preparations for east, 20.4.1; 8.1
- Caesarea 20.9.1 f. decisions 9.3 (Arsaces, 20.9.3)
- Singara
- Bezabde 20.6-7
- reception of envoys 20.9.6-8 ← envoys and appointments 20.9.4f
- Lupicinus returns 20.11.4
- Atthuarii 20.11.1-3
- Melitene / Lacotena / Samosata / Edessa
- Amida 20.11.4
- Bezabde 20.11.6-32 'post equinoctium autumnale' 20.11.4
- Vienne 20.11.3 cf. 21.1-2
- Antioch 20.11.32 cf. 21.1.1

Winter (left) — **Winter** (right)

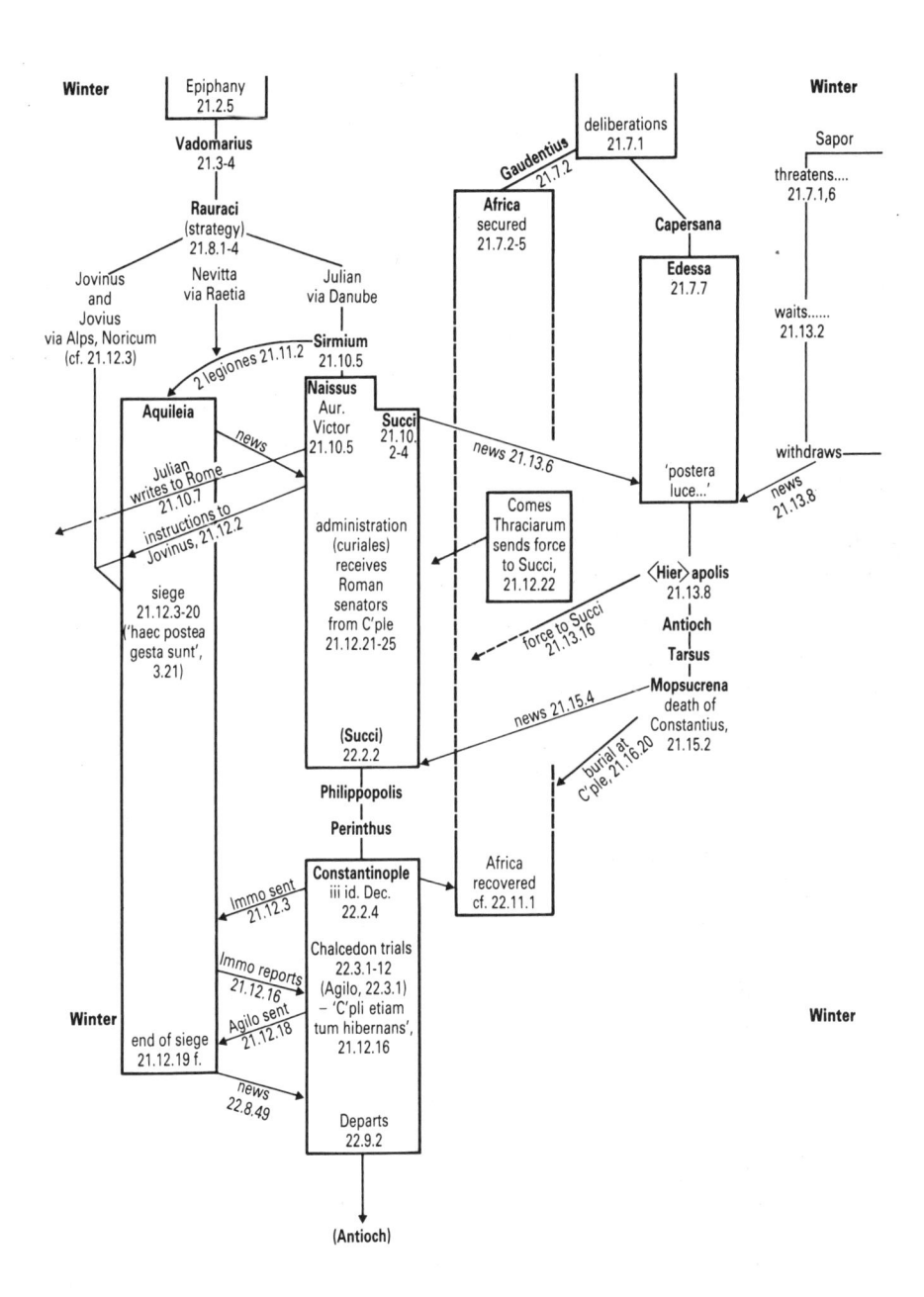

Winter	Epiphany 21.2.5				deliberations 21.7.1		Winter
	Vadomarius 21.3-4			Gaudentius 21.7.2			Sapor threatens.... 21.7.1,6
	Rauraci (strategy) 21.8.1-4			Africa secured 21.7.2-5	Capersana		
Jovinus and Jovius via Alps, Noricum (cf. 21.12.3)	Nevitta via Raetia	Julian via Danube			Edessa 21.7.7		waits...... 21.13.2
		2 legiones 21.11.2	Sirmium 21.10.5				
Aquileia	news	Naissus Aur. Victor 21.10.5	Succi 21.10. 2-4	news 21.13.6	'postera luce...'		withdraws news 21.13.8
Julian writes to Rome 21.10.7 instructions to Jovinus, 21.12.2				Comes Thraciarum sends force to Succi, 21.12.22	⟨Hier⟩apolis 21.13.8		
siege 21.12.3-20 ('haec postea gesta sunt', 3.21)		administration (curiales) receives Roman senators from C'ple 21.12.21-25		force to Succi 21.13.16	Antioch Tarsus		
				news 21.15.4	Mopsucrena death of Constantius, 21.15.2		
		(Succi) 22.2.2			burial at C'ple, 21.16.20		
		Philippopolis					
		Perinthus					
	Immo sent 21.12.3	Constantinople iii id. Dec. 22.2.4		Africa recovered cf. 22.11.1			
	Immo reports 21.12.16 Agilo sent 21.12.18	Chalcedon trials 22.3.1-12 (Agilo, 22.3.1) – 'C'pli etiam tum hibernans', 21.12.16					
Winter	end of siege 21.12.19 f.						Winter
	news 22.8.49	Departs 22.9.2					
		↓ (Antioch)					

the narrative of these events but to show graphically the complexity and coherence of Ammianus' account of them; every detail there included is either stated in or can be directly inferred from his text. Taking for granted the accuracy of the narrative, we are free to analyse the conflict in terms of the respective strengths of the two sides.

In his *Letter to the Athenians*, Julian mentions Constantius' supply depots, three million 'medimnoi' of grain stored at Brigantia (Bregenz) to the east of Lake Konstanz, and the same quantity near the Cottian Alps. Constantius, who on this evidence planned to mount an attack upon Julian from both Italy and Illyricum, had also written to his supporters in Italy to impose a blockade against any troops from Gaul and had sent instructions to the praetorian prefect of Italy (*Ep. ad Ath.* 286A-C). Julian seized the corn supplies and intercepted the letters to Taurus. He also alleged Constantius' readiness to use barbarian allies against him, an allegation borne out by Ammianus' description of the arrest of king Vadomarius of the Alamanni while at dinner with the Roman commander at Kaiseraugst (21.3-4). A Roman *notarius* had been intercepted by Julian's guards bearing letters from Vadomarius to Constantius reporting on his Caesar's 'lack of discipline', while he simultaneously addressed Julian as 'dominus' and 'Augustus'. Ammianus also stated that Vadomarius had been instructed to cause sufficient unrest in the regions adjoining his own principality to prevent Julian from leaving the Gallic frontier (21.3.4f.).[30] The westerly penetration of Constantius' power, and the fragility of Julian's support there, are further shown by the hostile reception by the Roman senate of Julian's letter addressed to that body from Illyricum (21.10.7); while he also received at Naissus (and promoted) two leading senators who had been sent as envoys to Constantius and were now returning – disconcerted, no doubt, to find Naissus already in the hands of the usurper (21.12.24).[31] The attachment of the senate to Constantius must be seen in the light of its relations with an emperor who had visited Rome with such success only four years previously; these things were remembered. Two 'legiones Constantiacae' that Julian found at Sirmium, sent with a cohort of archers to serve in Gaul because he did not trust them, entered Aquileia on their way there and declared the city and its region loyal to Constantius; this was a serious problem, and one only resolved – and even then not immediately, for the defenders of Aquileia were reluctant to believe it – by the arrival of the news of Constantius' death (21.11.2ff.).

Julian's most effective manoeuvre in face of the massive territorial and military advantage of Constantius was speed – such speed as would frustrate the emperor's hope that he could both patch up his differences with Sapor and meet Julian before his campaign had gathered momentum (21.7.1). All sources – Julian himself, Zosimus (from Eunapius) and the panegyrist Mamertinus as well as Ammianus – emphasise the extraordinary speed of Julian's advance down the Danube to Sirmium, using a fleet of river-boats that he either found by chance (according to Ammianus) or had ordered to be constructed (in the version

VI. The Rise of Julian

of Eunapius).[32] He also split his army into three divisions in order, as Ammianus says, to allow rumour to exaggerate the size of his forces as they advanced along different routes. In doing so, he was imitating Alexander the Great and other expert generals who had done the same when need arose (21.8.3) – a rather 'literary' interpretation of a manoeuvre permitting Julian to strike quickly for Illyricum while the supporting divisions advanced by way of north Italy and Raetia respectively (21.8.3). In the event the manoeuvre was partly undermined by the adherence of Aquileia to Constantius, to which Julian was obliged to divert the division marching under Jovinus by way of north Italy (21.12.2). The speed of Julian's advance is shown also by the flight to the court of Constantius of the praetorian prefects of Italy and Illyricum, Taurus and Florentius, and by Julian's dramatic night-time capture of Constantius' general Lucillianus at Bononia near Sirmium. Lucillianus was in bed expecting nothing of the sort, when he was woken up by a commotion and found himself surrounded by total strangers who escorted him to the young pretender (21.9.4-8)!

In one sense, Julian had overstretched his resources. He had no difficulty advancing past Naissus and seizing the strategic pass of Succi leading down into Thrace, but did not have the forces to advance beyond it.[33] The Thracian armies had been mobilised against him by the *comes Thraciarum* (21.12.22), while Constantius was preparing an attack as soon as he could free himself from his problems in the east (21.6.6). Further, Constantius controlled Africa (21.7.2-5), Aquileia was loyal to him, and an eastern field army was being prepared for an advance into Thrace ahead of Constantius' own arrival (21.13.16). Ammianus is justified in portraying Julian at this time as apprehensive and anxious (21.12.21); a state of mind in which we should imagine his conduct of the sacrifices and divination performed at Naissus, among them rites that indicated the coming death of Constantius. Despite this (he did not know of Constantius' own premonitions of his approaching end), Julian dared not attempt to break out of the Dacian provinces into Constantius' dominions (22.1.1f.).

The tension was resolved, and the omens confirmed, by the sudden arrival of the news of Constantius' death, brought by two envoys who also told Julian that his rival had named him as his successor (22.2.1). The reign of Julian as sole Augustus effectively begins at this point, but Ammianus preserves a continuing sense of its character as a journey with digressions, beginning with his descent of Succi and rapid advance to Constantinople, then in a series of stages through Asia Minor to Antioch, and from there to the Persian campaign on which, still marching, he was killed.

Julian's periods of residence in the cities of the empire through which he passed on his journey are characterised by Ammianus through activities of government and administration picking out guiding themes of his reign. At Naissus he received embassies and made appointments, heard litigation and, at the instance of town councils, imposed civic burdens on many individuals, an act criticised by Ammianus (21.12.23-5). It was from Naissus that Julian wrote to the Roman senate and probably also his letter to the council and people of the Athenians, as we have seen a crucial source for the events of his usurpation.[34] It was one of a series of missives sent to the cities of Greece, a region that with the occupation of the prefecture of Illyricum now fell under his control. The letters to Sparta and Corinth are also mentioned in our sources, though with the exception of a brief citation from the letter to the Corinthians describing his father's residence in the city, they do not survive (Zosimus 3.10.4; Libanius, *Or.* 14.29f.).

Julian's sojourn at Constantinople is portrayed in a series of episodic chapters describing aspects of his regime: the trials at Chalcedon at which, in the intimidating presence of the military, several unjust as well as just sentences were imposed (22.3.1-12);[35] the reform of the palace administration by an onslaught upon elimination of ostentation and waste, in which Ammianus, while permitting himself an eloquent digression on luxury that occupies most of the chapter, thought that Julian went further than befitted a true philosopher (22.4.1-10), the treatment of Christians and, in an ironically juxtaposed chapter, of some litigious Egyptians (22.5-6). The Egyptians were sent to Chalcedon on the pretence that the emperor himself would come to hear them, and orders then issued that no man must transport an Egyptian from Chalcedon to Constantinople. The litigants eventually became disheartened and returned home (22.6.1-4). The Christians were granted a freedom of belief that, in Julian's opinion, would ensure their rapid decline into squabbling sectarianism (22.5.3f.). It is in this context that Ammianus makes his explicit avowal of Julian's early adherence, 'a rudimentis pueritiae primis', to the gods, and describes his open declaration of support for the old religions, with instructions that the temples should be reopened and sacrifice restored (22.5.1f.).

These chapters are followed by a description of Julian's conduct in the senate of Constantinople, introduced by his behaviour on the Kalends of January 362, when the new consuls, Mamertinus and Nevitta, were admitted to office (22.7.1-6). Ammianus' comment that Julian, in a gesture praised by some but criticised by others as cheap and affected, processed with the consuls on foot, is confirmed by the panegyric of Mamertinus delivered on the occasion.[36] There is then a rapid transition to Julian's conduct of military affairs, including his famed rejection of the advice to make war against the Goths (22.7.8), and his reception of various embassies. In rising degrees of implausibility they came from the Transtigritane regions and Armenia, from India and Ceylon and from Mauretania in 'the south', and, in the solitary northern regions of the Black Sea, from the Bosporani and 'hitherto unknown' peoples, petitioning that they be allowed to live in their ancestral lands (22.7.8). Perhaps such embassies (or some of them) did arrive, but the whole passage is an essentially 'literary' collection of peoples, whose main function is to dramatise the extent of Julian's power and to furnish a

VI. The Rise of Julian

transition to the long digression on the Pontic regions with which the rest of Julian's sojourn at Constantinople is occupied (22.8.1-48). The digression ends, incongruously, with the arrival of yet more good news (in addition, that is, to the arrival of the envoys), the surrender of Aquileia and the burning alive of those who had inspired its rebellion (22.8.49).

That is the end of Julian's sojourn at Constantinople. Only upon his departure does Ammianus indicate such an important matter as the emperor's benefactions to the place, 'incrementis maximis fultam'; other sources mention a harbour with a portico in the form of the Greek letter sigma – a semi-circle – leading to it, and a library (built in fact by Constantius), to which Julian donated all the books he possessed (Zosimus 3.11.3).[37] Only now, too, does Ammianus specifically mention Julian's affection for the city as his birthplace – though this might of course have been explained in one of the lost books (22.9.2). His departure from Constantinople took him by Chalcedon and Libyssa – the burial place of Hannibal, adds Ammianus in a characteristically erudite note (22.9.3) – and on to Nicomedia, whose recent devastation by earthquake provided another opportunity for the exercise of civic munificence by Julian, 'pari modo ad reparanda ... abunde praestitis plurimis' (22.9.5). Again, we saw earlier how it is only at this point that Ammianus mentions Julian's boyhood residence at Nicomedia under the tutorship of bishop Eusebius (22.9.4; p. 85).

The journey continues, in Ammianus' presentation a typical combination of itinerary and encyclopaedia. On the boundaries of Galatia (for literary purposes styled 'Gallograecia' by Ammianus), a diversion from the main route takes Julian to the shrine of Magna Mater at Pessinus. It also provides the historian with the opportunity for a learned remark on the Second Punic War and the Cumaean Sibyl, a back-reference to his description of the reign of Commodus, in which he had narrated the arrival of the image of the goddess in Italy, and a little piece of etymology in which Ammianus unusually specifies Latin rather than Greek as his 'own' language. The place was called Pessinus, 'apo tou pesein, quod cadere nos dicimus', for it was there that the image of the goddess had fallen to earth: though other writers gave different explanations (22.9.5f.).[38] Julian sacrifices to the divinity and returning to the main route proceeds to Ancyra, where he is besieged by crowds of litigants demanding the return of confiscated property or complaining that they were unjustly added to the lists of city councillors. Some even went so far as to accuse their opponents of *maiestas* (22.9.8) – a charge for which recent events gave considerable scope, if what was meant by 'maiestas' was publicly declared support for Constantius; many men in the east were so committed (above, p. 101). Amid all the rancour Julian held fast to the cause of justice, but is again criticised by Ammianus because petitions by city councillors for additions to their number were hardly ever refused, whatever the force – through privilege, military service or origin – of claims for exemption (22.9.12). The passage through 'Pylae', that is the Cilician Gates separating the provinces of Cappadocia and Cilicia, allowed Julian to renew an acquaintance with a fellow-student at Athens, now governor of Cilicia, whom he conveyed with him in his imperial carriage to Tarsus; the man obviously knew of the emperor's approach and was waiting at the provincial boundary to greet him (22.9.13). Then, pursuing in reverse the fatal journey of Constantius the previous year (one would love to have had described the reception given him at Mopsucrena), Julian came to Antioch, the 'Crown of the Orient; 'orientis apicem pulchrum' (22.9.14). He was received 'like a god' by welcoming crowds acclaiming him in almost Messianic terms as a 'star of salvation' come to shine upon the east, in an example of the traditional 'adventus' ceremony described elsewhere in this book (pp. 231ff.); the same thing, in the same fashion, had happened at Sirmium (21.10.1f.) and at Constantinople (22.2.4), and doubtless, on a lesser scale, everywhere along the emperor's route. Since his arrival at Antioch coincided however with the celebration of the festival of Adonis (on 18 July), it was also marked by ill-omened cries of mourning for the stricken youth (22.9.15); it will be recalled that Ammianus had used the same image of lamentation in describing the funeral of the Chionite prince at Amida (p. 61). It is the first hint of the religious foreboding that will from now attend Ammianus' description of the reign of Julian until the moment of his death in Persia, and can in that sense be seen as a turning point in the narrative.[39]

It is not surprising that Julian's stay at Antioch should be pervaded by the atmosphere of the approaching campaign; it is, after all, why he was in the city in the first place – as is earlier hinted by Ammianus' description of the rejection of war against the Goths in favour of a more worthy enemy (22.7.8) and, in a context immediately preceding the move from Constantinople to Antioch, by his evocation of the undying success bestowed by Fortune upon her favourite; quite apart from his past victories, Julian was throughout his sole reign free of the threat of civil war and foreign invasion (22.9.1). Now, Julian's stay at Antioch was extremely eventful, particularly in religious controversy and in the emperor's dispute with the city over problems of the corn supply. Ammianus' description of it is however barely more substantial than that of the few (perhaps six) months spent at Constantinople; and it contrasts markedly, in detail and in emphasis, with Julian's own account in his pamphlet the *Misopogon* or 'Beard-Hater' in which the emperor, by a brilliant inversion of literary postures reflecting the ritual impersonations and masquerades characteristic of the New Year festivities at which it was composed, denounces the people of Antioch through a sustained double parody of their judgment upon him.[40]

Compared with this vividly subjective impression, Ammianus' presentation of Julian's regime at Antioch is a model of studied caution. History is not satire, and Ammianus' verdict on the *Misopogon* is that it 'added many things to the truth' (22.14.2). There is a point of contact, in Ammianus' introductory comment on the emperor's resistance to the 'seductive pleasures in which all Syria abounds' (22.10.1) before he passes

VI. The Rise of Julian

on to his determined commitment to the conduct of law. The connection of thought is that Julian avoided frivolity in order to devote himself to serious concerns. Even here, Ammianus offers criticism. Julian tended to be impulsive, and sometimes asked litigants what was their religion – not that this could ever be shown to have led to an untruthful or unjust outcome (it is however a curious view of legal impartiality) (22.10.2). Under Julian it was almost as if, in the emperor's own words, the goddess Justice herself had descended from heaven to earth – were it not that he did sometimes permit legal decisions to be swayed by his own will rather than the strict rule of law, and so clouded many fine achievements (22.10.6). Julian made many improvements in the laws, removing ambiguities so that they declared clearly what was allowed and what was not – but against this was his intolerable prohibition of adherents of the Christian faith from acting as professors of rhetoric and grammar; 'illud autem erat inclemens, obruendum perenni silentio, quod arcebat docere magistros rhetoricos et grammaticos ritus christiani cultores' (22.10.7).[41] Setting aside this specific complaint, Ammianus' reservations in this passage are in striking contrast to the unqualified admiration for Julian's financial and judicial administration expressed in similar digressions on his rule in Gaul. In this they are consistent with his view that it was the earliest phase of Julian's rule that was the most remarkable (16.1.5; cf. above, p. 89f.).

The next substantial episode in the narrative of Julian's regime at Antioch, the murder of bishop George of Alexandria by a seditious crowd there (22.11.2-11), is loosely connected with Julian's legal activities by the arrest, trial and execution of the former *dux Aegypti* Artemius, which encouraged the Alexandrians to turn against Artemius' ecclesiastical ally (22.11.2). This is however an invalid connection, since the riot at Alexandria and the murder of George can be clearly dated to the end of 361, before Julian had come to Antioch and before the Alexandrians had had the opportunity even to petition for the removal of their hated commander, let alone secure his trial and execution.[42] Ammianus follows this misplaced episode with an account of Julian's preparations for the Persian campaign, and of his excessive sacrifices at Antioch, which led to disgraceful scenes as his soldiers were carried to their lodgings incapable from their indulgence in the left-overs from the sacrifices, and caused a proliferation of fortune-tellers of all sorts who sprang forth, eager to exploit the emperor's passion for divination (22.11.6f.). Julian further encouraged the atmosphere of religious 'curiositas' by ordering the purification and reopening of the oracular shrine of Castalian Apollo at Daphne, an event followed by the destruction by fire, on 22 October 362, of the beautiful shrine of the god and his magnificent image (22.12.8-13.1).[43] Ammianus' brief account of the restoration of the oracle and the burning of the temple is however remarkable for his failure to make the causal (as opposed to merely chronological) connection between these events that is certified by our other sources (below, pp. 439ff.).

Equally unrelated to its historical context is his description, which follows the burning of the temple, of the failure of the autumn rains which led to the running dry of normally perennial streams (22.14.1). This is seen by Ammianus as an omen and is linked to the further devastation of Nicomedia and damage to Nicaea in an earthquake, all of which added to the emperor's anxieties. He makes no specific connection between the failure of the rains and the already existing corn shortage which it aggravated, setting Julian's policy of fixing food prices merely in the context of his desire to win popularity and seeing this as a distraction from the serious business of preparing the Persian campaign (22.14.1f.). It is in the setting of Julian's dispute with the city council of Antioch over this issue that Ammianus mentions the *Misopogon*, in which the emperor denounced the Antiochenes (22.11.2), in return being made to suffer insults for his odd physical appearance and mannerisms, and his excessive religiosity. All of this is quite well conveyed by Ammianus and the chronology (the New Year festivities of 363) is accurate, but it remains curiously remote from its actual historical context. The *Misopogon* provides a partisan but coherent account of the origins and the development of the corn crisis in the winter of 362/3. If Ammianus (as we may assume) had read it, he remains remarkably indifferent to the evidence it provides (below, p. 409).

There is little more to say about Julian's stay at Antioch. After a brief description of his ascent of Mount Casius to see the sunrise and sacrifice to Jupiter – an occasion that provided an opportunity to forgive the supporter of Constantius from Hierapolis mentioned earlier – Ammianus reports the discovery in Egypt of the sacred bull Apis and turns this into a long digression on that country which carries him through to the end of Book 22 (14.6-16.24). Despite the claim that the context 'demands' ('videtur ... flagitare') the digression, it does not fit naturally into its context. It should be seen as a parallel to the digression on the Pontic regions that concludes the narrative of Julian's sojourn at Constantinople (22.8.1-48; above, p. 106). In both cases, the transition is of a literary rather than a substantive character, the motive being to add scale to a narrative that might otherwise lack it.

Book 23, the first on the Persian campaign, begins with the abortive restoration by Julian of the Temple at Jerusalem – an act which again, despite its obvious connection with the emperor's religious policies, Ammianus describes as expressing merely Julian's ambition to leave behind some worthy monument of his reign; 'imperii sui memoriam magnitudine operum gestiens propagare' (23.1.2). It is another somewhat detached perspective in which Ammianus seems deliberately to ignore the most obvious and most widely held, that is to say the religious, interpretation. The failed attempt to restore the Temple, which may be misplaced in Ammianus' narrative, is followed by a group of appointments to high office, and by the deaths of Julian's uncle and of a *comes sacrarum largitionum* which usher in a series of adverse omens.[44]

Only two aspects of the actual preparations for the Persian campaign are relevant at the moment. The first is Julian's writing to Arsaces of

VI. The Rise of Julian

Armenia, which foreshadows the role of that king in the strategy of the campaign (below, p. 138); and the second, Ammianus' remark that orders were issued for troops to assemble from their winter quarters in all parts of the east, and to await the emperor's arrival at their various postings; 'dispersi per stationes varias adventum principis exspectabant' (23.2.3). Ammianus, we shall see, makes his first personal appearance on the campaign near Zaitha on the Euphrates, a day's march below the junction with the Khabur and so already in Assyria (23.5.7; p. 132). It remains a matter of speculation what the historian had been doing between Ursicinus' departure from office in 360 and the Persian campaign of 363. Whether he rejoined the service after a spell in private life, or was attached to the campaign from some more distant assignment, Ammianus can have joined the army at any of a wide variety of possible locations. It is by no means certain that he was actually with the army of Julian as it left Antioch on 5 March 363.

*

Between the two detailed military narratives of the usurpation of Julian and his Persian campaign, Ammianus' account of the actual reign of his hero is surprisingly inconclusive. As suggested earlier, it might almost be described as a journey (with digressions) from Naissus to Antioch, Julian's brief sojourns both at Constantinople and at Antioch being 'filled out' by digressions on the Pontic regions and on Egypt, introduced with more literary than historical purpose, in the middle and at the end of Book 22. (In Book 23, an immense digression on Persia, with more obvious justification but far exceeding what is needed for Ammianus' purpose, has a similar effect in expanding the scale of his treatment). Further, the episodic nature of Ammianus' description of the domestic reign of Julian contrasts with the fluency and complexity of his narrative of the military events that flank it on either side.[45]

Important aspects, especially of the religious personality of the emperor, are presented by Ammianus in a curiously oblique manner. It is not that the historian is inexplicit or evasive. We saw that he mentioned Julian's studies in Asia Minor and Athens, his early 'conversion' to the cause of the old gods and his interest in divination, then the initial dissimulation and the gradually emerging openness of his religious policies, especially in the restoration of sacrifice and of the temples of the gods. This is coherent and convincing, but none of it is stated in any detail, and certain aspects only in retrospect. As to the restoration of the oracle and subsequent destruction of the temple of Apollo at Daphne and the attempted rebuilding of the Temple at Jerusalem, Ammianus seems to reject the opportunity to adopt a dimension of religious controversy that is clearly recognised in other sources. The restoration of the oracle is presented in its broadest sense as part of a perspective looking back to the Athenians' purification of Delos in the fifth century BC, and not as part of the intensely controversial setting at Antioch that we know did exist

(Chapter XVII.2, pp. 439ff.). Although it is chronologically connected, the destruction of the temple is causally separated from the restoration of the oracle, the 'envy of the Christians' that was suspected as the cause of the fire being acknowledged but given the least possible emphasis. According to Ammianus, they simply objected to the building of a peristyle there – not false, but a mere fragment of the true situation (23.13.2; p. 439). The restoration of the Temple at Jerusalem, placed emphatically and perhaps with dramatic licence at the beginning of Book 23, is given a context in Julian's munificence rather than forming any part of a religious policy such as the emperor's own writings help to define; the Jewish God fits perfectly, indeed pre-eminently, into the theory of 'national divinities' expounded in his tract *Contra Galilaeos*.[46] The 'balls of fire' that broke out and put an end to the work on the Temple are given no explanation, human or divine, but are attributed simply to the 'determined opposition of the element' (that is, fire). In a fascinating piece of understatement, their repeated blows made the place 'inaccessible to the workmen'; 'fecere locum exustis aliquotiens operantibus inaccessum' (23.1.3)!

Ammianus' only direct comment on the religious personality of Julian, apart from his interest in divination, relates to his superstition. Ammianus notes this both in his own person, and as a reaction assigned to the people of Antioch (22.12.6f.; 14.3). Perhaps thinking them no part of the public policy of a Roman emperor, he says nothing of matters as important to Julian as his institution of a revived provincial priesthood organised on a hierarchical basis (rather like the Christian clergy), nor of his promotion of charitable activities connected with the temples to rival those associated with the Christian church.[47] In all this, although Ammianus' account by no means lacks a religious dimension, it remains detached from the emperor's own perceptions and even, on occasion, hostile to them. How is this to be explained?

A puzzling feature of Ammianus' obituary of Julian is the lack of connection there made between the emperor's virtues, which are discussed in terms of the four 'cardinal' and other subordinate virtues defined by the philosophers, and his shortcomings, presented briefly in the form of a series of separate observations (25.4.16-21). The discrepancy can be viewed in various ways, for example in terms of literary technique and the structure of Ammianus' account (p. 468f.); what is important for the present is the extent to which the historian seems careless of the force of the shortcomings he adduces. Julian is criticised for his impulsiveness and his love of popularity, for his excessive interest in divination and for a religiosity that seemed to broach the borders of superstition; for the law forbidding Christians to teach rhetoric and grammar unless they adopted the cause of the old gods, and for his over-insistent imposition of the burdens of town-councillors upon men who possessed valid exemptions. It amounts to a criticism of every major aspect of Julian's policies, religious, cultural and civic, and in his archaically restrained treatment of the imperial office.

An additional feature of Ammianus' presentation is that he repeats his

VI. The Rise of Julian

criticisms almost verbatim from narrative text to obituary – almost as if he were deliberately denying to the latter the more generalised quality that might enable the shortcomings of Julian to be weighed against his virtues.[48] This is true of his description of Julian's edict on professors of rhetoric, where the general clarity of his legislation is also mentioned in both contexts (22.10.7, cf. 25.4.20), and of the enforcement of membership of curial orders (22.9.12, cf. 25.4.21), as well as of his general administration of justice, where both passages allude to Julian's claim that the goddess Iustitia had returned to earth, in each case with an allusion to the poet Aratus, who had described her flight to heaven to avoid the wickedness of men (22.10.6, cf. 25.4.19).

That the shortcomings of Julian remain peripheral to Ammianus' judgment of the emperor would in a way be more serious if it were confined to the obituary notice in Book 25. In fact, as we have seen, it pervades the articulation of Ammianus' view of his hero. It is not that certain aspects are not made clear; they are simply not made central to Julian's character, in a way that the emperor himself and our other sources would lead us to expect. The origins of Julian's apostasy in his youth and the steady development of his religious predilections are mentioned, but in retrospect; his sojourns in Asia Minor and at Athens contain no indication of their intellectual implications; the personal religiosity of Julian during his stay at Antioch is connected with his interest in divination and sacrifice, but the restoration of the oracle at Daphne and the burning of the temple, and the attempted restoration of the Temple at Jerusalem are described in such a way as to minimise the air of religious controversy that surrounded them; all this has been mentioned and need not be repeated.

It is therefore not simply that the faults assigned to Julian remain unintegrated in Ammianus' obituary of the emperor; they are not a 'load-bearing' feature of his narrative text either, where they occur as incidental remarks that are clearly not intended by Ammianus to cast fundamental doubt on his portrayal of the positive qualities of Julian's reign. The problem can be solved most simply and radically by asking what, in Ammianus' judgment, were the positive virtues of the reign. The answers are clear – indeed, they can be read from the first and dominant section of the obituary of Julian. Apart from his personal asceticism and self-control, Julian is praised for his administration of law and justice, for his financial management which enabled him to reduce and even to abolish taxes, and for his skill, courage and authority in all aspects of war; that is to say, for Ammianus, Julian was not primarily a religious figure. In fact, intensity of religious feeling forms no part of Ammianus' view of what makes a good emperor. Both Julian and Constantius are criticised in their obituary notices for their 'superstition' (21.16.8; 25.4.17), while the Christian Valentinian is praised for his religious neutrality (30.9.5).

Ammianus' emphasis on the administration of justice, finance and war conforms closely to his own experience of Julian, focussed as it was on the beginnings of his regime as Caesar and upon the Persian campaign. It also conforms to the restrained proportions of a narrative of Julian's 'peacetime' government which, crammed in between the proclamation and its sequel in Books 20 and 21 and the Persian campaign beginning in Book 23, is itself inflated by long digressions on the Pontic regions (22.8) and Egypt (22.15-16); these digressions, as we saw, are appended to accounts of Julian's sojourns at Constantinople and Antioch that are themselves no more than episodic and, without the digressions, might look insubstantial. Whether his emphasis conforms also to Ammianus' own personality is a subjective question, and unanswerable because it can only be posed in relation to a text that is itself the sole evidence for his personality; yet merely to pose the question may help to remind us that the late Roman empire was not merely a hot-house of religious piety but that it did contain its pragmatists, men more interested in the necessities of finance and administration and in the course of justice than in the self-indulgencies of religious introspection.[49] In setting religious piety at the margin of his account of Julian, Ammianus may have presented the emperor as he wished to remember him rather than as he actually was; unless it really was possible for men of Ammianus' persuasion to view the emperor in the light of his public policies rather than his private beliefs, and to see the latter as a relatively unimportant flaw – when taken to excess – in a reign of overwhelming integrity and virtue. Something has in any case been omitted that was extremely important to Julian himself and to many hostile and friendly observers, and that in the last resort left a profound impact on the outcome of his reign. Readers of this book who, like Ammianus, are eager to pass directly to an account of the Persian campaign of Julian, may do so (Chapter VIII); those who wish to attempt an impression of religious influences set on one side by Ammianus – and, in the process, come to a fuller and more complex assessment than he offers of the reign and personality of Julian – may begin by considering in a new perspective some of the events described or referred to in the first part of this chapter.

CHAPTER VII

Julian and the Philosophers

In his *Lives of the Sophists*, Eunapius refers to an incident which took place in Gaul before Julian's declaration of civil war against Constantius in 360.[1] In this incident, Julian met with three men including his doctor Oribasius and the hierophant of the goddesses at Eleusis, whom Julian had summoned from Greece, and 'by performing certain rites known to them alone' gained the courage to abolish Constantius' tyranny (*V. Soph.* p. 476). Eunapius explains that he had narrated the affair in more detail in the books about Julian in his *History*: the passage does not occur in any surviving version or fragment of that lost work. So, too, Eunapius had told in the *History* how, according to another passage in the *Lives of the Sophists* (p. 498), Oribasius had 'through his outstanding excellence' made Julian emperor. It is more than possible that this is a veiled allusion to the same episode.[2]

Eunapius' account is tantalising in what it does not tell the reader. The question as to the nature of this transaction between Julian, Oribasius and the hierophant, is however partly answered by a letter which Julian wrote from Gaul to another Greek friend, the philosopher Priscus. Julian asks his friend to send him a book, of which he knows that Priscus can get a corrected copy from his sister's father-in-law (a person otherwise unknown, no doubt also a philosopher). He describes the book as 'the commentaries of Iamblichus on the works of my namesake' (*Ep.* 12; p. 19 Bidez).

Identification of this 'namesake' presents no problem. He was the so-called 'Julianus the theurgist', said to have lived in the time of Marcus Aurelius and to have been the author of works listed in the Byzantine lexicon, the Suda (I, 642), as '*Theourgika, Telestika*, Oracles (*Logia*) in verse, and other occult works relating to such arts'. Julianus is said in other sources to have composed also commentaries on the 'Oracles' and a work on the heavenly 'Zones'; a reference is given by one of these sources to Book 7 of this work. He is claimed in the Suda, how credibly we do not know, to have been the son of another Julianus, known as the 'Chaldaean', who lived under Trajan and wrote a work in four books 'On Demons' (*Peri daimonôn*).

It has been suggested that the word '*theourgos*', or 'theurgist', was actually coined by (the younger) Julianus. Formed by analogy with such Greek words as those for 'metal-' or 'stone-worker' (*chalkourgos, lithourgos*), it would imply that Julianus was not merely a speculative writer on the gods and the occult, but that he could put his knowledge to practical use; like a blacksmith or stone-mason, he could 'work' his material, in this case the gods, by performing miracles. Julianus the theurgist, an Egyptian magician, and Christian prayers are rival claimants for the 'Rain Miracle', a famous episode, commemorated on the Column of Marcus Aurelius, when Marcus' army was saved from disaster in his Marcomannic wars by a sudden rainstorm.[3] Another story has Julianus obstruct the attempt of another magician, Apuleius, to make the 'seven-rayed' Sun come down and meet him – an ungenerous performance which, as we shall see, is much more closely allied in its technique to 'theurgy' as later philosophical tradition understands it.[4]

Power over the weather and other natural phenomena was part of the standard repertoire of a late Roman miracle-worker. The hierophant Nestorius on one occasion, following instructions given to him in a dream, consecrated a little image of Achilles in a miniature temple, which he placed beneath the statue of Athena in the Parthenon and by joint sacrifices to image and statue saved Attica from an earthquake: this was in the year 375. Zosimus, who tells this story (4.18), had as his source a hymn to Achilles written by the fifth-century Neoplatonist philosopher Syrianus. Nestorius, a 'very old' man when he saved Athens from the earthquake, was none other than the hierophant of the goddesses summoned to Gaul by Julian, the participant with Oribasius in the secret rites mentioned by Eunapius. He was probably also the same as a 'priest' Nestorius who had once cured of depression a Roman senatorial lady who was convinced that her soul had in previous incarnations occupied in turn the bodies of a slave-girl to a family of inn-keepers in Attica, a dog, a serpent, and a female bear. As the slave-girl, she had been cured of forgetfulness (an inconvenient failing in a barmaid!) by an encounter with a spirit; the dog and the serpent, she – that is, her soul inhabiting their bodies – had in shame forced to suicide by making them throw themselves respectively from the roof of a house and under the wheels of a cart. The poor lady could remember all this very clearly.[5]

Apart from his power over the elements and gift for psychoanalysis, Nestorius was known as a prophet and astrologer. He had in another dream received an astrological formula linking the seven vowels of the alphabet with the seven planets, and the consonants with the signs of the zodiac. The first of these at least was a technique known to magicians and theurgists; Ammianus tells of the fate of a young man in the time of Valens, executed for magic because he was seen to perform certain gestures in the public baths while reciting to himself the seven vowels of the Greek alphabet (29.2.28; below, p. 222). As for his skill at divination, the hierophant was once questioned by the Athenian sophist Prohaeresius whether Julian's tax reforms would be permanent, and was told that they would not. Prohaeresius, a Christian, made his enquiry in a spirit of irony, combined with a personal interest in whether Julian would last for long; he had lost his chair in consequence of Julian's edict

VII. Julian and the Philosophers

forbidding Christians to practise as teachers of rhetoric (*V. Soph.*, p. 493). The accumulation of Neoplatonic and (in the question of the transmigration of souls) Pythagorean doctrines, and of the priestly duties of a hierophant with skill as a diviner and miracle-worker, is not exceptional, but a typical illustration of religious tendencies of the late Roman period. Through his grandson Plutarch and his greatgranddaughter Asclepigeneia, Nestorius was further instrumental in the transmission of theurgical doctrine to the Athenian Neoplatonic school of Syrianus and his pupil Proclus in the fifth century. Even before his initiation by Asclepigeneia into what his biographer Marinus calls the 'perfect theurgical art', Proclus had by the use of *iunges* – magical spinning discs – relieved Attica from drought and, like Nestorius earlier, given protection against earthquakes. It is not surprising in view of these successes that Proclus too had a dream, in which he was informed that he belonged to the 'chain of Hermes' and that he possessed the soul of Nicomachus, a famous Pythagorean philosopher.[6] The 'chain of Hermes', originally the golden chain by which in Homer's *Iliad* (8.19) Zeus threatened to show his strength to the other gods by hauling them up to heaven in a sort of cosmic tug-of-war, had come to symbolise for Neoplatonists the authentic lineage of philosophers who had received from heaven their knowledge of divine truth.

For the Neoplatonists, theurgy was however not simply a technique for 'working the gods' in the sense of achieving miracles by magic: at a more profound level, it was one of the means by which the soul, wrapped in the envelope of the physical body, could achieve purification and re-unification with the divine principle from which it had descended into the world of the senses. Theurgy could operate at various levels, from the white magic used in the 'affairs of human life', as in the rainmaking and prevention of earthquakes just mentioned, through the preparation of the mind for divine knowledge by ritual and divination, to an all-encompassing 'theurgy' employed in the achievement of mystical union with the divine principle, or the One.[7] According to Proclus, theurgy in this higher sense was 'greater than all human wisdom and knowledge, comprising the benefits of divination and the purifying powers of initiation (*telesiourgikê*); in a word, all the operative functions (*energêmata*) of divine inspiration'. God was not to be sought as if he were the object of definite knowledge, but by 'abandoning oneself to the divine light', by 'shutting the eyes' like a religious devotee. Being unknowable, God was not to be conceived by 'those who know about divine matters', nor expounded in normal discourse. He was to be understood only by 'analogy' – or, to put this in more practical terms, by magical 'symbols' and procedures. By these 'symbols', Proclus meant the physical objects and substances, the words (as we might say, the spells) of regular magic as used for the enlightenment and elevation of the soul, and also, at the highest level, the metaphysical 'analogies' by which the divine essence could be grasped and union with it achieved.[8] The soul has an affinity with God and the divine world, just as physical objects – stones, herbs, animals, and so on, as well as words – have their own affinity with and potentiality to 'return' to the Ideas, or Forms, from which they are derived. It is these lines of 'sympathy' – symbols, or *sunthêmata* – running through the Platonic universe, which the theurgist can exploit by magic ritual. 'Relying on these divine symbols', wrote Julian's revered Iamblichus, 'theurgy ascends to the superior beings to which it is united' (*De Mysteriis* 4.2).

Such, in outline, is the theoretical basis of the 'telestic' art, the art of spiritual purification as practised by the theurgists.[9] A particular aspect of their skill relevant here concerned the acquisition of knowledge concerning the nature of the gods and the religious and moral conduct required of their observer, or knowledge of the future. This could be done by the animation of statues. 'The practisers of the telestic science', wrote the Byzantine Michael Psellus, after Proclus, 'fill the cavities of statues with substances belonging to the powers (*dunameis*) presiding over them: animals, plants, herbs, seals, engravings, sometimes also sympathetic spices, and set up together with them mixing bowls, vessels for offerings, censers: they animate the images and move them with a secret power' (*Ep.* 187 Sathas). Whatever theatrical special effects – as some contemporaries believed – clever use of lighting and mirrors or sheer fraud were involved in such feats, the animation of statues was another of the regular techniques of ancient magic, mentioned also by the magical papyri.[10] 'Theurgy,' according to Proclus, 'through certain symbols applied to the "illumination" of artificial statues calls forth the unbounded goodness of the gods.'

Through oracles, given by animated statues and in other ways, the divine powers revealed their nature and declared the future. Such revelations might occur spontaneously to divinely-inspired individuals. One of the philosophers described in Eunapius' *Lives* had a dream in which the god gave him an oracle in hexameter verse. Waking up, he found that he could remember the general sense of what he had been told but not the 'divine meaning', until a slave attendant showed him that writing had appeared on his left hand. It was, of course, the oracle (*V. Soph.*, p. 464). Eunapius tells also the fascinating story of a young man, the son of Julian's friend the philosopher Chrysanthius, who had only to put on a crown and face the sun in order to produce oracles which were always truthful and 'composed according to the most beautiful form of divine inspiration', although (an unlikely claim) he had never been trained in grammar or metre.[11] The gods clearly loved this young man. Without having had a single day's illness in his life, he died at twenty (*V. Soph.*, p. 504).

Ammianus cited 'oracles and famous writers' as authorities for the way in which a very few men had through their virtues been granted acquaintance with their 'genius', the personal guardian spirit that is born with every man and attends him through life: such, among philosophers, were Pythagoras, Socrates, Hermes Trismegistos (Latinised by Ammianus as 'Termaximus'), Apollonius of Tyana and Plotinus. Ammianus went

VII. Julian and the Philosophers

on to explain how Plotinus had written profoundly on the origins of these *genii* who, 'linked with human souls, protect them as if they held them to their bosom, and teach higher truths, if they see them to be pure and preserved from the taint of sin by undefiled association with the body' (21.14.5; below, p. 434). According to his biographer Porphyry, Plotinus on one occasion attended a seance in the temple of Isis at Rome, at which an 'Egyptian priest' promised to secure for him a vision of his *daimôn* (the Greek equivalent of 'genius').[12] The priest brought with him birds 'for protection' (as an apotropaic symbol) and the *daimôn* appeared, turning out however to be not a mere *daimôn* but an actual god – thus showing how elevated was the soul of Plotinus. The potentially interesting discussion between Plotinus and his god was prevented when for some reason – 'either through envy', says Porphyry, 'or because he was afraid of something' – the friend of Plotinus who was holding the birds throttled them so that they died (*V. Plot.* 10). Had the god's replies been forthcoming they might well have been expressed, or at least recorded, in oracles in hexameter verse.

With this transition we return to the figure of Julianus the theurgist, the author or editor of the 'oracles in verse' on which the commentary written by Iamblichus was requested from his friend Priscus by Julian the Apostate. There is not much doubt that these oracles were in fact the so-called 'Chaldaean Oracles' of which fragments survive, as preserved by the later Platonists, especially by Proclus, and by Michael Psellus, who knew well the works of Proclus and his contemporaries.[13]

*

The *Chaldaean Oracles* were a collection of propositions in hexameter verse about the nature of God and the universe, and prescriptions as to how the deity was to be approached and comprehended. Their interpretation presents many difficulties. They would not deserve the name of oracle if they had been invariably lucid, direct and free from ambiguity; and further, since we owe our knowledge of the oracles to selections and quotations made from them by other writers, we rely on these writers to have produced a reasonably accurate representation of their contents, and one that is not distorted by being forced to serve their own, often polemical ends. Yet it would be evasive not to attempt some summary of their theological content, and we may begin with the First Principle or 'Father' whose nature is evoked by the oracles. This Supreme Deity is said to exist beyond all knowledge in a 'transcendental abyss' (Fr. 18), in a 'god-sustaining silence' (Fr. 16). He is associated with, yet at the same time remote from, the other members of a triad, or Trinity, of gods or 'Fathers'; these other two are called 'Intellect' (*nous*) and 'Power' (*dunamis*). Hidden in himself, unknown and unknowable, the Supreme God is so profoundly secluded as to be separated even from his own creative aspects:

he does not enclose even his own Fire in the Power of his Intellect. (Fr. 3)

The second member of the divine triad, 'Intellect', has a double nature, since it contemplates at once the First Principle and the universe of which it is apparently itself the creator:

> ... By the Father resides a Dyad;
> it has these two functions, to conceive by intellect the Intelligibles,
> and to introduce sensation to the worlds. (Fr. 8)

The third member of the triad, 'Power', is the animating force by which 'Intellect' (the creator, or Demiurge) expresses its creative purpose. 'Power' seems in some Oracles to be identified with Hecate, from whose right side

> leaps the swelling stream of the primordial Soul,
> animating light, fire, ether, stars. (Fr. 51)

There is no need to stress the magical role of Hecate, mistress of the Underworld, in Greek and Roman religious belief – as in her invocations in Book Six of the *Aeneid* and especially the *Second Idyll* of Theocritus, a prime source for ancient magical practices, and in the mystic cults adopted by the members of pagan nobility of Rome in the later fourth century.

In addition to this triad of 'Father', 'Intellect', and 'Power', the *Chaldaean Oracles* describe divine beings of lower status, especially the 'spinners' (*iunges*), which are themselves the thoughts, or perhaps the bearers of the thoughts, of the Father:

> They, themselves thought of by the Father, also think,
> moved to do so by his unutterable counsels. (Fr. 77)

'*Iunges*' are in another context – as in Theocritus' *Second Idyll* – the spinning discs or 'rhomboi' of ancient magical ritual. In Chaldaean theology they form a lower triad with entities described as the 'connectives' (*sunocheis*) and the 'masters of initiation' (*teletarchoi*); these latter are described in one Fragment as the 'masters of souls' (Fr. 86).[14] In these beings is inherent the theoretical justification of the notion of initiation and purification by magic, by means of the symbols or 'sympathies' which 'connect' the physical world with the realm of Ideas and, correspondingly, the human soul with the divine:

> The Intellect of the Father has planted symbols through the universe,
> He who contemplates the Intelligibles: they are called the unutterable
>   beauties. (Fr. 108)

VII. Julian and the Philosophers

The theurgist used the magical 'symbols' of physical objects and substances, and devices such as spinning discs, which operated by analogy on the *iunges* or 'spinners' of the theology of the Oracles; these are normal techniques of ancient magic, here applied to the religious purposes of the Neoplatonists.

It is essential to recognise that the use of these methods was justified in relation to the central issue in later Platonic thought, that of the descent of the soul and its longing to conceive, and ultimately to return to, the world of the Intelligible Ideas from which it came. This could not be done, according to the *Oracles* as also to Iamblichus and Proclus, by rational thought:

> There is a certain Intelligible, which you must conceive with the flower of
>   the intellect;
> For if you intensify your mind and contemplate that Intelligible
> as a particular object, you will not conceive it...
> ...
> You must not conceive that Intelligible with vehemence,
> but with the refined fire of a refined intelligence, which may measure
>   everything
> except that Intelligible. You must think of it
> not with concentration, but with the holy gaze of an averted eye.
> Extend to the Intelligible the emptied intellect of your soul
> in order to learn the Intelligible, for he exists outside the grasp of intellect.
>   (Fr. 1)

Another Oracle calls for the exercise to the same end of ritual act and incantation:

> Seek the channel of the soul, from where it comes in a certain order
> to do hired labour for the body, and how you will again lead it up
> to its ordered place, uniting act with sacred word. (Fr. 110)

'Uniting act with sacred word': it would be difficult here to mistake the reference to magic arts.

This conception of the 'Intelligible' as beyond the grasp of a purely intellectual contemplation was fundamental to the use of magical techniques by the theurgists. In the view of Iamblichus, the soul's descent to the world of the senses was so complete that it had lost all affinity with the Intelligible, in a thorough-going dualism that reflected the human experience of sin and suffering. The chasm between the two could *only* be crossed by magic. This opinion was however not that held by the founder of Neoplatonism, Plotinus. For Plotinus, the higher part of the soul still retained an affinity with God, who could on this basis be approached by sustained intellectual effort in the Platonic manner. But it was a real objection to Plotinus' method that even he, throughout his life of rational contemplation at the highest possible level, had only four times experienced 'ecstasy' – moments in which, in a glimpse of heaven his soul had 'stood outside' his body and been united with God – and Porphyry only once (*V. Plot.* 23). It was evidently an exclusive ideal. How many ordinary men were granted the opportunities – material as well as spiritual, for the life of the philosopher presupposes his economic independence – to reach such a goal?

Ancient commentators undoubtedly over-simplified the situation in seeing it in this way, but for them the division in the Platonic school between the 'intellectual' tradition of Plotinus and the 'theurgical' tradition of Iamblichus was fundamental to its history. According to a sixth-century Neoplatonist, 'some put philosophy first, such as Porphyry, Plotinus, and so on; others the priestly art (*hieratikê*), like Iamblichus, Syrianus, Proclus and all the priestly school' – meaning the theurgists; and Michael Psellus, reflecting the views of a sixth-century opponent of the Platonists, noted that after reading the *Chaldaean Oracles* Iamblichus and Proclus had abandoned 'Greek' – that is philosophical – for 'Chaldaean' – or magical – doctrine.[15] Iamblichus is said by Eunapius occasionally to have prayed privately to God, 'performing certain rites' – but to have discouraged his pupils' belief that he levitated to a height of ten cubits and turned a lovely golden colour while he did so. He did on one occasion consent as a demonstration of his powers to evoke two divine beings from the hot springs in the baths at Gadara. With a clever touch of historical scruple Eunapius admitted that he had no eye-witness account of this scene (*V. Soph.*, p. 458f.).

*

The division between the supporters of Plotinus and of Iamblichus, between the 'philosophers' and the 'priestly school', is essential for understanding the position of Julian the Apostate. As a young man, 'travelling around wherever he wanted', as Eunapius drily noted, 'accompanied by the emperor's suspicions and a bodyguard', Julian came to Pergamum in Asia Minor to see the great philosopher Aedesius, a former pupil of Iamblichus; it was Aedesius who had found miraculously written on his hand the words of the oracle which he had dreamed (above, p. 118). Aedesius, an old man, recommended Julian to consult certain of his pupils, now themselves teachers of philosophy. (To read between the lines of Eunapius' account, Aedesius had found the persistent Julian a rather wearing experience; in going to these pupils, Julian would, he reckoned, 'cease to harass my old age'). He named four such pupils, of whom one, Maximus, had gone to Ephesus, while Priscus, to whom Julian later wrote from Gaul for Iamblichus' commentaries on Julianus the theurgist, had gone to Athens. Two others, Eusebius and Chrysanthius,

VII. Julian and the Philosophers 123

were still at Pergamum (*V. Soph.*, p. 474).

Eusebius and Chrysanthius presented a contrast, which we can understand at once in terms of the two Neoplatonic traditions just described. Chrysanthius, like the absent Maximus, was 'passionately involved in working marvels, and studied the science of divination'. Eusebius, on the other hand, used to add an epilogue to his lectures, to the effect that the only true realities lay in dialectical argument. The impostures of witchcraft and magic that deceive the senses, he would say, were the works of conjurers, 'insane men led astray into the exercise of material powers'. The words here used for 'material powers', *hulikas ... dunameis*, are technical expressions for the use of physical materials as magical 'symbols'.

Julian, puzzled by Eusebius' epilogue, at Chrysanthius' suggestion asked him what it meant. Eusebius then told Julian of an experience of his own, in order to show how Maximus' genius had led him to despise logical proof in favour of the 'acts of a madman'. Maximus had taken Eusebius and some others to a temple of Hecate at Pergamum – not a random choice of goddess. He had there consecrated and burned some incense, recited to himself 'some hymn or other' (magical papyri sometimes stress the need to mutter the incantation so that it cannot be overheard), and succeeded in making the image of Hecate smile and even laugh aloud. Maximus then announced that the torches in the goddess's hands would break into flame. Before the words were out of his mouth, they did so (*V. Soph.*, p. 475).

For Eusebius, the whole occasion was a piece of 'theatrical wonder-working'.[16] This does not mean that he disbelieved the authenticity of what Maximus had done, any more than Plotinus, despite his indifference to it, actually disbelieved the effectiveness of magic; simply that he was unmoved from his conviction that the highest aim of philosophy was the elevation of the soul by reason. In this whole narrative, in fact, Eusebius was declaring his commitment to the tradition of Plotinus and Porphyry against that of Iamblichus and the theurgists. Julian, anxious as ever for quick results, had other ideas. 'Farewell', he said to Eusebius, 'devote yourself to your books: you have shown me the man I wanted', and off he went, dragging his bodyguard (not to mention the emperor's suspicions) to Ephesus to find Maximus.

Julian's commitment to the theurgists, after the choice presented to him so explicitly by Eusebius, is no flirtation with some vague exotic mystery, but a declaration, with serious consequences, in favour of a specific tradition in late Platonism. This also emerges from the letter to Priscus (*Ep.* 12 Bidez), in which Julian requested the commentary of Iamblichus on Julianus the theurgist. He referred in the letter to the libels against Iamblichus of the 'supporters of Theodorus' (*Theodoreioi*). Theodorus of Asine believed, like Plotinus, that part of the human soul had remained unfallen from its divine state, and so implicitly rejected theurgy in favour of the intellectual approach of Plotinus and Porphyry.[17]

It would be difficult to over-emphasise the importance of the theurgical tradition of Neoplatonism in Julian's mentality. At the end of his allegorical *Hymn to the Mother of the Gods* (180 B), Julian offers a prayer in which he asks to be given true knowledge about the gods and made perfect in theurgy. Earlier in the same tract, having written in a piece of pure theurgical doctrine of the growth of plants as caused, like the rising up of the soul, by the attractive power of solar rays, he goes on; 'if I should mention the unutterable mystery of the seven-rayed God of whom the Chaldaean spoke ecstatically, as through his agency he caused the souls to ascend, I should speak of unknown things, unknown especially to the vulgar crowd, but known to the blessed theurgists' (172 D). The word here used for the 'seven-rayed' Sun, *heptaktis*, occurs in the *Chaldaean Oracles* (cf. Fr. 194), and also in the source that described how Julianus the theurgist had prevented the Sun from coming down from heaven to meet Apuleius.[18]

This discussion of certain aspects of Neoplatonic religious practice has had little to say of Ammianus Marcellinus; but it is important to recognise that Julian was devoted to theurgy, not as a dilettante to something he happens to find colourful and exotic, but as a serious philosopher to a technique central to his philosophy. We can look more closely now at some possible effects on his reign, and at Ammianus' view of them.

During his studies at Ephesus with Maximus and Chrysanthius (who joined them there), Julian was told of a man of still greater wisdom in Greece, the hierophant of the goddesses at Eleusis, and went to visit him. Eunapius, who records this, was unable to reveal the name of the hierophant, since he himself had been initiated by him into the mysteries of Eleusis. The hierophant, in fact Nestorius, had prophesied in Eunapius' presence the destruction of the temples and of Greece, and other misfortunes, all of which in later years came to pass (*V. Soph.*, p. 476).

When he was appointed Caesar in Gaul, after some victories over the barbarians Julian sent for the hierophant, who came to Gaul; and it was with him and others, in the incident with which this chapter began, that Julian mustered the courage to attack Constantius, after 'performing certain rites known to them alone'. The reference to theurgical acts is by now surely unmistakable. In so far as any chronology can be inferred from Eunapius' account, the incident took place at a time when Julian had as yet no explicit intention of claiming the imperial throne for himself (above, p. 99).

At a later stage, according now to Ammianus, while Julian was spending the winter at Vienne after his proclamation and debating his policy towards Constantius, he inferred Constantius' imminent death, both by the use of divinatory techniques, 'in which he was expert', and from dreams (21.1.6). Ammianus digresses at this point to defend Julian, 'a learned *princeps*, and a student of all forms of knowledge', against

VII. Julian and the Philosophers

those malicious critics who asserted that he employed corrupt arts in order to learn the future; 'praenoscendi futura pravas artes assignant'. In reply to these critics, Ammianus will explain briefly how a 'wise man' ('sapienti') may possess skill in learning the future, a 'not inconsiderable branch of learning'; 'doctrinae genus haud leve' (21.1.7).

The passage in which Ammianus does this (21.1.7-14) is extremely interesting for the light which it casts on Ammianus' own theological learning, and is analysed in this sense in a later chapter of this book.[19] As far as Julian's conduct is concerned, Ammianus confines himself in the digression to a description of traditionally accepted modes of divination – augury and *haruspicina*, the inspection of entrails, oracles uttered by divinely-inspired media, the interpretation of apparently random sounds and sights, thunder, lightning, shooting stars and dreams. These techniques, none of which could be described as 'corrupt', Ammianus regards as fully accredited, subject only to the imperfection of men's skills in interpreting them (21.1.13f.; pp. 428ff.). Julian himself, while still at Vienne before the march against Constantius, had a dream in which a splendid figure appeared to him, many times repeating in heroic verse, of which Ammianus gives the Greek text, a prediction of the exact date of Constantius' death. In consequence, Julian was convinced that no more harm could be done to him (21.2.2).

For the time being, Julian kept his activities quiet and maintained his pretence of Christianity. In private, however, with 'a few accomplices in secret rites' ('arcanorum participibus paucis'), he devoted himself to *haruspicina* and augury, and to 'the other things which believers in the gods have always done'; 'et ceteris quae deorum semper fecere cultores' (21.2.4). It is unlikely that Ammianus is here referring to theurgy or to any other activity that might pass under the rubric of 'pravae artes': it is simply that anything to do with the worship of the old gods had to be treated by Julian as a secret and performed in private with accomplices.

Later, coming to the east after Constantius' death, Julian wrote to his teachers, Maximus and Chrysanthius, and invited them to join him at court. The two men conferred and took the omens, which were hostile. Chrysanthius decided to conform to the will of the gods, but Maximus was recalcitrant. It was the duty of Greeks, especially of educated Greeks, he argued to Chrysanthius, 'not to submit feebly to the first obstacles they meet, but to wrestle with the heavenly powers until you make them yield to their servant'. Chrysanthius still refused, but Maximus 'tried every means, until he secured what he wanted and desired'; and so he went to Constantinople surrounded, as Eunapius describes, by an escort of admirers and fêted wherever he passed (*V. Soph.*, p. 477). Maximus and Julian induced Priscus to join them from Athens, but Chrysanthius remained unmoved in his obedience to the gods, stayed in Lydia and was in the end entrusted with the high-priesthood of the province. Here too Chrysanthius read the future more accurately than most, and did not use his office in aggressive support of Julian's religious policies. He built no temples and was not harsh, as others were, to Christians. Indeed so mild was he that 'throughout Lydia the restoration of the temples almost passed unnoticed' (*V. Soph.*, p. 501). But it was Chrysanthius' reading of the future that proved accurate, and because of his mildness, when Christian emperors again took over there were no reprisals in his province.

The philosophers retained their influence upon the emperor, even during the Persian campaign of 363. Writing to Libanius, Julian recalled his journey as far as Hierapolis by the Euphrates, noting in particular the signs of traditional religious practice in cities on the route (*Ep.* 98 Bidez; below, p. 144). At Hierapolis, he had a happy meeting with a co-religionist of whom he had heard but never met. This man, presumably a philosopher, had married a daughter of Sopatros, and he in turn had been a pupil of the 'most divine Iamblichus' (p. 182 Bidez). About Iamblichus enough has been said; Sopatros also is well-known. Like Iamblichus a Syrian, he had come to Constantinople in or soon after 330 in the hope of restraining the 'impulsiveness' of the Emperor Constantine – that is, of moderating the Christian policies which were increasingly dominating his reign.[20] But how did Sopatros intend to achieve this – by writing polite notes to the emperor and seeking audiences in which he might persuade him? or by theurgical magic? Sopatros in any case met an appropriate end. He was denounced by a Christian supporter of Constantine and beheaded; the charge was that he had by magic 'fettered the winds' which brought the corn-ships from Alexandria to Constantinople (*V. Soph.*, p. 463). It was a splendid finale, a piece of weather-making well worthy of the tradition of Julianus the theurgist, Nestorius the hierophant and Proclus the Neoplatonist philosopher.

The course of the Persian campaign brings out, in two episodes in particular, the impact of the theurgical tradition on Julian's conduct as emperor, and lends an extra dimension to Ammianus' assessment of his religious policies.

The unique quality in Ammianus' account of the Persian campaign that distinguishes it from others is precisely its emphasis on the role of the divine in its conduct and outcome.[21] Ammianus underlines the omens which made it clear that the campaign was doomed to fail; he has them dominate his narrative and makes clear from the beginning the truth of what they portended. On the second day of the march was brought to Julian the body of a huge lion which had attacked the army but been shot down. Then a soldier of the 'lofty name' Jovianus was killed by lightning, together with the two horses he had been watering in the Euphrates. The official seers, *haruspices*, who were travelling with the army, set to work on the interpretation of the omens. Getting out their books, which Ammianus specifies as the 'libri exercituales' and 'libri fulgurales', the seers pronounced that the omens were adverse; the gods were advising against the campaign. Their opinions were however 'trodden underfoot' by the 'philosophers', whose authority was 'at that time revered'. These philosophers, 'persisting long in matters that are little understood'

VII. Julian and the Philosophers

declared that the omens were either indifferent or were actually in favour of the campaign (23.5.10ff.). Later, in the early hours of the day of Julian's death, a spectacular shooting star was seen. The *haruspices*, again consulting their books, 'Tarquitiani libri, in titulo de rebus divinis', declared that nothing must be done that day or that at the very least there must be a delay (25.2.7f.). Again, their advice was overruled by the philosophers, with the consequence that within a few hours the latter found themselves acting in another professional capacity – sharing Julian's death-bed reflections on the immortality of the soul.[22]

These 'philosophers' were of course none other than Julian's old friends Maximus and Priscus, and it would be completely against their previous record if on these occasions too they were not producing their opinions after theurgical rites designed, as Maximus had put it to Chrysanthius, to 'force the heavenly powers to yield to their servant'. At this point a fragment of the Chaldaean Oracles comes very firmly into the reckoning, for it explicitly denies the value of traditional *haruspicina*:

> Let go the humming circuit of the moon; it always runs by force of necessity;
> the course of the stars was not brought forth to favour you.
> The broad heavenly flight of birds is never truthful,
> nor the incisions of offerings and entrails; these are all but games,
> sustaining a corrupt deception. Avoid these things,
> if you would open up the holy paradise of piety,
> where virtue, wisdom and good order meet together. (Fr. 107)

If so, then to be strictly consistent with his own philosophical views and those of his advisers, Julian would be committed to a trust in theurgical *as opposed to* traditional modes of divination: a position difficult to reconcile with the religious duties of a *pontifex maximus* and Roman emperor. There is no need to interpret Julian's position quite as strictly as this. Ammianus, after all, has explained that Julian was an expert in all forms of knowledge, which should and does mean that none was excluded. Further, it is not as if the *Chaldaean Oracles* were such a coherent body of texts that one pronouncement, however emphatic it may seem to be, can be made to yield a single general conclusion without risk of contradiction by others. Nevertheless, the difficulties that might arise in the case of a direct conflict of opinion, such as occurred during the Persian campaign, should be evident. We have seen that Ammianus gave the actual titles of the priestly books which the *haruspices* brought out in order to give their interpretations of the omens. He contrasted these with what he showed as the spontaneous inventions of the philosophers, supported by some pseudo-scientific rationalisation (24.5.14). Now, Ammianus must have known enough about the philosophers to have been aware that behind their pretensions as prophets lay an extensive literature of religious and philosophical exposition. What then should we make of his assertion that the philosophers 'persisted long in matters that are little understood': 'in parum cognitis perseverantium diu'

(23.5.11)? Did he mean that they held out for hours against the *haruspices* until they got their way – or that they had wasted their whole lives in pointless speculation?

*

Ammianus' summary of Julian's religious attitudes, classified among the shortcomings briefly set out in the obituary of the emperor, was that he was 'superstitious, rather than a legitimate observer of divine matters'; 'superstitiosus magis quam sacrorum legitimus observator' (25.4.17).[23] 'Superstition' is a notoriously difficult word to define; Ammianus also writes of Constantius' 'old woman's superstition' in his obsessive treatment of the disputes of the Christian religion (21.16.18), and the emperors themselves used it in their legislation of anything to do with the practice of pagan cults or magic arts. It might be possible to get further with the word 'legitimus', as applied to Julian's religious conduct.

It was partly a matter of degree. Julian drenched the altars with the sacrifices of hundreds of victims – Ammianus cited as parallel a mock letter of the 'white cattle' to Marcus Aurelius, protesting that if he went on winning victories they, the white cattle, would be exterminated! Julian's sacrifices at Antioch were so lavish, and the meat provided by them so plentiful, that his soldiers had sometimes to be carried home to their billets incapable from food and drink (22.12.6). The more precise nuances of 'legitimus' might be inferred by analogy from certain of Ammianus' attitudes to the political system of his day. Ammianus does not formulate any general 'theory of kingship', but he took a definite stand as to the proper behaviour of emperors in certain situations. They should operate within the framework of institutions and rules by which individual rights, as well as the emperors' interests, were protected, and it was in contempt for these procedures that unconstitutional power found its expression (below, pp. 250ff.). The word 'legitimus' should mean something analogous when applied to an emperor's religious conduct. Ammianus criticised Julian for accepting the views of the 'philosophers' in his entourage and for rejecting those of the *haruspices*. For a Roman army on campaign, led by a Roman emperor, the *haruspices* were the proper interpreters of the information provided by the gods. In a case of conflict, it was on their understanding of the signs, rather than on that of the 'philosophers', that the 'conjectures of men', in a phrase of Cicero's approved by Ammianus, were more securely based (21.1.14).[24] Ammianus brings out this point of view by his references to the books on which the authority of the *haruspices* rested, citing their titles (in one case also the chapter in question), and by contrasting this with the unyielding ignorance of the philosophers. In their own context, the books of the *haruspices* were the equivalent of the public institutions such as the courts of law, whereby the emperors preserved legitimate constitutional government and avoided personal despotism.

VII. Julian and the Philosophers

Julian's rejection of the *haruspices* on the Persian campaign brings out the ambiguities in his position as emperor and as restorer of the ancient gods; ambiguities which were not trivial or superficial, but part of the essential nature of his religious position. They were also inherent in the nature of late Roman paganism. The philosophy to which Julian and the 'philosophers' to whom he committed himself adhered, was concerned less with matters of common interest to late Roman society than with the position of the individual in relation to the divine world from which he had descended. The practice of magic, too, tends to be connected with the personal interests of an individual, and owes its efficacy to the preservation of its occult, or hidden, nature. Neoplatonic theurgy was not an approach well adapted to the service of a restored public paganism, and Julian showed great (and characteristic?) unsureness of judgment in letting the 'philosophers' acquire the influence which they did in the public counsels of a Roman emperor. He was to some extent, no doubt, the victim of circumstances in allowing the contradictions to appear so openly as in the disputes between the philosophers and the *haruspices* on the Persian campaign; but such conflicts must have arisen sooner or later, and if an admirer like Ammianus had such doubts as he expressed or implied on these episodes and in general on Julian's religious policies, the most serious questions must attach to the coherence of these policies and to their prospects, in the best of all possible worlds, of success. The 'best of all possible worlds' included, it goes without saying, a successful outcome to the Persian campaign of 363, and it is to the conduct, and to the failure and consequences of this, that we must now turn.

CHAPTER VIII

The Invasion of Persia

(1) Historical perspectives

At the beginning of April 363, Julian's army crossed the river Khabur near its confluence with the Euphrates at Circesium. The passage took some time, and only when every man had gone over did the emperor cross the Khabur himself and have the bridges dismantled behind him (23.5.4). The army then advanced to Zaitha, 'the Olive Tree', and a further day's march in the direction of Dura, before Julian gathered the troops together and addressed them. This was not the first time, he reassured them, that Romans had entered the realms of Persia. Setting aside those Republican generals who had been successful in those regions, Julian recalled his predecessors among the Roman emperors. Trajan, Verus and Septimius Severus had each of them returned victorious from Persia. So too would the Emperor Gordian have returned, had he not fallen victim to the treachery of Philip and his supporters, struck down in the very place where he now lay buried. Julian reminded his army of the tomb of Gordian, which they had just seen as they passed it on the march (23.5.16f.).

The authenticity of speeches in ancient historians is a notoriously difficult problem. The distinction between the words actually spoken on any occasion, and what could be convincingly attributed to it, is in the nature of things a very fine one. Thucydides was unusually scrupulous in asserting as a principle that he would make some attempt to convey what was actually said in the speeches he included in his history or at least to respect their specific historical circumstances (1.22.1), and he was not generally followed by his successors in his observance of it. A speaker would normally try to say what was fitting for a particular occasion, and a literate historian – one accomplished in rhetoric, the art of persuasion – would be no less competent to make up something suitable. There was little reason for a historian to attempt more, and his audience would not expect it. Zosimus, narrating Julian's campaign from the lost *Histories* of Eunapius, merely says of this speech that the emperor addressed the troops with 'fitting' words (3.13.3). Zosimus' comment must simply mean that he found here in Eunapius nothing out of the ordinary – and this was in a passage of narrative more detailed in some respects than Ammianus' own.[1]

A speech in the manner of that ascribed by Ammianus to Julian was evidently given to an army which, on crossing the Khabur, had effectively

VIII. The Invasion of Persia

entered Persian territory. The army's advance did indeed take it by the tomb of the Emperor Gordian, who had died in Persia and been succeeded by Philip (in AD 244). Ammianus located the tomb at or near the place called Zaitha. Exactly how near is not immediately apparent, for, as Ammianus noted, the tomb could be seen from far off; 'longe conspicuum' (23.5.7). Other writers give its precise position as twenty miles from Circesium, which would seem to concur with what Ammianus says.[2] There is however a difficulty. Ammianus has described how Julian went to pay his respects to Gordian at the tomb, after which, pressing on towards Dura, he was brought the body of the huge lion which had attacked the army and been shot down (23.5.8). In the evening of the next day, 7 April, the soldier Jovianus was killed by lightning as he returned from watering horses by the Euphrates' edge (23.5.12f.). Only at this point of his narrative, between Zaitha and Dura and at the end of the second full day of the march, does Ammianus place Julian's speech and its reception by the army; yet he introduces the speech with a second reference to the dismantling of the bridge over the Khabur and describes the need to make it as Julian's most urgent priority ('antiquissimum omnium') upon crossing the river (23.5.15).

If we accept the implications of these last remarks, Julian actually delivered his speech immediately after crossing the Khabur. This is of course where such an address would have been expected by the army and where, on the evidence of Zosimus, it was placed by Eunapius. Ammianus' subsequent narrative supports this interpretation, in apparent contradiction of his first sequence.[3] After an immense digression on the districts and peoples of the Persian empire (23.6.1-88), Ammianus resumes his story at the beginning of Book 24 by mentioning again the joyful reception by the army of Julian's speech (24.1.1). He then marks formally the entry into Assyria at the dawn of the following day, surveys the dispositions of the army and describes for a second time, but more briefly, the two-day march to Dura (24.1.1-5). From this alternative sequence it would appear that Julian's speech was in fact delivered immediately after the army had assembled beyond the Khabur, when Julian himself had crossed and the bridges had been dismantled.

For reasons which may appear later (p. 178f.), Ammianus has in Book 23 displaced Julian's speech in its narrative context. He has achieved this by bringing forward certain events of the first two days of the march so that in his narrative they appear to precede a speech made in fact at the outset of the campaign. He has then given a corrected sequence at the beginning of the next book of his history, in which the invasion is narrated continuously from its outset. One consequence of this double presentation is of particular interest. If Julian's speech was in fact delivered not after, but before, the army had come to Gordian's tomb twenty miles from Circesium, then its reference to that monument, 'which we have just seen with respect' (23.5.17), cannot have been made in this form. Being consistent with a distorted narrative sequence, it is the work not of Julian himself, but of his historian.[4]

In this case, Julian's – or rather Ammianus' – allusion to the betrayal and death of Gordian can be linked directly with the reference the historian has made to Gordian in his narrative, shortly before coming to Julian's speech. At Zaitha, he wrote, suggesting for the first time his own presence on the campaign, 'we saw (*vidimus*) the tomb of Gordian the emperor, conspicuous from a far distance: of whose deeds from earliest boyhood, successful leadership of armies and death by treachery I have told in the proper place' – that is, of course, in one of the lost books of the history (23.5.7).

The notion that Gordian died as a result of Roman treachery, though shared by other Classical historical sources and, in part, by the thirteenth so-called *Sibylline Oracle* (vv. 13ff.), is not totally unchallenged. The 'official' Persian view, assuming this to be what is given in the trilingual inscription at Naqsh-i-Rustam near Persepolis known as the *Res Gestae Divi Saporis*, was that Gordian had been killed in battle with the Persians, and his successor Philip forced to treat for terms. This is the version also illustrated in the great rock sculptures at Bishapur, which show Philip as a suppliant before Sapor, whose horse treads down the prostrate corpse of Gordian.[5] The battle at which Gordian met his death, according to the *Res Gestae*, was fought at a place called Misichê, now renamed (in its Greek transliteration on the inscription) 'Pêrôs-Sabour'. It is the Persian city of Peroz-Shapur on the Euphrates, Pirisabora in Ammianus, which was besieged and taken by Julian in the campaign of 363. Its name meant 'Sapor Victorious' (it has been thought of as a sort of Persian 'Nicopolis'), and it was described by Libanius as the city named after the Persian king (*Or.* 18.227). For Zosimus, Pirisabora was after Ctesiphon the greatest city in Assyria (3.18.6). It stood over two hundred miles from Gordian's tomb, in true Babylonia, below the division of the Euphrates and the great canal leading direct to Ctesiphon.[6]

It is therefore by no means certain that Gordian was in fact killed, as Ammianus had Julian claim, at the place where he was buried, and frustrating that, with the loss of the book of Ammianus' history in which it was described, we cannot be sure whether he deliberately intended his allusions to Gordian's death to be read as a prefiguration of that of Julian himself. But Ammianus' entire account of Julian's expedition is pervaded by doom and foreboding, punctuated by omens, prophecies and portents whose significance he makes no attempt to disguise, but emphasises.[7] If the historian can remind us that he had written in one of his lost books of Gordian's 'deeds in first boyhood and glorious leadership of armies' and then of his 'death by treachery' while on a Persian campaign, it is beyond belief that he should not have seen, nor intended, the parallel with Julian. As often with such allusions, it is not clear how far he meant the parallel to be pursued. Ammianus gave no hint in his account of Julian's death that the emperor had fallen by treachery to a Roman hand; but even if he did not himself accept this, he must have known that there were many others who did believe it.

However we understand Ammianus' intentions here, the precedent ascribed to Julian's speech, of the Persian campaign of Gordian, was at best ambiguous. So was another, which is not in Julian's speech but appears by implication in Ammianus' later narrative. After reducing a Persian fortress not far from Ctesiphon, Julian went forward with a small party to survey the ruins of the once great city of Seleucia, destroyed (so Ammianus believed) by the Emperor Carus. The bleak scene which met Julian's eyes as he viewed the ruins was made still more desolate by the corpses of relatives of the garrison commander who had given up Pirisabora to Julian. They had been searched out and crucified in the ruined city (24.5.3).

The Persian campaign of Carus was not mentioned in the speech ascribed by Ammianus to Julian, though it had in fact been used by Julian in a genuine oration, his first panegyric to Constantius (*Or.* 1.18A). The expedition had become an object-lesson in the proper limits of Roman ambition in the east. Carus had taken Seleucia and Ctesiphon, but had then been struck dead, either by plague or, in an alternative but less plausible version, by lightning. One writer, contemporary with Ammianus, canvassed the idea that Carus had ignored oracles warning him not to go beyond Ctesiphon; another thought that his death showed the envy of the divine power for too great prosperity among mortals.[8] These notions are elaborated by the late fourth-century author of the *Historia Augusta* into an allegedly current belief that fate had forbidden Roman emperors from advancing beyond Ctesiphon. The belief is challenged by the writer and ascribed to timidity, and he calls on the Emperor Galerius, to whom he purported to dedicate the *Life of Carus*, to provide the remedy. It could be done, said the author darkly, if the promised favour of heaven were not betrayed by Roman neglect.[9]

Whether the author of the *Historia Augusta* intended his words to evoke Julian rather than Galerius and, if so, what he intended by them, are not easy questions to answer. It is not as if Julian, for all the 'promised favour of heaven', had in true conscience overcome the inhibitions of fate: he had rather confirmed them. Evidence that Galerius campaigned in this part of Assyria, and a curious link between Galerius and Julian are however provided by the discovery by Julian's army in the town of Anatha on the Euphrates of an old soldier of Galerius who had fallen sick and been left behind by the Roman army. Ammianus told his story as witnesses had heard it: the soldier had settled down in Persia, married several wives in native fashion and raised a large brood of children. Now aged, he had for long known and had predicted that he would be buried in Roman soil (24.1.10).[10]

With the exception of Galerius, the more recent precedents in Roman history were therefore not unambiguously favourable; an emperor might as plausibly expect sudden death as spectacular conquest – or, worst of all, captivity in Persia. The Emperor Valerian had met Sapor I in battle and been taken prisoner, his captured legionaries being deployed by the Persians as builders and technicians in such exemplary projects as the construction, about thirty miles east of Susa, of the new city of

Gundeshapur and of the 'King's Dyke', a dam to control the waters of the river Karun. This victory, like that over Gordian, was magnificently celebrated in the rock sculptures at Bishapur and Naqsh-i-Rustam.[11] For later emperors of the Roman east, it was an image of humiliation which they were not allowed to forget, and of which Ammianus must necessarily have written something in his lost books.

Strictly speaking, the fate of Valerian was not a precedent for an emperor planning an invasion of Persia, since he had been defeated not in Persian territory but in the Roman empire, near Edessa in Osrhoene. But it was not less ominous for that, given the aggressive pretensions currently shown by Sapor II. Edessa was the city from which the general Sabinianus had been instructed to co-ordinate the defence of northern Mesopotamia against the great attack which in 359 saw Amida, and in the next year Singara and Bezabde, besieged and captured. Indeed, it was in part to relieve the pressure on this northern region, constantly threatened by Sapor's declared intention to win back his 'ancestral dominions' in Mesopotamia, that Julian undertook his ambitious strike into Assyria and Babylonia. If successful, his expedition would transform the balance of power in the region and shift the diplomatic initiative as decisively in Rome's favour as had Galerius' victory over Narses (p. 53). In the case of Julian, we may add another, more personal though no less potent, motive – to discredit the inglorious eastern policy of the dynasty of Constantine in favour of the more assertive one of the emperors of the first two centuries, upon whom he modelled himself.

*

Few Roman military enterprises were so surrounded by discussion and criticism as Julian's Persian campaign. It could hardly have been otherwise – the emperor's ambition was so transparent, the possibility of success so seductive and the risks of failure so obvious, while the directness of Julian's personality and his informality as emperor invited the free, and sometimes provocative, expression of opinion. Ammianus thought Julian's critics defeatist and malign, as they expressed indignation at the disruption of the entire Roman world which had taken place merely because of a change of emperor – views which, in their eagerness to get the campaign put off, they deliberately expressed in the hearing of those whom they knew would taken them to Julian (22.12.3). Some criticism was more directly expressed. While waiting at Circesium for his army to cross the Khabur, Julian received a letter from the praetorian prefect of Gaul, imploring him not to persist with the campaign. Ammianus mentioned the letter among omens and portents through which the gods also were expressing their opinion, concluding for his part that Julian was held immovably by the decrees of fate (23.5.4). It was of course too late now to turn back, even had the emperor wished to; but Ammianus might have recalled Julian's own protest, when Constantius insisted on recalling troops from Gaul for the eastern campaign of 360, that the defences of Gaul were being weakened (20.4.7). The prefect's anxiety can well be understood, as he saw a huge army, including many troops from the west, committed to a reckless gamble on the Euphrates. He was proved right by the outcome. When Valentinian became emperor in 364 he found renewed chaos on the Rhine frontier – so soon after Julian's successes there. Indeed Valentinian's own financial severity could be defended by the extent of his needs after the 'Parthian disaster' of Julian; 'post procinctus Parthici clades magnitudine indigens impensarum' (30.8.8). Ammianus was frank enough to report this, but could only raise against it the argument that there were no circumstances whatever which could have justified the degree and methods of Valentinian's avarice. That the campaign of Julian had been a disaster was not in doubt.

Ammianus offers his most explicit defence of Julian's Persian policy at the end of his obituary of the emperor. Those critics, he here wrote, who believed that Julian had provoked 'new tumults of war to the detriment of the state' should know the plain truth. It was not Julian but Constantine who had kindled war with Persia, when, as Ammianus had explained fully in an earlier book, his greed had led him to believe the 'lies of Metrodorus'; 'non Iulianum sed Constantinum ardores Parthicos succendisse, cum Metrodori mendaciis avidius acquiescit, ut dudum rettulimus plene' (25.4.23). It was for this that armies had been defeated, generals and troops captured, cities and forts destroyed, provinces exhausted by taxation.

The story of Metrodorus happens to be known, for a version of it is preserved by an eleventh-century Byzantine writer, Cedrenus (pp. 516-17 Bonn). Metrodorus was a philosopher, supposedly of Persian descent, who in the time of Constantine had visited the Brahmin wise men of India. He had there been held in honour and had been permitted to enter sacred shrines of the Brahmins, from which he had taken precious stones and pearls. He had received more from the king of the Indians, to present to Constantine; but Metrodorus offered the treasures to the emperor as a personal gift, alleging that there had been more, which had been confiscated as he passed through the country of the king of Persia. Constantine was provoked to write to Sapor demanding the return of the jewels, and this was the cause of the breaking of the peace between Rome and Persia.[12]

This is essentially the same episode as that mentioned by Ammianus. He shares with Cedrenus the allegation that Metrodorus' story was the cause of the ending of the peace, while the theme of Constantine's greed, stated by Ammianus and implied by Cedrenus, was a regular feature of pagan criticism of the Christian emperor. It was Constantine, wrote Ammianus in another context, who first opened wide the jaws of his associates, while Constantius stuffed them with the vital substance of the provinces. These, in Ammianus' eyes, were well-attested facts; 'ut documenta liquida prodiderunt' (16.8.12).

Ammianus' attribution of the collapse of the peace to the 'lies of

Metrodorus' must be explained by the convergence of two strong sentiments, his dislike of Constantine and a wish to defend Julian at any cost against his critics; for on any reasonable assessment of the circumstances, the attribution seems trivial and irrelevant. The journey of Metrodorus took place in the late 320s, when Constantine's relations with Sapor were peaceful and Sapor himself, who had assumed the throne in childhood in 310, was still a young king; to this fact can perhaps be ascribed the extremely patronising tone in which (if the letter is genuine) Constantine wrote to proclaim his piety to Sapor and to commend to his protection the Christians in the land of Persia (Eusebius, *Life of Constantine*, 4.9-13). It was in the mid-330s, as Sapor's authority and ambition grew, that his relations with Rome became more warlike. There arrived in the Roman empire, appealing to a treaty with Constantine, a faction of Armenian noblemen whose king had been seized, blinded, and taken to the Persian court, and whose country had then been invaded by Sapor's army.[13] Constantine's response to this appeal was vigorous. It involved the bestowal of the title 'King of Kings' upon his nephew Hannibalianus and his dispatch to Caesarea in Cappadocia; the fortification by Constantius Caesar of the city of Amida, which is mentioned by Ammianus (18.9.1; p. 54); and, in 337, a military campaign against Persia, which Constantine was preparing when he died.[14] From the moment of his accession, as Julian himself said in his first panegyric to Constantius (*Or*. 1.20B-21D) Constantine's successor was preoccupied by the Persian threat to Mesopotamia. Every year they came, beginning in 337 or 338 with an unsuccessful two-month siege of Nisibis, the first of the three sieges which it suffered between Constantine's death and 350.[15]

It is obvious that far more was at issue in Constantine's relations with Persia than a fit of avarice induced by the lies of a philosopher. Nor could Ammianus fairly maintain that Constantine's policy, however provocative he believed that to have been, made Julian's Persian enterprise any less disruptive of the Roman empire than its critics claimed. Julian inherited the Persian problem from Constantius, as Constantius had from Constantine. Something had to be done; but nothing emerges more clearly from Ammianus' account than the force of Julian's personal obsession with the invasion of Persia, and his belief in his own unique ability to pursue it successfully.

These facets of Julian's personality had been shaped by his recent experience. His successes in Germany, achieved against all expectation, and his bloodless victory over Constantius in the civil war, had encouraged his confidence that he was the special favourite of fortune and the gods. The news of Constantius' death had filled him with elation, not only because it had resolved a military situation which he feared was not in his favour (21.12.21f., cf. 22.1.3), but because it fulfilled the public reading of the omens which he had conducted for the first time in Illyricum. Julian was already convinced by dreams, by private divination and by various experiences of the time of his proclamation, that he was in

VIII. The Invasion of Persia

the hands of a divine power, and this belief was now confirmed by the first public declarations of his apostasy (22.5.1f.). Elated by success, wrote Ammianus in a later passage, Julian breathed more exalted air than ordinary men. Fortune had never failed him in her generosity, bestowing glory without end; and Ammianus endorsed the emperor's conviction, adding as further proof of the gifts of Fortune that in the time of his sole reign Julian was troubled neither by foreign invasion nor by any civil disturbance (22.9.1). Ammianus has not at this point of his narrative mentioned the Persian campaign, but it is implied immediately by the move from Constantinople to Antioch (9.2). In moving east, Julian had ignored advice to turn his attention to the Goths. They had often proved unreliable, Julian was told; but he replied that he was in search of a 'better enemy' ('hostes ... meliores'), and would leave the Goths to Galatian slave-traders, by whom they were sold everywhere, well-born and humble alike (22.7.8). Julian did in a way manage to find a 'better enemy', but given the progress of events after his death, few of his judgments on the contemporary situation were so spectacularly misconceived.

Ammianus' fullest description of Julian's mentality in this period is reserved for the account of his stay at Antioch (22.12.11ff.). Then, wrote Ammianus, Julian strenuously prepared the campaign, which his noble mind had 'long before' conceived, passionately determined to avenge sixty years of destruction which the Persians had inflicted on the Roman empire – Ammianus is evidently not at this moment thinking to blame Constantine for 'kindling war with Persia'. Julian burned with desire for war; impatient of inactivity, he dreamed battles and the blare of trumpets, while the pleas of supposedly intractable German kings, still fresh in his mind, fed his ambition to add 'Parthicus' to the glorious titles which he already held (12.12).

Ammianus clearly accepted Julian's belief in his mission and in his unique capabilities to fulfil it; so that it is welcome confirmation that the emperor spoke for himself in his work, the *Caesars* or *Kronia*, composed at Antioch towards the end of 362. In this mock-contest of emperors, held before the assembled gods at the festival of the Saturnalia, the winner is of course Julian's model, Marcus Aurelius; the loser, stigmatised with terrific ferocity for his self-indulgence, prodigality and moral wickedness, is Constantine.[16] There is an intruder among the contestants, Alexander the Great, who is made to excel even Julius Caesar in martial achievement, especially by virtue of his eastern conquests. It is Alexander whom the warlike Trajan joins at the end of the contest, seeing in him a kindred spirit. Trajan had argued on his own behalf that he had tried for the same achievements as Alexander, but more prudently (*Caesars*, 333A).

The reason for the intrusion of Alexander, and for this emphasis on military prowess, is obvious. The *Caesars* was written while Julian was in the heat of preparations for the Persian campaign, and Trajan and Alexander reflect his preoccupations – Alexander being imported also to give expression to Julian's Hellenism, to associate Roman with Greek triumphs over the Persian empire. Yet the spirit of Alexander rose before any emperor who turned his ambitions to the east. Cassius Dio had told how Trajan went to Babylon during his Parthian campaign, to offer sacrifice in the room where Alexander was believed to have died, and how he stood on the shore of the Persian Gulf, watching a boat sail away to India. The ageing emperor was moved to a nostalgic reflection: so would he too have crossed the sea to India, if he had but been a young man (Dio 68.29f.).[17]

*

Julian's recollections of the submission of those German kings, who had been supposed readier to accept defeat than to face surrender, might suggest that the object of the Persian campaign also was to extract from Sapor a negotiated peace. This would no doubt be too strict an interpretation of a train of thought attributed to Julian at this time by Ammianus (22.12.2), but it raises the question already touched on, of the precise aims of the campaign and Ammianus' understanding of them.

The strategic design of the campaign is intelligible from Ammianus' narrative, though he nowhere sets it out explicitly. Certain crucial details have to be recovered from other sources, and at one point his text seems to have suffered damage. The idea of a double strike by both Tigris and Euphrates routes into Assyria had already been exploited by Trajan, who in Dio's fragmentary narrative first appears supervising the crossing of the upper Tigris in boats taken in pieces to the river and assembled there, then later at Hit on the Euphrates, from where he went on to attack Babylonia (Dio 68.26).[18] Likewise Julian marched first to Carrhae to give the impression that he was going to attack Sapor in the familiar battlegrounds in northern Mesopotamia, but then struck south by the Euphrates route into Assyria. Meanwhile a substantial army under Procopius and Sebastianus was deployed in the north, to secure the Tigris frontier against attack and later, if possible, to link up with Arsaces of Armenia and ravage parts of Media before joining the main army in Assyria (23.3.5). Exactly what was implied by this last provision is unclear. Ammianus seems at one moment to represent the dispatch of the army of Procopius simply as a response to an unexpected attack by the Persians on the Tigris frontier (23.3.4f.), but he notes at the same time that the army had formed part of Julian's earlier plans, and twice mentions the supply depots prepared for its use in those regions (23.3.6; 25.8.7).[19] This army was obviously a major element in Julian's strategy, being intended at least to distract Sapor and occupy him in the north, in order that the main advance to Ctesiphon should be unimpeded by serious opposition, and do what further damage it could. The importance of this design is reflected in Julian's haste to reach Ctesiphon quickly, as he pressed sieges and sometimes passed by fortresses without trying their strength, and in his mounting anxiety as he approached Ctesiphon

VIII. The Invasion of Persia

that the Persian army would arrive prematurely. The failure of the army of Procopius to achieve the more limited of its objectives was crucial to Julian's failure at Ctesiphon: it is not however Ammianus (as his text survives) but a fragmentary Greek source which tells how Sapor realised that he had been deceived into committing his main army to the north, and describes – or invents – some of the measures which he took to retrieve the situation.[20]

While this omission may possibly be attributed to a fault in the textual transmission of Ammianus' history (p. 159), it is a more serious deficiency in his account that he fails anywhere to state explicitly what political aims Julian's military strategy was designed to achieve. Libanius, who might conceivably have known, asserted in a letter that Julian intended to install Hormisdas on the Persian throne in place of Sapor (*Ep.* 1402). Hormisdas was a Persian prince who had fled to the court of Constantine in an earlier dynastic conflict in Persia, and was highly favoured by that emperor, as by Constantius.[21] The strength of his claim to the Persian throne should not be discounted, but it seems unlikely that this renegade could have hoped to supplant the great Sapor, now at the height of his immense authority. Hormisdas plays a prominent role in Ammianus' narrative, as a general, and as the recipient of insults from beleaguered Persian garrisons and captured Persians, but with no suggestion that he figured in any wider plans of Julian. It is not impossible that he played such a role, if only as one of several contingencies. Ammianus may simply not have known if this were the case; equally, Libanius may have been indulging in speculation, in an attempt to deduce such plans where none were immediately apparent to the outside observer.

It is after all possible that Julian's campaign had no such precise object. A military campaign with diplomatic aims will always be less easy to characterise than one whose aim is conquest, though the physical methods used might not differ much from one case to the other. There could be no doubt of Sapor's ambition to recover and hold by military action what he regarded as his ancestral dominions in Armenia and Mesopotamia; but no one could seriously have envisaged the permanent annexation by Rome of the regions overrun by Julian's army in 363. Julian's desire to capture Ctesiphon is as clear as that of Sapor to take Nisibis, but there can have been no question in Julian's case of holding such a prize permanently. The capture of Ctesiphon would be the splendid climax of the campaign, Julian's guarantee of a safe withdrawal (the Persians would not allow their capital to be destroyed) and his chief weapon in the negotiation of a favourable, lasting peace. It would show too that Julian could match the emperors of earlier times – those emperors mentioned in the speech ascribed to him by Ammianus at the outset of the campaign. Trajan, Verus and Septimius Severus had taken Ctesiphon and departed safely (it does not matter for these purposes that Trajan's successes were fragile and short-lived). They had adopted the title 'Parthicus' coveted by Julian, increased their own prestige in Roman eyes and demonstrated the enemy's weakness to surrounding peoples –

Saracens, Armenians and others whose attitudes were much affected by the success of the postures adopted by their imperial neighbours. Julian could hardly hope to achieve more than these predecessors. The real danger was that, in his own eyes at least, he had more to prove. To an eastern public, Julian's victories in Germany, the work of a gifted amateur rather than a true professional, must still have seemed distant and parochial in their importance, and they had not been fairly represented in Constantius' propaganda. Success against Persia, the historic enemy, would surely transform the prospects for Julian's domestic policies, in the religious sphere and others. It was easy for Ammianus' 'malign critics' to point to the dangers; but what if the gods were to declare themselves for Julian and he returned victorious? 'It could be done, if the promised favour of heaven were not betrayed by Roman neglect'. Julian had satisfied the condition: what might he not expect in return?

(2) Historical geography

Roman historians' descriptions of military campaigns are often our best evidence for the character and way of life of those less civilised peoples against whom they were directed:[22] this is true of the *Gallic War* of Caesar, of the account given by Tacitus of the suppression of the African rebel Tacfarinas in the time of Tiberius, and of Ammianus' own richly detailed narrative of the defeat by Theodosius of the Moor Firmus in the early 370s.[23] Julian's Persian campaign, by contrast, was a journey to the origins of civilisation itself, to a land of ancient culture fully equal in material resources and complexity of social organisation to the Classical Near East of Ammianus' birth and upbringing. For Ammianus, Mesopotamia was in a sense the natural extension of the Classical world. The town of Circesium, where Julian's army crossed the Khabur into Assyria, and where Ammianus may have joined the campaign, was already half-way from Antioch to Ctesiphon. The Persian capital itself stood towards the far end of the 'Fertile Crescent', a politically divided but culturally and linguistically homogeneous band of territory of which Ammianus's native city was the pivot.

As Ammianus well knew, the conquests of Alexander the Great and the work of his successors had long ago planted the landscape of Mesopotamia with Greek cities, which were within the intellectual horizons of men of the Classical world, even when they were outside its political boundaries.[24] Among the finest and most successful of these cities was Seleucia on the Tigris, which in the days of Strabo and the elder Pliny, who describe it, was one of the greatest cities of the east, inside or outside the Roman empire. Founded by Seleucus Nicator in the late fourth century BC to outrival Babylon, Seleucia had by Strabo's time (16.1.16) replaced it as the metropolis of Assyria. Pliny ascribed to the city a population of 600,000, a later estimate suggesting 400,000 for the mid-second century.[25] Such calculations in ancient authors must always

VIII. The Invasion of Persia

be viewed sceptically, but figures like these would make Seleucia at its height a really great city, of the order in size of Syrian Antioch – a comparison actually made by Strabo (16.2.5). It had from the beginning possessed a mixed character, since it contained not only the Macedonian Greeks involved in its foundation by Nicator, but the Semitic and Iranian populations of Opis and Babylon, who were moved there, and many Syrians. The result was a city of notorious volatility and periodic violence, especially between Jewish and Syrian inhabitants, and one, from a Parthian point of view, of dubious loyalty. Towards the middle of the first century AD. Seleucia held out for seven years in revolt against its enfeebled Parthian masters.

Close by Seleucia across the Tigris lay Ctesiphon, built up by the Parthian kings as their winter residence, as Strabo explains, in order to spare the people of Seleucia the nuisance (and no doubt, given their political temper, the provocation) of quartering the 'Scythian people and soldiery' employed by them (16.1.16). It was with a nice sense of Graeco-Roman civic proprieties that Strabo described Ctesiphon as a 'large village'. He meant by this that it had no formal civic constitution in the Greek manner; yet, as Strabo made clear, it was in all respects of size and importance a city, since apart from its function as a royal residence, it was a trading centre for goods that 'suited the Parthians' and so was an assertion of Iranian cultural identity in contrast with the Hellenistic character of Seleucia. When Julian confronted the place in 363 it had been further developed by the Sasanians and seemed impregnable (24.7.1; below, p. 158).

As for Seleucia, it was by then an abandoned site, referred to by Syriac sources as 'Sliq Kharawta', 'empty' or 'deserted Seleucia': so too by Ammianus (24.5.3; p. 157) who, like the Syriac writers, shows it as a place of execution outside a new city, Coche (or Kôkhê). This is the city also known as Veh Ardeshir, so named after Artaxerxes I (c. 226-c. 241), the Sasanian monarch who had built it. Coche-Veh Ardeshir, not Ctesiphon as was earlier assumed, is the 'round city' that appears in archaeological plans beside the rectangular Hellenistic plan of Seleucia, across an old bed of the Tigris that seems, in this respect misleadingly, to separate them.[26] It is here necessary to understand the true sequence of events. The Tigris had indeed once flowed by the walls of Seleucia, but had already receded when Coche-Veh Ardeshir was founded in the third century; it then flowed, with the assistance of walls and dykes, round the eastern side of the new city, separating it from Ctesiphon. Then, in a further shift of the river-course that must at the time have caused a major urban disaster, Coche-Veh Ardeshir had itself been cut in two, the segment of the city left on the eastern bank of the new river course being absorbed into Ctesiphon. It was possible, according to a passage in the Babylonian Talmud, to go to the water's edge at Veh Ardeshir and see there ruined walls running down into the water where part of the city had once stood;[27] a reminder of the day when flood had divided it in two. For the purpose of defining Sabbath limits, Veh Ardeshir and Ctesiphon were

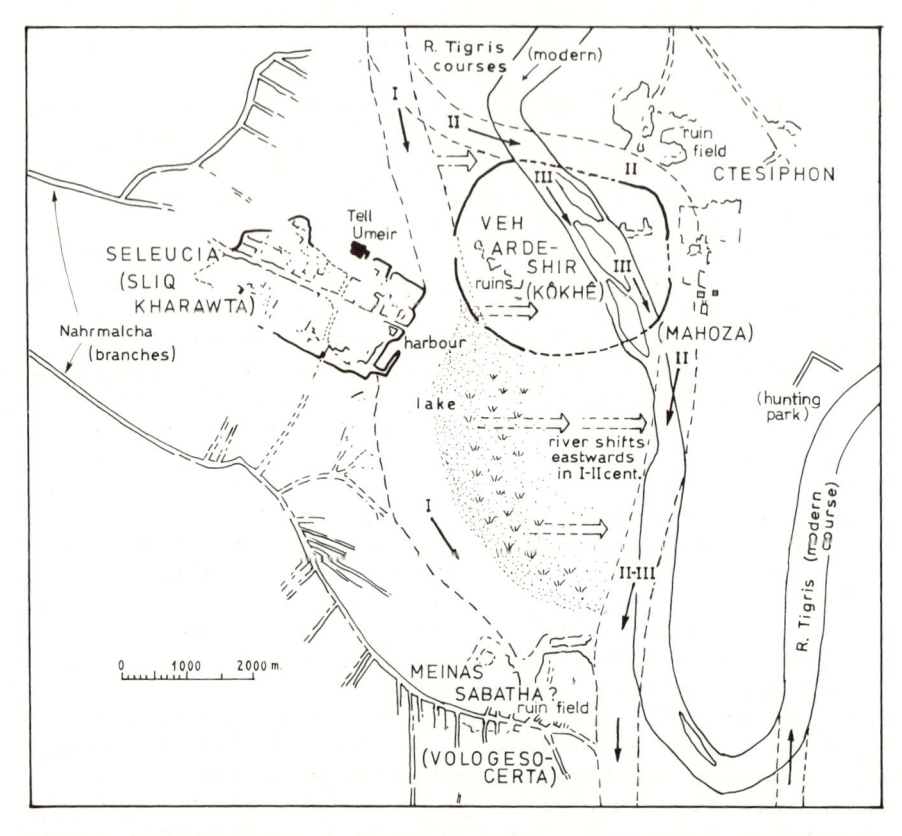

Map 4. Seleucia and Ctesiphon. Drawn from the plan in Clark Hopkins (ed.), *Topography and Architecture of Seleucia on the Tigris*, 164, with amendments from G. Gullini, *Mesopotamia* 1 (1966), 7-28, J.M. Fiey, *Sumer* 23 (1967), 3-38, and A. Oppenheimer, *Babylonia Judaica in the Talmudic Period*, 179ff. (plan at 233).

regarded in the Talmud as one city, being divided only by the Tigris, and this, as in effect a single city with the river running through it, is how they were described by some Classical accounts of the Persian campaign of Julian.[28]

The decline of Seleucia, initiated perhaps by the first-century Parthian foundation of yet another city, Vologesias or Vologesocerta, to serve as the port of Ctesiphon and undermine its dissident rival, was ensured by the shift eastwards of the course of the Tigris.[29] The role of repeated Roman attack was, relative to these events, of lesser significance, although the sack of Seleucia by the army of Avidius Cassius in AD 165 was particularly destructive – gratuitously so, since the population had received the Romans inside under promises of friendship. Even after that, the city was rebuilt. Its archaeological history is one of progressive

VIII. The Invasion of Persia

decay rather than sudden destruction. By the mid-third century Seleucia had declined, Coche-Veh Ardeshir had been founded, and Classical sources begin to refer to the place indifferently by its old and new names – as indeed does Ammianus: 'Coche, quam Seleuciam nominant' (24.5.3). It must have been an eerie sight, quite apart from the corpses gibbeted in the abandoned city; the walls of Coche-Veh Ardeshir, round which the Devil himself had once been seen running,[30] overlooking huge sand-swept ruins, the old harbour of Seleucia (clearly visible in aerial photographs) enveloped by the still swampy river bed abandoned by the Tigris, the once busy water-courses neglected and choked with silt (below, p. 151). The decline in modern times of nineteenth-century industries has familiarised us, in very different circumstances, with the image of archaeological sites emerging from fading communities, disused canals and railway tracks reverting to a 'natural' state that does not disguise their artificial origins. It is not an inappropriate image to have in mind as we contemplate the end of the once great city of Seleucia: always remembering that in terms of the region as a whole we are looking not at decline but at shifts of population and economic activity from one urban centre to another under the influence of a locally unstable physical environment.

*

For those with eyes to see, an advance down the Euphrates to Ctesiphon was a journey to one of the richest, most ancient and most complex areas of civilisation of the Near Eastern world. This fact should encourage us to view Julian's campaign in its cultural and geographical setting, even if it had not been attended by such an observant and alert participant as Ammianus. Not that Ammianus was the only one of his kind to accompany the campaign. Julian's doctor, Oribasius, kept a memoir which he made available to his friend, the historian Eunapius (cf. fr. 8). Libanius referred to the many men who came back from the campaign with notes on it, and himself composed a well-informed and detailed account in his *Funeral Oration* for Julian (*Or.* 18.204ff.).[31] There were too those 'philosophers' travelling with the camp, whose opinions on omens were so eagerly sought by Julian; whatever the quality of the advice which they proffered the emperor, one would expect them to have been observant men, interested in what they saw around them.

The presence of such men on Julian's campaign would lend it, like its predecessors and especially the eastern campaigns of Alexander the Great, something of the quality of a 'study tour'. The philosopher Plotinus had, according to his biographer Porphyry, actually joined the Persian campaign of Gordian in order to find out more about Persian and Indian philosophy (*V. Plot.* 3), a transformation of military campaign into intellectual venture which may seem eccentric but is far from unique. Julian himself conveys a fitting tone of curiosity in his last letter to Libanius, in which he describes the opening stage of the journey, from

Antioch to Hierapolis near the Euphrates (*Ep.* 98 Bidez).[32] He passed on the way a ruined site, which he took to be the remains of an 'Antiochene winter camp' (whatever he understood that to mean) perhaps to be located at Imma; then travelled along a rough road to a marshy place where stones appeared to have been assembled and laid deliberately, but not by any usual building procedure. It has been convincingly suggested that his description answers to a bed of volcanic lava, broken by natural process into regular shapes to give the appearance of a made-up road. The emperor went by a place called Litarba (El-Terib), where he received in audience the Antiochene senate, which had accompanied him so far, and came to Beroea. Here he visited the acropolis, sacrificed a white bull to Zeus and lectured an apparently indifferent – no doubt because Christian – local council on the virtues of piety. Next on the road was Batnae, where traces of sacrifice and proper religious practice were to be seen. Batnae reminded Julian of Daphne near Antioch, with its fertile landscape dotted with young cypresses; a simple lodging had been prepared for the emperor, made of wood with no painted decoration, and there was a pleasant garden, with fruit and vegetables growing in little plots, cypresses and other trees neatly planted in rows.

Here too Julian sacrificed, before going on to Hierapolis, to be delightedly received there by an adept of Neoplatonist philosophy whom he had never before met – though the philosopher's father-in-law was none less than Sopatros, pupil of the 'divine Iamblichus' (see p. 126). The philosopher had often met Constantius and Gallus Caesar, without yielding to their inducements to abandon his piety to the gods.

It is difficult, in reading this little *journal de voyage* addressed to an intellectual friend, to visualise the actual circumstances of Julian's journey – the dust, the clatter of wagon wheels, the hordes of troops and officials who accompanied him. In Hierapolis itself, a portico by the main gate collapsed on Julian's army as it passsed underneath, causing heavy casualties, fifty dead and many injured (23.2.6). Julian understandably omits to mention this episode in his letter to Libanius; yet in general the details included by Julian are not unlike those often picked out by Ammianus and other sources on the journey down the Euphrates to Ctesiphon – matters of an antiquarian rather than a military interest, but adding variety to the account and showing the curiosity of an eye-witness. Ammianus describes an elegant royal palace near Seleucia, spared by the army because it was constructed in the 'Roman style', and the hunting park adjacent to it (24.5.1f.; below, p. 157). Both were mentioned also by Eunapius and, in confused but colourful detail, by Libanius (*Oratio* 18.243). Ammianus remarks on the buildings of a suburban estate near Ctesiphon, with the interesting comment that the Persians never showed anything in their paintings and sculpture except 'various forms of slaughter and battle scenes' (24.6.3).[33] He recalls too the ruins of ancient walls seen near the place where the Euphrates divides into the first of its great navigable canals. They had been built long ago to protect Assyria from foreign invasion (2.6).

VIII. The Invasion of Persia

In one brief reference to a weakly fortified town sacked by the Roman army, having been abandoned by its Jewish inhabitants (24.4.1), Ammianus touches a fact of great importance about the population of central Mesopotamia. The position of the town may be consistent with that of the famous Rabbinic academy of Neardea,[34] but there is no need to press the identification in order to seize the interest in Ammianus' remark. Pronouncements in the Babylonian Talmud assume that in many communities in the area a substantial part, sometimes a majority, of the population was Jewish. So: a barrel of wine is found floating in the Euphrates, and the question arises, has it been prepared by Jews and so can be consumed by them, or is it libation wine of the gentiles? The verdict: if the barrel was found near a town with a Jewish majority, it may be consumed; otherwise, it must not be used. In the light of this decision, a later rider that the barrel might after all have floated down-river from Hit and is therefore untouchable, seems pedantic and grudging – though it has the merit of making it clear that the town of Hit, lying above the edge of the alluvial plain of the Euphrates, was beyond the strict limits of Babylonian Jewry or 'area of pure lineage'.[35]

It is a little surprising that the Talmud, with all its emphasis on particular situations, real or hypothetical, has no specific reference to the Persian invasion of Julian. Problems arising for the Jewish community from military mobilisation in Persia are occasionally discussed, with reference to Sapor's internal wars against Arabs and others, but it seems that the invasion of Julian, which caused very great damage to persons and property, both by the direct action of the Roman army and because of the efforts of the inhabitants to resist it, did not raise the problems of legal and religious propriety with which Talmudic sources concerned themselves.[36] To the Jewish populations of Babylonia Sapor was a tolerant king, who ruled firmly but did not restrict their religious freedom nor subject them to oppressive taxation – he could hardly, given their numbers, have done otherwise. It is unlikely that Julian would have been able to undermine the Persians by making of the Jews a dissident faction among them, and we can view with reserve the possibility that any of Julian's domestic policies, in particular his attempted restoration of the Temple, were intended to attract the sympathies of Jews living in Mesopotamia.

*

The progress of Julian's march, from the Khabur crossing to Hit and beyond, was, for the army at large, relatively uneventful. Not that it was entirely free of incident, as in the fate of the soldier Jovianus, struck by lightning while leading horses from the Euphrates' edge (23.5.12). Another soldier swam over the river while drunk, to be seized on the other side by Persians and killed in full view of the Roman army (24.1.16). A more general mishap was caused by a sudden gale which blew up and caused destruction and chaos in the Roman camp. It was impossible to keep a steady footing, says Ammianus, so strong were the gusts (1.11). Yet more ominously, on the same day the Euphrates overflowed when some sluices broke and some grain-ships were sunk in the deluge. In view of what was to happen later in the march, it is surprising that Ammianus ever imagined that the breaking of the sluices could be due to an accident; though he was observant enough to remark that the sluices themselves, built to control the water for irrigation, were made of stone in the customary manner.

The first major town to be encountered was Anatha, which stood like many Euphrates settlements on an island in the river (24.1.6). Anatha was surrounded overnight by a fleet sent on ahead with a picked detachment of 1,000 men, and quickly surrendered.[37] Other towns, such as Thilutha and Achaiacala, were passed by since they declined to yield instantly, but preferred to wait and see what happened, while Julian had no time to spend on them. Ammianus describes in stately language how their inhabitants gazed respectfully over their walls at Julian's fleet as it slipped by; 'verecunda quiete spectabant immobiles' (2.1f.). Other deserted settlements were sacked and burned, their people having fled rather than trust their defences (2.2f.).

The nature of the landscape and habitation of the country are well suggested by the account written by Captain (later General) F.R. Chesney of the journey by raft down the Euphrates, which he undertook in 1831 as an exploratory mission for the British Government to see whether an overland route could be found to India and the Far East.[38] Captain Chesney recorded how, beginning his descent of the river at Anah (Anatha), he passed on his raft between 'well-wooded banks, and along islands of various dimensions', past the 'still perfect walls of ancient Tilbus' (Ammianus' Thilutha) and Hadisa, 'built on high ground, surrounded by a defensible wall washed by the river'. Hadisa was perhaps the same as Achaiacala, since Ammianus too mentions its difficulty of access, with a suggestion of its height; 'arduumque transcensu' (24.2.2). Other island settlements were El-Oos, a town of some importance, 'with two mosques, some flourmills, and about 250 houses', where Chesney's raft grazed the walls as they came down into the water; and Jibba, 'with some 500 houses ensconced in a date-grove, which extends for more than a mile along the centre of the river, which is here shut in by high ranges of hills ...'.

> Throughout the whole distance from Anna to Hit (131 miles) [wrote Chesney in summary], we passed though a constant succession of watermills and aqueducts, villages and hamlets, which succeed each other at almost every fresh sweep of the river; now showing themselves between the low hills which skirt the river's banks, now enlivening the wooded islands which frequently divide the stream – which, in this part of its course, has an average width of 350 yards, a depth of 11 feet, and a current of three knots per hour in the season of floods. I counted fourteen islands during this part of our descent, many of which have small towns upon them, often built upon some ancient site. (*Euphrates Expedition*, 75f.)

VIII. The Invasion of Persia

Contemplating this and other accounts of travel in Assyrian Mesopotamia, one wonders whether on surveying the site of Anatha in preparation for its siege, Julian shared the reaction of a French traveller of the seventeenth century, Jean Baptiste Tavernier, who was reminded of Paris, 'for it is built upon both sides of the River Euphrates; and in the midst of the River is an island, where stands a fair Mosquee'.[39] Tavernier was writing for a Parisian audience; it is unlikely that despite his affection for Paris, Julian was struck by any such resemblance, even allowing for the replacement of the temple which no doubt stood in Roman times on the Ile de la Cité, by the cathedral of Notre Dame. Writing of another town, Diacira (Hit), Ammianus does however happen to mention that there could be seen over the river a high temple, placed on the summit of the hill round which the town was clustered; 'Diacira civitas ..., in qua templum alti culminis arci vidimus superpositum' (24.2.3).

The town of Hit marked the end of the first stage of Capt. Chesney's journey down the Euphrates, as it did of Julian's. It was overhung by a pall of smoke from the boiling bitumen springs for which it was famous; Chesney was greeted by the governor, Sheik Mohammed, 'whose attire accorded well with the murky atmosphere of the place' (*Euphrates Expedition*, p. 76)! At Hit, Chesney had a boat made in the age-old manner: a wooden frame was staked out on the ground, the flat bottom and sides of the boat were constructed of lattice-work, the sides held firm with ties and the whole vessel coated inside and out with layers of pitch – just as Noah was instructed to 'make an ark of gopher wood ... and pitch it within and without with pitch' (*Genesis* 6.14); the result was a boat light in construction, with a large capacity and shallow draught, ideal for its purpose. The Assyrian name for Hit, Id, comes from the word for pitch, *iddu*, just as its Aramaic name, Ihi Dekira (Ammianus' Diacira, Dakira in Eunapius) means 'place of asphalt'.

Ammianus too mentions the 'bubbling well of bitumen' ('fonte scatenti bitumine', 24.2.3) seen by Julian's army opposite the town of Hit. It was an imposing sight. 'Near unto the river Euphrates,' wrote a sixteenth-century traveller through Mesopotamia to the East Indies, Cesar Fredericke –

> there is a city called Heit, nere unto which city there is a great plaine full of pitch, very marvellous to beholde, and a thing almost incredible that out of a hole in the earth, which continually throweth out pitch into the aire with continuall smoake, this pitch is thrown with such a force that being hot it falleth like as it were sprinckled all over the plaine in such abundance that the plaine is always full of pitch, the Mores and the Arabians of that place say that that hole is the mouth of hell and in truth it is a thing very notable to be marked: and by this pitch the whole of the people have their benefit to pitch their barks.[40]

Shorter but no less evocative is the description given in the account of the Assyrian King Tukultu Enurtu II, who in 884 BC made his encampment 'opposite Id, close to the sources of bitumen ... where the great gods speak'.[41] The springs were the same as those inspected by Trajan during his campaign of AD 116. It was from them, the emperor was correctly informed, that the bitumen had been taken for building the walls of Babylon (Herodotus 1.179.4); they were made of brick cemented with bitumen, just as Ammianus and Eunapius described the formidable double walls of Pirisabora, built by a Persian monarch a millennium later. It was, wrote Ammianus, the most durable manner of building known; 'quo aedificii genere nihil esse tutius constat' (24.2.12).

A detachment of Julian's army was sent over the river to take Diacira.[42] They killed the women found there and took large quantities of the salt which in modern times too is an important product of the region. After Diacira was Ozogardana, where a tribunal was shown, built for Trajan to address his troops in the campaign of 116 (24.2.3). This town, like Diacira left undefended, was taken and burned, and it was soon after this (two days being allowed for rest) that the Persian army was first seen in the open. An ambush laid for the general Hormisdas was almost successful. Ammianus, alert as ever to the dramatic possibilities, used the occasion to introduce briefly the Persian commanders, and to convey the impact on the Romans of their previously elusive enemy. There they stood, arrayed for battle in the first light of day, with their glinting helmets and bristling armour; 'visi tunc primitus corusci galeis et horrentes indutibus rigidis' (2.5). Their commanders were a splendidly assorted pair – Surena, a Persian nobleman whose ancestors had led the king's armies for centuries (it was a Suren who defeated Crassus at Carrhae in 53 BC), and Malechus, a lawless desert chieftain whose customary delight it was to terrorise Roman frontier regions; 'famosi nominis latro, omni saevitia per nostros limites diu grassatus' (24.2.4). We shall in a later chapter see something of the wider significance of this most interesting figure.[43]

After a skirmish, in which the Romans closed quarters and prevented the enemy from using its strength in archery, the army came to Macepracta, where ruins of the great walls were seen, built in ancient times to defend Assyria against invasion (24.2.6); and below this, to the point where the Euphrates divided into the first of its main derivative channels. It was an important moment in the campaign.[44] The river had now, a few miles below Hit, entered its alluvial plain. The physical geography of the region, in terms of the relationship between the river and its surrounding lands, had crucially changed; the natural resources available for Persian resistance were multiplied, and Julian's enterprise became ensnared in difficulties for which the journey so far had given little preparation.

*

In the book of the Babylonian Talmud called *Berakoth*, 'Blessings', the following pronouncement is recorded:

VIII. The Invasion of Persia

He who sees the Euphrates up to the Babylonian bridge says 'Blessed be thou who has made the Creation'; but nowadays, since the Persians have altered it, that Benediction is only to be pronounced above Be Shapur. Rab Joseph said: 'Only above Ihi Dekira'.[45]

This means that there was a point on the Euphrates below which it was not right to bless the Creator, since his handiwork had been effaced by changes made by man to the nature of the river. Differing opinions were offered as to where this point was located, the strictest view picking out Ihi Dekira, or Hit. The less rigorous alternative, Be Shapur ('place of Sapor') is to be identified with Peroz-Shapur, Ammianus' Pirisabora, the next major town to be attacked by Julian. Piri-sabora, the Arab city of al Anbar, 'the Arsenal', contained or was very close to the famous Rabbinic academy of Pumbadita, an Aramaic word suggesting the separation of the waters of the Euphrates. As we have seen, it was just above Pirisabora that the Roman army came to the first of the great canals of the Euphrates.[46] Here, wrote Ammianus, the river divided, one part going to inner Babylonia to irrigate the land and provide water for its cities, while the other branch flowed past Ctesiphon. This channel, according to Ammianus, was called the Naarmalcha, or 'King's river', and at the point where the waters divided stood a tall tower like a lighthouse (24.2.7).

The channel so described by Ammianus, and now crossed by Julian's army, was at least in its earlier sections the ancient predecessor of the Saqlawiyah canal, through which Captain Chesney in 1838 sent a steamer to the Tigris a little below Baghdad. The Saqlawiyah canal, as Chesney noted, was undoubtedly 'one of the most ancient commercial communications in the world', though this observation applies, as relevant to Ammianus' account, only to the first part of its course.[47] The channel as seen by Ammianus, and as described by the elder Pliny in the first century (*Hist. Nat.* 5.90), like the Saqlawiyah had its inlet above Pirisabora and followed the course of the Saqlawiyah to the north of the ridge that extends eastwards for about twenty miles behind that city. The channel must then have turned south round the end of the ridge, leaving the course of the Saqlawiyah canal to join by one of many possible routes the waterway which Classical and Talmudic sources more usually know as the Naarmalcha or King's river ('basileios potamos' in Greek), running from the Euphrates past the site of ancient Sippar and on to the Tigris at Seleucia. Ammianus' account raises a problem as to the correct location of the Euphrates inlet of the Naarmalcha. The problem is best solved by the supposition that there were more than one. Beginning with the most southerly, an inlet was located by Ptolemy (5.17.5) on the same latitude as Sippar and Seleucia. Near the inlet, according both to Ptolemy and to Talmudic texts, stood the Jewish city of Neardea; this is no doubt represented by the ruin mound shown on modern surveys as Tel Nihar or Tel Quhr Nahar, on the left bank of the Euphrates due west of Seleucia just where Ptolemy placed it.[48] It is however implied by Eunapius' account of the campaign that the Naarmalcha also possessed an inlet

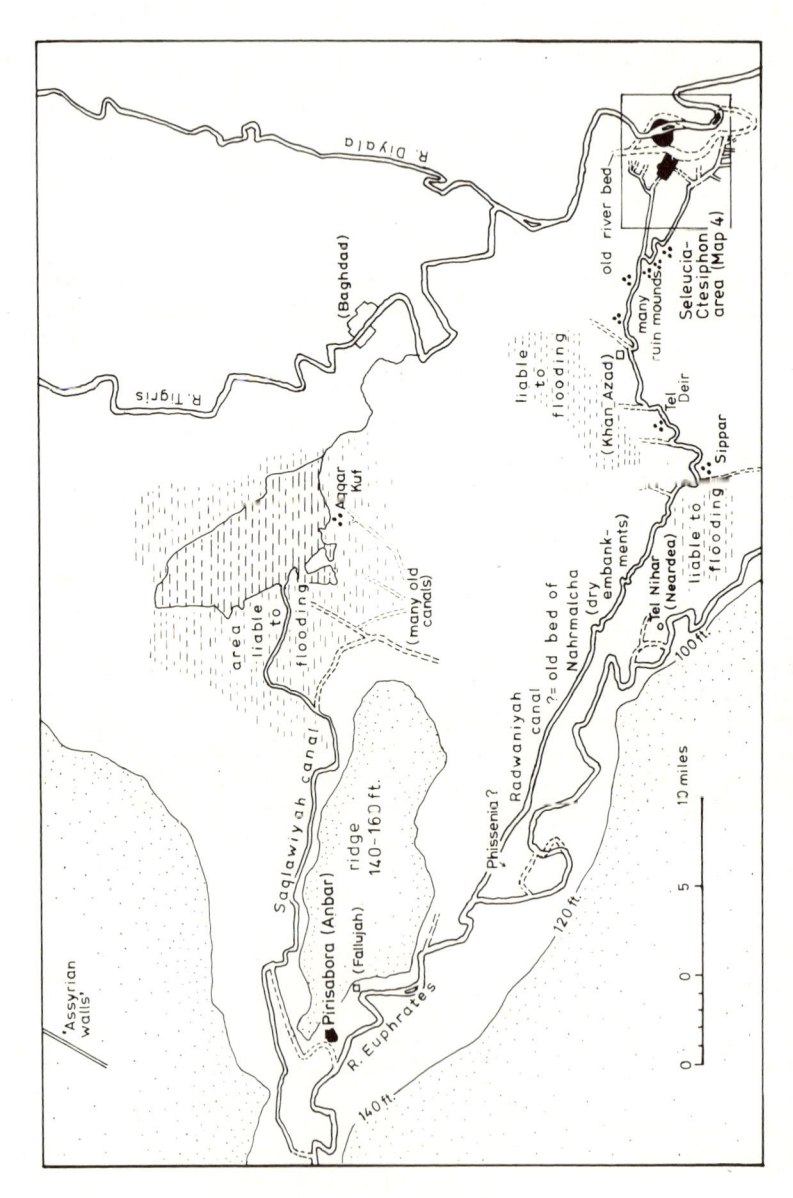

Map 5. Julian in Mesopotamia (Pirisabora-Ctesiphon). Drawn from maps prepared by the British Mesopotamian Expeditionary Force, ¼-inch scale (1917-19), sheet TC 87 Baghdad-Saklawiyah, with details added from 1-inch map (1918-20), sheets 85-6, 100, 102-3.

VIII. The Invasion of Persia

further to the north, possibly on the alignment of the later Radwaniyah canal (below, p. 153); while as we have seen, Ammianus assigned the name Naarmalcha to a third, still more northerly channel leaving the Euphrates above Pirisabora. In this he has the support of Pliny's statement that the channel drawn from the Euphrates near Massice (Parthian Mšyk or Misichê, later renamed Pirisabora) was called the Naarmalcha by 'all the Assyrians'.[49] The source of the ambiguity in locating the Euphrates inlets of the Naarmalcha may well be that the original 'King's river' (*nâr šarri* of Babylonian texts) had run from Sippar to the Tigris at the time when Sippar lay on the Euphrates, and that all three later inlets which connected the Euphrates with the ancient canal as the bed of the river shifted westwards came to share its name. The cuneiform name for the Euphrates is, precisely, 'river of Sippar', though very early texts suggest that the river was already receding from the city. The site of Sippar (Abu Hubbah) is now waterless, as is the ruin mound of Tel Ibrahim, linked with Sippar to the south by the dry but once heavily settled riverbanks known in Arabic as Habl-Ibrahim ('Abraham's Rope'), which mark the old course of the Euphrates.[50]

It is evident that description of settlement in this region has to accommodate frequent, and sometimes quite marked, shifts in the river-courses, the distribution of urban sites being inexplicable without the assumption that the great rivers and their derivative channels once took water to places now isolated in the desert. One such change, on a smaller physical scale than the abandonment of Sippar by the Euphrates but quite as dramatic in its consequences, has already been discussed as relevant to the local context of Ammianus' narrative (p. 141). The bed of the Tigris had shifted eastwards as it passed Seleucia and Ctesiphon, leaving Seleucia isolated from the river that had sustained it. It had then, in a subsequent change of course, cut in two the new city of Coche-Veh Ardeshir which had succeeded Seleucia, to form the configuration visible in Ammianus' day.

This is a landscape subject in both larger and smaller dimensions to constant change, caused both by natural process and by human intervention, as watercourses become silted and have to be cleared or replaced, and in which what is a 'natural' and what an 'artificial' river-bed are not clearly distinguished one from the other. Strabo wrote of the continuous labour and the difficulties involved in clearing and maintaining the canals, especially at their inlets, 'for the soil is so deep, soft and yielding that it is easily swept away by the currents; and so the plains are eroded, the canals filled and their inlets choked by silt' (16.1.9). The consequence of damage or inadequate maintenance is that the land is liable to flooding and, lacking natural drainage, can degenerate into insect-ridden swamps and marshes.

A lively glimpse of some of the arrangements necessary for the maintenance of the canals is given in the Talmud. We read there, for instance, of the arrival of a Sasanian canal official – even if the vision of his methods of enforcement seems over-dramatised:

152   Part One: Res Gestae

R. Zera's father was tax collector for thirteen years. When the head of the canal came, he would advise, 'Come, my people, enter into thy chambers' [*Isaiah* 26.20, which continues: 'and shut thy doors about thee: hide thyself for a little moment, until the indignation be overpast'], and to others he would say, 'The head of the canal is coming to town, and he will slaughter the father in the presence of the son, and the son in the presence of the father'. So they all hid. When the officer came, he would say, 'Of whom shall I make the demand ... ?' (*b. Sanhedrin* 25b)

The demand is no doubt for some sort of corvée or tax devoted to canal maintenance. Herodotus had noted (1.193.2) that Babylonia was like Egypt in being divided by canals, and papyri from Oxyrhynchus illustrate the obligations laid on farmers to take their part in the maintenance of the dykes (*P. Oxy.* 1409, 2847), record accusations of bribery of the canal superintendent by individuals who wish to avoid their obligations (3264), and mention other abuses (1469, 2853). References in the Talmud show the elaborate arrangements surrounding the rights of usage by landowners of water from irrigation channels, and such details as their obligation to maintain and keep clear a towpath of specified width beside canals used for barge transport.[51]

To the use of canals for irrigation and transport, a third function should be added, that of defence: and with this, we return to the campaign of Julian. The city of Pirisabora is described by Ammianus as 'protected by water like an island' ('ambitu insulari circumvallatum', 24.2.9), though in this case it is the more systematic description of Eunapius, as preserved by Zosimus, which shows that the city was defended to the north by a wide channel drawn from the river, which also provided its water (3.17.4; p. 174).[52] Another place several miles further on, called Phissenia by Eunapius but unnoticed by Ammianus, had a deep ditch by its walls, into which the Persians had admitted water drawn from the nearby 'King's river', evidently below the second of the three inlets identified earlier. In consequence, the Roman army passed it by without offering siege. Later, at an unnamed place near Ctesiphon, Ammianus noted two towns formed into island sites by the stream – here the ancient Naarmalcha between Sippar and the Tigris. The inhabitants of these settlements, less sure of their defences than the people of Phissenia, had made off for Ctesiphon, some through the 'dense woods', some by circuitous routes through the nearby marshes, carried on boats made of hollowed-out trees (24.4.8). The marshes in question were no doubt connected with the 'immense lake' debouching into the Tigris near Seleucia, alluded to by Ammianus (5.3) and other writers. It was formed, not strictly as Ammianus thought by the waters of a 'constant source' but by the Naarmalcha and its branches as they tried to enter but were held back by the swift-flowing Tigris, and so were heavily silted at their outlets.[53]

The last episode at Phissenia illustrates another use of water as a defensive resource, fully exploited by the Persians in their resistance to Julian. Beyond the settlement the entire countryside had been

VIII. The Invasion of Persia

transformed into a swampy morass (24.3.10f.; Zosimus 3.19.3). The Persians had achieved this by the simple but drastic method of deliberately flooding the plain, both from the main channel of the Euphrates and also (Eunapius was precise on this, even if Zosimus' summary of him is confused) from the Naarmalcha: the army was marching between the two.[54] Eunapius used the difficulties now faced by the army to show the resources and determination of Julian in getting his men over the morass, having experts build bridges over water channels and crossing the shallower parts of the inundation on woven mats. Libanius also wrote at some length of the emperor's courage and ingenuity, and of the determined patience of the army during this part of the march (*Or.* 18.223ff.). Ammianus was content with a brief description of the difficulties experienced in getting the army over, which was done by using pontoons, boats and inflated bladders, and rafts of woven palm-branches (24.3.10f.). Both Zosimus and Ammianus make clear that the army had to camp overnight in this uncongenial and obviously unhealthy country, though for some the conditions were eased by the discovery at a place called Bithra of a palace and buildings in which they could stay (Zosimus 3.19.4). It was after this that the army reached huge palm-groves, extending as far as Mesene (Maišan) and the Persian Gulf. Here, stated Ammianus, the main stream of the Euphrates divided into many small branches; 'pars maior Euphratis in rivos dividitur multifidos' (24.3.14).

Julian's predicament is to be understood in the context of two basic features of Mesopotamian geography. The first relates to the habits of alluvial rivers, as in their seasonal flooding they deposit at their edges quantities of debris, which is left there as the waters of the river spread over the flood-plain and in due course recede. The banks of such rivers are gradually built up by such deposits until the river-course is guarded, like Mark Twain's Mississippi, by embankments (known as levées) which generally contain the river when it is full but are broken from time to time. When the Mississippi overflowed its embankments, the landscape became like that of a 'vague dim sea that is shoreless, that fades out and loses itself in the murky distances', the embankments themselves being visible like thin ribs in the water. It was just such an embankment of river or canal of which Libanius wrote, when he described how some of Julian's men made their way precariously along a steep and narrow bank, with the floodwaters lapping up to each side (*Or.* 18.224).[55]

In such a terrain, the banks of canals are built up by human agency more quickly than those of natural river-courses, as their beds are dredged to keep them clear and the sludge is dumped on the edge of the canals. Eventually the banks become so steep and high that the operation is impracticable, and when this happens a channel will be abandoned to silt up, and a new one started. By repetition of this process the whole of this part of Mesopotamia is littered with the remains of old canals that have been replaced by new courses. The ancient Naarmalcha itself is dry between still huge embankments, while the modern Mahmudiyah canal runs on a parallel course to the south of its ancient predecessor.

At the same time as the banks of such water-courses are built up in this way, deposits of silt raise their beds as well, so that in due course the maximum water level may be higher than the surrounding plain. The prospect of flooding in such circumstances can be imagined, as the river or canal spills over its banks and down onto the land around. More pertinent to Julian's experience, when a deliberate breach is made in the walls of a watercourse, the flooding will be progressive, as the water runs down from its higher level over the plains; and since drainage back into the water course is impossible until its natural level falls, and is at best extremely slow, large tracts of land are reduced to a swampy condition which, without effective remedial action, may rapidly destroy good soil.

The second factor of Mesopotamian geography therefore concerns the regime of the river Euphrates. Rising in the Armenian mountains, the river increases its flow as the snows melt in spring, adding their volume of water to the seasonal rainfall. In the two months from the middle of March, the Euphrates doubles its rate of flow, producing at Hit by mid-May in a typical year over 50,000 cubic metres of water (nearly 400,000 gallons) per second.[56] The rise in its level in the same period, measured at Ramadi just below Hit, is almost two metres, though the difference can in some years be much more than this. The contrast in the conditions experienced by Julian's army and by Xenophon's Ten Thousand in 401 BC is instructive. When Cyrus reached the Euphrates at Thapsacus in Syria and found the boats there burned to prevent his crossing, his men were actually able to wade over the river (*Anabasis* 1.4.17f.). Local people remarked that the level of the river was unnaturally low; in fact no one could remember its ever being crossed in this way before. The conditions, certainly very rare, were unimaginable except during late summer, when the Euphrates flows at its lowest. Julian's campaign, on the other hand, took place when the river was rising to its highest level. Ammianus remarked, as the army left Callinicum at the end of March, on the swelling of the Euphrates from the waters of its tributaries; 'aquis adolescentibus undique convenis' (23.3.8). And so it continued; by early May, when the army encountered the flooding in the region beyond Pirisabora, the Euphrates had still to rise over half a metre before it reached its maximum. The inundation was progressive, and would not abate in time for the army to leave Mesopotamia by the same route as that by which it had entered.

The use of water to provide large-scale strategic as well as local defence of Babylonian cities was a very ancient device. The best-known instance is Nebuchadnezzar's Babylon, which according to Herodotus was protected by a large lake drawn off from the Euphrates at some distance north of the city (Herodotus 1.185). In consequence, the approach to Babylon was made more indirect and tortuous for an enemy planning an attack from the north:

> To strengthen the fortification of Babylon I continued, and from Opis upstream to the middle of Sippar, from Tigris bank to Euphrates bank I

VIII. The Invasion of Persia

heaped up a mighty earth-wall and surrounded the city for 20 *beru* [80 miles] like the fullness of the sea. That the pressure of the water should not harm the dike, I plastered its slopes with asphalt and bricks.[57]

On the reconstruction accepted here of the route of Julian's army, the emperor had crossed the inlet of what Ammianus calls the Naarmalcha (the Saqlawiyah canal) and continued his advance along the left bank of the main channel of the Euphrates. Crossing other canals drawn from the Euphrates, the army proceeded to and then followed what Ptolemy and other sources knew as the 'Royal river'; this, as we have seen, left the Euphrates at the same latitude as Seleucia. In this case the army, advancing along the Royal river by the ruins of ancient Sippar, will have passed to the west and then to the south of the area covered by Nebuchadnezzar's lake; yet it remains an intriguing reflection that the Persians defended their capital against Julian by recreating in more improvised fashion the water defences designed by Nebuchadnezzar for the protection of Babylon.

*

One major obstacle, a waterside fortress called 'Maiozamalcha' by Ammianus, still stood between Julian and Ctesiphon. The same place, not named but described as a fortification ('phrourion') near a city called Besouchis, was located by Eunapius ninety stades, or just under twelve miles, from the Persian capital (Zosimus 3.20.4f.).[58] It is clear too that the fortress lay by the Naarmalcha, but despite these indications neither its location nor that of Besouchis has been positively identified. This is in itself not so surprising. Habitation along the great waterways of Mesopotamia was often very intense, neighbouring sites being occupied successively over a long period of time. As with modern urban growth that absorbs nearby villages as a city expands along its lines of communication, it might not always be easy to tell by observation just when one had left one community for another, the whole district being a rather indeterminate mixture of urban and rural settlement.

The name 'Maiozamalcha' given to the fortress by Ammianus, however, raises a more particular problem. 'Mahoza' – 'market' or 'town' – was the Aramaic name for the seat of one of the four Rabbinic academies of Babylonia; two of the others, Pumbadita-Pirisabora and Neardea (the fourth is Soura), have already been mentioned in this narrative of Julian's campaign. Now Mahoza stood, as Talmudic references make absolutely clear, by the Tigris. It was because they drank the waters of the swift-running Tigris, said one pronouncement, that the people of Mahoza were so shrewd (*Berakoth* 59b, adding, in less complimentary terms, that they had blotchy faces because they indulged in sexual intercourse in the daytime, and weak eyes because they lived in dim, dark houses, while the women liked jewellery and 'ate without working'!). Mahoza is Coche-Ctesiphon, the twin city formed when Coche, or Veh

Ardeshir, was built in the third century to replace Hellenistic Seleucia (p. 141). The place-name 'Maiozamalcha' – the second element meaning 'royal', as in 'Naarmalcha' and the personal name 'Malchus' – ought to represent a fuller Aramaic designation of Coche-Ctesiphon: for it would be strange if unadorned 'Mahoza' meant Coche-Ctesiphon while *'royal* Mahoza' were some other place than the Persian capital. It looks as if Ammianus has misnamed the fortress besieged by Julian, either by simple error or possibly by confusing the name of the district in which the fortress stood with that of the fortress itself. A Greek source called the district round Ctesiphon the 'land of the people called the Mauzanitai' – that is, of Mahoza – and some such description as this may be the source of Ammianus' confusion.[59]

Eunapius' Besouchis, near which the fortress stood, also looks like an Aramaic place-name, in some such form as Bê Saukhê, 'place of branches' – just as Ammianus' Bezabde represented the Syriac Beth Zabde (above, p. 53). That it has not been located might again reflect the density of the urban development of this region, in which cities and townships present themselves so frequently, and under so many names, as to baffle systematic description. Besouchis must in any case be distinct from the strong 'castellum' near Ctesiphon assaulted and taken, with losses on the Roman side, after the capture of 'Maiozamalcha' (24.5.6ff.). Unnamed by Ammianus, the 'castellum' was identified by Eunapius as Meinas Sabatha and located thirty stades, less than four miles (Besouchis was twelve miles), from Seleucia (Zosimus 3.23.3). Meinas Sabatha is clearly the city known to the Arab geographers as Sabat or Sabat al-Mada'in;[60] far from being a mere fortified outpost, it is none other than Vologesias or Vologesocerta, Parthian Valashapat, founded in the first century by Vologeses I to outface Seleucia as a trading centre and obviously a major city. We should also take account, in forming our impression of the socio-economic character of this region, of the two unnamed settlements on the Naarmalcha whose inhabitants, not trusting their defences, had escaped through woods and marshes (24.4.8).

Al-Mada'in was the name given by Arab writers to this land of 'the great cities', the 'cities of the country of the Arameans', and we can begin to see just what was so remarkable about it. The whole region must, if we knew more about it, have been one of the most amazing exercises in urban development ever known in the ancient world, a staggering expression of a mastery of the arts of production, transportation and communications, achieved by social organisation allied to the experience of centuries.[61]

Ammianus' 'Maiozamalcha' was protected, like so many other strongholds encountered by Julian, by water as well as its walls. The army had to be conveyed across the Naarmalcha in order to begin the siege (Amm. 24.4.6), and Libanius adds a particularly vivid and picturesque detail: the place stood on an island and was surrounded by a thick bed of reeds, which concealed the path from the walls to the river's edge (*Or.* 18.235). After intense fighting, the place was taken in the small

VIII. The Invasion of Persia

hours of the third day of the siege by a famous exploit, a tunnel being dug to within its inner fortification. This achievement, and the daring of the three soldiers who first leapt out of the tunnel inside the city and were later decorated by Julian before the assembled army (24.4.23f.), was universally reckoned to be one of the outstanding moments of the campaign.[62]

While the fall of the fortress was awaited, an advance party went on to test Persian resistance to the crossing of the Tigris (24.4.31), and in the two days' rest given to the army after its capture, Julian visited the deserted site of Seleucia; nearby were palaces built in the 'Roman' style – that is, presumably in a Hellenistic style derived from the architecture of Seleucia – and the great hunting park of the Persian king, into which Julian let his cavalry to enjoy themselves (24.5.1ff.). Resuming its march, the main army crossed more canals, evidently irrigation canals derived from the Naarmalcha, and, under increasingly effective threat from the garrisons of Coche and other strongholds (24.4.31; 5.5ff.), reached an old, now dried-up and blocked channel of the Naarmalcha to the Tigris. Ammianus thought that this channel had been excavated by Trajan and re-used by Septimius Severus in their respective campaigns against Ctesiphon, and that it was itself called the Naarmalcha, but this view was mistaken. The channel with its control sluices ('cataractis', 24.6.2) was undoubtedly more ancient, excavated originally to take the Naarmalcha to the Tigris above Seleucia. What is more, Trajan had not actually had the channel opened, being advised that its level was higher than the Tigris and fearing that, once opened, it would cause the Naarmalcha to run dry and become unnavigable (Dio 68.28.1ff.). The cut had long been disused; indeed Libanius reports that its blocked inlet was cultivated – which is presumably why it was so hard to find – but Julian, who knew of its existence 'from books', had it cleared (*Or.* 18.245ff.). The waters of the Naarmalcha then carried the Roman fleet quickly through the channel to the Tigris, a distance of thirty stades, or less than four miles (24.6.2). It is Libanius, again, who notes that the inhabitants of the 'two cities', Coche and Ctesiphon, were apprehensive for the safety of their walls when they saw bearing down on them the waters of the Tigris swollen by those released from the Naarmalcha – fears for which, as we have seen, they had the best possible justification, for it was through just such a disaster that their cities had been formed as they were (*Or.* 18.247; above, p. 141).

Meanwhile the Roman army relaxed in an elegant and shady park near Coche, fresh with the beauty of fruit trees, vines and green cypresses; 'in agro arbustis et vitibus et cupressorum viriditate laetissimo' (24.6.3). The whole landscape, with its parks, gardens, retreats and frequent townships, has in Ammianus taken on a distinctly suburban character, reminiscent even of the ideal of a 'garden city'. It was here, in referring to the 'diversorium', or pavilion, in the middle of the park near Coche that Ammianus remarked on the violent subject-matter of the paintings and sculptures with which the Persians enlivened their buildings,[63] and this may be an apt moment to note that the word 'paradise' comes to us, through Greek sources, from the Persian word for a garden – potent symbol, both for desert- and for city-dweller, of peace and rest, reflecting however no innocent state of nature but the expression of a social ideology through highly sophisticated techniques of environmental control.

Ctesiphon itself now lay opposite and Julian, convinced as ever that all difficulties would yield to his touch, decided against his generals' advice to force a night crossing. A strike force got across the Tigris, a fierce battle secured the other bank, and the Persian resistance was driven back into Ctesiphon (24.6.4ff.). But the euphoria was short-lived. Julian's generals prevented their men from entering Ctesiphon in pursuit of the Persians, for they would only get caught inside (24.6.13). A note of sudden uncertainty is struck by Julian's sacrifice of ten fine bulls to Mars, which was rejected by the god (24.6.17), and for the first time the military aims of the campaign fall under a shadow of doubt and perplexity.

Perhaps the most striking aspect of Ammianus' description of the council of war now held to decide whether or not to besiege Ctesiphon, is the readiness with which Julian's generals were prepared to abandon as a 'rash and untimely enterprise' ('facinus audax et importunum', 24.7.1) what had obviously been the prime object of the campaign.[64] If the city really did seem, as Ammianus now says, to be impregnable in its situation ('situ ipso inexpugnabilis'), then Julian had clearly underestimated its capacity for resistance. He had perhaps been misled by the experience of previous emperors, who had found the place a relatively easy prize – though intelligence on the current state of its defences was surely not hard to come by. More ominously, it was believed that the Persian king, escaping from whatever entanglements had been devised for him in the north, was about to arrive with a great army (24.7.1).

It was at this point, in order to press further inland and away from the river, that Julian made his sensational decision to burn his boats and pursue the campaign without them, keeping only what would be needed for the construction of bridges. Protest broke out in the army, suspicion falling upon the Persian deserters who were now guiding it. The deserters, indeed, confessed under torture to misleading the army, and Julian's order was countermanded (24.7.5). The impact on the morale of the army, when it proved impossible to quell the flames and save the ships, was catastrophic; yet Julian knew that something like twenty thousand men had been occupied in managing and protecting the boats (24.7.4), and Ammianus seems somewhat uneasily to agree that, without the encumbrance, the army was more coherent and stronger for its advance into the interior (24.7.6). It would in any case have been impossible to haul ships upstream against the strong current of the Tigris, and it may be, too, that with the opening of the old channel to the Tigris the Naarmalcha itself had, exactly as Trajan had once feared, run empty and become unnavigable.

It is unfortunate that Ammianus' text may have suffered damage precisely where it would have enabled Julian's decision to be better

VIII. The Invasion of Persia

understood (24.7.2). Other sources mention at this point such important matters, absent from Ammianus, as the reception by Julian of envoys from Sapor;[65] and it was perhaps here also that Ammianus set out the reasons, which he later said he had given but which appear nowhere in his text as it now stands, for the failure to appear of the army sent to the north under king Arsaces and the Roman generals, Procopius and Sebastianus (24.7.8, 'ob causas ... praedictas'). It is therefore uncertain whether the burning of the boats, however symbolic it may appear of Julian's predicament, followed from a decision to advance further into Persia (whatever this could have achieved), or to retreat. Ammianus clearly believed the former, in showing Julian's eagerness to press on (24.7.6), and his impatience with his generals' inertia in urging him to release his grip on a country which was practically won (24.7.3). The decision to retreat by Corduene is reported in a different and later context (24.8.5).

By then, circumstances had changed still further. Procopius and his colleagues had failed to show up, while, as might have been expected, the Persians had burned their standing crops, the fires forcing the Romans to stay in a fixed camp and depriving them of food, and began to harass the army (24.7.7). Retreat by way of Assyria was impossible, as Julian and others made clear in argument to the discontented soldiers. The terrain was stripped, the ground sodden and flooded, the rivers still rising beyond their banks. Moreover, the whole land was filled with gnats and mosquitoes, rising in such clouds that, in Ammianus' words, 'they obscure the light of day and the glitter of stars at night' (24.8.3). There were also those cities which in his haste Julian had passed by without reducing, and which would now be only too happy to turn out to oppose his retreat.

It has been suggested that the later development by the Sasanians of the region of the Diyala river east of the Tigris, made possible by a massive and complex system of canal irrigation, was a consequence of the devastation and economic decline of the districts overrun by Julian's army in 363.[66] This view is probably an exaggeration. Unlike the feeble Abbasid rulers of the thirteenth century, unable after long decline to make good the destruction wrought by the Mongols to dykes and canals, the fourth-century Sasanians possessed the political organisation and will to undertake the rehabilitation of the land. The prosperity of the Diyala region should be associated with the further development of Ctesiphon as the Persian capital in the fifth and sixth centuries, a period which witnessed the highest degree of urbanisation and the most sophisticated economic organisation ever known in the regions east of the Tigris. Yet the damage caused by the invasion of 363 must have been extremely severe, no less from the flooding and the destruction of dykes and canals than from the ravages directly caused by the Roman army. No account of any previous Roman campaign against Persia mentions the tactic of deliberate flooding being used against it, and it is possible that Julian's most serious miscalculation in his Persian campaign was his failure to anticipate the readiness of the Persians to damage their own land in order to resist him. This was itself a consequence of Julian's successful diversion of Sapor to the theatre of war in the north, a strategy of which his own delay, because of the flooding, in reaching Ctesiphon had lost him the advantage.

*

Julian's army broke camp on 15 June, to try to secure retreat by the Tigris route to Corduene. For Ammianus, it was a moment of especial significance, which he registered with emphatically formal solemnity: 'sextum decimum Kalendas Julias, promotis iam signis, progresso imperatore cum lucis exordio ....' (24.8.5). The army had scarcely moved when a halt was sounded, because of the appearance in the distance of a cloud of dust or smoke. As to what it might be, opinions differed. Perhaps it was a herd of wild asses, travelling close together to deter attack by lions. Some thought that Arsaces and the Roman generals were arriving, attracted by rumours of a great siege of Ctesiphon: others, that it was a Persian force, lying in wait for the Roman march.

In the uncertainty the army encamped for the night in a valley near a watercourse, adopting a heavily defensive formation. The cause of the cloud of dust, which could only be dimly seen as the evening mists rose, could still not be determined (24.8.7).

At this point, Ammianus ends Book 24 of his history. He begins the next in unbroken continuation of the narrative ('et hanc quidem noctem ...'), proceeding at once to the suspense of the waiting army. The night was black and starless, and the men spent it (or as Ammianus actually says, 'exegimus'; 'we spent it') as one would expect in a tense and uncertain situation: no one dared sit down, or close his eyes in sleep, for fear. In the first light of dawn the metallic glint of armour, and breastplates gleaming in the distance, showed the truth. The king's army had arrived (25.1.1).

It is a moment as arresting as any in Roman historical writing, contrived with great craft, and it conveys what is most obviously characteristic of Ammianus' presentation of the campaign (of which it was, of course, a crucial turning point): the immediacy and sense of involvement deriving from his own experience of it, and his awareness of the dramatic significance of particular moments. The word 'dramatic' is here used strictly. From the very beginning of his account of the campaign, Ammianus wrote with explicit recognition that it was destined to fail, and that the emperor would die. From this recognition, his work draws a sense of tragedy which, carefully worked out in the technique of his composition, is what most clearly distinguishes his narrative of the campaign from others that survive.

It is with this quality of Ammianus' in mind that we may now go on to assess the relations between this part of his history and other descriptions of the campaign which may have been available to him. The question is not merely to what extent Ammianus may or may not have

VIII. The Invasion of Persia

used written sources to supplement his own observation, or for clarification on matters of fact. This would of course be worth knowing: far more important, however, is the way in which he used such sources within the framework of his own distinctive presentation of Julian and his fated enterprise.

(3) Ammianus and other sources

The manner in which a historian handles the written material available to him is always relevant to an understanding of his principles of writing and to any judgment of his reliability.[67] It is often the only control of these matters that we have, and since the procedures of textual comparison that are involved are relatively straightforward and objective, it is not surprising to find that much, especially of the earlier modern, writing on Greek and Roman historians is devoted to enquiry into their written sources. The method is most apt when a historian is clearly inferior to his sources in knowledge and judgment, when he draws his information from materials that are limited in number and variety, and especially when he is describing a remote period of which he has no personal experience. In such cases source criticism is less a method of research into the secondary authority than the recovery of original material that will, once recovered, become the object of study; so with the raising of the Greek historians Ephorus or Hieronymus of Cardia from the voluminous pages of Diodorus and – relevant to the subject of this book – of the history of Eunapius from Zosimus.[68] In neither case is the dependence on or the inferiority of the surviving writer to his source in any doubt. Both Diodorus and Zosimus were compilers or summarisers without valid claims to originality as historians, and both were without direct personal experience of the subject-matter of their books.

The dangers of source criticism when these conditions do not apply – as when a historian uses many different sources and types of source, or combines personal research and testimony with his written material – are obvious. As applied to Ammianus' account of the Persian campaign of Julian, the technique fails to encompass the complexity of a historian's problems in assembling and ordering information on a subject as large in scale, as well documented, and as controversial as this was. Further, it ignores the plain evidence of Ammianus' involvement in such earlier episodes as the suppression of the usurper Silvanus, the fighting on the Tigris front during the invasion of 359, the siege of Amida, as well as the Persian campaign itself. In his preface to Book 15 Ammianus promised to set down what he was old enough to have witnessed himself or could by interrogation learn from others, and nothing is more obvious than the depth of his interest in the personality and fate of Julian. It would be paradoxical if such a historian should, after such experiences and having made such declarations, produce an account of the tragic climax of the reign of Julian that essentially derived from other written accounts.[69]

This is not to deny that Ammianus made any use at all of other sources of information, and the Persian campaign provides an opportunity to consider some of the material which was available to him. The campaign was a sensational enterprise which attracted interest from many different points of view. Its failure and the death of Julian provoked reactions of extreme and lasting intensity, from the jubilation of the emperor's Christian opponents to the bitter grief of his supporter, Libanius. Libanius remarked that many men had come back from the Persian campaign with notes and memoirs on it. In a letter he complains that men who had promised to give him written material and verbal accounts had failed to do so, interest in the emperor's deeds having died with the emperor himself. Some soldiers, unknown to him before, had provided information about times and distances on the journey, and the names of places, but nothing worthy of a proper history of the emperor's achievements (*Ep.* 1220). Despite his complaint in this letter, Libanius did not find information hard to come by. His *Funeral Oration* in Julian's honour (*Or.* 18) shares common ground with other accounts in its narrative of the campaign but also, as we have seen, provides circumstantial details which are not in other sources and add touches of colour of their own.[70]

One of the returning witnesses of the campaign whom Libanius (*Ep.* 1434) shows to have kept notes on it, was surely known to Ammianus. This was Philagrius, who had served in Germany under Julian and was then the central figure in an episode for which he must have been Ammianus' source, since it features a confidential letter given by Julian to Philagrius, to be opened only under the particular circumstances which in fact occurred (21.4.2f.).[71]

Another such figure was Eutropius the historian, who accompanied the campaign, little though he has to say of it in the *Breviarium* of Roman history which he dedicated in about 370 to the Emperor Valens (cf. *Brev.* 10.16.1). Eutropius' book will have held scant interest for Ammianus, at least as far as contemporary events were concerned. Its author was however mentioned in Ammianus' account of the treason trials conducted at Antioch and other eastern cities in 371, in which he narrowly escaped the fate of other former friends of Julian (29.1.36). Ammianus could clearly, if he wished, have consulted Eutropius on the Persian campaign and discussed it with him – much as he surely learned from another historian, Aurelius Victor, who happened to be there, the circumstances of Julian's advance upon Sirmium in 361 (21.10.6).

That it should be possible to suggest the names of certain individuals with whom Ammianus may, if he chose, have talked of Julian's Persian campaign, is not particularly significant, for it is obvious that in the years after 363 the eastern provinces were full of such men, making their way home with reminiscences of what they had seen. The 'philosophers' such as Priscus and Maximus, who in Ammianus' opinion had so much to answer for in the advice which they gave to Julian, were doubtless articulate in narrating their experiences and justifying their actions, and there were many others. The Roman empire must in these years have

VIII. The Invasion of Persia

resounded with recrimination and with justifications of Julian's policy; both attitudes are reflected in Ammianus' defence of the Persian campaign, which he appended to his obituary of the emperor, and in phrases from handbills and graffiti denouncing Jovian which are cited in a passage of the Suda perhaps to be assigned to Eunapius.[72] The campaign must for a time have been the dominating subject of conversation in the streets, bars and dining-rooms of Antioch and every other eastern city. It would be unrealistic to limit Ammianus' contacts with witnesses of the campaign to those whom it may be possible to name and identify: the problem would rather have been to hold to one's own opinion among the welter of those expressed.

The issue is not quite the same in the matter of what written sources existed for Ammianus' possible use. Here again, far more was available to Ammianus than his modern reader can ever know of. In the second century, Lucian had satirically described the flocks of histories inspired by the Parthian campaigns of L. Verus, by authors aspiring to be a second Thucydides, Herodotus, or Xenophon; how true it was, he wrote, that 'war was the father of all things', if it had at one stroke generated so many histories (*On the Writing of History* [Libell. 59], 2)! The situation was no different after the Persian campaign of Julian. Yet Lucian's point would be missed unless most of what was written were rubbish; and in discussion of Ammianus, we may look most profitably at two particular writers of the many who existed: Magnus of Carrhae, of whom a summary of about 700 words survives in the sixth-century chronicler, John Malalas; and Eunapius of Sardis.

*

The fragment of Magnus which is preserved by Malalas is not sufficient to define his qualities as a historian. Yet Magnus was a real person, who stood in an intelligible relationship with Julian's campaign, even if he was not, as has been argued, one of the three soldiers who leapt out of the tunnel at 'Maiozamalcha'.[73] His native city, Carrhae, was crucial to Julian's strategy, for it was from there that the roads to the east divided, one going to Nisibis and northern Mesopotamia, the other to Circesium and the confluence of the river Khabur with the Euphrates.

As we have seen, Julian's initial strategy was to convince the Persians that he was about to launch a major attack by the northerly route and to draw the enemy to that battle-zone while he took his main army south in a rapid strike at Ctesiphon. Magnus' narrative made clear the purpose of the army of Sebastianus and Procopius to act as a diversion. He described Sapor's manoeuvres when he realised he had been deceived and, descending from history to romance, told the story of two Persians who allowed their noses to be cut off (in the manner of a famous tale in Herodotus) and were sent mutilated to Julian's camp to lead him astray into the desert and gain time for the army of Sapor to make its way south. Ammianus either did not know or did not believe this story, though he described how the burning of the boats was inspired by misleading information given by Persian deserters, and mentioned the guides to whom Julian proposed to entrust himself in a further march into the interior beyond Ctesiphon (p. 158). In general Julian's strategy, though ambitious, was not obscure, and one would not have thought that Ammianus, who offers an intelligible account, would have needed to consult Magnus in order to produce it. He mentioned the projected rendezvous of Procopius and Sebastianus with Julian from the point of view of the main army in its predicament at Ctesiphon, and the absence in Ammianus of any account of its failure must be due to a deficiency in his text as it survives, for he explicitly claims to have done so (p. 159). The only similarity between Ammianus and Magnus on which any sort of argument can be based is the description of the parting of the roads at Carrhae, and even this is not conclusive (below, p. 169f.).

A more productive comparison with Ammianus is the history of Eunapius of Sardis. Eunapius was a young student at Athens at the time of the death of Julian and never knew him personally;[74] but through his interest in medicine he later came to know Julian's doctor and intimate friend, the famous Oribasius, who made available to him a detailed personal record or 'memoir' (*hupomnêma*) of the reign – including, of course, an account of the Persian campaign.[75] Traces of the information provided by Oribasius have been found in the works of fifth-century writers whose own use of Eunapius, and above all that made of him by Zosimus, enables us to assess the nature of his work. Zosimus' epitomator, the ninth-century patriarch Photius, commented that he differed from Eunapius only in his brevity and greater clarity, and in his freedom from the extravagant figures of speech of which Eunapius was fond (*FHG* IV, p. 9f.). Photius knew and could compare both texts: his testimony is explicit and should be accepted.

The suggestion that Magnus of Carrhae rather than Eunapius was the source for Zosimus' *New History* can be discounted, not least because it contradicts the direct evidence of Photius. It is of course possible that Eunapius himself, writing some years after the Persian campaign, used such a narrative history as that of Magnus, especially if the memoir of Oribasius was of a relatively informal nature and Eunapius preferred also to work with a source that already provided an explicitly historical framework. But the state of preservation of the texts does not permit this possibility to be tested, and although we should bear it in mind we can seriously discuss the question of Ammianus' use of his sources on the Persian campaign only in terms of his relationship with Eunapius, as he is preserved by Zosimus.

*

We find here a detailed and precise narrative of the Persian campaign, which even in Zosimus' summary (3.12-29) is at many points a supplement to that of Ammianus. Zosimus produces the names of places

VIII. The Invasion of Persia

not mentioned by Ammianus or presented by him in different forms, describes incidents and episodes which Ammianus does not record, and offers many differences of detail and in presentation.[76]

To begin with discrepancies in the names of places, Zosimus records two settlements, Sitha and Megia, in the neighbourhood of 'Dakira' (Ammianus' Diacira, or Hit), which are not registered by Ammianus, and, further south, the towns of Bithra, identical with or near to the unnamed Jewish settlement mentioned by Ammianus (24.4.1); Besouchis, near which Ammianus' 'Maiozamalcha' was situated; and Meinas Sabatha. 'Maiozamalcha' is referred to by Zosimus as a 'fortress' (*phrourion*). Whether Eunapius also did this is not known, but it is possible that Ammianus' form of the name was itself based on a misunderstanding (above, p. 155f.). We saw earlier how Magnus of Carrhae, referring to the same place, mentioned the 'district of the Mauzanitai'; that is, the region of the town of Mahoza, or Ctesiphon.[77]

The names of places mentioned by both writers can appear in Zosimus in forms clearly independent of those given by Ammianus. The island fortress of Anatha is described by Zosimus as located 'near Phathousa', the explanation in this case perhaps being that Eunapius was referring to the settlement on the bank of the Euphrates opposite Anatha rather than to the site on the island. Ammianus' Ozogardana, where the Emperor Trajan's tribunal was shown (p. 148), appears in Zosimus as Zaragardia, and the city of Coche is given by Zosimus as Zochasa.[78] It is of course possible that the name has been affected in its transmission from Eunapius to Zosimus. As we saw earlier, the settlement patterns and nomenclature of this region of Mesopotamia are immensely complicated, and discrepancies between different authors are the least to be expected. Where they do occur, however, they are proof of the independence of these authors, one from the other.

A more substantial omission in Ammianus is the town of Phissenia south of Pirisabora, surrounded according to Zosimus by a ditch flooded from the nearby channel of the 'King's River' or Naarmalcha. This part of Julian's advance is covered by Ammianus merely by a reference to a journey stage of fourteen miles beyond Pirisabora, upon which the floods were encountered (24.3.10). Ammianus makes no mention, as Eunapius did, of Julian's determination and ingenuity in getting the army across the morass, nor of the 'palace' near Bithra which, for some, made their overnight stay in the swamps less unpleasant. He leaves unstated the source of the flooding, and located what he called the Naarmalcha well to the north, above Pirisabora. On the assumption that the Naarmalcha had more than one inlet to the Euphrates, Ammianus' account is compatible with that of Eunapius, but clearly independent of it.[79]

The forcing of the canal at Pirisabora, summarily presented by Ammianus (24.2.8), was described in detail by Eunapius as a major engagement. The Romans met severe resistance, which they overcame by a tactical manoeuvre inspired by Julian, and by the soldiers' tenacity and bravery in action. Eunapius described the difficulties caused by the muddy ground, which especially hampered the cavalry, and by the depth of the channel, as well as by harassment from Persian missiles. Julian himself has the motion of sending Lucillianus' task force of 1,500 picked men to cross the channel lower down, while Victor is to make a night crossing out of sight of the Persians, and effect a rendezvous with Lucillianus. The manoeuvre is carried out and the Persian defenders are taken in the rear and overcome by the combination of Roman forces.

The greater detail in this account, compared with Ammianus' summary notice, is evident. Ammianus mentions the Persian missiles and the crossing of the Naarmalcha on pontoon bridges, but he gives no indication of the difficulties described by Eunapius, nor of the manoeuvre by which they were countered. This is interesting, for Julian's military expertise and ingenuity are repeatedly emphasised in Ammianus' history, and 'scientia rei militaris' is one of the set of virtues around which his obituary of Julian is constructed (25.4.11). If Ammianus knew Eunapius' history and was accustomed as a matter of course to use it, why should he have neglected an episode so illustrative of the emperor's military genius?

So much for specific divergences – more could easily be found – in individual details and episodes of the campaign. The differences between Ammianus' and Eunapius' accounts can be explored in more continuous fashion in their descriptions of the earlier stages of the invasion. Eunapius began with a different selection of details from that furnished by Ammianus in describing Julian's march from Antioch to the Euphrates; this was, of course, a part of the campaign which Ammianus may not have known at first hand, if he joined it at a later point. Where Ammianus merely records that Julian marched to Hierapolis 'by the usual route' and from there moved on hurriedly ('propere', 23.2.6f.) across the Euphrates to Batnae, Eunapius noted that the journey to Hierapolis took five days and that this city was the assembly point for the military and transport ships coming down the Euphrates from Samosata and other places (Zosimus 3.12.1f.). The name of the commander of the fleet is given as Hierius, who is nowhere mentioned by Ammianus, and since the river Euphrates runs in an arc a good twenty miles to the east of Hierapolis, that city cannot be where the fleet was actually assembled. The apparent anomaly may in fact confirm Eunapius' accuracy, if, as Zosimus implies, he described how Hierius was 'sent on ahead' from Hierapolis while the emperor delayed there, in order to supervise the assembly of the fleet on the Euphrates, detaching him from his command in the land army for this purpose (Zosimus 3.12.1).[80] Ammianus explains how the assembled fleet later rejoined Julian below Callinicum (23.3.9). After three days at Hierapolis, Eunapius continued, the army moved on to Batnae in Osrhoene, where Julian received a deputation from Edessa, offering him a crown and inviting him to visit the city. The embassy is not mentioned by Ammianus, and Eunapius was mistaken if he believed that Julian accepted the invitation; in fact he refused to visit the city on account of the excessive Christian piety of its inhabitants, with which he had become acquainted as emperor.[81] This error may however have been

VIII. The Invasion of Persia

introduced by Zosimus. From Batnae, the army proceeded to Carrhae, where the roads to the east divided in the manner already mentioned.

Eunapius now gave a story which, if it was known to Ammianus, was rightly rejected by him. Having dispatched the army of 18,000 men (which Ammianus gave as 30,000 and Magnus of Carrhae as 16,000) to defend the Tigris frontier under Sebastianus and Procopius, Julian is alleged to have conceived a desire to inspect the army from a secret vantage point, for the sheer pleasure of seeing it (Zosimus 3.13.1). The story is surely no more than a rhetorical fabrication to enable Eunapius to describe the army, whose total numbers, infantry and cavalry, are given in this context as 65,000 men. The army then left Carrhae, as Ammianus also describes (23.3.6f.), advanced by way of various intermediate stations to Callinicum, and from there to Circesium on the Euphrates. Julian then crossed the Khabur and embarked on his journey down the Euphrates, followed by the boats carrying supplies and the soldiers guarding them.

Eunapius next introduced the fleet, with more discrepancies between himself and Ammianus (13.1-3). It consisted of 600 wooden and 500 skin-covered boats, with 50 troop-ships as well as 'other' (Eunapius may have meant 'another fifty') flat-bottomed vessels for crossing rivers, and many others to carry siege machinery and timber for building engines. The fleet was commanded by 'Lucianus' and 'Constantius'. For Ammianus, who described the fleet not here but earlier (23.3.9), its strength was 1,000 ships for transport, supplies and siege machinery – a figure differently classified and lower than that given by Eunapius, whose total of 1,100 excluded the ships carrying siege machinery. In addition, there were 50 warships and 50 vessels for the construction of bridges; in these figures Ammianus agrees with Eunapius. Their commanders, given by Ammianus in reverse order from that in Eunapius – and in reverse order of seniority – were Constantianus (a mere tribune) and Lucillianus. These, and not those given by Zosimus, were the correct forms of their names; although it is easy for such variations to occur in the process of transmission of a text.[82]

If Ammianus here knew Eunapius' account, or any other from which it derived, he was clearly not dependent upon it either in points of detail or in his disposition of the material. In locating his description of the fleet near Callinicum rather than after the crossing of the Khabur, for instance, Ammianus supplied a more subtly integrated narrative context than that of Eunapius. Instead of a formal enumeration of the fleet, on which Eunapius was actually more specific, Ammianus has the reader visualise the impact of its arrival among the rest of Julian's preoccupations; 'while he was addressing the Saracen envoys ... the fleet arrived, commanded by the tribune Constantianus together with the *comes* Lucillianus, packing solid the great width of the river Euphrates. It contained a thousand transport ships constructed in various fashions, carrying great quantities of supplies, weaponry and siege machines, fifty other warships and another fifty boats necessary for the assembling of bridges' (23.3.9). Eunapius continues by referring to Julian's address to the assembled army, which he locates at its natural (and correct) place immediately after the crossing of the Khabur, and mentions the donative of 130 silver pieces for each man which was made by the emperor (Zosimus 3.13.3). Ammianus has no donative, and the complexity of his presentation of the speech of Julian has already been noticed (p. 131). Whatever the explanation of his treatment, it has nothing to do with any use of literary sources. Ammianus is writing in his own terms, making his own stylistic and rhetorical calculations, and independently of any such account as that of Eunapius.

As to the marching order of Julian's army, Ammianus and Eunapius are in broad agreement, the main differences being of arrangement and presentation. Eunapius began with the names of Victor and Hormisdas, the commanders of the cavalry, and Arintheus, commander of the infantry, and then went on to explain the marching order, with the cavalry on the left (protecting the army on the side exposed to the desert, from where mounted raids might be expected) and part of the infantry on the right, while the rest of the army followed on, the pack animals being grouped in the middle. In his subtler, more flexible manner, Ammianus incorporated the names of the commanders in his description of the order of march, adding that the right flank of the army, marching by the river, was led by Nevitta, that Dagalaifus, Victor and last of all the *dux Osrhoenae* Secundinus brought up the rear (evidently in command of cavalry forces), and that the fleet kept pace, proceeding along the winding reaches of the river (24.1.2ff.). Ammianus' additional names and details of the disposition of the army are clearly important for the understanding of Julian's marching tactics. Such apparent omissions by Eunapius cannot be pressed, since they may be due to Zosimus' attempts to summarise him, but the greater freedom with which Ammianus presents his material is a significant point of contrast.

Both Eunapius and Ammianus noted the extension of the army as it moved into Assyria. It spread over seventy stades, according to Eunapius (Zosimus 3.14.1); 'almost as far as the tenth milestone' ('decimo paene lapide', 24.1.3) in the words of Ammianus, who thereby provides his description with a touch of traditional Roman vocabulary, such as we find frequently in his account of the campaign (cf. 23.2.6). Ammianus compares Julian's strategy to that of king Pyrrhus, who spread out his forces to give the impression that they were greater than they really were. In a similar allusion, he compared a tactic used by Julian in the march against Constantius in 361 with one employed by Alexander the Great 'and other skilled generals' when need arose; he had sent his army over the Alps in three divisions, to create rumours and give an impression of great numbers (21.8.3; p. 105). Whether this was Julian's intention on the Persian campaign is questionable. From the standpoint of an interested observer of the campaign, a different aspect may be stressed – the difficulty of securing a coherent view of the experiences of an army spread out over ten miles of country, with a fleet that because of the

VIII. The Invasion of Persia

winding course of the Euphrates must often have been completely out of sight and was sometimes deployed independently of the land forces.

*

If Ammianus knew of Eunapius' account, or any other from which it derived, he was clearly not dependent upon it. He omits places and some quite significant geographical details which were mentioned by Eunapius, and leaves aside opportunities to include anecdotes which would have confirmed his heroic conception of Julian; and where he shares information with Eunapius, he deploys it with a freedom of presentation, and sometimes with a rhetorical purpose, which differ from those of the Greek writer.

There remain a few passages where the subject-matter and similarity of language between Ammianus and Eunapius, even as preserved by Zosimus, are close enough to suggest a specific connection between them. The argument needs to be conducted with care. When two ancient authors share a known error, this may be inexplicable unless one derives from the other: the possibilities of error being boundless, an error shared is significant. Similarities of language where the subject-matter is the same and there is no reason to suppose error are much more difficult to interpret, and conclusions based on the similarities must often be a matter of judgement rather than of proof. In the case of Ammianus' relationship between Eunapius and other sources, a basis for judgment can be offered by setting out the passages in question, in translations which reflect the language and word order of the originals.

(1) The division of the roads to the east beyond Carrhae is presented in similar terms by Ammianus, Zosimus, and Magnus of Carrhae, as summarised by John Malalas:[83]

> ... and from there he found two roads, one leading off to the city of Nisibis [then held by the Romans], and the other towards the Roman camp (*kastron*) called Circesium, which lies between the two rivers, the Euphrates and the Aboras (Khabur). This camp was founded by Diocletian, emperor of the Romans. (Magnus, in *FHG* IV, p. 4; the words in square brackets were presumably added by Malalas)

> Now from that point two roads lay before him, one leading in the direction of the river Tigris and the city of Nisibis and the satrapy of Adiabene, the other in the direction of the Euphrates and Circesium (this is a fortress (*phrourion*) encircled by the river Aboras and the Euphrates itself, and adjoins the borders of Assyria). (Zosimus 3.12.3)

> ... from where two royal roads ('viae regiae') lead in separate directions to Persia, to the left in the direction of Adiabene and the Tigris, to the right in the direction of Assyria and the the Euphrates. (Ammianus 23.3.1)

In such brief accounts of a well-known geographical situation, it is not clear that any of these writers need necessarily have known any of the others. Although it is clearly possible that the versions of Eunapius and Magnus are related and that Ammianus knew one or the other, the similarities between them are not sufficiently precise to demonstrate this. Ammianus included in a later passage a description of the site of Circesium, as mentioned also by Magnus and Eunapius:

> ... its walls are encircled by the rivers Aboras and Euphrates, which form it into an area like an island. This fortress, formerly weak and suspect, was provided by Diocletian with walls and lofty towers, when he was arranging the inner frontiers on the actual borders of the barbarian territory ('cum in ipsis barbarorum confiniis interiores limites ordinaret') (Ammianus 23.5.1f.)

Ammianus' description has in common with both other sources the encirclement of the site by the Khabur and the Euphrates, but it is unlikely that he would have needed to consult either Magnus or Eunapius for the geographical nature of a place which he had seen himself, and whose essential defensive qualities lay in its protection by the two rivers. Further, Ammianus deploys his description of Circesium more freely than Eunapius and, as in the case of the arrival of the fleet near Callinicum, gives it a more closely integrated narrative context. It forms part of a small digression in Ammianus' account of the arrival of the army at Circesium at the beginning of April, and is followed by an explanation of Julian's delay there while he allowed the entire army to cross the Khabur before having the bridges dismantled, and by his receipt of the letter from the prefect of Gaul attempting to dissuade him from the expedition (23.5.4f.).

Ammianus' note, which he shares with Magnus, on the fortification of Circesium by Diocletian, is also freely deployed, being followed by an anecdotal digression on a Persian attack made on Antioch a century before Ammianus' time. In the time of Gallienus, before Circesium was strengthened and when the Persians could make raids into Syria at will, the people of Antioch were on one occasion sitting in the theatre, intently watching a scene from married life being acted in a mime. The wife in the mime suddenly broke the audience's concentration on the performance by a startling exclamation: 'Unless I'm dreaming, the Persians are here!' (it was evidently a bedroom scene). Turning their heads as one to look up, the spectators saw the Persian arrows pouring down on them, and scattered in all directions. In the sack of the city which followed very many were killed, and nearby places as well as Antioch itself were set on fire and pillaged by the Persians, who met no opposition and left without suffering any harm. Mareades, an Antiochene deserter who had led the Persians to his own city, was burned at the stake (23.5.3). The story of the deserter Mareades (or Cyriades) is variously told in other sources, but two particularly colourful details not recorded elsewhere – the surprising of the people at the theatre and the execution of the traitor – occur in

VIII. The Invasion of Persia

other Antiochene writers, namely in speeches of Libanius (*Or.* 24.38; 40.2) and an entry in John Malalas (p. 295f.) respectively. The latter adds that Mareades, councillor of Antioch, fled to the Persian through debt – he had embezzled funds entrusted to him for the preparation of racehorses at Antioch – and that his execution was by order of King Sapor I for betraying his own city.[84]

If Ammianus knew of Eunapius' or of Magnus' histories, it can hardly be shown that he depended on either of them for his description of the most obvious feature of the town of Circesium, its situation between the Euphrates and the Khabur. This, and his account of its fortification by Diocletian, which Ammianus shares with Magnus, occur in a context that reflects independent knowledge on Ammianus' part, and in the second case the personal interest of an Antiochene, which leads him to tell a story of essentially local interest, in a form and with a chronology which it does not possess in non-Antiochene sources.

(2) The second passage concerns the capture of the Euphrates fortress of Anatha.[85] The similarity of expression is here between Ammianus and Eunapius, as he is summarised by Zosimus:

> Sending Lucillianus against this fortress with the thousand assault troops under him, (Julian) laid siege to it. As long as it was night, the besiegers were undetected, but when day came they were seen by one of the men in the fortress when he came out to fetch water, and threw into panic those inside .... (Zosimus 3.14.3)

> At the onset of evening, the *comes* Lucillianus was sent by the emperor with a thousand assault troops embarked on ships, to storm the fortification of Anatha, which like many others is surrounded by the waters of the Euphrates. In accordance with instructions, the island was besieged by the vessels, disposed around it in appropriate places, the night mists keeping the assault secret and hidden from view. But when daybreak came, someone coming out to fetch water suddenly saw the enemy and with cries and shouts warned the defenders, roused by the excited din of voices. (Ammianus 24.1.6)

Later, after Julian had received the surrender of Anatha:

> he sent the men, with the children and women, under armed guard to territory under Roman control, and gave to their commander Pusaeus the rank of tribune and held him among his friends, having made trial of his loyalty. (Zosimus 3.14.4)

> Pusaeus their commander, later *dux* of Egypt, was granted the rank of tribune. The rest meanwhile were treated generously and sent off with their families and household possessions to the city of Chalcis in Syria. (Ammianus 24.1.9)

172   Part One: Res Gestae

The additional information provided by Ammianus is not necessarily significant, in that Eunapius may have been abbreviated by Zosimus – though some of Ammianus' details, like the reference to the later rank of *dux Aegypti* held by Pusaeus, the settlement of the inhabitants of Anatha at Chalcis, and the comparison of Anatha with other Euphrates strongholds, are characteristic of him. The discrepancy between the names given to the place by Ammianus and Eunapius has already been explained (p. 165); Eunapius was referring to the settlement on the bank opposite Anatha, Ammianus to the fortress on the island. It is however in the light of this and other discrepancies, suggesting the independence of Ammianus and Eunapius, that the similarities between their narratives of the capture of Anatha must be explained.

The possibility that the Greek Eunapius would have made use of the Latin history of Ammianus, even if their respective dates of publication permitted it, can be disregarded.[86] What needs to be accounted for, if the similarity of the parallel passages is agreed to require explanation, is Ammianus' use of Eunapius. The explanation is in the nature of the attack on Anatha. The fleet was dispatched ahead of the main army, leaving in the evening from a point four days' easy marching, say 55 miles, below Dura (24.1.6). Sailing with the current of the Euphrates, the ships covered overnight the distance of about 35 miles by the winding route of the river, arriving at Anatha before dawn, while the Roman army (as well as the Persian garrison of Anatha) slept peacefully.[87] The fortress was surrendered on the same day, and it would be late on the next that the main army would begin to arrive, having since the departure of the fleet marched a distance by land of about 25 miles. Anatha was therefore taken by the fleet and its thousand assault troops a full day before the army reached the place. Unless Ammianus had happened to be a member of the task force under Lucillianus, he could not himself have been in a position to observe its capture. He therefore referred, for this particular purpose, to the account of a writer who was in a position to tell him exactly what had happened. But Ammianus does not leave it at this. Having narrated from this source the capture of Anatha, he reasserted his independence by introducing the aged veteran of the campaign of Galerius, found among the surrendered population of the place. The old man himself told his story ('ut aiebat'), affirming to witnesses ('testibus adfirmans') that he had long predicted his return to Roman soil (24.1.10). It is easy to imagine the interest the old soldier would have attracted in the Roman camp – and to see Ammianus himself among those gathering around to hear what he had to say.

(3) A similar explanation resolves a third similarity between Ammianus and Eunapius, relating in this case to the capture of Diacira:[88]

> After some days' marches, he came to Dakira, a city lying on the right to one sailing (down) the Euphrates. Finding it deserted of inhabitants the soldiers seized the large amount of corn stored there and a considerable quantity of salt; and killing the women left behind in the city, they destroyed it so

VIII. The Invasion of Persia 173

thoroughly that no one looking at it would believe a city had ever been there. On the opposite bank to that on which the army was travelling was a source emitting asphalt. (Zosimus 3.15.2f.)

From there (Baraxmalcha) the river was crossed and the city of Diacira, lying at a distance of seven miles on, was attacked. The place was empty of inhabitants, but full of corn and pure salt, and in it we saw a shrine of great height, built on the citadel. When this city had been put to the flames and the few women found there killed, passing a bubbling source of bitumen we took possession of Ozogardana.... (Ammianus 24.2.3)

Diacira stood on the right bank of the Euphrates, opposite the main army as it marched down beside the river. Obviously, not the entire army but only a detachment of it was sent over to reduce an almost unoccupied town. As in the case of Anatha, unless Ammianus were himself in the party sent to reduce the place, he could not know from personal observation what was found at Diacira or happened there. Again, Eunapius offered a practical way of finding out, well-placed through Oribasius' memoir to give an authoritative version of what took place. And again, as in the case of the old soldier found at Anatha, Ammianus seems deliberately to reassert his own standing as a first-hand observer. The attack on Diacira, in which Ammianus did not take part, is described in the third person ('*invaditur*'); the capture of Ozogardana, which lay further down on the left bank of the Euphrates, in the first person ('*occupavimus*'). The lofty shrine at Diacira could be seen from over the river by Ammianus and the main army, as is also noted in the first person ('in qua templum alti culminis arci *vidimus* superpositum' 24.2.3). In all this, Ammianus distinguishes what he had himself observed and taken part in, from what he owed to others.

(4) The forced crossing of the canal above Pirisabora, which Ammianus knew as the Naarmalcha, was narrated, as we have seen, in quite different terms by the two authors – Ammianus being content with a brief notice, Eunapius giving a lengthy account of the difficulties of the terrain, the Persian opposition, and the Roman manoeuvre used to overcome it. The assault on the fortress of Pirisabora and its capture produce certain similarities which may be thought to show derivation of Ammianus from Eunapius. One in particular is persuasive, the experience of Hormisdas, who advances to the walls at the inhabitants' request to parley but is then rejected with insults:

Sometimes they requested Hormisdas to be sent forward to discuss terms, but then heaped insults on him as a deserter, an exile and a traitor to his country. (Zosimus 3.18.1)

Sometimes, urgently requesting discussions with Hormisdas as a native of the country and of royal family, when he approached they assailed him with insults and reproaches as disloyal and as a deserter. (Ammianus 24.2.11)

In their descriptions of the site of Pirisabora the two sources naturally have much in common. The place was there for all to see and enough time was spent there for an observer to note its obvious and most important features – the double walls and great towers of brick and bitumen, surrounding a high citadel, the watercourse on the northern side offering protection. But there are differences. Eunapius' remark that from half-way up the towers were made of brick and gypsum (rather than bitumen) gives a detail not noted by Ammianus. The watercourse protecting the north side is described by Eunapius as an artificial channel used also for watering the city (Zosimus 3.17.4): Ammianus regards it as part of the Euphrates (24.2.12). The difference was perhaps not clear to one simply looking at the site. The fighting lasted two days according to Eunapius, for Ammianus the best part of three, though the first was largely taken up with the negotiations involving Hormisdas (24.2.12ff.). Eunapius gave a much fuller account of the food supplies and arms taken after the surrender of the place, before the remainder, 'suitable only for the use of Persians' (Zosimus 3.18.6), were burned or thrown into the river. Ammianus is content with a formal note that the Romans burned what was of no use to themselves when they set fire to the town, 'unde necessariis sumptis, reliqua cum loco ipso exussere' (24.2.22). Ammianus differed widely from Eunapius in the number of prisoners taken; 2,500 against Eunapius' 5,000. Both writers remark that the rest of the inhabitants had escaped in boats, but Ammianus, unlike Eunapius, suggests that this had happened in anticipation of the siege and not after its conclusion; 'nam cetera multitudo obsidium ante suspectans ...', (24.2.22). The name of the commander of the garrison, Mamersides in Ammianus, appeared in Eunapius as Momoseiros; this was the man whose relatives were found crucified at Seleucia (24.5.3; cf. above, p. 133).

In his description of the site of Pirisabora, Ammianus, as in other cases, handles his material with greater freedom.[89] Eunapius began with a formal description of the site in which, as we have just seen, he presented certain details not included by Ammianus. Ammianus' information is deployed more selectively, and as it becomes relevant to his narrative. The only physical detail which he presents at the outset is the protection of the fortress by watercourses, which surrounded it like an island; this is relevant, and sufficient to give the setting for Julian's initial survey of the city (24.2.9). The description of the citadel, and of the construction of its walls in brick and bitumen ('the strongest means of building known') is deferred, to the moment when the defenders abandon the double walls of the outer city for the citadel, which on the northern side fell sharply to the waters of the Euphrates. With the exception of this side, which broke off an arc of the circular rim, the citadel presented the appearance of an Argive shield; 'cuius medietas in sublime consurgens tereti ambitu Argolici scuti speciem ostendebat' (24.2.12). The comparison, appealing to the visual imagination of the reader, is surely also intended to convey Ammianus' personal impression of the site of Pirisabora.

A closer study of the text of Ammianus in relation to that of Eunapius,

VIII. The Invasion of Persia

even as he is preserved by Zosimus, would no doubt produce more expressions and details in which derivation of Ammianus from Eunapius might be suspected. The purpose of this selective discussion has not been to establish for its own sake the likelihood of Ammianus' use of Eunapius but to suggest more precisely the extent of this use and its implications. These can be quite closely defined. Ammianus used Eunapius' history to gain knowledge of specific circumstances, such as the surrender of Anatha and the capture and sack of Diacira, which he considered essential for his narrative but was unable, for particular reasons, to have witnessed for himself. In other cases, such as the forcing of the canal at Pirisabora and the crossing of the swamps below Phissenia, he took no notice of Eunapius' presentation, even when one would have thought this congenial to him in the evidence which it provided of Julian's character and military abilities. On many occasions when he could have added from Eunapius more precise details of geography and narrative than he himself possessed, he did not do so. Sometimes he seems deliberately to declare his credentials as an independent observer after passages in which Eunapius has been used, and he deploys descriptive and explanatory material more freely and in a manner more integrally linked with his narrative.

We can now with more confidence see some of Ammianus' other details for what they are – the observations of an eye-witness, writing of the campaign of Julian in his own terms and from his own point of view. The stone irrigation sluices, built in the local manner, which caused the Romans' first experience of flooding near Anatha (24.1.11), the old survivor of the campaigns of Galerius discovered in the city (24.1.10), the walls of Macepracta, built in ancient times to protect Assyria from invasion (24.2.6), the engineer killed by a misfiring artillery machine, whose body was so violently shattered that it was unrecognisable, and whose name Ammianus was unable to recover ('cuius nomen non suppetit', 24.4.28) – these and many other passages show Ammianus observing and recording details for himself and using them to add circumstantial colour to his account of the campaign.

A class of details particularly prominent in Ammianus' history has been held back, as expressing that aspect of his writing which most clearly distinguishes him from Eunapius and his other Greek counterparts. It is in his moral and dramatic intention that the true measure of Ammianus' independence of the contemporary Greek tradition appears most clearly. In relation to this, the limited and severely practical use to which Ammianus put Eunapius or any other written source that might be identified or postulated, is an issue of secondary importance in the understanding of his historical purpose.

*

Photius, introducing his summary of Eunapius' history, remarked that the part of it relating to the reign of Julian was more like panegyric than true history.[90] We can see something of what he had in mind by comparing

Eunapius' account, as it is preserved by Zosimus, with that of a genuine panegyrist, Libanius, in his *Funeral Oration* for Julian (*Or.* 18). The advance of Julian is presented in these versions as a triumphal progress, punctuated only by the reduction of fortresses and cities and the defeat of Persian armies in battle (*Or.* 18.214ff.). Problems such as those experienced in passing over the inundated area south of Phissenia, crucial as they were in the failure of the campaign by delaying Julian's progress and allowing the main army of Sapor to make ground in its approach from the north, could be presented as difficulties, there to be overcome by the emperor's persistence, bravery and ingenuity.

It was above all the failure to force the siege of Ctesiphon, as Ammianus was uneasily aware (p. 158), that left something for the supporters of Julian to explain; and this they signally fail to do. Neither Libanius nor Zosimus offers any convincing explanation of the decision to turn away from the Persian capital, nor acknowledges the change in the prospects of the campaign which it implied. Indeed, Zosimus contrives to record the crossing of the Tigris and subsequent advance northwards without mentioning Ctesiphon at all (3.26.1f.), an omission which it is presumably impossible to attribute already to Eunapius, especially since the latter cited an oracle mentioning Seleucia (Fr. 26) and named a place called Abouzatha, presumably north of Ctesiphon, which is not in any other source (Zosimus 3.26.1). The withdrawal from Ctesiphon, presented not as a retreat but as a further advance of indeterminate purpose, is narrated in an atmosphere of continuing but progressively more unreal glory, and Julian's death in battle comes with total unexpectedness and is the sole cause of the failure of the expedition when it was at the brink of success. The aftermath, the agonising march back to northern Mesopotamia and the humiliating surrender of territories under duress by Jovian, is ascribed to the impact of this one accident. At the death of Julian, wrote Libanius, the Persians behaved as if their enemies had been swallowed up by the earth (*Or.* 18.271)!

This interpretation ignores the extreme predicament into which Julian had led his armies, and makes no attempt to allow for the skill and resource with which the Persians had after initial embarrassment recovered their position in opposing Julian's advance and hampering his retreat. Above all, it lacks that sense of the transformation of the mood of the campaign from optimism through ominous uncertainty to sure disaster which is so central to the account of Ammianus.

Ammianus from the beginning regarded the Persian enterprise, in all its ambitious splendour, as doomed to failure, the fates having willed that it should be so (23.5.4). In a presentation full of rhetorical contrivance he develops this conception, marking with heavy and often dramatic emphasis the moments at which the inevitability of failure became ever more apparent.

Ammianus' account of the reign of Julian is laden with signs and portents, which emerge with an ironic persistence from the emperor's own religious piety. His entry to Antioch had coincided with the festival of

VIII. The Invasion of Persia

mourning for Adonis, the air being full of cries and wailing (22.9.15). Ammianus' first mention of the Persian campaign is accompanied by a reference to Julian's excessive sacrifices (22.12.6) and by his decision to purify and restore the oracle of Apollo at Daphne (22.12.8). The omens become more sinister; the temple of Apollo at Daphne burns down (22.13.1-3), there is a shortage of water, normally plentiful springs running dry, and an earthquake destroys what was left of Nicomedia and part of Nicaea (22.13.4f.).

The catalogue resumes, after a description of Julian's worsening relations with the people of Antioch and a digression on Egypt, provoked by the discovery there of the bull-god Apis (22.14-16). The failed attempt to restore the Temple at Jerusalem is presented as an example of Julian's manifold diligence and energy in the midst of the preparations for the campaign, rather than as possessing in itself a particularly ominous character (23.1.2f.); but the death of the emperor's uncle Julian, following that of the *comes sacrarum largitionum* Felix, gave a sinister meaning to the imperial titulature displayed to the people on placards and inscriptions, 'Felix Iulianus Augustus', suggesting that the emperor would be the next to die. As Ammianus remarked, the outcome was not long delayed (23.1.5). When Julian entered his consulship on New Year's Day 363, an aged priest collapsed and died while ascending the steps of the temple of Genius with Julian and the members of his college. The death of a consul seemed to be portended – but of which: the older, or the senior in power? As it turned out ('ut apparuit'), the latter (23.1.6). There was an earthquake at Constantinople, which inspired expert advice to call off the campaign. The Sibylline Books at Rome were consulted, and warned that the Roman emperor should not leave his domains that year (23.1.7).

Ammianus not only registers the omens; he makes absolutely clear what they portended. As Julian left Antioch for the campaign, his parting threat to the Antiochenes was that when he returned from Persia he would not see them again but would set up his residence at Tarsus in Cilicia; he had written to the governor instructing him to make all appropriate arrangements ('cuncta usui congrua'). And that is what happened, for after Julian's death his body was taken to Tarsus and buried there in accordance with his instructions (23.2.5). After the disaster which occurred at Hierapolis when a portico by the city gate collapsed, killing fifty soldiers passing underneath and injuring others (23.2.6), at Batnae a huge pile of chaff stored there slipped, suffocating fifty of the crowd of attendants who had gone there for fodder. This was a 'woeful portent', wrote Ammianus ('illaetabile portentum', 23.2.7), and after it the emperor left 'sadly' for Carrhae; '*maestus* inde digressus ...' (23.3.1).

At Carrhae, Julian made sacrifice to the Moon, 'who is devoutly worshipped in those parts' (23.3.2), but was disturbed by dreams suggesting some unhappy outcome. As was discovered later, it was on the same night that the temple of Palatine Apollo at Rome caught fire, the

178 Part One: Res Gestae

Sibylline Books themselves only being saved by the great numbers of those who came to help (23.3.2f.). At the point of his departure from Carrhae, Julian's horse Babylonius was seized by an attack of gripe as it was led to him and fell, scattering its regalia. The occasion was saved by Julian's presence of mind. 'Babylon has fallen', he pronounced, 'and is stripped of her ornaments' – but he delayed a little before leaving, to confirm by sacrifice that the omen was favourable (23.3.6f.). At Circesium, the letter was received from the praetorian prefect of Gaul, attempting to dissuade Julian from making the campaign. It was in this context that Ammianus offers his most decisive comment on its outcome, that the fates, once decided, cannot be swayed by any human force or virtue (23.5.4),[91] and the army's departure from Circesium was attended by yet another 'woeful portent' ('omen illaetabile'). It passed the corpse of an official executed by order of the praetorian prefect Salutius because the supplies which he had promised had not appeared. The ships carrying them arrived on the following day, when the poor man was already dead; 'miserando homine trucidato advenit, ut ille promiserat, alia classis ...' (23.5.6).

Immediately, Ammianus describes the arrival of the army at Zaitha, near which the tomb of the Emperor Gordian could be seen, and its march from there towards Dura (23.5.7f.). During this stage of the march Julian is brought the body of the huge lion, which seems to portend the death of a king, and the soldier Jovianus is struck by lightning. Both omens provoked dispute between the *haruspices* travelling with the army and the 'philosophers' of Julian's entourage. Ammianus' sympathies are with the *haruspices*, who brought out their ritual books on the different classes of omen and demonstrated that the signs were against the campaign; but their views were 'trodden underfoot' by the philosophers with their objections (23.5.10f., 13f.; p. 126f.).

It may now become clear why Ammianus only at this point introduces the speech of Julian to the army, which was in fact delivered immediately after the crossing of the Khabur.[92] By holding it back, he has been able to pursue his sequence of omens continuously into the first days of the march into Assyria. In the disputes between the seers and the philosophers, Ammianus has shown not only that the campaign was doomed and that the emperor would die, but that this outcome itself was somehow a consequence of Julian's lack of judgment in listening to the wrong advice – or rather, we might say that his character as shown in this lack of judgment was the vehicle through which the 'fatal order', which had declared itself against the campaign, was expressed. Following these two omens in Ammianus' narrative (but in fact preceding them), Julian's speech to the army, with its air of hesitant optimism, acquires an edge of dramatic irony. In a speech that can be proved to be essentially his own invention, Ammianus has Julian hint at his own death (23.5.19), and the reference in the speech to Gordian's tomb and to his death during a Persian war connects with Ammianus' own reference to the lost books of his history, in which he had told of Gordian's youthful exploits, successful

VIII. The Invasion of Persia

leadership of armies, and treacherous murder (above, p. 132). For Ammianus, the price of some temporary narrative distortion, made good at the beginning of Book 24 of the history, was a price well worth paying for the dramatic effect which he gained by displacing Julian's speech from its correct position.

The omens, with Ammianus' explicit interpretations, pursue Julian through the failure at Ctesiphon to his death in the skirmish beyond the Tigris. The change in the atmosphere of the campaign, as the attempt on Ctesiphon is abandoned, is marked by the failure of Julian's sacrifice to Mars. The emperor's exclamation that he would never again offer sacrifice to Mars was fulfilled, for his death followed swiftly (24.6.17). His glimpse, of which he told his closest associates, of the figure of his tutelary deity, or Genius, whom he had first seen at the time of his proclamation in Gaul, now creeping sadly away through the imperial quarters, was followed by the appearance to the sleepless emperor of a shooting star. The seers, summoned before dawn in their last appearance in the history and on the morning of Julian's death, warned that nothing must be attempted that day (25.2.7). But this interpretation, and the plea of the *haruspices* for at least a few hours' delay, were alike rejected.

That Eunapius as well as Ammianus said something about the attitude of the gods towards Julian's campaign is implied by Zosimus' remark that as he left Antioch the sacred signs were unfavourable, 'but as to how this was so, though I know I will pass over' (3.12.1).[93] Among the Byzantine excerpts attributed to Eunapius is a fine hexameter oracle predicting the emperor's re-union with the gods after subjecting Persia by sword as far as Seleucia.[94] Yet Ammianus was surely always unique in the sheer weight of emphasis which he devoted to this aspect throughout his narrative of the Persian campaign and in the manner in which he allowed it to dominate his interpretation and to carry its rhetorical articulation. He constantly moves between one level and the other, the divine and the human. The abortive sacrifice to Mars is followed, in Ammianus' narrative, by the conference held to decide whether or not to press the siege of Ctesiphon, a conference overshadowed by the first open mention of the imminent appearance of the army of Sapor; then follow in rapid sequence the burning of the boats, 'as if Bellona herself had applied the torch' (24.7.4), the impact on the Romans of the Persian scorched-earth policy which was to deprive them of food, the book ending with the sighting of the mysterious dust-cloud and the next beginning with the dramatic appearance of the Persian army of Sapor (p. 160). For the reader of Ammianus, his entire narrative has as its counterpoint the premonition of failure, most clearly conveyed in the repeated signs of divine opposition to the campaign, which haunt the departure from Antioch, attend the successful early phases and the critical turning point at Ctesiphon, and escort Julian, the servant of the gods, to his ordained death.

CHAPTER IX

Legitimacy and Usurpation: Jovian to Procopius

Ammianus' account of the retreat from Ctesiphon is compelling in its expression of hardship, intensely conveyed, for it was shared by the author. The reader will also gain an impression of defeat and demoralisation. The army could no longer live off the land, since the Persians destroyed the crops (24.7.7, cf. 25.1.10; 2.1), and it suffered miserably from hunger. It was constantly harried by the Persians, who could attack as they chose, slowing down the Roman retreat and making it extremely difficult to establish secure encampments. The Tigris was in spate and the Romans were unable to make a crossing. There were desertions, and cowardice in the line of battle, which Julian dared not punish with the usual rigour (25.1.7ff.). Ammianus remarks more than once on the Persian unwillingness to take on the Romans in set battles, but they can hardly be blamed for fighting in the manner that best suited them – rapid attacks on exposed parts of the Roman army, and swift withdrawals before effective counter-attacks could be mounted. The Persians held every tactical and strategic advantage, and time was on their side as the physical state of the Roman army declined.

The catastrophe of Julian's death came early in the retreat. The army had broken camp on 16 June, but halted immediately when (as it turned out) the king's army was sighted in the distance, and it was on the morning of 17 June that the Romans got under way, with a foray in which a Roman officer, Machameus, was killed (25.1.2). The army moved slowly, spending two days at a well-stocked place called Hucumbra, and three days in truce after a fierce battle in which Persian losses were heavy (25.1.4-2.1). It was on the night of 25-26 June that Julian, unable to sleep, imagined that he glimpsed the veiled figure of the Genius Publicus 'creeping sadly away' through the tents and, leaving his bed, saw the ominous shooting star interpreted by the seers (25.2.3f.). The departing spirit makes a good story, either told to or invented by Julian's intimates (25.2.3), complementing its appearance before the proclamation at Paris (cf. 20.5.10). Yet a military camp at night will be full of silent, creeping figures who might lend themselves to this construction; Julian was perhaps simply looking at a deserter or, still more humbly, a soldier slipping off to relieve himself away from his tent. As for a shooting star, that is a common and rather beautiful spectacle on a clear night – not

IX. Legitimacy and Usurpation

pleasant, however, for an anxious man who believes in the gods and divination, and knows that he is in trouble.

On the next day the army was marching in defensive formation, though not very compactly (it emerges later that it covered four miles of ground). Julian was surveying the way ahead, unarmed, when he was told of an attack on the rear of the army. Grabbing a shield and hastening there (but not thinking to put on a breastplate), he then learned of an attack on the vanguard, where he had just been, and trying typically to be everywhere at once, rushed off there. The Persian onslaught was clearly a calculated effort, for a heavy attack of cataphract troops and elephants was now launched at the middle section of the army. It was repelled by a counter-attack and the Persians turned in retreat. Julian threw himself into the pursuit, shouting and waving his arms to excite his men, but also making himself conspicuous. His bodyguard, now scattered – Ammianus attributes this to fear, but confusion, and the emperor's own indiscipline, are likelier explanations – shouted at him from all sides not to expose himself to such a 'tottering mass' of fugitives, but he ignored them and was struck by a spear loosed from horseback; it grazed his arm, passed through his ribs and lodged in the lower liver. Julian tried to pull it out, but cut through the tendons of his fingers on the sharp edges. Falling from his horse, he was hustled away for medical treatment while the battle continued. Encouraged by an easing of the pain, he demanded weapons and a new horse, but the extent of his wound became apparent to him as his strength failed. He realised his last day had come when he asked what the place was called; its name was 'Phrygia', where, in one of those ambiguous forecasts so beloved of ancient historians, it had been predicted that he would die.[1] The place-name is not much use to the modern historian (it was perhaps not genuine anyway, or at best an approximation of some Aramaic or Persian name). The next location to the north reached by the high command of the army was Sumere, or Samarra (6.4); Julian died about fifty miles north of the site of Baghdad.

The death-bed speech now provided by Ammianus for Julian is in the circumstances one of staggering complacency, or so one would conclude if the reported words were in fact those of the emperor; if Ammianus' own, then they are a vivid illustration of the force of literary convention in a situation of whose gravity the historian was certainly conscious.[2] Now that the emperor was ready to repay his debt to nature (so Ammianus has him begin) how could he not prefer the better condition to the worse, given the universal belief of philosophers that the spirit is more blessed than the body? Death, he observed, was sometimes given by the gods as a supreme reward to the pious. He repented of nothing he had done, either in his years of obscurity or after he had become emperor. In civil affairs he had sought moderation, in military aggression or defence the most rational course of action (this is certainly not a full account of his motives in the Persian campaign, as Ammianus himself presents them); granted, the success and utility of his projects had not always run hand in hand, the ultimate outcome of human ventures lying always with the gods (as if it were not also an emperor's duty to match utility with the prospects of success). He would not hide it from his listeners that he had long ago learned by prophecy that he would die by the sword (so he should have been more careful about the breastplate). He thanked God that he had not succumbed to conspiracy, long disease or the death of a condemned man, but was departing in the midst of his glory, a noble exit; and he had not done the cowardly thing of wishing for death when times were hard, or shrinking from it when the right moment came (it is hard to think of a less opportune moment except, from Julian's point of view though of little consolation to the army, that his glory was palpably coming to an end in the chaos that now surrounded him). More he would not say, as his strength was failing; as for a successor, he would recommend no one, for fear of passing over a worthy man or, in nominating one, exposing him to mortal danger if another were preferred. So justifying his neglect of an obvious contingency, he made certain dispositions of a personal nature, asked for Anatolius the *magister officiorum* and wept when told that he was dead. He then fell to discussing with the philosophers Maximus and Priscus certain matters pertaining to the sublimity of souls, but was seized by an aggravation of his wound. Feverish and gasping for breath, he asked for a drink of water and died at about midnight. It is an eloquent but astonishingly unreal scene, and an effort to recall the actual circumstances – a tent in the desert, an army not only grieving (when it heard the news) but thirsty, hungry, desperate for escape from the dreadful situation into which its emperor had led it.

Ammianus' is by far the fullest account of the death of Julian that we possess.[3] He wrote from a personal acquaintance with the circumstances, and had clearly made himself well informed on many of the more intimate details. He told how Julian was carried from the field for medical attention, how the spear, wielded from horseback, drove down through the ribs into his liver, and he gave an adequate account of the development of Julian's condition. It is however in the medical aspects of the situation that we might expect Eunapius to have been particularly well informed, because of his access to the personal material collected by Oribasius. The influence of Oribasius has been detected in one most striking detail, preserved in a fifth-century writer who can be shown to have used Eunapius, the ecclesiastical historian Philostorgius (p. 101 Bidez). When the spear that killed Julian was pulled out, explains Philostorgius in a nice point of medical observation, the flow of blood drawn from the wound was accompanied by 'kopros', or faeces. A specific point of vocabulary in Philostorgius surely also derives from Oribasius, when he reports that the spear drove down into the emperor's 'peritonaion'. This, in its Latin form 'peritoneum', is the modern term for the membrane which lines the abdominal cavity.

Eunapius also preserved more precise information than Ammianus in the matter of the identity of the man who killed Julian. Ammianus specifically says in narrating the episode that the source of the fatal spear was not known – 'incertum <unde>, subita equestris hasta ...' (25.3.6)[4] –

IX. Legitimacy and Usurpation 183

but he later has Persians taunting the Romans with having killed their own emperor, having heard from deserters that Julian had fallen to a Roman weapon (25.6.5). This version appealed also to ideological supporters of Julian such as Libanius, who wished to impute their hero's death to treachery by a Christian Roman (*Or.* 18.274). According to Philostorgius, however, Julian's assailant was a Saracen spearman on the Persian side, who having struck Julian was himself pursued and killed. Indeed, Libanius himself in a later speech identifies Julian's killer as a 'Taienos', that is a Tayy Arab – what Ammianus would call a Saracen – instructed by the Persians to kill the emperor (*Or.* 24.6). Ammianus remarks on Saracens fighting with the Persians during this phase of the campaign; they preferred this service to the Roman because, in another triumph of tact and commonsense, they had been told that Julian, a warlike emperor, possessed no gold, but only iron (25.6.10). A Bedouin horseman fighting with the Persians, immediately slain in the battle: so much for Libanius' earlier argument that Julian's killer must have been a Roman, because no Persian had ever come forward to claim the reward offered by Sapor in a proclamation (*Or.* 18.274)!

*

The succession crisis following Julian's death shows the late Roman decision-making process at its most accident-prone – though to be fair, nothing like it had happened for a very long time; the dynasty of Constantine had been founded long before most of those present were born, and one had to go well before that to find a real parallel. The generals met (on 28 June) with the commanders of infantry and cavalry units and were divided, some looking for a good candidate from the survivors of the regime of Constantius, others for someone from the Gallic army establishment (25.5.2). In the deadlock they turned unanimously to Julian's praetorian prefect Salutius Secundus, but he demurred, pleading old age and ill-health. It was not a good moment at which to become philosopher-emperor and Salutius' reluctance, which has been variously interpreted, is not hard to understand.[5] At this point an unnamed soldier of some distinction ('honoratior aliquis miles') asked the generals, and Salutius in particular, what they would have done if, as sometimes happened, the emperor had committed the war to them in absence? Would they not put all other considerations aside in order to get the army out of its predicament? Then, if they ever saw Roman territory again, an emperor could be chosen by the united suffrage of armies of east and west; 'utriusque exercitus consociata suffragia legitimum principem declarabunt' (25.5.3).

It is a schematic, but not necessarily an unrealistic, presentation of the course of the meeting. As to the identity of the 'honoratior aliquis miles', Gibbon suspected that this was Ammianus himself, discreetly indicating his own presence (and good judgment) in the situation.[6] But this seems unlikely. At no other point in his narrative does Ammianus stand in such close relation to the central command of the campaign. He writes as an alert observer rather than an active contributor at this level, recording no personal exploit of his own from beginning to end of the campaign. It seems more probable that the 'honoratior miles' is to be envisaged as a respected soldier of long service putting forward the soldiers' point of view to the council: get out of Assyria, then think about an emperor, and do not waste time now in partisan argument and professions of reluctance. In fact, despite its appearance of practical sense it is not a particularly realistic point of view. Historical experience would show that it was very hard to prevent emperors being made in these circumstances, in fact difficult to control the situation at all; and wise heads surely knew that an agreement with Sapor would have to be made, and that nothing less than an emperor would be able to make it. The Persian king would wish to be sure that any peace agreement made with the Romans would be honoured.

It was all futile. The discussions had not taken long, says Ammianus, considering the importance of the matter, when somewhere else in the army a candidate was put up, clothed in the imperial purple and shown to the army. It was Iovianus, first in rank of the *domestici*, and son of Varronianus, a well-known general who had recently retired. Jovian was, says Ammianus, 'paternis meritis mediocriter commendabilis' (25.5.4), an expression one can ponder for hours without knowing whether the 'mediocrity' is to be understood primarily of the son or the father. The point is that Jovian was a familiar figure; his father well-known to the army, Jovian's accelerated promotion in the *domestici* had kept him in the public eye and near the emperor. More particularly, he had escorted the remains of the dead Constantius for burial at Constantinople, the sort of honorific duty that would tend to draw attention to a man, and for which one would need to look the part. Jovian was young, affable and vigorous, and nothing was known against him except that he liked food, drink and sex – all of which emerges shortly in his obituary notice in Ammianus, together with the remark that he might have corrected these shortcomings, had he lived, out of respect for the imperial office (26.10.15). Ammianus writes of the proclamation of Jovian as 'disorderly' ('tumultuantibus paucis', 25.5.4), and has a deserter who feared Jovian's enmity tell Sapor that it was accomplished by a mutiny of camp attendants ('turbine calonum concitato', 25.5.8); but it is hard to see how he can have known of allegations made to the Persian king. It is more reasonable to suppose that the proclamation was plotted by relatively junior officers excluded from the generals' deliberations. The army was about to move, something had to be done, and Jovian was produced; 'subitoque productus e tabernaculo per agmina iam discurrebat proficisci parantia' (25.5.5).

The reign got off to an unfortunate start when the name 'Iovianus', acclaimed back in the army, was misheard by those in front as 'Iulianus' – the difference, as Ammianus remarked, only amounted to a single letter, 'o' being for these purposes equated with 'u' – but they were quickly

IX. Legitimacy and Usurpation

disabused when they saw approaching an immensely tall, stooping figure in no way to be confused with Julian. The death of Julian made no difference to the sacrifices now made and omens sought; and when these urged an immediate start and not the delay envisaged by Jovian, the new emperor, though a Christian, concurred.

The army was soon under way, harried as usual by the Persians. On the approach to Samarra was discovered the body of the *magister officiorum* Anatolius, killed in the same battle as that in which Julian had been fatally wounded, and from which the prefect Salutius had narrowly escaped with his life (25.3.14). The passage gives a rare indication of Ammianus' own deployment in the army, for in the same place, he writes, 'we received' ('recepimus') sixty soldiers and some officials who had taken refuge from the battle in a fortification called 'Vaccatum' (25.6.4; 3.14). Ammianus was thus with the part of the army that now approached Samarra, at which a battle had already been fought by the vanguard; it is painfully slow progress in which an army cannot cover the extent of its own deployment in a day's march. On the next day they came to Charcha, then (on 1 July) a place named Dura, where the Romans were unable to move for three days through constant harassment from Persians and their Saracen allies (25.6.10). The soldiers were desperate and, misled by a rumour that the Roman frontiers were now not far away, clamoured to be allowed to cross the Tigris. Some Germans and Gauls, familiar from childhood with strong north European rivers, were chosen to swim across at night, and managed to get to the opposite bank. The army in general, frantic to make the crossing, was restrained by the promises of engineers to construct floating bridges supported on bladders, a forlorn project to which they now devoted their efforts while the army waited (25.6.11-7.1). The river was too fast, there was a lack of materials for the operation, and two more days were spent in miseries of hunger (25.7.4).

Having so vividly portrayed Roman misfortunes, Ammianus now tries, unconvincingly, to show Sapor as equally troubled, reflecting on his losses in men and beasts, the determination of the Romans and their desire for revenge rather than safety (this directly contradicts what has just been said about their desperation to cross the river); considering also the ease with which a new army could be summoned from the Roman provinces by a simple command for mobilisation, and the fact (which Sapor is presented as 'discovering') that another army was left in Mesopotamia, hardly smaller than the one that faced him now; while five hundred men had safely crossed the Tigris, killing its defenders and inspiring their colleagues to like exploits.

Only by such misrepresentation of Sapor's position can Ammianus justify his view that what happened next showed the favour of heaven for the Roman side; 'erat tamen pro nobis aeternum dei caelestis numen' (25.7.5). Against all expectation the Persians were the first to sue for peace, but Ammianus' assertion that they too were despondent in view of the growing Roman supremacy in battle is belied by the terms they offered, 'difficiles et perplexas' as he describes them. In the name of humanity, said the envoys, their most clement king was prepared to let the Romans return to their own territory, if Caesar and his associates would comply with his demands. The praetorian prefect Salutius and the *magister militum* Arinthaeus were sent to consider the terms, and in the four days then spent in negotiations, the Roman army suffered further torments of hunger (25.7.7).

In Ammianus' opinion, the emperor could have taken advantage of the time wasted before the Roman envoys were sent (this must mean while the attempts were being made to construct the bridges), to extricate the army gradually from Persia to the safety of Corduene, which Ammianus alleged to be only a hundred miles from where they now were. It is true that every day that passed was to the Persians' advantage, but the argument does not show Ammianus at his most persuasive.[7] The true distance to Corduene was nearer two than one hundred miles, and Ammianus had made it clear how the Persians could at will prevent the Roman retreat by the lightning tactics at which they were adept, in one case for four whole days. On that occasion the rumour that the Roman frontiers were not far away is described as a fiction welcome to men in desperate fear, and the army had hardly moved at all since then (25.6.11). Further, a dash for Corduene was hardly consistent with the physical condition of soldiers whose sufferings from hunger Ammianus repeats like an incantation; 'attenuata rerum omnium copia, herbis frumentisque crematis...' (25.1.10); 'commeatibus nos destitutos inedia cruciabat iam non ferenda' (25.2.1); 'furebat inedia iraque percitus miles, ferro properans quam fame, ignavissimo genere mortis, absumi' (25.6.4); 'dies quattuor sunt evoluti inedia cruciabiles et omni supplicio tristiores' (25.6.7); and, even after the signing of the peace treaty with Sapor, '... multorum, qui fame ad usque spiritum lacerati postremum' (25.8.1) – and so on, for the army's sufferings did not stop when, by agreement with the Persians, it had crossed the Tigris and marched unharassed. The seventy-mile march from the derelict desert city of Hatra towards the Roman frontiers was devoid of fresh water, and no edible vegetation was found; the army survived on the water taken from Hatra and was reduced to eating slaughtered camels and pack-animals (25.8.6). At a Persian site called Ur the *dux* of Mesopotamia and a tribune met the army with what was left of the food stockpiled for the force led by Procopius and Sebastianus (25.8.7), but this did not last for long. Soon a single *modius* of barley, if it happened to be found, might be sold for ten gold pieces at least – a rhetorical exaggeration no doubt, but effective, for it happens to be a hundred times the famine price of wheat (not barley) recorded elsewhere by Ammianus (25.8.15; cf. 28.1.18).[8] The situation was not relieved until the army reached the city of Nisibis, a longed-for sight; 'Nisibi cupide visa' (25.8.17).

There is no need to revert now to the terms and conditions laid down for the Romans' safe departure from Assyria; the surrender of the five Transtigritane satrapies, with fifteen Roman *castella* and Nisibis, Singara and castra Maurorum (25.7.9). Ammianus presents Jovian as

IX. Legitimacy and Usurpation

inspired by his fear of a proclamation by Procopius to agree without delay to Sapor's demands; yet Procopius turned up loyally to meet the emperor south of Nisibis (25.8.16), and Ammianus inconsistently remarks that Jovian's envoys achieved it as a 'difficult' concession that Nisibis and Singara be evacuated before they were handed over, and that the garrisons of the surrendered forts be permitted to return to Roman territory rather than become Persian prisoners (25.5.7, 11). The negotiations took four days to complete, during which the Roman army suffered extremes of hunger; it was hardly then a case of 'hasty' capitulation on Jovian's part.

Ammianus' final judgment on the peace treaty of Jovian is to question whether in the entire recorded history of Rome territory had ever been surrendered to an enemy by an 'imperator' or consul. Further, on occasions agreements made in humiliating circumstances had been disowned, even after oaths were exchanged, and war renewed (25.9.9f.). On the first point, it is no doubt pedantic to note Aurelian's abandonment of Dacia in the 270s, and various other occasions on which less significant territories, such as the 'Agri Decumates' beyond the Rhine[9] (p. 308), had been given up and never recovered by Rome. Tacit abandonment is not the same as deliberate surrender. On the second point as on the first, Ammianus' examples are taken from ancient Republican days, when agreements reached by commanders in the field might be disavowed by a senate that was the ultimate arbiter of the making and breaking of war and treaties. Present circumstances were very different. What did Ammianus really suppose should happen when the emperor himself was the commander in the field, and had left it with a thirty-year treaty of peace which only he, and no longer the senate, was competent to make? His implied suggestion is not only in principle (as is obvious) but also in practical terms most questionable.

*

Little more need be said of the short reign of Jovian, except to note the procedures undertaken to secure his position in the Roman empire at large. He had already, from Ur in Mesopotamia, sent agents to Gaul and Illyricum to inform those regions of the death of Julian and his own accession. They were to travel night and day, wherever they went spreading the rumour that the Persian campaign had ended successfully. They were also to deliver into the hands of military commanders and civil governors letters from the new emperor, and to convey back swiftly both their replies and what could be divined of their true sentiments (25.8.12). At Sirmium they were to find Jovian's father-in-law Lucillianus, a military officer also (like Jovian's father) now in retirement, give him letters of promotion as *magister equitum et peditum* and ask him to go to Milan and settle matters there.[10] Lucillianus did so, taking with him two tribunes, Seniauchus and Valentinianus; the second of these was also at leisure in Illyricum, having earlier been relieved of his duties in Gaul by

Julian (16.11.7). From there they made haste to Rheims to secure the Gallic army; Malarichus, offered the insignia of *magister militum* in Gaul, had declined that office, which remained in the hands of Jovinus, a distinguished general whom Jovian (if Ammianus is to be believed) would have preferred out of the way (25.8.11).

At Rheims a junior financial official for reasons of his own went to the army alleging that Julian was still alive and that this was rebellion against him, and Lucillianus and Seniauchus were killed in a military demonstration in Julian's favour. Valentinian was protected by an old friend, named Primitivus (25.10.7). The truth soon emerged, however, and Jovinus sent elite soldiers to Jovian to declare the allegiance of the Gallic army to his regime. Jovian received the delegation at Aspuna in Galatia, rewarded its members and sent them back to their service in Gaul. His general Arintheus went there also, with instructions to confirm Jovinus in his office, arrest the authors of the sedition at Rheims and send them to the imperial court. Valentinian was made commander of the second Schola Scutariorum, went on with Jovian to Ancyra and remained there while the emperor continued his journey towards Constantinople, with instructions to follow later (26.1.5). He was no doubt glad of this unexpected opportunity to resume his interrupted career.

Jovian entered the consulship at Ancyra with due ceremony, marred ominously by the screaming refusal of his colleague, his little son Varronianus, to be conveyed on the curule chair (25.10.11). The emperor proceeded to Dadastana on the borders of Galatia and Phrygia, had a good dinner, went to bed, and was found dead during the night. As to the cause of death, no enquiry was made. Over-indulgence, for which Jovian was well known, was thought possible, alternatively poisonous fumes filling the room in which he slept, which had been newly plastered (25.10.13). The likeliest explanation is carbon monoxide poisoning caused by fumes from a charcoal brazier; Julian had once nearly met a similar fate at Paris (*Misopogon*, pp. 340D-342A).[11] One must feel sympathy for the citizens of Dadastana, whose efforts to dine their emperor and to prepare elegant lodgings at such short notice (the freshly plastered room) had issued in such disaster. Rarely can the excitement of an imperial 'adventus' have collapsed with quite such awful finality.

Ceremony of another sort followed: of mourning while the body was prepared, to be escorted this time to Constantinople for burial, 'inter Augustorum reliquias' (26.1.3). And again the high civil and military officials met to choose a suitable candidate; 'moderatorem quaeritabant diu exploratum et gravem'. Some had hopes for themselves – which, given the recent history of the imperial office, must be seen as a tribute to human optimism as well as ambition. The process did not take long. The name of Aequitius, tribune of the first Schola Scutariorum, was hesitantly mentioned but turned down by the more influential of those present because of his abrasive and uncultivated character, an interesting point of discrimination; 'displicuisset ut asper et subagrestis' (26.1.4). Some support went to a relative of Jovian, Januarius, but he was

IX. Legitimacy and Usurpation 189

rejected as too far away (he was military commander in Illyricum). Preference then fell, with no dissentient voice, upon Valentinian.[12] One can understand why. He was the right age and his recent activities had made him known and given some indication of his resource and capacity for survival (he might easily have been lurking in unseen retirement in Illyricum, or at the other extreme of fortune have been killed in Gaul). Valentinian was at Ancyra commanding the second Schola Scutariorum, and while he was fetched Aequitius and a Pannonian colleague named Leo took measures to ensure that the army would not bid for a candidate of its own from among those present; this was a precaution conspicuously neglected at the time of the proclamation of Jovian. For ten days the Roman world was without an emperor, as was divined at the time by the *haruspex* Marcus, consulting the entrails at Rome (26.1.5).

Valentinian arrived at Nicaea on the eve of the 'bissextile day' of February, an intercalated day believed to bring bad luck, and he refused to appear in public until it had passed. Ammianus cleverly reproduces the delay in his text by inserting a careful account of the origin and vicissitudes of the bissextile day, ending after centuries of arbitration by priests with its regularisation by Augustus, following the calculations of Greeks; so, Ammianus concludes rather incongruously in the circumstances (except that in doing so he reminds us again of Rome and of the gods), 'with the help of the divinity, eternal Rome, which will live with the centuries', established the principles of calculation' (26.1.14). The next day Valentinian was presented to the army. Ascending the tribunal in full imperial regalia with a prepared speech, he was greeted with murmurs of discontent, the soldiers agitating for the appointment of a second emperor. The unrest grew, inspired, some thought, by the bribery of overlooked candidates but more likely the result of genuine anxiety in the army, fostered by recent events. Valentinian seized the occasion and after an address of unexpected authority was escorted to his quarters already secure in his position; 'ambitiose stipatum iamque terribilem' (26.2.11). He did however concede the need for a colleague to be appointed.

As to who the colleague should be, Valentinian again called together the senior statesmen and asked them their opinion. No one spoke – an ominous silence, since everyone knew that Valentinian had a younger brother in the army. The general Dagalaifus broke it, no doubt speaking for all when he told Valentinian that 'if he loved his own, he had a brother; if the *res publica*, he should look around for someone to clothe in the purple' (26.4.1). Valentinian was annoyed but kept his counsel, and after the army had entered Nicomedia, on 1 March he appointed Valens to the rank of *tribunus stabuli*; was this to ease the transition to empire, or did Valentinian still wish to delay, while keeping his options open? He continued to ponder, or to give the appearance of it until, on 28 March, after his arrival at Constantinople, he pronounced Valens Augustus at the military suburb of Hebdomon and, in a time-honoured gesture (Constantius had done it for Julian), took him up into his carriage as his colleague.

The emperors must have made a curious pair, if one had seen them at close quarters; Valentinian tall and well-built, healthy, clear-eyed and forbidding in expression, Valens dark, sluggish in movement, slightly pot-bellied and with bow-legs. This however is how Ammianus described Valens' appearance fourteen years later at the time of his death (31.14.7); advancing middle age does not lend majesty to everyone, and Valens perhaps looked better at thirty-six than at fifty. Though not personally distinguished, he would not necessarily make a bad emperor. The trouble with choosing the 'best man', as Valentinian realised, was that it left too many disappointed candidates; the advantage with brothers is that no one can question that this is what they are. No one challenged the elevation of Valens, nor doubted his submissiveness to the superior authority of Valentinian.

The emperors spent the summer quietly, except for a feverish illness affecting them both and for a time bringing the supporters of Julian under suspicion; and towards the end of the year they went together to the imperial residence of Mediana just outside Naissus (26.5.1). There they split the empire, distributing generals, army and palace staff between them – Ammianus referring in very exact terms to the categories of the division; 'partiti sunt comites ... et militares partiti sunt numeri ... diviso palatio' (26.5.1-4). This was all done according to the wishes of Valentinian, who chose the west and went to Milan to hold the consulship of 365 while Valens went to Constantinople as his colleague (26.5.2ff.). Of the generals claimed by Valentinian the most important for future events was Aequitius as *comes* of Illyricum.

The division of the empire is rather succinctly described by Ammianus, and it is easy not to appreciate what a significant undertaking it was. Traces of the division of the 'comitatensian' or 'field' army can still be detected in the *Notitia Dignitatum*, which lists the units of this army as they were after a further generation's often turbulent use. Existing units were divided in two, the new formations, which were no doubt intended to be brought up to regular strength by intensive recruitment, bearing the titles 'seniores' and 'iuniores' associated respectively with Valentinian in the west and with Valens in the east. A mark of the division appears almost immediately in Ammianus. Among the units acquired by Procopius at the outset of his rebellion of 365 were the 'Divitenses Tungrecanique Iuniores' (26.6.12; the term 'Iuniores' is to be understood of both units). Sent by Valens to meet an anticipated Gothic invasion in Thrace, they were intercepted and used by Procopius in his proclamation. Their counterparts, the Divitenses and Tungrecani Seniores, take part in Valentinian's early Alamannic campaigns, contemporaneous with the rebellion of Procopius (27.1.2), and in the early fifth century are listed, still together and now serving in Italy under the command of the *magister peditum*, in the western *Notitia*.[13] The Divitenses and Tungrecani Iuniores are nowhere to be found, in eastern or in western *Notitia*. They had either been disbanded for treason by Valens, or else were among those units annihilated at the battle of Hadrianople. The year 395 is often

IX. Legitimacy and Usurpation 191

taken as that in which the Roman empire was divided into eastern and western 'partes', leading to the separate and divergent developments of each in the post-Roman period. In the closer perspective of the late empire itself, the division of 364 was quite as significant.

*

From the death of Julian until the accession of Valentinian and Valens less than a year later, Ammianus has twice described, with much circumstantial detail, the transfer and establishment of imperial power in the late Roman world. He says much about the legitimacy of power, the diffusion of information and rumour, the control and deception of public opinion that attended the transfer of power, about political ambition and the workings of chance. The modern historian of Ammianus' time has nothing remotely comparable at his disposal. And it is not yet over, for even before Valentinian had settled down to the wars against the Alamanni to which he had elected to give his attention, and before Valens had left Asia Minor for the eastern frontier, rebellion had broken out at Constantinople. The usurpation of Procopius repays attention, not only as a most elegantly constructed narrative but as a commentary on imperial power no less telling than the legitimate accessions described so far.[14]

To begin as Ammianus does with the individual, Procopius was an introverted, taciturn man, gloomy in manner and strict, not to say repressed, in his personal behaviour. Though not marked by any particular disability, he would probably not have advanced far in the imperial government, if he had not been connected with the imperial family. But as he was so connected, he rose high in the ranks of *tribuni et notarii*. He took part in Constantius' second embassy of 358 to Persia (Ammianus has him responsible for the famous coded message in the sword scabbard sent to Ursicinus), and under Julian was at the rank of *comes* put in joint command of the troops sent to the northern sector of the Mesopotamian frontier during the Persian campaign (above, p. 138). The rendezvous which they were supposed to effect with the main army of Julian failed, however, and Procopius and his colleague managed only to meet the Roman army, now the army of Jovian, on its return across the desert (p. 186f.). Procopius was given the duty of escorting the body of Julian for burial at Tarsus, after which he may have reported back to Jovian and then retired to his family estates in the territory of Cappadocian Caesarea. This at least is the version of Zosimus, derived from Eunapius, but Ammianus makes Procopius go immediately into hiding without returning to Jovian, for fear that he was being hunted down by the new emperor; 'nec inveniri usquam potuit studio quaesitus ingenti' (25.9.13). There is every reason to believe Ammianus' account rather than that of Eunapius.[15] A dangerous rumour was abroad that Julian had named Procopius for the succession (despite Ammianus' explicit assertion that Julian had made no such nomination), a rumour that will scarcely have been quieted by his selection for the ceremonious duty of escorting the remains of the dead emperor for burial. Jovian had himself as *primicerius domesticorum* performed the same duty for the remains of Constantius, and he was now emperor; these duties tended to put one in the public eye. Procopius had also heard (who had not?) of the fate of another Jovianus, a hero of the storming of 'Maiozamalcha'; behaving with foolish indiscretion after the death of Julian, he had been escorted from dinner in the camp at Nisibis, hurled down a well and buried with stones (25.8.18). There was clearly much to be said for not being in the public eye.

Ammianus' description of the usurpation of Procopius is a minor masterpiece of construction, falling into several stages which are well represented by the modern chapter divisions of his text. The first phase, discussed in more detail below, introduces Procopius and narrates the earliest stages of his rise and proclamation (26.6). The second explains the manoeuvres by which Procopius established a civil and military regime and the initial response of Valens – both sides acting with a hesitancy and confusion quite understandable in the circumstances (26.7). Next (26.8) is a phase of success for Procopius as he secured Bithynia, Pontus and the Hellespont and began to extend his control into Asia. In an act of rash over-confidence, Procopius offended the retired general Arbetio, who was provoked to lend his authority to the cause of Valens; and by the spring of 366 Valens, having organised his response with effective support from the commanders of the east and of Illyricum, overcame Procopius, whose supporters handed him over for execution to Valens near Nacolia in Phrygia (26.9). Then are narrated the subsidiary proclamation of Marcellus and its prompt suppression by Aequitius, commander in Illyricum, followed by a description of, and reflections on, the judicial enquiries that were the natural sequel to the civil war. The book actually ends (27.10.15f.) with a description of the earthquake and tidal wave of 365 and the destruction wrought by them. The effect, surely deliberate, is to suggest a counterpart in the natural elements to the political turmoil among humans, and Ammianus is able to make Book 26, after its frantic activity and transfers of power, close quietly with his own role in later years as observer of the ship cast two miles inland by the tidal wave at Mothone in Laconia. 'Ut nos transeundo conspeximus' (26.10.19); it is like the signature on a painting.[16]

Ammianus has created a dramatic structure of classic type from the historical circumstances of the rebellion of Procopius. What is remarkable is the manner in which he has been able to convey this effect by artful deployment of the factual material available to him. This is particularly evident in the first of the phases mentioned above, describing the earlier career of Procopius, his disappearance after the accession of Jovian, and his proclamation at Constantinople. Ammianus begins with Procopius' background and earlier career, explaining how after Julian's death he came to be suspected and sought by the new emperor. He therefore goes into hiding, suffering hunger, squalor, and a life without

IX. Legitimacy and Usurpation

human contact (and so, if this is taken literally, beyond the reach of authentic evidence as to his activities), until he decides to seek refuge with an old friend living at Chalcedon. From there he begins to make visits to Constantinople. Ammianus' claim that Procopius' unshaven face and emaciated look made him physically unrecognisable (like a spy) involves an element of romance, for his friend was a former soldier, now a senator of Constantinople, who could no doubt afford to look after his friend; but the fact of the visits to the capital was beyond doubt, for it was established, as Ammianus specifically notes, in the enquiries that followed his fall (26.6.5). The statement that Procopius used the visits to gather rumours of discontent about Valens, though of its nature beyond specific documentation, provides a link between Procopius' movements bringing him to Constantinople incognito, and a digression on the state of opinion there, particularly hostile to Valens' father-in-law Petronius, a military officer suddenly raised to patrician rank. Petronius' eagerness to raise money led him to search out debts as far back as the reign of Aurelian, and to torture, and to fine quadruple, men who owed tax or were claimed to owe it (26.6.7). Ammianus is careful to cover all sectors of opinion in his description of the complaints; rich and poor houses alike were closed, both provincials and military men were afraid of worse to come, and there was a widespread wish, at present whispered only darkly, for change, 'with the help of the Supreme Power' (26.6.9). Ammianus admits some literary embellishment to his picture, in the form of comparisons of Petronius with the prefects Cleander and Plautianus under their emperors Commodus and Septimius Severus, but he guides the digression firmly back to Procopius with the reminder that he observed all these things from his hiding-place; 'quae Procopius latenter accipiens ...' (26.6.10). Narrative and explanatory digression, drawn together into a connected whole; it is a beautifully ingenious piece of writing that stays strictly within the bounds of authentic history.

For the time being Procopius lay low, 'like a beast of prey waiting to leap on its victim' (26.6.10), but the opportunity for action soon arose. It is an opportunity also for Ammianus to broaden his narrative, which he does by recalling Valens' departure from Constantinople for the east at the end of the previous winter (26.6.11). On the journey Valens was informed of a Gothic threat to the Danube frontier, and dispatched part of his army to meet it. It was these troops, the Divitenses and Tungrecani Iuniores, that were solicited by Procopius as they passed through Constantinople, spending two days there in the usual fashion; they were billetted in the Anastasian Baths, named after a sister of Constantine (26.6.12, 14). We have already seen how up to date is Ammianus' designation of these units (p. 190). Their arrival at Constantinople not only provides Procopius with the opportunity to initiate his usurpation, but from the point of view of Ammianus' narrative links the pretender with the wider military situation.

Procopius' elevation by these troops is described in terms designed to emphasise the ill-fated nature of the enterprise; it is characterised as a ridiculous piece of burlesque, as Procopius is dragged to the tribunal pale-faced and trembling, clothed in a parody of the imperial vestments and looking more like a slave apprentice than an emperor (p. 236f.). In portentous language derived from a well-known passage of Sallust, Ammianus drives home the absurdity of the occasion, and piles on dramatic colouring to emphasise its doomed outcome.[17] Procopius is presented as a 'disturber of public tranquillity' ('quietis publicae turbatorem'), although this can scarcely have been evident, as Ammianus claims it to have been, at the time of his promotion to the rank of *comes* by Julian; his withdrawn temperament, as there described, does not make Procopius look like a potential usurper (26.6.1). His proclamation is a hollow image of the real thing, Procopius trembling with fear on a platform to which he had been taken by his soldiers as if he were their captive; 'in modum obsessi' (26.6.14). As they escorted Procopius through the narrow streets, the soldiers protected him by holding their shields over his head to ward off stones and tiles that they feared might be hurled down at them from roof-tops. As they did so, their shields clashed together 'mournfully'; 'horrenti fragore scutorum lugubre concrepantium' (26.6.16). Ammianus surely means us to recall his descriptions of how soldiers expressed their sentiments in parade-ground demonstrations. They declared their support for the elevation of Julian as Caesar by clashing their shields against their armour, 'horrendo fragore' (15.8.15). They greeted Julian's speech on the occasion of his proclamation as Augustus by fiercely clashing spears against their shields, 'hastis feriendo clipeos sonitu adsurgens ingenti' (20.5.8), and another speech of Julian, as he set out against Constantius, was received by the soldiers 'immani scutorum fragore' (21.5.9). In their efforts to protect their leader from physical harm, Procopius' soldiers unwittingly produced, as it were, an ominous variant of these noisy demonstrations: '*lugubre* concrepantium'.

The people's reaction to Procopius' appearance was indifferent, in so far as they were not motivated by a normal desire among common folk for novelty and change – together with dislike of Petronius, of whom Ammianus adds an effective reminder at this point (26.6.17). The usurper's words are heard in an 'unhappy silence' ('silentium triste'), though one might wonder whether the silence was not simply attentive, and the acclamations in his favour begin hesitantly, led by men bribed for the purpose (26.6.18). Acclamations were normally initiated by cheer-leaders, and Ammianus is unlikely to have had specific information that they had been paid by Procopius, however safe it was to assume it. Procopius then enters the senate, which is described as being ill-attended, and only by men of inferior distinction, no 'clarissimi' being present. The proclamation, arranged at overnight meetings among the military officers concerned, was early in the day and not expected by anyone; Procopius could not expect both the element of surprise and a crowded senate waiting to greet him. He then hurriedly entered the imperial palace 'with ill-omened footsteps'; 'palatium pessimo pede

IX. Legitimacy and Usurpation

festinatis passibus introiit' (26.6.18). The date, we happen to know from another source, was 28 September 365.[18] Ammianus concludes the section with historical parallels, for the benefit of those who could not believe that events so ridiculous and embarked upon so incautiously could produce such woeful disasters to the state; 'irrisione digna principia incaute coepta et temere, ad ingemiscendas erupisse rei publicae clades' (26.6.19).

For all its rhetorical colour, so cleverly worked into the texture of his narrative, Ammianus' account of the rebellion is as it progresses a model of exact historical analysis. He exposes the 'anatomy' of power, seen in its civil and military, its strategic, financial and geographical dimensions, and with a considerable and most interesting attention to the modes and limitations of communications between individuals and bodies of men, and between different regions of the empire. This last emphasis is not surprising, if we recall some of Ammianus' own experiences as a serving officer under Constantius. At times, orders given in the best of faith by a distant authority could seem incomprehensible to recipients closer to the field of operations (p. 41).

After his proclamation, Procopius set about the selection of a civil and military administration, choosing first a prefect of Constantinople, a *magister officiorum* and a pair of generals, then a praetorian prefect, and securing the arrest of supporters of Valens (26.7.4ff.); this was all done quickly, not to omit any means of causing fear and apprehension among his opponents (26.7.4). Ammianus remarks on the motivation of the men who now came forward to offer service. They were from the lowest social ranks, driven by desperation and blind ambition, together with men of good birth who were about to fall low, some to exile or death (26.7.7). At the outset of the rebellion, small-time profiteers, men who served or had served in the palace, and some retired soldiers, joined Procopius, either willingly or under some sort of compulsion: others, who did not like the look of things, took themselves off to the camp of Valens. Among these was the *notarius* Sophronius, the first to reach Valens at Caesarea and inform him of the uprising: perhaps he was also an informant of Ammianus, who mentions that he was later – in about 382 – prefect of Constantinople (26.7.1-2).[19] There were also the grievances against Petronius, twice already and now for a third time mentioned by Ammianus. These united rich and poor, civil and military, against the regime of Valens (26.6.9, 17; 8.14).

Ammianus explicitly distinguishes between the formation of an administrative establishment, which he calls 'factio' or 'party', and the assembling of military support (26.7.8). In this matter Valens played helplessly into Procopius' hands, for in addition to the Divitenses and Tungrecani Iuniores responsible for his proclamation, more (unnamed) units of horse and foot also passed through Constantinople on their way to Thrace, and were won over (26.7.9). The motives of the soldiers are presented with a different emphasis from those of Procopius' civilian supporters. Swayed naturally by money and the promise of rewards

(26.6.13; 7.9), they were susceptible also to Procopius' prestige and connections. He gained the Divitenses and Tungrecani by approaching men among their number whom he already knew, and accepting their promises to bring over the rest (26.6.12f.). No doubt his acquaintance with them went back to the Persian campaign of Julian. Still more interesting is the effect of Procopius' claim to be linked with the house of Constantine.[20] He took around with him the posthumous baby daughter of Constantius, and was sometimes also accompanied by her mother, Constantius' second wife Faustina. Their presence helped Procopius win over the second of the groups of troop units referred to by Ammianus (26.7.10), and they were with him too in the military campaign of early 366 (26.9.3). In a remarkable early *coup* near Nicaea, Procopius was able to win over more of Valens' troops, the Iovii and Victores (again, though Ammianus does not say so, the 'Iuniores' of those names), by running before their lines, greeting a soldier called Vitalianus and appealing to him to abandon the 'unknown emperors' whom he now served in favour of a representative of the old regime (26.7.16). He also received help, too late in the event, from three thousand Goths, they too attracted by the reputation and name of Constantius (26.10.3).[21]

Ammianus shows the importance of finance, both by incidental allusion and by deliberate statement. An agent of Valens, sent to Nicomedia for money to pay the troops of the eastern garrisons, found the city (and its mint) already in the hands of Procopius and made haste for Cyzicus, where Valens' *comes domesticorum* Serenianus had been sent to guard the treasuries (26.8.7). The city was powerfully fortified, but its harbour was penetrated by the valorous exploit of the tribune Aliso, Serenianus being captured and imprisoned at Nicaea (26.8.9f.). Having secured these cities, with Helenopolis, Nicaea and Chalcedon, Procopius was master of Bithynia. He now cast his eyes upon Asia, and to win over its wealthy cities sent there, in an ominous expression, men 'skilled in extracting gold'; 'eruendi peritos auri' (26.8.14). Ammianus regarded this phase of the campaign as blunting Procopius' effort, begun with such energy but now allowed to fade. It is true that Valens was able to regroup his forces in the meantime, but he would have done that in any case, being secure in his control of the east and not dislodged from the possession of Anatolia. Winter had come, and no one would advance then to meet him. There was little choice for Procopius but to embark upon a period of consolidation, and an expansion of influence to the rich cities of Asia by what one might broadly call 'diplomatic' means.

The provinces of Thrace fell to Procopius by the simple device of arresting their military commander, enticed to Constantinople by letters extorted by force ('violenter') from Valens' imprisoned praetorian prefect (26.7.5). The acquisition of Thrace gave Procopius a further claim on the troops sent by Valens to face the anticipated Gothic invasion, and the city of Philippopolis remained loyal to him until the end (26.10.6). He tried to secure Illyricum, further west, by the interesting ploy of sending there men with gold coin minted in his name and image, but Valentinian's

IX. Legitimacy and Usurpation 197

commander in Illyricum, Aequitius, caught and killed them (26.7.11). Ammianus regarded the failure to secure Illyricum as a serious impediment to Procopius' chances of success (26.7.12), and lays repeated stress on the passes that led from Illyricum into Thrace, particularly the pass of Succi bringing the military high road down past Philippopolis (26.7.12; 10.4). The same point was crucial in Julian's march against Constantius; he delayed at Naissus while Constantius grouped his forces in Thrace, and was very lucky not to have to face battle there (p. 105).

Seen from Valens' point of view, the rebellion of Procopius shows the sheer diversity of an emperor's preoccupations.[22] After the division of the empire late in 364, Valens had entered his consulship for 365 at Constantinople (26.5.4ff.). Recent events however made his presence on the eastern frontier seem imperative, and he set off there at the end of the winter. His progress through Anatolia was measured, for he did not prepare to leave Caesarea until the summer heat had waned, making the journey through Cilicia a more tolerable prospect (26.6.11; 7.2). He had already received reports from his provincial commanders of a prospective Gothic invasion, to which he had to send troops, who passed by Constantinople with the results already noted. The rebellion of Procopius in late September was a third field of action, compelling Valens to defer his march to the east and return to Bithynia. After his initial failures there he established a holding position in Galatia (26.7.2, 13), making his base at Ancyra (26.8.4). Ammianus presents Valens as totally disconcerted by the turn of events, and ready to surrender the imperial regalia if his associates had not encouraged him to carry on (26.7.13). This is no doubt exaggerated, but one can readily see the situation from Valens' point of view; here was an emperor seriously involved on both eastern and lower Danube frontiers, but distracted from both of them through civil war in Asia Minor.

Valens was encouraged to hope for better things by the prospect of reinforcements from the east, and these in due course arrived, permitting an advance to Pessinus in old Phrygia (26.8.4; 9.1). He had in the meantime been able to mount attacks on Procopius' forces in Phrygia, forcing the departure from his province of the archaically styled 'proconsul' Hormisdas (26.8.12).[23] The emperor's resources were clearly superior, and so, when it came to a crisis, was his authority. The general Arintheus had at an early stage won over detachments from Procopius by simply ordering them to arrest and hand over their useless commander (26.8.4). A similar intervention by Arbitio in Lydia achieved the defection of Procopius' general Gomoarius (26.9.6), and at the confrontation near Nacolia the majority of Procopius' forces turned down their spears and joined the emperor (26.9.7). Procopius was tied up by two of his own officers and delivered to Valens for execution (26.9.9).

*

Throughout Ammianus' account, questions arise of time, distance and communications, and their effect on the conduct of the civil war. Procopius produced so-called 'messengers' from the west, claiming that they had come from Gaul and reporting the death of Valentinian there (26.7.3); this was a clever move on Procopius' part, for nothing was better calculated to undermine the standing of Valens than the loss of his senior colleague and author of his dignity. Meanwhile Valentinian did not know what had happened to his brother. Rumours of a usurpation reached him, but left it unclear whether or not Valens was dead. A firm report was sent in by Aequitius in Illyricum, who had got his information from a military tribune in Dacia Mediterranea (26.5.10). Again there was little detail beyond confirmation of the fact of rebellion. Valens' fate remained unclear – naturally enough, since Constantinople was between Valentinian and Cappadocia, and Procopius sat astride the direct routes of communication with the west.

Valentinian responded by raising Aequitius to the rank of *magister militum*, with instructions to secure Illyricum against a rapid attack from Thrace; he did not want the equivalent of a march of Julian against him (26.5.9ff.). In the meantime he sent agents with a select force to secure Africa in case Procopius should attempt to win that province – a practical and economical action, precluding the usurper at an early stage from control of the corn supply of Rome (26.5.14). If Valens were eliminated, Procopius might use such control to blackmail Valentinian into recognising him. Aequitius easily overcame Procopius' attempt to subvert Illyricum (26.7.11), no further action being required of him for the moment. As the rebellion neared its close he hesitated, uncertain what was going on in Asia Minor, where he knew, without any detail, that the war was now being fought. He moved into Thrace and attacked Philippopolis, thinking that he might have to outflank Procopius and advance through Haemimontus (on the European coast of the Black Sea) to bring help to Valens and not daring, if he did so, to leave Philippopolis loyal to Procopius. In performing these manoeuvres, remarks Ammianus, he had 'not yet heard what had happened at Nacolia' – that is, the death of the usurper (26.10.4). As for the defenders of Philippopolis, they refused to yield their city until they had actually seen the head of Procopius being carried to the Gallic provinces (26.10.6). Just so, the citizens of Aquileia had refused to yield to Julian until they had proof of the death of Constantius (above, p. 104). In both cases, the leaders of the resistance were punished with a severity that drew comment from Ammianus (21.12.20; 26.10.6).

Ammianus' narrative is studded with allusions to modes of communication and expressions of opinion indicating the sentiments at work in the usurpation of Procopius. The ceremonial installation of the usurper was attended by acclamations in his favour, beginning hesitantly, but gradually encompassing the populace of Constantinople. It was preceded by the hustled progress through the streets of the city, and followed by a speech to a sparsely attended senate. The soldiers too make acclamations, swearing mighty oaths by Jupiter (26.6.13; 7.17); they lower their spears and standards as a sign of defection, in one case

IX. Legitimacy and Usurpation

from Valens, in another from Procopius (26.7.17; 9.7). In the first case their gesture of submission comes instead of the fearsome battle roar, known as 'barritus', which was expected (26.7.17). Procopius could win over a detachment by greeting and personally addressing (in Latin) a soldier whom he claimed to know (26.7.15f.), and with equal aplomb Arintheus could scorn battle and bring troops over to his side by addressing them with the full weight of his authority, ordering them to throw in chains their despicable commander, an ex-palace attendant (26.8.5). Both are interesting indications of the 'face to face' contact expected between commanding officers and their troops, and indeed in social relations generally in Ammianus' time.[24]

Particularly notable is the immense influence on the formation of opinion of the reputation of the house of Constantine.[25] This is especially true of the army. His possession of the baby daughter of Constantius, and the presence on one occasion of her mother Faustina when Procopius received some element of the imperial insignia, had a real effect, specifically linked by Ammianus with Procopius' bids for military support (26.7.10). At a later stage, Faustina and her daughter attended Procopius in the field before he committed himself to battle. The idea was to get the troops to fight with the enthusiasm due to a member of the house of Constantine (26.9.3), but Procopius was outdone by the emergence from retirement of Arbitio, angry at the stripping of his house of its priceless furniture (26.8.13). The appearance before one of Procopius' armies of this distinguished general swayed opinion towards Valens, especially when he reminded them of their shared labours of old; let them follow him, a general known for his famous victories, rather than a worthless profligate bound to be deserted and fail (26.9.5)! Respect for a general of the time of Constantine was expected to calm the soldiers' eagerness for war, and so it turned out; 'ut Constantiniani ducis verecundia truces animi lenirentur, neque secus evenit' (26.9.4).

Procopius' propaganda made much of the lack of distinction of the obscure Pannonians now raised to the imperial throne. Addressing Vitalianus before the front line of the Iovii and Victores, he denounced the 'Pannonius degener' who dared to crush beneath his heels a empire to which he had never in his prayers dared to aspire – Procopius himself claiming to be of the highest in the state, that is to say a member of the house of Constantine; 'culminis summi prosapiam' (26.7.16). Still more stinging sneers were reserved for Valens personally, when he tried unsuccessfully to prise Chalcedon from Procopius' hands by siege. Among the taunts hurled down at him from the city-walls was the slang-name 'Sabaiarius'. 'Sabaia', as Ammianus explained, was a cheap drink made in Illyricum from barley or wheat (26.8.2). A century-and-a-half earlier, the Bithynian Greek Cassius Dio, who had governed Pannonia as consular legate and claimed to write from personal knowledge, had described Pannonians as a violent people who possessed nothing to induce them to an honourable life. They had only a little wine of poor quality, and instead drank beer made from barley and millet (49.36.2ff.).

It is remarkable to see the very same Mediterranean prejudice against the north repeated after such a lapse of time by Dio's Bithynian compatriots at Chalcedon. To the modern historian, nothing seems more natural than that imperial dynasties should be replaced, when they come to an end, from the military classes of Pannonia. It is the story of the third century, culminating in the rise of Constantine the Great, born in the military city of Naissus and proclaimed in Britain. It clearly looked different in the later fourth-century east; the dynasty of Constantine had shaken off its origins and, after two generations of rule from Constantinople, was the very image of civilised imperial power. The insults flung from the walls of Chalcedon take us close to an interpretation of Procopius' rebellion as an expression of class and cultural prejudice of eastern urban dwellers against rural upstarts from the west – at the same time as they provide a commentary on the essential narrowness of Procopius' power base. If he could not control Illyricum he could not control the empire, as Ammianus well understood; 'magna perdidit instrumenta bellorum' (26.7.12). The observation is as relevant on the ideological level as on the strategic: so much for contempt for beer-drinking Pannonians!

Two other aspects of the 'public imagery' of the rebellion will repay a moment's reflection. The first is Procopius' attempt to win over Illyricum by sending there men to distribute gold coin bearing his image and to embark on a policy of subversion by corruption; 'aureos scilicet nummos effigiatos in vultum novi principis, aliaque ad illecebras aptantes' (26.7.11). It would have been neglectful to do less; although Procopius may have over-estimated the appeal his name would have in Illyricum (the swift response of Aequitius ensuring that it would not be put to the test), there was much to be said for trying such measures, if they were not too expensive, in areas beyond his current military capacities. Procopius' appreciation, and Ammianus' recognition, of the propaganda value of coinage in such circumstances, are telling items of evidence in the modern historian's understanding of this important general issue. The coinage itself, struck at the group of mints in the Hellespontine region – Constantinople, Nicomedia, Cyzicus, and (in bronze coin only) Heraclea in Thrace – displays in gold and bronze denominations a variant of a legend much used in the second half of the reign of Constantius, but never employed by Valentinian and Valens: 'REPARATIO FEL(icium) TEMP(orum)'.[26] The issues of silver, struck in the first instance for donatives to the army, look forward hopefully to the fifth anniversary of the reign, 'VOT(a) V'. The image of Procopius, who is shown as an ascetic, lean-faced and bearded figure, is an obvious reminiscence of the portraiture of Julian. So too, on a closer inspection than the soldiers of Illyricum are ever likely to have given the coins, are certain of the mint-marks employed on them, but it is more likely that these, if not also the choice of legends, have more to do with routine minting procedures than with active propaganda. There is however no doubt about the portrait, and this is the detail noted by Ammianus.

IX. Legitimacy and Usurpation

The second aspect is in a grotesque way connected; no longer the coin image, but the actual head of Procopius being transported from Asia Minor to Gaul, on its way by dumb appeal persuading the citizens of Philippopolis to end their resistance to Aequitius (26.10.6). So on later occasions, the heads of the usurpers Maximus and Eugenius, successively defeated by Theodosius, wound their way across the Roman empire mounted on the end of a pike, to be displayed on the walls of Carthage.[27] The scene is easy to visualise: a detachment of mounted troops brandishing banners and devices, the head of the usurper held aloft with a painted placard, like an increasingly macabre parody, as its condition deteriorates, of the imperial standard; trumpeters and a herald to make a proclamation before the walls of cities, whose populations send out envoys with loyal addresses, make acclamations to the legitimate emperor, and donations in celebration of his victory. The end of the usurpation of Procopius matched the beginning, politics as dramatic scena or tableau; 'ut in theatrali scaena simulacrum quoddam insigne per aulaeum vel mimicam cavillationem subito putares emersum' (26.6.15).

*

Ammianus' attitude to the rebellion of Procopius is interesting for his categorical endorsement of legitimate power. It is clear that he sympathised with the widespread dislike of the regime of Valens, and especially of Petronius, whose oppressive financial administration and nasty character are repeatedly brought to our notice (26.6.7f., 17; 8.14). Of the general Serenianus, imprisoned at Nicaea and murdered there by Marcellus after the fall of Procopius, Ammianus remarks that his death was the saving of many lives, for he would have killed many innocent men had he lived to be on the winning side. Serenianus came like Valens from Pannonia, was uncultivated and cruel, and resembled his master as much as he was congenial to him; 'Valentique ob similitudinem morum et genitalis patriae vicinitatemque acceptus' (26.10.2). Procopius on the other hand is in personal terms favourably treated. Quiet and respectable, strict in his personal conduct and inclined to depression (Procopius lived, says Ammianus in a marvellous phrase, 'amid the shadows of a sad nature'), he was well educated and, what was especially remarkable, throughout his life untainted by the shedding of blood (26.6.1; 9.11).[28] The short obituary notice of Procopius, in which this last point is added to what Ammianus had said earlier, immediately precedes the character-sketch of Serenianus in Ammianus' text, in a clearly deliberate rhetorical contrast: 'sed, quod est mirandum, quoad vixit incruentus' of Procopius (26.9.11), is followed by the description of Serenianus; 'occultas voluntates principis introspiciens ad crudelitatem propensioris, multas innocentium ediderat strages' (26.10.2).

Yet, distasteful as it might be, it was Valens who was the legitimate emperor and Procopius the usurper, venturing an illegal assault on the imperial throne and justly defeated and executed. Despite his lack of capacity for the office, low origin and unpleasant character, it was the cause of Valens that was 'piissima' (26.10.13) and Procopius, far superior in birth, character and temperament, who was a 'disturber of public calm' (26.6.1), a 'usurper of improper power'; 'usurpator indebitae potestatis' (26.7.12). He was a 'praesumptor' (26.8.24), his cause a 'criminal outrage'; 'proterviae totius auctore' (26.8.4). Procopius' captors, his own officers Florentius and Barchalba, were themselves executed, but this was for Ammianus an ill-considered act. If they had betrayed a 'princeps legitimus', Justice herself would have applauded their execution. As it was, they had surrendered a 'rebel and assailant of civil tranquillity' ('rebellem et oppugnatorem internae quietis') and should have been generously rewarded for a noble deed; 'amplas eis memorabilis facti oportuerat deferri mercedes' (26.9.10). It was no doubt what they had hoped for themselves.

Ammianus evoked the social confusion spawned by civil war, the prospects of gain attracting ambitious palace officials and men who had retired from imperial service, some former soldiers (26.7.1). Procopius failed to appreciate that a happy man may by a turn of Fortune's wheel be most wretched before the evening (26.8.13), and people committed themselves to his cause not knowing what the future would bring, and not always of their own volition (26.7.1). Some (Ammianus is thinking here of the people of Constantinople) liked change for its own sake, which is not to say that there were no complaints with the present state of affairs (26.6.17). The judicial enquiries which followed the suppression of the rebellion were among the instruments by which this social upheaval was achieved, and Ammianus dwells on them, with more rhetorical intensity than precision of detail, emphasising the emperor's cruelty, the tortures and penalties, proscriptions and exiles that ensued – their purpose being, in Ammianus' eyes, to transfer the wealth of the defeated into the pockets of the victorious party (26.10.14). The victors' cause was just, but tainted by the manner of its celebration; 'causae quidem piissimae, sed victoriae foedioris' (26.10.13).

It is disconcerting to find Ammianus' endorsement of legitimate power so undisturbed by the moral quality of those who now exercised it, but he gives no indication that he regarded such judgments as relevant to the circumstances. The overriding consideration seems to be the formal legitimacy of the government in office. That being so, it is not easy to feel totally satisfied with Ammianus' criticism of Valens' conduct of the judicial enquiries which followed the suppression of Procopius. Procopius knew, and Ammianus knew, what was the nature of power in the fourth-century Roman empire, and what happened to those who, whether by magic arts, subtle conspiracy or armed rebellion, challenged it unsuccessfully. It was precisely through the judicial pursuit of such challenges that good men were brought down, suffering death or exile in a manner that seemed to Ammianus quite normal in times of civil war; 'ut in certaminibus intestinis usu venire contingit' (26.7.7).[29] Legal processes were no mere incidental adjuncts to situations that had been resolved

IX. Legitimacy and Usurpation

elsewhere. The emperors took their duties seriously and had to be equipped against the possibility of attack, and the courts of law were as integral to the maintenance of their position as was the capacity to take military action against a rebel. All emperors, including Julian, used them, and Ammianus recognised their necessity (p. 252). Nor is it as if the emperors were disinterested observers of threats to their own position. Not for the first time, Ammianus has failed to take the imaginative step of putting himself in the emperor's position. But then, what realistic man of conscience could have chosen without unease between principles of judicial conduct apt for an ideal world in which people did not rebel, and support of legitimate government in a real world in which they did? If Ammianus seems at times to want the best of both worlds, the maintenance of legitimate government without the judicial processes necessary to defend it, that is not in human terms surprising, nor is it morally absurd to argue that legitimate power should be defended by the minimum of necessary force. The difficulty lies in establishing what degree of force constitutes the minimum, and on this point emperors, their historians and their victims might easily take different views.

CHAPTER X

Valentinian and Valens: Sex, Magic and Treason

In a brief preface to Book 26, Ammianus had referred to the dangers of composing the history of an age that now lay within the reach of living memory, and to his hesitation in embarking upon a period that was so well known, in a narrative so open to the attentions of untimely critics; 'convenerat iam referre a notioribus pedem, ut et pericula declinentur veritati saepe contigua et examinatores contexendi operis deinde non perferamus intempestivos' (26.1.1). A historian may give offence by the omission of unimportant trivialities – the reasons for the punishment of common soldiers, what the emperor said at dinner, the names of minor fortifications and of those who paid court to the urban praetor, and so on. On such matters Ammianus turns his back, in favour of the true claims of history, which is accustomed to run among 'high places' and not scuffle about after irrelevant details; 'praeceptis historiae ... discurrere per negotiorum celsitudines assuetae, non humilium minutias indagari causarum'. What other 'dangers' might be involved apart from the giving of offence by untimely omission, has been the subject of much speculation relating to such issues as an author's freedom of speech under an autocracy and the expression of religious dissent in an age of prejudice;[1] but it is possible that Ammianus' declaration amounts merely to a promise that he will be as open and frank as he has been before, not in defiance of any physical threat to his own person but of the risks to a literary reputation that might be incurred by the writing of contemporary history. Current affairs were, after all, the proper field of the panegyrist, whose claims to truth can only in special cases, such as that of Julian, be compared to those of the historian (16.1.3; p. 468). A renewed invocation of truth, integrity and a lofty purpose was appropriate as one approached living memory, and it was a neat touch to conciliate the audience by acknowledging the risks of adverse criticism that were involved.

It is often argued that the preface to Book 26 indicates an extension of an original design that had not been intended to go beyond the death of Julian and its immediate sequel.[2] It is however difficult to believe that the usurpation of Procopius was not from the beginning an integral part of Ammianus' plan. Not only is the information of a sustained quality, the writing as artful and controlled, the portrayals of character as penetrating and varied as ever; the whole book is arranged with a

X. Valentinian and Valens

symmetry perhaps equalled only in Book 14 of the history. It consists of ten divisions of subject-matter, the first five, after the preface and other preliminaries, narrating the election of Valentinian and his choice of Valens as colleague, as described above (p. 190). The division of the empire completed at Mediana near Naissus and at Sirmium is then immediately expressed in practice by the invasion of Alamanni which took Valentinian to the west, and the revolt of Procopius. These two events, introduced together at the centre of the book, are followed by a statement of Ammianus' method in the new circumstances, east and west with their separate histories (26.6.7-15). The Alamanni are deferred to Book 27, the second half of Book 26 being devoted to the usurpation of Procopius and the punishment of his supporters – a work of art in itself, as we have just seen.

Ammianus knew from the outset that, once it had happened so soon after Julian's death, he would have to describe the rebellion of Procopius. Granted this, to terminate with the rebellion would offer some advantages. It would allow the aftermath of the Persian campaign of Julian to be satisfactorily resolved, it would mark the true end of the dynasty of Constantine, and bring the new emperors to power without committing the historian to a detailed account of their rule. In a sense Ammianus' remarks about the hazards of writing contemporary history would read more convincingly at the beginning of Book 27, for that is where the contemporary age really began. Did Ammianus in effect transpose his preface from Book 27, in order to punctuate his work for formal reasons at the beginning of Book 26, the second half of his third decad? If this were so, by parity of reasoning he should have put his earlier preface not at the beginning of Book 15 but of 16; as for Book 27, we have just seen that it is in substance as well as structure linked with its predecessor, invasions of Alamanni, which are integral to Ammianus' presentation of the attitude taken by Valentinian to Procopius and so to the history of the rebellion, being deferred to it. Ammianus' transition at the beginning of the book is explicit in connecting the two issues; 'dum per eoum haec, quae narravimus, diversi rerum expediunt casus, Alamanni ... supra Gallicanos limites ... iam persultabant' (27.1.1).

We should conclude that the preface to Book 26 declares no more than the author's realisation that he is now approaching the generally more controversial field of contemporary history, without implying that what follows should be read as an amendment to any 'original' plan. We must however allow for contingency, and for the tendency of events to take unexpected directions. When Ammianus first embarked on his research for the history of the period after Julian's death he cannot have known how far he would have to go, nor that Valentinian and Valens would die within three years of each other, making possible a relatively well-defined termination to the history; nor did he then know that the death of Valens would be in circumstances so portentous, permitting a final book of such power. The climax of Ammianus' history, the Gothic wars culminating in the battle of Hadrianople in August 378 and the death of Valens, was a catastrophe for the Roman empire but historiographically a gift of Fortune, who also provided the author, in the outlandish Huns and the Alani, with a marvellous opportunity for picturesque description with which to begin his final book (below, Chapter XIV.2).

Despite these observations, Books 27-31 of Ammianus' history differ from their predecessors, not only in the less expansive scale of their narrative – two-and-a-half years per book rather than one year per book in 14-26. The division of army, court and provinces between the two emperors meant that a historical narrative must for practical purposes be similarly arranged, in order to preserve the coherence of events that were contemporaneous but had for clarity to be described, as east and west were governed, separately.[3] Ammianus explains this with care, having mentioned Valentinian's refusal to help Valens against Procopius and just before embarking on his narrative of the usurpation: events in east and west took place simultaneously and only confusion would be caused by jumping all the time from one to the other; 'ne dum ex loco subinde saltuatim redire festinamus in locum, omnia confundentes squaliditate maxima rerum ordines implicemus' (26.5.15). What was true in particular of the revolt of Procopius was true also of the general character of the reigns of Valentinian and his brother.

The division of the empire under these emperors was essentially a reversion to previous practice, the reign of Julian being a brief and inconclusive exercise in unity. In the time of Constantius, Ammianus had had to co-ordinate events between east and west, while preserving the coherence of each. Yet there was a difference between this and the contemporary age. In the earlier books, Constantius' relations with his Caesars, Gallus and Julian, provided a link between the two halves of the empire, effective even in its demonstration of Constantius' failure to maintain the loyalty of his subordinates. The rise of Julian and his march against Constantius bound together east and west in a pattern converging dramatically upon a civil war averted only by Constantius' death.[4] The reigns of Valentinian and Valens on the other hand brought about a divergence of the two parts, with only occasional links between them, such as the appointment of a protégé of a western praetorian prefect as governor of Syria and proconsul of Asia (29.2.22), or the presence of an Antiochene as prefect of Rome (28.4.3). The march of Gratian to help Valens at Hadrianople might have been an expression of unity, but in the event proved not so, for the emperor was detained by an invasion of Alamanni, and failed to arrive in time (31.10; 12.4-7).

There is also the contribution of Ammianus' own career to the unity of his history. From 354 until the return of Julian's army to Antioch in 363, with the exception of the 'lost' years after the dismissal of Ursicinus, Ammianus had himself been involved in many of the events he described. His movements around the empire and beyond its frontiers had even in their more unpredictable phases given coherence to the histories of the widely separated regions of which they formed a part. After the accession of Valentinian and Valens, this narrative and dramatic focus deriving from Ammianus' own participation is lost. Instead we find scattered allusions, such as his presence at Antioch during Valens' treason trials there (29.1.24; 2.4), and the victimisation in the trials of some men whom he knew: moments of intense involvement but passive in nature and not forming part of a wider pattern.

Without these elements of unity between the two parts of the empire, the reigns of Valentinian and Valens assume in Ammianus a less cumulative, more episodic, air than those of their predecessors. Certain themes provide continuity with what has gone before. Ammianus still gives accounts of the tenures of office of urban prefects – though he omits some (below, p. 212). He has an excursus on the senate and people of Rome (28.4) which complements his digression in Book 14 and links these widely separated parts of his text.[5] So too there is a second digression on Thrace and the Pontus (27.4) to set beside one in an earlier book (22.8). His account of the Huns and Alani is not only pertinent to its context, but in style and manner reminiscent of other descriptions of foreign peoples, such as the Saracens, in earlier books. The promotion of the young Gratian to the rank of Augustus, after his father had recovered from a serious illness in which there was much talk of the succession, balances and adds a certain ceremonial variety to other accounts of the elevations of imperial candidates (and usurpers) – Julian, Jovian, Procopius, and Valentinian and Valens themselves (27.6.1-16).

The most important issue of the reign of Valentinian of which Ammianus gives any sort of continuous narrative is his campaigns against the Alamanni. Although his chronology is not always exact year by year, he has chapters on this subject under the campaigning seasons 365 and 366, 368, 369, 370, 371-2, and 374.[6] After this, the emperor was forced to attend to invasions of the Quadi on the Danube frontier, in the course of which he died; he had nevertheless determined to return to the Rhine as soon as he was able to, believing this to be the more important frontier (30.5.17). Military operations elsewhere, as in Britain (27.8; 28.3) and against the Saxons (28.5.1-7), are dealt with in separate chapters, not always with an exactly stated connection with other areas of activity. Close study of Ammianus' text is needed to elicit the chronology of the campaigns of Count Theodosius in Britain (367-8),[7] and the transition from this subject to events in Tripolitania carries a statement of the precedence of thematic over chronological arrangement, with a back-reference to the beginning of Valentinian's reign to make it clear that the origins of the African episode are given out of sequence; 'haec in Britannis agebantur. Africam vero *iam inde ab exordio Valentiniani imperio* exurebat barbarica rabies ...' (27.9.1). After this brief indication that something is amiss in Africa, Ammianus moves to a short digression on Valentinian's excessive favour to the military, and defers a full narrative of the Austurian uprising to a separate treatment; this occurs, after many other matters have intervened, in the last chapter of the following book (28.6.1-30). The origins of the uprising are here traced still

208   *Part One: Res Gestae*

further back in time by the statement that the first signs of unrest actually took place under Jovian (28.6.4). Events are then followed through from the ceremonial acceptance by the provincial council of Valentinian's rule ('ob imperii primitias', 28.6.7) and are only resolved when a report was submitted to his successor Gratian by the then proconsul and *vicarius* of Africa (28.6.28): that is to say, the events described in this chapter cover a full twelve or thirteen years, and extend both before the accession and after the death of Valentinian. The final outcome, the suicide of the court official Remigius, is in the very last sentence of Book 28 further deferred to a still later passage (30.2.9-12), where it occurs as part of a brief western diversion in a predominantly eastern narrative.

Another substantial episode, the rebellion of Firmus in Mauretania in Book 29, does not cover the same wide chronological range as events in Tripolitania, but here again the narrative of the episode, whose origins lay in a dispute over the inheritance of a Moorish king, incorporates the events of a full three campaign seasons (29.5.1-56).[8] Although his text has suffered damage at this point, Ammianus begins his description of the affair with an explanation of its thematic nature, as remote in subject-matter and location from other events described in the same part of his history, and to avoid confusion best kept separate from them, 'ne, dum negotiis longe discretis et locis alia subseruntur, cognitio multiplex necessario confundatur' (29.5.1).

Ammianus' decision in such cases to present his narrative in consolidated 'blocks' of material covering several years of narrative, was in the best interests of coherent exposition. The Tripolitanian episode dragged on through embassy and petition, complaint, evasion and sordid conspiracy: no need to present under their exact year, even had this been possible, the separate elements of the episode, when their internal connections were clear and nothing elsewhere hung on the outcome or chronology. In the case of the Mauretanian rebellion, one needed only to know that by the beginning of 373 Theodosius, after successful campaigns in Britain and on the Rhine frontier, was available to take the command (29.4.5; 5.4). At no other point, save only the involvement of the *comes Africae* Romanus in this as in the Tripolitanian episode, was there need of co-ordination with any other sequence of events. Ammianus would gain nothing by separating the affair mechanically into an annalistic framework, and there were great possibilities of confusion in trying to do so. Ammianus similarly put Valens' campaigns against the Goths in 367-9 into a single narrative covering all three years of operations (27.5.1-10). That he prefaced this narrative with a digression on Thrace, of clear relevance to its subject-matter (27.4.1-14), adds further to one's sense of reading a little monograph, excursus followed by narrative in a miniature anticipation of Book 31, within the main structure of the book; though the narrative is 'tied in' to what has preceded by a reminder of the still recent suppression of Procopius. It was the military support offered to Procopius by the Goths that gave Valens

X. Valentinian and Valens

his opportunity to make war on them when after enquiry he professed himself dissatisfied by their excuses (27.5.1).

*

In the case of one particularly important episode, of domestic rather than foreign policy, Ammianus' account compacts the events of many years into a single narrative, but without providing the points of integration with other parts of his text necessary to have made it fully intelligible. Since this episode, the trials for magic and adultery conducted in senatorial circles by Valentinian's agents, is central to the impression conveyed by Ammianus of the reign of this emperor, and since the issue of magic in its social context is important to our general understanding of Roman society, it will be worthwhile to indicate Ammianus' treatment of the subject and some of the problems that attend it.[9] The discussion may also, as it does in Ammianus, balance the equally severe investigations into conspiracy and magic conducted at Antioch under Valens in the same years.

Ammianus introduces his subject with ostentatious hesitancy as one of extreme delicacy, in words reminiscent of the 'pericula ... veritati contigua' mentioned in the preface to Book 26. He recoils from the events that lie before him, and relies upon the 'moderation of the present age' to make possible a selective account (in 57 sections) of the most memorable aspects of the affair; 'tamen praesentis temporis modestia fretus, carptim, ut quaeque memoria digna sunt, explanabo' (28.1.2). Ammianus adds a parallel from ancient times to help explain his position. The Athenian playwright Phrynichus had been punished by his countrymen for telling them the truth in a play about the sack of Miletus (during the Ionian Revolt of 499-4 BC). He had upset his audience by his imputation that their city was to blame for the sack by its failure to help its fellow-Ionian allies against the Persian siege (28.1.3f.). Ammianus presumably intended his remark as a general illustration of the courage of a writer who dared to tell the truth, without implying a more precise analogy between himself and Phrynichus. The tale does little to show how the Romans could have helped their fellow-citizens who were victims of the prosecutions conducted by Valentinian's agents, nor into what danger Ammianus could fall by writing of them in later years.

Ammianus dates the troubles to 'the sixteenth year and more' after the destruction of Nepotianus; 'anno sexto decimo et eo diutius post Nepotiani exitium' (28.1.1) – he means that they began in 365 or 366 and continued thereafter. A surviving source on the rebellion at Rome of Nepotianus has corpses piled in the streets after its suppression by Magnentius (Aur. Victor, *Caes.* 42.7), an account which no doubt resembles that furnished by Ammianus in one of his lost books (12 or 13). Yet, if the reader of Book 28 was intended to apply such a description to the more recent troubles, it is curious that the chronology implied by the fall of Nepotianus for the prosecutions of Valentinian is not supported in

Ammianus' narrative. They began when a senator named Chilo and his wife alleged to the urban prefect Olybrius that their lives had been threatened by sorcery, naming a musician, a wrestler, and a fortune-teller (28.1.8). Q. Clodius Hermogenianus Olybrius held the prefecture of Rome from the autumn of 368 until 370, being last recorded in August of that year.[10] Since he suffered from a protracted illness, the enquiries were transferred at the plaintiffs' request to the *praefectus annonae* Maximinus. These circumstances do not fit Ammianus' chronology, for it was certainly not before late 369, in view of the delay caused by Olybrius' illness, that the affair was transferred to Maximinus.

Another indication might be provided by an early victim of the trials, the proconsul of Africa Julius Festus Hymetius.[11] Hymetius was accused of consulting a diviner in order to make the emperor lenient to him. His offence was that to meet a famine at Carthage he had released from imperial granaries there corn destined for Rome, selling it at a high price and replacing it at a third the cost when corn was plentiful (28.1.17ff.). For this service he was thanked by a statue and inscription set up in his honour after Valentinian's death (*ILS* 1256), but the emperor was less well pleased and complained that Hymetius had made insufficient restitution for what he had taken. Yet Hymetius remained in office as proconsul until 367 or 368, and his consultation of the soothsayer must come after this; given the attitude of Valentinian to such matters, he would not have been allowed to remain as proconsul with any suspicion of fraud hanging over him. Neither the complaints of Chilo and his wife nor the case of Hymetius can provide the basis for Ammianus' dating of the outbreak of the prosecutions. If this is to be found, it must be sought elsewhere than in Ammianus, by far the most precise of the other evidence being provided by the legislation of Valentinian.

A law of 8 October 367 addressed to the urban prefect Praetextatus refers to punishments of 'exceeding severity' ('austerior ... ultio') inflicted on senators for proportionately serious offences, requiring that the emperor be consulted in such cases (*CTh* 9.40.10). This law, and whatever circumstances give rise to it, accord better with Ammianus' dating of the beginnings of the trials at Rome, although they bear no relation to his account of the manner in which they actually arose. The desire to protect the reputation of Praetextatus if he were in some way connected with the origin of the troubles might conceivably explain Ammianus' embarrassment in narrating them; but if so, he would have achieved his result by a misleading presentation of the facts that seems both uncharacteristic and unnecessary. There was no need to be so precise in the first place; if Ammianus' motive were to protect Praetextatus, he need never have invited trouble by writing that the prosecutions began in the sixteenth year after the suppression of Nepotianus, when his own narrative suggested a different chronology.

Ammianus connects the trials primarily with the tenures of office of successive *vicarii* of Rome. Maximinus, the evil genius of the prosecutions, with whose background and character Ammianus sets the

X. Valentinian and Valens 211

tone of his narrative (28.1.5-7), was promoted to the vicariate from the post of *praefectus annonae* when his report on the situation at Rome was accepted by the emperor.[12] He received as assistant a fellow-Pannonian Leo, subsequently *magister officiorum* at the court of Valentinian, where Maximinus himself became praetorian prefect of Gaul after his vicariate (28.1.12); it is in Gaul that he is later found, inciting the emperor to further acts of cruelty, of which Ammianus gives a selection (29.3.1ff.). Maximinus' successor at Rome, Ursicinus, was replaced for undue mildness in referring a difficult case to the imperial court (28.1.44); to fill his office came another supporter of Maximinus, Simplicius of Emona, formerly a schoolmaster, devious and sinister (28.1.45). Finally was sent a Gaul, Doryphorianus, chosen for his wild audacity, claims Ammianus, to execute a senator of high standing (28.1.53f.). In the end, as Ammianus concludes his narrative by explaining, they paid with their lives for their presumption. After the death of Valentinian, Maximinus was executed for 'overbearing conduct' under Gratian, Simplicius beheaded in Illyricum and Doryphorianus thrown into the Tullianum at Rome, to be seized from there by the advice of the emperor's mother, taken to his home town in Gaul and put to death there 'amid immense tortures' (28.1.57). Something is known or can be reconstructed of a political reaction under Gratian connected with these violent events, and of the rise to power of a new court faction based on the influence of the poet Ausonius, Valentinian's quaestor and the tutor of his son.[13] Ammianus says nothing of any of this. He nowhere even mentions Ausonius, and never fulfils his intention, stated in this passage, to tell of the fates that befell Maximinus and his colleagues; 'ut postea tempestive dicetur' (28.1.57). This is one of Ammianus' only two unfulfilled promises, no casual omission, since he introduces Maximinus with the remark that his father, a man skilled in divination, had told him that he would rise high but fall to the executioner's sword (28.1.7). It is possible, and has often been argued, that the omission has to do with events after the death of Valentinian that Ammianus may have thought embarrassing or dangerous, notably the execution at Carthage, in mysterious circumstances, of the *magister militum* Theodosius, the father of the reigning emperor.[14] This may be so; on the other hand, if there were dangers in what he had discovered, Ammianus could easily have avoided them simply by deleting the promise he had made. If he were completing his text towards the year 390, he had ample opportunity to do so (p. 30f.).

By contrast with this sequence of *vicarii*, the prefects of Rome play only a minor role in Ammianus' narrative. He acknowledges Olybrius' involvement in his account of the prosecutions (28.1.8f.), but not in his formal notice, only three chapters later, on the prefecture of Olybrius. This he describes as peaceful and quiet, its holder as an overconscientious official, anxious to avoid any harsh deed or word, a rigorous opponent of calumny and fraud, insistent on the distinction between justice and injustice, and restrained in his conduct towards those under his authority (28.4.1); not a word, directly or by implication, of the complaint laid before him by Chilo and his wife.

Olybrius' successor, P. Ampelius, is described in the account of his prefecture as an excellent choice and pleasing to the people, sometimes rigorous except that he failed to maintain his rigour as he should; the reference however is not to capital jurisdiction but to regulations on licensing hours and the sale of food in the streets of Rome (28.4.3f.; p. 414). In Ammianus' narrative of the trials, the former proconsul Hymetius is judged by Ampelius as prefect, sitting in court with Maximinus as *vicarius*. Hymetius seemed on the brink of condemnation and appealed to the emperor, who remitted the case to the senate. Valentinian was infuriated when this body merely exiled him to a Dalmatian island, but allowed the sentence to stand (28.1.22f.). Further, Ampelius was the recipient of a law of Valentinian issued on 6 December 371, of obvious relevance to the circumstances (*CTh* 9.16.10). It specified that those members of the senatorial order ('nonnulli ex ordine senatorio') who were currently accused of magical practices were to be heard by the *praefectus urbi* and remitted to the emperor, with full transcript of the proceedings, when the prefect's court was unable to reach a decision.

It seems clear that the involvement of the prefecture in the judicial hearings at Rome was deeper than is stated or suggested by Ammianus.[15] It may then be significant that none of Ampelius' immediate successors as prefect, Bappo, Principius and Eupraxius, gains any notice in the history; but if so, it is the more puzzling that the last of them receives praise from Ammianus for his integrity and courage on earlier occasions at the court of Valentinian. On one of these occasions, when Valentinian answered the complaint of a senatorial embassy that senators were being tortured against the provisions of the law by claiming that he had given no such instruction, Eupraxius as quaestor corrected his emperor (28.1.25). The quaestor had responsibility in the administration for the drafting of law and imperial rulings on legal questions. Those laws of Valentinian that may conjecturally be attributed to Eupraxius' hand have been described as possessing an 'even and moderate tone', as 'calm, dignified and restrained' – qualities fully consistent with Ammianus' description of Eupraxius' character.[16]

The petition of the embassy, which was composed of three high-ranking senators led by Vettius Agorius Praetextatus,[17] arose from the 'relatio' of Maximinus to Valentinian in which, after enquiries into the state of affairs at Rome, he reported that serious crimes were afoot, requiring severe penalties, and received in reply the ruling that they be considered under the heading of *maiestas* (28.1.11). It would in consequence of this ruling be permissible to apply torture even to those normally exempt, like members of the senatorial order, for in the case of *maiestas*, as Valentinian said in a law of 8 July 369 addressed to the urban prefect Olybrius that may embody part of his reply to Maximinus' *relatio*, 'there is only one and the same condition for all'; 'in qua [*sc.* maiestatis causa] sola omnibus aequa condicio est'. In no other circumstance was anyone to be stripped of office or rank in order to allow him to be tortured, at least

X. Valentinian and Valens

without consultation of the emperor (*CTh* 9.35.1). Ammianus elsewhere alleges a provision of the ancient Leges Corneliae that in cases of *maiestas* torture might be applied to men of high social rank (19.12.17). In his discussion of Valentinian's ruling to Maximinus he presents an opposite opinion, in stating that certain categories of people were exempted from torture 'by ancient law and the rulings of emperors' (28.1.11); nor does he know of a partial precedent of Constantius covering cases of magic found at the imperial court (*CTh* 9.16.6; 5 July 357). It is perfectly possible that Valentinian himself was unaware of the law in insisting to the senatorial legation that he had not ordered the torture of senators. As Eupraxius advised him, he had sanctioned it in allowing Maximinus to proceed under the heading of *maiestas*.[18]

The intrusion of *maiestas* into the affair should not mislead us into believing that Ammianus has tried to describe a conspiracy.[19] Individuals, men and women, were executed and exiled (or sometimes acquitted) on accusations of magic arts and, especially in the later years of the prosecutions, for sexual offences. A senator convicted of adultery, one exiled for 'a slight error', another beheaded because he had copied a book on magic 'in the infirmity of youth' (28.1.26) – such miscreants are hardly plausible conspirators. Most of the recorded victims were senators and senatorial women, together with characters like musicians, diviners and charioteers, persons only too familiar in Ammianus' own account as clients and hangers-on of senatorial households (p. 415). As for these men of lower social rank, Ammianus here as elsewhere excuses himself for omitting certain things that happened 'per squalidas personas', not everything that happens being worthy of record (28.1.15). He does however preserve some trace of the penal distinction between the upper and lower classes, senators being beheaded while members of other ranks are beaten to death or burned alive (28.1.16; 28f.).

Ammianus' account of the trials, as he concedes (28.1.15), is imprecise in its chronology – inevitably so, as it is punctuated only by changes in the vicariate of Rome as cases dragged on for years, often involving the pursuit of information laid by men of low estate such as the musician, wrestler and diviner mentioned at the outset. Though named at the beginning of the trials (28.1.9) they were not executed until much later, no doubt when they had said what they had to say and were of no further use to the inquisitors (28.1.29). The execution of the diviner consulted by the proconsul Hymetius is mentioned just before the latter's exile, together with the exile to Britain of an adviser, but in fact fell later (28.1.21). The case of the senator Aginatius, who first quarrelled with Maximinus by disputing the latter's judicial competence as *praefectus annonae* – and so not later than 370, by which time Maximinus was *vicarius* (28.1.30-33) – did not come to fufilment until several years had passed and Maximinus had after long reflection devised a way to take his revenge. This is in fact the last event in the trials to be recorded (28.1.50-56).

As if to compensate for its chronological imprecision, Ammianus'

214 Part One: Res Gestae

narrative is at various points illuminated by external evidence in the form of imperial legislation. In addition to the law addressed to Olybrius already mentioned, two laws of 19 May 371 addressed 'to the senate', may form part of the emperor's reply to the senatorial embassy led by Praetextatus. In one of them (CTh 9.16.9) Valentinian distinguished legitimate divination ('haruspicina') from magic, a clear reference to the diviners and fortune-tellers caught up in the prosecutions, as well as testimony to the ease of confusion between the categories of legal and outlawed practices in this area. The other law (CTh 9.38.5) pardons one or two accused persons, while observing that such leniency 'brands those persons whom it frees' and concluding ominously that 'he who pardons the senate, condemns the senate'; 'qui indulgentiam senatui dat, damnat senatum'. The act of pardon can in logic be extended only to the guilty, and it has often been noted that Ammianus at no point maintains the innocence of any of those convicted in the trials; his complaint is only that the punishments went far beyond the seriousness of the offences.[20] This was also the argument of the senatorial embassy to Valentinian; 'ne delictis supplicia sint grandiora' (28.1.24). A law posted at Rome on 23 March 374 by the *vicarius* Simplicius refers to the harbouring of guilty persons, exactly as happened in the case of the senators Avienus and Anepsia (28.1.49; CTh 9.29.1). Another law, addressed after Valentinian's death to Maximinus just before the latter's downfall and execution, prohibits the taking of evidence from slaves and freedmen against their masters except in cases of treason (CTh 9.6.1-2;15 March 376). Anepsia had been informed upon by a slave in a case of sexual misdemeanour associated with her protection of Avienus (28.1.49). Since Maximinus was at the time prefect of Gaul, the law may not apply to Italy or Rome; on the other hand, the next (and last) law addressed to Maximinus was actually posted at Rome on 16 April 376 (CTh 9.19.4). It is therefore possible that the earlier law also applied to Rome, and if so, that it arose from the case of Anepsia.[21]

Not the least among many puzzling aspects of Ammianus' account is his failure to draw any structural or thematic connection between the trials and his own digressions on the moral conduct of the senate and people of Rome. The long account of the trials, in 57 sections, concludes with an emphatic formal statement: 'is urbanarum rerum status, ut ita dixerim, fuit' (28.1.57). Then follow two much shorter chapters (fourteen and nine sections respectively) on Valentinian's military activities on the Rhine frontier and the campaigns of Theodosius in Britain, before Ammianus returns to Rome, in a digression of thirty-five sections introduced by the strange remark that he has long neglected the city, being distracted by the great mass of foreign affairs; 'diu multumque a negotiis discussus urbanis, adigente cumulo foris gestorum ...' (28.4.1). It is as if he had totally forgotten his account of the prosecutions. The digression, in which Ammianus denounces the association of senators precisely with charioteers and fortune-tellers, and criticises their addiction to horoscopes and magic arts (below, p. 420), actually begins

X. Valentinian and Valens

with the successive prefectures of Olybrius and Ampelius, whose connections with the prosecutions at Rome have already been noted; yet we saw that Ammianus makes no mention of the subject, no cross-reference of any kind. Further, Ammianus had earlier endorsed the strict action of Apronianus, *praefectus urbi* under Julian, in a case involving a charioteer who had taught magic arts to his son and was executed. On a later occasion, it is alleged, a senator had taught similar secrets to a slave, but escaped punishment by bribery and could long afterwards be seen parading, as if in total innocence, in the streets of Rome (26.3.4f.). In remarking how 'long impunity' made possible this state of affairs, Ammianus again seems to ignore the trials conducted on just this issue by the agents of Valentinian.[22] Even if, on the most schematic account of his methods of composition, he had not come round to composing Book 28 when he wrote down his comment on the prefecture of Apronianus in Book 26, he had surely begun to collect his material for the later events and was aware of their significance.

Ammianus' narrative of the trials is therefore a fitting comment, except that he fails to make it, on his own opinion of the conduct of that minority at Rome who sank themselves in immorality, ignorance and vice (14.6.7). It is difficult to understand in its lack of integration with other aspects of his text; not only with the digressions on Rome in Books 14 and 28, but with what he says elsewhere about magic and treason, and with his accounts of the prefects of Rome whom he shows to have been involved; and his initial chronology relating the trials to the fall of Nepotianus finds no trace in his text as it was written. Finally, he even makes no connection between the trials and his presentation of the character of the regime of Valentinian.

In two passages, Ammianus gives examples of Valentinian's cruelty; they are illustrative episodes of a varied character and chiefly affect the court – such as, in a sequence of actions allegedly inspired by Maximinus, the fate of an incautious petition for a change in a provincial assignment, the execution of the superintendent of an arms factory for offering short weight in a piece of armour manufactured under his supervision, the stoning of another official for substituting horses he was inspecting in Sardinia for military use (29.3.4-6). In an earlier passage, before Maximinus has arrived on the scene, Ammianus had mentioned the burning alive of a former head of the state treasuries in Illyricum for 'minor offences', and the execution of four officials who were complained of by a superior officer (27.7.5).[23] In such cases the emperor was perhaps being unduly censorious – and Ammianus rather tolerant – of corruption in the administration, but this austere consideration of justice does not excuse the clubbing to death of a groom for releasing a dog prematurely on a hunting expedition (29.3.3), or the amputation of the hand ordered for a stable boy who failed to control the emperor's horse as he was mounting it. This punishment was held back by the official instructed to implement it, presumably in the belief that Valentinian would relent; in the event there was no need, for the emperor died the following day

(30.5.19). Another court official, Eupraxius, had by a timely exposition of the theory of martyrdom saved the curial orders of three towns from summary execution (27.7.6), and there is always the paradigm of the emperor's pet bears, an anecdote of court life told also of the Emperor Galerius.[24] Despite opportunities to do so, nowhere does Ammianus adduce Valentinian's prosecutions at Rome as an example of his cruelty or any other facet of his character or policy, even when the cases present some similarity. A court official was accused of having killed a donkey in the hope of procuring from some part of its remains a magical cure for his baldness, which Ammianus reports without making any connection with the prosecutions at Rome (30.5.11). Nor does he revert to them in his obituary of Valentinian, unless it is in the comment that the emperor hated the well-dressed, the educated, the opulent and the noble; 'bene vestitos oderat et eruditos et opulentos et nobiles' (30.8.10). The first, third and fourth of the hated categories indeed concur with Ammianus' opinion of the senatorial aristocracy at Rome – not however for approval, but for criticism of the ostentation, idleness and fraudulent pretensions of its members.[25] The comparison which follows of Valentinian with Hadrian refers to that emperor's envious pretensions to cultural superiority, not to any political or judicial campaign against the upper class; 'ut solus videretur bonis artibus eminere'. It would help to have known what Ammianus wrote in detail of Hadrian. He does not say that Valentinian expressed his hatred by having the objects of his jealousy executed and exiled, and it is possible that in this passage Ammianus is not thinking of senators at all.

Ammianus' account of the trials is thus both chronologically and thematically detached, as if it had little to do with other situations described, and other opinions held, by the historian. He makes no connection between the trials and his description soon afterwards of the conduct of the senators of Rome, nor with the character of Valentinian; he neglects to make clear the role of the prefects of Rome in the prosecutions, and gives an account of their origins that is either deficient or misleading. Not only does he fail to carry out his promise at the end of his narrative to tell of the fall of Maximinus and his colleagues, but in remarking only a few paragraphs later, at the beginning of his digression on Rome, that he had long neglected urban in favour of foreign affairs, Ammianus writes momentarily as if the long first chapter of Book 28 did not exist at all.[26] As to the cause of his confusion – political or personal inhibition, sensitivity to his informants or to surviving victims of the trials, fear of their or their descendants' anger – this seems impossible to determine. Perhaps this is because the explanation does not lie in this direction at all. The anomalies in Ammianus' narrative are not all of one order. They involve both major and minor issues, and apply both to its content and to its place in the structure of the history. They might best be explained by some facet of the process of composition, for example by the supposition that the historian failed fully to master, or to revise thoroughly – or both – his complicated source material. Hurried composition or lack of revision

X. Valentinian and Valens

are unlikely, however, to be the complete explanation of the anomalies in Ammianus' account, since the chapter occupies a conspicuous place in his text, and is introduced with an elaborate rhetorical flourish clearly intended to amplify, not to diminish, its dramatic importance (p. 209). It is precisely this emphasis, and the role of the chapter in the broader economy of Ammianus' work, that may give us the clue that we need to seek the explanation of its character not in isolation but in its relationship with other descriptions of similar subjects, notably the account of the prosecutions conducted by Valens at Antioch, described at the beginning of Book 29 of the history.

*

Ammianus' account of the trials conducted by Maximinus and his successors at Rome is in fact the second of three main instances of the prosecution of magic arts and divination which he describes, in diverse but equally interesting circumstances. The first of them, in the time of Constantius (19.12.1-17), arose from the practice of consultation of an oracular shrine of the god Besas at Abydus in the Thebaid. Enquirers there were accustomed to put their questions, personally or through others acting for them, in writing, and many of these documents were left at the shrine after the replies had been given (19.12.4). Some were collected and sent to the emperor, who summoned his famous inquisitor, Paul 'the Chain', and prepared to hold hearings at Scythopolis in Palestine.[27] It was chosen as the venue because it was out of the way, and equidistant from Alexandria and Antioch, from which cities came a large proportion of those accused.

Ammianus' account of the trials of Scythopolis is coloured by emotive references to manacled prisoners from all parts of the world and all social classes, to exiles, tortures and executions (19.12.7f.; 13). It actually names only four accused men, two of whom were exiled, the other two acquitted since nothing could be proved against them. One of those acquitted, a philosopher named Demetrius from Alexandria, proclaimed under torture that of course he had sacrificed to the god, whom he had worshipped from childhood, but he had never consulted the oracle on his prospects for the future, nor did he know anyone else who had done so. The other acquitted man, a well-known poet, was guilty of nothing at all and was released (19.12.18). Of those convicted, Simplicius, the son of Constantius' famous praetorian prefect Fl. Philippus, was accused of enquiring about his own chances of power and tortured by imperial order (being otherwise exempt), but survived to go into exile; so little, said Ammianus, did Constantius care for the claims of 'pietas' (12.9)![28] The other named victim, Parnasius of Patrae in Achaia, had often been heard to say that when he had once left his home to seek a public office he had dreamed that he was escorted by 'many figures in tragic dress' (19.12.10). He was sent into exile, in a way fulfilling his dream. He was no doubt unwise to tell it to anyone, but this would be to underestimate the seriousness with which such signs were regarded by late Roman men.

In terms of the law as it stood, there was nothing unusual about the conduct of these cases. Fourth-century legislation, confirmed at the outset of his reign by Valentinian – and perhaps also by Valens, since the law, which survives only in a later reference to it, has the look of an agreed statement of policy[29] – had generally prohibited private divination with the severest penalties, but permitted the public expression of piety to the gods in any recognised fashion (CTh 9.16.1-2); while consultation of the gods about the prospects of one's own advancement would at any time, and not only in the later empire, have been severely dealt with. If Simplicius, with his connections and background, really had asked about his own prospects, Constantius would with more reason have been accused of negligence, than praised for loyalty to the son of an old friend, in overlooking it.

Without giving any actual cases, Ammianus describes the extension of the accusations to cover men incriminated because they wore amulets to repel fevers and other illnesses, or executed for sorcery and communion with the dead because they were seen passing a tomb at evening (19.12.14). Raising the ghosts of the dead was naturally visited in the law by capital punishment (CTh 9.16.5), Ammianus' complaint being of the flimsiness of the actual evidence adduced. As for innocent magical charms designed to achieve favourable weather, the well-being of crops and the health of the body, these were permitted in a law of Constantine condemning only magic designed for harmful purposes (CTh 9.16.3). In responding to such accusations, claims Ammianus, Constantius was indulging his obsessively distrustful temperament. Allegations of disloyalty could be fed into his ears, while serious matters were neglected, by servile flatterers who persuaded him that he was thereby exempt from all evils (19.12.16).

If the trials at Rome reveal magic arts and divination at work in the private lives of senatorial society and its sordid underworld, those at Scythopolis show how, by wilful misrepresentation, innocent loyalties to ancestral belief and harmless old customs could lead to suspicion of dissent. It was at the best of times a matter of interpretation. On an earlier occasion, not described by Ammianus, the Christian sophist Prohaeresius of Athens, deprived of his chair by the edict of Julian, had enquired of the goddesses of Eleusis, whom he had learned would tell the future to anyone who asked, whether the emperor's tax reforms would be long-lasting, and was told that they would not. It was a clever question, but Prohaeresius might have found himself severely exercised in a court of law to prove that he was not asking about the emperor's prospects of survival. In such circumstances, though a clement emperor like Julian might have spared him in order, as he used to put it, to increase the number of his friends (22.14.5), he would be lucky under a suspicious one to escape with torture and exile.[30]

*

In contrast with the trials at Scythopolis and Rome, the prosecutions conducted under Valens at Antioch in the early 370s were a clear case of divination in league with conspiracy; though here too this led, through mutual acquaintance and shared intellectual tastes, to the involvement of many who, though not unsympathetic, were in no true sense conspirators, and of others who were totally innocent. The affair began, as often happened, with trivial allegations unconnected with the serious matters that ensued. A certain Procopius denounced two court officials as having used magic arts against the *comes rei privatae* Fortunatianus, who was exacting from them money they had 'intercepted' (that is, embezzled) from the treasury. Questioned by Fortunatianus, the officials named as their accomplices Palladius, a sorcerer of obscure origin, and Heliodorus, a reader of horoscopes. The case was now, magic arts being involved, laid before the praetorian prefect of the east, the same Domitius Modestus who as *comes Orientis* had presided over the trials at Scythopolis (19.12.6). Faced with the prospect of torture in the prefect's court, Palladius announced that what had been discovered was trivial in comparison with what else he knew, and was encouraged — apparently by promise of an amnesty, for he never was punished but on the contrary revelled in his notoriety (29.2.7) — to reveal more. What now emerged was in Ammianus' words an 'endless coil' of crime (29.1.6), an amazing story of dissent and conspiracy: fascinating too for the modern historian interested in the manner and techniques of private divination.[31]

Several men of high rank, including an ex-provincial governor and another who was a court official as well as expert in divination, had made secret enquiries as to who would succeed Valens. By secret methods of enquiry ('motasque secretis artibus sortes') they had learned that they would acquire an 'excellent princeps' but that they, the enquirers, would come to a miserable end (29.1.7). When they asked themselves who was the man in question, the name of Theodorus, second in rank in the corps of *notarii*, came to their mind: and rightly, says Ammianus, for Theodorus, a Gaul, was distinguished in ancestry, educated and erudite, liked by everyone, and in all the virtues superior to the rank and office which he held; 'locoque, quem retinebat, superior videbatur'. This in itself, if it were expressed publicly, comes very close to a treasonable statement. He was also extremely discreet (29.1.8). Other conspirators were named, including a recent *vicarius* of Asia, who also was arrested and placed in custody. The records of the proceedings were in the usual way shown to Valens, who was infuriated — encouraged, Ammianus claims, by the prefect Modestus, who was afraid of losing his post (29.1.11). This may be so, but Modestus would have been guilty of negligence if he had not pressed his view upon the emperor, and such influence and motive are hardly needed to explain the strength of the emperor's reaction.

The preliminary hearings continued ('praeiudicia varia', 29.1.12).[32] Theodorus was fetched from Constantinople, where he had gone on family business, suspected accomplices were rounded up from distant provinces, clapped in irons and put in prison. Theodorus himself, who wore black, having abandoned hope of living ('praemortuus et atratus', in Ammianus' bleakly expressive words) was held in a remote place in the countryside of Antioch until the trials were ready to begin.

All of this Ammianus describes with a rhetorical intensity that tends to divert attention from his admission that Valens actually was subject to a conspiracy and had now and earlier been in danger of his life (29.1.15). In particular he had escaped the attack of a *scutarius* called Sallustius as he took his afternoon siesta on the road between Antioch and Seleucia. Other emperors too had escaped such attacks (Commodus and Septimius Severus, adduced at this point, are not the most enticing of parallels) and Valens was entitled to defend himself – but not with cruelty or malice, nor without attempting to distinguish guilt from innocence, driving harmless men into beggary and exile in order to lay hands on their property. We have seen much of this before, as in the suppression of the supporters of Procopius (p. 202). Again, we may sympathise with Ammianus' sentiments without feeling that he has presented the case with much understanding of the emperor's position. It was not as if the guilty and the innocent fell into two neatly separated groups, predestined as in the eye of God for punishment or reward; this was the 'civitas terrena', the 'earthly city', in which the guilty and the innocent had by the fallible judgment of men to be separated amidst contradiction, recrimination and the playing-off of old scores, and in which much of the behaviour under investigation lay in uncertain territory between the legal and the illegal.[33]

Ammianus' description of the trials at Scythopolis began, in keeping with this imagery of Judgment, with the sound of trumpets; 'inflabant litui quaedam colorata laesae crimina maiestatis' (19.12.1). So too at Antioch, a fanfare of trumpets ('internarum cladum litui iam sonabant'), interrupted by a diversion on the emperor's cruelty, then develops into a grotesque fantasia of clanking irons and shouted instructions to apply the tortures, while the various machines, the 'horse', lead weights and lashes, are prepared (29.1.23). As elsewhere, Ammianus renounces the obligation to give a full account of matters so confused and so hard to recall, passing on to a more summary account of what he can remember (29.1.24). He does not however ignore the presence of judicial procedures, reminding us of them in a series of remarks that punctuate the rhetoric and emotional intensity with which events are described. The case of one Pergamius, accused of learning the future by 'criminal imprecations', was dealt with first: he was tortured to the point of expiry and then, almost as if to keep him quiet, executed. Before the judges had yet decided in what order to deal with the cases before them, he had in a flood of terrified eloquence poured out the names of 'thousands' of accomplices the world over; an excessive task for the judges, as Ammianus drily remarks. We then come, 'quasi ad Olympici certaminis pulverem' (29.1.25), to the case of Theodorus.

Ammianus pauses again to add rhetorical intensity to the scene, but

X. Valentinian and Valens 221

without losing sight of the procedural development of the trials. The court was formally instituted and the judges declared the law; 'constituto itaque iudicio, et cognitoribus praescripta ostentantibus legum' (29.1.27). What follows is worth waiting for, as the official Hilarius offered to the court a detailed account of the seance in which he had participated. His evidence is presented by Ammianus in the unusual form of an address to the judges in direct speech.[34] They had made and consecrated a tripod of laurel wood (it stood before them in the courtroom, having been brought in before Hilarius began to speak) and then, in a house purified by incense, had placed on it a circular plate made of various metals, around the rim of which were engraved at carefully calculated intervals the twenty-four letters of the Greek alphabet. A man performing the role of priest then propitiated by incantations the god of divination and began to swing a metal ring suspended over the centre of the metal plate; the ring too had been consecrated by mystic ritual. The letters on the rim of the plate, marked out by the movements of the magic pendulum, then spelled out a sequence of perfectly formed Greek hexameter verses. They were an oracle revealing the circumstances, as Ammianus indicates a moment later with a citation of three lines, of the emperor's death in war on the 'plains of Mimas' (29.1.31; 33).

When the participants in the seance next enquired who would succeed Valens, the ring indicated the three letters theta, epsilon, omikron. It then added a fourth letter, delta, which seemed enough to indicate the name of Theod(orus); and with that the session ended. Hilarius added, with 'kindly' intent ('benivole'), that Theodorus himself did not know what was being done. When asked by the judges whether the conspirators also had foreknowledge of what was now happening to them, Hilarius quoted the oracle to show that they did, but that the emperor and the judges themselves were also threatened (29.1.33).

After further, conflicting evidence from others, Theodorus was allowed to speak. He began with a prostrate appeal for pardon but in another brusque indication of the actual conduct of the trial was told by the judges to get up and address himself to the point at issue. He then claimed that he had only heard of the affair through someone else and had repeatedly tried to tell the emperor but was dissuaded, on the legally futile but philosophically interesting ground that no actual attempt on the throne was required, since fate would bring about the outcome without anyone's intervention (29.1.34). Theodorus' story was however refuted by the evidence of a letter from him to Hilarius, in which he sought an opportunity to obtain his desire, having conceived hope from soothsayers that he might be successful. The seance was evidently not the only divination that was going on. Theodorus had been making his own enquiries, not being content, as he claimed, to leave the affair passively in the hands of fate; 'spe iam firma concepta ex vatibus, de re non cunctabatur sed tempus patrandae cupidinis quaeritabat' (29.1.35).

There is no need to follow Ammianus into the widespread enquiries that now ensued: Eutropius the proconsul of Asia accused but acquitted;

the philosopher Simonides, who admitted knowledge of the fateful oracle but had told no none, laughing at the instability of fortune while burning at the stake; the theurgist Maximus, similarly but perhaps more deeply implicated (he knew the oracle and its interpretation), beheaded at Ephesus, his home city; Alypius, *vicarius* of Britain under Julian, exiled and seeing his son reprieved from execution at the last moment by popular demand while their informer, a lower-class man, was burned alive (29.1.37-44); two brothers who had been joint consuls punished with exile and fines, though later recalled and restored to honour (29.2.9-11).[35]

It is easy to see how the trials involved matters only indirectly connected with the conspiracy and others far removed from it. If there was any suggestion, as the action of Theodorus implied, that the plan of the fates required human assistance to bring it about, consultation of the fates might well be taken to show that the enquirers were prepared to cast themselves in the role of conspirators, and a favourable response as encouragement to them to do so. A senior *notarius* suffered confiscation of his property for enquiring about the future – on his own account, to find out the sex of a child expected by his wife – being defended from a worse fate by his influential kinsmen. A philosopher was executed by the proconsul of Asia because he had asked his wife in a letter to 'crown the door of the house', a proverbial expression signifying that something unusually important is to be done (29.2.25). Also in Asia, a distinguished citizen was put to death because he had cast the horoscope of a man called Valens – his brother, so he said, though the court did not wait for the proof of his claim (29.2.27). Since the brother (assuming that he had existed) was dead, it would appear, ironically, that the horoscope had predicted correctly; had the brother been alive, and the horoscope therefore a failure, he would still have been executed for predicting the death of the emperor.

In all these cases, unjust though the executions may have been, one can see how they came about. The same cannot be said of the punishment of a simple old woman who (again in Asia) was put to death because she cured fevers with a charm, having used the technique, with his knowledge, to cure the daughter of the very proconsul who condemned her (29.2.26); or of a young man beheaded because he was observed in the public baths to touch the wall of the building, and then his breast, while reciting the seven vowels of the Greek alphabet as a remedy for a disorder of the stomach (29.2.28). The seven vowels, mystically connected with the seven planets, figure frequently in Graeco-Roman magical procedures.[36] By the terms of the law of Constantine of 318 mentioned earlier (*CTh* 9.16.3), both victims should, if they were telling the truth, have been exempt from execution because they were using magic to benefit the health of the human body, and not to do it harm.

It is not surprising that fears of implication in the prosecutions spread widely, especially among the literate classes of the east. Ammianus writes from his own experience of the atmosphere at Antioch, in which men crept about 'as if in the shadows of the underworld', 'velut in

Cimmeriis tenebris reptabamus' (29.2.4) – recalling the image of darkness with which he earlier described the trials as hidden in the confused shadows of memory; 'ut in tenebrosis rebus confusione cuncta miscente' (29.1.24). Not only were there indiscriminate executions in the eastern provinces, 'like the slaughtering of cattle' in Ammianus' expression, 'like hens at a banquet' in the colourful phrase of Eunapius referring to the same events (*V. Soph.*, p. 480); whole libraries of books and scrolls were piled up and burned, although most had nothing to do with magic, but were works of literature and legal tomes (29.1.41). Men were so terrified that they even burned their own books for fear of their being examined when their houses were searched, and interpreted maliciously (29.2.4). A familiar story told by John Chrysostom described how when he was young he and a friend one day, when the authorities were searching Antioch for books on sorcery and magic, fished out from the river Orontes a half-written book, to be struck with terror when they saw a soldier nearby; its owner had thrown the book away in fear of being arrested (*PG* 9.273f.).[37] It will be recalled that a young senator at Rome was executed for having 'written down' – that is, copied out ('descripsisse') – a book on magic arts (28.1.26).

For the modern observer, one of the most interesting features of the trials of Scythopolis and Antioch is the diverse modes in which knowledge of the future was sought; by written consultation, in person or through agents, of the god at Abydus and, at Antioch, by the use of an ouija board first to produce an oracle in verse and then the name of the favoured successor to Valens. We have already seen one of the purposes of theurgical magic as the eliciting of oracles. Theurgy involved the use of normal magical techniques for religious enlightenment, and the tripod of laurel was constructed by the conspirators at Antioch precisely as set out in a surviving magical papyrus.[38] There was naturally some division of opinion as men tried to escape involvement or to pass the blame on to others. One group of defendants maintained that, once the oracle had declared that the 'best man' would become emperor, the enquirers had themselves considered who this might be and had thought of Theodorus: another, that the name of Theodorus was revealed by the ouija board, in the same session that had first produced the oracle. Indeed the description of the seance was only given after conflicting reports had been eliminated by torture and the actual tripod produced in court (29.1.28). The claim that Theodorus was only told afterwards about the consultation was refuted by the letter to Hilarius in which he professed himself ready to secure what he knew 'from soothsayers' was in store for him. We saw that Theodorus' letter also revealed an interesting difference of opinion as to whether it was necessary for men to take active steps to secure what was promised by fate: did human intention itself form part of the fated pattern? The judges posed an equally interesting question to the conspirators, in asking whether they had foreseen the fate that had befallen them. The problem of the failure of men to anticipate, and so to avoid, what would happen to them if divination were a valid form of knowledge was discussed by Ammianus in his digression on divination, and answered in terms of human error in the interpretation of the divine signs (21.1.13; p. 430). In this instance the conspirators informed the judges that they had indeed known of their fate. Whatever the cost to themselves, the 'conjectures of men' were not in their case at fault.

There was, as in all the best predictions, an element of genuine ambiguity. The oracle that Valens would die in war 'on the plains of Mimas' was taken by the emperor – as, no doubt, by the conspirators – to mean a place near Erythrae in Asia Minor rather than the plains of Thrace near Hadrianople, associated with Mimas by the post eventum 'discovery' of an inscription bearing the name (31.14.9).[39] As for the name Theodorus, of which the first letters were produced by the ouija board, perhaps that too was the name already expected and somehow elicited from their seance by the enquirers. It should not have been too difficult to swing the magic pendulum in such a way (in a series of shifting ellipses) that all the letters engraved on the board were indicated in sequence: it would then be for the officiating priest to determine, from his observation of the movements of the pendulum, which were the significant letters of those picked out. This is perhaps how we should reconcile the claim that the conspirators themselves thought of Theodorus with the claim that it was revealed in the seance (29.1.8; 32): both were true, the conspirators already having in mind what they expected to be told. 'THEO...', the letters first produced by the magic ritual, made up one of the commonest elements in Greek proper names, the addition of 'delta' – Ammianus distinguishes this final stage in the revelation (29.1.32) – seeming to be enough to identify Theodorus. It was of course not conclusive. No one thought (how could he?) of the young Spaniard Theodosius, currently an unknown military officer in the west (cf. 29.6.15). Pure coincidence (of course) but it is an important facet of Ammianus' description of the magical procedures, and of his own views on divination, that the conspirators had got the answer right. They should simply have waited for two more letters beyond the 'delta'.

The intensity of Valens' response to the conspiracy of Theodorus is intelligible in another perspective, when we consider it as part of the still active legacy of the reign of Julian. The philosopher Maximus, indefatigable in his pursuit of subversive oracles, is an obvious, and perhaps not deeply regretted, victim of the connection. The proconsul of Asia, Festus of Tridentum (the historian Festus) who came to Ephesus and effected the execution of Maximus and others, is criticised by Ammianus for his cruelty and denounced by Eunapius – falsely, it seems – for his rabid Christianity;[40] though it was Maximus who in his career had done the greater harm, Ammianus being at best ambiguous on his role under Julian, clearly instrumental with that of the fates in leading the emperor to destruction. The former *vicarius* of Britain Alypius, exiled in the trials, had assisted Julian in his abortive restoration of the temple of Jerusalem (23.1.2f.); like others, he perhaps found his connections with

X. Valentinian and Valens

the emperor hard to shake off. Theodorus himself, an educated and well-born Gaul, can be seen as an early supporter of Julian, who had come to the east with him in 361 and stayed there after the emperor's death. He might then belong to the same political nexus as the historian Eutropius, a cultivated Gaul who had joined Julian in the west and accompanied him on the Persian campaign (*Brev.* 10.16.1); he too fell into danger at the time of the conspiracy of Theodorus (29.1.36). If there was a faction here, it had raised its head earlier. Two supporters of Procopius, Euphrasius and Phronimius, are earlier described as noble and educated Gauls by Ammianus (26.7.4):[41] perhaps they believed, as later did the friends of Theodorus, that the eastern empire could do better than the rough Pannonian who now occupied the throne, and saw in Procopius a more sympathetic successor to Julian, whom they had followed from Gaul to the east in the march against Constantius.

*

The involvement of intellectuals in the enquiries conducted at Antioch was one aspect of the manifold nature of late Roman attitudes to philosophy and magic, science and astrology, religion and the occult. Given also the unifying function of ancient culture and the mobility of the educated classes which this made possible, it is not surprising to find the investigations spreading out from Antioch and Syria to other parts of the east, notably to the cities of Asia. Connections between Syria and Asia Minor were especially strong in the tradition of theurgical Neoplatonism associated with Iamblichus and his followers and adopted by Julian. It was in Asia Minor, not in Syria, that Julian had his 'conversion' to this tradition in Neoplatonism (p. 122f.), and it was back to Syrian Antioch that he took his philosophical supporters from Asia, such as Maximus, when he went east to prepare the Persian campaign.

The role of religion in the affair is much more difficult to define. Despite the involvement of intellectuals and philosophers and its connections with the reign of Julian, in no sense was the conspiracy any sort of 'pagan revival' in the east, nor were the prosecutions an attack on paganism as such. The emperors recognised, and still expressed in their legislation, the difference between the pursuit of magic arts and the worship of the old gods, between astrology and legitimate divination, and (except in the case of Julian, for which he was criticised by Ammianus), between a Classical education and religious belief. But the distinctions cannot in practice be drawn so clearly, there was much scope for distortion, and for genuine as well as wilful misunderstanding. Christians as much as pagans believed in the efficacy of magic, the disagreement between them being one of attitude – whether or not the use of magic was legitimate, whether the deities whom it invoked were true gods (or *daimones*), or evil spirits to be repelled and exorcised. Christians as well as pagans, in the gleeful opinion of the latter and to the embarrassment of Christian bishops, indulged in magical superstitions, wearing amulets and charms, carrying around sacred texts, 'crossing' themselves – not unlike the young man in the public baths mentioned above – to avert ill-health and misfortune.[42] The case of the eastern court official who consulted diviners on the sex of the child expected by his wife, has a ready parallel in a long account in Augustine's *Confessions* of discussions in Christian court circles at Milan of the horoscopes of the progeny expected by the wife of a court official and by one of his slaves (*Conf.* 7.6.8f.). Even bishop Athanasius could be accused by his enemies of an illicit interest in the art of foretelling the future, as Ammianus himself records (15.7.8; p. 441).

It is difficult, though not absolutely impossible, to imagine a professed Christian taking an active part in the magical enterprises described to the court at Antioch. Yet many a dutiful bureaucrat no doubt attended church as was expected of him – as did Julian at Vienne before he had declared his apostasy – while reserving his opinion on astrology and divination, and harbouring an interest (forbidden by his bishop) in the occult arts. Fragments of Eunapius preserved by the Suda give in addition to Theodorus the names of three, possibly four, of the conspirators named by Ammianus, adding a further name, Jacobus, which is either the name of a Jew – or of a Christian; he is alleged, how plausibly seems impossible to say, to have drunk poison on the advice of Libanius because he had enquired into the identity of Valens' successor.[43] Nothing is positively known of the religious beliefs of Theodorus, but it would be strange to imagine that the conspirators against Valens were connected with Julian the Apostate as shown above, without being connected, at least in public estimation, with his religion.

However one interprets them in this sense, the affairs of Scythopolis and Antioch, ranging in the information they reveal from seances, oracles and their interpretation, to magical charms, harmless superstitions and the raising of ghosts, give a fascinating insight into the variety of pagan belief and its still vigorous residue in east Roman society. As for Rome itself, magic arts in the pursuit of success at the races and in the beds of married women, nothing so creditable can be said; nor, for all his criticism of the conduct of Valentinian's agents there, does Ammianus try to say it.

*

Most of the remainder of Book 29 and the greater part of Book 30 of Ammianus' history are taken up with narrative of western events, although eastern ones are not neglected. Book 31, beginning with a digression on the Huns and Alani, describes the crossing of the Danube by the Goths, culminating in the battle near Hadrianople in Thrace in which the emperor Valens was killed and two-thirds of the eastern field army were destroyed. Ammianus does not waste the opportunity in his obituary of the emperor to remind us of the oracle revealed in the seance at Antioch, quoting again one of the three lines cited in the earlier passage and explaining how the 'plains of Mimas' on which Valens perished were not, as Homer and Cicero seemed to have indicated, near Erythrae in Asia Minor, but in Thrace (31.14.8, cf. 29.1.33). Circumstantial 'evidence' was naturally provided of the truth of the oracle. An inscription 'was said' to have been found near the place where Valens 'was thought' to have fallen (of course, no one, as Ammianus himself makes perfectly clear, actually knew where this was) bearing the name of one Mimas; the actual text, identifying Mimas as a Macedonian general, being duly produced by later Byzantine sources. Another, longer oracle, of which Ammianus again provides the Greek text, forms part of the sequence of omens with which he actually opened Book 31 of the history. The lines were read on an inscription dug out of the 'ancient walls' of Chalcedon when they were dismantled – in punishment, as other sources tell, for that city's support of the usurper Procopius.[44]

Ammianus further draws together his story in the last episode which he narrates. Julius, *magister militum* in the eastern provinces, in a carefully co-ordinated plan assembled in the parade-grounds of the cities in which they were garrisoned all the Goths already in Roman service, as if to receive arrears of pay. He then had them massacred, an 'efficacious' action by which the eastern provinces were saved from great peril (31.16.8). Eunapius also narrated this episode, alleging that the action was approved by the senate of Constantinople. If this were true, it would be an interesting indication of one of the ways in which the eastern provinces coped with the crisis of authority caused by Valens' death; but the manner and context in which the story is presented inspire little confidence (Zosimus 4.26).[45] Ammianus for his part describes Julius as *magister militum* 'trans Taurum', thereby locating himself and his reader west of the mountain range that divided Asia Minor from Syria. But we cannot miss the significance of the episode for Ammianus himself. He is describing the liberation from danger of his own native provinces by the initiative of a military commander normally resident in Antioch. It is an unspoken fragment of autobiography, in which Ammianus for the last time enters obliquely into the events he describes. This is immediately confirmed by the epilogue in which Ammianus, the 'soldier and Greek', vainly entrusts the history of the present age to writers of a new generation.

Although in comparison with the earlier books they lack a degree of continuity, the last six books of Ammianus' history are notable for their use of balance and contrast. After the accession of Valentinian and Valens, their division of the empire and the rebellion of Procopius in Book 26, and the campaigns of the two emperors in west and east in Book 27, Books 28 and 29 begin respectively with accusations of magic in upper-class society in west and east; while 30 and 31 close with the deaths and obituary notices of the two emperors. It is indeed possible that some of the difficulties, seen earlier, in Ammianus' narrative of the trials conducted at Rome by Valentinian's agents arise because the historian has tried to present them as a counterpart to the Antiochene trials of Valens, in a way that their substance will not bear; he has tried to describe as a unified episode with a single meaning events that were in fact disparate, and generally less significant than he makes them.

The more schematic formal character of these books reflects the greater detachment of the historian from the events he describes and the more intractable nature of his source material, not least the division of the empire into western and eastern units of government. It is these considerations rather than any change in the plan of composition that best explain the less integrated, more episodic quality of these in contrast to the earlier books: more like a series of narrative and discursive essays (though Book 31 is a masterpiece of both) than continuous history.

So far, Ammianus the historian has been presented in relation to the events in which he was to different degrees involved as participant or observer, biographical interpretation alternating with excursus within a strict overall structure in a manner that partly reflects his own. It will be obvious that he is a wonderfully eloquent witness of almost every aspect of the life and society of his times. In breadth of interest, wealth of circumstantial detail and power of observation he rivals any other Greek or Roman historian known to us from any period, and outclasses most. As contemporary historians only Thucydides and possibly Polybius have any prior claim to our admiration, and Ammianus' world is so much vaster, its political structures more forbidding, and its cultural complexity far greater than theirs: all seen with the observant eye of an individual fascinated by all forms of human conduct, a still living challenge to the modern historian of his age. In Part Two of this book we therefore turn from Ammianus himself to the description, beginning with the emperors and their office, of the society in which he lived, and for which he provides such a comprehensive wealth of material.

Part Two
Visa vel Lecta

CHAPTER XI

The Office of Emperor

A Roman history running from the principate of Nerva to the death of Valens will naturally assign the central role to the emperors. The personalities and exploits of the emperors of Ammianus' own day dominate his surviving books, just as – to judge by the nature of his back-references – did those of the second, third and early fourth centuries the books that preceded. It may seem impractical to isolate Ammianus' views on the nature of the imperial office, and the documentation of such an all-pervasive issue will inevitably be selective and arbitrary. But that Ammianus did have opinions on the matter will be obvious, and the risk of arbitrary documentation is worthwhile if we may hope to see what they were. The subject is incomplete, however, without a corresponding description of the impact in practice of government on the society of Ammianus' time. 'The Office of Emperor', 'The Character of Government' and 'The Practice of War' are complementary subjects, and should be be taken together. If there is some overlap between them, this is justified by the different perspectives that are involved. The first sees the emperors as far as possible in their own right, the second sees them, as it were, from the point of view of their late Roman beneficiary or victim, the third portrays them in their most important single activity. We begin with an occasion notable for the convergence of all three aspects.

*

On 28 April 357 the Emperor Constantius came to Rome on an official visit to his capital city.[1] Ammianus' description of his entry to Rome is classic, both as a demonstration of the historian's technique and visual power, as an evocation of the late Roman imperial office at its most ceremonious, and as a description of one of its best-known actual ceremonies, the imperial arrival or 'adventus'. Constantius approached the city enthroned in a golden carriage, immovable as a statue, amid the glitter of precious stones. He was attended by the emblazoned standards of his army, dragon ensigns fluttering in the breeze;[2] on either side were mailed infantrymen, their armour fitting as closely as if they too had been bronze statues (16.10.7f.). The emperor was acclaimed by the massed crowds lining the route, while he himself, amid the din, 'never flinched, but showed himself as immobile as he was normally seen in his provinces.

Fig. 1. The Emperor Constantius, seated in consular robes and holding a sceptre, performs the gesture of 'liberalitas'. From his open hand pours coin for the populace, behind his throne are stacked oblong dishes or 'lanxes', intended as largesse for select recipients. The dais, throne and curtains are familiar elements in the imperial iconography of this type. The illustration is from an early seventeenth-century copy of a lost ninth-century MS of the so-called 'Calendar of the Year 354' (H. Stern, *Le Calendrier de 354* [Paris, 1953], pp. 19, 325ff., and pl. XIV). Constantius shared the consulship of 354 with Gallus Caesar, whose corresponding (though standing) image also appears in the Calendar.

He bent his body low when he entered lofty gateways, and kept the gaze of his eyes straight ahead, turning his face neither right nor left, as if his neck were held in a clamp. Like a graven image of a man ('tamquam figmentum hominis') he neither allowed his head to shake when the wheel of the carriage jolted, nor was he at any time seen to spit, wipe or rub his face or nose, or to move his hands' (16.10.9f.). The idea was to give an impression of superhuman endurance, granted alone to the emperor, 'as was given to be understood'; 'ut existimari dabatur' (16.10.11). The whole passage, one of the most famous in Ammianus, is anticipated in remarkably similar terms in Xenophon's book *Cyropaedeia* or 'Education of Cyrus', where the author, writing of Cyrus' methods in establishing his royal power, comes to his recognition of the need to 'bewitch' his subjects by certain facets of deportment:[3]

> Rulers ought not to differ from their subjects simply by being better than they, but ought as it were to cast a spell on them. At any rate [Cyrus] elected to wear Median dress himself and persuaded his associates also to do the same; the purpose of this being to conceal any physical defect and make its wearers look tall and handsome. They have footwear so designed that by adding something beneath the soles they can appear taller than they are without this being realised. He also encouraged the making up of the eyes to enhance their beauty and the use of cosmetics, to make the complexion seem finer than it really is. He taught his associates also *not to be seen spitting or wiping the nose in public, nor to turn their heads round to gaze at anything – as if they were men whom nothing could surprise.* (Cyrop. 8.1.40-2)

According to Herotodus (1.99), who claims it to have been an offence for a subject to laugh or to spit in the royal presence, Persian regal ceremonial had been established by Cyrus' ancestor Deioces, with the purpose of exalting the king and setting him apart from potential rivals, equal in birth and virtue. The tendency of the prescribed behaviour is to eliminate spontaneity in favour of a static symbolism of power, and to suggest in the monarch reserves of self-control beyond normal human possibilities – to impose him as if by magical force upon his subjects.

The political and ceremonial setting of Constantius' visit to Rome was actually rather complex. Within its span, on 22 May, fell the twentieth anniversary of the death of Constantine the Great, and so of the accession as full Augustus of Constantius. One source indeed reports of the visit to Rome that he 'celebrated his vicennalia' there (*Cons. Const.* s.a. 357); he had already, at Arles on 10 October 353, given public games to commemorate the thirtieth anniversary of his first promotion to the rank of Caesar by Constantine (14.5.1). The specific opportunity for the visit to Rome was provided by Constantius' continued presence in the west after the defeat of Magnentius, followed by the need for political and military reconstruction there. It is this military and triumphal aspect of the *adventus* that Ammianus emphasised. He saw the visit as a celebration of victories in civil war, by an emperor whose record in foreign campaigns did not merit it.[4] Constantius never defeated any foreign people that made war on him, nor did he ever stand in the first line of battle, nor add to the territory of the empire; he merely wished to demonstrate imperial power to a Roman people living in peace and quiet, neither expecting nor desiring to see anything like it (16.10.2). The emperor carried himself 'as if he were off to intimidate Euphrates or Rhine with a show of arms', and his motionless, imperturbable posture was such as it was commonly seen in the provinces (10.6.9). In effect a triumph over Roman blood shed in civil war, the procession was inappropriate for the seat and shrine of empire, the residence of peace, civility and freedom. Once he was inside the city, indeed, Constantius' behaviour was transformed. He addressed the senators in the senate-house, the people from the tribunal in the forum, he held equestrian games and delighted in the friendly shouts of the people, who managed to respect both due modesty and their traditions of liberty. The emperor on his side maintained proper decorum, even allowing the chariot races to reach their own outcome. In other cities, it is implied, he imposed his own discretion on the results of races, presumably by indicating in advance which result he would prefer (10.13f.).

Many of these features of imperial behaviour were obligatory for the occasion, and appear as such in other sources. The acclamations of the people assembled to receive the emperor, mentioned by Ammianus (16.10.9), are described by the poet Claudian, in his panegyric on Honorius' sixth consulship of 404; so too the cheerful exchanges between emperor and people alluded to by Ammianus:[5]

>   quantamque rependit
> maiestas alterna vicem, cum regia circi
> conexum gradibus veneratur purpura vulgus
> adsensuque cavae sublatus in aethera vallis
> plebis adoratae reboat fragor, unaque totis
> intonat Augustum septenis arcibus Echo!
>   (VI Cons. Hon. 612-17)

As for the emperor's relations with the nobility of Rome, not only did he address its members formally in the senate-house; according to the panegyrist Pacatus, Theodosius during his visit of 389 attended senators in their own homes. The emperor would dismiss his military escort and enter the senatorial mansion in what Pacatus significantly – because it excludes precisely what Ammianus found *in*appropriate, at least in Constantius' initial posture – calls 'civili' progressu' (*Paneg.* 47.3).[6] Not only the individual elements in imperial behaviour, but also the transition, on reaching Rome, from 'military' to 'civil' modes of conduct, were aspects of the recognised protocol of such occasions.

No one would suppose that these modes of conduct were more than relics of the past, handed down from the distant days when an emperor's reputation had stood or fallen on the quality of his relations with the

XI. The Office of Emperor

senate and people of Rome. Fourth-century emperors rarely visited Rome, and impinged only occasionally on the life of the city. In his panegyric of 404, Claudian only recognised three such occasions (*VI Cons. Hon.* 392-5); he was referring, no doubt, to one of the visits of Constantine the Great, the visit of Constantius, and that of Theodosius in 389.[7] Ammianus was for his part too much of a realist to suppose that an emperor should be judged merely, or even primarily, in the context of his relations with the city of Rome and its senatorial class. Yet the senate attached importance to the manner of its treatment by Constantius. We saw earlier how, three years after the visit, in the course of his march against Constantius Julian wrote to the senate a letter of self-justification for his action in proclaiming himself against the emperor, and added sharp comments directed against him. The senate resented this, and demanded in acclamations that Julian should respect the author of his dignity; 'auctori tuo reverentiam rogamus' (21.10.7). This, said Ammianus, was a fine demonstration of the independent spirit of the nobility, and showed its affection for Constantius. The orator Symmachus, addressing the Emperor Valentinian II in 384, recalled another aspect of Constantius' visit; apart from the admiring inspection of old temples also mentioned by Ammianus, Constantius had in his capacity as *pontifex maximus* filled vacancies in the colleges of priests by appointing nobles to them (*Rel.* 3.7). In so doing, he allowed his personal commitment to the Christian religion to yield to the public duties of *pontifex maximus*; another among many instances of the pressures still exerted by ancestral traditions on the developing institutions of the new empire of the fourth century.

Ammianus is unsympathetic to one particular innovation of imperial protocol that was prevalent in his own day. He criticised Constantius for his ambition to model his rule on that of the 'civiles principes' of earlier times, while styling himself in dictated letters as 'Aeternitas Mea' and, in letters written with his own hand, 'Master of the entire world'. This, thought Ammianus, was a departure from 'justice' indulged in by Constantius after the execution of Gallus, when his courtiers persuaded him that his virtue and fortune were without limit, and that he was free from the normal inconveniences of mortality (15.1.3).

Ammianus' objection is a curious one. Apart from its triviality as an instance of the point of principle at stake, he must have known that the style to which he refers was commonplace in imperial pronouncements of the times.[8] In his obituary notice of Constantius, Ammianus produced a more considered assessment of the public aspects of an emperor's position. He here wrote that Constantius treated the imperial office with the dignity due to it. In an allusion to the raised boot worn by dramatic actors – reminiscent of the raised 'Median shoe' mentioned by Xenophon – he remarked that Constantius always kept on the trappings of imperial authority and despised the pursuit of mere 'popularity'; 'imperatoriae auctoritatis cothurnum ubique custodiens popularitatem elato animo contemnebat et magno' (21.16.1). This, the first of the points offered in favour of Constantius in the obituary notice, contrasts sharply with Ammianus' judgment of Julian, that he fed on the applause of the multitude, seeking praise without restraint even on the most trivial of matters, affecting in his thirst for popularity to converse with the unworthy; 'vulgi plausibus laetus, laudum etiam ex minimis rebus intemperans appetitor, popularitatis cupiditate cum indignis loqui saepe affectans' (25.4.18).

Ammianus had illustrated this opinion in narrating a number of episodes that occurred at Constantinople in the early part of 362. On the first day of the consular year, Julian appeared in public in humble guise, processing on foot among the 'honorati' rather than riding apart from them. Some liked this, wrote Ammianus, others thought it a cheap affectation, 'affectatum et vile' (22.7.1).[9] Then, when the consul presided over circus games and slaves were led in according to custom to be manumitted, Julian pronounced the appropriate formula himself, forgetting that on this occasion the jurisdiction belonged to the consul. Julian fined himself ten pounds of gold, as having committed a breach of legal propriety (22.7.2). In the same months, Julian often took his seat in the senate of Constantinople to consider problems of government and to hear cases at law. On one such occasion, the arrival from Asia was announced of the philosopher Maximus. Julian leapt up unceremoniously and, *forgetting who he was* ('qui esset, oblitus') went charging out of the senate to greet his friend, whom he then kissed, received with reverence (that is, as an equal or superior, and not as an emperor receives a subject), and escorted into the senate (of which he was not a member). For Ammianus, the episode seemed to show Julian as an ostentatious seeker for glory, like those philosophers who, according to Cicero, wrote books denouncing fame and ambition, yet put their names to them (22.7.3f.). It is interesting that Maximus' progress from Asia to Constantinople was viewed, from the standpoint of a provincial writer, as a demonstration of pomp and ostentation just as unsuitable for a philosopher as Julian's spontaneous humility was for an emperor (Eunapius, *V. Soph.* p. 442). To each his proper mode of conduct – an ironic reflection on Julian's dream of being like a Platonic philosopher-king. The two modes of life were, in late Roman conditions, simply incompatible.

An emperor ought in his public appearances to set a certain standard of dignified behaviour, to do otherwise being a perverse ostentation. The worst aspects of a lack of dignity are brought out in Ammianus' description of the usurpation of Procopius in 365. Procopius was put up by soldiers in the Anastasian baths at Constantinople, and awaited his public presentation pale and nervous, as if he had been dragged up from the underworld.[10] Since no proper cloak could be found, he was dressed in a gold-threated tunic, so that above his waist he looked like a palace attendant, below it like a slave from the palace training school. He wore purple slippers, carried a spear and held in his hand a piece of purple cloth. Pursuing the dramatic metaphor of the 'cothurnus' used of Constantius, Ammianus remarked that Procopius resembled a stage

XI. The Office of Emperor

apparition, a fancy-dress mockery of the real thing; 'ut in theatrali scaena simulacrum quoddam insigne per aulaeum vel mimicam cavillationem subito putares emersum' (26.6.15). The affair was a ludicrous disgrace, deserving scorn and hilarity had not the outcome been so disastrous; 'ad hoc dehonestamentum honorum omnium ludibriose sublatus ... irrisione digna principia incaute coepta et temere, ad ingemiscendas erupisse rei publicae clades' (26.6.16; 19). Ammianus' expressions carry portentous weight, further increased by their allusion to some famous words of the historian Sallust. In a speech assigned to the consul Lepidus, Sallust referred to one Fufidius, a centurion promoted senator by the dictator Sulla — an unsuitable parallel, no doubt, for a relative of Constantine made emperor, but the basis for a magnificently resonant allusion instantly recognisable to Ammianus' more literate readers; 'quibus praelatus in magistratibus capiundis Fufidius, ancilla turpis, *honorum omnium dehonestamentum?*' (*Hist.* 1.55.21). Ammianus confirms the allusion to Sallust by adding the phrase '*ancillari* adulatione' to describe the self-abasing manner in which Procopius addressed his supporters (26.6.16).[11]

The proper conduct of Roman emperors, like any question of protocol, was a matter of what was fitting for time, place and company. That it was necessary to accept certain restraints upon personal conduct is no more than one would expect. A *magister militum* made emperor in 421 is said to have regretted his promotion because he was no longer free to come and go as he chose and was unable to play games as he was used to; he had formerly enjoyed himself hugely at banquets, often joining in the antics of mime dancers as they performed before the guests![12] According to Ammianus, the Emperor Jovian was known for his drinking and eating habits, and for his over-indulgence in sex — faults which he would perhaps have corrected had he lived, out of respect for the imperial office; 'quae vitia imperiali verecundia forsitan correxisset'. He is also said to have been of vivacious expression and is compared with Constantius in that he often worked in the afternoons (the usual time for rest and relaxation) and did not mind being seen joking with his friends; 'iocarique palam cum proximis assuetus' (25.10.14f.). Ammianus' comparison of Jovian with Constantius on this point of *in*formality well emphasises what was exceptional in that emperor's public conduct during the ceremonial visit to Rome in 357.

The personalities and tastes of emperors as they appear in Ammianus can indeed be at variance with his descriptions of their conduct in office. The most striking instance is that of the formidable, warlike Valentinian, who is said to have liked 'elegant but not extravagant' dinner-parties. He wrote in an attractive hand, painted and modelled 'charmingly' ('venuste' is Ammianus' unexpected word); perhaps more in keeping with one's expectations, he liked inventing new types of military equipment, but in general was rather fastidious in his taste; 'amator munditiarum' (30.9.4). One might see the emperor as a connoisseur of miniatures, something of an amateur artist and draftsman — an impression hard to reconcile with that of an emperor who could be described as 'roaring' his objections to the presence of a petitioner, could order the head of another to be struck off importunately, have clubbed to death a young groom who released a hound prematurely and kept man-eating bears outside his bedroom, making sure that they were otherwise not over-fed (29.3.3ff.; p. 260). The poet Ausonius, employed by Valentinian to tutor his son in the literary arts, flattered the emperor as a man of erudition, capable of exchanging Vergilian tags around the dinner-table; 'vir meo iudicio eruditus' (*Cento Nuptialis*, praef.).[13] In striking contrast is his brother Valens, described by Ammianus as 'uncultivated, untrained in liberal studies', as 'uneducated and rude'; 'subagrestis ingenii, nec bellicis nec liberalibus studiis eruditus ... inconsummatus et rudis' (31.14.5; 8). Yet Valens accepted literary dedications from the historians Eutropius and Festus, and consulted 'learned men' on the interpretation of the prophetic verses that indicated where he would meet his end (31.14.8). Julian was in all respects a special case; as for Constantius, his literary ambitions were frustrated by bluntness of intellect. After failing in rhetoric he turned to writing poetry but did not achieve much in that field either (21.16.4).

The physical appearances of the emperors are described by Ammianus in the authentic manner of Classical biography.[14] Constantius was dark, with soft hair and smoothly shaven cheeks, had rather bulging but sharp-sighted eyes, was long in the body and short in the legs and good at running and jumping (21.16.19); Julian of medium height with strong neck and shoulders, keen eyes, pendulous lower lip and – his personal eccentricity – a long beard, trimmed to a point (25.4.22); Jovian was very tall and dignified in bearing, with a slight stoop, grey eyes and the vivacious expression just mentioned (25.10.14, cf. 5.6). Valentinian was powerful and well-proportioned, with regular features, healthy complexion, grey-eyed with a severe, observant expression and of great physical presence when addressing a crowd (30.9.6, cf. 26.2.5); his brother was of average height with a protruding stomach, dark complexion and a defect in one eye, not apparent from a distance (31.14.7). Ammianus allows us to see his emperors as human beings despite the pressures and constraints of their office. They are required on appropriate occasions to show an almost superhuman endurance but do not conform to any stereotype of character or physical appearance, in which some imperfections, studiously disguised in their more ceremonious performances, were only perceptible at close quarters and in more intimate circumstances.

*

That Ammianus recognised the complexity of the relationship between the personal character of an emperor and the nature of the imperial office is clear at once from those 'faults' which Jovian would have corrected had he lived, from a sense of respect ('verecundia') for his new position. Ammianus cited Valentinian's opinion on the tendency of the strict exercise of power to provoke envy and misinterpretation (30.8.10),[15] and,

XI. The Office of Emperor

introducing his obituary notice of Valentinian, observed in a beautiful phrase how the possession of power is liable to lay bare the intimate reaches of the soul, revealing there good and bad alike; 'vitiorum ... vel bonorum, quae potestatis amplitudo monstravit nudare solita semper animorum interna' (30.7.1)

It was especially in these obituary notices that Ammianus gave his most concentrated statements of the qualities shown by emperors and the expectations held of them.[16] The obituaries are valuable for another reason, for it is here that he is likely to assume a consensus of opinion among his readers against which to measure his judgment of their virtues and shortcomings. In general, he offers in these passages candid verdicts on the achievements and shortcomings of emperors – which is not to say that they are free from normal techniques of rhetorical presentation designed to influence the reader's opinion.

The techniques are particularly evident in the obituary notices of Constantius and Julian. In the case of Constantius (21.16.1-18), the register of virtues, stated plainly without much elaboration, runs to seven sections of text (16.1-7); the shortcomings add up to eleven sections (8-18), an ascendancy of vice over virtue achieved largely by the accumulation of rhetorical parallels ranging from Manlius (in a citation of Cicero) to Gallienus, to illustrate the vices. As we saw earlier the obituary of Julian deters objective analysis by its presentation, in the long discussion of Julian's virtues, in terms of the four cardinal virtues defined by the 'philosophers', supported by four corresponding 'external characteristics' of virtue (25.4.1). The obituary has also to be read as the culmination of at least two preceding passages which bear many of the features of panegyric (16.1.1ff.; 5.1ff.). Julian's shortcomings, on the other hand, are presented briefly, and as of little significance compared with the virtues. They have to be considered very carefully by Ammianus' reader if he is to understand how important they are in the context of the emperor's aims and policies, and how insufficiently emphasised by the historian.[17]

In these passages, setting virtues against vices in balancing sections, Ammianus writes in the manner of the Classical biographers, sharing their tendency to attribute to the personal characters of rulers actions that are better understood in terms of the situations in which they found themselves. To take an obvious example, the need to raise money may have the best possible justification in terms of the external pressures upon emperors, but will be seen as an expression of their personal greed, 'avaritia'. Ammianus wrote that Valentinian was avaricious, without distinguishing between good and evil; 'aviditas plus habendi sine honesti pravique differentia' (30.8.8). Some excused this by reference to the situation in which Valentinian was placed, that is the immense waste of Julian's Persian campaign, which had left his successor short of troops and the money to recruit and pay them. Ammianus rejected this argument, on the grounds that whatever the circumstances there are limits to what is permitted, even when the power exists; yet his use at this point of an anecdote showing Themistocles' contempt for personal gain merely repeats a confusion of private avarice with the public stringencies that emperors were from time to time forced to impose.

We cannot expect Ammianus, or any ancient writer, to have seen such issues other than in terms of the personal character of emperors. The Christian apologist Lactantius had similarly attributed Diocletian's financial strictness to his 'avarice' (*Mort. Pers.* 7.2), much as that emperor had himself, in his *Edict on Maximum Prices*, blamed monetary inflation on the 'avarice' of tradesmen aimed, we are asked to believe, at victimising his innocent, defenceless army (praef. 12f.). Ammianus does however imply a distinction between certain irregular ways of raising money frequently resorted to by emperors, such as the confiscation of the wealth of the rich by political prosecutions, and the conduct of regular taxation. Perhaps this is what Ammianus intends to convey in his phrase quoted above, 'sine ... honesti pravique differentia'. Unless he intends some such distinction, Ammianus is guilty of inconsistency, for in their obituaries he records among the virtues of both Valentinian and Valens that they were noted for their restraint in the taxation of provinces. Valens was an 'extremely fair protector of the provinces, whose indemnities he maintained as if they were part of his private household, while urgently attempting to ease the burdens of taxation'; 'tributorum onera studio quodam molliens singulari' (31.14.2). Valentinian is similarly said to have lightened tax burdens; 'tributorum ubique molliens sarcinas' (30.9.1).

This is an interesting judgment even when confined to the domain of taxation, given the exceptions recorded by Ammianus. In the opening years of his reign, Valens is alleged to have raked in tax arrears dating back almost a century, to the days of the Emperor Aurelian, a policy assigned not directly to Valens himself but to his father-in-law Petronius, to escape whose rapacity many men were said to have favoured Procopius (26.6.7ff.). The chief exception to the otherwise moderate policy of Valentinian was his praetorian prefect, Petronius Probus, whose financial ravages in Illyricum Ammianus is not the only author to denounce (30.5.4ff.). It is difficult to see this passage as other than a contradiction of Ammianus' conclusion that Valentinian was sparing of his provincials and tried always to lighten their tax burdens; except that when he heard of it the emperor tried, but failed, to put a stop to Probus' conduct.[18] Of other emperors described by Ammianus, Constantius was ruthless in raising and exacting taxes, the inexhaustible rapacity of his demands bringing him more unpopularity than money; 'plus odiorum ei quam pecuniam conferentium' (21.16.17). Added to this, he never heard an appeal against a tax assessment nor offered any indemnity: he had of course to finance his interminable civil and foreign wars. Julian, by contrast, remitted many overdue taxes ('diuturnitate congesta') and refused the imperial treasury any advantage over private plaintiffs in cases of dispute at law (25.4.15). We may recall his reduction of the tax assessment in Gaul at the beginning of his regime as Caesar there from

XI. The Office of Emperor

twenty-five to seven *solidi*. The justification of the reform, that it was better to set a modest rate of taxation and collect it successfully than to make excessive demands and be forced to grant indulgences, tells as much about the ability of better-placed provincials to defend their interests as about the pressures exerted on them by imperial authorities (16.5.14f.; p. 89).

On a different matter, Valentinian was rather inclined to severity – forgetting no doubt that a man holding great power must avoid all forms of excess 'like headlong cliffs'; 'omnia nimia velut praecipites scopuli sunt evitanda'. He never remitted a death sentence, as even the most savage of emperors sometimes did, and was inclined to order the use of torture in judicial enquiries (30.8.2f.). So too Constantius was suspicious and harsh in cases of *maiestas*, again tending to permit torture and even devising new forms of execution (21.16.7ff.). In such cases, wrote Ammianus, Constantius hated 'with a capital hatred' the right course of action, though anxious to be known as a just and clement emperor (21.16.11). Here again, Ammianus has allowed interpretations of the personality of emperors to become confused with judgments of public policy, attributing to shortcomings of personal character a procedure, the use of torture, that was long established in the public law of the Roman empire. Ammianus understood this perfectly well, as is clear from his short digression on the treason laws of the Republic (19.12.17). As in the case of finance, a distinction can be made that helps to preserve Ammianus' consistency. He regarded these emperors as having crossed the borderline between true discipline and vindictiveness, or to have allowed their quest for gain (by confiscating the property of the condemned) to override the restraints of the laws. He makes the distinction explicit in saying on one occasion that Constantius pursued cases of *maiestas* more severely than was correct or proper; 'acrius exsurgens quam civiliter' (21.16.9).[19]

Among the examples adduced by Ammianus to illustrate the conduct of the emperors of his own day, the holders of that office in the earlier period of Roman history are naturally given a prominent role. Constantius II provides a rich selection, particularly as regards his shortcomings of character and policy. In other ways a moderate emperor, in his pursuit of charges of treason Constantius easily surpassed in cruelty Caligula, Domitian and Commodus, especially at the beginning of his reign, when he murdered all his relations – an interesting hint of what Ammianus had written, in one of the lost books, of the events following the death of Constantine the Great in 337 (21.16.8; p. 84). He exceeded even Gallienus, an emperor who, frequently harassed by actual plots and conspiracies (Ammianus cites those of Aureolus, Postumus, Ingenuus, Valens also named Thessalonicus, and 'many others'), was nevertheless often lenient in judging them. Constantius on the other hand invented capital accusations from quite trivial circumstances. In this he was unlike Marcus Aurelius, who burned documents incriminating supporters of the rebel Avidius Cassius in order to avoid making unnecessary enemies (16.11). In a slightly different perspective, when Ursicinus fell under the threat of accusation at the court of Constantius, his prospects are indicated by reference to the fate of Domitius Corbulo, who 'is said' to have been killed 'in the polluted depravity of the age of Nero'; 'in colluvione illa Neroniani saeculi' (15.2.5). The allusion is picked up again by Ammianus in referring to the *magister militum* Theodosius, who achieved distinction under Valentinian. He is here compared with Domitius Corbulo and Lusius Quietus 'of olden times, of whom one flourished under Nero, the other under Trajan' (29.5.4). Ammianus does not need to say that both these generals were killed (or forced to suicide) by Roman emperors; Corbulo by Nero, Lusius Quietus in the turbulence attending the succession of Hadrian in AD 117. The allusions enable Ammianus to acknowledge the fact of the execution of Theodosius in 376 without having to explain the circumstances.[20]

Of Constantius' successors, Valentinian is similarly equipped with a range of historical *exempla*, including emperors of earlier times, to help define and illuminate aspects of his character.[21] Among Valentinian's faults was his cruelty, a shortcoming which the emperor could have corrected had he contemplated the example of the Persian king Artaxerxes known as Macrochira, the 'Long-handed'; he devised symbolic punishments so as to avoid penalties characteristic of the government of kings, like beheading, or lopping off the ears of victims (30.8.4). The Republican magistrate Papirius Cursor spared a praetor of Praeneste who had failed to bring reinforcements rapidly in the Samnite Wars, but did not through his clemency sacrifice respect or martial glory. He alone, it was believed, could have resisted Alexander the Great had he invaded Italy – an untestable hypothesis but relevant to Valentinian, who was known both for his military achievements and for his tendency to punish in haste (30.8.5). As to his avidity for financial gain, some justified this by the parallel of Aurelian, who had found the treasury empty after the reign of Gallienus. In his hatred for the upper classes, Valentinian wanted for himself a monopoly of 'bonae artes', a fault which 'we read' was particularly severe in the case of Hadrian; 'quo vitio exarsisse principem legimus Hadrianum' (30.8.10). Valentinian was also overbearing in manner but could be reduced to submission by the emotion of fear. Knowing this, a *magister officiorum* on one occasion mentioned the subject of barbarian incursions in order to curb the emperor's anger: upon which he was as calm and kindly as Antoninus Pius (30.8.12)! In all, there was much in Valentinian's reign worthy of emulation. Had he restrained his shortcomings, indeed, he would have been 'like a second Trajan or Marcus'. This is said with particular reference to his care for the well-being of provincials, his restraint in matters of taxation, and the strictness of his military discipline (30.9.1).

The case of Julian, who is compared in foresight with Titus, in warlike prowess with Trajan, in mildness with Antoninus Pius, and in his pursuit of true reason with his admired model Marcus Aurelius, is discussed elsewhere, as fundamental not only to Ammianus' conception of an ideal emperor but to his entire intellectual and historiographical development

XI. The Office of Emperor

(pp. 468ff.). A brief digression on the character of Gratian – whose death in 383 closely precedes the period in which Ammianus was composing his history – shows him as 'eloquent, restrained, warlike and tolerant', indeed emulating the conduct of the best emperors, until he was led astray by obsequious advisers and turned to the 'vain pursuits of Caesar Commodus': though Gratian, unlike Commodus, was not known for the letting of human blood. Ammianus comments that the situation of empire (the context is the preliminaries of the battle of Hadrianople, with Gratian bringing reinforcements to Valens) required rather a Marcus Aurelius than an insubstantial dilettante. Not that even Marcus could in Ammianus' opinion have remedied the situation 'without colleagues after his own character and sober wisdom in counsel'; 'sine collegis similibus et magna sobrietate consiliorum' (31.10.18f.).[22]

These parallels were no mere literary exercise. They provided a framework within which Ammianus' readers were expected to judge the conduct of the emperors of their own day and to compare them with their counterparts in earlier ages. Further, as instances of correct behaviour they were accessible in literature to contemporary emperors, who should permit themselves to be guided by them. If Valentinian failed to imitate the clemency of Papirius Cursor or the restraint of Themistocles, it was because he 'did not know' the example or 'pretended not to know' that certain things, though possible for one holding supreme power, are not permitted; 'haec forsitan Valentinianus *ignorans*' ... '*dissimulans scire* quod sunt aliqua quae fieri non oportet, etiam si licet ...' (30.8.6; 9). There is nothing more profoundly Classical in Ammianus than the belief, implied by these words, in the relevance of historical models of behaviour, and in knowledge as the source of true moral action.

If the actions of earlier emperors were guides to the contemporary conduct of the imperial office, we have evidently to assume a compatibility at some level between emperors of the early and later periods of Roman history, and it is worth asking how Ammianus saw the relationship between them. The age of Augustus was indeed far in the past (as far from Ammianus, it is a sobering thought, as Elizabeth I is from us), and Ammianus' expressions can reflect this. Comparing efforts made in early and recent times to transport obelisks from Egypt to Rome, he designates Augustus (whom he calls 'Octavianus Augustus') as an 'emperor of old'; 'veterem principem' (17.4.12). He praises Domitian's prohibition of the practice of castration as an event, as we might say, of 'olden times'; 'iuvat veterem laudare Domitianum ...' (18.4.5). On the other hand, the episode in which Diocletian made Galerius walk before his carriage after his Persian defeat is described as 'not such an ancient example'; 'non adeo vetus exemplum' (14.11.10). The phrase, interesting for its hint that an *exemplum*, a model of correct behaviour, would normally be expected to be 'vetus', is here attributed by Ammianus to the Emperor Constantius, in trying to persuade Gallus Caesar to leave Antioch and return obediently to him. Ammianus can similarly contrast what he saw as the military indiscipline of his own day with the situation under Galerius, characterising that as a 'recent' period of history; 'contra quam *recens memoria* tradidit; notum est enim sub Maximiano [*sc.* Galerio] Caesare ...' (22.4.8). Coming to an end in 305, the Tetrarchy was indeed, for Ammianus as a young man, within reach of the living memory of many who had seen it. One of the minor delights of the Persian campaign of Julian was the discovery in the Persian town of Anatha of an old soldier of Galerius who had been captured by the Persians as a young man, stayed in Persia and raised a family. He was now a bent old man claiming nearly a hundred years; 'centenario iam contiguus' (24.1.10; p. 172).

To see a continuity, in which Greek and early Roman, occasionally even foreign parallels, are no less relevant to his own age than those from the earlier imperial period, Ammianus must clearly be expressing himself in a moral rather than in a political or institutional sense. For he well understood that the institutional character of the imperial office had changed much since the early empire. Ammianus makes clear that he knew this in describing the restoration to favour of Ursicinus at the time of the rebellion of Silvanus in 355. The general is summoned to the consistory and introduced by the 'Master of Admissions'. He is then 'offered the purple': that is, he is invited to kiss the edge of the imperial robe in the ceremony known as 'adoratio' (*sc.* 'purpurae'). The ritual marks Ursicinus' restoration to favour after a phase in which his reputation has been under a cloud. As we saw earlier, he was encouraged by the gesture to embark on a speech of self-defence, but was cut short by the emperor's observation that this was no moment for recrimination, but for concord and co-operation.

The introduction of the custom of *adoratio* is attributed by Ammianus, in explanation of this passage, to an emperor who had brought it in as a 'foreign rite and royal custom' ('extero ritu et regio more'), emperors of earlier times having, 'as we read', been greeted in the manner of civil governors; 'cum semper antea ad similitudinem iudicum salutatos principes legerimus' (15.5.18).[23] The name of the emperor responsible for the innovation does not now stand in Ammianus' text as we have it, but comparison with other writers, using language closely similar to his, makes it clear that it was Diocletian. Aurelius Victor wrote that Diocletian was the first emperor since Caligula and Domitian to allow himself to be openly addressed as 'dominus', to be 'adored' ('adorari') and to be called a god. He too, expressing in this a despotic and overbearing arrogance, first had gold thread woven into silken robes, adorned himself with purple and his shoes with precious stones (*Caesares* 39.2f.). A similar though much briefer notice in Eutropius' *Breviarium* of about 370 (8.26) permits the inference on technical grounds that the source of information on the matter was a lost Latin imperial history written in the time of Constantine and used by Aurelius Victor and Eutropius.[24] Whether Ammianus knew this history at first hand or depended on Eutropius' or some other version of it is not clear, nor need we pursue the question here in order to establish two fundamental points; first, that the

XI. The Office of Emperor

more resplendent ceremonial deportment of the Roman emperors, as introduced by Diocletian, was for contemporaries a point of distinction between the emperors of the earlier and those of the later period; and second, that the ceremonial was itself perceived to be of foreign origin. For all the uncertainties surrounding the late fourth-century collection of imperial biographies known as the *Historia Augusta*, its author expresses a contemporary attitude in alleging that Alexander Severus prohibited 'adoration' of himself, which his predecessor Elagabalus had encouraged, 'in the manner of Persian kings'; 'regum more Persarum' (*Alex.* 18.3). The contrast was symbolic of the distinction between the ideal Roman 'princeps', Alexander Severus, and the grotesque Oriental despot whom he succeeded. According to Herodian (5.6.10) Elagabalus used to go out in public with made-up eyes and cheeks painted with rouge, in a curious and possibly even conscious evocation of the Persian habit mentioned at the beginning of this chapter.

Now it is not true, or at best it is over-simplified, to say with Aurelius Victor that emperors were not regarded as gods before the time of Diocletian.[25] So, too, early emperors other than Domitian were addressed as 'dominus', and without provoking objection; it is the standard form of address used by the younger Pliny in his letters to Trajan, that most respectful and 'civil' of emperors. Expressions of the 'sacredness' of the imperial person are also found much earlier than the Tetrarchy, by which time they are commonplace in panegyric. The *Digest* refers more than once to 'sacrae constitutiones' in the sense of 'imperial' constitutions cited by the Classical lawyers (e.g. 41.1.5 praef.). That these references need not be late interpolations is shown by part of the reply to a petition to Commodus referring to a 'sacra subscriptio domini nostri' (*ILS* 6870), and there are other such instances.[26] The statements of Aurelius Victor and other writers as to the extent of the innovations introduced by Diocletian and their historical origins are therefore factually questionable, but as to the meaning and function of late Roman ceremonial one thing is clear, and very important: that late Romans themselves believed, both that the ceremonial itself was brought in by Diocletian, and that it was of foreign, specifically of Persian, origin. Their view of the elaborate ceremonial forms surrounding the emperors and dividing them from their subjects reflected their own conviction that they were living under an Oriental, or despotic, system of government, removed both in time and in principle from the tolerant equality, or *civilitas*, in social and political relations maintained by the best of the early emperors.

It is then interesting that Ammianus, in saying merely that he had 'read' of the origins of the ceremony of *adoratio*, and introducing the subject only to explain the act of protocol in which Ursicinus was invited to participate, seems not to imply that he attached any particular importance to it. He gives no indication of having mentioned the matter – as would have been easy for him to do, by adding a short phrase such as he often uses to indicate a back reference – in his lost books on the reign of Diocletian. He reports the origin of *adoratio* dispassionately and without personal commitment, an absence of feeling that is worth reflection – especially when we consider that not only Ursicinus, but Ammianus himself on his promotion as *protector domesticus*, will have taken part in the ceremony.

The ceremony of *adoratio* is on one level an act of submission to an Oriental despot. For Ursicinus, however, the act marked his restoration to favour after a period of uncertainty. This aspect is made very clear by Ammianus. Ursicinus was 'honourably' admitted by the *magister admissionum* – 'qui mos est honoratior' – and 'calmly' offered the purple to kiss; 'multo quam antea *placidius*'. When he embarks on his speech of self-defence he is 'gently' stopped by the emperor; 'oratione *leni* prohibet imperator' (15.5.18ff.). The atmosphere after the act of *adoratio* is far more relaxed than before it.

In another case mentioned by Ammianus, an official called Thalassius is accused of having plotted against Gallus Caesar and in consequence excluded from Julian's favour. More precisely, he is prevented from 'adoring and being present among the *honorati*'; 'adorare adesseque officio inter honoratos prohibito'. In due course, Julian was reconciled with Thalassius and he returned to the emperor's favour; 'rediret in gratiam' (22.9.16). At this point he is presumably allowed again to adore the purple. On another occasion, during Julian's march against Constantius in 361 his men caught the general Lucillianus totally unprepared and brought him to Julian in a state of shock. He was at once offered the opportunity to adore the purple and, emboldened by this gesture, began to express doubts to Julian as to his wisdom in attacking Constantius. Julian cut him short; 'I offered you the symbols of majesty to put an end to your fear, not to enrol you as an adviser'; 'maiestatis enim insigne non ut consiliario tibi, sed ut desinas pavere porrexi' (21.9.8)! Leaving aside Julian's sarcasm, the purple would be offered to a potential intimate or adviser and the opportunity to kiss it was one to seize and welcome: it was a symbol of reconciliation, of inclusion in the charmed circle of the emperor's friends, those *honorati* privileged to show him respect.[27] In the same spirit, a law of 387 concedes to *domestici* and *protectores* the right to greet *vicarii* with a kiss, a gesture implying equality between its participants, as *adoratio* implies subjection; for 'it would be tantamount to sacrilege, if this honour were not granted to those who are thought worthy to touch Our purple'; 'qui contingere nostram purpuram *digni sunt aestimati*' (*CTh* 6.24.4).

The ritual of *adoratio* is not merely a symbol of the remoteness of an Oriental despot before his subjects, but a demarcation, acted out before one's eyes, of those imperial supporters entitled to a place in the emperor's presence, and of an order of precedence within their number. The circle of those so permitted to 'touch Our purple' was by no means narrow, if it were to include *protectores domestici* like Ammianus, not to mention a plain *protector* like Fl. Abinnaeus, or the four officers whom the tribune Fl. Gaiolus sent from Egypt to Constantinople to 'adore the divine purple of the emperors' (above, p. 77). We should add to the privileged

XI. The Office of Emperor 247

band, among many others, the officials listed in the *Notitia Dignitatum* who, having served as 'princeps' in their *officium*, adore the purple and receive promotion to *protector*; 'principem de eodem officio, qui completa militia adorat protector' (*Not. Dig., Or.* 39.37, etc.).[28]

Observers of late Roman public life from Ammianus onwards have seen it in terms of theatrical performance, a sort of ceremonious masque in which power, rank and privilege were proclaimed by courtly gesture, uniform and accoutrement.[29] Gibbon wrote in just such language of the insignia of public office preserved in the illustrations to that fine monument to a self-conscious bureaucracy, the *Notitia Dignitatum*:

> By a philosophic observer, the system of late Roman government might have been mistaken for a splendid theatre, filled with players of every character and degree, who repeated the language, and imitated the passions, of their original model. (*Decline and Fall*, Ch. XVII; ed. Bury, II, p. 160)

We have seen how Ammianus uses theatrical imagery in describing the public comportment of emperors. He wrote that Constantius always kept on the *cothurnus*, or 'tragic buskin' symbolising the majesty of his position. The usurper Procopius, by contrast, was like a figure brought up from the underworld, a theatrical performer in a comedy, even some striking image of stage decor (26.6.15; above, p. 236f.). So too the 'Median shoe' and facial makeup recommended for a king in Xenophon's *Cyropaedeia*, part of an attempt to bewitch the public into regarding its princes as a superior race of men.

Not only the public comportment considered appropriate for the imperial office, but that of late Roman society at large, displayed a taste for the theatrical, for pictorial gesture and pageantry, that is perhaps their most obvious distinguishing feature in relation to the early empire.[30] Ammianus describes the airy, light clothing worn by senators, which they would lift up with excited movements so as to show off the fringes and multi-coloured decorations of the tunics beneath (14.6.9). The bishops of Rome went around in a carriage, wearing conspicuous clothes so as to be seen by all; 'procedant vehiculis insidentes, *circumspecte vestiti* ...' (27.3.14). One senator, years after escaping from an accusation of magic arts, could still be seen in Rome, and

> as if he alone were innocent of any crime, mounted on a caparisoned horse rides over the pavements followed by columns of attendants. One would think that he was trying to attract to himself some particular interest by a new sort of distinction; 'per novum quoddam *insigne*, curiosius *spectari* affectans'. (26.3.5)

'Insigne', with 'simulacrum', was a word used by Ammianus of the public presentation of the usurper Procopius (p. 236). It is the language of gesture, image and stage-play, such as are met at all turns in the political life and social relations of the later Roman empire.

When Julian entered Sirmium in 361, he was received with lights and flowers, with expressions of good fortune ('votisque faustis') and hailed as 'Augustus' and 'dominus' (21.10.3). Just so had the people of Autun received Constantine in 311, filling the streets with the 'standards of the city guilds, statues of all the gods, the sounds of clear-toned musical instruments' (*Pan. Lat.* 7.8.4).[31] In the senate at Rome, ritual acclamations had superseded political discussion, at least as regards the relations between senate and emperor. No longer do we find sharp questions on the division of power between the two such as had confronted Tiberius in AD 14 (Tacitus, *Ann.* 1.12.2), or discussions on the issues of senatorial prerogatives and 'liberty', but series of organised acclamations. The best-documented example is the meeting of 438 that promulgated in the west the newly compiled Theodosian Code. The series begins:

> Augusti Augustorum, maximi Augustorum (repeated 7 times)
> Deus vos nobis dedit, deus vos nobis servet (repeated 27 times)
> Romani imperatores et pii felices, multis annis imperetis (repeated 22 times)
> Bono generis humani, bono senatus, bono reipublicae, bono omnium (repeated 24 times)
> Spes in vobis, salus in vobis (repeated 26 times)
> Ut vivere delectet Augustos nostros semper (repeated 22 times)

The grand total of acclamations, which go on to cover such mundane questions as the safekeeping of the new volume and the prevention of interpolation in its text, adds up to seven hundred and eighty-seven, divided between forty-three separate acclamations.[32] At a modest estimate of five seconds for each acclamation, we may imagine over an hour of continuous performance. No longer than a panegyric or public lecture, perhaps, but that is not the point. The actual substance of the acclamations, set out as a traditional *senatus consultum* – as could easily be done – would barely take a couple of minutes to read. The rest was pure theatre.

Ceremonial, in sight and sound, is a mode of communication. It was not new in the late empire; it is obvious, and clear from the evidence, that processions, ceremonial receptions, the expression of both popular and senatorial will by acclamations, go back to the early empire and in some cases well before that. Yet the fourth century undoubtedly saw an increase in the frequency and in the elaboration of public ceremonial, and assigned to it a more central role in the relations between emperors and their subjects, whether of the upper or the lower classes in Roman society. It is clear too that contemporaries thought themselves to be in the presence of an innovation, in likening the ceremonial procedures of Diocletian and his successors to those of an Oriental despot. It may be helpful to consider two possible reasons why this had come about.

XI. The Office of Emperor

First, the military commanders of the early empire, like the emperors of that period, had been men of property from landed aristocratic backgrounds in the countries around the Mediterranean, who shared the interests and civilian culture of the senatorial class to which they belonged. They combined military and civil posts in their careers, alternating both types of post with substantial periods in private life, and were not, by any rigorous standard, 'professional' soldiers.[33] The question of their place in and integration with Roman society did not arise in that period, for, by birth, economic background and education, they were already integrated. Subsequently, however, the constant military crises and civil wars of the third century had prompted the evolution of a military ruling elite originating from the frontier provinces – and from distinctly 'non-senatorial' backgrounds – from which first the Roman high command, and in due course the emperors themselves came;[34] and these were men sharing little, in background or cultural affinities, with the Mediterranean-based ruling classes of the early empire. The gulf between them is indicated by the historian Cassius Dio, a Bithynian Greek who governed Pannonia in the early third century. In a passage discussed in a previous chapter, Dio could still write of Pannonians as a warlike people who lived in prolonged winter, grew no olives, drank beer, made only a little poor wine and in general possessed nothing that made an honourable life worth while (49.36.3f.; p. 199). His words, expressing a Mediterranean city man's prejudice against those areas and peoples from whom the military ruling classes and emperors of the third century came, represent a failure of communications of formidable proportions. In the new circumstances, and in the stable conditions bequeathed to the fourth century by the Tetrarchs, ceremonial may have provided a mode of 'rehabilitation' between the emperors and civilian society, not on the basis of old ideals of relations among social equals aspired to under the early empire, but on the simplified but workable basis of the relations of an autocrat with his subjects. Modes of popular communication replaced at every level the more literary, philosophical debates about freedom and political rights which, within a much narrower social milieu, had characterised these relations in the early empire.

Secondly, as we shall see more fully in the next chapter, the Tetrarchy was responsible for a great expansion of government, both in intensity and in its sheer scale, that is in the numbers of active – and, in due course, of inactive – participants in its operations. Imperial ceremonial, in such acts of protocol as *adoratio purpurae*, provided a focal point, and a sense of identity, to a new and enlarged governing class, the members of the imperial *militia*. It included them, by visible gesture, in the new order and at the same time differentiated the various ranks among them. Late Roman ceremonial functioned in two ways: to isolate the emperor and show him as different from the ordinary run of mortals, but also to include a large and ever-expanding political and social grouping, those privileged men who, at their various levels and in their various capacities, were the emperor's friends.

This chapter began with Constantius' visit to Rome in 357, and it is appropriate to bring it to a conclusion with a reminder that Ammianus' most explicit statement of the origins of the imperial system links it organically with the institutions and traditions of the city of Rome. He introduces the topic to explain why it should be that whenever his narrative turned to Rome there was nothing to tell but of 'riots, drunkenness and other such unworthy matters' (14.6.2). The dignity and grandeur of Rome, symbolised by the glory of its ancient assemblies, were betrayed by the unrestrained frivolity of a minority of the population; 'levitate paucorum incondita' (14.6.7).[35] Ammianus showed the 'splendour of the assemblies' by presenting the growth to power and maturity of Rome as a life-span. From birth to the end of childhood, a period of three hundred years, Rome sustained local wars and in early adulthood and maturity spread influence over the entire world, bringing home laurels and triumphs and establishing the rule of law for all the peoples of her empire. In present times, now approaching old age and 'conquering in name only', Rome has withdrawn to a quieter life, but is everywhere respected as mistress and queen, the white hair of senators and the name of the *populus Romanus* being revered and honoured (14.6.6). Having achieved in maturity the mastery of the world, she has now in old age, like a shrewd parent, yielded her birthright – the exercise of power – in trust to the emperors; 'Caesaribus tamquam liberis suis regenda patrimonii iura permisit' (14.6.5). This is not an image of decline, far from it; as Rome enters old age, her 'children' in the pugnacious shape of the Roman emperors, carry on the mission.[36]

That this mission was in essentials a military one is clear not only from Ammianus' formulation of the growth of Roman power, but from the sheer weight of narrative – not to mention the professional interest – that he devotes to warfare in all its aspects: it is an emphasis that merits a separate discussion, in the third of this group of related chapters (Chapter XIII). Yet Ammianus' interest in the subject does not prevent him from recognising that war and armies, like the imperial power itself, are not an end in themselves, but are the precondition of the peace under which all wise men wish to live, protected by law and free from alien domination. Writing of Valentinian, Ammianus gave his understanding of the rightful exercise of imperial power. It was, as the philosophers had defined it, to preserve the interests and security of loyal men; 'finis enim iusti imperii, ut sapientes docent, utilitas oboedientium et salus' (30.8.14). He expressed this sentiment in very similar terms elsewhere, again ascribing it to 'men of wisdom'. The purpose of empire, he here explained, was to preserve the safety of others: an emperor should restrain his exercise of power to this end, resisting personal enmities and the opportunities for profit; 'nihil aliud esse imperium, ut sapientes definiunt, nisi curam salutis alienae, bonique esse moderatoris

XI. The Office of Emperor

restringere potestatem, resistere cupiditati omnium rerum et implacabilibus iracundiis ...' (29.2.18).

Ammianus' conception best emerges on those occasions when correct principles of imperial conduct were violated.[37] In the prosecutions under Gallus Caesar at Antioch, men were executed, exiled, forced to live on the charity of others, no resources left to them but 'complaints and tears'. Rich houses were closed, as a 'civil and just empire' was turned over to the bloody whim of one man; 'civili iustoque imperio ad voluntatem converso cruentam' (14.1.4). Not even suborned prosecutors were heard in court to preserve that semblance of legal propriety which the most notoriously cruel emperors had sometimes conceded. Whatever Gallus determined was treated as right and lawful and immediately carried out; 'id velut fas iusque perpensum, confestim urgebatur impleri' (14.1.5). No attempt was made to examine the truth of allegations, nor to tell apart the guilty from the innocent. The rule of law was expelled and driven from the courts; 'velut exturbatum e iudiciis fas omne discessit' (14.7.21). At one point, two men were accused before Gallus. One of them, 'a philosopher in name alone, as became apparent', confessed complicity in treason which never existed, when put to the torture and threatened with death. He was in addition, said Ammianus (himself, it will be recalled, an eye-witness of the proceedings), totally ignorant of legal procedure. His colleague, who knew his rights, and proclaimed that the affair was an act of brigandage and not a court of law, demanded a proper accuser and the usual formalities. It did him no good. He was dreadfully tortured for his insolence and dragged out for execution (14.9.5f.).

Other emperors are criticised for the same fault, perversion of the courts of justice for personal ends. Valens professedly wished cases at law to be determined in proper legal fashion, but he committed them to specially chosen judges and allowed nothing to happen against his will. He permitted accusations to be made without distinguishing truth from falsehood – a fault to be shunned in private, everyday affairs, let alone in courts of justice (31.14.6). Constantius was roused by fear of treason to actions more severe than correct ('acrius exsurgens quam civiliter'); he too appointed judges chosen for their harshness (21.16.8f.). Under Julian, an uncompromising judge of right and wrong but inclined to mercy in his application of the law (18.1.2; 16.5.12f.; 22.10.4f.), the goddess Justice herself seemed, as Ammianus twice remarked, to have returned to earth – except that Julian sometimes acted arbitrarily and in haste, following his own inclination rather than the law (22.10.6; 25.4.19). At such times Julian was 'unlike himself', and where his hasty temperament had betrayed him he allowed himself to be corrected by his associates (22.10.3). This is not the whole story, for Ammianus mentions another tendency of Julian, that he sometimes in courts of law asked people their religious opinions. This, Ammianus concedes, was 'untimely' ('intempestivus'), adding however that on no occasion could this practice be shown to have produced a result inconsistent with equity (22.10.2). As regards capital jurisdiction, despite Julian's well-known mildness the trials of

Chalcedon brought unjust sentences on some of Constantius' supporters, partly because among those whom the emperor put in charge of the trials was a man of known deviousness and arrogance, 'semper ambiguum et praetumidum' (22.3.9). Most of the punishments meted out at these trials Ammianus found entirely justified (p. 93), but it is hard to see how Julian's conduct was in principle better than that of Constantius and Valens, who appointed specially chosen judges when it suited them.

Ammianus was prepared to admit the need for a law of treason. He discussed the matter in narrating inquiries made by Constantius in 359, when an affair came to light involving alleged consultation of oracles, exaggerated by Constantius' suspicion and the pressure of his courtiers into a great affair of state (19.12.1ff.; p. 217f.). Ammianus agreed that strict inquiries in such circumstances were in order; any sensible man, he wrote, would agree to that (19.12.17). A lawful emperor, the protector and champion of men of good will ('propugnator bonorum et defensor') was entitled to the support of those whose safety he was appointed to defend. To this end the Cornelian laws on *maiestas* had permitted the torture of men without respect of social standing. But it was wrong that an emperor should take pleasure in such affairs, so that his subjects appeared to be living under despotism rather than lawful power.[38] Cicero had written that excuses should be sought to pardon rather than to punish (19.12.18); as Julian said in the same spirit, an emperor should always seek to 'increase the number of his friends' by clemency (22.14.5).

Ammianus was no abstract theorist on political, any more than he was on philosophical or religious matters. His views of the imperial office and its duties are in this sense not original, but they are straightforward and serviceable. The emperors had inherited the protection of law and settled life from the senatorial government of the Republic. Their function was to defend men of good will, and they were entitled to protection by a law of treason from the machinations of the wicked. But men were not to be hounded down and punished to satisfy the personal whim or avarice of an emperor; there were properly instituted courts of law and regular procedures, and in the observance of these was the essence of what Ammianus, in just this context, called a 'civil and rightful empire'; 'civile iustumque imperium' (14.1.4).

CHAPTER XII

The Character of Government

Imperial government in Ammianus' time was unmatched in Graeco-Roman history in its scale and complexity of organisation, in its physical incidence upon society, the rhetorical extravagance with which it expressed, and the calculated violence with which it attempted to impose its will. Its expansion of scale, though it had begun earlier, derived essentially from the time of Diocletian and his colleagues in the late third and early fourth centuries. The challenges to government and authority posed by the disorders of the third century had been met by a combination of submission to the force of circumstances and greater assertiveness, in quantity and in character, in the governing that was done.[1] Problems of response in an empire under constant threat of military invasion on widely separated frontiers were met by the division of imperial power. This came about, first by repeated usurpations, resisted by 'legitimate' emperors at immense cost to the resources of the empire, and subsequently, and far more sensibly, by the recognition of the need for a collegiate system of imperial power. Under the new arrangements, which in practice were quite flexible, regional emperors in east and west, with Italy, Africa and the Illyrian provinces as a third region between, financed and organised their military operations in relatively compact areas in which the lines of communication were not unduly extended and the possibilities of rapid troop movement were not precluded by sheer distance.[2] Within these areas, later systematised as the regional praetorian prefectures of the fourth century, the provinces were progressively increased in number and reduced in size – again, more likely for ease of administration than (as has been supposed) through fear of the excessive power that might be acquired by individual governors. By a further definition of powers, carried through by Constantine, military and civilian (including financial) spheres of administration were separated, under the supervision respectively of new *magistri militum* and praetorian prefects. With exceptions in particular cases or circumstances – some of them mentioned by Ammianus, as when a *notarius* was joined with a *dux* in an attempt to build a fort in barbarian territory (28.2.5ff.), or when the military command of Tripolitania was temporarily assigned to the *praeses* of the province (28.6.11) – this separation between the two hierarchies of power was respected in the fourth century.[3] Ammianus praised Constantius because he rigorously

253

kept apart civilian and military personnel and functions; conversely, it was a criticism of Valentinian that, first of all emperors, he raised the military to a point beyond what was good for the public interest, bestowing on them honours and wealth (21.16.1f.; 27.9.4).

By the increase in the 'incidence' of government, by the multiplication of the imperial office, and by their own willingness to travel the frontiers of the empire – 'ultro citroque discurrentes', as Ammianus wrote, in a phrase attributed to Constantius describing the Caesars of the Tetrarchy (14.11.10) – the late emperors offered to their subjects that personal concern and 'presence' (*praesentia*) to which panegyrists of the early fourth century attached particular importance. The panegyrists, and the communities for which they spoke, well knew that, despite the expenditure and risks involved in direct exposure to imperial power, it was through the 'presence' of the emperor that the cities of the empire stood to gain privileges, and exemptions from the very burdens that the government laid upon them. Hence the importance of one particularly well-documented ceremony, that of the emperor's *adventus*, or arrival in a city (pp. 231ff.). An orator from Augustodunum (Autun) in Gaul, addressing the young Constantine at Trier in 310, picked up the theme in urging the emperor to visit his city; this, he said, 'will immediately be restored, *once you see it*' (*Pan. Lat.* 7.22.7). And so it was. Two years later another orator, also speaking at Trier, recalled Constantine's visit to Autun, commemorating benefactions for rebuilding and the resettlement of land earlier offered the city by the emperor's father Constantius (*Pan. Lat.* 8.4.4) and, from Constantine himself, a five-year tax remission and a reduction of its assessment from 32,000 to 25,000 *capita* (ibid. 11; 13).[4]

The reign of Diocletian was characterised by Lactantius, in a thorough-going onslaught on the administrative innovations of the Tetrarchy, as a time when the numbers of tax-payers in the Roman empire were exceeded by those of tax-collectors (*De Mort. Pers.* 7.3). Like the rest of Lactantius' account it is a caricature, but the genuinely increased scale of late Roman government implied by it can readily be illustrated: by modern estimates ranging from 446 to 834 officials in the palatine office (that is, excluding its provincial departments) of the eastern *comes sacrarum largitionum*;[5] by the seventy members of curial families currently serving as imperial officials, who are listed on the municipal register of the city of Timgad in Numidia in 362 or 363 – five serving in the office of the *vicarius* of Africa, thirty-seven in that of the *consularis* of Numidia, twenty-three in that of the *praefectus annonae* of Africa, and five in that of the *rationalis* of the fiscus, or imperial treasury, of the province; by the fifty or more civil servants and retired military officers who lived and owned property at Hermopolis and Antinoopolis in mid-fourth century Egypt (*P. Flor.* 71);[6] or by the lists of the *Notitia Dignitatum*, such as (taken at random) that of the *vicarius* of Asiana (*Or.* 24), consisting of a '*princeps*, serving at the rank of *ducenarius* from the corps of *agentes in rebus*, who [on promotion] adores the clemency of the emperor and departs with the insignia [of *protector*]', below him a

XII. The Character of Government

cornicularius, a *commentariensis*, an *adiutor*, an *ab actis*, *numerarii*, a *cura epistularum* and, at the base of the structure '*exceptores* and the other *officiales*'. Members of this category, in the case of *consulares*, *praesides* and *correctores* of provinces, are not permitted to transfer to any other service without the specific assent, or 'annotation', of the imperial clemency (*Or.* 43-4; *Occ.* 43-5). Such examples, to which others could easily be added, make clear the enhanced scale of government in the late empire, and also the bureaucratic mentality with which it functioned, in its preoccupation with lists and procedures, grades of appointment, salaries, rules of promotion and the titles of status.

Another innovation assigned by contemporaries to the time of Diocletian was the enhanced ceremonial surrounding the office and person of the emperors; it was taken, as we have seen, to symbolise the transition of the emperor from the 'civil magistrate' of the early empire to Oriental despot. This aspect of the public presentation of the late Roman emperors, expressed in their dress, their comportment and gestures, and the physical setting in which they appeared, applies also to their officials. A late Roman governor or palatine official would receive his letter of appointment in the form of a scroll or bound book, or, in the most senior positions, an ivory diptych – a pair of hinged leaves decorated with figures in carved relief, edged with gold and containing inside the codicils of office. On the cover of the diptychs was a portrait of the emperor or emperors, on the books an acclamation addressed to the recipient of office and wishing him good fortune and success in its tenure. These insignia he would place on a table covered with a blue cloth, which stood in his office. In the case of the more elevated civil appointments a set of candlesticks stood with the insignia on the table, and sometimes on the floor beside can be observed a tall baton-shaped object with carved panels on its sides tapering down towards a tripod base; this is a ceremonial inkstand, symbolising the judicial powers of the prefect or governor in question. The document in which these and other insignia are shown, the *Notitia Dignitatum*, as we have already seen (p. 247), seemed to Gibbon in just this context to evoke a theatrical performance rather than the more prosaic realities of public administration.[7] At all levels of the governmental system, both within its ranks and in its relations with the public, that *civilitas*, or pretence of equality with which, according to Ammianus and others, earlier Roman emperors had been accustomed to receive their officials, had been replaced by an array of ceremonial relationships, expressed in the stylised 'instant language' of gesture, decor, pose, and acclamation.

The same is true in the field of legislation, for here too the Roman government had left far behind the measured, persuasive style of the early empire. The emperors now proclaim their intentions in strident rhetoric, with moral outrage and threats of violence. So, in a law of Constantine of 331, 'Let the rapacious hands of officials now cease; let them cease, I say: unless they do heed this warning and cease, they shall be cut off with swords .... If any should imagine that a bribe may be demanded in cases of civil jurisdiction, armed vengeance shall be present to sever the head from the neck of the wicked offender' (*CTh* 1.16.7). By a law of Theodosius, posted in 390 in public places at Rome, male prostitutes, 'whose criminal practice it is to pervert the male body in the masquerade of a woman's, to submit themselves to the passive sufferance of the other sex and regard themselves as no different from women' shall expiate their crime by being burned alive before the people: 'so that all may understand that no man may without the supreme penalty seek to adopt the opposite sex, having so disgracefully rejected his own'.[8] Another law of Constantine with horrific aptness orders the execution of nurses who connive at the abduction of girls in their care: their mouths and throats are to be stopped by pouring in molten lead. So shall be repaid the 'fables and wicked persuasions of nurses' (*CTh* 9.24.1, of 320). In a similar outburst of what has been splendidly called the 'didactic symbolism' employed by the late Roman government, false accusation is to be 'stopped in the very throat of the calumniator, the tongue of envy torn out by the roots' (*CTh* 10.10.2, of *c.* 319).[9] The language here may indeed be rhetorical, an unhappily chosen metaphor – it is the vice of calumny that is to be removed rather than the actual tongue that utters it. However, two *curiales* mentioned by Ammianus in his narrative of Tripolitanian embassies to Valentinian fled into hiding, the emperor having ordered their tongues to be torn out for making false accusations to one of his officials (28.6.20; 28).

It is not surprising that Ammianus, remarking in praise of Valentinian that he was tolerant in religious matters, can observe that he did not force his subjects 'by menacing prohibitions' to bend their necks to his own belief; '*ne interdictis minacibus* subiectorum cervicem ad id, quod ipse coluit, inclinabat' (30.9.5). The laws of the fourth century make it awfully clear what is meant by 'menacing prohibitions'. They refer constantly to the 'severity' of judges, the 'terror' of punishment, to the strictures of the 'avenging' sword and flames, to the 'carefully devised tortures' with which execution should be embellished, to the horrors of 'prisons dark with filth', where iron manacles rend the flesh to the bone and men may die through the inhuman conditions there. This fate is 'considered pitiable for the innocent but not severe enough for the guilty' (*CTh* 9.2.15, of 320), a hollow reminder of the fact that in Roman penal custom prison was used as a mode of confinement for those awaiting trial and, where it was not carried out immediately, execution, but not in its own right as a form of punishment. Similarly, torture was supposed to be used only to extract truthful information in a court of law and not as a mode or refinement of punishment;[10] yet the most cursory reading of Ammianus Marcellinus, or many another late Roman source, will show how unreal this distinction had now become.

The atmosphere of intimidation and violence conveyed by much fourth-century imperial legislation meets the reader of Ammianus at every turn.[11] Imperial inquisitors are sent out to provinces to conduct trials for treason, throwing men of good birth into fetters and herding

XII. The Character of Government

them to court like captured beasts, loaded down with chains, to await exile or execution (14.5.3ff., 15.3.10, etc.): a philosopher smiles with contempt for the flames that consume him while his companions are strangled, all in full view of the multitude (29.1.38): courageous individuals suffer on the rack without revealing the names of alleged 'accomplices' (14.9.6; 15.6.1f.): sides are 'furrowed' by iron claws (14.9.4; 28.1.10) and men stand bent double under the instrument known as the 'horse', or *eculeus* (28.1.19). Instruments are prepared – the 'horse' and its lead weights, lashes and rods – while the courtrooms resound with truculent voices, shouting grim instructions to 'seize: fasten: tighten up: take him away', amid the clash of chains (29.1.23). Instances can be multiplied at will: two *curiales* of Aquileia are beheaded for holding their city loyal to Constantius against Julian (21.12.20); an official of Valentinian is after his emperor's death imprisoned in the Tullianum at Rome, then taken to his home city in Gaul and there executed 'after immense tortures' (28.1.57); a charioteer is burned at the stake, a minor official stoned to death, a senator 'hauled aloft' and hanged (28.1.56; 29.3.5); two women are led to execution for adultery, their executioner being later burned alive because he had not allowed one of them to remain decently clothed while she was being led to her death (28.1.28). This last episode is a vivid illustration of the fierce puritanism with which late Roman government conceived its duty.

At times, whole cities lived in dread of judicial vengeance because of their connection with cases of high treason, especially when linked with the conduct of magic arts, or for some other reason. Ammianus recalls of his own city of Antioch how men 'crept around in deathly gloom' while the emperor conducted investigations into magic and treason there (29.2.4; above, p. 222f.). In the same city eighteen years earlier, Gallus Caesar ordered the execution of all the leading members of the curia in a dispute over the price of corn, a threat that would have been carried out, claims Ammianus, had not the *comes Orientis* stood against it (14.7.2). On a later occasion in the west, only the intervention of the *quaestor sacri palatii* Eupraxius prevented Valentinian from ordering the execution of the curial orders of three entire towns (27.7.6). Eupraxius' grounds were that the victims would be regarded as Christian martyrs, as had indeed already happened at a place near Milan known as 'Ad Innocentes' after the executions there of four imperial officials (27.7.5).[12]

On at least three occasions during Ammianus' later lifetime the lives of hundreds, even thousands of men in major cities of the empire hung by the thread of an imperial decision. At Milan in 386 the Catholic congregation occupied a basilica, refusing to hand it over to the Arian community as the emperor instructed. In pulling down the imperial hangings that denoted the building as confiscated property, the Catholics had committed a technical act of treason, but the emperor backed down before Ambrose's power and the urban disorders he could, if he wished, provoke (Ambrose, *Ep.* 20).[13] In 387 Ammianus' Antioch awaited retribution after riots over taxation in which imperial statues and images had been overturned.[14] Men fled from the city, while city council, bishop, clergy and local monks spoke on its behalf to the imperial commission of inquiry. There were arrests and confiscations, executions 'by sword, fire, and the jaws of wild beasts' (Libanius, *Or.* 19.37), but in the end the emperor was merciful: the city had feared the worst. At Thessalonica in 390 the worst happened. The people there had killed their garrison commander in riots over the imprisonment of a popular charioteer for homosexuality. A retributive killing was ordered for the death of the commander: the countermand was too late, and thousands of spectators at the races (a later source puts the figure at 7,000) were massacred in the streets of the city.[15]

To the modern eye, such acts of judicial violence, individual and collective, appear as reflections of the general temper of the age. Ammianus saw them as something more specific than this – as expressions also of the personal characters of the officials and agents appointed, and sometimes specifically instructed, to enforce the emperors' requirements. The official of Velentinian just mentioned, Doryphorianus, was while in office 'aggressive to the point of insanity', devoted to seeking out ways in which he might ruin a senator, even when no one would help him. In his prosecution of the senator Aginatius, he showed himself to be more a bandit than a judge; 'iudex, quin immo praedo nefandus' (28.1.54f.). His predecessors were Ursicinus, replaced because of his undue mildness in wishing to appear careful and to respect proper procedures by remitting a case to a higher court (28.1.44), and Simplicius, a man of modest demeanour and tactful in expression, but devious and terrifying, 'obliquo aspectu terribilis' (28.1.45).

Ammianus often uses images derived from the behaviour of wild beasts to convey the characters of hostile or aggressive officials.[16] This is more than a merely stylistic affectation. We must also see it in the context of the Classical view of man's rational faculty as that which pre-eminently sets him apart from the world of animals. The comparison of the behaviour of men with that of animals so enables Ammianus to underline, in a manner faithful both to the Classical elements in his own intellectual tradition and to the expressive conventions of his own age, the 'un-human', the excessive or irrational, in the behaviour of men. Instead of allowing the different facets of his character to be moderated by rational reflection, an individual embarks upon a distorted mode of action, a wilful narrowing of the imagination leading, by what we would call irrational obsession, to results more characteristic of animal than human behaviour. In the extreme case, we find ourselves in a sort of nightmare, in which rational, sane and innocent men are made subject to the control of raging beasts. The first of Valentinian's series of *vicarii* of Rome, Maximinus, began mildly, partly through fear, it was alleged, of an associate who might betray him, partly through diffidence at the lowliness of the public offices he then held. He behaved at that time 'like a subterranean serpent, creeping through low places'; 'tamquam subterraneus serpens per humiliora reptando' (28.1.7). Upon Maximinus'

XII. The Character of Government

promotion from these 'low places' to the vicariate of Rome, he gave vent to the natural savagery implanted in his cruel nature, 'as you often see with wild beasts in the amphitheatre, when the gates are broken aside and they are released'; 'ut saepe faciunt amphitheatrales ferae, diffractis tandem solutae posticis' (28.1.10). What actually happened, as we saw earlier (p. 212), was something rather more prosaic; Maximinus' preliminary enquiries at Rome prompted him to submit a *relatio* to court, in response to which he was instructed to treat cases of magic and adultery under the law of *maiestas* (28.1.10f.).

The metaphor of the snake is applied also to Gallus Caesar (14.7.13), to Constantius' general Arbetio (15.2.4) and, more elaborately, again to Maximinus, when as praetorian prefect of Gaul he directed enquiries against the senator Aginatius like a 'wild man', with the vicious anguish of an injured snake (28.1.33). Meanwhile his successor Leo had come to Rome like a 'funeral gladiator, a Pannonian bandit breathing out cruelty from a wild beast's jaws, as greedy as his colleague for the taste of human blood'; 'efflantem ferino rictu crudelitatem, etiam ipsum nihilo minus humani sanguinis avidum' (28.1.12). In the same terms one of Valentinian's proconsuls of Africa, Julianus Rusticus, conducted himself in his province with the raging thirst of a wild beast for the blood of humans; 'quasi adflatu quodam furoris bestiarum more humani sanguinis avidum' (27.1.6). Gallus Caesar, having ordered the execution of two Antiochene *curiales*, is compared to a man-eating lion; 'ut leo cadaveribus pastus' (14.9.9).

In a similarly colourful metaphor the eunuch Eusebius is like a poisonous viper, sending out its numerous offspring – the junior eunuchs – to inflame Constantius against the general Ursicinus; 'ut coluber copia virus exuberans, natorum multitudinem excitans ad nocendum' (18.4.4). The informer Paul 'the Chain' was a sort of snake, expert at scenting hidden roads of danger for others (14.5.6), and his adjutant Mercurius, nicknamed 'Count of Dreams' (*comes somniorum*) because of the all-pervading reach of his intelligence network, is compared to an untrustworthy dog, wagging its tail as it begs for scraps of food at banquets but inclined to bite without warning (15.3.5). This is a good metaphor, for it was as a guest at banquets that Mercurius picked up much of his incriminating information.

We should not exaggerate the importance of Ammianus' use of these metaphors, nor try to confine it narrowly within the Classical philosophical tradition mentioned earlier. Men have always seen affinities between the behaviour of humans and that of animals, and attributed to animals the moral qualities that their behaviour, so interpreted, seems to merit. Wild beasts provide a repertoire of images of human character and behaviour, opportunities not neglected by the authors of propaganda whether literary or visual, the latter including the formalised symbolism of heraldry. Ammianus' own professional environment, if we can go so far as to call it that, the Roman army, had always exploited such images, not only in the famous legionary eagle and emblems of the early empire, but more especially in the names and shield devices of the army of Ammianus' own day.[17] Their figures can be seen in the rows of shield devices illustrated in the *Notitia Dignitatum*: a lion's head, birds of prey, dogs or wolves, serpents, wild boars, a bull, a bear and so on, often in hybrid forms such as a serpent with a dog's head or the famous 'horned' design (*cornuti*), of heads emerging from a single trunk and turning to face each other. One of the images is mentioned by Ammianus, in the passage discussed earlier (p. 231), describing the dragon standards on the banners of Constantius' army as it entered Rome in 357. The banners stretched out in the breeze so that the dragons themselves, rather than merely the emblazoned emblem, seemed to hiss angrily, while their coiled tails were borne aloft behind them; 'hiatu vasto perflabiles, et ideo velut ira perciti sibilantes, caudarumque volumina relinquentes in ventum' (16.10.7).[18]

Some of Ammianus' images, one may suspect, were, like the furious broken-backed snake of Vergil's *Aeneid* (5.273ff.), more familiar to his urban, literate readership from their knowledge of Classical literature than from encounters in real life: perhaps also in a very different field of cultural experience with which they were no less familiar, the artificial presentation of 'wild life' in the amphitheatres of Rome and other cities of the empire.[19] Some of the most telling images refer explicitly to hunting and gladiatorial games, as with the frustrated Gallic soldiers shut inside the walls of Amida during the siege of 359 like savage wild beasts in their cages, awaiting combat (19.6.4); or Ammianus himself and his colleagues, dreading their fate at Cologne at the hands of Silvanus as if they were prize-fighters about to be exposed to savage wild beasts; 'ut bestiarii obiceremur intractabilibus feris' (15.5.23). The simile of combat in the arena is applied, as we have just seen, to Maximinus' conduct in the prosecutions at Rome of the late 360s; so, too, Valens, in the trials of Antioch 'raged with an extreme frenzy, as if practised specifically in doing harm, like a beast of the arena' (29.1.27). The ultimate, quite literal, application of all this is Valentinian's two pet she-bears, which he kept in cages near his private quarters and had 'looked after with the greatest care, lest their savagery be impaired'; perhaps he was afraid of their being fed titbits by passing visitors. In the end one of the bears, by a nasty turn of humour named 'Innocentia', the emperor ordered to be released into the forest. She had earned her freedom by 'the burials of many men she had torn to pieces'; 'post multos, quas eius laniatu cadaverum viderat, sepulturas'. No doubt the emperor was used to exhibiting her in the amphitheatre at Trier, perhaps at private shows also (29.3.9). Her name is not exactly easy to parallel for a man-eating bear, as Valentinian's were alleged to be ('Simplicius', the name of a performing bear on a north African mosaic, is not too far distant); more typical, no doubt, are names like 'Omicida' and 'Crudelis', which appear on a fourth-century mosaic at Carthage commemorating hunting displays in the arena.[20]

In this as in other ways, Ammianus' language is notable for the strength of its visual effect and the over-literal, often grotesque

XII. The Character of Government

exaggeration of its imagery. Human activity and character are seen no longer in the measured, analytical terms of Classical philosophy but in the instant, universal language of symbolism and didactic posture. The 'ravening wild beasts' jaws' of Ammianus' murderous officials are seen as if part of the artificial combat of the arena rather than in a state of nature – a comparison that reaches to the heart of Ammianus' conception, and in many ways to the reality, of late Roman social and political life.

The violence and brutality with which late Roman government and law enforcement were conducted are no doubt exaggerated by concentration on individual instances, as Ammianus and other sources provide them. Yet it is clear that the impression given by these sources is not totally false. Such things could happen, often in ways unpredictable and inexplicable to the victims of judicial investigation. Of the four members of two successive Tripolitanian embassies to Valentinian – pursuing perfectly normal activities for leading members of Roman provincial communities – two died of natural causes while abroad, a third was executed with three alleged accomplices for lying to the emperor, and the fourth ambassador was imprisoned but escaped (28.6.21f.; 24). In the same affair, two imperial officials committed suicide rather than face the emperor's anger (28.6.27; 30) and another was executed (28.6.22). Two *curiales* of Lepcis went into hiding for fear of having their tongues cut out for lying; 'cum sibi iussos abscidi linguas didicissent ut prodigas' (28.6.28). Against those whose social position or profession exposed them to it, an imputation of treason, or an accusation of magic arts or adultery, might be levelled on the slenderest of evidence; a chance event or passing comment might in an instant expose to judicial processes of an extraordinarily refined violence men whose life had been spent in discreet obscurity and untroubled ease.

Ammianus was moved by the injustices that descended upon those whose discreet obscurity proved insufficient to avoid the inquisitiveness of the laws. He was not, it must be emphasised, against the laws themselves, from which cases of unjust victimisation could spring. He denounced the conduct of magic arts (26.3.3f.), thought adultery a typical expression of the unworthy social conduct of senators (28.4.2), regarded a good flogging followed by exile as a sound punishment for a riot leader (15.7.5) and, in a carefully measured passage, defended the need of the emperors for the protection of a law of treason, with all the consequences that this implied for the nature of the judicial processes involved (19.12.17).[21]

With certain recondite exceptions, some of them mentioned above, the penalties inherent in the laws were not in themselves new, but the harshest of them had by the fourth century come to be imposed at higher points on the social scale than was customary in the early empire. According to the system of punishments graded by social status, as developed in the Classical age of Roman law, execution by burning at the stake, clubbing, or exposure to wild beasts (crucifixion was abolished by Constantine) were accepted as fitting for members of the lower and servile classes in Roman society, those broadly categorised as 'humiliores'; for the more privileged, those of the 'more honourable' classes ('honestiores'), less brutal modes of execution, usually beheading, were thought appropriate.[22] Although he preserves traces of the distinction (pp. 213; 222), we should find it difficult to read in Ammianus' accounts of judicial procedures any such rigorously self-denying an application of the law as this. His narrative is full of examples of propertied, cultivated men of the Roman provinces – paradigm cases of what is meant by 'honestiores' – being subjected to tortures and methods of execution to which, two centuries earlier, they would never legally have been exposed.

Apart from the wider extension of more brutal penalties, what is new about fourth-century legislation is the intensity of the rhetoric with which the laws were expressed, as the emperors strove with ever-increasing urgency to win over Roman society at large to their own view of the need for lawful behaviour, and the exemplary punishment of those who deviated from it. Though understandable, it is facile and misleading to read the legislation merely as if from the point of view of those who through guilt or misfortune found themselves the victims of its attentions. In fact, the terror and moral didacticism of its tone were intended to stir a sympathetic response in a public united with its emperor in opposition to criminal, subversive and immoral behaviour. Nor did the emperors exempt themselves from the standards they set for others. According to the Christian preacher John Chrysostom, anyone who brought a prostitute into the imperial palace, or was found drunk there, or did any other such disgraceful thing, was liable to the penalty of death. If such things are not allowed in the palace (Chrysostom went on) how much more shall we incur the ultimate punishment from the king of all, who is present everywhere and sees all (*Hom. in Joh.* 5.4; *PG* 69.60)! It is sometimes popularly believed that the Roman empire declined because of its immorality, but as far as the facts are concerned the opposite is the case; it suffered, if from anything, from an excess of self-righteousness.

*

The working institutions of the late Roman state appear frequently in Ammianus' narrative, in episodes which, while not adding up to a systematic description, can give a lively impression of the impact of the government and its agencies upon the population of the empire. He has occasion to remark, for instance, that among those executed during Valentinian's prosecutions for adultery and magic was the procurator of the imperial mint at Rome (28.1.29). Ammianus' description of treason trials at Antioch incorporates references to the imperial purple-dye and weaving shops at Tyre, together with two arms factories ('fabricae') at unspecified locations; the tribunes in charge of these were named as accomplices in a plot, though in the event innocent namesakes were

XII. The Character of Government 263

arrested by mistake (p. 34). An equally incidental reference brings in the arms factory at Hadrianople in Thrace. A civic magistrate there, angered because the Goths encamped around the city had ravaged one of his estates, raised a force against them from the lower-class population and the workers in the arms factories, 'of whom there are very many living in the city'; 'cum fabricensibus, quorum illic ampla est multitudo' (31.6.2). As this and other evidence shows, the imperial arms factories were considerable establishments, and their workers, organised in trade guilds, a powerful force in the lives of the cities in which they were situated. The 'fabricenses' of Hadrianople had on an earlier occasion demonstrated against a church council held there (Athanasius, *Hist. Arian.* 18), and at Caesarea in Cappadocia they and the textile workers once joined together in popular riots in favour of their bishop (Gregory of Nazianzus, *Or.* 43.57). In a later chapter some metalworkers of Antioch will be found in a similar role, being prominent in leading popular demonstrations during a corn shortage at Antioch.[23]

The distribution of *fabricae* through the provinces of the empire is recorded, for the late fourth century, by the *Notitia Dignitatum* – fifteen in the eastern empire, twenty in the west.[24] One of the latter, the shield factory at Cremona in north Italy (*Occ.* 9.27), happens to be mentioned by Ammianus. The instigator of the plot against the *magister militum* Silvanus pursued his design by sending letters in the name of Silvanus and his colleague Malarichus to the tribune in charge of the arms factory at Cremona, addressing him as an accomplice and urging him to 'have everything ready quickly' (15.5.59). The tribune was baffled and sent the letter on to court by the same courier who had brought it, adding that he had no idea what it meant. Whatever the truth of the tribune's protestations there is no mystery about the role of a shield factory at Cremona in a threatened military proclamation allegedly involving highly-placed generals at Cologne and Milan.

Co-ordination of the arms factories of the late empire, with their rather specialised production – in north Italy for instance, shields, bows, arrows, swords and cuirasses were manufactured in different establishments spread over the whole region from Luca to Concordia – presupposes well-organised transport facilities, both for the supply of the workshops and for the assembly and distribution of their products. One imagines the roads of north Italy and other areas as constantly busy with the 'heavy goods' service of the imperial administration, a situation evidently too banal to be mentioned by a historian with pretensions to Classical style and elevated subject-matter (cf. 26.1.1).[25] The imperial courier service, or *cursus publicus*, is a different question, for it will often impinge on politics. Ammianus on several occasions mentions it, as in his comment that in the time of Constantius the system nearly collapsed because of the hordes of bishops whom the emperor permitted to use it on their journeys to frequent synods (21.16.18). In a more ominous context, when Gallus Caesar was recalled from Antioch and had passed through Constantinople into Thrace, he was taken on from Hadrianople in a convoy of ten vehicles of the public transport service, retaining only a few members of his palace staff, and hurried non-stop to Poetovio by continuous changes of horses for the successive stages of the journey (14.11.16; 19). It was a sign of his final humiliation when he was conveyed to Pola in a private carriage, wearing none of the imperial insignia (14.11.20).

The *cursus publicus* was a physical resource without which the defence and administration of the Roman empire could simply not have been conducted. Ammianus himself, with Ursicinus and his other aides, used the system to travel from the east to Milan on the emperor's orders in 354. The access of a *magister militum* and his staff to these facilities need occasion no comment; Ammianus uses the allusion rather to explain the great speed with which his party was able to hurry to its destination; 'copia rei vehicularia data Mediolanum itineribus properavimus magnis' (14.11.5). Speed was one advantage, and security for the private or 'semi-official' traveller, if he was able to gain the privilege from an influential contact. So Augustine was authorised in 384 to use the *cursus publicus* to go from Rome to Milan to take up the appointment as public orator there awarded him by Symmachus (*Conf.* 5.23). An episode narrated by Libanius shows how he had been promised use of the *cursus publicus* to travel from Constantinople to Athens on his way to take up studies there. When he got to Constantinople he discovered that the friend on whose influence he had relied had fallen from favour; he was unable to provide the service he had promised, and Libanius had to continue by boat, paying the captain to put to sea in the close season (*Or.* 1.14f.).

We encounter from time to time in Ammianus the 'roving officials' whom the public transport service delivered with such efficiency into the unsuspecting lives of the inhabitants of the empire – like the *agens in rebus* who attended a dinner given at Sirmium by the governor of Pannonia Secunda, heard treasonable comments uttered there under the influence of drink and informed the *princeps* of the administrative staff of the praetorian prefect. The *princeps*, bearing the news 'as if carried on wings' to the imperial court, brought down the governor and his associates and secured for himself two further years in his evidently advantageous employment (15.3.8f.).[26] Another *agens in rebus*, a guest at a dinner-party in Spain, wilfully or through excess of zeal misinterpreted a harmless custom of the house – slaves calling 'vincamus', 'may we conquer', as they lit the lamps for the evening – and destroyed a noble house of the province (16.8.9). The episode provides another instance of the unpredictable, and no doubt to its recipients inexplicable, impact of the law of treason on men whose social position exposed them to its more far-reaching operations.

The most disquieting illustration of the impact on local communities of the imperial bureaucracy 'at large' takes the form of a successful parody of the real thing. It is that of the Maratocupreni, bandits from a village near Apamea in Syria who impersonated merchants and officials in order to plunder estates and towns, and the houses of the wealthy (28.2.11ff.).[27]

XII. The Character of Government

On one occasion they came to the walls of a town disguised as the *rationalis* of the province and his staff, and made a proclamation through a herald that they had been sent by the emperor to confiscate the property of a wealthy citizen. The ploy worked like a dream: the bandits got inside the town, ransacked the fine mansion of the local worthy, and made off with their booty before being suspected. It was evidently, give or take a little, the behaviour to be expected of the *rationalis* and his staff. On another occasion described by Ammianus, an official of Constantius, sent to recall the *magister equitum* Silvanus immediately before his usurpation, in the event joined forces with the *rationalis* of the province in order to undermine Silvanus' position among his dependants by pretending that he was already condemned and his property marked down for confiscation (15.5.8). The references make ominously clear one of the functions of the *rationalis*, to supervise the confiscation of proscribed property. As for those bogus officials the Maratocupreni of Syria, a comparison at some points is provided by the journey, recorded in a papyrus dossier, of the *scholasticus* Theophanes from Egypt to Antioch and back around 320.[28] He too travelled, evidently on public business and so using the public transport service, with a retinue of officials and slave assistants and a considerable amount of baggage. Theophanes, like the Maratocupreni, had a 'herald' (*praeco*) among his staff (*P. Ryl.* IV.644). The Maratocupreni, and so presumably the *rationalis* and entourage whom they impersonated, were a substantial body of men; 'impiorum hominum globus', as Ammianus describes the bandits (28.2.13). As an individual the *rationalis* was evidently an imposing figure. Julian could use him as a symbol of glamorous ostentation when commenting on the appearance of a barber whom he had summoned; 'ego ... non rationalem iussi, sed tonsorem acciri' (22.4.9).

The operation of part of the provincial administration – possibly again that of the *rationalis* – is seen in a not dissimilar perspective in an episode involving Martin, bishop of Tours, as told by his biographer Sulpicius Severus (*Dial.* II.3). During a tour of his diocese, Martin encountered on the public high road an official carriage of the Gallic treasury (*fiscalis raeda*), drawn by a team of mules and carrying a party of military men or civil servants (*militantes viri*). Passing them on his donkey, Martin somehow startled the mule team of the imperial carriage – 'those long lines into which, *as you often see*, the poor animals are yoked together' – making them shy away and causing a holdup while their traces were untangled. In annoyance at the delay, or perhaps fearing that they had fallen into a trap set by bandits, the officials leapt down and set about Martin, beating him with rods and lashes until he fell unconscious, to be picked up by his companions as they followed along the road a little way behind.

The *rationalis* (and similar officials) and their staffs made up considerable retinues, whose progress through the provinces of the empire was a familiar sight to their inhabitants; but they were as nothing compared with the emperor himself when on the march.[29] The impact of the arrival of an emperor with all his assorted impedimenta is well illustrated in the preparations for the battle of Hadrianople in 378. The Goths were drawn up to besiege the city, having heard from deserters that the emperor was there with his high officials, the treasuries and the insignia of the imperial office; 'potestatum culmina maximarum et fortunae principalis insignia thesaurosque Valentis' (31.15.2). All had been left there before the great battle, together with the prefects and members of the imperial consistory, protected by the walls of the city while the baggage and pack-animals were left outside with a military guard (31.12.10).

It is perhaps surprising that this is the only occasion on which Ammianus gives any true impression of the sheer scale and physical impact of the emperor and his *comitatus* when on the move. It is a scene that he must simply have taken for granted, as must we in other, less specifically detailed descriptions of late Roman emperors on the march from city to city. It was one of the most distinctive sights of the later empire. We may think of the impact on the city of Antioch of the preparations for a Persian campaign, and of Libanius' remark that it was a sign of his recovery from illness when, on the arrival at Antioch of Valens and his army in 371, he could stand the 'glint of arms and standards and the raucous blare of trumpets', though previously he could not have borne even to hear them mentioned (*Or.* 1.144). Ammianus wrote of the triumphal arrival of Constantius at Rome in 357 that, inappropriate as it was for the Eternal City, the home of freedom, Constantius' conduct was as it was often seen in the provinces; it was as though he were off to intimidate Euphrates or Rhine by a demonstration of armed strength: 'tamquam Euphratem armorum specie territurus aut Rhenum' ... 'talem se tamque immobilem, qualis in provinciis suis visebatur' (16.10.6; 9). Ammianus here leaves out of account in favour of its ceremonial aspect the more mundane side of the emperor's arrival – the crowds of officials, columns of horses, mules, carriages and wagons that conveyed the imperial administration and its accessories around the provinces. In the course of one such attempt to 'intimidate Euphrates by a demonstration of armed strength' the Persian campaign of Julian, the press of men and wagons entering Hierapolis caused a portico by the city gate to collapse, with the loss of fifty men marching under it and many injured (23.2.6; cf. p. 144).

So far we have considered the emperor and his supporters as at various levels and in various ways they impinged upon the lives of provincial communities. It is natural that a history devoted so largely to the Roman emperors and their activities should reveal much also of the institutions and procedures of the central government itself. Although the circumstances in which they arise in Ammianus' narrative are usually exceptional, it does not follow that the institutions themselves are seen in such a way as to distort or falsify their character; government, after all, largely consists of reducing the exceptional to the manageable by the use of regular procedures, in dealing with crises without sacrificing the

XII. The Character of Government

essentials. The institution closest of all to the emperor, the imperial consistory (*consistorium*), features in several episodes. Some of these concern formal circumstances, as when Julian passed a sarcastic comment on an *agens in rebus* who, summoned on a ceremonial occasion of some sort ('quadam sollemnitate') to the consistory to receive a payment of gold coin, cupped both hands to receive it rather than take it in a fold of his mantle, as was more usual; 'agentes in rebus know how to grab, not how to receive', said the Caesar (16.5.11). Other occasions were more contentious, sometimes pressing to its limits the pervading atmosphere of formality. An embassy of senators, sent to court to protest at the imposition of torture on their colleagues at Rome, is admitted to the consistory to speak its case, to be met by loud complaints from Valentinian that he had made no such order as was alleged and was being calumnied. This could have been awkward, had not the emperor been contradicted by the quaestor Eupraxius and induced to restore the immunity, which he was perhaps not aware of having removed in instructing Maximinus to conduct his prosecutions under the heading of the law of *maiestas* (p. 213). It was an act of bravery on Eupraxius' part, for which Ammianus praises him warmly (28.1.24f.). On another occasion Eupraxius, with equal skill and courage, dissuaded Valentinian from ordering the execution of the *curiales* of three towns, on the obviously calculated grounds that the victims would be venerated as martyrs (27.7.6).[30]

One particularly well documented meeting of the consistory has already been described in some detail, the occasion on which Ammianus' patron Ursicinus was restored to favour and instructed to bring down Silvanus at Cologne (p. 37). The meeting was summoned to consider the crisis at the dead of night, and Ursicinus introduced to it by the *magister admissionum*, a formal mark of honour on which Ammianus specifically comments. Granted the renewed privilege of kissing the purple, Ursicinus began to embark on a speech of self-defence against the suspicions entertained of him, but was mildly prevented by Constantius: now was not the time for recrimination, when all should be restored to their former concord. This 'diplomatic' prelude was followed by a long discussion as to what should be done; 'habita igitur deliberatione multiplici ...' (15.5.18ff.).

Apart from his description of the actual conduct of the consistory, a notable feature in Ammianus' account is the effectiveness with which he evokes its atmosphere – the meeting summoned in the depths of night, Ursicinus' tension, resolved by his sudden change of prospects, his over-anxious attempt to justify himself, the emperor's calm rejoinder. The most dramatic of Ammianus' descriptions of the *consistorium* is however the death of the Emperor Valentinian while hearing an embassy from the Quadi. The barbarians are brought into the consistory and embark on an unconvincing defence of their compatriots' actions. Stirred to anger, Valentinian accuses them of ingratitude, his voice resounding with contempt and abuse. He then subsides and seems more inclined to be considerate, but is suddenly overcome by his fatal seizure. His voice and breath fail and the emperor is hurriedly taken out by attendants to a private room, 'lest he be seen falling in the presence of so many men of low estate' (30.6.3). After struggling massively for his life, the emperor died some hours later (30.6.6). Less sensational though no less vivid is Ammianus' portrayal of the scene in which Julian's general Marcellus, replaced by Constantius for failing to relieve the Caesar when besieged at Sens, went to court to accuse Julian of 'higher ambitions' than was proper. Arriving at Milan in an agitated state of mind ('strepens et tumultuans') Marcellus was admitted to the consistory and there accused Julian, as he put it, of 'fitting out more powerful wings for himself'. These accusations he made with great vigour, at the same time gesticulating 'with huge movements of his body' (16.7.2). 'Ita enim cum motu quodam corporis loquebatur ingenti'; Ammianus' words are precisely intended to connect Marcellus' metaphor with his physical gesture. He pictures Marcellus (and Ammianus had an eye-witness of the scene, the eunuch Eutherius who was there to defend Julian) as standing before Constantius and his officials in the consistory, mightily waving his arms about in imitation of the flight of a bird! It is not exactly how one would expect to imagine the conduct of this solemn and formal assembly.[31]

The imperial *consistorium* is normally visualised as dominated by formality and protocol. This it no doubt was, but it is clear at the same time that there was another aspect to the conduct of its meetings, as participants get involved in intense exchanges of conversation and dispute, in which matters of substance are under debate, their outcome genuinely in doubt. To judge by Ammianus' descriptions, the meetings might be lively occasions, in which opinions are exchanged without inhibition, an emperor may be criticised and change his mind, and will conduct himself, not with the timeless 'tranquillitas' of much official language and iconography of the period, but with strong emotion, a sense of the needs of a specific situation, and a preparedness for the unexpected.

From the emperor's point of view, ceremonial and protocol offered a positive advantage, in their capacity to function as a mode of defence against over-insistent subjects. The usurper Maximus sought to gain tactical advantage by insisting on receiving in the consistory Ambrose of Milan, who came as envoy from the Italian court of Valentinian II in 384, to ask for the return of the corpse of the murdered Gratian. In his letter to Valentinian on the subject (*Ep.* 24) Ambrose gave an extremely interesting account of the exchanges between himself and Maximus, beginning with a combat of rival forms of protocol when the bishop refused, despite the exhortations of *consistoriani*, to receive the kiss of greeting offered by the emperor. In the exchanges that follow, Maximus at one point 'burst out' angrily ('erupit') in response to a provocative remark by Ambrose, the bishop replying 'gently' ('leniter') before embarking on his prepared speech. Allowance must be made for Ambrose's apologetic purpose in composing his account for Valentinian,

XII. The Character of Government

to whom Ambrose had to justify his conduct of the embassy; yet the exchange of opinions, spontaneity and contrasts of manner between the participants in the proceedings are what we have come to anticipate from Ammianus' descriptions of meetings of the consistory.

One wonders whether it was before the assembled *consistorium*, though we are not specifically told this, that another outspoken bishop, Martin of Tours, brought off a notable *coup* over (or under) Valentinian I. Excluded from the palace by Valentinian's order, Martin gained access with the help of an angel after no less than seven days and nights of fasting and prayer. Upon his unexpected appearance in Valentinian's presence, emperor and bishop are, like Ambrose and Maximus, locked in a conflict of dignities. Each refuses to yield to the other, Valentinian by rising to his feet or Martin by doing obeisance to the emperor. The impasse was resolved when Valentinian's throne miraculously burst into flame under him, forcing him abruptly to his feet (Sulpicius Severus, *Dial*. II.5.5f.)! At Martin's first entrance Valentinian is described as 'roaring' ('frendens') his demand to be told how he had come to be admitted. We are left to imagine for ourselves what noise he uttered at the climax of the scene.

Even as described by a hagiographer, seven days and nights of prayer is a considerable tribute to the inaccessibility of the emperor to the most insistent of his subjects, if he should decide that to be in his best interests. Apart from his privileged access to the power of prayer, a courageous or obstinate bishop was in a position to challenge protocol with protocol, to match his dignity against the emperor's. This was however exceptional. In normal circumstances, an emperor might often be glad to use the ceremonious formality of the *consistorium* to bring discussion to a close and maintain his dignity in the presence of his associates; even so, as we have seen, the members of the consistory were quite used to frank exchanges of opinion and substantive discussion of matters of genuine importance. For all his powers as an autocrat and his remoteness, enshrined in protocol and ceremony, an emperor was capable of and accustomed to taking the advice of his associates, and of receiving correction from them.

*

Among the virtues recognised by Ammianus in the Emperor Constantius was his observance of correct principles of good government, notably in his selection of high officials. In this matter he was very sparing and allowed few new increases in administrative powers (21.16.1). Most of the other emperors described by Ammianus merit similar praise. Jovian would have shown good judgment, as was apparent from the few appointments he made in his short reign (25.10.15). Valentinian and Valens were similarly cautious in bestowing high office. Valens indeed was hesitant to a fault in doing so, though it was much to his credit that he allowed no one to claim advantage because of a connection with the imperial family (31.14.2). Whether this observation is entirely borne out in Ammianus' narrative is open to question (p. 193); this does not affect the importance of the principle as ground for praise in a regime. Valentinian prohibited that common abuse of flourishing bureaucracies, the sale of office – except at the beginning of his reign, a time when, through the distractions of a new emperor and in the hope of impunity, certain improper things do happen (30.9.3).[32] Constantius in particular observed one central canon of late Roman government; he restrained the power of the military classes and confined their influence to the spheres proper to them. All officials, military as well as civil, respected the praetorian praefects as the 'summit of all honours' according to the ancient custom; 'honorum omnium apicem priscae reverentiae more praefectos semper suspexere praetorio' (21.16.2). Ammianus cited personal knowledge in affirming that under Constantius no military commander of the rank of *dux* was admitted to the clarissimate, nor was a *magister militum* received by the civil governor on arrival in his province or allowed to interfere in any matter of civil administration – all necessary safeguards in a system open to the extension of improper forms of patronage (21.16.1f.). Of Valentinian on the other hand it is noted that he controlled his minor military officers well but was weak in restraining the powerful; from which ensued disaster in Britain, Africa and Illyricum (30.9.1).

It would not have occurred to Ammianus or his contemporaries to deny the propriety of influence – *suffragium* – in the promotion of perceived and reliable virtue.[33] Indeed, his own early advancement to the rank of *protector domesticus* surely owed something to a personal connection with the *magister militum* Ursicinus (pp. 78ff.). A corrupt or unjust appointment, for Ammianus, was not one in which all possible candidates had failed to be considered before an appointment was made; it was one in which an individual was promoted ahead of the specific claims of a better candidate. On his dismissal from service, Ursicinus was replaced by Agilo, at that time only a tribune. This, thought Ammianus, was an 'excessive leap' to high command; 'Agilone ad eius locum *immodico saltu* promoto ex ... tribuno' (20.2.5). When Julian met at Naissus two senators who had been sent as envoys to Constantius, he passed over the 'better man', Symmachus, and made Valerius Maximus prefect of Rome. This was to please the latter's uncle, the influential Vulcacius Rufinus (21.12.24). There was of course no objection to the proper exploitation of opportunity, such as was provided for instance by participation in an embassy to the emperor. From the point of view of Julian's encounter with them, it was entirely by chance that either senator was at Naissus; it was simply that, of the two men, Julian ought to have chosen Symmachus.[34] Ammianus approved entirely of Julian's appointments of three senators, sent to him as envoys to Antioch in 363, to various high offices (23.1.4), and of Vettius Agorius Praetextatus, whom he had earlier happened to find at Constantinople on private business, as proconsul of Achaia. This appointment was specifically attributed by Ammianus to

XII. The Character of Government

Julian's personal initiative; 'arbitrio suo'. Julian had evidently found the senator congenial, for obvious reasons given his religious tastes, and Ammianus had no complaint, for Praetextatus was a man of 'true excellence and ancestral gravity'; 'praeclarae indolis gravitatisque senator' (22.7.6). The case of Praetextatus is to be distinguished from such as that of Terentius, a baker from the city of Rome who owed promotion under Valentinian to his successful denunciation of a former prefect of Rome for embezzlement. Terentius' arrival as governor of Tuscia was portended in the town of Pistoria by a donkey that ascended the public tribunal and proceeded to bray loudly, to the amazement of all who saw it (27.3.1f.).

Elsewhere Ammianus shows the system of advancement by patronage at work at lower levels of the political system. The plot against Silvanus was hatched by one Dynamius, an *actuarius*, or accountant, in the imperial baggage department (one imagines him, in different circumstances, checking inventories and lists in preparation for one of the emperor's departures on campaign or on a tour of some frontier region). Dynamius had forged his incriminating letters over Silvanus' signature, having earlier requested from him letters of recommendation to certain friends, which he then retained in the hope that he might one day put them to some ulterior purpose; 'commendaticias ab eo petieret litteras ad amicos, ut quasi familiaris eiusdem esset notissimus' (15.5.3). The ninth book of Symmachus' letters, largely containing just such letters of recommendation, was so labelled by its early editors: 'continens commendaticias' (ed. Seeck, p. 235). Dynamius' action in retaining the letters from Silvanus was not in itself especially remarkable. The papyrus dossier of the travelling official Theophanes mentioned earlier contained two copies of a Latin letter of recommendation from a superior official, probably the *rationalis*, addressed respectively to the governor of Syria and the prefect of Egypt. Theophanes evidently hoped to put them to use as opportunity arose but for some reason never did – for they survive in the dossier.[35]

No less revealing than the case of Dynamius is Ammianus' account of an unsuccessful case of patronage. One Africanus, who had been a lawyer at Rome, obtained a provincial governorship but wanted to change it for another, no doubt of a more exalted rank. A petition was presented to Valentinian on his behalf by Theodosius, then *magister equitum* at the imperial court and so, one would have thought, a man of unimpeachable influence. The general, who is described by Ammianus as Africanus' 'suffragator', was met with an unexpected reply: 'Go, general, and change his head, since he wishes to change his province!' This, remarked Ammianus, was the end of an eloquent man whose only fault was in hastening, like many, to secure his advancement; 'ad potiora festinans, ut multi' (29.3.6).

It was on the foundations of patronage, or *suffragium*, that cliques and factions were able to form at the imperial court, of men often – though this was not the only criterion – from the same provincial background.

The most obtrusive case presented by Ammianus is that of the Pannonian compatriots of Valentinian, men taken to possess that temperamental brutality exemplified by Maximinus and Leo, successive *vicarii* of Rome. An exception, Viventius from Siscia, is described as an 'honest and wise Pannonian'; 'integer et prudens Pannonius' (27.3.11).[36] It is not clear whether Ammianus simply regarded Viventius as unlike other Pannonians whom he knew, or whether he intended to imply that his origin and virtues somehow presented a contradiction in terms. Viventius was certainly an unusual case. He rose to the prefecture of Rome in 367, having been *quaestor sacri palatii*, and so, given the duties of that office in drafting legislation and imperial replies, was a man of some literary cultivation. Maximinus' patronage brought in also Simplicius, a Dalmatian from the city of Emona (modern Ljubljana). Before his elevation to the vicariate, Simplicius had been an adviser of Maximinus; he was a former schoolmaster. 'Maximini consiliarius ex grammatico' (28.1.45). Another of Maximinus' promotions was Festus from the north Italian city of Tridentum (Trento), a man in Ammianus' view of the very lowest birth; 'ultimi sanguinis et ignoti' (29.2.22). He reached the peak of his notoriety in the trials conducted by Valens at Antioch; but he too was a man of at least some literary pretension, if one can judge by his modest *Breviarium* of Roman history, dedicated to that emperor in about 370.[37]

Maximinus' son, Marcellianus, was *dux* of the Pannonian province of Valeria – an appointment that did not turn out very well – while Maximinus himself held the praetorian prefecture of Gaul (29.6.3f.); and a brother of Maximinus, by name Valentinus, having been exiled to Britain for some serious offence, was executed by order of the *magister militum* for subversive conduct there (28.3.3ff.). This family of such varied distinction came from Sopianae (modern Pécs) in Valeria. Ammianus described Maximinus as descended from a refugee Dacian people settled by Diocletian on the Roman side of the Danube; unless he is writing with more imagination than factual material, this will have been after the occupation of Dacia by the Goths (cf. below, p. 318). Maximinus' father had been a minor official (*tabularius*) on the staff of the provincial governor of Valeria, and Maximinus himself had after a modest literary education become an undistinguished pleader of cases at law (28.1.5f.). His career is a paradigm of social mobility in the imperial service, of political influence built up from small beginnings – and, one may add, of native talent obscured by prejudice and laid waste by circumstance.[38]

Though that of the Pannonians was the most notorious, it was by no means the only provincial cabal to be found, even in the time of Valentinian and Valens. Under the latter emperor there was an outcrop of Cappadocians at the eastern court, men revealed to us not by Ammianus but by the writings of the famous Cappadocian bishops with whom they were connected. In the time of Valentinian there were the 'Galli qui aderant in commilitio principis' who in 367 produced an imperial candidate when Valentinian fell ill and seemed likely to die

XII. The Character of Government 273

(27.6.1).[39] This was the *magister memoriae* Julianus Rusticus, who in his later proconsulship of Africa behaved in his province with the 'savage fury of a wild beast' (above, p. 259). He was also a friend of the poet Ausonius and, through him, of Q. Aurelius Symmachus (cf. *Epp*. 1.32; 3.6). Possibly still more remarkable than this variety in his characterisation, is his survival of a period in which he was presented as a possible candidate for the imperial throne. The prominence of Gauls under Valentinian, symbolised if not led by Ausonius, yielded an outright dominance when Valentinian died and was succeeded by his son, the more pliable Gratian. Ausonius is one of the more intriguing omissions from Ammianus' history; his son Hesperius gains a single, purely incidental mention when, as proconsul of Africa under Gratian, he helped produce the report that found in favour of the Lepcitanian upper class against the former *comes Africae* Romanus and his associates (28.6.28; p. 386f.).

It seems likely also that the group of military men and court officials with Spanish connections, whose influence lay behind the selection of Theodosius as imperial candidate after the battle of Hadrianople in 378, had first formed in the time of Valentinian. Its members included Theodosius' father, the famous *magister militum*, and one Cl. Antonius, a relative by marriage who held under Valentinian the office of *quaestor sacri palatii*.[40] Theodosius himself, 'princeps postea perspectissimus' as Ammianus calls him on his one appearance in the history, was in 373 *dux* of the province of Moesia, evidently benefiting from his father's patronage; he was at that time a mere twenty-six years old (29.6.15). We should also include in the group a Spanish relative (in what degree is not clear), Magnus Maximus, who after serving with the elder Theodosius in Africa (29.5.6; 21) and Britain, declared war against the regime of Gratian while commander in Britain in 383; he was probably hoping for recognition from Theodosius' son, then eastern emperor. The combination of civil and military offices among members of the group, connections of marriage among themselves and with other factions in court circles – and indeed the alternations of good and bad fortune which they suffered – present a pattern not unlike that of the family of the Pannonian Maximinus. He, like the elder Theodosius, was executed in the political turbulence of the time of Gratian, when Theodosius' son thought it prudent to retire to the family estates in Spain (28.1.57; cf. p. 382).

Viewing the possibilities in another perspective, one wonders about the group of Africans (a good half-dozen of them, including relatives and the women of the group) surrounding the orator of Milan Augustine at the court of Valentinian II.[41] Augustine himself, the son of a modest *curialis* from Thagaste in Numidia, had been educated at Madauros and Carthage. He had practised rhetoric at Thagaste, and at Carthage and Rome, and was then recommended to the city of Milan by the *praefectus urbi* Symmachus, having delivered a sample oration before him (*Conf*. 5.23). His fellow-townsman Romanianus was a wealthy citizen of Thagaste – he was a generous benefactor of that city – now in Italy to pursue litigation (6.24). Another member of the group, Alypius, who came from a town near Carthage, gained appointment as an assessor on the staff of the Italian department of the *comes sacrarum largitionum* (6.16), and Augustine himself was able to contemplate an advantageous marriage arranged by his mother, and the prospect of a provincial governorship (6.19; 23ff.). At one point the group was visited by a fellow-African, an *agens in rebus* named Ponticianus, who came to them with tales of life at another great imperial capital, Trier (8.14ff.).[42] It was this arrival that with other events turned the minds of Augustine and his friends from politics and secular concerns. But for this, we can reasonably ask whether, had any of the more important members of the group — Augustine himself, Romanianus, Alypius — been offered an opportunity and broken through to a position of real political influence, we might have found ourselves able to talk of a 'faction of Africans' at the court of Valentinian II, as the recipient of good fortune took good care to spread it more widely among his friends. But this is a remote contingency; more likely the party, had it remained in politics, would like most others have done so obscurely and on the fringes of court life — in the spreading foothills, as it were, of the bureaucracy. In those regions took place a vast, largely unsung competition for small advantage and minor promotion. At any time a man might, through random opportunity but at some danger to himself, ascend near the very summit of the system from an origin hidden in its lower reaches; but these — men like Maximinus, Leo, or some of the great praetorian prefects recorded by Ammianus — are a tiny proportion of the total numbers of those who worked in the imperial service. It is at the same time clear that considerable power and influence were exercised at much lower levels of the system, and Ammianus' narrative is remarkable for what it shows of this, and of the workings of patronage and favour at all levels, not merely the highest, of the apparatus of government.

In contemporary eyes, the most scandalous case of improper influence at the imperial court among those described by Ammianus was that of Constantius' eunuchs.[43] Ammianus viewed this aspect of the late Roman system with undisguised prejudice. He shared the conventional notion, much aired in rhetoric, that the absence of normal sexual and family affections disposed eunuchs, in compensation, to an overwhelming love of riches, 'which they embrace, as if they were their little daughters' (18.5.4). 'Lizards and toads', bishop Basil of Caesarea called eunuchs, in a rhetorical onslaught on their character of a most un-Christian ferocity (*Ep.* 115); while legislation issued in the name of Arcadius described the influence of Eutropius, who had disgraced the consulship, as the 'stigma of our age', the sight of whose portraits might 'pollute the sight of those who look at them', and so on (*CTh* 9.40.17, of 399). Such imagery is a pale reflection of the abuse poured on Eutropius by Claudian in his long poem of 399 denouncing the eunuch. At the head of Constantius' palace eunuchs was the *praepositus sacri cubiculi* Eusebius 'with whom, if the truth may be told, Constantius possessed much influence', as Ammianus

XII. The Character of Government

remarked in a memorable expression; 'apud quem, si vere dici debeat, multa Constantius potuit' (18.4.3).[44] Eusebius' activities were, indeed, manifold and delicate, requiring both subtlety of touch and confidentiality. Ammianus records how in 354 he averted a revolt in the Gallic army by judicious payments to the ringleaders (14.10.5). Earlier in his career it was maintained that he had in 337 concealed the will of Constantine the Great, and that through him the Arians had first won over Constantius to their cause; through him also that they later plotted against Athanasius of Alexandria. These are rather unlikely, and certainly polemical, allegations. Better founded are his role in negotiations between Constantius and the Catholic bishop of Rome, Liberius, in 354 and, in the same year, his appearance at Pola as one of the judges of Gallus Caesar (14.11.21).[45] The death sentence passed on Eusebius himself at the trials of Chalcedon in 361 was welcomed by Ammianus as the belated operation of all-seeing Justice (22.3.12). He had devoted his influence to enriching himself (16.8.13), and to harming others by weaving webs of calumny and suspicion (14.11.2). In particular, he had prejudiced Constantius' receptive ears against the excellent Ursicinus, Ammianus' patron.

With Eusebius very much in his mind, Ammianus referred favourably to a law of Domitian prohibiting castration; but for this, he wondered how mankind could have borne the swarms of eunuchs that would have existed, when even their relative rarity was so hard to bear (18.4.4)! His view implies both prejudice and excessive faith in the influence of legislation in the field of social control; and Ammianus should in any case have conceded that the presence of eunuchs was not a mere personal failing of some emperors, but a normal aspect of the imperial office of the period. Ammianus mentions eunuchs also in the personal entourage of Valens (30.4.2; 31.13.12), and the eunuch *praepositi* assigned by their emperors to the Caesars Constans, Gallus and Julian, by name Gorgonius (15.2.10) and Eutherius (16.7.1ff.). The former was guilty as an instigator of Gallus' crimes, from the consequences of which he was protected after Gallus' fall, in an interesting exercise of group solidarity, by the concerted action of the other eunuchs in court service (15.2.10). Eutherius on the other hand provided Ammianus with material for a digression showing how, by way of a preternatural exception to the normal rule, there might be such a thing as a good eunuch. Even a wild beast, he reflected in a passing allusion to a range of metaphors much used elsewhere, may be tamed, and a rose grow among thorns (16.7.4)! Brought into the empire in childhood from Armenia – eunuchs were imported from the east as castrated children – Eutherius advanced at the court of Constantine the Great by his sharpness of intelligence and phenomenal memory (16.7.5). Appointed to the staff of Constans, he would have restrained that Caesar's excesses had he been listened to, just as he corrected the excessively 'Asiatic' manners and inconsistency of Julian; and he loyally defended Julian when he was criticised at court by one of the generals set over him by Constantius. This is the occasion when the general Marcellus is glimpsed in the *consistorium*, flapping his arms like the wings of a mighty bird (above, p. 268).

In their employment of eunuchs, the emperors were reflecting, if they were not initiating, a more general custom in aristocratic Roman society. Ammianus described how Roman matrons were attended in public by columns of eunuchs, ranged young and old in order of age; 'multitudo spadonum, a senibus in pueros desinens' (14.6.17): it is a facet of social conduct mentioned also by Jerome, in an exhortatory letter to a young ascetic devotee, telling her what contemporary forms of conduct she should avoid (*Ep.* 22.16). A single reference in Ammianus specifying the 'adulti', the grown-up eunuchs at the imperial court (18.4.4), shows by implication that here, too, were cadet eunuchs, awaiting their turn in palace training establishments to serve the emperors' and empresses' private domestic needs and to become their confidants.

The importance of the eunuchs in late Roman court life may be viewed in various ways. They may, it has been suggested, have functioned as a 'lubricant' at points of friction in the late Roman system of government, popular distaste for their physical deformity enabling them to absorb resentment between conflicting interests at the imperial court and thereby to avert the weakening of the structure that would otherwise have ensued.[46] Though this is a rather schematic view, there is much to be said for it. To 'personalise' differences of opinion by assigning them to envy or dislike has the salutary effect of neutralising, of rendering subject to social control, what might otherwise be divisive issues of principle.[47] To make an enemy of a court eunuch might pose short-term difficulties, but, given the traditionally envious character of that breed and the relative insecurity of their power, it need neither reflect badly on oneself nor have damaging permanent consequences. From the emperors' standpoint, the eunuchs were a group among their supporters with whom they were able to establish confidential personal relations without the risk of their being able to form dynasties of officials occupying the most sensitive and intimate positions of power – an advantage the emperors will have appreciated the more keenly, the more they made themselves inaccessible to other sources of advice. The most convincing explanation is in a combination of these factors. The sexual indifference of eunuchs enabled them, in an age of high official morality (above, p. 262), to serve emperors and empresses in their most intimate personal and domestic requirements without suspicion of impropriety; while their physical condition, by convention repulsive to most Romans, and their lack of family connections, rendered them unable to transform their personal intimacy with the emperors into a firmly based and lasting political influence.

Eunuchs were able to dispose as they wished of the wealth and property they had acquired through their influence (*CJ* 6.22.5, of 352), and there is no denying the reality of this influence, at least in the limited sphere of court politics, while it lasted.[48] They were sometimes able, like Eutherius, to win for themselves a respected social position – though this,

XII. The Character of Government

in Ammianus' view, was an exception, most eunuchs hiding themselves away 'like bats' from the eyes of an offended public (16.7.7). But their position was unlike that of the founders of the great dynasties whose growth and consolidation through political influence is a central aspect of this as of any other period of Roman history – men such as Constantius' praetorian prefect Fl. Philippus, mentioned once by Ammianus (19.12.9), a new politician whose virtues of industry, loyalty and vigilance in the emperor's service are elaborately praised by Constantius in an inscription in his honour, and whose descendants formed one of the great senatorial dynasties of later fourth- and fifth-century Constantinople.[49] The eunuchs did not bring to political life the interests of any great families to which they belonged; it was the essence of their position that they came into the empire from outside in childhood, grew up and were trained in the imperial palace, and lacked known family connections, with all that this implies as to the intrusion of entrenched forms of influence into the imperial administration.

Ammianus gives a classic example of this form of influence in his description of the senator Sex. Petronius Probus, who died in about 390 after holding four praetorian prefectures and, in 371, the consulship; he was a rare exception to Valentinian's almost exclusive promotion of the military, and members of his own family, to this supreme office. Ammianus' account of Probus is justly admired both for its portrayal of personal ambition and character, and (less commonly) for its exact appreciation of the 'structural' aspects of his position as representing the interests of a great senatorial family at the imperial court (27.11.1-6).[50] Probus' yearning for political power left him miserable – as Ammianus says, gasping like a fish out of its natural element – when deprived of it. Yet even while enjoying the peak of wealth and political power he was always anxious and troubled and suffered 'therefore' (Ammianus makes just this connection) from minor illnesses; '*ideoque* semper levibus morbis adflictus' (27.11.6). Overbearing to the weak, Probus was easily intimidated by those who stood up to him, and, depending on whether he was confident or afraid, varied in manner between extremes of arrogance and humility. Never the man to instruct a client or slave to commit anything illegal, he would nevertheless support them through thick and thin, and with no regard for right and wrong, if they were caught in illegal acts of their own devising (27.11.4). He possessed immense power as long as he lived, by the scale of his largesse, and by holding continuous prefectures; 'largiendo et intervallando potestates assiduas'. Into these he was forced, says Ammianus in a penetrating phrase, by the insistence of the senatorial clans to which he belonged and which pursued unrelentingly their quest for ever-greater possessions, never innocent in their immense acquisitiveness; 'familiarum ... numquam innocentium per cupiditates immensas'.[51] It was to preserve their impunity in doing so that they immersed their 'master' ('dominum suum') in affairs of state (27.11.3). Ammianus does not deny that Probus possessed huge wealth 'throughout almost the whole Roman world', on the justice of which he affects to reserve judgment; 'iuste an secus, non iudicioli est nostri' (27.11.1). Yet the most striking aspect of his presentation of Probus' influence is in his location of the initiative for his public career, not so much with Probus himself as with the families whom he represented. One of the 'familiae' in question, the Anicii, had already arisen in Ammianus' narrative. They were mentioned, in an unfortunately damaged passage of the text, among those who benefited from Constantius' enrichment of his associates at the expense of the provinces, Constantine the Great having set the pattern by 'opening the jaws' of his supporters. These members of the latter-day nobility, Ammianus seems to have said, in trying to match their famous ancestors were never content with what they had, though their possessions were actually far greater; 'satiari numquam potuit, cum possessione multo maiore' (16.8.12f.).[52]

It is significant, and may be deliberate on Ammianus' part, that he presents the economic ambitions of the Anicii at a point in his text before he comes to the personal political ambition of their 'dominus' in the next generation. The modern historian will surely agree with him, in seeing Petronius Probus not merely as an example of personal power, but as the representative of aristocratic influence on an imperial regime that required the support of the landed classes in order to survive, and was then unable to break free of the political influence to which their dependence exposed them. Valentinian was astonished to learn from a provincial ambassador of the extent of Probus' depredations in Illyricum, but was obliged to proceed against him with such circumspection that he was unable to remove him before his own death (30.5.10).[53] It is an ominous sign of the ascendancy which, despite their apparent political subjection, the great landed families enjoyed in the late empire, and which enabled the strongest of them to survive into the fifth and sixth centuries, long after the power of the Roman emperors had declined and, in the end, had been replaced by that of barbarian kings.

CHAPTER XIII

The Practice of War

The central characters of Ammianus' history are the emperors and their supporters. That its central subject is war is obvious, defies summary and requires little explanation. It is clear not only in the narrative emphasis given to the subject, which far outweighs any other in the text, but in the deployment of some of Ammianus' most substantial digressions – on Gaul and Persia (among his longest), on Thrace, on Huns and Alans and, preceding Julian's Persian campaign, on artillery and siege machinery. All are presented as relevant to war, an emphasis which is not simply a matter of Ammianus' own background and experience, but of the place of war in the Roman mind.[1]

If war is at all times an expression and a determinant of social organisation, in the case of the Romans of all people, war, and the systematic application of its results, were the specific achievement of their social order, and the central feature of their history and ideology. For Ammianus, the subjection by Rome of 'proud and savage nations' was the precondition for her gift of laws, the 'eternal foundations of liberty', to the peoples of her empire; 'post superbas efferatarum gentium cervices oppressas, latasque leges, fundamenta libertatis et retinacula sempiterna' (14.6.5). The process, beginning with the 'circummurana bella' of early Rome and the conquest of her local enemies, had passed in her maturity through the expansion of Roman power in the Mediterranean and the north, to the defence of the massive, embattled system of empire that Ammianus knew, while Rome and her senate grew old in tranquillity.[2] It was to maintain this condition of sustained and necessary war that Rome had in advanced years transferred her inheritance to the Caesars, 'as to her children', being content to conquer from time to time, in Ammianus' day, 'by name alone'; 'nomine solo aliquotiens vincens' (14.6.4).

Apart from their contemporary application, there is nothing very original in these sentiments. They are reminiscent of, and may be intended to evoke, Vergil's famous lines written four centuries earlier, conceding to 'others' (that is, to Greeks) the finer things of life and reserving for Rome the arts of government and war and a more solemn duty, the imposition of peace and the subjection of pride:

279

> tu regere imperio populos, Romane, memento
> (hae tibi erunt artes), pacisque imponere morem,
> parcere subiectis et debellare superbos. (*Aen*. 6.851-3)

For Ammianus, the eternity of empire was symbolised by the eternity of Rome, expressed in a sort of providential pun, 'victura, dum homines erunt, Roma' (14.6.3). 'Victura': 'which will live'? – or 'which will conquer'? – as long as there are men; Ammianus can hardly have been unaware of, or failed to intend, the ambiguity. There is also an irony in the historical pattern, one known to Ammianus no more than to Vergil, in fact beyond all but the most speculative of fourth-century visions. Just as the history of Rome began with 'circummurana bella' against her Latin neighbours, so it was with 'circummurana bella', the sieges of Alaric the Visigoth in 408-410 and of Geiseric the Vandal in 455 that it would come full circle, survival in Italy replacing foreign conquest as her main preoccupation. In a final irony, the arts of government and war were left to the Byzantines, those 'Greeks' to whom Vergil would have denied them; but that part of Vergil's prophecy – it has rather been seen as a renunciation – was already falsified by the second century.[3]

The dominance of war, with all that this implies, in Greek and Roman historiography had been established by its founders, Herodotus and Thucydides, in the first case in terms of the cultural identity in defence of which the Greeks overcame their weaknesses and went to war against barbarians, in the second for its exposure of the deepest truths about human nature and society. By the time that Livy had documented the emergence of Rome in the Italian peninsula and Polybius the growth of Roman power in the eastern Mediterranean, the centrality of war had been established in such a way that no future historian would be able to ignore; or, if he did so, it was by adopting a new genre of writing, the biographical, against which, whether (in its various forms) philosophical, erudite, or scandalous, Ammianus firmly set his face (p. 459). For the traditional historian an age without war would be, as Gibbon wrote of the reign of Antoninus Pius, an age without history.[4]

For the Roman, war was then a cultural and a historiographical issue of central importance, in both respects as a legitimate expression of his culture. The converse of this observation is that war and warfare, as the proper subject of history, are to be described in the literary manner appropriate for the broader cultivated audience; that is to say without undue use of technical language. Ammianus' expression in his epilogue that he had written 'as a soldier and a Greek' can be read on many levels, of apology and of justification. One of the latter is surely that he had felt entitled, in his choice of history as a mode of writing, to subject military history to the conventions of a literary style.

Apart from its cultural and historiographical role, no one will doubt the actual significance of war in the structure of the late Roman state and the preoccupations of its rulers. One might even define the state, without gross exaggeration, as a system for the financing of war. Finance and taxation are not in themselves enticing subjects for a historian with

Classical literary ambitions. That is no reason to exclude them as they arise, however, and Ammianus is too circumstantial a writer not to allow them their relevance to the events he describes. We saw how the comment of the *comes sacrarum largitionum* Ursulus before the ruins of Amida earned him the enmity of the military classes and his execution at the trials of Chalcedon;[5] he contrasted what he saw as the lack of spirit with which the military were defending the cities with the economic exhaustion of the empire in face of the military budget; 'en quibus animis urbes a milite defenduntur, cui ut abundare stipendium possit, imperii opes iam fatiscunt' (20.11.5). The vast expenditure of Julian on the Persian campaign was argued by some to justify the financial severity of Valentinian, again with reference to the need to provide soldiers' pay, 'ut militi supplementa suppeterent et stipendium' (30.8.8). The same justification is not explicitly offered for Valens, although it could have been, for the cost of the Persian campaign fell both on east and west, and Valens too was known, at least initially, for the harshness of his financial exactions (p. 193). When at the end of his reign Valens was persuaded to accept the settlement of Goths in the Roman empire, he was attracted by the argument that with these new recruits he could cease to levy peasants for military service, taking cash in lieu from landowners who had had to supply men. Although Ammianus presents this as an argument offered by court sycophants to please the emperor, it is in the circumstances of the late Roman state an extremely important consideration (31.4.4). Manpower was a constant problem, and the claims of military need and agricultural production were not always easy to reconcile; given the frequent comment that the Roman empire suffered from an excess of idle mouths, it is hard to blame an emperor for trying to turn consumers into producers, to return the peasantry to the land and recruit soldiers from outside the system.

The relationship between taxation and war, explicitly stated in these passages, is implied in all references to the furnishing and transport of supplies, and to such matters as the billetting of troops in local communities. Julian's soldiers at Antioch were not only responsible for disgraceful scenes as they were carried through the streets to their lodgings drunk and incapable (22.12.6); they were unedifying beneficiaries of another of the many varieties of direct taxation in the late Roman state. Further, the presence at Antioch of many thousands of extra mouths to feed, of people connected with the court and army, had an adverse effect on two occasions in the mid-fourth century upon the food supply of the city, leading to shortages affecting the local population, and to civic unrest (p. 409). An issue of taxation lies behind the dispute between the *comes Africae* Romanus and the citizens of Tripolitania who requested his help against the inroads of desert tribesmen. Romanus demanded 4,000 camels before he would undertake the campaign, and departed without offering help when they were not provided (28.6.5f.). The demand seems, and perhaps was, excessive, but inscriptions have shown the obligation, going back to the time of Constantine, of landowners in the vicinity of the Roman frontier in Africa to provide it with supplies.[6] We cannot say how conscientiously the obligation had been met in a period of peace for the province – a law on the subject addressed in 365 to the *vicarius Africae* ominously mentions collusion by 'tabularii' (*CTh* 11.1.11) – nor whether the provision of camels had ever been envisaged rather than simply supplies of grain; but it is by no means impossible that Romanus, in making his demand, was reminding the provincials of years of neglect of their legal obligations. Initially supported by the emperors (*CTh* 11.1.11) and of course by his soldiers in the province (28.6.23), he maintained his innocence to the end of the affair, and claimed that the enquiry which ultimately closed it was biassed in favour of the provincials (28.6.29). Modern historians, excited by the episode as a case study of corruption in the late Roman administration, have been reluctant to consider it from the commander's point of view.[7] Circumstances were different when the *magister militum* Theodosius promised to support his campaign against the rebel Firmus by using the enemy's own resources; his announcement was greeted with gladness by the landowners of the region: 'laetitia possessorum' (29.5.11). The expression is significant for what it implies of the alternative, the requisitioning of supplies from 'possessores' and the widening of the gulf of economic interest between the landowning and military classes.

Roman generals naturally supported themselves, when they could, on the profits of their campaigns. It was a frequent preoccupation of Julian in his Alamannic wars – sometimes frustrated by circumstances or errors of judgment, as when his attack was made so early in the year that the crops in barbarian country were not ripe for Roman use (17.9.2f.). Otherwise grain supplies – the product of taxation – were brought to the German front from Aquitania and from Britain, and (in the latter case) stored in granaries rebuilt by Julian (17.8.1; 18.2.3f.). It was clearly for reasons of supply rather than military capability in the narrow sense that the normal campaigning season in the north-west began only in July (17.8.1). Supplies for campaigns, as is obvious, had to be arranged to make sure they were adequate for predictable contingencies, depots set up and properly guarded, and severe penalties threatened (the Theodosian Code is full of examples) to inhibit the massive opportunities that existed for maladministration. Ammianus tells of a minor official executed by the praetorian prefect of the east (who was in charge of taxation and supply) because some supplies promised by him for the Persian campaign of Julian had not arrived when he said they would; they turned up the following day, too late to save the poor man's life (23.5.6). The Persian campaign needs no special mention at this point. Apart from the thousand or more ships devoted to the transport of supplies, weaponry and siege machinery, stockpiles were laid down for the army's use along its routes of advance into and predicted withdrawal from Assyria. Supplies were also taken as opportunity arose from captured fortresses, and from Persian lands not damaged by flooding or fire. It was the latter, together with constant harassment in the districts

XIII. The Practice of War 283

east of the Tigris, that reduced the Roman army to extremes of starvation on its journey home, until they were met by an army bringing provisions from Roman Mesopotamia (p. 186).

That the role of the emperors was in the first instance a military one is made clear at all turns of Ammianus' narrative. The military setting dominates their lives, from their earlier careers, their selection by cabals of officers, their presentation to and acclamation by the assembled troops, through the events of reigns spent tramping the frontiers of empire from one scene of warfare to another, to their deaths in camp (or in battle) and escort for burial by squads of selected officers. What is true of legitimate emperors is also true of usurpers, whether (like Julian and Procopius) they are proclaimed by soldiers, in camp or passing through at a timely moment, whether in the end (like Silvanus) they are murdered by troops suborned for the purpose or (like Procopius) are abandoned by them on the field of battle.

It is natural to find military expertise among the central virtues, and a deficiency of it among the shortcomings, of the emperors described by Ammianus. 'Scientia rei militaris' was the first of the practical virtues assigned to Julian in his obituary, ranging in specific terms from his skill at siege warfare and arranging lines of battle, to the selection of safe places for encampments and the posting of advance (or frontier) guards and pickets (25.4.11). It was a measure of Julian's 'fortitudo' (the last of the cardinal virtues assigned to him, immediately preceding military knowledge in the text) that he was willing to expose himself to danger in the front line of battle, and of his 'auctoritas' that because he shared the dangers faced by his men he could discipline cowards, control his soldiers even when (because of Constantius' policy to him) he had no pay to give them, and raise their morale by addressing them in speeches (25.4.10; 12f.). The survey which introduces the obituary of Valentinian concerns his suppression of the various military threats posed to the Roman empire, beginning with his fortification of strongholds and cities on the Rhine frontier and his increase in the military establishment there against the threat of the Alamanni (30.7.5ff.): in addition to which, he was excellent in preserving military discipline and most skilled in the practice of war (30.9.1; 4). He also invented new kinds of military equipment (30.9.4). The reference in this passage to the maintenance of frontier defence recalls Ammianus' statement, under the year 369, that Valentinian re-fortified the entire Rhine frontier from Raetia to the North Sea with camps, forts and watch-towers (28.2.1).[8] Ammianus thereby sets out under a single year the policy of Valentinian's entire reign, shown also by epigraphic and archaeological evidence on the middle Danube frontier – though only once mentioned for this region by Ammianus, in explanation of Valentinian's wars against the Quadi (29.6.3f.). All this was a 'great and useful enterprise' of Valentinian's; 'magna animo concipiens et utilia' (28.2.1). Ammianus' judgment is supported by a careful and very interesting description of the construction of a fort on the banks of the river Neckar by the efforts of soldiers and hydraulic engineers, with the emperor's personal encouragement. At times the men had to work chin-deep in the water in order to secure the piles on which the fort rested (28.2.2-4).

Although it was among Valentinian's virtues that he was a strict guardian of military discipline, it could be said against him that this was more evident in his treatment of the lower ranks, the emperor allowing complaints against the high-ranking to go unchecked (30.9.1): whether Ammianus has in mind more than the specific cases of Romanus in Africa and of Marcellianus the son of Maximinus in Valeria (for his inhospitable murder of king Gabinius of the Quadi) is not clear, but he remarks elsewhere as a general truth that Valentinian was the first emperor to raise the military to a pitch of untrammelled insolence, to the detriment of the common interest (27.9.4). It was of course difficult, given their awareness of their own importance, to keep the military in check, but Constantius had achieved it, maintaining a strict separation between military and civil powers and – a point Ammianus could certify from his personal knowledge – always confining 'duces' to the rank of 'perfectissimus'; he did not allow them to achieve senatorial rank (21.16.2).

The separation both in central bureaucracy and in provincial administration of civil and military powers, is a hallmark of the late imperial system. The process, described in Chapter XI (p. 248f.) in connection with the growth of ceremony as a mode of communication between the new military ruling classes and a civilian society from which they were potentially alienated, has many implications for the reading of Ammianus, and for the general understanding of the Roman empire of the fourth century. As far as concerns Ammianus, it has meant that the vast amount of evidence which he provides for the military power-structure and personnel of the empire has tended to be studied in terms of the specialist history of the late Roman army and high command rather than for its more general interest.[9] As for the late empire itself, the polarisation of social classes and culture implied by this specialisation is well illustrated by the visit to the court of Valentinian in 369-370 of the senatorial orator and envoy, Q. Aurelius Symmachus. The episode is not mentioned by Ammianus, and there is no particular reason why it should be, though there is an intriguing convergence in the fact that the year of Symmachus' journey to Trier was also that under which Ammianus placed his general assessment of Valentinian's frontier policy in the north (28.2.1ff.): almost as if it had somehow been agreed that this would be an appropriate year in which to commemorate this aspect of the emperor's work.

Symmachus attended court to present to the emperor the anniversary gold voted by the senate to celebrate the completion of his first quinquennium in power, and (politely passing over the cost to the senate) to express hopes of more.[10] His second panegyric, addressed to Valentinian on New Year's Day 370, can be compared with the history of Ammianus for its explicit and detailed recognition, rare in a civilian writer, of the military aspects of Valentinian's governmment. One reads in this panegyric the sorts of thing that constantly occur in Ammianus: fortified posts, bridgeheads and landing-stages built, river-fleets equipped, Alamann tribesmen settled on the land, Burgundian embassies received with petitions of peace, forays into unsafe barbarian country. Symmachus, like Ammianus, described the emperor's personal contribution to the building of a new fort at the junction of two rivers (*Or.* 2.18ff.). On topographical grounds, this should be a different fort from that described by Ammianus, again lending support to the notion that there was some calculation of a public response in the presentation of Valentinian's policy, as the emperor symbolically associated himself, surveying instruments in hand, with its implementation. Symmachus departed from Trier with the honorary rank of 'comes ordinis tertii' and could refer in a letter to a court friend, the poet Ausonius (and be similarly flattered in reply), to the days when he had 'attended the imperial standards', and to the fine dinners they had enjoyed when they had been together 'at headquarters' in the frontier region (*Epp.* 1.14; 32; cf. Ausonius, *Griphus*, praef.). Ausonius, in his best and most famous poem, the *Mosella*, describes a journey made while returning from campaign with the emperor, from Bingen via Neumagen to Trier, and composed two epigrams in honour of the sources of the Danube in territory once, but no longer, held by the Romans (*Epigr.* 28, 31). The 'discovery' of the Danube sources, allegedly 'unknown in Roman annals' (*Mosella* 424), by a Roman visiting party corresponds with the rebuilding by Julian of a 'Trajanic fort' beyond the frontier, described by Ammianus (17.1.11f.), and with the visit, mentioned also by Symmachus in his second panegyric, to the Roman 'ghost town' of Lopodunum (Ladenburg), in an area of earlier occupation long since abandoned (*Mosella* 423; *Or.* 2.16). In a strange glimpse of a 'post-Roman' future in the west (below, p. 308f.), remains of its buildings and inscriptions could still be seen there; 'Romanae coloniae antiqua vestigia et tituli' (*Or.* 2.16). Valentinian could have restored the city, but preferred not to, being content with the implication, suitably conveyed by Symmachus, that it had been unwisely founded in the first place!

Such documents are more than unreal attempts to associate their writers with a world of warfare and action to which they did not belong. They are part also of the efforts made by remote and ill-understood military rulers to represent themselves and their activities favourably to a civilian society on whose financial resources their continued efforts depended, and in whose interests they undertook them. After his reception at court and promotion there (known most explicitly from his inscriptions, and so clearly a source of pride to him) Symmachus was no doubt intended to convey to the senate the reassurance that the emperor was indeed devoting his crown gold and the proceeds of other taxation to the defence of the frontiers of the empire. In Symmachus' speeches, delivered and circulated at Rome, senators could hear and read accounts of the background and earlier career of their emperor, and of the virtues of the young heir to the throne – that is Gratian, whose elevation in a predominantly military setting was fully described by Ammianus (27.6.4ff.). They could learn from these speeches of the submission of barbarian tribes and the restoration of the frontier regions, explained in language that evoked heroic parallels and achieved the ultimate in elevating warfare to the untechnical. For all its artificiality, this was no pointless exercise. It was because of their exemption from direct involvement in the emperors' efforts that the senate and people of Rome could live in peace as Ammianus described them, having conveyed the duties of war to younger men (14.6.5). It was right that some attempt should be made to show them the reality: whether they were ever willing to face it is quite another question.

*

The actual range of military action described by Ammianus is comprehensive in type, scale and setting. He includes accounts of campaigns against Alamanni (in no less than nineteen chapters of his work), Sarmatians, Franks, Saxons and Quadi, not to mention the great wars with Persia conducted by Constantius and Julian and the Gothic war of Valens that dominates the last book of the history. There are 'internal wars' against Isaurian bandits and Moorish rebels, and complex operations of civil war involving in turn Julian and Procopius. Ammianus' descriptions range from the great confrontations of Julian against the Alamanni at Strasbourg and of Valens against the Goths at Hadrianople, through significant episodes like the storming of the Alamann hill-fort near Solicinium by Valentinian and the battle of Ad Salices against the Goths, to a variety of smaller operations, ambushes, commando raids and skirmishes by the score. There are fine accounts of sieges: apart from the marvellous description of the Persian attack on Amida in 359, the sieges of Singara, Bezabde (on two occasions, the town changing hands on the first), of Pirisabora and 'Maiozamalcha' in Julian's Persian campaign and, in the civil war of Julian and Constantius, of Aquileia.

Some writers on Ammianus are critical of the clarity and accuracy of his military narratives. This chapter is in part an attempt to test this criticism, but it can fairly be claimed at the outset that, for all the selection of detail and the rhetorical colouring that have seemed to compromise his accuracy, Ammianus never leaves unexplained the specific character of a battle or the strategy of a campaign, even though he may not always be so clear as to its purpose. For all his reluctance to set out formally the general topography of cities besieged, he invariably notes the features relevant to the events that actually occurred, and he explains the diplomatic contexts that were involved in the actions he describes – the exchange of messages, the conduct of intelligence, the role of envoys and hostages, the installation of friendly kings over foreign nations, political assassinations sometimes approved, sometimes (if the outcome were unfavourable) disclaimed by the Roman authorities. All this has occurred frequently in the preceding chapters of this book and will recur in the next, and there is no need to repeat it here: as Ammianus would say, 'ut saepius dicta, praetermitto'.

That Ammianus' military narratives should be modelled in a rhetorical fashion is not surprising. As we saw, it was precisely the central role of war in Roman ideology that qualified it for literary description, in history as in epic poetry. It was after all to introduce the Gallic wars of Julian, using the words with which Vergil introduced the Italian wars of Aeneas, that Ammianus evoked the 'higher order of things' now awaiting his reader – beginning with the long digression on Gaul, which Ammianus saw as directly relevant to his narrative of Julian's campaigns (15.9.1). It is of course true that the technical parameters of warfare – space, time, topography, the calculation and provision of resources, the design and manufacture of equipment, the efficiency of administration and transport, and so on – are, of all subjects, least suited to the high style of poetic language. Yet to say this is only to remark on the general character of the Classical literary tradition. There were such things as military handbooks, works on organisation and tactics, technical descriptions of machinery. Some survive, and they are often very interesting (especially in translation); but they are not the same as works of history and they observe different conventions.[11]

In considering the conventions of history, we must also admit what we might call the 'moral role' of war, seen as providing a measure of character in confrontation with physical danger and pain, of courage and cool judgment in extreme circumstances and, at the most general level, of cultural and political allegiance in conflict with those who would destroy them. Despite the particular nature of Ammianus' own military service, which tended to emphasise the role of the individual and of personal enterprise in action, nothing was more obvious to him than that armies were large, and largely prosaic, institutions, and that wars were won by collective effort, by the accomplishment of the plain necessities of administration and supply, by routine, discipline and the elimination of the finer feelings as much as by individual acts of heroism. This was not however how the literary tradition would encourage him to present them. The vast weight of historiographical precedent, Greek and Roman, would show that the historian's duty was to describe the event rather than the situation, to single out the specific, the individual and the outstanding from the drably monotonous, in the case of battle the sheer confusion, beyond accurate description, that surrounded it. This could be left to descriptive rhetoric of a more impressionistic order – the dust of conflict, clash of metal, the hissing of arrows, cries of pain, varied forms of death, piles of corpses, rivers running with blood – and to the imagination, with which the reader is of course expected to approach the rhetoric, allowing himself to engage the emotions it was designed to provoke. And Ammianus has a better claim on our imaginations than some. He had been in battles, had fought for his life, had seen people killed and had undoubtedly killed some himself, not at a distance but hand to hand, knowing just what he was doing and seeing the effect of it. He is better qualified than many ancient historians to convey not only the strategic and tactical shape of war and battles, but a sense of what it was actually like to take part in them. We can help ourselves to understand his rhetoric if we see him as describing not only the conduct, but also the experience, of war.

Paradoxically in view of his personal involvement at Amida, it is above all in his narratives of sieges that Ammianus can most readily be suspected of writing to a structural and rhetorical pattern.[12] From them, we may assemble a sort of composite account of the normal sequence of events. The enemy comes up, the local people take refuge in their overcrowded city. Having reconnoitred the terrain and the defensive outworks, the besieger encircles the city with armed pickets two (21.12.4), three (20.11.21; 24.2.9; 4.10) or (at Amida) five ranks deep (19.2.2). He will try to persuade the occupants to give themselves up by making announcements below the city walls, usually receiving a dusty reply (and worse), as at Amida (19.1.5), Bezabde (on two occasions, 20.7.3f.; 11.7) and Pirisabora (24.2.9). Ladders are then carried up and siege engines prepared, as at Singara (20.6.3) and Bezabde (20.7.6). These 'men carrying ladders' make regular appearances in sieges (20.11.21; 21.12.6, 13), including mention in a slightly different context of a legendary combatant, taken from Valerius Maximus, in the wars of C. Fabricius Luscinus against the Lucanians. A huge man seen carrying a scaling ladder was nowhere to be found in the next day's roll-call; from which it was concluded (other explanations apparently being neglected) that he was the god Mars himself (24.4.24; Val. Max. 1.8.6). The siege machinery is then brought up, battering rams and the artillery devices described more fully below; this was a lengthy operation, since the more elaborate devices were conveyed in sections and had to be put together, and suitable emplacements constructed. Much sheer hard work was involved in making the preparations ('labore multiplici', 24.4.13). At Bezabde the Romans had a huge Persian battering ram used against them a century earlier and abandoned by its Persian owners at Carrhae;[13] it was an ancient device, which came apart for ease of transport ('aries vetustus et dissolutus, ut facile veheretur') and was re-assembled for use by the Romans (20.11.11f.). As Ammianus also notes, either for its pictorial effect, or possibly because the Persian workmanship was in itself of interest, its iron point was actually shaped in the form of a ram's head; 're vera formam effingit arietis' (20.11.15). In the event it was entangled by nets thrown down from the walls and rendered inoperative.

The actual fighting is fierce and resourceful, as defenders counter the tactics employed by the besiegers, and there is some repetition of rhetorical, as surely of actual, situations. The defenders vow to die with glory (19.2.4, 13; 20.11.22), arrows fly like hail or rain (19.1.8; 20.7.6), attackers and defenders suffer various forms of death, transfixed by arrows and bolts or shattered by stone missiles (19.1.8; 21.12.6, etc.). The

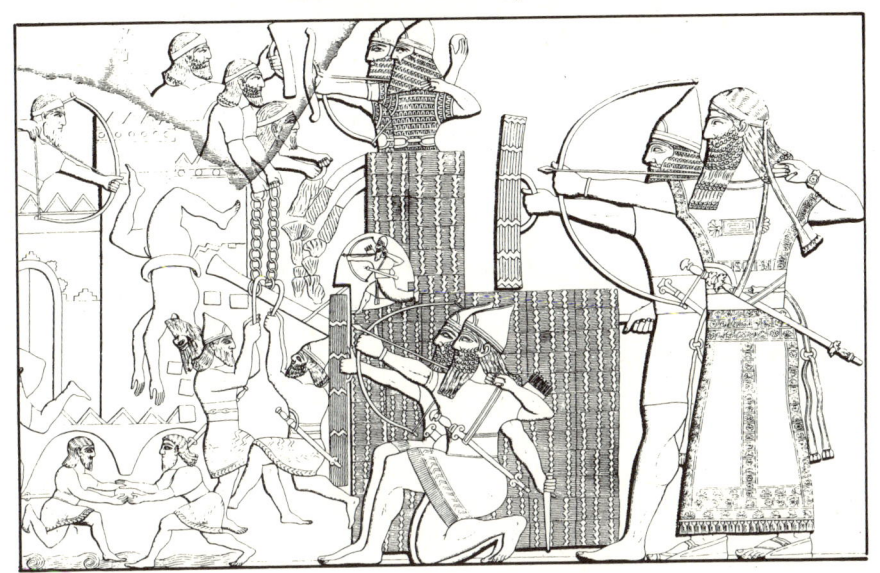

Fig. 2. The Face of Battle (1). The Assyrian king Ashurnasirpal II assaults a city; an illustration (pl. 19) from the first volume of Austen Henry Layard's *The Monuments of Nineveh, from Drawings made on the Spot*, published in 1849. The original relief, in fact from Nimrud, c. 850 BC, is now in the British Museum, Assyrian Sculpture Galleries, Room 19; cf. Julian Reade, *Assyrian Sculpture* (British Museum Publications, 1983), p. 30. The details well illustrate the text of Ammianus. The Assyrians bring up a siege engine with projecting ram, which has been caught by chains let down from the walls but is being held in position by Assyrian soldiers with hooks, and has made a breach. The defenders are throwing down flares to set fire to the machine, but these are being dealt with by water directed by flexible hoses from a reservoir inside it (the form of attack is evidently expected). Below, Assyrian soldiers are engaged in tunnelling, or have found an underground passage, into the city. See the continuation of the scene on p. 292 below.

fighting continues until a weak point in the walls (usually a tower) is found and breached by rams, or a successful stratagem is devised or the besiegers, for a variety of possible reasons, retire unsuccessful. In the case of a 'successful' siege there follows the sack, the killing of defenders and the taking of prisoners, the acquisition of supplies and the firing of the city. This phase allows for a certain variety, depending upon circumstance. At 'Maiozamalcha', the defenders took refuge in subterranean tunnels around the city and were smoked out (24.4.29f.), at Amida the leaders of the resistance were crucified by king Sapor (19.9.2)

That there is a regularity, even a certain ceremonious repetition, in these narratives, is undeniable: which in no way excludes the likelihood that the regularity was part of the events themselves, the conditions of siege warfare being by their nature repetitive; indeed, it was precisely the similarity in the actual conduct of sieges that facilitated the element of ceremony attached to them. This being so, Ammianus' accounts of sieges are as notable for the sheer variety of their outcomes, and for their sense of the individual circumstances involved, as for any repetitions they contain. The Persians took Singara by attacking with a ram a part of the city wall that had recently been repaired, so that the cement was not yet thoroughly dry (20.6.6f.), and the Romans were then as always unable to send an army to recover the city because of the waterless terrain surrounding it (20.6.9). At Bezabde the Persians attacked a weak point in the fortifications, suspicion for their knowledge falling groundlessly, so Ammianus said, upon its bishop, who had recently gone to Sapor's camp as an envoy (20.7.9).[14] In a creative use of local materials the Roman defenders of Bezabde used their mural artillery to hurl blazing baskets coated with pitch and bitumen, the Persians countering the fire by covering their biggest ram with wet bull's hide (20.7.10, 13). Its Persian defenders in turn held the city against Constantius, when he came to recover it, by entangling the huge battering ram assembled and brought to the city walls, and were ultimately saved when bad weather caused the Romans to abandon the siege (20.11.15; 25ff.). After equally resourceful opposition, Aquileia was surrendered to Julian's men when its inhabitants learned of the death of Constantius, in whose interests they had defended it (21.12.18f.); so Philippopolis yielded to Aequitius when its defenders saw the head of the usurper Procopius being carried aloft on a pike to the northern provinces (26.10.6; p. 201). In another episode mentioned earlier, Cyzicus fell to Procopius when the tribune Aliso broke the chain across the harbour mouth with a huge axe (26.8.8ff.; p. 196). On the Persian campaign of Julian, Anatha was given up by negotiation on being surrounded unexpectedly by the water-borne assault force conveyed ahead of the main army (24.1.6-9), the defenders of Pirisabora surrendered when they saw the siege tower known as 'helepolis' ('city-taker') being prepared against their inner fortification, the fortress of 'Maiozamalcha' fell when three soldiers led an assault party out of a tunnel mined under its walls into the city (24.4.21ff.). In his narrative of this episode, Ammianus even mentions the fact that props were used to support the roof of the tunnel (24.4.21), a detail entirely characteristic of his narrative of the Persian campaign, especially when compared with other accounts of it (p. 175).

Above all, Ammianus' account of the siege of Amida of 359, though as we saw it contains some difficulties of selection and chronology, is from start to finish full of circumstantial and personal details, effectively observed and narrated. Such details do not exclude elements of rhetorical colouring, but co-exist with them. The besieged suffer the usual forms of death, 'diffractis capitibus multos ... moles saxeae colliserunt, alii traiecti sagittis, pars confixi tragulis ... vulnerati alii' and so on, the passage yet culminating with a specific detail, the use by the Persians of Roman artillery captured at Singara (19.2.7f.). Another rhetorical passage, in which only night brings an end to slaughter (we may imagine the rest), resolves into the exact comment that the city was overcrowded, 20,000 people being inside, including seven 'legiones' – only one of them, he has

XIII. The Practice of War

told us earlier, forming the regular garrison, the rest being additional (19.2.14; 18.9.3). Ammianus' account of the siege of Amida, certainly the most circumstantial of his siege narratives, is by no means the least rhetorical. The two facets do not contradict, but complement each other.

It is in a different way a reflection of the claims of rhetorical over strictly factual considerations, that Ammianus' digression on artillery and siege machinery occurs as part of his description of the preparations for Julian's Persian campaign (23.4.1-15), where it actually comes later than most of the sieges to which it is relevant; Amida, Singara, both sieges of Bezabde and that of Aquileia all precede it in his text. One must therefore read back as well as forward in the history in order to apply to the actual events described by Ammianus his information about the equipment used in attacking and defending cities.[15]

Ammianus begins with the 'ballista', a versatile instrument in both attack and defence, which could project heavy pointed missiles at a rapid rate of fire. A battery of five light *ballistae*, 'ocius lignea tela fundentes', was used at Amida with lethal effect against the seventy Persian archers who occupied a tower, picking them off, sometimes two at a time, until none were left (some threw themselves down from the tower in sheer terror); the machines were then restored to their normal place on the battlements (19.5.6f.). With such a machine the skilled operator shot down the son of king Grumbates, riding by his father's side as he advanced to view the city – a narrow miss no doubt, but still impressive documentation of its accuracy at a distance (19.1.7). A similar fate nearly befell Julian at Meinas Sabatha as he rode up to its walls to survey it (24.5.6). For those attacking cities, the main use of the *ballista* was to provide covering fire, to clear battlements of defenders while the walls below were breached by battering rams. For this purpose it was important to gain an angle of fire from above; the Persian siege-towers at Amida had *ballistae* encased in iron-clad turrets (19.7.5).

Ammianus' description of *ballistae* is followed by the so-called 'scorpion', known in his own day by the slang name 'onager' or 'wild ass' – the physical violence of its action having replaced the visual image of the raised sting tail in the naming of the instrument (23.4.4; cf. 31.15.12). It was a device with a single throwing arm operated, like the moving slider of the *ballista*, by torsion springs of sinew. It could throw heavy projectiles with a certain accuracy over considerable distances (a modern reconstruction could hurl an eight-pound missile nearly 500 yards), its main defensive use in sieges being to weaken the machinery, especially siege-towers, brought against cities, and to demoralise and keep at a distance encircling armies.[16] At Amida, the advancing Persian siege-towers were first broken by this heavy artillery, then destroyed by fire-arrows shot from the walls into their exposed timbers (19.7.6f.). The mural artillery of Amida had earlier been used to cover the entry of refugees into the city and, operated unloaded, for the sake of their noise, the night foray of the Gallic soldiers against the Persian camp (18.8.13; 19.6.10); and we have seen the scorpion used at Bezabde to project

Fig. 3. The Face of Battle (2). The scene (Layard, *The Monuments of Nineveh*, pl. 20) adjoins that shown on p. 289 above. The city is being assaulted by soldiers ascending scaling ladders, while another crawls through a tunnel under the walls. A vulture hovers overhead. Like Ammianus' Pirisabora (above, p. 174) the city under attack has a double, even a triple, ring of fortifications, and stands by a water-course.

flaming baskets against the Persian siege equipment (20.7.10). The *onager*, explains Ammianus in his digression, required a firm emplacement from which to operate, for its recoil could break apart a stone base. Bonded brick emplacements were needed or, in less permanent circumstances such as encampments, platforms of compacted turf (23.4.5).[17] Ammianus notes the skill required to adjust the direction of fire of the four such machines deployed against the Persian siege towers at Amida, and it is this narrative rather than the digression on artillery that best shows the effectiveness with which, handled skilfully, they could be brought to bear (19.7.6f.). Another episode shows the fearful power which their torsion springs could generate. On Julian's Persian campaign an engineer standing behind such a machine was killed when it misfired and hit him. Such was the force of the impact of the missile (Ammianus perhaps exaggerates a little) that his body was smashed into many pieces, none of them recognisable. Ammianus did not know his name either, a point worth mentioning for its implication that he would normally expect to name the victim of such a notable accident – unless the disappearance of the name is intended as a grimly pedantic comment

XIII. *The Practice of War*   293

on the dissolution also of his body (24.4.28).[18] Ammianus' account in his digression of the mode of operation of the machine makes one wonder whether there were more such accidents then we know of, for it seems very dangerous. The operator had in some way to stand 'above' the mechanism ('sublimis') and hit a retaining key with a large hammer to release the spring (23.4.6).[19]

Ammianus briefly passes over battering rams, in order to reach the 'helepolis', a siege tower invented and deployed to great effect in the wars of the Hellenistic age (23.4.10). Yet the digression here goes wrong, for what Ammianus actually describes under this name, a mobile armoured shed used to protect the backs of soldiers attacking the base of walls, is different both from the Classical *helepolis* and from the machines named as such in his narrative; it is a much more humble device, and it misses one of the most important functions of the *helepolis*, to operate against the walls of cities from a superior height. Invented in earlier times but perfected by Demetrius Poliorcetes ('the Besieger'), the true *helepolis* was an iron-clad wooden tower mounted on great pivoted casters, its wheels driven by a capstan in the base of the tower turned by gangs of soldiers, the whole device rising to a height of a hundred feet and more.[20] It was divided into storeys linked by ladders, a one-way system for ascent and descent being mentioned by Plutarch in his description of one of the most famous of these devices (*Demetrius*, 21.1f.). From the separate floors gangways and bridges led outwards, for armed men and engineers to work at various levels on the walls of beleaguered cities, while archers and artillery at the top cleared the battlements of their defenders. The fantastic contraption was (to a modern eye) surprisingly effective; it evoked the admiration of writers both technical and literary, and offered a challenge to their descriptive powers. The account of the *helepolis* used by Demetrius at Rhodes in 304 BC by a writer called Diocleides was famous, and may have influenced others. Plutarch, in his *Life of Demetrius*, for example, describes that king's masterpiece in suitably imposing language. A multi-storeyed structure 66 – or even, if his text be suitably emended, 99 – cubits high (alternatively 99 or 144 feet) and tapering from a broad square base of 48 cubits to a narrower summit, the *helepolis* could by the capstan just mentioned be driven to the walls of cities without leaning or tottering at all: an awesome sight, but also one to give pleasure, thought Plutarch – this point of appreciation presumably depending on one's point of view (*Demetrius* 21.1f.). Caesar told in his *Commentaries* how the contempt of the beleaguered Aduatici for the Romans turned to dread when they saw the siege tower, whose construction at a distance they had derided, being brought up against them. They did not suppose, their envoys told Caesar, that such a machine could be moved so quickly without the help of the gods (*Bell. Gall.* 2.30-31)! The Aduatici (of Tongres) were sheer novices at this sort of warfare, but the far more experienced defenders of Pirisabora surrendered the inner citadel to which they had resorted at the mere sight of the *helepolis* being assembled by the engineers of Julian's army;

the outer wall of the city having been taken by an orthodox attack on a corner tower by a battering ram (25.4.12). Countermeasures could be taken, but they required considerable resources of technique and imagination. The Persian siege-towers used at Amida, equipped with light *ballistae* which from their superior height could fire down on the battlements of the city, were broken by the skilful use of the four *onagri* mentioned earlier. At Aquileia Julian's men devised a variation of the *helepolis*, admired by Ammianus with an enthusiasm rather out of proportion to its effectiveness. Prevented by difficulties of the terrain from bringing a tower to the walls of the city, the engineers mounted one on boats lashed together in groups of three, and floated it up by the old harbour frontage, which now formed part of the fortified circuit of Aquileia (below, p. 396). The enterprise failed when the defenders ignited the two-storeyed device with fire-arrows, so that the soldiers inside all ran to the other side and capsized it (21.12.9f.) – a predictable outcome, though it would have been neglectful not to make the attempt, so few other options being available.

Against technologically inferior enemies, properly manned city defences were impregnable. Alamanni and Goths (and, at a still lower level of expertise, the Austurian desert tribesmen of Tripolitania) cursed themselves for their stupidity in attempting to attack city walls, and a famous anecdote in Ammianus shows the Goths, victorious on the battlefield, hesitating before the walls of Hadrianople when a missile projected by an *onager* hit the ground in their midst; no one was hit, but the Goths were thoroughly cowed and had to be urged back into line by their leaders (31.15.12f.). It had earlier been part of Roman policy towards the Goths in Thrace to deprive them of supplies by storing these in walled cities which, as Ammianus remarked, the Goths were totally incapable of reducing; 'haec et similia machinari penitus ignorantes' (31.8.1).[21] Siege warfare between Romans and Persians was however conducted on a technically equal basis. To the modern eye their efforts, however spectacular, seem laboured and antiquated – the *helepolis* had nearly eight centuries of use behind it, with no significant improvements of design or materials in that period – as they deploy artillery operated by springs of twisted sinew and siege towers constructed of massive wooden frameworks (which must over time have worked loose as they were assembled and dismantled), treated with alum to make them fireproof and clad in iron, with fleeces and felt draped over their sides to absorb the impact of missiles and to reduce the echoing clatter for those inside. With their windlasses and wheels also made of wood, connected to the driving wheels by ropes and wooden gears, all but the newest machines must have creaked and groaned pitifully as they were laboriously winched to city walls by grunting soldiers hidden inside: then, the crashing and the flying dust as the rams came into action along the gangways, and the howling and thumping of artillery at the upper levels. Ancient sieges must from a mechanical and every other point of view have been very noisy affairs. As we saw in the case of Amida, Ammianus frequently

XIII. The Practice of War

mentions the noise wrought by the artillery devices and at sieges in general, a topic which recurs in his narrative of the siege of 'Maiozamalcha'. Within a few sentences, artillery is set up, ready to burst out in its 'deadly din'; 'in funestos sonitus proruptura' (24.4.12): the *ballistae* fire off their arrows, which hiss as they speed on their way; 'flexus stridore torquebantur' (24.4.16): a tower broken by a battering ram brings down its adjoining curtain wall with a 'tremendous crash'; 'cuius ruina contiguum latus secum immani fragore protraxit' (24.4.19). (All these expressions can easily be paralleled from other siege narratives.) The city is furiously attacked on two sides to distract the defenders, and to drown the sound of pickaxes as the tunnel under the walls nears completion (24.4.22). As at Amida, the action begins with the sound of trumpets, with shouts and roars on both sides (24.4.15), and the efforts of besiegers and besieged issue in splendid deeds by both; 'obsidentium labor obsessorumque industria vicissim facinoribus speciosis inclaruit' (24.4.20). In this narrative above all others, the 'set piece' of the siege is the framework for individual exploits symbolised by the three soldiers who in one of the high points of the entire Persian campaign led the raiding party out of the tunnel inside the city, and were later decorated for their bravery by Julian in a ceremony before the army (24.4.24). Again, it is difficult to separate precisely observed detail from the effects of rhetoric, for they support each other; and here as at Amida and elsewhere, Ammianus conveys very well the contrast, factual rather than rhetorical but rhetorically most effective, between the laborious preparation of sieges with their clumsy but awesome mechanical support and building operations, and the violence and abruptness of the actual fighting.

*

The patterns in Ammianus' accounts of sieges in no way weaken his sense of the particularity of individual episodes or his ability to differentiate between their circumstances. The same, in a less organised way (they were less organised affairs) is true of battles. If we had possessed Books 10-13 of Ammianus' history, we might know how he presented the Persian army in set formation, at the drawn battle of Singara, to which he refers – although the battle was fought, or at least concluded, at night (18.5.7). The Persian army appears in the surviving books in a series of recollections of disparate encounters, reflecting Ammianus' experience of it as described in earlier parts of this book: the fires of raiding parties around Nisibis, the masses of allies as they assembled in the plains beyond the Tigris, the ritual solemnity of the encirclement of Amida, cavalry brigades leaping without warning from the landscape like the 'Spartoi' of Greek legend – warriors growing instantly from sown teeth (19.8.10f.); then, on the Persian campaign of Julian, the shining helmets and glittering arms of the first Persian ambuscade, cataphract horsemen looking like burnished statues in their fitted armour and, with that wonderful sense of dramatic tension mentioned earlier, the approaching dust cloud near Ctesiphon, revealed in the light of dawn as the army of the great king (p. 160). The nearest approach in the surviving books to a set battle against the Persians is the fighting at the place called 'Phrygia' where Julian was killed. As we saw, Ammianus' account indicates the strategic context, in which the Persians harried the retreating army, the sequence of events in the actual engagement, and the manner – Ammianus did not know the agent – of Julian's fatal wound (p. 181). He makes clear in general terms, and often in exact detail, the terrain relevant to the manner in which campaigns, notably those against Isaurians, Moors and Alamanni, were conducted (below, Chapter XIV). He shows how Valentinian's attack by the most difficult route of access to the Alamannic position near Solicinium was successful because of the Roman soldiers' ability to press their attack uphill against defenders in an advantageous position (27.10.12ff.). In only one of many such touches, he notes the ingenuity of Julian in having boats rowed up and down the river Meuse, carrying men armed with poles to prevent the water freezing and allowing Franks who had occupied an abandoned Roman fort to escape to their own territory (17.2.2f.). In another winter campaign, he records a detail of startling immediacy; the bodies of men contorted with pain as the overnight frost shrivelled their wounds while they lay dying; 'semineces et constrictos, quos vulneribus asperitate contractis dolorum absumpserat magnitudo' (27.2.8). At such moments it seems wrong to pose a distinction between rhetorical image and stark reality.

The two greatest set-piece battles recorded by Ammianus, those of Strasbourg and Hadrianople, were decided by the success or failure of Roman armies in maintaining their discipline against the onslaught of less controlled adversaries. (That the difference was a matter of training, or cultural adaptation, and not national character is clear when one considers the largely German composition of the Roman armies. The 'barritus', the famed battle-cry of the Roman armies, rising from murmur to awesome roar in a long crescendo, was itself of German origin; at the battle of Strasbourg it was actually raised by the Romans against the Alamanni (16.12.43), as at the battle of Ad Salices against the Goths (31.7.11); on the latter and on another occasion (26.7.17) it is specifically said by Ammianus to be a 'barbarian' word.) At Strasbourg, after the unexpected collapse of the Roman cavalry, the infantry charge which threatened to break the Roman centre was held, the Germans were turned and chased to the Rhine where many drowned, in an unequal conclusion to a battle that had been evenly poised. At Hadrianople, the battle was delayed by the Goths to give time to their cavalry to return from a plundering expedition.[22] Meanwhile they lit fires in order to make conditions even more unbearable for the Romans than they already were, as they waited in full armour in the heat of an August day. The acrid smell of smoke and sweat, mixed with that of human and animal bodies in the dense formations (the soldiers would have to relieve themselves as they stood where they were posted) need only be imagined. Further, all, men and horses, were tormented by hunger (31.12.13). More time was consumed in negotiation and an abortive exchange of hostages, and battle was joined untidily, in an undisciplined skirmish between the lines. It quickly turned against the Romans when their cavalry charge against the Gothic wagon encampment was repelled. This mishap exposed first the Roman left, then the centre to a flank attack from the Gothic right. The Romans were so densely packed that they could not wield their weapons, but fell to missiles as they stood there helpless. Nor, for the same reason, could they get away. They had had nothing to eat or drink all day, and their armour weighed them down, baking them alive under the scorching sun (31.13.7). When they came close, the barbarians had the advantage in hand-to-hand conflict, being fresher, more adaptable in movement, and better motivated than their opponents. The Emperor Valens fell fighting among the infantry; no one knew the exact circumstances, though a survivor of the day claimed to have seen how Valens had taken refuge in the upper storey of a farmhouse, which was burned down by the Goths in ignorance of the emperor's presence (31.13.12ff.).

Although it is not altogether easy to follow the marching and countermarching manoeuvres which preceded the battle of Hadrianople, no difficulty arises as to the nature of the terrain on which it was fought, a plain just south of the Haemus mountains; while the general configuration of the field near Strasbourg is quite well conveyed, with references to the banks of the Rhine behind the Alamanni, rolling cornfields, low hills and nearby woods (16.12.19, 59, etc.). It takes a little help from Libanius, with his allusion, derived ultimately from Julian's own account, to an artificial watercourse on the battlefield, to locate the actual site (*Or.* 18.56).[23]

Ammianus' description of the engagement of Strasbourg, a long chapter of seventy sections, is divided in roughly equal proportions into the preliminaries of battle and the actual fighting; then comes an epilogue on Constantius' reaction to Julian's victory, the credit for which he claimed for himself (16.12.67-70). The episode is set up with speeches by Julian, unsuccessfully urging delay before the battle is fought, exhorting his troops in preparation for it, later haranguing the faltering Roman cavalry during its progress (16.12.9-12; 30-3; 39-41). The conclusion, as retreating Germans struggle for their lives in the Rhine, is compared to a piece of decorative stage scenery, the personified river, in continuation of the imagery, being shown as astonished at its own increase by the blood of the dead; 'spumans denique cruore barbarico decolor alveus insueta stupebat augmenta' (16.12.57). 'Alveus', strictly the bed of the river rather than the stream itself, is in this context a rather poetic usage. After his defeat, king Chnodomarius is taken to Julian in trepidation, his tongue held fast by consciousness of his crimes, a pathetic transformation – 'quantum ab eo differens!' – from the great king who had terrorised the provinces of Gaul and crowed over their ashes (16.12.61).

As for the battle itself, few tactical indications are provided: only the initial dispositions, the opening of the engagement, the retreat of the Roman cavalry, halted by Julian, the furious attack on the central position by Alamanni, held in check by the 'Primani' (16.12.23-6; 36; 37-41; 49). Apart from these Primani, only four Roman detachments are named, fighting as we often find them in pairs; Cornuti and Bracchiati, Batavi and 'Reges' (better, Regii) (16.12.43; 45).[24] Otherwise, there is the usual evocation of the atmosphere of battle; the sound of trumpets, rising clouds of dust and 'various forays', assorted manners of death of Alamanni and, in a series of contrasts more literary than technical, the difference between the fighting character of the two sides (16.12.37; 53; 47). We are given no exact indication of why the battle turned in the Romans' favour, and the casualty figures only add to the air of rhetorical disproportion; 243 Roman dead including four officers of whom three are named (the name of the fourth, a 'tribunus vacans' being, in a touch of scrupulous documentation, 'unavailable'), 6,000 Alamanni counted on the field of battle and untold numbers drowned in the Rhine (16.12.63).

On these last two points, the turn in the fortunes of the battle may simply have followed from the failure of the Alamann attack on the Roman centre – having failed to break it, there was little the Germans could do but withdraw, but no way in which they could do so safely – and the inequality in casualty figures is not inconceivable, as the Germans tried only to escape from the battlefield while the better-armed Romans pursued them, their bloodlust inflamed by the slaughter they were inflicting. It is when men are running away unable to defend themselves that they are most likely to be killed, and in many ancient battles the greatest casualties were suffered in the closing stages of hard-fought conflicts.

The narrative of the battle of Hadrianople, also, is full of touches of rhetorical and dramatic technique. As at Strasbourg, clouds of dust arise, obscuring the sky; 'nec ... caelum patere potuit ad conspectum' (31.13.2). In a contrasting metaphor, the armies clash together like rows of warships, an awkward image somewhat redeemed by the vivid allusion to movements 'like waves' among the armies as they struggled. Again, death in many forms and, above all, hopeless confusion (31.13.4f.). At one point the general Victor sent for reinforcements of Batavi, posted in reserve, to go to help the emperor, but they could simply not be found, either having disappeared from the field of battle, or having become helplessly involved in it (31.13.9).

In circumstances of such genuine confusion, and such variety of individual experience, it is reasonable to ask what a historian could be expected to do other than describe initial dispositions, indicate the terrain and therefore the type of battle that would be fought, give a general outline of its main phases, select notable individual events and exploits (this was relevant, the role of morale being crucial as men strove not to seem less brave than those around them), describe the result, with casualty figures if they were available, and give some impression of the atmosphere of battle. That this was in practice a largely literary procedure is obvious, if only for the reason that the vast majority of a historian's public would compare a description of a battle, not with battles which they had experienced, but with battles of which they had read, in books which glorified the suffering, simplified the outcome and drew an undisputed moral.[25] While by no means rejecting these influences, Ammianus always adds the particular observations which help to 'fix' a battle and avoid its being interchangeable with any other. The rhetorical transformation of king Chnodomarius from arrogance to tongue-tied submission is matched by the transformation of his physical state from majestic asset to gross liability, as, without his horse and impeded by his bulk, he vainly seeks refuge in neighbouring woods (16.12.59). On another level, there is the confidence of a section of the Alamanni because they recognised in the Roman battle array the shield devices of units they had recently chased off their territory (16.12.6). And the poignant detail reminding us (as if we had forgotten) that battles are a human affair; the son of Ammianus' patron Ursicinus, a still young officer who back in the 350s had lent substance to fears that Ursicinus might be thinking of imperial power for himself, was killed at Hadrianople (31.13.18).

Given the literary conventions within which he wrote, it is hard to feel seriously dissatisfied with Ammianus' portrayal of the 'face of battle'. A more powerful criticism is that his interest in dramatic structure and moral contrast in his narration of battle leads him to distort the wider strategic setting of the campaigns both of Strasbourg and of Hadrianople: though if so, it is to his credit that he himself provides the material from which his misrepresentations can be corrected.

To take first the battle of Strasbourg, the campaigning season of 357 involved an ambitious pincer movement against the Alamannic federation, in which Julian's army approaching from the north-west would converge, 'forcipis specie' in Ammianus' expression, with an army of 25,000 men led by Constantius' general Barbatio advancing northwards from Raetia (16.11.3). The whole design, conceived by the high command of Constantius, required the good faith and co-operation of its participants. In the event Julian allowed himself to be distracted by subordinate (though lucrative) operations on the Rhine, which Barbatio refused to support (16.11.8-12).[26] Julian's delay left Barbatio isolated, and the latter had to content himself with a limited raid into Alamannic territory opposite Raetia. When he withdrew (or was forced out) he burned the supplies prepared for the larger campaign to prevent them falling into the hands of the Alamanni, thereby incidentally depriving Julian of their use (16.11.12). This at least is a more persuasive explanation of his action than that offered by Ammianus, for whom the burning of the supplies was a deliberately malicious attempt by Barbatio to undermine Julian (16.11.12f). Yet one can imagine the reaction at Constantius' headquarters when the whole plan of campaign was ruined by what must have been interpreted there as wilful neglect by

Constantius' Caesar of his clear instructions; in Ammianus' account of Julian's activities during the summer, his part in the proposed pincer attack on the Alamanni seems entirely to have left his head (16.12.8-12). A central theme of Ammianus' presentation of Julian was his success in transcending the obstacles placed before him by Constantius. It is therefore no objection to the historian's point of view, that Julian was victorious at Strasbourg without the assistance he expected from Constantius' generals. It is however an affront to the coherence of Constantius' plan of campaign. The Alamanni were delighted to learn from a deserter that they were facing an army of only 13,000 men; they had expected far more (16.12.2f.). The victory of Julian, in itself a triumph effectively exploited in the sequel, was in the context of 357 a fortunate outcome of a strategy which had collapsed because of Julian's failure to implement his share of its requirements. Even though his forces seem to have included some of Barbatio's men (theirs were the shield devices recognised at Strasbourg by the Alamanni), they were only a fraction of the 25,000 whom the general had had with him before their dispersal. It would not be surprising if, as Ammianus alleges, Barbatio returned to court framing accusations against the Caesar (16.11.15).

At Strasbourg, Julian wished to delay the fight but was overruled by his advisers, as it turned out wisely (16.12.14). At Hadrianople, Valens is presented as over-eager for confrontation with the Goths, reluctant to await the arrival of the army of Gratian from Illyricum and even, in a way reminiscent of the alleged attitude of Constantius to Julian, grudging his young colleague a share in the glory he confidently expected (31.12.7).[27] At the council of war held before the battle, delay was urged by the general Victor, a Sarmatian who showed true Roman caution in the advice he gave; 'Sarmata, sed cunctator et cautus' (31.12.5). The contrary view, that of Sebastianus, is associated with that of the court flatterers who wished to please the emperor, and with Valens' own fateful determination; 'funesta principis destinatio et adulabilis quorundam sententia regiorum' (31.12.7). In his presentation of the arguments, Ammianus has failed to give due weight to the absence of the Gothic cavalry, which was away on a plundering expedition and expected to return by the hour (31.12.12f.). It was in the Goths' interests to delay the engagement in order to allow this to happen, as well as to make the Romans' physical conditions less tolerable; the countervailing strategy on the Roman side, naturally, to force the issue to a conclusion. Ammianus may also have given less than proper consideration to reports received by Valens from scouts that the Gothic army was only 10,000 strong (31.12.3). On any rational calculation, the Romans had the advantage. Until it had actually came about, one would assume that Roman resources, discipline and fighting skills would have made the actual outcome impossible. The last thing – or, given the experience of Strasbourg, almost the last thing – one would expect was that the Roman heavy cavalry would turn before the resistance of barbarians, inferior in equipment, technique and organisation. Something very serious, Ammianus does not say what,

XIII. The Practice of War

happened at the Gothic stockade. Yet, once it had happened, his description of the physical conditions in which the battle was fought makes it painfully clear both why the Romans lost and what it was like to be there, on the losing side. All that is required, and Ammianus would expect it, is a contribution from the imagination of the reader.

*

We should finally consider the question of Ammianus' standpoint as a military participant and observer. Did he from his own experience possess knowledge of any particular aspect of Roman military policy that would lend special authority to his information and judgment on this aspect?

It has been argued that Ammianus shows a special interest in artillery and that his position in the army concerned this aspect of its activities.[28] It is true that he is interested in the subject. His descriptions of the siege and defence of cities are well documented in detail, and he is aware of the general role of siege warfare in military strategy. Ammianus was among those who planned the defence of Amida, with the deployment and use of its artillery, and he first introduces the city as a depot or strongpoint ('conditorium') of mural artillery (18.9.1; p. 54). The role of artillery in the siege is one of the most vivid features of Ammianus' description of it.

These observations are not decisive. Warfare on the eastern frontier turned on the possession of cities. Any account of it would involve a proportion of siege warfare, and Ammianus' emphasis does not necessarily reflect more than this inescapable fact. Eunapius, whom none would accuse of expertise in siege or any other form of warfare, like Ammianus mentioned the ships of Julian devoted to the transport of machinery (Zosimus 3.13.3), and we saw earlier that Ammianus' involvement in the siege of Amida came about through his unplanned presence there as an officer, and need not reflect any particular expertise on his part (p. 64f.). And on closer inspection it is impossible to believe that for all its erudition and quasi-technical character the digression on artillery is the work of an expert in the subject. As we saw, Ammianus' description of what he calls the *helepolis*, a shed used to protect soldiers working at the base of walls from missiles thrown down at them, bears no relation to the machine made famous by Demetrius Poliorcetes, nor to the towers actually named as such and described on two occasions in his narrative. Further, Ammianus' descriptions of both *ballista* and *scorpio*, whether through genuine lack of understanding or from obscurity caused by a wish to avoid technical language, make it seem (his words are not very clear) as if the torsion springs which provided their power were simply part of the binding which held the machinery together. It is confused to write that the fixed stock (the guiding channel) of the *ballista* was 'bound in' ('illigatus') by the twisted sinews that propelled the moving part (23.4.2), and perverse to suggest that the spring which drove the arm of the *scorpio* or *onager* was inserted to prevent the framework of the device from 'springing apart', 'ne dissiliat' (23.4.4): rather as if one were to say that the fuselage of an aircraft were put there to hold the wings together. Although Ammianus appreciated, for instance, that it was not the dead weight but the recoil – 'concussione violenta, non pondere' – of the *onager* that tended to break apart its emplacement if it was not constructed of the right materials (23.4.5), his confusion on the central issue of the motive power of the machinery makes it difficult to believe that he wrote as a practising expert on the subject.

Ammianus appreciates the role of supply and commissariat in military operations, and frequently mentions the subject, particularly but not only in his narrative of the Persian campaign from which especially it has been inferred that this was his sphere of responsibility.[29] The same observation can here be made as in the case of artillery. The importance of supply, its provision, transport and co-ordination in the conduct of campaigns was obvious to any intelligent observer, and it is not clear that Ammianus' awareness of the subject is more than we should expect of the general knowledge of a serving officer. He had after all experienced the deprivation of the retreat from Persia, in which the shortage of supplies and their rediscovery in Roman Mesopotamia were matters whose appreciation was in no sense reserved for the specialist.

A more recent suggestion that Ammianus was concerned with the assembling and interpretation of intelligence and the preparation of tactical and strategic plans on the basis of it, has the real merit that it reflects what Ammianus can be seen to be doing in the course of his narrative – notably in his visit to the satrap of Corduene but also on many other occasions when, in the service of Ursicinus, he is observed receiving information in various forms from envoys, deserters and spies, and helping to judge the best course of action in accordance with what was discovered.[30] His interest in the subject is evident also in passages of his history when he was not personally involved, as for instance in his many narratives of Roman relations with the Alamanni.

The difficulty with this theory is of a more general nature. The gathering and application of intelligence were in Ammianus' day not specific functions defined as it were by department, but something that must be undertaken by any commander or military officer who held responsibility in a field of action. We saw how Ursicinus was appointed to the eastern front to take charge of local defensive arrangements in the light of whatever developed in a constantly changing situation (p. 40f.). For this he needed as much detailed and accurate information as he could get, and it is not surprising that this, from the interrogation of deserters and captives and the interpretation of coded messages to planned missions of espionage, forms a prominent part of Ammianus' presentation of his activities: it was a true reflection of their importance. His interest in intelligence was not a consequence of any special duty or deployment, but of his service as aide to an active general, involved in situations that of themselves required the collection and use of information.

There is the problem of Ammianus' employment in the years 360-63, after the retirement of Ursicinus from public life, and of his role during the Persian campaign of Julian. Of the former, nothing secure can be said that does not involve the circularity of inferring what Ammianus was from what he seems to know, and the obviously fallible assumption that this must depend on personal experience when so much information was available by intelligent enquiry of those who were involved, 'versatos in medio' (15.1.1); it does not seem possible, for example, to argue from his description of it that he was present at the siege of Bezabde in 360.[31] As for the Persian campaign, we saw earlier that, although Ammianus witnessed much and gives a fair account of the strategy of the campaign, he does not stand in the same close relationship to the highest circles of decision-making as he had in the earlier phase; he says nothing definite, for example, of the overall purpose of the enterprise, of what Julian was trying to achieve. On the contrary, it seems possible that Julian's Persian campaign was Ammianus' last opportunity to make for himself the really distinguished military career that might, in the early days, have been predicted for him but had not been fulfilled, and that the death of Julian, followed by the elevation of a different type of imperial candidate, marked his definitive retirement from public service.

More generally, it was from his close relationship to Ursicinus at the beginning of his career that Ammianus gained his perspective of the political and military history of his time. Devoted to Ursicinus and his cause, he was inclined to see changes of policy, promotions and assignments of authority affecting his patron in terms of alliances and enmities, real or imagined, at the court of Constantius – when in fact the emperor was only doing his best to respond to circumstances. Similarly with Julian, sent off to Gaul to be surrounded by officials instructed, as was reasonable given his inexperience, to control him: it was only too easy for Ammianus to adopt Julian's own view of his advisers and collaborators as personal enemies motivated by envy, spite and conflicts of personality. It is a view with which one can sympathise, but it does not lead to the fairest judgment of the circumstances in which imperial policy was made.

Ammianus' view of military policy was intense and sharply defined but sometimes narrow, and gained from an unreliable vantage point – the more so, the more intimately he felt himself to be involved. In this it does not lack a personal and authentic reality. It would be a bold assertion that politics at the imperial court in Ammianus' day were not conducted for much of the time as he describes them. His mistake was to assume that nothing was ever decided on the merits of the case and, where interests clashed, to fail to consider in their true light those of the emperor. Yet, if Ammianus does less than justice to the broad setting and rationale of imperial policy, that would be a far more serious shortcoming were it not for the immensely detailed and vivid range of circumstantial information which he makes available to his reader. This is true not only of the aspects of Roman military policy that he describes, but of the character of the barbarian and other enemies against whom it was devised.

CHAPTER XIV

Barbarians and Bandits

Above all it must be recognised that wild nations are pressing upon the Roman Empire and howling about it everywhere, and treacherous barbarians, covered by natural positions, are assailing every frontier. For usually the aforesaid nations are either covered by forests or occupy commanding mountain positions or are defended by snow and ice, while some are nomadic and are protected by deserts and the burning sun. Others are defended by marshes and rivers and cannot easily be tracked down; yet they mutilate our peace and quiet by unexpected forays .... (Anon., *De Rebus Bellicis* 6.1f.; tr. E. A. Thompson)

With these words, addressed to 'clementissimi principes' usually identified as Valentinian and Valens, an anonymous author recommended his ideas for modernising the army by adopting new inventions in order to give the Roman empire the advantage over the enemies that beset it.[1] He also offered various suggestions – like his inventions, some were practical, others wildly implausible – for reforming the administration, reducing taxation, improving the standard of the coinage, eliminating corruption, securing recruitment without incurring great expense, and clarifying the law. From a different point of view, the anonymous writer's image of 'wild nations' pressing upon the Roman empire[2] is a good starting point for a survey of some of these peoples as Ammianus presents them. Throughout his work, the historian narrates military campaigns against foreign peoples protected by deep forests, by the snow and ice of northern winters, by mountain and desert, river and marsh. Enough has been said in earlier chapters of the wars of Rome with her eastern enemy, the Sasanian Persians, to whom the anonymous writer made allusion in his reference, following those quoted above, to enemies defended by city and fortress walls and, in another passage (19.2), to their guile and physical courage. Other nations, such as the Picti, Scotti and Attacotti of northern Britain, gain only passing mention in Ammianus as his text survives (26.4.5; 27.8.5), and little can be done with them.[3] Some, like the Sarmatians and their former subjects the Limigantes (17.12-13; 19.11), are the subject of substantial narratives that do not characterise their mode of life in any detail – though Ammianus' description of Constantius' campaign of 358 against the Limigantes provides a pertinent example of a people defended by the

XIV. Barbarians and Bandits

natural obstacles of river and marsh at the confluence of the Danube and the Tisza, or Theiss (17.13.4).

In the case of other foreign peoples, Ammianus offers descriptions rich in such material. Merely to name them is to catch a glimpse of a 'post-Roman' future. Across the frontier of the middle and upper Rhine lived the Alamanni, a relatively recent association of Germanic tribes, who both provided the emperors with their most sustained military challenge in the north, and Romance languages with their word for Germany. Next to the Alamanni to the north and east respectively were the Franks and Burgundians, peoples whose impact on European history would be no less profound than that of their neighbours. Likewise, across the Danube to the east of the Sarmatians and Quadi were the Goths, living in part of the old province of Dacia but on the brink of the migration into the Roman empire that would bring them to settle in south-western Gaul and in the Iberian peninsula. Like their Germanic counterparts of the north, the Goths were a settled agricultural people, displaced from their homes and thrown into conflict with the Roman empire at the cost of the near-destruction, for nearly two generations, of their normal way of life. Pressing upon the Goths from the east were the Huns and Alani, nomadic steppe peoples of whom the former were totally new to the Romans, while the Alans, though already known to the Classical world and less outlandish than the Huns, were still formidable and wild, lacking the social refinement and stable morality of settled folk. Another nomadic people, the Saracens or desert Arabs, enter marginally into Ammianus' narrative in the context of Roman relations with Persia, and receive only a short digression from the historian; yet despite the brevity of his treatment, Ammianus touches developments in Arab society which, apart from their intrinsic interest, have a far-reaching relevance to the future.

Writing of the 'wild nations' threatening the Roman empire and, elsewhere in his treatise (2.3), of 'brigandage' caused by the oppression of the poor by the rich, the anonymous author might also have reflected on enemies living inside as well as outside its boundaries. The activities of such peoples, appearing in Graeco-Roman eyes as campaigns of banditry or rebellion, when seen in a more objective light represent conflicts of interest – between Roman and native, town and country, mountain and plain – at times when for whatever reason their ways of life did not follow their usual pattern of mutual toleration and support. Ammianus presents two such episodes, in different parts of the empire; uprisings of Isaurians in southern Asia Minor and, with a similarly detrimental effect on the settled communities around, the insurrection of an allied native prince in western north Africa. Ammianus' narratives of these events are full of the observations and touches of detail that, even though this is not their purpose, enable his reader to learn something of the lifestyle and social structure of the rebellious peoples.

This chapter is designed to exploit to this end the information provided by Ammianus on these various nations, and is arranged in three main sections corresponding to the general character of their subjects: first, Alamanni and Goths, settled farming peoples of Germanic origin; second, Huns and Alani (taken together, as they are by Ammianus), and Saracens, nomadic peoples existing in diverse physical circumstances but all outside the social and moral framework of settled life; and third, Isaurians and Moors, living within the empire in areas not totally penetrated by the Romans and offering the possibility of some independence of culture and social organisation. Together with this topical arrangement, the chapter moves in geographical sequence from the Rhine to the Danube and the south Russian steppe, then (in reverse order) to Asia Minor and the Syrian desert, lastly back to the far west of the Roman empire south of the Mediterranean. Its object is not to advance knowledge in their own right of the peoples described – that would hardly be possible, each being a specialised, and in some cases widely discussed, subject in itself – but to help bridge the gap between the knowledge of his world that Ammianus possessed and took for granted, and that of his modern reader. Within the overall structure, each section is self-contained, without transition from one to the next though with obvious links between them, and a final section reviews the whole chapter in the form of a brief discussion of Ammianus' source material on this subject.

(1) Farmers: Alamanni and Goths

(i) Alamanni

There is no digression on the Alamanni in the surviving books of Ammianus, and if he gave one in the lost books (as is unlikely, there being nothing mysterious or exotic about a plain Germanic people) he does not refer to it. Yet his narrative contains nineteen sections on diplomatic and military relations with the Alamanni, ranging in the case of military operations from a great set battle to the most trivial of skirmishes. Such emphasis would even on a narrow view make this one of the most important single issues described in Ammianus' history, but its interest extends much further than this. It is typical of his richly detailed style of narrative that he should in the course of it reveal many aspects of the social and economic situation of the Alamanni, even though this is not the central interest of his text.[4]

The Alamanni lived in what Ammianus in common with other sources calls 'pagi', or rural cantons. The location of some of these can be identified by reference to the Roman settlements and communities adjacent to them. The most south-westerly 'pagus', that of king Vadomarius, lay opposite the city of Augusta Raurica (Kaiseraugst) (21.3-4; p. 315). We may infer from the modern name of the district, the Breisgau, that this canton belonged to the division of the Alamanni known as the Brisigavi (not actually named by Ammianus). Another canton, which emerges in the course of the narrative as that of the

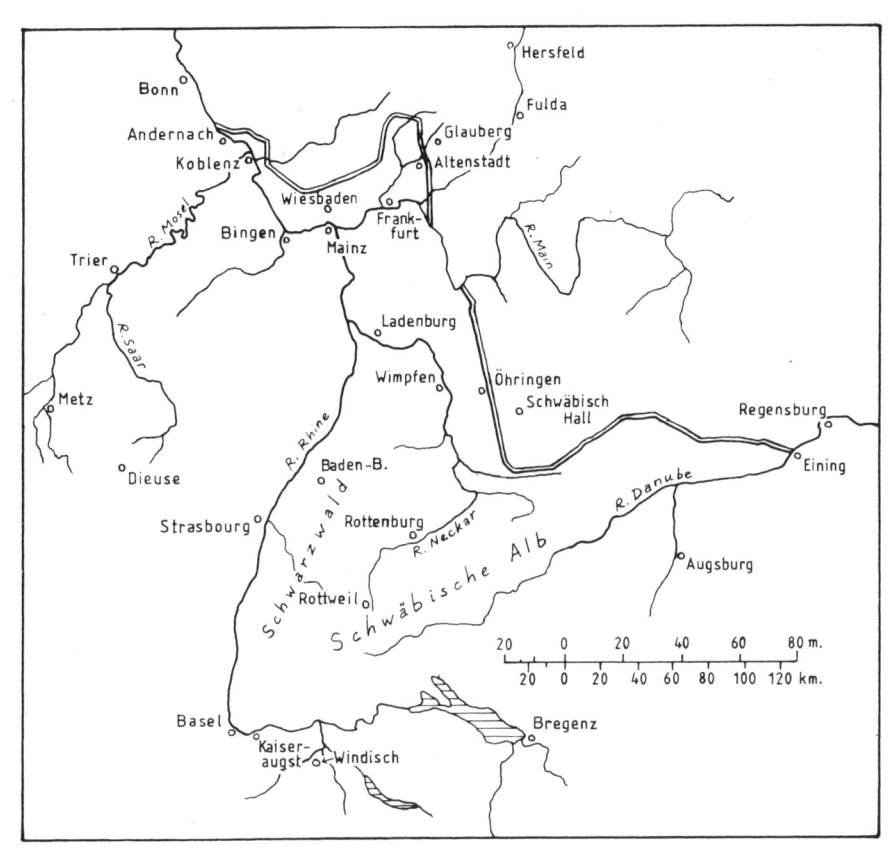

Map 6. The territory of the Alamanni. Place-names are given for convenience in their modern form. Most of the ancient forms are either in familiar usage or are made clear in the text. Of those that are not, Wimpfen is Roman civitas Alisinensium, Rottweil is Arae Flaviae, Rottenburg is Sumelocenna, Baden-Baden is Aquae, Metz is Mediomatrici and Eining is Abusina.

Bucinobantes, lay to the south of the Taunus mountains, in the valley of the lower Main opposite Moguntiacum (Mainz) (29.4.7); it was approached from the Roman side by way of Aquae Mattiacae, modern Wiesbaden (29.4.3). In the south-eastern corner of 'Alamannia', as Ammianus and other sources call it (20.4.1; 30.3.1), were the Lentienses, who were approached from the south by the fringe of Lake Konstanz (15.4.2ff.). The Lentienses too have left their name to a modern district, the Linzgau.

To the north of the Alamanni were the Franks, to their east the Burgundians. The borders between Alamanni and Burgundians, marked according to Ammianus by boundary stones (18.2.15), were not far from, and may have followed, the old Roman 'limes' frontier of the second and early third centuries; the two peoples, like their German predecessors centuries earlier, disputed the possession of salt deposits, in this case those near Schwäbisch Hall and Öhringen, in its vicinity (28.5.11; below, p. 313).

The whole region was that known to Tacitus (*Germania* 29), and hence to modern historians, as 'Agri Decumates', annexed by the Flavian emperors, consolidated in the second century, and held until its abandonment to German occupation in the 250s. The annexation had been designed to provide a better military frontier between Rhine and Danube by eliminating the re-entrant angle between the upper courses of these rivers (modern Baden-Württemberg). Near the south-western apex of the re-entrant – ominously close, until its annexation, to the developing provinces of Gaul and to routes over the Alps to north Italy – had stood the early legionary fortresses of Vindonissa (Windisch, near Brugg), and Argentorate (Strasbourg). It was of course near Strasbourg, one of the strategic points of 'Agri Decumates' and once again a frontier city after their abandonment, that Julian encountered the Alamannic federation of king Chnodomarius in the great battle of 357. To the west of Strasbourg, on the road to Mediomatrici (Metz) was the community or district of 'Decem Pagi', or 'Ten Cantons' (modern Dieuse) (16.2.9), persuasively identified as the settlement area of the occupants of 'Agri Decumates' when that region was evacuated.[5] This suggestion would both help to solve the archaeological mystery of what happened to the Romanised Celtic inhabitants of Agri Decumates after nearly two centuries of Roman occupation, and provide a parallel to the case of Dacia, where the Roman inhabitants – or as many of them as wished or were able to – were transferred to a new Roman province, by tacit deception named 'Dacia', on the south bank of the Danube.

Like the Goths in old Dacia, the Alamanni, inhabiting their cantons among the roads, towns, villas and military posts that had comprised the provincial territory of Agri Decumates, dwelt in a sort of 'post-Roman twilight' that on its local level foreshadows the end of the western empire itself. Among Julian's enterprises was the recovery of seven ruined 'civitates' in the middle Rhine area, from Bingium (Bingen) to Novaesium (Neuss) (18.2.4). Towns, remarked Ammianus, writing of the districts around Strasbourg but expressing himself in general terms, are avoided by Alamanni 'like tombs encircled by nets'; 'ipsa oppida ut circumdata retiis busta declinant' (16.2.12). This may be a rhetorical convention, and the nets are a mystery, but it is not impossible that the Alamanni did actually regard towns with apprehension, much as the post-Roman inhabitants of Britain, viewing the physical relics of Roman rule there, could think of them as the 'works of giants' and imagine the life that had gone on inside. The most famous expression of this attitude of haunted admiration is the Anglo-Saxon poem, 'The Ruin', preserved in a manuscript in the cathedral library at Exeter (the original words are quoted in order to evoke, in however shadowy a form, the language spoken by Ammianus' Alamanni):[6]

> Hrofas sind gehrorene,   hreorge torras,
> hrungeat berofen,   hrim on lime,
> scearde scurbeorge   scorene, gedrorene,
> aeldo undereotone ....

XIV. Barbarians and Bandits

> The roofs have fallen,   towers lie in ruins,
> the barred gate abandoned.   Hoar-frost on the lime,
> gaping roofs   are shattered and decayed,
> eaten away by age .... ('The Ruin', 3-6)

The Rhine-Danube frontier, the so-called 'Pfahlgraben' or 'palisaded ditches', which enclosed Agri Decumates on their eastern side, could hardly match the ruins of Bath or the great walls of northern Britain for monumental grandeur, but must still have been an imposing and mysterious physical feature to barbarian onlookers, implying resources and techniques beyond their imaginations, as it sped on its direct line across the Odenwald and south, before swinging east to reach the Danube at Eining. In this eastern section the works were later known as 'Teufelsgraben' or 'Devil's Dykes', with fine folk-tales to match the name. The Devil was granted by God as much of the earth as he could enclose by a wall in one night, and began constructing one around the whole world. The cock crowed as the last stone was about to be set in place, and the Devil in frustration knocked down the entire wall he had built – except for the Teufelsgraben, which remained as a monument to his enterprise. Once a year, on Christmas Eve, the Devil came to visit it, and local householders were well advised to take a tile off the flue of the family stove, so that if the Devil came inside the house he would not have to break it down in order to get out.[7]

The 'limes', a continuous earthwork topped by a wooden palisade or (in these eastern sections) a stone wall, and accompanied by frequent watchtowers, had once, by the most definitive of static gestures, divided Roman from barbarian. One would not be surprised to find that it now formed the boundary between Alamanni and Burgundians, if the salt sources disputed by them were near Öhringen, for this town – 'vicus Aurelii', or some such name – lies exactly on the *limes*: in which case one begins to wonder further about the boundary stones ('terminales lapides') which supposedly marked the limits of their territories, and their possible connection with Roman inscriptions and milestones of the old frontier system. It has been said that it would be unusual to find barbarian peoples separated by artificial markers rather than by natural features such as hills and forests, but such a remarkable physical feature as the old boundary of the Roman empire surely presents a special case.[8] There is no reason to think that artificial boundaries were as such beyond German comprehension. In the early first century, in an admittedly rather different landscape, the Angrivarii had distinguished their territory from that of the Cherusci by a substantial linear earthwork (Tacitus, *Annals* 2.19.3; 20.2f.). Ammianus may even support the interpretation offered here, in remarking that the boundary lay in a region which he calls 'Capellatii vel Palas' (18.2.15). Whatever the meaning of 'Capellatii', it has long been conjectured that 'Palas' is a derivative of the Latin 'palus' (German 'Pfahl', as in 'Pfahlgraben'): a stake or, collectively, palisade.[9]

We enter an atmosphere of Roman civilisation at the very limits of its diffusion, in various passages of Ammianus on this region and its people, as for example when he refers to the feat of 'ancient, sober virtue of the Romans' which had driven a road through the impenetrable country by Lake Konstanz, used by a general attacking the Lentienses (15.4.3). He elsewhere alludes in a most intriguing passage to the habitation by some Alamanni of houses in the Main valley 'carefully built in the Roman style', 'curatius ritu Romano constructa' – that is, Roman villas precisely, reoccupied by the Germans (17.1.7). This situation has some archaeological support, as in a modest Roman villa at Ebel bei Praunheim (Frankfurt), occupied and extended with dry-stone walling in the fourth century by an Alamannic optimate, who was buried there with military grave-goods (long-sword, lance, arrow-heads, shield) and an assortment of wares of both Roman and German manufacture: belt-fastenings, Rhineland glassware, pottery vessels and a bone comb.[10] Exactly what is meant in the same passage of Ammianus (17.1.11) by the fort in barbarian territory built by and named after Trajan, now restored by Julian, remains unclear, nor can we say on what basis Ammianus' assertion rests, unless there were inscriptions on which the emperor's name occurred, read and perhaps misunderstood by someone who was present at the site; the name of Trajan would also occur in the full nomenclature of his successors Hadrian and Antoninus Pius. The occasion is reminiscent of the visit of Valentinian and his court to the abandoned Roman town of Lopodunum (Ladenburg), described in the previous chapter; here too ruins could be seen and inscriptions read (p. 285). Still more remarkably in considering the memory of Rome in this area of German occupation, it appears from Ammianus that the Burgundians actually 'know' themselves ('sciunt', in the present tense) to be descended in ancient times from Romans (28.5.11)! The early fifth-century historian Orosius, perhaps making the poor best of a bad job and with a ridiculous etymology – 'Burgundians' connected with 'burgus', the late Roman word for fort[11] – has them descended from Romans left behind after the German campaigns of Drusus in the time of Augustus (*Hist. adv. Pag.* 7.32.11f.). Ammianus tells how their descent from Romans was pressed upon the Burgundians by Valentinian in an attempt to get them to attack the Alamanni. It may therefore be an invention of Roman diplomacy, the inspired conjecture of some erudite courtier; yet who can tell what ancient folk memories or heroic tales among the German peoples such a belief might indicate?

The pattern of life of the Alamanni emerges in details from Ammianus' descriptions of the impact of war upon it. They lived a sedentary agricultural existence in their 'pagi', as is shown by the frequently mentioned destruction by Roman raiding parties of the crops and herds which they raised there (e.g. 16.11.14; 18.2.19; 27.10.7). The raids sometimes reduced them to the point of total impoverishment (17.10.9;

29.4.7). The cantons were located in the more fertile parts of the river valleys and in cleared forest areas, particularly in the Neckar and Main basins; the Wetterau opposite Mainz, where Julian found the reoccupied Roman farmsteads, is good land for both cereals and grazing – 'opulentas pecore villas et frugibus', as Ammianus says (17.1.7). The terrain is conventionally but adequately described by Ammianus – river valleys, hills and dense woods, their pathways and routes blocked against the Romans by great felled trees – and differentiating the more mountainous country accessible to the Lentienses in the extreme south-east of Alamannic territory (31.10.12, 16). On campaign the Alamanni lived, naturally enough, in tents (27.2.9); in their own country, except for those of their optimates who were able to occupy the old Roman villas, in flimsy wooden cottages ('saepimenta fragilium penatium', 18.2.15), which the Roman attackers set fire to in the manner immortalised by the columns of Trajan and Marcus Aurelius at Rome (17.10.6; 27.10.7).[12] The Sarmatian Limigantes, whom Constantius successfully attacked in 358, lived in similar wooden shacks, which suffered the same fate at the hands of the Roman army (17.13.12f.).

We must envisage one further element in the pattern of occupation, for the Alamannic settlers of the third and fourth centuries sometimes reoccupied ancient hill-forts, as strongpoints commanding the landscape around and as refuges for the local populations. The most notable of these sites, Glauberg near the old Roman fort of Altenstadt on the Wetterau-*limes* east of Frankfurt, was a hill-fort dating back to the prehistoric (Urnfield and La Tène) age. It was now given additional defences of dry-stone walling, built in a manner and with materials reminiscent of those used at the re-occupied villa of Ebel bei Praunheim, and, as there, suggesting the work of Roman inhabitants remaining in the area who found themselves under Alamannic 'protection'. The site of Glauberg, occupied through the fourth and fifth centuries, yielded clear archaeological evidence of relations with the Roman side of the Rhine and has been plausibly assigned to the Bucinobantes, in whose territory it stood. It is not clear how Ammianus would describe a hill-fort, nor indeed whether he would recognise it as anything as specific as the modern designation implies, but he narrates in suggestive fashion the storming by Valentinian of a hill-top position occupied by Alamanni in the campaign of 368 (27.10.7ff.). The Romans boldly attacked the position by the steeper approaches, forcing the defenders back down the gentler and more vulnerable route of access to the north, where a Roman army awaited them. Ammianus mentions no earthworks or walls at the site, only natural obstacles, and its location, near a place called Solicinium, possibly Sülchen near Rottenburg am Neckar, is not identified; but a configuration such as he describes, with three steep sides and a gentler approach on the fourth, is a characteristic hill-fort formation, combining defensive possibilities with reasonable but controlled ease of access. Indeed, its configuration resembles that of Glauberg, where the gentler ascent possessed the most formidable artificial barriers. The Alamanni

312 Part Two: Visa vel Lecta

did not choose at random where to make their stand, and since the reoccupied hill-fort seems a more than incidental form of settlement in this period (about a dozen are identified in their territory, mostly beyond the old Roman frontier but some inside it), it is natural to wonder, without any proof, whether the site near Solicinium was one.[13]

Despite the claim of the anonymous author *De Rebus Bellicis*, cited at the beginning of this chapter, that the 'unlearned barbarians' were no strangers to mechanical invention (praef. 4), Alamannic technology was not advanced. Archaeology indicates the working of iron, simple decorative jewelry and combs of bone (Germans were very fond of combing their hair, which they wore long, as many Classical sources observe), and hand-formed pottery – that is pottery not turned on the wheel, a classic index of technological limitation. Ammianus speaks in one passage of retreating Alamanni taking with them their families, supplies and native artefacts; 'opes barbaricas' (16.11.10). One of the terms of a treaty made by Julian with king Hortarius involved the provision and transport by cart of timber for the reconstruction of Roman forts at Novaesium, Bonna and other Rhineland cities; beams more than fifty feet long were delivered, surely not without use of the old Roman roads in Alamannic territory (17.10.9; 18.2.6). On this occasion the Alamanni were unable to provide corn, for the Romans had destroyed it all. Another king on whom this provision was imposed had to deliver it and obtain receipts as if he were an ordinary contractor, 'susceptorum vilium more' (17.10.4). As for further economic activities, Ammianus provides a case of that market enterprise characteristic of relations between unequal cultures, slave-trading. The episode concerns another of Valentinian's raiding-parties, which encountered a band of slavers escorting their wares somewhere beyond the Rhine.[14] The traders were killed to prevent their carrying ahead news of the Romans' movements. As for who they were, Roman or German, and who the slaves, presumably Saxon or other barbarian captives taken by the Alamanni (Ammianus does not write of them as if they were Roman prisoners of war), what their sex and what happened to them, not a word (29.4.4). Since Ammianus mentions only that they were 'taken from' the traders, they were presumably not killed with them, but kept by the Romans themselves as legitimate booty of war.

Ammianus reveals little of the religious customs of the Alamanni, unless their aversion from Roman cities 'like tombs' is an indication of such. One would like to think of them entering battle, as did the Goths, singing praises of their ancestors (31.7.11), but Ammianus does not actually say this of the Alamanni. They did however perform divination, as Ammianus suggests without indicating the techniques employed, in explaining their willingness on one occasion to make peace rather than take on the Romans in battle (14.10.9). The Byzantine historian Agathias, writing nearly two centuries after Ammianus, described how the Alamanni worshipped certain trees, rivers, and mountain crests and valleys, to which they sacrificed horses and other victims by beheading

XIV. Barbarians and Bandits

(Agathias 1.7.1f.). Agathias' description is in part reminiscent of Tacitus' account of the sacrifice by the Hermunduri in the mid-first century AD of horses and men from their defeated Chattan enemies to 'Mars and Mercury' – that is, to Tiw (Thor) and Woden (*Annals* 13.57.3). The worship of woods and groves is very widely reported in ancient sources on the Germans, and not hard to understand of people whose lives were spent among them. It also transpires that the dispute over salt sources which brought about the first-century war between the Hermunduri and Chatti was intensified by a religious aspect. Both peoples believed the site to be 'closer to heaven', for the gods had provided the gift of the salt, and were nowhere else more willing to listen to the prayers of men (*Annals* 13.57.1f.). Tacitus' words, though inevitably reduced to an alien conceptual idiom, lend some imaginative force to the religious mentality surrounding what an archaeologist might call an 'indigenous cult centre', and perhaps help to explain the dispute mentioned by Ammianus between Alamanni and Burgundians over the salt springs of Schwäbisch Hall or Öhringen.

As far as Ammianus is concerned, in this matter of religious custom the Burgundians are more forthcoming than the Alamanni. He gives the native titles both of their priest and king, 'sinistus' and 'hendinos', stating of the latter that he was deposed in time of adversity in war or if the crops failed (28.5.14). If this is true, the Burgundian king had a symbolic religious function and was subject to a religious sanction, as is nowhere said of the Alamanni. This is an interesting difference, for the Burgundians too were a Germanic people, Ammianus' terms for both 'priest' and 'king' being closely paralleled in Gothic.[15] If there is any question here of the origins of the 'sacral kingship' of medieval times, it is in the historical development of the institution itself, for it is not implicit in its nomenclature.

To contemporaries, the most distinctive physical feature of the Alamanni was their long, flowing hair, as mentioned in the prelude to the battle of Strasbourg (16.12.26) and attested by the frequent appearance of combs in their grave deposits;[16] their most distinctive custom, their fondness for drink. These facets appear together in an episode recorded by Ammianus, in which a Roman raiding party surprised a band of Alamanni relaxing in the forest. Some were bathing, some dyeing their hair 'in the usual manner', others just drinking (beer, of course); 'lavantes alios, quosdam comas rutilantes ex more, potantesque non nullos' (27.2.2). 'Drunken Alamanni' were a by-word for many a later writer, notably the fifth-century moralist Salvian, who thought them no worse than drunken Christians – he means Romans, the Alamanni being still pagan in his time (*Gub. Dei* 4.68). A taste for drink was a German characteristic already noted by Tacitus (*Germania* 22.2, etc.); one thinks of the feast given 'in native style' by king Hortarius, disturbed by Roman raiders well after midnight and still in full swing (p. 315). Cultural prejudice against beer-swilling northerners was, as we have seen, characteristic of a Mediterranean man's point of view; could it even be a lingering sign of barbarian deference for the ways of Rome, that for the Anglo-Saxon poet cited earlier it was wine, not beer, that the proud lords of Roman Bath supped in their once splendid halls ('The Ruin', 33ff.)?

As for Alamann social structure, the 'kings' ('reges') of their cantons appear frequently in Ammianus' narrative, whether acting independently or in concert with others; the most telling instance of the latter being the twelve 'reges', seven of them named, mentioned as allies of Chnodomarius in the confederation which faced Julian at Strasbourg (16.12.1, 26). They, with their 35,000 fighting men 'ex variis nationibus', were drawn there by pay and promises of mutual support, that is to say not by sentiment alone (12.26). Ammianus frequently mentions also nobles, or 'optimates', in his narrative, as attendants of kings and as their envoys (14.10.9), or as the parents of hostages to Rome (28.2.6,8); there sometimes occur also lesser kings or princes, such as ten 'regales' mentioned as part of a clearly articulated social progression between five 'reges' of the second rank and a numerous array ('series magna') of 'optimates' present in the engagement at Strasbourg (16.12.26). It is hard to be sure whether the 'regalis' Rando, head of an Alamannic canton near Moguntiacum, was the same as a 'rex' or something less elevated, the Strasbourg reference implying the latter (27.10.1). Whatever the position of king within his own canton, the emergence of a leader of a confederacy of numerous divisions of the Alamanni was often, as with the Goths, a response to some threat or other circumstance which fostered unity, exacted charismatic leadership and placed a premium on success. Physical and moral authority, not any form of constitutional sanction, created the figure of Chnodomarius, imposing himself on his compatriots at Strasbourg, later when his fortune failed escaping from the battlefield with his 'attendants' ('satellites'), and finally, in another well-differentiated social microcosm, coming forward to surrender together with two hundred 'companions' ('comites') and three 'very close friends' ('amici iunctissimi'), all of whom had sworn to follow him to the death (16.12.60). It is a clear example, and Ammianus gives others, among both Alamanni and Goths, of the 'following' or 'Gefolgschaft' familiar from Classical writers, and from early medieval German history.[17]

As such institutions imply, German kings and nobles were much attached to their pride, and reacted strongly to any suggestion of belittlement of themselves or their people. The invasions under Valentinian began because Alamannic envoys to court had not been properly treated nor received the accustomed gifts and presents (26.5.7). On a later occasion the Burgundians killed their captives and dispersed in an angry mood, feeling themselves 'put to scorn' when Valentinian failed to turn up for a rendezvous against the Alamanni and then refused to cover their retreat (28.5.13). The same emperor had to go to the most ceremonious lengths to make peace with king Macrianus in a manner that did justice to his adversary's sense of dignity. Ammianus describes the scene, in which Valentinian crossed the Rhine on a boat to meet Macrianus with his retinue on the far side, with a vivid and authentic appreciation of its theatrical potential (30.3.4f.). Macrianus' loyalty was however assured, and, in a fascinating transformation of loyalties, he later died fighting for the Romans 'in Francia' (3.7). The political attitude of the kings was as versatile as one would expect of a people within reach of Roman diplomacy and military action at their most subversive. On one occasion king Hortarius, at that time favourable to Rome, gave a banquet to other German kings who were not. He gave the party, not plotting rebellion but simply being friendly to his neighbours; 'non novaturus quaedam, sed amicus finitimis quoque suis' (18.21.13). A Roman raid broke up the festivities in the small hours of the morning, the kings managing to leap on horseback and escape into the forest, while their humbler attendants – not necessarily less sober, but lacking horses – were caught and killed. The engagement arose from Julian's attempts to build a bridge across the Rhine without violating the territory of kings with whom he had concluded peace: one of these kings, Suomarius, was 'threatened' by his Alamannic colleagues in other cantons to stop the crossing, his treaty with Rome having alienated his suspicious neighbours (18.2.8). The loyalty of another king, Vadomarius of the Brisigavi, was suspect in Julian's eyes since he had been caught sending letters critical of him to Constantius (21.3.1).[18] Vadomarius had earlier been received by Constantius into the 'clientela' of Rome and confirmed as joint king with his brother Gundomades. After the latter's murder and the adherence of his people to the Alamann cause, Vadomarius alleged – if this can be inferred from Ammianus' here fragmentary text – that his own tribesmen's support of Chnodomarius was not according to his will (16.12.17). Whatever his explanation, it was apparently accepted, for in 359 he came to plead before Julian for three other kings who had joined Chnodomarius (18.2.18). Vadomarius' arrest was accomplished when he crossed the Rhine to Kaiseraugst to have dinner with the Roman commander there; the 'comites' who had come with him (another 'Gefolgschaft') were allowed to return home, since the sealed instructions which ordered Vadomarius' arrest said nothing about them (21.4.2ff.). The king had come to Kaiseraugst in all innocence, alleging that the Alamannic raid from his canton which was the immediate cause of his arrest had been conducted without his knowledge. He probably believed himself to be doing no more than his duty in reporting to Constantius on the behaviour of his Caesar, not appreciating the consequences for himself of the worsening relations between them.

Seen at all its levels, the relationship between Germans and Romans along their 'collimitia' or common boundaries (15.4.1; 21.3.4; 31.10.1) was one of great complexity. As part of peace agreements, the Germans provided hostages who spent time and received education among the Romans. One of the kings who fought at Strasbourg, Agenarichus son of Mederichus, had earlier, while a hostage with the Romans, become initiated into a Greek mystery cult and taken the most un-Germanic name Serapio in commemoration (16.12.25). Ammianus describes him and Chnodomarius (his uncle) as pre-eminent among the German leaders at Strasbourg (16.12.23). A particularly interesting episode described by Ammianus shows the contrasting reactions of two Alamannic kings to the camp of Julian when they were received there (in the heart of their own country). Macrianus, seeing them for the first time, was amazed at the standards and assorted weaponry on display, while Vadomarius, who lived close to the frontier and was used to the Romans, admired what he saw but was not overawed, being familiar with it from his youth; 'utpote vicinus limiti mirabatur quidem apparatum ambitiosi procinctus sed vidisse se talia ab adolescentia meminerat prima' (18.2.17). The same sort of familiarity led some Alamanni at Strasbourg to look down on detachments of Romans, which they knew they had recently turned to flight since they recognised their shield devices (16.12.6).

Upon the conclusion of peace treaties it was usual for the Alamanni to provide the best of their youth for the Roman armies (18.2.19; 21.4.8; 31.10.17), and many also signed up as individuals, attracted by the sophistication and the prospects of advancement provided by life with the Romans. The infiltration of Alamanni into the Roman army, and hence into Roman society, was extensive.[19] The names of Alamannic cantons – Brisigavi, Bucinobantes, Raetobarii – are preserved as the names of troop units in the *Notitia Dignitatum* in both east and west (*Or.* 5.58; 6.58; *Occ.* 5.201-2), and many generals and officers were of German origin. Ammianus is full of examples. An Alamann notable was sent to command a highly successful troop of his countrymen in Britain, when it turned out that the canton over which he had been made king, that of the Bucinobantes, had been too severely devastated to be viable (29.4.7). Three German officers in Constantius' army in 354 were thought to 'wield the commonwealth in their right hands' (14.10.8); their names were Scudilo, Agilo – whose daughter married an eastern official and senator (26.7.6; 10.7) – and 'Latinus'. A German soldier killed in Valentinian's attack on the Alamann position near Solicinium bore by contrast the wonderful name Natuspardo, 'Born-again Panther' – presumably, like the name of a Red Indian brave, a translation from his own language. Unperturbed by the name, Ammianus compared his courage with that of Republican Roman heroes (27.19.16). In one case, mentioned by Ammianus without particular comment, Alamanni, and in another case Taifali (Gothic allies) were settled on farming land in the Po valley (28.5.15; 31.9.4). Settlement of this nature, which had been going on for centuries, was a sort of economic exchange for the Roman prisoners of war put to work as farm labourers in the Alamannic cantons. Their return was a frequent, and frequently evaded, issue in Roman peace negotiations (17.10.4, 7; 18.2.19).

Apart from such large-scale settlement – though often, no doubt, arising from it – individual movement back and forth across the frontier was commonplace, and for all sorts of reasons. A tribune in Roman service, Hariobaudes, was sent on an intelligence mission to an Alamannic canton near Moguntiacum because of his excellent German – his native language, of course (18.2.2). The resolve of the Alamanni

XIV. Barbarians and Bandits

assembled at Strasbourg was strengthened by a Roman soldier who took news to them of Julian's unequal resources; he was afraid of being punished for some crime he had committed and so deserted, a situation not unparalleled on other frontiers (16.12.2; p. 68). The Lentienses acquired foreknowledge of Gratian's imminent journey to the east in 378 from a talkative member of the imperial guard who returned home on a visit, was questioned what was going on 'in palatio' and was only too pleased to show off his knowledge (31.10.3). Yet, as Ammianus also makes clear, the Lentienses had as immediate neighbours of Rome observed it for themselves; 'ipsi quoque haec quasi vicini cernentes' (31.10.4). The guardsman was punished for his indiscretion, but one suspects that there was little of importance that did not somehow come to their attention.

The dangers of disloyalty in all this cannot be ignored, but taken in context do not seem very significant.[20] Ammianus reports fears that the three German officers who 'held the commonwealth in their hands' were in collusion with their compatriots in 354 (14.10.7f.). Even though Ammianus clearly indicates that these fears were groundless, it is significant that they were entertained; but in general the Romans had little to fear, and much more to gain, from the German officers and men in their employ. They were, as was proclaimed of Franks by one of their compatriots in the imperial service, devoted to the empire; 'homines dicatos imperio' (15.5.6). The most prominent of them, Silvanus, accepted his proclamation at Cologne partly because he was warned by a German officer on his staff that if he took refuge with his countrymen they would kill him (15.5.16). His father, Bonitus, had been a general of Constantine, and had married a Roman woman (15.5.33).

It is a measure of the familiarity between Alamanni and Romans along the northern frontier, and of the wealth of information available to a historian from men who had served there, that so many Alamanni are individually characterised by Ammianus; certainly more than for any other barbarian people. The most memorable is obviously Chnodomarius, appearing at the battle of Strasbourg hugely imposing in his massive bulk but reduced in defeat to physical helplessness, his horse lost, muddy from scrambling on the ground, corpulence hindering his escape (16.12.23, 65). Yet he could still summon up the spirit in defeat to address Julian in German before submitting to exile and old age at Rome, a notable addition to the already considerable variety of the human condition on display there. Chnodomarius is run close for personal interest by various other candidates: by Macrianus, who had Valentinian cross the Rhine to make peace with him; by the young king Agenarichus who was an initiate into the rites of Serapis; and above all by the versatile Vadomarius, who survived his ambiguous relations with Constantius and Julian, his arrest at the dinner-party at Kaiseraugst and exile to Spain, later to become *dux* of Phoenicia, an office in which he had ample opportunity to display his native cunning; 'ad perstringendum fallendumque miris modis ab aetatis primitiis callens, ut postea quoque ducatum per Phoenicen regens ostendit' (21.3.5).[21] Sadly, Ammianus says nothing further of this strikingly imaginative appointment. It is probably Julianic, even though Vadomarius, already 'ex duce et rege Alamannorum', was sent by Valens (in the event without success) to recover Nicaea from Julian's relative Procopius (26.8.2). He is later found with the general Traianus engaging the Persians in Mesopotamia in 371 (29.1.2). Vadomarius' supple realism clearly permitted an extraordinary degree of cultural and political adaptation. Once he had made or been manoeuvred into it, he was not deflected from his choice of loyalty even by the Roman-inspired murder of his son and successor Vithicabius by a personal attendant who, having stabbed his master to death, fled to the Roman side. Vithicabius, as Ammianus remarks in another brief but lively sketch, was physically frail and sickly ('specie quidem molliculus et morbosus'); but he was bold and brave and warlike, and his death offered promise of better things for Rome; 'inopina rei Romanae spes laetiorum affulsit' (27.10.3). The murder of Vithicabius is one of the approved actions of Valentinian in Ammianus' obituary notice, a sharp reminder of the unvarying expediency of Roman political methods (30.7.7). His father perhaps thought himself lucky, on reflection, to have suffered nothing worse than arrest at a dinner-party at Kaiseraugst.

(ii) Goths: Thervingi and Greuthungi

The Germanic invaders known as the Goths had appeared at the Danube frontier of the Roman empire before the middle of the third century, when they raided the Balkan provinces as far south as Dalmatia, descending upon Asia Minor and even parts of Syria, and finally occupying part of the evacuated Roman province of Dacia about twenty years after the Alamanni had overrun the Rhine-Danube *limes* and taken possession of the so-called Agri Decumates (p. 308).[22] Defeated by Constantine the Great in 332, the Goths then lived at peace but with gradually increasing strength on the Danube frontier until the middle of the fourth century, when, impressed by the name of Constantine with whom they had concluded a treaty of friendship, they offered support in 365 to the usurper Procopius (26.10.1; 27.5.1).[23] With the retaliatory war conducted by Valens in 367-9, and with their great crossing of the river Danube into the Roman empire in 376, they enter the historiographical domain of Ammianus; not like the Alamanni in many dispersed fragments but in two concentrated blocks of narrative, the second of them very extensive (31.3ff.). In surveying what Ammianus has to say of this barbarian people, it will be worth keeping in mind what he has written of their Germanic counterparts the Alamanni, in both cases anticipating the contrast that will follow when we come to the enemies of both Goths and Romans, the non-Germanic Huns and Alani.

The geographical extension of the Goths in their settlements beyond the Danube is reflected in Ammianus' accounts both of the campaigns of Valens, and of the events preceding the great crossing of the river in 376.

Map 7. Gothia and the Roman Danube.

In the first of his campaigns, in 367, Valens crossed the Danube by a bridge of boats at Daphne (27.5.2). The Goths avoided battle and took refuge in the inaccessible 'montes Serrorum', except for those families who were caught before they could reach the mountain country. In the next year Valens assembled his army at 'vicus Carporum' but was unable to cross the Danube because of floods and withdrew for the winter to Marcianopolis, a strategic centre at the eastern end of the Haemus mountains (Stara Planina) (27.5.5). In his third and most extensive campaign, the emperor started from Noviodunum and, again crossing by a bridge of boats, attacked a 'more distant' division of the Goths known as the Greuthungi and concluded an agreement with Athanaric, a powerful Gothic leader styled by Ammianus 'iudex potentissimus', before returning again to Marcianopolis.

The areas under attack are well defined by these indications. They comprise in the first instance the plains lying between the Danube and the southern Carpathians ('montes Serrorum'), that is the region known in more modern times as Wallachia; subsequently the more easterly regions of Moldavia and Bessarabia, in the river systems of the Prut and Dniester. The easterly shift in Valens' campaigns is apparent from the successive crossing-points and winter quarters mentioned by Ammianus, though the compression of his narrative fails to make clear either the scale or the achievement, especially of the third phase of the campaigns. His account obscures the fact that Athanaric, as emerges in a later context, was the leader not of the Greuthungi, named in the campaign of 369, but of the nearer section of the Goths known as the Thervingi (31.3.4). Valens reduced to submission one of the main divisions of the Gothic people and attacked the lands of the other; it was clearly an ambitious, and largely successful, operation.[24]

The location of the two peoples and the distinction between them are further defined by the events preceding the Gothic crossing of the river into the Roman empire in 376. To the east, Ammianus alludes to those Alani customarily called 'Tanaitae' or 'Don people' (p. 336), remarking that they adjoined the Greuthungi; 'Greuthungis confines' (31.3.1). The lands of the Greuthungi therefore ran up to the steppe country that began at the river Don and was inhabited by nomadic peoples. The description which follows of the Hun attack on the 'broad and fertile cantons (pagi)' of king Ermenrich of the Greuthungi underlines an essential feature of Gothic as opposed to Hunnish life; not nomadic or pastoral but, like that of their Germanic counterparts the Alamanni, sedentary and agriculturalist.

As for their western limits, in the defence that they now offered against the Huns, the Greuthungi fell back 'ad amnem Danastrum' (the Dniester), a river 'flowing through wide plains between the Danube and the Dnieper'; 'inter Histrum et Borysthenen per camporum ampla spatia diffluentem' (31.3.3). At the Dniester Athanaric of the Thervingi also made his stand against the Huns – pitching camp, as Ammianus remarks, at some distance from the Greuthungi – but was surprised by the swiftness of the Hun attack, which ignored his advance parties and made directly for his main position (31.3.5f.). The natural reading of Ammianus' account is that the Dniester formed the division between the two main Gothic folk, and furthermore that they were not necessarily inclined to act in concert.

After his setback, Athanaric tried to build a physical barrier 'from the banks of the river Gerasus as far as the Danube'; 'a superciliis Gerasi fluminis ad usque Danubium ... muros altius erigebat' (31.3.7). These 'walls' are described as skirting the lands of the Taifali, an account of

XIV. Barbarians and Bandits

their course not helped by the uncertainty as to the identification of the river Gerasus; was it between the Prut, or some more westerly river such as the Siret or Buzaul and the Danube that Athanaric attempted to run his line of defence? The location of the Taifali to the west in Oltenia in any case makes the geography difficult to visualise, nor is it clear what proportion of his own territories Athanaric was thereby hoping to defend. In the event, his power broken by his defeat and by his people's privation, Athanaric took refuge with the minority of the Thervingi that still supported him in inaccessible mountain regions, expelling their Sarmatian inhabitants (31.4.12f.). That is, he abandoned the plains for mountain uplands somewhere in the south-eastern Carpathians, a safer but less productive environment, in which his followers would find it much harder to live far above subsistence level.

To summarise the information provided by Ammianus, the Goths had settled the country to the east and to the south of the Carpathian mountain chain, their two main divisions, Thervingi and Greuthungi, being divided by the river Dniester. Their agricultural lifestyle is made clear not only by reference to the 'fertile and broad pagi' of king Ermenrich, but by the constant emphasis in Ammianus' accounts of their negotiations with the Romans in and after 376 on their need for fertile soil on which to settle as farmers in Thrace, 'quod et caespitis est feracissimi' (31.1.8; 4.5; 12.8, etc.). The contrast with the nomadic life-style of the Huns is further indicated by those tales, mentioned in the next section of this chapter (p. 337), of the circumstances in which the two people first came into contact, and attested by the still accumulating archaeological evidence from the regions of Gothic occupation.

The nature, date and extent of Gothic settlement in the lands north of the Danube makes it seem certain that theirs is the archaeological culture known in Romanian archaeology as the 'Sîntana de Mureş culture' after the site in north-eastern Transylvania from which its features were described, and in Russian work as the 'Chernyakhov culture' after a corresponding site in southern Russia.[25] The settlement sites are described as typically located on hillside terraces and gentle slopes or on low plateaux, with some concentration in river-valleys and around water sources. The dwellings in the settlements consist of huts, built either at ground level or partly dug into the ground, with some but limited variation of size and very simple in design, arranged in 'necklace rows' to form open villages, more or less dispersed in configuration and never fortified. That the villages were devoted to agricultural exploitation is shown not only by the location of the sites, but by the inventory of finds: grinding mills and pots for grain storage, farming tools including ploughshares of the Roman type, technically better than those of the indigenous populations of the region and showing the effect of contact with Rome. Domestic finds conform to this picture of simple village life, with pottery – generally turned on the wheel and in this sense superior to Alamannic ware of the same period (p. 312) – clothing accessories and simple adornments in stone, clay, bone, metal and glass, weaving implements and household utensils. The presence of stock-raising is shown by the bones of cattle, sheep, horses and poultry found at the sites; but this activity took place in the villages and there is no clear evidence for pastoralism in the broader sense, involving the Carpathian uplands and transhumance between mountain and plain. This picture may be distorted by a number of factors; by the lack of archaeological discovery of mountain settlements if these existed, and by the likelihood that transhumance was conducted still by indigenous peoples of the region, for example Sarmatians, whose lifestyle was little affected by the advent of the Goths and leaves little definite archaeological trace.

As for the chronology of the settlements, the earliest sites in Romania appear to be east of the Carpathians, in the regions of Moldavia and Bessarabia, where they existed by the later decades of the third century. Slightly later, if the archaeological data are reliable, came settlement in eastern Wallachia, followed by penetration of the Carpathians into south-eastern and then into north-eastern Transylvania, with little or no indication of settlement in the more westerly regions of Wallachia and Transylvania, Oltenia (the land of the Taifali) or Banat. The zone of occupation, that is to say, encroached upon the old Roman province of Dacia from the east and south-east but did not reach its more westerly portions beyond the river Olt. The archaeological material does not indicate a specific ethnic type, but a blend of indigenous and immigrant features in varying proportions. Burial grounds show mixed rites with both inhumation and cremation, a phenomenon which may well reflect a mixed ethnic population. There was some basis for this variety, since the area in question included peoples of Carpic and Sarmatian origin, and also Dacian, both the 'free Dacians' sometimes identified with the Carpi, who were excluded from the Roman annexation of the province of Dacia, and, west of the Carpathians, the Romano-Dacians included by it. At one site is an emphatic reminder of a favourite Germanic custom mentioned earlier, grooming of the hair: there was found near Bîrlad in southern Moldavia a craftsmen's settlement with no less than sixteen workshops devoted to the production of combs manufactured from bone and antler.[26] The artefacts were found in all stages of manufacture from the prepared raw material to the finished article: clear evidence not only of Germanic social customs at their most distinctive but of the presence of specialised production techniques (as is also exemplified by the wheel-turned pottery) and, by implication, of economic exchange among the villages.

*

The picture of social life among the Goths suggested by the archaeological evidence is given circumstantial force by a literary text deriving ultimately from Gothic society itself, the *Passion of St. Saba*.[27] The narrative, of the trials and execution of a Gothic martyr in the year 372, needs handling with even more than the usual caution appropriate for a text of this nature. It was written in Greek for a Christian audience in

XIV. Barbarians and Bandits 323

Roman Asia Minor and contains all the ideological and polemical conventions normal for the genre. In its details of everyday life and social relations, however, it provides an 'inside perspective' such as is rarely available of a barbarian people.

The story of St. Saba unfolds in a village adjacent to woods and thickets, through the burned remains of which the future martyr is at one point whipped by his persecutors (4.6). The village has an assembly or council (*sunedrion*), before which Saba is denounced and defends himself (3.4). There is a neighbouring settlement, or *polis*, where Saba, a lector of his own village church, wishes to celebrate Easter with its presbyter – his own priest, Sansala, having left for 'Romania' in order to escape the persecution (4.2). Saba tries to go there on foot, but finds the road blocked by an unseasonable fall of snow and is forced to return to his own village, where he finds that Sansala has returned home (4.1ff.). Upon his conviction in the renewed persecution, Saba is tied up and flogged, but freed by a woman preparing food at night for the occupants of the house to which she belonged; the most natural interpretation of this is that she was baking the next day's bread for the household, and that the household was a substantial one (5.3). It seems that before the outbreak of persecution Saba had been able to conduct his religion freely with the presbyter of his village; indeed, so unwilling are the villagers to cause him harm that they first attempt to trick him into eating the sacrificial meat brought by the persecutors, and later defend him against his accusers by declaring him to be a man of no possessions, who can do them 'neither good nor ill' (3.1, 5).[28]

The narrative assumes throughout that the persecution is imposed from outside the village community: specifically by the tribal magnates, or *megistanes*, whose representatives the villagers attempt to mislead in order to defend Saba, and whose leader engages in an altercation with the village council (3.1,4f.). The 'great persecution' which ensues is implemented by an agent called Atharidus, 'the son of Rothesteus of kingly rank, and a company of lawless bandits', as the *Passion* describes them (4.5). It is Atharidus who, through emissaries, again orders Saba to eat sacrificial meat (6.1). These emissaries include one of Atharidus' own 'sons' who, angered by Saba's contempt for his father's authority, tries, in what is perhaps one of the more circumstantial scenes in the *Passion*, to fell him with a wooden pestle which he seizes and hurls at him (6.4). It is when Atharidus 'learns' of the insult to his standing – he is evidently not present in person at any stage of the inquisition – that he orders Saba's execution (7.1). The martyr is taken and drowned in the river 'Mousaios'; that is, possibly, the Buzaul, which emerges from the eastern flank of the Carpathians into the Wallachian plain, joining the Danube just above Noviodunum. As we have seen, it was an area of well-attested Gothic settlement, Noviodunum being the point from which Valens launched his third and final campaign against the Goths. The death by drowning is another element in the story that may be authentically Germanic.[29]

The portrayal of a village community in the *Passion of St. Saba* can hardly be called a specific representation of the Sîntana de Mureş/ Chernyakhov culture; it might be true of village life at more or less any time or place. But it is compatible with it, not least in its picture of the relations between the village and the tribal authorities who impose the persecution, against the wishes of the villagers themselves. They come from outside, bringing with them the entourage described as 'a gang of lawless bandits' – surely a dismissive reference to a Germanic institution known from many other sources and from Ammianus himself, the Gefolgschaft or 'following' of a tribal magnate (pp. 314, 315). A tribal aristocracy has not specifically emerged in the archaeology of the Goths, but its presence is clear from the literary sources, and is implicit in such 'royal' possessions as the magnificent, though sadly incomplete, treasure hoard found near Pietroasa (Buzău) in north-eastern Wallachia. Surely Gothic, and possibly fourth-century, the hoard shows a glimpse of an altogether different social milieu from that of the villagers of the Sîntana de Mureş culture or the *Passion of St. Saba*. At Pietroasa, near Ploesti to the south and at other places, have further been identified agglomerations of settlement which may indicate relative concentrations of population associated with the presence of elements of the tribal aristocracy.[30] One would not expect to find a Gothic 'capital city' but, rather as in the case of the fifth-century Huns in the later, more settled phase of their existence, an area of more intensive village settlement in which the leaders of the people had their residences (p. 342). However this may be, in the archaeology as in the *Passion of St. Saba*, the tribal nobility, with its treasures, its court life, its horse-riding and its 'Gefolgschaften', speaks of a different and in many ways more familiar world than the humble village communities of the Goths.

*

From Ammianus, it is naturally the world of the kings and aristocracy that emerges most clearly, evidence of the way of life of the Gothic people at large being only indirectly presented. As we saw, the Goths fall into two groups, the Thervingi and, to the east of the river Dniester, their neighbours the Greuthungi. In describing the impact of Hunnish invasion on them, Ammianus gives a brief 'dynastic history' of the Greuthungi. He begins with king Ermenrich (Hermanaric in our other main literary source, Jordanes' *Getica*), who was defeated in battle against the Huns and either ended his own life in despair or, in the variant version of Jordanes, suffered a lingering death from wounds he had received (31.3.1; *Getica* 129f.).[31] To succeed him was chosen as king ('rex creatus') Vithimir, who was killed in battle with the Alani and followed by his son Viderich; he, a minor, ruled under the regency of two leading nobles, Alatheus and Saphrax, 'duces exerciti et firmitate noti' (31.3.3). Viderich, like his father, is explicitly called 'king' of the Greuthungi (4.12); it is clear that the royal succession among this section of the Goths was essentially dynastic, although it may be that when there was no direct

XIV. Barbarians and Bandits

succession a king could, like Vithimir, be chosen.

The political organisation of the Thervingi appears differently, or perhaps merely in a different perspective from that of the Greuthungi. They live under Athanaric, their 'judge' or 'iudex', described on his first appearance in 369 as 'iudex potentissimus' and retaining the title in the later context (27.5.6; 31.3.4). The use of the word 'iudex' by Ammianus and in other Latin sources, and in Greek writers of its equivalent, *dikastês*, shows it to be a technical term relating to some sort of federal overlordship of the Thervingi rather than to kingship of any individual 'pagus' or group of 'pagi' that comprised them.[32] If the position of 'iudex' — like that of Chnodomarius among the Alamanni — was in some sense elective or an expression of prestige and consent among the kings and aristocracy, the kingship among the thervingi was and remained hereditary; Ammianus mentions the mighty oath sworn by Athanaric to his father, also a king, never to enter the Roman empire (27.5.9). Abandoned by the majority of his people in consequence of its misfortune against the Huns and for other reasons, Athanaric took refuge in the Carpathians with his remaining followers (31.4.12). The majority, placing themselves under Alavivus and Fritigern, successfully petitioned Valens for settlement in Thrace. Whether Athanaric continued to be 'iudex' over his people after his loss of authority among them is very difficult to say; he did not cease to be king. When, 'expelled by a faction of his associates' he came over to the empire in 381 and died shortly afterwards, he was buried with great honour by Theodosius, and many Goths came to witness the funeral, as that of a king (*Cons. Const.*, s.a. 381). Ammianus mentions the event, in one of those passages looking forward to a moment after the terminal point of his history (27.5.10).

Ammianus does not designate king Ermenrich of the Greuthungi or any of his successors as 'iudex', although he was ruler of many 'pagi' and is clearly seen as the most important leader of this division of the Goths. The absence of the term may reflect not any real difference in the political organisation of the Greuthungi from that of the Thervingi, but their greater distance from the Romans, and incompleteness in the information about them available to a Roman observer. Ermenrich is described on his first appearance as a terror to the 'nationes' living around (31.3.1), but Ammianus does not say who or what these 'nationes' were, whether other branches of the Goths, divisions of the Greuthungi, or the indigenous inhabitants of the surrounding territories. Perhaps he means nothing as definite as any of these things, but is using the phrase simply as a general illustration of Ermenrich's power. It would in any case be a mistake to force the political and social organisation of the Goths into a rigid pattern, in a period when they were under the strain of foreign attack, experiencing a variety of relations with their neighbours, and in transition from one way of life to another. On two occasions, they are described as enrolling Huns, on one occasion Alans also, as allies against other enemies, in return for payment or the promise of great booty (31.3.3; 8.4). It has even been argued that the guardians of the boy king Viderich, Alatheus and Saphrax, were not Germanic but respectively Sarmatian, and Alan or Hunnish, in origin.[33] It would not be surprising if the Gothic federations, like their settlements, were more varied in composition than first impressions might suggest. According to Ammianus, the Huns killed and despoiled many of their Alan rivals and took the rest into alliance (31.3.1) – a pattern of warfare and accommodation among the barbarian peoples that must have been very frequent in the turmoil of this unsettled period.

Below the 'rex' or 'iudex' were the Gothic aristocracy, or 'optimates'; though these too may be described as the leaders of 'peoples', as in the case of Sueridus and Colias, two Gothic notables who had earlier been received into the empire by Valens and were stationed at Hadrianople, 'cum populis suis ante suscepti'. After a fracas with the people of Hadrianople, they joined Fritigern of the Thervingi, apparently without making more than marginal difference to his forces (31.6.1). Ammianus has many other references to 'optimates', like Farnobius of the Greuthungi and Munderichus and others of the Thervingi (31.9.2; 3.5), including some where the word is not actually used but implied, as when it is replaced by such words as 'duces' or 'principes' (31.3.3; 4.1; 7.8, etc.). In one passage, Ammianus writes of the 'satellites' or 'followers' who attended Gothic leaders as a guard of honour and for their safety; 'qui pro praetorio honoris et tutelae cause duces praestolabantur' (31.6.6). The 'duces' here are Alavivus and Fritigern, the leaders of the majority of the Thervingi who had abandoned Athanaric; the occasion their reception at Marcianopolis by the Roman general Lupicinus. The attendance on a tribal magnate of his 'Gefolgschaft' is, as we have seen both of Alamanni and of the Gothic magnates of the *Passion of St. Saba*, a characteristic institution of Germanic society.

Ammianus' allusions to other classes of Gothic society tend to be confined to passing references of a rather general nature. They are there nevertheless, as in the mention of the 'familiarum partem' captured in the Roman invasion of 367 before they could reach the safety of mountainous country (27.5.4), and in references to the selling of captured Goths into slavery in the Roman empire. By 378 the Gothic forces in Thrace were swollen by returning tribesmen who had been sold into slavery, a outcome which Julian had been content to entrust to 'Galatian slave traders' when urged by his advisers to make war on the Goths (31.6.5; 22.7.8). For Ammianus, it was cause for comment when among Goths sold by the Roman commanders in 376 were some optimates (or their children); 'inter quae quidam ducti sunt <filii?> optimatum' (31.4.11). The Danubian provinces had for long been the centre of a slave trade of prisoners taken in barbarian territory beyond the river, as a fourth-century source remarks of the Pannonian provinces.[34] We saw earlier a slaving party operating beyond the Rhine frontier (p. 312), and a decade after Hadrianople the senator Symmachus is found writing to his colleague Nicomachus Flavianus commenting on the reasonable price of slaves in the frontier regions (*Ep.* 2.78). Given the administrative office

XIV. Barbarians and Bandits

then held by Flavianus – the prefecture of Italy, Africa and Illyricum – the Danube frontier must be what is meant. It is likely that in the balance of trade between the Goths and the Roman empire, human beings were by far the most important export. We should not however think only of export into slavery. Like other less advanced neighbours of Rome such as Alamanni and Sarmatians, Goths had as individuals entered Roman military service for many years before the migration of 376. Ammianus speaks of the many Goths previously accepted into the Roman empire and stationed in the east in 'civitates' and 'castra' in the year of Hadrianople, when their expectation that they would receive their pay was treacherously deceived (31.16.8). A proportion of what such volunteers earned in the Roman service no doubt found its way back to their families in Gothia, helping to finance those imports of food and clothing from the Roman empire mentioned by the orator Themistius.[35]

The common people of the Goths appear otherwise in brief allusions revealing little except by implication, and little of this reassuring, of the quality of their lives. They appear as potential recruits for the Roman armies of Valens (31.4.4); as a 'hostile mob' ('plebem ... truculentam'), transported over the Danube together with their wagons (31.4.5), and as later prevented by Lupicinus from entering Marcianopolis in order to purchase essential provisions, despite the fact that they were now friends of Rome; 'ad comparanda victui necessaria ... per preces assidue postulantem'. A brawl between them and the people of Marcianopolis ensued, culminating in the murder at Lupicinus' orders of the 'satellites' of Fritigern and other optimates (31.5.5). We see them crammed inside the wagon circle frequently described by Ammianus and once given its popular name, 'carrago' (31.7.7ff.; 12.11); he must mean that it was so named by Romans, since it is derived from an ordinary Latin word for cart or wagon.[36] After the inconclusive battle at Ad Salices, the Goths stayed inside their 'wagon walls' for seven days, not daring to step outside their protection (31.8.1, cf. 7.5). The wagon circle was the vital focus of the battle of Hadrianople, for it was in its defence that the Goths repelled the Roman heavy cavalry, thereby causing the disorder among the infantry that led to the defeat of the army (13.2; p. 297). The similarity of Ammianus' description of the Gothic wagon circle to that of the Alani, 'like cities loaded on carts' (2.18; p. 337), is a reminder of the extent to which the Goths had been forced in their migration to abandon their normal sedentary way of life in favour of one resembling that of the steppe nomads. It left them at a great disadvantage in respect of their productive capacity. Unable to pursue agricultural exploitation and ill-equipped to adopt the life of steppe nomads, they were reduced to scavenging and plunder, modes of acquisition insufficient to provide their needs.

Just as it was the manpower of the Goths that encouraged Valens to accept their entry into the Roman empire, so it was their numbers that constituted their main weakness against the Roman authorities, once the latter had turned oppressors. They attempted systematically to use the

Goths' desperate need for food to manoeuvre them into submission through starvation.[37] Through food shortage in Gothia ('attenuata necessariorum penuria') the majority of Athanaric's people had deserted him under the impact of Hunnish attack, and Roman policy after the crossing of the Danube was to reduce the Goths to slow starvation by confining them within the more unproductive tract of territory between the river and the Haemus mountains, 'ut in locis incultis nusquam repperientes exitus diuturna consumeret fames' (31.7.3). They applied this policy with particular severity while waiting for the general Frigeridus to come with reinforcements from Gratian, blocking off the routes of exit from the mountains to the fertile plains by physical barriers, 'aggerum obiectu celsorum' (31.7.3, cf. 8.1). The *magister militum* Saturninus supported the policy by establishing posts for the defence of the countryside ('stationes agrarias'), everything that could provide sustenance for the Goths having been transported into the cities and kept under guard there. It was well known that the Goths were unable to attack walled cities, and to deprive them also of control of the countryside was from the Roman point of view an effective tactic, if it could be sustained (31.8.1ff.). Saturninus in the event relaxed the blockade of the mountain passes, apparently fearing that he would be unable to control the explosion that would ensue, and hoping to achieve something like an ordered dispersal into the countryside. Some Goths then made for the region of Cabyle in order to be free of ambush and starvation in the open terrain around it; 'ut in regionibus patulis nec inedia nec occultis vexarentur insidiis' (31.11.5).

The critical dependence of the Goths on food supplies provided by the Roman authorities is shown by their repeated demands for them in negotiations with the Romans, as well as by the scene at Marcianopolis when Lupicinus refused to let them enter the town to buy provisions (31.4.8, 11; 5.1, 5, etc.). At Hadrianople something similar occurred. The two Gothic leaders admitted earlier to the Roman empire and so far uninvolved in more recent events, joined Fritigern when their request for travelling supplies was turned down and they were attacked by a force of workers from the arms factories in the city, raised by a civic leader who was angry because his estates near the city had been ravaged by the barbarians (31.6.2ff.). If the truth behind the episode can be conjectured, it is probable that the Goths had simply commandeered from his land the food supplies which had been refused them. The events at Hadrianople and Marcianopolis give some notion of the fears entertained in Roman communities even of Gothic bands that were officially friendly; 'dicioni nostrae obnoxiam et concordem', as Ammianus said of the Goths at Marcianopolis (31.5.5). The Goths of Sueridus and Colias had kept themselves to themselves, thinking it in their own interests not to get involved in what was going on; 'salutem suam ducentes antiquissimam omnium, otiosis animis cuncta contuebantur' (31.6.1). As on other occasions, notably of course the great crossing of the Danube, the Goths were forced by Roman reactions to them into more hostile postures than they would otherwise have adopted.

In another situation described by Ammianus, relations between Romans

XIV. Barbarians and Bandits

and Goths appear in a different light, one that illuminates the class history of the Roman empire itself. The Goths in Thrace found themselves assisted in their search for supplies of food by their compatriots who had surrendered to the Romans or been taken captive by them, and now returned with other barbarians earlier sold into slavery. To these, Ammianus adds a new category of refugee, Roman gold-miners who fled to the barbarians to escape from the weight of taxation which they were unable to bear; 'vectigalium perferre posse non sufficientes sarcinas graves' (31.6.6). These people were of great assistance to the Goths in a terrain new to them, pointing out supplies of food and settlements and places where men might lie hid. The Roman who prefers a simple and honest life with the barbarians to the corruption of Roman society makes other appearances in Classical sources, and is not always an entirely convincing character: but Ammianus' reference is more circumstantial than most.[38] In choosing the Goths at this time, the miners were not exactly opting for the easy life.

Gothic economic dependence upon the Roman empire was an issue that underlay their wars with Valens in the late 360s. In 369, as Ammianus remarks in words whose tone will by now be familiar, the war was likely to come to an end because, with the prohibition of their commerce with the Roman empire, the Goths fell under pressure of extreme hardship; 'quod commerciis vetitis ultima necessariorum inopia barbari stringebantur' (27.5.7). What is implied by this is indicated by Themistius' allegation in a panegyric addressed to Valens after his victory, that until 369, when they were prohibited from trading at any but two specified locations on the Danube, the Goths had freely imported grain, clothing and other articles as well as minted coin from the Roman empire – no doubt in exchange for the human merchandise mentioned earlier as well as through subsidies paid to them by the Roman government (*Or.* 10.135B). Between their defeat by Constantine in 332 and the treaty with Valens which restricted their access to the two points mentioned (but unfortunately not named) by Themistius, the Goths had managed to enhance both the scope and the freedom of their trade with the Roman empire to a point beyond that achieved by almost any other barbarian tribe known to us in its relations with the Romans. Tacitus mentions the unique privilege of the Hermunduri in the first century that they were able to trade freely with the Romans anywhere they chose without restriction or supervision (*Germania* 41). Part at least of what the Hermunduri had gained by treaties of friendship, the Goths had for a period of more than thirty years secured by political ascendancy on the lower Danube frontier.[39] Against this background, their defeat by Valens in 369 seems the more damaging.

*

The slender indications provided by Ammianus on the religious practices of the Goths can be supplemented from other sources, but the result is no more than the sketchiest of impressions. Ammianus happens to mention that they went into battle (at Ad Salices) chanting praises of their heroic forebears (31.7.11) – Jordanes adding that the Goths worshipped the spirits of their legendary ancestors, to whom he gives the name 'anses' (*Getica* 78). Ammianus also records the 'fearful oath' sworn by Athanaric, and the mandate of his father, that he would never set foot in the Roman empire: by what dire divinity he swore the oath is not stated, nor again by what deity the Goths swore 'ex more' as they entered upon the battle of Ad Salices (27.5.8; 31.7.10). The *Passion of St. Saba* describes how the Gothic authorities ordered the villagers to partake of sacrificial meat as a ritual test, while the church historian Sozomen has a wooden image (in Greek, *xoanon*) wheeled on a cart through the villages – and, presumably, from village to village – to be worshipped in the time of persecution (6.37.13). Neither custom says anything very exact about the nature or objects of Gothic worship; the suggestions that the first is a symbolic enactment of a communal meal and the second a rite to fructify the land are attractive conjectures but no more than that.[40] A fragment of Eunapius (Fr. 55) has been taken to indicate that the 'tribe' (*phulê*), was the organisational basis of Gothic religion – but whether Eunapius meant by *phulê* an entire section of the Goths such as the 'natio omnis Thervingorum' mentioned at one point by Ammianus (31.5.8), some lesser division with it – or anything definite at all – is not clear; all he actually says is that many *phulai* crossed the Danube, and that each brought its own priests and priestesses and ancestral cult objects.[41] One would assume the unit to be larger than the individual 'pagus', or canton, but we have no indication what intermediate position between 'natio' and 'pagus' was occupied by the 'tribe', nor again how it was defined, whether by locality, kinship, or in some other way.

Eunapius also remarked that the Goths shrouded their cult objects in the greatest secrecy, and neither he nor Ammianus nor any other contemporary source has anything positive to say about the organisation of Gothic religion, nor about its priesthood. We are less well informed about the actual objects of Gothic worship and the nature of their cult than we are about the Alamanni or the Huns. We even know from Ammianus the title of the Burgundian chief priest, 'sinistus' (p. 313); it is the same word as that used in the Gothic Bible for 'elders' in the phrase 'chief priests and elders' (e.g. Mt. 27.3; 'guðyans, yah sinistam'), but this does little more than confirm for us that the Goths, like the Burgundians, had priests, even if they used the word more widely. Jordanes remarks in a curious passage that after the enactments of the fabled Gothic lawgiver Dicineus the priests of the Goths were called 'pilleati' after the word 'pilleus' (a tiara or hat), while the rest of the people were called 'capillati' – that is, they went bareheaded (*Getica* 71f.).[42] This account is certainly contaminated by earlier Classical sources, in particular by a lost work of Dio Chrysostom describing the Getae, some of whom are said in another work of the same author to have worn a 'pilos', or felt cap (*Or.* 72.3). The habit is extended by the historian Cassius Dio to the Dacians, among whom it was a symbol of rank (68.9.1). Jordanes' reference might be

XIV. Barbarians and Bandits

dismissed as a piece of antiquarian propaganda – neither Getae nor Dacians have anything whatever to do with Goths, and neither Chrysostom nor Cassius Dio mentions priests – except for his statement that the Goths still in his time retained the word 'capillati' in their songs; 'adhuc hodie suis cantionibus reminiscent' (*Getica* 72). This might in turn imply that the word was no longer in common use, but a law of Theoderic in Cassiodorus' *Variae* happens to be addressed to 'all provincials and *capellati, defensores* and *curiales* in the regions of Siscia or Savia', announcing a new governor among them (*Var.* 4.49). This looks like a complete register of the classes whom Theoderic, or Cassiodorus on his behalf, thought it appropriate to address. Whether these 'capellati' in Pannonia are the 'bareheaded ones' or laymen mentioned by Jordanes, and whether his reference has any bearing on the Goths of the time of Ammianus or is an antiquarian reconstruction of a later period, seems impossible to say: one suspects the latter, as Jordanes (and Cassiodorus) strove to give the Goths an erudite mythological background to compare with that of the Romans among whom they now lived. Similar doubt attaches to the laws allegedly given by 'Dicineus' and, in their written form, surviving in Jordanes' day under the name 'belagines' (*Getica* 69).

That the Goths as a nation were still heathen up to the time of their entry to the Roman empire in 376 is widely accepted, nor does Ammianus imply otherwise.[43] It is evident that they contained some Christians, the missionary work of Ulfila, especially among prisoners of war and other Roman expatriates among them, having produced a considerable number of converts and Christian communities; but one would not imagine that these formed more than a minority of the population at large, nor that they penetrated to any great extent the higher echelons of Gothic society. Many Christians would have been the expatriates just mentioned, their names having been identified as Asian or Syrian, rather than Gothic, in origin. Gothic converts are however recorded, such as the Inna, Rema and Pinna, Wereca and Batwin and others mentioned in Gothic martyrologies.[44]

It is a reflection both of the modest size of Christian communities and the unassuming social status of their members that apart from Ulfila, who after a seven-year mission abandoned Gothia under persecution in 347/8 and never returned (Constantius settled him and his followers near Nicopolis in Moesia),[45] the Christians among the Goths were led by presbyters rather than bishops; we saw that this was the case in the village communities mentioned in the *Passion of St. Saba*. Though limited in its numerical impact, however, the achievement of the early missionaries among the Goths was by no means negligible. If the Gothic leaders had found Christianity worthy of persecution, they cannot have considered it entirely harmless. Like Roman emperors of earlier times, they would assess the danger not by any simple calculation of the numbers of Christians among them, but by the extent to which the religious integrity of their society seemed threatened at moments of crisis: for example, when under attack by Rome. Conversely, it is not impossible that the extent of Christianisation among the Goths achieved by the fourth-century evangelists was sufficient to influence the 'official' conversion of the people to Arian Christianity that followed at some point their encounter with Rome. When Fritigern confronted Valens at Hadrianople, he conveyed his wish to avert the battle by sending a Christian presbyter as an envoy to the emperor 'cum aliis humilibus' (31.12.8). Ammianus may mean by this phrase simply to point the contrast with the normal status of envoys; Valens is said to have refused to listen to a second mission sent to him later in the day, on the grounds that they were men of low rank, not the 'optimates' he would expect to receive in deference to his own status (31.12.13). Despite this, it is reasonable to think that the 'alii humiles' of the first embassy were also plain Christians, possibly other members of the clergy, or even Gothic monks in the company of their presbyter. The presbyter himself is described as a trusted associate of Fritigern, who knew his plans ('conscius arcanorum et fidus'). His role would assume an added importance if it is correct, as has recently been argued, that the Thervingi of Fritigern accepted Christianity upon their acceptance into the Roman empire by the agreement of 376.[46] It would be a natural assumption on Fritigern's part that if he wished now to influence the Roman emperor, he had best attempt to do so by sending a trusted representative of the religion that his agreement with Valens had forced him to accept.

(2) Nomads: Huns and Saracens

(i) Huns and Alans

Ammianus begins Book 31 of his history with the portents that indicated the forthcoming Gothic wars and the battle of Hadrianople. Wolves howled, night birds lamented, the sun rose dim in the sky. Ominous acclamations and cries were made at Antioch, the ghosts of the king of Armenia and of judicial victims of Valens appeared; a heifer was found with its windpipe cut, and an inscribed oracle was dug out of a wall at Chalcedon (31.1.1ff.). We miss only the birth of babies portentously deformed, like the infant born at Daphne in 359 with 'two mouths, two sets of teeth and a beard, four eyes and two tiny ears' (19.12.19).

The deficiency is soon remedied, the Huns being, one might say, their own prodigy – 'prodigiosae formae', as Ammianus says (31.2.2). In one of the fullest of all his digressions, Ammianus gives a memorable portrait of these creatures, their faces scarred and beardless as eunuchs' from the gashes scored in them at birth, with thick necks and powerful limbs, resembling two-legged beasts, or the crudely carved wooden stumps erected at the parapets of bridges (31.1.2).[47] They wear clothing of linen and skins, never changing or washing it but keeping it on until it falls in pieces from their backs, trousers of goatskin cover their hairy legs, and their shoes are so roughly made as to prevent them from walking easily. This characteristic of Huns was as memorable as their physical

XIV. Barbarians and Bandits 333

appearance, to the point of caricature: the Suda gives as a gloss on a rare Greek word *akrosphaleis*, 'people who trip up while walking, that is the Huns'! Another entry reveals a different image, the word *kanchazein* being illustrated by a phrase explicitly assigned to the history of Eunapius (= fr. 41); 'and the Huns went away, roaring with laughter'.

The physical appearance of Huns became more familiar to Romans in time, but continued to strike fear into those who saw or read about it.[48] Jordanes describes their misshapen heads, their ugly faces, scarred (as Ammianus also says) at birth, their eyes, like little holes in the head, the sound of their speech, scarcely human at all (*Getica* 127). Gothic propaganda preserved by Jordanes – it cannot be genuine legend, for the Huns were as novel to the Goths as they were to the Romans – told how the race was begotten by wild spirits upon witches expelled from the Gothic kingdom in ancient times (*Getica* 121f.). A modern observer would interpret the matter more prosaically: whether Mongol or Turkish, the Huns were certainly no Indo-European physical type.

In addition to the physical appearance of the Huns and their origin, vaguely placed in the frozen lands beyond lake Maeotis and its marshes (the Sea of Azov), Ammianus describes the social, economic and cultural conditions of Hunnish life. It is a description naturally influenced, but not overwhelmed, by rhetorical convention. Their dietary regime matched their appearance, so uncouth that they neither cooked nor seasoned their food, but ate wild roots, and meat which they warmed a little (claims Ammianus in a famous misunderstanding) by putting it on the backs of their horses and sitting on it as they rode (31.2.3). They roamed at large, inured from infancy to cold, famine and thirst, and had no fixed buildings but avoided these 'like tombs', even fearing to be indoors. Their dress was the filthy garments just described, with the addition of round caps, and in compensation for their inability to walk properly they lived on horseback as if fastened there, sometimes sitting side-saddle to perform everyday chores. On horseback they transacted all their business, even slept. The horses themselves were like their owners, hardy but ugly; 'duris quidem sed deformibus' (31.2.6).

In planning action, they consult in common, submit themselves to the irregular guidance of their leaders and have no established monarchy (31.2.7). Their mode of fighting is rapid and fleeting, as they enter battle in masses but then divide into smaller bands, attack and disappear; and they will never take on a camp or fortification. As for equipment, they conduct the preliminaries of battle with long-distance archery, gallop to close quarters and use swords, with lassoes to entangle their opponents (31.2.8f.; cf. Sozomen 7.26.8). They conduct no agriculture, but live in wagons, in which they move around and in which all household and marital activities are conducted – sexual intercourse, the raising of the young, and the sewing together of the nasty garments. They are unreliable in making agreements, submit to passing impulses, and are greedy for gold – an instinct which they would in the course of time adeptly switch from booty to Roman subsidies. They recognise no

334   *Part Two: Visa vel Lecta*

difference between right and wrong and are deceitful and ambiguous, for they totally lack religion of any kind; 'nullius religionis vel superstitionis reverentia aliquando districti'. They are quarrelsome and volatile, and will make enemies and be reconciled to them with incredible rapidity (31.2.11).

Ammianus follows with a similar digression on the (H)alani or Alans, a race, or federation of races, overcome by the Huns.[49] Resembling the Huns but less savage and quite unlike them in physical appearance, being tall, handsome and fair where the Huns were (in the translated words of Jordanes) 'stunted, foul and puny', the Alans live by hunting and plunder (31.2.21). Like the Huns, they have no houses or agriculture, but live in wagons, moving around in search of the fertile pasture plentiful in the damp climate of those regions, a terrain watered by many streams; the region in question is that defined to west and east by the Don and the Volga, to the south by the Caucasus and the vast low-lying wastes of salty semi-desert that adjoin the northern shores of the Caspian Sea.[50] Ammianus' words imply a conscious contrast with the climate of the Mediterranean area, and perhaps also with the nomadism described elsewhere with respect to the Saracens of the Arabian desert (below, pp. 344ff.), but he does less than justice to the seasonal and periodic aridity that can afflict the steppe, the more acutely as one moves east into the Asian continent; the hunger, cold and thirst to which the Huns were used from birth were no mere literary flourish, but part of the reality of the steppe environment. As for the pattern of life of the Alani, the women and children perform the domestic tasks, while male children are brought up to the mounted warfare, in the practice and ideals of which they excel; no fate more contemptible than a peaceful death in old age (31.2.22). The Alans, like the Huns, have no temples, but they do have a religion, for they plant a sword in the ground where they come to rest and worship it as the martial deity of the land; and they conduct divination in a strange manner, with willow branches and incantations (31.2.24); both of these customs are reminiscent of but not precisely the same as rites assigned by Herodotus to the Scythians (Hdt. 4.62, 67).[51] They have no slavery, all of the tribe are of 'noble blood' and they select as their chiefs men of known reputation as warriors (31.2.25).

Now Ammianus is writing here of historical processes at the very edge of the civilised world, which he naturally tries to bring into some relation to what was known to his Graeco-Roman public from their more familiar reading; in this case mainly, but not exclusively, Herodotus.[52] From this source no doubt derive, directly or indirectly, Ammianus' references to Nervi, Vidini – the 'Neuroi' and 'Boudinoi' of Herodotus – and Geloni, Agathyrsi, the 'black-cloaked' Melanchlaenae and the nomadic and cannibal Anthropophagi; all these are neighbouring peoples supposedly conquered by the Alans (31.2.14f.; Hdt. 4.102ff.), while the Alans themselves are identified as the former Massagetae, whom Herodotus places east of the Araxes or Volga (31.2.12; Hdt. 1.201). Readers familiar with Herodotus' Scythian excursus might at this point divert themselves

XIV. Barbarians and Bandits

with the tale, disbelieved by Herodotus, that the Neuroi turned into wolves for a few days each year and then back again into men, and with the information that the Boudinoi ate lice, that the Anthropophagoi had a language all their own, and that the easy-living Agathyrsoi shared their women to avoid hatred and envy among themselves (4.104-9). It would all add to their sense of the barbarous exoticism combined with the literary familiarity of what they were reading; as to what historical relationship the peoples named by Ammianus bore after eight centuries to those whose ancient customs were so remarkably described by Herodotus, there seems no point in asking. He presumably named them for no better reason (though he would think it a good one) than that they were believed to have lived in the area overrun by the Alani, *alias* Massagetae, and could be presumed to have been absorbed by them. In any case, Ammianus' knowledge of Herodotus' excursus may be indirect, or reflect only what, with additions from other sources, had entered the general ethnographical tradition. For example, the Alans are said by Ammianus to have beheaded and then skinned their defeated victims to provide decorations for their war-horses, a custom not unlike that of his Geloni, who in a manner not mentioned by Herodotus but by a secondary Latin writer (Pomponius Mela 2.1.14), stripped skin from their enemies to clothe themselves and their horses (31.2.14, 22). The Scythians likewise indulged in head-hunting and in scalping and flaying their enemies (Hdt. 5.64f.) – widespread social customs enjoyed by native folk from the Indians of the New World to the Dayaks of Sarawak, though perhaps not always with the cheerful insouciance of the latter; 'the white men read books, we hunt for heads instead' (E. B. Tylor, *Primitive Culture*, I, p. 459)!

That Ammianus neither attempts nor implies any such comparisons with previously attested peoples in the case of the Huns is a measure of their sheer novelty in Roman eyes; 'Hunorum nova feritas', wrote Jerome in a work of the year 393 (*Adv. Jovinianum* 2.7; PL 23.308). It was a view shared by the Goths, in a reaction assigned to them by Ammianus; 'inusitatum hominum genus' (31.3.8). As Ammianus remarks in introducing his digression, they had hardly been touched on by earlier writers; 'monumentis veteribus leviter nota' (31.2.1). 'Monumenta vetera' implies more than the single very doubtful reference in Ptolemy's *Geography* which is all that now survives (3.5.10),[53] but can hardly refer directly to a contemporary writer like Eunapius, who had recently produced a description of the Huns in order to familiarise his Greek audience with this hitherto unknown people. It might however be an allusion to that writer's attempt to combine poetic and other literary 'evidence' about people identified as the Huns, with more recent testimony (Fr. 41). What survives of Eunapius' procedure enhances the impression given by Ammianus' far superior account. Eunapius connected the Huns alternatively with the 'Royal Scyths' of Herodotus, who thought all others their slaves (Hdt. 4.20.1), with some alleged 'simoi' or 'snub-nosed' people who lived beyond the Danube (5.9.1f.) and apparently also with the 'Nebroi' or 'Neuroi', also mentioned by Herodotus but associated by Ammianus with the Alani (Zosimus 4.20.3; Philostorgius, p. 123 Bidez). However plausibly in view of their facial appearance, Eunapius had achieved his identification of the Huns with the 'snub-nosed' people through a plain misreading of Herodotus – it is the horses, not the men, who are there described as 'simoi' – not to mention a wildly inaccurate displacement of the Huns from their correct location.[54]

Once the Huns had intruded so rudely upon the civilised world, one would naturally expect the more recondite corners of Classical ethnography to be ransacked by writers anxious to discover plausible identifications. It would have been better to admit that within a Graeco-Roman perspective their origin was indefinable, and it is somewhat to Ammianus' credit that he attempts no such identification in their case. The Alani had by contrast a well-documented and authentic existence in Classical literature. Josephus already knew that they lived in the region of the river Don and the Sea of Azov, from where they launched attacks against Parthia and Armenia through the Caucasian Iron Gates (*Bell. Iud.* 7.244-51); we saw how Ammianus gives the commonly used name of a section of the Alani, that neighbouring the Gothic Greuthungi, as the Tanaitae or 'Don folk', 'quos Greuthungis confines Tanaitas consuetudo nominavit' (31.3.1). The historian Arrian, who as governor of Cappadocia in the mid-second century composed a treatise on the military character of the Alani and how to counter it, described their tactic of the 'feigned retreat', in some respects anticipating Ammianus' description of the manner in which the Huns attacked in 'wedge' formation but suddenly broke apart and fought without any set order of battle; 'subito dispersi vigescunt, et incomposita acie cum caeda vasta discurrunt' (31.2.8; Arrian, *c. Alanos* 25ff.). Used either by Alani or by Huns, it is an obvious tactic of mounted steppe warfare, a military application of that expertise in horsemanship that has been described as the 'basic economic skill of the nomadic pastoralist'.[55]

It is not surprising that Ammianus should have described Hunnish and Alan nomadism in terms partly repeated from his digression on the Saracens (p. 344). It was of course common to such peoples that they should know little of agriculture or farming tools, should feed on meat, milk, and herbs and roots gathered in the wild, that they live a wandering life, so that their children may be said to be conceived, born and brought up in different places (14.4.3, 5; 31.2.10). Ammianus can write in this way of Huns and Saracens, as may a modern writer of the notions of 'nomadic pastoralism' and 'hunter-gatherer economies' of which Ammianus' rhetorical patterns are the equivalent, without being taken to imply that he has confused the south Russian steppe with the Arabian desert.

A more interesting problem concerns the extent to which we may combine details from Ammianus' descriptions of Huns and Alans to produce a composite picture of the social and economic life of both

XIV. Barbarians and Bandits

peoples. He does after all regard the Alans as in all respects similar to but less wild than the Huns; 'Hunisque per omnia suppares verum victu mitiores et cultu' (31.2.21). He happens to mention hunting in the case of the Alani, for example, but not in that of the Huns (31.2.21); but no one will doubt that hunting was also an occupation of the Huns. It is central to one version of those popular stories of the manner in which the wandering Huns first encountered the settled Goths, by following a deer through the lagoons of lake Maeotis; in another version it is a heifer, bringing out the pastoral element in their mode of life (Jordanes, *Getica* 123ff.; Sozomen 6.37.3f.). It is said of both Huns and Alans (as of Saracens) that they gather food as they find it growing wild (31.2.3; 19). Alans but not Huns are said (again like the Saracens) to feed on plentiful supplies of milk. To call nomads 'drinkers of milk' may be a rhetorical stereotype, but milk is obviously characteristic of the diet of pastoralists, and there is no need to deny it to the Huns.

The pattern of life of the Huns and Alani is described by Ammianus in language particularly expressive of the latter. The Alani, he writes, move about on wagons, which they cover with round roofs of bark and form into circles when they reach their pasture; and there they live off the land 'in the manner of wild beasts', that is to say by collecting what they can find; 'cumque ad graminea venerint, in orbiculatam figuram locatis sarracis ferino ritu vescuntur' (31.2.18). When the resources of one location are exhausted, they carry away their 'cities loaded on carts'; 'absumptisque pabulis velut carpentis civitates impositas vehunt' (31.2.18). Wherever they move they drive before them their herds and flocks, and their horses, to which they devote especial attention; 'armentis prae se agentes cum gregibus pascunt maximeque equini pecoris est ei sollicitior cura' (31.2.19). Ammianus' Huns are assimilated to this pattern of pastoral nomadism without this being made explicit, except in the detail of their use in battle of the lasso, an obvious martial application of a technique of pastoralism.[56] The Alani also used the lasso in battle, as appears from an incidental reference in Josephus' account of their invasion of Armenia in c. AD 73; king Tiridates was caught in one but cut himself free (*Bell. Iud.* 7.249f.). The Huns also have their wagons (31.2.10), and domesticated animals, if their domestication can be inferred from Ammianus' use of the word 'pecus' for 'herd'; 'semicruda cuiusve pecoris carne vescantur' – this item of their diet being added to the gathering of wild root crops; 'radicibus herbarum agrestium' (31.2.3). So too the Saracens feed on the flesh of wild animals and birds, milk, and 'herbae multiplices' (14.4.6).

None of this is meant to suggest that Ammianus is free of mistakes and misunderstandings. That Huns warmed up their meat by sitting on it on horseback and so ate it 'half-cooked', is a characteristic exaggeration, to the point of incongruity, of a barbarian habit, widely assumed in Classical sources, of consuming meat in its raw state and with only the slightest preparation (a custom with a modern legacy, from a later race of nomads, in Steak Tartare).[57] In fact, as the discovery of many copper cauldrons shows, the Huns were quite capable of cooking meat. Like Herodotus'

Fig. 4. A herding and hunting community in southern Russia, as shown in rock drawings from the region of Minusinsk; M. Davlet, *Sovietzkaya Arkheologia* 1965.3, pp. 128-9, cf. (the right-hand picture only), O. Maenchen-Helfen, *The World of the Huns*, 327. The connection with the Huns is conjectural, based on the location of the drawings and on the similarity of the cauldrons shown on them with those associated archaeologically with the Huns (see n. 57 of this Chapter). Some of the huts of the community are shown as made of wood, others of a different material, perhaps skins, on a wooden frame.

Scythians (4.60), they did it in large stews, from which soup was taken in ladles and chunks of meat were lifted with tongs, as is shown in rock drawings (if they relate to the Huns) from south-central Russia. The explanation of Ammianus' misunderstanding is not that the Huns were cooking meat by sitting on it as they rode, but that they were curing it, or else that they carried pieces of meat under their saddles to eat on excursions away from their encampments. Either is a better explanation than they they used the meat as poultices, to prevent their horses' backs developing sores through chafing – a nation born to live on horseback could do better than this! Archaeology does not support Ammianus' assertion that the Huns used arrows tipped with sharpened bone (31.1.9); none have been found, but many tipped with iron. His explanation may still be partially if it cannot be exclusively correct, but would be more persuasive if transferred from arrows to bows, for bone inlay formed an important part of the complex structure and the decoration of these sophisticated instruments, made by craftsmen, effective, and highly prized; only broken, useless bows are found in grave deposits. The physical appearance of the Hunnish hordes was no doubt more varied than Ammianus implies if, like the Alani, they had absorbed their neighbours by conquest into a sort of federation;[58] yet, as we saw, the Hunnish physiognomy remained distinctive until long after Ammianus' time (p. 333). It has been argued that the scarring of the faces of Huns was a consequence, not of the slashing of the faces of infants, but of rituals of grief, as attested in many societies. Yet Jordanes, like Ammianus, assigns the practice to infancy, while assigning a different (though mistaken) motive in saying that its purpose was to inure the Hun against pain from his earliest years (*Getica* 127). There is no good reason to doubt that the marking was done in infancy.[59]

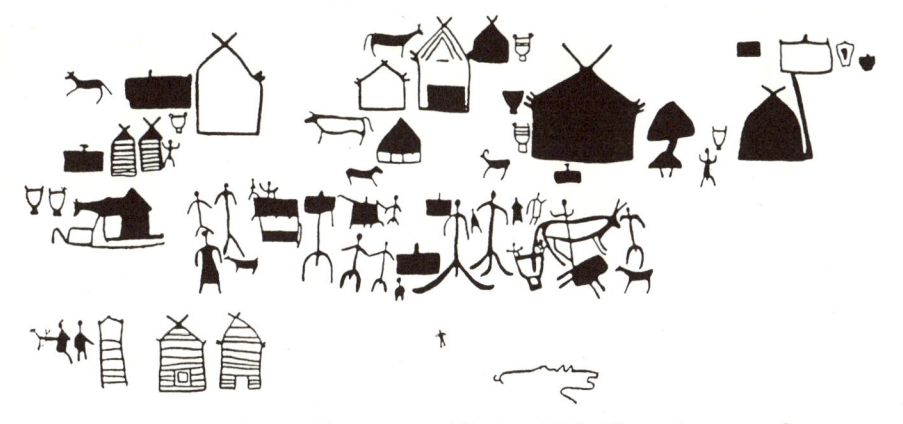

In describing how both Huns and Alani lived in wagons which – as stated only in the case of the Alani, but clearly true of the Huns – they drew up in defensive circles when they rested anywhere, Ammianus may have confused their style of life when migrating with that when settled in their pastures; for the Huns lived, when so settled, not on their wagons but in encampments of tents made of fur and skins, which they loaded onto their wagons when they were on the move, as mentioned above (p. 337). The reason for Ammianus' misunderstanding may be that his information concerned the barbarian peoples during a major period of migration, when they were moving west across the Don and attacking the Goths, and was in this respect not typical. The same inference might have been made from observation of the Goths during the years of their migration across the Danube to the Roman empire, but wrongly; the Goths were no pastoral nomads but a displaced agricultural people.

In one detail, Ammianus may give an insight into a different aspect of Alan, and perhaps also of Hunnish, society. He notes that all Alani were 'of noble birth'; 'omnes generoso sanguine procreati' (31.2.25). This is difficult to interpret, unless Ammianus were referring to a clan system in which the identity of all members of the clan was defined in terms of kinship with an actual or legendary ancestor. This would resemble the practice among another nomadic people, the desert Arabs, who were identified within their tribal structure as common descendants of a named ancestor; hence the importance of genealogy in their oral culture (p. 347). Ammianus is surely correct in denying to the Huns an established system of kingship over the whole nation, which is not to deprive them of any sort of aristocracy, or any tendency towards the acquisition by inherited prestige of positions of influence among them.[60] Like the Alani, and indeed the Goths and Alamanni, the Huns submitted themselves as occasion arose, and particularly during periods of stress such as occurred during migration, to the leadership of assertive and successful individuals. There is no contradiction in this, for qualities of leadership, which are naturally favoured by accidents of social origin and upbringing, would tend to coincide with the inherited prestige of the more notable kindreds and their acknowledged leaders. It is not just a rhetorical stereotype, but the actual spontaneity of their decision-making processes, and the fact that they so often operated in separate groups not necessarily bound by each others' agreements, that made them appear to the Graeco-Roman observer to be so untrustworthy and faithless. It does not imply that they were incapable of collective aims or a common plan of action when these were required.

It is impossible that, as Ammianus claims, the Huns had no religion of any kind. A nomadic people, they built no temples at fixed sites, as Ammianus specifically records of the Alani: these had no shrine or temple, not even a roofed hut served as such (31.2.23). The Alans nevertheless venerated a sword ritually planted in the ground which they occupied at any time, and conducted divination with twigs in the strange manner mentioned earlier (31.2.24). The Huns too attached divine attributes to the sword, as can be seen from Jordanes' story, cited from Priscus of Panium, of the herdsman who was led by one of his cattle to find one hidden in the pasture and presented it to Attila; it was received with delight as the sword of Mars (*Getica* 183, cf. Priscus, fr. 8; pp. 280-1 Blockley). By some form of divination, Attila had learned to favour one of his sons rather than the others (Priscus, pp. 288-9 Blockley), and it has been suggested that the rites of 'haruspicina' conducted before Toulouse in 438 by the Roman general Litorius were pressed upon him in this late season by his Hunnish federate troops. One can hardly imagine that the Huns had acquired a religion between the time of Ammianus and that of Attila. Ammianus has picked up details of the religion and practice of divination of the Alani, without seeing the implication for the Huns that a lack of temples does not of itself imply a lack of religious custom or belief. It is perhaps relevant that he presents the lack of religion of the Huns in the specific context of their faithlessness in keeping to agreements. There is an element of circularity in Ammianus' view: what the Huns lacked was just the sort of religion that would have led them to keep their promises. He sees it in a Graeco-Roman moral perspective that does not lead him to consider how Hunnic religion may have functioned within its own society.

What remains difficult to assess, both from Ammianus and the somewhat imprecise archaeological evidence, is the extent of manufacturing and technological expertise available to, and the productive capacity achieved by, these nomadic pastoralists.[61] The use of linen together with skins in the clothing of the Huns might be, but is not necessarily, a proof, against Ammianus, of agricultural exploitation, for Herodotus mentions how a cloth very like linen could be made from a hemp plant resembling flax, which grew wild in his 'Scythia' (4.73). The use of wagons however requires access to skill in carpentry and wheel-making, the use of Hunnish bows the considerable craftsmanship required for the construction of these complex, and often artistic, items of equipment. As for swords, nomadic peoples do not readily possess the

XIV. Barbarians and Bandits 341

resources or the metallurgical techniques of a level required for the manufacture of high quality articles of this nature; yet it is impossible that the Huns and Alans acquired such equipment, so essential to their life-style and social ideology, merely through casual plunder or occasional barter. Attila received the sword brought to him by the herdsman so gladly because he believed it to be sacred, not because this was the normal way of acquiring such things. Further, the copper cauldrons associated archaeologically with the Huns are too homogeneous in style to be explained as merely casual acquisitions. That Ammianus should say that the Huns made no use of fire (31.2.3) may be intended as a symbol, to convey their lack of a basic resource of civilised life, rather than a plain statement of fact, and he associates it, mistakenly, with their lack of any cooked food. His statement might however be more true of manufacturing than it is of domestic uses, and we should not ignore the difficulty of finding sufficient heating materials for large-scale production in the treeless grasslands over which the Huns normally roamed – those bare tracts of country occupied by Herodotus' Massagetae, 'stretching out interminably before the eye' (1.204, tr. Rawlinson). We must surely envisage more settled Hunnish or allied communities of carpenters, metalworkers and other craftsmen, with whom their nomadic pastoralist counterparts were in regular contact for barter and exchange, or whose services and skills were extorted by conquest.

Herodotus remarks of his 'Boudinoi' (identified by Ammianus, as we saw, with the Vidini, part of the Alan federation) that they possessed a wooden city in which Greek religious rites were celebrated and a mixture of Greek and Scythian spoken, the Greek element having been taken there by migrants from the *emporia* of the Black Sea coast (4.108).[62] The Greek culture of the Boudinoi may (who knows?) be a myth, but the city was real enough; it was burned by Darius in his invasion of Scythia (4.123). Despite their city, the Boudinoi are described by Herodotus as a 'nomadic' people, while their neighbours the Gelonoi enclosed their land and cultivated it (4.109.1). That the city of the Boudinoi was called 'Gelonos', while Herodotus emphatically denied the Greek view that the Boudinoi and Gelonoi were the same people, adds to the peculiarity of the situation; we might explain it by supposing that adjacent peoples, one largely settled and one largely nomadic, had achieved an economic symbiosis, the more settled people establishing a city, or trading post, in the territory controlled by the other. The relevance to Ammianus of the situation envisaged here should be clear; it is to give form to the possibility of a greater variety of settlement patterns among the Huns, Alani and their associated peoples than his excursus strictly allows for. The picture of 'pure' nomadism presented by Ammianus, though it conveys what could readily be perceived by an outside observer, over-simplifies the actual pattern of life among the steppe peoples; this, as in the case of the Saracens (pp. 344ff.) – and indeed the Scythians of Herodotus – combined sedentary with nomadic elements over an area in which both were present, in a constant interplay of social and economic relations.

In the mid-fifth century, the classic account given by the Byzantine diplomat, Priscus, of his visit to the court of Attila, shows the Hunnish leader living among his people in a 'very large village', in a wooden residence surrounded by a palisaded courtyard.[63] Both residence and palisade were noted by Priscus for their excellent carpentry; the palisade was even, in his judgment, designed for elegance rather than security. It also had towers, perhaps in imitation of Roman frontier building style. In the same village, which was apparently unfortified and may in that respect have preserved in semi-permanent form the configuration of an open encampment, stood the residence and palisaded courtyard (without the towers) of another Hunnish leader, and other Huns lived around in more villages in the same region. It is merely an assumption, though of course it may be true, that the carpentry was the work of Gothic prisoners of war. In one of the more poignant individual experiences of the period, described in the same passage of Priscus, a Roman who had been taken prisoner at Sirmium and was employed by the Huns to build a bath-house (for which he imported the materials from ruined cities in Pannonia), found himself after its completion made bath-attendant rather than, as he had hoped, being given his freedom. That particular change of custom on the part of the Huns to cleanliness, if not to any recognisable form of godliness, would have surprised Ammianus (p. 332), and is a measure of the influence even of declining Roman ways upon the most intractable of neighbours. A similar recognition was assigned by Procopius to a Hunnish leader of the sixth century, who complained to Justinian of his generous treatment of an enemy faction whom he had defeated on the emperor's behalf. The emperor should beware of treating his enemies better than his friends, in case the latter, '[having gained] the mastery by the gift of fortune ... may see the vanquished faring more splendidly than himself at your hands, seeing that we eke out our existence in a deserted and thoroughly unproductive land, [while] the Cutrigurs are at liberty to traffic in corn and to revel in their wine-cellars and live on the fat of the land. And doubtless they have access to baths too and are wearing gold ... and have no lack of fine clothes embroidered and overlaid with gold.'[64] As so often, these are sentiments put into the mouth of a barbarian envoy by a Roman historian, but they are not inept as a description of the attractive – some would say destructive – force of the wealth of the empire over these, the least favoured of its neighbours.

(ii) Saracens

In his digression on the eastern provinces of the Roman empire, Ammianus describes Arabia as neighbouring on one side Palestine, on the other the country of the Nabataeans (14.8.13). This is not an entirely straightforward definition, for historically the province of Arabia was not distinct from but essentially the same as the Nabataean kingdom, as annexed by Trajan in AD 106.[65] Ammianus' statement reflects changes in provincial organisation that in the early fourth century had added the

XIV. Barbarians and Bandits

southern part of Trajan's Arabia – namely Sinai and the Negev, with the area east of the Wadi Araba – to Palestine. The new province, later known as 'Palaestina Salutaris' or 'Tertia', extended southwards to the Gulf of Suez and touched the Mediterranean near Rhinocolura (El Arish); it therefore incorporated much of what had in earlier times been the kingdom of the Nabataeans, including their famous city of Petra, which is explicitly assigned to Palestine in early fourth-century sources. Late Roman 'Arabia', by contrast with the maritime provinces of Palestine, was an inland zone running east from the Jordan valley between lines drawn from the Golan Heights and the southern end of the Dead Sea; it included the Nabataeans' other chief city of Bostra, mentioned in Ammianus' digression together with Gerasa (Jerash) and Philadelphia (modern Amman) (14.8.13).[66] This restructuring of inland and coastal commands might explain how Arabia comes in Ammianus to be separated from the Nabataeans, but his province of Palestine receives no advantage. The most southerly cities assigned to it are Ascalon and Gaza (14.8.11), and it includes no Nabataean settlement. The omission of Petra is immediately obvious, and there might have been a case, at least as to size and economic importance, for the inclusion of Elusa in the Negev.[67] The anomaly is best explained by the supposition that Ammianus was compiling his digression from earlier sources on the second- and third-century eastern provinces without considering any but the most immediate implications of more recent changes in their boundaries. His separation of the Nabataeans from Arabia conveys a sufficiently accurate indication of the scope of 'provincia Arabia' in the fourth century, an inland zone looking to the desert, even if his reference to the Nabataeans themselves has by this date a strong air of archaism.[68]

Arabia, Ammianus continues, was rich in commerce, and had forts and castles built at suitable points in ancient times to check the incursions of neighbouring peoples, 'ad repellendos gentium vicinarum excursus'. By these 'gentes vicinae' he must mean the desert peoples to the east of the old Nabataean kingdom and of the Roman *limes* or frontier zone, running from Aila (Eilat) to Bostra, Damascus, Palmyra and beyond, that succeeded its annexation. The road that formed the spine of this frontier zone, 'Via Nova Traiana' as it is called on inscriptions, was itself the culmination of a half-century of Roman consolidation in the east from the upper Euphrates to Sinai, to which the annexation of Arabia provided the finishing touch.[69] By the fourth century the road had been superseded by a route a little to the east known as the 'strata Diocletiana', but its military purpose remained the same, to unify a defensive zone directed against brigands and desert nomads rather than any foreign enemy. It was a system of proven inadequacy when later, with the Islamic expansion, the desert nomads actually became the foreign enemy; it had never been designed to meet this sort of threat.

The province of Arabia, according to Ammianus, was reduced to Roman jurisdiction by Trajan; 'obtemperare legibus nostris Traianus compulit imperator' (14.8.13). Ammianus implies by his use of the word 'compulit' that the subjugation of Arabia was forcible and violent, referring to the unruly behaviour of the inhabitants that had led to it, but his connection of the annexation with the Parthian wars of Trajan almost ten years later does not inspire confidence in this conclusion. Ammianus seems to be using conventional language without reference to the specific circumstances of the case. The evidence suggests that the annexation of Arabia followed many years of diplomatic and commercial relations between Rome and the Nabataean kingdom, and took place smoothly and without violence.[70] Client kingdom evolves into province, native dynasty into local aristocracy; it is a pattern familiar to observers of the eastern policy of Rome.

Ammianus was however correct to view Arabia as a normal urbanised province of the Roman empire. Quite different is his image of the other category of Arabs, or Saracens as they were called in Ammianus' time (below, p. 349): the nomads of the desert. He presents their customs in a brief digression inspired by their raids on eastern communities, having earlier written of them, so he says, in his account of the emperor Marcus Aurelius and elsewhere (14.4.1, cf. 31.16.5); an excellent opportunity for such a digression would be provided by the journey of Marcus (in AD 175) through Palestine to Egypt, to which oblique reference is made in a later book (22.5.5). Desirable neither as friend nor foe, the Saracens were spread all over the east, from the cataracts of the Nile to Assyria. All warriors, and equal to each other in fortune or lifestyle ('omnes pari sorte bellatores'), they range widely on horses and camels, whether in times of peace or war. They cultivate neither cereal crops nor fruit-trees, have no fixed abode or laws, and take wives as it were 'on hire'. A wife brings a spear and a tent as dowry but may leave her husband at any time; and they perform sexual intercourse with unbelievable passion – 'incredibile est quo ardore' – in both partners (14.4.4). They live on game and milk, herbs, and whatever wild birds they can catch: Ammianus had himself seen Saracens acquainted with neither grain nor wine (abstention from alcohol is an attested though far from universal feature of pre-Islamic Arab society). Enough, says Ammianus, of this 'pernicious' race, 'de natione perniciosa', ending his digression with a neat play on the word for 'speed', that central theme of Saracen life (14.4.7).

If Ammianus' explanation of the origins of the province of Arabia is in detail confusing, his digression on the Saracens gives a seriously oversimplified impression of their social and economic character. It is only in the broadest terms true to say that nomadic peoples do not conduct agriculture in settled places, and that their rules of living are unlike those of urbanised communities with written laws; the real situation is much more complex than this. Desert Arabs existed in different degrees of nomadism, and engaged in a wide variety of inter-dependent relationships among themselves and with their settled counterparts, and with the peoples around them.[71] They raised crops at favoured sites and seasonal locations in the desert. They came to towns at the desert edge and traded there, controlled the supply routes on which

XIV. Barbarians and Bandits

the towns depended and extorted protection money from defenceless communities and passing travellers. Strabo tells how merchants travelling from Syria to Babylonia chose the direct route across the desert, where the 'Skenitai', or desert Arabs, offered protection to the camel-drivers and charged only moderate dues, in preference to the route by the Euphrates, where the chieftains exacted extortionate tolls for the passage through their territories (16.1.27). Without making a sharp distinction between them, Strabo's language nevertheless indicates that the Arabs of the river zone – not prosperous country, as he explains, but less unproductive than the desert – were more sedentarised, in the sense of being more closely based on defined territories, than the desert peoples; each chieftain possessed his 'dunasteia', or sheikhdom, through which travellers had to pass.

In the conditions of the Roman empire and the more settled relations that for long periods ensued with its eastern neighbour, some desert Arabs became urbanised, building the spectacular oasis cities of Palmyra and Hatra, and using their command of the desert to escort the caravans that plied between the eastern fringes of the Roman empire, Parthian Babylonia and the maritime *emporia* of the Persian Gulf; this is in the period after that described by Strabo, Palmyra having assumed the role of the Scenite Arabs as guardian of the caravan routes as well as becoming patron, protector and market for the migrant Arabs inhabiting the desert around. We glimpse their movements in a remarkable inscription, the 'tax law' of Palmyra of AD 137 in which, among many details that illuminate the life of this extraordinary desert city, it is said that the tax collector may 'if he wishes' mark animals brought into the territory from outside for the purpose of grazing.[72]

This provision of the tax law is one of the rare insights given to us, in Classical sources, into the nomadic movements which brought desert Arabs into contact with the settled lands adjoining or within their territories. It is an issue we encounter more frequently as the Arabs enter more closely into the conduct of Romano-Persian relations, and so attract the attention of historians and other literate observers. In the sixth century Procopius describes king Chosroes' attempt to contrive a *casus belli* between himself and Justinian by provoking a dispute between pro-Roman and pro-Persian Arab factions over rights of pasture on land south of Palmyra (*Wars* 2.1.1-11). The pro-Roman Arab, Arethas, argued that the territory was Roman, as was shown by its name, 'Strata', the Latin word for road; presumably the relevant section of the *strata Diocletiana*, which passed through the territory, is what is meant. The pro-Persian Arab, Alamoundaros or al-Mundhir, did not dispute the meaning of the name but claimed that he had for long received tribute for pasturage in the area from the owners of the flocks who used it. Both sides cited the evidence of antiquity in favour of the situation they claimed to exist in the present, Arethas adducing 'testimonies of men of ancient times' and al-Mundhir the long established nature of the tribute allegedly paid to him. The Roman representatives appointed by Justinian to resolve the dispute differed as to what should best be done. One argued that the Romans should not abandon their claim to the territory as vested in their support for Arethas, while the other recommended the emperor not to give the Persians a pretext for war 'for the sake of a little tract of land that is of no account whatever, but completely unproductive and unable to bear crops' – a sentiment anticipated in his narrative by Procopius himself: 'nowhere does it bear a tree or any of the good things of farmed land, for it is intensely scorched by the sun, but from ancient times has been given over to occasional grazing for flocks of sheep'.[73] The whole situation is a classic illustration of the complexities of life in the steppe (al-Mundhir, for instance, did not claim to use the pasture himself, but to let it out for the use of others), and of the profound gulf of misunderstanding that could exist between the urbanised Roman, used to sedentary agriculture, and his nomadic pastoral ally, whose interests he could only appreciate in terms of a stereotype familiar to himself.

Contact between the nomadic and the settled territories at the desert edge was naturally more extensive at times when, for climatic or other reasons, the steppe pasture was in short supply. This would extend the area sought by the nomads for seasonal grazing and increase their need for food from other sources, and so could result in the conflicts with the settled country that Classical sources categorised under the broad definition of 'latrocinium', or brigandage.[74] For Strabo, the Scenite Arabs – the same who in his very next paragraph appear as 'offering peace' to the caravan riders – were 'brigands and shepherds, who simply move from one location to another when their pasture and booty give out' (16.1.26). It is of course very difficult in the case of a people who live by seeking pasture and by gathering what other resources they can in and around the desert, to draw a strict line between what is and what is not theirs to take. This is particularly so in view of the different criteria according to which settled and nomadic peoples view questions of the land and its use. For the pastoral nomad, herds and not land form the standard of wealth, the land itself being seen, not in terms of demarcation and ownership, but of its collective appropriation by the social unit. Rights of transit rather than settlement, of customary use rather than legal possession, are the essential criteria.[75]

Despite the risk of accepting a stereotype, it would be wrong to be too dispassionate on this subject. The Classical perspective, though partial and to a degree uncomprehending, is not totally false.[76] Raids are raids, people – mainly defenceless peasants – are killed or enslaved, their homes are destroyed, their crops and possessions seized and their animals driven off. Brigandage for plunder, even construed as an economic necessity, generated an ideology of approbation among the Saracens – as was equally necessary if it was to be carried out successfully.

It is in the image of bandit that the desert Arab constantly recurs in Classical sources; among many such passages, the elder Pliny wrote of the 'innumerable tribes' of the Arabs as engaging equally in trade and

XIV. Barbarians and Bandits

brigandage (*Hist. Nat.* 6.162). An episode narrated by Jerome in vivid and on the whole persuasive detail tells of a travelling party of seventy people attacked and taken prisoner by Saracen bandits 'on horseback and camel' on the road between Beroea and Edessa (*Vita Malchi* 4; *PL* 23.57). Jerome's informant, the Syrian hermit Malchus, was on his way from his monastery at Chalcis to claim an inheritance at Nisibis and was travelling in convoy precisely in order to avert the Saracen raids which were always expected. It was especially when Rome and Persia suffered poor relations with each other that the desert Arabs situated between them were able to indulge in plunder, with the frequent encouragement of their imperial patrons, as Ammianus several times states or implies (p. 352), and whatever its exact date the raid described by Jerome fell in such a period. Its victims were disposed of by their captors to a variety of masters, and after a long and precarious journey by camel across the desert and beyond the 'great river' with only camel's milk to drink and 'half-raw flesh' to eat, Malchus found himself bending his neck 'ex more gentis' before the mistress and children of his new owner's family.[77] He was then set to work herding sheep on the steppe, his consolation being that in his solitude he rarely saw his masters or fellow slaves and could devote himself, as he later imagined it, to reproducing his monastic way of life at Chalcis. In order to foster his loyalty and to assist his integration into Saracen society, he was even made to marry by Arab custom his companion in misfortune, an already married woman whose husband, a member of the same travelling party, had been taken off by a different owner and was never seen again (*Vita Malchi* 5f.); his disappearance is evident from the fact that after his escape to the Roman empire Malchus lived with the woman as a chaste companion at Maroneia near Antioch, where Jerome saw them and heard their story.

To return to Ammianus' digression, the 'equality of fortune' ascribed to the desert Arabs may have been the impression they gave as they descended onto settled communities or travellers as war-bands in search of plunder or, in another common situation, were encountered in their territories in peaceful encampments of a few families surrounded by their animals; such, no doubt, was the desert community to which Malchus was brought. Nothing is however more important to the society of desert Arabs than the prestige of their chiefs, enshrined in social custom, commemorated in song and legend, genealogy and feud. Arab society, fluid and egalitarian as it might appear to the outside observer, was shaped from within by social prestige and ancestral distinction, and the observation that the Saracens lacked a code of written law, though true, fails to appreciate the force of unwritten custom among them.[78]

Ammianus has offered a partial stereotype of a nomadic people, one differentiated by every criterion of social, economic (and sexual) behaviour from the ordered ways of civilised urban dwellers. Certain of his expressions, especially among those relating to diet and family life, can as we saw be paralleled in his much fuller excursus on the Huns and Alans (p. 336). That is not to say that his description is irrelevant to the specific circumstances of Arab life, but the moral dimension in Ammianus' digression is undeniable; indeed, it is introduced as part of a series of disasters to afflict the eastern empire – beginning with the Isaurians – in addition to the juridical abuses of Gallus Caesar at Antioch (14.2.1). The gulf in civilised conduct between Roman and Saracen is further illustrated in a later episode which is nothing if not circumstantial in content. An Arab in Roman service after the battle of Hadrianople charged almost naked among the Goths then besieging Constantinople, with blood-curdling war-cries killed one of them with a dagger and then, to the horrified consternation of Gothic onlookers, sucked the blood from his throat. The Saracen's conduct seemed portentously barbarous, even to 'barbarian' witnesses; 'quo monstroso miraculo barbari territi ...'.[79] Ammianus' description of the bloodthirsty Saracen as long-haired and naked but for a loin-cloth, 'crinitus quidam, nudus omnia praeter pubem' (31.16.6), resembles Jerome's description of the raiders who captured Malchus and his party on the road from Beroea to Edessa – 'crinitis vittatisque capitibus, ac seminudo corpore' (*Vita Malchi* 4) – as well as the dress adopted by Malchus himself in the desert (ibid. 5). Both authors mention also the flowing cloaks sported by the Beduin as they rode (14.4.3; *Vita Malchi* 4).[80] As we saw, the consumption of uncooked or 'half-raw' meat is another rhetorical motif of the life of nomadic steppe people, being assigned in similar terms by Ammianus to the Huns as by Jerome to the Saracens (p. 337).

*

Confusion between the two sorts of 'Arab' described by Ammianus, settled and nomadic, persists in and is somewhat encouraged by Classical writers, for whom all of the race were described at will as robbers and bandits; this is perhaps how Ammianus could assume that the province of Arabia was formed because of the disorder of its people. The confusion is not entirely without foundation, any more than the distinction between the settled and the nomadic can be drawn with absolute clarity. In another saint's life, Jerome wrote of the Nabataean city of Elusa in the Negev as a 'largely semi-barbarian' settlement ('oppidum ex magna parte semibarbarum') on account of its location; it was frequented by Saracens, who came there with their wives and families to worship at the shrine of their national goddess Venus or Lucifer (Arab al-'Uzzâ), and were once heard chanting the word for 'bless' in what Jerome took to be Syriac but may in fact be the Arabic language; 'voce Syra "barech", id est benedic clamantes' (*Vita Hilarionis* 25; *PL* 23.42).[81] The Emperor Philip (244-9), a member of a family of equestrian rank from the Arab town of Shahba in Auranitis (the Hawran), is described with painstaking sarcasm in one fourth-century source as the obscurely-born son of a most distinguished bandit leader 'humillimo ortus loco ... patre nobilissimo latronum ductore' (*Epit. de Caes.* 28.4). Shabha, renamed Philippopolis by its favourite son, stood, to be sure, by the Jebel Druz, an area of notoriously

XIV. Barbarians and Bandits

endemic banditry; a much earlier inscription from nearby Canatha spoke of people who 'hide in caves like animals', a clear reference, among others in the region, to bandits (*OGIS* 424). A little to the north, in the region of Apamea, we find in Ammianus the robber village of the Maratocupreni; the first part of their name refers in the Syriac language to the caves in which they lived, or once had lived and found refuge.[82] Philip 'the Arab' was however no grizzled bandit chief, but a prominent citizen of a local community – which is not to rule out the possibility or even likelihood that, like many an otherwise respectable Isaurian (below, p. 365), he was a local dynast with connections and authority among the robber gangs. In general terms, there was no less reason why an emperor should come from a town of 'provincia Arabia' than, as others did, from villages in Thrace or Pannonia; it is all part of the widening franchise of political and social advancement in the Roman empire, bestowed on its more outlying regions by the military pressures to which the empire was increasingly subjected in the later period.

In his digression on Egypt Ammianus adds an interesting detail, in remarking that to the east the country faces the Red Sea and the 'Scenite Arabs, whom we now call Saracens'; 'Scenitas Arabas, quos Saracenos nunc appellamus' (22.15.2). He repeats the information also in his digression on Persia, where the same subject arises (23.6.13). The old name, 'Scenitae', means 'living in tents' (Greek *skênai*), that is nomadic desert Arabs; it was so used both by Pliny (*Hist. Nat.* 6.143) and Strabo, in a passage mentioned earlier (16.1.28; p. 345). It is possible that in recording the change of name Ammianus reflects a significant aspect of the recent development of Arab society. The use by a Roman observer of an Arabic proper name, 'Saraceni', to denote all desert Arabs, rather than a Greek descriptive epithet, *skênitai*, may relate to the emergence by the fourth century of larger groups in the form of confederations of desert peoples. That such a consolidation of power did occur is widely agreed by historians of pre-Islamic Arabia.[83] It is located in the third and fourth centuries of our era and is germane to the shifts in Arabic social and political organisation upon which the Islamic expansion was ultimately based.

A contributory feature in this process of consolidation was surely the decline of the great cities of Palmyra and Hatra in the third century. The deserted ruins of Hatra were seen by the Roman army of Julian as it retreated across the desert in 363 (p. 392). In the surviving books of the history Palmyra is never mentioned by Ammianus, though he would have had to take account of it in considering in the lost books the rise and fall of the dynasty of Odaenathus and queen Zenobia. Although resettled as a frontier garrison by Diocletian after its destruction by the armies of Aurelian, the city never achieved more than a fraction of the spectacular urban growth, based on commerce with the east, which it had seen in the first centuries of the Roman empire. At Palmyra as at Hatra, the urbanised Arab populations, caravan leaders and all, should be seen as reverting to the desert in this phase of 'de-urbanisation' in the third century. It is difficult to imagine that the social structures created by the cities would have long survived exposure to the desert. The decline of the cities would leave a vacuum of power, to be filled by new alignments among the Beduin peoples.[84]

The defeat of Palmyra, in Roman eyes achieved by Aurelian to restore unity to the eastern provinces of the Roman empire after the 'usurpation' of Odaenathus and Zenobia, was seen quite differently in Arab legend. It is here presented as an act of vengeance for the treacherous murder by Zenobia (Arabic al-Zabbâ) of sheikh Jadhima of the Tanukh. Something is known of the Tanukh. They were a confederation of tribes which had migrated northwards from the Arabian peninsula in the early third century, leaving some of their number in the region of al-Hira near the Euphrates, while the rest moved on to the west Syrian desert.[85] Here, at the Roman settlement of Umm al-Jimal near Bostra, sheikh Jadhima is described as 'king of the Tanukh' on an intriguing bilingual inscription in Greek and Nabataean at the tomb of his Arab tutor or 'tropheus'.[86] Jadhima was succeeded by his nephew 'Amr ibn 'Adî, who (in legend now, not fact) avenged his uncle's murder by killing Zenobia. 'Amr ibn 'Adî was succeeded by his son Imru'l-qais, and Imru'l-qais in turn is styled 'king of the Arabs' on his tomb inscription of AD 328, written in Arabic but in Nabataean characters, at Nemara in the Hawran.[87] Nemara was a town formerly part of the Roman province of Arabia. Even if the town and its region were not abandoned by the Romans, they were clearly subject to a substantial increase of Arab power in the locality; again, the situation tells against any irrevocable distinction in this border region between the ways of settled and those of nomadic Arabs. 'King of the Arabs' is of course a claim of overlordship, not a statement of fact. The Nemara inscription however mentions settlements and tribes extending to the borders of the Yemen (the ancient kingdom of Sheba), indicating a consolidation of tribal influence under the Tanukh on the edges of Roman rule in western Arabia. This phenomenon was surely connected, as the Zenobia legend in its broadest sense implies, with the decline of Palmyra and the retrenchment of the Roman frontier in the east as Arabic power in the desert grew in coherence and comprehensiveness.

Another possible illustration of this process concerns the Saracen queen known to Classical sources as Mavia or Maouia (Arabic Mâwiya), whose raids on the borders of Palestine, Phoenicia and Egypt after the death of her husband culminated in a great battle against the Romans in which the *magister militum* of the east, summoned to help by the military commander of Palestine and Phoenicia, was lucky to escape with his life.[88] The events of the battle, wrote Sozomen in the fifth century, were in his day still remembered in those districts, and celebrated in Arab song (*Hist. Eccl.* 6.38.4). The insurrection of Mavia, if it can be called that, was ended by a treaty involving the marriage of her daughter to an east Roman general. In addition, the queen received into her dominions a Christian monk as bishop, with a view to the conversion of her people to Christianity. Despite the battle, which was clearly no trivial affair, the

XIV. Barbarians and Bandits

scale and duration of the Saracen raid of Mavia are not clear, and we are informed neither of the reasons for her breaking of the existing treaty with Valens (it no doubt lapsed with the death of her husband, but it did not follow that Mavia would at once attack Roman provinces), nor of the terms of this or of her new treaty with the Roman government; the latter at least, comprising a dynastic marriage and the giving of a bishop, seems consonant with, although it does not prove, Roman rather than Saracen initiative. The story of queen Mavia is told by ecclesiastical historians with emphasis upon a religious dimension, and in later sources with a foray into romantic fiction – the captured Christian slave through her beauty becoming the consort, and after his death the successor, of an Arab sheikh. None of this is true, nor does it express what was the most important aspect at the time.[89] This was political and social, with military and diplomatic implications; again, we have a semi-legendary historical figure who can plausibly be seen as more than the head of an individual Arab grouping, the leader, perhaps, of an association of tribes – even if, by the standards of Imru'l-qais 'king of the Arabs', it was a modest one. Despite the remark of a mid-fourth century source that the Saracens accepted the rule of women (n. 77 above), it is going far beyond the evidence to see Mavia as the actual successor of Imru'l-qais; the scope of her raids, and the extension of her power, were much more limited than this suggestion would imply. As for the Christian conversion of her people, this had presumably not progressed far by 378, for it was a Saracen provided by Mavia to the Roman service by the terms of her treaty with Valens who so shocked the Goths by his barbarous conduct before Constantinople (p. 348). This is the sole aspect of the relations of queen Mavia with Rome to be mentioned by Ammianus. He describes the Saracen detachment at Constantinople as a recent arrival there (31.16.5), but does not indicate from where or from whom it had come, nor the circumstances in which it had entered Roman service.

Saracens otherwise participate in Ammianus' narrative in relation to the Persian campaign of Julian. Their chiefs approached Julian to present a crown and offer their services at Callinicum, the assembly point for the fleet and army. The fleet, indeed, arrived with exquisite timing just when the Saracens were being heard by the emperor. No doubt they were impressed; it was not often that desert Arabs saw a thousand ships launched upon the Euphrates (p. 167)! Their services were accepted as suitable for the more clandestine aspects of warfare; 'ut ad furta bellorum appositi' (23.3.8). Both sides in the conflict, Roman and Persian, made use of, and were used by, the desert populations between them. At an early stage of the campaign the Romans encountered the Persian general Surena accompanied by a Saracen chief in alliance with him; this was 'Malechus son of [or, also known as] Podosac(i)s', phylarch of the Saraceni Assanitae, a notorious bandit long accustomed to ravaging Roman frontier regions with great violence; 'Malechus Podosacis nomine, phylarchus Saracenorum Assanitarum, famosi nominis latro, omni saevitia per nostros limites diu grassatus' (24.2.4; p. 148). Leaving aside its now familiar stereotype of brigandage, Ammianus' language suggests important aspects of Malechus' position, possibly also of Arab society. His name (if Ammianus has not confused it with a title) is the Semitic 'malik', or 'king'; as a title, it is used of Imru'l-qais in the inscription of Nemara. 'Phylarchus' is the Greek term used to designate those sheikhs whose position as head of their tribe was recognised for political purposes by the Roman (in this case the Persian) government. The description of the phylarch as a 'bandit' who ravaged Roman frontier districts means little more than that his people conducted a normal Saracen lifestyle in a context defined by his allegiance to the Persian interest.

The most interesting, if perhaps the most speculative, detail is however the name of his people, the 'Saraceni Assanitae'. It is entirely possible that this is the first surviving reference in any source to the Ghassanids of sixth-century relations between east Rome and Persia.[90] By then they had migrated to the western fringes of the Syrian desert and are found in the employ of the Romans. There is nothing strange in such a migration, considered either geographically or politically. In a complementary shift of location and political allegiance, the pro-Persian counterparts of the Ghassanids, the Lakhmids of al-Hira, connected themselves by descent with that sheikh Jadhima who was murdered by Zenobia, and whose Arab 'tropheus' was buried near Bostra; his nephew and successor, the father of Imru'l-qais 'king of the Arabs' of the inscription from Nemara, is described in later Arab sources as the founder of the Lakhmid dynasty. The validity of this claim is in the present context not critical; its effect is to document the region from which the later Lakhmids believed themselves to have come, and to attest the possibility of these great tribal movements in the desert zone.

It will also be recalled, though Ammianus is not our source for it, that Julian was killed in battle in Persia by a 'Taiênos', that is to say a Tayy Arab fighting on the Persian side (p. 183). Ammianus remarked in the same general context that the Persians had one particular group of Saracens fighting for them because Julian, when approached by them for the payments and gifts they were used to receiving, had turned them away with the words that he had plenty of iron but no gold to give (25.6.10). Julian's reply, and the Saracens' choice of the Persian allegiance, need to be understood from the point of view of desert tribesmen, for whom war between Rome and Persia was one of the relatively few ways available to them to enrich themselves, add variety to their lives, and provide a wider arena for their feuding. Writing in just such terms of a later period, the Persian wars of Anastasius, a Syriac chronicler, Joshua the Stylite, commented that 'to the Arabs on both sides this war was a source of much profit and they wrought their will upon both kingdoms'.[91] The sentence could serve as a motto on the relations of the desert Arabs with the Roman and Persian empires.

Brief and rhetorical as they are, Ammianus' descriptions of Arabs preserve the distinction between the urbanised Roman province of Arabia, and the Saraceni, nomadic Beduin who ranged over the whole

XIV. Barbarians and Bandits

region from Nile to Euphrates, herding and where necessary raiding for a livelihood, and cleverly exploiting the disagreements of the imperial powers at the settled fringes of their country. Ammianus describes them largely in a literary stereotype (though he had seen them), as lawless brigands who lived outside the physical and moral framework of Graeco-Roman life. The result is an over-simplification rather than a rank falsification of their character. It has been observed that desert Arabs of any degree or category of nomadism actually lived near subsistence level, with little disparity of wealth between individuals and little functional specialisation in their society,[92] which is at least partly consistent with Ammianus' description of them as warriors of equal standing or fortune; 'omnes pari sorte bellatores' (14.4.3). 'Bellatores' is however too narrow a criterion even for Ammianus' own description, for his account is not only of war-bands, but of the pattern of life of the social groups that supported them. As for the more subtle forces of tribal prestige, ancestral distinction and honour sustained by legend and protected by the blood-feud, forces which provided Beduin society with its internal coherence, such matters lay beyond the mere observation of physical conduct, and so beyond the range of perception available to Ammianus. In their essence, Beduin society and its rules and conventions, like those of the Huns and Alani, were for the urbanised Graeco-Roman observer a profound mystery.

*

It is obvious that in viewing both Huns and Saracens through the eyes of Ammianus, we are presented with stereotypes of social conduct, especially in the sharp distinction that he, like his predecessors, draws between the nomadic and the settled.[93] As in the story of Cain and Abel (such is the depth of ancestry of the stereotype), keepers of sheep do not till the ground and plant corn, nor do they build cities (cf. Genesis 4:2f., 17). They have no written laws, they do not cook their food, they dislike roofed buildings, they conceive, give birth to and rear their children on mobile wagons and, in the case of the Saracens, conduct their sexual relations with abandoned passion; that is, they lack civilised restraints in every form and are defined by contrast with those who possess them.

For Ammianus and other Classical writers, the image of the settled Arab tends to be confused with or contaminated by that of the Beduin of the desert, through such concepts as brigandage and banditry, themselves stereotypes of the behaviour of rootless, marginal people in their impact upon the settled. In the case of the Alani, Ammianus relates them to Classical order by identifying them with people already mentioned by Herodotus and subsequent ethnographers. That Ammianus is here performing a rhetorical exercise, and that the language of Herodotus in describing such folk already involves stereotypes is evident, but it is important not for this reason to underestimate the value of their accounts as perceptions of the pastoral-nomadic world, very unlike that of the Greeks and Romans, that existed north of the Black Sea. In the case of the Huns, Ammianus makes no such comparisons. The Huns were novel and outrageous to Goths and Romans alike, and Ammianus conveys this not only by the character of his descriptions, but by refusing even those ethnographical allusions that might have incorporated the Huns as an exotic part of the barbarian world. The Huns, 'inusitatum hominum genus' (31.3.8), cannot be compared to anybody.

Both in the east and on the Danube, the Roman empire came into contact with nomadic peoples. There are however important differences in the historical character of the confrontations in the two areas. The Arabs impinged directly upon the existing borders of the Roman empire. Here, the settled desert fringe, where rainfall and water conservation begin to make possible Mediterranean-style agriculture in the territories of the cities, adjoins the areas of nomadism – which, as we saw earlier, might periodically expand to bring the nomads into conflict with the settled areas, but normally permitted a *modus vivendi* acceptable to both sides. From the Roman point of view, the frontier systems of our archaeological knowledge were designed to counter the socio-political situation existing immediately beyond them; beyond that, relations were maintained not by direct intervention, but by constantly fluctuating friendships and alliances, depending on the self-interest of the participants. The desert Arabs were for their part located in the gravitational field of the two empires of Rome and Persia, a situation that helps define the nomadic region from all sides of the settled Fertile Crescent; while the rivalries between the two empires gave focus, incentive and impetus to a Beduin lifestyle, which could be exploited by one side or the other. If it is also true, as suggested above, that the third century saw developments in the coherence of desert society in the form of incipient federations of Arab peoples, then this phenomenon, when set in the context of the rival postures of the Roman and Persian empires that continued into the early Byzantine period, enables us to see the rise of Islam partly in terms of developments already inherent in pre-Islamic Arab society.

Unlike that of the Arabs, the Huns' first impact upon the Romans was indirect, for it was mediated by the Goths, to whom the Huns were as outlandish as they were to the Romans. Even the Goths were at first shielded from direct contact with the Huns by the Alani, a pastoral people but one relatively well known to them, as to the Romans, from their long presence east of the Don; in fact, they were there long before the Goths arrived in the country to the west (p. 336). Only when, in a classic stage of the growth of empires of steppe peoples, the Huns combined with the Alans and adopted a more predatory posture, were the Goths confronted by nomadic invasion.[94] In consequence of their own displacement in this process, the Goths themselves appeared to the Romans, when they came to the Danube in 376, as a wandering people. They came with their wagon trains, as if they too were nomads of the steppe; but this, we have seen, is a superficial impression. The Goths were displaced agriculturalists

XIV. Barbarians and Bandits

looking not for rights of transit and seasonal grazing, but for land to settle and farm.

Unlike the desert Arabs, the Huns as we see them were not caught in the fields of influence of rival empires. They approached the Roman empire in the final phase of a long westward movement through the steppe corridor north of the Aral and Caspian Seas, and were far removed from the regions of their origin and first expansion; whether or not the Huns were the same as the 'Hsiung-Nu' of Chinese sources of the period is an interesting question but not one with any relevance to their contemporary situation in the west.[95] Further, when they enter our perception in their attacks on the Alani and then, with the Alani, on the Goths, they have already made the transition from a nomadic to a predatory phase of existence. Subsequently, as they enter the Danubian basin the Huns become in part sedentarised, until we see them, or at least their upper orders, living in the loosely organised village society described in the memoir of Priscus mentioned earlier. Such a development – the divergence of Hunnish society from its pastoral nomadic state, first in a more predatory and then in a more sedentary phase – may help to account for the rapid collapse of the fifth-century Hunnish 'empire'. The social ties that had unified the Huns in a period of migration and conquest were weakened as a more settled lifestyle based on the extortion of tribute and services from the conquered populations, which was adopted at least by the tribal elite and their followers, diverged from the pastoral economic base of the mass of the people: in addition to which, the Huns were never able to impose themselves demographically upon their subject populations.[96] Hunnish society disintegrated into its constituent clans and tribes under the impact of military defeat and the death of its charismatic leader, Attila. Above all, the Huns lacked that age-old balance between the nomadic and the settled, both within their own society and with their neighbours, that characterises the Arabs of the Syrian and Arabian desert, and is an essential element in the rise of Islam.

(3) Rebels: Isaurians and Moors

(i) Isauria and Isaurians

The territory of the Isaurians lay in the mountain hinterland of the coast of southern Asia Minor extending between the cities of Side in the west and Seleucia (modern Silifke) in the east, overlooking to the north the territories of Iconium (Konya) and Laranda (Karaman).[97] Defined geographically, the region forms part of the western Taurus, the mountain chain which provides the southern limit of the Anatolian plateau, and in its eastern extension continues past Commagene into Armenia and Kurdestan. The mountains in the Isaurian sector of the Taurus, created by complex folding against the Anatolian plateau, are broken and irregular in pattern, geologically too young to have been

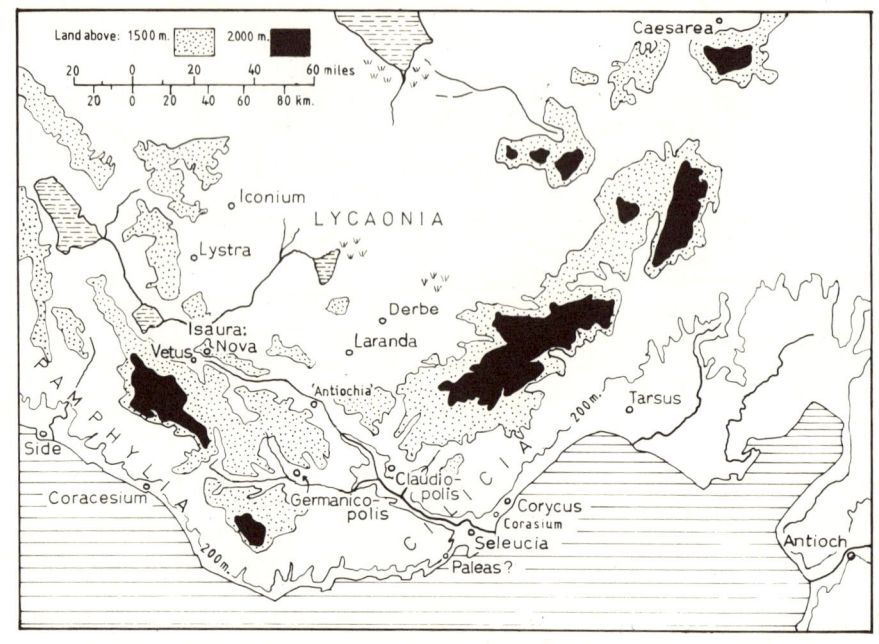

Map 8. Isauria and its neighbours.

penetrated by rivers from the interior, which drain inland into marshes and shallow lakes of varying and indeterminate size. Here, to the north of the mountains, lay the high plains of Lycaonia, bleak and spare, grazing rather than agricultural country (Strabo has there sheep and wild asses), but easy of transit and containing well-established cities such as Iconium and Laranda with their territories, and smaller towns such as Lystra and Derbe, known from a famous visit of St. Paul described in Acts of the Apostles; in the former town, Paul and Barnabas were acclaimed by the local populace in the Lycaonian language – the apostles' visit also flushing out a local priest of Jupiter who believed that his god had come to town, and hostile Jews from the metropolis of Iconium, who were clear that he had not (Acts 14:6ff.).

The narrow coastal strip, not strictly part of Isauria but of Pamphylia and Cilicia, has few harbours, and those that exist are difficult of access from the interior; hence their importance, in the late Republic, as the base of operation of the famous Cilician pirates, operating from harbour towns such as Coracesium (Alanya), where they were finally defeated by Pompey. The northern slopes of the Taurus, more precisely the districts around Sugla Gölü (Lake Trogitis), were the homeland of other neighbours of the Isaurians who enter early into Roman history, the Homonadenses. These were an intransigent and well-organised federation of peoples, possessing, according to Pliny, an 'oppidum' called Omana and forty-four strongpoints ('castella') among the mountains

(*Hist. Nat.* 5.94). Their pacification by the Romans was only completed, and then with difficulty, in the time of Augustus.[98] Subsequently the area was not actively occupied by Roman forces, but rather 'picketed' by military settlements and emplacements controlling the valleys and points of access, in a policy of containment that was not invariably successful but offered a more satisfactory return than any other.

The administrative organisation of the area was complex, perhaps deliberately so, for the effect was to break up its unity by denying to the peoples of the region their natural boundaries. Confined by Pisidia to the east, Lycaonia to the north and Cilicia to the east and south, but ethnically distinct from all three, the region of 'Isaurikê', as Strabo called it (12.6.2), fell in the early empire under the provincial jurisdiction of Lycaonia; it had earlier been part of the client kingdom of that Amyntas of Galatia who founded the new city of Isaura Nova (below, p. 358). In the second century, as part of Cilicia Tracheia ('Rough Cilicia') the region comprised one of the three divisions, the others being Lycaonia and Cilicia Pedias ('Level Cilicia'), of an enlarged Cilician province governed by a legate of consular rank (*ILS* 8827: Zengibar Kalesi). Not until the late empire was the name Isauria actually applied to a province, and then it covered more than the Isaurian region, extending to the coast which did not properly belong to it. From the early fourth century if not before, the province was administered by a military governor or 'dux et praeses', sometimes at the rank of 'comes'. The governor, later styled in full 'comes rei militaris per Isauriam et praeses', by exception from normal practice combined civil and military powers (*Not. Dig., Or.* 29.6).[99] The nature of the province was thereby conceded. It had a garrison and an internal defensive system, to protect the settled country from the depredations of the mountain folk. The illustration in the *Notitia Dignitatum*, more individually characterised than most, shows the city of Tarsus on a plain by the sea, and behind it mountains with wild beasts and fortress towers.

This description, combined with the reputation of the area for endemic banditry, may yet give a misleading picture of its economic character. Isauria is not simply a secluded mountain fastness. It is also the region drained by the river Calycadnus (Göksu Nehir) and its tributaries, which provide a wide variety of possibilities for rural and urban development. In addition, although their rapid drainage tends not to promote agriculture, its beds of porous limestone contain supplies of fresh, pure water, providing perennial springs and, at higher altitudes, lush mountain pasture. Although it does not encompass the economic complexity of the country, Ammianus' formulaic description of Isauria in his digression on the eastern provinces as 'rich in the vine and in the fruits of the earth – 'uberi palmite viret et frugibus multis' (14.8.1) – is not misleading as an indication of local conditions. Roman cities such as Claudiopolis (modern Mut), the two Isauras Vetus and Nova, and Germanicopolis (Ermenek), occupied sites by the main river valleys, commanding fertile, well-watered territories and routes of communication. Below the town of Ermenek, wrote a nineteenth-century visitor, the Rev. E. J. Davis, a long declivity of fertile and well-cultivated land extends to a distance of one and a half hour's ride down the Ermenek river. All the newer portion of Ermenek is built here, and some of the houses in this quarter are really good, and surrounded by fine gardens and orchards. The supply of water is extremely abundant in the upper town, almost every second street having its fountain, ice-cold and pure .... On the opposite side of the river, facing the town, there is a vast declivity, well cultivated and full of villages. Some of them seem of considerable size .... At the top of the declivity is a great mountain plateau, in which are the yailas [summer pasturages] of the various villages; but in winter it is impassable from snow. (*Life in Asiatic Turkey*..., 352f.)

Another traveller, William Leake, had seen the site of Claudiopolis as indicative, despite its depressed state when he went there in 1800, of a once great prosperity. After a description of the then extensive ruins of the Classical city, Leake goes on to give an almost lyrical description of the beauty and fertility of the site,

in a valley which promises the greatest abundance and fertility, and which is certainly capable of supporting a large population. Its scenery is of the greatest beauty; the variegated pastures, groves and streams are admirably contrasted with the majestic forms and dark forests of the high mountains on either side. (*Journal of a Tour in Asia Minor*, 109)

Such passages can be multiplied many times over in the descriptions of these and other travellers in the region.[100]

In his digression on the eastern provinces, in addition to the 'many towns' ('oppida') of the province, Ammianus names the cities of Seleucia and Claudiopolis, setting aside Isaura Vetus as previously powerful but overcome as rebellious and now showing but few traces of its former greatness; 'antehac nimium potens, olim subversa ut rebellatrix interneciva, aegre vestigia claritudinis pristinae monstrat admodum pauca' (14.8.2). The site of Isaura Vetus is now located by an inscription at or near the modern town of Bozkir, in the valley of the river Çarsamba which was diverted to facilitate the capture of the place by P. Servilius Isauricus in 75 BC (Sallust, *Hist.* 2, fr. 87; Frontinus, *Strat.* 3.7.1; cf. Amm. 14.8.4). The fine hilltop city visited by William Hamilton in 1837 a few miles to the east at Zengibar Kalesi, with extensive ruins including a monumental arch in honour of Hadrian and a gateway dedicated to Marcus Aurelius, and inscriptions commemorating magistrates, priests, and a provincial governor, is therefore not, as assumed until recently, Isaura Vetus, but its nearby successor in prosperity, Isaura Nova (a place not mentioned by Ammianus).[101] Isaura Nova had been given by Octavian to Amyntas of Galatia, who, abandoning Isaura Vetus, built himself a palace in his new city but had not finished fortifying it when he was killed in war with the Homonadenses (Strabo 12.6.3). The security so important to Amyntas may explain the continued success of Isaura Nova after the decline of its neighbour, the city being protected by its hilltop

XIV. Barbarians and Bandits

site and enabled from its position right on the watershed of the Çarsamba and the Calycadnus to dominate and provide stability to an area whose pacification was never quite certain. Ammianus' phrase 'antehac nimium potens' of Isaura Vetus looks back to the Hellenistic period, when Diodorus (18.22) attests its prosperity in a description of the attack on it by king Perdiccas in 322 BC, and his reference to its 'subversion' is to its capture by Servilius Isauricus in 75 BC. Ammianus is not pointing to any decline that had occurred in his own day or since the early Roman empire. As often in a digression, he is looking far back in history, in this case to the days when Isaura Vetus had, in truth, been a regional capital as opposed to the mere provincial city that it now was.

In a letter written in 374 to the bishop of Iconium, who had some responsibility for Isauria when its churches were disrupted by the Arian policies of Valens (*Ep.* 190), Basil of Caesarea referred to the 'small towns or chief villages' ('*mikropoliteiai* or *mētrokōmiai*') of Isauria that were accustomed in normal times to have a bishop. In seeking the secular counterpart of these arrangements – a province internally organised by towns and village communes of less than municipal status – we should direct our attention to lesser townships (Ammianus' 'oppida') such as Dalisandos, and of village communities like that of the Gorgoromeis, revealed by recent archaeological surveys. The town of Dalisandos, known from documentary sources as one of twenty-five 'cities' of Isauria but not previously located, has been identified as a site in a small but fertile upper valley not far from the historic 'capitals' of Isaurian country, the two Isauras, but clearly coexisting with them. It was built in a 'typical upland basin, set in karstic limestones of the Toros mountains, well-watered ... surrounded by juniper and oak forest, cool in summer, rich in grazing – the environmental attributes characteristic of a Toros yayla'.[102] The Gorgoromeis for their part cultivated the land on the northern edge of Sugla Gölü, their centre being near the modern village of Akkisse. With their neighbours the Sedaseis, and no doubt other erstwhile fractions of the Homonadenses so far unknown to us, they formed village settlements connected to each other by social and economic ties now hidden, but important in their day and suggesting the possibility that in Isauria also the communities might have formed groups capable, like the Homonadenses, of concerted action. This conclusion is also implied by the ease with which Ammianus' Isaurians moved across the entire region in the first of the three rebellions that he describes (p. 363f.): this could not have been done without support from the villages and in the countryside. Strabo had written of the two Isauras, Vetus and Nova, as masters of many other villages, all of them settlements of bandits (12.6.2). While Strabo's use of the concept 'bandit' may be open to reinterpretation, his implication that their communities were interconnected through the cities of the region should be accepted. It would help to explain how it was that, after one uprising mentioned by Ammianus, the people of Germanicopolis could offer to intercede between the rebels, 'with whom they at all times had great authority', and the Roman government (27.9.7; below, p. 365).

In its combination of city and village settlement, river valley and mountain pasture, the Isaurian landscape offers an environment that may prove as elusive to the traveller – and to the archaeologist and historian – as it was difficult for the Romans. 'Our halting place that night', wrote the Rev. E. J. Davis, 'should have been the village of Bejeh, in the valley between Sarchizalana and Adrass, but we were told that all the villages would either be employed harvesting, or in their yailas, and we should find the place quite deserted.' In the event Davis and his party stayed with the village miller, 'who was bivouacking in the valley below, and gathering his harvest' (*Life in Asiatic Turkey*, 340f.). Strabo mentioned a fertile valley system of the Taurus which was cultivated by people who lived not actually on their land but on mountain edges overlooking it, some of them in caves (12.6.5). These people too lived under arms and from the safety of their mountains were wont to make inroads on the territories of others.

It is within this complex dynamic of settlement and land use that we must imagine the social patterns of Isaurian life. As is also borne out by more recent habitation in the area and by the frequent observations of travellers, apart from the cities, townships and villages, there was much dispersed settlement and seasonal transhumance, as families and entire communities moved between summer and winter farmsteads, in a manner characteristic of mountain dwellers of many regions and times;[103] the Turkish 'yayla' gives its name to a standard category of seasonal migration, and the patterns of social organisation and inter-communication that are involved, as the villagers of an entire district will pack up their belongings for a festive summer journey to the high pastures, and, in less festive mood, down again for the winter, are complex as well as in their detail delightful.[104] One can see too how an economic balance consisting of so many interrelated factors – mountain and valley, pastoral and agricultural, rural and urban – operating seasonally and in marginal climatic conditions, might in unfavourable circumstances break down, causing the hardship and social disruption which could express itself, in the eyes of surrounding city-dwellers and the Roman authorities, in brigandage. Classical sources repeatedly, and not without reason, connect the shepherd and the bandit. The resemblances between them, in terms both of observed behaviour and a functional understanding of their way of life, were considerable. Both made their living outside the settled framework of urban civilisation, and at the limits of the law-enforcing capabilities of the civic authorities. Shepherds were classic non-urban types, real outsiders who nevertheless depended (as did bandits) on the support of the town and village communities through which they passed, and they could not always be too fussy about the manner in which they secured their pasturage or, in hard times, found something to eat for themselves. The boundary between the legal and illegal, like that between the settled and unsettled territories traversed by the shepherds, must have constantly been crossed and re-crossed, and individual decisions whether or not to enforce

XIV. Barbarians and Bandits

the law made in a spirit of tolerant pragmatism. There must have been a willingness to accept as inevitable a certain level of violence at the fringes of settled life, and the risks of provocation had always to be weighed by the law-enforcing authorities. The consequence of an unwise or excessive punishment in ill-chosen circumstances or in an area of marginal security could, as we shall see in two cases mentioned by Ammianus (p. 362), be something close to insurrection, damaging to the settled life of a province and expensive to control.

For all its unruliness, Isauria was part of the Roman empire, and it is an error to think of it as a permanent enclave of dissension. Its young men served in the Roman, and later the Byzantine, armies, as had their predecessors as mercenaries of Hellenistic kings; while in the fifth and sixth centuries Isaurians acquire some reputation as builders, particularly during and after the reign of their compatriot Zeno, born Tarasis son of Kadisos from the village of Rousoumblada – true Isaurian names for a true Isaurian dynast.[105] But one would be hard pressed to show that the contribution of Isauria to the economy and culture of the empire matched that of its neighbours, who thought of it as a wild, inhospitable place. A friend and former pupil of Libanius, appointed governor of Isauria in 364, wrote from his province to his old teacher regretting his absence from the public baths of Antioch, where he could converse with others and hear what happened everywhere. Libanius demurred. Better be praised by visitors to the baths for his achievements elswhere, he replied, than sit there idly and extol the praises of others: besides which, his brother too had written to Libanius to say how much he disliked Arabia, where he was governor (*Ep.* 1133)! Libanius' letters to the brother show that he was having a hard time in his province, with troublesome cities, a painful journey there, bad weather and the fear of brigandage, even 'barbarians' – presumably desert Arabs – to fight (*Epp.* 1127, 1136). We may wonder at the literal truth of all this, but Libanius and his correspondents reflect clearly the educated man's view of such 'uncivilised' provinces as Isauria and Arabia. Comparing them with Asia, Syria, or even the less urbanised Cappadocia, one can understand such sentiments, while observing that there are few things more annoying to provincial folk or more likely to increase their suspicion and undermine their wish to be hospitable than the self-assumed superiority of metropolitan types.

Though one cannot believe everything written on the subject either in ancient or in modern times, the connections of Isauria with the empire had during the third century become more fragile. Zosimus, following Eunapius, describes at some length a rebellion under the Emperor Probus, in which an Isaurian bandit called Lydius raided the provinces of Pamphylia and Lycia and seized the old Roman colony of Cremna in Pisidia, which was then besieged by the Romans.[106] Lydius had sustained his enterprise by digging a tunnel from the city to a point outside the lines of investment and, when this failed, by reducing the numbers of unproductive inhabitants by expelling or killing them. His rebellion

362   *Part Two: Visa vel Lecta*

ended when, in a typical bandit's death, he was killed by one of his supporters (Zosimus 1.69).

For all the picaresque character of this episode, its basic historical authenticity is assured. No such credence can be attached to the pretender or 'archipirata' Trebellianus, alleged by the *Historia Augusta* to have declared himself emperor at the Isaurians' request, to have minted coins and established a palace stronghold 'in arce Isauriae', and to have ruled also in Cilicia before being tempted to the plain from the shelter of his mountains and defeated by a blatantly fictitious general of Gallienus (*Tyr. Trig.* 26.2-4). Yet some elements in the story may have value in relation to events of the fourth century, notably in the conception, reminiscent of the quotation from the *De Rebus Bellicis* with which this chapter began, of the role of their landscape in providing the Isaurians with a novel sort of 'limes', or frontier defence; 'regio eorum novo genere custodiarum quasi limes includitur, locis defensa, non hominibus'.[107] Then follow aspersions on the poor physique, feeble courage and lack of military and intellectual sophistication of the Isaurians: only their inaccessibility, it is alleged, could save them (ibid. 6f.). Since their rebellion under 'Trebellianus', they had been susceptible to the humanity of no emperor, but were treated as barbarians; 'pro barbaris habentur'. However unfair that judgment, few cultivated Romans of the fourth century would have disagreed with it.

*

Ammianus' account of the first and most extensive of the three Isaurian insurrections of the fourth century which he records, distinguishes between the general background of insecurity and the causes of the specific outbreak in question; 'olim quidem perduelles spiritus irrequietis motibus erigentes, hac tamen indignitate perciti vehementer, ut iactitabant ...' (14.2.1). These causes were very similar to those of the attacks of the Austuriani of the Sahara against the cities of Tripolitania, which will be described in the next chapter (pp. 383ff.). The Austuriani took to arms when one of their leaders was burned at the stake for illegal acts including what Ammianus regarded as conspiracy against the province; 'provinciam omni fallaciarum via prodere conabatur' (28.6.3). The Isaurians maintained that some of their number had been thrown to the beasts in the amphitheatre of Iconium in Pisidia (14.2.1); much as we see the same fate befalling wretched desert tribesmen in a series of mosaic pictures from a villa at Zliten in Tripolitania, east of Lepcis Magna.[108] In such cases, we have the authorities' response to acts of 'brigandage' perpetrated by men living outside the assumptions and outside the protection of civic life and Roman law. The penalties of burning alive and exposure to wild beasts, used respectively for the Austuriani and the Isaurians, were among those reserved for the lower-classes and unprivileged – ideal in fact for bandits, for all that the Isaurians alleged the execution of their colleagues to go beyond normal

XIV. Barbarians and Bandits 363

practice. It was, they claimed, 'praeter morem' (14.2.1). Their insistence on this point is unpersuasive, given the provision of a later law in the Theodosian Code that Isaurian bandits could be tortured during Lent and even on Easter Day – for God would certainly understand when the safety and welfare of many were thereby secured (*CTh* 9.35.7, of 408)! There would be interesting implications for the social standing at least of some of the 'bandits', if the punishments were 'praeter morem' in the sense that the rebel leaders belonged to the classes normally exempt from such penalties. This is no doubt to make too much of the phrase, but Ammianus must have meant something by it. Perhaps it was simply that the punishments had been meted out in circumstances or for offences that were normally overlooked, or treated more leniently according to the spirit of tolerant pragmatism mentioned earlier on the part of the authorities (p. 360f.).

The outbreaks of Isaurian aggression recorded by Ammianus fall under the years 353, 359, and 368. The first two outbreaks are linked by references to the abortive siege of Seleucia (14.2.14ff.; 19.13.1), but only the first is described in any great detail. It however provides Ammianus with material for a substantial narrative, which makes clear its geographical range and social origins, names regions and cities, describes terrain and the conditions of communication, and almost achieves the status of a campaign history, with separate phases and opposing strategies. It is in respect of scale, and not in terms of any declared aims of the insurgents, that the episode can be seen as a case of rebellion or civil war. The Isaurians had no such grandiose aims in mind; but equally, the episode went far beyond a sporadic outbreak of banditry, and acquired something of the character of a general movement.

The Isaurians were provoked into insurrection, as just explained, by the execution of some of their number at Iconium. Their first manoeuvre, however, was not in any direct sense an act of revenge against Iconium, for it took them in the opposite direction from that city. They descended from their mountains to the coasts and made night attacks on ships anchored there, killing the crews and making off with the cargoes of the vessels.[109] When news of this activity got around and ships abandoned the Isaurian harbours for the north coast of Cyprus, the insurgents made over the mountains for the open country of Lycaonia, where they barricaded the roads and robbed residents of the province and travellers through it (14.2.4). The terrain, and their mobile tactics, easily enabled the Isaurians to evade the military resistance from Roman 'municipia' and 'castella'. They could overcome footsoldiers sent against them by taking to the heights, but were at a disadvantage on the level ground of the plateau, and if caught there were massacred without difficulty (14.2.7).

To avoid the open terrain the Isaurians now by circuitous routes made for Pamphylia to the west, a province so far unaffected by the raids but strongly garrisoned against their eventuality; 'magnis undique praesidiis communitam' (14.2.8). They crossed the hills and descended to the river

Melas (Manavgat Çay), which they tried to cross on fishermen's boats and improvised craft but were prevented by 'legions' brought up from their winter quarters at nearby Side and stationed opposite, on the western bank of the river. After some isolated losses as some of their number tried to force the bank, the bandits re-crossed the mountains back to Laranda in Lycaonia, attacked villages in its vicinity but withdrew before a cavalry force and sent home for reinforcements. They now made again for the sea and spent three days and nights trying unsuccessfully to reduce a fortified place called Paleas, where, as was still the case when Ammianus wrote, were stored the supplies distributed to the soldiers who defended the Isaurian borders; 'ubi conduntur nunc usque commeatus, distribui militibus omne latus Isauriae defendentibus assueti' (14.2.13).[110] In increasing frustration they then made for Seleucia, which was protected by the regular garrison of the province, three hardened 'legiones' under count Castricius. If this was a bold move against the major and best guarded city of the region, it was justified in the event, for the Roman troops, having advanced from the city, declined battle and withdrew inside it. It was now the defenders of Seleucia who began to suffer shortage, while the Isaurians controlled the river Calycadnus and captured grain-ships sailing on it. They withdrew, however, and the insurrection came to a close, when Gallus Caesar ordered Nebridius, *comes Orientis*, to collect troops and relieve Seleucia. At this, the bandits returned to their native mountains, content perhaps with the supplies which their capture of the grain-ships had delivered into their possession.

The second episode, no more than a brief notice in Ammianus (19.13.1f.), reminds us of the abandoned siege of Seleucia, to tell how the Isaurians came down again from the mountains in 'dense companies' of men, using their knowledge of the country to avoid Roman military opposition. The appointment of Lauricius as *comes Isauriae* effectively subdued the outbreak. A capable man, Lauricius inhibited the Isaurians by threats of action rather than violence, and secured a period of quiet. Rather more than this was in fact involved, since an inscription also happens to record how Lauricius recovered from 'long occupation by bandits' and garrisoned a fortified post by the upper Calycadnus river on the hills to the north of Germanicopolis; 'castellum diu ante a latronibus possessum et provinciis perniciosum... occupavit' (*ILS* 740).[111] The circumstances in which the Isaurians had come into possession of this strongpoint, which gave them something approaching permanent control of the vicinity, are lost to us.

In the third episode (27.9.6-7), the Isaurians attack towns and estates of Pamphylia and Cilicia; that is, they are moving both east and west from their mountain enclave. Provoked to retaliation, the *vicarius* of Asia, Musonius, rushed from Sardis and raised against them the local militia, called Diogmitae or 'Pursuers', but was caught in an ambuscade and killed with his men. A former rhetorician at Athens, Musonius was hopelessly out of his depth in military operations such as had proved difficult for the best Roman generals. In the eyes of literary colleagues, his death was the most notable event of the uprising. It was mentioned in this sense in the history of Eunapius (Fr. 45), with citation of a Greek epitaph composed by one Theodorus, who summoned Eunapius to his presence in order to predict the catastrophe; the epitaph incongruously compared Musonius to Homeric heroes who had died in battle.[112] The bandits were then confined to the mountains by regular Roman forces and, with no food, asked for peace. This was conceded, and hostages given for good behaviour, the city of Germanicopolis being instrumental in pressing for these arrangements. In Ammianus' remark that the opinions of the Germanicopolitans 'always carried great authority with the Isaurians' – 'quorum apud eos ut signiferae manus semper valuere sententiae' (27.9.7) – we can glimpse the role of a city, seated in the rebellious area and able to act as intermediary in a conflict with which, through location, economic interest and social connections between themselves and the rebels, its citizens must have felt themselves to be closely involved.[113]

A common feature of all three episodes described by Ammianus is their military inconclusiveness. The Romans mobilise their forces, but are unable or unwilling to engage in set battles; this is especially conspicuous before Seleucia, where Castricius is not prepared to risk three regular 'legiones' against a less well equipped and organised, but presumably far more numerous, enemy. Though the Romans have much the better of the Isaurians on open ground, especially if they can use cavalry, they are unable to penetrate the mountains native to the Isaurians and are repelled with losses when they try. On the other side, the Isaurians deploy considerable numbers, far more than can simply be called a robber band, and more than can have operated as they did without substantial support from the countryside. They are described as advancing both in large groups and in smaller raiding parties. They are able to call for reinforcements, to move across the terrain and to negotiate, in the end giving hostages in the manner of a fully-fledged enemy of Rome. They are unable to force sieges, but share this inability with almost all adversaries of Rome except the Persians. Despite their apparent ability to plan their movements, at no point does Ammianus name any of their leaders, nor any Isaurian at all (nor indeed any Roman, except for military commanders), nor mention any individual exploit; in this respect his narrative is unlike that of Zosimus of the uprising of Lydius in the third century. This is no disadvantage if one feels that the details of Zosimus' account are more picturesque than credible, but the lack of reference to any individual Isaurian in Ammianus' narrative remains an interesting feature of it. The Isaurians must have had their leaders; their giving of hostages indicates that they were not all of negligible social rank, or at the very least that they contained some sort of hierarchy that could, from the Roman authorities' point of view, be effectively controlled in such a fashion.

Despite this lack of information from Ammianus about their personnel and leadership, the Isaurian targets in banditry are set out in all their resourceful variety and in their physical setting: ships at harbour, travellers on the road, towns, villages, country estates. The bandits attempt without success a military supply depot and seize grain-ships on the Calycadnus. Ammianus makes clear and relevant (as he should) the diversity of terrain over which the insurrections ranged: mountainous country overgrown with shrubs and thickets and divided by glens and ravines, rapid swirling rivers. The language is the normal historian's language for mountain warfare, but is effective, and can be very accurate in its detail. The river Melas, for example, reached by the Isaurians after crossing high mountains, deterred them by its depth and current as it ran between its banks through the plain near Side; 'cum, superatis difficultatibus arduis, ad supercilia venissent fluvii Melanis, alti et verticosi ...' (14.2.9). The Isaurians sought to cross it on fishermen's boats and hastily constructed rafts but were prevented by the legions brought up from winter quarters at Side. The Manavgat Çay is in fact navigable for light craft for some distance inland. It is swift and too deep to ford, and, until modern times having no bridge, could be crossed only by ferry. The river does, as Ammianus indicates, run in a curve and protect the inhabitants of the coastal plain beyond; 'qui pro muro tuetur accolas circumfusus' (14.2.9).[114] In contrast with river and mountains, there is then the open country of the Anatolian plateau, over which horsemen could range widely and where the Isaurians were at a disadvantage. Ammianus mentions the fortified towns and 'castella' surrounding the Isaurian country, the regular 'legions' of Seleucia under the *comes Isauriae* as well as those wintering at Side; the 'municipia' which could send out troops against them – specifying in one instance the local militia, or 'Diogmitae', taken into battle by Musonius; the harbours of the coast, abandoned for ports in Cyprus by sea-captains who heard what was afoot in Isauria (an indication of trade between Asia Minor and the Levant conducted by ships which could use either route); the travellers through Lycaonia whom the Isaurians made their victims when their coastal raids had driven away their sea-borne booty. The diplomatic initiative of Germanicopolis is mentioned, the response of Roman governors and commanders and, more distantly, of Gallus Caesar when he was told 'by frequent reports' what was happening in Isauria (14.2.20).

The point of view of the Isaurians themselves is left unspoken, though an insight is given by the execution in the arena of some of their leaders at Iconium and, in more than one passage, references to the hunger to which they were reduced. This too was how P. Sulpicius Quirinius had overcome the Homonadenses in the time of Augustus (Strabo 12.6.5).[115] If the Romans could not safely penetrate the mountains, they could blockade the exits from them and deprive the enemy of the food resources of the plains – as they did the Goths in 376-8 (above, p. 328). It was to seize imperial supplies stored there that the Isaurians attacked Paleas; and when reduced to submission after their defeat of Musonius, it was through hunger that they were forced to accept the Germanicopolitans' suggestion that they treat for terms. We saw that the first insurrection

XIV. Barbarians and Bandits

ended when the Isaurians withdrew from Seleucia before the approach of imperial forces – having taken supplies from the grain-ships on the river Calycadnus.

Isaurian incursions – or rather excursions, as they issued in all directions from their mountain enclave to the sea-coast and the adjacent provinces – are repeatedly presented in Classical sources as outbreaks of banditry or brigandage. Against this perspective should be put another, one with an equal social reality to those who were its victims: the alternation of economic success and failure in the life of the mountain people. For such men, the affluence of the cities and the fertility of their cultivated territories, if not envied in times of plenty, were a provocation in times of hardship. Seen in this way, 'brigandage' is less a description of fact than a commentary imposed by the urban Graeco-Roman observer on an economic situation that lay beyond his perception; it was not the last period in history in which uncaring governments have reduced to a simple question of 'law and order' – that is to say to the point of view of the governing classes – the social consequences of economic deprivation. It is a corollary of this situation that we have to visualise for ourselves what the real causes of outbreaks of disaffection may have been. It seems clear both of the Isaurian uprisings and of the attacks of Austuriani on the cities of Tripolitania, that they were not random, meaningless events or gratuitous outbursts of aggression against the Graeco-Roman cities and their territories, but expressions of some more profound economic adversity, producing a response of a more general character.[116] The Isaurians did not first retaliate against the lands of Iconium, the city where the execution of their leaders had taken place, but moved in the opposite direction, and even Ammianus believed that the execution of Stachao was not the true reason for the incursions of the Austuriani in Africa; 'hanc causam praetendentes ut seriam' (28.6.2). The true reason, for Ammianus, was that they were liable to such conduct by their nature, for that was how they lived; 'vivereque adsueti rapinis et caedibus'; but if this is any more than another statement of the prejudice of city dweller against desert people, it leaves unexplained why the latter were ever at rest, 'paulisper pacati'. Stachao, indeed, is said to have plotted against the province while moving freely about it in a time of peace, 'ut in otio nostra peragrando licentius' (28.6.3). There is an unstated mode of causation here, operating in the relations between city-dwellers and inhabitants of the hinterland, mountain or desert. It is economic and social in character, and not to be waved aside by casual reference to banditry and lawlessness, for that is simply to adopt the perspective of the city-dwellers and their spokesmen, the government authorities. For Ammianus to have adopted this perspective is natural, but it would be wrong for the modern historian to be content with it.

(ii) Moors and Mauretania

The Grande Kabylie, extending between the cities of Icosium (Algiers) and Saldae (Bougie), is a moist and in modern times heavily populated coastal massif, part of the series of mountain ranges which, beginning with the Tell Atlas in the west and ending in the east with the Aurès Mountains and the hills of Proconsular Africa, determine the geophysical structure of north Africa.[117] Conforming to this pattern, and in this respect like the Taurus mountains of Isauria, the Grande Kabylie lies from west to east, with few, and no easy direct routes of penetration from the hinterland to the coast. As in the case of Isauria, the massif is surrounded by Roman urban settlements, both on the coast and placed inland at river-valley sites and along the main route from Sitifis (Sétif) to Auzia (Aumale) and its lateral offshoots into the foothills. The Romans had not tried to occupy the mountains intensively, being content to surround them with military emplacements and veteran colonies connected by good roads; and here again, as in Isauria, uprisings of mountain peoples had threatened the cities and townships located in their vicinity. In the third century, rebellions of the tribal federation known as the Quinquegentiani, first in mid-century and later in the time of the Tetrarchy, were significant events, requiring intervention from Roman military authorities at a high level – in the second case the presence of the Emperor Maximian, who campaigned there in 297. These were the most general instances of a tendency to disorder widely attested in individual episodes. Q. Gargilius Martialis of Auzia is claimed in an inscription to have secured the capture and death of 'the rebel Faraxen'. The same inscription, set up by the town council of the colony of Auzia, commemorated his subsequent death at the hands of the Bavares, a local tribe; 'insidiis Bavarum decepto' (*ILS* 2767).

In other ways, the situation in Mauretanian Africa was unlike that in Isauria, the disturbances there being linked to a tribal organisation that still persisted in the late empire and is not to be detected in Isauria. The advance westwards of Roman power into Mauretania had been largely achieved not by the suppression but by the exploitation in Roman interests of the indigenous tribal structure – under the supervision, often, of 'praefecti gentis' appointed by the Romans[118] – and insurrection may more readily take the form more of organised rebellion than of the banditry characteristic of Isauria. The difference is to some extent one of definition, and of the extent of our knowledge; the effect on local communities was much the same in either case, and the mass of the surviving evidence reveals the organisation of Moorish society as it does not reveal that of Isaurian, to which it was possibly more similar than appears at first sight. The different nature of our background knowledge, and of Ammianus' own information (p. 380f.), must be borne in mind in considering his accounts of insurrection in the two areas.

One difference meets the eye immediately. If the outbreaks in Isauria and among the Austuriani of Tripolitania had as their immediate cause the punishment of some of their number in Roman cities by methods reserved for the lower classes, the rebellion in Mauretania originated at an entirely different social level. It arose from dynastic disputes following the death of a powerful Moorish chief, Nubel – 'regulus per nationes Mauricas potentissimus', as Ammianus describes him (29.5.2). Nubel had left numerous offspring, legitimate and by concubines, and one of the latter, Zammac, was murdered by a legitimate son, Firmus, no doubt in pursuit of his inheritance. No consequence need have arisen, but for the fact that Zammac enjoyed good relations with the *comes Africae* Romanus (the same who was involved in the complaints of the Tripolitanians to Valentinian). Denounced by Romanus in reports to the emperor for his murder of Zammac, and unable to defend himself against Romanus' connections at court, Firmus was forced into revolt; 'ab imperii dicione descivit' (29.5.3).

Valentinian took the outbreak seriously, appointing the *magister equitum* Theodosius to lead an expeditionary force, which sailed from Arles to Igilgili in Mauretania Sitifensis in the early summer of 373 (29.5.5).[119] Theodosius went first to Sitifis to organise his campaign, which can conveniently (while omitting in detail the actual fighting described by Ammianus) be presented in four main strategic stages. First, linking his forces with the army of the province, he marched north-west from Sitifis to Tubusuctu on the edge of 'Mons Ferratus', the Grande Kabylie. Rejecting an embassy from Firmus because it had not brought hostages whose surrender had been agreed, Theodosius engaged the enemy and stormed 'fundus Petrensis', a strongpoint once owned by Zammac but now occupied by the supporters of Firmus, and then advanced to 'Lamfoctense oppidum' in the midst of tribal territory (29.5.13).[120] Christian priests now came from Firmus escorting hostages, after which Firmus presented himself to Theodosius and was received with a formal gesture of reconciliation. This, says Ammianus, was merely in the public interest, 'quoniam id rei publicae conducebat', implying that even then Theodosius did not trust his adversary's good faith (29.5.16). Whatever Firmus' own attitude, the tribes were still in rebellion, and Theodosius advanced westwards to Tipasa and Caesarea, the chief city of the second of the Mauretanian provinces. Caesarea had been sacked and Tipasa besieged unsuccessfully by Firmus' supporters, the neighbouring city of Icosium (Algiers) being given up to Theodosius as part of the agreement between them, together with the return of military standards and the crown of a provincial priest. What had happened to the priest is not stated.

At Caesarea, Theodosius established that Firmus' submission had been a tactical ploy and that he was still encouraging rebellion (29.5.19); so the second phase of the campaign began with further advances along the Oued Chélif, which runs to the west and enters the Mediterranean not far from Oran. Ammianus names among the settlements that were involved 'municipium Sugabarritanum' (Zucchabar/Miliana), 'Tigaviae' or Tigava castra, and, if his text is reliable at this point, 'Tingitanum castellum' (Orléansville). After these and other operations, Theodosius returned to Tipasa in February (of 374) and conducted negotiations with a number of tribes of the region; Baiurae, Cantauriani, Avastomates, Cafaves,

'Davares' (perhaps the Bavares, the tribe that killed Q. Gargilius Martialis) and unnamed 'neighbours' of theirs (29.5.33).

In the third phase, seeing the war turning against him, Firmus fled to the remote and inaccessible 'Caprarienses montes', where Theodosius pursued him, able to do so safely because Firmus' support began further to disintegrate upon his departure (5.34f.). A passing reference to 'Ethiopians' with whom Theodosius made a truce would lead far to the south, to the regions of the Hodna, or even to the Aurès Mountains and the Sahara edge; but how precisely is Ammianus (or his source) using the expression? Firmus had installed Roman captives in a place called 'civitas Contensis', a fortified site in a remote and high location, but its name is not otherwise known and the place could be anywhere in a mountainous terrain (29.5.39).

The final phase of the campaigns finds Theodosius back in the north, in and around the fortified town of Auzia (29.5.44). He then returned to Sitifis by way of the towns of Mauretania Caesariensis (29.5.50). If this was by the main route from Auzia to Sitifis, then these will have been such settlements lying on and near it as Equizeto, Thamallula, Sertei and Sava. Near Sitifis, Theodosius received the surrender of Firmus' last allies. To the frustration of the chieftain who betrayed and imprisoned him in hope of a reward, Firmus committed suicide and his corpse was brought to the Roman camp on a camel. As a final, calculated mark of humiliation, it was transferred to a pack-animal for its actual delivery to Theodosius (29.5.55). Not long before, Firmus had displayed himself on horseback in a purple cloak, exhorting Theodosius' soldiers to surrender their commander to him as a brutal martinet (29.5.48).

The campaigns had in these well-defined stages encompassed the mountain mass of the Grande Kabylie and the Mitidjian Atlas, first advancing by the Oued Soummam through the Kabylie and, after the western excursion along the course of the Chélif and the pursuit of Firmus to distant parts, returning by the axial road from Auzia to Sitifis. The physical relationship of Roman cities with mountain massif which characterises settlement in the area is not coincidental, but a direct expression of the cities' need for the water collected and distributed by the mountains. Therein lay a problem of security, for unrest in the mountains would express itself in raids and incursions, on a smaller or larger scale, into the city territories. The Romans had not penetrated the Grande Kabylie in the full sense of military occupation and control. As in the case of the Hodna and, in essentials, the Aurès Mountains north of the Sahara (not to mention Isauria), their procedure was one of containment by roads, by garrisons at points of access to the mountains and strongpoints in the valleys. At the Sahara edge, the strategy was reinforced by the so-called 'fossatum Africae', a visible demarcation, supported by the capacity to take military action, of the extent of the settled territory to the north.[121]

Ammianus' account directly or indirectly incorporates several of the features of these arrangements. Of the places named by him, Tubusuctu,

XIV. Barbarians and Bandits

'castellum Tingitanum' and Auzia are listed in the *Notitia Dignitatum* as the central points of internal *limes* sectors in Mauretanian Africa (*Occ.* 25.27, 34; 30.17): another, Bida – 'limes Bidensis' in the Notitia (*Occ.* 25.35; 30.13) – is not named by Ammianus, but Theodosius would have passed it on his first march through the Kabylie from Tubusuctu to Caesarea and Icosium. The troops of the province which Theodosius joined to his own at the outset of the campaign ('consociato indigena milite', 29.5.9) were presumably the troops listed in the *Notitia* under the command of the *comes Africae*. One of their units, Equites Armigeri Iuniores (*Occ.* 6.37=80; 7.198), had been commanded, as an inscription shows, by none other than the 'regulus' Nubel whose death created the circumstances for the rebellion (*ILCV* 1822; p. 373). The integration of tribal power within the Roman defensive system implied by the inscription is fundamental to an understanding of the structures of authority in Mauretanian Africa.

Alongside the army and *limes* sectors, Roman policy in Mauretania depended on the co-operation of the tribal dynasts, whom the Roman occupation had not removed from their position; at one and the same time they guaranteed their own loyalty to the Roman power, and, through their control of the attitude of their tribesmen, the peace of the province. These chiefs and princes, and their seats of power, figure prominently in Ammianus' narrative of the campaigns of Theodosius. Apart from the main protagonists, Nubel, Firmus and Zammac, he mentions Mascizel and Dius, leaders of the 'Tyndenses' and 'Masinissenses' in the region of Tubusuctu (29.5.11). They are described as 'brothers' of Firmus, but this is perhaps not exact for the extended family of a Moorish prince, and, even if taken strictly as denoting a blood relationship, does not distinguish the 'legitimate' from the 'illegitimate' among Nubel's offspring. A 'sister' of Firmus was Cyria, another dynastic figure who contributed to his support 'great riches and feminine determination'; 'abundans divitiis et destinatione feminea' (29.5.28). It was with Igmazen, chief of the Isaflenses, that Firmus and his 'brother' Mazuca took refuge when the rebellion began to crumble (29.5.40ff., 51f.), while from the Mazices come Bellen, described as 'princeps', and Suggen, a 'leader' (ductor), of the tribe (29.5.21, 27). A *praefectus gentis* named Fericius was executed with Bellen for supporting the rebellion (29.5.21, 24). While Firmus' 'brother' Mascizel joined the rebellion, another prince, Gildo, fought with the Romans against his own people; he is found operating with Maximus – perhaps Magnus Maximus, the later usurper (29.5.21).[122] By an irony, when Gildo, then *magister militum* in north Africa and allied by marriage with the house of Theodosius, later rebelled against the government of Honorius and Stilicho in 395, it was Mascizel who was sent to suppress him. He was thanked, on his return to Italy, by being pushed to his death from a bridge, or so it was alleged (Zosimus 5.11.4f.).

We are reminded often in the details as well as the general pattern of Ammianus' narrative, that this was a relatively un-Romanised part of the empire, where native culture and social structure survived and exercised great influence on the life of the Roman province. The 'regulus' Nubel, according to Ammianus, had been born among the tribe of the Iubaleni, amid the 'high mountains and tortuous paths' near Auzia (29.5.44); though, as his inscription from Rusguniae shows, he had extended his influence through the Kabylie to the coast (*ILCV* 1822) and, of course, to the tribes of the surrounding regions; he was after all, as Ammianus remarks, 'potentissimus'. It was a land of diverse cultures and languages, 'dissonas cultu et sermonum varietate nationes plurimas', as Ammianus described a Moorish army drawn up against Theodosius (29.5.28). Similar though less explicit phrases are used of the babel of languages spoken among other 'barbarian' armies, Persian and Gothic (19.1.8; 31.7.11), but this is not to say that they have no circumstantial validity; especially in the case of the Persians, the contrary is the case. The names of some of the Moorish leaders, Igmazen, Suggen, Bellen, like 'the rebel Faraxen' in the third century (p. 368), have the termination in '–en' or '–in' characteristic of Libyan personal names, as recorded on inscriptions from end to end of Roman north Africa, and even in literary references in Roman writers.[123] On another point of tribal structure among the Moors, we have already seen the possibility that the designation 'brother' (and 'sister'), applied to several leaders in their relationship with Firmus, may have a broader meaning in the setting of the extended family of a Moorish prince than it would have in the context of Roman family relations.

We further encounter the power-centres of these tribal chieftains, fortified rural seats such as the 'fundus nomine Mazucanus' where Theodosius brutally punished Roman deserters; it was no doubt a possession of the prince Mazuca, a supporter of Firmus (29.5.31, 41f.). Another such settlement, 'fundus Gaionatis' near Tigaviae, was fortified by a strong wall and served as a refuge for the rebels. It was a substantial place, for in order to capture it, Theodosius brought up battering rams, and levelled the walls to the ground before moving on; 'muro circumdatum valido, receptaculum Maurorum tutissimum, arietibus admotis evertit ...' (29.5.25). Such 'castella' of local chiefs are a feature of the archaeology and epigraphy of the region from the fourth century and earlier, and reflect the fundamental and unchanging social structure of the region.[124] It has been argued that we find the same thing in Isauria in the form of towers and enclosures apparently built by the landowners to secure local control of the country. This is a quite possible, and in general terms persuasive, interpretation, though the epigraphic evidence, and the supporting social situation, are less explicitly formulated than in the case of Mauretania.

Most interesting of all these power-seats of the Moorish nobility is 'fundus Petrensis', once the possession of Zammac and occupied by Firmus after his murder. As Ammianus says in describing its destruction by Theodosius, its master Salmaces had built it up 'like a city'; 'fundi Petrensis ... quem Salmaces dominus, Firmi frater, in modum urbis exstruxit' (29.5.13).

XIV. Barbarians and Bandits

By extreme good fortune there survives an inscription from 'fundus Petrensis' which sets the establishment, here named as 'Petra', in its geographical and diplomatic context. The inscription is a double acrostic in hexameters, in which the first and last letters of each line, read vertically, yield the words 'Praedium Sammacis'; its verses describe a fortified mountain site by a river (the Oued Soummam), established to secure peace among native peoples willing to set aside war and join in alliance with Sammac, and through him with the Romans, in whose 'triumphs' they then share (*ILS* 9351).[125] Ammianus names the brother murdered by Firmus first as 'Zammac' and then, in the context of his ownership of 'fundus Petrensis', as 'Salmaces' (29.5.2, 13). Why this should be so, and whether Ammianus even failed to realise the identity, are questions relating to his possible use of different sources for the two passages (p. 381); the identity itself is beyond any doubt. Sammac (Zammac, Salmaces) appears in his inscription just as Ammianus presents him, as a native prince inclined to favour, and to be favoured by, the Roman authorities. Ammianus' expression that Zammac was 'comiti Romano acceptus' (29.5.2) is an implicitly political definition of the Moorish prince's attitudes, and with his entire narrative shows how a tribal dispute could involve the issue of loyalty to the Roman power, to which the princes were allied and to the maintenance of which they were indispensible.

As for the father of Zammac-Salmaces, the adherence of Nubel to Roman ways is revealed in extraordinary diversity by another inscription (now lost, but preserved in a transcript) from the coastal town of Rusguniae (*ILCV* 1822). Here called Flavius Nuvel – the name 'Flavius' proclaiming him as a client of the house of Constantine – the Moorish 'regulus', as Ammianus called him, is described as the son of Saturninus, 'vir perfectissimus' and formerly 'comes', and his wife, 'honestissima femina'; the form of her name, not clear from the transcript, looks as if it were native rather than Roman. Fl. Nuvel was not only, as mentioned earlier, commander of the Equites Armigeri Iuniores of the *Notitia Dignitatum*; in fulfilment of a vow, with his own wife Nonnica and 'his entire family' (presumably including Firmus, if not his children by concubines!) he built a church at Rusguniae and dedicated there a fragment of the True Cross brought from the Holy Land; 'de sancto ligno crucis Christi Salvatoris adlato adque hic sito ... basilicam voto promissam adque oblatam cum coniuge Nonnica ac suis omnibus dedicavit'. It is a remarkable glimpse of the connections of a Moorish prince with the wider world, and, on a surprisingly precise level, with the religious ideology of the house of Constantine. The 'True Cross' is first mentioned in sermons of Cyril of Jerusalem in the later 340s, and the inscription of Fl. Nuvel is one of the very earliest attestations of its wider diffusion. Another, as it happens, is an inscription from a martyr's shrine near Sitifis of the year 359.[126]

The complexity of the issues of loyalty and personal motivation that were involved in the rebellion of Firmus is not surprising in a movement inspired, as this was, by the natural leaders of the country and directly involving the Roman authorities. The situation must have presented some difficult choices, as men calculated which was the more considerable danger – Moorish chief, corrupt Roman official, or distant and unpredictable imperial court. One of Theodosius' first actions was to send agents to arrest the deputy of the *comes Africae* for collaborating in his superior's maladministration; 'qui curans Romani vicem, incivilitatis eius erat particeps et furtorum' (29.5.6). The official in question and some others made themselves scarce, but emerged from hiding later (29.5.19). A company of mounted bowmen, perhaps themselves African, had gone over to the rebel together with some infantry of the Constantiani, one of whose tribunes had actually 'crowned' Firmus with a neck-chain for a diadem as if in an imperial proclamation; 'torquem pro diademate capiti imposuit Firmi' (29.5.20). Not only prince Bellen of the Mazices, but also their *praefectus gentis* or 'tribal commissioner' appointed by the Roman government, had joined the rebellion (29.5.21, 24). Two *curiales*, father and son, apparently of Caesarea, were convicted with others of having helped the rebel 'by secret counsel' (29.5.44), and two other men, Castor and Martinianus, were executed for participating in the depredations of Romanus; 'rapinarum flagitiorumque Romani participes' (29.5.50).

Theodosius' response to acts of collaboration was ruthless in the extreme. Having been first mildly dealt with by demotion, upon later 'consultation' with the army the offending infantry and bowmen were executed, the infantry by the ancient military ritual of clubbing by their fellows, the commanding officers of the bowmen merely having their hands cut off, no doubt in recognition of their superior rank and for the 'didactic symbolism' (p. 256) of the destruction of the skill they had abused in supporting the rebellion. These punishments were compared, and defended by Ammianus against possibly imaginary detractors of Theodosius, by reference to ancient precedent and the example of conduct they had set (29.5.23). The collaborating councillors of Caesarea and their accomplices were burned at the stake (29.5.43), as on two recorded occasions were deserting soldiers while others, like the bowmen's officers, lost their hands (29.5.31, 49). Romanus' accomplices, Castor and Martinianus, were tortured to the point of death before suffering the same mode of execution as the *curiales*, burning alive (29.5.50). This is discipline by terror, in a manner savagely reminiscent of the contemporary court of Valentinian, from which Theodosius had come to north Africa, and of many pages of Ammianus. One can see why Firmus preferred suicide by hanging to the 'protracted torments' to which Theodosius, and then no doubt Valentinian, would have subjected him (29.5.54).

Reactions of the Roman occupants of the cities are sometimes recorded; the joyful response of landowners ('laetitia possessorum') when Theodosius announced that he would supply his campaigns not from the provincials' resources but from what he took from the enemy (29.5.10f.) – an announcement in marked contrast with the demand for 4,000 camels

XIV. Barbarians and Bandits

made by Romanus in reply to the request of the Tripolitanians to campaign on their behalf (p. 281f.). We are told of the gladness of the citizens of Caesarea who saw the head of Mazuca when it was brought to their city, 'cum magno visentium gaudio' (29.5.42), and of the inhabitants of a town near Sitifis when the body of Firmus was displayed there. Theodosius called together and asked his soldiers and the inhabitants of the place whether they recognised the features – pure public relations, since he had met the man himself and even kissed him in greeting (29.5.56, cf. 15)! Assured of the identity, Theodosius entered Sitifis in triumph, and was received with the commendation of every age and rank of society; 'aetatum ordinumque omnium celebrabili favore susceptus' (29.5.56).

These episodes may also be considered under the domain of social relations (p. 405), and are part of the complexity of the social and political issues that were involved in the rebellion of Firmus. This was of a rather special order, something between a tribal uprising and a usurpation. Despite his 'crowning' by a Roman tribune and his subsequent appearance before the army dressed in a purple cloak, there is no obvious way in which Firmus could have converted either his tribal ambitions or his instinct for self-preservation into a claim for Roman imperial power, and it is difficult to imagine what he would do with such power, were he to obtain it. But the rules of the game are not always of one's own choosing. The high level of the response of the Roman authorities, and the urgency of their methods, show that the rebellion was viewed as a significant matter; and this it was, not simply in its scale, but because it threatened the essential structures of Roman control in western north Africa. In this respect, despite their common features as involving mountain peoples, the insurrections in Isauria and Mauretania were in their social and political dimensions rather dissimilar. The uprisings in Isauria were certainly a severe test of Roman military capabilities in a peculiarly intransigent area, but were in the last analysis a question of one side against the other, Roman forces against insurgents. Ammianus' description of the Isaurian attacks gives little indication of their organisation beyond what is implied by their capacity to move about the country, to call up reinforcements and conduct basic diplomacy. No Roman unit is reported to have deserted to the Isaurians, and despite the mediating role of the city of Germanicopolis (p. 365), no member of a curial order of any Roman city nor any Roman official is mentioned as having collaborated with the rebels. Ammianus says nothing of their leadership, and very little of the basic cause of the uprising; if we are to recover these, we have to work on a level not explicitly covered by Ammianus, though as we saw he provides us with much material that helps us, with the other evidence, to do so.

The case of Mauretania is rather different. The mass of the people were naturally involved with their leaders in the rebellion – the size of Firmus' armies, able to conduct pitched battles, is an indication of the scale of his support – but Ammianus' account, supported by epigraphy, makes it clear that the insurrection had a specific origin and cause among the tribal nobility of the province. It was generated at the highest level of Moorish society and involved instances of collaboration in every aspect of the affair of which we are informed – army, imperial administration, curial order – in an area in which peace for the Roman cities was maintained by a combination of military occupation and alliances of the emperor's interests with those of the local dynasts, in whose hands lay the social control of the territory.

(4) Conclusion: Ammianus and his sources

The subjects of this chapter represent a great variety of peoples, physical environments and lifestyles, and to submit them to a uniform manner of description is to risk ignoring the diversity in Ammianus' treatment which is one of his main qualities as a historian. This diversity is a reflection of many factors: the intrinsically different nature of the peoples and events described, the functions and literary character of narrative and digression in Ammianus' text, the quest for variation as a purely literary aim and, not least important, the manifold nature of his source materials. These ranged from personal observation and scrutiny of eye-witnesses – those 'versati in medio' mentioned in the preface to Book 15 – to other literary records, written reports and documentary archives, and involved these and other resources in various combinations.[127] The chapter ends therefore with a brief survey of Ammianus' source materials, taking each section in turn, with a view not to ascertaining the exact nature of the source in each case, but to suggesting the range of possibilities at the historian's disposal.

The effect of this arrangement is to be confronted first by the most complex situation, for the range of sources available for Ammianus' accounts of Roman relations with the Alamanni was very wide. To begin in the most literal sense with 'versati in medio', the ultimate authority for one episode can be identified with certainty, for his knowledge was unique. Philagrius, the *notarius* who received the sealed orders to arrest king Vadomarius if he were seen on the Roman side of the Rhine, was clearly the source for the contents of a confidential letter which he saw only when he opened it in private, making an excuse to leave the banquet at which Vadomarius was a guest in order to read it (21.4.2ff.). The letter became public after the arrest of Vadomarius, when Philagrius supported his action by reading out the orders it contained ('textu lecto iussorum', 21.4.5); but Ammianus' account puts Philagrius at the very centre of the episode and tells it largely from his point of view, from his seeing Vadomarius and remembering the emperor's words to him, to his withdrawing to a private room ('diversorium') to read the letter, and then ordering the arrest. Philagrius could very well be Ammianus' direct source, for he is described in the same passage as 'comes postea Orientis', an office normally held at Antioch. It is not certain that in 382, when Philagrius is attested in the post (*CTh* 8.5.41, 20 September), Ammianus

XIV. Barbarians and Bandits

was still in his native city, but Philagrius had lived in the east for many years before that;[128] having gone there with Julian in 361, he gave to Libanius information from his journal of the Persian campaign in which, like Ammianus, he had participated (p. 162). King Vadomarius, whom Philagrius arrested at Kaiseraugst, became *dux* of Phoenicia and is also found in operations against Procopius and serving in Mesopotamia under Valens. Ammianus' not altogether flattering reference to Vadomarius' cunning as *dux Phoeniciae* (21.3.5) implies that he knew more about his conduct in the east than actually appears in the history, but makes it unlikely, fascinating though it would be to think of it, that Vadomarius was a source for Ammianus. There would be no shortage of eastern observers interested in the career of an Alamann king among them. Vadomarius was never less than an intriguing figure, in every sense of that word.

Another Roman official, the *notarius* Syagrius, was the only survivor of an Alamann attack on a Roman building party operating over the Rhine in the time of Valentinian. In consequence of the defeat he was dismissed from the imperial service (28.2.5ff.). As sole survivor, Syagrius must ultimately be the unique source for the episode, which Ammianus narrates with explanation of the background, both diplomatic and military, and with considerable circumstantial detail. There is some possibility of confusion, there being two Syagrii, consuls in 381 and 382 respectively, but a good chance that the *notarius* of Valentinian, 'postea praefectum et consulem', was Ammianus' direct source.[129] This need not necessarily be so, for Syagrius would have to explain his conduct to Valentinian and, as his dismissal implies and as Ammianus more or less states, he was made to take public responsibility for the defeat. But often when Ammianus alludes to the later careers of individuals whom he names, there are grounds for thinking that he may have known them personally. As in the case of Philagrius, the narrative is told from the participant's point of view, and with more sympathy for his predicament than would be found in an official version of the episode.

Ammianus frequently mentions reports ('relationes') submitted by field commanders to emperors and to each other, whether directly, or indirectly by use of the verbal form ('referente ...').[130] It does not follow that on such occasions he knows the actual contents of a report, nor that when he does know it, it forms his main source for events that may also have been otherwise recorded. In some cases, however, the use of a more formal source can be inferred from Ammianus' manner of writing. The account of Valentinian's attack on the Alamann position at Solicinium, complete with the loss of the emperor's 'cubicularius' and the ceremonial helmet which he was carrying, reads like a communiqué in which, while working within its framework of information, Ammianus has transformed an originally favourable reference to Valentinian's personal role in the engagement to criticism of the emperor's almost fatal over-estimation of his own abilities; 'ut erat sui arrogans aestimator' (27.10.10).[131] That such communiqués were in fact issued at least for important episodes (of which this was certainly one) is shown by Ammianus' references to 'laureatae litterae' sent out to provinces (16.12.69) and by references of Symmachus to accounts of imperial victories composed by literary men at court and read out in the senate and to the people (*Epp.* 1.95; 3.18; *Rel.* 47). The authors of these dispatches – 'orationes', as Symmachus described the versions read in the senate – would have composed them on the basis of reports received by the emperor from his officers in the field. In doing so, they achieved an elevation of official report ('relatio') to literary account ('oratio') which, allowing for their different purpose, was not unlike Ammianus' own procedure when he enjoyed the use of such sources. We saw earlier the possibility that his review of Valentinian's frontier works entered under the year 369 may be connected with a more widely concerted attempt, visible in speeches of Symmachus and poems of Ausonius, to present the emperor's military policy to the cultivated public (pp. 284ff.).

The authority of one written account of an admittedly special type, Julian's memoir of his triumph at the battle of Strasbourg, deterred the historian Eunapius from essaying one of his own.[132] Ammianus refers to other letters and pamphlets composed by Julian, and may have ensured that he knew his account of Strasbourg, particularly since he had himself been posted away from Gaul by the time the battle was fought. Yet if he did use it, Ammianus would have so adapted this material to a Roman historiographical and moral framework that it ceased to bear much resemblance to the original – much as he gave to the Persian campaign of Julian a totally different flavour from that of the contemporary Greek sources, even when he can be shown to have used them (pp. 175ff.). One wonders a little about such events as the surrender to Julian of king Chnodomarius; yet this was a scene which anyone who saw it – such as Julian's eunuch supporter Eutherius, whom Ammianus came to know as an old man – would remember for the rest of his life.[133]

In addition to his personal memoir, there would also be formal reports of the battle submitted by Julian to Constantius. Ammianus mentions the derision of Constantius' courtiers for Julian's reports claiming victories whenever he commanded against the Germans (16.12.67), and he may be indulging in a subtle stroke of historiographical irony when he places the full weight of 'documentary' reference in his narrative of Strasbourg, not on Julian's reports but on the reaction of Constantius. In communiqués on the battle preserved as edicts in the 'tabularia publica', the emperor arrogated to himself his Caesar's triumph, claiming in an evidently detailed account that he had personally arranged the battle-lines, fought in the front ranks and received the submission of Chnodomarius – when he was actually forty days' journey away at the time (16.12.70)! Ammianus thought this an expression of Constantius' delusions of grandeur and his susceptibility to adulation. He illustrated his view by an ironically disingenuous example; if the emperor were in Italy and a general enjoyed some success in the east (the relationship between Constantius and Ursicinus will of course not cross our minds), no mention would be made of the general's name in the 'lengthy text' of laureate letters sent out to the provinces. Ammianus should have acknowledged the normal conventions that would at any time in the fourth century have claimed the successes of his subordinates, whether generals or Caesars, to the credit, and to the titulature, of their Augustus; but his description is excellent evidence of the practice of emperors to inform their subjects of their military successes by issuing communiqués, and of the preservation of such documents in state archives where, presumably, they were available for consultation.

No such communiqué would be issued or expected after the battle of Hadrianople, although some numbers and names, at least of the more notable casualties, were available (31.13.8). There would in any case be no shortage of comment and information on the battle and many stories, such as that of the survivor who claimed to have witnessed the immolation of Valens in the burning farmhouse, would have circulated (31.13.14-16). Ammianus specifically, indeed rather emphatically, mentions how the survivor came back and told his story; 'is ipse iuvenis occulte postea reversus ad nostros haec ita accidisse narravit' (31.13.16). As with Julian's Persian campaign, the difficulty with such stories would be knowing what to reject rather that what to believe. As to the earlier history of Romano-Gothic relations, the wars of Valens of 367-9 and some of the engagements immediately preceding Hadrianople were undoubtedly the subject of reports, easily available to those who wished to know more. Yet far outweighing these in importance and interest were the many men of all ranks with personal experience of the campaigns. The Gothic point of view would also be widely disseminated, particularly after the reception of Athanaric at Constantinople in 381. Although the king died soon after his reception, there would be many companions and humbler tribesmen who stayed with the Romans and would be willing to impart their knowledge to an interested enquirer who could claim experience of war – and whose former patron's son had been killed at Hadrianople (31.13.18). As hinted earlier, one may wonder whether Ammianus' reference to the splendid burial 'in Roman fashion' of Athanaric at Constantinople reflects personal observation (27.5.10; p. 16). This might explain why he mentioned it at all: as to the event itself, the number of potential informants ran into the thousands who witnessed it. Ammianus' knowledge of the intelligence brought to Roman commanders during the wars of 376-8, and of their varying responses to it – as of the emperor's reaction when first offered the opportunity to receive so many recruits – would demonstrate his access to highly-placed informants; for this material, revealing errors of judgment, disputes in councils of war and the false interpretation of intelligence, can have formed no part of any official announcement.[134]

Ammianus' digression on Huns and Alani reflects in presentation as well as in its factual material the relative degrees of knowledge available of these folk. The origins of the Huns are vaguely described, being located in the far north rather than the east, from which they came along the steppe corridor north of the Caspian Sea. Ammianus no doubt assumed that they had followed the Goths from the north rather than converged on them from a different direction; in any case his statement does not look as if it were specifically researched. His description of the Huns repeats stereotypes of a pastoral nomadic people, but he still achieves a specific description of their physical appearance, pattern of life and social customs. That he offers no comparison of the Huns with any hitherto known peoples is perhaps a deliberate expression of their outlandish novelty. The customs of the Alani are also presented in lively style, comparisons with peoples of Scythia familiar from Herodotus here reflecting the fact that unlike the Huns the Alani were already known, by name and in respect of their basic culture, to the Romans. By the late 380s, Huns were serving as cavalrymen in the Roman armies (they took part in Theodosius' campaign against Maximus in 388); information about them, both from Roman and from Gothic sources such as the supporters of Athanaric, would become available progressively from the time of their first apparition to their terrified neighbours.

The Saracens, or desert Arabs, present no difficulty of content or source material. As Ammianus remarks, he had himself observed Saracens who knew neither grain nor wine, and he had encountered them in various warlike postures on the Persian campaign of Julian. The rest came from general knowledge. Ammianus' account is not highly detailed, nor of central importance in his history; nor were the Saracens, extending as Ammianus says 'from Assyria to the cataracts of the Nile', an especially exotic subject for a Syrian Greek who had travelled to Egypt. To find Isaurians, one had only to travel from Antioch to Tarsus and Seleucia, then up the road into the Calycadnus valley and through the Taurus to Iconium – a route which Ammianus must have taken more than once in his life. In a sense, one might have expected the last of the three campaigns recorded by Ammianus, that in which the *vicarius* Musonius was killed, to have been the best reported, given the notoriety of that event. Ammianus' praise of the *comes Isauriae* Lauricius, who in the second outbreak achieved much by restraint and commonsense (and by re-occupying a strategic fort) could suggest that excellent man as a source of his information.[135] It is however the first invasion, that of 353, which is in fact the best documented, setting the scene for those that followed. There would never be any shortage of official and unofficial information coming across the Cilician plain to Antioch when trouble was afoot in Isauria. Ammianus says as much, in recording how the first insurrection subsided when Gallus Caesar heard rumours and received reports from the *comes Isauriae* Castricius, and organised the sending of reinforcements; 'haec ubi latius fama vulgasset missaeque relationes assiduae' (14.2.20). The character of Ammianus' narrative of the first insurrection, very full and clear although composed some years after the occurrence of events that in themselves were disparate and confused, explaining the specific origins of the outbreak but lacking individual detail on the Isaurian side, might be best explained if he were guided by a

XIV. Barbarians and Bandits

contemporary account written from the Roman point of view and concentrating on military and other events, such as the exchange of diplomatic messages, that were on public record. The initiative during the third uprising of the civic authorities of Germanicopolis, followed by the giving of hostages by the Isaurians, was a sequence of events that would remain on record in the city and appear in any official account of the insurrection (27.9.7).

The narrative of the uprising in Mauretania and its suppression has every appearance of deriving closely from an official report submitted to the emperor by the general Theodosius or issued by the court on the basis of it. This seems implied by Ammianus' detailed but rather formal exposition, from the departure of Theodosius from Arles to north Africa to his final return to Sitifis, 'triumphanti similis'. At one point his arrival at Tipasa is noted as having taken place 'mense Februario', a detail that seems most likely to have been recovered from some sort of report or journal. Notable too is the very full register of proper names, of people, places, and tribes and their leaders, in Ammianus' account. It has been observed that the places and tribes are disposed almost as if in an official itinerary in which places are named, sometimes with the most routine of descriptive attributes – 'Lamfoctense oppidum, inter gentes positum ante dictas'; 'municipium Sugabarritanum, Transcellensi monti adcline'; 'fundum nomine Gaionatis, muro circumdatum valido ...', and so on (29.6.13; 20; 25). These were surely not places that Ammianus had seen himself, but are presented with an unadorned adequacy and lack of individual colour characteristic of military reporting.[136] If we look for a contrast, Ammianus' descriptions of places seen on Julian's Persian campaign are distinguished from those of Eunapius precisely by their greater immediacy and informality, and by his selection of facets of the situation that were of special relevance to what actually occurred (cf. pp. 167ff.). Ammianus also names, with a thoroughness and attention to formal detail best explained as deriving from a documentary record, the names of military units and individuals punished for various offences and in various ways by Theodosius. It is all very scrupulous, and a unique source for the history of the province, but lacks the points of observation, the idiosyncrasies and insights into character that mark Ammianus' narratives when he was a witness of the events described, or wrote of them from the information provided by witnesses.

A specific detail in favour of the inference that Ammianus is here using an official documentary source is the change in the form of the name of the Moorish prince murdered by Firmus from 'Zammac' in his introductory remarks to 'Salmaces' in the body of his narrative (above, p. 373). Ammianus seems not to notice, and certainly does not comment on, the obvious identity of the person. The two versions of his name seem to come from different layers of information, as if Ammianus were in his first reference providing an explanatory introduction to a written account that did not possess one, without seeing the point of contact between the two.

As for what Ammianus may have added to such a report apart from introductory comments to give the setting, that seems unproblematic: rhetorical colouring in such matters as the description of military engagements and the nature of the terrain, the attribution of contrasting moral character to the main protagonists – devious cowardice to Firmus and his supporters, heroic grandeur to Theodosius. Comparisons of Theodosius with Republican heroes and, possibly, the defence against 'obtrectatores malevoli' of his severity in meting out punishments are other and very clear additions made by Ammianus. Like similar critics assigned to Julian (above, p. 134), one suspects that they have been conjured up for the occasion, just in order to enable Ammianus to frame his defence.

An official report of the kind suggested here, to which Ammianus added an introduction, some rhetorical colouring and historical parallels, concluding with an account of the triumph of Theodosius taken from this source, will obviously not have provided information on a baffling sequel; the execution of Theodosius at Carthage in the following year (Orosius 7.33.7; Jerome, *Chron.*, s.a. 376). It is often suspected that the death of Theodosius in such circumstances was an event from which Ammianus recoiled as too dangerous to narrate, even in the 'praesentis temporis modestia' of the reign of Theodosius' son – 'princeps postea perspectissimus' as Ammianus styled him on his one appearance in the history (28.1.2; 29.6.15).[137] This could be so, but there might be an alternative explanation, of a more formal character. The death of Valentinian in November 375 while on campaign against the Quadi, and the succession of his younger son Valentinian II as colleague of Gratian, provided a decisive terminal point for the western parts of Ammianus' history; while events in the east in 376-8, culminating in the death of Valens at the battle of Hadrianople, formed the most dramatically powerful conclusion that could be imagined – certainly more so than Ammianus can have anticipated when, with the achievements of Julian in mind, he began collecting his material and considering the scale and structure of his work. The modest discrepancy of terminal dates in west and east was of no significance, provided that the relations of Gratian with his uncle Valens were explained, as they were, in sufficient detail to make intelligible Valens' actions in the approach to the battle of Hadrianople. That it was Valens' death at Hadrianople which made an emperor of the son of the *magister militum* Theodosius was true but best left to a future historian, if one were forthcoming, to describe in a manner fitting for the occasion (cf. 31.16.9). Events at Carthage in 376, the execution of the emperor's father and its connection with the turbulent politics of the early reigns of Gratian and Valentinian II, were a subject not covered in Ammianus' source material on the rebellion of Firmus, and they fell beyond the chronological limits of his history of the west. They would involve difficult enquiries with a risk of awkward revelations, and they contributed nothing to the force of the climax of the history as it stood. One cannot blame Ammianus for leaving them alone.

CHAPTER XV

The Physical Environment: Town and Country

To turn from Valentinian's wars against northern barbarians to the sufferings inflicted upon Lepcis Magna and its African neighbours by desert tribesmen was, Ammianus remarked, 'like migrating to another world'; 'tamquam in orbem migrantes alium' (28.6.1). This vivid phrase, rather more than a mere formal transition, touches our imagination at various levels – most obviously in terms of the physical contrast which, between the landscape of forests and rivers over which the late Roman emperors conducted their northern wars and the sand-blown cities on the coastal plain of modern Libya, could not be more striking. But there is more than this to Ammianus' expression. The material and symbolic distance between these emperors, locked in their incessant wars in the north, and the ancient cities of the Mediterranean, is a distinctive mark of the political and social structure of the late empire. The Tripolitanians found this to their cost, as we shall see, in trying to make their complaints known to a remote and otherwise preoccupied emperor at Trier. One feature, however, the two 'worlds' had in common, the distinction each of them made between what passed for 'Roman' and 'non-Roman', and the inferences they drew from this. Before passing to Tripolitania, Ammianus had described the deception and massacre of a band of Saxon raiders on the lower Rhine. Treacherous and shameful though it might seem, he wrote, a fair judge of the matter would not disapprove of the suppression of a band of destructive brigands, if the opportunity presented itself (28.5.7).[1] The Tripolitanian misfortunes began, in a fashion similar to those in Isauria, when a leader of the Austuriani, Stachao, convicted 'by most evident proofs' of conspiring against the province, was burned at the stake (28.6.3). To avenge his execution, his tribesmen attacked the territory of Lepcis, seizing a leading citizen – in fact the head of the curial order – whom they found with his family on his country estate and provoking the city authorities to complain to the emperor of their misfortunes.

The 'affair of the Tripolitanian embassy', as Ammianus had described it in anticipation (15.5.36), has generally, and rightly, been taken as an illuminating example of the relations between provincial communities, imperial officials in the provinces, and the imperial court itself.[2] On an equally circumstantial level, the episode is revealing also of the life of a fourth-century city in relation to its agricultural hinterland and of the functioning of its civic institutions, and so can well serve as introduction to this and the next chapter, on the cities of the empire in their physical context and on social relations within them.

Provoked by the execution of Stachao, the Austuriani overrun the rich lands of Lepcis, fearing to attack the city because of its solid walls and large population: 'civitatem muris et populo validam' (28.6.4). For three days they plunder, killing the country folk who fail to reach safety in the 'caves' – these were presumably in the lower reaches of the Jebel escarpment which rises behind Lepcis and, because of the water it conserves and delivers, is crucial to the agricultural development of the area.[3] It is now too that the leading *curialis* of the city, Silva, is taken captive, no doubt with the idea of trading him off for a fat ransom. In a second raid, on the territories of Lepcis and its neighbour Oea (modern Tripoli), more plunder is taken and decurions killed, among them two civic officials, namely a provincial priest (*sacerdotalis*) and an aedile (28.6.10). Later, in a third raid another leading townsman of Lepcis, Mychon, is surprised on his estate outside the city. Prevented by lameness from getting away, Mychon is thrown down a well, but on second thoughts pulled up still living and taken to the city gates. There he is ransomed by his wife and lifted inside the walls on a rope, only to die two days later (28.6.14). Lepcis is besieged for eight days, but the attackers are unable to press their advantage. Some of the desert tribesmen are wounded and they retire in subdued mood to their own habitations: 'redierunt ad propria tristiores' (28.6.15). Like other barbarian enemies of Rome, they had found it easy to win possession of the countryside and force the Roman population behind their walls, but did not have the resources or the organisation either to take the cities, or to exploit fully the economic advantage which their command of the countryside might have given them. The difficulty for the Roman Africans of coming to terms with this particularly mobile enemy is well shown by the initial demand made by the *comes Africae* Romanus for 4,000 camels if he was to conduct the campaign (p. 281). Whether the demand was excessive or not, it shows the nature of the problem that confronted them. It would in any case be an error of perspective to regard the incursions as arbitrary or wilful, or the execution of Stachao as their real cause. The harm for the province which he was allegedly plotting arose no doubt from some more deep-seated cause of tension between the desert peoples and the Roman cities of the provinces – some economic adversity which forced the tribes into their confrontation with the Roman communities.[4] 'Brigandage' can in such circumstances be classified, as it was by Aristotle (*Politics* 1256a), as a mode of production resorted to in the absence of more regular resources such as hunting, fishing or agriculture, or when these suffer critical deterioration.

With the departure of the desert people from the walls of Lepcis, the rest of the story concerns the attempts made by the provincials to get a

XV. The Physical Environment 385

fair hearing at the imperial court, and by imperial officials to prevent their success – in which the latter were so effective that the full truth of the matter may well have been suppressed beyond recovery. But it is worth pausing to survey the evidence provided by Ammianus' account of the episode for the civic institutions and procedures which enabled the Tripolitanians to register their complaint.

The first incursions were made while Jovian was still emperor (28.6.4), and the first opportunity for the Tripolitanians to approach the emperor arose from the annual provincial council – 'die concilii, quod apud eos est annuum' – envoys being deputed to present gold statues of Victory to the new emperor, Valentinian, to celebrate his accession (28.6.7). The council is the regular annual *concilium* of the province, attested for all periods and regions of the Roman empire, and the statues of Victory are an example of the *aurum coronarium* – 'crown gold', offered as a quasi-voluntary goodwill contribution to mark the accessions and anniversaries of emperors.

The envoys were instructed by the council at the same time to inform the new emperor of the lamentable state of the province, and this they did, making speeches to him and presenting their *decreta*, the 'decrees' of the council containing a full account of the affair (28.6.9). This again was regular practice, as was the envoys' use of a formal occasion such as the recognition of an imperial accession to present in addition a matter of substantial interest to themselves. The *decreta* would embody the 'mandate' of the embassy – the terms of reference entrusted to it by the council, which the ambassadors were obliged to observe scrupulously on pain of legal penalties – and it was usual to accompany the formal presentation of the degree with an oration designed to attract the emperor's sympathy. A third-century handbook of rhetoric offers advice exactly appropriate for the situation of the ambassadors from Tripolitania;[5] in fact, Ammianus' account could serve as a text-book example of the situation envisaged. The envoy approaching an emperor on behalf of a distressed city, the handbook suggests, should inspire his sympathy by picturing its present sad plight, contrasting this with its former greatness. The example in the handbook, ancient Ilium or Troy, gives some idea of the historical perspective thought admissible for such parallels. The Lepcitanian envoys, for their part, need look back a mere three centuries, to a time when the munificence of its Punic-descended aristocracy had made their city one of the finest and best-appointed of the western empire. The ambassador (continues the handbook) must speak for his city, evoke its youth and old men, picture its mothers and children as they pour forth their tears and plead for compassion. And when he has done this, he will request the emperor to accept the decree. In response to the Tripolitanian petition, indeed, the military command of the province was transferred to the civil governor, though it soon reverted by collusion to the *comes Africae*, the original cause of the provincials' complaint (28.6.11). By a process equally familiar to those who had dealings with the imperial government, an official enquiry promised into the affair was deferred 'amid the more important preoccupations which are apt to play on the attentions of heads of state'; 'eo more, quo solent inter potiorum occupationes ludi potestates excelsae' (28.6.9).

The third invasion, in which the *curialis* Mychon lost his life, and the continued absence of their embassy, provoked the civic authorities of Lepcis to send a second legation to inform the emperor of their latest sufferings (28.6.16). At Carthage the deputation met the returning members of the first embassy, but continued its journey to the imperial court. At the same time, an imperial official, Palladius, arrived in the province with arrears of pay for the soldiers and was shown the devastation by two leading citizens, 'distinguished and eloquent men' as Ammianus calls them; 'facundos municipes et insignes' (28.6.18). Palladius seemed sympathetic; he went to Romanus and denounced him for his inactivity, but the provincials were undermined by further manoeuvres of the *comes Africae*, and on his return to Lepcis the surviving member of the second delegation (his colleague having died at Trier) was disowned by his fellow-citizens. They claimed that he had exceeded his mandate in what he had told the emperor (28.6.21). Disputes about mandates are not uncommon in the provincial history of the Roman empire, and the existence of legal penalties for failing to observe them has already been indicated.[6] On this occasion the ambassador was also induced to admit that he had deceived the emperor, and in consequence he and three alleged accomplices – presumably *curiales* who supported him – were executed at Utica by sentence of the *vicarius* of Africa, while the *praeses* of the province met his death at Sitifis in Mauretania for being too outspoken in a report to the emperor (28.6.22f.).[7] The survivor of the first legation also (its second member having died at Carthage), made to defend his conduct before the *vicarius* and *comes Africae*, was assailed by angry acclamations of the soldiers present, objecting that the Tripolitanians could not be defended because they had not provided what was necessary for the campaign; they were referring to the 4,000 camels required by the *comes Africae*. The ambassador was imprisoned but managed to bribe his guards and escape to Rome, where he lay low and died a natural death (28.6.24). In view of the carnage around them – not to mention the express threat to cut out their tongues as the purveyors of false information – it is not surprising that the two 'distinguished and eloquent townsmen' who had shown Palladius the devastation of the province made themselves scarce. After Valentinian's death they re-emerged to tell their story to the proconsul and *vicarius* of Africa appointed by Gratian (28.6.28). The 'full report' made by these officials delighted the *curiales* of Lepcis, who set up public statues in their honour with inscriptions praising them as patrons, and in one case for the 'justice' he had shown in the case of the Tripolitanians delegated to him. The report did not however please the *comes Africae*, who continued to maintain that the proconsul and *vicarius* were 'inclined to favour the province' (28.6.29). So too, it may be felt, was Ammianus, whose expression in praise of the 'equity and authority' of the proconsul and *vicarius* is an uncanny echo of the Lepcitanians' inscriptions in their honour;[8] but it would be naive of a modern reader of Ammianus to attribute blame or distribute imputations of wickedness among the various participants in this unhappy business – whether imperial authorities, provincials, or indeed the desert tribesmen who first provoked it. Once the first steps were taken, all were trapped in a cycle of violence and retribution beyond any of their powers to control.

The affair of the Tripolitanian embassies of course involves exceptional circumstances. Yet it was just the purpose of these institutions and procedures – councils, embassies, decrees, mandates, and so on – to make a city's or a province's opinions known to the authorities in circumstances which were by their nature exceptional. The affair of the embassies shows normal patterns of civic and provincial life, not as history in their own right, but as they happen to impinge upon events which provide materials for history. Such evidence is furnished by Ammianus at all turns of his narrative, in episodes which may owe their inclusion to political, moral or some other special interest but reveal a normal style of life, caught momentarily but in exact detail by the passing light of circumstantial events.

The case of the merchant and former official Antoninus, who deserted to the Persians in 359 with his wife and family, has already been examined for what it has to tell about the social background of Ammianus and the eastern lands extending towards Mesopotamia.[9] A similar case is that of Craugasius of Nisibis – a man, as Ammianus writes, 'distinguished in the municipal order by reason of his family, reputation, and influence'; 'in municipali ordine genere fama potentiaque circumspecti' (18.10.1). So might one write of a leading notable of any city, but Craugasius' social position as a prominent *curialis* could hardly be defined more exactly. In one of Ammianus' more romantic episodes, Craugasius' wife was captured by Sapor in an attack on a Roman fort near the Tigris and taken off into captivity, but got news to her husband that she was alive and well treated, and begged him to join her (19.9.3ff.). To allay the suspicions of the authorities at Nisibis, Craugasius behaved as if he had given up his wife for lost and was planning to remarry. His projected bride was a girl of 'splendid' family; 'matrimonium alterius splendidae virginis affectavit' (19.9.7). Like Craugasius she belonged to a leading family of the curial order of Nisibis. The preparations for the wedding feast were made at a country estate owned by Craugasius eight miles from the city, and it was while visiting it, supposedly for this purpose, that he made off on horseback to join a Persian raiding party 'which he had learned was coming' (19.9.7): another case of the private intelligence which men of his class could acquire on the movements of the eastern enemy of Rome. He joined Antoninus at the Persian court, being a man 'less intelligent [or, less devious] than his predecessor, but no less well known'; 'natura simplicior, nominis tamen itidem pervulgati' (19.9.8). Like the affair of the embassies, the story of Craugasius is in many respects a typical scene of provincial life, the normality of its social setting rather belied by the unusual circumstances which give Ammianus reason to tell of it. It was not to attract attention but to allay it that Craugasius prepared his wedding feast on his country estate near Nisibis, and that Antoninus bought the farm in which he installed his family near the river Tigris before crossing over to the Persians. Both had special reasons, but their behaviour was not such as to raise suspicion.

Although we should not forget such episodes as noble houses of Gaul and Spain destroyed by indiscreet conduct at dinner-parties (16.8.8f.; p. 264), it is as one might expect, that Ammianus' most vivid descriptions of the social life of town and country should concern the eastern regions of the empire of his own background and upbringing. The fairs held at Batnae and Amida, for example, are mentioned because they were relevant at certain points to Ammianus' narrative of the Persian wars of Constantius. In the case of the annual September fair at Batnae the crowds of people of all classes assembled there to trade in imports from every part of the known world attracted the attention of an opportunist Persian frontier commander (14.3.3); at Amida, the multitude of country folk who, undeterred by the obvious threat of Persian invasion, had come to the fair, swelled the population of the besieged city (18.8.13).[10] Another episode relating to Batnae occurs during the Persian campaign of Julian; fifty men died when a huge pile of chaff stored there 'as is the manner in those regions' collapsed and overwhelmed them as they went there for fodder (23.2.8). And yet again, there are the Maratocupreni, the bandits whose village near Apamea was the base of raids which they conducted in the guise of imperial officials or traders. We saw earlier how, coming to a town on one occasion they made a 'proclamation' outside its walls that they had come to confiscate the property of a leading citizen whom the emperor had proscribed (p. 265). The raiders obviously knew what they were doing, in going for the 'spectacular mansion' of this local dignitary ('ambitiosam domum cuiusdam primatis') and their ploy stood no chance of success unless in the eyes of the local population he had been sufficiently prominent to have attracted the emperor's attention (28.2.13). The Maratocupreni are notable for the sophistication of the methods of their banditry and, as we shall see later, for the luxury of the community that they had built for themselves on its proceeds; 'quos [sc. lares] ambitiose luctuosis aliorum dispendiis construxerunt' (28.2.4).[11] From a different point of view their story, like that of the Tripolitanian envoys with which this chapter began, is a sobering illustration of the possible impact of the imperial government upon a provincial community.

*

Ammianus came from and knew well this world of urban communities and country estates, of municipal worthies dividing their time, as frequently in the episodes mentioned so far, between the city and their rural properties; and he described it with the circumstantial detail and sense of occasion which are his most characteristic qualities as a historian. Yet for Ammianus the cities of the empire were far more than the accidental backdrop for events of circumstantial interest. There was a powerful 'ideological' element in his conception of the cities and the societies which they contained. This is as we should expect. As an educated product of Classical society, Ammianus would instinctively regard cities as the institutions in which Roman civilisation was enshrined and its cultural values invested. The countryside and its labouring classes existed, one might even be aware of their importance – armies marched over them, their taxes, manpower, rents and profits sustained the imperial government and made possible the exuberant life of the cities – but that was no reason for a historian to say much on the subject. It would emerge as and when relevant to the narrative as it progressed.

Ammianus' attitude to cities comes out most explicitly in his various digressions on the provinces of the empire.[12] In a highly formalised mode of presentation, he will write that a region or a province is 'ennobled' or 'made splendid' by its greater cities and will enumerate these, passing over the less significant towns ('oppida'), perhaps adding a word or two on the ancient founders of a city or on its historical distinction. There is no need to do more than illustrate his manner. The province of Thrace, for instance, is 'adorned by Philippopolis (ancient Eumolpias) and Beroea, prosperous cities' (27.4.12), Marcianopolis in the same province is named after the sister of Trajan, and Nicopolis celebrates that emperor's victory over the Dacians (27.4.12; 31.5.16). Viennensis in southern Gaul glories in the splendour of many cities, among which Vienna itself, Arelate and Valentia (Vienne, Arles, Valence) are outstanding; to which should be added Massilia (Marseilles) 'on whose friendship and support we read that Rome sometimes relied in times of danger' (15.11.14). Arabia possesses together with certain 'oppida' the 'huge cities of Bostra and Gerasa, together with Philadelphia, strong and well-fortified with walls' (14.8.13). One of the fuller entries concerns the province of Phoenicia, 'a region full of charming attractions, enhanced by great and lovely cities, among which Tyre is outstanding in its pleasant character and in the fame of the names associated with it; there are also Sidon and Berytus and, matching them, Emesa and Damascus, founded in ancient times' (14.8.9). So too the cities of Palestine rival each other in distinction, including Caesarea, established by king Herod to honour Octavian the *princeps* (14.8.11).

Some cities, less famous than in their heyday but still flourishing in Ammianus' time, are mentioned in the digressions only for their historical importance: Massilia, as we have just seen, for its ancient treaty with Rome and in another passage for its foundation centuries ago by Phocaean colonists (15.9.7), Corinth for its employment of the future tyrant Dionysius as a schoolmaster (14.11.30). Apart from a reference to a *vicarius* of Asia who had once taught rhetoric there (27.9.6) and, indirectly, to the sojourn of Julian as a student in the city (15.2.8; 8.1),[13] Athens features only in its role in ancient Greek history, and Carthage, except for a couple of incidental allusions referring to a corn shortage and to the death there of one of the Tripolitanian envoys (28.1.17; 6.16), only in connection with the Punic wars. Yet in Ammianus' time Carthage was still one of the half-dozen greatest cities of the Roman empire, and Athens still a considerable centre of learning, as the writings of Libanius and Eunapius make clear. Their absence from Ammianus' pages is a reflection of the isolation of these cities from the political scene which was the historian's main concern.

Particularly revealing of the artificial formality of Ammianus' digressions as compared with the circumstantial detail of his narrative, is the case of Nicomedia in Bithynia. In his digression on the Pontic regions, Ammianus merely remarks in his usual fashion that the city once called Astacus was later renamed Nicomedia 'after the king' – he means the Hellenistic monarch Nicomedes I of Bithynia, who had refounded the place in 262 BC after the destruction of its predecessor (22.8.5). In 358 Nicomedia was largely ruined by an earthquake. Describing Julian's reaction to the condition of the city when he passed through it four years later, Ammianus sets its history in terms both historically more relevant and closer to contemporary experience. Nicomedia, he writes here (in the very next chapter after his digression), was a city 'famous in former times, but so increased by the great expenditure of earlier emperors that in the profusion of its private and public buildings it might on a correct estimate be compared to a region of the Eternal City itself'; 'recte noscentibus regio quaedam urbis aestimaretur aeternae' (22.9.3ff.). Nicomedia had in the late third century been developed as an imperial residence and showpiece, the predecessor of Constantinople itself. It had gained from the unbridled 'passion for building' ascribed to Diocletian by Lactantius, who like Ammianus makes the comparison with Rome; 'studens urbi Romae coaequare' (*Mort. Pers.* 7.8ff.). This facet of its history was of far more practical relevance to the circumstances of Ammianus' day than the details of its foundation by Nicomedes, as set out in his digression.

A similar observation applies to Ammianus' own Antioch, which in his digression on the eastern provinces is described simply as 'a city known throughout the world, incomparable in the resources imported and produced there' (14.8.8) – despite its touch of pride and obvious truth, a rather colourless expression. It is in the nearby narrative context of the conduct of Gallus Caesar that Ammianus mentions a more interesting detail, the street lighting for which the city was famous (14.1.9); its provision was one of the liturgies which fell on the upper classes of the city. Not that Antioch is generally neglected by Ammianus, far from it: in other narrative settings, notably in the economic troubles under Gallus Caesar and Julian, and in the political trials conducted there by Valens in the early 370s, he reveals many more aspects of the life and society of the great metropolis.[14] It is simply that, as in the case of Nicomedia, the formal character and extreme brevity of the reference in the digression bear little relation to the nature of the city as he knew it, and as he described it elsewhere.

XV. The Physical Environment

Even in a digression, Ammianus can let fall a detail of circumstantial value: on occasions, a moment of personal experience. Aventicum (Avenches) in Gaul has no place in the surviving narrative but is described in a digression as a 'deserted town, but once not undistinguished, as its half-ruined buildings demonstrate to this day'; 'ut aedificia semiruta nunc quoque demonstrant' (15.11.12).[15] Ammianus had no doubt seen them himself. The province of Lugdunensis Prima is 'adorned' by the cities of Cabillona, Senones and Bituriga (Cavaillon, Sens, Bourges) and 'the huge old walls of Autun', 'moenium Augustoduni magnitudo vetusta' – an allusion which well anticipates the description, not many chapters later, of improvised local defence being mounted from the walls of this ancient city 'of spacious circuit, but insecure through the decay of centuries'; 'muros spatiosi quidem ambitus, sed carie vetustatis invalidos' (15.11.11; 16.2.1). Augustodunum, the 'civitas antiqua' of Ammianus' description, was a foundation of the time of Augustus, supplanting the native hill fortress of Bibracte (Mont Beuvray, 25 miles west of Autun in the Morvan). Its walls, of which considerable parts, with two fine monumental gateways, still stand, were designed to reflect the prestige of the settlement as a centre of Roman culture in the newly pacified province.[16] A panegyrist of the time of Constantine described it as 'that city which first made Roman cities of the others' (*Pan. Lat.* 8.4.4) – with some justification, for it had from the earliest days been a centre of Roman culture in Gaul. In AD 21 sons of the Gallic nobility receiving a liberal education there were taken hostage by a rebel leader (Tacitus, *Ann.* 3.43). In the conditions of the late empire the walls of Autun were an anachronistic luxury, grandiose but impracticable. Many cities had acquired smaller, more easily defended circuits, built in the late third or early fourth centuries (below, p. 394).

As we have seen in these cases of Avenches and Autun, and earlier of Isaura Vetus, Ammianus observed the contrast to be found between the ancient glories of some cities and their present, less distinguished appearance. The actual destruction of cities by war and natural catastrophe is evoked in a number of passages, the most intense being in the reaction of Constantius and his courtiers before the ruins of Amida after its capture by Sapor in 359 (20.11.5). So did Mauretanian Caesarea, attacked and burned by the rebel Firmus, appear to the army of Theodosius, with the traces of widespread fires and pavements white with ash (29.5.18). A military force was instructed to clear away the rubble and stand guard against renewed attack. The city continued, for a few years later its bishop is found as an envoy to the court of Gratian, seeking a tax exemption for the community in view of the damage it had suffered.[17] Some cities had disappeared altogether, succumbing to hostile action, natural decay, or economic decline. Dura-Europus on the Euphrates was a 'deserted town' when Julian's army passed it by in 363 (23.5.8); it had never been re-settled after its capture by the Sasanians in 256. Indeed, its desertion was so complete that it was not until 4 May 1920, with the appearance to excited archaeologists of its name on a now famous wall-painting, that the city was even located in modern times on the correct side of the river.[18] Until that moment it had been placed – partly through a natural though misleading interpretation of the text of Ammianus – on the south bank of the Euphrates. The old metropolis of Seleucia on the Tigris, which had once, according to the elder Pliny, had a population of 600,000, was now a 'deserted city' (above, p. 141). Though often attacked by Roman armies, Seleucia owed its decline more to shifts in the course of the river Tigris, which had affected its commercial prosperity, and to the foundation nearby of the rival city of Parthian Vologesias. The tremendous complexity of urban settlement of this part of Mesopotamia, as reflected in Ammianus' description of the Persian campaign of Julian, has been discussed in an earlier chapter (VIII.2). As a final example of a ruined Mesopotamian city mentioned by Ammianus, which had joined the register of abandoned sites of that region, on its retreat through the desert the Roman army of Julian passed Hatra, an ancient caravan city, 'vetus oppidum in media solitudine positum'. As Ammianus notes, it had in former times been attacked without success by the Emperors Trajan and Severus, but was now for long deserted, 'olimque desertum' (25.8.5). It too had been destroyed by the Sasanians in the mid-third century.[19]

Ammianus' most detailed description of urban ruin (apart from that achieved by war) concerns the destruction of the greater part of Nicomedia by the earthquake of 358. Most of the city and its suburbs were flattened by the tremors, and many of the temples and private houses which would otherwise have survived were destroyed by fires, which raged for five days and nights. Built on hillside terraces, collapsing houses fell on others and dragged them to ruin, and the bodies of many dead were never recovered from the debris (17.7.1ff.). Visiting the city a few years later, Julian mourned its great buildings 'reduced to ashes': 'moenia ... in favillas miserabiles consedisse' (22.9.4). What remained of the city was destroyed by a further tremor on the eve of the Persian campaign (22.13.5).

*

For Ammianus as for any educated man of his class, a city was the tangible expression of many more abstract sentiments on the nature of civilised life. Its residences and public buildings expressed the wealth and public spirit of its leading citizens, housed its institutions and deities, and generally stood for the amenities of Graeco-Roman culture in contrast with the ignorance, illiteracy and unending toil of the countryside – a subject of which few Classical writers have much to say, unless it is to endorse the morally improving nature of the physical labour in which they did not participate. Ultimately, a city's walls themselves provided the barrier between 'Roman' and 'non-Roman', between the 'civilised' and the 'barbarian'. The defenders of Autun, anxiously viewing their German assailants from behind the walls built in

XV. The Physical Environment

the first century as symbols of the Roman ideal in a recently conquered province, have something in common with the people of Lepcis Magna, confronted at their very walls by outlandish desert tribesmen. The famous pronouncement of the Goth Fritigern that he was 'at peace with walls' (31.6.4) was fully justified both by his people's success in winning control of the Thracian countryside in 376-8, and by their total failure when on rare occasions they tried to attack Roman cities. They did so after the battle of Hadrianople and after heavy losses sustained at the walls of the city concluded that they had been mad to invite the miseries of siege warfare against the advice of their king (31.15.15). Earlier, a German war-band had given up a thirty-day siege of Sens in Gaul, cursing themselves for their stupidity for ever having tried to take the place (16.4.2).[20]

The cities that feature in Ammianus' narrative invariably possess fortified wall circuits: there would scarcely appear to have been any such thing in his day, either in the Roman empire or in Persia, as an 'open city', one not surrounded by walls. The structures can be placed in different categories, reflecting the circumstances of different historical periods. Sometimes they were the ancient fortifications of famous cities, dating from centuries earlier. This, as we have seen, was true of Autun, as of Cyzicus in Bithynia. It was here that Venustus, an official of Valens, took refuge against the supporters of Procopius in 365. It was guarded by Serenianus, a general sent there by Valens to defend the imperial treasures, the city being 'impregnable by reason of its wall circuit, and known also for its ancient monuments' (26.8.7). The harbour entrance of Cyzicus was blocked by a heavy chain stretched across it; the breaking of this chain won an amnesty for the officer who achieved it when the rebel faction was defeated by Valens, and he survived to die later in Isauria (8.10).[21] The walls of Lepcis Magna vainly attempted by the Austuriani were built not so long before Ammianus' time, in the later third or possibly the early fourth century, and were constructed of re-used material taken from tombs in their vicinity; the refortification of a much smaller circuit was undertaken by the Byzantines in the sixth century, when the city had declined and large parts of its previously inhabited area were overrun by sand dunes (Procopius, *Buildings* 6.4.1ff.). The fourth-century wall circuit however included almost all the built-up area of the earlier city, and its effectiveness in practice is shown by the reluctance of the Austuriani to attack it, and by the panic, as Ammianus describes it, of the women of the city when they did so; it had never happened to them before (28.6.15).[22] Tarsus in Cilicia had its local counterpart to the Austuriani, though more persistent and dangerous, in the 'bandits' of the Isaurian mountains. Like the other cities of the region such as Seleucia and the coastal depot of Paleas (or Palaia), mentioned by Ammianus (14.2.13, 15),[23] Tarsus was fortified and its gates guarded. When an Armenian prince interned in the city by Valens broke out with three hundred supporters, the gate attendant on duty warned the provincial authorities, who set off in pursuit of their escaping hostage

(30.1.6). There is no need to repeat here what was said earlier about the foundation and defences of Amida. It had been established under Constantine as a local stronghold and refuge, with an armament of mural artillery (18.9.1; p. 54). By contrast, the city of Carrhae was at Ursicinus' order evacuated in 359, its walls being distrusted as insecure; 'oppidum invalidis circumdatum muris' (18.7.3).

In some parts of the Roman empire, the cities had been refortified on a less expansive scale than before in response to the barbarian invasions and unsettled conditions of the third century. At many urban sites in these areas, from Athens through north Italy to Gaul and Spain, the courses of these walls, often with substantial parts of the actual structures, can still be traced. They defend the monumental areas of the cities, enclosing only a small proportion of the urbanised area of the first two centuries and, as in two famous cases, Le Mans and Carcassonne (there are many others), forming the basis of the medieval defences.[24] When Julian was besieged at Sens in the winter of 356/7, it was within these late third-century walls that he was confined (16.4.2; above, p. 90); so too at Tricasini (Troyes), when the citizens hesitated to admit Julian inside their gates because of the barbarians swarming everywhere, it is the third-century fortifications of the city that are meant (16.2.7). Ammianus' description of 'Rauracum' (otherwise 'Rauraci') as standing right on the edge of the Rhine ('ad supercilia fluminis Rheni') shows him to be referring to the fortified settlement that had supplanted the ancient colonial foundation of Augusta Raurica; Constantius came there through difficult country and wet spring weather with snow, on a campaign against the Alamanni in 354 (14.10.6), and it was there that king Vadomarius was arrested at a dinner-party with the Roman commander (p. 315). The fine old *colonia* of Augusta Raurica stood on a natural platform between two small tributaries of the Rhine, some distance back from the banks of the river towards which it spread as it developed, attracted by the lines of communication focussed on the bridges over the Rhine to the now annexed territory beyond it. It was the later settlement, in essence a defended bridgehead, that was the nucleus of the medieval and modern town of Kaiseraugst, while the old site was abandoned. Ammianus might appropriately, as in the case of nearby Avenches, have regarded the 'half-ruined buildings' of Augusta Raurica as a sign of its earlier grandeur. The old site was not necessarily quite deserted in Ammianus' time, but any lingering population there had little connection with the now derelict amenities of the earlier city and none with the economic situation that had sustained them. The place was once again a frontier post.[25]

Ammianus occasionally has reason to comment, and does so in a highly interesting fashion, on the contemporary state of city defences. His remarks usually form part, and are discussed elsewhere in the context, of his narratives of military events, especially sieges; such (again to leave aside Amida) is his description of how the Persians smashed their way into Singara by attacking a part of the wall which had recently been

XV. The Physical Environment

repaired, so that the mortar was still damp (20.6.5; p. 290). Ammianus reports on Sirmium in Pannonia almost like an archaeologist, in telling of the fortifications set in hand there by the praetorian prefect of Illyricum, Petronius Probus. At first terrified by the threat of barbarian attack, Probus pulled himself together to repair the city walls. He cleared the ditches (*fossae*) of their accumulated rubbish and rebuilt the walls and defensive towers.[26] For this purpose he was able to use materials collected some time before to build a theatre; 'impensas aedificandi theatri dudum congestas sufficientes ad id, quod efficere maturabat, invenit' (29.6.11). 'Dudum' is a vague word; Ammianus does not say, and can scarcely have known, how long before 373 this venture had been conceived or abandoned, but his description is apt commentary on a situation well-known to archaeologists. The wall circuits of later Roman cities frequently involve the re-use of materials taken from the monuments of the early empire, especially theatres and amphitheatres; those of Lepcis, as we saw, were made from old grave monuments. The situation at Sirmium is unusual only in that, although the materials had been laid in store for the project, the theatre had never actually been built. Elsewhere Ammianus produces another example of the re-use of building materials from an earlier period. A Greek inscription predicting the death of Valens at Hadrianople was dug out of a wall at Chalcedon, where it lay hid ('structura latebat in media'), having already been put to secondary use at an earlier time. It was now, with the demolition of the walls of Chalcedon, to be re-used again in the construction of a bath-house at Constantinople (31.2.4).[27]

Another once splendid Pannonian city, Carnuntum on the Danube, Valentinian found in 375 to be 'deserted and unkempt' though still suitable for military use (30.5.2), and spent three months there before passing by way of Aquincum to spend the winter at Brigetio (30.5.11; 13ff.). As with Augusta Raurica, one wonders what Carnuntum now looked like. Founded as a legionary base in the Julio-Claudian period, the settlement had expanded quickly until in its prime, with the development of the adjacent municipality, it measured over 4,000m from eastern to western ends and possessed extensive monumental, residential and trading quarters; their traces can be seen in fascinating aerial photographs of the fields that now cover the site. 'Desertum quidem nunc et squalens', says Ammianus (30.5.2): what had happened to all of that? In the same year, 375, Valentinian visited another Pannonian city, Savaria, where two interesting episodes took place.[28] An owl settled on the roof of the imperial bath-house ('culminibus regii lavacri insidens') and could not be stopped from its ominous hooting, though pelted with stones and arrows (30.5.16).[29] More germane to the present subject is the frustration of Valentinian's wish to leave Savaria by a particular gate in order to create a favourable omen. The gate was cleared of the rubbish impeding it, but it proved impossible to shift a massive iron grille which had fallen into position and blocked the way, forcing the emperor to use a different exit (30.5.17). Gate and portcullis had evidently been unused for some time, and indeed Ammianus remarks of the ruinous walls of Sirmium that they had been 'neglected in long years of peace'; 'murorum maximam partem, pacis diuturnitate contemptam et subversam' (29.6.11). The picture is a surprising one, of cities which despite their apparent exposure to barbarian threat and, in the case of Sirmium, regular occupation by the emperors and their praetorian prefects, had not maintained their defences to a basically adequate standard. Ammianus' descriptions of neglect and dilapidation – not to mention the panic of a praetorian prefect when threatened with attack – cast a far from reassuring light on Roman military preparedness in the years preceding the battle of Hadrianople and the Gothic penetration of the eastern Balkans.

One famous western city receives a particularly full account of its siege by the armies of Julian in 361, yielding details that illustrate far more than the strictly military aspects of its situation. The loyalty of Aquileia to Constantius caused Julian much anxiety, for the place, he was 'told and had read', had never been taken by siege or storm (21.12.1). Further, its influence was such as to induce its Italian neighbours, by which Ammianus must mean the smaller towns and villages of the locality, to behave with concerted loyalty to Constantius (21.11.3). Aquileia was one of those cities re-fortified in response to the uncertain conditions of the third century.[30] The historian Herodian, a contemporary, describes how the walls were repaired after long neglect to meet the attack of Maximinus in the civil war of 238 (8.2.3ff.); monumental inscriptions of the first century, and beautifully carved pieces of architrave from a portico, are among the materials put to secondary use then or later, in order to fortify the old harbour frontage by the addition of a defensive wall and bastions. The experience of Julian's men before Aquileia confirmed its reputation for impregnability. Failing to carry the city by direct assault, they devised a water-borne siege engine which was capsized by the defenders as it floated down the river by the walls – that is, along the now fortified quayside just mentioned (21.12.8ff.; cf. p. 294). The besiegers then cut the aqueducts, an obvious though not a very effective manoeuvre, since the inhabitants were able to use wells for their supply; in his account of the siege of 238, Herodian too had mentioned the limitless supplies of water from wells available for those living in the city (8.2.6) – the site is low-lying and the water-table not far below ground level. Julian's men then scoured the 'suburbs' ('suburbana omnia') to find a way of bringing siege machinery to the walls, but failed to find a convenient place of access (21.12.14f). The interest of this detail is in its indication that the fortified part of Aquileia was surrounded by an intensively built-up area; it was not the terrain in itself, a flat alluvial plain, that presented the difficulty of access.

The 'suburbana' of Aquileia should be visualised in the most obvious sense of this word, as a built-up area lying immediately outside the walled core of the city – which might in its own right, as in the case of Aquileia though not of all re-fortified cities, be quite extensive. At

XV. The Physical Environment

Sirmium, Julian was greeted by crowds who met him as he approached the 'fine, extensive suburbs' of the city; 'suburbanis propinquantem amplis nimiumque protentis' (21.10.1). If Sirmium, like Aquileia, was surrounded by a large built-up area, one can begin to appreciate how in a period of peace the defensive walls, tucked away in the middle of houses and streets, and no doubt in the absence of effective building control often used as a structural element in later development, had come to be so neglected and the defensive ditches (or what was left of them) filled with rubbish. At Aquileia the city wall hurriedly repaired in 238 was, as Herodian notes, 'very ancient', *palaiotaton* (8.2.4). Built in the late Republic and early empire to consolidate a crucial strategic point in the expansion of Roman power into central Europe, the defences had simply been neglected and forgotten in the long years of peace and commercial prosperity which then ensued (cf. Strabo 5.1.8).

*

Ammianus' 'suburbs' represent a variety of settlements in the economic and social dependance on a city which the term implies. It can refer, as in the cases just mentioned of Sirmium and Aquileia, to the built-up area immediately outside and adjoining the walls of a city. It may also by progressively broadening definition indicate urban districts in the vicinity of their parent but separable from them, and agricultural properties situated within a certain distance from a city.

A 'suburb' within the first of these categories might be a substantial settlement distinct from the main city, with its own name, and constituting with its parent a genuine conurbation.[31] When Valentinian and Valens entered Pannonia to divide the empire between them in 364 they came to Naissus, 'copiosum oppidum', as Ammianus describes it elsewhere (21.10.5), and held their conference in the imperial suburb called Mediana, three miles from the city (26.5.1). Antioch had a suburb known as Hippocephalus ('Horse's Head'), three miles out of the city on the road to Tarsus (21.15.2) and, most notably, the famous resort of Daphne with its temple of Apollo, burned down by accident in the time of Julian (22.13.1ff.). Daphne, 'amoenum illud et ambitiosum Antiochiae suburbanum', as Ammianus proudly calls it (19.12.19), is lyrically praised also by Libanius for its lovely gardens and cool, abundant waters (above, p. 70). A fifth-century mosaic from a villa at Daphne gives a schematic view of the route from Antioch to its stylish suburb; on it are shown the springs of Daphne, named after the nymphs Pallas and Castalia, the *nymphaeum* or ornamental pool built in the time of Hadrian to receive their waters, then in sequence the 'baths of Ardaburius' (an establishment later than the time of Ammianus, named after a fifth-century general), the Olympic stadium, an *ergasterion*, or workshop, by the shrine of the martyred saint Babylas, a public bath-house and other buildings, including a *xenodocheion*, or hostel.[32]

Another 'suburb' mentioned though not named by Ammianus,

Hebdomon ('seventh milestone') was the scene of Valens' proclamation as Augustus in 364 (26.4.3) and retained through Byzantine times its character as a military parade ground and setting for imperial ceremonies. Hebdomon was by its nature a special case, but its military and ceremonial role recurred on a more local scale in the vicinity of many other cities, such as Paris, where Julian went out to greet 'in suburbanis' soldiers arriving there before his proclamation as Augustus (20.4.12).[33] The same situation is implied by the action of Sabinianus in conducting military exercises 'among the graves' of Edessa – the graves being naturally outside the city – and by that of the *magister militum Orientis* who in 378 ordered Gothic soldiers in Roman service to be taken to the 'suburbs' of the cities where they were stationed as if to receive their pay; he had given secret instructions that once there they should be massacred in order to safeguard the eastern provinces after the battle of Hadrianople (31.16.8). It would be an essential part of the plan, both that the cities should be closed against the Goths while the soldiers carried out the massacre, and that the Goths should until the onset of their catastrophe have no cause for suspicion that anything unusual was happening. The 'suburbana' in these and other cases should be visualised as regular military quarters or at least as centres of military activity (for, especially in the east, the soldiers were often actually billeted within the cities), with the resources and installations that we should expect in such situations – barracks, stores and granaries, parade-ground with tribunal, stables, watering facilities, and so on.

The 'suburban region' was defined by the simple criterion of distance from a city and dependance on it rather than by any specific physical or economic character through which this dependance was expressed; this might be very diverse from one case to another, the examples given by Ammianus naturally tending to reflect the political and military emphasis of his history. The area comprises also agricultural holdings which happened to be located within the same spatial limits. Two of the decurions taken by the Austuriani were surprised on their estates in the 'rich suburban regions' of the city (28.6.4, 14), which the desert people had overrun while avoiding the walls of Lepcis itself. In 378, a leading magistrate of Hadrianople armed the people and the numerous workers in the imperial arms factories, and led a foray against Gothic allies encamped in the country around it. He was angry because the barbarians had ravaged his estate in the suburban district; 'ob rem suam in suburbano vastatam' (31.6.2).[34]

The cities of the Roman empire symbolised much of what a man of Ammianus' class understood as a properly conducted social and cultural life. Yet they cannot be separated from their territory, the agricultural hinterland from which their prosperity was drawn. The *curiales* of Lepcis Magna caught on their estates by desert raiders, however unfortunate they might have been to be so surprised, were living as they had always lived, as well-to-do farmers frequenting their estates and country residences, dividing their time between town and country. We saw how

XV. The Physical Environment 399

one Lepcitanian *curialis*, the leader of his order, had his family with him in the country when he was captured (28.6.4; p. 382). At the other end of the Roman empire, Craugasius of Nisibis, arranging his 'marriage' to a young girl of curial family on a country estate some miles from the city, was behaving just as the widow Pudentilla of Tripolitanian Oea had in the second century, when she married at her 'villa suburbana' her new husband, Apuleius from Madauros. Craugasius' motive was the need to avert scrutiny and suspicion among his compatriots; Pudentilla's, according to Apuleius' speech of defence, to avoid wearisome dinner-parties in the city, and the townspeople's expectations of largesse to celebrate the occasion.[35]

We saw earlier that Classical authors in general show little appreciation of the countryside in its own right, viewing it, and the people, culture and languages found in it, with the self-conscious disdain of city folk. It is a disdain that can fall far short of the real social experience of men whose wealth derived from the land and the labours of its inhabitants, and who must in the nature of things have had constant dealings with them.[36] Such admissions are however rarely made in literary sources, nor is it surprising that Ammianus should as a historian show little interest in the physical or economic character of the countryside except when it is relevant to military action or to questions of transport and communication associated with military action, to food shortages and similar problems affecting the cities from the standpoint of public order, to political misfortunes involving the upper-classes in their role as landowners and men of power, and to other situations that give rise to concrete events yielding narrative in the traditional manner. Even on this basis, the countryside and its settlements occur in Ammianus in a variety of contexts that repay mention from a social and economic point of view.

The settlements comprise in the first instance what Ammianus calls 'villas', and 'farms' ('fundi'); by which he usually means something more like a country estate than an individual farmstead, often in effect an entire rural community. In 354 the two Apollinares of Antioch, father and son, were convicted of treason under Gallus Caesar and sent into exile. They came under escort to a place twenty-four miles from Antioch called Craterae which, it so happened, was an estate ('villa') of their own. Here the two men's guards, carrying out their orders, broke their legs and then executed them (14.9.8). The location, as well as the nature, of the punishments, was no doubt specified in the orders. Craterae is to be visualised as a community consisting of the dependants whom the brutal killing of the Apollinares was meant to intimidate. In other words, it was the rural centre of the social and economic influence of these leading *curiales* of Antioch.[37] We should imagine the 'villa' eight miles from Nisibis, where Craugasius set up his preparations for his remarriage, in the same way – not simply as a personal residence but as a working estate containing a community of country folk. Together with other properties which he may have had, it provided the wealth that sustained

Craugasius' status as a leading *curialis* of his city.

Such a perspective would agree, at least in terms of their physical character and economic role, with other references made by Ammianus to 'villas' in this region; such as Bebase, which lay on the invasion route taken by Sapor in 359. From Bebase to the city of Constantia a hundred miles away, wrote Ammianus, the terrain was arid except for the scanty water available in desert wells (18.7.9). Bebase was a water-point in the desert – hardly therefore a single 'villa' or farmstead but a rural community dependent on and exploiting the oasis.[38] In a not far distant region the Armenian king Papa, having escaped from internment at Tarsus, was able to get himself and three hundred supporters across the Euphrates and return to his own country, finding at 'villas' devoted to the cultivation of vines the materials for making rafts supported by inflated bladders (30.1.9).

The economic circumstances suggested by these episodes may throw light on some 'villas' mentioned by Ammianus outside the limits of the Roman empire, in the first instance the villa known as Hucumbra east of the Tigris, which supported the Roman army of Julian for two days on its retreat from Ctesiphon; it provided all the food and stores that could be wanted, and was burned down when the Romans left (25.1.4). Hucumbra was obviously no isolated country house, more a substantial agricultural community. We should visualise Hucumbra as an agglomeration of working as well as residential buildings, with storage facilities for the locality; in eating what they could, taking away what could be carried and then burning the place, Julian's army treated it as more or less like a regular town or village – which is how it was described in the parallel narrative of Eunapius.[39] The physical situation is more explicit with the palaces built 'in the Roman manner' near Seleucia on the Tigris – probably mansions constructed in a Hellenistic style derived from the architecture of the great city, complete with gardens and pavilions (24.5.1; p. 144). At the other end of the Classical world, the 'domicilia curatius ritu Romano constructa' found by Julian's soldiers in Alamannic territory beyond the Rhine (17.1.7) are identified as old Roman villas re-occupied by Alamannic notables, and presenting a mixture of Germanic and Roman artefacts of the Rhineland area.[40] After the description in the previous chapter there is need only to refer briefly here to a further category of rural domains in a frontier or 'near-frontier' region, though it is a distinctive one; the 'fundi' of Moorish chieftains as they arise in the campaigns of the *magister militum* Theodosius against the rebel Firmus and his supporters.[41] These formidable establishments belong to a specific socio-economic as well as military and strategic context alongside the Roman and indigenous towns and villages of Mauretanian Africa; fortified rural settlements acting as focal points, and in certain circumstances as refuges and centres of rebellion of relatively un-Romanised native peoples. In the light of Ammianus' descriptions and the supporting archaeological evidence, they must be seen as more like castles or fortified townships than the plain farmsteads ('fundi') that his

XV. The Physical Environment

choice of word might be taken to imply.

A special category of 'villas' mentioned by Ammianus is that of the official residences occupied from time to time by Roman governors and by members of the imperial family travelling between their capital cities in the northern provinces. In one such establishment, the 'publica villa' known as 'Pistrensis', the daughter of Constantius, destined for marriage to Gratian, nearly fell into the hands of marauding barbarians but was got out to Sirmium twenty-six miles away by the initiative of the provincial governor; he took her with him on his official carriage (29.6.7). At another, the 'villa Caesariana' Melanthias, Valens lodged shortly before the battle of Hadrianople; he had his army with him, for it was from there that he 'struck camp' to the place called Nice, and thence to the battlefield (31.11.1; 12.1). Most characteristic of these establishments, it was from an imperial residence a hundred miles from Brigetio that the little boy Valentinian was fetched, with his mother Justina, to be made emperor in 375. The place bore the name Murocincta, 'girt by walls' (30.10.4) and has reasonably been compared – indeed identified – with a great country house with walled enclosure known from archaeological excavation at the village of Parndorf near Carnuntum.[42] Imperial residences of this type, substantial establishments which complement the capital cities of the northern provinces, may well account for some of the more obscure places in which emperors from time to time issued laws, such as 'Contionacum', from which Vaientinian sent out five laws between 29 June and 16 August 371 (CTh 9.3.5-4.6.4); the first of them was dispatched on the day after Valentinian is known to have been at Trier (CTh 12.1.75; 10.20.5). Contionacum is probably to be identified with the remains of a substantial fourth-century villa, semi-fortified and with apsidal audience hall, at Konz, a short distance from Trier at the confluence of the Saar and the Mosel. The 'suburb' of Naissus known as Mediana also falls within this category of imperial retreats situated within easy reach of the great military frontier cities. Valentinian and Valens went there to arrange the division of the empire between them in 364 (26.5.1).[43] A special case even within this category of imperial residences was the best known of them, the palace at Spalato (Split), built not to launch a refreshed emperor against the barbarian enemies of Rome but to receive him in well-earned retirement in an agreeable part of his native province.[44] Diocletian's palace makes a single incidental, though in its own way only too typical, appearance in Ammianus' surviving books: a charge of treason was laid against an innocent man by his estranged wife, who accused him of stealing and hiding away with accomplices the purple covering that lay on the tomb of Diocletian (16.8.4). This was in the famous octagonal mausoleum that in medieval times, as the settlement at Split grew and nearby Salona declined, was transformed into the cathedral of the new city. Considering Diocletian's reputation as a persecutor of Christians, the outcome does not lack irony.

Ammianus' socio-economic landscape includes one more category of settlement worthy of attention, that of townships and village communes, or 'vici' (in Greek, *kômai*) subordinate to the cities in whose territories they were established,[45] but largely self-governing and often enjoying considerable prosperity. Ammianus' most explicit descriptions of *vici* relate to special cases within the empire, and indeed to communities altogether outside its boundaries and obviously not subject to any Roman legal or social definition, like the '*vici* constructed like cities' mentioned in his digression on the Persian empire, in Media and around the mouth of the Euphrates (23.6.11, 31), and the settlements destroyed by Julian's army during its march down the river (24.8.2); but he evidently uses the word by analogy with what would be familiar to his readers by its terms of reference within the empire. His most detailed description of an individual *vicus* is again in the east, and could be seen as unusual. It is the settlement of Abarne in the rich and fertile cultivated country of Gumathena, to the west of Amida; the *vicus* was known for the curative hot springs there, which were presumably what gave the place its prosperity and special character (18.9.2). Also untypical, in the sources of its wealth as well as the nature of its independence, was the *vicus* of the bandits called the Maratocupreni near Apamea in Syria. The name of the Maratocupreni is itself of interest, being composed of elements from an Aramaic dialect meaning respectively 'caves' (*m'ârâtâ*) and 'village' (*kapra*, the equivalent of the Greek *kômê*).[46] The derivation is perfectly intelligible in an Aramaic-speaking area that produces examples of local banditry, in one case, some distance to the south, based on the caves of the Hawran (*OGIS* 424; p. 348f.). Whatever their original mode of life, the Maratocupreni had clearly advanced far beyond that stage of development, having built up their houses in splendid style ('ambitiose') on the proceeds of their long unpunished brigandage – a prosperity which came to an abrupt end in 369, when the Maratocupreni were suppressed by imperial order, their village destroyed and their families put to the sword (28.2.14). Another settlement in northern Mesopotamia is not actually called a 'vicus' by Ammianus, though that might well be the best description of it: Meiacarire in the Tur Abdin, a shady place on the road between Nisibis and Amida, with vines and fruit trees. Its name, as Ammianus explains, meant 'place of the cool waters' (18.6.16); he does not explain that this meaning is derived (like that of the Maratocupreni) not from the Greek but the Aramaic language.[47] The local people had taken refuge there during the invasion of 359, among them being found a spy, discovered hiding in a remote part of the settlement ('in remoto secessu latentem'). This was evidently not simply a cluster of houses, but a substantial village or modest township.

    Ammianus' references to 'vici' correspond well to a class of settlements well documented in the civic structure of the Roman empire. The term is used to designate townships which, though established in the territory of another city to which they were attributed, possessed a degree of self-government and a quasi-municipal system of internal organisation, and might even include substantial urban amenities. In the time of

XV. The Physical Environment

Constantine, Orcistus in Phrygia successfully petitioned for independence from the nearby municipality of Nacolia: an inscription preserves the terms both of its petition and of the emperor's favourable reply (*ILS* 6091). Among the arguments advanced by its representatives were its possession of a large population, magistrates and a curial order – just as if it had been a self-governing community – an excellent water supply, public and private baths, a lodging house, and location at a major crossroads.[48] In presenting the petition, the delegates of Orcistus described their community as a 'vicus'. It was evidently a considerable township, whose promotion to the status of municipality was – once it had carried its argument – a simple transaction based on the physical realities of the case.

Ammianus' narrative in one way or another touches the full range of established urban and rural communities of the provinces of the Roman empire – and, as we saw in the last chapter, of regions beyond its borders. He portrays these communities in terms which the social historian of the empire will recognise, and he shows leading members of provincial society moving across the landscape, between town and country, in a manner which reflects their position as urban magnates whose prosperity came from the countryside, and provides many other insights into the nature of their economic life. His descriptions cover both east and west, with some intensity of documentation for parts of the Roman empire as widely dispersed as northern Mesopotamia, Tripolitania, Isauria and Mauretania, and in scattered but significant detail for many other areas. He also provides evidence for the functioning of the civic institutions of the cities of the empire, for their modes of communication with the imperial authorities, for the ideology with which they were viewed, and for the nature of social relations that existed within them. In turning now in more detail to what Ammianus has to say on these subjects, the next two chapters will also touch an important issue so far deferred – the economic life and social relations, and then the religious life in its social dimension, of the great cities of the empire, especially Rome, Ammianus' own Antioch, and Alexandria.

CHAPTER XVI

Social Relations

The communities of the Roman empire – cities, groups of cities or associations within them, even villagers and peasants – were long used to expressing their interests to the ruling power by instructing and dispatching embassies. The procedures that were involved can be seen from the embassy of the provincial council of Tripolitania sent to the Emperor Valentinian and its sequel, as described in the previous chapter.[1] On another occasion, the leader of a delegation sent to Jovian by Nisibis with its gift of crown gold, just as the city was about to be surrendered to the Persians, burst out angrily, 'So, emperor, may you be crowned by your other cities!' (25.9.4). This was clearly no part of his mandate. Almost as disconcerting was an embassy sent by the provincials of Epirus to Valentinian. Following the example of other provinces, they were forced to send an embassy of thanks by the praetorian prefect of Illyricum, Petronius Probus. It happened however that Valentinian recognised the leader of the embassy, a philosopher named Iphicles whom he had apparently met before, and asked him (in Greek) whether the provincials' thanks were sincere. Then the truth came out. They had come, replied Iphicles, not gladly but unhappily and under duress; 'gementes ... et inviti' (30.5.9). Like the episode before Nisibis, the outcome of the embassy was a deviation from its normal pattern of a civic duty, performed in this case with a certain unenthusiasm on the part both of provincial council and of Iphicles, who had not wanted to undertake it; 'adegere, non sponte propria, pergere ad id munus implendum'. In this detail too we see a familiar aspect of the social history of the Roman provinces, for Iphicles would not have been the first philosopher to try to use his status to evade a civic obligation; it was a repeated preoccupation of imperial legislation to prevent their doing so.[2] Behind the whole incident we must imagine a council in the metropolis of the province, a vote of delegates and the selection of envoys with a decree and mandate to convey thanks to the emperor; at its head the philosopher, chosen for his eloquence and reluctantly accepting the duty, but in the event displaying the true integrity of his profession before the emperor's questioning. The story could be told of any period or region of the Roman empire.

Within individual communities, upper classes and populace declared their opinion in the manner appropriate for each, councils passing

404

XVI. Social Relations

decrees and the people making their will known by acclamations in their places of assembly, or when they received a governor at the gates of their city, in theatre or circus, or as he passed through the streets. Acclamations made in this way had a quasi-official standing, and might be communicated to higher authority as an expression of the popular will.[3] A law of Constantine, addressed 'ad provinciales', referred to acclamations both in praise and criticism of governors and officials, and instructed that praetorian prefects and their deputies 'shall refer to our knowledge the utterances (*voces*) of our provincials', so that the emperor might honour or censure governors as appropriate (*CTh* 1.16.6). Acclamations of the people of Rome, a special case no doubt, were conveyed to court by the imperial transport service, a sign of their formal status (*CTh* 8.5.32). In these terms of procedure should be seen the expressions of support for Ursicinus by eastern cities protesting at his recall to the court by Constantius in 359. Distressed at the prospective loss of their defender of many years' standing, the cities tried to keep him for themselves by decrees and acclamations; 'ordines civitatum et populi decretis et acclamationibus ... detinebant paene publicum defensorem' (18.6.2). Ammianus is characteristically exact in naming decrees and acclamations as the modes of expression respectively of city councils ('ordines civitatum') and popular assemblies ('populi'). He was with Ursicinus at the time and described events as they happened, in the social and political order with which he was familiar. His account also casts a revealing light on the local popularity of a general, of whom the emperor had cause to feel apprehensive.[4]

In the nature of things, Ammianus' history will present social relations, not as a topic suitable for analysis in their own right but as they happen to arise in contexts of circumstantial interest. He provides a rich array of examples, momentary images indicative of general situations. A slave in a senatorial household informs on his master because his wife, a slave in the same household, has been whipped for some offence (28.1.49); a trusted servant comes to Nisibis with a message for a leading *curialis* from his captured wife in Persia, while the *curialis* feigns re-marriage into another leading family of the city (20.9.4ff.; p. 387). There are the two 'companions' who escape with Ammianus himself from Amida, men used to walking while he rides on horseback – a telling mark of the social distinction between them (19.8.5ff.); or the lost child, found crying in the road during the invasion of 359 and taken back to Nisibis by Ammianus because he wore a neck-chain and seemed to be of good family (18.6.10).[5] A Roman baker becomes governor of Tuscia after his successful prosecution of a former prefect of Rome for embezzlement, later being executed for fraud in an affair concerning the *navicularii*, or guild of shipowners (27.3.1f.); rival notables of Asian cities, afraid of being assigned as city councillors by Julian, divert attention from themselves and pay off old scores by accusing each other of conspiracy (22.9.8ff.); a proconsul relieves famine at Carthage by releasing corn destined for Rome from imperial granaries, replacing the stocks at a third the price when supplies are plentiful (28.1.17f.).

If we seek more fully articulated accounts of social relations, Ammianus most often shows them as they arise in situations of disorder, of which a repeated and well-documented cause, especially in the greater cities of the empire, was food and wine shortage, above all of the corn supplies which had to be imported in large quantities, and in sometimes unreliable conditions of transport, to meet the demands of their populations. Ammianus describes several such situations, particularly at Rome, and in successive crises at Antioch, under Gallus Caesar in 354 and, eight years later, under Julian. The Antiochene crises should be understood in relation to each other. While the first is narrated in some detail by Ammianus, the second, summarily mentioned by him, is more fully documented in other sources; they are therefore complementary. In neither case does Ammianus directly confront the social and economic issues that were involved, emphasising rather the personal conduct and characters of Gallus and Julian. Yet in both instances he makes the circumstantial comments and chooses the terminology from which his attitude can be inferred.[6]

In the first instance, intent on his subject, the oppression by Gallus of all classes of eastern society – 'nec honoratis parcens nec urbium primatibus nec plebeiis' (14.7.1) – Ammianus does not specify the causes of the food shortages except to say that they were 'manifold and intractable'; 'multas difficilesque' (14.7.5). No easy solution was available, either for the city council, whose leading members were lucky to escape sentence of death merely for stating the truth to Gallus too bluntly, or for the *consularis* of Syria Theophilus, totally undeserving of the fate that overtook him. Declared responsible by Gallus for the corn shortage, he was attacked by a mob and murdered (14.7.8). For Ammianus, the council was correct in opposing Gallus' demand for the promulgation of lower prices as inopportune ('vilitatem intempestivam urgenti'); circumstances did not permit it. A similar observation was made by Libanius on the situation under Julian. The poor harvests, he said, had made impossible respect for the law (*Or.* 15.21).

An additional cause of the shortages is hinted at by Ammianus, though he does not make the connection explicit, and its effect is to complicate still further the question of responsibility as between imperial government and city council. The protest which led to the death of Theophilus came as Gallus was about to leave for Hierapolis on a campaign against Persia (14.7.5). Preparations for a military campaign may have contributed to a shortage of supplies at Antioch as they were diverted to frontier districts. This was not a situation in which a provincial governor could intervene effectively, for he could hardly lay his hands on military stockpiles. The remedy for the shortage, thought Ammianus, should have been forthcoming from Gallus himself, the 'diffusa potestas' of imperial authority making possible the alleviation of local misfortunes by the use of outside aid. He could for instance have imported corn from neighbouring provinces (14.7.5).[7] Such action too was

XVI. Social Relations

beyond the powers of a provincial governor, and if Gallus was blaming Theophilus for not performing it, this was clearly unjust. There was a tradition, commemorated in honorific inscriptions of the early empire, for governors and leading citizens to provide at their own expense corn for cities to save them from hardship;[8] but again, it is not clear that governor or leading citizens had an obligation to provide this service for a city swollen by the imperial court, with all its extra consumers. It seems clear nevertheless that Theophilus owed his death to suspected collusion with the landowning councillors of Antioch, and that this was what Gallus Caesar meant by his repeated assertion ('id assidue replicando') that there need be no famine but for the conduct of the governor. That the people of Antioch so interpreted the situation is shown by their reaction. Having murdered the governor, they turned their attention to the house of a leading city councillor, Eubulus, whose house they burned down when they found that he had fled to the foothills of mount Silpius, which came down into the eastern suburbs of the city (14.7.6; Libanius, *Or.* 1.103).

Ammianus' presentation of the crisis is essentially thematic, his main intent being to demonstrate the character of Gallus Caesar and the injustice of the fate of Theophilus. Its chronology emerges indirectly, in the progression from fears of shortage to the actuality and the increasing severity of hunger. At the time of Gallus' first approach to the city council, shortage was impending rather than actual, though prices were already rising; 'vilitatem intempestivam urgenti, cum impenderet inopia' (14.7.2). At a later stage, indicated as such by Ammianus ('post haec'), when Gallus was challenged by the people before his planned departure for Hierapolis and in response blamed Theophilus, famine was still feared, but now acutely and as imminent; 'inediae metum, quae ... adfore iam sperabatur ... ultima metuenti multitudini' (14.7.5). It seems to be a distinct and later phase when Theophilus was attacked and murdered and the house of Eubulus burned down, for by then the famine was 'getting worse' and the people were driven to violence by 'famine and fury' (14.7.6). If this is so, the attack did not take place on the same occasion as Gallus' remarks about the *consularis* but later, the Caesar's words being remembered as a sort of sentence of death against him; 'ut sibi iudicio imperiali addictum' (14.7.6).

Ammianus' account reveals, if it does not state in detail, the articulation of social relationships implicit in an outbreak of civic disorder. Gallus 'presses his view' ('urgenti') on the council of Antioch that prices should be reduced; the council replies 'more severely than was wise' ('gravius rationabili'), and its chief men come under threat of execution (14.7.2). The *comes Orientis* Honoratus, who defended the *curiales* from this fate, can be seen, like other officials in similar circumstances recorded by Ammianus,[9] as moderating through personal intervention an outburst of anger by the Caesar, when confronted by frank criticism.

When the Antiochene populace expressed its anxieties to Gallus about the impending shortages, this would be done by acclamation at a place of public assembly, such as the Hippodrome. Here, too, would be registered Gallus' complaints about the *consularis* of Syria, words remembered until the food shortage was worse and the onset of famine was actually felt. The rioting broke out in an expression, as Ammianus says, of lower-class violence ('vulgi sordidioris audacia', 14.7.6), but it is Libanius who many years later reveals the fact, not mentioned by Ammianus, that the attack on Theophilus was led in the Hippodrome by five metalworkers (*Or.* 19.47). If the metalworkers were, as is possible, from the imperial arms factories at Antioch (*Not. Dig., Or.* 11.21-2), then we might see them as combining the interests of imperial establishment and populace against the alliance of *consularis* and the leading member of the city council whose mansion was burned down.[10] From Libanius as well as from Ammianus we learn of the further consequences of the rioting – trials and executions under Constantius' praetorian prefect Strategius Musonianus. These were less ruthless than might have been feared. Not too many mothers were made to grieve, remarked Libanius, indicating by this statement that the guilty metalworkers were residents of Antioch (and, indeed, since he mentions mothers and not wives, that they were young men).[11] Ammianus reverts in due course to the enquiries made into the murder of Theophilus, adding unexpectedly that, while men of low estate (Libanius' metalworkers) were on tenuous evidence executed for the offence, certain 'rich men' escaped the consequences of their involvement, suffering only confiscation of property; 'exutis patrimoniis absoluti sunt divites' (15.13.2). What role in events was played by these 'divites' – supporters of Gallus Caesar among the Antiochene upper-class – is left unexplained by Ammianus, who was clearly aware of complexities in the affair that escape us. The murder of Theophilus was not simply the result of a sudden outbreak of violence by a 'vulgar mob', acting for no other reason than basic instability and love of disorder. It was an event with complex ramifications in Antiochene society and its relations with the imperial court. Commenting on the situation in the light of his own experiences eight years later, Julian adds the revealing observation that although its actions were excessive, the attitude of the people had in itself been justified (*Misopogon*, 370C).

This view comes as no surprise, for Julian's response to the similar situation which he encountered on his arrival at Antioch was very like that of Gallus Caesar in 354. Ammianus explicitly makes the comparison between the two – 'Galli similis fratris, licet incruentus', he writes of Julian (22.14.1) – but his summary description of the no less complex and otherwise far better documented circumstances than those that faced Gallus is less satisfactory. This is not only because it is less detailed than his account of the earlier episode – in fact it is hardly narrated at all – but because of the oblique perspective in which he portrays it. Ammianus regarded Julian's attempt to enforce reduced prices at Antioch merely as a distracting interlude in the preparations for the Persian war. It was part of a quest for a popularity which had eluded Julian since his first

XVI. Social Relations

entry to Antioch, and now seemed ever less likely to be his, as the altars ran with the blood of slaughtered animals and his drunken Gallic soldiers were carried insensible to their billets (22.12.6). Consistently with his view of the crisis under Gallus Caesar, Ammianus observed that legislation to enforce low prices will often be ineffective unless done with the support of proper arrangements, otherwise tending to produce only shortage and hunger (22.14.1); and he states that the city council of Antioch made plain to the emperor – as it had to Gallus – that his aim could not be attained ('non posse, aperte monstrante'), but without deflecting him from it (22.14.2). In anger at their obstinacy, and in general disillusionment with his reception at Antioch, Julian wrote his pamphlet, the *Misopogon* or 'Beard-Hater', at the end of which he justified his handling of the food crisis.[12] Julian's account is all the more interesting in that Ammianus must have read it, yet ignores its partisan but perfectly serious attempt at economic analysis, referring instead to the *Misopogon* as an expression of Julian's volatile character and his worsening relations with the city of Antioch. No more than in the case of Gallus Caesar does Ammianus engage the question of the food supply in its true dimension, as a problem of economics, social organisation and government.

*

When Julian came to Antioch in July 362, he was received in the theatre with acclamations complaining of the high prices of food: 'Nothing scarce, nothing cheap', was the shout of the people (*Misopogon*, 368C).[13] This was as much allegation as statement of fact, but on the next day Julian called together the leaders of the city council and asked them 'to reject unjust profits and to benefit the citizens and strangers in the city'. His remark conveys his own suspicion that the councillors' conduct was a cause of the shortage, and concedes a factor mentioned by other sources, the impact on the local economy of large numbers of visitors arriving with the imperial court and army. The councillors' failure to take any action for the next three months convinced Julian that the people's allegation was correct; supplies were plentiful and prices high, only because of the collusion of the propertied classes in keeping food off the market (*Misopogon*, 368D). Whether he was justified in this conclusion is an open question. Its answer lies not in the statement of any objectively agreed set of facts, but in the economic relations between social classes, transformed into conflict in the adverse circumstances. These were indeed complex. As in the disorders under Gallus Caesar, preparations for an eastern campaign must have distorted local markets and diverted supplies from Antioch to military depots not accessible to the city authorities. We have seen references in Ammianus to corn supplies laid up at Batnae and elsewhere, and Julian's army was the size of a considerable city on the march.[14] Further, the *Misopogon* refers to the poor harvests of recent times (359A) – which we might add to the 'causas multiplices difficilesque' mentioned but not explained by Ammianus on the earlier occasion (p. 406). There is also a tendency for rises in the price of one staple product, such as corn, to force up the price of others, and we must take account of the panic that sets in when, for whatever reason, food shortages are anticipated and individuals try to lay in stocks for themselves and their families.[15] One such reason for panic in the east Mediterranean economy is the failure of the rains necessary for a successful autumn sowing. Ammianus notes, and Julian confirms, that the early winter of 362/3 was unnaturally dry, even perennial sources of water failing for a time (22.13.4). He does not associate the drought with the food crisis, and it came too late to explain the origins of the crisis in the summer of 362; but fear of the failure of the next year's crop may well be relevant to its aggravation, especially when one recalls, yet again, the preparations for the Persian campaign. The roads of northern Syria must at this time have been crowded with wagons transporting corn – away from Antioch towards the frontier region.[16]

Julian's response to the crisis, after the three months allowed to the council had elapsed (we are now in late October), was to impose price controls not only on corn but on all foodstuffs (*Misopogon*, 369A). This point is touched upon by Ammianus, with his remark that unless supported by 'proper arrangements', price regulations will often produce the opposite effect to that intended; 'vilitati studebat venalium rerum, quae non numquam secus quam convenit ordinata inopiam gignere solet et famem' (22.14.1). It is not easy to see what in Ammianus' view would constitute such 'arrangements'. As we have seen, he criticised Gallus Caesar for not using his wider powers to import corn from neighbouring provinces (p. 406); but Julian actively used his powers in this way. He brought in 400,000 'measures' ('metra') of corn from Chalcis, Hierapolis and other cities, and when these were exhausted he contributed further quantities of 5,000, 7,000 and 10,000 *modii* from his own estates, together with a delivery of corn imported for his use from Alexandria (*Misopogon*, 369A-B). This last contribution was no doubt a consignment which would normally have gone to Constantinople but had been diverted for Julian's court at Antioch, and the emperor 'gave it to the city' at the fixed price of a unit of currency, which he first calls an 'argurion' or piece of silver but seems later to indicate as the gold *solidus*, for fifteen 'metra'. Julian argued in the *Misopogon* that this was a cheaper price than the city had enjoyed even at the best of times, ten 'metra' per 'argurion' being a normal summer's price, and a mere five measures the price now to be expected, the winter having set in so hard. However these claims are to be interpreted, Julian's policy did not amount to a fundamental attack on the retail market; on the contrary, he had decided to operate through it. His success depended on whether the additional supplies were adequate to support the low price, and on what measures were taken to control the operation of the market and speculation by landowners and corn-merchants.

Serious difficulties confront us in trying to resolve these questions. On

XVI. Social Relations 411

the first point, the quantities of corn supplied, Julian does not help his historian by giving them variously in 'metra' and 'modii' without providing a rate of conversion between them; the *Misopogon* was of course addressed to Antiochenes, who knew, as we do not, what their 'metron' was worth in terms of the Roman *modius*. The latter – the enhanced 'modius castrensis' of 31.25 lb in regular use in the fourth century administration – is used in Julian's text exclusively for consignments of grain from imperial estates, to which Roman rather than local standards of measurement were applied by the department of the bureaucracy which administered them. The corn from Chalcis, Hierapolis and elsewhere is given in the 'metra' used in the city territories.[17] Julian also seems to refer to a silver as well as a gold currency unit to indicate what he evidently thinks of as the same price of fifteen 'metra' per unit (*Misopogon*, 369B, D). The word 'argurion' is however often used in Classical texts to mean coin in general; Classical Greek cities did not mint in gold, and the need to distinguish gold from silver currency does not arise in their literature. Julian's text is barely intelligible without the assumption that he is using the word 'argurion' in an untechnical sense to mean, in effect, the gold *solidus*.[18]

Any calculations on the basis of Julian's text must remain extremely hypothetical. We might however infer from other recorded prices indicating a figure of 30 *modii* per *solidus* in times of plenty (cf. Amm. 28.1.18), that the 'metron' referred to by Julian at a bottom price of 15 'metra' per *solidus* was considerably larger than, possibly double, the Roman *modius*. If so, then Julian's contribution to the solution of the crisis was predominantly one of organisation – the diversion of supplies from other regions to Antioch – rather than of personal generosity. The total of 22,000 *modii* (687,500 lb) brought in from the emperor's own estates and an unspecified amount from Alexandria (based on standard figures, a shipload might be about 35,000 *modii castrenses*, but we do not know how many ships arrived)[19] would provide only a small supplement to the 400,000 'metra' imported from Chalcis, Hierapolis and other places; taking them together we have a figure approaching 1,000,000 *modii*. The arrangements would provide enough grain, on an estimate of consumption of 3 lb per man per day, and half that quantity for women and children, to feed a city of a quarter of a million inhabitants for about two months.[20] This would be a significant contribution against which to measure the extent, as Julian saw it, of the city's maladministration. (It should not however be forgotten that in view of the failure of the winter rains as well as the needs of the Persian campaign, he had in effect to make good a deficiency in two years' supply.)

As for distribution and control, the emperor's phrase that he 'gave' the corn 'to the city' means that apart from setting a price he entrusted the management of the corn to the free market, to the corn-merchants and in particular to the city councillors, who were already suspected, by the people and by Julian himself – as on the earlier occasion by Gallus Caesar – of forcing up prices by hoarding grain.[21] Not surprisingly, they did so again, apparently by selling their own stocks out in the countryside where price control was ineffective and forcing country people closer to Antioch to crowd into the city to compete for the supplies put on the market there by Julian (*Misopogon*, 369C-370A).

Libanius described the corn crisis under Julian in a series of speeches, more or less sympathetic to the emperor depending on the point of view he was representing (none of them being published at the time); that of Julian against his detractors in the Funeral Oration or *Epitaphios* (*Or.* 18), of the council to Julian (*Or.* 15), of Libanius to the council (*Or.* 16), or of his disillusioned old age, to a private audience (*Or.* 1).[22] According to the account closest to Julian's own, the councillors used the supplies contributed by Julian while hoarding their own (*Or.* 18.195). In a less sympathetic version he noted that Julian's measures to control prices – the inspiration, in his most hostile judgement, of some malicious spirit (*Or.* 1.126) – had the effect of emptying the market not of only corn but of all other foodstuffs. To remove profit, he observed, was in effect to put an end to trade altogether (*Or.* 15.21). While being careful, in an interesting piece of economic analysis, to divert the blame from his landowning colleagues to the corn-merchants,[23] Libanius conceded that insufficient controls might have been imposed by the council upon the bakers, and that some Antiochenes, showing 'human frailty and error', had possibly been too greedy for profit (*Or.* 15.23). It also appears from remarks in a letter of Libanius to the *consularis Syriae* Alexander (*Ep.* 1406), that after his departure on the Persian campaign Julian's officials actively supervised shopkeepers at Antioch, compelling them with threats of punishment to produce audited accounts of their transactions in the crisis. The traders professed this to be an impossible demand. Not expecting ever to have to produce accounts, they had not kept them.

Price control, special imports of grain and diverted supplies, supervision of shopkeepers and traders – it is difficult, picking up Ammianus' criticism of Julian's policy, to see what other arrangements to deal with the crisis could be envisaged, unless it were to transfer the administration of the grain supply from the city council altogether into the emperor's own hands. This would in contemporary terms have been a very radical solution, but Julian appears to have moved some distance along this path. Resentment at such direct intervention by the government in the administration of Antioch may be what lies behind Ammianus' remarks in describing the *consularis* Alexander, whom Julian left in office on his departure on the Persian campaign. A harsh and turbulent man, Alexander was a fitting match for the greedy and aggressive Antiochenes, as Julian described them in justifying his appointment; 'dicebatque ... Antiochiensibus avaris et contumeliosis huius modi iudicem convenire' (23.2.3). The presence in Julian's words of the themes of 'avarice' and 'insolence' is not arbitrary, but an expression of the conflicting interests of which he was the victim.[24] 'Insolence' represents the outspoken conduct of the people of Antioch. It was however the 'avarice' of the propertied class of the city that had frustrated

Julian's policy on the corn supplies, undertaken from a desire, as Ammianus saw it, to be well thought of by the people. On this issue of 'popularity' Ammianus stands with Libanius (in the orator's more sincere moments) against Julian, against Gallus Caesar – and against Christian bishops, those eloquent spokesmen for the poor – in his defence of the interests of the upper classes of Antioch.

If Ammianus' attitudes are hidden away in passing hints and choices of phrase, Libanius was quite frank in his support of the free market against government intervention. Writing to the *comes Orientis* Aradius Rufinus after the latter's departure with Julian to the Persian frontier, Libanius urged him 'in the matter of the corn' to allow the economy of the city to function freely and without interference. The interventionist policies supported by Rufinus, reflected Libanius, were more suitable for Rome than for Antioch; here, people preferred the market to be 'autonomous' – 'it being better to suffer a little, than to live amid reproach and accusations of responsibility' (*Ep.* 1379). There, it may be said, speaks a man who does not have to suffer very much himself. Libanius' correspondent was a Roman senator, later *praefectus urbi* under Gratian. It would not be surprising if, used to the problems of the city of Rome, he was prepared to take a more authoritarian approach to the questions of corn supply and market control than Libanius would think appropriate.[25]

The experiences of Antioch in 354 and 362 are no tribute either to the effectiveness, or to the social justice, of the free market economy at a time of crisis. Yet the problem is only partly the general one of government control in relation to private enterprise. Antioch had never fully adjusted to its role as part-time imperial capital. Its ancient civic institutions and their spokesmen were ill-adapted to the demands made on their city and its resources by the emperors and their supporters, and by those imperial officials, civil and military, who were resident there and formed a significant part of its population (p. 72ff.). Antioch was not simply, as many still liked to think, a metropolis of the Greek east. It was an imperial capital city, which had not yet accepted the structures of power and authority that its status in the end made inevitable.[26]

The stage of the food crisis at Antioch associated with Julian's fixing of maximum prices coincides almost exactly with the burning, on 22 October 362, of the temple of Apollo at Daphne: that disaster itself being the sequel of Julian's attempt to purify the sacred site by removing burials from its precincts, including the relics of the martyred saint Babylas. The events at Daphne are best described in the context of Ammianus' religious opinions, but here establish the point, not only that the particular experience of Julian at Antioch was an extremely diverse one, but that social relations in the city presented themselves in a variety of expressions, religious as well as economic.[27] The same is true of Alexandria, notable for disorder and riots over religious dissension, and of course of Rome, the scene of the most varied and richly documented of all Ammianus' portraits of social relations in a big city. Ammianus' descriptions of Rome, to which he gave very great importance in the

414　　　　　　　*Part Two: Visa vel Lecta*

design of his history, take a variety of forms, literary and circumstantial. We begin with the first of these before moving on to the historian's more particular accounts of social relations in the Eternal City.

*

Ammianus' two digressions on social life at Rome occur at widely separated points in his surviving text (14.6 and 28.4). Introduced in similar fashion, and in each case presenting the faults of senate or nobility followed by those of the common people, the digressions can easily look like two attempts to achieve the same result.[28] Yet there are differences of presentation in the two digressions. The first is more selective in choice of material, more thematic in its emphasis and more measured in its presentation, its various topics are introduced with a greater variety and resource of language and style. The second digression, perhaps even more lively in specific detail, is less coherently organised, its often arresting images are more arbitrarily related to each other and the general considerations that lie behind Ammianus' choice of examples are not made clear. It is as if Ammianus were filling out his first digression with a further selection of examples, using left-over material he had not included earlier; or perhaps the second passage, less polished than the first, never received the revision intended for it. It is however worth asking whether the two digressions are differently presented because they express different preoccupations on Ammianus' part. The first is occasioned by his reflections on the evolution of Rome from infancy and youth, through maturity to an old age in which her historic mission is inherited by the emperors.[28] Only the citizen assemblies of the Eternal City now represent her greatness in earlier ages, were they not betrayed by the frivolous tastes of men 'who do not reflect where they were born' (14.6.7). Ammianus' digression, with a thematic emphasis reflecting this heavily 'ideological' introduction, moves from the ostentation in the public conduct and self-advertisement of the senatorial class, to their treatment of foreigners, their lack of culture, their insularity, their lack of interest in anything that comes from outside Rome, their hypochondria – a sort of perverse ostentation in disease reflecting the arrogance of their social position.

The second digression is introduced, more prosaically, by licensing laws brought in by the urban prefect Ampelius. No one may open a tavern before the fourth hour of the day, or heat water for mixing drink or cook meat before the appointed time, and no respectable person must be seen eating in public (snacks bought from street kiosks and cookhouses) – excellent measures, in Ammianus' view, had not Ampelius lost his nerve and failed to enforce them (28.4.4).[30] In keeping with this very down-to-earth introduction, Ammianus' digression, leaving ideology aside, presents aspects of senatorial and popular taste in a series of specific images. Some topics, repeated from the first digression, are now given added colour by this emphasis on circumstantial detail. Lack of

XVI. Social Relations 415

cultural interest, 'libraries closed like tombs' in the earlier digression, becomes a liking for Marius Maximus and Juvenal at the expense of any other writer (14.6.18; 28.4.14); the 'peregrinus' treated with arrogant disdain in the first digression now finds himself closely interrogated about which bathing establishment he uses and which house he frequents (14.6.19f.; 28.4.10); the lack of social finesse in the first digression is transformed in the second into the wonderfully visual image of senators averting their foreheads 'in the manner of threatening bulls', from visitors attempting to greet them with the kiss that would indicate their claim to social equality (14.6.13f.; 28.4.10)! Public processions of senators with columns of attendants now materialise as expeditions to Puteoli or Lake Avernus in painted barges with silk screens to keep out mosquitoes and the rays of the sun (14.6.16f.; 28.4.18), or forays into public baths to seek out the latest courtesan or prostitute (28.4.9).

The second digression adds abuses not mentioned in the first: passion for horses and charioteers (28.4.11), the capricious treatment of slaves (28.4.16), gaming with dice (28.4.21), the elaborate dishes paraded at dinner-parties – a topic rhetorically passed over ('praetermitto') in the first digression (14.6.16; 28.4.13) – godless superstition (28.4.24), sordid litigation and disputes over wills between husband and wife (28.4.26). In some of these vignettes, social relations between the nobility and other classes are stated or implied; as in senatorial houses crowded with singers, dancers, musicians and their monstrous mechanical inventions (14.6.18), flatterers and leisured parasites (28.4.12), or the visitors to Rome, to whose experience Ammianus reverts with the natural interest of one who had suffered it himself (14.6.19ff.; 28.4.11), encounters in baths with lower-class prostitutes (28.4.9), lifelong friendships forged in gambling saloons (28.4.21), charioteers and magicians recruited to conduct blackmail in cases of debt (28.4.25); above all, in a splendid combination of the rhetorical and the circumstantial, those columns of attendants who followed them in their excursions, entire households marching like armies through the streets of Rome, complete with kitchen staff and the family buffoon, and idle hangers-on picked up in the streets ('otiosis plebeiis de vicinitate coniunctis') – the procession winding up with the household eunuchs, carefully arranged in order of age.[31]

Not that Ammianus minimises the differences in culture and the physical resources of life between the upper and lower classes of Rome. While senators commission gilt bronze statues to secure their name for posterity (14.6.8) and import sycophants to admire the columns of their mansions, their walls gleaming with variegated marble colours (28.6.13), the people squat in poverty under the awnings of the theatre (14.6.25) and quarrel at street corners and in forums and squares over the rival merits of teams of horses (28.4.29). Senators produce fantastic dinners of fish, fowl and dormouse, and have secretaries standing by, pen in hand, to note down the delicacies served (28.4.13) – while the common people haunt taverns and soup-kitchens and, drawn by the odour of cooking and the shrill street-cries of women, bend over to inspect the revolting concoctions, standing on tip-toe and biting their fingers impatiently until the food is cool enough to taste (28.4.34). Intent on the dice, they vent their excitement with vulgar snorting noises through the nostrils (14.6.25). In both digressions, Ammianus emphasises the people's passion for the races; incredible it was, he writes, to see the minds of so many men hanging as one on the outcome of a race (14.6.26). The Circus Maximus is 'their shrine, their abode, their meeting place, their very heart's desire' (28.4.29). There and in the theatre they express their feelings, hissing the performers presented to them unless reconciled by payments of money, or shouting for strangers to be expelled (28.4.32), screaming their opinions at comedy or hunting show, horse-race or theatrical performance with acclamations aimed at 'the major and minor magistrates, even matrons', who provide them (28.4.33).[32]

*

The element of satirical distortion in Ammianus' portrayal needs no emphasis, nor the visually exuberant, even theatrical, quality of his choice of detail. The result is a caricature of the social manners of the classes of Rome, resembling not so much serious analysis as the parodies of popular comedy, less photographic archive than portfolio of cartoons.[33] For all that the cartoon is a powerful and valid form of social comment, this is not all that Ammianus provides. He offers descriptions of actual episodes of late Roman social life, to set beside the literary constructions presented so far. To judge from these episodes, the relationship between the senators and people of Rome was intense, intimate, and volatile; it could shift from high popularity to a hostility expressed in riots and disorder, and, with equal abruptness, back again to popularity.

The case of L. Aurelius Avianius Symmachus, prefect of Rome in 364-5, illustrates this volatility, and the roots in social behaviour from which it sprang.[34] As prefect of Rome, Avianius Symmachus supervised the building of a new bridge over the Tiber. He was allowed by the emperors to dedicate the bridge after his departure from office, the popularity that accrued from the new amenity being granted to him personally rather than to the office of *praefectus urbi* (*ILS* 769). Ammianus records that the dedication was greeted by the 'great joy' of the populace, presumably in some form of organised celebration; 'magna civium laetitia dedicavit' (27.3.3). A few years later, however, a rioting mob set fire to his splendid house in Trastevere because he had been heard to say, at a time when wine was in short supply, that he would sooner use the surplus produce of his estates to quench lime-kilns than sell it at the low prices demanded. The 'vilis quidam plebeius' who heard this knew what he was talking about; for it has been pointed out, on the evidence of the elder Pliny, how wine could be used to slake lime as part of the preparation of waterproof cement for building 'piscinae', or bathing-pools.[35] Symmachus' comment was an allusion to the building works mentioned also by Q. Aurelius Symmachus in letters of the same period to his father. The elder

XVI. Social Relations

Symmachus was on this occasion forced to leave Rome because of the rioting, but by the following New Year's Day (of 376) he was back among his colleagues, having been recalled by a decree of the senate and popular acclamations (Symmachus, *Epp*. 1.44; 2.38).

Avianius Symmachus' successor as urban prefect, C. Caeionius Rufius Volusianus Lampadius, had acquired popularity as praetor by giving games, by public building and by indiscriminate largesse to the people; pressed by the people to distribute money to the unworthy, 'in order to show himself both generous and contemptuous of the multitude', and apparently combining this with a sarcastic comment upon papal charity, he summoned and arbitrarily enriched a collection of paupers 'from the Vatican' (27.3.6).[36] He also suffered frequent public tumults in his prefecture, during one of which a mob 'of the lowest sort' tried to burn down his house near the baths of Constantine. Lampadius retreated to the Milvian Bridge waiting for the riot to subside, while his household slaves and other inhabitants of the locality ('vicinorum et familiarum') repelled the demonstrators by climbing to the rooftops and pelting them with stones and tiles (27.3.5ff.). This alliance between the slave 'familiae' of Lampadius and his neighbours against the rioters is an interesting projection of the distinction earlier drawn by Tacitus between the 'respectable part of the populace, connected with the great houses' ('pars populi integra et magnis domibus adnexa') who welcomed the death of Nero in the hope of better things to come, and the 'plebs sordida et circo ac theatris sueta' who had depended on the emperor for its amusements, regretted his fall and, together with the 'worst of the slave population', feared its consequences for themselves (*Hist*. 1.14).[37] The slave attendants of the great families belong by implication to the more respectable part of the urban populace, and so it is still in the time of Ammianus.

One more story of a riot reveals another type of social relationship between a prefect and the people of Rome, and another cause of unrest. The prefect Fl. Leontius (356) had provoked riots by his arrest of a popular charioteer, whom he held in custody despite the attempts of a crowd to get him released.[38] The outburst died down, but a few days later came more disorder, on the occasion this time of a wine shortage. Leontius amazed his attendants by advancing boldly on the crowd. Sitting in his carriage he looked sharply about him until he saw someone he recognised; this was a large man with red hair, 'vasti corporis rutilique capilli'. The prefect asked him if he was in fact Petrus Valvomeres, 'as he had heard' (15.7.4). Receiving an aggressive reply in the affirmative, he had the man grabbed as a known trouble maker and hoisted aloft, hands bound behind his back. The sight of their leader forlornly calling for their help as he hung there cowed the people, who now melted away through the streets of the city; 'per varia urbis membra diffusum ita evanuit'. Petrus Valvomeres was let down, given a scourging and exiled to Picenum, where in a further, flagrant violation of social conventions (not to mention the law) he seduced a girl of good family, and was executed (15.7.5).

*

In all this, it is almost as if rioting and disorder were exaggerated forms of normal social relations. The people express their reactions to events, in however simplified a form, yet articulately, making it clear exactly what their response is. If they turn to rioting, it is possible for Ammianus to say what was the cause of it, and apparent that this was understood at the time. In the case of Symmachus' comment about using wine to slake his lime-kilns, it has taken modern research to show by learned reference what was known at the time by a lower-class Roman (27.3.4); and on the occasion just described, disorder about the detention of a charioteer turns to demonstrations about a wine shortage, it being perfectly clear what the successive situations were. Further, despite the size and vast population of the city of Rome, the episode of Leontius and the popular leader Petrus Valvomeres reveals a mutual recognition of a remarkable intimacy. 'Are you Petrus Valvomeres, as I have heard?' says the prefect, face to face, and the man can assent with resounding insults before being arrested; 'cum esset, sonu respondisset obiurgatorio' (15.7.6).

From the earliest of their public magistracies, senators were obliged to play a full part in the ceremonial and festive life of the city, especially through their obligation to provide commemorative games. A historian of the early Roman empire will scarcely recognise the quaestorship, praetorship and suffect consulship as the significant offices they had once been in the career of a senator, leading to governorships of provinces, curatorships and military commands. They are now held by a young man hardly out of his teens, their main duties to do with the public games it was his – in practice his father's – obligation to provide to commemorate the office.[39] The sums laid out in this regularised largesse were huge. The senator Petronius Maximus, 'one of the rich ones', laid out 4,000 pounds of gold on his son's praetorship in the early fifth century, according to the well-informed Greek historian Olympiodorus (Fr. 44); and Symmachus, described in the same passage of Olympiodorus as a senator of 'middling' rank, spent 2,000 pounds of gold on his son's praetorship in 401. It is these games that Symmachus can be seen organising in many of his latest letters: importing horses from Spain, antelopes from north Africa, bears from Africa and Dalmatia, Scottish dogs, Egyptian crocodiles ... not to mention Saxon prisoners to be displayed as gladiators, a 'race worse than Spartacus', who upset Symmachus' sensibilities by committing suicide rather than face humiliation (and in any case be killed) in the arena (*Ep.* 2.46). To secure these resources, in a culmination of a life spent in a patient, unremitting garnering of influence, Symmachus mobilised friends and contacts in all quarters of the Roman world and the imperial administration.[40] The Spanish horses, for instance, he arranged to have stabled at Arles for the duration of the winter (9.20), and the Dalmatian bears can be traced in Symmachus' letters at all stages of their journey, across the Adriatic to Apulia, then by road through Italy to

XVI. Social Relations 419

Rome (7.121; 9.135, 142). To his friends and colleagues Symmachus sent invitations to the games – one standard form of letter bears the heading 'multos ad praeturam invitat' (8.71) – and gifts in the form of ivory diptychs, silver canisters and penholders (2.81). To the people, no doubt, were distributed the bronze medallions now known as 'contorniates', showing figures of the early empire known for their munificence (Trajan, Nero), assorted literary figures (Sallust, Apuleius), even Alexander the Great – not with any aim of systematic 'pagan propaganda', as has been argued, but with a generalised appeal to the glorious past of Rome and her empire, and the romantic appeal of antiquity.[41]

Senators did not shrink into the background of the visible social life of Rome: far from it. We have seen how Ammianus describes them, parading through the streets of the city and journeying through Italy, wearing gorgeously coloured apparel, which they would allow to float in the wind to display the emblems embroidered on their under-garments (14.6.8): behaviour well associated with the 'theatrical' aspects of late Roman life so often stated or implied by Ammianus and our other sources.[42] Ammianus presents a particularly vivid image to add to those mentioned earlier: of an unnamed senator who, escaping by bribery (so it was said) from involvement in an accusation of magic, so far from trying to improve himself flaunted a display of innocence and could still be seen, when Ammianus wrote nearly thirty years later, clattering around the streets of Rome on a caparisoned horse, dragging after him armies of slave attendants. Ammianus' staccato rhythms rattle across the page in fine imitation of the senator's progress; 'equo phalerato insidens, discurrensque per silices, multa post se nunc usque trahit agmina servulorum' (26.3.5).

It is impossible to state any 'scientific' conclusion as to the moral standards and general seriousness of the senatorial class of Rome. Nor is it clear what any such conclusion could signify, when such a variety of conduct is on show, expressing the tastes of a class of such diverse social and cultural backgrounds, from landed millionaires to retired bureaucrats only recently adlected, from ancestral Roman clans to provincial gentry hanging on to their status by the mere skin of their teeth; the indispensible letters and orations of Symmachus well express the range of social experience in question.[43] Ammianus felt no such inhibitions in denouncing senators for ignoring serious concerns and high culture, instead filling their houses with the 'diversions of leisure and idleness', namely musicians, actors, organ-players and the dancing-girls mentioned earlier;[44] and he can adduce individual cases to fill out his picture, like that of Olybrius, a member of the great family of the Anicii, who spent 'almost his entire private life following the theatre and in love affairs' (28.4.1). Yet, if scientific objectivity is unattainable, certain episodes do allow us to place Ammianus' picture of waste and moral frivolity in the context of social relations at Rome. In one of these, the urban prefect L. Turcius Apronianus Asterius (362-3) has lost the sight of an eye, he suspects by sorcery (he was in Syria at the time), and for this and other reasons decides to conduct a purge. Among those punished was a charioteer, Hilarinus; the grounds for his execution were that he had given his son for training to a sorcerer, in the hope, evidently, that having learned these priceless but illegal arts the boy could conduct magic rites without involving outsiders and the risk of blackmail.[45] This case is immediately followed by that of the senator just mentioned, who had had a slave trained in magic arts (26.3.3ff.). In his second digression Ammianus further alleges that a senator in debt will go to a charioteer, 'who will try anything, without inhibition', get him to accuse his creditor of magic, and then blackmail the creditor to escape his debt (28.4.25). In his particularly detailed account of prosecutions for magic and adultery at Rome under Valentinian, Ammianus describes how the whole affair began when a senator and his wife alleged before the *praefectus urbi* Olybrius (the amorous theatre fanatic just mentioned) that their lives had been attacked by magic arts.[46] They named three suspects, whose identity strikingly confirms Ammianus' allegations on the complicity of senators with prominent representatives of 'low life' at Rome: they were an organ-player (or -builder), a soothsayer and a professional wrestler (28.1.8). Other men, arrested and put to the torture, named certain nobles as having used 'experts in doing harm' – that is, sorcerers – through the agency of their 'clients and other men of low birth, known criminals and informers' (28.1.10). There is no need now to follow Ammianus into the seamy side of senatorial life that was now revealed, except to note that at one point four distinguished senators were accused not only of complicity in magic but of patronising a charioteer named Auchenius (28.1.27); and that, along with two other senators, the procurator of the Roman mint was executed for involvement in magic arts. His complicity is intriguing, given what was said earlier about the 'contorniates', commemorative medallions issued to the people on the occasion of public games. Perhaps his connection with the games was in one way or another how the procurator had found himself caught up with this aspect of senatorial life and social relations at Rome. Ammianus, it will be recalled, told how the people hissed performers off the stage unless they were appeased by payments of money; 'artifices scaenarii per sibilos exploduntur, siquis sibi aere humiliorem non conciliaverit plebem' (28.4.32; p. 416).

*

These connections, based both on material interests and on sentiment and ideology, between the nobility and people of Rome, were the setting for an aspect of the social relations of the time not so far discussed, the expansion of Christianity. As we shall see in the next chapter, Ammianus exploits this aspect of the situation in order to give an indirectly polemical emphasis to his descriptions of religious events at Rome and other great cities, by reducing them to secular terms. Whether in doing so he distorts the true nature of his material, or merely presents it in one of

XVI. Social Relations

its many possible perspectives, his testimony is extremely important. Whatever else was involved, the existing framework of social relations was that in which the Christian religion advanced in this century of its greatest relative growth. Here too are riots and disorder, meetings and processions, great public monuments, and a rising papacy expressing itself in the manner of the secular aristocracy, conspicuously, expensively, and with ostentation.

The place of Christianity in the affections of the people of Rome is pertinently illustrated in Ammianus' account of Constantius' attempt to induce bishop Liberius to support his efforts to force Athanasius of Alexandria into exile. Refusing to co-operate, Liberius was himself exiled, but had to be smuggled out of the city at night for fear of the people, who supported him avidly; 'populi metu, qui eius amore flagrabat' (15.7.10). Worse was to follow when a few years later Liberius died and a dispute broke out over the succession, an explosion of violence in which no less than 137 corpses were left on the floor of a Christian basilica. The *praefectus urbi* Viventius retired to the suburbs while the violence reigned, and stiff action was called for from his successor, Vettius Agorius Praetextatus (27.3.11f.; 8.8ff.). What an 'honest Pannonian' bureaucrat could not achieve was left to a great pagan senator of Rome – with conspicuously more successful results.

Allowance must be made for the irony, and for a certain polemical purpose in the way in which Ammianus describes these events.[47] Even so, on the facts he presents it becomes clear that, whatever spiritual values were at stake, the papacy and senators of Rome were involved in the same competition as each other for publicity and prestige, its arena the public places, now including the great churches, of Rome.

It is possible to glimpse the public role of the Christian church at Rome in similar terms, though in a far different perspective, in the poems of Prudentius on prominent martyr-cults of his day, the *Peristephanon Liber*.[48] The poet's images fit perfectly into the world of visual effect and ceremony summoned up by Ammianus. He pictures for instance the observance by the populace of the festivals of Saints Peter and Paul, as they crowd into the squares before their churches on their common feast-day, while the poet attends and sings hymns in both (*Per.* 12.57-60). The bishop of Rome, having done vigil in St. Peter's across the Tiber, will then cross to the left bank to attend the church of St. Paul, naturally leading a procession of the faithful on his way. The building of the church of Saint Paul on the via Ostiensis (S. Paolo fuori le Mura) was the subject of a *Relatio* of Symmachus of the year 384, and it was dedicated by a Theodosian *praefectus urbi* in 391. This was a spectacular monument of the new Rome, and one familiar to Ammianus; he must have seen the building site when he first arrived at Rome, and would pass it on any later trip he made to Ostia.[49] The church was badly damaged by fire in 1823 and its authentic form lost in the rebuilding. Its earlier appearance is however preserved in a fine engraving by Piranesi, and if this may seem to give an idealised impression, we may adduce the 'regia pompa', or 'royal magnificence' attributed to the church by Prudentius – gilded beams and triumphal arch decorated with mosaic frescoes of flowers, orders of marble columns (*Per.* 12.46-54).[50]

Prudentius tells in another poem how on the festival of St. Hippolytus, senate and people jostled together in their common devotion, the massed people breaking apart like a battle-line the ordered ranks of senators; and in this poem too we get a brief description of the lofty columns and gilded beams of the church (*Per.* 11.188ff.; 215ff.). In particular, the cult of St. Laurentius, the 'Roman martyr' *par excellence*, was favoured by the now converted senators, according to the long second poem in the *Peristephanon* (2.517-20). It is no coincidence that amid this choice of cults, it was at the shrine of St. Laurentius that the senatorial heiress Melania was spending night vigil before suffering the miscarriage that was to turn her thoughts away from family life and the married state.[51] Neither Prudentius nor the fascinating *Life* of St. Melania makes it clear which of the shrines of St. Laurentius was involved in the senatorial worship they describe, an ambiguity worth exploring briefly for the light it casts on the social role of the later fourth-century papacy.

Damasus, whose turbulent accession to the bishopric of Rome was mentioned above, was actually proclaimed bishop in the church of St. Laurentius known as 'in Lucina' or 'in Lucinis'. It lay to the north of the central area of Rome, not far from the mausoleum of Augustus. During his tenure of the papacy, Damasus founded another, more central church dedicated to St. Laurentius. (Like Damasus himself before his elevation, Laurentius had been a deacon of the Roman church. One of the poems written by Damasus for the shrine lays some emphasis on his subject's ecclesiastical career, and it is hard to imagine that the parallel with himself was not intended to be drawn). The new church, known as 'S. Laurentii in Damaso', is described in the sixth-century account of Damasus in the *Liber Pontificalis* as situated 'iuxta theatrum', that is the ancient theatre of Pompey. It was also known, according to a note in a manuscript edition of Damasus' poems, as the church 'in Prasino', which it does not take long reflection to identify as the nearby stables of the Green circus faction.[52]

It would be naïve to press this incidental connection between a fourth-century pope and the circus faction supported, among the Roman emperors, by Caligula, Nero, L. Verus, Commodus and Elagabalus. Nor need we here enter the dispute whether the Green faction was, as these imperial preferences imply, associated with a more 'popular' tradition in Roman political life – one connected rather with the 'plebs sordida et circo ac theatris assueta' than the 'pars populi integra et magnis domibus adnexa' mentioned earlier as categories of social organisation at Rome (p. 417). Descriptions of the districts of Rome place the stables of all six factions in the Ninth Region of the city, named 'Circus Flaminius',[53] and it is more likely that Damasus' new foundation, if it had any such purpose, was intended to reconcile the competing factions within the Christian church rather than to exploit any one of them in his favour. At

XVI. Social Relations

the same time, enough has been said of the involvement of the people of Rome in the religious life of their city and of charioteers as a medium of popular and senatorial taste, to suggest the potential role of a church dedicated to the 'Roman' martyr in the midst of the region of the city in which the circus factions were housed. More generally, through such church foundations, the religious life of the people of Rome was as it were physically diverted from the shrines of the old cults, standing vacant in the monumental area of the city, to centres of worship in the quarters and suburbs where the people actually lived. The conversion of 'urbs Roma' to Christianity was nothing if not a complex process, and one operating on many levels; but part, and an essential part, of the manner in which it was done concerns the social relations and the physical area within which the process took place. There may be an ironic affinity between the ceremonious ineffectiveness of pagan spokesmen before the advance of Christianity (Symmachus, let us say, against Ambrose of Milan), and the old monumental areas of the city, admired by visitors such as Constantius in 357, but lacking an actual resident population upon whose ordinary lives they impinged.[54] While the people of Rome found their place in the great new churches of the Christian faith, and as these gradually encroached on the central area of the city, paganism also shifted its ground. It moved from the public arena of its historic greatness to the patronage of a determined but diminishing minority of senators, and ultimately, with the disappearance of any actively 'religious' content in favour of a scholarly antiquarianism, from their public lives to their private libraries.[55]

CHAPTER XVII

Religion and Philosophy

(1) Divination and *daimones*

If there is a natural temptation to think of Ammianus' religious position primarily in terms of his attitude to Christianity, it must be resisted, for it will result in a badly distorted perspective. The subject bears far more broadly than on the particular issue of Christianity, and cannot be reduced to a closed set of questions within any conventionally accepted category, or categories, of fourth-century experience. What is at stake is the entire definition and role of that domain of human thought and conduct in which the gods and the divine have an interest, amid the many possibilities, Christian and other, that were available. Symmachus' assertion that there was more than one road by which to approach the mysteries of the Universe (*Rel.* 3.10) was not just a concession made in face of his adversary, Ambrose of Milan; it was controversial, precisely in that it denied to the Christians *their* claim – immediately made in reply by Ambrose – to be the possessors of the 'one true way'.

The same is true on the other side. It is well appreciated how Julian's attempts to emulate the Christian church by providing hospices, support for widows and orphans, and by creating a hierarchical priesthood whose members were required to subscribe to standards of conduct and belief defined by the emperor, were innovations within paganism itself.[1] The old religions, as known to Ammianus, did not place emphasis on 'correctness' of belief in matters that were by definition mysterious, better understood by symbol, myth and allegory, and maintained by the due performance of ritual acts rather than by theological assertions; while, rather than requiring, like Christianity, participation of the faithful in organised ceremonies of a 'spiritual' character, they penetrated, through a multiplicity of points of contact between the divine and the human worlds, every patch and corner of everyday life and social relations. There were of course the mystery cults of Graeco-Oriental origin, such as the mysteries of Serapis ('Graeca quaedam arcana') into which a German prince was initiated during his sojourn as a hostage in Gaul (16.12.25); or the cults of Mithras and Magna Mater, of which Julian was an initiate. The senator Praetextatus, a man probably known to Ammianus, was an initiate in no less than six mystery religions, to many of which he also introduced his wife.[2] These cults, with their personal 'baptisms' and their explicit anticipation of the life to come, trod the same ground as

Christianity and they, rather than the old gods, were recognised by many Christians as the main challenge to their own religion. But Ammianus was not writing a religious history. He mentions the conversion of the German prince only as a circumstantial detail to explain his change of name from Agenarich to Serapio, and says nothing about the initiations of Julian or of Praetextatus. The 'high places' where true history was accustomed to run (26.1.1) were of a secular, not a religious character.

We must avoid too the deliberately false perspective introduced by Christians in their use of the term 'pagan'.[3] This term, which was commonly used in this sense only in Ammianus' later lifetime, is for his earlier years anachronistic in its implication that the only remaining heathen were country folk ('pagani' – men of rural districts, or 'pagi'). This was simply not true in the middle years of the fourth century. Here we are looking at a mixed society, with a preponderance of Christians in all but the upper classes (and often there too), but with many supporters of the old religions still surviving vigorously, well organised and quite able to speak up for their own interests and those of their gods. In their use of the word 'pagan', Christians identified their antagonists as these would not have identified – indeed not even have recognised – themselves. Further, it is essentially a western perspective, radically different from the eastern in its assumption that 'paganism' was nothing but a rural survival. In the east, by contrast, the use of the term 'Hellene' to define a believer in the old gods implies an identification of religious conviction with devotion to Greek culture, in a way no less contentious than its identification in the west with rural ignorance. This view was encouraged, for example, by Julian and by Jerome, who for their opposite reasons regarded Christianity and Classical culture as contradictions in terms. It was shared by relatively few others, and was far from universal even among churchmen. In a series of orations against Julian, Gregory of Nazianzus justified use by Christians of a Greek culture that was part of their birthright as free men, and that provided the language in which political life and social relations among those of all religious persuasions were articulated. Ammianus, as we have seen, took the more tolerant view, and criticised Julian on just this point of his religious policies.[4]

Ammianus has no specific term for what later fourth-century Christians of west and east respectively categorised as 'pagans' and 'Hellenes'. He would of course include them among those 'true worshippers of the Divinity', mentioned in a passage referring to modest provincial clergy to whom he also accords this status (below, p. 445). Like Symmachus in the third *Relatio*, he might concede to Christians the knowledge of one of the many roads to the great mysteries of the Universe – even if the privilege of free travel was not extended by the Christians to those whose choice of route differed from their own. Avoiding 'pagani' (if he knew of the Christian use of the term) as inept and misleading, he might have written, as does Ambrose, of 'gentiles'. For Ammianus, this word and its cognates usually meant things foreign or native, more precisely barbarian soldiers in Roman service rather than religious outsiders, but even had this not been so, it would imply the same false perspective as before, putting the writer outside the system of belief in question and accepting that it was best viewed in a Christian perspective.[5] But 'pagans' have no need to define themselves only in relation to their opponents. Christianity was the newcomer, their own the ancestral religion, and it stood in no need of justification or apology.

Ammianus not only fails to reproduce the concept 'paganism' and to provide a simple terminology for it. He has no use either for the abstract term 'Christianity' – surprisingly rare, in fact, in Ammianus' day – to denote a religion or system of belief.[6] Like Symmachus, Ammianus uses institutional, in themselves neutral, terms like 'lex', 'religio', or 'secta', with the defining epithet 'Christiana', otherwise 'ritus Christianus'; or else he will simply say 'Christiani', that is a body or a group of Christians taken in a specific, definite, and not an abstract sense.[7] Ammianus would see the question of religion as involving an infinitely varied system of conduct, attitudes, customs and beliefs about the world and the divine powers that impinge on it, and one not capable of a single, fixed terminology. It emerges in the history through topics like divination, sacrifice, astrology and magic arts, linked by manifold transitions to intellectual and cultural issues, to science, mathematics and philosophy, to superstition. Any of these issues – for example horoscopes and magic in their association with treason – might at any moment become the central issue in relation to government action, but 'paganism', though it can be in part *characterised*, cannot be *defined* in any one of these ways: fear of magic, though connected with it, is not the same thing as hostility to paganism. What we call 'paganism' was linked with the institutions of social life, education and government much as Gibbon described it in a still fine chapter,[8] and this integration is precisely what made it so difficult for the emperors to deal with as a separate issue. They could ban nocturnal sacrifice and private consultation of soothsayers, close temples and confiscate their properties, follow their predecessors in suppressing magic arts, take a hundred other measures, but had constantly to make exceptions in favour of established practice and custom. The modern historian faces a no less intractable problem of definition and should not embark upon it with a vocabulary and conceptual framework that prejudge the issue.

*

Ammianus was born around the year 330, that is to say after the conquest of the east by Constantine and the council of Nicaea, at a time when Athanasius of Alexandria, sharply criticised for his ambition in one passage of the history (p. 441f.), was already a rising star, ready to try his strength with the emperor's; his first exile, to distant Trier, fell when Ammianus was a little boy. Ammianus' adult world bristles with Christians and their institutions, in the cities and in the government and administration, and this is reflected in the history; his towns contain

XVII. Religion and Philosophy

their Christian churches, the churches contain pious citizens and supporters of the emperors, religious policies are recognised as a central part of the emperors' interests. Whether or not a historian made an issue of any of these matters, they were prominent in the society that surrounded him, and must be acknowledged if he had any pretensions at all to be writing about the real world. As to emphasis and mode of presentation, these are matters in which a skilful writer may use his technique in order to retain some initiative in face even of unwelcome facts, and to indicate his preferences without becoming involved in controversy.

Although they are in general terms relevant to his attitudes, there is little point in cataloguing the allusions to the gods, fate and Fortune with which Ammianus equips his narrative. This facet of his style is clear to anyone who opens the text of the history, but it will often be difficult to show that a god or goddess (Mars, say, or Bellona), or an allusion to fate or Fortune, is more than a technical device useful, for example, in transition from one subject to another or to convey the enormity, or unexpectedness, of the events by which the Romans were confronted, but not implying any significant theological or philosophical reflection. There are exceptions, as when the Persian campaign of Julian is described as being determined by fate, when the emperor was convinced before the campaign that his 'Fortuna' was irresistible or tried during it to make a sacrifice to Mars (above, pp. 137, 158). Here, Ammianus is presenting in their true historical light aspects of the religious views of Julian, as relevant to the events in which they were involved. In certain contexts, Fortuna can acquire a purposive, even a moral role, as when, in a brief philosophical excursus, she is by implication seen as the agent of Adrastia or Nemesis – 'whom theologians of old imagined as the daughter of Justice, looking down at earthly affairs from some secret eternal vantage point' – in toppling Gallus Caesar from his heights of power and destroying him (14.11.25ff.). Yet this is an unusually elaborate passage, worked up, by rhetorical as much as by philosophical means, to suit the particularly intense sequence of tragic narrative, moral reflection and historical parallels with which Ammianus concludes his Book 14 (11.1-34). In the great majority of cases, fate, Fortune and the gods function in Ammianus as part of the normal equipment of a historian writing in the Classical manner.[9] To take an instance: at the opening of the obviously portentous Book 31, although one of his editors listed the passage under the index entry 'Fortuna dea', Ammianus' expression, 'inter haec Fortunae volucris rota, adversa prosperis semper alternans, Bellonam Furiis in societatem ascitis armabat' (31.1.1), is hardly more than an elaborate literary gesture designed to change the scene and indicate in epic language the nature of the great events now in prospect. It is a gesture which even a Christian audience would expect from a poet such as Claudian, and certainly does not imply that Ammianus is making any very forcible point on the other side. It is part of the machinery: what would Classical history and poetry, written with deference to epic style,

428   *Part Two: Visa vel Lecta*

have done without Fortune and the gods?

It will be more rewarding to look in closer detail at certain passages where Ammianus reflects on specific philosophical issues of his time. These passages concern, first, his discussion of divination in the narrative of the reign of Julian in Book 21; second and very briefly, some more scattered reflections on astrology and mathematics; and third, his digression on guardian spirits ('genii' or 'daimones'), also in Book 21.

*

As we saw earlier (p. 124f.), Ammianus defends Julian's interest in divination as proper for a learned man, one interested in all forms of knowledge; 'erudito et studioso cognitionum omnium principi'. Indeed, divination was itself a form of learning; 'doctrinae genus haud leve' (21.1.7). It is through the 'various forms of learning to which we aspire' ('ex his, quae per disciplinas varias affectamus') that the deity shares with mankind the gift of divination. Ammianus supports his interpretation by deploying in rapid succession many diverse points of erudition.[10] He offers in a form not exactly paralleled elsewhere a derivation of the name of Themis, the goddess of Fate, from the Greek word *tetheimena* (literally, 'things placed in position'), and assigns it to ancient writers on theology – 'theologi veteres', or poets who composed on divine matters (21.1.8). He refers to the legendary appearance from the earth of the Etruscan seer Tages, and appeals to 'physici', writers on the physical universe, on the affinity of the Sun with human souls (21.1.11). He cites Aristotle on the physiology of true dreams, though most assume this otherwise unknown reference to have come to Ammianus at second-hand (21.1.12); and, to round off the digression, Cicero, in a combination of two passages from different works of that author (below, p. 430).

As to the philosophical bearing of this flurry of erudition, the language and concepts used by Ammianus, which on first reading follow each other with bewildering rapidity, share a background in Neoplatonic doctrine. To take them in order, there is, first, 'elementorum omnium spiritus', the supreme God who, as just mentioned, shares with mankind the gift of divination. Below this Godhead are 'substantiales potestates', the intermediate deities or 'gods below the heavens', in Macrobius' expression, of the Neoplatonic universe (*Sat.* 1.17.2). These intermediate deities, 'placated by rites of diverse kind', are the actual givers of prophecy, articulate knowledge of the future. Their presiding spirit or 'numen' is Themis, who shares the bed and throne of Jupiter. Ammianus' reference to Jupiter as a 'life-giving force' ('vigoris vivifici') is a characteristic Neoplatonic abstraction, easily paralleled from Plotinus and, again, from Neoplatonic passages of Macrobius (cf. *Somn. Scip.* 1.17.4). Moving on to prophetic utterance by inspired mediums, Ammianus adduces the Sun, the 'world-soul' ('mens mundi'), from which human souls are derived as 'sparks' ('scintillae') which may burn fiercely

XVII. Religion and Philosophy

and prophesy; this notion of the Sun is also present, together with reference to the 'physici' cited as authorities for it, in Macrobius, commenting on an Orphic oracle (*Sat.* 1.18.15), and in that author's Neoplatonic *Commentary on the Dream of Scipio*. 'Heraclitus physicus' together with other philosophers is here cited by Macrobius, for the phrase 'scintilla stellaris essentiae' to describe the nature of the soul (*Somn. Scip.* 1.14.19); it is an early philosophical belief taken over and made part of their system by the Platonists.

As well as Neoplatonism, there is in Ammianus' digression more than a touch of Stoic theory. This is not surprising, elements of Stoic belief having long been incorporated in Neoplatonic philosophy. One effect of the Stoic admixture is to make the divine being more sympathetic of human needs, for the 'numen', in strict Neoplatonic belief a remote and imperturbable deity, is said 'in his kindness' to allow the future to be glimpsed by men, 'whether because they deserve it or because he is touched by their affection'; 'seu quod merentur homines, seu quod tangitur eorum affectione' (21.1.9). It was to the Stoics that Cicero, in his remarkable work *De Divinatione* (1.82) attributed the argument that the validity of divination is a logical consequence of the existence of the gods, because they are benevolent.[11] Ammianus elsewhere, in more Platonic vein, justified knowledge of the future as flowing from the affinity of human souls with the divine (18.3.5).

On certain points, Ammianus seems to go beyond the strictly philosophical implications of the doctrines he presents. His statement that 'sparks' flying from the Sun as 'mens mundi' actually ignite prophetic souls when they are said 'to burn with the mighty force of fire' ('ardere torrente vi magna flammarum') is not paralleled in any other surviving text, and looks more like an over-literal embellishment than a development of philosophical doctrine (21.1.4). Further, Cicero in *De Divinatione* (1.118) denies that the gods direct the flight of individual birds to give signs of the future, supposing that the prophetic meaning of their flight comes from a deeper sympathy with forces in the Universe. Ammianus seems to imply belief in divine direction, though his use of the singular, more abstract, form 'deus' instead of Cicero's 'gods' makes his attitude rather difficult to define; 'volatum avium dirigit deus ...'. Ammianus is perhaps not very interested in such distinctions. His main purpose is to dismiss the idea that birds themselves, ignorant of the future, can of their own intention predict it.

We have seen in all this that certain aspects of Ammianus' philosophical language are closely paralleled in western Neoplatonic sources, where we find them in Macrobius, Martianus Capella, and in allegorising interpretations of Vergil mentioned by his commentator Servius. Now Ammianus cannot himself have used any of these writers, for they all belong to the next generation; so that it seems necessary to suppose him to have been familiar with an earlier tradition of Latin Neoplatonist writing and translation, such as that known to us from the rhetorician Marius Victorinus and the earlier works of Augustine.[12]

There is no need to labour the interest of this for the understanding of Ammianus' philosophical formation. Why did he, as a Greek, look for his vocabulary in existing Latin adaptations of Neoplatonism? One possible explanation might be that Ammianus developed these interests later in life, when he had completed the transition to a Latin intellectual culture and had no wish to go back to Greek sources for something he was used to thinking of and, possibly, had first read in Latin. Or perhaps he was simply adapting his philosophical vocabulary to a form that he knew would be familiar to his western public. Yet a third possibility is that Ammianus was not profoundly interested in philosophy as such. His digression on divination is neither more nor less than a learned digression, employing technical language in a manner calculated not to offer his own views, but to inform his audience at a certain level of erudition, on a topic that he saw to be relevant to his theme. In philosophical terms, his digression on divination – well-informed, compact, even a little over-learned – is written in the same spirit as if he were describing artillery, the origins and causes of earthquakes or the rationale of the bissextile day. There is a difference, in the warmth of feeling in his opening remarks that reflects Ammianus' regard for Julian, but the digression itself does not betray a complete mastery of the actual philosophical issues that were involved.

The allusion to Cicero with which Ammianus concludes his digression is a direct quotation from that writer's work *De Natura Deorum* (2.12). Like Ammianus, Cicero compares the art of divination with medicine, a comparison for which many parallels exist. The similar argument in Cicero's own *De Divinatione* runs from divination to medicine, and then to helmsmanship, generalship, and statesmanship (1.24). These are all 'arts', *technai* in Greek, for which an informed skill is necessary and in which errors can be made. If this happens in the case of divination, it is not the gods but man who is at fault; in Cicero's words quoted by Ammianus, 'non deorum natura, sed hominum coniectura peccavit' (21.1.14). Now, the list of analogous 'arts' – grammar, music and medicine – adduced by Ammianus in support of this argument actually comes from a different work of Cicero, his *Tusculan Disputations* (2.12). Ammianus' language again derives from that of Cicero, but the latter's argument is different; if a grammarian may commit an error ('barbare loquatur') or a musician sing out of key ('absurde canat'), how much worse is the incompetent philosopher, who claims the knowledge relevant to the good life itself? Although Ammianus would have agreed with this argument and with its philosophical basis – the understanding of grammar, music and of life itself as arts that can be acquired – Cicero's argument is not the same as that presented by Ammianus. The historian has combined two passages of Cicero, sharing the conclusion offered by one, but taking his illustrations from the other, where the philosophical context differs from his own. Again, one may ponder the reason for this, but one possibility is that Ammianus' procedure is more literary than philosophical; not that this in any way reduces the warmth of his feeling on the subject. One more thing must be added, however. If Ammianus had paid equal attention to Cicero's most important work on the subject, the *De Divinatione*, he should have realised that although this work views the arguments from all sides, it is in the end a devastating attack on the validity of divination.[13]

*

In his digression on Alexandria, Ammianus gives a survey of the various forms of learning studied there, in which he moves from geometry and music to physics, astronomy ('mundani motus et siderum') and mathematics ('doctique sunt numeris non pauci'), and from this to astrology; 'super his scientiam callent quae fatorum vias ostendit' (22.16.17). This is followed by an emphatic account of the prestige of the Alexandrian schools of medicine.[14] As in the digression on divination, the study of the future is reckoned among other 'scientific' arts as a technique, or learned doctrine. On the science of astronomy, Ammianus has elsewhere a digression on eclipses and their causes, an extremely dense and complicated discussion ending with a reference to the nature of the universe, in the course of which it is stated that the heavenly bodies actually have a fixed location, their apparent movements in space being a consequence merely of the imperfections of human vision. In proportion to the universe, writes Ammianus – 'quantum ad universitatem pertinet' – the earth is but a tiny point in space; 'rerum magnitudini instar exigui subditum puncti' (20.3.12). The passage is striking for its reminiscence of Ammianus' earlier judgment of the emperor Constantius' pretensions to be 'master of the whole world', when he should instead have considered its insignificance. He should have so reflected, thought Ammianus, even if he had ruled the infinity of worlds postulated by Democritus and dreamed of by Alexander the Great when told of them by Anaxarchus. This outburst of commonplace erudition – Ammianus could have got it from Valerius Maximus (8.14. ext. 2) – is relevant to what Ammianus expected of his emperor. Even the circuit of the earth, which seems immense to humans, fills but a tiny point in the Universe; 'ambitus terrae totius, quae nobis videtur immensa, ad magnitudinem universitatis instar brevis optinet puncti' (15.1.4). This was agreed by astronomers ('ut docent mathematici concinentes'), as Constantius 'ought to have read or heard'. Ammianus means that this knowledge, if Constantius had possessed it, would have had a direct influence on his conduct. The knowledge of 'mathematici concinentes' is cited not as a merely 'scientific' issue nor as a gratuitous parade of erudition, but as relevant to the formation of correctly instructed moral attitudes on the emperor's part.

In the digression on eclipses, as in that on divination, elements of Ammianus' vocabulary have been found in a Latin Neoplatonist commentary (that of Calcidius on Plato's *Timaeus*), suggesting an acquaintance of the two writers with handbooks available in the west, or at least with expressions familiar there in more specialist discussion. It is however equally relevant to the character of his digression, that Ammianus can make what has been called an 'embarrassing mistake' in confusing two sorts of eclipses.[15] It seems that here, as in other digressions of a relatively advanced technical nature, Ammianus took care to consult the relevant scientific literature on the subject, but was capable of misunderstandings in its more abstruse aspects.

*

Ammianus' discussion of 'genii' or 'daimones' (21.14.3ff.) arises, curiously when we consider the emperor's Christian beliefs, from the approaching death of Constantius: the emperor suffered disturbing dreams, and confessed to feeling abandoned by a 'certain secret being' ('secretum aliquod') that he was used to seeing, though indistinctly ('squalidius'), in his company (21.14.2). It was supposed that Constantius' 'genius', or guardian spirit, was deserting him and that his life was nearing its end. In the same way, just before his death Julian saw leaving him in the camp in Persia that guardian spirit, the 'genius publicus', who had first appeared to him at Paris, bidding him seize the opportunity of his proclamation (p. 180).

By way of explanation, Ammianus briefly digresses on *genii*.[16] Like his discussion of divination, the digression is not original in subject-matter or interpretation, but interesting for its accumulation of themes: and, again, for idiosyncrasies that may imply a lack of appreciation of some of the finer points of its subject. As in his earlier digression, Ammianus cites 'theologians' ('theologi'), now as authorities for the doctrine that every man has a guardian spirit who, when the individual's 'many virtues' merit it, may even be perceived by him. This truth, says Ammianus, was attested also by oracles and by literary authorities; 'idque et oracula et auctores docuere praeclari' (21.14.4). Pursuing his 'auctores', Ammianus quotes Menander to the effect that a 'daimon' joins every man at birth, to lead him 'like a religious guide', or 'mystagogos', through his life. The lines of Menander (Fr. 714 Koerte) were widely cited, though, as with many well-known quotations, no one actually names the work from which they come. They are quoted, for instance, by Plutarch, more extensively by Eusebius of Caesarea. Eusebius owed his quotation to a survey of Classical learning written a century before his time by Clement of Alexandria; he omits some words but indicates that his citation is incomplete.[17]

Menander's argument is clear from the fuller versions of his words preserved by these authorities; it is that the wicked actions of men are of their own doing and there is no point in trying to pin the blame on an evil genius, for the *daimôn* that attends a man through his life is not evil but good, *agathos*. This word, *agathos*, in the emphatic place at the beginning of the line which gives Menander's passage its philosophical point, is omitted by Ammianus, who concludes his citation at the end of the previous line. In omitting it, he has ignored the essential argument of

XVII. Religion and Philosophy

Menander's lines, in order to appeal to him on the mere existence of personal *daimones* rather than on the consequences that flow from their character as good, and not evil, spirits. Once again literary aptness has taken precedence over philosophical rigour.

The interpretation which now follows of the gods of Homer as allegorical *daimones*, is a common feature of middle and later Platonic theory.[18] In his treatise 'On the God of Socrates', Apuleius allegorises Athena-Minerva, the divine companion of Odysseus, as the virtue of 'prudentia', or wisdom, that attended him (*De Deo Socratis* 24). Similarly, in Plutarch's work on the same subject, Socrates' relationship with his famous guardian spirit is, in the allegorising tradition adopted by the Platonic school, compared with that of Odysseus with Athena (*De Genio Socratis* 10: p. 580C).

Ammianus' list of those whose 'genius' made them great, including politicians as well as philosophers and mystics, is at first glance an odd mixture. As far as the philosophers are concerned, neither Pythagoras, Socrates, 'Hermes Termaximus' (a Latin version of the more familiar 'Trismegistos'), Apollonius of Tyana nor Plotinus presents any real difficulty except for some awkwardness in the case of Hermes Trismegistos; he was strictly a god, a Hellenisation of the Egyptian Thoth, originally the scribe of the sun-god and divinity of wisdom.[19] No doubt Ammianus was thinking of this Hermes as a sort of prophet, a divinely inspired medium, a teacher of divine revelation to men before he was promoted through self-purification to join the gods. As for Plotinus, we saw earlier how, according to Porphyry's *Life*, the *daimôn* of the philosopher, evoked at a seance in a temple of Isis, turned out on its appearance to be no mere *daimôn* but a god (above, p. 119). Ammianus gives no hint that he knew of this variation.

As for the politicians (more relevant than the philosophers, one might think, to the case of Constantius) the example of Octavianus Augustus is the least open to specific documentation. Augustus' general claim to divine support is beyond doubt, but there is no precise mention in surviving sources of his 'genius' or any divine agency that could be viewed as such. The other three politicians mentioned by Ammianus are however on record as having been aided by particular divine figures. According to Livy (1.19.5) king Numa established 'fear of the gods' ('deorum metum') among the Romans, alleging personal meetings with his protectress, the nymph Egeria. Scipio Africanus was well known for his claims of personal contact with the divine, presented both by Polybius (10.2.1; 16.12.9) and by Livy (26.19) as part of an attempt to attribute his achievement to the gods in order to rally the masses to his side. In this connection are variously mentioned Hercules, Neptune and Jupiter, though none of these is identified as a special guardian, and none of them is a 'genius' in the strict sense of that term. A Neoplatonist might, as we have seen, so regard them as allegorical extensions of the virtues of an individual, but this was a later approach not available to Polybius or Livy, and Ammianus gives no hint that he is aware of any such refinement. As for

Marius, there was a strong tradition, represented by Plutarch's *Life of Marius*, of support given by divine agencies, and by a Syrian prophetess named Martha (*Marius* 17.1).[20] Ammianus' view that Marius was helped by his 'genius' is sometimes taken as a variant of the tradition that he had a god, or gods, to assist him, but it is more likely that this and the other cases are examples chosen for their impact as well-known historical parallels rather than for their philosophical consistency.

Particularly intriguing, then, is an allusion to works of Plotinus himself on *daimones*, where Ammianus adduces points suggesting more careful reflection on certain issues. He remarks, for instance, on Plotinus' teaching that their guardian spirits protect certain favoured individuals 'as far as is permitted', 'quoad licitum est' – by this reservation conceding, as was proper, the prerogative of fate (21.14.5). Ammianus' remark here echoes the first sentence of the digression, to the effect that guardian spirits are attached to men at their birth 'without prejudice to the fatal outcome of their lives'; 'salva firmitate fatali' (21.14.3). The clearest application of this principle was of course Julian's Persian campaign, destined to fail despite the presence, until it abandoned him, of Julian's guardian spirit, the 'genius publicus', and despite the efforts of theurgists to raise their emperor beyond the reach of fate.[21]

Ammianus also acknowledges Plotinus' doctrine on the 'higher education' given by guardian spirits to those souls which they take more closely to themselves, 'if they see them to be pure and preserved from the taint of sin by undefiled association with the body'; 'si senserint puras [*sc.* animas] et a colluvione peccandi immaculata corporis societate discretas' (21.14.5). A distinction is implied between those favoured politicians who were merely assisted in their secular pursuits by guardian spirits, and the philosophers, immaculate in mind and body, who were taught higher truths by them. From the latter is required ascetic discipline and purity, a soul free from contamination by the body. This is not an ideal one would think helpful to a Roman emperor, and it would be surprising if Ammianus, for all his stern morality, attached it to himself. But what of Julian? With his ascetic demeanour, chastity, and much-publicised preference for the philosopher's cloak to the imperial robes, that emperor might seem a good candidate for the 'higher teaching' described by Plotinus. Ammianus does not say this, paradoxically linking his digression not with Julian (as he had opportunity to) but with Constantius. Yet connections are made, not only in the text as it is written but in the imagination of the reader, and the relevance to Julian of Ammianus' remarks is implied by the context, common to the digressions both on divination and on geniuses, of Constantius' approaching death and the omens that foretold it. Could anyone read of the departure from Constantius of his guardian spirit without recalling the appearance to Julian in the previous book (20.5.10) of the 'genius publicus', bidding him seize the opportunity that was about to present itself to him? The theme of Book 21 is the rise of Julian and decline of Constantius, not forgetting the divine indications that made the outcome

XVII. Religion and Philosophy

clear to both protagonists. This theme is in the broader sense the setting of the two philosophical digressions, at the beginning and near the end of the book, with their common ground in Neoplatonic learning, researched by Ammianus and presented by him in language, and with examples, that would be familiar to his western audience. It would be perverse to deny the relevance of both digressions, and not only that on divination, to the philosophical tastes of Julian.

On the main intellectual issue of Ammianus' time, the conflict of religions, he has contrived by skilfully deployed – if flawed – displays of erudition to declare his position without indulging in polemic. The complementary themes of the rise of Julian and the decline of Constantius are linked by strategic digressions to the religious personality of the new emperor, and so to the religious policies of his reign. Ammianus does not offer any such digression on the subject of Christianity. He does however succeed by a similarly calculated treatment in giving the issue prominence while depriving it, by a sort of 'polemic of distortion', of its authentic religious content.

(2) Christianity in Ammianus

Given the incidence of Christianity at all levels of the society of Ammianus' time, it is no surprise that the subject should enter into his narrative in purely circumstantial contexts, without implying any particular attitude on the part of the historian.[22] He reports no more than the facts in describing how the usurper Silvanus at Cologne, and on a later occasion a charioteer at Rome, unsuccessfully sought asylum in chapels of the Christian faith. Ammianus offers no comment on either situation, despite his own complicity in the suppression of Silvanus, and despite the fact that the charioteer was involved – incongruously, given his choice of refuge – in an accusation of magic arts, a subject in which Ammianus generally shows great interest (15.5.31; 26.3.3). Silvanus was on his way to early morning worship when he was attacked by the troops bribed by Ursicinus, and there are other occasions on which Ammianus mentions Christian services as bearing upon events which he described. In Africa the official Palladius, travelling under escort to stand trial before the emperor, hanged himself while his guards were spending the night at church in celebration of a Christian festival, possibly Easter; 'festo die Christiani ritus in ecclesia pernoctabant' (28.6.27). At Moguntiacum on the Rhine, an Alamannic raiding party was able to break into the town and take captives and booty without meeting the slightest resistance, the population and garrison being intent on a Christian service (27.10.1f.)! In describing how Julian, celebrating his 'quinquennalia' at Vienne and shortly after his proclamation as Augustus, attended church to observe the festival of Epiphany, Ammianus is the first writer of any persuasion to attest the existence of this holy day in the west, and to give its name; 'feriarum die, quem celebrantes mense Ianuario Christiani Epiphania dictitant' (21.2.4).[23]

Ammianus' description is interesting too for its clear implication that the city of Vienne, and Julian's entourage there, comprised a majority of Christians, whose support he dared not put at risk by an open declaration of his apostasy.

Other events reveal the Christian clergy acting in one of their more familiar and increasingly important secular capacities, as envoys and intermediaries.[24] The Moorish rebel Firmus used bishops to plead for peace with the *magister militum* Theodosius (29.5.15), and in August 378, before the battle of Hadrianople, the Gothic leader Fritigern unsuccessfully sent 'a presbyter, as they call them, of the Christian rite', to Valens, urging that war could be avoided if the Goths were allowed to settle peacefully in Thrace (31.12.8f.). In the most interesting of these episodes, the bishop of Bezabde on the Tigris went to the camp of king Sapor to persuade him to call off his siege of the city and go home to Persia, after the heavy losses suffered by both sides. On his return, the bishop was suspected of revealing the weak points of the fortifications of Bezabde to the Persians, since they immediately attacked them and took the place. Ammianus defends the bishop against this slander ('suspicio vana'), which was false although many repeated it; 'licet asseveratione vulgata multorum' (20.7.7ff.). The subsequent fate of the bishop and his followers after the capture of Bezabde and the deportation of its inhabitants to new homelands in Persia is told in the Syriac accounts of Persian martyrs. Nine thousand Christians (following common Persian practice, this probably means the whole population of Bezabde) were led into captivity and the bishop, Heliodorus, was one of many who died.

From time to time Ammianus' narrative involves him in explanations of aspects of the Christian faith. He describes the capture by Sapor of a community of Christian virgins in a fort on the Tigris frontier.[25] In a show of clemency notable in one who treated Bezabde so harshly, the king had them kept from harm and left free to serve their religion without hindrance, in a settlement that now passed into Persian hands. Ammianus' description of this is dispassionate, even sympathetic; 'virgines Christiano ritu cultui divino sacratas custodiri intactas, et religioni servire solito more nullo vetante praecepit' (18.10.4). The theme of martyrs and martyrdom appears twice, on both occasions with a word of explanation. On the first, in the course of describing the fate of bishop George of Alexandria and his supporters (below, p. 443), Ammianus defines martyrs as those who, under compulsion to abandon their religion, endured punishment and torture and, 'advancing with undaunted faith to meet a glorious death, are now called martyrs'; 'ad usque gloriosam mortem intemerata fide progressi, nunc martyres appellantur' (22.11.10). Ammianus could not have lived in the fourth-century east without knowing what martyrs were, but his expression is remarkable for its apparent sympathy with the courage of the victims of persecution. The phrase 'ad usque gloriosam mortem' is particularly notable from one of Ammianus' persuasion – if one did not suspect him of irony, the death of George being so conspicuously inglorious.

XVII. Religion and Philosophy

On the second occasion, Ammianus tells how Valentinian's impulsive threat to execute the entire curial orders of three Pannonian towns was averted by the observation of his quaestor, Eupraxius, that the only consequence would be that they would be regarded as martyrs, 'id est divinitati acceptos' (27.7.6). The more detached nature of Ammianus' explanation here is perhaps due to its being attributed to a court official trying to influence the emperor to mildness. One would be surprised if even an angry Valentinian needed a reminder of the meaning of 'martyr', but it is possible that Eupraxius is seen as pointing out to him a corollary of martyrdom in the present case rather than offering a general definition of the term; it was the victims, and not their persecutor, whom the Divinity would favour. It was in any case a fact that a number of officials wrongly executed by Valentinian on a previous occasion were now venerated at a place near Milan known as 'Ad Innocentes' (27.7.5).[26] Ammianus here touches indirectly an issue of some concern to the church authorities of the time, that of the integrity of the cult of martyrs against the claims of impostors – executed bandits and the like – which were sometimes supported by local communities. One such impostor in central Gaul was unmasked, in a personal confrontation with his spirit, by Martin of Tours (*V. Mart.* 11). 'Banditry' involves the perpetration of acts of robbery and violence with the support of the social orders from within which the bandit operates and whose protection he enjoys. It is easy to see how, given an appropriate ideology of the after-life, such support may survive the execution of the bandit, in a world in which the law operates primarily to protect the interests of propertied classes and of government, by processes of perceived inequity.

*

It is a mark of Greek and Roman historians writing in the Classical manner, to avoid the use of technical expressions belonging to specialised subjects where their inclusion would adversely affect the purity of literary style, and to introduce them, if at all, only with an apology and an explanation.[27] In Ammianus' time and even later, this convention applied to expressions and titles specific to the Christian religion, which were considered alien from the style, as was their subject from the content, of true history. Some examples of this inhibition have already been noted, as in Ammianus' references to presbyters 'as they call them' of the Christian faith, and to Epiphany as a festival 'so called' by the Christians: 'Christiani ritus presbyter, ut ipsi appellant' (31.12.8); 'feriarum die, quam ... Christiani Epiphania dictitant' (21.2.5). On the latter occasion, as we saw, Ammianus' artificiality is justified by his being the first writer of any persuasion to name the festival at all, but he tends also to use an apologetic expression in the case of words that were in much wider use, and often very well known. He twice excuses the word for a church council, or synod, describing in the first instance how Athanasius of Alexandria was removed from his episcopal office by an 'assembly of many colleagues of the same rank gathered together – a synod, as they call it'; 'synodus, ut appellant' (15.7.6f.); and in the second how the Emperor Constantius weakened the state transport service by issuing passes to bishops as they travelled to the church councils summoned by the emperor in order to make the whole faith, or 'rite', yield to his will – 'per synodos, quas appellant' (21.16.18).

Ammianus even holds back from the normal word for bishop, 'episcopus', sometimes preferring the more general term for priest, 'antistes', with a qualifying phrase to identify the cult in question as Christianity, as in the case of the bishop of Bezabde, mentioned above (20.7.7), and that of pope Liberius, 'Christianae legis antistes' (15.7.3). The bishops who approached the *magister militum* Theodosius on behalf of Firmus are similarly called 'Christiani ritus antistites' (29.5.15). The same convention governs Ammianus' expression for a church, 'conventiculum ritus Christiani', used in one case of Cologne and in another for one of the major churches of fourth-century Rome (15.5.31; 27.3.13). 'Ritus Christiani sacrarium' is the chapel sought as refuge by the Roman charioteer accused of magic, and 'aedicula' the chapel at Cologne in which Silvanus tried vainly to escape from his assassins (26.3.3; 15.5.31). The nuns taken by Sapor in Mesopotamia are described with similarly measured care as 'virgines Christiano ritu cultui divino sacratas' (18.10.4).

Ammianus' practice in this matter is actually more flexible than these examples suggest. He is prepared in certain circumstances to use the normal technical terms of the Christian religion: that is, when the context makes the issue clear, or when he has already introduced it with words of a non-technical character.[28] The reference to the bishop of Bezabde as 'antistes' is shortly followed by the usual term 'episcopus'; this is acceptable, the subject-matter having first been defined by the less technical expression (20.7.9). After Liberius of Rome has been introduced as 'Christianae legis antistes', Athanasius of Alexandria can appear without comment as 'episcopus' (15.7.7) and there is no difficulty about the conflict between Damasus and Ursinus for the see of Rome, 'ad rapiendam episcopi sedem ardentes' (27.4.12). Bishop George of Alexandria is designated immediately as 'episcopus', it being clear that the entire episode, and not just an incidental reference within it, concerns the Christian religion. By the same token, one of two officials at Alexandria lynched as supporters of George can without explanation be described as engaged at the time in building a church, 'dum aedificandae praeesset ecclesiae' (22.11.9). Once the Christian service at Vienne attended by Julian has been named as Epiphany, there can be no objection to saying that it was celebrated in a church; 'progressus in eorum ecclesiam ...' (21.2.5). Similarly, since the guards of the arrested official Palladius were observing all-night vigil in celebration of a Christian festival, no embarrassment arises from the use of the normal word for a church; 'festo die Christiani ritus in ecclesia pernoctabant' (28.6.27). The word 'basilica' does not yet carry a specifically Christian

XVII. Religion and Philosophy

connotation but requires definition in this sense; the worst of the fighting between the supporters of Damasus and Ursinus, discussed below, took place 'in basilica Sicinnini, ubi ritus Christiani est conventiculum' (27.3.11).

These examples mean no more than that Ammianus, faced by the presence of Christianity and its institutions in his society, allowed them their role in events, while observing certain conventions relating to the terminology of an institution that did not yet form part of Roman history as traditionally understood. The result is a quite substantial dossier of examples, interesting precisely for their unforced occurrence and sense of normality. Indeed, Ammianus is markedly less self-conscious in his presentation of the issue than other writers, even Christians, who were working within the Classical historiographical tradition. The Byzantine historian Agathias, for example, indulged in a periphrasis compared with which Ammianus' six words, quoted above, are a model of terse economy, in order to avoid imposing upon a literary work the familiar Greek word for nuns, *monachai*.[29] But Ammianus hardly needs at this stage a testimonial to his realism, or to his sense of the need to present detail in an intelligible circumstantial context. As in the case of philosophy, more can be learned of his attitude to Christianity from certain more extended descriptions of events affecting the new faith and its adherents.

*

In writing of Julian's religious and other preparations for the Persian campaign of 363, Ammianus describes how the emperor responded to the destruction by fire of the temple of Apollo at Daphne and its marvellous statue of the god by closing the 'greater church' ('maiorem ecclesiam') at Antioch. Ammianus reports without endorsing it Julian's suspicion, pursued by 'more strict enquiries than were usual', that Christians were responsible for the burning of the temple, resentful because of the building of a new peristyle around it (22.13.2).[30] He also records counter-allegations in the form of a 'groundless rumour' that the fire was started by Asclepiades, an aged philosopher who had taken a statuette of a goddess into the temple and lit candles there as usual, sparks from which had set fire to the ancient, dry timbers. If this were so, one wonders why it had not happened before, the risk was so obvious. In fact, Ammianus has told at best half the story. Other sources reveal how Julian, arriving at Antioch, had been grievously disappointed to find the temple at Daphne neglected by the now Christian senate of Antioch, and the famous oracles of the holy shrine silenced.[31] Accepting the diagnosis of a theurgist called Eusebius, he ordered to be removed from the site the remains of the martyred saint Babylas, installed there by Gallus Caesar. Christian sources describe vividly the efflux of Christians from Antioch to convey the remains to their new resting place just outside the city, with acclamations against Julian taken from Psalms:

Confounded be all they that serve graven images, that boast themselves of idols! (Ps. 97:7)

On the night of the fire, the shrine was crowded with theurgists, priests and temple acolytes, all of them striving 'by every means possible' to awake the stilled voice of the gods (*Passio Artemii* 56). No doubt Asclepiades was there among them – his statuette of the goddess is reminiscent of theurgical practices attested elsewhere (p. 116) – but it would surely be impossible to say whether he, or anyone in particular, was really to blame for the fire in the obviously confused circumstances.

Ammianus' description of the purification of the site of Daphne differs in detail and in emphasis from the version of the ecclesiastical writers.[32] These maintain that it was specifically the remains of St. Babylas that silenced the oracular voices and were diagnosed as the cause by the theurgist Eusebius. For Ammianus, the site was cleared of all human remains buried there, in a general purification compared with the Athenians' sanctification of Delos in the fifth century BC (22.12.8). On this account, the removal of the relics of St. Babylas will have been the reaction of the Christian community of Antioch to the particular aspect that concerned them of a general clearance of the site. Yet more surprisingly, Ammianus fails to make a connection between the silence of the oracles and the contamination of the site by burials; for him, the oracle had been silenced long ago and for quite different reasons, the Emperor Hadrian having blocked up the Castalian spring in the fear that the intimation of imperial rule given to him there might as readily be given to others. The purification is seen as part of Julian's desire for religious innovation, and presented in the context of his excessive sacrifices, of which Ammianus did not approve, during his stay at Antioch (22.12.6f.). Nor is the purification of the site connected at all closely by Ammianus with the burning of the temple; 'eodem tempore' is the only indication that is given. The fire is rather associated by Ammianus with other gloomy omens and portents given to Julian during the preparations for the Persian campaign. He cites a rare shortage of water at Antioch, and further destruction by earthquakes at Nicomedia and Nicaea, all of which added to the emperor's anxieties without deterring him from the project; 'quae tametsi maestitiam sollicito incuterent principi ...' (22.14.1).

It would no doubt be possible to reconstruct a full account of these far from straightforward events that exploited the authentic details and chronology both in Ammianus and in the ecclesiastical sources. For the present, it is enough to have shown how Ammianus, confronted with the same events and surely as well informed on them as the ecclesiastical writers, presented them with a thematic emphasis of his own choosing. His version is no less telling for what is omitted than for what is included. In remarking on the closure of the 'greater church' at Antioch in retaliation for the burning of the temple, Ammianus does not indicate how Julian's action actually went to the point of the decommissioning of

XVII. Religion and Philosophy

the church and confiscation of its treasures; and he is remarkably non-committal, given the attitude of the other sources, on the judicial enquiries made 'solito acriores' into the catastrophe. Even the priest of Apollo, alleges Sozomen (5.20.6), was put to the torture, in the suspicion that he had colluded with Christian opponents of Julian in setting fire to the temple. In Ammianus by contrast, between the sacrifices of Julian that precede the episode and the portents that follow it, the connection of the Christians with the destruction of the temple is hardly mentioned, and only in the uncertain setting of the emperor's suspicions. The effect of this dismantling of apparently authentic connections is to set aside the specific role of Christianity and its supporters in the affair, the purification of the site being presented in its most general aspect and the episode linked more closely with the theme of Julian's own religious development than with the external conflict with which other sources connect it.

*

In a further group of episodes, relating to the internal history of fourth-century Christianity, Ammianus again shows himself to be well-informed, but selective in his presentation of the issues.[33] The first concerns the emperor Constantius' attempts to persuade Liberius of Rome to endorse the expulsion of bishop Athanasius from Alexandria (15.7.6ff.). Liberius was summoned to court as an opponent of 'the emperor's orders and the decrees of the great majority of his colleagues', 'imperatoriis iussis et plurimorum sui consortium decretis' – a somewhat detached allusion, in the manner described earlier, to the decrees of church councils which had declared themselves against him. Constantius was eager for the support of Liberius 'because of the weightier prestige of the bishop of the eternal city' ('tamquam auctoritate potiore aeternae urbis episcopi') – an expression better taken as a general allusion to the greatness of Rome and natural authority of its bishop than as a premature assertion, in this most unexpected source, of the doctrine of papal supremacy. Liberius refused and was himself sent into exile, being smuggled by night out of the city because of his tremendous popularity there; 'populi metu, qui eius amore flagrabat' (15.7.10). We now see why the affair is raised under the administration of the urban prefecture of Leontius. It directly follows the flogging and exile of Petrus Valvomeres after the rioting which he had led, first over the arrest of a charioteer, and then over a wine shortage, the usual reasons for urban disorders (p. 417).

Throughout his narrative of the affair, Ammianus sets aside its theological aspects in favour of a 'secularised' picture of ambition, popularity and disorder. He remarks on Athanasius' widely rumoured expertise in telling the future, through which activity and others the bishop fell under suspicion of entertaining notions 'alien from the character of the law, over which he presided', and on his overbearing conduct at Alexandria, rising above the proper calls of his profession;

'ultra professionem altius se efferentem' (15.7.7f.). The expression forms a nice counterpart to the description of Liberius' popularity at Rome, itself impressive documentation of the progress of Christianity among the population of the city. Ammianus could not have got this far in his description without taking the trouble to inform himself of the circumstances. He has given a view of the motivation of the participants and indicated the essential procedures involved, imperial edicts and the decisions of church councils. In one expression describing Athanasius' removal from his bishopric, 'a sacramento quod obtinebat' he comes close to giving an equivalent for 'ordained office'. Beyond this there was no need to go, and no need to emphasise the religious content of the episode. This was partly, but not only, because of the secular complexion of Ammianus' history. By raising himself 'above his profession' Athanasius had himself subordinated the religious issue to the secular. No more (but no less) was involved than the ambition and self-interest of urban magnates, in the instantly penetrable disguise of prelates of the Christian faith.

The implications of such activities 'beyond the proper calling of Christianity' come out in two notorious cases of religious controversy leading to crises of public order in the cities of Athanasius and Liberius, Alexandria and Rome respectively. The violent murder under Julian of bishop George of Alexandria is narrated by other sources, with emphasis on ecclesiastical issues again neglected by Ammianus (22.11.3ff.). For him, the reasons for the murder were connnected in the first place with the well-known tendency of Alexandria to rioting and disorder.[34] Ammianus remarks, citing 'oracles' among his authorities, that no special cause was necessary, the city being 'suopte motu' liable to turbulent riots; in his digression on Alexandria, he was shortly to recall the destruction of the quarter of the city named Bruchion in the time of Aurelian (22.16.15). Nevertheless, there were actual causes, beginning with George's conduct as a political informer to Constantius against certain Alexandrians. The description of George's incriminations as conveyed 'apud patulas aures Constantii' assimilates the bishop's activities to those of the purely secular informers known to Ammianus from his own and Ursicinus' experiences under that emperor (pp. 34ff.). George was also said to have suggested to Constantius that the public buildings of Alexandria should be made to provide their share of revenues to the treasury. The decisive cause of George's downfall was, however, his remark, made after returning from a visit to the imperial court and while surrounded (as usual) by a crowd, directed against the temple of Genius at Alexandria: 'How long will this sepulchre remain standing?' (22.11.7). One would assume the crowd to be one of Christian supporters of the bishop, whom he was inciting to a bout of temple-smashing, but Ammianus takes the remark to have been remembered by the pagans of Alexandria, who hastened when opportunity arose to take their revenge; and this happened, according to Ammianus, when Julian's execution at the Alexandrians' request of the former *dux Aegypti* Artemius removed all restraint and fear from the

XVII. Religion and Philosophy 443

populace.[35] Having terrorised them while in office under Constantius, on his departure Artemius had threatened to return and do the same again. In particular, as other sources relate, he had occupied the temple of Serapis with an armed force and let soldiers loose upon the people; this, though not specified by Ammianus, is sufficiently covered by the 'mass of atrocious crimes' for which Artemius paid by his execution (22.11.2).

As well as bishop George, two imperial officials at Alexandria were murdered. One of them, the commandant of the imperial mint of the city, died because he had overthrown an altar recently erected there (by order of Julian?), the other because while building a church he had shorn the heads of boys as a suitable tribute, presumably calculated for its offensiveness, to 'the gods'. The bodies of all three, George and the officials, were dragged through the streets, their dismembered remains then strapped to camels and taken to the sea-shore, where they were burned and thrown into the sea to prevent any relics from being recovered and commemorated by a martyr's shrine (22.11.10). It is in this savage context that Ammianus offers his deceptively amenable definition of martyrdom (p. 436).[36]

George's conduct as bishop was resented no less by the Athanasian party of Christians at Alexandria than by the supporters of the old gods. Indeed, Sozomen (5.7.4) reported the opinion that the Athanasians were primarily responsible for his death. It is however the pagans whom Ammianus, not by explicit statement but by his presentation of the causes of the riot, makes primarily responsible for it. The threat against the temple of Genius, the attempt to make the public buildings of Alexandria liable to taxation, the deaths of the head of the mint for destroying an altar and of his colleague for shaving the heads of boys, not to mention the dispersal of the remains of the victims to prevent their being commemorated as martyrs – all these issues express the resentments of pagans at Alexandria rather than of disaffected Christians. In fact, Ammianus' connection of the murders with the execution of Artemius is historically invalid, for if George and his supporters were in fact killed on the attested date of 24 December 361, having been thrown into prison as soon as Constantius' death was announced at Alexandria on 30 November, there had not yet been time for the Alexandrians even to petition Julian for the punishment of Artemius, a procedure that involved the selection of an embassy of complaint to the emperor, and its journey to the imperial court.[37] Ammianus indeed sets the execution of Artemius and its alleged consequences at Alexandria in the context of Julian's judicial activities after his arrival at Antioch in the summer of 362. He gives no indication that the riots and the death of George actually took place several months before; nor does he allow for the fact that the victims were kept in prison for more than three weeks before being taken out to their deaths, a delay acknowledged by Julian in his letter of reproach to the Alexandrians (*Ep.* 60 Bidez).

Ammianus has presented a partial, and in one significant respect an incorrect, picture of the circumstances, and he has omitted the doctrinal and ecclesiastical issues that, if not the direct cause of George's murder, certainly contributed to his unpopularity. He also gives a distorted impression of George's activities in acting as an informer 'apud patulas aures Constantii', to the effect that men were resisting the emperor's orders (in his letter to the Alexandrians, Julian also remarked how George had 'embittered' the emperor against the city). The most natural interpretation of the bishop's conduct is that it related to opponents of Constantius' religious policies, whom he presented to the emperor's suspicious mind as potential political dissidents. Yet the careers both of Athanasius and of George had shown how closely related these categories could be.

Ammianus' construction of the situation involves a number of themes, mostly of a secular character: the judicial activities of Julian at Antioch (inaccurately), the turbulent urban history of Alexandria, resentment against a hated governor, measures and threats directed against the temples of the gods, the overbearing conduct of the bishop, his behaviour as a *delator*. As an account of causes it is convincing except for what is *not* described, divisions and controversies within the Christian faith. At this point, Ammianus no doubt felt that he had come to the limits of secular history, but even here he gives an indication, brief but telling, of this issue. The two officials lynched with the bishop might, says Ammianus, have been saved by the Christians from their pitiful death, save only for one thing, the universal hatred of George; 'ni Georgio odio omnes indiscrete flagrabant' (22.11.10). That is, Athanasian Christians and pagans made common cause against him, a factor allowed for by Ammianus in this single phrase, without affecting his overall emphasis on the hostility of the pagan community of Alexandria.

Lastly, there is the conflict between the supporters of Damasus and Ursinus, rivals who 'burned beyond human measure' in their ambition to succeed to the bishopric of Rome left vacant by the death of Liberius.[38] The rioting was bitter and prolonged, its bloody climax 137 dead bodies in one of the churches of Rome, the 'basilica Sicinnini, ubi ritus Christiani est conventiculum' (27.3.11ff.). There survives a considerable archive of administrative material relating to the episode, bringing out to the full its religious dimension. Ammianus makes no mention of this aspect. Instead, he permits himself to reflect on the worldly motives that brought about the conflict. Ambition for the prize of the bishopric he sees as natural, 'considering the ostentation of urban life', in which priests could enjoy the donations of matrons, eat dinners fit for kings, and parade in carriages, resplendent in the apparel of their office; 'procedantque vehiculis insidentes circumspecte vestiti, epulas curantes profusas adeo, ut eorum convivia regales superent mensas' (27.3.14). They would however do better and be 'truly happy' if they were to despise the magnificence of city life and live in the manner of humble provincial bishops, whose self-restraint in food and drink, rough clothes and downcast expressions commend them to the eternal deity and his true worshippers as pure and modest. Ammianus' expression here is in beautifully balanced contrast to the words just cited on metropolitan bishops; 'vilitas etiam indumentorum et supercilia humum spectantia perpetuo numini verisque eius cultoribus ut puros commendant et verecundos' (27.3.15).

Ammianus can hardly mean by this testimonial to the virtues of humble provincial clergy that their conduct recommended them only to *pagans* as pure and modest. His remark makes real sense only if he considered that Christians too might be counted among 'true worshippers of the eternal deity'. Ammianus does seem on occasion to concede this point. The nuns captured by Sapor in the town on the Tigris frontier were permitted to continue to serve God in their accustomed fashion ('religioni servire solito more'); Ammianus gives no indication that this was not, in its own way, a legitimate way to 'serve the deity'. When Julian celebrated Epiphany at Vienne, despite doubts about the emperor's sincerity the historian seems to allow that, for those who preferred it, this was a valid way to worship God; 'sollemniter numine orato' (21.1.4). Ammianus elsewhere wrote, no doubt with more than a touch of irony when one considers what had become of it, that in its true nature Christianity enjoined 'only what was just and mild' (22.11.5), and criticised the emperor Constantius for corrupting by excessive interference a religion that was in essence 'plain and simple'; 'absoluta et simplex' (21.16.18). His accounts of the episodes just described have a common theme in the blatantly secular conduct of the champions of their religion. Damasus and Ursinus 'burned above human measure' for the prize of the bishopric of Rome, an object of ambition for those seduced by the splendour of urban life; 'huius rei cupidos'. Neither for Christians nor for pagans was cupidity a virtue, but Christians at least professed to prefer the eternal rewards of the next life to the fragile charms of this. George of Alexandria forgot the 'gentle precepts' of his faith, while Athanasius had 'raised himself above his profession', involving himself in matters 'alien from the tenets of the religion over which he presided'. None of this should surprise in a historian who, describing how Julian invited bishops and laymen of the various Christian factions to the palace and suggested that they set aside their differences and live freely in peace, remarked that no policy was more likely to increase their dissension.[39] Even wild beasts, he added, are less savage to men than are Christians to each other (22.5.4)!

*

After all this, Ammianus was not a polemical writer in the manner, say, of Eunapius of Sardis – a Greek professor, fanatically devoted to his philosophy and to the memory of Julian the Apostate, seeing the Christian emperors, notably Constantine and Theodosius, through the all-distorting lens of religious prejudice. For Eunapius, every aspect of an emperor's moral character and of his policies, secular and military as well as cultural and religious, was judged in the light of his religious persuasion. This was not so for Ammianus, whose emperors, whatever they are, are never one-dimensional. Ammianus may on the contrary be accused of giving *in*sufficient weight to the religious preoccupations of emperors; yet there were historiographical and stylistic grounds for this, and in the last resort, whatever omissions and distortions there may be in his narrative, in all cases but one of the emperors he discusses (the exception is Valens), he produces in his obituary notice a clear indication, noted with approval or disapproval, of the emperor's religious belief and policies.

Eunapius sought his audience in Greek-speaking intellectual circles in the east, an audience of men committed to the same philosophical and religious views as himself, men who did not need persuading on the basic issues. In the event he achieved a broader appeal, for the version of the history known to us through fragments and citations, and more fully through the use made of it by Zosimus, represents a second, extended edition in which the polemical tone of the original version was apparently modified. What exactly is entailed, either structurally or in terms of polemical intensity, by this 'second edition' ('Nea Ekdosis'), and what its relation to the first, are questions which have not been, and perhaps cannot be, fully answered.[40] In any case Eunapius' history in its revised form became standard, meriting a systematic refutation, on the question of Constantine's conversion to Christianity, by the church historian Sozomen (1.5.1ff.), but used even by ecclesiastical writers, such as Sozomen and Philostorgius, as the basis of their secular narratives of fourth-century history.

Ammianus' circumstances were very different from those of Eunapius, and his success, it would appear, more uncertain – perhaps because his work, complex, challenging and varied, did not appeal with sufficient accuracy to any specific audience of known tastes: nor could it easily be epitomised, and the style can be disconcerting. To choose the Latin language, and to complete his history in Rome, meant that, unlike Eunapius, Ammianus sought his audience among men who did not know him already and share his own background and opinions; it may indeed, as we saw, have included Theodosian courtiers in Rome for the emperor's visit of 389 and staying there until his departure for the east in summer 391 (p. 8f.). It is hard to imagine that what appealed to this somewhat incalculable audience of visitors to Rome was the same as what would have appealed to Eunapius, or to Libanius, whom some of them informed of the recitations when they returned to the east. For his part, Ammianus was too pragmatic, too sensitive to individual detail and too observant of subtleties and contradictions of character, not to say too widely experienced in life and too ambitious a historian, to have narrowed his chances of success by risking the provocation of open polemic.

Ammianus expresses himself in similar terms on both sides of the religious issue. He criticises Julian, for whom his admiration is obvious, on aspects of his religious policies, just as he criticised Constantius for an equivalent 'superstition' in his obsessive pursuit of unity in the church.[41]

XVII. Religion and Philosophy

He passes over opportunities to show Christianity in a bad light, such as would not have been neglected by a truly polemical writer like Eunapius. Examples will come to mind from the material presented in this chapter. The bishop of Bezabde was not responsible, as some thought, for the capture of his city by the Persians; nuns may worship the Divinity in their own fashion, even martyrs, with no more than marginal irony, may be said to meet a glorious death, their faith unsullied. It was true that the absence of his guards at a Christian service permitted the corrupt official Palladius to hang himself, and the attendance at church of the garrison of Moguntiacum allowed the Alamanni to enter the city. Yet there might be all sorts of reasons for such negligence, and Ammianus may be doing no more than explain the circumstances relevant to these occasions without wishing to offer aspersions on the Christian faith in general. One wonders a little about the general Terentius, described as humble in gait and always gloomy ('demisse ambulans semperque submaestus'), but as long as he lived a great inciter of dissensions (30.1.2). These might be sectarian, for Terentius, a correspondent of Basil of Caesarea, was a pious Christian, who as a reward for his services in Armenia under the Arian Valens requested the emperor to build a church for the orthodox, and whose daughters were consecrated deaconesses in a religious community at Samosata (Basil, *Ep.* 105). Yet Terentius' downcast manner may have been a personal idiosyncrasy, and the dissensions he fomented may, as Ammianus gives grounds to believe, have been strictly diplomatic.[42] As for the emperors, Ammianus never, even in the case of Julian, implies that their religious policies were more than one of the many criteria by which they should be judged.

We may infer from the handful of references in the surviving books that this was true even of Ammianus' attitude to the first Christian emperor, Constantine the Great. In most of these cases, the polemical opportunities that did exist and are pursued by other writers were not taken up by Ammianus, whose own remarks, if he considered the reign of Constantine in a primarily religious dimension, are curiously inconsequential.

To take first the briefer and less significant allusions, Ammianus mentions the execution of Crispus Caesar at Pola in Istria and, in a digression, the birthplace of Helena the mother of Constantine. The second of these is a passing reference only, the town of Drepanum being renamed Helenopolis, and Ammianus does not give the explanation (26.8.1); the first is adduced as a parallel to the execution at Pola of Gallus Caesar (14.11.20). This is an allusion that might, but does not in Ammianus, possess a context in religious polemic; in the history of Eunapius and in other Greek sources, the execution of Crispus, and the murder soon afterwards of his stepmother Fausta, are seen as the prime motives in Constantine's conversion to Christianity, as the emperor found, after fruitless consultation with pagan priests, that only Christianity could provide absolution for such appalling crimes (Zosimus 2.29.3). This hostile version lies behind the denunciation of Constantine at the end of the *Caesars* of Julian, where the emperor seeks the company of Jesus, who proclaims absolution to all who want it, whether adulterers or murderers (336A-B); and it is specifically refuted by Sozomen (1.5.1ff.) as the misguided view of certain 'Hellenes', or pagans – meaning specifically Eunapius.[43] Ammianus gives no hint of this background: it is not even clear that he had mentioned the execution of Crispus in the proper place of his history (p. 29).

In another allusion containing unrealised polemical possibilities, Ammianus describes how it was Constantine who first 'opened the greedy jaws' of his supporters while Constantius rammed the wealth of the provinces down their throats (16.8.12). The double motif of munificence and avarice might carry a hint of anti-Christian progaganda, given Constantine's reputation for prodigality – another aspect of Julian's denunciation in the *Caesars* (336A) – financed by his confiscations of temple treasures. Ammianus, however, assigns the avarice not to Constantine but to Constantius, connecting it primarily with the emperor's exploitation of the laws of *maiestas* in order to lay hands on the property of the wealthy and only partially, and in retrospect from the reign of Julian, with the depredation of the temples (22.4.3). Nor, in the same context, does he imply a religious aspect – as he could easily have done, given the conspicuous promptitude of their conversion – to the insatiable cupidity of the Christian senatorial clan of the Anicii; their behaviour forms part of an orthodox sequence of political abuses involving Constantius' chief civil and military officers, as it is later associated with the conduct in office of their 'dominus', Petronius Probus, under Valentinian (16.8.13; 27.11.3; p. 277f.). Similarly elusive is Ammianus' allegation that Constantine went to war with Persia, misled by the lies of the philosopher Metrodorus (25.4.23; p. 135). His motive, according to Ammianus, was the quest for financial gain; 'cum Metrodori mendaciis *avidius* acquiescit'. In the hands of Eunapius, Constantine's cupidity forms part of a general assessment of the reign, based on a hostile perception of his religious policies.[44] It is impossible to say whether, in the lost book to which he refers ('ut dudum rettulimus plene'), Ammianus took over this connection or not, though in view of his caution elsewhere it seems unlikely: he certainly does not state it in any part of his text as it survives.

Ammianus incorporates an indirect back-reference to Constantine, in narrating how Julian, writing to the Roman senate during his march against Constantius, denounced Constantine as a 'destroyer of ancient laws and established custom', adding the accusation that he appointed barbarians to the consulship (21.10.8). The first part of Julian's denunciation possesses religious implications – other writers, such as Aurelius Victor and Eutropius, set Constantine's religious innovations in the context of his radical secular policies in order to avoid addressing them directly[45] – but these implications are offset by Ammianus' criticism of Julian's appointment of Nevitta as consul, a man far less distinguished than those whom Constantine had made consul, being uncultivated, rude

XVII. Religion and Philosophy 449

and, worst of all, cruel in his high office. Further, the whole passage on Constantine follows the senate's hostile reaction, expressed in acclamations, to what Julian had written about Constantius; 'auctori tuo reverentiam rogamus' (21.10.7; p. 104). If there are elements of 'pagan propaganda' here, then Ammianus has gone to considerable trouble to deflect their force, concealing a possible religious allusion within a reference to the secular policies of Constantine, and setting the whole passage in a context of express disapproval of Julian's own conduct.

There remain two episodes in which a religious dimension to the reign of Constantine is made explicit by Ammianus. In both cases, he does so in a curiously oblique fashion if he were aiming to criticise the religious policies of that emperor. Ammianus described how Constantine employed the later praetorian prefect of Constantius, Strategius Musonianus, to help him interpret those 'superstitious sects' into which he was making 'careful enquiries'; 'cum limatius superstitionum quaereret sectas' (15.13.2). Another source, namely Eusebius' *Life of Constantine*, relates how Strategius was among those 'friends' whom the emperor dispatched to church councils in order to make his views known to them (*V. Const.*, 3.62.1).[46] As his example of 'superstition', however, Ammianus chooses not any of the major Christian heresies that beset the reigns of Constantine and his son, but the Manichees; 'Manichaeorum et similium'. It implies no disrespect to the Manichees to say that they are a peripheral example, had Ammianus wished to express distaste for Constantine's interference in church politics or hostile attitude to the pagan cults. Since Ammianus must have known of both, one might almost think that in choosing the Manichees he is deliberately avoiding mention of either. The historian is much more direct in his allegation that Constantius destroyed the imperial transport service in permitting bishops to use it to travel to constant synods, his 'old wives' fancies' making him more interested in fomenting than in resolving their disputes, thereby encouraging endless wars of words; 'in qua [*sc.* Christiana religione] scrutanda perplexius quam componenda gravius, excitavit discidia plurima, quae progressa fusius aluit concertatione verborum' (21.16.18; p. 128). The criticism of Constantius' involvement in such matters that is stated here is not levelled against Constantine, although it was surely no less relevant. Indeed, the notion of 'superstition' here applied to Constantius is in the earlier passage addressed not to Constantine but to the objects of his 'careful' religious enquiries. Nor is the word 'limatius', applied to these enquries, in itself pejorative; Ammianus uses it, in a not far distant context, of his own historical method (15.1.1).

Lastly, there is Constantine's decision to move an obelisk from Egypt to be re-erected at Rome (an enterprise completed by Constantius, the context in which Ammianus describes it). Making light of the inhibitions attributed by Ammianus to the Emperor Augustus against disturbing a monument sacred to the Sun-god, Constantine supposed that no 'religio' would be violated by the removal of the obelisk, Rome being nothing less than the 'temple of the whole world'; 'in templo mundi totius' (17.4.13).[47] Though consonant with Ammianus' own views as expressed in many passages of the history, this is a strange attribution of motive to Constantine, when we consider him not only as a Christian emperor, but as the founder of Constantinople as a 'second Rome' and, partly at least on the basis of the Christian ideology upon which it was founded, rival of the old.[48] If Ammianus was here writing with polemical intent in attributing the motives he does to Constantine, then it can only be said that he expressed it with the most abstruse irony. It is much more natural to conclude that, in writing of the obelisk, Ammianus simply attributed to Constantine motives that arose from his own, rather than the emperor's way of thinking. He did this, not with polemical intent or in a spirit of irony, but innocently, seeing no reason to regard the emperor's action as inconsistent with his profession of Christianity. Though Eunapius may have subscribed to it, it was never Ammianus' view that an emperor's activities were dominated in every aspect by a single overriding motive, religious or other, in the light of which all others could be interpreted. This was so of every emperor whose reign he describes in the surviving books of the history. It is true even of Julian, where the emperor's administrative, financial, judicial and military achievements are at least as important as his religious policies in Ammianus' assessment of his personality and government. There is no need to suppose that the reign of Constantine was judged by criteria that were any less complex. The role of a Christian emperor in a pagan world was no less full of contradictions than that of a pagan emperor in a Christian.

*

Though he can hardly be said (as has occasionally been argued) to have favoured it, Ammianus' expressed attitude to Christianity was not one of indiscriminate hostility: though it might be better to say that his criticism was reserved for cases and circumstances in which it was undeniably justified. Beyond this, it is a matter of how one reads his text without help from the tone of voice, the raising of the eyebrows or the subtle gesture that would, in specific passages, have revealed his intention to his hearers – or that might, if Ammianus doubted his audience, be withheld. Yet there is surely irony when he writes that Christianity enjoined 'only what is mild and just', given the actual conduct of its practitioners as described in his text; so too in his remark that Constantius distorted a 'plain and simple religion' (was it ever that?) by excessive intervention in doctrinal matters, and in his appeal to the conduct of modest provincial clergy against that of their ambitious metropolitan counterparts. Was the Christianisation of the Eternity of Rome to be achieved through ostentation, riot and disorder – those aspects of life there which he had excused to surprised visitors as unworthy of the great traditions of the city, and as the conduct of a minority there who 'did not reflect where they were born'?[49]

XVII. Religion and Philosophy

Perhaps Ammianus was simply criticising the excesses of their faith in a way that Christians too, if they were honest with themselves, would have approved: even challenging them to do so. Jerome, after all, proposed to write (though never did) a history of the church which would show how, under the protection of the Christian emperors, it had become richer in possessions and power, but poorer in virtue.[50] Had Ammianus known of this project, as he surely did not, it would have been a clever and still subtler irony to challenge Christians to side with Jerome, their self-appointed conscience. Not all Christians would have welcomed the opportunity so to align themselves: the harshness of Jerome's strictures (and other reasons to do with his character) had got him drummed out of Rome by the ecclesiastical establishment.

These are the polemical techniques of all times – if we could be sure that Ammianus intended them. A similar uncertainty accompanies the more extended passages discussed in the later part of this chapter, in which Ammianus advances resolutely secular interpretations of what, for those involved, were intensely religious issues. Just as it is a standard polemical technique to undermine one's adversaries by showing them that they do not live up to the standards that they ought (and know that they ought) to set for themselves, it is hard to resist the implications of Ammianus' refusal to Christians of the religious motives that were actually central to their conduct, in favour of profane and less edifying ones.

In the end, a certain ambiguity, in which critical comment may be veiled in irony and a distortion of motive from religious to secular be explained as a consequence of literary form, is part of Ammianus' manner. Open hostility to Christianity, if Ammianus felt it, might be counterproductive, deterring rather than attracting an audience, and denying the common ground that a writer must try to establish if he is to communicate effectively; but who would deny to a historian of serious moral intent (and proven satirical skills, as in his digressions on senate and people of Rome) the right to criticise what was palpably wrong in a system of conduct and belief, whether he subscribed to it himself or not? In the last resort, Ammianus' personal opinions, set in a literary tradition of such complexity, cannot simply be read from his text. In religious as in other matters, they must be drawn out with the most careful finesse from the layers of convention and technique that surround them.

CHAPTER XVIII

The Roman and the Greek

As Ammianus would be the first to agree, writing history is a difficult and a very complicated matter.[1] Its aims are serious, its standards exact, its modes of exposition, argument and organisation complex and artificial. Its conventions vary with the temperament of historians and the environment in which they work, as they attempt to pose new questions, to exploit advances made in other areas of study, to offer new insights, to keep up with the times; but whatever they are – narrative or analytical, documentary or anecdotal, quantitative or impressionistic, empirical or theoretical – they remain conventions, ways of ordering and making less intractable a study, that of human society in action, which far exceeds one person's gifts of comprehension.

The finished product, it will be evident, is no spontaneous outburst of personal opinions. It is a text, something 'woven' – that is to say an intellectual construction founded on specific methodological and structural procedures. For an ancient rather more than for a modern writer but to some extent for both, the procedures are also defined by the literary and historiographical – and, in Ammianus' case, the linguistic and cultural – traditions within which he sets his activity. These traditions assign a role to the various components of his work; its structure and mode of exposition, its moral, political or other purpose, its starting point and terminus. The result is a calculated and highly artificial framework within which are contained the attitudes he expresses, and through which they are given form and made articulate.

This may be an over-stated point of view, in that all coherent discourse, and not just the professional discourse of historians, is a function of the assumptions current, the language (or languages) used and the forms of communication adopted in the society which generates it. Its consequence is however a problem of comprehension of some importance: how is the modern reader to be sure that he can detect the 'opinion' of an ancient writer through the layers of convention in which he writes? The answer is that he cannot be sure. It is an illusion to think that we can simply take an ancient writer off the shelf and read him as if he were of our own time and culture. Even if his expressed attitudes seem clear to us, we cannot know that we have correctly re-created the mentality to which they belong, except in so far as this 'mentality' is itself a construct of the text we have read; and even if we can break the circularity of this argument, there remains the problem of relating his mentality to our own and communicating it to others without distorting either to a point beyond recognition.

The problem is at its least intractable when the personality of a writer is expressed in action – just as the least intractable history is the history of action. This is certainly true of Ammianus, especially in the more sharply defined personal nature of the earlier of the surviving books. We here see Ammianus, as if in intense but often marginal sequences from a much larger subject: sharing the political uncertainties of his patron Ursicinus, reflecting (with literary elaboration) on his prospects of survival from the journey to meet Silvanus at Cologne – not to mention the cool professionalism with which he records the outcome; later, in a series of microcosms of action, taking the little lost boy back to Nisibis, on his way to rejoin his party waving his cloak to warn of the approach of the enemy, then struggling to keep up with them on his tired horse and escaping by moonlit night across the desert; we witness the encounter, during a half-hour's skirmish, of Ursicinus with the renegade Antoninus as the latter walks backwards from the general's presence, bowing deeply and doffing his tiara as he goes; the curtailed attempt to pull the arrow from the wound of Verinianus; the struggle into Amida and the escape from it when the city fell and other *protectores*, men of Ammianus' rank, were led into captivity; the exhausting journey from the city with the two companions more used than was Ammianus to walking; the unexpected return to Antioch. The Persian campaign of 363 emphasises less the historian's personal exploits, but still we catch him in glimpses, more of an observer than a participant – on the journey to Ctesiphon, documenting the change of mood in the campaign from optimism to uncertainty and despair and sharing the grim retreat to Nisibis, then leaving its service when it again reached Antioch.

These are personal insights, worth a fortune to the modern historian in his attempts to translate Roman military policy into the actualities of battle-ground experience, and in many other ways. Yet they remain the insights of a soldier, and although this is what Ammianus was, it cannot express his entire personality; it does not begin to account for his role as a historian, which is how we know anything about him at all. We are not told the sort of personal details that would seem essential if one is really to know someone as an individual (one is generally told them in a novel). What did Ammianus look like? Was he short or tall, well-built or wiry? Was he married (perhaps more than once)? Did he have children? Let us assume that when he came to Rome in the 380s he was accompanied – though he nowhere mentions them – by personal attendants, such as the two companions of lower social rank who escaped with him from Amida; did he also bring with him a wife or, perhaps, like the young Augustine at about the same time, a devoted concubine?[2]

Skill in horsemanship is presupposed by his military role and consistent with his social background, but what more can we say? We can guess, but do not actually know what sort of man his father was.

Ammianus notes the smartness in dress even of poor Gauls, and had seen the ruins of Avenches; had he also witnessed an enraged Gallic housewife 'raining blows like a catapult' in defence of her man, or is this just another theatrical image (from low comedy), of no personal importance for himself? He remarks on the uninhibited passion of both sexes in Saracen love-making; does this imply that the Graeco-Roman upper classes to which he belonged were (as may well be the case) sexually more decorous than desert Arabs, or is he simply offering a rhetorical image of Saracen lawlessness? And what of the physicians of Alexandria, whose ministrations are so often needed 'in this life of ours, neither sparing nor sober'; 'in hac vita nostra nec parca nec sobria' (22.16.18)? This gentle, reflective phrase goes a little beyond what one needed to say; is Ammianus associating himself with the common lot of humanity, is he hinting at some more personal interest in the subject, or is he again evincing a moral attitude that does not connect in any particular way with his own experience?

More broadly, what Ammianus' reader may take as personal opinions on issues of the time – his praise of moderation and common sense,[3] his support for restraint in matters of religion and his opposition to bigotry and superstition, his respect for law and the institutions of law, his views on fate and divination, his admiration for modest provincial clergy, his dislike of eunuchs – are based on statements made and implications conveyed in a text of an artificial and formal character, that to a large extent creates its assumptions and makes its choice of subjects according to literary convention. In this sense, Ammianus' 'personality' can only be a construct of his text – an unbroken series, *par excellence*, of 'successful gestures' – for nothing is known of him in any other way. The one certain external reference to Ammianus, Libanius' letter to him of late 392, shows him as a successful historian and as an Antiochene, but adds no further detail. Yet even in the field of gesture there are alternatives of style, structure and language. In order to appreciate these it is important to know something of the nature of the text and of the historiographical traditions within which Ammianus wrote. It is with these questions that this book will end, in a discussion that will also take the opportunity to summarise certain themes mentioned in earlier chapters but so far not considered together.

*

With the loss of the first thirteen books of Ammianus' history we are without the preface to his entire work, in which he would have described its contents and scope, indicated its central theme and the historiographical tradition in which he conceived it. We do however possess the epilogue added to the very end of Book 31, in which Ammianus states the starting point of the work as the reign of Nerva and goes on to entrust its continuation to successors. These will be men with youth and learning on their side, who must raise their style, in Ammianus' very last words, to something appropriate for the present age; 'procudere linguas ad maiores moneo stilos' (31.16.9). The oblique reference (it is no more than this) to panegyric as the appropriate vehicle for contemporary history is reminiscent of what was written by Eutropius, concluding his *Breviarium* at the outset of the reigns of the 'inclyti principes' Valentinian and Valens; 'reliqua stilo maiore dicenda sunt' (10.18.3).[4]

Ammianus was probably acquainted with Eutropius, and wrote of his escape as proconsul of Asia from a treason accusation involving eastern court officials with whom he had been connected while serving Valens at Antioch (p. 225). But it is extremely unlikely that Ammianus' closing words were meant as a literary compliment to Eutropius. Nor is it likely that Ammianus' descriptions of the reigns of Valentinian and Valens, with their treason trials involving, in the case of Valens, just such literary men as Eutropius, answered what that author had in mind in his phrase 'stilo maiore dicenda sunt'; their eloquence, powerful though it was, was of a very different order. In any case, as both Eutropius and Ammianus imply, no literary successor could tackle the present age until, with the death of the reigning emperor, it had vacated the field of panegyric for that of authentic history. If Ammianus' epilogue is any more than a purely formal gesture, it is better seen as an attempt to suggest to his readers that predominantly Greek tradition of historiography in which authors, taking over from their predecessors, hand on the continuance of their work to younger men in order to produce continuous history written, as time goes on, by successive contributors. So Xenophon, self-appointed continuator of Thucydides, ended his *Hellenica* with the invitation to another to take up the story from there (7.5.27). Polybius thought of himself as the successor of Aratus of Sicyon and Timaeus of Tauromenium (1.3.2; 5.1), and was himself continued by Poseidonius and then by Strabo. In Ammianus' own time, Eunapius of Sardis had taken up his history (in fourteen books) with the reign of Claudius Gothicus, where his predecessor Dexippus had left it.[5]

In taking us back to AD 96, 'a principatu Caesaris Nervae exorsus' (31.16.9), Ammianus raises the question in his own case of the individual integrity of works composed in sequence to form continuous history. Neither Xenophon's *Hellenica* nor other continuators did justice to the intensity of Thucydides' theme, if we consider that writer's masterpiece not simply as a sort of 'measured length' of narrative, but as a historical study of a particular subject;[6] and it was the splendid Polybius' good fortune to find a subject, the rise of Rome to world empire, in which unity of theme, grandeur of conception and spacious narrative coincided to form a unified whole. But what next? Polybius' theme might be extended to show Rome's worthiness of the dominion she had acquired – a great theme in its way, but one that could hardly without degeneration into panegyric sustain the historiography of the Roman empire to the days of early Byzantium.[7] It is in no obvious sense the central theme of Ammianus, though as we shall see his account of the rise of Rome does incorporate it.

The problem of defining the theme of a Roman history running from AD 96 to 378 is made more acute by the difference of scale between Ammianus' later and his earlier, now lost, books. To summarise what was argued earlier, if we suppose that (say) the years 96-337 were dealt with in the first ten books, it will follow that the next three books covered 15 years, while the surviving eighteen books, on the period 353-378, cover a mere 25 years.[8] The changing ratio of something like 24 to 1.5 years per book (with some decrease of concentration in Books 27-31) represents an expansion of scale which at some point or in some part of the work must have begun to look conspicuous. This reflects what seems evident from the surviving books, that Ammianus' main preoccupation was the recording of contemporary history from personal enquiry. At the same time it poses the question of the relationship imagined by Ammianus between the earlier and the later books, and so between his own and earlier times.

It is hard to imagine that the preface to Ammianus' entire work, beginning with the principate of Nerva, made no allusion to Tacitus, who was known to Ammianus' contemporary Jerome to have written 'Lives of the Caesars, in thirty books' – *Historiae* and *Annales* being taken as a single work ending with the death of Domitian.[9] Ignoring Jerome's grossly offhand description of Tacitus as a writer of biographies, one wonders how Ammianus effected the junction between his predecessor and himself. The problem is both literary – neither in scale nor in manner would the opening of Ammianus' history bear much resemblance to the last pages of Tacitus – and thematic. In a programmatic, carefully written and obviously very important passage in Book 14, Ammianus set out his conception of the progress of Roman power from the 'circummurana bella' of the early Republic to the acquisition of world empire. During this period the senate, growing old, had passed on the rule of empire as a 'careful, wise parent' passes on an inheritance to the next generation, in this case the emperors (14.6.5).[10] Ammianus later explained how these emperors, the 'protectors and defenders of all men of good faith', were entitled to the protection of a law of treason, and might even apply torture to men of high estate when their own safety was at risk (19.12.17). If Ammianus was in any sense Tacitus' successor, he achieved it largely by neutralising the central theme of the earlier writer, the conflict between emperor and senate, focussed precisely on the political use of the law of *maiestas*. He might have effected the actual transition by remarking that the tyranny of Domitian was the end of the days of oppression before the reconciliation of 'libertas' and 'principatus' hailed in the first chapters of Tacitus' *Agricola*, and indicated in the preface of the *Histories*;[11] but whatever its force in its own day, that was not really a sufficient theme to sustain a Roman history over almost three centuries of change since the time of Domitian. Its influence on Ammianus can hardly be more than residual.

*

In the absence of Ammianus' preface to his entire work, we have the benefit

XVIII. The Roman and the Greek

of two other statements in which he sets out his procedure. In the first, introducing Book 15, he records his claim to have set out as clearly and truthfully as he could the events of more recent years that he was able to witness himself or could find out by 'earnestly cross-questioning' ('perplexe interrogando') those who had taken part. He then announces his intention to continue in the same spirit, recording events as carefully as he is able, without fear of seeming prolix.[12] Brevity is commendable only when it avoids unnecessary delays without detracting from the knowledge of events; 'tunc enim laudanda est brevitas cum moras rumpens intempestivas nihil subtrahit cognitioni gestorum' (15.1.1).

The preface to Book 26 makes a similar point, but with a rather different emphasis. Ammianus here hesitates, unsure whether to go on to the more recent age for fear of the 'dangers that attend the truth'; 'pericula ... veritati saepe contigua' (26.1.1). We saw earlier the possibility that Ammianus has in mind, not so much the fear of physical danger to himself from displeased emperors or politicians, as of complaints from readers who, before events with which they are familiar, wonder why certain details, of trivial importance for history, are omitted. Such fears had provoked some historians, as once observed by Cicero in a (lost) letter to Nepos, not to publish accounts of their own lifetime while they survived (26.1.2). History, Ammianus continues, keeps to the high road, 'negotiorum celsitudines', not troubling itself with insignificant trivialities; for who would wish to count the atoms – ' "atomos", ut nos appellamus' (26.1.1)?

Both prefaces, accounting in terms of method for the whole of the surviving part of Ammianus' history and for the books more immediately preceding 14, express a preoccupation with recent history; and nothing is clearer than that, in the context of the literary production of the mid-second to fourth centuries, this was a preoccupation of Greek rather than Latin historical writing. Ammianus' appeal to the authority of personal experience and eye-witness accounts – 'perplexe interrogando' – is reminiscent of Polybius' careful explanation of the role of an interlocutor who 'contributes as much to the interview as the informant', by the 'discipline which the trained interviewer brings to the occasion'.[13] It is not difficult to find such informants in Ammianus. The historian was surely acquainted with Aurelius Victor, who became prefect of Rome in 388-9, when Ammianus was living and writing there. He mentioned the bronze statue with which Victor was honoured by Julian as a literary man, and briefly acknowledged his reputation as a historian. It would not be surprising if in answer to Ammianus' enquiries what was worth reading on earlier Roman history, Aurelius Victor had directed him to or lent him a copy of the lost Latin history now known as 'Enmann's Kaisergeschichte' from the nineteenth-century scholar who demonstrated its existence by comparison of the writers, including Victor, who used it:[14] but Ammianus' real interest in Aurelius Victor was surely that, being at Sirmium when Julian advanced upon it in 361, he was able to furnish information about the advance, and especially the attack upon nearby

Bononia, which found the general defending it in an embarrassing state of unpreparedness (21.10.6). Aurelius Victor belongs to that class of participants, 'versati in medio', of whom other examples can be found – such as Philagrius and Syagrius, sources for episodes in the Alamannic campaigns of Julian and Valentinian respectively, Vettius Agorius Praetextatus, witness of certain events at Constantinople in 362, and Julian's eunuch supporter Eutherius of the 'immense memory', who was still living at Rome when Ammianus was there himself in the 380s.

Other historical writers are mentioned by Ammianus, but with no reference to their literary work: Eutropius, as we saw, for his involvement in suspicion of high treason under Valens, Festus for his role as scourge of eastern philosophers and others connected with Julian. Ammianus may have consulted Festus' *Breviarium* for some details of fourth-century provincial organisation, but probably in ignorance that the historian and the supporter of Valens were the same.[15] It is characteristic of ancient historians' practice that one literary source which Ammianus can be shown to have used, he should not have acknowledged. This is the history of Eunapius of Sardis, to which Ammianus had recourse in specific circumstances for certain episodes of the Persian campaign of Julian (Chapter VIII.3). As we saw, Ammianus' use of Eunapius has the effect, when seen in context, of emphasising the first-hand quality of his narrative in general, and it would be surprising if it were extensive. Although Eunapius' reputation may be due for re-assessment, he is primarily known for his highly rhetorical and polemical manner of writing (Photius, *Bibl.*, cod. 77), and when he can be compared directly with Ammianus he is usually much inferior. Ammianus is certainly a rhetorical writer, and the admiration of Julian and dislike of Constantine which he shared with Eunapius are manifest; yet he did not embark on the uncritical elevation of the one and denigration of the other that marked Eunapius' treatment. Indeed, Ammianus' praise of Julian is offset by some quite serious criticism, a complexity of view influenced, no doubt, by the fact that his personal experience, not confined to lecture rooms and libraries, involved him in the real world and required him to accommodate to a wide variety of contacts and opinions, amid many divergences of ideological belief.

Ammianus' manner of organising his material was annalistic, though in the circumstances this was not, and could not have been, applied rigorously throughout. Nor does it carry the heavily 'ideological' implications with which Tacitus, in his linking of 'consulatus' and 'libertas' after the expulsion of the kings (*Annales* 1.1) had invested this manner of structuring his material. In an empire governed separately in its different regions, the annalistic framework was satisfactory only to a certain point. Especially after 364, with the reigns, in practical terms autonomous, of Valentinian and Valens, it provided very incomplete guidance. Much is narrated outside it in the form of digressions, and many problems of chronology, and some of more general interpretation, emerge from this manner of presentation.[16] As for the lost books, it is

XVIII. The Roman and the Greek

clear that if they were written on the limited scale postulated here they can in no true sense have been annalistic in structure.

As to the alternative mode of composition, the biographical, Ammianus' opinion of Marius Maximus, the successor of Suetonius, is well known; he classified him with Juvenal among the unworthy reading matter of members of the Roman nobility; 'nulla volumina praeter haec in profundo otio contrectantes' (28.4.14). This does not mean that Ammianus rejected all biographical elements, far from it. His history is full of descriptions of character, individual conduct and physical types. Yet in general, biography, especially Latin biography, confused precisely that distinction between the trivial and the important that Ammianus asserted in his reference to the 'negotiorum celsitudines' at the beginning of Book 26. We would not expect Ammianus to have rejected all aspects of biographical technique, and there is nothing he does better than pick out the significant detail illuminating the wider theme; but he is unlikely to have favoured a mode of writing that of its nature gave equal status to the serious and the insignificant.

If in the hands of Suetonius and Marius Maximus biography had acquired an erudite, somewhat antiquarian character (not excluding the scandalous and the prurient), with the Greeks, and especially with Plutarch, it had taken on a more philosophical air: how was character formed, how did it develop through experience and habit, why did similar characters turn out differently in different social and political contexts? There is much of this too in Polybius, but it is not what preoccupied Ammianus, who is never afraid to judge character but does not indicate any philosophical theory as to how its development and expression should be analysed.[17] Ammianus is more concerned with virtue and vice as shown in action than with theories on the origins and development of character. In particular he is concerned with the pathology of human conduct when exposed to the tensions, threats and prizes of power. The Emperor Valentinian used to reflect that the correct exercise of power was always liable to expose its holder to the opprobrium of severity (or, depending on how one reconstructs the text, that due severity in its exercise laid him open to enmity and malice; 30.8.10).[18] It was of the same Valentinian that Ammianus remarked that the holder of supreme power must 'avoid all forms of excess like headlong cliffs' (30.8.2f.) and, in a powerful phrase, described the possession of power as liable to 'lay bare the innermost secrets of the soul'; 'nudare solita semper animorum interna' (30.7.1). Ammianus may be thinking here of the notion that a man's character is revealed by circumstance – as Aristotle put it, after an old saying, 'power will show the man'[19] – but if so it is not in a strictly philosophical sense but as part of common wisdom. Ammianus' diagnoses are based more on observation of behaviour than on theoretical analysis. We see this in his description of the senator Petronius Probus, forced into his prefectures by the avarice of the families of which he was head, but, in what has been called a 'masterly diagnosis of morbid ambition', always anxious, and so subject to minor ailments:[20] and of the general Marcellus coming to court to defend himself against allegations that he had not defended Julian as he should by claiming that Julian was 'fitting out for himself more powerful wings, so as to rise higher in the sky' – 'for thus he spoke, with a huge movement of the body', 'cum motu quodam corporis ingenti' (16.7.2). It is a wonderful scene, the over-excited general enacting before an astonished consistory the flight of a mighty bird. Julian's supporter, the eunuch Eutherius (surely Ammianus' source for the scene) refuted Marcellus' claims. He spoke 'verecunde et modice', Ammianus' phrase contrasting his calm manner with the general's mad turbulence; 'strepens et tumultuans, ut erat vanidicus et amenti propior'. Contrasting temperaments and emotions, on both sides, are expressed in appropriate physical gesture.[21]

It is unsatisfactory to consider such portrayals merely in relation to the conventions of biography. If there are moments in Ammianus when one can imagine oneself back in the more reflective, ironic world of Plutarch or Theophrastus, in doing so one misses the peculiarly expressionistic manner of his time. It was an age of what, in a phrase quoted in an earlier chapter (p. 256), has aptly been called 'didactic symbolism'; one in which the hands of thieving civil servants may be cut off by the 'avenging sword', the tongue of calumny torn out by the roots, the mouths of conniving nurses stopped with molten lead, the purveyor of false premises suffocated over a slow-burning fire.[22] It is hard always to be sure when penalties are literally and when figuratively intended: a significant ambiguity in an age in which gesture and reality are so closely related. Late Roman dress is flamboyant, signifying wealth, rank and status to the most casual glance, the emperor is surrounded by a protocol of theatrical elaboration, he is addressed and refers to himself in abstract periphrases to convey the timelessness of his virtues in a world of violence and change. Pursuing this pictorial idiom, Ammianus' characters are sometimes described in animal metaphors. They creep like serpents, prowl like caged lions, run amok like beasts in the amphitheatre, snap like vicious dogs, hide (in the case of eunuchs) like bats from the eyes of men (p. 258f.). Their jaws drip with human blood as, like hungry beasts, they secure the downfall of men of repute through savage torture and execution. In a literal enactment of the imagery, Valentinian kept pet bears near his quarters, one of whom, named 'Innocentia', he ordered to be released into the forest. She had won her freedom by the 'burials of many men she had torn to pieces' (29.3.9). It does not matter that Ammianus may here be misled by a misunderstanding of a practice also ascribed to Galerius, for we are talking not only of factual reality but of a symbolic mode of representing it: or was it that, in certain contexts, factual reality had adopted a symbolic form?

In Ammianus, the portrayal of character as found in biography, whether erudite or philosophical, has been further subjected to an imagery of public display and theatre, his descriptions of persons and situations resembling (sometimes by deliberate choice of language) scenes from a play or masque. This is consistent with an age in which

XVIII. The Roman and the Greek

'instant' visual and ceremonial communication have come increasingly to dominate the relations between government and governed, and in which the word of authority is increasingly domineering, relying more on the stirring of emotions than on rational exposition. We do not need to ask whether Ammianus owes his conception and portrayal of character to any specific tradition, whether of Suetonius or of Plutarch: both have been overtaken by a different, more symbolic mode of expression.

*

It has been suggested that in his statement that he had written 'as a former soldier and a Greek' ('ut miles quondam et Graecus'; 31.16.9), Ammianus is claiming a double qualification as a historian. As a 'soldier', he has the practical experience required of the historian of contemporary affairs; as a 'Greek', the cultural equipment necessary for their eloquent exposition.[23] There is some force in this view. The purpose of history was after all as a moral lesson drawn for contemporaries from the past or from present times for the future, and nothing was more relevant to the pursuit of this essentially persuasive task than the deployment of those rhetorical skills first developed by the Greeks. It was not for nothing that oratory and history were considered as related and adjacent arts, nor that Ammianus could in one passage refer to his narrative as 'oratio' (14.6.2), and in another compare his history, though true and based on the best evidence, with panegyric (16.1.3).

Despite these considerations, it is unlikely that Ammianus is making such a claim. His very next remark, that he had written to the utmost of his abilities, 'pro virium explicavi mensura', implies rather that he is offering an apology rather than staking a claim – the apology of a *mere* soldier ('ut', in a concessive sense) to have ventured on an occupation more characteristic of civilian, even aristocratic, pursuits than of the military profession, and of a native-born Greek to have written in the Latin language.

Ammianus' contemporary reader would at once see what was paradoxical in the writing of history by a soldier. Ammianus presented many soldiers in his history, and for all their variety they do not generally emerge as potential historians, combining the depth of literary culture and subtlety of understanding that this art required. They range from his patron Ursicinus, 'a warrior, always a soldier and a leader of soldiers but far removed from the subtleties of legal dispute' (14.11.11), to men of 'subagreste ingenium' and worse – an expression defined in one case, that of a career bureaucrat who supported Valens, in such a way as to exclude in principle the writing of history; '*nullis vetustatis lectionibus* expolitum' (30.4.2). Ursicinus' rival Sabinianus may by exception (if the text is correct) have been a 'cultivated old gentleman' – 'cultus quidem senex et bene nummatus'[24] – but he lacked all other qualifications of character and temperament, being indolent and timid, a small man in every way (18.5.5; 6.7).

Ammianus' statement that he had written as a 'Greek' would also at this ultimate stage of his history have declared an obvious paradox, though the fact of his origin would have emerged in hints that he came from Antioch and was familiar with the landscape and peoples of Syria and northern Mesopotamia, and in his occasional proprietary use of the Greek language, especially in contexts of scientific or other technical interest; so, 'visions of the night, which we call "phantasies" ' (14.11.18): 'the limits of the lands below, which we call "horizons" ' (18.6.22): 'minute channels in the earth [the source of earthquakes], which we call in Greek "syringes" ' (17.7.11): and many other cases. He quotes in Greek several sections of the translation made by Hermapion of the hieroglyphs on an obelisk installed at Rome by the Emperor Constantius (17.4.18ff.), and gives lines of poetry and parts of oracles in their original language (15.8.17; 21.2.2, 14.4; 29.1.33, etc.).[25]

Such passages point to a deeper affinity of Ammianus with Greek historiographical ideals. The affinity appears above all in his use of digressions, on a wide variety of subjects: on regions of the empire (the eastern provinces, Egypt, Gaul, the Pontus) and its neighbouring regions (Persia, Saracens, Huns and Alani). He digresses on the conduct of the senate and people of Rome (twice), on earthquakes, shooting stars, rainbows, the various forms of divination, 'geniuses' or 'daimones', the origins of pestilence, the wickedness of lawyers, artillery machines, the sextile day, obelisks (including the Greek translation just mentioned of long extracts from a hieroglyph inscription).[26] He steps aside to remark on all sorts of things, both in digressions and in narrative contexts: how palm-trees love and embrace each other, and reproduce themselves by physical intercourse, how the corpses of Romans and Persians were counted after the siege of Amida (those of the Romans decomposing more quickly), how fodder is stored in great piles in Mesopotamia, and stone sluices built in the Euphrates river: the qualities of naphtha when used in fire-arrows (twice, in almost identical language: 23.4.15; 6.37, cf. 6.16) and (repeatedly) the terrifying appearance of elephants: the quarrelsome nature of Egyptians (22.6.1, cf. 16.23). Although he may have read the details in Pliny or Solinus, it is hard to think of anything more 'Herodotean' in spirit than Ammianus' description of how the hippopotamus confuses its hunters by walking backwards, leaving many tracks, lets its own blood and plasters the cuts with mud until the flesh is healed over (22.15.22f.). Hippopotami, according to Ammianus, had taken refuge in the land of the Blemmyes 'through weariness at being hunted' – or so at least the local inhabitants conjecture, 'ut coniectantes regionum incolae dicunt' (22.15.24). Like Herodotus and some Roman writers, Ammianus mentions the migrating winged snakes of Arabia which encounter the Egyptian ibis in aerial battle and are vanquished by them (22.15.25f.; Hdt. 2.75), and in another passage describes how the lions of Mesopotamia, plagued in summer by myriads of gnats, in desperation throw themselves into rivers or scratch out their own eyes and so die (18.7.5).

XVIII. The Roman and the Greek

It is essential to realise that, for Ammianus, such digressions and asides were not extraneous, but integral to his historical purpose. They served a variety of functions, rhetorical as well as practical: not only to interest and inform the reader but to vary the pace of the narrative, to enlarge its scale, to enrich it by allusion, to define his own viewpoint. A short excursus on the causes of pestilence in his account of the siege of Amida enables Ammianus, without labouring the point, to recall Thucydides' classic description of the Great Plague of Athens of 430 BC (Thuc. 2.47-54).[27] His descriptions of the Christian attitude to martyrdom, and of the ostentatious behaviour and ruthless ambition of the bishops of Rome permit Ammianus to assert his distance from the Christian religion without having to attack it directly. A short excursus on the law of *maiestas* enables him without fear of giving offence to lay down the conduct expected of a good emperor in relation to the courts of law.

Digressions might, as in Book 14, enable Ammianus to achieve symmetry of structure in an individual book ranging widely over east and west, or in a larger context elevate a subject to a greater prominence than seems entirely justified by its narrative content. The reign of Julian is an extreme example of this. To leave aside for the moment the digressions on Gaul and Persia with which Ammianus introduces particular phases of the achievements of Julian, his account of Julian's reign as sole emperor (Books 22-24.4) is equipped with long digressions on Egypt, occasioned by a reference to the bull Apis (22.15-16), and on the regions of the Pontus, artificially brought in by mention of an embassy from the 'Bosporani and other hitherto unknown people' as among those who came to Julian at Constantinople in 362 (22.8; p. 106f.). There is a digression on artillery (23.4), suggested by the ships carrying such equipment, as they were assembled at Callinicum in readiness for the Persian campaign of 363. In strictly historical terms this is not the best place for it, for as we saw, Ammianus' books 19-21 contain accounts of five sieges, of Amida, Bezabde (two sieges), Singara and Aquileia, for any of which the digression on artillery would have been more directly relevant than it turns out to be for the Persian campaign. It is natural to wonder whether the inclusion of so many digressions in the books devoted to Julian expresses Ammianus' wish to elevate this part of his work to a still higher level than it already possessed in the 'rerum celsitudines' of the preface to Book 26.

This emerges particularly from the two digressions so far passed over, those on Gaul (15.9-12) and Persia (23.6). The first of these is introduced with an allusion in Vergilian terms to the 'higher theme', that of war, now awaiting the reader; 'ut Mantuanus vates praedixit excelsus, "maius opus moveo, maiorque mihi nascitur ordo"' (15.9.1). The digression has been judged relevant and helpful to Ammianus' narrative of the campaigns which follows, and this is no doubt true; yet the description of the mythology, history and cities of Gaul goes far beyond what would be needed to understand in any strictly military sense the Gallic campaigns of Julian. So too, in its context, does the digression on Persia, ending (23.6.85-8) with a description of pearls and a comparison of the Persian and the British varieties.

Ammianus in both cases justifies the length of his digression. He anticipates that his description of Persia may seem on the long side ('prolixior'), but argues that this will be in the interests of 'full knowledge'; 'ad scientiam proficiet plenam' (23.6.1). A writer who aims at brevity about the unknown will find himself worrying more about what he should omit than what he should explain more clearly (23.6.1). As for the digression on Gaul, he should avoid putting himself in the position of a mariner who has to make running repairs in a storm when he could have put affairs in order before setting out. Others had left an incomplete account – 'notitiam reliquere negotii semiplenam' – of the origins of the Gauls, a situation rectified by Timagenes, 'in diligence and in language, a *Greek*'; 'et diligentia Graecus et lingua' (15.9.2).[28] The expression 'scientia plena', so contrasted with the 'notitia *semi*plena' achieved by earlier writers on Gaul, has rightly been taken to exemplify Ammianus' ideals as a historian, but it is important to appreciate that he uses it to justify, not a lengthy political or military narrative, but a digression.[29] This sense of the need to place a narrative in nothing less than its entire geographical and cultural context, is itself enough to establish Ammianus' claim to belong to the tradition of Greek historiography. There were of course digressions in the Latin historians of the Classical age, but not of the number, scale or variety of those offered by Ammianus, nor displaying his range of erudition. As for the contrast between Ammianus and the Latin historiographical tradition of his own day, that is too obvious to state.

*

A true historian, Greek or Roman, was expected to write of his own times as one who had played a role in them. The expectation had two facets, concerned with the nature and quality of the material a historian could collect from personal recollection and by enquiry of contemporaries, and with his role as a man of experience qualified to pass judgment on events, possessing an understanding of the realities of political experience and of the motivations of men involved in public life. This aspect, expressed or implied in the writings, say, of Thucydides, Polybius and in the later books of Cassius Dio, comes out a little differently in the Latin tradition of Tacitus. Here, a writer's social rank and status give him the authority and the right to be heard – such as a 'vir consularis' enjoyed in the senate – and an awareness of the often arcane circles in which imperial policy was now devised. As we might expect, the Greek attitude had more to do with intellectual, the Roman with social and political, authority.[30]

As far as Ammianus is concerned, nothing is clearer than the extent of his personal involvement with some of the events he describes. It is an involvement of an often disconcerting intensity which can lead his narrative into personal memoir of a somewhat idiosyncratic nature. Now

XVIII. The Roman and the Greek 465

Ammianus lived a dangerous life which might have ended on any of a number of occasions – at Cologne, in the fighting on the Tigris banks or at Amida during the campaign of 359, during the retreat from Persia, at many other times. He had witnessed much, had been in danger of his life, had seen death dealt out and had doubtless dealt it out himself. He remarks in a powerful phrase that the siege of Amida focussed upon a single region all the misfortunes of the Roman world – a reflection provoked by the sight of Sapor's army before its walls (19.1.4) – and the events he describes in that book of his history were clearly central to the course of Roman history of the time. Yet this highlighting of Ammianus' personal experiences is unusual. The element of memoir when it is found in Greek and Roman historians (such as Polybius and his predecessors), generally reflects the experience of a higher social level than that of a young field officer. To some extent Ammianus compensated for this by adopting as his own the judgments of his superior officer Ursicinus; hence the rather narrow and personal basis of some of his opinions. Ursicinus lost his command after the fall of Amida, particularly after his sarcastic remarks about Constantius' eunuch advisers. Ammianus' opinion of the eunuchs is coloured by Ursicinus' view of their influence, as is his opinion of the general Sabinianus, who in refusing to commit the eastern field army to the relief of Amida was following Constantius' specific instructions.

Despite Ammianus' frequent declaration of the paramount importance of objective truth, 'veritas', in history,[31] his judgments in other contexts also are often characterised by the personal standpoint, notably his admiration for Julian, from which they are made. His views on the suppression of magic arts, on the conduct of judicial enquiries and on other matters are inconsistent and tend to vary with the emperor responsible, whether Julian or some other. Again in order to defend Julian, he offers a contradictory account of the origins of Roman wars with Persia in the fourth century, and his admiration for Julian is undermined, without his seeming to realise and certainly without his acknowledging it, by reservations on all major aspects of Julian's policies.

Together with personal experience, some historians, notably Thucydides and Polybius, had used absence from their own countries, even through exile, to give their writing a greater detachment and to increase their understanding of the point of view of the other side; in the case of Herodotus an invigorating sense of the variety and relativity of human custom and experience.[32] Ammianus travelled as widely as any historian whom we know – from northern Mesopotamia to Cologne and Ctesiphon in the course of his active career; to Egypt, southern Greece, the Pontus, possibly Thrace and of course to Rome after his retirement from it. His visit to Rome in the 380s has seemed to some critics to show Ammianus as a lonely, isolated figure, particularly if we take him to have been among those 'foreigners' expelled during the corn crisis of 383 or 384, of which he writes with such distaste (14.6.19), and to lurk under the guise of the 'honestus advena' who found senatorial houses so inhospitable, and their occupants so lacking in genuine cultural interests (14.6.12f.; 28.4.14). It is true that Ammianus occurs in no literary or social milieu at Rome known to us, but that does not mean that he had no friends there. The richness and variety of social life at Rome far exceeds even our generous documentation of it. There is no reason to assume that Ammianus must have belonged to any particular circle at Rome about which we happen to know – for example that of Symmachus – nor that any such circle must necessarily have been 'senatorial'.[33] There were certainly others, and other social levels, and it is unlikely that the historian, after so many years of gregarious company and widespread travel, suddenly went into his shell when he arrived there. What of the eunuch Eutherius of the 'immense memory', who, living in old age at Rome, was 'cultivated and admired by all classes of men'; 'colatur a cunctis ordinibus et ametur' (16.7.7)? Did his admirers not include Ammianus? Libanius' letter to Ammianus, written late in 392, shows him making successful recitations to an audience which, since it included men who would take the news of his success to Libanius, clearly contained visitors to as well as residents of Rome.

Ammianus' travels and visit to Rome did not distance him from or give him new perspectives in later years on an earlier, less developed concept of Roman history; they were themselves a part of his concept. Rome and the empire were linked, as Ammianus made clear both in his description of the ceremonial entry of Constantius in 357 and his subsequent conduct before senate and people, and in his analysis, conducted in profoundly Roman terms, of the transmission of the powers of the senate and ancient assemblies to their heirs, the Caesars.[34] Ammianus often balances Greek with Roman 'exempla': Artaxerxes and Papirius Cursor, Isocrates and Cicero, Themistocles and 'Romani duces' (all from the obituary of Valentinian); Pyrrhus and Scipio Aemilianus (in the Persian campaign of Julian, the latter seen through the eyes of Polybius; 24.1.3; 2.16f.). The Greek and the Roman are kept in equipoise: Julian's famous Homeric quotation on being made Caesar – 'Purple death has seized me, and fate imperious' (*Il.* 5.83) – is within a few lines balanced by the evocation of Vergil's *Aeneid* mentioned above. Cicero comes in at all times, on the sense of relief after the removal of danger (15.5.23), the vanity of philosophers who put their names to the books they have written despising glory (22.7.4), human fallibility in divination (21.1.14), the use of power to save rather than to destroy (30.8.7), and so on. It is in similarly 'Roman' fashion that Ammianus formulates the proper exercise of imperial power in terms of respect for the law and its established procedures (pp. 250ff.) and, in the Persian campaign of Julian, prefers the forecasts of *haruspices*, drawn from their learned books, to the 'inspirations' of Greek philosophers, 'persisting long in matters that are little understood' (23.5.11). There is more here than can be explained as a late addition to an originally different way of thinking.

It is still possible that Ammianus achieved distance and objectivity between himself and his material at the most fundamental level of all, in

XVIII. The Roman and the Greek

his choice of the Latin language. For a Greek to write of the Roman empire in the traditional language of Roman historiography – though it had not been used for this purpose for nearly three hundred years – might indeed encourage a certain detachment of thought. Is there any chance that the adoption of the Latin language was Ammianus' 'exile', a detachment from his native culture that enabled him to stand back and reflect more dispassionately on his subject-matter?

In considering this question, we must remind ourselves that the context of Ammianus' choice was not the same as it would have been in the late Republic or in the first or second century of the empire. In that period, what we have to reckon with is the mastery of Greek by members of the Roman governing classes, to produce a sort of cultural bilingualism much admired in recent times, perhaps because it allows critics to contemplate both what they most admire in the Greek and least dislike in the Roman character. In the fourth century, the reverse process, for some reason less admired by modern critics, had taken place, in the growth in the Greek east of the franchise of Latin, a consequence of the expansion of the administration initiated by Diocletian, with its roots in Latin-speaking court centres. It was possible to survive in the Greek world as an exclusive Greek-speaker, but at the expense of a distinct parochialism and narrowness of aim. The politically ambitious among the pupils of the Hellenist Libanius disappeared into the local administration of the eastern provinces and, with few exceptions, not to the imperial court; Libanius' recorded travels, from Antioch to Constantinople to Athens to Nicomedia and back to Antioch, hardly bear comparison with those of his compatriot and neither does his breadth of sympathy.[35] Greek teachers are also found in the west, for instance the famous Prohaeresius whose career is described by Eunapius (*V. Soph.*, pp. 485-93); Palladius of Athens, mentioned as a professor of rhetoric of Rome in the letters of Symmachus (*Ep.* 1.15); and others. Of particular interest is Hierius, an orator at Rome to whom the young Augustine dedicated his early work *De pulchro et apto*, knowing him by reputation only. Hierius had become famous first in Greek and then in Latin eloquence and, of especial relevance to Ammianus, he came from Syria (Augustine, *Conf.* 4.21). Most brilliant of all, there was Claudian of Alexandria, who, achieving mastery of the Latin language placed himself, in Gibbon's words, among the poets – as Ammianus placed himself among the historians – of ancient Rome.[36]

These men were the tip of an iceberg, for the west was full of such Latin-speaking Greeks, men active in public life: such as Hypatius of Antioch, prefect of Rome in 378-9; Ampelius the father of the usurper Priscus Attalus and prefect in 371-2; at a later date the father-in-law of Claudian's young friend Palladius, who as *primicerius notariorum* at the court of Milan had under his supervision that most Roman of documents, the *Notitia Dignitatum*, in the edition known to us from Renaissance copies of a lost Carolingian exemplar.[37] We see their counterparts in the east, in the pages of Ammianus, such as Strategius Musonianus, 'facundia sermonis utriusque clarus', who helped Constantine in his enquiries into Manichaean and other heresies, and under Constantius rose to the praetorian prefecture; it was his knowledge of the languages, Ammianus clearly states, that brought him to this distinction (15.13.1f.). The deserter Antoninus, a former merchant turned bureaucrat, took to the Persians detailed intelligence on Roman military dispositions and the preparations that were being made. He owed his access to this information, as Ammianus again makes clear, to his knowledge of Latin as well as Greek (18.5.1).

In this context, we can see that Ammianus' choice of the Latin language was no eccentricity but a natural option for one of his class. Perhaps it seemed natural to him precisely as an expression of his own career, which had been largely conducted in Latin, the language of administration and the army; if 'Graecus' defined the literary character and scale of the history he wrote, 'miles' largely determined the language in which it was written. Considered in relation to his historiographical purpose, Ammianus' choice of language gave him the opportunity to connect Greek and Roman traditions in the manner described in this chapter. Once this step was taken, the existence of a primarily Greek convention that a historical work might link with others to form part of a continuous series would suggest to him, having observed what the Latin tradition had to offer, the starting point of AD 96. This, the terminal point of Tacitus' *Histories*, was the obvious date for Ammianus to choose if the Greek convention were applied to Latin historiography across the empty centuries that lay between Ammianus and his predecessors.

But we still have to ask why Ammianus conceived of writing on this scale at all. The precedent of Tacitus in itself seems insufficient to explain the essential concept of a history of Rome reaching back from Ammianus' lifetime to the principate of Nerva. If a single explanation is to be sought for the transition in Ammianus' mind from contemporary to early Roman imperial history, it is provided, as it surely must be, by Julian.[38]

The importance of Julian in Ammianus' historical conception is obvious, and can be demonstrated, not so much from the actual attitudes towards the emperor expressed by the historian (which are far from simple), as from the formal aspects of his presentation. We have seen how, introducing the excursus on Gaul with which he follows Julian's elevation as Caesar, Ammianus summons up Vergil to set the scale of the higher theme now awaiting the reader. Ammianus' allusion is to the words with which Vergil brought in the wars fought by the followers of Aeneas after their landing in Italy (*Aeneid* 7.44f.) – an appropriate introduction to the heroic military exploits upon which Julian, and Ammianus, are about to embark. After the digression, Ammianus resumes his narrative, remarking that he will require the full resources of his modest talent; 'instrumenta omnia mediocris ingenii, si suffecerint, commoturus'. He adds that what will follow will read as panegyric, though based on the best documentary evidence (16.1.2f.).

This rhetorical introduction to the regime of Julian is balanced by a

XVIII. The Roman and the Greek

similarly elaborate presentation of its close. Ammianus' obituaries of emperors generally proceed by setting out the virtues of the emperor in question, followed by his shortcomings – the latter often illustrated by 'exempla' which make them appear more substantial than is justified by the actual content of what is said. This device is particularly obvious in the obituary of Julian's predecessor, Constantius (21.16.1-18; p. 239). The obituary of Julian has a more elaborate scheme, one that from the start determines its form as panegyrical.[39] Ammianus begins by listing the four cardinal virtues defined by the philosophers, 'temperantia, prudentia, iustitia, fortitudo'. To these are added four subsidiary virtues, or rather, external manifestations of virtue; 'eisque accedentes extrinsecus aliae, scientia rei militaris, auctoritas, felicitas atque liberalitas' (25.4.1). Julian's actions are then set out to illustrate in turn his possession of these virtues (in fourteen sections), and this is followed by a brief statement of the emperor's 'few shortcomings' (in six sections). Ammianus then appends a defence of the Persian campaign against its critics, arguing that it was not Julian but Constantine who had provoked war with Persia, and that Julian would have been successful had the fates been in his favour (25.4.23-7). That this argument is so unconvincing – as well as inconsistent with a view earlier attributed to Julian himself (p. 137) – detracts nothing from its significance in Ammianus' attitudes.

In fact, Ammianus' account of Julian's shortcomings raises difficult questions as to his attitude towards one whom he almost literally heroised ('vir ... heroicis connumerandus ingeniis', 25.4.1); for his criticisms strike at the fundamental principles of the emperor's attempt at the restoration of traditional practices and beliefs, based as this was on the total renewal of the civic life and culture, secular as well as religious, of the Roman empire. Whether Ammianus himself fully realised the effect of his remarks is very hard to say. A possible explanation is that he held at bay his disappointment in Julian by elevating his hero to a level at which normal judgments did not apply, for one effect of presenting the emperor's shortcomings separately from the literary framework of his virtues is to divert their impact by removing them from the same formal dimension as the virtues. Similarly though on a different plane, the attribution of Julian's failure to the working of fate, even if the emperor's personality was among its instruments, has the effect of placing him beyond the reach of a merely human judgment.

Whatever the explanation of the ambiguities in Ammianus' attitudes, Julian was a challenging figure, and remained so despite his failures of judgment and the ultimate collapse of his policies. He exacted comparison with the past – with the dynasty of Constantine the Great, whose religious and military policies he had tried to reverse, with the Tetrarchy of Diocletian and his colleagues and, looking further back, with Marcus Aurelius, for whom, in his work the *Caesars* (written at Antioch in the winter of 362/3) he expressed such admiration. In his preface to Book 16, Ammianus also referred to Marcus, as the emperor whom, above all others, Julian tried to emulate in every way; 'ad cuius aemulationem actus suos effingebat et mores' (16.4.1). Perhaps then for Ammianus the figure and personality of Julian were the link between his own experiences as described in the earlier of the surviving books, and the broader course of Roman history. This was the emperor who – to quote the prophecy of the old woman of Vienne when Julian first entered that city – would 'restore the temples of the gods' (15.8.22), would put the barbarians to flight and restore old standards of integrity to the imperial office and provincial government. The earlier stages of this project, witnessed by Ammianus during his tour of duty in Gaul in 356 and 357, seemed to demonstrate all that was best and most admirable in the reign of Julian – the more remarkable because, as he put it, his success was so totally unexpected (16.1.5).

Both Ammianus' original conception, based on the events and experiences of his own lifetime, and its expansion to include the earlier centuries of the Roman empire, were integral to his own thinking and do not require the intervention of other historiographical models, however influential these were in determining the precise form his work would take. In a sense the enlargement of a preoccupation with Julian to the context of Roman history at large, like the formal separation of the virtues and shortcomings in the obituary of the emperor, has the effect of 'neutralising' what was uncomfortable about him when viewed at closer quarters. It is a distancing, both in formal presentation and in historical perspective, that helped to make him easier to live with in one's memory, and more convincing to a later, more dispassionate audience for whom he was either a heroic failure, or a misguided irrelevance.

*

Having brought us so far, Ammianus would not object to our asking of him one further question: how would he have viewed the future? We may begin, in fact can only begin, to answer this by looking at his view of the past. Introducing his digression on Rome in Book 14, Ammianus wrote of the achievement of the city in establishing laws, 'the foundation and eternal guarantees of liberty', before handing on her inheritance of power to the Caesars 'as to her children' (14.6.5).[40] The role of liberty in relation to autocracy was, as we have seen, the central question of the *Annals* of Tacitus, the reconciliation of 'principatus' and 'libertas', as expressed in his *Agricola* (3.1), being a formulation of the relationship between senate and emperor under a benevolent, respectful and tolerant emperor. We also saw however that Ammianus goes further than this, writing not of conflict nor of mere reconciliation, but of a positive alliance between the two, achieved through the emperors' acceptance of a birthright entrusted to them by the senate. Ammianus is talking not of decline, but of a rejuvenation of Rome in the persons and office of the emperors; through their efforts in conducting successful wars in her name, Rome will live (or conquer: again that ambiguity in the word 'victura') as long as there are men.

XVIII. The Roman and the Greek

Ammianus' entrusting to the emperors of the defence of Rome and her values conforms to the emphasis which he places throughout on their personal qualities, and to the role of human planning implied by this in the securing of the future (it also conforms, of course, to the pattern of his own career). Criticising the conduct of Gratian in the year of Hadrianople, Ammianus reflects on the predicament of the empire, which required an unremitting concentration on important issues without the distraction of trivial forms of behaviour. Even had Marcus Aurelius been emperor, the situation could only with difficulty have been saved, with the help of colleagues of like character, and sober counsels; 'aegre sine collegis similibus et magna sobrietate consiliorum lenire luctuosos rei publicae poterat casus' (31.10.19).[41] What can in practice be meant by 'sobriety of counsel' comes out at one level in the aftermath of Hadrianople, when the *magister militum* of the east ordered to be assembled in the suburbs of the cities where they were stationed all the Goths presently in imperial service, and then had them massacred (31.16.8; p. 16). The experience of modern man renders him helpless before the morality of this action, of which Ammianus took a cruelly uncomplicated view. For him, the initiative of Julius saved the eastern provinces from disaster. It was an 'effective and salutary action, quickly taken', 'efficacia ... salutaris et velox'; a 'prudent counsel, smoothly and promptly put into effect', 'quo consilio prudenti sine strepitu et mora completo ...' (31.16.8). In the same spirit he had defended the massacre of a band of Saxons after a peace agreement had been made with them. A strict judge of the circumstances might think the affair treacherous and ugly ('perfidum et deforme'), but on reflection would not object to the destruction of a dangerous enemy, the opportunity having once presented itself (28.5.7). It is in a way remarkable that Ammianus posed the question from a moral point of view at all; it would have worried very few of his predecessors, or contemporary Romans of any social class.

From these examples, but more important from the whole tenor of the history, it is clear that Ammianus attached the highest value to the determination and physical energy with which the emperors and their supporters performed the duty entrusted to them. The emperors spent their lives marching back and forth along the frontiers where military challenges were set; like the Caesars of the Tetrarchy, they devoted themselves to 'running here and there' in loyal obedience to necessity or, where appropriate, their superiors' will (14.11.10). The outstanding example, or rather the limiting case, of Ammianus' pattern is again that of Julian. His early career in Gaul was noted for the amazing military success that expelled the Alamanni to their lands beyond the Rhine, and for the reforms in administration and taxation which Julian achieved, even against his associates' advice: all as expressions of relentless personal activity, and of the conviction that by energy shown in action, by virtue and discipline, by the refusal to be distracted from central issues by bureaucratic obfuscation, one could turn back the tides of misfortune, mismanagement and corruption that had seemed irresistible. More than this, one might even turn back the religious and cultural decline of the Constantinian era in favour of a renewal of the Golden Age of the Antonines and restore the military glories of the early empire. The Persian campaign, surely the most damaging possible legacy an emperor could leave to his successors, is presented by Ammianus as a continuation of the personal inspiration of Julian, thwarted only by the decrees of fate. If on this occasion the alliance of Virtue and Fortune that had made Rome great broke down, it was a failure of Fortune; there was no doubt of the emperor's virtue. It is an awkward argument, but the whole of Ammianus' obituary of Julian in Book 25 is designed in content and structure to convey it.

This emphasis on the autonomy and effectiveness ('efficacia') of the human will, as shown, among other ways, in the actions of the emperors appointed to inherit the historical mission of Rome, is one of the characteristic features of Ammianus' history, and what ultimately defines him as a man of the Classical world. So too did Ammianus' nearest successor, the Greek historian of western affairs, Olympiodorus of Thebes, see the disintegration of the western empire in the early fifth century as the consequence of a failure of human policies in adverse circumstances provided largely by chance or Fortune, 'Tyche'; while a recovery, beginning with the installation of Valentinian III as emperor in 425, was based on the active intervention of the eastern court in his favour, as an expression of a restored harmony in the Roman empire.[42] This harmony was fortified by the marriage of Valentinian to the eastern princess Eudoxia in 437, and by the compilation, and the publication in that and the following year, of the Theodosian Code: the first time since the Twelve Tables, it is astonishing to note, that the Roman state had, as an act of public policy, devoted itself to the codification of its law. Apart from the unity of east and west declared by the actual process of compilation of the Code – the gathering of material over a period of several years from its scattered sources – the publication of a book of law is nothing if not an assertion of confidence in the power of man by effort and will to affect the circumstances that surround him. Looking further ahead, it is not a coincidence that the preparation a century later of the Digest and Code of Justinian preceded the reconquest of the west. Both are statements of the confidence of a government, and Ammianus' phrase that Rome 'will live as long as there are men' is more than a rhetorical gesture. Nowhere is Ammianus more Classical in his perspective than in so connecting the eternity of Rome with human will and human effort. Ammianus' career, his morality and his history alike express the conviction that, whatever the crisis and whatever the scope of accident, something can be done, and that it is in the nature of man to attempt it.

Notes

The foundations of modern work on the text of Ammianus were laid by the critical edition of C. U. Clark (2 vols., Berlin 1910 & 1915). The Loeb edition of J. C. Rolfe (3 vols., Cambridge, Mass. 1935-40, repr. 1956-8) added nothing to our understanding of the text; yet its translation, though inelegant and on occasions inaccurate, was a heroic effort that must not go unrecognised.

In recent years have appeared in sequence the volumes of the Budé edition of the text, with French translation and commentaries of a consistently high standard. Vol. 1 by E. Galletier (with the collaboration of J. Fontaine) covers Books 14-16 and was published in 1968; Vol. 2 by G. Sabbah (1970) covers Books 17-19; Vol. 4 by J. Fontaine covers Books 22-25 (this is the fullest of the series, in two volumes with extensive commentary: publ. 1977); Vol. 5 by Marie-Anne Marié covers Books 26-28 (1984). Still to appear are Vols. 3 (Books 20-21) and 6 (Books 29-31). Wolfgang Seyfarth published a new text with German translation and commentary in four volumes (Berlin, 1970-71) and, in 1978, the two volumes of his fully-documented Teubner edition of the text, with extensive critical apparatus. This supersedes the earlier Teubner text of V. Gardthausen (2 vols., 1874-5; repr. 1967). There is a text with Italian translation by Antonio Selem (Turin, 1965). The Variorum edition of Wagner and Erfurdt (3 vols., Leipzig & London, 1808; repr. Hildesheim, 1975) retains value for its presentation of the annotations of earlier editors of Ammianus.

From a more general point of view and for English readers of Ammianus, the most important recent development has been the appearance of the late Walter Hamilton's Penguin translation, with introduction and notes by Andrew Wallace-Hadrill, *Ammianus Marcellinus: the Later Roman Empire (A.D. 354-378)* (Harmondsworth, etc., 1986). Although it is a selective translation, the great majority of the text does appear, the omissions consisting mainly – though with some regrettable exceptions – of digressions and narrative passages of lesser importance. This book has done wonders for the accessibility, and for the appreciation, of Ammianus.

There are no less than three recent concordances: by Maria Chiabò, *Index Verborum Ammiani Marcellini* (2 vols., Hildesheim, Zürich & New York, 1983); G. Viansino, *Ammiani Marcellini rerum gestarum Lexikon* (Hildesheim, Zürich & New York, 1985); and Geoffrey J. D. E. Archbold, *A Concordance to the History of Ammianus Marcellinus, in 49 microfiche* (University of Toronto, 1980). Of these, the first is essentially a word-list; the second takes more the form of a conventional dictionary, with analytical subdivisions of entries. The concordance of Archbold displays the immediate context of the word in question and is invaluable, despite the inevitable awkwardness of the microfiche format and the trivial inconvenience, also deriving from computer preparation, that separate word-forms are listed individually.

Among commentaries, in addition to those in the Budé series and the relatively brief annotations of Seyfarth's earlier edition, of particular value for particular facets or sections of Ammianus' text are M. F. A. Brok, *De Perzische Expeditie van Keizer Julianus volgens Ammianus Marcellinus* (Groningen, 1959); cf. the commentary by Fontaine on Books 23-25), and J. Szidat, *Historischer Kommentar zu Ammianus Marcellinus, Buch XX-XXI* (Historia, Einzelschriften 31 and 38; 1977 and 1981 – in fact ending with 21.4). The enterprise of P. de Jonge, *Philological and Historical Commentary on Ammianus Marcellinus* (Groningen, 1935-1982), covering Books 14-19 (Book 14 in German, the rest in English) is being continued by J. den Boeft and H. C. Teitler of Utrecht University and D. den Hengst of Amsterdam; the first instalment of their continuation, on Book 20, appeared late in 1987. I would also mention with particular warmth the Budé edition of Zosimus by François Paschoud of the University of Geneva; esp. Vol. II, in two parts (1979), on Zosimus Books 3-4, which cover the period described in much greater detail by Ammianus. The narrative of Zosimus is far inferior to Ammianus', but Paschoud's notes, extensive, critical and informative, shed a flood of light on both authors, as on Eunapius, from whom Zosimus essentially derives.

It is a familiar aggravation to late Roman historians that editions of late Classical texts, especially Greek, tend to use divergent systems of reference. It may help if I set out my practice with regard to the most important of these. I have generally referred to the works of the **Emperor Julian** in the Budé edition by J. Bidez, G. Rochefort and Ch. Lacombrade (in two vols., each in two parts; 1924-32 and 1963-4), which, particularly in the case of the *Letters* (Vol. I.2, by Bidez; 1924, repr. 1972) is superior in every way to the Loeb ed. of W. C. Wright (3 vols., 1913-23; repr. 1954-61). For convenience, I have in the case of the *Letters* added page references to Wright's edition: not however to her numeration of the letters, which differs from that in the Budé edition. For the other works of Julian, references are to the marginal numbers, which cause no ambiguity and are included in all editions. For **Eunapius'** *Lives of the Sophists* (*V. Soph.*) I have used the Loeb ed., again by W. C. Wright (with Philostratus' work of the same title; 1921, repr. 1961); here too references are to the traditional marginal numbers, which will permit them to be traced also in the critical edition of J. Giangrande (Rome, 1956). The fragments of the *History* of Eunapius are conventionally referred to in the numeration of C. Müller, *Fragmenta Historicorum Graecorum*, Vol. IV (Paris, 1851), pp. 7-56. They have been re-edited, with translation and some commentary, by R. C. Blockley, *The Fragmentary Classicising Historians of the Later Roman Empire: Eunapius, Olympiodorus, Priscus and Malchus* (ARCA: Classical and Medieval Texts, Papers and Monographs 10; Liverpool, 1983). Apart from its cumbersome title, this generally very useful book inconveniently changes the numbers of Müller's fragments. To avoid ambiguity and to preserve consistency with the mass of modern secondary literature, I give the numbers of Greek historical fragments as in Müller, adding page references to Blockley's edition. The references can be completed by use of Blockley's Concordance of Fragments at pp. 485-9 of his edition.

The works of **Libanius** are referred to in the standard Teubner edition of R. Foerster (11 vols., 1903-22; Vols. X-XI, the Letters, were reprinted in 1963). Most of the Orations relevant to this book are published, with translation, in two excellent volumes by A. F. Norman; (*Libanius: Selected Works* I and II, ed. Loeb, 1969 and 1977: Vol. III to follow); the first oration, also by Professor Norman, in *Libanius' Autobiography (Oration I): the Greek text, edited with introduction, translation and notes* (London, New York, Toronto, 1965). In the Liverpool series, Translated Texts for Historians, have appeared two volumes of particular relevance to this book; S. N. C. Lieu, *The Emperor Julian: panegyric and polemic* (1986), with translations from Syriac (Ephraim's *Hymns against Julian*) as well as Greek (John Chrysostom on Saint Babylas) and Latin (the panegyric of Mamertinus); and C. E. V. Nixon, *Pacatus: Panegyric to the Emperor Theodosius* (1987). My own and Peter Heather's collection of sources on *The Goths in the Fourth Century* will appear shortly in the same series, and a selection of the orations of Themistius is also anticipated. The Byzantine chronicler **Malalas** is cited by page in the 1831 Bonn edition of Dindorf (*Corpus Scriptorum Historiae Byzantinae*); the same system will also locate a passage in the invaluable translation by Elizabeth and Michael Jeffreys, Roger Scott and others (Melbourne, 1986). The Byzantine lexikon known as the **Suda** is cited by letter and numbered entry in the edition of A. Adler (5 vols., 1928-38). References to other Classical and Patristic texts, and to inscriptions and documentary sources, are to standard editions and series, some of which are shown in the following list of abbreviations and short titles.

Abbreviations

Acta Antiqua	*Acta Antiqua Academiae Scientiarum Hungaricae*
AE	*L'Année Epigraphique*
AJP	*American Journal of Philology*
BAR	*British Archaeological Reports* (International and Supplementary Series; Oxford)

BZ	Byzantinischer Zeitschrift
CAH	Cambridge Ancient History
Chron. Min.	Chronica Minora I, II (ed. Th. Mommsen, MGH auct. ant. IX, XI)
CIL	Corpus Inscriptionum Latinarum
CJust	Codex Justinianus (ed. P. Krueger, Berlin, 1877, repr. 1895)
CQ	Classical Quarterly
CSEL	Corpus Scriptorum Ecclesiasticorum Latinorum (Vienna)
CTh	Codex Theodosianus (ed. Th. Mommsen, P. Meyer, Berlin, 1905)
Dig.	Digesta Iustiniani Augusti (ed. Th. Mommsen & P. Krueger, Berlin, 1870)
FIRA[2]	Riccobono (et al), Fontes Iuris Romani Antejustiniani (2nd ed. 1940, repr. 1968); Vol. II by J. Baviera
GCS	Die Griechischen Christlichen Schriftsteller der ersten drei Jahrhunderte (Berlin)
HAColl, Bonn 1963-	J. Straub and others (edd.), Bonner Historia-Augusta Colloquium (publ. Bonn, 1964-)
HSCP	Harvard Studies in Classical Philology
ICUR	G. de Rossi (ed.), Inscriptiones Christianae Urbis Romae
IGLS	L. Jalabert and R. Mouterde (edd.), Inscriptions Grecques et Latines de la Syrie III (Paris, 1950)
ILS	H. Dessau (ed.), Inscriptiones Latinae Selectae
IRT	J. M. Reynolds and J. B. Ward-Perkins (edd.), The Inscriptions of Roman Tripolitania (Rome & London, 1952)
Jacoby, FGrH	F. Jacoby, Die Fragmente der Griechischen Historiker (Berlin, 1923-)
JHS	Journal of Hellenic Studies
JRS	Journal of Roman Studies
MAMA	Monumenta Asiae Minoris Antiqua
MEFR	Mélanges de l'Ecole française de Rome
Mél. Carcopino	Mélanges d'archéologie, d'épigraphie et d'histoire offerts à J. Carcopino (Paris, 1966)
Mél. Piganiol	Mélanges d'archéologie et d'histoire offerts à A. Piganiol (Paris, 1966)
Mél. Seston	Mélanges d'histoire ancienne offerts à William Seston (Paris, 1974)
MGH auct. ant.	Monumenta Germaniae Historica, auctores antiquissimi (Berlin)
Müller, FHG	C. Müller, Fragmenta Historicorum Graecorum IV (Paris, 1851)
Mus. Helv.	Museum Helveticum
Not. Dig., Or./Occ.	Notitia Dignitatum, pars Orientis/Occidentis (ed. O. Seeck, Berlin, 1876; repr. Frankfurt, 1962)
P. Abinn.	H. I. Bell et al, The Abinnaeus Archive: papers of a Roman officer in the reign of Constantius II (Oxford, 1962)
PBA	Proceedings of the British Academy
PBSR	Papers of the British School at Rome
PG	J.-P. Migne, Patrologia Graeca
PIR	Prosopographia Imperii Romani
PL	J.-P. Migne, Patrologia Latina
PLRE	The Prosopography of the Later Roman Empire I (edd. A. H. M. Jones, J. R. Martindale, J. Morris, Cambridge, 1971); II (ed. J. R. Martindale, Cambridge, 1980)
P.Oxy.	The Oxyrhynchus Papyri (London, 1898-)
P.Ryl.	Catalogue of the Greek and Latin Papyri in the John Rylands Library, Manchester, Vol. IV (edd. C. H. Roberts and E. G. Turner, Manchester, 1951)
RAC	Reallexikon für Antike und Christentum
RE	Pauly-Wissowa, Realencyclopädie der Classischen Altertumswissenschaft

REA	Revue des Etudes Anciennes
REL	Revue des Etudes Latines
RhM	Rheinisches Museum für Philologie
RIC	The Roman Imperial Coinage (edd. H. Mattingly, C.H.V. Sutherland, R.A.G. Carson), Vols. VIII (1981), IX (1951)
Röm. Mitt.	Mitteilungen des Deutschen Archäologischen Instituts, Römische Abteilung
SChr	Sources Chrétiennes
Seeck, Regesten	O. Seeck, Regesten der Kaiser und Päpste (Stuttgart, 1919; repr. Frankfurt/M., 1964)
TAPA	Transactions of the American Philological Association
ZPE	Zeitschrift für Papyrologie und Epigraphik
ZSS	Zeitschrift der Savigny-Stiftung für Rechtsgeschichte

I. Introduction

1. The hymns of Ephraim are translated (by Judith Lieu) with commentary in S.N.C. Lieu, *The Emperor Julian: Panegyric and Polemic* (1986), pp. 90–124. The quotation at the head of this Chapter is from the *Third Hymn against Julian*, stanza 4 (Lieu, p. 118).

2. For an excellent discussion of the third siege and its attendant traditions, see now C. S. Lightfoot, 'Facts and fiction — the third siege of Nisibis', *Historia* 37 (1988), 105–25; cf. also Lieu, 97–9. The events are documented in the *Nisibene Hymns* of Ephraim, translated by J.T. Sarsfield Stopford, in J. Gwyn (ed.), *Nicene and Post-Nicene Fathers (Second Series)*, XIII (Oxford, 1898), 167–72.

3. *Third Hymn against Julian*, stanza 1 (Lieu, p. 117). The banner is specifically mentioned by Ammianus; 'gentis suae signum ab arce extulit' (25.9.1).

4. See Chapter IX, p. 186f..

5. Alan Cameron, 'The Roman friends of Ammianus', *JRS* 54 (1964), 15–28, is particularly good, on both the specific and the general aspects of Ammianus' position at Rome. The letter addressed to Ammianus is Libanius, *Ep.* 1063 Foerster (Chapter II.1, p. 8f.); Symmachus, *Ep.* 9.110 was clearly addressed to someone else (Cameron, at 15–18). Its recipient was no Greek, and a Roman senator; Ammianus was one, and not the other. See also the careful discussion, supporting Cameron, by Sergio Roda, *Commento Storico al Libro IX dell'Epistolario di Q. Aurelio Simmaco* (Pisa, 1981), 242–5. The same conclusion was reached independently by François Paschoud, *Roma Aeterna: études sur le patriotisme romain dans l'Occident latin à l'époque des grandes invasions* (1967), at 66 n. 169, and is now very generally accepted.

6. R. Syme, *Ammianus and the Historia Augusta* (1968), argues that in certain passages the Historia Augusta makes allusion to Ammianus (esp. Book 15). This may be so (my own preferred dating of Ammianus' publication, c. 390 rather than 395, eases the chronological limitations discussed by Syme in his earlier chapters): still more valuable is his characterisation of the Historia Augusta (and of Ammianus), and of the general quality of fourth-century literary life at Rome. Syme's argument is pursued in a further particular by D. den Hengst, 'Die romeinse Keizerbiografie', *Lampas* 17 (1984), 367–80, at 377–8, comparing phrases in Ammianus 31.7 with Historia Augusta, *Aurelian* 11; the references at *Aurel.* 10.1 to 'friviola,' 'levia' and 'curiositas' would be a parody of professions of seriousness made by Ammianus, e.g. at 26.1.1. There are also general similarities, and some striking verbal resemblances, between Ammianus and the so-called *Epitome de Caesaribus* written shortly after 395 (cf. esp. *Epit.* 42.18 and Amm. 21.16.4; 45.2 and 30.7.2; 45.5f. and 30.9.4; 45.8 and 30.6.6), and between Ammianus and the *Getica* of Jordanes (*Get.* 128 and 31.2.2; 135 and 31.4.11). The effect of these is to grant Ammianus some — highly selective — readers, but not significantly to widen the scope of his impact as a historian. Nothing is known of the author of the *Epitome*, and Jordanes does not take us outside the literary milieu of Cassiodorus and Priscian (see next note). Jörg Schlumberger, *Die Epitome de Caesaribus: Untersuchungen zur heidnischen Geschichtsschreibung des 4. Jahrhunderts n. Chr.* (1974), ch. IX, pp. 208–32, postulates a common source, namely the *Annales* of Nicomachus Flavianus (p. 224), to explain the resemblances between Ammianus and the Epitome.

In a subsequent article, 'Die verlorenen Annalen des Nicomachus Flavianus: ein Werk uber Geschichte des römischen Republik oder Kaiserzeit?', *HAColl, Bonn 1982/1983* (1985), 305–25, Schlumberger argues, in view of the different social milieux of Ammianus and Nicomachus Flavianus, and accepting a later date for Flavianus, that the latter's work was intended as a senatorial riposte to Ammianus' history. This is all very interesting, but adds nothing to what we actually know. I remain as sceptical as ever as to the relevance of these 'Annales' of Nicomachus Flavianus.

7. Priscian XI 51 (Keil, *Grammatici Latini*, II, p. 487) gives the citation 'ut indulsi indulsum vel indultum, unde Marcellinus rerum gestarum XIIII; "tamquam licentia crudelitati indulta" ' etc.; the reference is to 14.1.4. The computer concordance prepared by Geoffrey Archbold shows nine occurences of the usage in the surviving books, 14–31. Since it seems unlikely that there were none to be found in Books 1–13, it may be inferred that the text of Ammianus available to Priscian already began at Book 14. What remains unclear is whether this text was itself the (indirect) source for the earliest known MS of Ammianus, from Hersfeld (see next note), which also began with Book 14, or whether Priscian's and the Hersfeld traditions derived separately from a truncated fifth- or early sixth-century text. While regretting the partial and tenuous nature of the survival of Ammianus' text, we should reflect that the goddess of chance to whom we owe it could very well have made the author a prisoner-of-war in Persia rather than a historian at all (19.9.1; Chapter III, p. 46).

8. *Note on the MS tradition*

A technical account of the MS and early editorial history of Ammianus is given by W. Seyfarth in his Teubner edition, Vol. I (1978), Praefatio, pp. vi-xv, with documentation for the brief acount in this note; for a clear summary, L.D. Reynolds, in Reynolds (ed.), *Texts and Transmission: a survey of the Latin Classics* (Oxford, 1983), 6–8. We owe the survival of the text to two ninth-century Carolingian MSS from the closely linked Benedictine Foundations of Hersfeld and Fulda in Germany showing traces of a 'continental insular' parentage from the same milieu; on which see L.D. Reynolds and N.G. Wilson, *Scribes and Scholars: a guide to the transmission of Greek and Latin literature* (2nd ed., Oxford, 1974), ch. 3, esp. pp. 80–90. The Fulda MS of Ammianus, now in the Vatican Library (Vat. lat. 1873, known as V), is now agreed to be a copy of the MS of Hersfeld; the latter, known as M, was dismembered for book-binding in the late sixteenth century, and its six surviving leaves rediscovered at Marburg in 1874: they were published by H. Nissen as *Fragmenta Marburgensia* at Berlin in the following year. From V derive four direct copies of the fifteenth century:

D   Vat. lat. 1874
E   Vat. lat. 2969
N   Par. lat. 6120
F   Florent. S. Marc. I.V. 43.

From F were copied or derived all the other known MSS, including W, now at Venice, which is discussed below.

With the possible exception of W, none of the direct copies of V, nor of the later MSS, nor of the early printed editions, adds anything but editorial conjecture (of widely varying quality) to the authority of V, which is itself highly imperfect (Reynolds, *Texts and Transmission*, p. 6 n. 1). However the edition of 1533 by Gelenius benefited from the use, especially for Books 26–30, for which it was the prime source, of M, which had been lent by the abbott of Hersfeld and was still intact from Book 14 as far as 30.9.6; this was where Gelenius' edition also stopped (cf. Seyfarth, xii, citing Gelenius; 'reliqua in archetypo [=M] desiderantur'). The value of Gelenius as a witness to the readings of M is however offset by his editorial methods, evident in other texts to which he set his hand as well as Ammianus. In particular, he left out words without indicating that he had done so, ignored textual lacunae where they existed in the MSS, and inserted his own conjectures without distinguishing them from MS readings (Reynolds, 8).

It is argued by Rita Cappelletto, *Recuperi Ammianei da Biondo Flavio* (1983) on the basis of a marginal note added by the fifteenth-century humanist Biondo to the Venetian MS W and transcribed also by the copyist of N, that an entire folio was missing from V at 16.10.4, where editors mark a lacuna of c. 17 letters. Biondo claims that he had seen a fuller version, containing significant material, in an old copy of the text of Ammianus:

> hic deest unius folii scriptura ex iis qu(a)e in exemplari vetusto legisse memini. et est pars multi facienda. (Bibl. Naz. Marciana, lat. Z.388, f. 48v.; Cappelletto, 18ff. with Tav. I,2; cf. 28 with Tav. III,1 for the note in N)

If this is true, then the space left at this point by the copyist of V (cf. Cappelletto, Tav. II) indicates a much larger lacuna, and editors' attempts to restore c. 17 letters are misled. Cappelletto identifies the substance of the missing passage in a marginal note inserted by Biondo c. 1453/5 to an early version of his *Italia Illustrata* and subsequently incorporated in MS and printed versions of that work (see her p. 35 with Tav. IV for the insertion), and traces it to a reading of a fragment of M conjecturally brought to Italy in 1452/3 (pp. 90-1).

The addition concerns the role of the Persian Hormisdas in the entourage of Constantius during the visit to Rome of 357, and the nature of the town of Ocriculum as in effect a built-up part of Rome (cf. Amm. 16.10.4, after the lacuna; 'transcurso Ocriculo'): other appropriate material to occupy the lost folium is suggested by Cappelletto, 40ff. Unfortunately, Biondo's recollection of his reading of M, if it is this, remains impressionistic. It is no doubt a venial error that he has Constantius visit Rome from Constantinople – any knowledge of the context of the journey would make it clear that it was Milan. As regards the content of Biondo's additional material, it seems unlikely that Ammianus would have described Hormisdas, a member of the Persian royal family, as 'Persarum gentis architecturae peritissimum', or indeed that Constantius would have assigned him the role alleged by Biondo, of 'architectural adviser' to the emperor on the occasion of his visit to Rome; this looks more like an inference from the tale told by Ammianus about Hormisdas and the Forum of Trajan at 16.10.16. Nor does it seem seriously plausible that the emperor should have withheld from Hormisdas the right to hold converse with anyone, in order that the Persian should enter Rome from the built-up area beginning at Ocriculum without realising it; the 'Herodotean' flavour of this story (cf. Cappelletto, 41) seems very inconsequential. Further, Ammianus writes at 16.10.16 as if this were the first appearance in a recent context of Hormisdas, 'cuius e Perside abscessum supra monstravimus'. This is more likely to be an allusion to a lost book describing his desertion from Persia under Constantine (see Chapter VIII.1, note 21), than to the passage supplied at 16.10.4 (so Cappelletto, 40-1). A back-reference to such a recent passage would be superfluous, and it would be more natural to describe Hormisdas' desertion in the context, for instance (there were other opportunities), of Constantine's wars with Persia (cf. 25.4.23). The difficulties with Biondo's reminiscence of the 'exemplar vetustum' of Ammianus, whether or not the 'exemplar' is M, are therefore considerable. The implication that there may be substantial lacunae in the text of the historian is however salutary (cf. 24.7.8 with Chapter VIII.3, p. 158f.).

It will be clear that modern editions of Ammianus, notably those of Clark and Seyfarth, represent a considerable achievement, both for their authors and for the science of textual criticism; the historian may be thankful that, in these terms at least, he can use the text with only occasional inhibition. In cases where inhibition is in order I have tried to ensure that I have never adopted readings that are less than seriously defensible. On one or two occasions where the exact reading of the text seems beyond editorial reconstruction I have indicated in my notes the lines of my preferred solution, and I have also given my reasons in some cases where I have adopted a reading against specific alternatives.

II. Ammianus and his History

(1) The political setting

1. Libanius, *Ep.* 1063; tr. (from Gimazane) in P. M. Camus, *Ammien Marcellin*, 278-9. For the date of the letter, securely located towards the end of 392, Seeck, *Die Briefe des Libanius*, pp. 202 (Marcellinus VII) and 463. In a paper given at Oxford in February 1987, Charles Fornara argued that the recipient of the letter was not the historian Ammianus,

but another Marcellinus of Antioch, a rhetorician practising at Rome. It is true that the word *sungraphê* used in Libanius' letter does not necessarily refer to historical writing; but this is its common meaning, and Libanius' letter indicates a single work divided into sections rather than, as Fornara's argument requires, a number of separate oratorical pieces made into a collection. Histories also were recited and the name Marcellinus, and the date of the letter addressed to him, would be doubly coincidental if the historian were not the recipient. A corollary of Fornara's argument is that the historian Ammianus need not come from Antioch, Libanius' letter being the only explicit proof. It is true that no specific passage of the history formally attests its author's origin, but taking the work as a whole his links with that city are very strong.

2. On the political background referred to in this Chapter, see my *Western Aristocracies and Imperial Court*, ch. IX.1. For the movements of Theodosius in 391, Seeck, Regesten, 278f. The laws of 19 June and 18 July are *CTh* 10.17.3 (Aquileia); 13.9.4 (Constantinople).

3. See Chapters XVI, p. 414f. and XVII, p. 446.

4. *Western Aristocracies*, ch. VII. For the metaphor, cf. 22.1.1, 'dum haec in diversa parte terrarum fortunae struunt volubiles casus'; 26.1.3, 'hac volubilium casuum diritate'; 3.1. See also Chapter II, n. 45.

5. *Western Aristocracies*, 225. For Theodosius at Milan, *CTh* 15.14.7, cf. 15.14.6 (22 Sept., Aquileia).

6. *Western Aristocracies*, 229. The ecclesiastical text is Socrates 5.14.5ff. (an otherwise circumstantial account); cf. Seeck's ed. of Symmachus (*MGH, auct. ant.* VI.1), pp. lvii-viii.

7. I maintain my opinion that Nicomachus Flavianus was quaestor in 388/9 and praetorian prefect for the first time in 389/90 (rather than in 383); *Western Aristocracies*, 231 and *PLRE* I, pp. 347f. (Flavianus 15). I will argue my position, against Callu, O'Donnell and Vera, in a forthcoming article to be published in collaboration with Professor A. M. Honoré (see Bibliography). The *Annales* of Flavianus are referred to on the inscr. of 431 in honour of his son (*ILS* 2948). Neither their scope nor their character is known, largely in consequence of which they make frequent appearances in modern literature, in relation not only to Ammianus but also to the Historia Augusta, the *Epitome de Caesaribus*, and even the Hellenist Eunapius; cf. F. Paschoud, *Cinq Etudes sur Zosime* (1975), 149-54. See Chapter VIII, n. 21 and the salutary remarks of Syme, *Ammianus and the Historia Augusta*, 110-11. The editorial work on Livy is referred to by Symmachus, *Ep.* 9.13, and commemorated in subscriptions to MSS of the first decad; see the apparatus criticus to the OCT or Budé editions at the end of Books I, II, IV, V, etc. Cf. Seeck, *Symmachus*, p. li n. 181 and *Western Aristocracies*, 374.

8. Cameron, 'The Roman friends of Ammianus', *JRS* 54 (1964), 15-28, at 24.

9. Chastagnol, *Fastes*, No. 92 (pp. 230-2).

10. The panegyric is now translated, with introduction and selective commentary, by C. E. V. Nixon, *Pacatus: Panegyric to the Emperor Theodosius* (1987).

11. For the 'adventus' ceremony, see Chapter XI, pp. 231ff.

12. See Chapter I, n. 8 for discussion of the material relating to Hormisdas found by Rita Cappelletto in a work of Biondo, and assigned to his recollection of a now lost passage of Ammianus.

13. For the date 384 (when Symmachus was urban prefect), see Cameron (above, n. 8), at 27f.

14. 15.1.1; 'utcumque potuimus veritatem scrutari, ea quae videre licuit per aetatem, vel perplexe interrogando versatos in medio, narravimus ordine casuum exposito diversorum'. Ammianus goes on to explain that he will continue to narrate with care, 'limatius': that this word does not have a strictly comparative sense and does not imply a change of procedure is argued at Chapter II, n. 36 (nor could it easily do so, if Ammianus has already embarked on narrative from personal experiences and the questioning of witnesses).

15. See Chapter II.2, pp. 27ff. with n. 36 for the relevance of this to Ammianus' use of digressions, and to the question of the lost books.

16. See Chapter XVIII, p. 462 for the historiographical implications of this.

17. On Ammianus' sources for the digression, I. Gualandri, 'Fonti geographiche di Ammiano Marcellino XXII.8', *Parola del Passato* 23 (1968), 199-211: cf. Chapter VI, p. 106f. for its function in Ammianus' text and XV, p. 389 and n. 12 for its character.

18. Chapter X, pp. 219ff.
19. Chastagnol, *Fastes*, No. 82 (pp. 204-6); *PLRE* I, Hypatius 4, pp. 448f. See also Chapter X, p. 222.
20. 31.16.8; Julius' action showed 'efficacia'; see Chapter XVIII, p. 471 for the relevance of this to Ammianus' attitudes.
21. Cf. 18.6.5, where the phrase 'cis Taurum' should from the context mean north of the Taurus (it forms part of a hurried journey to Italy which brings Ammianus next to the river Hebrus in Thrace). At 21.15.2, the phrase 'hinc pergentibus' of a journey from Antioch to Cilicia might seem to imply an eastern perspective, except that Ammianus seems to relate it specifically to the stage from Tarsus ('hinc') to Mobsucrenae: this was the last station in Cilicia to one travelling from the east, as Constantius then was.
22. *Consularia Constantinopolitana*, s.a. 381, 382; Mommsen, *Chronica Minora* I (*MGH, auct. ant.* IX), p. 243.
23. See bishop Ambrose's letter of winter 381/2 to the Emperor Theodosius, *Ep.* 14.6-7 (*PL* 16.955; ed. Zelzer, *CSEL* 82(3), p. 200); 'cum unus Constantinopolitanae presbyter ... intra Achaiam synodum orientalium iuxta atque occidentalium postulaverit, advertit clementia tua non fuisse irrationabile postulatum, quod etiam orientalibus est petitum. sed quia Illyrici suspecta movetur (moverunt *Zelzer*), ideo maritima ac tutiora quaesita sunt'. Still more vivid is *Ep.* 15.2, of 382/3, to the bishops of Macedonia on the death of Acholius of Thessalonica: it was a near miracle that the news of his death had arrived, 'occupatis terrarum barbarica infestatione regionibus, cum deesset qui advenire potuerit', etc. (*PL* 16.956, referring a few sentences later to the treaty of October 382). For the chronology, J. R. Palanque, *Saint Ambroise et l'empire romain* (Paris, 1933), 504-9.

(2) Composition

24. The purpose of this section is to set out the evidence for the date of composition of Ammianus' history and the essential implications of this, and at the same time to introduce the contents of the history; cross-references are given only when there is specific purpose in doing so. Much of the same material is presented in more substantive fashion in Chapter XVIII.
25. The passages are conveniently set out in the old Teubner ed. of V. Gardthausen (1874, repr. 1966), pp. 2-3. The most important are: Constans in Britain, 20.1.1; 27.8.4; 28.3.8, cf. 15.5.16 (his death). Eastern wars of Constantius, 14.7.7; 18.9.3. Rebellion of Magnentius, 16.6.2, 21.8.1; 22,13.3, cf. 21.8.1 (revolt of Vetranio). For a revolt in Palestine, possibly narrated in Book 13, see Chapter III, n. 2. The narratives of Silvanus and Gallus Caesar, and the aftermath of the rebellion of Magnentius, are given in Chapter III; Ammianus' experiences on the eastern front and the siege of Amida in Chapter IV.
26. See esp. Chapter VIII.1, pp. 134ff. for discussion of Ammianus' view of the Persian campaign.
27. Petronius Probus was alive in c. 389 and dead by 395; see my *Western Aristocracies and Imperial Court*, at 230 n. 5. I have been suggesting since 1967, and still believe, that Symmachus, *Ep.* 3.88 to Fl. Rufinus, of c. 390, refers to the death of Probus; *Historia* XVI (1967), 487-8; *Western Aristocracies*, 230; 'Symmachus and his enemies', in *Symmaque: Colloque Genevois* 1984 (1986), 174-5. For the character and influence of Probus, Chapter XII, p. 277f.
28. There are other cases where such phrases may indicate that the individual in question was known to Ammianus, possibly as a source: so, Philagrius, 'notarium, orientis postea comitem' (21.4.2; Chapter VIII, p. 162 and XIV, p. 376f.); Aurelius Victor, 'Pannoniae secundae consularem praefecit et honoravit ... multo post urbi praefectum' (21.10.6; Chapter XVIII, p. 457f.); Sophronius, 'tunc notarius, praefectus postea Constantinopoleos' (26.7.2; Chapter IX, p. 195); and Syagrius, 'tunc notarium, postea praefectum et consulem' (28.2.5; Chapter XIV, p. 377).
29. For Praetextatus as a source, G. Sabbah, *La Méthode d'Ammien Marcellin*, 230-1, citing Klein and Ensslin and emphasising the phrase 'aderat his omnibus Praetextatus' (22.7.6), followed by remarks that seem to authenticate his authority and objectivity. For the death of Praetextatus, Symmachus, *Rel.* 10-12, Jerome, *Ep.* 23.2f. with Chastagnol,

Fastes, 177.
30. Chastagnol, *Fastes*, 232-3. For the events in question, Chapter VI, p. 104f.
31. Sabbah, 183f., proposes diverse forms of archival material connected with the prefecture rather than more formal documentation such as 'acta populi et senatus', combined with enquiry of the prefects themselves. The idea of a formal 'Stadtchronik' envisaged by earlier writers, including systematic accounts of the prefectures (as Klein, *Studien zur Ammianus Marcellinus*, 53), should be regarded as a historiographical relic. A plain list of prefects, as supposed by Seeck, 'Die Reihe der Stadtpräfecten bei Ammianus Marcellinus', *Hermes* 18 (1883), 289-303, and Ensslin, *Zur Weltanschauung*, etc., 25, would of course be readily available; the notion however that this was transmitted to Ammianus by an intermediate literary source was satisfactorily dealt with by E. A. Thompson, *The Historical Work of Ammianus Marcellinus*, 26f.
32. 'anno sexto decimo et eo diutius post Nepotiani exitum, saeviens per urbem urebat cuncta Bellona' (28.1.1). The chronological and other difficulties associated with this remark are discussed at Chapter X, pp. 209ff.
33. Eutherius' role as a source for Ammianus seems assured; Sabbah, *La Méthode d'Ammien Marcellin*, 228-230 and Syme, *Ammianus and the Historia Augusta*, 95.
34. The idea that Books 26-31 represent a second instalment of Ammianus' history seems to be generally agreed by his commentators; see for instance Thompson, *The Historical Work of Ammianus Marcellinus*, esp. ch. 7, 'The composition of the last six books', and in his article, 'Ammianus Marcellinus', in T. A. Dorey (ed.), *Latin Historians* (1966), 144 (where it is stated definitively); H. T. Rowell, 'Ammianus Marcellinus, soldier-historian of the late Roman Empire', *Semple Lectures 1961-1965* (1967), at 280, and in *Mél. Carcopino* (1966), 839-48; Syme, *Ammianus and the Historia Augusta* (1968), at 7, 11 and ch. III; and at *JRS* 58 (1968), 217-8 (reviewing Demandt); R. C. Blockley, *Ammianus Marcellinus: a study of his historiography and political thought* (1975), 12-16. The preface to Book 26 seems to me not to be decisive in this sense. It is hard to believe that the usurpation of Procopius was not part of Ammianus' original plan, and Books 26 and 27 are organically connected; see Chapter X, pp. 204f. for these and other complications. I much prefer a single design running to Book 31 – or to Book 30, if 31 is seen as an originally unplanned addition, containing massive events that no one could have predicted.
35. So too Alan Cameron, *JRS* 61 (1971), at 259-62 (reviewing Syme, who argued for a date of completion of c. 395). A date in the later 380s is supported, with arguments of variable quality, by C. P. T. Naudé, 'The date of the later books of Ammianus Marcellinus', *American Journal of Ancient History* 9 (1984), 70-94. The 'obituary' of Petronius Probus at 27.11.1-6 (cf. above, n. 27) could, he thinks, be a late insertion. See further Chapter X, pp. 204ff.
36. The theory of an entirely separate work for the earlier period, proposed by H. Michael in a dissertation of 1880, was strongly criticised by L. Jeep, 'Die verlorenen Bücher des Ammianus Marcellinus', *RhM* 43 (1888), 60-72, on the basis of a study of Ammianus' practice in making cross-references within the surviving books. There is no 'objective' system of values; a 'long' or 'full' digression can consist of a few sentences, a 'brief' or 'summary' one can cover several pages. The theory has however been re-stated by H. T. Rowell in his two studies cited at n. 34, esp. (1967), at 276-81; this was opposed by Momigliano, 'The lonely historian Ammianus Marcellinus', *Studies in Ancient and Modern Historiography* (1977), 130, and by Blockley, 23f., adducing the practice of Procopius, where relatively long digressions can co-exist with a summary narrative. See also Alanna Emmett, 'The digressions in the lost books of Ammianus Marcellinus', in Croke and Emmett (edd.), *History and Historians in Late Antiquity* (1983), 42-53 – after a thorough critique of the arguments of Jeep and others concluding (with undue hesitancy) in favour of a single work in 31 books. I would add at this point that the word 'limatius' in the preface to Book 15 ('residua quae secuturus aperiet textus, pro virium captu limatius absolvemus') should not be seen as strictly a comparative (the Loeb and Penguin translations are in this respect misleading) and does not entail a promise to write 'more exactly' or 'in greater detail' than before. The preface links Book 15 with its predecessor(s) and indicates no change in historical method or procedure. It may occur at this point because Ammianus is now (since 14.9.1) a participant in his own narrative.

37. This theme is pursued more substantially at Chapter XVIII, pp. 464ff.
38. On this point, Jeep, at 71f.; see also Seeck in *RE* 1 (1894), 1848, adducing 31.16.8 (the epilogue) and 23.6.24 (cited in my text).
39. Syme, *Emperors and Biography* (1971), has a typically acute chapter (XI) on Maximinus. His wife was Caecilia Paulina (ibid. 192).
40. J. F. Gilliam, 'Ammianus and the Historia Augusta: the lost books and the period 117-284', *HAColl, Bonn 1970* (1972), notes the passage at 142-3 (No. 47), adding that 'chronology is largely ignored' and suggesting a common source for this passage and the *Lives* of Gallienus and Claudius in the Historia Augusta.
41. This would be the 'Kaisergeschichte' (KG) postulated by Alexander Enmann in 1883/4 to account for this and other similarities between Aurelius Victor, Eutropius and the Historia Augusta. See the full discussion of T. D. Barnes, 'The lost Kaisergeschichte and the Latin historical tradition', *HAColl, Bonn 1968/9* (1970), 13-43 and his brief account in *The Sources of the Historia Augusta* (1978), 91-4 (though I do not accept his conclusion that KG must have been composed after the death of Constantine in 337); also Syme, *Ammianus and the Historia Augusta*, 105f.
42. This conclusion emerges from the careful study of J. F. Gilliam, cited above in n. 17. M. F. A. Brok, 'Un malentendu tenace (Les rapports entre Hérodien et Ammien Marcellin)', *REA* 78-9 (1976-7), 199-207, gives reasons to doubt the extent of Ammianus' knowledge of Herodian. He would no doubt have read the Greek author, but there is very little connection and many divergences between them, and much ground is common to other Greek sources. According to S. A. Sterz, 'Ammianus Marcellinus on the Emperor Gallienus: his sources', *The Ancient World* 2.2 (1979), 69-71, Ammianus combined a hostile 'senatorial' view of Gallienus with a more favourable one derived from Greek sources. This however was exceptional, Ammianus depending generally on the Latin sources for this period.
43. This book has relatively little to say on Ammianus' digressions in their own right. See however Chapters XIII, pp. 291ff. (on artillery), XVII, pp. 428ff. (on divination, astronomy, and geniuses or *daimones*) and, in somewhat different spirit, XIV.3 (Huns and Saracens), and some remarks on provinces and cities in Chapter XV, pp. 389ff. On the purpose of Ammianus' digressions, see Sabbah, *La Méthode d'Ammien Marcellin*, esp. 525-8; Emmett, cited above in n. 36, with much of broader interest on the subject. R. L. Rike, *Apex Omnium: Religion in the Res Gestae of Ammianus* (1987) brings the digressions into play as evidence for Ammianus' religious views, but without sufficient recognition of the differences between Ammianus' style of writing and source materials in narrative and digression respectively; see my Chapters XV, n. 12, XVII, n. 10 and XVIII, p. 462f.
44. Fergus Millar, *A Study of Cassius Dio* (1964), 30-3, with suggested amendments, which do not substantially affect the issues as relevant here, by T. D. Barnes, 'The composition of Cassius Dio's Roman History', *Phoenix* 38 (1984), 240-55, esp. 251f. Two or three stages of composition can be surmised (Millar, 32f.; Barnes, 252): (i) the collection of the material; (ii) the compilation of a rough draft in the form of a 'commentarius', or (as in the case of Oribasius: Chapter VIII.3, p. 164) *hupomnêma*. This is no doubt what Olympiodorus of Thebes meant by *hulê sungraphês* or 'materials for history', diffidently referring to his own finished version which – as Photius observed – was nevertheless divided by books with 'prooimia', or literary prefaces (Müller, *FHG* IV, p. 58); (iii) composition of the final version, presumably incorporating the division by books with prefaces mentioned by Photius. Evidently these stages may overlap; stage (ii) may be truncated or omitted by a confident writer, and finished versions of individual sections may be produced at any time, for recitation or critical discussion. The introduction of literary allusion, relevant to Ammianus' relations to his Latin predecessors, presumably occurs mainly at stage (iii); much progress in the compilation and organisation of material, and in the formulation of leading ideas, can be made without it.
45. The main efforts to detect stylistic traces of Tacitus in Ammianus were by Ed. Wolfflin, 'Stilistiche nachahmer des Tacitus', *Philologus* 29 (1870), at 559-60: H. Wirz, 'Ammians beziehungen zu seinem vorbilden, Cicero, Sallustius, Livius, Tacitus', ibid. 36 (1877), at 634-5: and G. B. A. Fletcher, 'Stylistic borrowings and parallels in Ammianus Marcellinus', *Revue de Philologie*, 3rd ser., 11 (1937), at 389-92; cf. J. F. Gilliam (above, n. 40), at 127, n. 5. The difficulty – as Mommsen observed, in a remark noted by Gilliam – is

that so many of the parallels detected seem casual, indifferent, or even incongruous in relation to the contexts in which they are used or from which they are drawn. Why for instance should Ammianus, recommending his work to others to continue, 'aetate et doctrinis florentes' (31.16.9) wish to remind his readers of Titus' mistress Berenice, 'florens aetate formaque' (*Histories* 2.81)? Gilliam noted the relevance of Ammianus 22.1.1 (cited above, n. 4) in relation to *Histories* 2.1 ('Both are the opening words of a book dealing with the transfer of imperial power'), but Ammianus later develops the phrase in his own fashion (26.1.3; 3.1). I am essentially in agreement with R. C. Blockley, 'Tacitean influences upon Ammianus', *Latomus* 32 (1973), 63-78, noting (at 65) that 'the great majority of "Tacitean" phrases in Ammianus (about 60 of 65 counted) gain nothing by reference to the model. There is no parallelism of subject, and in some cases the linguistic similarity is slight', and (78) 'that Tacitus was a major historiographical influence upon Ammianus is not borne out by analysis. Many of the apparent points of contact are in the traditional procedures of ancient historical writing which both [Tacitus and Ammianus] share with many surviving historians, and doubtless shared with many who do not [survive]'. My own studies of the material fully support this conclusion, to which I would add the absence of Tacitean reminiscences in contexts where one would expect to find them. It is different with Cicero and Sallust: Cicero is clearly cited (passim), Sallust echoed in distinct phrases, such as an audience would recognise and of relevance to the context. The best is at 26.6.16, cf. Chapter XI, p. 237. The significance of Cicero in Ammianus' writing is noted by (among others) H. Tränkle, in a fine article, 'Ammianus Marcellinus als römischer Geschichtsschreiber', *Antike und Abendland* 11 (1962), 21-33, at 25-6. Other writers, notably L. E. Wilshire, 'Did Ammianus Marcellinus write a continuation of Tacitus?', *Classical Journal* 68 (1972-3), 221-7 (sceptical also on the relevance of Ammianus' 'literary borrowings' from Tacitus), Dieter Flach, 'Von Tacitus zu Ammian', *Historia* 21 (1973), 333-50 (particularly emphatic), and I. Borszák, 'Von Tacitus zu Ammian', *Acta Antiqua Academiae Scientiarum Hungaricae* 24 (1976), 357-68, have noted the entirely different political, ideological and historiographical circumstances in which Tacitus and Ammianus worked, and concluded, as would I, that the relationship between them can be little more than formal.

III. Ammianus and Constantius

1. In a chapter designed merely to introduce Ammianus and survey his early career, there is no need to give extensive documentation, or more than occasional cross-reference to the use made of the same material in later parts of this book. The regime of Gallus Caesar is seen in different ways by historians: by E. A. Thompson, *The Historical Work of Ammianus Marcellinus*, ch. 4, in terms of Gallus' support for the lower classes of Antioch, to which Ammianus was generally hostile: by R. C. Blockley, *Ammianus Marcellinus: a study of his historiography and political thought*, ch. 1, as a rhetorical study in tyranny, the fate of Gallus arising from his misunderstanding of the limitations inherent in the office of Caesar; cf. also his article, 'Constantius Gallus and Julian as Caesars of Constantius II', *Latomus* 31 (1972), 433-68. Hermann Tränkle, 'Der Caesar Gallus bei Ammian', *Mus. Helv.* 33 (1976), 162-79, shows how Ammianus' treatment, selective and rhetorical, is built around the personalities of Constantius and Gallus, and how it fails to give due emphasis to issues that are not contained within these categories. Anna Maria Tassi, 'Costanzo e la difesa della maestà imperiale nell'opera di Ammiano Marcellino', *Critica Storica* 6 (1967), 157-80, gives a lively account of this aspect of Ammianus' account, without adding much that is not already implicit in the text. In general terms, Book 14 is a model of symmetry, perhaps more so than any other book (Book 26, on the rebellion of Procopius, is a partial parallel; cf. Chapter X, pp. 204f.). It opens with a description of Gallus' savagery and closes with his execution (14.1; 11). At its centre is a long digression on the senators and people of Rome (14.6) while, preceding this and the final section, are relatively brief western narratives (14.5; 10); and each half of the book contains substantial sections on the east (14.2 on Isauria and 8 on the eastern provinces). Unrest in Isauria is rhetorically linked with the miseries caused by Gallus (14.2.1; 'nec sane haec sola pernicies orientem diversis cladibus affligebat') and the digression on the east similarly with the extent of these misfortunes throughout the eastern provinces (14.7.21). Sabbah, *La Méthode d'Ammien Marcellin*, 526,

points out with characteristic finesse how the digression on the eastern provinces, 'calme et savante' as he describes it, helps to add conviction to the violent chapters on Gallus that precede and succeed it (14.7-9) – while noting the artificiality of the way it is introduced. It is important to recognise from the start that the digressions are not extraneous, but an integral part of Ammianus' conception. (This does not mean that there are no differences of manner between narrative and digression).

2. Josef Geiger, 'Ammianus Marcellinus and the Jewish revolt under Gallus: a note', *Liverpool Classical Monthly* 4.4 (1979), 77, adduces Talmudic evidence for the suppression of this revolt by Ursicinus, who is named in several passages. The revolt could have been described in Book 13 of Ammianus. It is mentioned by Aurelius Victor 42.11, Jerome, *Chron.* s.a. 352 (ed. Helm, p. 238), and by the church historians Socrates (2.33), Sozomen (4.7.5f.) and Philostorgius (ed. Bidez, p. 222). The revolt was centred at Diocaesarea and was directed against 'Hellenes' and Samaritans. Diocaesarea, Tiberias, Diospolis and 'many towns' (Jerome) were taken by Roman forces, and Diocaesarea destroyed. Tränkle, (cited above in n. 1), at 167-9, notes the seriousness of the episode, and the success of Gallus as agent of the eastern policy of Constantius.

3. On this aspect, Blockley, *Latomus* 31 (1972), at 434-8 argues for the reality of a plot against Gallus without acknowledging the extent of Constantius' own complicity; at 465 Domitianus' actions are seen as exceeding Constantius' instructions (cf. in the same vein E. A. Thompson, 64-6). On the technical question of food supplies and the praetorian prefect, Blockley, 465. Julian's relations with his prefect Florentius can be seen in similar terms: Chapter VI, p. 89f.

4. The effects of Ammianus' loyalty to Ursicinus upon his narrative of this and subsequent events, are very well discussed by Thompson, ch. 3.

5. For the techniques involved in Gallus' removal (his isolation from his supporters), cf. Blockley, at 464-7 (except that in my view Domitianus' actions were approved by Constantius). Ammianus remarks on the occasion of his mention of Pola that it was there that Constantine had executed his son Crispus (14.11.20). So foreshadowed, Gallus' own death comes a few lines later (23). Robert N. Mooney, 'Gallus Caesar's last journey', *Classical Philology* 53 (1958), 175-7, assesses the respective calculations of Gallus and Constantius in the episode, observing that Ammianus too 'reads minds rather freely'.

6. With similar intent, Ammianus compared the general Theodosius with Lusius Quietus and Corbulo – both of whom had achieved distinction and come to grief under earlier emperors (29.5.4). R. C. Blockley, 'Constantius II and his generals', in C. Deroux (ed.), *Studies in Latin Literature and Roman History*, II (Coll. Latomus 168; 1980), 467-86, sees Constantius' policy in terms of the need to keep in check potential rebellious senior generals by playing one off against another; cf. his broader discussion in 'Internal self-policing in the late Roman administration. Some evidence from Ammianus Marcellinus', *Classica et Medievalia* 30 (1969), 403-19, arguing that the emperors used internal rivalries in order to maintain discipline in the administration, encouraging subordinates to inform against their heads of department and senior generals and bureaucrats against each other. If so, then Ammianus could well be said to illustrate the dangers of the policy (Blockley allows, at 416-19, that it was not always successful, citing the examples of Petronius Probus in Illyricum and of Romanus and his supporters in Tripolitania).

7. For these forgeries see further the discussion of patronage in Chapter XII, p. 271. W. den Boer, 'The Emperor Silvanus and his army', *Acta Classica* 3 (1960), 105-9, argues that Silvanus was forced into rebellion by his army, and that the claim of innocence made on his behalf by a supporter (15.6.2) was genuine. This is doubted by D. C. Nutt, 'Silvanus and the Emperor Constantius II', *Antichthon* 7 (1973), 80-9 – arguing that Silvanus led his army into rebellion through unjustified doubts as to Constantius' attitude to him, fostered by the manoeuvres of the emperor's emissary Apodemius (15.5.8). Either interpretation would justify professions of innocence.

8. This passage too is discussed later, in illustration of the conduct of the imperial consistory; Chapter XII, p. 267. For the possible date of the proclamation as 11 August, see the article of den Boer (previous note), p. 107, n. 10 (the suggestion of Seeck); below, Chapter VI, n. 3.

9. This early indication of the fundamental importance of Cicero for Ammianus should be

noted. The passage is not found in any surviving work (not surprisingly, the sentiments can be paralleled).

10. Cornuti and Bracchiati, again mentioned together, play a more heroic role at the battle of Strasbourg: 16.12.43 and Chapter XIII, p. 298. See too *Not. Dig., Occ.* 5.14-15 = 7.9-10. The episode has occasioned some modern disquiet, expressed for example by E. A. Thompson, at 42 ('utterly dishonourable') and 45 (a 'sordid story'). Ammianus himself was less squeamish when faced with conspiracy, even when he admired the conspirator; something of the same attitude recurs in his discussion of the usurpation of Procopius; Chapter IX, p. 201f. See esp. on the episode René Martin, 'Ammien Marcellin ou la servitude militaire', in R. Chevallier (ed.), *Colloque Histoire et Historiographie, Clio* (Coll. Caesarodunum XV bis, 1980), 203-13 – the 'servitude' being precisely the absolute duty of a soldier, at whatever cost to his own feelings ('la grandeur et la servitude militaires', p. 211), to defend legitimate power against usurpation. At Chapter VI below, pp. 82-4, is discussed Ammianus' possible involvement in the aftermath of the suppression of Silvanus.

11. As Thompson remarks, at 4: 'In what manner he found this out he does not say.' For the ruins of Avenches and other 'quasi-archaeological' material preserved by Ammianus, see Chapter XV, pp. 393ff.

12. It is important to note that Ammianus does not claim to preserve the actual words of these letters (which would in any case be written in Greek). His words introducing them are '[litteras], quarum *hunc fuisse accepimus sensum*' (17.5.2) and 'responsum est *hoc modo*' (5.9). I have described Ammianus' perspective upon the events that follow in 'Ammianus and the eastern frontier: a participant's view', in P. Freeman and D. Kennedy (edd.), *The Defence of the Roman and Byzantine East (Sheffield Colloquium, 1986)* (BAR Intern. Series 297, 1986), 549-64.

13. The text of Ammianus is not quite secure here; see below, Chapter XVIII, n. 24, where it is more directly relevant.

14. Presumably the letter was received at or near Hadrianople, for that is where the high road from Constantinople to Illyricum crossed the Maritza; for this and my general understanding of the situation, see 'Ammianus and the eastern frontier', 554 and n. 6.

15. Ursicinus' collaboration with Marcellus in Gaul seems not to have produced such conflicts, or at least none were mentioned by Ammianus; 16.2.8 and Chapter VI, p. 90f. Thompson, 45-7, is suspicious on this point and in general unduly hostile to Ursicinus, though he may be justified in seeing him as a 'capable soldier' but 'impossible as a subordinate' (52).

16. Amudis, on the road from Nisibis to Meiacarire, cannot be the place 'Ammuda' mentioned at *Not. Dig., Or.* 33.30 (Syria or Euphratensis); see my 'Ammianus and the eastern frontier', 562 n. 4.

17. 'Ammianus and the eastern frontier', 558f., with the interpretation of the message now offered by R. C. Blockley, 'The coded message in Ammianus Marcellinus 18.6.17-19', *Echos du Monde Classique* 30, n.s. 5 (1986), 63-5.

18. This episode is discussed in its geographical and social dimensions in Chapter IV.1.

19. The point is that the Roman generals were informed, 'unum e navalibus pontem transisse reges absque ulla circumitione' (18.7.2), but that Ammianus' information showed this to be a mistaken belief; see 'Ammianus and the eastern frontier', 560 and n. 13, where the reconstruction of Dillemann is criticised.

20. The graves of Edessa among which Sabinianus carried out exercises are often and (it must be said) very attractively, taken to be the famous martyrs' memorials of the place: so J. B. Segal, *Edessa, The 'Blessed City'* (1970), 172ff., cf. S. d'Elia, *Studi Romani* 10 (1962), 389 and E. D. Hunt, *CQ* 35 (1985), 195. In this case, Ammianus' reference could be construed as subtle anti-Christian polemic. I once accepted this, but am now inclined to think that it simply refers to the parade-ground at Edessa, which like the cemeteries was naturally outside the walls: Chapter XV, p. 398.

21. 'quem scissis collibus molinae ad calles artandas aedificatae densius constringebant'. In his commentary on the passage (n. 214 at p. 205), Sabbah suggests that the 'molinae' are large blocks resembling millstones placed deliberately in order to constrict passages and inhibit the approach of hostile cavalry. Clark's 'aptandas' for V's 'artandas' is an unnecessary change.

22. 18.8.12; 'miles ante me quidam discriminato capite, quod in aequas partes ictus gladii fiderat ["had split"] validissimus, in stipitis modum undique coartatus haereret'. It seems grudging to question such a circumstantial allusion, but (i) how did the soldier get there in the first place with such a wound? and (ii) similar victims appear among the slain at the battle of ad Salices; 'quorundam capita per medium frontis et verticis mucrone distincta in utrumque umerum magno cum horrore pendebant' (31.7.14). Waiving the first objection, one might then speculate on the second that the visual image stayed with Ammianus, for rhetorical use on the later occasion. In Chapter XIII, I try to illustrate how rhetorical embellishment and circumstantial detail are not contradictory but complementary facets of Ammianus' writing, often found in close juxtaposition – as if defying the reader to claim that a given passage is *merely* rhetorical.

23. Arnaldo Momigliano commented wryly and perhaps unfairly on this escape that 'It is symbolic [of Ammianus' alleged personal reticence] that the greatest feat of his military career was to escape unnoticed from besieged Amida while the Persians were breaking into the city' (*The Conflict between Paganism and Christianity in the Fourth Century*, 97 = *Essays in Ancient and Modern Historiography*, 122). See the more detailed account in Chapter IV.2.

24. Constantius' actions, as Ammianus' full narrative makes clear, are also bound up with his response to the usurpation in Gaul of Julian; see Chapter VI, p. 100f.

25. See Chapter XIII, n. 31 (and p. 303) for the question of Ammianus' presence (or otherwise) at the siege of Bezabde in 360.

26. A posting to Isauria has been conjectured on the basis of Libanius, *Ep.* 233 (of 360) mentioning an Ammianus, described as a 'soldier in dress but in deeds a philosopher', who was on his way from Antioch to Cilicia; Syme, *Ammianus and the Historia Augusta* (1968), 45, cf. Thompson, *Historical Work*, 10f. and Ensslin, 4f. (reserving judgment). The word 'soldier' can however refer to a court official rather than a military person and, as Seeck pointed out (*Die Briefe des Libanius*, 58, s. Ammianus II, cf. 374), Libanius' terminology makes his Ammianus look more like a financial agent. A further (no doubt surmountable) difficulty is that Ursicinus was dismissed from Constantinople (19.11.17, cf. 20.2.5; 4.1), while the Ammianus of Libanius' letter was travelling from Antioch to Cilicia. Others, notably G. A. Crump, 'Ammianus and the late Roman army', *Historia* 22 (1973), 91-103, at 102f. and in his *Ammianus Marcellinus as a Military Historian*, 8-11, think it more likely that Ammianus (the historian) was explicitly or tacitly allowed to withdraw from the scene until his return to active service in 363. H. T. Rowell, 'Soldier-Historian', at 284f. scouts this notion, citing the case of Fl. Abinnaeus (on whom see Chapter V, p. 75), but in the end concludes that Ammianus probably continued in active service.

IV. North-East Frontier

(1) The satrapy of Corduene

1. Austen H. Layard's famous *Discoveries in the ruins of Nineveh and Babylon, with Travels in Armenia, Kurdistan and the Desert* (1853) is an illuminating and relevant account of the physical and human geography of the region, and L. Dillemann's *Haute Mésopotamie Orientale et pays adjacents* (1962) is a closely and variously documented study, not always easy to use and sometimes confusing in detail. David Oates, *Studies in the History of Northern Iraq* (1968) describes lucidly (ch. I) the geographical background and (chs. IV-V) the Severan and late Roman/Byzantine frontier. I have learned much also from Christopher Lightfoot's unpublished D.Phil. thesis on the eastern frontier policy of Constantius (Oxford, 1982), and from discussion with Michael Whitby, now of St. Andrews University, on the topography of northern Mesopotamia.

2. On the validity of Ammianus' estimate see esp. N. J. E. Austin, 'In support of Ammianus' veracity', *Historia* 22 (1973), 331-5.

3. The view from Mardin, Layard, p. 252n.

4. K. Rosen, *Studien zur Darstellungskunst und Glaubwürdigkeit des Ammianus Marcellinus* (1970), 45, expresses forcible doubts as to the strict accuracy of this item; 'wahrschainlich interpretiert Ammian einer persischen Brauch, vor den er erfahren hatte,

nach seiner eigenen Vorstellung um', cf. de Jonge's commentary, p. 223: 'Ammianus can not possibly have seen this'. This does not prove that Ammianus was simply engaging in rhetorical embellishment. He *could* state it as a fact, believing it (even mistakenly) to be true; that is, he could have seen it, 'nisi deficeret acies' (18.6.21, with Sabbah's comment, n. 198). Everything was visible, if only the eyes had been sharp enough.

5. For this interpretation, see Chapter III, p. 43f.

6. The site of Nimrud is illustrated in M. E. Mallowan, *Nimrud and its Remains* (1966), I, plates 2-4 (at pp. 34-5); less spectacularly, in Martin Beek, *Atlas of Mesopotamia* (1962), pl. 71 (p. 38). Mallowan gives the perimeter of the site as five miles, enclosing 884 acres = 357 ha, including an acropolis (ziggurat) of 60 acres = 24 ha.

7. For these settlements and their possible identification, Dillemann, 84f., 110-12. Ammianus on various occasions gives Bezabde its 'ancient' name of Phaenica (20.7.1, 16; 11.24), hence a connection is inferred with the modern place-name Finik or Finyk – a place 15 km above Djezireh, with a chateau overlooking the Tigris (Dillemann, 84, cf. Layard, 53f.) – and, more speculatively, with Strabo's Pinaka. I do not know how plausible is the transference of place-name entailed by this obviously attractive identification.

8. On the geographical conditions of the region, see Oates, ch. I; also J. B. Segal 'Mesopotamian communities from Julian to the rise of Islam', *PBA* 41 (1955), 109-39, at 117-19.

9. J. B. Segal, *Edessa: 'the Blessed City'* (1970), ch. I and esp. plates 8(b) and 10(b).

10. For the coins of Resaina, G. F. Hill, 'The mints of Roman Arabia and Mesopotamia', *JRS* 6 (1916), at 166f.

11. For a description of Singara, see Oates, 97-106 (with plates). The annual rainfall at Singara is given as 19.5 inches in 1936-9 in the B.R. Admiralty Handbook, *Iraq* (1944), at 623 (with an aerial photograph of Singara, plate 23, opp. p. 78). See also W. B. Fisher, *The Middle East* (7th ed., 1978), 375.

12. Cf. Robert N. Mooney, 'Nature lore in Ammianus Marcellinus', *Classical Bulletin* 33.6 (1957), 61-3; 67-8, at 68. Lions of course figure frequently both on Sasanian and on Assyrian hunting reliefs; see for some examples of the latter the British Museum handbook, by Julian Reade, *Assyrian Relief Sculpture* (1983), 53-60.

13. For the ecclesiastical district of (Beth) Arbaye under Nisibis, see Dillemann, 113-14 (with refs.).

14. The campaign and triumph of Galerius are discussed (and dated 298/9) by T. D. Barnes, 'Imperial campaigns, A.D. 285-311', *Phoenix* 30 (1976), at 182-6, and in *The New Empire of Diocletian and Constantine* (1982), 63 The 'satrapies' listed in the text are given by Peter the Patrician, Fr. 14 (Müller, *FHG* IV, p. 189). 'Supra ripam Tigridis' is the expression of Festus, *Breviarium* 14, to be taken with 25; 'Mesopotamiam cum Transtigritanis regionibus reddiderunt [*sc.* the Persians to Galerius]': see the ed. of Festus by J. W. Eadie (1967), 57. See now the excellent work of Engelbert Winter, *Die sāsānidisch-römischen Friedensverträge des 3. Jahrhunderts n. Chr.* (1988).

15. The quotation is from the Syriac *Life of James the Hermit*, French translation by F. Nau, in *Revue de L'Orient Chrétien* 20 (1915), at 7. I am grateful to Andrew Palmer for discussion of this passage.

16. For the orientations of Amida, see the commentary of de Jonge, at 280-2; for Abarne/Çermik, de Jonge 286f., Sabbah, n. 217 (p. 206); the word derives from a Persian word meaning hot water or baths. Ammianus' account of the often fetid quality of the water-source at Amida is borne out by the geology of the region, cf. Dillemann, 63.

17. For Rhabdion, see Dillemann, 212-14: Hisn Kef, 228f., with S. Ory, in *Encyclopaedia of Islam* (2nd ed., 1971), III, 506-9 (s. Hisn Kayfa). The place is recorded as Cefa at *Not. Dig., Or.* 36.13, 30. For Bezabde, Dillemann, 84-5 with pl. IX.

18. G. Hoffmann, *Abhandlungen für die Kunde des Morgenlandes* 7.3 (1880), 22-4, cited by Dillemann, 110, and (with Hoffmann's German translation of the relevant paragraph), by Aharon Oppenheimer, *Babylonia Judaica in the Talmudic Period* (1983), p. 231, n. 29. The text is the *Life* of the Syriac saint, Mar Sabha.

(2) The siege of Amida

19. Ammianus' account of the siege of Amida, here seen from a biographical point of view, is set in the context of his presentation of war, and military affairs generally, in Chapter XIII of this book; see especially (on sieges), pp. 288f. and (on artillery), 291f. In that chapter is also discussed the question of Ammianus' use of rhetorical technique in relation to the circumstantial aspects of his narrative, the two being shown as complementary, not contradictory, facets of his presentation. It seems futile to deny that, despite its obviously rhetorical character in many respects (on which see Rosen, *Studien zur Darstellungskunst*, etc., 51-68), Ammianus' account is based on personal experience; the question relates therefore to his use of rhetoric within this framework. On the topography of Amida, the best general account is that of M. van Berchem, in van Berchem and J. Stzrygowski, *Amida: matériaux pour l'épigraphie et l'histoire Musulmanes du Diyar-Bekir* (1910), at 6-12, 'Enceinte, porte et tours'; see also the commentary of de Jonge and Sabbah's n. 216, at pp. 205-6.

20. The chronological inference is not invalidated if the estimates of the tribune and notary Discenes as to the number of casualties at Amida (19.9.9), based on the assumption that Persian and Roman corpses decomposed at different rates, are rejected as unfounded. Its logic flows from Ammianus' belief in the truth of Discenes' observation. There is an excellent article on the 'plague' of Amida; G. Sabbah, 'La "Peste d'Amida" (Ammien Marcellin, 19,4)', in Sabbah (ed.), *Médecins et Médecine dans l'Antiquité* (Centre Jean Palerne, Mémoires III; 1982), 131-57, cf. esp. 139-45 on the literary context of Ammianus' description (particularly the works of Oribasius) and 146-7 on the 'moral dimension' of sickness and medicine. Part of Ammianus' intention is clearly to give his work epic stature; Thucydides and Homer are cited at 19.4.4, 6.

21. For this emphasis on 'res gestae', see the very good article of C. P. T. Naudé, 'Battles and sieges in Ammianus Marcellinus', *Acta Classica* I (1958; publ. 1959), and G. A. Crump, *Ammianus Marcellinus as a Military Historian* (1975); and my Chapter XIII, p. 287f.

22. The content of this paragraph (and of those at pp. 288ff.) well illustrates Ammianus' use of rhetorical gesture in combination with (and not as opposed to) his circumstantial veracity.

23. For the detail of Sapor's head-dress see below, n. 25.

24. E. B. Tylor, *Primitive Culture* (1903), I, 458-67. For the non-Zoroastrian burial rite of the Chionitae see Sabbah's n. 229 (p. 209); and A. D. H. Bivar, in *The Cambridge History of Iran* 3(1), 211f. See further n. 26 below.

25. The point about the ram's-head emblem is made by Bivar, at 210f., with illustrations of royal head-dresses at p. 135 and plates 25-30 (from the coins). The head-dress of Sapor is there said to be a mural crown, the ram's head to be the emblem of the Shah of the Kushans. It seems more likely that Ammianus has misremembered, or misreported, the emblem on the head-dress than that he has confused the Shah of Shahs himself with one of his vassal kings; or he may have added a mistaken touch of erudition when he came to write up his description, for the passage in which the head-dress occurs (19.1.3) refers to Sapor's leading of his armies to Amida, without the specific appeal to eye-witness experience that comes a little later (19.1.5). The army of Sapor also contained Albani (from Georgia) and Segestani (from Seistan or Sistan in eastern Iran); see 19.1.6; 2.3.

26. The identity of the Chionitae with the Hephthalites or 'White Huns' of Procopius was maintained by Roman Ghirshman in his classic study, *Les Chionites-Hephthalites* (1948), taking both names, which are found on their coins, as dynastic rather than ethnic in nature. Ghirshman's denial that the people was in any ethnic or cultural sense Hunnish was upheld by Joachim Werner, *Beiträge zur Archäologie des Attila-Reiches* (1956), at 11; there is no trace of skull deformation either in their physical remains or their coin images. However, both A. D. H. Bivar, *Cambridge History of Iran* 3(1), 211, and R. M. Frye, ibid. 137, take the Chionitae to be Hunnish, on the basis of a Middle Persian word *xiyon* for 'Hun', possibly with the addition of a Greek tribal suffix (*-itai*). N. S. Nyberg, *A Manual of Pahlavi* (Wiesbaden, 1974), Part II, p. 218, gives under the word *Xion*, 'Turkish peoples in Central Asia and East Iran' comparing Chinese Hiung-Nu = Huns. This last identification is however far from certain (Chapter XIV, n. 95), and this is not the only difficulty. The word is

also connected by Nyberg with a New Persian word *hayan*, meaning 'a dromedary used by express messengers'(!), and the Pahlavi text from which the Xion are identified is itself problematic, since it 'includes remnants of an epic cycle certainly of Parthian origin' (Nyberg, Part I, p. xiii). (I am grateful to Dr Zeev Rubin of Tel Aviv University for providing these references, and for discussing the problem with me). The evidence might be consistent with the Chionitae being perceived as Hunnish by outsiders, except that it seems unlikely that their coinage would so use an outsider's perception to designate themselves. In this respect and in general, Ghirshman's interpretation seems to me more convincing.

27. Also, in a similar expression, of the Gothic nations at the engagement of ad Salices (31.7.11; cf. p. 372). In each case, a rhetorical point is being made, not excluding the circumstantial truth of what is said.

28. On Pirisabora or Peroz-Shapur, see Chapter VIII.1 (p. 132).

29. This 'graded' use of the first-person singular is a further aspect of the circumstantial validity of Ammianus' narrative. See J. Vogt, 'Ammianus Marcellinus als erzählender Geschichtsschreiber der Spätzeit', *Abhandlungen der Akademie der Wissenschaften und der Literatur in Mainz* (1963/8), at 811-13, pointing out (812) the uniqueness in ancient literature of Ammianus' '*evado*-Bericht'. In his unique mixture of 'narrative' and 'historical' modes, Ammianus narrated his own escape from Amida, adding later how the city was plundered, prisoners were taken and Roman commanders crucified.

30. For a sceptical view of Ammianus' expertise in artillery, see Chapter XIII, at p. 301f.

31. The social implications of the story of the horse are indicated at Chapter V, p. 78.

32. An inscription recording rebuilding of the city in the time of Valens was subsequently incorporated into the north gateway of Amida, cf. A. Gabriel, *Voyages archéologiques dans la Turquie orientale* (Paris, 1940), I, p. 136 ('La Porte de Kharput'):

> VIRTUTE PRECIPUIS INVICTIS
> INPERATORIBUS SALVI[S]
> VALENTINIANO V[ALENTE ET]
> GRATIANO PERPETUIS [DUCIBUS(?)]
> AC TRIUMFATORIBUS SEM
> PER AUGGG CIVITAS DISPOSITIO[NE]
> PIETATIS EORUM A F[UNDA]MENTI[S]
> FABRICA[TA ES]T

The surviving (medieval) walls of Amida are at best indirectly related to those known to Ammianus.

V. The Young Ammianus

1. For the historical (Classical and non-Classical) background of urban life in Syria and Mesopotamia, see A. H. M. Jones, *Cities of the Eastern Roman Provinces* (2nd ed., 1971), chs. IX-X; esp., for the cities mentioned in my text, 215-22. On Edessa, J. B. Segal, *Edessa: the 'Blessed City'* (1970). There is relevant material in G. F. Hill, 'The mints of Roman Arabia and Mesopotamia', *JRS* 6 (1916), 135-69, at 150-67 and especially, on the cultural and linguistic background, in Fergus Millar, 'The Church, local culture and political allegiance in third-century Syria', *JRS* 61 (1971), 1-17. On Antioch itself see the fine studies by Paul Petit, *Libanius et la vie municipale à Antioche au IVe siècle* (1955) and J. H. W. G. Liebeschuetz, *Antioch: city and imperial administration in the later Roman Empire* (1972).

2. The captivity of the inhabitants of Bezabde is described by the Syriac *Life of Mar Sabha*, in Hoffmann (cited above, Chapter IV, n. 18) at 24; cf. J. Labourt, *Le Christianisme dans l'empire Perse sous la dynastie Sassanide (224-632)* (1904), 78-9, and esp. A. Vööbus, *History of Asceticism in the Syrian Orient*, II (1960), 204. See further Chapter XVII.2, p. 436 with n. 25.

3. For the activities of the satrap Jovinianus (also from the *Life of Mar Sabha*) see my Chapter IV.1, p. 57.

4. On the Syriac language, Jones, *Cities*, 222f. and *The Later Roman Empire*, II, 994; and esp. Millar, *JRS* 61 (1971), at 2-8. On the evidence of the *Digest*, Tony Honoré, *Ulpian*

(Oxford, 1982), 4, 20, etc. (Ulpian was himself from Tyre, cf. Honoré, 9-15).

5. John Chrysostom, *Ad populum Antiochensem*, Hom. 19.1 (*PG* 49.188); see also Jerome, *Vita Hilarionis* 22, 25 and *Vita Malchi* 2, 'Syrus natione et lingua' (*PL* 23.41-2, 56). Ammianus' reference to the 'cool waters' of Meiocarire may for local interest be contrasted with his description of the thermal springs of Abarne near Amida, and the often fetid supplies of Amida itself (18.9.2 and my Chapter IV.1, n. 16).

6. The quotations are from Liebeschuetz, *Antioch*, 62, and S. R. F. Price, *Rituals and Power: the Roman Imperial cult in Asia Minor* (1984), 91.

7. The relevant passages of the *Antiochikos* are translated, with archaeological commentary, by Roland Martin, in A. J. Festugière, *Antioche païenne et chrétienne: Libanius, Chrysostome, et les moines de Syrie* (1959), 23-61. For praise of cities, see Treatise II.xiv *Peri klêtikou* ('Speech of Invitation') in D. A. Russell and N. G. Wilson, *Menander Rhetor* (1981), 183-93.

8. This assessment of Libanius' role as a teacher is sketched in my *Western Aristocracies*, 105-7. It is based, with some change of emphasis, on the researches of Paul Petit, *Les Etudiants de Libanius* (1957), esp. 166ff. For Latin at Antioch, Liebeschuetz, 242ff., 'The rival studies'; Petit, 363-70.

9. Strategius Musonianus (Liebeschuetz, 248); *PLRE* I, pp. 611-12 and below, pp. 449 and 467f.

10. For the Tetrarchic palace at Antioch, Glanville Downey, *A History of Antioch in Syria* (1961), 318-23; its third-century origins, 259, n. 126.

11. The food crises under Gallus Caesar and Julian are discussed in detail in my Chapter XVI, pp. 406ff.

12. See on these officials Liebeschuetz, 110-18, Petit, 253-60; also Roger A. Pack, *Studies in Libanius and Antiochene Society under Theodosius* (diss. Michigan, 1935), esp. 56-61, and A. F. Norman, 'Notes on some *consulares* of Syria', *BZ* 51 (1958), 73-7. On Libanius and the *consulares*, Downey, *A History of Antioch*, 423-5.

13. On *protectores*, see H.-J. Diesner, 'Protectores (domestici)', *RE* Supplementband XI (1968), 1113-23, and (for the essentials) A. H. M. Jones, *Later Roman Empire*, II, 636-40; for the foundations of the epigraphical evidence, Mommsen, *Ephemeris Epigraphica* 5 (1884), 121-41 (= *Ges. Schr.* VIII 419-46).

14. For a similar story about wrestling, see Historia Augusta, *Maximinus* 2.6f. (there is a social connotation, as in the story about stamina at running, cf. below, n. 21).

15. This fascinating archive was edited with translation and full commentary by H. I. Bell and others, *The Abinnaeus Archive: papers of a Roman officer in the reign of Constantius II* (1962); see ch. II, pp. 6-12 on his career. The passage alluded to in my text (the service of 33 years) is at p. 34f.

16. *Not. Dig., Or.* 15; *Occ.* 13, with line drawings: though one needs the colour slides produced by the Bodleian Library from its MS of 1436 (Canon. Misc. 378) to realise the true splendour of the device.

17. Cf. Augustine, *Conf.* 7.1(1) with Brent Shaw, *Past and Present* 115 (1987), 40-1 for the end of 'adolescentia' at the age of about thirty.

18. For adoration by 'protectores', see *The Abinnaeus Archive*, 10. For the ritual itself, my Chapter XI, pp. 244-7.

19. For the term 'ducenarius' applied to *protectores*, cf. Mommsen's inscriptions, nos. 5 (= *ILS* 569), 8, 11 (= *ILS* 2778), 12, 14, 22, 39, and his remarks before Nos. 49-52. It ceased in such cases to refer to a salary and became a definition of status.

20. The contrast between Ammianus and Abinnaeus is made in just this spirit (from the point of view of Abinnaeus) at *The Abinnaeus Archive*, 11; but without the important distinction between 'protectores' and 'protectores domestici'.

21. Again, compare the stamina at running (a lower-class achievement) assigned, fictitiously, to the Emperor Maximinus; Historia Augusta, *Maximinus* 2f.

22. These comparisons are adduced by Jones, *Later Roman Empire*, 638.

23. For the 'honorati' see Liebeschuetz, 175, 186-92, 'The new aristocracy'; Petit, 370ff.

VI. The Rise of Julian

1. The position of Ursicinus is discussed by E. Frézouls, 'La mission du "magister militum" Ursicin en Gaule (355-357) d'après Ammien Marcellin', in *Hommages Grenier* (1962), II, 673-88 – demonstrating with painstaking care what is obvious from Ammianus: throughout this period Ursicinus was 'on secondment' from the eastern theatre of war, never having been replaced there.

2. In a book not about Julian but his historian, it will be enough to mention the most important works, and those most closely relevant to Ammianus. Among the biographical studies of Julian, Joseph Bidez's *La Vie de l'empereur Julien* (1930, repr. 1965) is still unsurpassed for its range and perception, though its attitude to Julian might be thought over-favourable; while in emphasising the intellectual aspects of Julian's development, the book diverges markedly from Ammianus' own perspective. Robert Browning, *The Emperor Julian* (1975) is broad-ranging and wise, though with some lapses of accuracy, and G. W. Bowersock, *Julian the Apostate* (1978) is acute in its analysis of Julian's character (and critical of Ammianus). Polymnia Athanassiadi-Fowden, *Julian and Hellenism* (1981) is the work of an admirer, but with much of interest on the intellectual side of Julian's personality. The collection edited by R. Braun and J. Riché, *L'Empereur Julien, de l'histoire à la légende 331-1715* (1978) contains (at pp. 31-65) Jacques Fontaine's very interesting 'Le Julien d'Ammien', and there are valuable chapters in E. A. Thompson, *The Historical Work of Ammianus Marcellinus*, and in R. C. Blockley's *Ammianus Marcellinus: a study of his historiography and political thought* (1975). On Julian's civic and religious policies, there is now above all Edgar Pack, *Städte und Steuern in der Politik Julians: Untersuchungen zu den Quellen eines Kaiserbildes* (Coll. Latomus 194; 1986). Biographical elements in Ammianus' writing are discussed by Christa Samberger, 'Die "Kaiserbiographie" in den Res Gestae des Ammianus Marcellinus. Eine Untersuchung zur Komposition der ammianeischen Geschichtsschreibung', *Klio* 51 (1969), 349-482, esp. at 433ff. On the circumstances of the usurpation of Julian I have learned much from reflection on J. F. Drinkwater, 'The "pagan underground", Constantius II's "secret service", and the survival, and the usurpation of Julian the Apostate', in C. Deroux, *Studies in Latin Literature and Roman History*, III (1983), 348-87. Of constant value are the commentaries on Ammianus 20-21.4 by J. Szidat, and on Zosimus by François Paschoud. The Letter to the Athenians is translated by W. C. Wright in the Loeb ed. of Julian's works, II, 241-91, and Mamertinus' panegyric by Marna Morgan in S. N. C. Lieu (ed.), *The Emperor Julian: panegyric and polemic* (1986).

3. W. den Boer, 'The Emperor Silvanus and his army', *Acta Classica* 3 (1960), 105-9, argues, perhaps rightly, that Proculus was telling the truth; Silvanus had been forced into rebellion by his army. den Boer cites Seeck's suggestion that the donative paid by Silvanus was in honour of Constantius' birthday (7 August). If so, the proclamation was on 11 August.

4. Sabbah, *La Méthode d'Ammien Marcellin*, 228-30, and Fontaine, 'Le Julien d'Ammien', 48, agree in seeing Eutherius as a prime source for Ammianus; see also Chapter II.2, p. 25 and n. 33.

5. Browning, *The Emperor Julian*, 87, supposes Ammianus to have been a participant at Strasbourg, but this fails to consider 16.10.21. For Ammianus' sources on the battle, Chapter XIV Conclusion, p. 378f.

6. Cf. on this 'psychologising tendency' Peter Brown, *Society and the Holy in Late Antiquity* (1982), at 90-2. An example is A.-J. Festugière, 'Julien à Macellum', *JRS* 47 (1957), 53-8.

7. Constantius may not have been responsible for the murders, but a group of generals and senior officials, possibly believing themselves to be carrying out the wishes of Constantine; cf. T. D. Barnes, *Constantine and Eusebius* (1981), 262.

8. For biography and the study of character see D. A. Russell, *Plutarch* (1972), esp. 100-6. The question is further discussed at Chapter XVIII, pp. 459ff.

9. A. Hadjinicolaou, 'Macellum, lieu d'exil de l'empereur Julien', *Byzantion* 21 (1951), 15-22. The place was in the vicinity of Caesarea, near the church of St. Mamas to the north-east of the city, founded in their youth by Gallus and Julian (Sozomen 5.2.9, etc.). Its

name is of course the Latin for 'market' – Latin perhaps being used because of the connection of the estate with the imperial house.

10. The two articles of Noël Aujoulat, 'Eusébie, Hélène et Julien. I: Le témoignage de Julien', *Byzantion* 53 (1983), 78-103 and 'II: Le témoignage des historiens', ibid., 421-52 are unnecessarily expansive and at many points groundlessly speculative. Their most interesting pages are 438-45, suggesting that Eusebia's death (cf. 21.6.4) was brought about by 'metromania', a hysterical condition induced by sexual frustration (her husband Constantius being 'anormalement insuffisant') and barrenness, finally resulting in death from anorexia.

11. On Julian's 'apostasy', Athanassiadi-Fowden, *Julian and Hellenism*, esp. 24-7. On Julian's activities in Asia Minor, Chapter VII, p. 122f.

12. *Itin. Burd.* 555.7 (p. 6, ed. Geyer). For the locations mentioned in the text, see Galletier's ed. of Ammianus, ed. Budé I (1968), n. 246 at p. 258.

13. On Julian's character (beginning with the evidence of Gregory of Nazianzus), Bowersock, *Julian the Apostate*, 12-32; also J. Bernardi, 'Un réquisitoire: les Invectives contre Julien de Grégoire de Nazianze' in *L'Empereur Julien, de l'histoire à la legende* (n. 2 above), 89-98.

14. For the system of 'capitatio', Jones, *Later Roman Empire*, I, 63-5, cf. (on this episode) 119-20, describing Julian's feat as 'incredible, if it were not vouched for by Ammianus'; cf. now the detailed discussion of Edgar Pack (n. 1 above), 62ff. Two laws of Constantius, both issued at Milan and addressed 'ad populum' and to the *PPo (Italiae)* Taurus on 2 April 356 and 1 April 357 respectively (*CTh* 11.16.7-8) prohibit the exaction of extra taxes by provincial governors except in cases of dire urgency and with the consent of the praetorian prefect, referred by him to the emperor for confirmation. The phrases 'nostrae intimari clementiae' ... 'referri ad scientiam nostram' in laws issued in the names of Constantius and Julian would seem technically to give them equal standing, but Florentius would (if he received the laws) interpret them in the light of Constantius' known seniority and his own mandate from the emperor. Julian was asking Constantius, in the terms of these laws, to withhold confirmation of his prefect's decision, in a case where his own prerogative had been challenged. It was a genuine conflict of authority.

15. Belgica Secunda, approximately the regions of Artois and Picardie, with the northern edges of Ile-de-France and Champagne, included the towns of Rheims, Soissons, Châlons-sur-Marne, Vermand, Arras, Cambrai, Tournai, Senlis, Beauvais, Amiens, Thérouanne, Boulogne; *Notitia Galliarum* VI (ed. Seeck, 1876, 265f.), with J. D. Harries, *JRS* 68 (1978), 40-1. Amm. 15.11.10 (in his digression on Gaul) mentions Amiens, Châlons, Rheims.

16. Norman Austin, *Ammianus on Warfare*, at 55f., takes the place in question to be Senon, not Sens, following in this C. J. Simpson, 'Where was Senonae? A problem of geography in Ammianus Marcellinus XVI,3,3', *Latomus* 33 (1974), 940-2; cf., more fully and independently of Simpson, Jean Nicolle, 'Julien apud Senonas (356-357). Un contresens historique', *Rivista Storica dell'Antichità* 8 (1978), 133-60. The place in question (its ancient name is not known) is a village between Metz and Verdun, near which is a late Roman castellum, 'le Bourge de Senon'. I cannot imagine that Constantius would have his Caesar spend the winter in a *castellum* 50 m square (even adding the outer 'enceinte' of 100 m square described by Nicolle), nor that Ammianus could describe such a place as an 'oppidum'; cf. 16.2.4, 'clausa ergo urbe' (Nicolle, 154, has difficulty with this). One cannot but be intrigued by a site excavated by German archaeologists in 1917 during the battle of Verdun (Nicolle, 148-51).

17. Thompson, *The Historical Work of Ammianus Marcellinus*, 79, comments on this episode.

18. *PLRE* I presents the material on these characters. Add Honoratus (*PLRE* I, Honoratus 2, p. 438f.), who as *comes Orientis* conveyed an order for the execution of one of Gallus' victims (14.1.3, cf. 7.2), and became Julian's *praefectus praetorio Galliarum*.

19. For brief comment on the trials of Chalcedon, p. 106 and n. 35 below.

20. R. C. Blockley, 'Constantius Gallus and Julian as Caesars of Constantius II', *Latomus* 31 (1972), 433-68, esp. 461ff. A. Selem, 'A proposito del comando militare di Giuliano in Gallia secondo Ammiano', *Rivista di Cultura Classica e Medioevale* 13 (1971), 193-200,

argues that Ammianus deliberately emphasised Julian's subordination in order to highlight his 'heroic character' in contrast with the character of Constantius. It is true that, as at Strasbourg (16.12.14), advice might be offered to Julian in polite terms; but this was not always so, and in general Selem seems to underestimate the extent of Julian's actual subordination to Constantius.

21. Cf. J. F. Drinkwater, art. of 1983 (n. 2 above), Appendix, pp. 383-7; 'Was Constantius' request for troops genuine, or born of envy of Julian's new-found reputation?'

22. The theory is that of Ilsa Müller-Seidel, 'Die Usurpation Iulians des Abtrünnigen im Licht seiner Germanenpolitik', *Historische Zeitschrift* 180 (1955), 225-44; favourably regarded by Drinkwater, at 370f. (with references also to Rosen, Szidat, and Blockley). A. Selem, 'L'atteggiamento storiografico di Ammiano nei confronti di Giuliano dalla proclamazione di Parigi alla morte di Costanzo', *Athenaeum*, n.s. 49 (1971), 89-110, ascribes alleged contradictions in Ammianus' account to his use of both pro-Julianic and pro-Constantian sources, influenced also by his own respect for the senate. This is an interesting idea that would account for most imaginable complexities, but it understates the intrinsic ambiguity of Julian's position as a usurper against his Augustus. For the more 'institutional' aspects of the proclamation see Kl. Rosen, 'Beobachtung zur Erhebung Julians 360-1 n. Chr.', *Acta Classica* 12 (1969), 121-49.

23. On Lupicinus' (and Florentius') absence, Drinkwater, 378f. – the more suspicious view of Julian's motives.

24. S. S. Frere, *Britannia: a History of Roman Britain* (3rd ed., 1987), 247-8; 339-48; Stephen Johnson, *Later Roman Britain* (1980), 94-8.

25. Decentius' quandary is well put by Drinkwater, 379. Like Drinkwater (382, n. 128), I find it hard to follow Blockley, *Latomus* 31 (1972), 451, in seeing Decentius as a (pagan) supporter of Julian.

26. Cf. for this meaning Blockley's fr. 29.1 of Eunapius (p. 46; from Suda I 401); 'They [the Antiochenes] mocked him [Jovian] in ditties, parodies and in the so-called "famosi" because of the abandonment of Nisibis' (cf. Chapter VIII, n. 72). In the Greek text, the word 'famosi' ('lampoons') is a transliteration of the Latin.

27. Browning, *The Emperor Julian*, 101, well expresses this aspect: '[a move to Mesopotamia would mean] ... that men who still depended on close links with an extensive kindred would be isolated in a distant land.'

28. On this dream, see also Bidez, *La Vie de l'empereur Julien*, 177f.: dating the episode to 359. Would the young sapling die with the fallen tree, or would it grow in its place? An (unknown) interpreter assured Julian that as long as the root (of the Flavian dynasty) remained in place, Julian would survive. After the battle of Strasbourg, the political reflections implied by such premonitions cannot have been uncommon.

29. Eutherius as source, above n. 4.

30. E. A. Thompson, 'Three notes on Julian in 361 A.D.', *Hermathena* 62 (1942), 83-95, at 83-8 discusses (and accepts the validity of) these exchanges between Constantius and Vadomarius. The arrest of Vadomarius is described at Chapter XIV.1, p. 315.

31. The senators were L. Aurelius Avianius Symmachus, the father of the orator; and (Valerius) Maximus, nephew of Vulcacius Rufinus, to please whom Julian appointed Maximus prefect of Rome, 'potiore [*sc.* Symmacho] posthabito'. Cf. *PLRE* I, pp. 582 (Maximus 17) and 863-5 (Symmachus 3); and Chastagnol, *Fastes*, Nos. 64 (154-6) and 66 (159-63; Symmachus became urban prefect in 364-5). See also Chapter XII, p. 270 with n. 34 for Ammianus' attitude to the promotion.

32. Zosimus' account must be taken seriously as representing for us the lost history of Eunapius. Its intrinsic quality is however a different question, as can be seen from the following statements made by Zosimus in the first eleven chapters of Book 3: he misreports Constantius' movements in 355 (1.1) and antedates by four years his return to the east (3.1). He has Julian spend a 'long time' at Athens (2.1) and describes barbarians in Gaul as advancing 'to Ocean' (3.1). He puts the battle of Strasbourg immediately after Julian's arrival in Gaul (3.3ff.), and gives the numbers of German dead as 60,000 plus 60,000 drowned in the Rhine (3.3; it is not impossible that these figures come from Eunapius). Without any obvious awareness that he is writing of the same event, he repeats his reference to the battle in the next chapter (4.2), he confuses king Chnodomarius with

Vadomarius (4.2ff.), reverses the order of operations of 358 (4.4-8.1), and makes the Quadi a subdivision of the Saxons (6.1,3; 7.5f.; 8.1, etc.). He transfers Persian operations in Mesopotamia of 350 to 359 (8.2), calls Paris a 'small town of Germany' (9.1). has Julian assisted by 'etesian winds' on his journey down the Danube (10.3), and has a *praefectus praetorio Illyrici* flee to Constantius from Rome (10.4); and he makes Julian the founder of the senate of Constantinople (11.3).

33. Thompson (cited in n. 29 above), at 88-93, and Selem (cited in n. 22 above), 101f., rightly emphasise the fragility of Julian's position, suggesting that Ammianus was critical of Julian's temerity and reliance on good fortune (cf. 21.5.13; 9.1, 8): so too R. Seager, *Ammianus Marcellinus: seven studies in language and thought* (1986), at 79. However, I am not sure that such reflections are relevant at this stage. Despite Seager's assertion that 'in this case Lucillianus' estimate merely echoed Ammianus' own', the word 'temere' at 21.9.8 is spoken by a humiliated opponent of Julian, and the context makes clear that the same word at 21.5.13 cannot be unambiguously pejorative. In fact Ammianus seems to be making the best case for bold action: 'ut poscebat negotii magnitudo, praestructis expertus, quid in rebus tumultuosis anteversio valeat et praegressus ... temere se fortunae commisit ambiguae'; cf. 21.10.1, 'in rebus trepidis'. Fortune favours the brave, and for the time being Julian was successful. W. E. Kaegi, 'The Emperor Julian at Naissus', *L'Antiquité Classique* 44 (1975), 161-71, emphasises (at 163) the strategic advantages of the place and (164ff.) its Constantinian connections, which served (in Kaegi's view) to intensify Julian's hostility against the house of Constantine. I do not see why this should be their effect.

34. Thompson, at 93-5, argues that the letter to the senate, less conciliatory than the others, was written earlier; Kaegi, at 169, is sceptical. Other sources mention without any detail letters to Italy, Macedonia, Illyricum, the Peloponnese (Thompson, 54f.).

35. For the trials at Chalcedon, Thompson, *The Historical Work of Ammianus Marcellinus*, at 73-8, seeing them as a conflict between 'civil' and 'military' factions. They were conducted 'in a spirit of narrow military partisanship' (78).

36. For the panegyric of Mamertinus, see the translation by Marna Morgan (n. 2 above). For Praetextatus as a source for Ammianus, Chapter II.2, p. 23 and n. 29.

37. Paschoud, in his ed. of Zosimus (Budé II.1, 1979), n. 29 at pp. 97-9, describes Julian's contributions to Constantinople (with earlier references). Zosimus' statement that Julian provided the city with a senate is a gross error in an already extremely confused account (above, n. 32).

38. Ammianus' attitude to Latin and Greek is discussed at Chapter XVIII, pp. 461ff.

39. See Chapter VIII.3, pp. 176ff., for the religious foreboding of Ammianus' presentation of the reign of Julian.

40. Julian's stay at Antioch, and the changing mood of his reign, are well described by Polymnia Athanassiadi-Fowden, *Julian and Hellenism*, ch. VI (pp. 192-225); and by Edgar Pack, *Städte und Steuern* (n. 2 above), Kap. IV. The *Misopogon* itself is brilliantly interpreted by Maud W. Gleeson, 'Julian's *Misopogon* and the New Year at Antioch', *JRS* 76 (1986), 106-1; see esp. 111-13 for the role-reversals that characterise the New Year Festival – as also, on a literary level, they do the *Misopogon*. The problems of the corn supply are discussed under the domain of social relations in Chapter XVI, p. 409f. Glanville Downey, 'Julian the Apostate at Antioch', *Church History* 8 (1939), 305-15, argues that the *Misopogon* was deliberately contrived to arrest the attention of the 'undignified and coarse' Antiochenes, and that it in fact contains clear statements of his programme. Downey is however ambivalent on the reason for Julian's presence at Antioch, arguing that he saw it as a volatile city, ripe for 're-conversion' to paganism. This is no doubt a possible motive, but the emperor had to be at Antioch in any case, in order to mobilise a campaign against Persia.

41. Julian's letter concerning Christian teachers is *Ep.* 61a in the ed. of Bidez (pp. 73-5 with comment, 44-7; ed. Loeb, pp. 116-22). A related (not identical) document is *CTh* 13.3.5, issued on 17 June and received at Spoletium in Italy on 29 July 362 – that is to say, it was issued before Julian had come to Antioch. The measure was cancelled by *CTh* 13.3.6, 11 Jan. 364.

42. See Chapter XVII, pp. 442-4 for the death of George and its chronology.

43. 'curiositas' picks up Ammianus' phrase, 'multorum curiosior Iulianus novam consilii

viam ingressus est' (22.12.8). The restoration of the oracles and associated events are described in Chapter XVII, pp. 439ff.

44. The chronology of the Temple restoration is discussed by Bowersock, *Julian the Apostate*, Appendix I (pp. 120-2); cf. S. P. Brock, 'A letter attributed to Cyril of Jerusalem on the rebuilding of the Temple', *Bulletin of the School of Oriental and African Studies* 40 (1977), 267-86, publishing a supposed letter of Cyril that is certainly not genuine as such, but may yet incorporate historically valid material – with an Appendix (pp. 283-6) setting out and translating other sources describing the abortive restoration and the events surrounding it. The date assigned in the new text to the restoration, Monday 19 Iyyar (May) 363, conflicts with Ammianus' implied chronology at the very beginning of the year (23.1.1, 5), but the chronology may serve a dramatic function, or else Ammianus may have wished to avoid interrupting a continuous narrative of the Persian campaign, once it had begun (at 23.2); or, Julian may have issued the order at the beginning of the year, the actual restoration attempt falling later, when the materials and workmen had been assembled. For the ominous deaths of early 363 (23.1.5f.), see Chapter VIII.3, p. 177.

45. The military emphasis of Ammianus' narrative is noted by Fontaine, 'Le Julien d'Ammien', at 60f.

46. For the theory of 'national divinities' (*c. Galilaeos* 115D-143B; tr. Wright, ed. Loeb, pp. 345ff.) see Bidez, *La Vie de l'Empereur Julien*, 307-9; Athanassiadi-Fowden, *Julian and Hellenism*, 177f.

47. *Ep.* 84 Bidez (*Ep.* 22 Wright); *Ep.* 89 a-b Bidez (*Ep.* 20 Wright, together with the *Fragment of a Letter to a Priest*; Wright, Vol. II, pp. 296-339). See esp. 289A-291D, 452D, with Bidez, 102ff., for the arguments for regarding these texts as a single document.

48. On Ammianus' obituary of Julian, Fontaine, 'Le Julien d'Ammien', at 53ff., is especially interesting, though I would emphasise more the formal contrast between the presentation of the virtues and the vices. Fontaine is however correct (at 55) in describing the presentation of the latter as 'cette page très dure ...'. S. d'Elia, *Studi Romani* 10 (1962), 380-2 gets the force of the panegyrical elements, but misses that of Ammianus' criticisms.

49. I am pleased to be able to appeal to Fontaine's judgment on Ammianus' pragmatism, cf. 56 with his whole discussion, 54-64; so, too, that of H. Tränkle, 'Ammianus Marcellinus als römischer Geschichtsschreiber', *Antike und Abendland* 11 (1962), at 30-3: Ammianus' panegyrical allusion at the outset of the reign of Julian is confined to the early part of the reign, he admired Julian's government and administration before his religious policies, seeing even the restoration of the Temple as an ominous sign to Julian rather than as an aspect of these policies, and he criticised the emperor's addiction to sacrifices.

VII. Julian and the Philosophers

1. In this chapter I claim no originality except in one or two points of emphasis, and in my attempt to define Julian's theological position in relation to Ammianus' lack of appreciation of it; it is a study of issues absent from Ammianus but relevant to Julian and indicative therefore of the limitations of Ammianus' understanding of his hero; my presentation will be more novel to readers of Ammianus than to those of Joseph Bidez's *La vie de l'empereur Julien*. I can do no more here than set out the works from which I have gained my hesitant understanding of this subject: notably, apart from Bidez, E. R. Dodds, 'Theurgy and its relationship to Neoplatonism', *JRS* 37 (1947), 55-69, reprinted as Appendix II in *The Greeks and the Irrational* (1951; repr. 1968), 283-311, from which I cite it. For the *Chaldaean Oracles*, published with annotation in the edition of E. des Places (Budé, 1971), see also the fundamental study of H. Lewy, *Chaldaean Oracles and Theurgy: mysticism, magic and Platonism in the later Roman Empire* (1956; the 2nd ed. of 1978 prints reviews of the first publication by Dodds and P. Hadot). For the relevant evidence of the sixth-century Platonist Proclus, E. R. Dodds, *Proclus: The Elements of Theology* (1933; 2nd ed. 1968) and the later texts printed by Bidez, 'Proclus, Peri tês hieratikês technês', in *Mél. Cumont* (1936), 85-100; also A. J. Festugière, 'Contemplation philosophique et art théurgique chez Proclus', in *Studi di Storia Religiosa della Tarda Antichità* (1968), 7-18 and, with much circumstantial documentation, E. Evrard, 'Le maître de Plutarque d'Athènes et les origines du Néoplatonisme Athénien', *L'Antiquité Classique* 29 (1960), 108-33 and 391-406. For

emphasis on the magical elements, S. Eitrem, 'La théurgie chez les néo-platoniciens et dans les papyrus magiques', *Symbolae Osloenses* 22 (1942), 49-79. Discussion of the strictly philosophical aspects is raised to new levels in recent work, as by Anne Sheppard, 'Proclus' attitude to theurgy', *CQ* n.s. 31 (1982), 212-24, discussing among much else Andrew Smith, *Porphyry's Place in the Neoplatonic Tradition* (The Hague, 1974); and in the remarkable study of Garth Fowden, *The Egyptian Hermes: a historical approach to the late pagan mind* (1986), esp. (on theurgy), 126-34. For the whole 'thought-world' that was involved, focussing on the theme of the 'presence' of the gods, see Robin Lane Fox's brilliant *Pagans and Christians* (1986), esp. chs. 4 (pp. 102-67), 'Seeing the Gods' and 5 (168-261), 'Language of the Gods'. Statues speak at p. 135f., Julian 'sees the gods' at 149 and admires the Chaldaean Oracles at 199.

2. *V. Soph.* pp. 476, 498. J. F. Drinkwater (cited at Chapter VI, n. 1) takes a secular view of this affair, but a religious interpretation is surely preferable. Barry Baldwin, 'The career of Oribasius', *Acta Classica* 18 (1975), 85-97, surveys the evidence for the life of this formidable intellectual figure and for his connections with Julian, but does not mention theurgy, nor make clear the force of Eunapius' belief that it was through his *virtues* that Oribasius made Julian emperor.

3. On Julianus, Dodds, 'Theurgy', 283f.; Kroll, *RE* X (1919), 15-18, s.v. Iulianus 8 and 9. It is possible that the theurgist (as, almost certainly, his father) was a fictitious character invented to explain the existence of the Oracles, but the Emperor Julian did not think so; Lane Fox, 197-200. On the term 'theurgy', Dodds, 283f. (citing Bidez, *La Vie de l'Empereur Julien* 369, n. 8). For the 'Rain Miracle', Garth Fowden, 'Pagan versions of the Rain Miracle of A.D. 172', *Historia* 36 (1987), 83-95 (cf. esp. 90-4, on the historicity of Julian the theurgist), followed at 96-113 by Michael M. Sage, 'Eusebius and the Rain Miracle: some observations'; C. Caprino and others, *La Colonna di Marco Aurelio* (Rome, 1955), Tav. XII (Scenes xvi-xvii).

4. For Julianus and Apuleius, see the text of Psellus cited by Bidez, *Mél. Cumont*, 93 (Text I). For the term *heptaktis*, Dodds, 'Theurgy', 301 n. 18 and esp. Julian, *Hymn to the Mother of the Gods*, 172D.

5. Nestorius; Paschoud's ed. of Zosimus, II.2. p. 367-9. The story referred to in the text is told at Proclus, *In Rempublicam* II 324-5 Kroll; cf. Evrard, *L'Ant. Class.* 29 (1960), 124ff.

6. Proclus and Asclepigeneia: Marinus, *V. Procli* 28 (ed. Boissonnade, p. 22); cf. Evrard, at 128-31.

7. For the 'levels' of theurgy (a technical and very difficult question), see the absorbing discussion of Anne Sheppard (n. 1 above), esp., on this passage of Proclus, 218-20.

8. On these 'affinities' or 'likenesses', see Sheppard, 220; Dodds, *Proclus: The Elements of Theology*, at 219, 222-3, 275-7 (on Propositions 32, 39, 145); also his Introduction at xxii-iii, including the passage from Proclus' *Platonic Theology* cited in my text (so too his 'Theurgy', at 291).

9. The 'telestic art' (Dodds, 'Theurgy' 291-5) is briefly documented by Lewy, *Chaldaean Oracles and Theurgy*, Exc. X (pp. 495-6).

10. On the use of mirrors, see the diagrams in Hero's *Katoptrika* 18 (ed. L. Nix and W. Schmidt, Teubner 1900, II.1, pp. 358, 361, figs. 91a,b); the animation of statues, Lewy 495f., and the splendidly circumstantial discussion in Lane Fox, *Pagans and Christians*, 133-5. For the Psellus reference cited in the text, Bidez, *Mél. Cumont*, 95 (Text III(b)); Dodds, 'Theurgy', 292.

11. S. Eitrem, *Symbolae Osloenses* 22 (1942), at 57-60 discusses the solar context and language of this episode.

12. On the seance, Dodds, 'Theurgy', at 289-91 – criticising Eitrem and also doubting the historical authenticity of the episode; its 'patterning' of course remains important.

13. Reference throughout the next section of the chapter is to the critical and fully annotated edition of the *Chaldaean Oracles* by E. des Places (n. 1 above) who refers to the commentary by Lewy on the interpretation of the individual fragments and prints at the end of the volume relevant texts by Psellus and Proclus. Lewy remains fundamental on the theological content of the Oracles. See also Lane Fox, at 195-200, describing the Oracles as an 'influential fraud' that later provided a 'jousting ground for the hyperintelligent', and connecting the texts with Numenius and the Middle Platonists.

14. See on these entities Lewy, 129-37.
15. Cf. Dodds, *Proclus*, p. xxiii. It is clear in the light of recent work, especially that of Anne Sheppard and Garth Fowden (*The Egyptian Hermes*, 126ff.), that this contrast between two Neoplatonic traditions is too schematic; equally clear, however, that Julian saw it as a real one.
16. For the use of mirrors and other technical aids, see above, n. 10.
17. On Theodorus of Asine, R. T. Wallis, *Neoplatonism* (London, 1972), 95, 120.
18. The term *heptaktis*, above, n. 4; cf. des Places, *Oracles Chaldaïques*, Fr. 194.
19. Ammianus' digression on divination is discussed in its own right in Chapter XVII, pp. 428ff. I am still uncertain whether by 'pravae artes' Ammianus means rites that he himself would find disreputable (such as theurgy) or whether he is assigning the attitude to Julian's religious opponents. In the former case, the digression would be a defence of certain, in Ammianus' opinion 'legitimate' sorts of divination, in the latter a defence of the entire art as such, without implying any further distinctions.
20. For Sopatros, *PLRE* I, p. 846 (Sopater 1).
21. This theme too is discussed elsewhere; see Chapter VIII.3, pp. 176ff.
22. The discussion of Julian's relations to the philosophers and haruspices on the Persian campaign is one of the most convincing aspects of R. L. Rike's *Apex Omnium: religion in the Res Gestae of Ammianus* (1987); cf. esp. pp. 61-7. I do not however share his view of Oribasius and Eunapius as sharing Ammianus' antipathy to Maximus; Eunapius had his doubts, but they were connected more with Maximus' unphilosophical conduct under Julian than with his doctrines. On the issue of theurgy they should be classed against Ammianus (cf. Rike, p. 41 on the secret rites in Gaul with which this Chapter began). The whole question of Ammianus' thoroughly 'Roman' attitude to traditional divination is extremely well discussed by Liebeschuetz in his recent article cited at Chapter VIII, n. 3 below; see esp. pp. 199-204. Ammianus 'reported omens and prodigies of general warning rather than oracles' (201).
23. For the obituary of Julian, Chapter VI, p. 112f. and XVIII, p. 468f. On the evolution to the fourth century of the term 'superstitio' in Latin usage, see Denise Grodzynski, *REA* 76 (1974), 36-60. Originally connected with the notion of fortune-telling and divination, it incorporates notions of excess and empty or irrational fear of the gods (the Greek *deisidaimonia*) – irrational, because a rational man will see that there is no need to fear them. The term comes to denote the religious beliefs and practices of one's opponents, and is used in this sense in fourth-century legislation. Ammianus' use of the notion of 'legitimacy' to help define it is entirely characteristic of the 'Roman' tendency of his writing, see Chapter XI, pp. 250ff.
24. On the 'conjectures of men', see Chapter XVII, p. 430.

VIII. The Invasion of Persia

(1) Historical perspectives

1. For the relationship of Zosimus and Eunapius, Chapter VIII.3, p. 161.
2. The location of the tomb of Gordian is given by Eutropius 9.2; Festus 22.5. *Epit. de Caes.* 27.3 has the emperor killed at Ctesiphon and buried 'prope fines Romani Persicicue imperii'.
3. W. R. Chalmers, 'An alleged doublet in Ammianus Marcellinus', *RhM* 102 (1959), 182-9, gives the history of this problem. His solution is that Ammianus crossed the Khabur as part of a reconnaissance party under Julian, advanced 'towards Dura' as far as Gordian's tomb, then returned to the main army as it completed mustering and resumed the advance in its company. Thus Ammianus twice covered the ground of the first two days' march and his narrative is strictly accurate from his own point of view. I see many objections to this, among them Ammianus' explicit statement (23.5.4f., 15) that Julian crossed the Khabur bridge after the entire army had gone over. Further, the scale of Cumont's map, cited by Chalmers, is inaccurate. Dura is not 45 but only a little over 30 miles from Circesium; the first two days' march took the army a distance towards Dura measured not from Gordian's tomb (this, a distance of 11/12 miles, would be an intolerably slow rate of progress in the

circumstances), but from the Khabur crossing. My own view on this and broader aspects of Ammianus' treatment (cf. Chapter VIII.3, pp. 175ff.) is very close to that of W. Liebeschuetz, 'Ammianus, Julian and divination', in M. Wisseman (ed.), *Roma Renascens: Festschrift Ilona Opelt* (1988), 198-213; on this point, 198-9.

4. Mommsen's conclusion, cited by Chalmers at 183, was that Ammianus altered the narrative sequence in order to be able to mention Gordian's tomb in 'Julian's' speech (*Ges. Schr.* VII 427). For my own slightly different view, see Chapter VIII.3, p. 178f. and Rosen, *Studien zur Darstellungskunst und Glaubwürdigkeit des Ammianus Marcellinus*, at 154-5; and esp. Liebeschuetz, at 198-9. These views assume a deliberate narrative deformation rather than inaccuracy or confusion in Ammianus, my own adding that Ammianus, aware of this, clarified his narrative at the beginning of Book 24.

5. E. Honigmann and A. Maricq, *Recherches sur les Res Gestae Divi Saporis* (1952), ch. IV, pp. 111-22; 'La bataille de Pērōz-Šāhpuhr ('Victorieux-Sahpuhr') et la mort de Gordien III', esp. at 113, 118-22. For the rock carvings of Bishapur, R. Ghirshman, *Iran: Parthians and Sassanians* (1962), plates 196-203, (a composite scene: Gordian lies dead, Philip sues for peace, Valerian is captive); cf. the similar representation at Naqsh-i-Rustam, plates 204-5.

6. On Misiche/Pirisabora (Mšyk/Pērōz-Šāhpuhr), Honigmann and Maricq, at 112-18; my Chapter VIII.2, p. 149 and VIII.3, p. 174.

7. This facet of Ammianus' presentation is discussed at Chapter VIII.3, pp. 176ff. For Julian's death, Chapter IX, pp. 181ff.

8. The spectacular end of Carus, 'fulmine tactu' (Aurelius Victor 38.4f.; 'ictu fulminis', *Epit. de Caes.* 38.2), or 'vi divini fulminis' (Eutropius 9.18.1), characteristically elaborated in the Historia Augusta, *Carus* 8-9, forms part of standard accounts of third-century history. It is possible that the 'fulmen' is not a literal thunderbolt but a metaphor for divine intervention, e.g. in the form of death by plague.

9. See on the oracle J. Straub, *Studien zur Historia Augusta* (1952), 123-32, and esp. Norman Baynes, *The Historia Augusta: its date and purpose* (1926), at 62, 103-4. Baynes was unduly anxious to see contemporary allusions in the Historia Augusta (this one is oddly described as 'a prophetic vision of Julian's success [sic]' in his Persian campaign'), and his theory of the work as a piece of Julianic propaganda directed to a popular audience has not gained acceptance. Nevertheless, given a late fourth-century date of composition, an allusion to Julian is hard to evade; cf. T. D. Barnes, *Phoenix* 30 (1976), at 184.

10. On the campaign of Galerius, Chapter IV, p. 53 and Barnes, 'Imperial campaigns, A.D. 285-311', *Phoenix* 30 (1976), 174-93, at 183-5, adducing the passage of Ammianus to support a return journey of Galerius along the Euphrates; *The New Empire of Diocletian and Constantine* (1982), 63.

11. A. Christensen, *L'Iran sous les Sassanides* (2nd ed., 1944), at 220-1. For the building of Gundeshapur, see also Girshman (cited above, in n. 5), 135-7 with a photograph of the Karun bridge, plate 174. For the name 'Band-e-Kaisar', 'King's Dyke', Christensen, 220. For the Bishapur and Naqsh-i-Rustam reliefs, see above, n. 5.

12. The most recent discussion of this episode is by B. H. Warmington, 'Ammianus Marcellinus and the lies of Metrodorus', *CQ* n.s. 31 (1981), 464-8, arguing that the story comes from a pagan tradition hostile to Constantine, presumably from Eunapius (the relevance of the passage for the quality of Ammianus' lost books is mentioned at Chapter II.2, p. 29, and for the question of his stance as a pagan polemicist, at Chapter XVII, p. 448). Despite Warmington's argument that the story was pure fiction, it is not impossible that some such episode contributed to diplomatic tensions in relations between Rome and Persia; the element of fiction or propaganda consists in assigning it the major role in the outbreak of war. The journey of Metrodorus is mentioned also by Rufinus, *Hist. Eccl.* 10.9. For the cultural background of such contacts, W. Schmitthenner, 'Rome and India: aspects of Universal History during the Principate', *JRS* 69 (1979), 90-106.

13. This (the orthodox view) is in essence that reconstructed on the evidence of Faustus of Byzantium by N. H. Baynes, 'Rome and Armenia in the fourth century', *EHR* 25 (1910), 625-43, reprinted with important revisions in his *Byzantine Studies* (1960), 186-208, at 188-90, with the further arguments of W. Ensslin, 'Zu dem vermuteten Perserfeldzug des rex Hannibalianus', *Klio*, n.s. 11 (1936), 102-10. Warmington, at 466, describes it as resting on 'insecure foundations', offering the prospect of a fuller discussion (not so far published).

The passage of Faustus is at 3.20f. (French tr. in Langlois, *FHG* V.2, pp. 229-31); the campaign described in the second part of 3.21 (p. 232) is a 'doublet' of the campaign of Narses against Galerius, but it is preceded by a mention of Constantine. The confusion arises from the fact that a brother of Sapor named Narses later campaigned against Rome (Ensslin, at 106f.; he is *PLRE* I, Narses 2, p. 616)

14. The parallel with the situation in 361 is relevant. Then, Constantius reaffirmed an alliance with Arsaces of Armenia in order to prevent his adherence to the Persian interest, adding a dynastic marriage with the daughter of a supporter of Constantine (20.11.1-3); all this was done at Caesarea (9.1ff.). The forthcoming campaign was to be fought in northern Mesopotamia, cf. Eutropius 10.8.2 on the last campaign of Constantine; 'bellum adversus Parthos moliens, qui iam Mesopotamiam fatigabant'. Armenia and Mesopotamia were strategically connected, cf. Chapter IV.1, pp. 53ff. T. D. Barnes, 'Constantine and the Christians of Persia', *JRS* 75 (1985), 126-36, also accepts (at 132 and 136) a Persian invasion of Armenia in 336. I am however reluctant to accept Barnes' view that Constantine was preparing a religious crusade on behalf of the Christians in Persia. The sequence of events, the evidence of Eutropius just cited, and (for what it is worth) Eusebius, *Vita Constantini* 4.56 – and indeed the predictions of Aphrahat of Mar Mattai, as presented by Barnes (pp. 130 and 134) – show Sapor as the aggressor. To argue that in doing so he had merely decided to strike first before Constantine attacked him seems arbitrary, and is not adequately supported by the considerations adduced by Barnes (p. 132). See also B. H. Warmington, 'Objectives and strategy in the Persian War of Constantius II', *Akten des XI Internationalen Limeskongresses 1976* (1977), 509-20, esp. 512; Sapor was planning a major strike against the Romans, Constantine was preparing to meet it.

15. Despite Barnes' confident exclusion (p. 133) of 338, either that year or 337 is chronologically possible for the first siege of Nisibis. The earlier date might be preferable if Sapor were at the time of Constantine's death already mobilised for an attack on Roman territory. The article of Warmington, cited in n. 14, offers a more positive appreciation of the policy of Constantius, as designed precisely to divert Sapor into expensive and unproductive sieges (it was, of course, a policy with risks).

16. *Caesars*, 336A-B; ed. Lacombrade, Budé II.2 (1964), pp. 70-1, cf. 27-30 for the date and circumstances of composition, and in general Barry Baldwin, 'The *Caesares* of Julian', *Klio* 60 (1978), 449-66. Constantine's prodigality is a leitmotif of hostile views of the emperor, present in Ammianus' reference to the 'lies of Metrodorus' cited earlier (cf. Chapter XVII, p. 448). G. W. Bowersock, 'The Emperor Julian on his predecessors', *Yale Classical Studies* 27 (1982), 159-72, is sceptical as to the extent of Julian's historical knowledge; so too Baldwin, who rightly regards it as very conventional.

17. For this episode see F. A. Lepper, *Trajan's Parthian War* (1948), at 10, 89-90 (a 'picturesque scene'), 151-5, 210 ('the pleasures of sight-seeing and display'). Arnaldo Marcone, 'Il significato della spedizione di Giuliano contro la Persia', *Athenaeum*, n.s. 57 (1979), 334-6, discusses this and other aspects of the 'ideological' setting of Julian's campaign (for Alexander, pp. 342-4). Particularly telling is his description (at 345) of its widespread unpopularity.

18. Lepper, 9-10, 133-6: making the comparison with Julian at 135.

19. R. T. Ridley, 'Notes on Julian's Persian Expedition (363)', *Historia* 22 (1973), 317-30, at 319, points to this uncertainty in Ammianus' presentation, but it must be emphasised that Ammianus does see the broader issue. Zosimus 3.12.4 alleges the need to protect Nisibis against incursion, but in a back-reference at 4.4.2. mentions the larger strategic scheme; see n. 33 of Paschoud's edition (Budé II.1, pp. 106-9). Perhaps the more limited version was put out by the high command, in order to prevent warning of the larger design being conveyed prematurely to Sapor. W. E. Kaegi, 'Constantine's and Julian's strategies of strategic surprise against the Persians', *Athenaeum*, n.s. 59 (1981), 209-13, presents evidence cited by John Lydus (3.33-4) from the *De Bello Parthico* of Cornelius Celsus and *sungrammata* of Constantine; both authorities, recommending a policy of sudden surprise attack, might well have been known to Julian.

20. Namely the epitome of Magnus of Carrhae preserved by Malalas (Müller, *FHG* IV, p. 5); cf. Chapter VIII.3, p. 163f. and note 73.

21. The essential relationships (no more) are given by *PLRE* I, pp. 443-4, esp. s.

Hormisdas 2. Hormisdas was son of king Hormisdas (Hormiz) II (302-309/10), who is seen in vigorous action on a relief at Naqsh-i-Rustam, unseating an adversary with a lance; Ghirshman, *Iran: Parthians and Sassanians* (above, n. 5), plates 219-220. He appears at Rome in 357 with Constantius (16.10.16; 'regalis Ormisda'), where Ammianus says that he had earlier described his departure from Persia; cf. Chapter I, n. 8 for discussion of material concerning Hormisdas detected by Rita Cappelletto in a marginal note of Biondo. Zosimus 2.27 has a highly colourful story of Hormisdas' imprisonment in and escape from Persia, the chronological and other difficulties of which seem insuperable: cf. Paschoud's ed., Budé I, n. 37 at pp. 218-19 – though there scarcely seems enough evidence in Ammianus' brief remark to justify the assertion that he and Zosimus were dependent on the same source. If they were, this would (as in the case of the lies of Metrodorus) be Eunapius, and certainly not, as argued by Paschoud, Nicomachus Flavianus. Alternatively, one might ask whether Ammianus' acquaintance, the eunuch Eutherius, an Armenian, might have some special interest in the desertion of a Persian prince of the line. The role of Hormisdas in relation to the aims of the campaign, is discussed by, among others, Marcone (cited above in n. 17), at 343-5.

(2) Historical geography

22. In following the course of Julian's march, the commentaries of Jacques Fontaine and François Paschoud on Book 24 of Ammianus and Book 3 of Zosimus respectively, and of M. F. A. Brok, *De perzische Expeditie van Keiser Julianus volgens Ammianus Marcellinus* (1959) are of immense value – while making clear how much, in terms of precise topographical interpretation, remains difficult and controversial. In more general terms, there is much to be learned from the observations of nineteenth-century and other travellers: for example Gen. Francis Rawdon Chesney, *Narrative of the Euphrates Expedition* (1868); Lt. J. B. Bewsher, 'On part of Mesopotamia contained between Sheriat-el-Beytha, on the Tigris, and Tel Ibrahim', *Journal of the Royal Geographical Society* 37 (1867), 160-82; Alois Musil, *The Middle Euphrates: a topographical itinerary* (1927). For more systematic presentation of the geography and ecology of the region, I have gained much from the war-time Naval Intelligence Division Geographical Handbook, B.R. 524; *Iraq and the Persian Gulf* (1944) and, in relation to the regimes of the Tigris and Euphrates and the construction and behaviour of the canal systems, from Robert McC. Adams, *Land behind Baghdad: a history of settlement on the Diyala Plains* (1965). On the historical development of the canal systems, in addition to Bewsher's survey and Appendix VI of Musil (pp. 267-74), see R. D. Barnett, 'Xenophon and the wall of Media', *JHS* 83 (1963), 1-26. The first part of Julian's route was traced, with identification of the sites, by F. Cumont, 'La marche de l'empereur Julien d'Antioche à l'Euphrate', *Etudes Syriennes* (1917), 1-33. References to individual sites are given in the notes below, but a special mention is due to J. M. Fiey, 'Topography of Al-Mada'in (Seleucia-Ctesiphon area)', *Sumer* 23 (1967), 3-38; while there is an excellent reference work, with full citation of sources (with translations), fascinating detailed comment, and bibliography, in Aharon Oppenheimer (with Benjamin Isaac and Michael Lecker), *Babylonia Judaica in the Talmudic Period* (1983). Musil's *The Middle Euphrates* has an Appendix on the route of Julian (App. IV, pp. 232-42, with many speculative identifications), and others on various places relevant to it, e.g. App. XIV (Zaitha), XVI-XVIII (Anatha, Hit, Pirisabora).

23. For description of the Mauretanian episode (29.5), see Chapter XIV.3, pp. 367ff., with p. 381 for the chance that it derives from a written campaign report.

24. The foundation of Greek cities in Mesopotamia is described at Chapter V, p. 67.

25. For archaeological research at Seleucia, see R. G. McDowell, 'The excavations at Seleucia on the Tigris', *Papers of the Michigan Academy of Science, Arts and Letters* 18 (1933), 101-19; and, by the same author, a survey of its history from literary sources, in Clark Hopkins (ed.), *Topography and Architecture of Seleucia on the Tigris* (Ann Arbor, 1972), 149-63; cf. Oppenheimer 179-235 ('The Mahoza Area'). The population estimates, to be treated with due caution, are by Pliny, *Hist. Nat.* 6.122 (600,000) and Eutropius 8.10.2; 'Seleuciam, Assyriae urbem nobilissimam, cum quadringentis milibus hominum cepit [*sc.* L. Verus in 165]'. Festus, *Brev.* 21 has an almost identical notice, replacing 'hominum' by

'hostium'; ed. J. W. Eadie (1967), p. 141. Adams, *Land behind Baghdad*, 175, n. 7 suggests 80,000 on the basis of comparative estimates of population density; this seems low, but the figures given by Pliny and Eutropius may make some allowance for territory outside the city. (I cannot verify Adams' statement that Cassius Dio gives a figure of 300,000, and McDowell's statement (1972, p. 161), that Eutropius mentions 40,000 captives is based on an inferior text. Festus confirms that 400,000 is the figure intended).

26. On Coche/Veh Ardeshir (the 'round city'), Giorgio Gullini, 'Problems of an excavation in northern Mesopotamia' and Marianzola Cavallo, 'The excavations at Choche (presumed Ctesiphon) – Area 2': both in *Mesopotamia* 1 (1966), pp. 7-38 and 63-81 respectively: cf. Antonio Invernizzi and others, in *The Land between Two Rivers: twenty years of Italian archaeology in the Middle East* (1985), 'Seleucia on the Tigris', at 87-99 (the foundation of Coche at 87), and R. V. Ricciardi and Maria Mancini, 'Coche', at 100-10; Oppenheimer, *Babylonia Judaica*, 223ff., with map at 233. For local topography, see also O. Reuther, 'The German excavations at Ctesiphon', *Antiquity* 3 (1929), 434-51 (with map at 435), and Clark Hopkins (cited above in n. 25), with map at 164, on which my Map 4 is chiefly based. Both Reuther and Hopkins mark the 'round city' as Ctesiphon, but the Italian excavations reported above now show that this cannot be correct. Excavation revealed a stratified sequence of 10 layers of occupation, all Sasanian (not a single Parthian coin was found). They were sealed by a silt layer and below this was a necropolis. The city must be a Sasanian foundation, hence Veh Ardeshir, with Ctesiphon to the east of it. For another 'round city' founded by Ardashir, Firuzabad, see R. Ghirshman, *Iran: Parthians and Sassanians* (1962), p. 123 (pl. 160).

27. For the old river course to the east of Coche/Veh Ardeshir, J. M. Fiey, 'Topography of Al-Mada'in' (n. 22 above), 4f., with map, at 37. The Talmud ref. is to *b. Eruvin* 57b; Oppenheimer, p. 198 (s. Ctesiphon, Source 1).

28. See p. 157 of this Chapter. The clearest references are Libanius, *Or.* 18.244 and Gregory of Nazianzus, *Or.* 5.10 (*PG* 35.676BC). For the decline of Seleucia, McDowell, art. of 1933 (cited above in n. 25), p. 112.

29. Pliny, *Hist. Nat.* 6.122 mentions the foundation of Vologesocerta, and its motive. A. Maricq, 'Vologésias, l'emporium de Ctesiphon', *Syria* 36 (1959), 264-76, identifies Vologesias and Vologesocerta as one city, which he places near Ctesiphon; Marie-Louise Chaumont, 'Les villes fondées par les Vologèse: Vologésocerta et Vologésias', *Syria* 51 (1974), 77-81, distinguishes them, placing Vologesocerta near Ctesiphon, Vologesias on the Euphrates south of Babylon. For further identification, see below, n. 60.

30. The Devil on the walls; Fiey, 21.

31. For the influence of Oribasius, Chapter VIII.3, p. 164, and (on the death of Julian), IX, p. 182. For Libanius, cf. Chapter VIII.3, p. 162.

32. See on this phase the article of Cumont cited at n. 22 above.

33. This remark evokes the many extant Sasanian hunting-dishes, not to mention monumental Assyrian reliefs and the Sasanian rock-sculptures described at Chapter VIII.1, p. 132; cf. A. Christensen, *L'Iran sous les Sassanides*, 469-72. Fontaine's n. 434 (p. 182) refers to various illustrations in Ghirshman's *Iran: Parthians and Sassanians*; cf. esp. the fine boar hunt at pp. 194-6 (pl. 236). For frescoes on a more 'domestic' scale, Ghirshman, pp. 182-3 (pls. 223-4, from Dura and Susa) – citing Ammianus, at 182.

34. For Neardea (Oppenheimer, *Babylonia Judaica*, pp. 286-7 on the site), see p. 149. Oppenheimer, at 290, cites Herzfeld's opinion that the Jewish settlement mentioned by Ammianus was Neardea.

35. Oppenheimer, p. 165 Source 3 (s. Ihi de-Qira), with comment at 168.

36. J. Neusner, *A History of the Jews in Babylonia* (Leiden, 1965-70), IV, 44-9.

37. The relevance of the capture of Anatha to the question of Ammianus' use of sources is discussed at Chapter VIII.3, p. 171f.

38. *Euphrates Expedition*, 75f. The journey by raft began on 2 January 1831 as a preliminary to the later expedition. See also Naval Intelligence Handbook, *Iraq and the Persian Gulf*, 24-32 for a description of the regime and topography of this section of the Euphrates.

39. *The Six Voyages of J. B. Tavernier* (Eng. tr. by J. P(hillips), 1678), p. 119.

40. Cesar Fredericke is cited from R. J. Forbes, *Bitumen and Petroleum in Antiquity*

(Leiden, 1936), 26: compare the description of John Eldred (of 1583), also quoted by Forbes; 'every one of these springs makes a noise like unto a smiths forge in blowing and puffing out of this matter which never ceaseth night or day'.

41. Tukultu Enurtu II; cf. Musil, *The Middle Euphrates*, 199ff., 350.

42. For the relevance of the capture of Diacira to Ammianus' use of sources, Chapter VIII.3, p. 172f.

43. On Malechus the Saracen, see further Chapter XIV.2(ii), p. 351f.

44. Here and in what follows, see the article of R. D. Barnett cited above, n. 22; p. 7f. for the ancient walls mentioned by Ammianus.

45. *Berakoth* 59b: tr. Rev. A. Cohen (Cambridge, 1921), p. 391; Oppenheimer, s. Ihi de-Qira, Source 2 (p. 165), with 167 for the interpretation.

46. For the intricate question of the canals of the Seleucia-Ctesiphon area, see Barnett, 8-15 and the refs. cited at nn. 22 and 50 of this chapter, on the Naarmalcha and other canal systems. For general descriptions, see for instance Naval Intelligence Handbook, 30 and 431-3; S. A. Pallis, *The Antiquity of Iraq* (Copenhagen, 1956), 7-13. Pirisabora/Pumbadita, Barnett, 13-15, Oppenheimer, 341-68 (362-4 for the site) and below, n. 52.

47. Chesney, *Euphrates Expedition*, 33; cf. Naval Intelligence Handbook, 30 on this channel as a possible prehistoric course of the Euphrates; cf. the map at p. 44 (fig. 13).

48. For Neardea, Oppenheimer, 276-83; esp. 286-7 for its location, and Source 12 (p. 279) for the proximity of the Royal Canal.

49. Pirisabora as Persian Mšyk/Misiche (= Massice of Pliny, *Hist. Nat.* 6.120, cf. 5.90), Barnett, 13f.; Oppenheimer, 363f., based on the detailed arguments of E. Honigmann and A. Maricq, *Recherches sur les Res Gestae Divi Saporis* (1953), 111-18. Pliny agrees with Ammianus in drawing off the Naarmalcha at this point.

50. On the Naarmalcha, or 'King's River', see Paschoud's n. 44 (pp. 127ff.) with Appendix B (pp. 246-50); Fontaine's nn. 172 (p. 77f.) and 325 (p. 145); also L. Dillemann, in *Syria* 38 (1961), 153-8. For the original starting point at Sippar, Barnett, 13ff. The shift of the Euphrates westwards away from Sippar is noted by Barnett, 10f., cf. Pallis, *The Antiquity of Iraq*, 10. For Tel Ibrahim, Bewsher (cited above in n. 22), at 117, 178f.; 'by far the largest mound in this part of Mesopotamia'.

51. J. Newman, *Agricultural Life of the Jews of Babylonia* (1932), 161-86 discusses the Talmudic evidence for canal regulation. The passage cited is given by Neusner (cited above in n. 36), III, 25-6.

52. A description of the site of Pirisabora (Arabic al-Anbar) based on aerial survey is given by A. Maricq, *Syria* 35 (1958), at 353-6 [= *Classica et Orientalia*, 95-8]; cf. esp. the aerial photographs, pl. XXIV a-b and fig. 4. The cliffs referred to by Ammianus as on the north ('e septentrione', 24.2.12) of the site are clearly visible: in fact on the north-west, overlooking an old river-bed.

53. The lake is also mentioned by Magnus of Carrhae, in Malalas (Müller, *FHG* IV, p. 5). McDowell, 1933 (cited above in n. 25) associates it with the decay of irrigation systems, and perhaps also with the (then derelict) harbour of Seleucia.

54. This detail tells against Paschoud's opinion (n. 50 and pp. 138-42) that Julian's army parted from the Euphrates at (that is, just above) Pirisabora and approached Seleucia by following Ammianus' Naarmalcha (the Saqlawiyah canal). A location 14 miles along this route, to the north of the ridge shown on modern maps east of Pirisabora/Fallujah, can hardly have been flooded from the waters of the Euphrates. The situation is more easily envisaged if the army were marching along the left bank of the Euphrates, below a second inlet of the Naarmalcha, at a point where the water-courses were still running close to each other. See my Map 5, p. 150.

55. There is an excellent description of the behaviour of alluvial rivers in Adams, *Land behind Baghdad*, 7ff. For Mark Twain's Mississippi, see *Old Times on the Mississippi*, ch. 4 (in *Great Short Works of Mark Twain*, paperback ed. of 1967, p. 36).

56. For the regime of the Euphrates, Pallis, *The Antiquity of Iraq*, 4-6: Naval Intelligence Handbook, 24f., providing the figures cited in my text. The figures are broadly similar to those shown in the chart of W. B. Fisher, *The Middle East* (7th ed., 1978), 366, though the figures mentioned in his facing text are at variance, both with the chart and with each other.

57. The Wadi-Brisa inscription; Barnett, *JRS* 83 (1963), 18-20 (with translation).
58. The topography of Ammianus' rather summary narrative at this point is not entirely clear; see Fontaine's n. 370 (p. 162f.) and Paschoud's n. 52 (p. 145f.), giving previous refs. Oppenheimer, 231, notes that the Aramaic name Maiozamalcha means 'royal capital', inferring that Ammianus must have heard the name Mahoza for Coche-Ctesiphon. However, the statement at p. 290 that 'Maiozamalcha is Maḥoza-Be Ardešir' (cited as the opinion of Herzfeld), imports a possible confusion. Ammianus has not confused the actual place 'Maiozamalcha' with Ctesiphon, but its name with the Aramaic name for the Persian capital – possibly, as suggested in my text, through confusion with the name of the district in which both stood. It is not possible (cf. Oppenheimer, 231, n. 28) that Maiozamalcha is Sippar, nor that Zosimus' Besouchis can have anything to do with Massice of Pliny, *Hist. Nat.* 5.90. Massice was miles away, at or near Pirisabora; cf. p. 132 of this Chapter, with n. 49 above.
59. For the 'land of the Mauzanitai' (*chôra Mauzanitôn*) see Magnus of Carrhae, in Malalas (Müller, *FHG* IV, p. 5). See for fuller detail the discussion of sources in Chapter VIII.3, p. 165. For the slander about the people of Mahoza, *Berakoth* 59b, tr. Cohen (cited above in n. 45), p. 391.
60. For Meinas Sabatha as Sabat al-Mada'in, see Paschoud's note on Zosimus 3.23.3 (n. 65 at p. 157f.); Fiey, p. 12. Oppenheimer questions (at p. 392) the identity with Valasapat/ Vologesias or Vologesocerta (cf. above, n. 29). However, Arabic sources make the identification and Zosimus 3.23.3 (Oppenheimer's Source 3, p. 391), is too confused to serve as evidence against it.
61. Fiey in his article of 1967 (cited above in n. 22) gives a vivid and fully-documented impression.
62. For these three soldiers, Chapter VIII.3, p. 163 (against the notion that one of them was the historian Magnus of Carrhae).
63. Cf. above, n. 33 for verification of this remark.
64. N. J. E. Austin, 'Julian at Ctesiphon: a fresh look at Ammianus' account', *Athenaeum* 50 (1972), 301-9, discusses this critical moment in relation to the different levels of information which he detects in Ammianus' narrative, that emanating from the 'high command' and the more apprehensive view prevalent among the troops. I agree entirely with Austin that Ammianus' ambiguities (Austin, 301-2) are not to be explained in terms of his use of different written sources (cf. Chapter VIII.3, passim); on the other hand it is possible that Julian's own actions were to a degree intrinsically ambiguous rather than reflecting different levels of information.
65. The embassy from Sapor (rejected by Julian) is mentioned or alleged by Libanius, *Or.* 18.257f. Libanius also stated (ibid. 249) that Julian held horse-races for his army outside the walls of Ctesiphon in order to distract the soldiers while the boats were unloaded (presumably to prepare them for burning, though Libanius does not make this connection) and while the crossing of the Tigris was prepared. (The similar version of Sozomen 6.1.6 derives from Libanius, whom he cites at 6.1.15f., and has no independent value). The games are also mentioned by Festus, *Brev.* 28 and Eunapius, Fr. 22.2 (Blockley, Frs. 27.3-4 and his notes, p. 134). Libanius reverts to the subject at *Or.* 1.133, but with a different and less credible narrative context, the games being here placed *after* the abortive attempt on Ctesiphon. Michael Di Maio, *Byzantion* 51 (1981), 502-10 suggests that the textual lacuna may be filled by material in Zonaras 13.13.2-9, in which Persian deserters promise to show Julian a safe route leading away from the river if he will burn the boats; they are believed by Julian but not by Hormisdas. It is true that the number of boats saved (12) and the total size of the fleet (1,100) are the same in Zonaras and Ammianus, but I would be reluctant to accept Di Maio's view, based on a theory of 1895, that Ammianus' version, mediated by another Greek source (John of Antioch), was known to Zonaras.
66. Adams, *Land behind Baghdad*, 70.

(3) Ammianus and other sources

67. This section may be read with the Conclusion of Chapter XIV, on Ammianus' sources for his descriptions of Roman relations with Alamanni, Goths, Huns and Alans, and other foreign peoples. The question of his sources for the Persian campaign has been, and

continues to be, intensively debated. I accept in essentials W. R. Chalmers, 'Eunapius, Ammianus Marcellinus and Zosimus on Julian's Persian expedition', *CQ* n.s. 10 (1960), 152-60, endorsed by T. D. Barnes, *The Sources of the Historia Augusta* (1978), at 117-19; certain textual parallels between Ammianus and Zosimus require that a common source be postulated, and by far the most economical and satisfactory solution is that, for these passages, Ammianus used Eunapius. My contribution is to suggest more precisely than has previously been done what were Ammianus' motives in (a) using Eunapius in certain passages, and (b) ignoring him otherwise. It is of course necessary that the first edition of Eunapius should have appeared by the time that Ammianus wrote Books 23-25, but that position seems to me fully defensible. Detailed arguments, and some discussion of alternative views, are given in my text and in the following notes.

68. On Hieronymus see the fine study of Jane Hornblower, *Hieronymus of Cardia* (Oxford, 1981). Zosimus' dependence on Eunapius for his fourth-century narrative is common ground; cf. the edd. of L. Mendelssohn (Leipzig 1887), xxxv-xlvii (excepting, however, the Persian campaign) and Paschoud, ed. Budé I (1971), xl-lxiii. In the later period (from 5.26) he is equally dependent on Olympiodorus of Thebes, cf. my article in *JRS* 60 (1970), 81f.; Paschoud, lvii-lxi. R. L. Rike, *Apex Omnium: religion in the Res Gestae of Ammianus* (1987), 128-32, is seriously awry in treating the Eunapian fragments and Zosimus as if they were separate sources. He cites only the opinion of Mendelssohn, and shows no acquaintance with the relevant recent literature on the subject.

69. Ammianus' independence as a witness of the Persian campaign was shown by E. A. Thompson, *The Historical Work of Ammianus Marcellinus*, ch. 2, esp. at 28-32 and Appendix I, pp. 134-7, and in detail by L. Dillemann, 'Ammien Marcellin et le pays de l'Euphrate et du Tigre', *Syria* 38 (1961), 87-158, at 98-135.

70. Sabbah, *La Méthode d'Ammien Marcellin*, 261-5, emphasises the divergences between Ammianus and Libanius' *Epitaphios*. For relevant details added by Libanius, cf. Chapter VIII.2, pp. 153; 156. Socrates, *Hist. Eccl.* 3.21.14 refers to one Kallistos, a *protector domesticus* of Julian, who wrote an account in heroic metre in which the emperor's death was ascribed to a demon! Such a man might well be known to Libanius – and to Ammianus.

71. For Philagrius as a source for Ammianus, see Chapter XIV Conclusion, p. 376f.

72. The notice (Suda I 401 Adler), not included in Müller's *FHG*, is Blockley, Fr. 29.1 (pp. 44-7): '... some of the pamphlets they threw on the ground, so that whoever wished could pick them up, others they posted on walls. These said such things as "You came back from the war, you should have perished there" and "ill-omened Paris, most handsome to look at", and so on ....'. See in general R. Turcan, 'L'abandon de Nisibe et l'opinion publique (363 après J.-C)', *Mél. Piganiol* (1966), 875-90.

73. The epitome of Magnus is at Malalas, pp. 328-33 (Bonn), cf. Müller, *FHG* IV, pp. 4-6, Jacoby, *FGrH* No. 225 (II B, pp. 951-4); cf. Paschoud's ed. of Zosimus, II.1, pp. 240-5 (with French translation). That Magnus, and not Eunapius, lies behind Zosimus' account of the Persian campaign and was a source for Ammianus was already argued by Mendelssohn, ed. of Zosimus, xxxix-xlvii (following a dissertation by H. Sudhaus of 1870). This theory was pursued by W. Klein, *Studien zur Ammianus Marcellinus* (Klio, Beiheft 13, 1914), who, by assembling parallel passages of Magnus as preserved by Malalas, together with Zosimus, Ammianus and sometimes Libanius, produced (often without the help of any actual citation of Magnus) a list of 81 so-called 'Fragments of Magnus of Carrhae'. This was described by Jacoby, *FGrH* II D, at 634 as 'eine etwas naive fragmentsammlung' and criticised still more pungently by Thompson (cited above in n. 69), 31-3; cf. also Chalmers, 154f. The identity of Magnus of Carrhae with the soldier Magnus of Ammianus 24.4.23 and Zosimus 3.22.4. accepted (after Seeck and others) by Jacoby, *FGrH* II B, 951f., was dispatched by Thompson, 31, and by Paschoud in his ed. of Zosimus II.1 (Budé, 1979), xlix-l.

74. R. Goulet, 'Sur la chronologie de la vie et des oeuvres d'Eunape de Sardes', *JHS* 100 (1980), 60-72, at 60-4; Eunapius arrived at Athens as a student only in 364, after the death of Julian.

75. Eunapius, Fr. 8 Müller (*FHG* IV, p. 15): Fr. 15 Blockley (p. 20f., with a possibly misleading translation; Eunapius says that Oribasius contributed the memoir for his use, not that he wrote it specifically for him). Eunapius' access to Oribasius' 'memoir' is supported by certain medical details preserved in later sources relating to Julian's death

(Chapter IX, p. 182). Paschoud suggests that the doctor's journal was also available to Ammianus (and to Libanius), and that it explains the textual similarities between Ammianus and Zosimus/Eunapius; cf. his ed. of Zosimus II.1, at xviii, and his article, 'Quand parut la première édition de l'Histoire d'Eunape?', in *HAColl, Bonn 1977/8* (1980), 149-62. Paschoud is right to observe (at 155f.) that the parallels are limited to the narrative of the Persian campaign, but I do not think that they are best explained by direct reference to the memoir of Oribasius: (i) it seems likely that the memoir was of an informal, private nature, made available to Eunapius as a favour to a student of medicine (cf. Chalmers, at 155); (ii) the theory of common derivation from Oribasius requires both Ammianus and Eunapius to have transcribed Oribasius' memoir more or less as it stood; the parallels are close enough to suggest a textual relation between one source and another rather than the mere informal exchange of information. Paschoud's suggestion of meetings at Antioch between Libanius, Ammianus and Oribasius is an intriguing hypothesis, but in my view is not the best explanation of the textual resemblances between Ammianus and Zosimus/Eunapius. Further, (iii) if Ammianus had access to the memoir he would surely have used it more extensively than the few parallel passages imply, not merely to inform himself on specific episodes of a military nature but to give himself greater access to the inner councils of the campaign than he in fact reveals.

76. Discrepancies are recorded also by Thompson, 28f., and in detail, and with emphasis on Zosimus' shortcomings, by R. T. Ridley, 'Notes on Julian's Persian expedition', *Historia* 22 (1973), 317-30 (tabulated at 327-9). The relevant issue is the additional material in Zosimus/Eunapius (cf. Ridley, at 324f.). Omissions and confusions in Zosimus are not necessarily relevant to Eunapius' relation to Ammianus (although they may be), for they may be due to Zosimus' own incompetence.

77. The nomenclature of 'Maiozamalcha' is discussed at Chapter VIII.2, p. 155f.

78. An eighth-century Syriac chronicle gives the form Kaukabā, which is nearer to Ammianus' Coche than to Zosimus' Zochasa; cf. Philostorgius, ed. Bidez (2nd ed. by F. Winkelmann, *GCS* 1972, p. 237).

79. The question of the inlets to the Naarmalcha is discussed at Chapter VIII.2, p. 149f.

80. The location of Hierapolis on the Euphrates is given as an error of Zosimus by Dillemann, 144; see also Ridley, 318; 'confusion or haste'. The confusion or haste may lie in modern readings of Zosimus' text, which is explicit that Hierius was sent on ahead of the army to supervise the fleet.

81. Sozomen 6.1.1 tells of Julian's refusal to visit the city. The emperor's acquaintance with the Christian character of Edessa is shown by his sarcastic *Ep.* 115 Bidez, with Intro., p. 127f. (*Ep.* 40, ed. Wright), responding to disorders between Arians and Valentinians there by confiscating the property of the church in order to encourage poverty in the clergy, and threatening the Edessenes with executions and exiles if disorder were repeated.

82. They are *PLRE* I, Constantianus 1 (p. 221); Lucillianus 2 (p. 517). To illustrate the ease of corruption of proper names, at 23.3.9 the MSS (VE) give 'constiano', corrected by a contemporary hand in E. Lucillianus occurs in his correct form at Zosimus 3.14.1,3 and at 3.16.2ff., so the first mention of his name at 3.13.3 could be subject to a simple fault in the transmission of the text.

83. Cf. Klein, *Studien zur Ammianus Marcellinus*, 63-7 (where this passage has become Fr. 2 of Magnus). As Thompson notes (p. 31), Magnus' narrative may have begun at Carrhae because he joined the campaign in his home town.

84. Malalas, p. 295 (Bonn) describes the exploits of Mareades; cf. Alan Cameron, *Circus Factions: blues and greens at Rome and Byzantium* (1976), 200-1, and G. Downey, *A History of Antioch*, 254-9, criticising Ammianus' narrative as chronologically and in other ways unsound. Historia Augusta, *Tyr. Trig.* 3 (ed. Hohl, Teubner, pp. 100-1), makes a fictional usurper of the historical figure. The evidence will be fully discussed in a forthcoming commentary on the Thirteenth Sibylline Oracle by D. S. Potter of Ann Arbor University. W. Seyfarth, 'Ein Handstreich persischer Bogenschützen auf Antiochia: sprachliche und historische Rechtfertigung einer Stelle bei Ammianus Marcellinus (23,5,3)', *Klio* 40 (1962), 61-4, accepts the historicity of the episode, retaining V's 'exacerbantia' in place of the emendation 'ex arce volantia' suggested by Petschenig and accepted by Clark.

85. Presented by Klein (though the episode is only in general terms mentioned in Malalas'

excerpt) as 'Fragments 12-13' of Magnus of Carrhae.

86. Thompson, 136f., supposed that Eunapius might have had direct or indirect access to Ammianus' text, a suggestion withdrawn in his 'Ammianus Marcellinus', in T. A. Dorey (ed.), *Latin Historians* (1966), 152f. This, and A. F. Norman's suggestion, *CQ* n.s. 7 (1957), 129-33, that Zosimus may have made use of Ammianus, were criticised effectively by Chalmers, 156-9, and by Alan Cameron, *CQ* n.s. 13 (1963), 232-6, esp. at 233. There are powerful general considerations against the Hellenist Eunapius' making use of a Latin source like Ammianus. Thompson was right, however, in observing that any theory of the relationship between Ammianus and Zosimus must explain the differences as well as the similarities between them.

87. For the geography, see esp. A. Musil, *The Middle Euphrates*, 238.

88. Klein, at 88f., gives this episode as 'Fragments 16-17' of Magnus. No trace survives in the actual extract of Magnus preserved by Malalas.

89. For the site of Pirisabora, Chapter VIII.1, p. 132. Zosimus/Eunapius' and Ammianus' descriptions of the site are discussed by Chalmers, 159, emphasising in a manner very like mine the greater informality of Ammianus' description and arguing that any derivation must be from Eunapius to Ammianus – from the more to the less formal – and not vice versa.

90. Photius, *Bibl.*, cod. 77, printed in Müller *FHG* IV, p. 9: Blockley, pp. 2-5.

91. See Chapter VII, pp. 125ff. for the force of this remark.

92. The argument here picks up the problem posed at Chapter VIII.1, p. 131, with the arguments of Rosen and Liebeschuetz. It is through the deliberate holding back of the speech until after the omens reported at 23.4.8-14, and not through narrative confusion or failure to use his sources coherently, that Ammianus produces the 'doublet' of 23.4.7f. and 24.1.5.

93. See on this passage Paschoud's n. 31, at pp. 103-4; Zosimus/Eunapius' avoidance of the issue is taken as intended to camouflage 'la conduite incohérente et inexplicable du héros païen' shown in his disobedience of the gods. This may be so: my point is that the result is a version of Julian's conduct quite unlike that of Ammianus, and one from which he cannot derive.

94. Fr. 26 in Müller, *FHG* IV, p. 25: Blockley, Fr. 28.6 (pp. 44-5), translating as follows:

> But, having driven the Persian race headlong with your sceptre
> Back to Seleucia conquered by your sword,
> A fire-bright chariot whirled amidst storm-clouds
> Shall take you to Olympus freed from your body
> And the much-enduring misery of man.
> Then you shall come to your father's halls
> Of heavenly light, from which you wandered
> Into a human frame of mortality.

The lines form a fine pendant to those of Ephraim the Syrian with which this book began.

IX. Legitimacy and Usurpation: Jovian to Procopius

1. In view of the controversy surrounding Julian's death (below, nn. 3, 5) it is not surprising that this prediction comes down to us in various versions. The historical fragment attributed to Magnus of Carrhae by Malalas (Chapter VIII.3, p. 163f.) calls the place not Phrygia but 'Asia', describing it as a deserted site near the ruins of 'Boubion'. Eutychianus, in the same passage, is reported as having described 'Asia' as a city near Ctesiphon, and this version has Julian, on hearing the name of the place, exclaim, 'O Helios, you have destroyed Julian' (*FHG* IV, p. 5; cf. Paschoud's n. 83 on Zosimus 3.19, at p. 202). Malalas, in a passage not cited by Müller, has Julian learn by a prophecy given him at Daphne that he would die 'in Asia' (p. 327 Bonn). One would suspect 'Asia' to be a later simplified variant of Ammianus' more recondite (and more accurate) 'Phrygia'. 'Boubion', if Babylon is meant (as Paschoud supposes, at 187), is in any case impossible, and 'near Ctesiphon' is too vague to import conviction.

2. On the philosophical (Socratic-Neoplatonic-mystic) pedigree of Julian's death-bed speech, see J. Fontaine, 'Le Julien d'Ammien Marcellin', 51-3, with his edition, nn. 544-58 (pp. 218-25). Fontaine understandably hedges his bets as to the extent to which the discourse can be considered genuine (that is, to represent Julian's own words). Julian was

well able to contrive such a scene; so too was Ammianus, and he knew that Julian was capable of doing so (he would of course have to represent it in a different language, for any discussions with the philosophers were certainly held in Greek). See also G. Scheda, 'Die Todesstunde Kaiser Julians', *Historia* 15 (1966), 380-3, pointing out the philosophical conventions that were involved but not denying the possibility that Julian himself may have behaved with a sense of the occasion. As Sabbah observes (*La Méthode d'Ammien Marcellin*, at 414), Julian's claim at 23.3.19 that he had not died 'in clandestinis insidiis' tells against any suggestion that his death was caused by Roman treachery in the battle; but he (or Ammianus) is probably thinking rather of conspiracies such as brought about the death of Gordian III, referred to in his initial speech – in this case, certainly Ammianus' own composition – to the army (above, p. 131f.).

3. The circumstances of Julian's death have naturally caused much discussion, summarised by Paschoud, ed. of Zosimus, II.1., n. 84, pp. 203-7; see esp. Th. Büttner-Wobst, 'Der Tod des Kaisers Julians: eine Quellenstudie', *Philologus* 51 (1892), 561-80 and the article of D. Conduché cited at n. 5 below. A. Selem, 'Ammiano e la morte di Giuliano (25.3.3-11)', *Rendiconti dell'Istituto Lombardo, Cl. di Scienze Morali e Storiche* 107 (1973), 1119-35 argues that Ammianus shared the view that Julian was killed by a 'Roman' hand but was obliged through the circumstances of his time of writing and the nature of his audience to indicate the truth only by hint and allusion (cf. Chapter VI, n. 22 for a similar theory with respect to the proclamation of Julian). It is obvious that Ammianus uses dramatic irony, particularly in presenting the ominous foreboding preceding Julian's death (the comparison with Gordian III is discussed above; Chapter VIII.1, p. 132). Beyond this I can only say that Selem's theory seems to me to contradict the natural reading of Ammianus (cf. the remarks of Fontaine, n. 528 at p. 214), and to treat other sources that describe this confused episode in an unduly insistent fashion (and to misreport them sometimes; for instance, Philostorgius, p. 101 Bidez does not say that Julian was killed by 'un Arabo disertore'). It is refreshing to be reminded (at 1119f.) that Gregory of Nazianzus mentions a barbarian buffoon from the imperial entourage as a possible assassin! It is possible however that Gregory has wilfully misunderstood the Latin word 'scurra': not here a 'buffoon' but a military slang word for a guardsman of barbarian origin; cf. Amm. 29.4.4 (slave traders in Alamann territory), 30.1.20 (the killers of king Pap of Armenia) – both in 'barbarian' contexts; see (with reservations on the connections postulated between sources), Barry Baldwin, 'Gregory Nazianzus, Ammianus, *scurrae*, and the *Historia Augusta*', *Gymnasium* 93 (1986), 178-80. See also, esp. on the evidence of Libanius' later speeches (24 and 30) and of Philostorgius, István Hahn, 'Der ideologische Kampf um der Tod Julians des Abtrünnigen', *Klio* 38 (1960), 225-32 – not however appreciating the connection between Philostorgius and Eunapius. On this, I would endorse the crisp remarks of Bowersock, *Julian the Apostate*, 116f.; so too on the medical details preserved by Philostorgius (117)

4. As indicated, there are textual difficulties with this passage, where V has 'fugientium molem tamquam ruinam male conpositi culminis declararet et incertum subitae questris has tacte brachii eius praestricta', etc. For the last group of words Gelenius' 'subita equestris hasta c<u>te brachii', etc. is the obvious correction, whether or not it has the authority of M; while 'declinaret' is universally accepted for V's 'declararet'. For the rest, most editors have supplied 'unde' after V's 'incertum' (for the expression 'incertum unde', cf. 16.8.3, 24.2.4, and esp. 19.8.10), thereby allowing to Ammianus explicit expression of the view that the origin of the fatal spear was unknown. Fontaine reads 'incertam' for 'incertum', attaching it to 'ruinam' in the sense of an 'uncertain tottering mass' of fugitives (n. 528, p. 213f.). This is an attractive suggestion requiring very slight amendment to V. The omission of 'et' after 'decl<in>aret' is a trivial correction, but so is the insertion of 'unde' after 'incertum'. Neither palaeographically nor in terms of meaning does there seem much basis for preference.

5. On the attitude of Salutius, the argument of J. J. O'Donnell, 'The demise of paganism', *Traditio* 35 (1979), at 46-7 and 53-4, that Salutius declined the opportunity to become emperor and continue Julian's campaign for paganism, since he believed in religious freedom and did not endorse Julian's intolerant policies, suggests too refined an attitude in the circumstances; taking these into account, the surprise would rather have been had he accepted the throne. So too the interpretation of Dominique Conduché, 'Ammien Marcellin et la mort de Julien', *Latomus* 24 (1965), 359-80 is very interesting in its working out of a

religious interpretation (Jovian as a neutral candidate who offered freedom from sectarian division) but seems to miss the actual nature of the occasion, and takes little account of the sequence of events reported by Ammianus. Raban von Haehling, 'Ammians Darstellung der Thronbesteigung Jovians im Lichte der heidnisch-christlichen Auseinandersetzung', in *Festgabe Johannes Straub* (1977), 347-58, shows how Ammianus over-emphasised the role of Salutius in order to emphasise the 'Julianic' connection, and distorted the character of the proclamation of Jovian in order to make it resemble a usurpation rather than a legitimate elevation; the Christian Jovian thus represents the ironic failure of Julian's dying wish (25.3.20) that a good successor be found (p. 358). This is by far the most convincing attempt to interpret the events within a religious dimension, and does justice to Ammianus' manner of writing as well as to the possible motives of individual actors; even so, I am more impressed by the objective predicament in which the army found itself, and the sheer difficulty of its achieving any coherent action in the circumstances.

6. *Decline and Fall*, ch. XXIV (Vol. III, p. 518, n. 104, in the edition of J. B. Bury (1897)). The identification is scouted by Haehling, at 353f.; the idea being to have Salutius as a caretaker emperor until it became possible, upon the army's return to Roman territory, to choose Julian's relative Procopius. It is of course quite possible that this rather impractical idea crossed the minds of some, but I find it hard to believe that Ammianus was thinking of it.

7. Ammianus' arguments are diffidently questioned by Gibbon, at p. 521 (accepting the distances but doubting an army's ability to cover them in the time alleged); see also Fontaine's ed., n. 645 at p. 257 ('Ammien prend un peu ses désirs pour les réalités'), citing Paschoud's n. 90 (at p. 217) and Dillemann, *Haute Mésopotamie*, 304. Paschoud also rightly calls Ammianus' assessment of Sapor's mentality as 'assez naive' (p. 217). Sapor was first to ask for negotiation because he could see the greater advantage to himself in doing so. R. Turcan, *Mél. Piganiol* (1966), 875-90, at 876f., is much too indulgent to Julian.

8. For prices of wheat, Chapter XVI, p. 410f.

9. For the 'Agri Decumates', Chapter XIV.1, p. 308.

10. For the personalities mentioned here and in what follows, see the notices in *PLRE* I.

11. The 'likeliest explanation' accepted in the text is in fact that offered by other sources, such as Orosius, Sozomen and Zonaras; cf. Fontaine's n. 725 (p. 286) – not however citing the passage of the *Misopogon*.

12. See esp. on the entire process Valerio Neri, 'Ammiano Marcellino e l'elezione di Valentiniano', *Rivista Storica dell'Antichità* 15 (1985), 153-82.

13. On this division, Roger Tomlin, 'Seniores-Iuniores in the late-Roman field army', *AJP* 93 (1972), 253-78, and Dietrich Hoffmann, *Das Spätrömische Bewegungsheer*, ch. 5 (pp. 117-30; 120f. on the Divitenses and Tungrecani). The year 364 is seen with good reason as the moment of division of the Roman empire by L. Valensi, 'Quelques réflexions sur le pouvoir impérial d'après Ammien Marcellin', *Bull. de l'Association Guillaume Budé* 4.4 (1957), at 102ff.

14. On the rebellion of Procopius, see R. C. Blockley, *Ammianus Marcellinus: a study of his historiography and political thought* (1975), ch. III (pp. 55-61), with selective discussion of earlier literature. There is a strategic analysis in Norman Austin, *Ammianus on Warfare: an investigation into Ammianus' military knowledge* (1979), and a discussion of the modes of propaganda employed, by the same author, 'A usurper's claim to legitimacy', *Rivista Storica dell'Antichità* 2 (1972), 187-94. A. Solari, 'La rivolta Procopiana a Constantinopoli', *Byzantion* 7 (1932), 143-8, argues (i) that the challenge to Valentinian before his brother's election (26.4.1) issued from a preference in the army for a pagan successor to Jovian, and (ii) that Procopius' rebellion – and the punishment of his supporters (below, n. 29) – had a significant religious dimension. I would not exclude this idea from the mind of everyone, but as a general explanation – and given what Ammianus actually says of these events – it seems arbitrary and unnecessary.

15. On the quality of Zosimus' narrative of this phase (4.4) see Paschoud's n. 114, at pp. 340-1. The most implausible allegation is that Procopius returned to Jovian the imperial purple earlier given him by Julian. This is against the clear and justified scepticism of Ammianus, 23.3.2; 26.6.2f.; cf. Sabbah, *La Méthode d'Ammien Marcellin*, 412.

16. On this 'literary collusion' of the elements, Sabbah, 555ff. has some characteristically

subtle remarks; but I find unnecessary his (hesitant) suggestion that the reference to Ammianus himself at the end of the book is intended to hint at his role as an eye-witness of the events he has described. The tidal wave and earthquake are characterised and discussed by François Jacques and Bernard Bousquet, 'Le raz de marée du 21 Juillet 365: du cataclysme local à la catastrophe cosmique', *MEFR* 96 (1984), 423–61; affecting in its consequences the southern Peloponnese and Alexandria, the earthquake had its epicentre south of Crete, 'dans le secteur central de la fosse hellénique, historiquement active' (cf. their map at pp. 442–3). The dating of 21 July is from the *Festal Index* of Athanasius. In the same volume (pp. 463–90), Cl. Lepelley, 'L'Afrique du Nord et le prétendu séisme universel du 21 Juillet 365', points to the absence of evidence, in literary sources or archaeology, for any effect of the earthquake in the north-west African provinces.

17. On the 'theatrical' elements in Ammianus' narration, see my Chapter XI, p. 247f. and Sabbah, 362f.; though I see no need to bring Themistius or any other written source into this aspect of Ammianus' presentation, which is integral to his own manner. For the Sallustian language Blockley, at 57f. and Syme, *Ammianus and the Historia Augusta* (1968), 127–8.

18. For the date, *Consularia Constantinopolitana*, s.a. 365 (*Chron. Min.* I, p. 240). The same source records the date of Procopius' death, 27 May 366.

19. Sabbah, at 203, envisages Sophronius as a documentary source for Ammianus on the basis of 26.7.2, 'textu narrato gestorum' (*sc.* to Valens). I would prefer to see him as an oral source (in this case, on Valens' response to the news of the rebellion), like Philagrius at 21.4.2; 'notarium, orientis postea comitem'; see my Chapter XIV, Conclusion, p. 376, cf. Chapter II.2, p. 23 and n. 28.

20. On this and other propaganda aspects, Austin, 'A usurper's claim to legitimacy', 189–91.

21. Cf. Chap. X p.208 for the *casus belli* adduced by Valens for his war with the Goths.

22. The situation of Valens presents points of similarity with that of Constantius facing Julian in 361; see my Chapter VI, pp. 100ff.

23. *PLRE* I, p. 443–4 (Hormisdas 3). He was the son of the Persian prince who accompanied the Persian campaign (26.8.12; cf. Zosimus 4.8.1). His appointment is explicitly characterised by Ammianus as archaic; 'civilia more veterum et bella recturo' (26.8.12).

24. A facet of social relations discussed in Chapter XVI, esp. pp. 416ff.

25. Austin, 'a usurper's claim to legitimacy', 189–91.

26. The coinage of Procopius; Austin, 192–3; for the issues, J.W.E. Pearce, in *RIC* IX, at 209–16 (Constantinople); 192–3 (Heraclea); 239–41 (Cyzicus); 250–2 (Nicomedia). As Austin points out (at 193), the fact that Procopius coined in gold with FEL. TEMP. REPARATIO supports his wish to exploit the Constantinian connection also in Illyricum (cf. 26.7.11).

27. Olympiodorus, Fr. 19 (Müller, *FHG* IV, p. 61). The imagery occurs as an illustration in an early chronicle; cf. Bernhard Bischof and Wilhelm Koehler, 'Eine illustriert Ausgabe der Spätantiken Ravennater Annalen', in W.R.W. Koehler (ed.), *Medieval Studies in Memory of A. Kingsley Porter* (1939), 123–38, Abb. 1 (p. 131). The illustration (an early sixth-century original?) shows three usurpers' heads on pikes, referring to the Chronicle entry s.a. 412; 'his consulibus occisi sunt in Galliis Iovinus et Sebastianus et venerunt capita eorum Ravennam III kal. Sep. et occissus est frater eorum Sallus(tius)'; cf. Prosper, in *Chron. Min.* I, p. 300. Below is shown the death of Heraclianus at Carthage (his body lies prostrate). The article was republished in Italian in *Studi Romagnoli* 3 (1952), 1–17.

28. For the characteristics of Procopius, see Sabbah, 362. For the (non-)relevance of Themistius' *Oratio* 7 to this portrait, see the next note.

29. On Ammianus' characterisation of these trials, cf. Sabbah, 361, who sees in his phrase 'proscriptiones et exilia et quae leviora quibusdam videntur, quamquam sint aspera' (26.10.14) an allusion to complaisant panegyrists of Valens, such as Themistius, who in *Oratio* 7 had praised the clemency of the emperor in the aftermath of Procopius' usurpation. As on other occasions (cf. above, n. 17 on its 'theatrical' quality), Ammianus' presentation is sufficiently part of his own manner to make external literary influences an unnecessary consideration. Solari (cited above in n. 14), 148, thought that the punishments were intensified by religious conflict. This seems to me an entirely superfluous notion.

X. Valentinian and Valens: Sex, Magic and Treason

1. The first few pages of this Chapter pursue suggestions as to Ammianus' time and circumstances of writing outlined in Chapter II above. The assertions of E. A. Thompson, *The Historical Work of Ammianus Marcellinus*, 109, as to Ammianus' lack of freedom as a writer seem to me too categorical; cf. his 'Ammianus Marcellinus', in T. A. Dorey (ed.), *Latin Historians* (1966), 148ff, where Ammianus is said to have been wary of the Emperor Theodosius (hence his praise of Theodosius the *magister militum* and his evasion of the promise to tell of the fate of Theodosius' alleged enemy Maximinus; below, n. 14), and especially doubtful of the emperor's religious policies. This may be so, but I do not believe that the political conditions of Ammianus' age are alone responsible for the anomalies that can be found in his historical writing. I have similar reservations about the arguments of C. P. T. Naudé, 'The date of the later books of Ammianus Marcellinus', *American Journal of Ancient History* 9.1 (1984), 70-94. I accept, with Naudé, a period of composition in the 380s rather than 390s, but do not accept that contemporary political circumstances provide a criterion for the definition of Ammianus' situation as a writer – especially when the criterion has variously been used to support a time of publication in the aftermath of the usurpation of Maximus (Naudé), under the usurpation of Eugenius, and after the death of Theodosius. My own view is based on the convergence of internal references in Ammianus' text upon a period up to and including 390 (Chapter II.2, pp. 22ff.).

2. See Chapter II.2, p. 26 and n. 34, with Alan Cameron, *JRS* 61 (1971), 255-67, at 262 (reviewing Syme's *Ammianus and the Historia Augusta*). If Libanius, *Ep.* 1063 looks forward to a new instalment of the history, that instalment is not necessarily Books 26-31; it might be a politely anticipated continuation after Book 31 – where Ammianus consigns the continuation of his task to others (31.16.9).

3. E. A. Thompson, *The Historical Work of Ammianus Marcellinus*, 25f., is good on this aspect (in the context of Ammianus' use of sources in the later books).

4. For the coherence of Ammianus' narrative of this phase, see Chapter VI, pp. 101ff., with the chart there printed of the movements of Julian and Constantius in 360 and 361.

5. For these digressions, see Chapter XVI, pp. 414ff. (Rome); XIV.2, pp. 332ff. (Huns and Alans); pp. 342ff. (Saracens).

6. The passages are 27.1-2; 27.10; 28.2; 28.5.8-15; 29.4; 30.3. The material is presented thematically in Chapter XIV.1.

7. Roger Tomlin, 'The date of the "Barbarian Conspiracy"', *Britannia* 5 (1974), 303-9. I find inconclusive the counter-arguments (supporting 368-9) of R. C. Blockley, 'The date of the "Barbarian Conspiracy"', *Britannia* 11 (1980), 223-5, but the difference of opinion is relevant to the nature of Ammianus' text. In a further article, 'Ammianus Marcellinus 26.4.5-6', *CQ* n.s. 29 (1979), 470-8, Tomlin rightly notes that the passage in question should be taken as a summary of the events of the whole reign of Valentinian and not as possessing any intrinsic chronological value.

8. For the Tripolitanian episode, Chapter XV, pp. 383ff.: Mauretania, Chapter XIV.3(ii).

9. A selective bibliography of studies of magic in the later Roman empire with relevance to Ammianus would include: J. Maurice, 'La terreur de la magie au IVe siècle', *Revue Historique de droit français et étranger*, IV.6 (1927), 108-20; F. Martroye, 'La répression de la magie et le culte des gentils au IVe siècle', ibid. IV.9 (1930), 669-701; A. A. Barb, 'The survival of magic arts', in Momigliano (ed.), *The Conflict between Paganism and Christianity in the Fourth Century* (1963), 100-25; Peter Brown, 'Sorcery, demons and the rise of Christianity: from Late Antiquity into the Middle Ages', in *Religion and Society in the Age of Saint Augustine* (1972), 119-46; and Denise Grodzynski, 'Superstitio', *REA* 76 (1974), 36-60. Directly relevant also to the processes under Constantius and Valentinian are A. Alföldi, *A Conflict of Ideas* (1952), ch. IV; W. Seyfarth, 'Glaube und Aberglaube bei Ammianus Marcellinus', *Klio* 46 (1965), 373-83; H. Funke, 'Majestäts- und Magieprozesse bei Ammianus Marcellinus', *Jahrbuch für Antike und Christentum* 10 (1967), 145-75; and R. von Haehling, 'Ammianus Marcellinus und der Prozess von Scythopolis', ibid. 21 (1978), 74-101. On the broader context in Roman history, see esp. Ramsay MacMullen, *Enemies of the Roman Order: treason, unrest and alienation in the Roman Empire* (1967), chs. III and IV.

10. Olybrius: Chastagnol, *Fastes*, pp. 178-84 (No. 70); Alföldi, *A Conflict of Ideas*, 71.
11. Hymetius: *PLRE* I, p. 447. The inscription to the statue in his honour erected at Rome in 376 refers to another statue at Carthage, also 'sub auro' (*ILS* 1256).
12. Maximinus: *PLRE* I, pp. 577-8 (Maximinus 7). *CTh* 14.17.6 was addressed from Trier to Maxim(in)us as *praefectus annonae* on 19 March 368, 370, or 373, but is classified in the Code between laws of 369 and 372. *CTh* 14.17.3 (365 or 368) was dated 365 by Seeck, on the basis of its companion, 14.17.4, to Mamertinus as praetorian prefect; if this is correct, 14.7.3 was addressed to a different *praefectus annonae* (*Regesten*, 32).
13. For this political reaction see my *Western Aristocracies and Imperial Court*, 64-9.
14. The death of Maximinus provides one of Ammianus' two, and his only significant unfulfilled promise (the other is at 22.8.35, something learned on the halcyon); cf. Alanna Emmett, 'The digressions in the lost books of Ammianus', in Croke and Emmett (edd.), *History and Historians in Late Antiquity* (1983), 43 with n. 22. The involvement of Maximinus in the death of the *magister militum* Theodosius is alleged, on what authority is not known, in an additional note to Jerome's *Chronicle*, s.a. 376 (edd. J. K. Fotheringham (1923), p. 330; R. Helm (*GCS*, 1956), p. 248 and Intro., p. xviii); cf. Thompson, *The Historical Work of Ammianus Marcellinus*, 93ff.; *Western Aristocracies*, 64; Naudé, (cited above in n. 1), 73ff. (adducing Symmachus and Petronius Probus as figures whom Ammianus would not wish to offend); and for further discussion this Chapter, p. 216, with Chapter XIV, p. 382.
15. This lack of correlation in Ammianus' account between the prefects and the trials is noted by Alföldi, *A Conflict of Ideas*, 71f.
16. Tony Honoré, 'The making of the Theodosian Code', *ZSS* 103 (1986), 133-222, at 194 (Eupraxius is discussed at 190-203).
17. Praetextatus: Chastagnol, *Fastes*, pp. 171-8 (No. 69). This would be one of the embassies mentioned on his inscr., *ILS* 1258: 'legato amplissimi ordinis septies et ad impetrandum reb(us) arduis semper opposito', cf. 1259, 'legatus a senatu missus V(II)'.
18. 28.1.11; 'uno proloquio in huius modi causas, quas arroganter proposito maiestatis imminutae miscebat, omnes quod iuris prisci iustitia divorumque [*sc*. previous emperors] arbitria quaestionibus exemere cruentis, si postulasset negotium, statuit tormentis affligi'. Ammianus' rhetoric apart, this is an accurate description of the legal situation.
19. Against the notion of political conspiracy and conflict, as argued by Thompson and Chastagnol, see my *Western Aristocracies*, at pp. 59, 63, with special reference to A. Demandt, *Historia* 17 (1969), 598-626, at 607f.; also Alan Cameron, *JRS* 61 (1971), at 260. Alföldi, *A Conflict of Ideas*, 76, refers to 'the hocus-pocus of witchcraft'. The article of Pierre Hamblenne, 'Une "conjuration" sous Valentinien?', *Byzantion* 50 (1980), 198-225 rightly emphasises the sheer variety of victims and situations described by Ammianus, but is marred by unclear presentation, and by the author's apparent belief (pp. 199, 211, 215) that Valentinian governed the empire from Constantinople.
20. As noted by Thompson, *The Historical Work of Ammianus Marcellinus*, 102. Alföldi, *A Conflict of Ideas*, 65ff., is less restrained, calling Ammianus' reports 'incredibly one-sided', with 'distortions of truth', 'wild prejudice' and 'boundless hatred', and suggesting, in one case chosen for close examination, that 'Aginatius was not the innocent lamb that Ammianus makes him out to be' (72). Alföldi agrees however that Ammianus was not indignant at the prosecution of these capital charges as a matter of principle, but because the senatorial oligarchy was under attack (76f.).
21. *CTh* 9.19.4, addressed 'ad Maximinum PPo' is given as 'p(ro)p(osita) Romae XVI Kal. Mai.' (of 376); cf. *PLRE* I, p. 578, concluding that the law 'must belong to the copy of the PPo Italiae'. *CTh* 9.6.1-2, addressed 'ad Maxim(in)um PPo', may be similarly interpreted, if the protocol of the first law, 'pp. Id. Mart.', is accepted rather than that of the second, 'dat. Id. Mart.' the place of issue and/or reception of neither law is preserved).
22. The inconsistency in Ammianus' attitudes when considering the actions of Apronianus is again noted by Alföldi, *A Conflict of Ideas*, 70-1. The inclusion of Apronianus tells against the possibility that Ammianus, reluctant to involve the prefecture in such disagreeable events, deliberately underplayed the role of the prefects. His expression that Bellona 'raged through the Eternal City' (28.1.1) and his remark in concluding the narrative that 'is urbanarum rerum status fuit' (1.57, cf. 4.1) seem too categorical for such sensitive distinctions. It is more likely that, influenced by the direct role of the *vicarii*, Ammianus

simply understated that of the *praefecti urbi*.

23. Alföldi, *A Conflict of Ideas*, 45f., assigns these cases (in a chapter entitled 'Corruption and its antidote, terrorism') to 'the awful severity with which Valentinian tried to further the welfare of his peoples' – a disconcerting but not unrealistic perspective, on which see further Chapter XII, pp. 256ff. The case of Faustinus, who killed a donkey in search of a cure for baldness (p. 216), is discussed by Seyfarth, 'Glaube und Aberglaube' (n. 9 above); Faustinus was not executed for this enterprise (cf. Pliny, *Hist. Nat.* 28.164), but for the maliciously alleged remark ('perniciose composito') that he would promote a friend Nigrinus as notary if the latter would make him emperor. For this treasonable wisecrack both men, and others, were executed (30.5.12). Cf. the further speculation of M. Clauss, 'Ein tödlicher Scherz (zu Ammian 30,5,11-12)', *RhM* 208 (1985), 97-8; the joke was dangerous because Valentinian had actually been made emperor by Pannonians, especially the *magister officiorum* Leo – present at Carnuntum, where the episode took place (30.5.1, 10f.). Clauss suggests that the charge was adduced by Faustinus' enemies when the first accusation failed.

24. For these bears, Chapter XII, p. 260.

25. Cf. on senatorial ostentation 14.6.9; 28.4.12, 18; opulence, 14.6.10, 12; fraudulent pretensions, 28.6.7 (claims of ancestry); cf. Chapter XVI, pp. 414ff. For intellectual impoverishment of the nobility, 14.6.18, 28.4.14 and the senator Orfitus, 'splendore liberalium doctrinarum minus quam nobilem decuerat institutus' (14.6.1).

26. 28.4.1; cited at p. 214 above.

27. The remarks on this episode of A. A. Barb, 'The survival of magic arts' (above, n. 9) are useful but patronising; 'the age-old and rather undefined and slightly comic god Besa ...' (p. 108f.); contrast Sabbah, ed. Budé (1970), pp. 220-1 (n. 287), '... un dieu de la toilette; il apparaît aussi dansant et jouant de la musique'. On Paulus 'Catena', my Chapters VI, p. 82 and XII, p. 259. By far the best and fullest discussion is that of R. von Haehling, 'Ammianus Marcellinus und der Prozess von Scythopolis' (n. 9 above), emphasising by means of a prosopographical study of the participants an element of religious partisanship in the trials which, he argues, was deliberately underplayed by Ammianus because of his own liking for toleration, and his wish to portray the trials as an expression of purposeless terror by the emperor and his supporters. It is true (Haehling shows this very clearly) that the judges were Christians and the defendants supporters of the old gods; the extent to which this lends the trials an explicitly religious dimension is a matter of perspective. However it appeared to the victims, I suspect that Constantius and his agents would have denied that they were were acting through religious motives; there was a real suspicion of treason in the information they possessed. The implicit connections with religious issues are clearly extensive (this Chapter, p. 225f.).

28. For the family of Simplicius, see n. 49 to Chapter XII; Haehling, 89-90. Parnasius (*PLRE* I, pp. 667-8; Haehling, 90-1) was prefect of Egypt in 357-9 and put on trial after laying down his office. Libanius reports (*Or.* 14.14f.) that he had consulted an astrologer, presumably during his tenure of office, and in *Ep.* 822 shows that he had ancestral property at (or in the territory of) Corinth. The poetic reputation of Andronicus (19.12.18) was considerable, though none of his work, in various genres, survives (Haehling, 91-2); he was in later years a correspondent of Symmachus (*Ep.* 8.22).

29. *CTh* 9.16.9 (a law of 371 distinguishing *haruspicina* from 'maleficorum causae' and asserting the rights of any 'concessa a maioribus religio'); 'testes sunt leges a me in exordio imperii mei datae, quibus unicuique, quod animo inbibisset, colendi libera facultas tributa est'. The law was no doubt issued before the separation of Valentinian and Valens at the end of 364 (Chapter IX, p. 190).

30. Eunapius, *V. Soph.* p. 493 (ed. Loeb, pp. 512-13); *PLRE* I, p. 731, s.v. Proaeresius.

31. See again Barb, 'The survival of magic arts', at 111-14. The notes (129-32) of François Paschoud on the parallel (but differing) narrative of Zosimus are valuable; II.2, pp. 356-62. In fact Zosimus (4.13.3f.) has the affair of Theodorus precede that of Fortunatianus and makes no causal connection between them. It is clear from Ammianus that this is an inaccurate sequence.

32. As in the case of the trials at Rome under Valentinian (p. 212), the presence in Ammianus of these procedural indications merits a word of emphasis.

33. At *Civitas Dei* 19.6, Augustine considers the quandary of a secular judge who knows that he must torture innocent witnesses to reveal the guilty, and that accused men may plead guilty in order to avoid torture. In consequence, it may never be clear whether the men he has executed are guilty or not.

34. Barb, 'The survival of magic arts', 111, considered that Ammianus studied the 'minutes of the proceedings' or else was an eye-witness. Sabbah, *La Méthode d'Ammien Marcellin*, does not discuss the passage, but remarks of the preceding sentence, 'aperiunt [*sc*. Patricius and Hilarius] negotii fidem ab ipsis exordiis replicatam' (29.1.28), that Ammianus uses the word 'fides' in cases where he 'garantit au lecteur que la version des faits presentée par un autre vaut aussi pour lui' (p. 21 with n. 52). The opening of Hilarius' speech is both arresting and circumstantial; 'Construximus, inquit, magnifici iudices ... infaustam hanc mensulam quam videtis'. Ammianus uses no such phrase as 'hunc in modum' or 'talia'. He begins, 'et prius Hilarius: Construximus', etc.

35. Fl. Eusebius and Fl. Hypatius were consuls in 359 (cf. 18.1.1). For Hypatius, summoned from Antioch to become prefect of Rome in 379, see Chastagnol, *Fastes*, pp. 204-6 (No. 82).

36. See on this episode Barb, 111, and my remarks on techniques used in theurgy, Chapter VII, pp. 116ff. Firmicus Maternus, *Mathesis* 2.30.4-7 (transl. Jean Rhys Bram, Park Ridge, N.J., 1975, p. 69) emphatically warns against an astrologer's consulting an imperial horoscope.

37. Barb, 116f., also describes this episode.

38. K. Preisendanz, *Papyri Graecae Magicae*, No. III, xi, lines 290ff. (Vol. I, p. 44).

39. See this Chapter, p. 227 with n. 44 below for the inscription.

40. Eunapius, *V. Soph.* p. 481 (ed. Loeb, pp. 458-61); *PLRE* I, pp. 334-5 (Festus 3); also *Western Aristocracies*, 46. Festus' religious beliefs remain unclear. The conclusion of his *Breviarium* addressed to Valens is non-committal – 'maneat modo concessa dei nutu et ab amico, cui credis et creditus es, numine indulta felicitas' (*Brev.* 30) – but this may be a gesture of literary detachment; while Eunapius is too polemical to be reliable on such a matter. For Maximus and Julian, Chapter VII, pp. 122ff.

41. See on these figures my remarks at *Latomus* 30 (1971), 1074f.

42. For Christian charms and talismans, see Barb, esp. 106-7 and 121-4. When I was a child in Leicester, to pronounce the word 'croggies' [?etym. 'crux', 'cruces'] while holding up crossed fingers was a means of gaining temporary asylum in an over-strenuous playground game: cf. Iona and Peter Opie, *The Lore and Language of Schoolchildren* (1959), 143, 150 (with variants).

43. Suda I 14, yielding Blockley's fr. 39.2 (p. 54f., with notes at 138ff.; not in Müller, *FHG*).

44. Zonaras 13.16 (Bonn III, p. 79-80); Cedrenus, 314B (Bonn I, p. 550). Socrates, *Hist. Eccl.* 4.8.6 (cf. Zonaras, p. 80 Bonn), provides a variant and slightly fuller text of the oracle cited by Ammianus, adding that the walls of Chalcedon were demolished at Valens' orders because the city had sided with Procopius and insulted him (cf. Amm. 26.8.2; Chapter IX, p. 199), and used to construct the baths called 'Constantianae' at Constantinople. According to another interpretation, also given by Socrates (4.8.8) the bath was that built by the prefect of Constantinople Clearchus after the completion of the aqueduct of Valens, in what later became the forum of Theodosius; Zonaras, p. 80, calls it a Nymphaeum in the 'place called Taurus', i.e. the Forum of Theodosius, cf. R. Janin, *Constantinople Byzantine* (2nd ed., 1964), 64-8. The oracle refers (v. 1) to the time when nymphs would dance in the streets of the city, and (v. 3) to the reluctant 'guarding' of baths by a (former city?) wall.

45. F. Paschoud, in his note on Zosimus 4.26.6 (n. 154 at p. 389f.) is justly sceptical: 'la version d'Eunape-Zosime doit donc être ici rejetée comme complètement falsifiée.'

XI. The Office of Emperor

1. See esp. Sabine MacCormack, *Art and Ceremony in Late Antiquity* (1981), esp. 34-45; Ramsay MacMullen, 'Some pictures in Ammianus Marcellinus', *The Art Bulletin* 46 (1964), 435-55, at 438ff.; Larissa Warren Bonfante, 'Emperor, God and Man in the fourth century: Julian the Apostate and Ammianus Marcellinus', *Parola del Passato* 99 (1964), 401-27, at 412-16. Much of the essential formal evidence for the political and ceremonial position of the

emperors of the fourth century, with particular emphasis upon Ammianus, and on the military base of imperial power, is assembled by Louis Valensi, 'Quelques réflexions sur le pouvoir impérial d'après Ammien Marcellin', *Bull. de l'Association Guillaume Budé* 4.4 (1957), 62-107. There is an equivalent study of the terminology of the imperial office by J. Béranger, 'La terminologie impériale: une application à Ammien Marcellin', *Mél. Collart* (1976), 47-60.

2. For the dragon standards, see further Chapter XII, p. 260.

3. This passage is discussed by M. P. Charlesworth, 'Imperial deportment: two texts and some questions', *JRS* 37 (1947), 34-8; for the comparison with Ammianus, p. 36. Such conduct was prescribed for performing artists, according to Tacitus, *Ann.* 16.4 – a close and significant parallel; 'ingreditur theatrum [sc. Nero] cunctis citharae legibus obtemperans, ne fessus resideret, ne sudorem nisi ea quam indutui gerebat veste deterget, ut nulla oris aut narium excrementa viserentur'; cf. MacMullen, 439.

4. The connection between *adventus* and triumph is well shown by MacCormack, 36f. She is right to observe (at 41) that there was no actual triumph in 357, but a broader connection of adventus with victory; yet, since Ammianus viewed the event in a 'triumphal' context, this is clearly a possible perspective (or plausible distortion). The 'triumphal' aspects are given prominence also by Y.-M. Duval, 'La venue à Rome de l'empereur Constance II en 357, d'après Ammien Marcellin (XVI,10,1-20)', *Caesarodunum* 5 (1970), 299-304; while Domenico Vera, 'La polemica contro l'abuso imperiale del trionfo: rapporti fra ideologia, economia e propaganda nel Basso Impero', *Rivista Storica dell'Antichità* 10 (1980), 89-132, pursues the notion of the 'false triumph' that formed the basis of 'senatorial' criticism of the Roman emperors (cf. Symmachus, *Rel.* 9). It is an interesting article but makes too many assumptions as to the 'senatorial' affinities of the sources, including Ammianus and the Historia Augusta. The extreme complexity of Constantius' relations with Rome in 357, and the very partial nature of Ammianus' presentation of the situation, are well conveyed by R. Klein, 'Der Rombesuch des Kaisers Konstantius II im Jahre 357', *Athenaeum* 57 (1979), 98-115. Constantius' ceremonial comportment was in no way unusual (cf. Julian at Sirmium and Constantinople), and his visit achieved a great deal to secure the goodwill of the Roman senate and people at a time when their position was under challenge from various quarters, notably Constantinople and Milan.

5. Alan Cameron, *Claudian: poetry and propaganda at the court of Honorius* (1970), at 382ff., discusses Claudian's description in relation to those both of Ammianus and Pacatus; emphasising at 383f. the 'popularity' of conduct expected, in this setting, of an emperor. Ammianus criticised Julian for seeking indiscriminate 'popularitas'. There was a time and place for such conduct, cf. Warren Bonfante (cited above in n. 1), 417-19; see further pp. 236ff. and below, n. 9.

6. See on Pacatus' panegyric A. Lippold, 'Herrscherideal und Traditionsverbundenheit im Panegyricus des Pacatus', *Historia* 17 (1968), 228-50; and the recent translation, with selective commentary, by C. E. V. Nixon of Macquarie University (1987)

7. Alan Cameron, 'Theodosius the Great and the Regency of Stilicho', *HSCP* 73 (1968), at 262-4, argued that Claudian may have overlooked Constantius' visit in order to include in his count a second visit of Theodosius alleged by some sources in 394. This seems to me a very forced reading of Claudian's text (in which no emperor is actually named).

8. This well-known phenomenon is set in context by MacMullen, 'Roman bureaucratese', *Traditio* 18 (1962), 364-78, at 372. My favourite example is *CTh* 5.16.31 (of 408), referring to the time 'since the father of Our Clemency [sc. Theodosius] exchanged earthly for heavenly eternity [that is, he died]'; 'ex tempore, quo clementiae nostrae pater iam humanam in caelestem aeternitatem mutavit'!

9. R. C. Blockley, *Ammianus Marcellinus: a study of his historiography and political thought* (1975), ch. V (esp. 77) sets this passage in the context of imperial virtues and shortcomings. Julian's gesture in processing on foot is mentioned also by Mamertinus, in his consular panegyric of 362; *Pan. Lat.* 11.30 (ed. Galletier); cf. the translation by Marna Morgan, in S. N. C. Lieu (ed.), *The Emperor Julian: panegyric and polemic* (1986), pp. 33-4.

10. For the circumstances, Chapter IX, p. 193f.

11. This Sallustian allusion, by far the most conspicuous in Ammianus, is also found at Historia Augusta, *Claud.* 5.4; cf. Syme, *Ammianus and the Historia Augusta* (1968), 127-8.

Notes to pp. 237–48

It is relevant to the extent and purpose of literary allusions in Ammianus, cf. Chapter II.2, p. 32.

12. Olympiodorus, Frs. 23, 34 (Müller, *FHG* IV, p. 62). This is the case of Constantius III; cf. my 'Olympiodorus of Thebes and the history of the West', *JRS* 60 (1970), at 91.

13. For the (literary and other) relations between Ausonius and Valentinian, see my *Western Aristocracies*, at 51-4.

14. The biographical element in Ammianus is discussed in Chapter XVIII, pp. 459ff.; see also (on Julian), Chapter VI, p. 84.

15. The text of this passage is not quite secure, though its general sense seems clear; see Chapter XVIII, p. 459 with n. 18.

16. On the character of Ammianus' obituary notices and their relation to his narrative text, see the remarks of G. Sabbah, *La Méthode d'Ammien Marcellin*, 449-53. They enable Ammianus to summarise and intensify, but also to correct and add nuance to the impression given by his narrative, and in general to reinforce his objectivity.

17. See Chapter VI, p. 112f., and XVIII, p. 469.

18. For Ammianus' view of the influence of Petronius Probus, see Chapter XII, p. 277f.

19. Cf. Ammianus' judgment on the trials held after the fall of Procopius; Chapter IX, p. 202.

20. For Ursicinus' predicament, see Chapter III, p. 36 with n. 6; the death of Theodosius, Chapter X, p. 231 with n. 14.

21. Blockley (cited above in n. 9), ch. IX and Appendix F (pp. 191-3), discusses and classifies Ammianus' use of 'exempla'. S. A. Sterz, 'Ammianus Marcellinus' attitudes toward earlier emperors', in C. Derox (ed.), *Studies in Latin Literature and Roman History*, II (Coll. Latomus 168; 1980), 487-514, is a full but rather schematic survey, emphasising Ammianus' dependance on the existing literary tradition.

22. On the model of Julian, see Chapter XVIII, pp. 468ff., with p. 471 for Ammianus' admiration of sobriety and above all effectiveness in action ('efficacia').

23. There is a full study of the ritual of 'adoratio' by W. K. Avery, 'The Adoratio Purpurae and the importance of the Imperial Purple in the fourth century of the Christian era', *Memoirs of the American Academy in Rome*, 17 (1940), 66-80; cf. Meyer Reinhold, *History of Purple as a Status Symbol in Antiquity* (1970), ch. VI (pp. 62-70).

24. viz. Enmann's Kaisergeschichte (cf. Avery, 70f.); see Chapter II.2, p. 29 with n. 41.

25. The continuity of Roman ceremonial, whether from Roman or earlier oriental sources, was emphasised by A. Alföldi in his two studies, 'Die Ausgestaltung des monarchischen Zeremoniells am römischen Hof', and 'Insignien und Tracht der römischen Kaiser', *Röm. Mitt.* 49 (1934), 4-118 and 50 (1935), 3-158; both reprinted in *Die monarchische Repräsentation im römischen Kaiserzeit* (1970). As a matter of archaeology this may be true, but it does not represent the extent to which contemporaries perceived in the ceremonial of their own day a point of distinction from the past. There is a fine description of Sasanian etiquette and court ceremonial of the time of Chosroes (sixth century) by A. Christensen, *L'Iran sous les Sassanides* (2nd ed., 1944), 397ff.

26. These examples are among those cited by W. Ensslin, *Cambridge Ancient History* XII (1939), 361-2.

27. The cases mentioned are set out by Avery, 66f. (for that of Lucillianus, see Chapter VI, p. 105), and interpreted in the sense suggested at 68: 'That the privilege of kissing the purple was a mark of distinction and that its concession indicated that the emperor was well-disposed towards the individual whom he so honored is evident ...'.

28. For the cases mentioned, see the discussion of Ammianus' own promotion at Chapter V, p. 77. The insignia of the *Notitia Dignitatum*, Chapter XII, p. 255.

29. On this whole topic, Ramsay MacMullen's 'Some pictures in Ammianus Marcellinus' (cited above in n. 1) is a now classic study, with a splendid visual sense. See further Chapter XII, pp. 255ff.

30. MacMullen, 'Some pictures ...', at 446f.; for theatrical imagery, 453.

31. These two occasions are discussed by Sabine MacCormack (cited above in n. 1), at 46f. (Sirmium) and 28, cf. 62-3 (Autun). The reception of Theodosius at Emona in 388 is also notable; Pacatus, *Panegyric* 37, tr. Nixon (cited above in n. 6), at 45-6 – a vivid description.

32. The acclamations form part of the 'Gesta Senatus', printed at the beginning of

Mommsen and Meyer's edition of the *Codex Theodosianus* (Berlin, 1905), pp. 2-4. For acclamations in general, Charlotte Roueché, 'Acclamations in the later Roman Empire: new evidence from Aphrodisias', *JRS* 74 (1984), 181-99 – with a survey of their historical development; cf. the reference article by Th. Klauser, *RAC* I (1950), 216-33; MacMullen, 'Some pictures ...', 437f. See also Chapter XVI, p. 416 with n. 32.

33. Cf. Brian Campbell, 'Who were the "viri militares"?', *JRS* 65 (1975), 11-31; esp. his remarks at 14 and 27 on the co-existence of literary talent and careers in public (including military) service; also his fine book, *The Emperor and the Roman Army, 31 BC-AD 235* (Oxford, 1984), ch. VII.3 (pp. 325-48), on the persistence of an 'amateur' approach even to military command – a theme most interestingly pursued in his further article, 'Teach yourself how to be a general', *JRS* 77 (1987), 13-29. Such arguments could never be applied to the fourth century.

34. See for the process R. Syme, *Emperors and Biography: studies in the Historia Augusta* (Oxford, 1971), 179ff. (on the background of the Emperor Maximinus).

35. See my 'Ammianus and the Eternity of Rome', in Christopher Holdsworth and T. P. Wiseman (edd.), *The Inheritance of Historiography* (1986), at 20ff.; the theme is further pursued in Chapters XIII, p. 279f. and XVIII, p. 470f.

36. For this imagery and its antecedents see esp. A. Demandt, *Zeitkritik und Geschichtsbild im Werk Ammians* (1965), 118-47. Passages of the historian Florus and of Seneca (cited by Lactantius) speak of Rome's 'second childhood' or 'rejuvenation' under the emperors. This is not quite the same as Ammianus' notion of an inheritance passed on by the senate to the emperors.

37. For a more general application of the notion of 'legitimacy', Chapter VII, p. 128f.

38. Compare Ammianus' attitude to the trials following the suppression of Procopius, Chapter IX, p. 202. The trials of Scythopolis (19.12.1ff.) are described at Chapter X, p. 217f.

XII. The Character of Government

1. Ramsay MacMullen, *Roman Government's Response to Crisis* (1976) is a characteristically lively picture of the changing character of the imperial government before the challenge of this unprecedentedly critical period of Roman history. In a very different perspective, Peter Brown, *The Making of Late Antiquity* (1978), writes (at 48) of the replacement of the 'soft' government of the early empire by the 'hard' government of the fourth century, and T. D. Barnes, *The New Empire of Diocletian and Constantine* (1982) provides a thoroughly researched formal framework for the study of the new age.

2. For an instance of the difficulties inherent in excessive distance between government and periphery, cf. the relations between Constantius and Ursicinus in 359; Chapter III, p. 40f.

3. For this central feature of late Roman administration, Jones, *Later Roman Empire*, at 43ff., 101, etc.; for adaptability in practice, R. S. O. Tomlin, 'Notitia Dignitatum omnium, tam civilium quam militarium', in R. Goodburn and P. Bartholomew (edd.), *Aspects of the Notitia Dignitatum* (1976), 189-209, esp. 195ff.

4. Sabine MacCormack, *Art and Ceremony in Late Antiquity* (1981), 17ff., on the imperial 'adventus' in its ceremonial aspects. For the practical implications, Fergus Millar, *The Emperor in the Roman World* (1977), esp. 31-40.

5. The estimates are those of Jones, *The Later Roman Empire*, 584f. (tabulated at 583); and MacMullen, 'Imperial bureaucrats in the Roman provinces', *HSCP* 68 (1964), 305-16, at 307.

6. A. Chastagnol, *L'Album municipal de Timgad* (1978), 33-9, esp. 37ff., arguing that they are Timgad residents (the sons of decurions of the city) in the imperial service, listed on the Album to prevent their evading municipal obligations. Officials with property at Hermopolis, etc., MacMullen, 309.

7. On the *Notitia Dignitatum*, Robert Grigg, 'Portrait-bearing codicils in the illustrations of the *Notitia Dignitatum*', *JRS* 69 (1979), 107-24, well demonstrates the elaboration and (given the hazards of transmission of such a document) the consistency of the insignia shown; cf. the full and interesting study of Pamela C. Berger, *The Insignia of the Notitia Dignitatum* (1981).

8. *CTh* 9.7.6. The fuller version of this law, preserving the strident rhetoric of the original, is preserved in the so-called *Mosaicarum et Romanarum Legum Collatio*, 5.3 (in *FIRA*² II, p. 557); this is a compilation by an unknown hand of c. 400 comparing Roman and Biblical law on various subjects. The version preserved by this text is addressed to the same recipient as *CTh* 9.7.6, the *vicarius* of Rome Orientius, but was posted at a different public place in the city and at a slightly different date.

9. Ramsay MacMullen, 'Judicial savagery in the Roman Empire', *Chiron* 16 (1986), 147-66 traces the development: the cases cited are at 157f. See also his article, 'Some pictures in Ammianus Marcellinus', *Art Bulletin* 46 (1964), 435-55, at 452f. (with the phrase quoted, 'didactic symbolism').

10. P. A. Brunt, 'Evidence given under torture in the Principate', *ZSS* 97 (1980), 256-65. Late Roman penal practice in this and other respects is illuminated (if that is the word) by two studies: J. J. Arce, 'El historiador Ammiano Marcelino y la pena de muerte', *Hispania Antiqua* 4 (1974), 321-44: and Denise Grodzynski, 'Tortures mortelles et catégories sociales: les Summa Supplicia dans le droit romain au IIIe et IVe siècles', in *Du Châtiment dans la Cité: supplices corporels et peine de mort dans le Monde antique* (Coll. de l'école fr. de Rome 79; 1984), 361-403.

11. A. Alföldi, *A Conflict of Ideas*, esp. ch. III, conveys the atmosphere; 'Corruption and its antidote, terrorism'.

12. For Gallus and the curia of Antioch, Chapter XVI, pp. 406ff.; Eupraxius and the martyrs, Chapter XVII.2, p. 437, with n. 26 for the shrine of the 'Innocents'.

13. For Ambrose and Milan, see the brief account in my *Western Aristocracies*, 189-91.

14. This is the so-called 'Riot of the Statues', on which the clearest general accounts are P. Petit, *Libanius et la Vie Municipale*, 238-44, and Glanville Downey, *A History of Antioch*, 426-33. See also R. Browning, 'The riot of A.D. 387 in Antioch', *JRS* 42 (1952), 13-20 and Liebeschuetz, *Antioch*, 104-5, 164, 215, etc.

15. For the riot at Thessalonica, see (briefly) my *Western Aristocracies*, at 234-6.

16. On animal images, see esp. MacMullen, 'Some pictures in Ammianus Marcellinus' (cited above in n. 9), at 441-5; R. C. Blockley, *Ammianus Marcellinus: a study of his historiography and political thought* (1975), 25-7 with Appendix B, pp. 183-4; and J. Fontaine, 'Valeurs de vie et formes esthétiques dans l'Histoire d'Ammien Marcellin', in *Le Trasformazioni della Cultura nella tarda Antichità* (1985), 781-808, at 797 with n. 48; 'Le bestiaire réel et figuré d'Ammien mériterait une étude particulière ...'. There is a rather mechanical but still interesting survey of the philosophical background to the imagery by E. C. Evans, 'Roman descriptions of personal appearance in history and biography', *HSCP* 46 (1935), 43-84.

17. On heraldry, MacMullen, 441f.; Pamela Berger, *The Insignia of the Notitia Dignitatum*, 50-53 (rather an antiquarian discussion).

18. It is worth pausing a moment on the rhythm and sounds of this passage: 'hiatu vasto perflabiles' is a sequence of long syllables conveying the gaping mouths of the dragons and the steady blowing of the breeze; 'et ideo velut ira perciti sibilantes', a much more rapid rhythm, expresses the agitation of anger (with the alliteration of 'sibilantes'); 'caudarumque volumina relinquentes in ventum' conveys in the first two words the intricacy of the coiled tails of the dragons; and the last three words, with their concluding long syllables, evoke the floating effect of the wind, the final phrase after 'relinquentes' forming a sort of 'syntactical tail' to correspond with the trailing tails of the banners. For the dragon standards of Julian at Strasbourg, cf. 16.12.39. Julian is recognised in the battle 'per purpureum signum draconis, summitati hastae longioris aptatum'.

19. On these amphitheatre images (common also on mosaics and wall-paintings), MacMullen, 'Some pictures ...', 443.

20. The Emperor Galerius is also reported to have had fierce pet bears (Lactantius, *Mort. Pers.* 21.5-6), but that does not mean that Valentinian had none (cf. Moreau's note ad loc., *SChr* 39, 1954, pp. 327-8; 'l'élevage d'animaux féroces est un des charactères typiques de l'époque impériale finissante'!). For their names (it is in a way reassuring that only 16 bear names are mentioned, as against 480 names of racehorses), cf. Jocelyn Toynbee, 'Beasts and their names in the Roman Empire', *PBSR* 16 (1948), 24-37, at 36 (Simplicius and others at pl. X, fig. 30): Katherine Dunbabin, *The Mosaics of Roman North Africa: studies in*

iconography and patronage (1978), 72-4. Galerius used to ask for his bears by name ('nominatim') but Lactantius does not say what the names were. According to R. Weijenborg, 'Zum Text und zur Deutung von Ammianus, Römische Geschichte 29,3,9', *Klio* 57 (1975), 241-7, the (female) bears are coded ciphers, intended for the appreciation of the Roman aristocracy, signifying the Empresses Marina Severa and Justina, Ammianus intending to ridicule the family of Valentinian as 'ein plattfüssige Bärenfamilie' (243). It is an amusing idea, requiring however a less than conclusive emendation of the text, a date of composition after 395 (the daughter of Justina married Theodosius), an extraordinary degree of insight on the part of Ammianus' readers, and a total neglect of the understanding of future generations. I do not think that private jokes like this are part of Ammianus' manner, or consistent with what he would regard as proper historical exposition.

21. For Ammianus' attitude to treason and the law, see the conclusions to Chapter IX, pp. 201ff., and Chapter XI, pp. 250ff.

22. The standard treatment of this subject is by Peter Garnsey, *Social Status and Legal Privilege in the Roman Empire* (1970), esp. Parts II and IV; see also his brief treatment, 'Legal privilege in the Roman Empire', *Past and Present* 41 (1968), 3-24, and 'Why penal laws become harsher: the Roman case', *Natural Law Forum* 13 (1968), 141-62: to be read with Ramsay MacMullen's 'Judicial savagery in the Roman Empire' (cited above in n. 9). The abolition of crucifixion ('vetus teterrimumque supplicium patibulorum et cruribus suffringendis') is stated by Aurelius Victor, *Caesares* 41.4. In a similar spirit, a law of Constantine forbad branding on the face 'quo facies, quae ad similitudinem pulchritudinis caelestis est figurata, minime maculetur' (*CTh* 9.40.2, of 316).

23. On *fabricae*, Jones, *The Later Roman Empire*, 834-6; for the metalworkers at Antioch, Chapter XVI, p. 408.

24. The distribution of *fabricae* at the end of the fourth century is given at *Not. Dig., Or.* 11.18-39; *Occ.* 9.16-39; cf. Jones, *Later Roman Empire*, 834.

25. For the effect of imperial arms and other establishments on the economy of north Italy, see briefly my *Western Aristocracies*, at 183ff. – heavily dependent on the book of Lellia Ruggini, *Economia e Società nell'Italia Annonaria* (1961).

26. This is the 'banquet of Africanus' of Syme's *Ammianus and the Historia Augusta* (1968), ch. XII (pp. 66-8). The occasion, relevant to the fortunes of the young Julian, is referred to in his *Letter to the Athenians*, 273C-D; cf. Chapter VI, p. 85. In another dining incident, an Aquitanian noble house was ruined after the provocative arrangement, in the presence of an inquisitive 'veterator quidam', of a purple-bordered tablecloth so that it resembled the imperial insignia; cf. M. F. A. Brok, 'Majestätsfrevel durch Missbrauch des Purpurs (Ammianus Marcellinus, 16,8,8)', *Latomus* 41 (1982), 356-61 – rather indulgent in regarding it as 'ein an sich harmloser Scherz mit den kaiserlichen Insignien'. Members of noble families should know better than to make jokes like that. A 'veterator' is a crafty fellow, a character from New Comedy ('ein schlagfertiger Kerl' is Brok's translation); in this case, an *agent provocateur* of malicious intent. The *agentes in rebus* are often described as though they were a form of secret police, but their attested duties are more to do with the supervision of the *cursus publicus*; see the collection of material from Ammianus and other sources by Narciso Santos Yanguas, 'El servicio policial secreto romano en el Bajo Imperio según Ammiano Marcelino', *Memorias de Historia Antigua* 1 (1977), 127-39.

27. The Maratocupreni are viewed in their socio-economic setting in Chapter XV, p. 402.

28. MacMullen, 'Imperial bureaucrats in the Roman provinces' (cited above in n. 5), at 308-9 is good on Theophanes; he adduces the Maratocupreni (without naming them) at 315, n. 28. The dossier, which would benefit from a full historical study, is published by C. H. Roberts, in Roberts and Turner, *Catalogue of the Greek and Latin Papyri in the John Rylands Library, Manchester*, IV (1952), 104ff.

29. The mobility of late Roman emperors can be seen in the Prolegomena of Mommsen and Meyer's edition of the Theodosian Code (1905), Vol. I, pp. ccixff., and in Seeck's *Regesten der Kaiser und Päpste* (1919); cf. T. D. Barnes, *The New Empire of Diocletian and Constantine*, ch. V, 'Imperial residences and journeys' (a purely technical reconstruction). On the historical background, Fergus Millar, *The Emperor in the Roman World*, 28ff.

30. For the consistory and its functions, see (as always) Jones, *Later Roman Empire*, 333-41; summarising at 334-5 the dispatch of Ursicinus to Cologne in 355 (cf. Chapter III, p.

37). For the intervention of Eupraxius, Chapter XVII, p. 437.

31. For the scene, and Eutherius' role, Chapter VI, p. 83.

32. There is a difficulty with the readings of this passage. To give the essentials, Seyfarth's Teubner text offers 'nisi inter initia ut solent occupationis spe vel †impuniae quaedam sceleste committi'. The word 'initia' was inserted by Gelenius (V has 'inter ut'), Heraeus more radically supplied 'inter imperandi exordia'. For the corrupt '†impuniae', Gelenius offered 'impunite', others 'inpunitatis' or 'incuriae [*sc.* spe]'. The general sense seems clear enough, though 'inter initia' seems abrupt and incomplete. 'inter imperandi initia' might be better, were it not that Ammianus has said 'imperante eo' only a few words earlier. H. v. Looy, 'Ad Ammianum Marcellinum XXX.9.3: notule de critique textuelle', *L'Antiquité Classique* 35 (1960), 210-12, reads 'nisi inter <imperatoris> ut solent occupationes spe impunitatis', etc. This eliminates any specific reference to the beginning of the reign.

33. On patronage, see G. E. M. de Ste Croix, 'Suffragium: from vote to patronage', *British Journal of Sociology* 5 (1954), 33-47. R. I. Frank, 'Commendabiles in Ammianus', *AJP* 88 (1967), 309-18, is a narrower study than its title suggests. The term sometimes indicates military men who advanced through paternal influence (25.5.4; 30.7.4; 31.13.18); but I cannot at all see that it functions as a technical term denoting the rise of a new (military) class. Frank himself cites 19.1.10 (of a barbarian prince) and 29.2.16 (of an aristocrat).

34. For the circumstances of the appointment, see Chapter VI, p. 104. It has been supposed – e.g. by Thompson, *The Historical Work of Ammianus Marcellinus*, 80, that Ammianus' attitude reflects his obligation to and favour for the family of the orator Symmachus, but in view of Alan Cameron, 'The Roman friends of Ammianus', *JRS* 54 (1964), 15-28, esp. 19-20, this no longer seems likely.

35. For Theophanes' Latin letters written on his behalf, Roberts and Turner (cited above in n. 28), pp. 104; 113 (No. 623). They are identical letters in the same hand, but to different addressees; 'Domino suo Achillio (*or*, Delfinio) Vitalis'.

36. For Pannonians, Alföldi, *A Conflict of Ideas*, ch. II (esp. pp. 13-27), and my *Western Aristocracies*, 43-9. For the characterisation of Viventius, G. Sabbah, *La Méthode d'Ammien Marcellin*, 421, with n. 59; 'homme honnête et clairvoyant, en dépit de son origine pannonienne'. He is a case of a character whose personality contradicts the 'objective' indication used to introduce him.

37. The *Breviarium* may have been used by Ammianus for certain details of provincial organisation; Chapter XVIII, p. 458 with n. 15.

38. For Maximinus' alleged origin, cf. 28.1.5; 'a posteritate Carporum, quos antiquis excitos sedibus Diocletianus transtulit in Pannoniam'. A similar allegation, in language almost worthy of Ammianus, was made by Lactantius of the Emperor Galerius; 'inerat huic bestiae naturalis rabies, efferitas a Romano sanguine aliena: non mirum, cum mater eius Transdanuviana infestantibus Carpis in Daciam novam transiecto amne confugerat' (*Mort. Pers.* 9.2). Thompson, *The Historical Work of Ammianus Marcellinus*, ch. 6, argues that Ammianus criticised Maximinus so harshly because of his involvement in the execution in 376 of the *magister militum* Theodosius, under whose son Ammianus was composing his history. This is avowedly conjectural (Thompson, p. 106), and probably exaggerates the extent of political inhibition felt by Ammianus. See Chapter X, nn. 1 and 14.

39. For Gauls and Spaniards at the courts of Gratian and Valentinian II, see my *Western Aristocracies*, at 65ff., 94ff. Cappadocians under Valens, Barnim Treucker, *Politische und Sozialgeschichtliche Studien zu den Basilius-Briefen* (1961), 43-8, esp. 45f.; cf. *PLRE* I, s.v. Aburgius (p. 5), Caesarius 2 (pp. 169-70), Martinianus 5 (p. 564), Philagrius 5 (p. 694), Sophronius 3 (pp. 847-8: he occurs at Ammianus 26.7.2, cf. Chapter IX, p. 195 with n. 18), Soranus 3 (p. 848); perhaps also Candidianus 2 (p. 178f.). See also the relevant entries in M.-M. Hauser-Meury, *Prosopographie zu den Schriften Gregors von Nazianz* (1960), and for the social and educational background, P. Petit, *Les Etudiants de Libanius*, at 124-9 – producing 12 from Cappadocia, 16 from Galatia and 20 from Armenia.

40. *Western Aristocracies*, 48; 51-5 (on the 'faction' of Ausonius).

41. The evidence for this is from the middle books (V-IX) of Augustine's *Confessions*. Despite Peter Brown's marvellous *Augustine of Hippo: a biography* (1967), and Brent Shaw, 'The family in late antiquity: the experience of Augustine', *Past and Present* 115 (1987),

3-51, the exploitation of the *Confessions* as a document of social history has scarcely begun.

42. Augustine's characterisation of Ponticianus is interesting; 'civis noster, in quantum Afer, praeclare in palatio militans' (*Conf.* VIII.vi.14).

43. For what follows, see esp. Keith Hopkins' brilliant study, 'The political power of eunuchs', *Proceedings of the Cambridge Philological Society* 189 (1963), 62-80; revised in his *Conquerors and Slaves: sociological studies in Roman history*, I (1978), 172-96.

44. The phrase produced the classically humourless emendation, 'apud quem ... multa Constantius *posuit*'. This entirely wastes the force of Ammianus' 'si vere dici debeat': there is clearly a surprise to follow.

45. For Eusebius' activities, *PLRE* I, pp. 302-3 (Eusebius 11).

46. Hopkins (cited above in n. 43), at 181ff. Roger Tomlin, in his article cited above in n. 3, modifies the schematism of Hopkins' picture.

47. Compare, in a very different context, the technique of Symmachus' letters in handling differences of opinion; see my 'Symmachus and his enemies', in F. Paschoud (ed.), *Colloque Genevois sur Symmaque* 1984 (1986), at 175.

48. On the limitations of eunuchs' power, both in scope and duration, see (briefly) Hopkins, at 179-80.

49. L. J. Swift and J. H. Oliver, 'Constantius II on Flavius Philippus', *AJP* 82 (1962), 247-64. See for his connections *PLRE* I, Philippus 7 and 8; Simplicius 4 (with stemma 25, p. 1145): *PLRE* II, Anthemius 1 and 3, Isidorus 9, Theophilus 7 (with stemma 5, p. 1311).

50. On Probus, *PLRE* I, pp. 736-40 (Probus 5), with W. Seyfarth, 'Petronius Probus: Legende und Wirklichkeit', *Klio* 52 (1970), 411-25, arguing that Ammianus' portrayal of Probus is a hostile caricature for reasons to do with his political affiliations at the court of Valentinian and possibly also with his religion – which I doubt: cf. the criticisms of Seyfarth offered by H. Drexler, *Ammianstudien* (1974), 74-8; Alan Cameron, 'Polynomy in the late Roman aristocracy: the case of Petronius Probus', *JRS* 75 (1985), 164-82 – with an Appendix (178-82) on his prefectures, to which Symmachus may be referring in his phrase, 'ament alii perpetuas potestates!' (*Rel.* 10.3).

51. There is some uncertainty about the text at this point. Seyfarth reads 'absque praefecturis, quas iurgiis familiarum ingentium capessere cogebatur'. 'iurgiis' is Henry de Valois' suggestion for 'iurgi' of V; others, including Gelenius and a contemporary correction to E (fifteenth century), suggest 'ob iurgia'. I am still attracted by the reading, suggested to me some years ago by Robert Ireland, of 'instantium' for V's 'ingentium'. Probus was forced into office by the quarrels – that is, the litigation, as at *CTh* 2.8.1 – of the importunate ('instantium') families to which he belonged.

52. For a case in point, Symmachus, *Rel.* 28; translated with some comment by R. H. Barrow, *Prefect and Emperor* (1973), 153-61.

53. The extent of Probus' maladministration of Illyricum is mentioned also by Jerome (himself a Dalmatian); *Chron.*, s.a. 372 (ed. Helm, *GCS*, p. 246). For the long-term ascendancy of the landed aristocracy, see the later chapters of my *Western Aristocracies and Imperial Court*, fortified by the welcome remarks of John Mann, *JRS* 69 (1979), at 183.

XIII. The Practice of War

1. Among general books on this subject I have found most useful G. A. Crump, *Ammianus Marcellinus as a Military Historian* (1975) and N. J. E. Austin, *Ammianus on Warfare: an investigation into Ammianus' military knowledge* (1979). K. Rosen, *Studien zur Darstellungskunst und Glaubwürdigkeit des Ammianus Marcellinus* (1970) emphasises the role of rhetoric in Ammianus' descriptions, cf. Norbert Bitter, *Kampfschilderungen bei Ammianus Marcellinus* (1976); and G. Sabbah, *La Méthode d'Ammien Marcellin*, esp. 572-88, studies the structural patterns of Ammianus' narrative. C. P. T. Naudé, 'Battles and sieges in Ammianus Marcellinus', *Acta Classica* I (1958; publ. 1959), 92-105 produces a well-judged balance of rhetorical and circumstantial elements in Ammianus' narrative. E. W. Marsden's two books on Roman artillery and its uses are invaluable: *Greek and Roman Artillery: historical development* (1969), and especially *Greek and Roman Artillery:*

technical treatises (1971); and I mention with particular warmth John Keegan's book *The Face of Battle* (1976). It does not discuss Ammianus, nor ancient warfare in general, but has many relevant observations on the historiography of war, and provides a rivetting imaginative introduction to the actual experience of battle. In that sense he is very close to Ammianus.

2. The 'embattled system' of empire known to Ammianus is described by A. H. M. Jones, *The Later Roman Empire*, ch. XVII (Vol. II, pp. 607-86), and in the monumental book by Dietrich Hoffmann, *Das Spätrömische Bewegungsheer und die Notitia Dignitatum* (Epigraphische Studien 7; two vols., 1969-70). For a brief but very knowledgeable account, Roger Tomlin, 'The army of the late Empire' in J. S. Wacher (ed.), *The Roman World* (1987), I, 107-35.

3. For Vergil's prophecy as a 'proud claim, but a fearful renunciation', Jasper Griffin, *Virgil* (1986), 90-1.

4. See the famous remark in *Decline and Fall*, ch. III (ed. Bury, I, 77); 'Antoninus diffused order and tranquillity over the greatest part of the earth. His reign is marked by the rare advantage of furnishing very few materials for history; which is, indeed, little more than the register of the crimes, follies, and misfortunes of mankind'.

5. Chapter IV, p. 66. The trials of Chalcedon are discussed in terms of a conflict between 'civil' and 'military' interests by E. A. Thompson, *The Historical Work of Ammianus Marcellinus*, 73-9. It certainly seems a justified view in the case of Ursulus.

6. Ch. Saumagne, 'Un Tarif fiscal au IVe siècle de notre ère', *Karthago* 1 (1950), 105-200, esp. 153-8. For billetting of soldiers as a form of taxation, Jones, *The Later Roman Empire*, II, 631-2.

7. B. H. Warmington, 'The career of Romanus, comes Africae', *BZ* 9 (1956), 55-64 provides the resources for a reconstruction; cf. Chapter XV, pp. 383ff.

8. For some material on Valentinian's military policies, see my *Western Aristocracies*, at 33; esp. H. von Petrikovits, 'Fortifications in the north-western Roman empire from the third to the fifth centuries A.D.', *JRS* 61 (1971), 178-218, at 184-6. A most interesting recent archaeological discovery is of a group of the river-boats used for patrolling the Rhine; O. Höckmann, 'Rheinschiffe aus der Zeit Ammians: neue Funde in Mainz', *Antike Welt* 13.3 (1982), 40-7 – narrow boats built for speed, about 18 m long with a length-breadth ratio of nearly 7:1, a single mast towards the bow and about 13 oars each side.

9. Examples of this emphasis are Dietrich Hoffmann's *Spätrömische Bewegungsheer* (cited above in n. 2); W. Ensslin, 'Zum Heermeisteramt des spätrömischen Reiches', *Klio* 24 (1930), 102-47. A well-balanced corrective is the monograph of G. A. Crump (cited above in n. 1) and his article, 'Ammianus and the late Roman army', *Historia* 22 (1973), 91-103.

10. Symmachus' visit to court in 369-70 is described in my *Western Aristocracies*, at 32f., and in 'The Letters of Symmachus', at 75-6.

11. E. W. Marsden, *Greek and Roman Artillery: technical treatises* (1971).

12. Cf. Crump, *Ammianus Marcellinus as a Military Historian*, 97-113, 'Sieges'. For the narrative patterns of Ammianus' sieges, Sabbah, *La Méthode d'Ammien Marcellin*, 579-82, 585-8. It is in respect of his military narratives that Ammianus' literary techniques have tended to attract adverse, or at least critical, comment; cf. L. Dautremer, *Ammien Marcellin: étude d'histoire littéraire* (1899), e.g. at 47, 116ff.; J. Vogt, 'Ammianus Marcellinus als erzählender Geschichtsschreiber der Spätzeit', *Abhandlungen der Akademie der Wissenschaften und der Literatur in Mainz* (1963), at 815-17; and many other works. That Ammianus used literary devices is of course obvious; the question is, what inference to draw from this.

13. David Potter has observed to me that there is a difficulty with Ammianus' account, in that Sapor appears not to have attacked Antioch and Carrhae in any single campaign. If found at Carrhae, the ram was probably used against that city and not, as Ammianus claims, against Antioch. The historian may well have been confused, for his knowledge even of local third-century history was apparently nothing special; cf. Chapters II.2, p. 29f. with n. 40 and VIII.3 n. 84 (p. 505 above).

14. The episode has implications for Ammianus' religious attitudes, see Chapter XVII, p. 436.

15. For artillery and its uses, see Crump, at 101-7 and Marsden, *Greek and Roman*

Artillery: historical development, esp. 195-8 on the late empire, and *Technical treatises*, 234-54 on Ammianus' digression and contemporary sources. Add two articles by M. F. A. Brok: 'Bombast oder Kunstfertigkeit: Ammians Beschreibung der ballista', *RhM* 120 (1977), 331-46, noting that even a contemporary would have found Ammianus' description of this device anything but clear; and, with a similar observation on the fire-arrow (23.4.14), 'Ein spätrömische Brandpfeil nach Ammianus', *Saalburg Jahrbuch* 35 (1978), 57-60.

16. Marsden, *Technical treatises*, 254-65 (262 for the performance cited in the text) describes the construction and operation of a modern 'scorpion'.

17. The construction of an emplacement is shown on Trajan's Column; C. Cichorius, *Die Reliefs des Traianssäule* (1896), I, Taf. LXVI (scenes 165-7); cf. (less clear) Lino Rossi, *Trajan's Column and the Dacian Wars* (1971) and (a detail) Marsden, *Technical treatises*, pl. 12.

18. Marsden, 260, describes this mishap.

19. Marsden's interpretation, at 262, of 'sublimis' as referring metaphorically to the rank of the officer in charge ('standing loftily beside it') seems to me frankly impossible.

20. For siege-towers, Marsden, at 84ff., commenting on the treatise of Biton, translated at 70-3. The tower built by Demetrius Poliorcetes is described at 84-5.

21. The technical inferiority of barbarians is well characterised by E. A. Thompson, 'Economic warfare', in *Romans and Barbarians* (1982), 3-19, esp. 6-10.

22. On the battle of Hadrianople, Crump, at 91-6, and T. S. Burns, 'The battle of Hadrianople: a reconsideration', *Historia* 22 (1973), 336-45, offer sensible analyses without surpassing the range of Ammianus' own account. The strategic background is discussed by Austin (cited in n. 27 below).

23. For the battlefield of Strasbourg, J. J. Hatt and J. Schwartz, 'Le champ de bataille de Oberhausbergen (357-1262)', *Bull. de la Faculté de Lettres de Strasbourg* 42 (1964), 427-30. On Ammianus' narrative, R. C. Blockley, 'Ammianus Marcellinus on the battle of Strasbourg: art and analysis in the History', *Phoenix* 31 (1977), 218-31, points to the rhetorical patterns that are used to reflect the (differing) outcome of the battles; it is not merely an observation about literary technique to note that precisely those Roman virtues of fortitude and discipline that were decisive at Strasbourg, were lacking at Hadrianople. Julian's own conduct at Strasbourg is the starting point for Jacque Fontaine's characteristically wide-ranging article, 'Un cliché de la spiritualité antique tardive: *stetit immobilis*', in G. Wirth (ed.), *Romanitas-Christianitas: Untersuchungen ... Johannes Straub zum 70 Geburtstag gewidmet* (1982), 528-52. (The allusion is to Amm. 16.12.3).

24. For Cornuti and Bracchiati as a pair of units, cf. *Not. Dig., Occ.* 5.14-15 = 158-59, with Hoffmann, *Spätrömische Bewegungsheer*, 133f. ('Schwestertruppe'). For 'Regii' (rather than 'Regenses'), *Not. Dig., Occ.* 5.80 = 229, *Or.* 6.8 = 49. The Batavi are not (or are no longer) found with them; *Not. Dig., Occ.* 5.19 = 163, *Or.* 5.34 = (58) = 186.

25. The literary characterisations of Ammianus' battles are analysed by G. Sabbah, *La Méthode d'Ammien Marcellin*, at 572ff. (note esp. the theatrical metaphor at 16.12.57; p. 297). For Strasbourg, Sabbah, 72-9; Hadrianople, 583-4. Cf. my comments at nn. 12, 15, and 23 above.

26. N. J. E. Austin, *Ammianus on Warfare*, 56-60 presents Julian's actions in 357 in this perspective. Jacques Fontaine, 'Le Julien d'Ammien Marcellin', in R. Braun and J. Richer (edd.), *L'Empereur Julien: de l'histoire à la légende* (331-1715) (1978), at 50, is of the same opinion, ascribing Julian's conduct to his 'levitas'. Contrast his actual conduct at Strasbourg: above, n. 23.

27. N. J. E. Austin, *Ammianus on Warfare*, 72-80, and 'Ammianus' account of the Adrianople campaign: some strategic observations', *Acta Classica* 15 (1972), 77-83 discusses Valens' policy in 378 in light of the quality of the information available to the high command. Roman policy towards the Goths in 376-8 is further discussed at Chapter XIV.1, pp. 327ff.

28. For Ammianus as an 'artilleryman', see E. A. Thompson, *The Historical Work of Ammianus Marcellinus*, 11 – referring also to Mackail, in *JRS* 10 (1920), 104, which is worth quoting; 'From his knowledge of machine-guns(!) and the evident interest he takes in them, it seems that he may have acted as an artillery officer'; cf. 112 on the digression. Better are Crump, *Ammianus Marcellinus as a Military Historian*, 12, arguing that

Ammianus 'displays no unusual competence in the subject' and, still more forceful, Marsden, describing Ammianus' phrase 'ne dissiliat' in his description of the scorpion (23.4.4) as 'ridiculous' (*Technical treatises*, 252). For R. C. Blockley (cited in n. 23 above), at 230, Ammianus' whole excursus is 'incomprehensible', either through incompetence or (more likely) as a 'failed attempt to encompass the subject without admitting the unseemly minutiae which everywhere he is at such pains to avoid'; even so, it is surely rather a matter of the avoidance of technical language. For the descriptions of the *helepolis, ballista* and *scorpio* see above, pp. 291ff. As M. F. A. Brok (1977; n. 15 above) remarks, Ammianus, though no expert, would have a reasonable working knowledge of the subject, at least to the extent of the deployment of the machines. This at least emerges from the narrative of the siege of Amida.

29. This was argued (e.g.) by L. Dillemann, 'Ammien Marcellin et le pays de l'Euphrate et du Tigre', *Syria* 38 (1961), 87-158, esp. 95f., 143.

30. That Ammianus was involved in the collecting and interpretation of intelligence is the thesis of N. J. E. Austin (who does not overstate it). I acknowledge with pleasure what I have learned from conversations on this subject with Norman Austin, and similarly with Doug Lee, of Trinity College, Cambridge (now of the University of Auckland).

31. Ammianus' presence at Bezabde in 360 was accepted by Thompson, *The Historical Work of Ammianus Marcellinus*, at 11, 36f.; contrast Dillemann (cited above in n. 29), 94-5, 104. I do not believe that Ammianus' presence at Bezabde is apparent from his writing, nor indeed that his career prospered at all after the dismissal of Ursicinus early in the year (p. 46f.; cf. Crump, 10f.)

XIV. Barbarians and Bandits

1. E. A. Thompson, *A Roman Reformer and Inventor* (1952); the translated passage is at pp. 113-14. Cf. Alan Cameron, 'The date of the Anonymous', in M. W. C. Hassall and R. Ireland (edd.), *Aspects of the De Rebus Bellicis: papers presented to Professor E. A. Thompson* (BAR Intern. Series 63, 1979), 1-10. The 'clementissimi principes' must be Valentinian and Valens, but I am not sure that Cameron has conclusively shown Valens rather than Valentinian to be the actual recipient of the treatise. For its survival as part of a late Roman archive (containing also the *Notitia Dignitatum*), see Thompson, 14: my *Western Aristocracies and Imperial Court*, 49. There is a new Teubner text of the Anonymous by Robert Ireland (1984); cf. his text, with translation and discussion, in Part 2 of the BAR volume mentioned above. The basic alternatives available to the Romans, between the direct and sustained assertion of military ascendancy over the barbarians (the policy of Julian) and the more accommodating policy of the negotiation of settlements with them (that of Constantius) are set in the context of their respective 'ideological' justifications by Edmond Frézouls, 'Les deux politiques de Rome face aux barbares d'après Ammien Marcellin', in Frézouls (ed.), *Crise et redressement dans les provinces européennes de l'Empire: Actes du Colloque du Strasbourg* (1983), 175-97.

2. The most telling of the Anonymous' 'inventions' is a *ballista* capable of firing a bolt across the Danube (18.5; Thompson, p. 120f.), concluding that 'the Ballista Fulminalis will be the guardian of your happy frontiers ("felicium limitum custos") ...' (Thompson, 121).

3. This is to refrain from pursuit of Jerome's allegation (based, he claims, on autopsy when he was a young man in Gaul) that the Attacotti indulged in cannibalism: *Adv. Iovinianum* 2.7 (*PL* 23.308-9); cf. R. Syme, *Ammianus and the Historia Augusta*, 19. Since I do not discuss Ammianus' accounts of Roman relations with Sarmatians and Quadi, I should refer to the recent published dissertation of Ursula-Barbara Dittrich, *Die Beziehungen Roms zu den Sarmaten und Quaden im vierten Jahrhundert n. Chr* (nach der Darstellung des Ammianus Marcellinus) (1984); cf. esp. her descriptions of the lifestyles respectively of the Sarmatians (19-25; sedentarised, but still showing traces of their nomadic origins) and Quadi (47-52; a typically sedentary Germanic folk).

(1) Farmers: Alamanni and Goths

4. On the Alamanni I owe much to conversation with and the unpublished work of my colleague, Dr Roger Tomlin of Wolfson College, Oxford, and to discussion with Dr John Hind

of Leeds University. There is an excellent survey of Alamannic settlement by J. Werner, 'Zu den alamannischen Burgen des 4. und 5. Jahrhunderts', in *Speculum Historiale: Festschrift für Johannes Spörl* (1965), 439-53; reprinted in Wolfgang Müller (ed.), *Zur Geschichte der Alamannen* (Wege der Forschung, Band C, 1975), 67-90; in the same volume, at 20-48, is printed K. F. Stroheker, 'Die Alamannen und der spätrömische Reich'. A magnificent inventory of the archaeological evidence is given by R. Roeren, 'Zur Archäologie u. Geschichte Sudwestdeutschlands im 3 bis 5 Jahrhundert n. Chr.', *Jahrbuch der römisch-germanischen Zentralmuseums, Mainz*, 7 (1960), 214-94. W. Veeck, *Die Alamannen in Württemberg* (1931), gives a generous and comprehensible sample of illustrations of artefacts. On Germanic society generally E. A. Thompson, *The Early Germans* (1965) is a typical combination of interpretative insight and vivacity. Alamannic and Gothic society are mutually illuminating, and my two sections should be taken together.

5. For the possible connection between 'Agri Decumates' and the 'Decem Pagi' of later sources (including Ammianus), see J. G. F. Hind, 'Whatever happened to the Agri Decumates?', *Britannia* 15 (1984), 187-92. For the Gothic occupation of Dacia, see this Chapter, pp. 318, 322.

6. 'The Ruin' is translated by Richard Hamer, *A Choice of Anglo-Saxon Verse* (1970), 25-9: and interpreted by Barry Cunliffe, 'Earth's grip holds them', in Brian Hartley and John Wacher (edd.), *Rome and her Northern Provinces (Papers presented to Sheppard Frere)* (1983), 67-83.

7. The stories retold here are taken from Thomas Hodgkin's early survey, *The Pfahlgraben* (1882; also in *Archaeologia Aeliana* n.s. 9, 1883, 73-161); attributed to a source of 1723. See for a more modern description of the same attitude to 'one of the most prodigious technical achievements of early Roman times', J. v. Elbe, *Roman Germany* (2nd ed., 1977), 243ff. (s.v. Limes), at 249.

8. Ed. Norden, *Alt-Germanien: Volker- und Namengeschichtliche Untersuchungen* (1934), 5-23, argued that the boundary in question is that between the Romans (not the Alamanni) and the Burgundians, reading at 18.2.15 (with MSS support), 'ubi terminales lapides Romanorum et Burgundiorum confinia distinguebant'; the reading was adopted by Seyfarth in his ed. of 1968 (cf. n. 32 at p. 176), and his Teubner text of 1978. But the geography of this interpretation is difficult to visualise; how did the Romans, beginning near Mainz (18.2.7), burn and pillage their way through Alamannic territory and come to their own frontiers with the Burgundians? Norden's arguments from the generally 'non-artificial' nature of Germanic frontiers are met in my text.

9. The significance of 'Palas' and 'Capellatii' is also disputed; cf. the extensive discussion of Norden, 85-136, arguing (surely inconclusively) that 'Palas' is the older form of a pair of names ('Doppelnamen') for the same place. 'Palas' would be pre-Celtic, while 'Capellatii' would be the (presumed) local name of an erstwhile Gallo-Roman 'gens'; see also Sabbah in his Budé edition of Ammianus Book 18, n. 147 at pp. 191-2. This is all too speculative. I also find unpersuasive Sabbah's view that the border in question is the original boundary between Romans and Burgundians, Alamannic occupation of the area between them being regarded by Ammianus (and Julian) as intermittent and without 'legal' title. Ammianus is describing the real world, not a legal fiction, and I remain of the view that the boundary is that between the Alamanni and Burgundians (cf. 28.5.11, where they are are said to fight 'salium finiumque causa'). The location is clearly somewhere 'am Ostrande des Decumanengebiets' (Norden, 136).

10. For the villa at Ebel bei Praunheim see Werner (cited above in n. 4), 77-8 (with plan at 76).

11. For 'burgus' see A. Ernout, A. Maillet, J André, *Dictionnaire étymologique de la langue latine* (4th ed., 1979), 78, where it is assigned a 'Germanic' origin. The word was however already in use in the late second century (*ILS* 395, cf. 8913, 5849), and others assign to it a Greek etymology (from *purgos*); E. Penninck, 'L'origine hellénique de burgus', *Latomus* 4 (1940/5), 5-21: *Thesaurus Linguae Latinae* 2.2250 (Ihm).

12. C. Caprino and others, *La Colonna di Marco Aurelio* (Rome, 1955), Tav. XIV 29, Scene xx (Taf. 28 in Domaszewski's edition). See also Scenes vii, xlvi, lxxi, cii and, on Trajan's Column, Cichorius, *Die Reliefs des Traianssäule* (1896), Scenes xxvi, lix, cxix, clii – though some of the latter are more like cities than country villages.

Notes to pp. 312–18 525

13. For the hill-fort of Glauberg see Werner, 'Zu den alamannischen Burgen' (cited above in n. 4), 84-9, with map at 86. For this and the other locations mentioned, see Map 6 (based in this respect on Werner, 82).

14. Slaving was characteristic also of Roman relations with the Goths; cf. this Chapter, p. 326f.

15. Despite the reservations reported by Seyfarth ad loc. (Vol. IV, pp. 334, n. 139), it is hard to doubt that *hendinos* is connected with Gothic 'kindins', 'ruler', used in the Gothic Gospels of Pontius Pilate, more generally of the Roman governor (Mt. 27:2, Luke 20:20, cf. 2:2), 'Sinistus' (pl. 'sinistans') is used of the elders (*presbuteroi*) in the phrase 'chief priests and elders' (Mt. 27:1, 3; Mk. 8:31). It is the superlative formed from 'sineigs', 'old' (cf. Lat. 'senex').

16. For Gothic 'comb-factories' in occupied Moldavia, see this Chapter, p. 322.

17. 'No Germanic institution has a longer history [than the *Gefolgschaft*]'; F. M. Stenton, *Anglo-Saxon England* (3rd ed., 1971), 302. Stenton's description is very close to Ammianus: 'the sanctity of the bond between lord and man, the duty of defending and avenging a lord, the disgrace of surviving him ...', cf. 16.12.60; 'flagitium arbitrati post regem vivere vel pro rege non mori, si ita tulerit casus, tradidere se vinciendos'.

18. For the role of Vadomarius in defending Constantius' interests during the usurpation of Julian, see Chapter VI, p. 104.

19. There is an excellent, fully illustrated account of Germanic archaeological penetration of the north-eastern Roman provinces in this period by H. W. Böhme, *Germanische Grabfunde des 4. bis 5. Jahrhunderts, zwischen unterer Elbe und Loire: Studien zur Chronologie und Bevölkerungsgeschichte* (2 vols., 1974); see esp. pp. 166-207, with excellent plates and maps. For the various patterns of recruitment and promotion of well-born barbarians in the Roman armies, see esp. D. Hoffmann, 'Wadomar, Bacurius und Hariulf; zur Laufbahn adliger und fürstlicher Barbaren im spätrömischen Heere des 4. Jahrhunderts', *Mus. Helv.* 35 (1978), 307-18.

20. For the low risks of disloyalty, A. H. M. Jones, *The Later Roman Empire*, II, 621-3; K. F. Stroheker, 'Zur Rolle der Heermeister frankischer Abstammung im späten vierten Jahrhundert', *Historia* 4 (1955), 314-30, reprinted in his *Germanentum und Spätantike* (1965), 9-29.

21. The vicissitudes experienced by Vadomarius and Macrianus (and others) in their transition to Roman service are well discussed by Hoffmann (cited above in n. 19), at 308-10.

22. The history of the Goths is covered in two studies by E. A. Thompson, describing respectively the periods before and after the crossing of the Danube in 376: *The Visigoths in the Time of Ulfila* (1966), and 'The Visigoths from Fritigern to Euric', *Historia* 12 (1963), 105-26; repr. in his *Romans and Barbarians* (1982), 38-57. Of these studies, the former concentrates more on material culture and social organisation, the latter more on political history. The comprehensive account of Herwig Wolfram, *Geschichte der Goten, von den Anfängen bis zur Mitte des sechsten Jahrhunderts: Entwurf einer historischen Ethnographie*, has now appeared in an English translation, as *History of the Goths* (tr. & rev. Thomas J. Dunlap from the 2nd German ed. of 1979; Berkeley, Los Angeles & London, 1988); for a brief survey, H.-J. Diesner, *The Great Migration: the movement of peoples across Europe, A.D. 300-700* (Eng. tr. by C. S. V. Salt, London, 1982), 90-123, is clear and well illustrated. The archaeological material from sites in modern Romania is surveyed in two articles in the volume edited by Miron Constantinescu, *Relations between the Autochthonous Population and the Migratory Populations in the Territory of Romania* (Bibliotheca Historica Romaniae, Monographs 16, 1975); they are by Ion Ioniţă, 'The social-economic structure of society during the Goths' migration in the Carpatho-Danubian area', at 77-89, and Gheorghe Diaconu, 'On the socio-economic relations between natives and Goths in Dacia', at 67-75; see also Ioniţă, 'Contributions à la connaissance de la civilisation de Sîntana de Mureş-Tchernéakhov sur le territoire de la Roumanie', in *Arheologia Moldovei* 4 (1966), 189-259 (in Romanian; French summary at 252-7). For more detailed archaeological reports, see, on the Romanian material, B. Mitrea and C. Preda, *Necropole din secolul al IV-lea e.n. in Muntenia* (with French summary; Bucharest, 1966), G. Diaconu, *Tîrgşor: Necropola din secolele III-IV e.n.* (with German summary; Bucharest, 1965), Cătălina Bloşiu, 'Necropola din secolul al IV-lea e.n. de la Leţcani (iud. Iaşi)',

Arheologia Moldovei 8 (1975), 203-80; and on the Russian, B. E. Rybakov (ed.), 'Chernyakhovskaya Kultura', *Materialy i Issledovniya po Arkheologii SSSR* 82 (1960). All are well illustrated, and the similarity of the Sîntana de Mureș and Chernyakov material seems evident. T. S. Burns, *A History of the Ostrogoths* (1984), discusses the early history of the people known to Ammianus as the Greuthungi, with brief reference to the archaeological material at 23f., 35. An important book on the Goths by Peter Heather, of Worcester College, Oxford, will be published shortly; among many other contributions, Heather shows that the 'Visigoth-Ostrogoth' division among the Gothic peoples, almost universal in modern writing about them, is essentially the creation of their sixth-century historian, Jordanes, and is anachronistic for the fourth century. Jordanes is translated with some commentary by C. C. Mierow, *The Gothic History of Jordanes* (1915; repr. 1966); for the Latin text, see Mommsen's edition in *MGH, auct. ant.*, V.1. *The Passion of St. Saba* was published with other material by H. Delehaye, 'Saints de Thrace et de Mésie', *Analecta Bollandiana* 31 (1912), 161-300, at 216-21 and (for comment) 274-91; also in G. Krüger, *Ausgewählte Martyrerakten* (4th ed., 1965), No. 33 (pp. 119-24). The text will be translated and commented, with other material, by Peter Heather and myself, in a book to be published by Liverpool University Press in the series Translated Texts for Historians. For a general account of the archaeological context, see Malcolm Todd, *The Barbarians: Goths, Franks and Vandals* (1972, repr. 1980); also his *The Northern Barbarians, 100 B.C.-A.D. 300* (1975). The emphasis of S. Teillet, *Des Goths à la Nation Gothique: les origines de l'idée de nation en Occident du Ve au VIIe siècle* (1984), is rather different, and the chronological focus later, than are directly relevant to this book.

23. See for the historical framework Thompson, *The Visigoths in the Time of Ulfila*, ch. 1 (pp. 1-23).

24. The location of Daphne is set at Pîrjoaia, 26/7 km downstream of Durostorum (Silistra), by P. Diaconu, 'În căutarea Dafnei (A la recherche de Dafné)', *Pontica* 4 (1971), 311-18 (with French and German summaries at 318). For the mountain range named by Ammianus, see Matei Cazacu, ' "Montes Serrorum" (Ammianus Marcellinus XXVII,5,3). Zur Siedlungsgeschichte der Westgoten in Rumanien', *Dacia* 16 (1972), 299-301, connecting the name with the modern designation, Siriul, of a mountain range in the Buzau region. Peter Heather, in his forthcoming book and in his article 'The crossing of the Danube and the Gothic conversion', *Greek, Roman and Byzantine Studies* 27 (1986), 289-318, argues that the settlement of 369 was not a total triumph for Valens, since he was unable to force Athanaric to cross to the Rome side for the agreement, which was compacted on a boat in the middle of the Danube. This rather depends on the extent to which Valens may have seen advantage in humouring his antagonist, or in rescuing him from the humiliation of defeat in order to keep him in power as a (relatively) docile client. One would not argue that Valentinian's crossing of the Rhine to meet Macrianus in 374 (30.3.4f.) was a sign of his submission to the German. Ammianus indicates on that occasion that a Roman campaign would have been preferable, but that both sides wanted an agreement.

25. This characterisation of the Gothic occupation of the Carpathian region is derived from the article of Ioniță (1975), and its chronological sequence from Diaconu, at 67f. (for both refs. see n. 22 above). A trace of the Roman evacuation of Dacia is found in Ammianus, in the background of Maximinus of Sopianae (28.1.5); above, Chapter XII, n. 38.

26. The comb workshops are described in articles by V. Palade: for instance 'Atelierele pentru lucrat piepteni din os din secolul al IV-lea e.n. de la Bîrlad-Valea Seacă', *Arheologia Moldovei* 4 (1966), 261-77; cf. Ioniță (1975), 79 nn. 4-5 for this and other references.

27. For a summary of the Passion of St. Saba, Thompson, *The Visigoths in the Time of Ulfila*, ch. 3, pp. 64-77; 'The Passion of St. Saba and village life'.

28. This passage is picked up by Thompson, 53, as indicating that 'sharp divisions of wealth had put an end to the general equality of the tribesmen' – wealth is associated in the chief's mind with power, but Saba had none. Whether this is so or not, the passage certainly suggests the villagers' reluctance to persecute one of their own number under orders from outside the community.

29. Cf. Tacitus, *Germania* 12.1, 'ignavos et imbelles et corpore infames caeno ac palude, iniecta super crate, mergunt', and the bodies of victims recovered in modern times from bogs. Another circumstantial detail may be the pestle mentioned at *Passio* 6.4, reminiscent

of the fire-hardened clubs hurled by Goths at the battle of ad Salices (31.7.13)

30. These agglomerations are mentioned by Diaconu (cited in n.22 above), at 73f., and brought into connection with the Pietroasa Treasure, presumably a Gothic royal, or at least aristocratic, possession. See on the treasure Radu Harhoiu (tr. N. Hampartumian), *The Fifth-Century A.D. Treasure from Pietroasa, Romania, in the light of recent research*, BAR Suppl. Series 24 (1977). Despite the title of this work, the fourth century is a possible date for the treasure.

31. On Ermenrich/Hermanaric, T. S. Brown, *A History of the Ostrogoths*, 37f.

32. For 'iudex/dikastês' as a technical term, Themistius, *Or*. 10.134c-d, and the *Letter* of Auxentius of Durostorum, 58 (ed. R. Gryson, *SChr* 267 (1980), p. 246-7; *PL* Suppl. 1.706); Thompson, 44ff.

33. Burns, at 38, offers this suggestion; cf. his refs. at 227, n. 75.

34. *Expositio Totius Mundi et Gentium*, 57; ed. J. Rougé, *SChr* 124 (1966), pp. 196-7; see this Chapter, p. 312, for slave-trading on the Rhine frontier.

35. The imports (cash, clothing, corn) are mentioned by Themistius at *Or*. 10.135a-b (ed. Downey, Teubner 1965, p. 205); cf. Thompson, 13f.

36. The word, of distinctly late fourth-century resonance, is used at Historia Augusta, *Gallienus* 13.9 (where it denotes a column of wagons drawn up for travelling); *Claudius* 6.6; 8.2, 5; *Aurelian* 11.6, cf. Vegetius, *De Re Militari* 3.10 (ed. Lang, p. 92.15f.); 'omnes barbari carris suis in orbem conexis ad similitudinem castrorum'. A 'carroballista' is a wagon-mounted artillery device, cf. Vegetius 2.25; 3.14.

37. G. A. Crump, *Ammianus Marcellinus as a Military Historian*, 60ff. is good on this aspect of Roman strategy.

38. A former Roman merchant now living with the Huns turns up in Priscus' famous Fr. 8 (Fr. 11.2 Blockley; pp. 266-73); and Salvian alleges that Romans took refuge with the barbarians against the iniquity of their own people (*Gub. Dei.*, 5.5ff.). This no doubt did happen, but, as Priscus demonstrates, the rhetorical potential of the situation was irresistible for a moralising writer. See nevertheless, for a full exploitation of this and other material, G. E. M. de Ste Croix, *The Class Struggle in the Ancient Greek World, from the Archaic Age to the Arab Conquest* (1981), 474-88 (the miners of Thrace, 479-80).

39. For the treaty of 332 and developments in the sequel, see Thompson, 12-17 and Heather, 'The crossing of the Danube and the Gothic conversion' (cited above in n. 24), 290 (the date is confirmed by T. D. Barnes, *The New Empire*, 79). The parallel of the Hermunduri is adduced by Thompson, 14f., cf. his *The Early Germans* (1965), 90 on the Roman practice of trade restriction. Tacitus specifically remarks that the Hermunduri were the *only* recipients of this trading privilege from the Romans.

40. Sozomen actually writes 'before the tents' (*kath' hekastên skênên*) of suspected Christians. This detail is anachronistic rather than simply inaccurate. The Goths were not at that time a migrating people, but lived in the settled villages described at p. 321f. of this Chapter. For the conjectured significance of the rites of sacrifice, Thompson, 61ff.

41. Fr. 48.2 in Blockley (pp. 74-7). The detail may be totally unreliable. Eunapius' point is that, although the Goths were pagan and brought with them their objects of worship and priests and priestesses, they subverted the Romans by pretending to be Christians; the passage is primarily polemical.

42. I assume that the resemblance of this name to Ammianus' description of the place on the borders of Alamannic and Burgundian territory named Palas or Capellatii (cf. this Chapter, p. 309f. with n. 9) is purely coincidental. An attempt to link the two passages would produce baffling possibilities.

43. The date and character of Gothic conversion to Arian Christianity, and its consequences, have been widely discussed. E. A. Thompson, 'Christianity and the Northern Barbarians', reprinted from *Nottingham Medieval Studies* 1 (1957), 3-21 in Momigliano (ed.) *The Conflict between Paganism and Christianity in the Fourth Century* (1963), 56-78, argued that the conversion of barbarian peoples essentially followed their entry into the Roman empire; so too in *The Visigoths in the Time of Ulfila*, ch. 4 (pp. 78-93). In the case of the Goths, this interpretation involves discounting the tradition in some ecclesiastical sources of a 'civil war' based on religious differences between the supporters of Fritigern and Athanaric. This tradition was supported by Zeev Rubin, 'The conversion of the Visigoths to

Christianity', *Museum Helveticum* 38 (1981), 34-54, but its inherent difficulties are pointed out by Heather, 'The crossing of the Danube and the Gothic conversion' (cited in n. 24 above). Thompson argued for a date of conversion of 382/95, following the treaty with Theodosius of October 382, but Heather's solution, an agreement between Valens and Fritigern in 376, is just as likely in terms of the evidence and gives the more economical interpretation of the Goths' choice of Arian, rather than Nicene, Christianity (see esp. his remarks at 315). Heather (at 293) usefully characterises the conversion of a people in this sense as not 'adherence body and soul to a new set of beliefs, but ... rather a determination to change public practice'; the extent of individual conversion among a people before any such event is of course a rather different issue.

44. For the names, Delehaye, 'Saints de Thrace et de Mésie' (cited in n. 22 above), 215-16; 276ff.; Thompson, *The Visigoths in the Time of Ulfila*, 84f.

45. The settlement in Moesia is attested by Philostorgius, p. 17-18 ed. Bidez, and by the *Letter of Auxentius*, 60 (ed. Gryson, cited n. 32 above, pp. 248-9); for the location near Nicopolis, Jordanes, *Getica* 267 (the descendants of the community were still there in the sixth century).

46. Cf. the comprehensive arguments of Peter Heather (cited in n. 24 above).

(2) Nomads: Huns and Saracens

47. E. A. Thompson, *A History of Attila and the Huns* (1948) gives a characteristically lucid and vigorous account, with emphasis on the socio-political development of the Huns rather than on their material resources; on the latter and on the archaeological material, J. O. Maenchen-Helfen, *The World of the Huns: studies in their history and culture* (1973) – the work of an enthusiast – provides a brilliant but in some ways idiosyncratic survey (the book was unfinished at its author's death, and much remains controversial). The most systematic account of the archaeology is Joachim Werner's *Beiträge zur Archäologie des Attila-Reiches* (Verlag der Bayerischen Akademie der Wissenschaften, Phil.-Hist. Klasse; Abhandlungen n.f. 38, 1956): for a brief summary, J. D. Randers-Pehrson, *Barbarians and Romans: the birth struggle of Europe, A.D. 400-700* (1983), provides the essentials; cf. H.-J. Diesner, *The Great Migration* (cited above in n. 22), pp. 70-85, stressing their mixed character and adaptability. In a broader perspective, E. H. Minns, *Scythians and Greeks: a survey of the ancient history and archaeology of the north coast of the Euxine from the Danube to the Caucasus* (1913), is a fascinating exploration of the physical and ecological environment. Perry Anderson, *Passages from Antiquity to Feudalism* (1974), Part II.2, 'The nomadic brake', analyses the transformations in northern nomad society in its relations with the settled peoples of the Classical world. Brent D. Shaw, ' "Eaters of flesh, drinkers of milk": the ancient Mediterranean ideology of the pastoral nomad', *Ancient Society* 13/14 (1982/3), 5-31, surveys the literary stereotypes that characterise Classical descriptions of pastoral-nomad society. On the Alans, B. S. Bachrach, *A History of the Alans in the West* (1973) is much better on the later than the earlier material. The Classical literary sources of the fifth century (especially Priscus of Panium) are translated by C. D. Gordon, *The Age of Attila: fifth-century Byzantium and the barbarians* (1960) and, with some commentary, by R. C. Blockley, *Fragmentary Classicising Historians*, II (1983).

Ammianus' digression, praised by E. A. Thompson, at 6-9, and by Maenchen-Helfen, at 9-15, is sharply handled by Brent Shaw, 25f., cf. W. Richter, 'Die Darstellung der Hunnen bei Ammianus Marcellinus (31,2,1-11)', *Historia* 23 (1974), 343-77 – setting out the earlier Latin parallels to Ammianus' language, and, still more broadly, T. E. J. Wiedemann, 'Between man and beasts. Barbarians in Ammianus Marcellinus', in I. S. Moxon, J. D. Smart, A. J. Woodman (edd.), *Past Perspectives: studies in Greek and Roman historical writing* (1986), 189-211; to judge by her English summary (at p. 117), Milena Dušanić, *The Geographic-Ethnographic Excursus in the Work of Ammianus Marcellinus* (1986; in Russian), is more sympathetic. That Ammianus employed literary stereotypes is obvious (and not only on matters of ethnography). The question is, to what extent, within this framework, does he characterise the Huns differently from other pastoral nomads?

48. On the physical appearance of the Huns, Maenchen-Helfen, at 360ff. The distribution of artificially deformed skulls – a facet of Hunnish social practice not mentioned by Classical

literary sources – provides some of the best evidence of Hunnish movements from east to west; on which Joachim Werner, at 5-18 with map (Karte 9; Tafel 73) shows a clear westerly movement between the third-fourth and fifth-sixth centuries. See his Tafeln 5 and 33-4 for photographs of the skulls and, for a brief account Randers-Pehrson, 42f. For 'akrosphaleis', Suda A 1019, cf. Thompson, 51; 'kanchazein', Suda K 11 (= Eunapius, Fr. 41).

49. Ammianus' MSS support the form 'Halani', but I use 'Alani' as the more familiar form.

50. For the geography of Astrakhan and the adjoining steppe, see the forbidding description of Minns, *Scythians and Greeks*, 3. The relative narrowness of the 'steppe corridor' along which ran nomadic migration to the west is made clear in *The Times Atlas of the World* (6th ed., 1980), plate 5, 'World Vegetation'. It is the zone (band 9) marked 'Steppe (Short Grass)'.

51. Herodotus' Scythians placed an ancient iron sword on the top of a vast pile of brushwood, to which they annually added more material to make up for loss of height by subsidence, and there sacrificed beasts and prisoners of war (4.62); the divination was conducted while the soothsayer untied a bundle of sticks, laid them on the ground, and then gathered them together and tied them up (4.67). Minns, *Scythians and Greeks*, 71, regards the sword worship of the Alani as a borrowing from Herodotus by Ammianus, but at the same time cites parallels from other peoples, 'the Bolgars, the Voguls, the Tangaz and the ancestors of the Magyars'.

52. Herodotus' Scythian digression has long fascinated scholars; see for instance Niebuhr's tract of 1828, translated in 1830 as *Researches into the History of the Scythians, Getae and Sarmatians* (Oxford), beginning: 'The internal history of the hunting and pastoral tribes in the north of Asia bears throughout an uniform character: that of the Huns and Mongols is the same, nor can that of the Massagetae have been different'. Compare also the first pages of ch. XXVI of Gibbon's *Decline and Fall*, and Tolstoi's description of the Bashkirs in his short story, 'How Much Land does a Man Need?': 'It was all just as the tradesman had said. The people lived on the steppes, by a river, on felt-covered tents. They neither tilled the ground, nor ate bread. Their cattle and horses grazed in herds on the steppe. The colts were tethered behind the tents, and the mares were driven to them twice a day. The mares were milked, and from the milk kumiss was made. It was the women who prepared kumiss, and they also made cheese. As far as the men were concerned, drinking kumiss and tea, eating mutton, and playing on their pipes, was all they cared about. They were all stout and merry, and all the summer long they never thought of doing any work ...' (tr. Louise and Aylmer Maude; Oxford World Classics, ed. of 1982, p. 220). I would not care to dismiss all such descriptions as stereotypes. How and Wells' notes on Herodotus contain many still fascinating remarks (e.g. on werewolves, p. 339; cf. Minns, 102f.).

53. On Ptolemy (and other alleged early sources), Thompson, 21.

54. So F. Paschoud, in his Budé ed. of Zosimus, II.2 (1979), n. 142 at p. 374f., arguing that the confusion is already Eunapius' own, not merely that of Zosimus. Eunapius declares at Fr. 41 that he is writing in order to develop, either what he had written about the Huns earlier in the text of his history, or what he had written about them in its first edition (*ta ... prôta tês sungraphês*). The second alternative leads to discussion of the possible date of the first edition and its points of difference with the second (so Paschoud, citing T. D. Barnes and W. R. Chalmers; cf. also Sabbah, *La Méthode d'Ammien Marcellin*, 36), but the first interpretation seems to me a preferable reading of the Greek. If so, the whole digression can be assigned to the first edition of Eunapius, which was known to Ammianus (he used it, selectively, in his account of the Persian campaign of Julian; see my Chapter VIII.3, pp. 169ff.).

55. The tract of Arrian is discussed by Bachrach, at 8f. and App. II, 126-32 (with translation). Bachrach's discussion of Historia Augusta, *Maximinus* 1.5f., and his note (p. 14 n. 28) on Syme's *Ammianus and the Historia Augusta*, 36f., may safely be ignored. My quotation on the 'basic economic skill of the nomadic pastoralist' is from Perry Anderson, 222.

56. On the lasso, Maenchen-Helfen, 239f.; Bachrach, 5f.

57. The 'half-cooked meat' has given rise to a scholarly debate bearing on the literary relations between Ammianus and Jerome (*Adv. Iovinianum* 2.7; *PL* 23.308); Syme, *Ammianus and the Historia Augusta*, 19, discussed by Alan Cameron, *JRS* 61 (1971), 259.

Neither brings into play Jerome, *Life of Malchus* 4; 'carnes semicrudae, cibus; et lac camelorum potus erat' (*PL* 23.58). For the cauldrons, Maenchen-Helfen, 306-37, Werner, Taf. 27-8 and (in brief) Randers-Pehrson, 43. The rock paintings, Maenchen-Helfen, 326f., Werner, Taf. 63: bows and arrows, Maechen-Helfen, 221-33.

58. For the possible (but very far from certain) Hunnish connections of the Chionitae mentioned by Ammianus in 359, see Chapter IV.2, pp. 61f. and n. 24.

59. The slashing of the face; Maenchen-Helfen, 361. For the archaeological evidence for skull deformation, see above, n. 48.

60. Hunnish kingship (or its absence) is discussed by Thompson, at 44f., 57-9.

61. Hunnish technological shortcomings (another controversial question) are briefly discussed by Thompson, 4-6, with citation of Minns, 'The art of the Northern Nomads', *PBA* 28 (1942), 47-99 (with plates) at 56; 'Metal-work, if not all art-work [this is far too categorical], was for slaves, tributaries, and neighbours to supply'. Contrast Brent Shaw, 25 n. 66.

62. For discussion of Gelonos (and other 'wooden cities'), see Minns, *Scythians and Greeks*, 103ff. Brent Shaw, at 11, regards Herodotus' Boudinoi and Gelonoi as representing contrasting stereotypes (the 'binary polarities' of agrarian and pastoralist), which the historian was unable to distinguish except in ethnic terms, the true situation being less schematic and more complex. I would not disagree with that, but would argue the force of Herodotus' attempt to characterise a complex situation by the interplay of *two* stereotypes.

63. Priscus' justly famous description of the camp of Attila (Fr. 8), discussed by Thompson, 102ff., is translated by Gordon, *The Age of Attila*, 72-101, and by Blockley (where it has annoyingly become Frs. 11.2; 12.1; 13.1, 3; 14, and 15.1). See also E. A. Thompson, 'The camp of Attila', *JHS* 65 (1945), 112-15. The prisoner of war turns up in Gordon, p. 84 and Blockley, 264-5. On the 'sedentarisation' of the Huns, see Perry Anderson, at 224f., and my remarks in this Chapter, p. 354f.

64. Procopius, *Wars* 8.9.16f. (tr. Dewing). The Cotrigurs are cited by E. A. Thompson, in his 'Economic warfare', in *Romans and Barbarians* (1982), 5.

65. The development of the Roman frontier in Arabia and its relation to changes in the Arab world are described with typical economy and perception by Glen Bowersock, *Roman Arabia* (1983); cf. his article, 'A report on Arabia Provincia', *JRS* 61 (1971), 219-42 (fuller on the archaeological evidence). Maurice Sartre, *Trois études sur l'Arabie Romaine et Byzantine* (1982) covers the third- and also the later fourth-century evidence not discussed by Bowersock (though see his article cited below in n. 88). The political situation is interpreted from the Arab side, with much vivid circumstantial detail and emphasis on the economic infrastructure of Bedouin life, by F. E. Peters, 'Byzantium and the Arabs of Syria', *Annales Archéologiques Arabes Syriennes*, 27-8 (1977-8), 97-113. Ch. I of Fred McGraw Donner's *The Early Islamic Conquests* (1981), is an excellent introduction to the social background from which the Islamic expansion grew. Irfan Shahîd, *Byzantium and the Arabs in the Fourth Century* (1984) covers the field with great verve and commitment (pp. 239-50 on Ammianus' digression). Shahîd's treatment is marked by his insistence on the early Christianisation of the desert Arabs and their role as federates of the (Christian) Roman government, by a tendency to use already difficult evidence speculatively, and to regard more and the less powerful arguments as possessing equal force; it remains however a most stimulating study.

66. For these changes in provincial organisation, see the geographically perceptive account of Bowersock, *Roman Arabia*, 142-4; and the more formal evidence assembled by T. D. Barnes, *The New Empire of Diocletian and Constantine*, 213-15.

67. For Petra, Aila (Eilat) and Phaeno as part of Palestine from the early fourth century, see Barnes, 205 and 214, Bowersock, 143 (with refs.). Phaeno, a settlement south of the Dead Sea, is linked with Petra at Eusebius, *Onomastikon*, ed. Klostermann (*GCS*), p. 168.10. There is no need to enter here into the awkward question of the appearance of a second 'Arabia' on the Verona List of c. 314 (cf. Barnes, 201ff.), but I doubt whether it is identical with the 'Nea Arabia' of a recent papyrus, as conjectured by Bowersock (cf. *Roman Arabia*, 145f.), followed by Barnes, at 204f., 213f. For Elusa, Avraham Negev, in *Aufstieg und Niedergang der Römischen Welt* II.8 (1977), at 634f.; and the reference to Jerome's *Vita Hilarionis* discussed later in this section.

68. Mommsen, 'Ammians Geographica', *Hermes* 16 (1881), 602-36 = *Ges. Schr.* VII 393-425, at 395, notes the schematic character of Ammianus' provincial excursuses; the entry on Arabia conforms to the pattern, and apart from its chronological confusion says nothing that would not be known from sources of the early empire.

69. On the Via Nova Traiana, Bowersock, 'A report on Arabia Provincia', 236ff.; *Roman Arabia*, 83.

70. For the annexation of Arabia, Bowersock's 'Report', at 228f., *Roman Arabia*, esp. 79ff. Despite Bowersock, *Roman Arabia*, 79 (he is more cautious in his 'Report', 228), Ammianus' Syrian background does not make him an especially good witness. For Roman economic penetration of the Nabataean kingdom before its incorporation as a province, see Benjamin Isaac, 'Trade routes to Arabia and the Roman army', *Roman Frontier Studies 1979* (1980), 889-901.

71. On this very large issue Donner, *The Early Islamic Conquests*, esp. 14-20 and 26-8, and F. E. Peters, 'Byzantium and the Arabs of Syria', are contrasting, but both excellent, studies.

72. J. F. Matthews, 'The tax law of Palmyra: evidence for economic history in a city of the Roman East', *JRS* 74 (1984), 157-80, at 173. The reference is to *Corpus Inscriptionum Semiticarum* II.iii, 3913 lines 233-7 (the end of the inscription).

73. See esp. Peters, 'Byzantium and the Arabs of Syria', citing this episode at 99, cf. n. 16 at p. 108: 'no one in Constantinople seems to have understood the issue in economic terms. They knew the steppe was not agricultural land and so dismissed it as worthless.'

74. Peters, at 102, describes the effects of these variations on the pattern of life of desert dwellers, referring to 'glimpses of what must have been a recurrent phenomenon: drought conditions forced the bedouin out of their normal migratory patterns and into other territories'. On one occasion recorded by a Roman source, 'drought drove the Lakhmid al-Mundhir and 15,000 of his tribe into Roman territory' (cf. Marcellinus Comes, *Chron.*, s.a. 536).

75. The formulation is that of Perry Anderson, *Passages from Antiquity to Feudalism* (1974), 220; there cited from Owen Lattimore, *Inner Asian Frontiers of China* (1951), 66.

76. See again Peters, 100, cf. n. 66 at p. 103f., referring to a nineteenth-century description of the 'expenses incurred by the farming villages for the bedouins' annual six-day mart east of Damascus'.

77. Irfan Shahîd, *Byzantium and the Arabs*, at 284-7 discusses this episode, bringing out, though rather vaguely, the implication as to the position of women among the Saracens: 'a matriarchal system of some sort' (286). See also on Mavia; p. 350f. with *Expositio Totius Mundi et Gentium*, 20 (ed. J. Rougé, *SChr* 124 (1966), p. 154f.): 'et mulieres aiunt in eos regnare.'

78. Donner, *The Early Islamic Conquests*, at 20-6 discusses a particularly important facet of these conventions, the genealogy, an instrument of tribal identity always open to judicious amendment in the light of changing political realities. See for western medieval parallels, David Dumville, 'Kingship, genealogies and regnal lists', in P. H. Sawyer and I. N. Wood (edd.), *Early Medieval Kingship* (1977), 72-104.

79. The effect on Gothic fighting spirit was noticeable; 'non ferocientes ex more ... sed ambiguis gressibus incedebant' (31.16.6)!

80. Ammianus' phrase 'coloratis sagulis pube tenus amicti' (14.4.3) suggests what I would consider a certain correction in the printed text of Jerome's *Vita Malchi* 4 (*PL* 23.57); 'latas caligas trahentes' should clearly be 'sagulas' ('cloaks').

81. On Elusa, the report of A. Negev (cited above in n. 67). Irfan Shahîd, *Byzantium and the Arabs*, 288-93, discusses the episode and the nature of the goddess, but characteristically exaggerates the extent of conversion achieved by Hilarion. It is unclear whether Syriac, as Jerome thought ('barech' for 'bless'), or Arabic ('barik') was the language spoken by the Saracens visiting Elusa; Shahîd, 291.

82. See the following section of this Chapter, p. 365, with the work of Keith Hopwood mentioned there. On the Maratocupreni, Chapters XII, p. 264f. and XV, p. 402.

83. The consolidation of power is argued in another article by F. E. Peters, 'Romans and Barbarians in Southern Syria', *Journal of Near Eastern Studies* 37 (1978), 315-26, esp. at 324-6: as by Maurice Sartre, *Trois études*, 134, and Bowersock, *Roman Arabia*, 131ff.

Taking up a suggestion of David Graf, Bowersock proposed (in an article cited below, n. 88), that the incomplete Nabataean word in the bilingual Ruwwāfa inscription, [SRK]T TMWDW (= Greek *to tôn Thamudênôn e[thnos]*) gave rise to 'Saracens', which would mean 'federation' or 'nation'; thus the word would itself document the process referred to. It will be evident that this is highly speculative. Apart from any etymological considerations, both the Nabataean word [SRK]T and the Greek *e[thnos]* are incomplete on the stone (the restoration of the Greek, however, seems probable). See Bowersock, 'The Greek-Nabataean bilingual inscription at Ruwwāfa, Saudi-Arabia' in *Le Monde Grec: hommages à Claire Préaux* (1975), 513-22, text and translation at 514f.; and also his 'Arabs and Saracens in Historia Augusta', *HAColl, Bonn 1984/1985* (1987), 71-80, esp. at 71-4, tracing the 'generalising use' of the word 'Saracens' to the third century.

84. On this phase of 'de-urbanisation', see my article on Palmyra, *JRS* 74 (1984), at 169 – taking up the implications of Ernest Will, 'Marchands et chefs de commerce à Palmyre', *Syria* 34 (1957), 262-77; also Peters, 'Byzantium and the Arabs of Syria', 97.

85. On the Tanukh, Bowersock, *Roman Arabia*, 132ff.; Sartre, *Trois études*, 134f.

86. The inscription (*Princeton Archaeological Expeditions to Syria* IV.A (1914), No. 41; pp. 37-40) reads:

> This is the tomb of Fihr,
> son of Shullai, the tutor of Gadhîmat,
> the king of Tanūkh.

87. For the Nemara inscription, discussed by Bowersock, *Roman Arabia*, 138ff. and Sartre, *Trois études*, 136-9, see above all the recent article by James A. Bellamy, 'A new reading of the Namārah Inscription', *Journal of the American Oriental Society* 105 (1985), 31-51. Bellamy provides the following translation (p. 46), based on a careful new inspection of the stone (plates I-III at pp. 49-51) and full discussion of the philological possibilities:

(1) This is the funerary monument of Imru'u l-Qays, son of 'Amr, king of the Arabs; and (?) his title of honour was Master of Asad and Maḏḥij,

(2) And he subdued the Asadîs, and they were overwhelmed together with their kings, and he put to flight Ma<d>ḥij thereafter, and came

(3) driving them into the gates of Najrān, the city of Shammar, and he subdued Ma'add, and he dealt gently with the nobles

(4) of the tribes, and appointed them viceroys, and they became phylarchs for the Romans. And no king has equalled his achievements.

(5) Thereafter he died in the year 223 on the 7th day of Kaslul. Oh the good fortune of whose who were his friends!

Cf. Peters (1977/8), 98; the King's claim 'signalled a new order on the steppe'.

88. On the career of Mavia (*PLRE* I, p. 569), there are three recent studies: again by Bowersock, 'Mavia, Queen of the Saracens', in *Studien zur Antiken Sozialgeschichte: Festschrift Friedrich Vittinghof* (1980), 487-95; Sartre, *Trois études*, 104-5; and Shahîd, *Byzantium and the Arabs*, esp. 138-69. Of these, Shahîd is over-influenced by his wish to see Mavia as a Christianised Roman federate (he even suggests, at 143, that the outbreak of rebellion against Valens may have had 'doctrinal grounds'); Bowersock's very interesting discussion exaggerates the extent of Mavia's power among the desert peoples. Sartre is well-balanced, and may be right in seeing the peace settlement with Mavia as being initiated from the Roman side.

89. See the scepticism of Bowersock (1980), 481f., and Shahîd, 190-2, dismissing the story as a 'Romanhaft'.

90. Bowersock (1980), 485, accepts without comment the identity of the Assanitae as the Ghassanids. Sartre, *Trois études*, 139-40, rejects it, on grounds that seem to me inconclusive.

91. Tr. W. Wright (Cambridge, 1882), p. 64. My attention was drawn to this passage by Ben Isaac of Tel-Aviv University.

92. Donner, *The Early Islamic Conquests*, 20.

93. This is to recall the salutary but in its own way doctrinaire article of Brent Shaw, cited above in nn. 47 and 62.

94. I owe the terms of the analysis that follows to Perry Anderson, *Passages from Antiquity to Feudalism* (1974), 222ff., referring to 'the fusion of rival clans and tribes on the steppe into confederations, for external aggression'. The subject is primarily the Mongols, but the pattern exactly fits the Huns and Alans of the fourth and fifth centuries.

95. The identification of Huns and the Hsiung-Nu of Chinese sources is part of scholarly mythology and, like most myth, difficult to interpret. Accepted by Gibbon, *Decline and Fall*, ch. XXVI (ed. Bury, III, p. 75) from the eighteenth-century scholar de Guignes, it was regarded with scepticism by Bury (ad loc. and Appendix 6, p. 493f.). E. A. Thompson, *A History of Attila and the Huns* (1948), 1, cf. 46, reserves judgment, referring however to Otto Maenchen-Helfen, 'Huns and Hsiung-Nu', *Byzantion* 17 (1944-5), 222-43, who seems to me to make a powerful case (or cases) against the identification.

96. Perry Anderson, 224f., discusses the structural disintegration of 'nomadic empires', with emphasis (225) on the demographic factor.

(3) Rebels: Isaurians and Moors

97. My understanding of the countryside and economy of Isauria is immeasurably indebted to my conversations (better called tutorials) with the late Dr Alan Hall of Keele University, and to discussion with and the published and unpublished work of Dr Keith Hopwood of the University of Wales at Lampeter. The geological and geographical background (overstating the inaccessibility of the region) is described by W. B. Fisher, *The Middle East* (7th ed., 1978), at 330-2, but for the ancient historian there is still more to be learned from the accounts of nineteenth-century travellers, especially the Rev. E. J. Davis, *Life in Asiatic Turkey: a journal of travel in Cilicia (Pedias and Trachea), Isauria and part of Lycaonia and Cappadocia* (1879); William Leake, *Journal of a Tour in Asia Minor* (1824); and William Hamilton, *Researches in Asia Minor, Pontus and Armenia*, Vol. II (1842). A. H. M. Jones, *The Cities of the Eastern Roman Provinces* (2nd ed., 1971), at 137-9 describes the urban development of the region; Keith Hopwood, 'Towers, territory and terror: how the East was held', in Philip Freeman and David Kennedy (edd.), *The Defence of the Roman and Byzantine East (Sheffield Colloquium, 1986)* (1986), 343-56 discusses problems of internal security in relation to a postulated transhumant pastoral economy; and R. Syme, 'Isaura and Isauria: some problems', in Ed. Frézouls (ed.), *Sociétés urbaines, sociétés rurales dans l'Asie Mineure et la Syrie hellénistiques et romaines (Colloque Strasbourg 1985)* (1987), 131-47 is a typically penetrating account, as, in its very different way, is L. Robert, *Documents de l'Asie Mineure Méridionale: inscriptions, monnaies et géographie* (1966), cited below for its description of the regions of Side and the river Melas. The fullest ancient description of 'Isaurikê' and neighbouring regions is that of Strabo, 12.6-77 (tr. H. L. Jones, ed. Loeb., V, 472-85). N. Santos Yanguas, 'Algunos problemas sociales en Asia Menor en la segonda mitad del siglo IV d.C.: Isaurios y Maratocuprenos', *Hispania Antiqua* 7 (1977), 351-78, gives a full account, respecting both the circumstantial detail provided by Ammianus, the geographical conditions of Isaurian life, and the need to find an economic explanation of Isaurian behaviour. Santos Yanguas' formulation of the situation as 'una manifestación separatista con un marcado carácter regional', with a tendency to local autonomy in relation to imperial power (371, citing modern opinions) includes too much to be really useful, but he well characterises the variation and volatility in Isaurian conduct, which consisted of extended periods of peace, or of isolated outbreaks of banditry that from time to time erupted into something more serious (cf. 14.2.1).

98. On the Homonadensian War, B. M. Levick, *Roman Colonies in Southern Asia Minor* (1967), App. IV, pp. 203-14; on the evidence of Pliny, R. Syme, 'Isauria in Pliny', *Anatolian Studies* 36 (1986), 159-64.

99. For the second-century province, Syme (1986), 159; for the government of late Roman Isauria, Jones, *Later Roman Empire*, III, 20f. (n. 26), and esp. Hansgerd Hellenkemper, 'Legionen in Bandenkrieg – Isaurien im 4. Jahrhundert', in *Studien zu den Militärgrenzen Roms III* (1986), 625-34.

100. For the travel journals of Davis and Leake, see n. 97 above. On Claudiopolis-Mut,

Stephen Mitchell, 'Iconium and Ninica: two double communities in Roman Asia Minor', *Historia* 28 (1979), at 426-35.

101. William Hamilton, *Researches in Asia Minor*, II, 330-6 (Zengibar Kalesi = Isaura Nova). For the site of Isaura Vetus, Alan Hall, 'New light on the capture of Isaura Vetus by P. Servilius Vatia', *Akten des VI Internationalen Kongresses für Griechische und Lateinische Epigraphik, München* 1972 (1973), 568-71; cf. L. Robert, *Bulletin Epigraphique* 1974, No. 603 and *AE* 1977, No. 816.

102. For the readings *mikropoliteiais* and *mêtrokômiais* see the Budé text of Basil by Yves Courtonne, II (1961), p. 142. The Loeb text has, mistakenly, *mikrokomiais*; accepted however by Jones, *Cities of the Eastern Roman Provinces*, at 137-9. The site of Dalisandos is described by D. H. French, *Epigraphica Anatolica* 4 (1984), 85-98 (the quotation in the text is at 89), and the Gorgoromeis by Alan Hall, *Anatolian Studies* 21 (1971), 125-64.

103. For modern transhumance in the area just to the west of Isauria, see the classic study of X. de Planhol, *De la Plaine Pamphylienne aux Lacs Pisidiens: nomadisme et vie paysanne* (1958), esp. 186ff. On shepherds as bandits (or putative bandits), see the article of Keith Hopwood mentioned above, n. 97, and Brent D. Shaw, 'Bandits in the Roman Empire', *Past and Present* 105 (1984), 3-52, at 30-2.

104. J.-P. Roux, *Les Traditions des nomades de la Turquie méridionale* (1970), at 52-68 (on the tribes of the Yörük). Roux studies traditions of nomadism deriving from the period of Turkish migration. There is no cultural continuity with ancient times; but the pattern of life he describes is one of seasonal transhumance over relatively short distances and in a specific environment. It may not be an accident that it is in the Isaurian region that it survives, and not impossible that something like it existed in the Roman period. I am grateful to Professor Martin Harrison for telling me about the work of Roux, and for his observations on the subject.

105. Cyril Mango, 'Isaurian builders', in P. Wirth (ed.), *Polychronion: Festschrift F. Dölger* (1986), 358-65. For the background of Zeno the Isaurian, R. M. Harrison, 'The Emperor Zeno's real name', *BZ* 74 (1981), 27-8.

106. For Zosimus' description, F. Paschoud's Budé ed., I (1971), at 60 and 175-6; cf. briefly, B. M. Levick (cited above in n. 98), 174. A full account by Stephen Mitchell of the siege of Cremna, and of relevant archaeological discoveries there, will be published in the proceedings of the Eastern Frontier Conference held at Ankara on 1-3 September 1988; see in the meantime his brief descriptions in *Anatolian Studies* 37 (1987), 46-7 with pl. VI and 38 (1988, forthcoming), with pls. IIIc and IV.

107. On the notice about Isaurians in the Historia Augusta, J. Rougé, 'L'Histoire Auguste et l'Isaurie au IVe siècle', *REA* 68 (1966), 282-315; R. Syme, *Ammianus and the Historia Augusta* (1968), ch. IX; Hopwood (cited above in n. 97), 344.

108. The Zliten mosaics are illustrated by Katherine M. D. Dunbabin, *The Mosaics of Roman North Africa: studies in iconography and patronage* (Oxford 1978), pl. XX (47-8) (with previous references).

109. Ammianus' description of the Isaurians scrambling aboard ships by climbing their anchor ropes in the light of the moon (14.2.2) is admittedly one of his more picturesque efforts; cf. J. Vogt, 'Ammianus Marcellinus als erzählender Geschichtsschreiber der Spätzeit', at 807 – with other examples of this highly coloured style of writing.

110. On the site of Paleas, identified as 'Palaia of Isauria' of the so-called *Acta Barnabae*, between Korasion (see next note) and Anemourion, cf. G. E. Bean and T. B. Mitford, *Journeys in Rough Cilicia 1964-1968* (1970), at 195; Hellenkemper (cited above in n. 99), at 629-30, with photographs, Abb. 7-9 (modern Tahtalimanı).

111. Lauricius also attended the church council of Seleucia in 359; *PLRE* I, p. 497 (Bassidius Lauricius). The fort was called 'Antioch'. For a similar rebuilding by Fl. Uranius, governor of Isauria under Valens, see *MAMA* III, p. 102 n. 1 with Taf. 41-3 (Korasion = Chok Ören, by the sea 10 km north of the mouth of the river Calycadnus); cf. Hellenkemper, 630 (with plan).

112. Eunapius, Fr. 45 Müller (Blockley, pp. 64-7); *PLRE* I, p. 613 (Musonius 2).

113. For the role of the Germanicopolitans as intermediaries in the conflict, Hopwood, at 350f.

114. The topography of the region of Side and the river Melas are described by L. Robert

(cited above in n. 97), at 44-52.

115. For the campaign of P. Sulpicius Quirinius, B. M. Levick, (cited above in n. 98), at 40; 211ff.

116. The Austurian invasions, their consequences and some possible causes are described in Chapter XV (pp. 383ff. with n. 4). N. Santos Yanguas (cited above in n. 97) offers some literary conceptions of banditry, with pertinent comments; the Maratocupreni of Syria (Santos Yanguas, 375-8) are however not a particularly good parallel to the Isaurians; cf. Chapter XV, p. 402.

117. I have little to add to the argument or bibliography of my article, 'Mauretania in Ammianus and the Notitia', in R. Goodburn and P. Bartholomew (edd.), *Aspects of the Notitia Dignitatum* (BAR Supplementary Series 15, 1976), 157-86: reprinted in *Political Life and Culture in Late Roman Society* (1985), ch. XI. I should however have mentioned T. Kotula, 'Firmus, fils de Nubel, était-il usurpateur ou roi des Maures?', *Acta Antiqua Academiae Scientiarum Hungaricae* 18 (1970), 137-46 – arguing against the notion that Firmus was in any true sense a usurper, and emphasising (as I do) the strength of the tribal background from which he came. Narciso Santos Yanguas, 'La Resistencia de las poblaciones indigenas norteafricanas a la romanización en la segunda mitad del siglo IV d.C.', *Hispania* 39 (1979), 257-300 is essentially a survey of the material provided by Ammianus (cf. his article on the Isaurians, cited above in n. 97). For the geographical setting, A. N. Sherwin-White, 'Geographical factors in Roman Algeria', *JRS* 34 (1944), 1-10. On the archaeological background St. Gsell's *Atlas Archéologique de l'Algérie* (1911), though now old, is still fundamental.

118. On *praefecti gentis*, see the survey of Cl. Lepelley, 'La préfecture de tribu dans l'Afrique du bas-Empire', *Mél. Seston* (1974), 285-95.

119. On the career of Theodosius, *PLRE* I, Theodosius 3 (pp. 902-4); R. Egger, 'Der Erste Theodosius', *Byzantion* 5 (1929/30), 9-23, reprinted in A. Betz and G. Moro (edd.), *Römische Antike und Frühes Christentum* I (1967), 126-43. On the geographical range of the campaign, see my 'Mauretania in Ammianus and the Notitia', at 150f., and St. Gsell, 'Observations géographiques sur la révolte de Firmus', *Recueil des Notices et Mémoires de la Société Archéologique de Constantine* 36 (1903), 21-46.

120. A bishop 'Vindemius Lemfoctensis' is mentioned in the Notitia Provinciarum et Civitatum Africae of A.D. 484 (in *CSEL* 7.118-34), s. Mauretania Sitifensis 21.

121. J. Baradez, *Fossatum Africae: recherches aériennes sur l'organisation des confins sahariens a l'époque romaine* (1949); cf. my 'Mauretania in Ammianus and the Notitia', at 167-9.

122. On the career of Maximus, *PLRE* I, Maximus 39 (p. 388); A. R. Birley, *The Fasti of Roman Britain* (1981), 349.

123. Augustine, *Ep.* 16.2 has 'Migginem' as a declined accusative from 'Miggin' (misrepresented in the Loeb translation as 'Miggo'); see *CIL* 8.20600 (Tixter, Mauretania Sitifensis, A.D. 359).

124. On the 'castella', my 'Mauretania in Ammianus and the Notitia', 174-7; for possibly analogous 'towers' in Isauria, K. Hopwood (above, n. 97) at 347ff.

125. For the site of Petra (M'lakou), Gsell, *Atlas Archéologique*, 6.148, with the observations of Kotula (cited above in n. 117), 142f. In the 1985 reprint of my 1976 article is shown (after p. 172) a photograph of the inscription, kindly provided by Professor John Wilkes of London University.

126. On the archaeological history of the 'True Cross', see above all E. D. Hunt, *Holy Land Pilgrimage in the Later Roman Empire, A.D. 312-460* (1982), at 37-42 and 128-30. The inscr., *CIL* 8.20600, is that mentioned above (in n. 123), bearing the name of the African martyr, Miggin.

(4) Ammianus and his sources

127. Ammianus' written and other sources on the Persian campaign are discussed above, Chapter VIII.3. Many of the older, more 'formalistic' assumptions as to Ammianus' possible use of earlier and contemporary written and documentary sources were swept away by E. A. Thompson, *The Historical Work of Ammianus Marcellinus*, ch. 2 (pp. 20-41). By far the

fullest account, with discussion of the bibliography, is now G. Sabbah, *La Méthode d'Ammien Marcellin*, Part II (pp. 115-239).

128. By September 382 Ammianus may already have left Antioch, en route for Constantinople and the west (Chapter II.1, p. 16f.).

129. The careers of the two Syagrii are discussed in my *Western Aristocracies*, at 75; cf. *PLRE* I, Syagrius 2 and 3 (pp. 862f.); see also Sabbah, 157-9.

130. For Ammianus' use of the word 'relatio' and derivatives ('referente' and such), see the suggestive but possibly over-refined discussion of Sabbah, at 160ff.

131. For an official report as the possible source of Ammianus' account of the engagement at Solicinium, see Sabbah, 208-10.

132. Eunapius, Fr. 9 (Fr. 17 Blockley) refers to a 'biblidion' composed on the battle by Julian (see Blockley, p. 131 n. 25). (The account of Zosimus, deriving from that of Eunapius, is irretrievably confused: see Chapter VI, n. 31). For documents of Julian referred to by Ammianus, cf. 20.8.18 (letters of Julian to Constantius); 21.10.7 (to the senate); 22.14.2 (the *Misopogon*). At 16.5.7 Ammianus acknowledges Julian's written works – 'orationes' and 'epistulae' – as signs of his literary tastes, but it is hard to trace a specific influence, cf. Sabbah, 294-6.

133. That Eutherius was a source of Ammianus seems assured; see above, p. 25, with Sabbah, at 228-30 and Fontaine (1978), 48.

134. Ammianus' information about the manoeuvres and discussions preceding Hadrianople is well discussed by N. J. E. Austin, *Ammianus on Warfare* (1979), 72-80, esp. 72f.; cf. Chapter XIII, p. 300.

135. That Bassidius Lauricius was a source for Ammianus is conjectured by R. Syme, *Ammianus and the Historia Augusta* (1968), 45.

136. Sabbah, 207 with n. 159 is very good on the relatively distant quality of these site descriptions, and of Ammianus' account in general of the Mauretanian episode; well-informed and precise, but showing no signs of personal involvement.

137. For Ammianus' reaction (or lack of it) to the death of Theodosius, cf. Chapters X, n. 14 and XII, n. 38; for the political circumstances, *Western Aristocracies*, 93.

XV. Town and Country

1. See on this passage P. Bartholomew, 'Fourth-century Saxons', *Britannia* 15 (1984), 169-85, at 171f. – an interesting but rather strained interpretation, arguing that Ammianus, far from condoning the action, is passing ironic judgment on the general responsible for it.

2. Detailed studies of this affair are given by J. Guey, 'Nicomaque Flavien et Leptis Magna', *REA* 52 (1950), 77-89; by B. H. Warmington, 'The career of Romanus, Comes Africae', *BZ* 49 (1956), 55-64; and by A. Demandt, in two articles: 'Die Tripolitanischen Wirren unter Valentinian I', *Byzantion* 38 (1968), 333-63; and 'Die Afrikanischen Unruhen unter Valentinian I', in H.-J. Diesner and others, *Afrika und Rom in der Antike* (1968), 277-92. Some of Demandt's chronological conclusions are challenged by Roger Tomlin, 'Ammianus Marcellinus 26.4.5-6', *CQ* n.s. 29 (1979), 470-8, at 475f. E. A. Thompson, *The Historical Work of Ammianus Marcellinus*, 129, refers to the 'fearful extortion and injustices' in late Roman administration, '... which reached a ghastly climax in the career of Romanus in Tripoli'. See also Chapter XII, p. 261.

3. For the economy of the region, see R. Goodchild, *Tabula Imperii Romani: Lepcis Magna* (Oxford, 1954), and 'Roman sites on the Tarhuna Plateau of Tripolitania', *PBSR* 19 (1951), 43-77, repr. with other relevant articles in his *Libyan Studies: select papers* (ed. Joyce Reynolds, 1976), 72-106; and esp. Ginette di Vita-Evrard, 'Quatre inscriptions du Djebel Tarhuna: le territoire de Lepcis Magna', *Quaderni di Archeologia della Libia* 10 (1979), 67-98, esp. at 67 and 87-91 on the role of the 'Djebel tripolitain' as the source of the agricultural prosperity of Lepcis, especially in the production of olive oil. Cf. her description of the physical nature of the Djebel (at 67): 'il se termine au-dessus de l'aride plaine cotière de la Djefara par une frange montagneuse, escarpée, coupée de vallées ....'

4. Cf. the discussion above (p. 363f.) of the Isaurian uprising of 353. The economic circumstances were however in themselves rather different in the two cases, if David

Mattingly is right in arguing that the aggression of the Austuriani was connected with their membership of a widespread tribal federation involved in a westward migration in the late Roman period; D. J. Mattingly, 'The Laguatan: a Libyan tribal confederation in the later Roman Empire', *Libyan Studies* 14 (1983), 96-108. In this case, a nearer affinity might be that of the Saracens also discussed earlier in this Chapter.

5. For the conduct of embassies, see my reference article, 'Gesandtschaft', in *RAC* X (1977), 653-88, esp. at 663-4; Fergus Millar, *The Emperor in the Roman World* (1977), esp. 375-85. For the handbook advice that follows, D. A. Russell and N. G. Wilson, *Menander Rhetor: edited with translation and commentary* (1981), Treatise II [xiii] (pp. 180-1).

6. A classic instance of such a dispute is from the so-called 'Thorigny Marble' (*CIL* 13.3162), recording the intervention of one Sennius Sollemnis of the Viducasses (Vieux) at the annual 'concilium Galliarum' in favour of a retiring governor of his province, under threat of prosecution; H.-G. Pflaum, *Le Marbre de Thorigny* (1948), p. 8 (côté droite, lines 20-26); 'Sollemnis iste [the honorand] ... proposito eorum [the governor's opponents] restitit, provocatione scilicet interposita, quod patria eius [the city of the Viducasses] cum inter ceteros legatum eum creasset, nihil de actione mandassent, immo contra laudassent [the governor]; qua ratione effectum est, ut omnes ab accussatione desisterent'.

7. Warmington (cited above in n. 2), 59, points out some chronological implications of the details mentioned by Ammianus. The affair was very protracted; Valentinian took up residence at Trier, where the first ambassador died, in 367, and Crescens is recorded as *vicarius* of Africa only in 370 (*CTh* 10.4.3).

8. On this see the articles of Guey and Warmington cited above in n. 2; the inscriptions are *IRT* 475 and 526. Note the similarity of sentiment between Ammianus 28.6.28, 'quorum aequitas auctoritate mixta iustissima' (continuing, 'torto Caecilio aperta confessione cognovit') and *IRT* 526, 'iustitiae quam causae Tripolitanae del(e)gatae ... exhibuit [*sc.* Hesperius]'.

9. For the case of Antoninus, see Chapter V, p. 68.

10. See Ramsay MacMullen, 'Market-days in the Roman Empire', *Phoenix* 24 (1970), 333-41. The fair at Batnae is registered at p. 336, n. 16.

11. On the Maratocupreni (also referred to by Libanius, *Or.* 48.35f.) see further below, p. 402 and n. 46.

12. There has been some discussion of the sources of Ammianus' digressions, notably by Mommsen, 'Ammians Geographica', *Ges. Schr.* VII, 393-425 (from *Hermes* 16 (1881), 602-36); criticising the views of Gardthausen, who supposed that Ammianus used a single handbook source, Mommsen indicated a multiplicity of possible sources. See also I. Gualandri, 'Fonti geographiche di Ammiano Marcellino XXII.8', *Parola del Passato* 23 (1968), 199-211 (above, Chapter II, n. 17), pointing to learned Greek sources in the digression on the Pontic regions ('un lavoro di mosaico', p. 211); and M. F. A. Brok, 'Die Quellen von Ammians Exkurs über Persien', *Mnemosyne* 4.28 (1975), 47-56 – arguing against Mommsen's postulation of Ptolemy as Ammianus' source, but with similar implications for the variety of materials available to him. My emphasis is rather on the 'ideological' pattern in Ammianus' presentation, and on his tendency to adopt a different cultural framework in digressions and narrative passages respectively; on which see also Sabbah, *La Méthode d'Ammien Marcellin*, 71f., 75 n. 53, 525ff., etc. Cf. Chapter XVIII, pp. 462ff.

13. Julian's sojourn at Athens is indirectly referred to, the city being actually named in neither passage; Chapter VI, p. 85.

14. Aspects of social and cultural life at Antioch are described elsewhere in this book, especially in Chapters V, X, and XVI.

15. Compare Isaura Vetus, described at 14.8.2; 'antehac nimium potens, olim subversa ut rebellatrix interneciva aegre vestigia claritudinis pristinae monstrat admodum pauca'; Chapter XIV.3, p. 358, with n. 101. For the archaeological sites mentioned in the following pages, the *Princeton Encyclopaedia of Classical Sites*, edd. R. Stilwell, W. L. MacDonald, M. H. McAllister (1976) is a constantly useful handbook (though out of date, as it happens, on Isaura). I generally also give for convenience a reference to a site handbook if I know of one. For Avenches there is G. T. Schwarz, *Die Kaiserstadt Aventicum* (1964) – though with few illustrations.

16. For Autun, E. Thévenot, *Autun: Cité Romaine et Chrétienne* (1932) is old but still serviceable; for the Augustan walls (well worth a visit), pp. 57-60. As Thévenot observes (at 127), it does not look as if Ammianus were describing at 16.2.1 the restricted 'castrum' site of Autun.

17. This is shown by Symmachus, *Ep.* 1.64: cf. Chapter XIV.3(ii), p. 369.

18. There is a vivid description in Clark Hopkins, *The Discovery of Dura-Europos* (ed. by Bernard Goldman, 1979), 1-4. (An added bonus is the marvellous photograph, at p. 198, of Cumont (with trilby hat and flowing beard) and Rostovtzeff (cloth cap and moustache) before the shrine of Mithras during the season of 1933-4).

19. On Seleucia, see Chapter VIII.2, pp. 140ff.; Hatra, J. B. Ward-Perkins, 'The Roman East and the Parthian West', *PBA* 51 (1965), 175-99, at 188ff.

20. The inadequacy of barbarians before Roman fortifications is a theme that occurs frequently in this book; as at Chapter XIII, p. 294, and XIV.2, p. 328.

21. The walls of Cyzicus (*Princeton Encyclopaedia*, 473-4 s.v. Kyzikos has nothing to say); see F. W. Hasluck, *Cyzicus* (1910), ch. 1, at 3-5 (harbours) and 5-10 (walls).

22. Lepcis Magna: R. Goodchild and J. B. Ward-Perkins, 'The Roman and Byzantine defences of Lepcis Magna', *PBSR* 21 (1953), 42-73.

23. On Paleas/Palaia, see Chapter XIV.3(i), p. 364 with n. 110.

24. The classic study of this subject for Gaul is still A. Blanchet, *Les Enceintes Romaines de la Gaule* (1907). R. M. Butler, 'Late Roman Walls in Gaul', *Archaeological Journal* 116 (1959), 25-50 gives an overall survey with some case studies and at *JRS* 48 (1958), 33-9 describes the city walls of Le Mans. See also Stephen Johnson, 'A group of late Roman city walls in Gallia Belgica', *Britannia* 4 (1973), 210-23, discussing Beauvais, Senlis and Soissons, but with allusions to other sites, and bibliography.

25. Augusta Raurica: R. Laur-Belart, *Führer durch Augusta Raurica* (4th ed., 1966).

26. For Sirmium, A. Mócsy, *Pannonia and Upper Moesia: a history of the Middle Danube provinces of the Roman Empire* (1974), esp. 310ff.; A. Lengyel and G. T. B. Radan (edd.), *The Archaeology of Roman Pannonia* (1980), 267-8.

27. See Chapter X with n. 43 for the circumstances (the walls of Chalcedon were taken down in punishment for the city's support of Procopius).

28. For Carnuntum, there is a beautifully illustrated account, with stunning air photographs showing the extent of (unexcavated) settlement at the site, by E. Vorbeck and L. Beckel, *Carnuntum: Rom an der Donau* (1973). See also Mócsy passim and Lengyel and Radan, 259f. The standard handbook is A. Obermayr, *Römerstadt Carnuntum* (1967). The archaeology of Savaria, a very important city, is summarised by Lengyel and Radan, 264-6, cf. Mócsy 313f. and *Princeton Encyclopaedia*, 232-3 (s. Colonia Claudia Savaria). There is a fuller account in A. Mócsy and T. Szentléleky (edd.), *Die römischen Steindenkmäler von Savaria* (1971), at 15-18 (by T. P. Buocz, on topography) and 19-34 (L. Balla, on the economy and history of the city).

29. The death of Valens was similarly, though less circumstantially, portended (31.1.2). The hooting of owls is a universal portent of death; see the references and parallel passages assembled by A. S. Pease in his commentary on one of the best of them, *Aeneid* 4.462 (1935; repr. 1963).

30. A. Calderini, *Aquileia Romana* (Milan, 1930) is still the basic handbook. Subsequent research is presented in the journal *Aquileia Nostra* (Aquileia, Museo Archeologico, 1930-) and in the series *Antichità Altoadriatiche* (Udine, 1972-).

31. Lengyel and Radan write (at 267) of 'suburban satellite cities which, although they became part of metropolitan Sirmium, developed separately rather than following the development of the main city of Sirmium'.

32. On this topographical map, see L. Jalabert and R. Mouterde, in *IGLS* 3 (1950), pp. 544ff. (the inscr. is No. 998c). It is also discussed in detail by Glanville Downey, *A History of Antioch in Syria* (1961), 30-2 and Excursus 18, pp. 659-64. Ammianus also mentions (21.15.2) the suburb of Hippocephalus ('Horse's Head'), three miles out of Antioch on the road to Tarsus; cf. Downey, 77 n. 108 with other refs. (but no detail).

33. On Hebdomon, R. Janin, *Constantinople Byzantine*, (2nd ed., 1964), 446-9; 'le lieu d'exercices et de concentration des troupes imperiales en Thrace'. For Sabinianus at Edessa, see Chapter III, p. 44f. with n. 20; Julian at Paris, Chapter VI, p. 98.

34. This passage is mentioned at Chapter XII, p. 263 in relation to the *fabricae* (arms factories) of Hadrianople.
35. On Pudentilla and Apuleius, A. R. Birley, *Septimius Severus: the African Emperor* (1971), 48-59; cf. the translation of Apuleius' *Apology* and *Florida* by H. E. Butler (1909, repr. 1970), p. 137 (*Apol.*, 88).
36. On this cultural dimension, see Chapter V, p. 69f.
37. I can find no reference to Craterae in any of the standard histories of Antioch (Petit, Downey, Liebeschuetz), nor in G. Tchalenko's classic *Villages Antiques de la Syrie du Nord: le massif de Bélos à l'époque romaine* (Paris, 1953-8) (though it was perhaps not in that direction). Ammianus' description might offer the chance that it could be found.
38. The site of Bebase is discussed inconclusively by L. Dillemann, *Haute Mésopotamie et pays adjacents*, 290-7; Dillemann's use of Amm. 18.7.2 is criticised at Chapter III, p. 44 with n. 19, and he almost certainly places Bebase (Beth Wasi in eastern sources) too far south. Earlier identifications locate it at Tell Bes, on a tributary of the W. Zergan – nearer to Constantia (Viranşehir) than the 100 miles given by Ammianus, 18.7.9.
39. Zosimus 3.27.2, who gives its name as 'Symbra', describes this place as a 'village' (*kômê*) located between two 'towns' (*poleis*) themselves separated by the Tigris. See Paschoud's n. 78 at p. 196 (ed. Budé 2.1) for the difficulties, and for possible identifications.
40. For the mansions near Seleucia, Chapter VIII.2, p. 157; Alamannic re-settlement of old Roman villas, Chapter XIV.1, p. 310.
41. See my 'Mauretania in Ammianus and the Notitia', at 175f.; Chapter XIV.3, p. 372f.
42. For Parndorf, E. B. Thomas, *Römische Villen in Pannonien: Beiträge zur pannonischen Siedlungsgeschichte* (1964), 177-92; Mócsy, *Pannonia and Upper Moesia* (cited in n. 26 above), pp. 135, 170f. with plan (on the first-century origins of the villa), 295 with n. 122, 302 (on its fourth-century development) and in Lengyel and Radan (cited in n. 26 above), indexed s. Murocincta. I do not know why the name of the 'public villa' Pistrensis (so V) should be changed to 'Pristensis' (so Seyfarth, after Heraeus).
43. For Konz, Edith Wightman, *Roman Trier and the Treveri*, (1970), at 165-8; and *Gallia Belgica* (1985), at 258: for Mediana near Naissus, Mócsy, 301-2 with pl. 43b.
44. J. J. Wilkes, *Diocletian's Palace, Split: residence of a retired Roman Emperor* (1986) is now the best and most accessible general account.
45. Compare the influence over its Italian 'incolae' exerted by Aquileia (21.11.3; p. 104).
46. For information on this point I have to thank Dr. Sebastian Brock, of the Oriental Institute of Oxford University, who responded very fully to my enquiry as to the possibility of identifying the village of the Maratocupreni. Referring also to the destruction of the Maratocupreni, Libanius, *Or.* 48.36 (translated by A. E. Norman, ed. Loeb, 1977, pp. 450ff.) calls their settlement a *kômê*; for the equivalence of this term with the Latin 'vicus', see L. Harmand, *Discours sur le patronage*, 126. N. Santos Yanguas, 'Algunos problemas sociales en Asia Menor en la segunda mitad del siglo IV d.C.: Isaurios y Maratocuprenos', *Hispania Antiqua* 7 (1977), 351-78, at 375-8, is disappointingly thin on the Maratocupreni: contrast his full and circumstantial discussion of the Isaurians, referred to at Chapter XIV, n. 97.
47. For the 'cool waters' of Meiocarire and the rancid hot springs of Abarne, Chapter V, p. 71 with n. 5.
48. *ILS* 6091 is not a complete version of the dossier; cf. *FIRA*[2] No. 95 (pp. 461-4), translated by A. H. M. Jones, *A History of Rome through the Fifth Century* (1970), II, No. 114 (pp. 250-2). Nacolia happens to be mentioned by Ammianus, as the place near which Procopius was betrayed (26.9.7; 10.4; p. 197).

XVI. Social Relations

1. The institution of the embassy is set in its historical context in my reference article 'Gesandtschaft' in *RAC* 10 (1977), cols. 653-85; and by Fergus Millar, *The Emperor in the Roman World* (1977), 375-85, etc. For the surrender of Nisibis, see Chapter I, p. 4; the Tripolitanian embassies, Chapter XV, pp. 383ff.
2. G. W. Bowersock, *Greek Sophists in the Roman Empire* (1969) is excellent on philosophers and their civic obligations. Compare *CTh* 13.3.7, addressed as it happens to Petronius Probus in 369, where the expressed irony in the law (that men who proclaim

themselves superior to fortune should not shun civic duties), recalls the rescript of Antoninus Pius, cited by Modestinus at *Digest* 27.1.6.7; 'I feel sure that those who are wealthy will voluntarily provide financial assistance to their cities. And if they quibble about the size of their estates, they will make it clear that they are not really philosophers' (cf. Bowersock, 34). The exemptions quoted by Modestinus include exemptions from service on embassies.

3. On acclamations as forms of civic expression, see J. H. W. G. Liebeschuetz, *Antioch*, 209-19: Charlotte Roueché, 'Acclamations in the Later Roman Empire: new evidence from Aphrodisias', *JRS 74* (1984), 181-99. Alan Cameron, *Circus Factions: blues and greens at Rome and Byzantium* (1976), ch. VII, puts the evidence from Rome in its historical context.

4. For this aspect of Ursicinus' career, see Chapter III, p. 40.

5. The episodes from Ammianus' career are described at Chapter III, pp. 65 and 41.

6. The Antiochene corn crises are discussed by various writers with different points of emphasis: e.g. by E. A. Thompson, *The Historical Work of Ammianus Marcellinus*, 60-3, 81; P. de Jonge, 'Scarcity of corn and corn-prices in Ammianus Marcellinus', *Mnemosyne* 4.1 (1948), 238-45; Glanville Downey, 'The economic crisis at Antioch under Julian the Apostate', in *Studies in Roman Economic and Social History in Honor of Allan Chester Johnson* (1951), 312-21; P. Petit, *Libanius et la vie municipale*, esp. 105-22 (on the corn crisis), and 235-8 (on social relations); J. H. W. G. Liebeschuetz, *Antioch*, esp. 126-32; Edgar Pack, *Städte und Steuern in der Politik Julians* (Coll. Latomus 194; 1986), 363-77. In developing my own approach I have gained much from advice given by Wolfgang Liebeschuetz and Dominic Rathbone and (on the numismatic evidence) by Cathy King and John Casey. For Libanius' speeches on the crisis under Julian, see pp. 412 and n. 22 below.

7. In view of his conflicts with the praetorian prefect Domitianus (Chapter III, p. 34), it is unclear that Gallus actually had the authority to do this; cf. R. C. Blockley, 'Constantius Gallus and Julian as Caesars of Constantius II', *Latomus* 31 (1972), 433-68, at 461-6.

8. On distributions made by governors and other notables in a spirit of munificence, see L. Robert, 'Epigrammes du Bas-Empire: IV. Epigrammes d'Aphrodisias', *Hellenica* 4 (1948), at 127-9.

9. Cf. the interventions of the quaestor Eupraxius before Valentinian; Chapters X, p. 212 and XII, p. 257.

10. Petit, *Libanius et la vie municipale*, 236, cf. *Not. Dig., Or.* 11.21-2. For arms workshops as a factor in urban social relations, cf. Chapter XII, p. 263 and n. 23 (Hadrianople and Caesarea).

11. See for this inference Petit, p. 237 n. 2.

12. For the *Misopogon*, see Chapter VI, p. 108, and the splendid article of Maud Gleeson, cited there at n. 39. Julian's description of the economic situation merits a fuller study than I can give it here.

13. 'Panta pollou, panta gemei' ('everything dear, everything plentiful') were the words of the acclamation, for which I attempt an idiomatically convincing paraphrase. For the date of Julian's entry to Antioch, at the time of the festival of Adonis just after the summer solstice but before 28 July 362 (*CTh* 1.16.8), cf. Seeck, *Regesten*, 210.

14. Zosimus, 3.13.1, gives the total numbers of Julian's army as 65,000. It is unclear in what proportions the army was divided (c.f. Paschoud's n. 34, pp. 110-11), but the question of supply is unaffected by this.

15. This point is noted by Petit, 113.

16. See again the fine discussion of Petit, 110f., emphasising (at 115) that the expectation of bad harvests may be the cause of panic in the markets. De Jonge (cited in n. 6 above), at 240-2 points to the effects of troop concentrations (cf. Petit, 110).

17. For the fourth-century 'modius castrensis' of 31.25 *librae* (10.09 kg) as opposed to the 21.8 *librae* (7.05 kg) of the 'modius italicus' of the early empire, see R. Duncan-Jones, 'The size of the modius castrensis', *ZPE* 21 (1976), 53-62. The distinction between 'metra' and 'modii' in this part of Julian's text reflects the distinction between the administration of the city territories (by the city authorities) and of imperial holdings (by the *comes rei privatae*; cf. *Not. Dig., Or.* 14.4 and, with more detail, *Occ.* 12). In *Ep.* 84 Bidez (ed. Loeb, p. 68) Julian defines in 'modii' the quantities of grain made available for distribution by the high priest of Galatia.

18. This variation in nomenclature is the most difficult facet of Julian's text to interpret. At *Misopogon* 369B he gives prices of 15, 10 and 5 *metra* for an *argurion* (a 'silver piece' or 'coin'), but at 369D, clearly referring to the same transaction, asks whether anyone can remember even a plentiful summer price of 15 *metra* for a gold piece (*chrusou*). At 369B (between the two references) he talks of a *nomisma*, a minted coin. The word is often used without comment to mean a gold *solidus*; and, as Dominic Rathbone has told me, corn prices were usually expressed in the form 'x *modii* per *solidus*'. If the price level intended by Julian is comparable with near-contemporary figures given by Ammianus of 30 *modii* and 10 *modii* per *solidus* in times of plenty and shortage respectively (28.1.18: Carthage), then the *metron* mentioned by Julian will work out at about two *modii*. (The figures given by Evelyne Patlagean, *Pauvreté économique et pauvreté sociale à Byzance, 4e-7e siècles* (1977), at 403-4 are unrepresentative, and in the case of Antioch in 362/3, unreliable, since she supposes Julian to be referring throughout to *modii*). The effect of taking Julian to refer to a silver coin (the light *miliarense* struck at Antioch at 72 to the pound) would be either to reduce drastically the size of the *metron* and the scale of Julian's intervention, or alternatively to indicate an impossibly cheap price for corn. See on the coinage J. P. C. Kent, *RIC* VIII, pp. 58 and 531, with 66 for the market relationship (about 18:1) of gold and silver coinages of equal weight. To take Julian's first reference (369B) to an 'argurion' as an untechnical reference to a (gold) coin may seem awkward, but the alternative involves taking his *chruson* at 369D as a silver coin, and altogether raises too many difficulties.

19. For the capacity of corn-ships see Geoffrey Rickman, *The Corn Supply of Ancient Rome* (Oxford, 1980), 123.

20. The calculation, which is intended not to give an exact result but merely to block out an order of magnitude, may be done in two ways: (i) by reducing estimates for the corn consumption of the city of Rome, taken by Peter Garnsey ('Grain for Rome', in Garnsey, Whittaker, Hopkins, *Trade in the Ancient World* [1983], 118-30) as up to 30 million *modii Italici* per annum, giving a daily intake, averaged for the different needs of men, women and children, of 1745 calories, to suit an estimated population of 250,000 for Antioch (cf. Liebeschuetz, *Antioch*, 92-6). This relatively generous calculation gives an annual grain consumption for Antioch of c. 7.5 million *modii Italici* (= 5.3 m. *modii castrenses*; Duncan-Jones, above, n. 17): (ii) by taking an estimated consumption of 3 lb grain per day for an adult male and 1.5 lb per day for women and children and applying this to a population of 250,000 broken down into 80,000 adult males and 170,000 women and children, on the proportions suggested for Rome by Keith Hopkins, *Conquerors and Slaves: sociological studies in Roman history* I (1978), 96-8; a daily consumption of 3 lb per day is the most plausible of the figures set out by Evelyne Patlagean (above, n. 18), 51-2. The resulting figure, 8.18 million *modii Italici* (= 5.8 m. *modii castrenses*) is sufficiently close to the 7.5 m. *modii Italici* (= 5.3 m. *modii castrenses*) produced under calculation (i). The basis of Julian's contribution was the 400,000 'metra' or c. 800,000 'modii castrenses' argued in n. 18, which produces just under two months' supply under both calculations. More cautious consumption figures would have the effect of increasing the relative scale of Julian's intervention.

21. On the 'mechanics' of upper-class exploitation of the situation, de Jonge, at 240; emphasising (at 242) the absence of any policy of rationing to accompany the distribution of supplies.

22. See on the evidence of Libanius, P. Petit, 'Recherches sur la publication et la diffusion des discours de Libanius', *Historia* 5 (1956), at 481-3, and his *Libanius et la vie municipale*, esp. 105-22; de Jonge (above, n. 6), 243f.

23. This distinction between the economic functions of *curiales* and corn-merchants in Libanius' analysis is noted by de Jonge, 243f.; cf. Petit, 116f.

24. Petit, 117, comments that Alexander 'a même accentué la politique tracassière de Julien: il a designé les controleurs des prix, 'logistai', qui persécutent les commercants en leur demandant leurs factures .... comme il arrive souvent, les subordonnés se montrent plus tatillons que leurs chefs'. That is to say, Alexander attracted the criticisms earlier levelled against Julian.

25. For Libanius as the apostle of free trade, cf. de Jonge, 243. On Aradius Rufinus (Petit, 117), see Chastagnol, *Fastes*, No. 78 (pp. 196-8). Ammianus records his appointment at 23.1.4.

26. Cf. my remarks at Chapter V, pp. 72ff.

27. The affair of the temple of Apollo is discussed at Chapter XVII, pp. 439ff.; so too the religious riots at Alexandria, pp. 442ff.

28. H. P. Kohns, 'Die Zeitkritik in den Romexkursen des Ammianus Marcellinus: zu Amm. Marc. 14,6,3-26; 28,4,6-35', *Chiron* 5 (1975), 485-91, makes clear (i) that the two digressions do not differ from each other in their purpose; (ii) that Ammianus asserts no moral distinction in principle between nobility and common people (the only difference is that 'diese arm, jene reich ist'; 488); and (iii) that his criticism relates to the longer time-scale of relations between senate and emperors 'seit Beginn der Kaiserzeit' (491), and not to an exact or exclusive concern with the conditions of his own day. None of this reduces the circumstantial interest of what he has to say. It is argued by Roger Pack, 'The Roman digressions of Ammianus Marcellinus', *TAPA* 84 (1953), 181-9, that Ammianus is in this passage inverting the rhetorical tradition of speeches in praise of cities by producing a sort of formal accusation owing more to literary tradition than to personal experience. As a strict line of argument this is unlikely, though no one would doubt the rhetorical element in Ammianus' writing. The passages are brought into relation with Ammianus' experience by Alan Cameron, 'The Roman friends of Ammianus', *JRS* 54 (1964), 15-28, at 26ff.

29. This theme is developed in my short paper, 'Ammianus and the Eternity of Rome', in Christopher Holdsworth and T. P. Wiseman (edd.), *The Inheritance of Historiography*, 350-900 (1986), 17-29, esp. 21f. See also Chapter XVIII, p. 470f.

30. Other aspects of Ampelius' prefecture are discussed at Chapter X, p. 212.

31. 'ne Sannione quidem, ut ait comicus, domi relicto'. The reference is to Terence, *Eunuchus* 780, where Sannio is the household clown. For eunuchs in the fourth century, see Chapter XII, pp. 274ff. There is another hint of Comedy in the sample of lower-class names alleged by Ammianus – as studied by Aldo Bartalucci, 'I "nomina culta" dei plebei urbani in Ammiano (Rer. Gest. XXVIII,4,28)', *Studi Classici e Orientali* 9 (1960), 147-60. The names are connected with a variety of popular tastes, notably to do with diet (sausages, soup, cheap vegetables, salt fish, etc.) and in general 'la vita di taverna'. Pictorial and colourful, the selection suits Ammianus' satirical intention.

32. Ammianus follows this with the citation of an acclamation, 'per te illi discant', which he alleges, unlike the witty remarks of earlier times, was understood by nobody; 'quid autem debeat disci, nemo sufficit explanare' (28.4.33; he is thinking of such acclamations as those discussed by Alan Cameron, *Circus Factions*, 158ff.). In an interesting note, 'Une "scie" à Rome au IVe siècle', *REL* 24 (1946), 75-6, G. Gougenheim suggested that the phrase was a more or less meaningless slogan adopted by the people in the manner of a nineteenth-century Parisian 'scie' (a 'catch-word' or 'gag'). It can however be understood as an encouragement to future givers of games ('illi') to 'learn from', and thereby improve, the quality of the present performance. Just this meaning is supported by a series of acclamations preserved on a mosaic from Smirat in Tunisia showing scenes from wild-beast combats; 'Adclamatum est: "exemplo tuo, munus sic discant futuri! unde tale? quando tale? exemplo quaestorum munus edes, de re tua munus edes" ', etc.; cf. Charlotte Roueché, *JRS* 74 (1984), at 183.

33. See the article of R. Pack, cited at n. 28. Also relevant is D. S. Wiesen, *Saint Jerome as a Satirist* (1964), e.g. 21, 15 (on Ammianus and Juvenal). In what follows I pick up themes outlined in my *Western Aristocracies and Imperial Court*, ch. I.2 (pp. 12-23); cf. my 'The Letters of Symmachus', 58-99, at 70-3.

34. On Symmachus' prefecture, *Western Aristocracies*, 22, and Chastagnol, *Fastes*, No. 66 (pp. 159-63). For his father's expulsion and return, *Western Aristocracies*, 20, 67.

35. J. Rougé, 'Une émeute à Rome au IVe siècle. Ammien Marcellin XXVII 3.3-4: essai d'interprétation', *REA* 63 (1961), 59-77. The reference (Rougé, 63-4) is to Pliny, *Hist. Nat.* 36.191, supported by Palladius, *Op. Agr.* 1,17 and 40.

36. The prefecture of Lampadius: Chastagnol, *Fastes*, No. 67 (pp. 164-71).

37. Cf. the discussion of this passage by Zvi Yavetz, 'Plebs sordida', *Athenaeum*, n.s. 43 (1965), 295-311, at 308ff.; and P. A. Brunt, 'The Roman mob', *Past and Present* 35 (1966), 3-27, at 21ff.; repr. in M. I. Finley, *Studies in Ancient Society* (1974), 74-102, at 95f.

38. I discuss this passage, with a sketch of its literary character in relation to Auerbach's famous chapter 'The arrest of Peter Valvomeres' (*Mimesis: the representation of reality in Western literature*, ch. 3), in 'Peter Valvomeres, re-arrested', *Homo Viator: classical essays*

for John Bramble (1987), 277-84.

39. On what follows, *Western Aristocracies*, 12ff. The levels of senatorial wealth and expenditure are well discussed by Rougé (above, n. 35), at 65-7.

40. J. A. MacGeachy, *Q. Aurelius Symmachus and the Senatorial Aristocracy of the West* (diss. Chicago, 1942), 103-9. The evidence, which can easily be recovered from Seeck's introduction to his edition of Symmachus' works, merits further study.

41. On the contorniates, see A. Alföldi's classic but tendentious study: *Die Kontorniaten: ein verkanntes Propagandamittel der Stadtrömischen Aristokratie in ihrem Kampfe gegen das christliche Kaisertum* (1942-3; 2nd ed. entitled *Die Kontorniat-Medaillons* (1976)). I am very doubtful of the religious interpretation offered by Alföldi (pagan propaganda connected with the New Year), on which the observations in Jocelyn Toynbee's review discussion, *JRS* 35 (1945), 115-21, retain their force.

42. On the 'theatrical' elements in late Roman life, see Chapters XI, p. 247, and XVIII, pp. 459ff.

43. An example of a retired bureaucrat in a senatorial milieu at Rome is Sextilius Agesilaus Aedesius, recorded in *ILS* 4152 as an initiate of Magna Mater, Mithras, Hecate and Liber Pater. His post as *magister memoriae* is mentioned also by Ammianus, who included him among the alleged conspirators against Silvanus (15.5.4). A financially straitened member of a provincial senatorial family is Valerius Fortunatus of Emerita, for whom Symmachus sought the quaestorship in *Or.* 8, with much reference to his 'poverty' (ed. Seeck, pp. 338-9).

44. Ammianus' observation is relevant not only to Roman society. For interest, and without pretension to scientific accuracy, I give the result of a survey of a (nearly) random sample of the professions of those notables recorded over a few weeks in late 1985 and early 1986 in the daily column 'Birthdays' in the *Guardian* newspaper: actors and actresses, 55; sports personalities and commentators, 35; popular authors and journalists, 24; pop singers, 22; politicians, 19; musical performers (pop and Classical), 14; comedians and entertainers, 10; film and stage producers and designers, 8; Classical/opera singers, 7; academics, 5; dancers and choreographers, 5; artists (including 1 architect), 5; royalty (domestic and foreign), captains of industry, Air Marshals, TV company directors, bishops (including 1 archbishop), 2 of each; judges, cartoonists, sexologists, record producers, chefs, Chief Rabbis, astronauts, 1 of each; serious historians, 1. This perspective is not unlike that of which Ammianus complains.

45. The charioteer, Hilarinus, had sought refuge in a church, 'confugit ad ritus christiani sacrarium', but was brought out and beheaded (26.3.3). For Ammianus' phraseology, and for this and another case of asylum sought in churches, see Chapter XVII, p. 438.

46. For the origins of the prosecutions at Rome under Valentinian, see Chapter X, p. 210.

47. The episode, and its significance in Ammianus' attitudes, are discussed at Chapter XVII, p. 441f.

48. See for a sketch my *Western Aristocracies*, 363-9. The poems of Prudentius are edited with translation by M. Lavarenne, ed. Budé, t. IV (1963), and by H. J. Thomson, ed. Loeb, Vol. II (1953). A fine study of the *Peristephanon* has just been published by Anne-Marie Palmer, *Prudentius on the Martyrs* (Oxford, 1989).

49. For the dedication of the church, see Chastagnol, *Fastes*, p. 238 (s. No. 96, Fl. Philippus; *PLRE* I, p. 697, Philippus 8). The Symmachan document is *Rel.* 25, referring to the excessive cost of the new basilica, and also of a bridge (cf. *Rel.* 26). The affair and its documentation are discussed by Chastagnol, 'Sur quelques documents relatifs à la basilique Saint Paul-hors-les-Murs', *Mél. Piganiol* (1966), I, 421-37.

50. The Piranesi engraving is shown, and the Prudentius text translated, in F. van der Meer and Chr. Mohrmann, *Atlas of the Early Christian World* (Eng. tr., 1966), No. 183 (184 is a drawing by Pinelli of the scene after its destruction, and 185 a photograph of the present-day church). See also Tim Cornell and John Matthews, *Atlas of the Roman World* (1982), p. 207; and John Wilton-Ely, *The Mind and Art of Giovanni Battista Piranesi* (1978), p. 31 and pl. 5.

51. V. Melaniae 5 (ed. D. Gorce, *Vie de Sainte Mélanie, SChr* 90 (1962) p. 134).

52. *Liber Pontificalis*, ed. L. Duchesne (1886), p. 212, with n. 7, pp. 213-14, gives the relevant texts. The eighth-century Sylloge Virdunensis preserves a poem of Damasus from the apse of the church: 'ad ecclesiam sancti Laurentii in Damaso, quae alio nomine appellatur in prasino. isti versiculi sunt scripti in illo throno: "Haec Damasus tibi, Christe Deus, nova tecta dicavi, / Laurenti saeptus martyris auxilio" '. See G. B. de Rossi, *ICUR* II, p. 134. No. 5, and A. Ferrua, *Epigrammata Damasiana* (1942), No. 58 (p. 212), with his notes on No. 57.

53. *Libellus de Regionibus Urbis Romae* (ed. A. Nordh, 1949), p. 86. The entry begins: 'Regio VIIII Circus Flaminius continet: stabula numero IIII factionum VI ....'

54. Richard Krautheimer, *Rome: profile of a city*, 312-1308 (1980), ch. 2, esp. 54ff., is fascinating on the evolution of the 'religious topography' of fourth- and fifth-century Rome; cf. at 29-31, where he remarks on the domination of the central area by the secular monuments of old Rome, the earlier fourth-century church foundations (St. Peter's, St. Paul outside the Walls, the Lateran, St. Lawrence, etc.) being peripheral. The habitation of this central area of 'theatres, porticoes and temples' (Krautheimer, p. 56) as the core of medieval Rome was a later development.

55. My reference to the libraries of senators is intended to pick up the *Saturnalia* of Macrobius, on which see my *Western Aristocracies*, 369-72 – assuming, as I still do, the fifth-century date, c. 430 or later, established by Alan Cameron, 'The date and identity of Macrobius', *JRS* 56 (1966), 25-38.

XVII. Religion and Philosophy

(1) Divination and daimones

1. In fact, these aspects of Julian's religious policies are barely hinted at by Ammianus; Chapter VI, p. 112. Ammianus' own attitude to Christianity is discussed in the second part of this Chapter.

2. *ILS* 1259: cf. my 'Symmachus and the oriental cults', *JRS* 63 (1973), 175-95, at 179f.; *Western Aristocracies*, 6f. For Ammianus' acquaintance with Praetextatus, see Chapter II.2, p. 23.

3. The term 'paganus' has been much discussed; others (e.g. Lane Fox, *Pagans and Christians*, 30-1), connect it with the notion of 'civil' as opposed to 'military', i.e. one not a member of the 'militia Christi'. This seems over-refined as a description of actual usage. By the later fourth century, writers seem agreed in believing it to mean country-folk or rustic: cf. J. J. O'Donnell, ' "Paganus": evolution and use', *Classical Folia* 31 (1977), 163-9, surveying the problem and pointing out (at 167) the rarity of the term between Tertullian and the mid-fourth century.

4. Esp. Greg. Naz., *C. Iulianum* II (*Or.* IV) 101ff. (*PG* 35.635ff.); J. Bernardi, *Grégoire de Nazianze, Discours 4-5 contre Julien* (*SChr* 309, 1983), 248f. For Ammianus' attitude, Chapter VI, p. 112.

5. I am thinking of Ambrose's reply to Symmachus, *Epp.* 17.10, 14, 16; 18.10, 15, 19, 31, etc. For Ammianus' usage, the microfiche concordance by Geoffrey Archbold (1980) is decisive; the word almost always means 'barbarian' or 'native'.

6. 'Christianitas' occurs in the Theodosian Code at 14.3.11 (365), 12.1.112 (386), 12.1.123 (391), 16.8.19 (409), 16.8.23 (416), 16.8.26 (423), 15.5.5 (426), 16.7.7 (426); also at *CJust* 3.12.6 (= *CTh* 2.8.19, 389, but the relevant phrase may be a later interpolation in *CJust* from *CTh* 15.5.5). The usages vary in meaning from the Christian clergy or clerical office (12.1.123) to something like Christendom (15.5.5; *CJust* 3.12.6), and the term is sometimes opposed to Judaism or apostasy (16.8.19, 23; 16.7.7). In general the term is 'objective' in tendency, connoting a religious allegiance rather than a system of belief.

7. For Symmachus' practice, see my brief remarks at *JRS* 63 (1973), 193; esp. *Ep.* 1.64, 7.51, recommending bishops to well-placed friends. Symmachus does not use the term 'Christianitas' at all. Consultation of Valeria Lomanto, *A Concordance to Symmachus* (1983) reveals just two instances of 'Christianae legis' – both in *Relatio* 21, in which Symmachus defends himself against sectarian attack.

8. *Decline and Fall*, ch. XV (ed. Bury, 1897, II, 16ff.).

9. W. Seyfarth, 'Ammianus und das Fatum', *Klio* 43/5 (1965), 291-306, sees Ammianus' use of this concept in terms of the 'high style' in which he wrote, adducing relevant parallels from the Historia Augusta and the Theodosian Code. The question is however not purely philological, and in a more far-reaching study C. P. T. Naudé, 'Fortuna in Ammianus

Marcellinus', *Acta Classica* 7 (1964), 70-89, sets Ammianus' use of the concept against its Greek and Roman philosophical and historiographical background. 'Fortuna' is seen either as a force working through external circumstance to a moral end – one ordained by the gods or fate, as at 14.10.25f. (Gallus Caesar) – or as a variable, unpredictable and usually adverse factor behind events (cf. Naudé, 72). These apparently opposing concepts can be partly reconciled by seeing Fortuna in terms of the external, unchosen factors by which men are overwhelmed, or against which they must strive in order to overcome them. Ammianus displays a variety of uses ranging from the merely metaphorical or stylistic, through the notion of 'Fortuna' as a state of affairs or social condition, to her role as protectress and associate of men or peoples and their 'genius'. Her most common occurrence is however as an unpredictable and generally hostile power impinging upon men. This relates to the moral conception fundamental to Ammianus, of the capacity of Rome to rise above misfortune by her unique 'virtus' (cf. 14.6.3, on the rise of Rome), 31.5.14; 10/19; 13.19, etc. (on the Gothic wars of 376-8). There is a characteristically full and sensible discussion of the material to be found in Ammianus on this and related topics, by Narciso Santos Yanguas, 'Presagios, adivinación y magia en Ammiano Marcelino', *Helmantica* 30 (1979), 5-49; cf. pp. 13-25 on Fate and Fortune, 25-43 on theurgy and other, more conventional forms of divination.

10. For what follows, I am greatly indebted, both in detail and in general interpretation, to the commentaries of Joachim Szidat on Ammianus Books 20 and (incomplete) 21; *Historia, Einzelschriften* 31 (1977) and 38 (1981), esp. (1981) at 71-84; also to his article, 'Der Neuplatonismus und die Gebildeten im Westen des Reiches: Gedanken zu seiner Verbreitung und Kenntnis ausserhalb der Schultradition', *Mus. Helv.* 39 (1982), 132-45. The subtitle of Szidat's article is important; his aim (cf. p. 144) is to use Ammianus and other sources to trace the influence of Neoplatonism outside professional circles to reach what one might call a 'lay' audience of non-specialists interested in philosophy. Ammianus' interest in Neoplatonism was already emphasised by Ensslin, *Zur Geschichtschreibung und Weltanschauung des Ammianus Marcellinus*, esp. ch. VI; on divination, pp. 83-96. Neglect of the work of Szidat and its implications diminishes the value of the recent work by R. L. Rike, *Apex Omnium: religion in the Res Gestae of Ammianus* (1937). There is much of interest in this book, but it is flawed by an unnecessarily obscure style, and by insecure technique in handling certain aspects of the text. It is true to say (Rike, p. 9) that the digressions are as much part of Ammianus' literary personality as his narrative history, but that does not mean that the two forms of writing are indistinguishable in manner, or in their sources of information. If Ammianus gained his knowledge of events from 'versati in medio', his digressions are characterised by 'bookishness'. It is essential that a 'theological synthesis' such as that attempted by Rike (cf. p. 11) should respect the difference between the two styles of writing. In general, I would prefer to look in Ammianus for a range of responses to complex and varied situations rather than for a single definable 'theology'.

11. Szidat's commentary, at 80; for Cicero, see the commentary of A. S. Pease on the *De Divinatione*, I (1920), p. 244 (citing this passage of Ammianus).

12. Szidat, at 75f. with the parallels adduced, and *Mus. Helv.* 39 (1982), 137f., sees Ammianus' relations with Macrobius in terms of a Latin handbook or handbooks consulted by both.

13. For Cicero's scepticism in its late Republican setting, see J. H. W. G. Liebeschuetz, *Continuity and Change in Roman Religion* (1979), ch. 1, esp. 29-39. In the *De Natura Deorum*, 'Cotta, Cicero's sceptical spokesman ... insisted that no amount of philosophical argument would induce him to desert the religious position of his ancestors' (Liebeschuetz, 31f.).

14. For Alexandrian science, see ch. 7 of P. M. Fraser's *Ptolemaic Alexandria* (1972) and esp. (on medicine) Vivian Nutton, 'Ammianus and Alexandria', *Clio Medica* 7 (1972), 165-76; on astrology, Fraser, 435ff. For a brief account, the splendid book of A. K. Bowman, *Egypt after the Pharaohs, 332 B.C.- A.D. 642* (1986), 223-33, at 227ff.

15. Szidat, in his commentary on 20.3.12 (1977, pp. 127-9), finds parallels to Ammianus' expressions in Calcidius' commentary on Plato's *Timaeus* 59 ('puncti quidem instar') and 78 ('languente visus acie'); cf. the ed. of J. H. Waszink, *Plato Latinus* 4 (1962), pp. 106, 125. The 'embarrassing mistake' is noted by D. den Hengst, 'Ammianus Marcellinus on astronomy',

546   *Notes to pp. 432–5*

Mnemosyne 4.29 (1986), 136-41 – also confirming Szidat's conclusion that Ammianus is using Latin sources. Cf. Chapter XIII, p. 301f., for comparable difficulties in Ammianus' digression on artillery devices.

16. On *genii* or *daimones*, Ensslin 62-9 and esp. A. D. Nock, 'The Emperor's divine *comes*', *JRS* 37 (1947), 102-16, esp. at 109-12: reprinted in Zeph Stewart (ed.), *Arthur Darby Nock: essays on religion and the ancient world* (1972), II, 653-75; also Camus, *Ammien Marcellin*, 160-5. I would be reluctant to assign to Ammianus direct acquaintance with Neoplatonic sources such as Porphyry's *Life of Plotinus*; as with the other cases (divination, astronomy) discussed in this chapter, his knowledge is – with the limitations implied by the term – 'encyclopaedic' rather than genuinely profound.

17. For the Menander citations, Plutarch, *Tranqu. An.* 15 (474B); Eusebius, *Praep. Ev.* 13.13.59; Clement, *Strom.* 5.14.13. As Nock observes (at 109-10) the formulation of the doctrine by Menander implies that it was not confined to philosophical circles, but had entered wider circulation.

18. For this allegorisation as part of Neoplatonic theory, Nock, at 110f.

19. See Garth Fowden, *The Egyptian Hermes: a historical approach to the late pagan mind* (Cambridge, 1986), esp. 22-31 on the origin and divine 'personality' of Thoth-Hermes, and 27-29 on his human connections. This reference and one other to Apollonius of Tyana (also in a digression; 23.6.19) do not justify the five pages devoted to that sage by Rike (n. 10 above), 80-4.

20. On Scipio Africanus and the divine, F. W. Walbank, 'The Scipionic legend', *Proc. Camb. Phil. Soc.* 13 (1967), 54-69, cf. H. H. Scullard, *Scipio Africanus: soldier and politician* (London 1970), 18-23. On Marius, Elizabeth Rawson, 'Religion and politics in the late second century B.C. at Rome', *Phoenix* 28 (1974), 193-212, at 202-6; cf. F. Chamoux, 'La prophétesse Martha', *Mél. Seston* (1974), 81-5 – on her costume and accoutrements rather than her religious accomplishments.

21. On Julian, the theurgists, and fate, see Chapter VII, esp. pp. 126ff.

(2) Christianity in Ammianus

22. I am freed of the necessity to survey in full the historiography of this very important subject by the appearance of E. D. Hunt, 'Christians and Christianity in Ammianus Marcellinus', *CQ* n.s. 35 (1985), 186-200. 'It is surprising [remarks Hunt, at 188] just how much reference to Christianity we find in Ammianus' pages – in stark contrast ... to others who were recording Roman history in Latin at around the same time.' See also V. Neri, *Ammiano e il cristianesimo: Religione e Politica nelle 'Res Gestae' di Ammiano Marcellino* (1985). Recent work, like that of Neri, has tended to emphasise the more active, even polemical, aspects of Ammianus' attitude to Christianity; cf. esp. S. d'Elia, 'Ammiano Marcellino e il cristianesimo', *Studi Romani* 10 (1962), 372-90; R. L. Rike, *Apex Omnium: religion in the Res Gestae of Ammianus*, e.g. at 1-7 (with a survey of modern interpretations). Yet d'Elia's view of the connections of Ammianus and the 'pagan senatorial aristocracy of Rome' now seems schematic and dated (as well as being inaccurate in some details), while Rike is insufficiently sensitive to the diversity of the literary conventions and historical preoccupations that comprise Ammianus' text. Iorgu Stoian, 'A propos de la conception historique d'Ammien Marcellin (Ut miles quondam et graecus)', *Latomus* 26 (1967), 73-81 emphasises the cultural, and in the end religious, implications of Ammianus' concluding motto, and this is developed, but also tempered, by some very well-judged remarks in J. Heyen's short article with the same title, *Latomus* 27 (1968), 191-6 – reviewing the contributions of Stoian, Rowell, and d'Elia. For another survey of modern opinions, L. Angliviel de la Beaumelle, 'Remarques sur l'attitude d'Ammien Marcellin, à l'égard du christianisme', *Mél. Seston* (1974), 15-23. I find myself often thinking along the same lines as A. Selem, 'Considerazioni circa Ammiano ed il cristianesimo', *Rivista di Cultura Classica e Medioevale* 6 (1964), 224-61, notably on the ironically detached manner in which Ammianus describes certain 'causes célèbres' of contemporary Christianity (cf. Selem, at 254-8). It is important not to convey too bland an impression of Ammianus' attitudes, which certainly leave room for a degree of calculated irony (this Chapter, p. 450f.). To say that Ammianus takes polemical opportunities is however not to say that he is

primarily a polemical writer on the subject.

23. On Epiphany; Hunt, 188, n. 18.

24. See on these activities my reference article 'Gesandtschaft', in *RAC* X (1977), 653-85, at 673-5.

25. Cf. Sozomen 2.13.7; J. Labourt, *Le Christianisme dans l'empire Perse sous la dynastie Sassanide (224-632)* (1904), 78f. and, more especially, A. Vööbus, *History of Asceticism in the Syrian Orient*, II (1960) – particularly pp. 224-32 for monastic foundations in and around the Tur Abdin in this period. After Sapor's capture of Bezabde, among the 9,000 souls led into captivity were its bishop and aged priests, also 'priests and deacons and the *qeiama* [an ascetic community or group] of men and women'. See Vööbus, I (1958), 204, and in general his whole discussion at 197-208, which could almost form a commentary, from a Christian ascetic point of view, on Ammianus' phrase 'ritu cultui divino sacratas ... et religioni servire solito more (praecepit)' (18.10.4). The episode is discussed by Angliviel de la Beaumelle (cited above in n. 22), 19-21, suggesting that Ammianus intended to convey criticism of the Christian pacifism implied by the bishop's attempt to make peace with Sapor rather than resist him.

26. For the cult at Milan, H.-I. Marrou, 'Ammien Marcellin et les "Innocents" de Milan', *Recherches de Science Religieuse* 40 (1951-2), 179-90: a monument, apparently an ancient sarcophagus lid, in the church of San Stefano Maggiore was since the fifteenth century called 'La Pietra degli Innocenti', the church itself deriving from a foundation of the mid-fifth century. On the episode in the *Vita Martini* see the extensive discussion by Jacques Fontaine, in *Sulpice Sévère, Vie de Saint Martin*, II (1968), at 703-12 – seeing in the bandit a local hero, possibly a leader of the third-century movement of Bagaudae.

27. See on this aspect Averil and Alan Cameron, 'Christianity and tradition in the historiography of the Late Empire', *CQ* n.s. 14 (1964), 316-28.

28. This nuance in the argument – the technical word as permissible after a non-technical introduction to the subject – is not to my knowledge brought out in existing studies.

29. Agathias 5.18. The example is cited by Averil Cameron, *Agathias* (1970), 86; see her entire discussion, 83-8.

30. A letter of Julian, written while on the road through Asia Minor to his uncle as *comes Orientis* (*Ep.* 80 Bidez: ed. Loeb, p. 98) contains instructions for the provision of pillars for the repair of the temple. They might be taken from imperial palaces where available, and from private houses – in the latter case clearly implying the pillaging of building materials from deserted temples. Columns of brick might be used as an emergency measure, to be clad later with stucco to give a marble effect.

31. The relevant sections of the homily of John Chrysostom against Julian and the pagans (*PG* 50.533ff.) are translated by Marna Morgan, with much helpful commentary on this and the other material, in the source-book edited by S. N. C. Lieu, *The Emperor Julian: panegyric and polemic* (1986), ch. 2, pp. 45-89. The paragraphs of the *Passio S. Artemii*, on which much of my narrative is based, are printed in Bidez's ed. of Philostorgius' *Ecclesiastical History* (*GCS*, 2nd ed. by F. Winkelmann, 1972), at 92-4; see also Sozomen 5.19.15-20.6 (ed. *GCS*, pp. 225-7).

32. See for Ammianus' perspective Hunt at 193-4, concluding: 'Ammianus is not content to label the incident in terms of a conflict between pagans and Christianity, as it was interpreted both by Julian and by his Christian opponents. The historian stands aside, distanced from their version of events'. I am in broad agreement with this, but the questions remain, whether in so 'standing aside' Ammianus has in effect falsified an inherently religious episode, and whether his detachment may itself be a form of polemical expression.

33. Hunt, 189-93 gives exemplary discussions of these episodes (with reference also to the church historians and general accounts).

34. For the propensity of Alexandria to civic disorder, P. M. Fraser, *Ptolemaic Alexandria*, esp. 71, 81-2, 90; A. K. Bowman, *Egypt after the Pharaohs*, 212ff. Ammianus reverts to the contentious character of Egyptians in his digression on their country (22.16.23); it was something of a literary stereotype, cf. Syme, *Ammianus and the Historia Augusta*, 28-9. The murder of George is well discussed by Selem (cited above in n. 22), at 254-6.

35. This chronology is in fact inaccurate, for Artemius was executed a year later; see n. 37 below.

Notes to pp. 443–50

36. The official, Diodorus, was presumably a Christian: hence Ammianus' remark that his action was intended as a tribute to 'the gods' must – unless he he is being maladroit and since he attributes the motive to Diodorus – contain more than a touch of irony. For remarks on the tonsure (22.11.9; 'cirros puerorum licentius detondebat'), Hunt, at 193, n. 46. D'Elia (cited in n. 22 above) well notes the implications of the disagreeable context of Ammianus' reference to martyrdom.

37. *PLRE* I, p. 112 (Artemius 2) gives the chronology. News of Constantius' death arrived at Alexandria on 3 November 361. Artemius was condemned to death, apparently at Antioch in winter 362/3 (22.10.1; 11.2); cf. Hunt, 191-2.

38. For accounts of this *cause célèbre*, see the refs. cited by Hunt, 191, n. 30; notably Ch. Piétri, *Roma Christiana* (1976), 407-18 and A. Lippold, 'Ursinus und Damasus', *Historia* 14 (1965), 119-28; to which I would add, with a note of caution, A. Alföldi, *A Conflict of Ideas*, 80-4. The ecclesiastical sources give a figure of over 160 dead (Pietri, 409); an indication that Ammianus' source, whatever its nature, was prefectoral, not ecclesiastical. The latter might have better information as to later deaths from injuries, thereby explaining the higher figure.

39. As d'Elia (cited in n. 22 above) shrewdly points out (390), the gentle and mild version of Christianity 'commended' by Ammianus would lose its political influence. I agree with d'Elia in seeing polemical implications in this.

40. Photius, *Bibl.* p. 77 (Müller, *FHG* IV, p. 9; Blockley, pp. 4-5). The questions of the successive editions of Eunapius' history, and of the availability of the first edition to Ammianus, are disputed; see esp. W. R. Chalmers, 'The NEA EKDOSIS of Eunapius' Histories', *CQ* n.s. 3 (1953), 165-70; T. D. Barnes, *The Sources of the Historia Augusta* (1978), ch. 9 (pp. 114-23, at 117-19) – both accepting Ammianus' use of Eunapius. Against, F. Paschoud, 'Quand parut la première édition de l'Histoire d'Eunape?', *HAColl, Bonn 1977/8* (1980), 149-62, argues for a later date of publication, c. 395. My own view is defined by my belief that Ammianus was in fact able to use Eunapius and did so, selectively, for aspects of the Persian campaign of Julian. For the arguments and parallel passages, see Chapter VIII.3, pp. 169ff. There is a recent study of Eunapius by Antonio Baldini, *Ricerche sulla Storia di Eunapio di Sarde: Problemi di storiografia tardopagana* (1984).

41. Hunt, at 198-9: see my Chapter VII above, at p. 128 with n. 23.

42. For Terentius' characterisation see Sabbah, *La Méthode d'Ammien Marcellin*, at 424 – comparing Procopius and Petronius Probus for other sorts of 'downcast' behaviour. That of Terentius is defined as 'hypocritical'.

43. Sozomen's refutation of Eunapius is discussed by F. Paschoud, *Cinq Etudes sur Zosime* (1975), ch. 2, pp 26ff. (although I do not believe that the 'Annales' of Nicomachus Flavianus enter into the argument).

44. Zosimus 2.38, with Paschoud's n. 51, pp. 241-4; cf. Eunapius, *V. Soph*, pp. 461, 462. At Julian, *Caesares* 336A, Jesus waits beside the goddesses Luxury and Prodigality, where he is joined by Constantine at the end of the contest; at 335B, Constantine's aim is said to have been to assemble all the wealth he could, in order to gratify his own and his friends' desires. When Ammianus remarks of Julian's dismissal of excess *palatini* that some of them had enriched themselves 'ex templorum spoliis' (22.4.3), it is only as one of the many means by which, through largesse and invasion of the property of others, they had raised themselves to the heights of opulence.

45. For Aurelius Victor, *Caesares* 41.4, 12, Constantine abolished crucifixion and was held 'pro conditore vel deo'; and he devoted his 'ingens animus', 'condenda urbe formandisque religionibus'. For Eutropius, 10.5-8, Constantine was 'vir ingens et omnia efficere nitens, quae animo praeparasset'. The religious implications of these expressions are calculated in their indirectness. *Epitome de Caesaribus*, 42, passes by the issue altogether.

46. *PLRE* I, pp. 611-12 (s. Musonianus); cf. T. D. Barnes, *Constantine and Eusebius* (1981), 228 (a summary reference).

47. Augustus had hesitated to move an obelisk 'deo Soli speciali munere dedicatus fixusque intra ambitiosi templi delubra, quae contingi non poterant, tamquam apex omnium eminebat' (17.4.12). The passage is discussed in typically oblique fashion by Rike (cited in n. 22 above), 28-30; 98-100. Garth Fowden points out, in a most interesting recent article ('Nicagoras of Athens and the Lateran Obelisk', *JHS* 107 [1987] 51-7) that

Constantius' dedicatory inscr. (*ILS* 736) claimed that Constantine had originally intended the obelisk for Constantinople. It is possible that this is Constantius' attempt to 'upstage' his father by asserting his own superior affection for Rome. Constantine may have intended the monument for Rome, but he had fallen out with the city.

48. See esp. Cyril Mango, *Le développement urbain de Constantinople (IVe-VIIe siècles)* (Travaux et Mémoires du centre de recherche d'histoire et civilisation de Byzance: Monographies 2; 1985), at 34-6 – minimising the explicitly Christian character of Constantine's city in relation to the Classical traditions inherited there from Graeco-Roman Byzantion, and in comparison with contemporary Rome, which possessed at least as many churches. Constantinople provides Ammianus with one of his most oblique references to Christianity, when he says that Constantinople was sent there for burial 'prope necessitudines eius' (21.16.20) – in the church of the Apostles.

49. See my discussion 'Ammianus and the Eternity of Rome', in C. Holdsworth and T. P. Wiseman (edd.), *The Inheritance of Historiography, 350-900* (1986), 17-29.

50. Jerome's promise is expressed at *V. Malchi* 1 (*PL* 23.55). Jerome would show 'quomodo et per quos Christi ecclesia nata sit et adulta, persecutionis creverit et martyriis coronata sit, et postquam ad Christianos principes venerit, potentia quidem et divitiis maior, sed virtutibus minor facta sit'.

XVIII. The Roman and the Greek

1. This chapter is retrospective and develops themes presented in earlier parts of the book. Back-references to this material are not given except for specific reasons or when something is added to what was said before. It will be obvious by now that I have more understanding of historiographical issues when they are related to specific writers and their situations than when they are posed in more abstract terms. Accordingly I would mention two books that I have found especially useful in this sense. F. W. Walbank, *Polybius* (Sather Classical Lectures 42, 1972) is a wise and penetrating study of the historical evolution of that splendid writer whom, of all his predecessors, Ammianus in many ways most resembles. Sir Ronald Syme's *Tacitus* (2 vols., 1958) is a masterpiece whose influence goes beyond any specific reference to page or chapter (though I reserve my position on the question of Tacitus' influence upon Ammianus). Between them, these two books provide much of what is relevant in assessing the Greek and the Roman influences in Ammianus' historical formation. In addition, I should mention the constant enlightenment I have gained from the writings, in a rather different tradition, of Arnaldo Momigliano.

2. On Augustine and his concubine, *Confessions* 6.15(25), with 9.6(14) for their son Adeodatus; with Brent Shaw, 'The family in Late Antiquity: the experience of Augustine', *Past and Present* 115 (1987), 3-51 at 45.

3. Ammianus' common sense is the central theme of many discussions, as recently of Robin Seager's semantic study, *Ammianus Marcellinus: seven studies in language and thought* (1986), esp. ch. 4, 'Caution, Prudence and Sobriety', cf. p. 131, 'a preoccupation with moderation and excess'. It would be difficult to think of a serious ancient writer who does *not* give his vote to moderation.

4. Eutropius continues: 'quae nunc non tam praetermittimus quam ad maiorem scribendi diligentiam reservamus'. Blockley, *Ammianus Marcellinus*, 96 n. 143 registers the parallels. Ensslin, *Zur Geschichtschreibung*, etc., 18, thinks that a compliment to Eutropius is intended; Sabbah, *La Méthode d'Ammien Marcellin*, 17f. compares Ammianus' words with the preface of Tacitus' *Histories* (1.1.6), which they do not seem to me to resemble very closely, either verbally or in theme. One of the most pertinent judgments of Ammianus' epilogue remains that of Gibbon: 'Ammianus Marcellinus ... recommends the more glorious subject of the ensuing reign to the youthful vigour and eloquence of the rising generation. The rising generation was not disposed to accept his advice, or to imitate his example ....' Gibbon goes on to write of 'fragments and chronicles, ... poetry and panegyric, and ... the precarious assistance of the ecclesiastical writers, who, in the heat of religious faction, are apt to despise the profane virtues of sincerity and moderation' (ch. XXVI; Vol. 3, p. 122, ed. Bury, London 1897).

5. On this tradition of 'universal history' as related especially to Polybius, Walbank,

Polybius, pp. 3, 42, 66f. For Polybius' continuators, Jacoby, *FGrH* 91 T.2 (Vol. IIA, p. 430). Eunapius and Dexippus, Eunapius Fr. 1, cf. Photius, *Bibl.* cod. 77 (ed. Müller, *FHG* IV, p. 9; Blockley, pp. 2-3).

6. Walbank, *Polybius*, 66 describes this double character of Thucydides' history.

7. Walbank, *Polybius*, 67f., 171-3 and 181 discusses Polybius' attitude to Rome's use and worthiness of empire; concluding that since Polybius does not face the question squarely, the last books of his history lack focus and direction.

8. For these conclusions, which are intended merely to outline the range of possibilities, see my Chapter II.2, at p. 27.

9. Jerome, *Comm. ad Zachariam* 3.14 (*PL* 25.1522). It is a passing reference only but shows how Tacitus was regarded in Jerome's time; cf. Syme, *Ammianus and the Historia Augusta*, 9, citing R. P. Oliver, 'The First Medicean MS of Tacitus and the titulature of ancient books', *TAPA* 82 (1951), 232-61. The MS contained both major works, numbered consecutively. On the broader issue Chapter II, n. 45, refers to articles by Tränkle, Wilshire, Flach, Blockley and Borzsák on the differences in the political and historiographical circumstances in which Tacitus and Ammianus respectively worked. Wilshire and Flach are particularly effective in indicating the biographical influences upon Ammianus' writing, as is G. Niccoli, 'Tradizione biografica suetoniana e orientamenti ideologici nei necrologi imperial di Ammiano Marcellino', *Critica Storica* 13 (1976), 610-20.

10. See on this passage A. Demandt, *Zeitkritik und Geschichtsbild im Werk Ammians* (1965), 118-47; and my 'Ammianus and the Eternity of Rome', in Christopher Holdsworth and T. P. Wiseman (edd.), *The Inheritance of Historiography, 350-900* (1986), at 21-3.

11. *Agricola* 3.1: 'Nerva Caesar res olim dissociabilis miscuit, principatum et libertatem'; cf. *Histories*, 1.1: 'rara temporum felicitate, ubi sentire quae velis et quae sentias dicere licet'. The phrases are often connected with the epilogue and with other passages of Ammianus in which he refers to his contemporary experience (e.g. 26.1.1; 28.1.2; cf. Chapter X, p. 209.); my point is that in terms of their substantive implications, they assert the distance between the two writers rather than their affinities.

12. Despite Sabbah, *La Méthode d'Ammien Marcellin* (and many others, including the Loeb and Penguin translators) the word 'limatius' at 15.1.1, 'residua ... pro virium captu limatius absolvemus' has in Ammianus' usage a certain emphatic force but is not a comparative. See Chapter II, n. 36.

13. Walbank, *Polybius*, 73f.

14. For Enmann's *Kaisergeschichte*, see Chapter II.2, p. 29 with n. 41.

15. The verbal parallels between Ammianus and Festus are close; Mommsen, 'Ammians Geographica', *Hermes* 16 (1881), 602-36 at 605-9 = *Ges. Schr.* VII, 393-425 at 396-400.

16. See my Chapter X, pp. 206ff. for this aspect of Ammianus' narrative of the more recent period.

17. On the character of Latin biography, Syme, *Ammianus and the Historia Augusta*, ch. XVIII, pp. 94-102, 'Biography against History'. On Suetonius and the biographical tradition Andrew Wallace-Hadrill, *Suetonius: the scholar and his Caesars* (1983), is especially revealing; cf. (for example) ch. 3, 'The scholarly biographer' and pp. 126-9, 'The antiquarian's view'. On the Greek tradition, my remarks at Chapter VI, p. 84 (relating to the Emperor Julian), and Wallace-Hadrill, 8; Walbank, *Polybius*, 91ff. There are formal analyses of Ammianus' character portrayals by D. A. Pauw, 'Methods of character portrayal in the Res Gestae of Ammianus Marcellinus', *Acta Classica* 20 (1977), 181-98, and 'Ammianus Marcellinus and ancient historiography, biography and character portrayal', ibid. 22 (1979), 115-29; Ammianus uses indirect methods of indicating character (e.g. through action, innuendo and reported opinion) rather than direct (e.g. in his formal necrologies), and in this respect, despite an obvious tendency to the biographical, shows himself more of a historian than a biographer.

18. As in other cases, Ammianus' general meaning is apparent although his text is uncertain. The version adopted by Clark and Seyfarth is as follows (readings of V are indicated in brackets): 'memorabat assidue (-ae) livorem severitatis (-em) rectae (-e) potestatis esse individuam (invidiam) sociam.' That virtues and vices were related was a commonplace sentiment (cf. Seneca, *Ep.* 45.7); since the sentiment is here attributed to Valentinian, the logic should be that a virtue (the correct exercise of power) is mistakenly

seen by some as a vice (undue severity). Valesius, preserving V's 'severitatem', deleted 'livorem', but this is the more drastic textual solution, the resultant reading is less powerful, and 'livor' is a good late Roman word often used of enmity and anger (cf. my 'Symmachus and his enemies', at 166f., 175): here the 'opprobrium of (incurred by) severity'. I would therefore favour 'livorem severitatis'. As for the rest, Ammianus begins the entire sentence emphatically with 'invidia', and it is unlikely that he would use the word twice, the second occurrence in the weaker position. Valesius' suggestion 'individuam' gives the excellent sense of severity as the 'inseparable companion' of strictness: the female gender of 'socia' being understood as substantive, in a sort of personification of 'livor severitatis'. Gelenius' attempt, 'memorabat ... livorem virtutum rectae potestatis invidiam esse sociam', like Valesius I find unintelligible, both in syntax and logic. It expresses over-ingenuity rather than any privileged acquaintance with an authoritative reading of M. As in the argument against two occurrences of 'invidia(m)', Ammianus also has 'virtutes' earlier in the same sentence (where V, as if to indicate what can happen, has 'veritotes'!).

19. Walbank, *Polybius*, 93 gives this reference.

20. Syme, *Ammianus and the Historia Augusta*, 149; Chapter XII, p. 277.

21. For similar contrasts of character, compare Ammianus' description of the general Severus, Marcellus' successor, 'nec discors nec arrogans, sed longa militiae frugalitate compertus' (16.7.2), with the passage quoted in the text; and the portraits of the usurper Procopius and Valens' general Serenianus, 26.9.11 with 10.2 (Chapter IX, p. 201).

22. Ramsay MacMullen, 'Some pictures in Ammianus Marcellinus', *Art Bulletin* 46 (1964), at 452f., cf. his 'Judicial savagery in the Roman Empire', *Chiron* 16 (1986), at 157-9 and Chapter XI, pp. 255f. See the article by E. C. Evans on the philosophical background, cited at Chapter XII, n. 16.

23. Ammianus' affinities with Greek culture, as implied in this phrase and in his historical manner in general, are another of the major issues in his interpretation, addressed more or less directly by all writers on him. See esp. H. Tränkle, *Antike und Abendland* 11 (1962), at 21-3 (citing the view of Wilamowitz, that Ammianus was in all essentials a Greek historian); and C. J. Clausen, 'Greek and Roman in Ammianus Marcellinus' History', *Museum Africum* 1 (1972), 39-47. For G. A. Crump, *Ammianus Marcellinus as a Military Historian*, 4, 'Ammianus cites these two elements ... because they constitute different sides of his preparation as a historian'. For the perspective argued above, see my articles, 'Ammianus Marcellinus', 1121f., and 'Ammianus' historical evolution', 30f.; R. Browning, in *Cambridge History of Classical Literature* II (1982), at 749: in making his claim at the very end of a long history in Latin, Ammianus is declaring an obvious paradox, and this facet must be present in the interpretation of the phrase. The cultural dimension of the phrase is emphasised and extended into a religious dimension ('Graecus' as equivalent to the word 'Hellene', a cultivated pagan; Chapter XVII.1, p. 425), by G. Stoian, Latomus 26 (1967), 73-81. I doubt whether, in this context, such a meaning is relevant, cf. Chapter XVII, n. 22. Sabbah, *La Méthode d'Ammien Marcellin*, 532ff., is characteristically illuminating. For Rike, concluding his book *Apex Omnium: religion in the Res Gestae of Ammianus*, the phrase shows Ammianus as 'Jason on the Black Sea, envisioning himself at one with those specifically bound by the gods to strenuous labour in a strange land' (p. 137). Waiving comment on this arcane remark, I would only ask how many meanings the phrase can be asked simultaneously to bear. For a further review of opinions, see G. Calboli, *Bollettino di Studi Latini* 4 (1974), at 71-5.

24. The text at this point is not secure. 'Cultus' is Heraeus' suggestion, adopted by Clark and Seyfarth, for 'victus' (V) and 'viduus' (E). Gelenius' reading 'vietus' is accepted by Sabbah and 'vegetus' by other modern editors. 'Vietus', meaning 'shrivelled, withered', loses the contrast with '*sed* inbellis et ignavus', etc.: the same objection applies to Walter's 'quietus'. 'Vegetus', which occurs in the name of the military writer Vegetius, means 'brisk, sprightly'. I must also mention with honour Bentley's suggestion, 'unctus', although I do not think Ammianus would have written that.

25. For Ammianus and Greek, see my 'Ammianus Marcellinus', 1122 and Sabbah, *La Méthode d'Ammien Marcellin*, 536, referring to 'l'usage systématique de la parenthèse pour affirmer sa qualité de Grec' (with references to Ammianus' citations of Greek as his own language). R. Moes, *Les Hellénismes de l'époque Théodosienne (Recherches sur le*

vocabulaire d'origine grecque chez Ammien, Claudien, et dans l'Histoire Auguste (1980), is a lexicographical study, of which the implications are not worked out. The conclusion (at 334) that the Historia Augusta contains 444, Ammianus 328 and Claudian 234 'hellenisms' indicates merely the scholastic erudition of the author of the Historia Augusta and the conscious literary 'Romanisation' of the two Greek writers.

26. Sabbah, 525-8, regards Ammianus' digressions as designed in part to establish his standing as a man of science and thereby increase the veracity of an often contentious political narrative. See also Helena Cichocka, 'Die Konzeption des Exkurses im Geschichtswerk des Ammianus Marcellinus', *Eos* 63 (1975), 329-40; and Alanna Emmett, 'The digressions in the lost books of Ammianus Marcellinus' (cited in Chapter II, n. 36), and 'Introductions and conclusions to digressions in Ammianus Marcellinus', *Museum Philologicum Londiniense* 5 (1981), 15-33. I much regret that I am unable to read the study (kindly lent to me by Helena Cichocka of Warsaw University) by Milena Dušanić, *The Geographic-Ethnographic Excursus in the Work of Ammianus Marcellinus* (1986: in Russian). Both the substantial English summary (at pp. 115-23) and the imaginative choice of illustrations, indicate that this is a work of great interest. Indicative of the conventional literary sources (notably Pliny and Solinus) of Ammianus' digressions in one respect is Robert N. Mooney, 'Nature lore in Ammianus Marcellinus', *Classical Bulletin* 33.6 (1957), 61-3, cont. at 67-8. The information about the cunning hippopotamus is partly derived from Solinus 32.30 – but Ammianus adds a reference to local opinion, which he had presumably heard himself. For the battling ibis, see again Solinus 32.32-3 as well as the Herodotus reference cited in my text. Amorous palm-trees, Pliny, *Hist. Nat.* 13.34-5.

27. This is one of Ammianus' only two direct references to Thucydides (see Chapter IV, n. 20). The other is at 23.6.75 (the digression on Persia), on the Athenians having been the first Greeks to give up the wearing of arms (Thuc. 1.6.1-3).

28. Timagenes, an Alexandrian Greek, had come to Rome in the triumviral period and made himself disliked by his rude and contentious manner. He finally, in an excessive attempt to combine the manners of a Roman with those of a Greek, choked to death while trying to vomit at a dinner-party; Jacoby, *FGrH* 88 T 1-3 (Vol. IIA, pp. 318-19); *PIR* T 156 and Sabbah, 71 n. 33.

29. So Sabbah, at 27-9, here taking the passage out of context, but rightly observing elsewhere (at 70) that Timagenes is used not as a historical but as an antiquarian source, and (at 527) that he supports Ammianus' own literary stance as a 'man of science' (see n. 26 above).

30. Polybius' statement of this principle, at 12.25g (ed. Paton, Loeb, Vol. IV, pp. 380-1) occurs as part of a polemical discourse directed against his predecessor Timaeus; see Walbank, *Polybius*, 51f. For the Roman view, Syme, *Ten Studies in Tacitus* (1970), ch. 1, 'The senator as historian' and in Tacitus, e.g. at 276, on Servilius Nonianus, 'by rank and attainments ... among the foremost in state and society – a nobilis, an orator, a consul, a proconsul of Africa', and at 299, 'Something much stronger [than "the assurance that derives from honesty and industry"] is conveyed by Tacitus – that authority of rank, weight and maturity which pronounces a consular verdict upon men and affairs, peremptory and incorruptible'. Applied to Ammianus, this would exaggerate his social position and authority, and overstate his place in the Latin tradition. For Ammianus as a Greek, see the refs. cited by Sabbah (above, n. 25), adding 26.1.1; ' "atomos", ut nos appellamus'.

31. On 'veritas' (and 'fides') in Ammianus, cf. Ensslin, 11f.; Syme, *Ammianus and the Historia Augusta*, 94 ('an obsession and a passion'); Sabbah, 19ff.

32. On this interesting theme of detachment or 'exile' from their own countries among Greek historians, see Momigliano, 'The historians of the Classical World and their audiences: some suggestions', *Annali della Scuola Normale Superiore di Pisa* III.viii.1 (1978), 59-75 = *Sesto Contributo* (1980), 361-75, at 363, 371 – contrasting with this the Roman tradition, in which 'accepted members of the ruling class were frequently its historians. This endowed historians in Rome with a halo of authority, which Pliny the Younger recognised in his friend Tacitus .... In Rome the relationship between historiography and government seems always to have been closer than in Greece'. Cf. Sabbah, 577: 'le choix du sujet, l'optique romaine de son oeuvre, le choix de latin l'ont "dégagé" premièrement et massivement de la Grèce'.

33. Alan Cameron, 'The Roman friends of Ammianus', *JRS* 54 (1964), 15-28, esp. at 25ff., dissociating Ammianus from any so-called 'circle of Symmachus'. For the mixed character of cultural circles at Rome, as implied by the *Saturnalia* of Macrobius, see the brief remarks in my *Western Aristocracies*, 372.

34. 14.6.5f.; see my 'Ammianus and the Eternity of Rome', at 21f.

35. The relatively limited scope of Libanius' influence is noted above, Chapter V, pp. 71ff.; cf. *Western Aristocracies*, 105f., and the biographical sketch of Libanius in A. F. Norman, *Libanius' Autobiography (Oration 1)* (1965), at vii-xii.

36. This is of course *Decline and Fall*, ch. XXX at end (ed. Bury, 1897, Vol. III, p. 284).

37. Claudian, *Epithalamium dictum Palladio v.c. tribuno et notario et Celerinae (Carmina Minora* XXV), 82ff., cf. *Not. Dig., Or.* 18.3-4, *Occ.* 16.4-5, 'Sub dispositione viri spectabilis primicerii notariorum: notitia omnium dignitatum et administrationum tam civilium quam militarium' (ed. Seeck, p. 160). The father-in-law of Claudian's friend is *PLRE* I, Anonymus 34 (p. 1011). I say 'in the edition known to us' because there must always have been such a document, updated as occasion arose.

38. On Ammianus and Julian, see again my two articles, 'Ammianus Marcellinus', at 1125 and (in similar terms)'Ammianus' historical evolution', 34-6.

39. Chapter VI, p. 112f., discusses the obituary of Julian in terms of a formal contrast between the two sections, on virtues and vices; see also Chapter XI, p. 239.

40. For what follows, cf. my 'Ammianus and the Eternity of Rome', at 22-4 and 27f. A. Demandt, *Zeitkritik und Geschichtsbild* (cited in n. 10 above) discusses the literary antecedents (Florus and Seneca) of the idea of the rejuvenation of Rome under the emperors; cf. J. M. Alonso-Núñez, 'The Ages of Rome', *Lecture delivered in the Free University of Amsterdam, 17th November 1981* (1982). Ammianus' notion of an inheritance handed down from senate to emperors is however a formulation without exact parallel in Seneca, Florus or any other source. W. Seyfarth, 'Vom Geschichtsschreiber und seinem Publikum im spätantiken Rom', *Wissenschaftliche Zeitschr. der Universität Rostock* 18.II.4/5 (1969), 449-55 notes (453) that in Ammianus' conception the eternity of Rome is linked with that of the emperors.

41. On 'sobrietas' and related virtues in Ammianus, Seager (cited in n. 3 above), 80-1. As Seager notes, the actual term 'sobrius' is not especially frequent in Ammianus (Archbold's *Concordance*, not cited by Seager, produces three examples of 'sobrietas' and ten of adjectival and adverbial forms of the word); but there are related concepts (such as 'prudentia'), and Seager's conclusion (at 81) that *'whatever its shades of meaning,* [sobrius] is not a major element in Ammianus' language and thought' (my italics) seems to me unjustified. Further, some of Seager's readings of individual passages fail to give to the term its true (moral) weight.

42. On Olympiodorus, *JRS* 60 (1970), at 96-7.

Bibliography

Recent surveys of work on Ammianus have been provided by Gualtiero Calboli, 'La credibilità di Ammiano Marcellino e la sua arte espositiva', *Bollettino di Studi Latini* 4 (1974), 67-103 – a review-discussion of the book by Klaus Rosen, *Studien zur Darstellungskunst und Glaubwürdigkeit des Ammianus Marcellinus* (1970); by Luciana Alfano Caranci, 'Alcuni orientamenti critici dei recenti studi su Ammiano Marcellino', *Bollettino di Studi Latini* 9 (1979), 71-82 – reviewing the work of Rosen, Selem and Arnaldi; by Miguel Alonso Núñez, 'Ammianus Marcellinus in der Forschung von 1970 bis 1980', *Anzeiger für die Altertumswissenschaft* 36.1/2 (1983), 1-20; and by Rosen in his later guide, *Ammianus Marcellinus* (Erträge der Forschung, 183; Darmstadt, 1982) – with a classified bibliography (more than 400 items) down to 1979 and some titles of 1980 and 1981. For more recent literature see works, on selected historiographical topics, Calboli, 'Ammian und die Geschichtsschreibung seiner Zeit', in P. Handel and W. Meid (edd.), *Festschrift für Robert Muth, zum 65 Geburtstag* (Innsbrucker Beiträge zur Kulturwissenschaft; Innsbruck, 1983), 33-53; G. Sabbah, 'Ammien Marcellin: quelques orientations récentes de la recherche', *Kentron* 3.4 (Caen, 1987), 173-88; and the recent issues (to 1986) of *L'Année Philologique*.

The Bibliography that follows lists the books, monographs and articles referred to in the notes, with the general exceptions of standard histories and reference books, of titles mentioned in the introduction to the Notes and in the Abbreviations, of certain works of incidental or decorative rather than substantial relevance to my subject, and of editions of ancient works used only for reference; such editions are however mentioned where a passage of a text is of particular interest or difficulty, or where its editor has contributed positively to its interpretation. In the hope of making it more manageable, the Bibliography is divided into three broad sections, of descending relevance to Ammianus himself. Problems of demarcation between the categories I have resolved by attributing to the doubtful cases the greatest degree of relevance to Ammianus that I could justify. So, the first section contains not only books and articles devoted specifically to Ammianus himself, but any works that contribute to the understanding of his text or subject-matter as such, the second section does the same for other sources, and the still substantial third section is devoted to the political, social and economic background – the Roman empire rather than Ammianus. No work is listed more than once, but an occasional cross-reference is given from one section to another.

(1) Works directly relevant to Ammianus Marcellinus

ALFÖLDI, A., *A Conflict of Ideas in the Late Roman Empire: the clash between the senate and Valentinian I* (tr. H. Mattingly, Oxford, 1952).

ALONSO NÚÑEZ, J. M., *La Visión Historiográfica de Ammiano Marcelino* (Departamento de Prehistoria y Arqueologia, Universidad de Valladolid; Studia Romana II, 1975).

—— 'The Ages of Rome', Lecture delivered in the Free University of Amsterdam on 17th November 1981 (Amsterdam, 1982) [pp. 5-28].

ANGLIVIEL DE LA BEAUMELLE, L., 'Remarques sur l'attitude d'Ammien Marcellin à l'égard du christianisme', *Mél. Seston* (Paris, 1974), 15-23.

ARCE, J. J., 'El historiador Ammiano Marcelino y la pena de muerte', *Hispania Antiqua* 4 (1974), 321-44.

AUERBACH, A., 'The arrest of Peter Valvomeres', in *Mimesis: the representation of reality in Western literature* (Eng. tr., Princeton, 1953; repr. 1958), ch. 3.

AUSTIN, N. J. E., 'Ammianus' account of the Adrianople campaign: some strategic observations', *Acta Classica* 15 (1972), 77-83.
—— 'Julian at Ctesiphon: a fresh look at Ammianus' account', *Athenaeum* 50 (1972), 301-9.
—— 'A usurper's claim to legitimacy', *Rivista Storica dell'Antichità* 2 (1972), 187-94.
—— 'In support of Ammianus' veracity', *Historia* 22 (1973), 331-5.
—— *Ammianus on Warfare: an investigation into Ammianus' military knowledge* (Coll. Latomus 165; Brussels, 1979).
BALDWIN, B., 'Gregory Nazianzenus, Ammianus, *scurrae*, and the *Historia Augusta*', *Gymnasium* 93 (1986), 178-80.
BARTALUCCI, A., 'I "nomina culta" dei plebei urbani in Ammiano (*Rer. Gest.* XXVIII,4,28)', *Studi Classici e Orientali* 9 (1960), 147-60.
BÉRANGER, J., 'La terminologie impériale; une application à Ammien Marcellin', *Mél. Collart* (Lausanne, 1976), 47-60.
BITTER, N., *Kampfschilderungen bei Ammianus Marcellinus* (diss. Erlangen; Bonn, 1976).
BLOCKLEY, R. C., *Ammianus Marcellinus: a study of his historiography and political thought* (Coll. Latomus 141; Brussels, 1975).
—— 'Internal self-policing in the late Roman administration. Some evidence from Ammianus Marcellinus', *Classica et Medievalia* 30 (1969), 403-19.
—— 'Constantius Gallus and Julian as Caesars of Constantius II', *Latomus* 31 (1972), 433-68.
—— 'Tacitean influences upon Ammianus Marcellinus', *Latomus* 32 (1973), 63-78.
—— 'Ammianus Marcellinus on the battle of Strasbourg: art and analysis in the *History*', *Phoenix* 31 (1977), 218-31.
—— 'Constantius II and his generals', in C. Deroux (ed.), *Studies in Latin Literature and Roman History*, II (Coll. Latomus 168; Brussels 1980), 467-86.
—— 'The date of the "Barbarian Conspiracy"', *Britannia* 11 (1980), 223-5.
—— 'The coded message in Ammianus Marcellinus 18.6.17-19', *Echos du Monde Classique* 30, n.s. 5 (1986), 63-5.
BOER, W. DEN, 'The Emperor Silvanus and his army', *Acta Classica* 3 (1960), 105-9.
BONFANTE, L. WARREN, 'Emperor, God and Man in the fourth century: Julian the Apostate and Ammianus Marcellinus', *Parola del Passato* 99 (1964), 401-27.
BORZSÁK, I., 'Von Tacitus zu Ammian', *Acta Antiqua* 24 (1976), 357-68.
BROK, M. F. A., 'Majestätsfrevel durch Missbrauch des Purpurs (Ammianus Marcellinus, 16,8,8)', *Latomus* 41 (1982), 356-61.
—— 'Die Quellen von Ammians Exkurs über Persien', *Mnemosyne* 4.28 (1975), 47-56.
—— 'Un malentendu tenace (les rapports entre Hérodien et Ammien Marcellin)', *REA* 78-9 (1976-7), 199-207.
—— 'Bombast oder Kunstfertigkeit: Ammians Beschreibung der ballista (23.4.1-3)', *RhM* n.f. 120 (1977), 331-46.
—— 'Ein spätrömischer Brandpfeil nach Ammianus', *Saalburg Jahrbuch* 35 (1978), 57-60.
BURNS, T. S., 'The battle of Hadrianople: a reconsideration', *Historia* 22 (1973), 336-45.
CAMERON, ALAN, 'The Roman friends of Ammianus', *JRS* 54 (1964), 15-28.
—— review of Syme, *Ammianus and the Historia Augusta*, *JRS* 61 (1971), 255-67.
—— and CAMERON, AVERIL, 'Christianity and tradition in the historiography of the late empire', *CQ* n.s. 14 (1964), 316-28.
CAMUS, P. M., *Ammien Marcellin, témoin des courants culturels et religieux à la fin du IVe siècle* (Paris, 1967).
CAPPELLETTO, R., *Recuperi Ammianei da Biondo Flavio* (Note e Discussione Erudite a cura di Augusto Campana, 18; Rome, 1983).
CHALMERS, W. R., 'An alleged doublet in Ammianus Marcellinus', *RhM* n.f. 102 (1959), 182-9.
—— 'Eunapius, Ammianus Marcellinus and Zosimus on Julian's Persian expedition', *CQ* n.s. 10 (1960), 152-60.
CICHOCKA, H., 'Die Konzeption des Exkurses im Geschichtswerk des Ammianus Marcellinus', *Eos* 63 (1975), 329-40.
CLASSEN, C. J., 'Greek and Roman in Ammianus Marcellinus' *History*', *Museum Africum* 1 (1972), 39-47.
CLAUSS, M., 'Ein tödlicher Scherz (zu Ammian 30,5,11-12)', *RhM* n.f. 208 (1985), 97-8.

CONDUCHÉ, D., 'Ammien Marcellin et la mort de Julien', *Latomus* 24 (1965), 359-80.
CROKE, B. and EMMETT, A. (edd.), *History and Historians in Late Antiquity* (Sydney, London, New York, etc., 1983).
CRUMP, G. A., *Ammianus Marcellinus as a Military Historian* (Historia, Einzelschriften 27; Wiesbaden, 1975).
—— 'Ammianus and the late Roman army', *Historia* 22 (1973), 91-103.
DAUTREMER, L., *Ammien Marcellin: étude d'histoire littéraire* (thèse, Paris, 1898: publ. Lille, 1899).
D'ELIA, S., 'Ammiano Marcellino e il cristianesimo', *Studi Romani* 10 (1962), 372-90.
DEMANDT, A., *Zeitkritik und Geschichtsbild im Werk Ammians* (diss. Marburg; Bonn, 1965).
—— 'Die Tripolitanische Wirren unter Valentinian I', *Byzantion* 38 (1968), 333-63.
—— 'Die Afrikanischen Unruhen unter Valentinian I', in H.-J. Diesner, H. Barth, H.-D. Zimmermann (edd.), *Afrika und Rom in der Antike* (Halle, 1968), 277-92.
DILLEMANN, L., 'Ammien Marcellin et le pays de l'Euphrate et du Tigre', *Syria* 38 (1961), 87-158.
DI MAIO, M., 'The Antiochene connection: Zonaras, Ammianus Marcellinus and John of Antioch on the reigns of the Emperors Constantius II and Julian', *Byzantion* 50 (1980), 158-85, and 'Infaustis ductoribus praeviis: the Antiochene connection, Part II', *Byzantion* 51 (1981), 502-10.
DITTRICH, U.-B., *Die Beziehungen Roms zu den Sarmaten und Quaden im vierten Jahrhundert n. Chr. (nach der Darstellung des Ammianus Marcellinus)* (diss. Bonn, 1984).
DREXLER, H., *Ammianstudien* (Spudasmata 31; Hildesheim & New York, 1974).
DRINKWATER, J. F., 'The "pagan underground", Constantius II's "secret service", and the survival, and the usurpation of Julian the Apostate', in C. Deroux, *Studies in Latin Literature and Roman History*, III (Coll. Latomus 180; Brussels, 1983), 348-87.
DUŠANIĆ, M. *The Geographic-Ethnographic Excursus in the Work of Ammianus Marcellinus* (Belgrade, 1986) (in Russian; English summary at 115-23).
DUVAL, Y.-M., 'La venue à Rome de l'empereur Constance II en 357, d'après Ammien Marcellin (XVI,10,1-20)', *Caesarodunum* 5 (1970), 299-304.
ELLIOTT, T. G., *Ammianus Marcellinus and Fourth-Century History* (Sarasota, Florida, 1983).
EMMETT, A., 'The digressions in the lost books of Ammianus Marcellinus', in Croke and Emmett (edd.), *History and Historians in Late Antiquity*, 42-53.
—— 'Introductions and conclusions to digressions in Ammianus Marcellinus', *Museum Philologicum Londiniense* 5 (1981), 15-33.
ENSSLIN, W., *Zur Geschichtschreibung u. Weltanschauung des Ammianus Marcellinus* (Klio, Beiträge zur alten Geschichte 16; Leipzig, 1923).
FLACH, D., 'Von Tacitus zu Ammian', *Historia* 21 (1973), 333-50.
FLETCHER, G. B. A., 'Stylistic borrowings and parallels in Ammianus Marcellinus', *Revue de Philologie*, 3.11 (1937), 389-92.
FONTAINE, J., 'Ammien Marcellin, historien romantique', *Bulletin de l'Association Guillaume Budé (Suppl. Lettres d'Humanité)* 28 (1969), 417-35.
—— 'Le Julien d'Ammien', in R. Braun and J. Riché, *L'Empereur Julien, de l'histoire à la légende 331-1715* (Paris, 1978), 31-65.
—— 'Valeurs de vie et formes esthétiques dans l'histoire d'Ammien Marcellin', in *Le Trasformazioni della Cultura nella tarda Antichità: Atti del Convegno tenuto a Catania, Università degli Studi, 27 sett.- 2 ott. 1982* (Rome, 1985), 781-808.
—— 'Un cliché de la spiritualité antique tardive: *stetit immobilis*', in G. Wirth, with K.-H. Schwarte and J. Heinrichs (edd.), *Romanitas-Christianitas: Untersuchungen zur Geschichte und Literatur der römischen Kaiserzeit, Johannes Straub zum 70 Geburtstag am 18 Oktober 1982 gewidmet* (Berlin & New York, 1982), 528-52.
FOWDEN, G., 'Nicagoras of Athens and the Lateran Obelisk', *JHS* 107 (1987), 51-7.
FRANK, R. I., '*Commendabiles* in Ammianus', *AJP* 88 (1967), 309-18.
FRÉZOULS, E., 'La mission du "magister equitum" Ursicin en Gaule (355-357) d'après Ammien Marcellin', in M. Renard (ed.), *Hommages à Albert Grenier* (Coll. Latomus 58; Brussels, 1962), II, 673-88.
—— 'Les deux politiques de Rome face aux barbares d'après Ammien Marcellin', in Frézouls (ed.), *Crise et redressement, dans les provinces européennes de l'Empire (milieu du IIIe –*

milieu du IVe siècle ap. J.-C.); Actes du colloque de Strasbourg (décembre 1981) (Strasbourg, 1983), 175-97.

FUNKE, H., 'Majestäts- und Magieprozesse bei Ammianus Marcellinus', *Jahrbuch für Antike und Christentum* 10 (1967), 145-75.

GÄRTNER, H., 'Einige Überlegungen zur kaiserzeitlichen Panegyrik und zu Ammians Characteristik des Kaisers Julians', *Akad. der Wissenschaften und der Literatur in Mainz, Abhandlungen der Geistes- und Sozialwissenschaftlichen Kl.* 1968.10 (Wiesbaden, 1968), 499-529 [3-33] (publ. separately).

GILLIAM, J. F., 'Ammianus and the Historia Augusta: the lost books and the period 117-284', *HAColl, Bonn 1970* (1972), 125-47.

GIMAZANE, J., *Ammien Marcellin: sa vie et son oeuvre* (Toulouse, 1889).

GOUGENHEIM, G., 'Une "scie" à Rome au IVe siècle', *REL* 24 (1946), 75-6.

GSELL, S., 'Observations historiques sur la révolte de Firmus', *Rec. des Notices et Mémoires de la Société Archéologique de Constantine* 36 (1903), 21-46.

GUALANDRI, I., 'Fonti geographiche di Ammiano Marcellino XXII.8', *Parola del Passato* 23 (1968), 199-211.

GUEY, J., 'Nicomaque Flavien et Leptis Magna', *REA* 52 (1950), 77-89.

HAEHLING, R. VON, 'Ammians Darstellung der Thronbesteigung Jovians im Lichte der heidnisch-christlichen Auseinandersetzung', in A. Lippold and N. Himmelmann (edd.), *Bonner Festgabe Johannes Straub zum 65. Geburtstag am 18 Oktober 1977* (Bonn, 1977), 347-58.

—— 'Ammianus Marcellinus und der Prozess von Scythopolis', *Jahrbuch für Antike und Christentum* 21 (1978), 74-101.

HAMBLENNE, P., 'Une "conjuration" sous Valentinien?', *Byzantion* 50 (1980), 198-225.

HATT, J. J. and SCHWARTZ, J., 'Le champ de bataille de Oberhausbergen (357-1262)', *Bull. de la Faculté de Lettres de Strasbourg* 42 (1964), 427-30.

HENGST, D. DEN, 'De romeinse Keizerbiografie', *Lampas* 17 (1984), 367-80.

—— 'Ammianus Marcellinus on astronomy', *Mnemosyne* 4.29 (1986), 136-41.

HEYEN, J., 'A propos de la conception historique d'Ammien Marcellin (*Ut miles quondam et graecus*, 31.16.9)', *Latomus* 27 (1968), 191-6.

HUNT, E. D., 'Christians and Christianity in Ammianus Marcellinus', *CQ* n.s. 35 (1985), 186-200.

JEEP, L., 'Die verlorenen Bücher des Ammianus Marcellinus', *RhM* 43 (1888), 60-72.

JONGE, P. DE, 'Scarcity of corn and corn-prices in Ammianus Marcellinus', *Mnemosyne* 4.1 (1948), 238-45.

KLEIN, R., 'Der Rombesuch des Kaisers Konstantius II im Jahre 357', *Athenaeum* n.s. 57 (1979), 98-115.

KLEIN, W., *Studien zur Ammianus Marcellinus* (Klio, Beiträge zur alten Geschichte 13; Leipzig, 1914).

KOHNS, H. P., 'Die Zeitkritik in den Romexkursen des Ammianus Marcellinus: zu Amm. Marc. 14.6.3-26; 28.4.6-35', *Chiron* 5 (1975), 485-91.

KOTULA, T., 'Firmus, fils de Nubel, était-il usurpateur ou roi des Maures?', *Acta Antiqua* 18 (1970), 137-46.

LIEBESCHUETZ, W., 'Ammianus, Julian and divination' in M. Wissemann (ed.), *Roma Renascens: Beiträge zur Spätantike und Rezeptionsgeschichte (Festschrift für Ilona Opelt)* (Frankfurt/M., Bern, New York, Paris, 1988), 198-213.

LOOY, H. VAN, 'Ad Ammianum Marcellinum XXX.9.3; notule de critique textuelle', *L'Antiquité Classique* 35 (1960), 210-12.

MACKAIL, J. W., 'Ammianus Marcellinus', *JRS* 10 (1920), 103-18.

MacMULLEN, R., 'Some pictures in Ammianus Marcellinus', *Art Bulletin* 46 (1964), 435-55.

MARCONE, A., 'Il significato della spedizione di Giuliano contro la Persia', *Athenaeum* n.s. 57 (1979), 334-56.

MARROU, H.-I., 'Ammien Marcellin et les "Innocents" de Milan', *Recherches de Science Religieuse* 40 (1951-2), 179-90.

MARTIN, R., 'Ammien Marcellin ou la servitude militaire', in R. Chevallier (ed.), *Colloque Histoire et Historiographie, Clio* (Coll. Caesarodunum XV bis; Paris, 1980), 203-13.

MATTHEWS, J. F., 'Mauretania in Ammianus and the Notitia', in R. Goodburn and P.

Bartholomew (edd.), *Aspects of the Notitia Dignitatum* (BAR Suppl. Ser. 15; Oxford, 1976), 157-86; repr. in *Political Life and Culture in Late Roman Society* (London, 1985), ch. XI.
—— 'Ammianus Marcellinus', in T. J. Luce (ed.), *Ancient Writers: Greece and Rome* (New York, 1982), II, 1117-38; repr. in *Political Life and Culture*, ch. I.
—— 'Ammianus' historical evolution', in Croke and Emmett (edd.), *History and Historians in Late Antiquity*, 30-41; repr. in *Political Life and Culture*, ch. II.
—— 'Ammianus and the eternity of Rome', in C. Holdsworth and T. P. Wiseman (edd.), *The Inheritance of Historiography, 350-900* (Exeter, 1986), 17-29.
—— 'Ammianus and the eastern frontier: a participant's view', in P. Freeman and D. Kennedy (edd.), *The Defence of the Roman and Byzantine East (Sheffield Colloquium, 1986)* (BAR Intern. Ser. 297(2); Oxford, 1986), 549-64.
—— 'Peter Valvomeres, re-arrested', in M. Whitby, P. Hardie, M. Whitby (edd.), *Homo Viator: Classical Essays for John Bramble* (Bristol, 1987), 277-84.
MESLIN, M., 'Le merveilleux comme langage politique chez Ammien Marcellin', *Mél. Seston* (Paris, 1974), 353-63.
MOES, R., *Les Hellénismes de l'époque Théodosienne (Recherches sur le vocabulaire d'origine grecque chez Ammien Marcellin, Claudien, et dans l'Histoire Auguste* (Assoc. des Publications près les Universités de Strasbourg; Strasbourg, 1980).
MOMIGLIANO, A., 'Pagan and Christian historiography in the fourth century A.D.', in Momigliano (ed.), *The Conflict between Paganism and Christianity in the Fourth Century* (Oxford, 1963), 79-99; repr. in *Essays in Ancient and Modern Historiography* (Oxford, 1977), 107-26.
—— 'The lonely historian Ammianus Marcellinus', *Annali della Scuola Normale Superiore di Pisa, Cl. di Lettere e Filosofia*, III.iv.4 (1974), 1393-1407; repr. in *Essays in Ancient and Modern Historiography*, 127-40.
—— 'The historians of the Classical World and their audiences: some suggestions', ibid. III.viii.1 (1978), 59-75; repr. in *Sesto Contributo alla Storia degli Studi Classici e del Mondo Antico* (Rome, 1980), 361-75.
MOMMSEN, T., 'Ammians Geographica', *Hermes* 16 (1881), 602-36; repr. in *Gesammelte Schriften* VII, 393-425.
—— 'Bemerkungen zur einzelnen Stelle Ammians', *Ges. Schr.* VII, 426-9.
MOONEY, R. N., 'Nature lore in Ammianus Marcellinus', *Classical Bulletin* 33.6 (1957), 61-3 and 67-8.
—— 'Gallus Caesar's last journey', *Classical Philology* 53 (1958), 175-7.
MÜLLER-SEIDEL, I., 'Die Usurpation Iulians des Abtrünnigen im Licht seiner Germanenpolitik', *Historische Zeitschrift* 180 (1955), 225-44.
NAUDÉ, C. P. T., 'Battles and sieges in Ammianus Marcellinus', *Acta Classica* 1 (1958: publ. 1959), 92-105.
—— '*Fortuna* in Ammianus Marcellinus', *Acta Classica* 7 (1964), 70-89.
—— 'The date of the later books of Ammianus Marcellinus', *American Journal of Ancient History* 9.1 (1984), 70-94.
NERI, V., *Costanzo, Giuliano e l'ideale del Civilis Princeps* (Studi Bizantini e Slavi 1; Rome, 1984).
—— 'Ammiano Marcellino e l'elezione di Valentiniano', *Rivista Storica dell'Antichità* 15 (1985), 153-82.
—— *Ammiano e il cristianesimo: religione e politica nelle 'Res Gestae' di Ammiano Marcellino* (Studi di Storia Antica 11; Bologna, 1985).
NICCOLI, G., 'Tradizione biografica suetoniana e orientamenti ideologici nei necrologi imperiali di Ammiano Marcellino', *Critica Storica* 13 (1976), 610-20 [26-36].
NICOLLE, J., 'Julien *apud Senonas* (356-357). Un contresens historique', *Rivista Storica dell'Antichità* 8 (1978), 133-60.
NORMAN, A. F., 'Magnus in Ammianus, Eunapius, and Zosimus', *CQ* n.s. 7 (1957), 129-33.
NUTT, D. C., 'Silvanus and the Emperor Constantius II', *Antichthon* 7 (1973), 80-9.
PACK, R. A., 'The Roman digressions of Ammianus Marcellinus', *TAPA* 84 (1953), 181-9.
PASCHOUD, F., *Roma Aeterna: études sur le patriotisme romain dans l'occident Latin à l'époque des grandes invasions* (Bibliotheca Helvetica Romana 7; Rome, 1957).

PAUW, D. A., 'Methods of character portrayal in the *Res Gestae* of Ammianus Marcellinus', *Acta Classica* 20 (1977), 181-98.

RICHTER, W., 'Die Darstellung der Hunnen bei Ammianus Marcellinus', *Historia* 23 (1974), 343-77.

RIKE, R. L., *Apex Omnium: religion in the Res Gestae of Ammianus* (Berkeley, Los Angeles & London, 1987).

ROSEN, K., *Studien zur Darstellungskunst und Glaubwürdigkeit des Ammianus Marcellinus* (diss. Heidelberg, 1970).

—— 'Beobachtung zur Erhebung Julians 360-1 n. Chr.,' *Acta Classica* 12 (1969), 121-49.

ROUGÉ, J., 'Une émeute à Rome au IVe siècle. Ammien Marcellin XXVII 3.3-4: essai d'interprétation', *REA* 63 (1961), 59-77.

ROWELL, H. T., 'Ammianus Marcellinus, soldier-historian of the late Roman Empire', *Semple Lectures, First Series, 1961-1965* (Princeton, 1967), 265-313.

—— 'The first mention of Rome in Ammianus' extant books and the nature of the "History" ', *Mél. Carcopino* (Paris, 1966), 839-48.

SABBAH, G., *La Méthode d'Ammien Marcellin: recherches sur la construction du discours historique dans les Res Gestae* (Paris, 1978).

—— 'La "Peste d'Amida" (Ammien Marcellin, 19,4)', in Sabbah (ed.), *Médecins et médecine dans l'antiquité* (Centre Jean Palerne, Memoires III; Saint Etienne, 1982), 131-57.

SAMBERGER, C., 'Die "Kaiserbiographie" in den Res Gestae des Ammianus Marcellinus. Eine Untersuchung zur Komposition der ammianeischen Geschichtsschreibung', *Klio* 51 (1969), 349-482.

SANTOS YANGUAS, N., 'Algunos problemas sociales en Asia Menor en la segunda mitad del siglo IV d.C.: Isaurios y Maratocuprenos', *Hispania Antiqua* 7 (1977), 351-78.

—— 'El servicio policial secreto romano en el Bajo Imperio segun Ammiano Marcelino', *Memorias de Historia Antigua* 1 (1977), 127-39.

—— 'Presagios, adivinación y magia en Ammiano Marcelino', *Helmantica* 30 (1979), 5-49.

—— 'La resistencia de las poblaciones indigenas norteafricanas a la romanización en la segunda mitad del siglo IV d. C.', *Hispania* 39 (1979), 257-300.

SCHEDA, D., 'Die Todesstunde Kaiser Julians', *Historia* 15 (1966), 380-3.

SCHWARTZ, J., 'Le champ de bataille de Oberhausbergen', see HATT, J. J.

SEAGER, R., *Ammianus Marcellinus: seven studies in language and thought* (Columbia, Missouri, 1986).

SEECK, O., 'Die Reihe der Stadtpräfecten bei Ammianus Marcellinus', *Hermes* 18 (1883), 289-303.

SELEM, A., 'Considerazioni circa Ammiano ed il cristianesimo', *Rivista di Cultura Classica e Medioevale* 6 (1964), 224-61.

—— 'A proposito del comando militare di Giuliano in Gallia secondo Ammiano', ibid. 13 (1971), 193-200.

—— 'L'Atteggiamento storiografico di Ammiano nei confronti di Giuliano dalla proclamazione di Parigi alla morte di Costanzo', *Athenaeum* n.s. 49 (1971), 89-110.

—— 'Ammiano e la morte di Giuliano (25.3.3-11)', *Rendiconti dell'Istituto Lombardo, Acc. di Scienze e Lettere (Cl. di Lettere e Scienze Morali e Storiche)* 107 (1973), 1119-35.

—— 'Ammiano XXV,2,8', *Athenaeum* n.s. 51 (1973), 399-402.

SEYFARTH, W., 'Ein Handstreich persischer Bogenschützen auf Antiochia: Sprachliche und historische Rechtfertigung einer Stelle bei Ammianus Marcellinus (25,5,3)', *Klio* 40 (1962), 60-4.

—— 'Ammianus und das Fatum', *Klio* 43/5 (1965), 291-306.

—— 'Glaube und Aberglaube bei Ammianus Marcellinus', *Klio* 46 (1965), 373-83.

—— 'Vom Geschichtsschreiber und seinem Publikum im spätantiken Rom', *Wissenschaftliche Zeitschr. der Universität Rostock* 18.2.4/5 (1969), 449-55.

—— 'Petronius Probus. Legende und Wirklichkeit', *Klio* 52 (1970), 411-25.

SIMPSON, C. J., 'Where was Senonae? A problem of geography in Ammianus Marcellinus XVI,3,3', *Latomus* 33 (1974), 940-2.

SOLARI, A., 'La rivolta Procopiana a Constantinopoli', *Byzantion* 7 (1932), 143-8.

STERZ, S. A., 'Ammianus Marcellinus on the Emperor Gallienus: his sources', *The Ancient World* 2.2 (1979), 69-71.

—— 'Ammianus Marcellinus' attitudes toward earlier emperors', in C. Deroux (ed.), *Studies in Latin Literature and Roman History*, II (Coll. Latomus 168; Brussels, 1980), 487-514.
STOIAN, I., 'A propos de la conception historique d'Ammien Marcellin (*Ut miles quondam et Graecus)*', *Latomus* 26 (1967), 73-81.
SYME, R., *Ammianus and the Historia Augusta* (Oxford, 1968).
—— review of Demandt, *Zeitkritik und Geschichtsbild im Werk Ammians*, JRS 58 (1968), 215-18.
SZIDAT, J., 'Der Neuplatonismus und die Gebildete im Westen des Reiches: Gedanken zu seiner Verbreitung und Kenntnis ausserhalb der Schultradition', *Mus. Helv.* 39 (1982), 132-44.
TASSI, A. M., 'Costanzo e la difesa della maestà imperiale nell'opera di Ammiano Marcellino', *Critica Storica* 6 (1967), 157-80.
THOMPSON, E. A., 'Three notes on Julian in 361 A.D.', *Hermathena* 62 (1942), 83-95.
—— *The Historical Work of Ammianus Marcellinus* (Cambridge, 1947; repr. Groningen, 1969).
—— 'Ammianus Marcellinus', in T. A. Dorey (ed.), *Latin Historians* (London, 1966), 143-57.
TOMLIN, R. S. O., 'The date of the "Barbarian Conspiracy"', *Britannia* 5 (1974), 303-9.
—— 'Ammianus Marcellinus 24.4.5-6', *CQ* n.s. 29 (1979), 470-8.
TRÄNKLE, H., 'Ammianus Marcellinus als römischer Geschichtsschreiber', *Antike und Abendland* 11 (1962), 21-33.
—— 'Der Caesar Gallus bei Ammian', *Mus. Helv.* 33 (1976), 162-79.
TURCAN, R., 'L'abandon de Nisibe et l'opinion publique (363 ap. J.-C)', *Mél. Piganiol* (Paris, 1966), 875-90.
VALENSI, L., 'Quelques réflexions sur le pouvoir impérial d'après Ammien Marcellin', *Bull. de l'Association Guillaume Budé* 4.4 (*Supplément: Lettres d'Humanité*, t. XVI) (Paris, 1957), 62-107.
VERA, D., 'La polemica contro l'abuso imperiale del trionfo: rapporti fra ideologia, economia e propaganda nel Basso Impero', *Rivista Storica dell'Antichità* 10 (1980), 89-132.
VOGT, J., 'Ammianus Marcellinus als erzählender Geschichtsschreiber der Spätzeit', *Akad. der Wissenschaften und der Literatur in Mainz, Abhandlungen der Geistes- und Sozialwissenschaftlichen Klasse* 1963.8 (Wiesbaden, 1963), 802-25 [3-27] (published separately).
WARMINGTON, B. H., 'The career of Romanus, *Comes Africae*', *BZ* 49 (1956), 55-64.
—— 'Objectives and strategy in the Persian Wars of Constantius II', *Akten des XI Internationalen Limeskongresses*, 1976 (Budapest, 1977), 509-20.
—— 'Ammianus Marcellinus and the lies of Metrodorus', *CQ* n.s. 31 (1981), 464-8.
WEIJENBORG, R., 'Zum Text und zur Deutung von Ammianus, Römische Geschichte 29.3.9', *Klio* 57 (1975), 241-7.
WIEDEMANN, T. E. J., 'Between man and beasts. Barbarians in Ammianus Marcellinus', in I. S. Moxon, J. D. Smart, A. J. Woodman (edd.), *Past Perspectives. Studies in Greek and Roman historical writing: papers presented at a conference in Leeds, 6-8 April, 1983* (Cambridge, 1986), 189-211.
WILSHIRE, L. E., 'Did Ammianus Marcellinus write a continuation of Tacitus?', *Classical Journal* 68 (1972/3), 221-7.
WIRZ, H., 'Ammians beziehungen zu seinem vorbilden, Cicero, Sallustius, Livius, Tacitus', *Philologus* 36 (1877), 627-36.
WÖLFFLIN, E., 'Stilistiche nachahmer des Tacitus', *Philologus* 29 (1870), 557-60.

(2) Works relevant to other sources

AUJOULAT, N., 'Eusébie, Hélène et Julien. I: Le témoignage de Julien', *Byzantion* 53 (1983), 78-103; and 'II: Le témoignage des historiens', ibid. 421-52.
BALDWIN, B., 'The career of Oribasius', *Acta Classica* 18 (1975), 85-97.
—— 'The *Caesares* of Julian', *Klio* 60 (1978), 449-66.
BARNES, T. D., 'The lost Kaisergeschichte and the Latin historical tradition', *HAColl, Bonn 1968/9* (1970), 13-43.

Bibliography

—— *The Sources of the Historia Augusta* (Coll. Latomus 155; Brussels, 1978).
—— 'The composition of Cassius Dio's Roman History', *Phoenix* 38 (1984), 240-55.
BARROW, R. H., *Prefect and Emperor: the Relationes of Symmachus, A.D. 384* (Oxford, 1973).
BAYNES, N. H., *The Historia Augusta: its date and purpose* (Oxford, 1926).
BELL, H. I., MARTIN, V., TURNER, E. G., VAN BERCHEM, B., *The Abinnaeus Archive: papers of a Roman officer in the reign of Constantius II* (Oxford, 1962).
BERGER, P. C., *The Insignia of the Notitia Dignitatum* (New York & London, 1981).
BERNARDI, J., 'Un réquisitoire: les Invectives contre Julien de Gregoire de Nazianze' in R. Braun and J. Riché, *L'Empereur Julien, de l'histoire à la légende, 331-1715* (Paris, 1978), 89-98.
—— (ed. and tr.), *Grégoire de Nazianze, Discours 4-5 contre Julien* (SChr 309; Paris, 1983).
BISCHOFF, B. and KOEHLER, W. R. W., 'Eine illustrierte Ausgabe der spätantiken Ravennater Annalen', in Koehler (ed.), *Medieval Studies in Memory of A. Kingsley Porter* (Cambridge, Mass., 1939), 123-38; republished as 'Un'edizione illustrata degli Annali Ravennati del Basso Impero', *Studi Romagnoli* 3 (1952), 1-17.
BOWERSOCK, G. W., 'The Emperor Julian on his predecessors', *Yale Classical Studies* 27 (1982), 159-72. See also below, §3.
BROCK, S., 'A letter attributed to Cyril of Jerusalem on the rebuilding of the Temple', *Bulletin of the School of Oriental and African Studies* 40 (1977), 267-86.
BÜTTNER-WOBST, T., 'Der Tod des Kaiser Julians: eine Quellenstudie', *Philologus* 51 (1892), 561-80.
CAMERON, ALAN, 'An alleged fragment of Eunapius', *CQ* n.s. 13 (1963), 232-6.
—— *Claudian: poetry and propaganda at the court of Honorius* (Oxford, 1970).
—— 'The date of the Anonymous', in M. W. C. Hassall and R. Ireland (edd.), *Aspects of the De Rebus Bellicis: papers presented to Professor E. A. Thompson* (BAR Intern. Ser. 63; Oxford, 1979), 1-10.
CAMERON, AVERIL, *Agathias* (Oxford, 1970).
CHALMERS, W. R., 'The NEA EKDOSIS of Eunapius' Histories', *CQ* n.s. 3 (1953), 165-70. See also above, §1.
CUMONT, F., 'La marche de l'empereur Julien d'Antioche à l'Euphrate', *Etudes Syriennes* (1917), 1-33.
DOWNEY, G., 'Julian the Apostate at Antioch', *Church History* 8 (1939), 305-15. See also below, §3.
FONTAINE, J. (ed. and tr.), *Sulpice Sévère, Vie de Saint Martin* (3 vols., SChr 133-5; Paris, 1967-9).
GLEESON, M. W., 'Julian's *Misopogon* and the New Year at Antioch', *JRS* 76 (1986), 106-19.
GORDON, C. D., *The Age of Attila: fifth-century Byzantium and the barbarians* (Ann Arbor, 1960).
GOULET, R., 'Sur la chronologie de la vie et des oeuvres d'Eunape de Sardes', *JHS* 100 (1980), 60-72.
GRIGG, R., 'Portrait-bearing codicils in the illustrations of the *Notitia Dignitatum*', *JRS* 69 (1979), 107-24.
HARMAND, L., *Libanius, Discours sur les Patronages* (Publications de la Faculté des Lettres de l'Université de Clermont; Paris, 1955).
HAUSER-MEURY, M. M., *Prosopographie zu den Schriften Gregors von Nazianz* (Theophaneia 13; Bonn, 1960)
HONORÉ, A. M., *Ulpian* (Oxford, 1982).
—— 'The making of the Theodosian Code', *ZSS* 103 (1986), 133-222.
—— 'Some writings of the pagan champion Nicomachus Flavianus', in *Xenia*, Heft 23, ed. W. Schuller (Konstanz, 1989), 9-48 (with Appendix A by J. F. Matthews, see below).
KAEGI, W. E., 'Constantine's and Julian's strategies of strategic surprise against the Persians', *Athenaeum* n.s. 59 (1981), 209-13.
KOEHLER, W. R. W., 'Eine illustrierte Ausgabe der spätantiken Ravennater Annalen', see BISCHOFF, B.
LIEU, S. N. C. (ed.), *The Emperor Julian: panegyric and polemic* (Liverpool, 1986).
LIGHTFOOT, C. S., 'Facts and fiction – the third siege of Nisibis (AD 350)', *Historia* 37 (1988), 105-25.

LIPPOLD, A., 'Herrscherideal und Traditionsverbundenheit im Panegyricus des Pacatus', *Historia* 17 (1968), 228-50.
LOMANTO, V. (with MARINONE, N. and ZAMPOLLI, A.), *A Concordance to Symmachus* (Hildesheim, Zürich, New York, 1983).
MacGEACHY, J. A., *Quintus Aurelius Symmachus and the Senatorial Aristocracy of the West* (Chicago, 1942).
MATTHEWS, J. F., 'Olympiodorus of Thebes and the History of the West (A.D. 407-425)', *JRS* 60 (1970), 79-97; repr. in *Political Life and Culture in Late Roman Society* (London, 1985), ch. III.
—— 'The Letters of Symmachus', in J. W. Binns (ed.), *Latin Literature of the Fourth Century* (London & Boston, 1974), 58-99; repr. in *Political Life and Culture*, ch. IV. See also below, §3.
—— 'Symmachus and his enemies', in F. Paschoud (ed.), *Colloque Genevois sur Symmaque, à l'occasion du mille six centième anniversaire du conflit de l'autel de la Victoire, 1984* (Paris, 1986), 163-75.
—— 'Nicomachus Flavianus' quaestorship: the historical evidence', in *Xenia*, Heft 23, ed. W. Schuller (Konstanz, 1989), 18-25. See also HONORÉ, A. M..
MIEROW, C. C. (ed. and tr.), *The Gothic History of Jordanes, in English version with an Introduction and a Commentary* (2nd ed., Princeton, 1915; repr. Cambridge & New York, 1966).
MILLAR, F., *A Study of Cassius Dio* (Oxford, 1964).
MOMIGLIANO, A.: see above, §1.
MOREAU, J. (ed. and tr.), *Lactance: De la Mort des Persécuteurs* (SChr 39.1/2; Paris, 1954).
PACK, R. A., *Studies in Libanius and Antiochene Society under Theodosius* (diss. Michigan, 1935).
PALMER, A.-M., *Prudentius on the Martyrs* (Oxford, 1989).
PASCHOUD, F., *Cinq Etudes sur Zosime* (Coll. d'Etudes Anciennes; Paris, 1975).
—— 'Quand parut la première édition de l'Histoire d'Eunape?', *HAColl, Bonn 1977/8* (1980), 149-62.
PETIT, P., 'Recherches sur la publication et la diffusion des discours de Libanius', *Historia* 5 (1956), 479-509. See also below, §3.
PLACES, E. des (ed. and tr.), *Oracles Chaldaïques, avec un choix de commentaires anciens* (ed. Budé; Paris, 1971).
RIDLEY, R. T., 'Notes on Julian's Persian expedition (363)', *Historia* 22 (1973), 317-30.
RODA, S., *Commento Storico al Libro IX dell'Epistolario di Q. Aurelio Simmaco: Introduzione, commento storico, testo, traduzione e indici* (Pisa, 1981).
ROUGÉ, J., 'L'Histoire Auguste et l'Isaurie au IVe siècle', *REA* 68 (1966), 282-315.
RUSSELL, D. A., *Plutarch* (London, 1972).
—— and WILSON, N. G., *Menander Rhetor: edited with translation and commentary* (Oxford, 1981).
SCHLUMBERGER, J., *Die Epitome de Caesaribus: Untersuchungen zur heidnischen Geschichtsschreibung des 4. Jahrhunderts n. Chr.* (Vestigia 18; Munich, 1974).
—— 'Die verlorenen Annalen des Nicomachus Flavianus: ein Werk über Geschichte des römischen Republik oder Kaiserzeit?', *HAColl, Bonn 1982/1983* (1985), 305-25.
SEECK, O., *Die Briefe des Libanius* (Leipzig, 1906; repr. Hildesheim, 1966).
STRAUB, J., *Studien zur Historia Augusta* (Dissertationes Bernenses I.4; Bern, 1952).
SYME, R., *Tacitus* (2 vols., Oxford, 1958).
—— *Ten Studies in Tacitus* (Oxford, 1970).
—— *Emperors and Biography: studies in the Historia Augusta* (Oxford, 1971). See also above, §1.
THOMPSON, E. A., *A Roman Reformer and Inventor: being a new text of the treatise De Rebus Bellicis with a translation and introduction* (Oxford, 1952).
TREUCKER, B., *Politische und Sozialgeschichtliche Studien zu den Basilius-Briefen* (diss., Frankfurt/M., 1961).
WALBANK, F. W., *Polybius* (Sather Classical Lectures 42; Berkeley, Los Angeles & London, 1972).
WALLACE-HADRILL, A., *Suetonius: the scholar and his Caesars* (London, 1983).

WIESEN, D. S., *Saint Jerome as a Satirist* (Cornell Studies in Classical Philology, 37; Ithaca, NY, 1964).
WILSON, N. G., *Menander Rhetor*, see RUSSELL, D. A.

(3) Political, social and economic background

ADAMS, R. McC., *Land behind Baghdad: a history of settlement on the Diyala Plains* (Chicago & London, 1965).
ALFOLDI, A., 'Die Ausgestaltung des monarchischen Zeremoniells am römischen Hof', *Röm. Mitt.* 49 (1934), 4-118: repr. in *Die monarchische Repräsentation im römischen Kaiserzeit* (Darmstadt, 1970), ch. I.
—— 'Insignien und Tracht der römischen Kaiser', *Röm. Mitt.* 50 (1935), 3-158: repr. in *Die monarchische Repräsentation*, ch. II.
—— *Die Kontorniaten: ein verkanntes Propagandamittel der Stadtrömischen Aristokratie in ihrem Kampfe gegen das christliche Kaisertum* (Budapest, 1942-3; 2nd ed. entitled *Die Kontorniat-Medaillons*, Berlin, 1976).
ANDERSON, P., *Passages from Antiquity to Feudalism* (London, 1974).
ATHANASSIADI-FOWDEN, P., *Julian and Hellenism: an intellectual biography* (Oxford, 1981).
AVERY, W. K., 'The Adoratio Purpurae and the importance of the Imperial purple in the fourth century of the Christian era', *Memoirs of the American Academy in Rome* 17 (1940), 66-80.
BACHRACH, B. S., *A History of the Alans in the West* (Minneapolis, 1973).
BARADEZ, J., *Fossatum Africae: recherches aériennes sur l'organisation des confins sahariens à l'époque romaine* (Paris, 1949).
BARB, A. A., 'The survival of magic arts', in Momiglièno (ed.), *The Conflict between Paganism and Christianity in the Fourth Century* (Oxford, 1963), 100-25.
BARNES, T. D., 'Imperial campaigns, A.D. 285-311', *Phoenix* 30 (1976), 174-93.
—— *Constantine and Eusebius* (Cambridge, Mass. & London, 1981).
—— *The New Empire of Diocletian and Constantine* (Cambridge, Mass. & London, 1982).
—— 'Constantine and the Christians of Persia', *JRS* 75 (1985), 126-36.
BARNETT, R. D., 'Xenophon and the wall of Media', *JHS* 83 (1963), 1-26.
BARTHOLOMEW, P., 'Fourth-century Saxons', *Britannia* 15 (1984), 169-85.
BAYNES, N. H., 'Rome and Armenia in the fourth century', *English Historical Review* 25 (1910), 625-43: repr. with revisions in *Byzantine Studies and Other Essays* (London, 1960), 186-208.
BEAN, G. E. and MITFORD, T. B., *Journeys in Rough Cilicia, 1964-1968* (Ergänzungsbände zu den Tituli Asiae Minoris, Nr. 3; Vienna, 1970).
BEEK, M., *Atlas of Mesopotamia* (Eng. tr., London, 1962).
BELLAMY, J. A., 'A new reading of the Namārah inscription', *Journal of the American Oriental Society* 105 (1985), 31-51.
BERCHEM, M. VAN, and STZRYGOWSKI, J., *Amida: matériaux pour l'épigraphie et l'histoire Musulmanes du Diyar-Bekr* (Heidelberg & Paris, 1910).
BEWSHER, J. B., 'On part of Mesopotamia contained between Sheriat-el-Beytha, on the Tigris, and Tel Ibrahim', *Journal of the Royal Geographical Society* 37 (1867), 160-82.
BIDEZ, J., *La Vie de l'empereur Julien* (Paris, 1930; repr. 1965).
—— 'Proclus, Peri tês hieratikês technês', *Mélanges Cumont: Annuaire de l'institut de philologie et d'histoire orientales et slaves* 4 (1936), 85-100.
BIRLEY, A. R., *Septimius Severus: the African Emperor* (London, 1971).
—— *The Fasti of Roman Britain* (Oxford, 1981).
BLANCHET, A., *Les Enceintes Romaines de la Gaule* (Paris, 1907).
BLOŞIU, C., 'Necropola din secolul al IV-lea e.n. de la Letçani (iud. Iaşi)', *Arheologia Moldovei* 8 (1975), 203-80.
BÖHME, H. W., *Germanische Grabfunde des 4. bis 5. Jahrhunderts, zwischen unterer Elbe und Loire: Studien zur Chronologie und Bevölkerungsgeschichte* (Münchener Beiträge zur vor- und frühgeschichte, 19; 2 vols., Munich 1974).
BOUSQUET, B., 'Le raz de marée du 21 Juillet 1965', etc., see JACQUES, F.
BOWERSOCK, G., *Greek Sophists in the Roman Empire* (Oxford, 1969).
—— 'A report on Arabia Provincia', *JRS* 61 (1971), 219-42.

—— 'The Greek-Nabataean bilingual inscription at Ruwwāfa, Saudi Arabia' in J. Bingen and others (edd.), *Le Monde grec: Hommages à Claire Préaux* (Université Libre de Bruxelles, Faculté de Philosophie et Lettres, 52, 1975), 513-22.
—— *Julian the Apostate* (London, 1978). See also above, §2.
—— 'Mavia, Queen of the Saracens', in W. Eck, H. Galsterer, H. Wolff (edd.), *Studien zur Antiken Sozialgeschichte: Festschrift Friedrich Vittinghof* (Köln & Wien, 1980), 477-95.
—— *Roman Arabia* (Cambridge, Mass. & London, 1983).
—— 'Arabs and Saracens in the Historia Augusta', *HAColl, Bonn 1984/5* (1987), 71-80.
BOWMAN, A. K., *Egypt after the Pharaohs, 332 B.C.- A.D. 642* (London, 1986).
BROWN, P. R. L., *Augustine of Hippo: a biography* (London, 1967).
—— 'Sorcery, demons and the rise of Christianity: from Late Antiquity into the Middle Ages', in *Association of Social Anthropologists, Monographs* 9 (London, etc., 1970), 17-45; repr. in Brown, *Religion and Society in the Age of Saint Augustine* (London, 1972), 119-46.
—— *The Making of Late Antiquity* (Cambridge, Mass. & London, 1978).
—— 'The last pagan emperor', review of Browning, *The Emperor Julian*, in *Society and the Holy in Late Antiquity* (London, 1982), 83-102.
BROWNING, R., 'The riot of A.D. 387 in Antioch', *JRS* 42 (1952), 13-20.
—— *The Emperor Julian* (London, 1975).
BRUNT, P. A., 'The Roman mob', *Past and Present* 35 (1966), 3-27; repr. in M. I. Finley (ed.), *Studies in Ancient Society* (London & Boston, 1974), 74-102.
—— 'Evidence given under torture in the Principate', *ZSS* 97 (1980), 256-65.
BURNS, T. S., *A History of the Ostrogoths* (Bloomington, Indiana, 1984).
BUTLER, R. M., 'Late Roman walls in Gaul', *Archaeological Journal* 116 (1959), 25-50.
—— 'The Roman walls of Le Mans', *JRS* 48 (1958), 33-9.
CALDERINI, A., *Aquileia Romana* (Milan, 1930).
CAMERON, ALAN, 'The date and identity of Macrobius', *JRS* 56 (1966), 25-38.
—— 'Theodosius the Great and the Regency of Stilicho', *HSCP* 73 (1968), 247-80.
—— *Circus Factions: blues and greens at Rome and Byzantium* (Oxford, 1976).
—— 'Polyonomy in the late Roman aristocracy: the case of Petronius Probus', *JRS* 75 (1985), 164-82.
CAMPBELL, J. B., 'Who were the "viri militares"?', *JRS* 65 (1975), 11-31.
—— *The Emperor and the Roman Army, 31 BC – AD 235* (Oxford, 1984).
—— 'Teach yourself how to be a general', *JRS* 77 (1987), 13-29.
CAPRINO, C., COLINI, A. M., GATTI, G., PALLOTTINO, M., ROMANELLI, P., *La Colonna di Marco Aurelio* (Rome, 1955).
CAVALLO, M., 'The excavations at Choche (presumed Ctesiphon) – Area 2', *Mesopotamia* 1 (1966), 63-81.
CAZACU, M., ' "Montes Serrorum" (Ammianus Marcellinus, XXVII,5,3). Zur Siedlungsgeschichte der Westgoten in Rumanien', *Dacia* 16 (1972), 299-301.
CHAMOUX, F., 'La prophétesse Martha', in *Mél. Seston* (Paris, 1974), 81-5.
CHARLESWORTH, M. P., 'Imperial deportment: two texts and some questions', *JRS* 37 (1947), 34-8.
CHASTAGNOL, A., *La Préfecture urbaine à Rome sous le Bas-Empire* (Paris, 1960).
—— *Les Fastes de la Préfecture de Rome au Bas-Empire* (Etudes Prosopographiques 1; Paris, 1962).
—— 'Sur quelques documents relatifs à la basilique Saint Paul-hors-les-Murs', *Mél. Piganiol* (Paris, 1966), I, 421-37.
—— *L'Album Municipal de Timgad* (Antiquitas, 3.22; Bonn, 1978).
CHAUMONT, M.-L., 'Les villes fondées par les Vologèse: Vologésocerta et Vologésias', *Syria* 51 (1974), 77-81.
CHESNEY, F. R., *Narrative of the Euphrates Expedition carried on by Order of the British Government during the Years 1835, 1836 and 1837* (London, 1868).
CHRISTENSEN, A., *L'Iran sous les Sassanides* (2nd ed., Copenhagen, 1944).
CICHORIUS, C., *Die Reliefs des Traianssäule* (2 vols. with plates: Berlin, 1896-1900).
CUNLIFFE, B. W., 'Earth's grip holds them', in Brian Hartley and John Wacher (edd.), *Rome and her Northern Provinces* (Papers presented to Sheppard Frere) (Gloucester, 1983), 67-83.
DAVIS, E. J., *Life in Asiatic Turkey: a journal of travel in Cilicia (Pedias and Trachea), Isauria*

and part of Lycaonia and Cappadocia (London, 1879).
DELEHAYE, H., 'Saints de Thrace et de Mésie', *Analecta Bollandiana* 31 (1912), 161-300.
DEMANDT, A., 'Der Tod des älteren Theodosius', *Historia* 17 (1969), 598-626.
DIACONU, G., *Tîrgșor: Necropola din secolele III-IV e.n.* (Biblioteca de Arheologie 8; Bucharest, 1965).
—— 'În cautarea Dafnei' ('A la recherche de Dafné'), *Pontica* 4 (1971), 311-18.
—— 'On the socio-economic relations between natives and Goths in Dacia', in Miron Constantinescu (ed.), *Relations between the Autochthonous Populations and the Migratory Populations in the Territory of Romania* (Bibliotheca Historica Romaniae, Monographs 16; Bucarest, 1975), 67-75.
DIESNER, H.-J., 'Protectores (domestici)', *RE* Supplementband XI (1968), 1113-23.
—— *The Great Migration: the movement of peoples across Europe, AD 300-700* (Eng. tr. by C. S. V. Salt, London, 1982)
DILLEMANN, L., *Haute Mésopotamie Orientale et pays adjacents: contribution à la géographie historique de la région, du Ve siècle avant l'ère chrétienne au IVe siècle de cette ère* (Inst. fr. d'archéologie de Beyrouth; Bibl. archéologique et historique, 72; Paris, 1962)
DI VITA-EVRARD, G., 'Quatre inscriptions du Djebel Tarhuna: le territoire de *Lepcis Magna*', *Quaderni di Archeologia della Libia* 10 (1979), 67-98.
DODDS, E. R., 'Theurgy and its relationship to Neoplatonism', *JRS* 37 (1947), 55-69: reprinted as Appendix II, 'Theurgy', in *The Greeks and the Irrational* (Berkeley & Los Angeles, 1951; repr. 1968), 283-311.
—— *Proclus: The Elements of Theology* (Oxford, 1933; 2nd ed. 1968).
DONNER, F. McG., *The Early Islamic Conquests* (Princeton, 1981).
DOWNEY, G., 'The economic crisis at Antioch under Julian the Apostate', in P. R. Coleman-Norton (ed.), *Studies in Roman Economic and Social History in Honor of Allan Chester Johnson* (Princeton, 1951), 312-21. See also above, §2.
—— *A History of Antioch in Syria, from Seleucus to the Arab Conquest* (Princeton, 1961).
DUMVILLE, D., 'Kingship, genealogies and regnal lists', in P. H. Sawyer and I. N. Wood (edd.), *Early Medieval Kingship* (Univ. of Leeds, 1977; repr. 1979), 72-104.
DUNBABIN, K. M. D., *The Mosaics of Roman North Africa: studies in iconography and patronage* (Oxford, 1978).
DUNCAN-JONES, R., 'The size of the modius castrensis', *ZPE* 21 (1976), 53-62.
EGGER, R., 'Der Erste Theodosius', *Byzantion* 5 (1929/30), 9-23, repr. in A. Betz and G. Moro (edd.), *Römische Antike und frühes Christentum: ausgewählte Schriften von Rudolf Egger*, I (Klagenfurt, 1967), 126-43.
EITREM, S., 'La théurgie chez les néo-platoniciens et dans les papyrus magiques', *Symbolae Osloenses* 22 (1942), 49-79.
ELBE, J. von, *Roman Germany: a guide to sites and museums* (2nd ed., Mainz, 1977).
ENSSLIN, W., 'Zum Heermeisteramt des spätrömischen Reiches', *Klio* n.s. 6 (1930), 102-47.
—— 'Zu dem vermuteten Perserfeldzug des rex Hannibalianus', *Klio* n.s. 11 (1936), 102-10.
EVANS, E. C., 'Roman descriptions of personal appearance in history and biography', *HSCP* 46 (1935), 43-84.
EVRARD, E., 'Le maître de Plutarque d'Athènes et les origines du Néoplatonisme Athénien', *L'Antiquité Classique* 29 (1960), 108-33; 391-406.
FESTUGIÈRE, A. J., *Antioche païenne et chrétienne: Libanius, Chrysostome, et les moines de Syrie* (Bibl. des Ec. fr. d'Athènes et de Rome 194; Paris, 1959).
—— 'Julien à Macellum', *JRS* 47 (1957), 53-8.
—— 'Contemplation philosophique et art théurgique chez Proclus', *Studi di Storia Religiosa della Tarda Antichità* (Messina, 1968), 7-18.
FIEY, J. M., 'Topography of Al-Mada'in (Seleucia-Ctesiphon Area)', *Sumer* 23 (1967), 3-38.
FISHER, W. B., *The Middle East* (7th ed., London, 1978).
FORBES, R. J., *Bitumen and Petroleum in Antiquity* (Leiden, 1936).
FOWDEN, G., *The Egyptian Hermes: a historical approach to the late pagan mind* (Cambridge, 1986).
—— 'Pagan versions of the Rain Miracle of A.D. 172', *Historia* 36 (1987), 83-95.
FRASER, P. M., *Ptolemaic Alexandria* (Oxford, 1972).
FRENCH, D. H., 'The site of Dalisandos', *Epigraphica Anatolica* 4 (1984), 85-98.

FRERE, S. S., *Britannia: a history of Roman Britain* (3rd ed., 1987).
GABRIEL, A., *Voyages archéologiques dans la Turquie orientale* (Inst. fr. d'archéologie de Stamboul; Paris, 1940).
GARNSEY, P. D. A., 'Legal privilege in the Roman Empire', *Past and Present* 41 (1968), 3-24; repr. in M. I. Finley (ed.), *Studies in Ancient Society* (London & Boston, 1974), 141-65.
—— 'Why penal laws become harsher: the Roman case', *Natural Law Forum* 13 (1968), 141-62.
—— *Social Status and Legal Privilege in the Roman Empire* (Oxford, 1970).
—— 'Grain for Rome', in P. D. A. Garnsey, C. R. Whittaker, K. Hopkins, *Trade in the Ancient World* (London, 1983), 118-30.
GHIRSHMAN, R., *Les Chionites-Hephthalites* (Mém. de la Délégation fr. en Afghanistan, 13/Mém. de l'Inst. fr. d'archéologie orientale du Caire, 80; Cairo, 1948).
—— *Iran: Parthians and Sassanians* (Eng. tr., London, 1962).
GOODCHILD, R., *Tabula Imperii Romani: Lepcis Magna* (Oxford, 1954).
—— 'Roman sites on the Tarhuna Plateau of Tripolitania', *PBSR* 19 (1951), 43-77; repr. in his *Libyan Studies: Select Papers*, ed. Joyce Reynolds (London, 1976), 72-106.
—— and WARD-PERKINS, J. B., 'The Roman and Byzantine defences of Lepcis Magna', *PBSR* 21 (1953), 42-73.
GRODZYNSKI, D., 'Superstitio', *REA* 76 (1974), 36-60.
—— 'Tortures mortelles et catégories sociales: les Summa Supplicia dans le droit romain au IIIe et IVe siècles', in *Du châtiment dans la cité: supplices corporels et peine de mort dans le monde antique* (Coll. de l'Ec. fr. de Rome 79; Rome, 1984), 361-403.
GSELL, S., *Atlas Archéologique de l'Algérie* (Algiers & Paris, 1911).
GULLINI, G., 'Problems of an excavation in northern Mesopotamia', *Mesopotamia* 1 (1966), 7-38.
HADJINICOLAOU, A., 'Macellum, lieu d'éxil de l'empereur Julien', *Byzantion* 21 (1951), 11-22.
HALL, A. S., 'The Gorgoromeis', *Anatolian Studies* 21 (1971), 125-64.
—— 'New light on the capture of Isaura Vetus by P. Servilius Vatia', *Akten des VI Internationalen Kongresses für Griechische und Lateinische Epigraphik, München 1972* (1973), 568-71.
HAMILTON, W., *Researches in Asia Minor, Pontus and Armenia* (2 vols., London, 1842).
HARHOIU, R., *The Fifth-Century A.D. Treasure from Pietroasa, Romania, in the light of recent research* (tr. N. Hampartumian, BAR Suppl. Ser. 24; Oxford, 1977).
HARRIES, J. D., 'Church and state in the Notitia Galliarum', *JRS* 68 (1978), 26-43.
HARRISON, R. M., 'The Emperor Zeno's real name', *BZ* 74 (1981), 27-8.
HASLUCK, F. W., *Cyzicus, being some account of the history and antiquities of that city, etc.* (Cambridge, 1910).
HEATHER, P., 'The crossing of the Danube and the Gothic conversion', *Greek, Roman and Byzantine Studies* 27 (1986), 289-318.
HELLENKEMPER, H., 'Legionen im Bandenkrieg – Isaurien im 4. Jahrhundert', in *Studien zu den Militärgrenzen Roms III* (13 Internationales Limeskongress, Aachen 1983; Stuttgart, 1986), 625-34.
HILL, F., 'The mints of Roman Arabia and Mesopotamia', *JRS* 6 (1916), 135-69.
HIND, J. G. F., 'Whatever happened to the Agri Decumates?', *Britannia* 15 (1984), 187-92.
HODGKIN, T., *The Pfahlgraben* (Newcastle-on-Tyne, 1882; reprinted from *Archaeologia Aeliana* n.s. 9 [1883] 73-161).
HOCKMANN, O., 'Rheinschiffe aus der Zeit Ammians: neue Funde in Mainz', *Antike Welt* 13.3 (1982), 40-7.
HOFFMANN, D., *Das Spätrömische Bewegungsheer und die Notitia Dignitatum* (Epigraphische Studien 7; 2 vols., Düsseldorf, 1969-70).
—— 'Wadomar, Bacurius und Hariulf: zur Laufbahn adliger und fürstliche Barbaren im spätrömischen Heere des 4. Jahrhunderts', *Mus. Helv.* 35 (1978), 307-18.
HONIGMANN, E. and MARICQ, A., *Recherches sur les Res Gestae Divi Saporis* (Acad. Royale de Belgique; Cl. des Lettres, Mém. 47.4; Brussels, 1953).
HOPKINS, C. (ed.), *Topography and Architecture of Seleucia on the Tigris* (Ann Arbor, 1972), 149-63.
—— *The Discovery of Dura-Europos* (ed. by Bernard Goldman, New Haven & London, 1979).

HOPKINS, K., *Conquerors and Slaves: sociological studies in Roman history* I (Cambridge, 1978).

—— 'The political power of eunuchs', *Proceedings of the Cambridge Philological Society* 189 (1963), 62-80; revised in *Conquerors and Slaves*, 172-96.

HOPWOOD, K., 'Towers, territory and terror; how the East was held', in P. Freeman and D. Kennedy (edd.), *The Defence of the Roman and Byzantine East* (Sheffield Colloquium, 1986) (BAR Intern. Ser. 297(1); Oxford, 1986), 343-56.

HUNT, E. D., *Holy Land Pilgrimage in the Later Roman Empire, A.D. 312-460* (Oxford, 1982).

INVERNIZZI, A. (et al.), 'Seleucia on the Tigris', in E. Quarantelli (general editor), *The Land between Two Rivers: twenty years of Italian archaeology in the Middle East: exhibition catalogue, Turin 1985, Rome and Florence, 1986* (Turin, 1985), 87-99.

IONIȚĂ, I., 'Contribution à la connaissance de la civilisation de Sintana de Mureș-Tchérneakhov sur le territoire de la Roumanie', in *Arheologia Moldovei* 4 (1966), 189-259 (in Romanian; French summary at 252-7).

—— 'The social-economic structure of society during the Goths' migration in the Carpatho-Danubian area', in Miron Constantinescu (ed.), *Relations between the Autochthonous Populations and the Migratory Populations in the Territory of Romania* (Bibliotheca Historica Romaniae, Monographs 16; Bucharest, 1975), pp. 77-89.

ISAAC, B., 'Trade routes to Arabia and the Roman army', *Roman Frontier Studies 1979* (BAR Intern. Ser. 71; Oxford, 1980), 889-901.

JACQUES, F. and BOUSQUET, B., 'Le raz de marée du 21 Juillet 365: du cataclysme local à la catastrophe cosmique', *MEFR* 96 (1984), 423-61.

JANIN, R., *Constantinople Byzantine: développement urbain et répertoire topographique* (2nd ed., Paris, 1964).

JONES, A. H. M., *The Cities of the Eastern Roman Provinces* (2nd ed., Oxford, 1971).

—— *The Later Roman Empire, 284-602: a social, economic and administrative survey* (3 vols. and maps, Oxford, 1964; repr. in 2 vols., Oxford 1973).

JOHNSON, S., 'A group of late Roman city walls in Gallia Belgica', *Britannia* 4 (1973), 210-23.

—— *Later Roman Britain* (London, 1980).

KAEGI, W. E., 'The Emperor Julian at Naissus', *L'Antiquité Classique* 44 (1975), 161-71.

KEEGAN, J. D. P., *The Face of Battle* (London, 1976).

KENT, J. P. C., in C. H. V. Sutherland, R. A. G. Carson (edd.), *The Roman Imperial Coinage, VIII: the family of Constantine I, A.D. 337-364* (London, 1981).

KLAUSER, T., 'Akklamation', *RAC* I (1950), 216-33.

KRAUTHEIMER, R., *Rome: profile of a city, 312-1308* (Princeton, 1980).

LABOURT, J., *Le Christianisme dans l'empire Perse sous la dynastie Sassanide (224-632)* (Paris, 1904).

LANE FOX, R., *Pagans and Christians* (Harmondsworth, New York, etc., 1986).

LAUR-BELART, R., *Führer durch Augusta Raurica* (4th ed., Basel, 1966).

LAYARD, A. H., *Discoveries in the Ruins of Nineveh and Babylon, with Travels in Armenia, Kurdistan and the Desert* (London, 1853).

LEAKE, W., *Journal of a Tour in Asia Minor* (London, 1824).

LENGYEL, A. and RADAN, G. T. B. (edd.), *The Archaeology of Roman Pannonia* (Lexington, Kentucky & Budapest, 1980).

LEPELLEY, C., 'La préfecture de tribu dans l'Afrique du Bas-Empire', *Mél. Seston* (Paris, 1974), 285-95.

—— 'L'Afrique du Nord et le prétendu séisme universel du 21 Juillet 365', *MEFR* 96 (1984), 463-90.

LEPPER, F. A., *Trajan's Parthian War* (Oxford, 1948).

LEVICK, B. M., *Roman Colonies in Southern Asia Minor* (Oxford, 1967).

LEWY, H. A., *Chaldaean Oracles and Theurgy: mysticism, magic and Platonism in the later Roman Empire* (Cairo, 1956; 2nd ed., 1978).

LIEBESCHUETZ, J. H. W. G., *Antioch: city and Imperial administration in the later Roman Empire* (Oxford, 1972).

LIPPOLD, A., 'Ursinus und Damasus', *Historia* 14 (1965), 105-28.

MacCORMACK, S., *Art and Ceremony in Late Antiquity* (Berkeley, California & London, 1981).

McDOWELL, R. G., 'The excavations at Seleucia on the Tigris', *Papers of the Michigan Academy of*

Science, Arts and Letters 18 (1933), 101-19.
—— 'The history of Seleucia from Classical sources', in Clark Hopkins, Topography and Architecture of Seleucia on the Tigris (Ann Arbor, 1972), 149-63.
MacMULLEN, R., 'Roman bureaucratese', Traditio 18 (1962), 364-78.
—— 'Imperial Bureaucrats in the Roman provinces', HSCP 68 (1964), 305-16.
—— Enemies of the Roman Order: treason, unrest and alienation in the Roman Empire (Cambridge, Mass. & London, 1967).
—— 'Market-days in the Roman Empire', Phoenix 24 (1970), 333-41.
—— Roman Government's Response to Crisis (New Haven & London, 1976).
—— 'Judicial savagery in the Roman Empire', Chiron 16 (1986), 147-66.
MAENCHEN-HELFEN, J. O., 'Huns and Hsiung-Nu', Byzantion 17 (1944-5), 222-43.
—— The World of the Huns: studies in their history and culture (Berkeley, California, 1973).
MALLOWAN, M. E., Nimrud and its Remains (London, 1966).
MANGO, C., 'Isaurian builders', in P. Wirth (ed.), Polychronion: Festschrift F. Dölger zum 75 Geburtstag (Heidelberg, 1966), 358-65.
—— Le développement urbain de Constantinople (IVe-VIIe siècles) (Trav. et Mém. du centre de recherche d'histoire et civilisation de Byzance, Monographies 2; Paris, 1985).
MANN, J., 'Power, force and the frontiers of Empire', review of E. N. Luttwak, The Grand Strategy of the Roman Empire from the First Century A.D. to the Third, JRS 69 (1979), 175-83.
MARICQ, A., 'Le tell d'Anbar', Syria 35 (1958), 353-6; repr. in Classica et Orientalia (Inst. fr. d'archéologie de Beyrouth, Publ. hors série No. 11; Paris, 1965), 95-7.
—— 'Vologésias, l'emporium de Ctésiphon', Syria 36 (1959), 264-76; repr. in Classica et Orientalia, 113-25.
MARSDEN, E. W., Greek and Roman Artillery: historical development (Oxford, 1969).
—— Greek and Roman Artillery: technical treatises (Oxford, 1971).
MARTROYE, F., 'La répression de la magie et le culte des gentils au IVe siècle', Revue historique de droit français et étranger, Ser. 4.9 (1930), 669-701.
MATTHEWS, J. F., 'Continuity in a Roman family; the Rufii Festi of Volsinii', Historia XVI (1967), 484-509; repr. in Political Life and Culture in Late Roman Society (London, 1985), ch. VI.
—— 'Gallic supporters of Theodosius', Latomus 30 (1971), 1077-99; repr. in Political Life and Culture, ch. IX.
—— 'Symmachus and the Oriental cults', JRS 63 (1973), 175-95; repr. in Political Life and Culture, ch. VIII. See also above, §2.
—— Western Aristocracies and Imperial Court, A.D. 364-425 (Oxford, 1975).
—— and CORNELL, T., Atlas of the Roman World (Oxford, 1982).
—— 'Gesandtschaft' in RAC 10 (1977), cols. 653-85.
—— 'The tax law of Palmyra: evidence for economic history in a city of the Roman East', JRS 74 (1984), 157-80.
MATTINGLY, D. J., 'The Laguatan: a Libyan tribal confederation in the late Roman Empire', Libyan Studies 14 (1983), 96-108.
MAURICE, J., 'La terreur de la magie au IVe siècle', Revue historique de droit français et étranger, Ser. 4.6 (1927), 108-20.
MEER, F. VAN DER, and MOHRMANN, C., Atlas of the Early Christian World (Eng. tr., London, 1966).
MILLAR, F. G. B., 'Paul of Samosata, Zenobia and Aurelian: the Church, local culture and political allegiance in third-century Syria', JRS 61 (1971), 1-17.
—— The Emperor in the Roman World (London, 1977).
MINNS, E. H., Scythians and Greeks: a survey of the ancient history and archaeology of the north coast of the Euxine from the Danube to the Caucasus (Cambridge, 1913).
—— 'The art of the Northern Nomads', PBA 28 (1942), 47-99.
MITCHELL, S., 'Iconium and Ninica: two double communities in Roman Asia Minor', Historia 28 (1979), 409-38.
MITFORD, T. B., Journeys in Rough Cilicia: see BEAN, G. E.
MITREA, B., and PREDA, C., Necropole din secolul al IV-lea e.n. în Muntenia (Biblioteca de Arheologie 10; Bucharest, 1966).

MÓCSY, A., *Pannonia and Upper Moesia: a history of the Middle Danube Provinces of the Roman Empire* (London, 1974).
—— and SZENTLÉLEKY, T. (edd.), *Die römischen Steindenkmäler von Savaria* (Budapest, 1971).
MOMMSEN, T. 'Protectores Augusti', *Ephemeris Epigraphica* 5 (1884), 121-41; repr. in *Ges. Schr.* VIII, 419-46.
MUSIL, A., *The Middle Euphrates: a topographical itinerary* (American Geographical Society: Oriental Exploration and Studies, No. 3; New York, 1927).
Naval Intelligence Division Geographical Handbook, B.R. 524; *Iraq and the Persian Gulf* (London, 1944).
NEGEV, A., 'The Nabataeans and the Provincia Arabia', in H. Temporini and W. Haase (edd.) *Aufstieg and Niedergang der Römischen Welt* II.8 (Berlin & New York, 1977), 520-686.
NEUSNER, J., *A History of the Jews in Babylonia* (5 vols., Leiden, 1965-70).
NEWMAN, J., *Agricultural Life of the Jews of Babylonia* (London, 1932).
NIEBUHR, B. G., *Researches into the History of the Scythians, Getae and Sarmatians* (Eng. tr., Oxford, 1830).
NOCK, A. D., 'The Emperor's divine *Comes*', *JRS* 37 (1947), 102-16; repr. in Z. Stewart (ed.), *Arthur Darby Nock: essays on religion and the ancient world* (Oxford, 1972), II, 653-75.
NORDEN, E., *Alt-Germanien: Völker- und Namengeschichtliche Untersuchungen* (Leipzig & Berlin, 1934).
NORMAN, A. F., 'Notes on some *consulares* of Syria', *BZ* 51 (1958), 73-7.
OATES, D., *Studies in the History of Northern Iraq* (London, 1968).
OBERMAYR, A., *Römerstadt Carnuntum* (Vienna, 1967).
O'DONNELL, J. J., ' "Paganus": evolution and use', *Classical Folia* 31 (1977), 163-9.
—— 'The demise of paganism', *Traditio* 35 (1979), 45-88.
OPPENHEIMER, A. (with ISAAC, B. and LECKER, M.), *Babylonia Judaica in the Talmudic Period* (Beihefte zum Tübinger Atlas des Vorderen Orients, Reihe B, No. 47; Wiesbaden, 1983).
ORY, S., 'Ḥiṣn Kayfā', *Encyclopaedia of Islam* III (2nd ed., 1971), 506-9.
PACK, E., *Städte und Steuern in der Politik Julians: Untersuchungen zu den Quellen eines Kaiserbildes* (Coll. Latomus 194; Brussels, 1986).
PALADE, V., 'Atelierele pentru lucrat pieptieni din os din secolul al IV-lea e.n. de la Bîrlad-Valea Seacă', *Arheologia Moldovei* 4 (1966), 261-77.
PALLIS, A., *The Antiquity of Iraq* (Copenhagen, 1956).
PATLAGEAN, E., *Pauvreté économique et pauvreté sociale à Byzance, 4e-7e siècles* (Ec. des hautes études en sciences sociales; Civilisations et Sociétés, 48; Paris, 1977).
PEARCE, J. W. E., in H. Mattingly, C. H. V. Sutherland, R. A. G. Carson (edd.), *The Roman Imperial Coinage, Vol. IX: Valentinian I – Theodosius I* (London, 1951).
PENNINCK, E., 'L'origine hellénique de *burgus*', *Latomus* 4 (1940/5), 5-21.
PETERS, F. E., 'Byzantium and the Arabs of Syria', *Annales Archéologiques Arabes Syriennes*, 27-8 (1977-8), 97-113.
—— 'Romans and Barbarians in Southern Syria', *Journal of Near Eastern Studies* 37 (1978), 315-26.
PETIT, P., *Libanius et la vie municipale à Antioche au IVe siècle après J.-C.* (Inst. fr. d'archéologie de Beyrouth: Bibl. archéologique et historique 62, 1955).
—— *Les Etudiants de Libanius* (Etudes Prosopographiques 1; Paris, 1957).
PETRIKOVITS, H. VON, 'Fortifications in the north-western Roman empire from the third to the fifth centuries A.D.', *JRS* 61 (1971), 178-218.
PFLAUM, H.-G., *Le Marbre de Thorigny* (Bibl. de l'Ec. des Hautes Etudes, 292; Paris, 1948).
PIÉTRI, C., *Roma Christiana: recherches sur l'église de Rome, son organisation, sa politique, son idéologie, de Miltiade à Sixte III (311-440)* (Bibl. de l'Ec. fr. d'Athènes et de Rome, 284; Rome 1976).
PLANHOL, X. DE, *De la Plaine Pamphylienne aux Lacs Pisidiens: nomadisme et vie paysanne* (Bibl. archéologique et historique de l'Inst. fr. d'archéologie d'Istanbul 3; Paris, 1958).
PREDA, C., 'Necropole din secolul al IV-lea e.n. in Muntenia', see MITREA, B.
PRICE, S. R. F., *Rituals and Power: the Roman Imperial cult in Asia Minor* (Cambridge, 1984).
RANDERS-PEHRSON, J. D., *Barbarians and Romans: the birth struggle of Europe, A.D. 400-700* (Oklahoma, 1983).

RAWSON, E., 'Religion and politics in the late second century B.C. at Rome', *Phoenix* 28 (1974), 193-212.
REINHOLD, M., *History of Purple as a Status Symbol in Antiquity* (Coll. Latomus 116; Brussels, 1970).
REUTHER, O., 'The German excavations at Ctesiphon', *Antiquity* 3 (1929), 434-51.
RICCIARDI, R. V. and MANCINI, M., 'Coche', in *The Land between Two Rivers* (see INVERNIZZI, A.), 100-10.
RICKMAN, G., *The Corn Supply of Ancient Rome* (Oxford, 1980).
ROBERT, L., 'Epigrammes du Bas-Empire: IV. Epigrammes d'Aphrodisias', *Hellenica* 4 (1948), 127-35.
—— *Documents de l'Asie Mineure Méridionale: inscriptions, monnaies et géographie* (Geneva & Paris, 1966).
ROEREN, R., 'Zur Archäologie u. Geschichte Sudwestdeutschlands im 3 bis 5 Jahrhundert n. Chr.', *Jahrbuch der römisch-germanischen Zentralmuseums*, Mainz, 7 (1960), 214-94.
ROSSI, L., *Trajan's Column and the Dacian Wars* (London, 1971).
ROUECHÉ, C., 'Acclamations in the later Roman Empire: new evidence from Aphrodisias', *JRS* 74 (1984), 181-99.
ROUX, J.-P., *Les Traditions des nomades de la Turquie méridionale* (Bibl. archéologique et historique de l'Inst. fr. d'archéologie d'Istanbul, 24; Paris, 1970).
RUBIN, Z., 'The conversion of the Visigoths to Christianity', *Mus. Helv.* 38 (1981), 34-54.
RUGGINI, L., *Economia e Società nell'Italia Annonaria* (Milan, 1961).
RYBAKOV, B. A., 'Chernyakhovskaya Kultura', *Materialy i Issledovaniya po Arkheologii SSSR* 82 (Moscow, 1960).
STE CROIX, G. E. M. DE, 'Suffragium: from vote to patronage', *British Journal of Sociology* 5 (1954), 33-47.
SARTRE, M., *Trois Etudes sur l'Arabie Romaine et Byzantine* (Coll. Latomus 178; Brussels, 1982).
SAUMAGNE, C., 'Un Tarif fiscal au IV siècle de notre ère (d'après des fragments épigraphiques découverts à Carthage)', *Karthago* I (1950), 105-200.
SCHMITTHENNER, W., 'Rome and India: aspects of universal history during the Principate', *JRS* 69 (1979), 90-106.
SCHWARZ, G. T., *Die Kaiserstadt Aventicum* (Bern & Munich, 1964).
SEGAL, J. B., 'Mesopotamian communities from Julian to the rise of Islam', *PBA* 41 (1955), 109-39.
—— *Edessa, The 'Blessed City'* (Oxford, 1970).
SHAHÎD, I., *Byzantium and the Arabs in the Fourth Century* (Washington D.C., 1984).
SHAW, B. D., ' "Eaters of flesh, drinkers of milk": the ancient Mediterranean ideology of the pastoral nomad', *Ancient Society* 13/14 (1982/3), 5-31.
—— 'Bandits in the Roman Empire', *Past and Present* 105 (1984), 3-52.
—— 'The family in late Antiquity: the experience of Augustine', *Past and Present* 115 (1986), 3-51.
SHEPPARD, A., 'Proclus' attitude to theurgy', *CQ* n.s. 31 (1982), 212-24.
SHERWIN-WHITE, A. N., 'Geographical factors in Roman Algeria', *JRS* 34 (1944), 1-10.
SMITH, A., *Porphyry's Place in the Neoplatonic Tradition* (The Hague, 1974).
STENTON, F. M., *Anglo-Saxon England* (3rd ed., Oxford, 1971).
STILWELL, R., MacDONALD, W. L., McALLISTER, M. H. (edd.), *Princeton Encyclopaedia of Classical Sites* (Princeton, 1976).
STROHEKER, K. F., 'Zur Rolle der Heermeister fränkischer Abstammung im späten vierten Jahrhundert', *Historia* 4 (1955), 314-30; repr. in *Germanentum und Spätantike* (Bibliothek der Alten Welt; Zürich & Stuttgart, 1965), 9-29.
—— 'Die Alamannen und der spätrömische Reich'; repr. in W. Müller (ed.), *Zur Geschichte der Alamannen* (Wege der Forschung, Band B, Darmstadt 1975), 20-48.
SWIFT, L. J. and OLIVER, J. H., 'Constantius II on Flavius Philippus', *AJP* 82 (1962), 247-64.
SYME, R., 'Isaura and Isauria: some problems', in E. Frézouls (ed.), *Sociétés urbaines, sociétés rurales dans l'Asie Mineure et la Syrie hellénistiques et romaines (Colloque Strasbourg, novembre 1985)* (Strasbourg, 1987), 131-47.
—— 'Isauria in Pliny', *Anatolian Studies* 36 (1986), 159-64.

Bibliography

TAVERNIER, J. B., *The Six Voyages of John Baptista Tavernier ... through Turkey into Persia and the East-Indies, finished in the Year 1670* (Eng. tr. by J. P(hillips), London, 1678).

TEILLET, S., *Des Goths à la Nation Gothique: les origines de l'idée de nation en Occident du Ve au VIIe siècle* (Paris, 1984).

THÉVENOT, E., *Autun: cité romaine et chrétienne* (Autun, 1932).

THOMAS, E. B., *Römische Villen in Pannonien: Beiträge zur pannonischen Siedlungsgeschichte* (Budapest, 1964).

THOMPSON, E. A., 'The camp of Attila', *JHS* 65 (1945), 112-15.

—— *A History of Attila and the Huns* (Oxford, 1948).

—— 'Christianity and the Northern Barbarians', *Nottingham Medieval Studies* 1 (1957), 3-21; repr. in Momigliano (ed.), *The Conflict between Paganism and Christianity in the Fourth Century*, 56-78.

—— *Romans and Barbarians: the decline of the Western Empire* (Madison, Wisconsin, 1982).

—— 'The Visigoths from Fritigern to Euric', *Historia* 12 (1963), 105-26; repr. in *Romans and Barbarians*, 38-57.

—— *The Early Germans* (Oxford, 1965).

—— *The Visigoths in the Time of Ulfila* (Oxford, 1966).

—— 'Economic warfare', in *Romans and Barbarians*, 3-19.

TODD, M., *The Barbarians: Goths, Franks and Vandals* (London & New York, 1972; repr. 1980).

—— *The Northern Barbarians, 100 B.C.-A.D. 300* (London, 1975).

TOMLIN, R. S. O., 'Seniores-Iuniores in the late Roman field army', *AJP* 93 (1972), 253-78.

—— 'Notitia Dignitatum omnium, tam civilium quam militarium' in R. Goodburn and P. Bartholomew (edd.), *Aspects of the Notitia Dignitatum* (BAR Suppl. Ser. 15; Oxford, 1976), 189-209.

—— 'The army of the late Empire', in J. S. Wacher (ed.) *The Roman World* (London & New York, 1987), I, 107-35.

TOYNBEE, J. M. C., review discussion of Alföldi, *Die Kontorniaten*, *JRS* 35 (1945), 115-21.

—— 'Beasts and their names in the Roman Empire', *PBSR* 16 (1948), 24-37.

TYLOR, E. B., *Primitive Culture: researches into the development of mythology, philosophy, religion, language, art and culture* (4th ed.; 2 vols., London, 1903).

VEECK, W., *Die Alamannen in Württemberg* (2 vols., Berlin & Leipzig, 1931).

VOOBUS, A., *History of Asceticism in the Syrian Orient: a contribution to the history of culture in the Near East, I (Persia), II (Mesopotamia)* (Corpus Scriptorum Christianorum Orientalium, Subsidia 14, 17; Louvain, 1958, 1960).

VORBECK, E. and BECKEL, L., *Carnuntum: Rom an der Donau* (Salzburg, 1973).

WALBANK, F. W., 'The Scipionic legend', *Proceedings of the Cambridge Philological Society* 13 (1967), 54-69.

WALLIS, R. T., *Neoplatonism* (London, 1972).

WARD-PERKINS, J. B., 'The Roman and Byzantine defences of Lepcis Magna', see GOODCHILD, R.

—— 'The Roman East and the Parthian West', *PBA* 51 (1965), 175-99.

WERNER, J., *Beiträge zur Archäologie des Attila-Reiches* (Verlag der Bayerischen Akad. der Wissenschaften, Phil.-Hist. Kl., Abhandlungen n.f. 38; Munich 1956).

—— 'Zu den alamannischen Burgen des 4. und 5. Jahrhunderts', in *Speculum Historiale: Festschrift für Johannes Spörl* (Freiburg i. Br. & Munich, 1965), 439-53; reprinted in W. Müller (ed.), *Zur Geschichte der Alamannen* (Wege der Forschung, Band C; Darmstadt 1975), 67-90.

WIGHTMAN, E. M., *Roman Trier and the Treveri* (London, 1970).

—— *Gallia Belgica* (London, 1985).

WILKES, J. J., *Diocletian's Palace, Split: residence of a retired Roman Emperor* (Univ. of Sheffield, Dept of Ancient History and Archaeology: Occasional Publications, No. 2, 1986).

WILL, E., 'Marchands et chefs de commerce à Palmyre', *Syria* 34 (1947), 262-77.

WINTER, E., *Die sāsānidisch-römischen Friedensverträge des 3. Jahrhunderts n. Chr.- ein Beitrag zum Verständnis der aussenpolitischen Beziehungen zwischen den beiden Grossmächten* (Frankfurt/M., Bern, New York, Paris, 1988).

WOLFRAM, H. (tr. T. J. Dunlap), *History of the Goths* (Berkeley, Los Angeles & London, 1988)

YAVETZ, Z., 'Plebs sordida', *Athenaeum*, n.s. 43 (1965), 295-311.

Index

Abarne, near Amida, curative springs at, 55 and n. 16, 402
Abinnaeus, Fl., *protector*, 75, 246
Abouzatha, settlement near Ctesiphon, 176
Abydus, in Thebaid, oracular shrine at, 217
Achaiacala (Hadisa?), Euphrates settlement, 146
acclamations: their status and recognition, 405; by cities, 40, 405; at Rome, 11, 231, 234, 405, 416 and n. 32; in senate, 248 and n. 32, 449; at Constantinople, 194, 198; at Antioch, 408, 409 and n. 13; military, 194, 198f.; at siege of Amida, 63; in Africa, 386; in *Notitia Dignitatum*, 255; Christian, 441f.
'ad Innocentes', martyrs' shrine near Milan, 257, 437
Adonis, rites of, 61; at Antioch, 108, 177
adoratio purpurae, Oriental custom, introduced by Diocletian, 29, 244; its origin, 244f.; function, 245-9; seen as privilege, 245f. and n. 27; grades of entitlement, 246f.; by *protectores*, 77, 246; Ursicinus and, 244
adultery: accusations of, 209-17; executions for, 257; *see also* magic
adventus ceremony, 11, 108, 188, 254; at Antioch, 108; at Sirmium, 248; at Autun, 248; of Constantius at Rome, 11f., 231-5, 266; and imperial 'praesentia', 254; triumphal aspects of, 233f. and n. 4, 375
Aedesius, of Pergamum, philosopher: and Julian, 122f.; and oracles, 118
Aequitius (or Equitius), *magister militum*: as tribune, imperial candidate, 188; role in accession of Valentinian, 189; in suppression of Procopius, 196f., 198; at Philippopolis, 198, 201; his character, 188
Africa: secured by Constantius in 361, 101, 105; by Valentinian in 365, 23, 198; Africans, at court of Valentinian II, 273f.
Africanus (1), governor of Pannonia II, executed, 36f., 92, 264 and n. 26
Africanus (2), protégé of Theodosius (1), executed for wanting change of province, 271
Agathias, Byzantine historian: on Alamanni, 312f.; on nuns, 439
Agenarichus, or Serapio, Alamann prince, nephew of Chnodomarius, 315; initiate into Greek mysteries, 315, 424f.
agentes in rebus: Julian on, 267; at Sirmium, 264; in Spain, 264; their duties, 518 n. 26
Agilo, *magister peditum*, successor of Ursicinus: his promotion, 270; German origin of, 316; his daughter, 316
Aginatius, *vicarius Romae* 368-70, dispute with Maximinus, executed, 213
'Agri Decumates': annexation and abandonment, 308; transference of population, 308
Alamanni (Map 6): in Ammianus, 207, 306-18; archaeology of, 535 n. 4, 525 n. 19
occupation of 'Agri Decumates', 308;

Index 573

inroads into Gaul in 350s, 81; their territorial boundaries, 307 and 524 nn. 8-9; *pagi* of, 306; settlement patterns and lifestyle, 310-12; use of hill-forts, 311f.; resettlement of Roman villas, 310, 400; attitude to Roman towns, 308; attack Moguntiacum, 435; inadequacies at siege warfare, 393; their economy, 312; as agriculturalists, 310, 312; kings and princes of, 314f.; federation of, at Strasbourg, 314; service in Roman armies, 316f.

fondness for drink, 313f.; hairstyles, 313; religious customs, 312f.; and divination, 312

Ammianus' sources on, 376-8; on battle of Strasbourg, 378f.

see also Agenarichus, Chnodomarius, Macrianus, Vadomarius

al Anbar, 'the Arsenal', *see under* Pirisabora

Alani, in Ammianus, 334f.; their location, 334; 'Don folk', 336; federation of, 334, 338; absorbed by Huns, 334; among Goths, 325; their pattern of life and customs, 334f.; nomadism, 334, 336, 339; pastoral economy, 337; horsemanship, 336; fighting techniques, 336; religion, 334f., 340; comparison with Huns, 337 literary comparisons, 334f., 353; in Classical literature, 336; identified as Massagetae, 334

Alatheus, 'dux', regent of Greuthungi, 324; possible origin, 326

Alavivus, Gothic leader, 325

Alexander the Great: eastern conquests of, 140, 143; in *Caesares* of Julian, 137f.; and the emperor Trajan, 137f.; and military strategy of Julian, in war against Constantius, 105; in Persian campaign, 168; and philosopher Anaxarchus, 431; as 'exemplum' applied to Valentinian, 242; his death at Babylon, 138

Alexander, *consularis Syriae*, appointed by Julian, his character, 412

Alexandria: visited by Ammianus, 14; in digression on Egypt, 26; in third century, 29; propensity to disorder, 29, 442

learning at, 431; schools of medicine, 14, 431 and n. 14, 454; and corn-supply, 126, 410

temples, of Genius, 442; of Serapis, 26, 443; church building at, 443 murder of bishop George, 442-4

see also Athanasius

al-Mada'in (Seleucia-Ctesiphon area), 156; topography of, 500 n. 22

al-Mundhir (Alamoundaros), pro-Persian Arab prince in sixth century, 345f.

Alypius, *vicarius* of Britain: supporter of Julian, 222, 224f.; role in attempted Temple restoration, 224; exiled under Valens, 222

Ambrose, bishop of Milan, 17 and n. 23; at court of Maximus, 268f.; and senator Symmachus, 424, 425

Amida (Diyarbekir): fortification by Constantius Caesar, 54f., 136; artillery at, 291f., 301; fair held at, 45, 388; siege of 359, 57-65, 288, 289, 290f., 295; its chronology, 58-60; pestilence, 58f. and n. 20; destruction of the city, 58, 66, 391; military consequences of its loss, 94f., 100; inquiry into, 46f.; rebuilding, 66; inscr. cited, 489 n. 32

Ammianus Marcellinus

his origin and social background, 8 and n. 1, 78-80, 453f.; age, 76f.; as *protector domesticus*, 76-9; and Ursicinus, 34f., 39, 47, 76, 78f., 100, 270, 303, 453; *tirocinium* under, 78

at Nisibis, 34; at Antioch under Gallus Caesar, 34f.; in Italy, 17, 35-7, 264; in Gaul, 38f., 81-3, 88; and rebellion of Silvanus, 37f., 76, 260; transferred to east, 39; visit to Corduene, 44, 48ff.; at Amida, 45f., 55, 57-65; after retirement of Ursicinus, 47 and n. 26, 100, 203;

on Persian campaign of Julian, 4, 108, 111, 160, 175-9, 180, 183f., 185, 186, 303; at accession of Jovian (??), 183f.; leaves army, 13
travels, 13-17; to Laconia, 14, 192; Alexandria, 14; Thebes, 14; Pontus, 14; Constantinople (?), 16, 379; at Antioch under Valens, 15, 220, 222f.; in 382 (?), 376f. and n. 128; at Rome, 8-13 and n. 5, 465f., 476 n. 5; relations with Eutherius, 25, 466; with 'circle of Symmachus', doubted, 466 and n. 33
military experience, 287f., 301f., 453, 465, 485 n. 10; imperfect understanding of artillery, 301f. and n. 28; supply, 302; military intelligence, 302; his role at Amida, 64f.; knowledge of desert terrain, 67, 462
survival and transmission of text, 6 and n. 8; in Priscian, 6 and n. 6; in Jordanes, 476 n. 6; textual problems discussed, 485 n. 21, 503 n. 65, 505 nn. 82 & 84, 507 n. 4, 519 nn. 44 & 51, 550 n. 18, 551 n. 24:
date of composition, 22-7 and n. 35, 31; his audience, 8f., 204, 446; the later books, 18 and n. 25, 20-5, 26 and nn. 34-5, 204-6 and n. 2, 226-8; problems in, 207f., 209f., 213, 214-17; the lost books, 27-30 and nn. 36-42, 456, 457, 498 n. 12; A. and contemporary history, 204-6, 209; its 'dangers', 204f. and n. 1, 457
character of the history, 18-20, 27; of the later books, 206f.; its unity, and Ammianus' career, 206f.; method of composition, 30-2 and n. 44; principles of history, 204, 455, 457, 459, 464; 'veritas' in, 465; limitations of annalistic technique, 206-9, 458f.; influence of biography, 280, 459; of oratory and panegyric, 455, 461, 468f.; history as memoir, 465, 489 n. 29
A.'s prefaces, 205, 456-8; his epilogue, 454-6 and n. 4, 461f.; 'miles et Graecus', 461f. and n. 23; A. and Latin, 80, 107, 429f., 466, 467f.; and Greek, 107, 125, 461 and n. 23, 462 and n. 25, 466; Latin and Greek balanced, 466;
narrative technique, 61, 64f., 178 and n. 92, 191-3, 497f. and nn. 3-4; symmetry in, 204f., 463, 483 n. 1; rhetorical technique in, 201, 427; in military narratives, 49 and n. 4, 286-91 and n. 12, 295-301, 486 n. 22, 522 n. 23; biographical elements, 238, 239, 280, 459-61, 491 n. 2, 550 n. 9; portrayals of character, 84, 268, 277f., 318, 459-61 and n. 17; obituaries, 84, 112f., 239-42, 469, 495 n. 48
digressions, their meaning and function, 27-9 and n. 36, 31 and n. 43, 111, 389-91, 462-4 and nn. 26-9, 483 n. 1, 537 n. 12; in later books, 207, 208; on eastern provinces, 342f., 389, 390; on Egypt, 14, 111, 431f., 462; on Gaul, 38f., 87, 389, 391, 463f.; on Huns and Alani, 207, 332-6 and 528 n. 47, 379f.; on Persia, 111, 464, 537 n. 12; on Pontus, 14 and n. 17, 106f., 111, 207, 390, 537 n. 12; on Rome, 207, 214f., 414-16 and n. 28; on Saracens, 207, 344 and n. 68; on Thrace, 207, 208, 389; on artillery, 291-4, 301f.; on divination, 428-31; on 'genii', 432-5; on pestilence, 59 and n. 20
treatment of 'letters' and speeches, 39f. and n. 12, 130f. and nn. 3-4, 168, 178f. and n. 92, 181f. and n. 2, 221 and n. 34; avoidance of technical terms, 437-9, 521 n. 15, 523 n. 28; dramatic technique, 160, 175-9, 192f.; picturesque effects, 534 n. 109; theatrical imagery, 193f., 201, 236f., 247, 297, 460f., 514 n. 3; satire, 416; animal images, 258f. and n. 16, 460; 'exempla', 239-44, 466; elements of style discussed, 260f., 419, 427f., 517 n. 18
sources: autopsy, 12f. and nn. 13-14, Chs. III-IV *passim*, 83, 144, 172-5;

Index 575

'versati in medio', 13 and n. 14, 21-5 and nn. 28-30, 100f., 161-3, 195 and n. 19, 268, 376f., 379, 457f.; reports and documents, 21, 24 and n. 31, 377f., 380f., 381f.
literary sources and influences: Eunapius, 164-75, 503 n. 67; A.'s use of him defined, 172, 175, 458; Magnus of Carrhae (??), 169, 504 n. 73; Oribasius (??), 504 n. 75; 'auctores' and 'oracula', 432; 'theologi', 428, 432; 'mathematici', 431; Homer, 87, 466, 488 n. 20; Herodotus, 14, 334f., 462; Thucydides, 59, 463 and n. 27; Menander, 432f., Terence, 415 and n. 31; Cicero, *q.v.*; Vergil, 17, 87, 287, 463, 468; Timagenes, 464 and nn. 28-9; Pliny and Solinus, 462; Valerius Maximus, 288, 431; Herodian, 482 n. 42; Enmann's 'Kaisergeschichte', 29 and n. 41, 244, 457; Eutropius, 455 and n. 4; Festus, 458 and n. 15; A. and Juvenal, 32, 415; and Marius Maximus, 32, 415; Historia Augusta, 6 n. 6; Epitome de Caesaribus, 476 n. 6; Priscian and Jordanes, *see above*
on the third century, 29f.; on Constantine the Great, 447-50; on Constantius II, 33-7; on Julian (*q.v.*), 83, 84, 110, 111-14, 166, 181-3 and nn. 1-3, 408f, 410, 412f.; importance of Julian for A., 463, 468-70; rebellion of Procopius, 191-203; A.'s attitude to, 193f., 195, 201-3; on Rome, 11-13, 24, 209-17, 250, 456, 470 and n. 40; prefects of Rome, 24, 211f., 215 and n. 22; senate, and senators, 213, 215, 216 and n. 25, 209-17, 278, 414-20; on cities and city life, 389-97; on *curiales*, 79f., 105f., 107; of Antioch, 406, 412
'political theory' of A., 128, 201f.; on imperial office, 235ff., 250-3; legitimacy and usurpation, 201-3; virtues of emperors, 450; their origins and character, 200, 249 and nn. 33-4; 'adoratio', 244-6;

justice and judicial procedures, 113f., 202, 209-17, 220, 241, 251f., 261, 466, 512 n. 27; on law of treason, 201-3 and n. 29, 252, 261 on omens and divination, 99, 105, 109, 124-8, 175-9, 180-1, 223f., 428-31; on 'legitimacy' and superstition, 128f. and n. 23; on fate and 'Fortuna', 178, 427f., 469; on 'paganism', 424f.; on 'geniuses', 432-5; on Christians and Christianity, (*q.v.*), 425f., 446f., 450f., 546 n. 22, 547 n. 32; terminology of, 426, 437-9; polemical aspects, 445-51, 463
A.'s morality and moral purpose, 431, 461; praise for moderation and commonsense, 454 and n. 3; 'sobrietas', 471 and n. 41, 243; 'efficacia', 471f.; pragmatism, 495 n. 49; inconsistency and prejudice, 215 and nn. 20, 22; omissions, 211 and n. 14, 382
Ampelius, P., *praefectus urbi* 371-2: character of his administration, 212; conducts trials under Valentinian, 212, 414; receives legislation, 212; his Greek origin, 467
'Amr ibn 'Adî, nephew of Jadhima, in Arab legend, kills Zenobia, 350
Amudis, fortification in Mesopotamia, 41 and n. 16
Amyntas of Galatia, client of Augustus, 357; founds Isaura Nova, 358
Anastasian baths, at Constantinople, 193
Anatha (Anah), Euphrates settlement, in Persian campaign of Julian, 146; aged soldier of Galerius found there, 133; its surrender, in A. and Zosimus, 171f., 290; as Phathousa, in Zosimus, 165
Anatolius, *magister officiorum*, killed in Persia, 182, 185
Ancyra (Ankara), Julian at, hears litigants, 107; Valentinian at, 189; Valens at, 197
Andronicus, poet, acquitted at trials of Scythopolis, 217 and n. 28
Anepsia, senatorial matron, her

adultery with Avienus, 214
Anicii, senatorial family, cupidity of, 278, 448; its Christianity, 448; *see also* Sex. Petronius Probus
animal metaphors, in A., 258-60; images, in *Notitia Dignitatum*, 260; and amphitheatre, 260
Anonymous, *De Rebus Bellicis*, text and character of, 304 and nn. 1-2; recommendations for reform, 304f.
Antinoopolis, in Egypt, civil servants at, 254
Antioch, in Syria (Map 2)
  origin of A., 8 and n. 1, 78-80; A. at, 13, 15, 34f., 222f., 376f. and n. 128; in Libanius' *Antiochikos*, 70-2; in digression, 390; in topographical mosaic at Daphne, 538 and n. 32
  third-century sack, 170f.; and traitor Mareades, 29, 170f. and n. 84; Constantius at, 100; Gallus Caesar at, 18, 406; trials held under, 15; Julian at, 108-11, 137; in A., 108f.; trials under Valens, 219-25; imperial court at, 72-4, 409f.; as military and administrative centre, 72f.; and Latin language, 71; army at, 266, 281, 409; 'riot of the statues', 257f.; *curiales* of, 79f., 406f., 409-13; council, attends Julian, 144; Apollinares of, 399; population, 541 n. 20; social relationships at, 407f.; Syriac language, 69; character of Antiochenes, 108f., 412
  corn crises, 281, 406-13; supplies and consumption, 411 and n. 20; bakers, 412, corn-merchants, 412, shopkeepers, 412; metalworkers, 408; *fabricae*, 408; imperial palace, 72; hippodrome, 171 and n. 84, 408; theatre, 170, 409; house of Ursicinus, 40, 73; baths and house of Hellebichus, 73f.; 'greater church', 439, 440f.; festival of Adonis, 108
Antoninus, former merchant and bureaucrat, renegade to Persia, 41, 43; his defection, 68; advises king Sapor, 41, 58; encounters Ursicinus, 45, 68; his cultural background, 68; knowledge of Latin, 68, 70, 468
Antonius, Cl., *quaestor sacri palatii* of Valentinian, Spaniard, relative of Theodosius, 273
Anzaba (Greater Zab), Persian crossing in 359, 43f., 50
Apamea, in Syria, 264, *see also* Maratocupreni
Apis, discovery of sacred bull, 110, 177
Apollinares, of Antioch, executed by Gallus Caesar, 399
Apollonius of Tyana, and his 'genius', 433
Apronianus, L. Turcius Apr. Asterius, *praefectus urbi* 362-3, 215; punishes magic arts, 215, 419f.
Apuleius, of Madauros: as magician, 116, 124; his marriage, at Oea, 399; his *Apology*, 399 and n. 35; *De Deo Socratis*, 433
Aquileia: supports Constantius against Julian, 104f., 396; its impregnability, 396; defences, 396, 397; siege and surrender, 104, 107, 290; *helepolis* used at, 294; its influence in locality, 104, 396; 'suburbs' of, 396; harbour frontage, 396; Herodian on, 396
Aquitania: in A., 39; dinner-parties in, 39; noble house destroyed, 264 and n. 26, 388; supplier of corn, 282; *see also* Ausonius
Aquitanians, as snappy dressers, 39
Arabia: in digression on eastern provinces, 342f.; province of, 343; its annexation, 343f. and n. 70; character and prosperity, 343f.; Roman roads in, 343; frontier, 530 n. 65; fourth-century reorganisation, 343
Arabs, *see* Saracens
Aramaic, *see* Syriac
Arbitio, Fl., *magister equitum*: presides over trials at Chalcedon, 252; relations with usurper Procopius, 197, 199
Arethas, pro-Roman Arab, in sixth century, 345f.
Arintheus (or Arinthaeus), Fl., *magister peditum*, relations with

Procopius, 197
Aristotle: on banditry, 384; on true dreams, 428; on human character, 459
Armenia: in frontier strategy, 53; in Persian war of Constantine, 136; Arsaces of, 99, 110f., 499 n. 14; supplier of eunuchs, 275; invasion of, by Alani, in Josephus, 337
arms factories ('fabricae'), 262f.; their distribution, in *Notitia Dignitatum*, 263; at Antioch, 408; at Caesarea in Cappadocia, 263; at Cremona, 263; at Hadrianople, 263, 328
Arrian, as governor of Cappadocia, 336
Arsaces, king of Armenia: and Constantius, 99, 499n. 14; in Persian campaign of Julian, 110f., 138f., 159
Artemius, *dux Aegypti*: his arrest and execution, 109, 442f.; chronology of, 443
artillery: digression on, 291-4, 301f. and n. 28; at Amida, 45, 54, 63f.; at Singara, captured by Persians, 290; Persians' use of, 288, 290, 294; *ballistae*, 291; *onager*, 291-3; accident with, 175, 292f.; *helepolis*, 293f.; collapsible ram, 288
Ascalon, in Palestine, 343
Asclepiades, philosopher: and burning of temple of Apollo at Daphne, 439f.
Asclepigeneia, of Athens, Neoplatonist philosopher, 117
astrology, *see under* horoscopes
Athanaric, 'iudex' of Thervingian Goths, 320, 325; oath sworn by his father, 330; wars, with Valens, 320; with Huns, 320f.; loss of authority, 321, 325; death and burial, at Constantinople, 16, 325, 379
Athanasius, bishop of Alexandria, 426, 438, 441f.; exile to Trier, 426; alleged interest in divination, 226, 441; his secular ambition, 441f.
Atharidus, son of Rothesteus, Gothic magnate, in *Passion of St. Saba*, 323f.

Athens, in digression, 389f.; sojourn of Julian at, 85; Neoplatonism at, 116-18
Attacotti, 304; cannibalism of, alleged by Jerome, 523 n. 3
Attila, Hunnish leader, his 'camp', 342; visit there, by Priscus, 342
Auchenius, charioteer, senatorial client, 420
Augusta Raurica (Kaiseraugst), 306; location, 394; early prosperity and evolution of site, 394; Vadomarius arrested at, 315
Augustine, St., in his *Confessions*: African origin and friends, 273f.; appointment as *orator*, 273; at Milan, 264, 273; promotion anticipated, 274; his concubine, 453 and n. 2; on horoscopes, 226; and Neoplatonism, 429
De Pulchro et Apto, dedication to Hierius, 467; *De Civitate Dei*, cited, 513 n. 33
Augustodunum (Autun), in A., 38; in digression, 391; its defences, 38, 391; visit of Constantine, 254; of Julian, 81; its early importance, 391
Ausonius, Decimius Magnus, poet and politician: *quaestor sacri palatii* under Valentinian, 211; tutor of Gratian, 238; 'faction' of, under Gratian, 211, 273; his son proconsul, 273, 386; relations with Symmachus, 273, 285; absent from A., 211, 273
on sources of Danube, 285; his *Mosella*, 285
Austuriani, desert people, incursions into Tripolitania, 362, 383f.; their outbreak and chronology, 362, 367, 385; unable to press sieges, 384; *see also* Laguatan
Auzia (Aumale), in Mauretania, 368; in campaign of Theodosius, 370; *limes* sector, 371; inscr. to Q. Gargilius Martialis, 368
Avenches (Aventicum), in digression, 391; its ruins, 38, 391
Avienus, senator, adultery with Anepsia, 214

Index

Babylas, St., shrine at Daphne, 439f.
Babylonius, Julian's horse, 178
ballista: description of, 291; on Trajan's Column, 522 n. 17; Ammianus' confusion on, 301f.; 'b. fulminalis', 523 n. 2
bandits, and banditry: defined, 367; in Aristotle, 384; in Gaul, 265, 437 and n. 26; in Isauria, 359, 360f., 365f.; Saracens and, 346-9; Austuriani and, 384; shepherds as, 360 and n. 103; execution of bandits, 362f.; *see also* Maratocupreni
Bappo, *praefectus urbi* 372, omitted by Ammianus, 212
barbarian troops: recruitment, 97, 316 and n. 19; families of, 97; commanders, 98; loyalty of, 317; on Persian campaign, 185; the 'barritus', 199, 296
Bashkirs, nomads, in Tolstoi, 529 n. 52
Basil of Caesarea, on eunuchs, 274; on Isauria, 359; correspondent of Terentius, 447
Barbatio, *magister peditum* of Constantius: relations with Julian, 91; failed co-operation with, 299f.; executed for treason, 40
Batavi, *see under* Heruli
Batnae, in Osrhoene: fair at, 70, 388; in Persian campaign of Julian, 144, 166, 388; pagan cult at, 144; Edessene embassy at, 166
bears, of Valentinian, 216, 238, 260 and n. 20, 460; bear names, 260
Bebase, in Mesopotamia: desert settlement, 400; its location, 539 n. 38
Belgica Secunda, administration of, 89f. and n. 15
Bellen, Moorish prince, chief of Mazices, 371, 374; his name, 372
Besa, oracular god in Thebaid, 217 and n. 27
Besouchis, Persian fortress, taken by Julian, 156; identification of, 156; in Eunapius, 165; *see also* Meinas Sabatha, Vologesias

Bezabde, on Tigris, 49; its site and name, 53f.; as 'Phaenica', 487 n. 7; garrison of, 53, 55; sieges of, 47, 288, 290; bishop of, 436; deportation of population, 68, 436 and n. 25, 489 n. 2
Bishapur, Persian city, rock sculptures near, 132, 134
bitumen: at Hit, 147f.; used in building, 148; at Pirisabora, 174; in siege warfare, 290
Bonitus, Frankish general, father of Silvanus, 38; supporter of Constantine, 38, 317; his Roman wife, 317
Bostra, Nabataean city, 343; in province of Arabia, 343; in digression, 389
'Boudinoi', in Herodotus, nomadic people, 341; as 'Vidini' in Ammianus, 334; 'wooden city' of, 341; *see also* 'Gelonoi'
Bracchiati, *see under* Cornuti
Brahmins, Indian wise men, 135
Brigantia (or Brigantium) (Bregenz), corn supplies at, 104
Brigetio (Szöny), in Pannonia, winter quarters of Valentinian, 395
Brisigavi, Alamannic people, 306; in Breisgau, 306; in Roman service, in *Notitia Dignitatum*, 316
Britain: Lupicinus in, 95f.; Theodosius in, 96, 207; supplies corn, 90, 282
Bruchion, quarter of Alexandria, destroyed under Aurelian, 29, 442
Bucinobantes, Alamannic people, 307; their location, 307; and Glauberg, hill-fort, 311; their 'pagus' reduced to impoverishment, 310, 316; in Roman service, in *Notitia Dignitatum*, 316
bureaucracy, imperial: expansion of, under Tetrarchy, 253-5; grades of promotion, 254f.; in *Notitia Dignitatum*, 254f.; separation of powers, 253, 284; the praetorian prefecture (*see under* taxation), 253
Burgundians, Germanic people, 307, 314; boundary with Alamanni, 307f., 309f. and nn. 8-9; religious

customs and terminology, 313, 330; alleged descent from Romans, 310

Caesarea, in Cappadocia, 99, 101; 'fabricenses' at, 263
Caesarea, in Mauretania, 369, 375; sacked by Firmus, 369, 391
Caesarea, in Palestine, in digression, 389
Calcidius, commentary on Plato's *Timaeus*, 431 and n. 15
Calycadnus river (Göksu Nehir), in Isauria, 357, 364; forts by, 364, 534 n. 111
camels, required by Romanus, in Tripolitania, 281, 384; at Alexandria, 443
canals, in Mesopotamia (Map 5), 149 and n. 46; maintenance of, 151f. and n. 51; embankments, 153f.; in Diyala region, 159; *see also* Nahrmalcha, Saqlawiyah
'Capellatii vel Palas', Alamannic boundaries at, meaning of term, 309f.
'capillati', Gothic laymen, in Jordanes, 330f.
Cappadocia, 99, 101; imperial estate at Macellum, 84f.; Procopius' estates in, 191; Cappadocians, in regime of Valens, 272 and n. 39
Carnuntum, on Danube, 395 and n. 28; early legionary fortress, 395; in fourth century, 395
'carrago', Gothic wagon circle, 327
Carrhae (Harran): Macedonian foundation, 67; Severan colony, 67; evacuated, 44, 394; in Persian campaign of Julian, 138, 169; worship of Moon at, 177; *see also* Magnus of Carrhae
Carthage: in digression, 389f.; statue of proconsul at, 210; corn shortage at, 210, 405f.
Carus, emperor: Persian campaign, 133; his death, 133; oracles relating to, 133
Cassiodorus, *Variae*, on classes of Gothic society, 331
'castella', in Mauretania and Isauria, 372
Castor, accomplice of Romanus, tortured and executed, 374
Castricius, *comes Isauriae*, 380; defends Seleucia, 364
cataphracti (mailed horsemen), in *adventus* of Constantius, 231; in army of Julian, 91; of Sapor, 61, 181
Celtae and Petulantes, *auxilia palatina*: transfer ordered by Constantius, 94; at Antioch, 72, 281
ceremonial, imperial, 231 and n. 1
at accessions, 87, 198f., 207, 374, 385; at anniversaries, quinquennial, 284, 435; vicennial, 233; burials, 184, 188, 549 n. 48; *adventus* (q.v.), 11, 231-5; in *Notitia Dignitatum*, 247, 255; shield devices and banners, 11, 231, 260 and n. 18, 299, 300, 316; in warfare, 63, 289; Persian, 62 and n. 25, 68, 233, 244f. and n. 25; Constantius and, 235; Julian and, 106, 236
its function, 248f.; as communication, 248f., 460f.; its origins and continuity, 245 and n. 25
see also acclamations, *adoratio*, *adventus*
Chalcedon: trials at, 66, 88, 92f., 106 and n. 35, 251f., 275, 280 and n. 5; secured by Procopius, 193; walls dismantled, 227 and n. 44, 332, 395; inscription found at, 395
'Chaldaean Oracles', their character and doctrines, 119-22 and 495 n. 1; sources, 119; commentary on, by Iamblichus, requested by Julian, 115, 119; on *haruspicina*, 127; *see also* 'Julianus the theurgist', Neoplatonism, theurgy
Chamavi, campaign of Julian against, 90
charioteers, and chariot-racing: at Rome, 213, 214f.; Constantius II and, 234; at Antioch, 8, 171; connection with magic, 215, 415, 420, 435; and rioting, 417; circus

factions, 422f.; charioteers as senatorial clients, 420
'Chernyakov culture', and Goths, 321f., 525 n. 22
Chilo, senator, allegations by, 210, 420
Chionitae, Persian allies, at Amida, 62f.; funeral rites of, 61f.; and Hephthalites of Procopius, 62 and n. 26
Chnodomarius, Alamann king: at Strasbourg, 314; his defeat, 297, 299; A.'s portrait of, 317
Christians, and Christianity, in A., 435-51; his attitude, 445-51; terminology of, 426, 437-9; 'Christianitas' in Theodosian Code, rarity of the term, 426 and n. 6; and 'paganism', 424-6; Constantine and, 447-50; Constantius and, 128, 449; his 'superstitio', 128; Gallus Caesar and, 439, 491 n. 9; Julian and, 86f., 106, 109, 112, 491 n. 9; Valentinian and, 256, 257, 267, 437
  at Alexandria, 26, 438, 442-4; at Antioch, 74, 439-41; at Cologne, 38, 435, 438; at Edessa, 166; at Moguntiacum, 435; at Rome, 421-3, 441f., 444f.; at Vienne, 86f., 435f., 437, 438, 445; among Goths, 331f. (see also Ulfila); among barbarian peoples, 527 n. 43
  bishops: of Alexandria, 438, 441-5; Antioch, 74; Bezabde, 436, 438; Rome, 421, 438, 441, 444f.; provincial clergy, in A., 445; priests, as envoys, of Goths, 332, 436; of rebel Firmus, 369, 436
  churches, and church services, 435-9; at Alexandria, 443; at Antioch, 439, 440f.; shrine of St. Babylas at, 439; at Cologne, 38, 435, 438; at Rome, 421f., 439, 444; at Rusguniae, 373; asylum in, 38, 435, 438, 543 n. 45; Epiphany, at Vienne, 86f., 435, 437, 438, 445; morning worship, at Cologne, 38, 435; Easter (?) vigil, in Africa, 435; at Moguntiacum, 435
  synods, 437f., 441, 449; martyrs and martyrdom, 216, 257, 267, 436f., 443; A.'s attitude to, 436, 443; tonsure (?), 443 and n. 36; monks, at Alexandria, 26; ascetic communities, in Mesopotamia, 436 and n. 25; at Samosata, 447
  dedication of True Cross, at Rusguniae, 373; crucifixion abolished by Constantine, 261, 518 n. 22, 548 n. 45
Chrysanthius, philosopher, and Julian, 123; declines invitation to Constantinople, 125; high priest in Lydia, his religious policy, 125f.; death of his son, 118
Chrysostom, John: on trials under Valens, 223; on conduct in imperial palace, 262; on Syriac language at Antioch, 69; homily against pagans, 547 n. 31
Cicero, in A., 37, 87, 239, 466, 483 n. 45; on divination, 128, 223f., 429, 430f. and n. 13; on fame and ambition, 236; on clemency, 252; letter to Nepos on contemporary history, 457; *Tusculan Disputations*, 430
Cilicia, 356; Cilician pirates, 356
Circesium, on Euphrates: fortified by Diocletian, 170; in Persian campaign of Julian, 131, 134, 140; in A. and Magnus of Carrhae, 169f.
Claudian of Alexandria: on imperial *adventus*, 234f. and nn. 5, 7; on Palladius, 467; Greek terms in, 551 n. 25; Gibbon's judgment of, 467
Claudiopolis (Mut), in Isauria, 357; description of site, 358
Coche (Veh Ardeshir) (Maps 4, 5), Sasanian city, 141; its urban history, 141-3 and nn. 26-8, 157; and Seleucia, 143; and the Nahrmalcha, 157; as Mahoza, 155f.; as Zochasa, in Zosimus, 165; as Kaukabā, in Syriac chronicle, 505 n. 78; in the Talmud, 141f.
coin, and coinage: exported to Goths, 329; in Julian's *Misopogon*, 410f. and n. 18; of Procopius, 196, 200; as propaganda, 196, 200;

Index

Procopius' image on, 200; mints, of Procopius, 200; at Antioch, 541 n. 18; at Alexandria, 443; at Cyzicus, 196, 200; at Rome, 262, 420; 'contorniates', 419, 420
Colias, Gothic leader, settled near Hadrianople, 326, 328
Collatio, Mosaicarum et Romanarum Legum, 517 n. 8
Cologne: and Silvanus, 37f.; taken by Alamanni, 88; recovered by Julian, 81; Christian chapel at, 38, 435, 438
consistory, 37, 267-9; protocol, 268f.; conduct of general Marcellus before, 460
Constans, emperor, in lost books of A., 18; and eunuch Eutherius, 25
Constantianus, tribune, commander of fleet in Persian campaign, 167
Constantine I (the Great), emperor birthplace, 200; as emperor, visits Arles, 248; at Trier, Autun, 254; Gothic policy of, 318; Persian war of, 135f. and nn. 12-14; motive, 499 n. 14; and 'lies of Metrodorus', 135, 448
his avarice and prodigality, 135, 278, 448; confiscation of temple treasures, 448; law on 'white magic', 218, 222; and Manichees, 449; removes obelisk, 449f. and n. 47; abolishes crucifixion, 518 n. 22, 548 n. 45
in A., 29, 447-50; in *Caesars* of Julian, 137, 448 and n. 44; in Eutropius and Aur. Victor, 448 and n. 45
eunuch Eutherius, as possible source on, 25
Constantinople, as 'second Rome': its ideology, 450 and n. 48; baths constructed at, 513 n. 44; Anastasian baths at, 193; mint, 200; Sopatros at, 126; Julian at, 23, 106f.; his birthplace, 107; benefactions, 107; elevation of Procopius at, 193-5; burial of Athanaric at, 16; witnessed by A. (?), 16, 379; Latin culture, in early sixth century, 6

Constantius I, emperor, father of Constantine: his early career, 75
Constantius II, emperor (Fig. 1) as Caesar, 54; after death of Constantine, 84 and n. 7, 86, 241; Persian wars of, 499 n. 15 and Chs. III-IV *passim*; in civil war, 100; relations with Gallus Caesar, 33-5, 243; with Julian Caesar, 84, 87ff.; and battle of Strasbourg, 378f.; *vicennalia* of, 233; visit to Rome, 11f., 104, 231-5, 266, 478 n. 8, 514 n. 4; his comportment there, 231f.; relations with senate, 104, 234f; as *pontifex maximus*, appoints to priestly colleges, 235; instals obelisk, 12, 462, 548 n. 47
regime and character, in A., 33f., 35f. and n. 6, 84, 218, 241; treatment of the imperial office, 235f.; and protocol, 235; pretensions of, 431; on Tetrarchy, 254; and division of powers, 253f., 270, 284; and law, 251; *maiestas*, 241, 448; selection of officials, 269; influence of eunuchs, 274; prodigality to supporters, 448; and rapacity, 240
physical appearance, 238; intellectual pretensions, 238; 'superstition' of, 128, 449; favours bishops, 438, 449; relations with Liberius, 441; attitude to divination, 218
Contionacum (Konz?), imperial residence, near Trier, 401
Corbulo, Domitius, general of Nero: Ursicinus compared with, 36, 242; and Theodosius, 242; suicide of, 36, 242
Corduene, 'satrapy' of, 44, 48ff., 53; relations with Rome and Persia, 55f.; its role, in Persian campaign of Julian, 56, 138, 159, 186
corn, and corn supplies, in military campaigns, 282f., 302, 406, 409f.; in Gaul, 90, 96, 282; granaries built by Julian, 90; in Isauria, 364; in Gothic wars of Valens, 327f., 329; at Brigantia, 104; in Persian campaign, 138, 177, 186, 406
shortages, at Antioch, 110; under

582 Index

Gallus Caesar, 406-8; causes, 406f.; and social relationships, 407f.; under Julian, 408-13; their causes, 409f.; and remedies, 410f.; distribution, 411-13; A.'s opinion, 412f:
consumption, at Rome and Antioch, 411 and n. 20; prices, 186; at Carthage, 210, 405f. and 541 n. 18; at Antioch, 406f., 409 and n. 13, 410f. and n. 18
Cornuti and Bracchiati, 38; at battle of Strasbourg, 298 and n. 24
Craterae, near Antioch, country estate of Apollinares, 399
Craugasius, *curialis* of Nisibis, 52, 387, 405; defection to Persia, 387f.; country estate, near Nisibis, 387, 399
Cremna, in Pisidia, in rebellion of Lydius, 361
Crispus Caesar, execution at Pola, 29, 447, 448
Ctesiphon, Persian capital (Maps 4, 5); its topography, 141f. and nn. 26-8; in Strabo, 141; its Iranian identity, 141; fortifications, 141, 158; abortive assault on, 158; games held at, 503 n. 65; council of war at, 158 and n. 64; further development in 5th-6th centuries, 159
curiales (city councillors), 79f., 107, 267; civic officials, of Oea, 384; Icosium, 369; provincial *concilia*, 385; statues and inscriptions, 210 and n. 11, 386f.; civic obligations, 404; exemptions, 79f.; benefactions, 273, 407; Julian's policy, in A., 105f., 107; A's. attitude, 79f.
in Asia, 405; of Antioch, 144, 257, 258, 399, 406-8, 409-13; of Aquileia, 257; of Auzia, 368; at Beroea, 144; of Mauretanian Caesarea, 374; of Hadrianople, 398; of Lepcis Magna, 383-7, 398f.; of Nisibis, 52, 387, 399, 404, 405; of Thagaste, 273; of Timgad, 254
see also Antioch, Craugasius, embassies, Tripolitania

cursus publicus, 263f.; use by A., 264; by bishops, 263, 438, 449; *agentes in rebus* and, 518 n. 26
'Cuseni', Kushans, in army of Sapor, 62, 63
Cyria, Moorish dynast; 'sister' of Firmus, 371
Cyzicus, taken by Procopius, 196; its fortifications, 196, 393; of harbour, 290, 393; treasuries and mint, 196, 200

Dacia, Roman province, occupied by Goths, 318, 322
Dadastana, on Bithynian-Galatian border, death of Jovian at, 188
Dagalaifus, *magister peditum*, on Persian campaign, 168; his role in elevation of Valens, 189
'daimones', *see under* 'genii'
Dalisandos, in Isauria, site of, 359
Damasus, bishop of Rome: accession of, 421, 422; rioting over, 444; church building of, 422; and 'Green faction', 422f.; secular ambitions of, 444f.; as deacon, 422; poem of, in St. Laurentius 'in Damaso', 543 n. 52
Daphne, suburb of Antioch: in Libanius' *Antiochikos*, 70; in A., 397, 440f.; topographical mosaic at, 397; shrine of Apollo at, neglected, 439; purified by Julian, 440; destroyed by fire, 109, 111f., 177, 397, 439-41; its priest, 441; shrine of St. Babylas at, 439f.
Daphne, Danube crossing, in campaign of Valens, 319f. and n. 24
'Decem pagi' (Dieuse?), 308
Decentius, Caesar of Magnentius, in lost books of A., 18
Decentius, *tribunus et notarius*, agent of Constantius, 94ff.
Demetrius 'Poliorcetes', *helepolis* of, 293
Demetrius, of Alexandria, philosopher, acquitted of divination, 217
Devil, athlete and builder, 143, 309
Diacira (Hit), 145; in Persian campaign of Trajan, 138; its capture by Julian, in A., and Eunapius, 172f.;

sacked, 148; temple at, 147, 173; bitumen springs, 147f.; salt, 148; its name, 147; in Eunapius, 165
'Dicineus', legendary Gothic lawgiver, 331
digressions, *see under* Ammianus Marcellinus
'dikastês', among Goths, *see* 'iudex'
Dio, Cassius, historian: on Pannonians, 199f., 249; on Dacians, 330f.; his manner of composition, 31
Dio Chrysostom, sophist, on Getae, 330
Diocletian, emperor: reforms of, 254; expansion of government under, 253; introduces *adoratio*, 29, 244; rebuilds Nicomedia, 390; his 'avarice', in Lactantius, 240; relations with Galerius, 243; mausoleum, at Split, 401
Diodorus, official (*comes et architectus?*) at Alexandria, builds church there, 443 and n. 36
'Diogmitae' ('Pursuers'), local militia, in Isauria, 364, 366
diptychs, letters of appointment, 255
divination, and diviners: A. on, 124f. and n. 19, 223f.; digression on, 428-31; techniques of, 217, 221, 222; its intellectual context, 225f.; and theurgy, 118; and Neoplatonism, 428-31 and n. 10; Cicero on, 430f.; law on, 218; relations with conspiracy, 219; trials for, at Antioch, 219-25; at Scythopolis, 217f. and n. 27
    Julian and, 86f., 99, 105, 109; Nestorius and, 116f.; philosophers and, 125; in Persian campaign, 126-8; at Rome, 210; and proconsul Hymetius, 210, 213; and father of Maximinus, 211; at Abydus, 217f.; among Alamanni, 312; among Huns, 340; among Alani, 334 and n. 51
    see also fate, 'Fortuna', *haruspicina*, horoscopes, theurgy
division of empire, by Valentinian, 190f.; in A., 206
Divitenses (and Tungrecani): Iuniores, in division of empire, 190; support

Procopius, 190, 193, 195f.; disappear from records, 190; Seniores, in Alamannic campaign, 190; in fifth-century west, 190
Dniester, river, as boundary between Thervingi and Greuthungi, 320, 325; line of defence against Huns, 320
domestici, see under protectores
Domitianus, *Ppo Orientis*, agent of Constantius, lynched at Antioch, 34
Doryphorianus, Gaul, associate of Maximinus, 211; as *vicarius* of Rome, 211; tortured and executed, 211; his character, 258
Dracontius, *praepositus monetae* at Alexandria, 443
Dura-Europus, on Euphrates: capture by Sasanians, 391; deserted site in fourth century, 130f., 178, 391; its rediscovery, 391f.
Dynamius, *actuarius*, in plot against Silvanus, 271

earthquake of 365; 192 and n. 16
Ebel bei Praunheim, near Frankfurt, Roman villa with Alamannic occupation, 310
eclipses, in A., 431f.
Edessa (Urfa), in Osrhoene, Macedonians at, 67; Severan colony, 67; defeat of Valerian near, 133f.; Sabinianus at, 41, 44f., 134, 398; embassy from, rejected by Julian, 166 and n. 81; its sacred pools, 51; graveyards, 485 n. 20; Christianity at, 166
Egypt, and Egyptians, in digressions, 14, 27f., 111, 462; and litigation, 106; canal systems, 152; obelisks, 14, 449f.
Elagabalus, emperor, in Herodian, 245
elephants, A. on, 63f.; at Amida, 63f.; in Persian campaign, 181
Elusa, Nabataean city, not in A., 343; its character, in Jerome, 348; cult of Venus at, 348
embassies, and envoys, their conduct, 385f., 539 nn. 1-2; decrees and mandates, 385f., 404f.; Menander

Rhetor on, 385; on Thorigny Marble, 537 n. 6; civic, 4, 8, 166 and n. 81, 256, 261, 383-7, 404, 443; senatorial, 10, 104, 105, 212 and n. 17, 267, 270, 284-6; with foreign peoples, 40, 42, 106, 159 and n. 65, 267f.; in civil war, 100f., 105; Christian priests as envoys, 268, 332, 369

Ephraim of Nisibis, *Hymns against Julian*, 3f.

Epitome de Caesaribus, 476 n. 6

Epiphany, Christian festival, at Vienne, 86f., 437, 438

Equites Armigeri Iuniores, in *Notitia Dignitatum*, 371; commanded by Fl. Nuvel (*q.v.*), 371

Ermenrich (or Hermanaric), king of Greuthungi, 320, 325; extent of his power, 325; defeat by Huns, and death, 324

Eubulus, *curialis* of Antioch, house burned down, 407

Eunapius, of Sardis, sophist and historian, as student at Athens, 164; his initiation by Nestorius, 124

History of, 115; summarised by Zosimus, 130, 161, 504 n. 68; Photius on, 458; editions of, 446, 529 n. 54, 548 n. 40; its audience, 446; style, 164; E. as polemical writer, 445f., 458; his relations with Oribasius, 143, 164 and n. 75, 182; and Magnus of Carrhae, 164, 504 n. 73; his knowledge of Ammianus, doubted, 172 and n. 86; use of by Ammianus, defined, 164-75, 458, 503 n. 67

on insurgent Lydius, 361; on battle of Strasbourg, 378; on Julian's war against Constantius, 104f. and n. 32; on Persian campaign of J., 152f., 155f., 164-75, 179, 499 n. 19; speech of J. in, 130, 168; J.'s army, 167; fleet, 167; geographical locations in, 164-7; omissions, 168; religious elements in, 179 and nn. 93f.; on death of J., 182; on rebellion of Procopius, 191; on death of Musonius in Isauria, 365; on trials under Valens, 223, 226; on Goths, 330; on Huns, 333, 335f.; misreading of Herodotus, 335 and n. 54:

Vitae Sophistarum, 115; on Julian in Asia Minor, 86, 122-4; on usurpation of J., 115, 124; on Iamblichus, 122; Sopatros, 126; Aedesius, 118, 122; Eusebius, 123; Chrysanthius, 123, 125f.; Maximus, 123, 125, 236, 497 n. 22; Nestorius, 115, 124; Prohaeresius, 218 and n. 30

eunuchs: A. on, 274-7; Basil of Caesarea on, 274; their origin and character, 274, 275; at imperial court, 274-7; nature of their power, 276f.; property of, 276; group solidarity of, 275; cadet eunuchs, 276; in senatorial households, 276, 415 and n. 31, *see also* Eusebius, Eutherius, Mardonius

Euphrasius, from Gaul, supporter of Procopius, 225

Euphrates, river, its regime and character, 146, 148f., 151, 153f.; sluices in, 146

Eupraxius, *quaestor sacri palatii*, 212f., 216, 267; praised by A., 212, 267; his character, as shown in legislation, 212; expounds theory of martyrdom, 216, 267, 437; as *praefectus urbi*, omitted by A., 212

Eusebia, wife of Constantius II: protects Julian, 36, 86, 87; J.'s oration in her honour, 86; allegations against her, 86

Eusebius of Caesarea, *Life of Constantine*, 136, 449, 499 n. 14

Eusebius, court eunuch: under Constantine, 275; under Constantius II, 274f.; hostility to Ursicinus, 40, 47, 275; compared to viper, 259; execution, 275

Eusebius, bishop of Nicomedia, tutor of Julian, 84f.

Eusebius of Mende, philosopher, pupil of Aedesius, 123; and Julian, 123; on Maximus, 123

Eusebius, Fl., *cos.* 359, exiled in trials of Antioch, 222 and n. 35

Eutherius, eunuch, supporter of Julian, 83, 93f., 100f.; in retirement at Rome, 25, 466; possible source for Ammianus, 25 and n. 33, 100f., 268, 378; on Hormisdas (?), 499 n. 21; his excellent character, 460

Eutropius, historian, 29, 455; his *Breviarium*, dedicated to Valens, 162, 238; his epilogue, and A., 455 and n. 4; and 'Kaisergeschichte', 29 and n. 41, 244; his origin, 225; as supporter of Julian, 225; attends Persian campaign, 162; in treason trials under Valens, 162; acquitted, 221, 455, 458; on Constantine, 448; on *adoratio*, 244

Eutropius, eunuch of Arcadius, consulship of, 274

Eutychianus, historian, on death of Julian, 501 n. 1

'famosi', lampoons, 97 and n. 26, 163 and n. 72

Faraxen, third-century rebel, in Mauretania, 368, 372

Farnobius, leader of Greuthungi, 326

fate, in A., as Themis, 428; as Nemesis, 427; and 'genii', 434; and 'Fortuna', 544 n. 9; and theurgists, 126f.; and Julian, 126f., 134f., 178, 427, 434, 472; see also divination, *haruspices*, horoscopes, theurgy, 'Fortuna'

Faustina, second wife of Constantius II, 196, 199.

Faustus of Byzantium, on Persian wars of Constantine, 498 n. 13

'Fertile Crescent', 69, 140

Felix, *comes sacrarum largitionum*, death of, 177

Fericius, *praefectus gentis* in Mauretania, executed for complicity in rebellion, 371

Festus, of Tridentum, historian, 224, 458; dedication to Valens, 238, 272; possible use by A., 458 and n. 15; protégé of Maximinus, 206, 272; proconsul of Asia, 206, 224; his execution of philosopher Maximus, 224; religious posture, in *Breviarium*, 224 and n. 40; in Eunapius, 224

Firmus, Moorish prince, rebellion of, 369-76; son of Nubel, 369; 'extended family' of, 371, 372; relations with Roman authorities, 369; 'crowned', 374; suicide, 370, 374; body displayed, 375; uses Christian priests as envoys, 369, 436

Flavianus, Virius Nicomachus, Roman senator; *vicarius Africae* under Gratian, 386f.; *quaestor* and praetorian prefect of Theodosius, 10, 479 n. 7; *Annales* of, 10 and n. 7, 476 n. 6; relations with Theodosius and Symmachus, 10

Florentius, *PPo Galliarum* and *Illyrici*: relations with Julian, 89f.; at battle of Strasbourg, 91; role in proclamation of Julian, 94-7; his motives, 96f.; joins Constantius, 99; made prefect of Illyricum, 99; flight to Constantius, 105

fortifications and defences, of cities, 393-7; in Gaul, 394 and n. 24

'Fortuna', in A., her function and character, 427f., 472; philosophical aspects, 427 and n. 9; Julian and, 137, 427; see also fate

Fortunatianus, *comes rei privatae* of Valens, 219

'fossatum Africae', see under 'limes'

Franks (cf. Map 3), their location, 307; 'Francia', 315; campaigns of Julian against, 95, 99; their occupation of Roman fort, 296; in Roman service, 37, 317; Silvanus and, 317

Frigeridus, general of Gratian, 328

Fritigern, Gothic leader, 325, 326; at Hadrianople, 332; and Christianity, 332, 436

'fundus Gaionatis', fortified place in Mauretania, reduced by Theodosius, 372; description in A., 381, cf. 400f.

'fundus Mazucanus', in Mauretania, 372, cf. 400f.

'fundus Petrensis' (Petra), near Tubusuctu, property of Zammac, taken by Firmus, 369, 372f.; inscr.

from, 373

Gaiolus, Fl., *protector*, 77, 246
Galerius, emperor: public humiliation by Diocletian, 243; defeat of Narses, 53, 133; route of his campaign, 133, 172; old soldier of, seen by A., 133, 172, 244; in *Historia Augusta*, 133; his character and origin, in Lactantius, 519 n. 38; pet bears, 517 n. 20
Gallienus, emperor, Persian invasion under, 170f.
Gallus Caesar, at Antioch, 18, 406; treason trials under, 34f., 251; and Jewish rebellion, 484 n. 2; Isaurian rebellion, 364, 366, 380; projected Persian campaign, 406; corn crisis under, 406-8; relations with *curiales*, 406f.; and *consularis* Theophilus, 406f.; his arrest and execution, 35, 263f.; his character, 259, 406; comparison with Julian, 408; and relics of St. Babylas, 439
Gaudentius, *notarius*, agent of Constantius: destroys Africanus, 92; with Julian in Gaul, 92; secures Africa for Constantius, 101; executed, 93
Gaul, and Gauls, A. and, 38f.; in digression, 38, 87, 389, 391, 463f.; domestic and social habits, 38f., 454; Gallic soldiers, at Amida, 59, 60, 65, 260; on Persian campaign, 185; Gauls, at court of Valentinian, 272f.
Gaza, in Palestine, 343
'Gefolgschaft': among Alamanni, 314, 315; among Goths, 324, 326
'Gelonoi', in Herodotus, 334; their settled lifestyle, 341; *see also* 'Boudinoi'
'geniuses', or 'daimones', their character and role: in digression, 432-5; in Plotinus, 434; their aid, given to philosophers and politicians, 433f.
Genius, temples of, at Antioch, 177; at Alexandria, 442
'Genius Publicus', deserts Julian, 180

Gentiles (palace guard), *see under* Scutarii
George, bishop of Alexandria, relations with Julian, 85; informer under Constantius, 442; his murder, 109, 442-4
Germanicopolis, in Isauria, 357; description of, 358; connections with Isaurian rebels, 359, 365, 381
Ghassanids, pro-Persian Arabs, in sixth century, 352; *see also* Saracens
Gibbon, Edward: on Ammianus, ix, 549 n. 4; on accession of Jovian, 183 and n. 6; on Claudian of Alexandria, 467; on reign of Antoninus Pius, 280 and n. 4; on ceremonial, 247; on 'paganism', 426
Gildo, Moorish prince, fights against Firmus, 371; rebellion of, 371
Glauberg, hill-fort, occupied by Alamanni, 311f.; in territory of Bucinobantes, 311
Gomoarius, *magister equitum*, betrays Procopius, 197
Gordian III, emperor, in lost books of A., 29; Persian campaign of, 143; killed in Persia, 130, 132, 178f.; his tomb, 130f. and nn. 2-4, 178; versions of his death, 132; as prefiguring that of Julian, 132
Gordyaioi, in Strabo, *see under* Kardouchoi
Gorgonius, eunuch, supporter of Gallus Caesar, 275
Gorgoromeis, village communities in Isauria, 359
Goths (Map 7), third-century invasions of, 318; occupation of Dacia, 272, 318, 322; area of settlement, 320-2; its character and chronology, 321f.; the archaeological evidence, 322, 525 n. 22

their treaty with Constantine, 318, 329 and n. 39; Julian and, 106, 108, 137; threaten Danube in 365, 193; support Procopius, 196, 208f., 318; campaigns of Valens against, 208, 318-20; their outcome, 320 and n. 24; wars against Huns,

320f.; enter Roman empire, 15-17, 281, 327; at Hadrianople, 15, 263, 296f., 300f., 379; in Roman service, massacred, 16, 227, 327, 471; occupation of Thrace, 17 and n. 23, 327-9; treaty with Theodosius, 17 their agricultural economy, 320, 321f., 327, 339; not nomadic, 327, 339; technological level, 321f.; incapacity at siege warfare, 294, 393; stock-raising, 322; villages, 321, 323f.; wagon circle, 327; comb workshops, 322; and Sîntana de Mureş culture, 321f.; divisions of wealth among, 526 n. 28; economic dependance on Rome, 329; enslavement by Romans, 326f.; kings and nobles, 324-6; dynastic succession, 324f.; other classes, 326f.; in Cassiodorus, 331 language of, 313 and n. 15, 330; 'laws' of, 330; religion of, 329f.; priesthood among, 330; Christianity among, 322-4, 331; its modest social level, 331f.; persecution of, by Gothic authorities, 322-4, 331; martyrologies, 331
see also Athanaric, Ermenrich, Greuthungi, Huns, *Passion of St. Saba*, Thervingi

Gratianus, of Cibalae in Pannonia, father of Valentinian, 75

Gratian, emperor: character of, 243, 471; education, 238; elevation as Augustus, 207; his regime, and influence of Ausonius, 211, 273; relations with Valens, 328; narrow escape of destined bride, 401

Greek: in A., 107, 457, 462 and n. 25; in Claudian and *Historia Augusta*, 551 n. 25; 'bilingualism', with Latin, 71f., 467f.; historiography, 455-61 and n. 23, 464 and n. 30; digressions in, 462; biography, 84, 459; Timagenes as Greek, 464 and nn. 28-9; *see also* 'Hellene', Latin

Greuthungi, Gothic people, 320, 324f., 326; neighbours of Alani, 320; political history of, 324; campaign of Valens against, 320; war against Huns, 320; *see also* Goths, Thervingi

Gregory of Nazianzus, on Hellenes and 'paganism', 425; on death of Julian, 507 n. 3

Grumbates, king of the Chionitae, 49; in Persian forces at Amida, 58, 62f.; his son killed, 58, 61-3, 291; burial rites, 61f.

Gundeshapur, Persian city, its construction by Roman prisoners, 133f. and n. 11

Hadrianople: 'fabricae' at, 263, 328; imperial court at, in 378, 266; Goths settled near, 263, 326, 328, 398; 'suburban' district of, 398 battle of, 15, 296-301, 332; tactics and character of, 296f., 300f.; Saracen federates at, 348; A.'s sources, 379

Hannibalianus, nephew of Constantine, in his Persian strategy, 136

Hariobaudes, German soldier in Roman service, 316

haruspicina, and *haruspices*, in A., 126-9; on Persian campaign, 126-8, 178f., 497 n. 22; at Rome, 189; among Huns, 340; distinguished from magic, 214, 218 and n. 29; *see also* divination

Hatra, desert city, 52, 186, 345; its decline, 349, 392; ruins, in fourth century, 52, 392

Hebdomon, suburb of Constantinople, 189; military character of, 189, 398

Hecate: magical role of, 120; statue of, at Pergamum, 123

Helena, mother of Constantine, and Helenopolis, 447

Helena, wife of Julian, 86, 87

helepolis, in digression on artillery, 293f.; description of, by Plutarch, 293; used at Pirisabora, 293f.; and Aquileia, 294; A.'s confusion on, 293, 301

Heliodorus, reader of horoscopes, 219

Hellebichus, *magister militum* of Theodosius, his munificence at Antioch, 73f.

'Hellene', as term for 'pagan', and Greek culture, 425; in Gregory of Nazianzus, 425; and Eunapius, 448
'hendinos', Burgundian word for king, 313; its etymology, 525 n. 15
Hephthalites ('White Huns'), see Chionitae
Hermes Trismegistos: 'genius' of, 118; as Thoth, divinity of wisdom, 433
Hermopolis, civil servants at, 254
Herodian, historian, on Elagabalus, 245; on Aquileia, 396; A.'s possible knowledge of, 482 n. 42
Herodotus, in Egyptian digression of A., 14, 462; his travels, 465; Scythian excursus, 334f. and nn. 51-2; on Persian ceremonial, 233; on hippopotami and winged snakes, 462
Heruli and Batavi, *auxilia palatina*, transfer ordered by Constantius, 94
Hesperius, son of Ausonius, proconsul of Africa under Gratian, 273, 386f.
Hierapolis, in Syria, 101; supplies corn for Antioch, 410; in Persian campaign, collapse of portico, 144, 177, 266; fleet assembled near, 166 and n. 80; Neoplatonic philosopher at, 126, 144
Hierius, fleet commander in Persian campaign, 166
Hierius, Syrian rhetorician, in west, 467; dedicatee of work of Augustine, 467
Hilarinus, charioteer, executed for magic, 420; seeks asylum in church, 435
Hilarius, palatine official, in trial of Theodorus, 219, 221
Hippolytus, St., festival at Rome, in Prudentius, 422
hippopotami, in A., 14, 462
Hisn Kef, see Kiphas
Historia Augusta, 6 and n. 6; on traitor Mareades (*q.v.*), 505 n. 84; on Persian campaign of Carus, 133; on Galerius, 133; its relevance to Julian, 133 and n. 9; on Isauria, 362; Sallust in, 514 n. 11; Greek terms in, 551 n. 25
Hit, on Euphrates, *see under* Diacira
Homer, quoted by Julian, 87; and Vergil, 466; mentioned by A., 488 n. 20; Neoplatonic allegorisations of, 433
Homonadenses, insurgent people under Augustus, 356; their suppression, 366; settlement patterns of, 356, 359
'honorati', 246; retired civil servants, at Antioch, 74, 406
Honoratus, *comes Orientis*, restrains anger of Gallus Caesar, 407; *PPo Galliarum* of Julian, 492 n. 18
Hormisdas (1), Persian prince, background, 499 n. 21; deserts to Constantine, 139 and n. 21, 478 n. 8; at Rome with Constantius, 12, 478 n. 8; role in Persian campaign of Julian, 139 and n. 21, 148; at Pirisabora, 173f.
Hormisdas (2), son of (1), 'proconsul' of Asia under Procopius, 197 and n. 23
horoscopes, reader of, 219; of Valens, 222; in Augustine's *Confessions*, 226; advice to astrologers, in Firmicus Maternus, 513 n. 36; astrological formula, 116; *see also* divination, theurgy
Hortarius, Alamann king, makes treaty with Julian, 312; gives party to his friends, 313, 315
Hsiung-Nu, and Huns, 355 and n. 95, 488 n. 26
Hucumbra, Persian settlement near Ctesiphon, 180; its character, 400; as 'Symbra' in Zosimus, 539 n. 39
Huns, their origin and migration, 333, 355, 379f.; physical appearance and manners, 332f.; in Eunapius, 333, 335f.; in Jerome, 335; in Jordanes, 333, 338f., 340; archaeology of, 528 n. 47; skull deformation, 528 n. 47
association with Alani, 334, 337; wars against Goths, 320f.; their impact, 335, 354; found among Goths, 325; in Roman service, 380 mode of life, 333f.; of fighting, 333,

336; horsemanship, 333, 336; leadership among, 339f.; implements and weapons, 340f.; nomadism, 333f., 336, 341; stereotype of, 336, 353; pastoral economy, 337; cuisine, 337f. and n. 57; sedentarisation, 342, 355; villages, 342; camp of Attila, 342; their lack of religion, alleged by A., 333f., 430; and *haruspicina*, 340 growth of power, 354; its collapse, 355; Cotrigurs, in sixth century, 342; and 'Hsiung-Nu', 355, 488 n. 26
see also Chionitae ('White Huns')
Hymetius, Julius Festus, proconsul of Africa, accusations against, 210; exiled, 212
Hypatius, Fl., *PPo Italiae* 382-3, of Antioch, exiled, 15, 222 and n. 35; *praefectus urbi* in 378-9, 467

Iamblichus, philosopher, Julian and, 126; and Sopatros, 126; on dualism, 121f.; alleged levitation of, 122; opposition to Theodorus of Asine, 123
Iconium, in Lycaonia, 355; Jews at, 356; execution of Isaurian leader at, 362
Igmazen, Moorish prince, chief of Isaflenses, 371; surrenders Firmus to Theodosius, 370
Illyricum: strategic importance of, 197, 198; administration of Petronius Probus in, 278; 'sabaia', cheap drink in, 199; *see also* Pannonia, Succi, pass of.
Imru'l-qais, 'king of the Arabs', in inscr. at Nemara, 350 and n. 87; his power, 350; title, 352; supposed founder of Lakhmid dynasty, 352
Innocentia, pet bear, 260, 460
Iovii (and Victores) Iuniores, won over by Procopius, 196, 199
Iphicles, philosopher from Epirus, envoy to Valentinian, 404
Isaura Nova, 357; at Zengibar Kalesi, 358f.; in Strabo, 359
Isaura Vetus, 357; in A., 358f., 537 n. 25; its site, 358; prosperity in Hellenistic age, 359; capture by Servilius Isauricus, 358; in Strabo, 359
Isauria (Map 8), territory of, 355f. and n. 97; and 'Isaurikê', in Strabo, 357; provincial government of, 357; in *Notitia Dignitatum*, 357; role in Roman empire, 361; in third century, 361f.; its garrison, 363f.; geography and settlements, 355-60; nature of terrain, 366; cities in, 359; '*mikropoliteiai*' and '*mêtrokômiai*', 359 and n. 102; transhumance, 360 and nn. 103-4; prosperity of, in A., 357; economy, 360; Isaurians, as mercenaries and builders, 361; rebellions, in A., 362-7; A's information on, 380f.
Islam, expansion of, 343, 354, 355
'iudex', title of Gothic leader, among Thervingi, 325

Jadhima (Gadhîmat), ruler of Tanukh, in Arab legend: murdered by Zenobia, 350; tomb of his 'tutor', near Bostra, 350 and n. 86
Januarius, general, relative of Jovian, rejected as imperial candidate, 188f.
Jerome: on eunuchs, 276; on Huns, 335; on desert Arabs, 347, 348, 529 n. 57; alleges cannibalism among Attacotti, 523 n. 3; unwritten history of the church, 451; on Tacitus, 456 and n. 9
Jerusalem, restoration of Temple by Julian, 110 and n. 44, 111f., 177
Jews, revolt of, under Gallus Caesar, 484 n. 2; at Seleucia on the Tigris, 141; in Mesopotamia, 145, 149; their relations with Sapor II, 145
Jordanes, historian of the Goths: on their tribal history, 525 n. 22; on king Ermenrich, 324; on Gothic religion and law, 330f.; on settlement of Ulfila in Moesia, 528 n. 45; on the Huns, 333, 338f.; on sword of Attila, 340; Ammianus and, 476 n. 6
Josephus, Jewish historian, on the Alani, 336, 337

Joshua Stylites, Syriac chronicler, on desert Arabs, 352

Jovian, emperor, son of Varronianus, 79, 184; as *primicerius domesticorum*, 79, 184; role in burial of Constantius, 184; elevation of, 183f.; treaty with Persians, 4, 185-7; his measures to secure regime, 187f.; at Antioch, 72; death, 188; his character, and conduct as emperor, 184, 237

Jovianus, soldier, killed on Persian campaign, 126, 131, 145

Jovianus, heroic exploit at 'Maiozamalcha', 157, 192; hurled down well, 192

Jovinianus, satrap of Corduene, known to A., 44; his background, 57, 68; hostage in Syria, 44; relations with Persia, 55f.; settles tribesmen in Beth Arbaye, 57; *see also* Corduene

Julianus, uncle of the emperor, recipient of letter on temple restoration, 547 n. 30; his death, 177

Julian (the Apostate), emperor
  born at Constantinople, 107; his education and upbringing, 84f. (*see also* Eusebius, George, Mardonius); loss of relatives in 337, 84; at Macellum, 84f.; maternal estates in Asia, 85; relations with Gallus Caesar, 36; at Constantinople, 23, 85; in Asia Minor, 85, 122-4; summoned to north Italy, 36, 85f.; protected by Eusebia, 86; at Athens, 85; elevation as Caesar, 87; marriage, 86; as Caesar, relations with Constantius, 84, 87ff., 299f., 493 n. 20

  regime in Gaul, 81-4, 87-93, 470, 471f. (and see below); relations with Florentius, 89f.; with Constantius' agents, 92f.; battle of Strasbourg, 91f., 297-300; acclamation by army, 92; policy in 359, 95 and n. 22; proclamation at Paris, 93-100, 115, 124

  war against Constantius, 100-5; strategy, 104f. and n. 33; and Vadomarius, 104, 315; at Sirmium, 104f., 248; at Naissus, 104-6, 270; writes to Rome and other cities, 104, 106, 448; at Constantinople, 106f.; and Goths, 106, 108, 137, 326; in Asia Minor, 107f.; at Antioch, 108-11 and n. 40, 408-13, 439-41; and corn crisis there, 408-13; temple of Apollo at Daphne, 109, 439-41

  Persian campaign (*q.v.*), 130-83; J.'s obsession with, 136-8; criticism of, 134; death of J., 127, 176, 180f. and nn. 1-3, 352; responsibility for, 182f. and n. 3; funeral cortège, at Nisibis, 3f.; burial at Tarsus, 177, 191; obituary, in A., 128, 239, 469, 495 n. 48; succession, 182, 183f.; J.'s appearance and character, 84, 88, 200, 238; his 'levitas', 522 n. 26; A.'s criticisms of, 112-14, 469; significance of J. for Ammianus, 469f.

  military policy in Gaul, 90-3; military virtues, 283, 522 n. 23; law and litigation, 109, 251f.; taxation, 89, 113, 240f.; of *curiales*, 105f., 107; treatment of imperial office, 23, 106, 236; quest for 'popularitas', 236; relations with Rome, 104, 448

  religious personality, 111f., 128, 494 n. 43; asceticism, 88, 434; apostasy from Christianity, 86f., 106; religious initiations, 424; interest in divination, 99, 105, 109, 124f., 127, 428; and theurgy, 124-8; sacrifice, 106, 107, 128, 144, 158, 177, 179, 283, 427; and fate, 134, 178, 434; 'Fortuna', 137, 427; 'genius publicus', 432, 434; his 'pagan restoration', 112, 424, 439f. and n. 30; in Lydia, 125f.; and temple at Daphne, 439-41; policy to Christians, 106, 109 and n. 41, 112, 445

  and 'Julianus the theurgist', 115f. and n. 3; and Iamblichus, 115, 122-4, 126, 144, 225; and 'philosophers', 122-9; and Neoplatonism, 122-4; on

Constantine the Great, 447f., 448f.; his historical knowledge, 499 n. 16; historical models, 242, 469f.; his writings, in A., 536 n. 132
Letter to the Athenians, 84-104 passim, 518 n. 26; *Oratio* 1 to Constantius, 133, 136; *Oratio* to Eusebia, 86; *Consolation on departure of Salutius*, 92; *Misopogon*, 108 and n. 40, 110, 188, 408-12 and 541 n. 18; *Caesares (Kronia)*, 137f., 448 and n. 44, 469f.; *Hymn to the Mother of the Gods*, 124; *Contra Galilaeos*, 112; letters, to senate of Rome, 104, 106, 235, 448; to cities of Greece, 106 and n. 34; to Constantius, 100f., 536 n. 132; *Epp.* 12 (to Priscus), 115; 14 (to Oribasius), 99; 61a (on Christian teachers), 494 n. 41; 80 (to Julianus), 547 n. 30; 84 (to Arsacius) and 89a,b (to Theodorus), 495 n. 47; 98 (to Libanius), 126, 144; 115 (to Edessenes), 505 n. 81; lost account of battle of Strasbourg, 378 and n. 132
Julian 'the theurgist', 115f., 119; his writings, 115; and 'Chaldaean Oracles', 119; historicity of, 496 n. 3
Julianus Rusticus, *praefectus urbi*, 10, 22; his origin, 273; as *magister memoriae*, possible candidate for throne, 272f.; friend of Symmachus and Ausonius, 273; his character, in A., 10, 273
Julius, *magister militum*, massacres Goths, 16, 227, 471; his 'efficacia', 471
Juvenal, satirist, 32, 415, 459

Kabylie, Grande, in Algeria, 367f., 370; as 'mons Ferratus', 369
'Kaisergeschichte', of Enmann, in A., 29 and n. 41, 244, 457; *see also* Eutropius, Aurelius Victor
Kallistos, *protector domesticus* of Julian, account in verse of Persian campaign, 504 n. 70
Kardouchoi: in Xenophon, 50; in Strabo, 50; *see also* Corduene
Khabur river, and Circesium, 169f.; in Persian campaign of Julian, 130f.
'King's River', *see under* Nahrmalcha
Kiphas (Cephas, Hisn Kef), on the Tigris, 54f.
Kushans, *see* 'Cuseni'

Lactantius, Christian writer, on reforms of Diocletian, 240; his 'avarice', 254; his building of Nicomedia, 390; on Galerius, 517 n. 20
Laguatan, Saharan tribal confederation, migration of, 536 n. 4
Lakhmids, pro-Persian Arabs, in sixth century, their ancestry and migration, 352
'Lamfoctense oppidum', in Mauretania, 369 and n. 120
Lampadius, C. Caeionius Rufius Volusianus, as praetor, largesse to people, 417; as *praefectus urbi*, suffers rioting, 417; burning of house, 417
Laranda, in Lycaonia, 355
Latin, A. and, 71f., 80, 461-6; as language of court, in fourth-century east, 71, 467f.; in army, 199; at Constantinople, 6, 71; at Nicomedia, 71; at Antioch, 71; 'bilingualism', with Greek, 71f., 467f.; historiography, 455-61 and 552 nn. 30, 32; biography, 459-61 and n. 17
Latinus, Germanic soldier, 316
Laurentius, St., 'in Damaso', Roman church, founded by Damasus, 422f.; its location, 422; as 'in Prasino', 422
Laurentius, St., 'in Lucinis', Roman church, proclamation of Damasus in, 422; its location, 422
Lauricius, Bassidius, *comes et praeses Isauriae*, checks rebellion and restores fortification, 364; possible source for A., 380
law, and legislation: language of, 255f.

and n. 8; violence of, 256-8, 261; its purpose, 262; 'didactic symbolism' of, 256, 262, 460; Julian, and clarity of law, 109; severity of enforcement, under Valentinian, 215f. and n. 23, 242, 374; good influence of Eupraxius under, 212, 267; his religious neutrality, 256

legal institutions, and administration of law, 250-2; under Gallus Caesar, 34f., 251; under Constantius, 251; under Julian, 109, 251f.; under Valens, 202f., 219-23; private litigation and litigants, under Julian, at Constantinople, 106; at Ancyra, 107, at Antioch; 108f.; Egyptians as, 106; Romanianus and, at Milan, 274

torture, judicial, 241, 256f.; under Gallus Caesar, 34, 251; under Constantius, 83, 217, 241; under Julian, 441; under Valentinian, 212f., 374; under Valens, 202, 219-23; under Gratian, 211; in the Theodosian Code, 256, 363, 460; instruments of, 83, 220, 257; exemptions claimed, 212f., 267

execution, modes of, 255-7, 260, 261, 460 and *passim*; 'didactic symbolism' of, *see above*; social distinctions in, 222, 261f. and n. 22, 362f.; Valentinian and, 215; military, 180, 374; Germanic, 323 and n. 29; crucifixion, abolished by Constantine, 261, 518 n. 22, 548 n. 45

see also adultery, divination, magic, *maiestas*

'Leges Corneliae', alleged exemptions from torture in, 213, 252

Lentienses, Alamannic people, 307, 310, 311; in Linzgau, 307; recruitment of, by Romans, 317; their knowledge of Roman movements, 317

Leo, Pannonian, *magister officiorum c.* 371-5: as *numerarius*, role in accession of Valentinian, 189; as *notarius*, assistant of Maximinus, 211; *vicarius* of Rome, 211; his character in A., 259

Leontius, Fl., *praefectus urbi* 355-6: riots during his prefecture, 417; their causes, 417, 418; and pope Liberius, 421

Lepcis Magna, in Tripolitania: territory and economy of, 384 and n. 3; walls of, 384, 393; Punic background, 385; attacked by Austuriani, 384f., 398; besieged, 384, 393; embassies to imperial court, 385-7; abandonment of site, in Procopius, 393

Libanius of Antioch, sophist, and Ammianus, 8f. and n. 1, 26, 476 n. 5, 510 n. 2; pupils of, 71 and n. 8, 467; parochialism, 467 and n. 35; and Latin language, 71; journey to Athens, 264; Jewish tenants of, 69 on Antioch, 70-4; in his *Antiochikos* (*Or.* 11), 70-2; Valens' army at, 266; on Daphne, 70, 397; on Antiochene corn crises, under Gallus, 407, 408; under Julian, 412; support for free market, 413; on Isauria and Arabia, 361; on battle of Strasbourg, 297; on Persian campaign of Julian, 139, 143, 153, 156, 157, 162 and n. 70, 176, 503 n. 65; his sources, 162; on death of Julian, 183

Funeral Oration (*Or.* 18), 143, 162, 176; on 'Jacobus', 226; letters to Parnasius, 512 n. 28; to Alexander, 412; to Aradius Rufinus, 413; *Or.* 47 'On Patronage', 539 n. 46

Liberius, bishop of Rome: popularity and exile, 421, 441; riots over succession to, 421

Libyan language, in Mauretania, 372

limes: in Germany, 309f.; in Arabia, 343; in Isauria, 362; 'interiores limites', on Euphrates frontier, 170; in Mauretania, 370f.; 'fossatum Africae', 370 and n. 121

Limigantes, former Sarmatian subjects, 304f., 311

lions: in Mesopotamia, 52; as omens, 126, 131

Litorius, fifth-century Roman general, Hunnish troops of, 340

Livy: text edited, 10; and emergence of Rome, 280; on king Numa, 433

Lopodunum (Ladenburg), in 'Agri Decumates', Roman 'ghost town', visited by Symmachus, 285, 310

Lucian, on the writing of history, 163

Lucillianus, *magister equitum et peditum* of Constantius, captured by Julian, 105; and *adoratio*, 246; father-in-law of Jovian, in retirement at Sirmium, 187; killed in Gaul, 188

Lucillianus, *comes*, commands fleet on Persian campaign, 166, 167, 171

Lupicinus, *magister equitum*, under Julian in Gaul, 94; in Britain, 95f.; arrested at Boulogne, 96

Lupicinus, general in Thrace, and Goths, 327

Lycaonia, second-century province, 357; its terrain, 363; Isaurian raids in, 363; Lycaonian language, 356

Lydius, Isaurian insurgent, 361f.

Lystra, in Lycaonia, visited by Paul and Barnabas, 356; Lycaonian language at, 356

Macedonians, city foundations in Mesopotamia, 67, 140

Macellum, imperial estate in Cappadocia, Julian at, 84f. and n. 9

Machameus, Roman officer, killed on Persian campaign, 180

Macrianus, Alamann king, 314f.; visits war headquarters of Julian, 316; negotiates with Valentinian, 314f.; killed 'in Francia', 315

Macrobius, in digression on divination, 428f.; his *Saturnalia*, date of, 544 n. 55

magic, and magic arts, techniques of, 117f. and n. 10, 223f.; 'white magic', not prohibited, 218, 222; theurgical, 115-19, 123, 126; distinguished from *haruspicina*, 214; books copied, 213, 223; amulets, 218; intellectual context, 225f.; and 'paganism', 217 and n. 27, 426; trials of Scythopolis, 217f.; of Antioch, 219-25; and adultery, trials at Rome, 209-17 and 510 n. 9, 227f., 420; and blackmail, 419f.; *see also* charioteers, *maiestas*, theurgy

Magna Mater, shrine of, at Pessinus, 107; mystery cult of, 424; Julian and, 124

Magnentius, rebellion of, in A.'s lost books, 18 and n. 25, 25; suppression of, 33

Magnus of Carrhae, historian, preserved in Malalas, 163 and n. 73; so-called 'fragments' of, 504 nn. 73, 83, 85, 88; on strategy of Julian's Persian campaign, 163f.; on roads to east, 169f.; on Circesium, 170; on the 'Mauzanitai', 156, 165; on location of Julian's death, 506 n. 1

Mahoza, 57, 155f. and nn. 58-9; Aramaic name of Coche-Ctesiphon, 156; Rabbinic academy at, 156; 'land of the Mauzanitai', 156

maiestas, and treason, accusations of, under Gallus Caesar, 34f.; under Constantius, 40, 241, 401, 448; under Julian, at Ancyra, 107; after suppression of Procopius, 212f.; under Valentinian, 212f.; under Valens, 219-25; at dinner-parties, 36f., 518 n. 26; as historical theme, in Tacitus and A., 456; 'leges Corneliae', 213, 252; A.'s attitude, 252, 261; *see also* law and legislation, 'Leges Corneliae', magic

'Maiozamalcha', fortress besieged by Julian, 155-7, 289, 290, 295; its name and identification, 155f. and n. 58; *see also* Mahoza

Malarichus, Roman officer, declines promotion, 188

Malchus, Syrian monk, captured by Saracens, 347, 348; informant of Jerome, 347

Malechus, Arab chieftain in Persian service, 148; his political and social position, 351f.

Mamertinus, Cl., *cos*. 362, 23, 106; his panegyric to Julian, 106
Manichees, Constantine and, 71, 449
Maratocupreni, inventive bandits in Syria, 263f., 349, 388, 535 n. 116; their name and settlement, 402 and n. 46; their destruction by Valens, 402
Marcellianus, *dux* of Valeria, son of Maximinus, 272; his murder of king Gabinius, 284
Marcellus, *magister equitum*, in Gaul, 81, 90; removed from office, 83; accusation of Julian, 83; his conduct in consistory, 268, 459f.; his character, 83, 268, 459f. and n. 21
Marcellus, under Procopius, usurpation of, 192, 201
Marcianopolis, in Thrace, in digression, 389; in Valens' Gothic campaign, 318f.; reception of Goths at, 327, 328
Marcus Aurelius, emperor, indulgence in sacrifice, 128; and 'Rain Miracle', 116; in *Caesares* of Julian, 137; his character, 243; as model for Julian, 242, 469f.
Mardonius, Armenian eunuch, tutor of Julian, 85
Mareades of Antioch, traitor, 29, 170f. and n. 84; in Libanius and Malalas, 170f.; in the *Historia Augusta*, 505 n. 84
Marius, 'genius' of, 433; and prophetess Martha, 434
Martialis, Q. Gargilius, of Auzia in Mauretania, exploits and death, 368, 370
Martianus, *comes Thraciarum*, supports Constantius against Julian, 101
Martin, bishop of Tours: fracas with imperial officials, 265; inflammatory encounter with Valentinian, 269
Martinianus, accomplice of Romanus, tortured and executed, 374
martyrs, and martyrdom, 216, 257, 267, 437; defined, 436, 437, 443; false martyrs, 437; shrine of, near Milan, 257, 437; Ammianus' attitude to, 436, 443
Mascizel, Moorish prince, 'brother' of Firmus, chief of Tyndenses, 371; participates in rebellion, 371; in Roman service, suppresses Gildo, 371; death, 371
Massilia (Marseilles), in digression, 389
Mauretania, Roman occupation of, 368; military policy and defensive system, 370f.; participation of tribal magnates in, 371, 373, 375; their strongholds, 400; Roman troops in, 371; cities and settlement, 368, 370; tribes and languages, 368, 369f., 371, 372 and n. 123; rebellions in, 368-70; of Firmus, 368ff.; its chronology, 208, 369, 381; social origins and tribal background, 368f., 371f., 535 n. 117; A.'s sources, 381f.
Mauretania Caesariensis, province of, 370
'Mauzanitai', land of, 156; *see also* Mahoza
Mavia (Mâwiya), Saracen queen, insurrection of, 350f.; receives bishop, 351; marriage of her daughter to Roman general, 350; provides troops for Valens, 351; her exploits celebrated in Arab song, 350
Maximian, emperor, campaigns in Mauretania, 368
Maximinus, emperor, character of, in A.'s lost books, 29 and n. 40
Maximinus, *PPo Galliarum* 371-6, origin and early career, 272 and n. 38; as *praefectus annonae*, investigates magic arts at Rome, 210; his *relatio*, to Valentinian, 212f.; as *vicarius* of Rome, 210f., 212; as *PPo Galliarum*, 214, 215; compared to snake, 258f.; his execution, predicted by father, 211, 273; omitted by Ammianus, 211 and n. 14, 519 n. 38
Maximus, of Ephesus, philosopher, pupil of Aedesius, 122; Julian and, 123; comes to Constantinople, 23,

125, 236; attends Persian campaign, 126f.; at Julian's deathbed, 127, 182; executed at Ephesus, 222, 224
Maximus, Magnus, usurper, Spanish origin and connections with Theodosius, 273; service in Africa, 371; in Britain, 273; court at Trier, embassy of Ambrose to, 268f.; relations with Symmachus, 9f.; suppression by Theodosius, 9
Maximus, Marius, biographer, mentioned by A., 32, 415, 459
Maximus, Petronius, senator, wealth of, 418; his son's praetorian games, 418
Maximus, Valerius, senator, appointed *praefectus urbi* by Julian, 270, 493 n. 31
Maximus, Valerius, antiquarian author, possible influence on A., 288, 431
Mazuca, Moorish prince, 'brother' of Firmus, participates in rebellion, 371; and 'fundus Mazucanus', 372; head of, received at Caesarea, 375
Mederichus, Alamann prince, father of Agenarichus, 315
Mediana, suburb of Naissus, imperial villa at, 190, 397, 401; empire divided there, 190, 401
Megia, Euphrates settlement, in Zosimus, 165
Meiacarire, settlement in Mesopotamia, 402; its name, 69, 402
Meinas Sabatha, Persian city, 156 and n. 60, 165; *see also* Besouchis, Vologesias
Mela, Pomponius, Latin ethnographer, 335
Melania, senatorial heiress, ascetic 'conversion' of, 422
Melanthias, 'villa Caesariana', in Thrace, 401
Melas river (Manavgat Çay), Isaurian insurgents at, 364; its physical character, 366
Melitene (Malatiya), near Euphrates, 46, 48, 65
Menander, on 'daimones', 432f.

'Menander Rhetor', author of rhetorical handbook, 71; on embassies, 385; on praise of cities, 490 n. 7
Mercurius, 'comes somniorum', adjutant of Paulus 'Catena', compared to dog, 259
Mesopotamia
  Assyrian, Roman control of, 51-5, 67; geography of, 48f.; agricultural exploitation, 51, 57; urban settlement, 51f., 67; Syriac language in, 69f.
  Babylonian, in Persian campaign of Julian, topography of, 140-60 and nn., *passim*; urban settlement, 140, 155, 157; river systems, 148-55, esp. 153-5 and nn. 55-6; Euphrates and Tigris, courses of, at Seleucia, 141-3 and nn. 26-8; Jewish populations, 141, 145
  see also canals, Euphrates, Tigris, Nahrmalcha, and under the individual cities
Metrodorus, philosopher, 'lies of', in Persian war of Constantine, 135f., 448; in Cedrenus, 135
Milan, court centre under Constantius: A. and Ursicinus at, 35-7; Julian at, 85-7; under Valentinian II, Augustine at, 273f.; 'ad Innocentes', martyrs' shrine, 257, 437; occupation of basilica, 257; *see also* Ambrose
Mimas, Macedonian general, 227; 'plains of M.', in oracle, 224, 227
mints, *see under* coins and coinage
Mithras, mystery cult, Julian and, 424
Mithridates VI (Eupator), in coded message, 43
Modestus, Domitius, *PPo Orientis* 369-77, presides at trials of Scythopolis and Antioch, 219; his character and lack of education, 461
'modius Italicus', 'castrensis', 410f. and nn. 17, 20
'Montes Serrorum', south-eastern Carpathians, in Gothic campaigns of Valens, 319 and n. 24
Mothone, in Laconia, A. at, 14

Murocincta, near Carnuntum, imperial villa, 401; as Parndorf, 401 and n. 42

Musonianus, Strategius, *PPo Orientis* 354-8, supporter of Constantine, 71, 449, 467; of Constantius, initiates negotiations with Persia, 39; conducts enquiries at Antioch, 408; acquainted with Libanius, 71f.; knows Latin, 71, 467f.; investigates Manicheism for Constantine, 449, 468; attends church councils, 449

Musonius, *vicarius Asiae*, killed in Isaurian rebellion, 364f., 380; death commemorated by Eunapius, 365

Mychon, *curialis* of Lepcis, captured by Austuriani, 384; ransom and death, 384

Nahrmalcha ('Royal canal'), course of, 149-51 and nn. 48-50; inlets, 149-51, 157, 165; and Tigris, 152, 157; passage forced, in A. and Eunapius, 165f., 173

Nabataea, and Nabataeans, 342f.; as 'provincia Arabia', annexed by Trajan, 342, 343f.; Roman roads in, 343; Roman relations with, 344

Nacolia, death of Procopius near, 197, 198; and Orcistus, 403

Naissus (Niš), birthplace of Constantine, 200; Julian at, 104, 105, 106; Valentinian and Valens at, 190; imperial palace at Mediana, 190, 397

Natuspardo, German soldier in Roman service, 316

Neardea, in Mesopotamia, Rabbinic academy at, located, 145 and n. 34, 149 and n. 48

Nebridius, *quaestor sacri palatii*, appointed by Julian, 96; promoted as praetorian prefect, 99

Nebuchadnezzar, and water defences of Babylon, 154f.

Neckar, river, building of fort by, 283f.

Nemara, in Hawran, inscr. of, 350; translated, 532 n. 87

Nemesis, in A., 427

Neoplatonism, in Asia Minor, and Julian, 85; at Athens, 117; and theurgy, 117-28; allegorising techniques of, 433; in digression on divination, 428-30; A.'s western sources, 429f; *see also* divination, Eunapius, philosophy and philosophers, theurgy

Neoterius, Fl., *cos.* 390, in A., 23; as *notarius*, secures Africa against Procopius, 23, 198

Nepotianus, rebellion at Rome, 25, 205

Nestorius, hierophant of Eleusis: initiates Eunapius, 124; with Julian in Gaul, role in his usurpation, 93, 115, 124; his accomplishments, 116

Nevitta, Fl., *magister equitum*, *cos.* 362, 106; appointed consul by Julian, 448; his character, 448f.; on Persian campaign, 168

Nicaea, in Bithynia, accession of Valentinian at, 189; recovered from Procopius, 318

Nicomedia, in digression, 390; developed by Diocletian, 390; mint at, 200; Eusebius of, 85; Julian educated at, 84f.; destruction in earthquakes, 85, 392; visit of Julian, and munificence towards, 107

Nimrud (Khalhu), Assyrian city, in Xenophon, 50

Nineveh, Assyrian city, 48f., 50

Nisibis (Nusaybin), in Mesopotamia: its name and origin, 67; as Severan colony, 67; agriculture in region of, 52, 387f., 399f.; sieges by Sapor II, 3, 136, 499 n. 15; in campaign of 359, 41; surrender to Persia, 4, 186; evacuation, 4; resettlement of population, 66; A. at, 4, 41

nomads, and nomadism, stereotypes of, 336, 347f., 352f., 538 n. 47, 530 n. 62; and Huns, 334, 337-41; their social evolution, 355 and nn. 94, 96; their migration route, 529 n. 50; and Saracens, 344-6 and nn. 73-6; migrant Arabs, at Palmyra, 345; transhumance (?), in Isauria, 360 and nn. 103-4; *see also* Huns,

Saracens
Notitia Dignitatum: division of empire in, 190; grades of bureaucracy in, 254f.; insignia in, 255; shield devices, 76 and n. 16, 260; on 'fabricae', 263, 408; Alamann units in, 316; Isauria in, 357; Mauretania in, 370f.; at western court, 467
Nubel (Fl. Nuvel), Moorish prince, 369, 371; origin and power, 372; his wife and family, 373; concubines, 369; Roman cavalry command, 371, 373; and 'True Cross', 373
Numa, 'genius' of, 433; and nymph Egeria, 433
nuns, in Mesopotamia, captured by Sapor, 436; their devotion, in A., 436 and n. 25, 445, 447
Nuvel, Fl., *see* Nubel

obelisks, seen by A. at Thebes, 14; erected at Rome by Constantius, 12, 449, 462; Constantine and, 449f. and n. 47; hieroglyph inscription, 462
Ocriculum, near Rome, 478 n. 8
Octavianus Augustus, 'genius' of, 433; honoured by Herod the Great, 389; as 'emperor of old', 243
Odaenathus, Palmyrene 'usurper', 350
Oea (Tripoli), Apuleius' marriage to woman of, 399; raided by Austuriani, 384
Olybrius, Q. Clodius Hermogenianus, *praefectus urbi* 368-70, 210, 215; hears complaint of Chilo, 210, 420; recipient of imperial legislation, 212f., 214; character of his administration, 211f.; passion for theatre and love affairs, 419
Olympiodorus of Thebes, historian, on senatorial wealth and munificence, 418; on fifth-century west, 472; his manner of composition, 482 n. 44
Omana, 'oppidum' of Homonadenses, 356
omens and portents, on Persian campaign, 126f., 134, 175-9; under Jovian, 185; at Pistoria, 271; and Gothic wars, 332; owls as, 395 and n. 29; Huns as, 332; *see also* divination, *haruspices*, Sibylline Books
onager, description of, 291-3; A.'s confusion regarding, 302
oracles, and emperor Carus, 133; on death of Valens, 221, 224, 226f.; their interpretation, 238; in Eunapius, 118, 179 and n. 94; found in walls of Chalcedon, 227 and n. 44; at Daphne, 439; on 'daimones', as source for A., 432; Sibylline, 132, 505 n. 84; Chrysanthius, Aedesius and, 118; *see also* 'Chaldaean Oracles', divination, theurgy
Orcistus, 'vicus' in Phrygia, petitions Constantine for independent status, 403; its amenities, 403
Orfitus, Memmius Vitrasius, *praefectus urbi* 353-6, 24; prosecuted for embezzlement, 405; his lack of culture, 512 n. 25
Oribasius, doctor, friend of Julian, 87f., 93; and Eunapius, 164; and Maximus, 497 n. 22; prophetic dream of, 99; role in usurpation of Julian, 115; attends Persian campaign, 143, 164; composes memoir, lent to Eunapius, 164 and n. 75; on death of Julian, 182
Orosius, alleged historian, 6; on Burgundians, 310
Ozogardana, Euphrates settlement: tribunal of Trajan at, 148; as 'Zaragardia' in Zosimus, 165

Pacatus, Latinus Drepanius, panegyrist of Theodosius, 11, 234 and n. 6
'pagan' and 'paganism': its character, 424-6; Gibbon on, 426; the term, 425 and n. 3; imperial policy towards, 426; priesthoods, at Rome, 235; connections with magic, 426; at Alexandria, 443
Paleas (or Palaia), fortified site in Isauria, 364; provisions stored at, 364; its location, 534 n. 110
Palestine, fourth-century provinces of,

343; incorporates part of Nabataean kingdom, 342f.; in digression, 389
Palladius, sorcerer, 219
Palladius, *tribunus et notarius*, in Tripolitanian affair, 386; suicide, 435
Palladius, Greek rhetorician in west, 467
Palladius, *primicerius notariorum* at Milan, in Claudian, 467
Palmyra, desert city, 345; and caravan trade, 345; and migrant Arabs, 345; 'tax law' of, 345; and 'strata Diocletiana', 343; its decline, 349
Pannonia, and Pannonians, in Cassius Dio, 199f., 249; as beer-drinkers, 199, 249; and origin of emperors, 200, 249; Valens as, in Procopius' propaganda, 199f., 225; under Valentinian, 272 and n. 36; Viventius as, 421; ruined cities of, in fifth century, 342; *see also* Carnuntum, 'Murocincta', Naissus, Savaria, Sirmium
Papa, Armenian king, escapes from Tarsus, 393, 400
Paris: Julian at, 94-9; parade-ground at, 98, 398; palace, 98
Parnasius, of Patrae, exiled for divination, 217f.; property of, in Achaia, 512 n. 28
Parndorf, possible imperial villa in Pannonia, *see* 'Murocincta'
patronage, in politics, 270-4
Paul, St.: visit to Lystra, 356; festivals of, at Rome, 421; basilica of (S. Paolo fuori le Mura), described by Prudentius, 421f.; in Piranesi, 421; its building and dedication, 421; destruction by fire, 421
Paulus 'Catena', judicial agent of Constantius, 82; relations with Julian, 92; conducts trials at Scythopolis, 92, 217f.; compared to snake, 259
Pentadius, *notarius*, involved in suppression of Gallus, 92; *magister officiorum* of Julian, 92, 96; acquitted at trials of Chalcedon, 93
'peregrini', at Rome, 12f.; their expulsion, 13, 24
Pergamius, executed for divination, 220
Persia, and Persians: in digression, 111; in *De Rebus Bellicis*, 304; expertise in siege warfare, 57-65 *passim*, 294; A. on their painting and sculpture, 144 and n. 33; rock sculptures, 132, 134 and nn. 5, 11, 499 n. 21; hunting dishes, 501 n. 33; Persian ceremonial, 233, 245 and n. 25
Persian campaign, of Julian, 3-5, 109-11, 130-83; precedents, 130-4, 135f., 139; Constantine and 'lies of Metrodorus', 135f.; aims and purpose, 134-40; criticisms of, 134f.; strategy, 138f., 163f., 499 n. 19; dispositions, 167f.; topography, 140-60 and nn. *passim*; route, 502 n. 54; Persian tactics, 138f., 152f., 158, 159, 180; aftermath, 135; defence of, in A., 135, 469; treaty of Jovian, A.'s judgment on, 187
Pessinus, shrine of Magna Mater at, 107; etymology of the name, 107
Peter, St.: Roman festivals of, in Prudentius, 421; basilica of, 421
Petra, in Arabia, Nabataean city, 343; assigned to province of Palestine, 343 and n. 67
'Petra', in Mauretania, *see* 'fundus Petrensis'
Petronius, father-in-law of Valens, financial exactions of, 193, 195
Petrus Valvomeres, riot-leader at Rome, 417, 418; exile and execution, 417
Petulantes, in proclamation of Julian, 97f; *see also* Celtae
'Pfahlgraben', Roman *limes* in Raetia, 309f.; folk-tales concerning, 309
Philagrius: as *notarius*, arrests Vadomarius, 376f.; as source for A., 376f., 480 n. 28, 509 n. 19; attends Persian campaign of Julian, 162, 377f.; as *comes Orientis* at Antioch, 376f.
Philip 'the Arab', emperor, in Persian campaign of Gordian III, 131f.; his origin and reputation, 348f.

Philippopolis, in Arabia, formerly Shahba, origin of Philip the Arab, 348

Philippopolis, in Thrace: sack of, in third century, 29; supports Procopius, 198, 201; surrender, 201; in digression, 389

Philippus, Fl., praetorian prefect of Constantius, virtues of, 277; *see also* Simplicius (1)

philosophy, and philosophers, under Julian, 122-9; A. on, 127f.; their vanity, in Cicero, 236; on Persian campaign, 143, 162, 178, 182, 497 n. 22; in trials of Antioch, 222; and theurgy, 117f., 496 nn. 1, 7; as civic ambassadors, 404 and n. 2; *see also* divination, Eunapius, Neoplatonism, Plotinus, theurgy

Philostorgius, church historian: on death of Julian, 182f.; use of Eunapius by, 182, 446

Phissenia, Euphrates settlement: in Eunapius, 152, 165; omitted by A., 165; its location, 152f. and n. 54

Phronimius, Gaul, supporter of Procopius: possible links with Julian, 225

'Phrygia', in Persia, death of Julian at, 181 and n. 1, 296

Phrynichus, Athenian dramatist, in A., 209

Picti, *see* Attacotti

Pietroasa Treasure, 324

Pinaka, fortified city in Corduene, 51

Pirisabora (Peroz-Shapur), Persian city, its name, 63, 132, 149; in Talmud, 149; as al-Anbar, 149; its site, 152 and n. 52; described, in A. and Eunapius, 174 and n. 89; fortifications of, 148; water defences, 152; besieged by Julian, 149, 288, 290; surrender, 133, 293f.; in A. and Eunapius, 173f.

'Pirosen', Persian acclamation at Amida, its meaning, 63

'Pistrensis', 'publica villa' near Sirmium, 401

Pliny, *Natural History*: on Seleucia, 140; on the Nahrmalcha, 149, 151, on Arabs, 346f.; on Homonadenses, 356f.; on waterproof cement, 416; on hippopotami, 462, on amorous palm-trees, 552 n. 26

Plotinus, philosopher: attends Persian campaign of Gordian III, 143; attends seance at Rome, 119, 433; lack of interest in magic, 119, 123; experiences 'ecstasy', 122; on 'daimones', 118f., 434; on dualism, 122; ascetic teaching of, 119, 434; A. and, 434

Plutarch, *Life of Demetrius*, description of *helepolis*, 293; *Life of Marius*, on divine supporters of Marius, 434; *De Genio Socratis*, 433

poets, as historical sources, 14

Polybius, historian, on growth of Roman power, 280, 455 and n. 7; on Scipio Africanus, 433; and Scipio Aemilianus, 466; in Greek historiography, 455, 465; on interviewing technique, 457; portrayals of character, 459

Ponticianus, *agens in rebus*, African, known to Augustine, 274

Porphyry, philosopher, 122; biographer of Plotinus, 119; experiences 'ecstasy', 122

praefecti gentis, in Mauretania, 368, 371, 374

Praetextatus, Vettius Agorius, at Constantinople, 23; as proconsul of Achaia, 23; appointed by Julian, 270f.; his character, 271; as prefect of Rome, receives legislation, 210; and accession of pope Damasus, 421; senatorial envoy to Valentinian, 212, 214; his religious initiations, 424; death as consul designate, 23; source for A., 23 and n. 29

praetorian prefecture, *see under* bureaucracy, taxation

prefects of Rome, in A., 24 and n. 31, 416f.; in trials under Valentinian, 210, 211f.; archival material from, 24 and n. 31

presbyters, among Goths, 323, 331f.; *see also* Christians and Christianity

'Primani', at battle of Strasbourg, 298

Principius, *praefectus urbi* in 373, omitted by A., 212
Priscian, grammarian, and text of A., 6 and n. 7
Priscus, Athenian philosopher, pupil of Aedesius, 122f.; letter from Julian to, 115; joins him in Gaul, 93; and at Constantinople, 125; attends Persian campaign, 126f.; at Julian's death-bed, 127, 182
Priscus of Panium, historian: on camp of Attila, 342; on his sword, 340
Probus, Sex. Petronius, senator: character of, in A., 22, 277f. and n. 50, 448, 459, 548 n. 42; his regime in Illyricum, 240, 278; at Sirmium, 395; insincere vote of thanks to, from Epirus, 404; defends interests of his 'familiae', their rapacity, 277f., 448; his death c. 390, 22 and n. 27
Proclus of Athens, Neoplatonist philosopher, 117-19; and theurgy, 117f., 122
Procopius, usurper, connections and early career, 191; envoy to Persia, 42f., 191; family property in Cappadocia, 191; in Persian campaign of Julian, 138f., 159, 163f., 186f., 191; escorts Julian's body for burial, 191; alleged choice for succession, 191f. and n. 15; rebellion of, 23, 191-203; proclamation, 193f., 236f., 247; attitude of Valentinian, 198, 206; extent of support, 194f.; motivation of his supporters, 195f., 225; support from Goths, 196, 318f.; his regime, 195f.; finance, 196; propaganda, 196, 198-200; and family of Constantine, 196, 199; the Julianic connection, 200, 225; his coin image, 200; mints, 200 and n. 26; betrayal and execution, 197; his head, displayed, 201 and n. 27; his character, in A., 191, 201, 548 n. 42; role of narrative, in structure of later books, 204-6
Procopius, historian: on 'White Huns' (*see also* Hephthalites), 62; on desert Arabs, 345f.; on Lepcis Magna, 393
Proculus, supporter of Silvanus, interrogated, 83
Prohaeresius, of Athens, Christian sophist, consults hierophant at Eleusis, 116f., 218; in west, 467
prostitution: in imperial palace, forbidden, 262; male, punishment of, 256
protectores, 74f.; their origin, 74; duties, 75; salary, 77; *prot. domestici*, 75-9; command and duties, 75f.; at Amida, 46, 65; *primicerius* of, 79, 184; *deputatio* of, 76; privileges of, 79; A. as, 37, 76-8; *adoratio* by, 77, 246f.
Prudentius, *Peristephanon*, on Roman Christianity, 421f.; on basilica of St. Paul, 421f.
Psellus, Michael, on theurgy, 118f.
Ptolemy, *Geography*: on site of Neardea, 149; reference to Huns, doubted, 335
Pumbedita, Rabbinic academy, 149, 155; at Pirisabora, 155
purple: dye-works at Tyre, 34, 262; treason and, 518 n. 26; *see also adoratio purpurae*
Pusaeus, Persian commander of Anatha, later *dux Aegypti*, 171f.

Quadi: lifestyle of, 523 n. 3; envoys to Valentinian, 267f.
Quinquegentiani, rebels in Mauretania, 368

'Rain Miracle', under Marcus Aurelius, 116
Rando, Alamann prince, 314
rationales, in provinces, 265; their function, 265; bandits masquerade as, 265
Remigius, *magister officiorum* of Valentinian, involved in Tripolitanian affair, his suicide, 208
Res Gestae Divi Saporis, on death of Gordian III and foundation of Pirisabora, 132
Resaina (Ras el Ain), in Mesopotamia,

Severan colony, 51f.
Rhabdion, in Tur Abdin, Roman fortress, 55
Rhine, river, 81; waterways of, 90; patrol boats on, 521 n. 8
rhetoric, and rhetoricians: Julian's edict on, 109, 112; Augustine as, 273
Romanianus, of Thagaste, friend of Augustine, 273f.
Romanus, *comes Africae*, in Mauretania, good relations with Zammac (*q.v.*), 369; his maladministration there, 374; and at Lepcis Magna, 281f., 384-7; his self-defence, 386
Rome, in A., 8f., 11-13, 23, 25, 465f.; visit of Constantius to, 11f., 231-4; Julian and, 104, 235; Valentinian and, 209-17; Theodosius and, 11, 234; digressions on, 207, 214f., 414-16 and n. 28; their character and purpose, 414; ideal of, 250, 279f., 450, 456, 470 and n. 40; growth of power, 279; in Polybius, 280, 455; 'ages of', 250, 279, 470 and n. 40; eternity of, 26, 280, 470; and emperors, 250, 231-5, 414, 456, 470; as 'temple of the world', 449f.
'populus Romanus': assemblies of, 414; passion for races, 415f.; acclamations of, 11, 234, 405, 416; and rioting, 416, 417, 444; relations with *praefecti urbi*, 416f.; with senators, 416f., 422; popular names, 542 n. 31; population and corn supplies, 541 n. 20; expulsion of 'peregrini', 13, 415
topography and cults, 11f., 423 and n. 54; priesthoods, 235; temple of Palatine Apollo, 177f.; Circus Maximus, 416; stables of factions, 422f.; bridge constructed, 416; obelisk raised, 12, 449f.
Christianity at, 420-3, 441f., 444f.; bishops of, 441, 444; pope Liberius, popularity of, 421, 441; rioting over succession, 421, 438, 444f.; churches, of St. Peter's, 421; S. Paolo fuori le Mura, 421f.; St.

Laurentius 'in Damaso' (*or*, 'in Prasino'), 422; 'in Lucinis', 422; 'basilica Sicinnini', 439, 444; liturgical processions, 421f.
see also Lampadius, Leontius, prefects of Rome, senate and senators, Symmachus (1) and (2)
Rousoumblada, Isaurian village, origin of the emperor Zeno, 261
Rufinus, Aradius, Roman senator: *comes Orientis* under Julian, addressed by Libanius, 413; *praefectus urbi* under Gratian, 413
'Ruin, The', Anglo-Saxon poem, on remains of Bath, 308f., 314
Rusguniae, in Mauretania, fragment of 'True Cross' in church there, 373

'Saansaan', Persian acclamation at Amida, interpreted by A., 63
Saba, Passion of St., as evidence for Gothic society, 322-4; village communities in, 323f.; relations with tribal authorities, 323f.; Gothic cult in, 330
'sabaia', cheap drink obtainable in Illyricum, 199
Sabinianus, *magister equitum*, criticised by A., 40, 44f., 46, 461 and n. 24; alleged failure to relieve Amida, 60
sale of office, under Valentinian, 270
Salian Franks, campaign of Julian against, 90
Sallust: in A., 32, 237; in *Historia Augusta*, 514 n. 11
Sallustius, Fl., *PPo Galliarum*, opposes Persian campaign of Julian, 134f., 178
Salmaces, Sammac, *see under* Zammac
Salutius, Saturninius Secundus: associate of Julian in Gaul, withdrawn by Constantius, 92; appointed *PPo Orientis*, 92; presides over trials at Chalcedon, 92; on Persian campaign, 178; after Julian's death, declines throne, 183 and n. 5
Salvian, Christian moralist, on Alamanni, 313
Samosata, Euphrates crossing, 40, 45;

naval station in Persian campaign, 166
Sapor I, Persian monarch: defeats Gordian III, refounds Pirisabora, 132; captures Valerian, 134f.; attacks Antioch, 170f., 288 and n. 13
Sapor II, Persian monarch: relations with Constantine, 135f.; with Constantius II, 39f.; attacks Nisibis, 3; invasion of 359, 40ff.; at Amida, 57ff., 61; at Bezabde in 360, 47, 436; displays clemency, 436; relations with his Jewish subjects, 145; his headdress, 62 and n. 25
Sansala, Gothic presbyter, 323
Saphrax, 'dux', regent of Greuthungi, 324; possible origin, 326
Saqlawiyah canal, described by Chesney, 149; its course, 149 and n. 47
Saracens, digression on, 344, 380; origin of name, 349 and n. 83; formerly 'Skênitai', in Strabo, 345, 346; their distribution, 344; at Elusa in Negev, 348; their control of desert zone, 344f.; and commerce, 344f.; nomadism, and relations with settled country, 51, 344f., 346, 354; urbanisation, 345 (*see also* Hatra, Palmyra); pastoral economy, 346, 347; brigandage, 346f.; social customs amongst, 347; dress, 348 and n. 80; sexual habits, 344, 454; social equality among, 344, 353; position of women, 347 and n. 77; importance of genealogy, 347 and n. 78; Arabic language, 348; Christianity among, 350f., 531 n. 81, 532 n. 88
envoys of, received by Julian, 167; in Persian campaign, 348, 351f.; in Persian service, 183, 185, 345f.; and death of Julian, 352; at Hadrianople, their impact upon Goths, 348, 351
growth of federations, in third century, 349f.; wars of Sapor II against, 145; 'Saraceni Assanitae', 352; expansion of Islam, 343, 354, 355

see also, 'Amr îbn 'Adi, Ghassanids, Imru'l-qais, Jadhima, Lakhmids
Sarisa, in Corduene, 50f.
Sarmatians, lifestyle of, 523 n. 3
Sasanians, *see* Persia and Persians
Satalka, in Corduene, 50f.
Saturninus, *magister militum*, policy towards Goths, 328
Savaria, in Pannonia, Valentinian at, 395; bath-house and city gate of, 395f.
Saxons: raiders, destroyed by Valentinian, 383, 471; prisoners, as gladiators at Rome, 418
Scipio Africanus, 'genius' of, and divine help, 433
Scutarii, and Gentiles, palace guard, transfer ordered by Constantius, 94, 98
Scotti, *see* Attacotti
Scythians, in Herodotus, 334f. and nn. 51f.
Scythopolis, in Palestine, trials of, 217f.
Sebastianus: *comes*, in Persian campaign of Julian, 138f., 159, 163f., 186; as *magister peditum*, at battle of Hadrianople, 300
Secundinus, *dux Osrhoenae*, in Persian campaign of Julian, 168
Seleucia, in Isauria, besieged by Isaurian insurgents, 363f.
Seleucia, on the Tigris (Maps 4, 5): its foundation and population, 140f. and n. 25; compared with Antioch, 141; harbour of, 143, 502 n. 53; sack by Avidius Cassius, 142; decline, 141-3, 392; as 'Sliq Kharawta', 141; executions at, 133, 141; hunting park and palaces near, 144, 157, 400
Seleucus Nicator, Macedonian monarch, founds Seleucia on the Tigris, 140f.
senate, and senators, in digression, 250, 279, 414-16; origins of, 419 and n. 43; magistracies, 416, 418; priesthoods, 235; jurisdiction, 212; embassies, 9, 10; acclamations in, 248; *aurum coronarium*, 284;

largesse and munificence, 418f.;
building, 416f.; games,
Symmachus and, 418f.;
Praetextatus as senator, 270f.;
Probus and Anicii, 277f.;
Symmachus, 9f., 284-6, 418f.;
senators and Christianity, 421f.
intellectual tastes of, 9, 32, 415;
moral standards, 216 and n. 25,
419f.; ostentation, 247, 419;
disreputable clients of, 213, 215,
415, 419f.; contempt for the lower
classes, 416f.; reception of
strangers, 12f., 414; and magic
arts and adultery, 210-17; in laws
of Valentinian, 210, 212f.
senate of Constantinople: and
philosopher Maximus, 23, 236; and
usurper Procopius, 193, 194, 198,
214; after death of Valens, 227;
acclamations in, 194, 198
relations with emperors: in Tacitus,
248; with Constantius, 234f.; with
Julian, 104, 235; with Valentinian,
209-16, 284-6; with Theodosius,
11, 234
see also prefects of Rome, Petronius
Probus, Symmachus (1) and (2)
Seniauchus, tribune, killed in Gaul,
187f.
Sens (Senones): Julian at, 83, 90; its
identification defended, 492 n. 16;
late Roman walls of, 394
Serapeum, at Alexandria, 14; its
destruction, 26
Serapio, Alamann prince, *see under*
Agenarichus
Serapis, Greek mysteries of, 315, 424
Serenianus, *comes domesticorum* of
Valens, defends Cyzicus, 196, 393;
his character, 201
Severus, *magister equitum*, in Gaul,
succeeds Marcellus, 83; his
character, 83, 91, 551 n. 21
Sibylline Books: consulted, 177; saved
from fire, 178
Silva, *curialis* of Lepcis, captured by
Austuriani, 384
Silvanus, *magister peditum* and
usurper, 37f. and nn. 7-8, 10; son of
Frankish general of Constantine,

38, 80; plot against, at Milan, 37,
263, 271; proclamation and
donative, 83; date of, 491 n. 3;
relations with Ursicinus, 80;
death, 38, 435; punishments of
supporters, 81-3; his character, in
A., 38
Simonides, philosopher, burned alive,
222, 257
Simplicius (1), son of Fl. Philippus,
exiled for divination, 217
Simplicius (2), of Emona, former
grammarian, associate of
Maximinus, 211, 272; as *vicarius*
of Rome, 211, 214; executed, 211;
his character, 258
Singara, in Mesopotamia, 43, 48;
climate, 52; battle of, 43, 295;
Roman artillery captured by
Persians, 290; besieged by Sapor,
47, 290; state of its defences, 394f.;
ceded by Jovian, 4, 53, 186
'sinistus', Burgundian word for priest,
313 and n. 15, 330
'Sîntana de Mureş culture', and Goths,
321f., 525 n. 22; and *Passion of St.
Saba*, 323f.
Sintula, *tribunus stabuli*, agent of
Constantius, 94, 98; 'Gintonius' in
Julian, 94
Sippar (Abu Hubbah): and Euphrates,
151; and Nahrmalcha, 151
Sirmium, in Pannonia: dinner-party of
Africanus at, 92, 264; Constantius
at, 39, 100; Ursicinus and A.
summoned to, 39; in civil war of
361, 104; Julian's *adventus* at, 248;
walls rebuilt, 395; after earlier
neglect, 396, 397; unfinished
theatre at, 395; 'suburbs' of, 396f.
and n. 31
Sitha, Euphrates settlement, in
Zosimus, 165
Sitifis (Sétif), in Mauretania, 368; in
campaigns of Theodosius, 369f.
'Skênitai', 345, 349; *see under* Saracens
slave-trading: in Alamannia, 312; and
Goths, 326f., 329
Socrates, 'daimon' of, 433
Solicinium, Alamannic hill-fort (?),
Roman attack on, 296, 377; its

configuration, 311
Solinus, on the hippopotamus, 462 and n. 26
Sopatros, Syrian Neoplatonist, pupil of Iamblichus, 126; at Constantinople, his attainments and execution, 126
Sophanene, satrapy on Tigris, 53, 56
Sophronius: *notarius*, informs Valens of Procopius' rebellion, 195; later prefect of Constantinople, 195; possible source for A., 195 and n. 19, 480 n. 28
Sopianae (Pécs), in Valeria, home city of Maximinus, 272
Spain, and Spaniards: Antiochene embassy to, 8; noble house of, destroyed, 264; at court of Valentinian, 273; origin of Maximus and Theodosius (*q.v.*), 9, 273
Sozomen, church historian: on temple of Apollo at Daphne, 441; on death of George of Alexandria, 443; on insurrection of Mavia, 350; on Gothic cult, 330; his refutation of Eunapius, 446, 448
Stachao, leader of Austuriani, executed, 367, 383
statues: dedicated, at Rome, to Aurelius Victor, 23f., 457; at Lepcis, to Nicomachus Flavianus and Hesperius, 386f.; at Rome and Carthage, to Julius Festus Hymetius, 210 and n. 11; animated, 118
Stoicism, in digression on divination, 429f.
Strabo, geographer: on Aquileia, 397; on Ctesiphon, 141; on Gordyaioi, 50; on Homonadenses, 366; on Isaura, Vetus and Nova, 359; on 'Isaurikê', 357, cf. 360; on Lycaonia, 356; on Mesopotamian canals, 151; on Seleucia by the Tigris, 140; on 'Skênitai' (desert Arabs), 345, 346; as historian, 455
Strasbourg, early legionary fortress at, 308; its strategic importance, 308; battle of, 91f., 296-300, 314; its site, 297 and n. 23; Alamannic confederation at, 314; Roman strength at, 300, 317; strategic context of, 299f.; tactics, 298; casualty figures, 298; A.'s sources, 378f.
'strata Diocletiana', road and frontier zone, 343; in territory of Palmyra, 345
'suburbs', in A., 396-9
Succi, strategic pass of, in Illyricum, 101, 105, 197
Sueridas, Gothic leader, settled near Hadrianople, 326, 328
Suetonius, principles of biography in, 459 and n. 17
Sumere (Samarra), in Persian campaign of Julian, 181, 185
Suomarius, Alamann king, 315
Surena, Persian nobleman, 148, 351
Syagrius, as *notarius*, sole survivor of Alamann attack, as A's. source, 377, 480 n. 28; later prefect and consul, 377
Symmachus (1), Q. Aurelius, the orator, *praefectus urbi* 384-5, son of (2): envoy to Valentinian, 10, 284-6; *Or.* 2, delivered at Trier, 284f.; on military policy of Valentinian, 378; *comes ordinis tertii*, 285; relations with Ausonius, 273, 285; on reports of military victories, 378; and expulsion of 'peregrini', 13; supports usurper Maximus, 9f.; apologises to Theodosius, and made consul, 10; organises son's praetorian games, 418f.; edits Livy, 10; on Christians and Christianity, 426 and n. 7; and 'paganism', 424; supposed 'circle' of, 466

Relatio 3, on altar of Victory, 235, 424, 425; *Rel.* 25, on S. Paolo fuori le Mura, 421; correspondence, 418f., 520 n. 47; to father, 416; on Palladius, Greek professor of rhetoric, 467; on Antiochene delegation to Spain, 8; *Epp.* 3.88 to Rufinus, 480 n. 27; 8.22 to Andronicus, 512 n. 28; 9.110 not to Ammianus, 476 n. 5; 'litterae

commendaticiae', 271
Symmachus (2), L. Avianius, *praefectus urbi* 364-5, father of Symmachus (1): as senatorial envoy to Constantius, meets Julian at Naissus, 104 and n. 31, 270; his prefecture of Rome, 416f.; building projects, 416; house burned down and driven from Rome, 416f.; recalled, 417
Syriac language, geographical and social diffusion, 69f.; in *Digest*, 69
Syrianus, of Athens, Neoplatonist, 116, 117; writes hymn to Achilles, 116

Tacitus, the historian: on the *populus Romanus*, 417; on the Hermunduri, 313, 329; on Germanic execution by drowning, 526 n. 29; on 'principatus ac libertas', 470; annalistic technique in, 458; and authority, 464; his influence on Ammianus, questioned, 32 and n. 45, 456 and n. 11, 468, 549 n. 4
'Taiênos' (Tayy Arab), and death of Julian, 183, 352
Taifali, Gothic allies, in Oltenia, 320f.; settled in Po valley, 316
Talmud, Babylonian, 145; on Veh Ardeshir, 141; on canal systems, 149, 151f.; on regime of Sapor II, 145
Tamsapor, Persian satrap, and defection of Antoninus, 68
Tanaitae ('Don people'), division of Alani, 320, 336
Tanukh, Arab federation, migration of, 350; *see also* Jadhima
Tarsus, in Cilicia, burial of Julian at, 177, 191; Armenian prince interned at, 393; its walls, 393f.
Taurus, *PPo Italiae*, partisan of Constantius against Julian, 104, 105
Taurus mountains, in Isauria, 355f.; in Ammianus' perspectives, 16 and n. 21, 227
taxation: and war, 66, 280-2; and imperial 'avarice', in Lactantius, 240; role of praetorian prefect in, 89f., 96f., 178, 253, 282; suggestions for reform, in *De Rebus Bellicis*, 304; *aurum coronarium*, 56, 284, 385; *superindictiones*, 89; billetting, 281; tax policy, under Tetrarchy, 254; under Constantine, 156; his confiscation of temple treasures, 448; under Constantius, 240; Julian and, 89f., 240f.; Valentinian and Valens and, 193, 240, 242; in Africa, 281f.; at Caesarea in Mauretania, 391; at Alexandria, 442f.; in Gaul, under Julian, 89 and n. 14; at Autun, remission by Constantine, 254; in Illyricum, 240, 277; in Thrace, 329
Terentius, former baker, promotion portended by donkey, 271; successful prosecution by, 271, 405
Terentius, gloomy general, his Christianity, 447
Tetrarchs, and Tetrarchy, reforms of, 249, 253f. and nn. 1-3; Lactantius on, 254; Constantius II on, 254, 471; *see also under* the emperors, Constantius, Diocletian, Galerius, Maximian
Thalassius, court official, reconciled with Julian, 246
Themistius, panegyrist of Valens, on Goths, 327 and n. 35, 329; his influence on A., questioned, 509 nn. 17, 29
Theodorus, *notarius*, from Gaul, accused of divination and conspiracy, 15, 219f.; possible supporter of Julian, 225; religious beliefs of, 226
Theodorus of Asine, Neoplatonist philosopher, and Iamblichus, 123
Theodosian Code, published in west, 248, 472; its 'ideology', 472; penalties and language in, 256, 460; on Isaurian bandits, 363; the term 'Christianitas' in, 544 n. 6; acclamations in, 248; *see also* law and legislation
Theodosius (1), *magister equitum*, father of the emperor: his Spanish origin, 273; campaigns in Britain,

207; their chronology, 510 n. 7; in Mauretania, 208, 282, 369ff.; his execution at Carthage, 211 and n. 14, 273, 382; not mentioned by A., 211 and n. 14, 382; compared by A. with Corbulo and Lusius Quietus, 242; his character and methods of discipline, 370, 374, 381, 382; at court of Valentinian, as 'suffragator' of Africanus, 271

Theodosius (2), the emperor, son of (1): Spanish origin, 273; as *dux Moesiae*, 16, 273, cf. 224; his reign predicted by divination, 224; accession and early campaigns, 16; treaty with Goths, 16; defeat of Maximus, 9; in west, 8-11; visits Rome, 11; his liking for history, 10

Theodotus, of Hierapolis, 101, cf. 110

Theophanes, *scholasticus*, papyrus dossier of, 265, 271

Theophilus, *consularis Syriae*, and corn crisis at Antioch, murdered by mob, 406-8; his collusion with *curiales*, 407

Thervingi, Gothic people, 320, 324f.; campaigns of Valens against, 320; defeat by Huns, 320; *see also* Athanaric, Greuthungi

Thessalonica, riot and massacre of, 258

theurgy, and theurgists, 115-19 and 495 n. 1; origin and meaning of the term, 115f.; theoretical basis of the art, 117f.; its influence on Julian, 124-8, 434; its uses, in weather-making, 116, 117, 126; and divination, 117f., 127f.; and spiritual purification, 117f.; theurgists, at temple of Apollo at Daphne, 439f.; *see also* Chaldaean Oracles, divination, 'Julianus the theurgist', Neoplatonism, Sopatros

Thilutha (Tilbus), Euphrates settlement, 146

'Thorigny Marble', 537 n. 6

Thoth, Egyptian god, as Hermes Trismegistos, 433

Thrace: visit of A. to (?), 16f.; digression on, 207, 208, 389; in war of Julian against Constantius, 101, 105; in usurpation of Procopius, 196, 198; occupation by Goths, 17 and n. 23, 328; goldminers of, 329

Thucydides, in A., 59 and n. 20, 463 and n. 27; speeches in, 130; historical character of, 455, 465

Tigris, courses of, at Seleucia, 141-3; and Mahoza, 155; and the Nahrmalcha, 157; crossing of, by Julian, 158; on retreat from Persia, 185

Timagenes, Greek writer on Gaul, 464; as antiquarian source, 552 n. 29; his character and end, 552 n. 28

Timgad (Thamugadi), municipal register of, 254

'Tingitanum castellum' (Orléansville), in Mauretania, in campaigns of Theodosius, 369; in *Notitia Dignitatum*, 370f.

Tipasa (Algiers), in Mauretania, in campaigns of Theodosius, 369

Tiridates, king of Armenia, lassoed by Alani, 337

Traianus, Roman general, in Mesopotamia, 318

Trajan, emperor, in Julian's *Caesars*, 137f.; Persian campaign of, 130, 148; at Babylon, 138; his yearning for India, 138 and n. 17

Trajan's Column, 522 n. 17, 524 n. 12

'Transtigritani', Roman troops at Amida, killed by Sapor, 56

treason, and treason trials, *see under maiestas*

'Trebellianus', alleged Isaurian rebel, in *Historia Augusta*, 362

Tricasini (Troyes), Julian at, 81; late Roman walls, 394

Trier (Treveri), imperial court capital: and Constantine, 254; exile of Athanasius to, 426; senatorial embassy to, under Valentinian, 10, 212, 267, 284f.; Symmachus and Ausonius at, 284f.; Tripolitanian embassy at, 386; amphitheatre at, 260; tales of court life, 274

Tripolitania: Austurian invasions in, 383-7; dispute with *comes* Romanus, 280f.; embassies to imperial court, 256, 261; their chronology, 207f., 536 n. 2, 537 n.

Index

7; military command of, 153
Tubusuctu, in Mauretania, in campaigns of Theodosius, 369; in *Notitia Dignitatum*, 370f.
Tukultu Enurtu II, Assyrian king, at Hit, 147f.
Tungrecani Iuniores (Seniores), *see* Divitenses
Tur Abdin, 52-5; settlements in, 55, 69, 402; ascetic communities, 547 n. 25

Ulfila, missionary among Goths, 331; settled at Nicopolis (ad Istrum), 331
Ulpian, Roman jurist, on native languages, 69; his origin, 489 n. 4
Ur, in Mesopotamia, 186, 187
Uranius, Fl., *praeses Isauriae*, under Valens, rebuilds fort, 534 n. 111
Ursicinus, *magister equitum*: at Nisibis, 34; at Antioch, role in trials under Gallus Caesar, 34f.; summoned to Milan, 36f.; his relations with Constantius, 35f., 40, 46f.; appearance in consistory, 37, 244, 246, 267; role in suppression of Silvanus, 37f., 80; commander in Gaul, 38, 81-3, 89f.; transferred to east, 39; his service there, 39-45; relations with Sabinianus, 40f., 60; encounter with Antoninus, 68; efforts to relieve Amida, 60; promotion to succeed Barbatio, 40, 46f.; his enmity with eunuch Eusebius, 40, 47; dismissed, 47, 65f., 100
service under Constantine, 80; his character, 34, 461: close relations with Ammianus, 34f., 39, 47, 78; house at Antioch, 40, 73; popularity in the east, 35, 40, 405; his sons, 35; son killed at Hadrianople, 299, 379
Ursicinus, *vicarius* of Rome under Valentinian, 211, 258
Ursinus, contender for bishopric of Rome, 444
Ursulus, *comes sacrarum largitionum* of Constantius, criticises military at Amida, 66, 281; supports Julian in Gaul, 88; executed at Chalcedon, 66

Vadomarius, Alamann king: relations with Constantius and Julian, 104, 315, 316; his 'pagus', 306; arrested at Kaiseraugst, 315, 317, 376f.; further career and character, 317f.; as *dux Phoeniciae*, 317f., 377
Valens, emperor, brother of Valentinian: promoted and elevated, 189; and rebellion of Procopius, 192-203; Gothic campaigns, 318-20 and n. 24; insurrection of Mavia, 350f.; death at Hadrianople, 297, 379; as predicted in oracles, 221, 224, 226f. and n. 44
his selection of officials, 269f.; Cappadocian supporters, 272 and 519 n. 39; financial policy, 193, 240, 281; administration of law, 251, 202, 220-3; his appearance and character, 190, 238; lack of education, 238
Valentinian, emperor, son of Gratianus, from Cibalae in Pannonia, 75; as *tribunus*, cashiered by Julian, 77; in retirement in Illyricum, sent to Gaul by Jovian, 187f.; escapes death there, 188; promoted, 188; imperial candidate after death of Jovian, elevated, 189; promotes Valens as colleague, 189; division of the empire, 190f.; his attitude to rebellion of Procopius, 198, 206
military policy and achievement, 207f., 283-5 and n. 8; its presentation, 284-6, 378; favours military, 254, 270, 284; conduct at Solicinium, 377; his selection of officials, 269; Pannonians and Gauls under, 272f.; financial severity, 135; justified, 239f., 281; his cruelty, 215f.; alleged 'conspiracy' under, 511 n. 19; conducts prosecutions at Rome, 209-17; law on divination, 214, 218
his death, 267f.; obituary, in A., 239-42; 'exempla' and, 242; his

physical appearance and character, 190, 237ff., 242; his views on imperial power, 238, 459
Valerian, emperor, captured by Sapor I, 133f.
Varronianus, *comes domesticorum*, father of Jovian, 79, 184
Vatican, paupers from, 417
Veh Ardeshir, *see under* Coche
Vergil, in A., 17, 87, 287, 463, 468; and Homer, 466; Valentinian and, 238; on 'Greeks', 279f.
Verinianus, *protector domesticus*, comrade of Ammianus, 45, 76, 453
vicarii of Rome, their role in prosecutions of Valentinian, 210f.
'vici', in A., characterised, 401-3
Victor, *magister equitum*, on Persian campaign, 168; his caution at Hadrianople, 300; Sarmatian origin, 300
Victor, Sex. Aurelius, historian, *praefectus urbi* 389/90, 29; meets Julian at Sirmium, 23, 457f.; bronze statue at Rome, 23f., 457; on 'adoratio', 244; on Constantine, 448; and 'Kaisergeschichte', 29 and n. 41, 244, 457; as source for A., 23 and n. 28, 457f.
Victores Iuniores, *see* Iovii Iuniores
Viderich, king of Greuthungi, 324
Vienna (Vienne), in digression, 389; Julian at, 86f., 435, 470; Florentius at, 94, 99; Christianity at, 435f., 438
'villas', in A., characterised, 399-401; imperial, 401; see also 'Contionacum', 'Mediana', 'Melanthias', 'Murocincta', 'Pistrensis'
Vindonissa (Windisch), early legionary fortress, 308
Vithicabius, Alamann king, son of Vadomarius, murdered, 318; his character, 318
Vithimir, king of Greuthungi, killed in battle, 324
Viventius, Pannonian, *praefectus urbi* 365-7, and riots over bishopric of Rome, 421; his character, 272 and n. 36
Vologesias (or Vologesocerta?), Parthian city (Maps 4, 5): foundation of, 142 and n. 29, 156; identified as Meinas Sabatha (Sabat al-Mada'in), 156; *see also* Besouchis, Meinas Sabatha

'White Huns', 62; *see under* Chionitae

Xenophon: on the March of the Ten Thousand, 50, 154; on Nimrud and Nineveh, 50; *Cyropaedia* of, on imperial deportment, 233; as continuator of Thucydides, 455
Xerxes, Persian king, his hosts compared to the army of Sapor, 44, 46

'yayla', mountain pasture, 359, 360
Yörük, in southern Turkey, transhumance among, 534 n. 104

Zaitha, on Euphrates: meaning of the name, 130; A.'s presence at, 111, 132; tomb of Gordian III near, 131
Zammac, Moorish prince: relations with *comes* Romanus, 369, 373; and 'fundus Petrensis' (Petra), 369, 372f.; murdered, 369; forms of his name, 373, 381
Zeno, Isaurian dynast and Roman emperor, his names and origin, 361
Zenobia, of Palmyra, 349; as al-Zabbâ, in Arabic legend, death of, 350
Zliten, villa in Tripolitania, mosaics from, 362
Zoroastrians, funeral rite of, 62
Zosimus, historian, 116; use of, by Eunapius, 104, 130, 161 and n. 68, 164f. and n. 76, 361; on Persian campaign (*q.v.*), 499 n. 19; on trials of Antioch, 512 n. 31; his qualities exemplified, 493 n. 32, cf. 508 n. 15